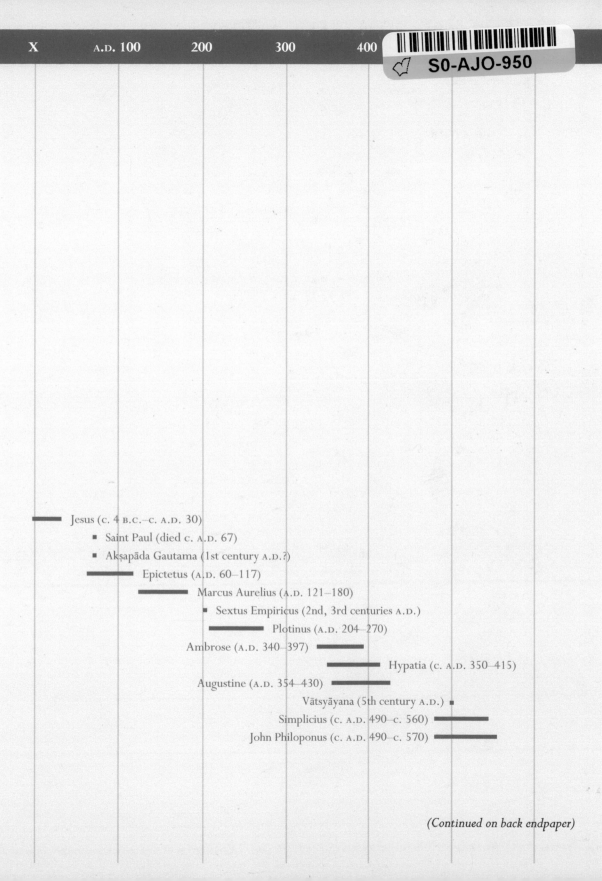

| X | A.D. 100 | 200 | 300 | 400 |

Jesus (c. 4 B.C.–c. A.D. 30)

Saint Paul (died c. A.D. 67)

Akṣapāda Gautama (1st century A.D.?)

Epictetus (A.D. 60–117)

Marcus Aurelius (A.D. 121–180)

Sextus Empiricus (2nd, 3rd centuries A.D.)

Plotinus (A.D. 204–270)

Ambrose (A.D. 340–397)

Hypatia (c. A.D. 350–415)

Augustine (A.D. 354–430)

Vātsyāyana (5th century A.D.)

Simplicius (c. A.D. 490–c. 560)

John Philoponus (c. A.D. 490–c. 570)

(Continued on back endpaper)

THE GREAT CONVERSATION

THE GREAT CONVERSATION

A Historical Introduction to Philosophy

EIGHTH EDITION

NORMAN MELCHERT
Professor Emeritus, Lehigh University

DAVID R. MORROW
Visiting Fellow, George Mason University

New York   Oxford
OXFORD UNIVERSITY PRESS

Oxford University Press is a department of the University of Oxford.
It furthers the University's objective of excellence in research, scholarship,
and education by publishing worldwide. Oxford is a registered trade mark of
Oxford University Press in the UK and certain other countries.

Published in the United States of America by Oxford University Press
198 Madison Avenue, New York, NY 10016, United States of America.

Library of Congress Cataloging-in-Publication Data

Names: Melchert, Norman, author. | Morrow, David R., author.
Title: The great conversation : a historical introduction to philosophy /
   Norman Melchert, Professor Emeritus, Lehigh University; David R. Morrow,
   Visiting Fellow, George Mason University.
Description: Eighth edition. | New York : Oxford University Press, 2018.
   | Includes bibliographical references and index.
Identifiers: LCCN 2018011655 | ISBN 9780190670610 (hardcover)
Subjects: LCSH: Philosophy–Textbooks.
Classification: LCC BD21 .M43 2018 | DDC 190–dc23
LC record available at https://lccn.loc.gov/2018011655

Printing number: 9 8 7 6 5 4 3
Printed in Canada by Marquis

CONTENTS

19. DAVID HUME: UNMASKING THE PRETENSIONS OF REASON 438

20. IMMANUEL KANT: REHABILITATING REASON (WITHIN STRICT LIMITS) 465

21. GEORG WILHELM FRIEDRICH HEGEL: TAKING HISTORY SERIOUSLY 496

22. KIERKEGAARD AND MARX: TWO WAYS TO "CORRECT" HEGEL 521

A WORD TO INSTRUCTORS

Philosophy is both argument and innovation. We try in this introductory text to provide students with excellent examples of both in the ongoing story of a basic part of our intellectual life. We aim to teach students how to think by apprenticing them to a succession of the best thinkers humanity has produced, mainly but not exclusively in the Western tradition, thereby drawing them into this ongoing conversation. So we see how Aristotle builds on and criticizes his teacher, Plato, how Augustine creatively melds traditions stemming from Athens and Jerusalem, how Kant tries to solve "Hume's problem," and why Wittgenstein thought most previous philosophy was meaningless.

This eighth edition continues to represent the major philosophers through extensive quotations set in a fairly rich cultural and historical context. The large number of cross-references and footnotes continue to make the conversation metaphor more than mere fancy. And the four complete works—*Euthyphro*, *Apology*, *Crito*, and *Meditations*—are retained.

New to This Edition

A number of new features will be found in this edition. Throughout, the text has been tightened up and minor sections were deleted to make room for new material. In addition, several larger changes have been made. These changes include the following:

- Three new chapters introduce students to the beginnings of philosophical conversations in India and China, with one chapter on ancient Indian philosophy and two chapters on ancient Chinese philosophy.

- A new chapter is devoted entirely to philosophy in the Islamic world.

- A section on Hildegaard of Bingen in a chapter on medieval thought and new sketches of Hypatia and Margaret Cavendish, and a profile of Émilie du Châtelet.

Again, for this edition, a student web page is available at www.oup.com/us/melchert. Here students will find essential points, vocabulary flashcards, sample multiple-choice questions, and further web resources for each chapter. The latter consist mainly, though not exclusively, of original philosophical texts. This means that if you want to assign students to read, say, Hume's *Enquiry* or parts of Plato's *Republic*, these texts are easy for them to find. An Instructor's Manual is available at the same site.

The text is again available both as a single hardback edition and as two paperback volumes, so it can be used economically in either a whole-year or a single-semester course. Although the entire book contains too much material for a single semester, it provides a rich menu of choices for instructors who do not wish to restrict themselves to the earlier or later periods.

In this era, when even the educated have such a thin sense of history, teaching philosophy in this conversational, cumulative, back- and forward-looking way can be a service not just to philosophical understanding, but also to the culture as a whole.

A WORD TO STUDENTS

We all have opinions—we can't help it. Having opinions is as natural to us as breathing. Opinions, moreover, are a dime a dozen. They're floating all around us and they're so different from each other. One person believes this, another that. You believe in God, your buddy doesn't. John thinks there's nothing wrong with keeping a found wallet, you are horrified. Some of us say, "Everybody's got their own values"; others are sure that *some* things are just plain wrong—wrong for everybody. Some delay gratification for the sake of long-term goals; others indulge in whatever pleasures happen to be at hand. What kind of world do we live in? Jane studies science to find out, Jack turns to the occult. Is death the end for us?—Some say yes, some say no.

What's a person to do?

Study Philosophy!

You don't want simply to be at the mercy of accident in your opinions—for your views to be decided by irrelevant matters such as whom you happen to know or where you were brought up. You want to believe for *good reasons*. That's the right question, isn't it? Which of these many opinions has the best reasons behind it? You want to live your life as wisely as possible.

Fortunately, we have a long tradition of really smart people who have been thinking about issues such as these, and we can go to them for help. They're called "philosophers"—lovers of wisdom—and they have been trying to straighten out all these issues. They are in the business of asking which opinions or views or beliefs there is good reason to accept.

Unfortunately, these philosophers don't all agree either. So you might ask, If these really smart philosophers can't agree on what wisdom says, why should I pay them any attention? The answer is—because it's the best shot you've got. If you seriously want to improve your opinions, there's nothing better you can do than engage in a "conversation" with the best minds our history has produced.

One of the authors of this book had a teacher—a short, white-haired, elderly gentleman with a thick German accent—who used to say, "Whether you will philosophize or won't philosophize, you *must* philosophize." By this, he meant that we can't help making decisions about these crucial matters. We make them either well or badly, conscious of what we are doing or just stumbling along. As Kierkegaard would say, we express such decisions in the way we live, whether or not we have ever given them a moment's thought. In a sense, then, you are already a philosopher, already engaged in the business philosophers have committed themselves to. So you shouldn't have any problem in making a connection with what they write.

Does it help to think about such matters? You might as well ask whether it helps to think about the recipe before you start to cook. Socrates says that "the unexamined life is not worth living." And that's what philosophy is: an examination of opinions—and also of our lives, shaped by these opinions. In thinking philosophically, we try to sort our opinions into two baskets: the good-views basket and the trash.

We want to think about these matters as clearly and rationally as we can. *Thinking* is a kind of craft. Like any other craft, we can do it well or poorly, with shoddy workmanship or with care, and we improve with practice. It is common for people who want to learn a craft—cabinetmaking, for example—to apprentice themselves for a time to a master, doing what the master does until the time comes when they are skillful enough to set up shop on their own. You can think of reading this book as a kind of apprenticeship in thinking, with Socrates, Plato, Kant, and the rest as the masters. By thinking along with them, noting their insights and arguments, following their examinations of each other's opinions, you should improve that all-important skill of your own.

This Book

This book is organized historically because that's how philosophy has developed. It's not just a recital of this following that, however. It is also intensively *interactive* because that's what philosophy

has been. We have taken the metaphor of a conversation seriously. These folks are all talking to each other, arguing with each other, trying to convince each other—and that makes the story of philosophy a dramatic one. Aristotle learns a lot from his teacher, Plato, but argues that Plato makes one big mistake—and that colors everything else he says. Aquinas appreciates what Aristotle has done but claims that Aristotle neglects a basic feature of reality—and that makes all the difference. In the seventeenth century, Descartes looks back on his predecessors with despair, noting that virtually no agreement has been reached on any topic; he resolves to wipe the slate clean and make a new start. Beginning with an analysis of what it is to believe anything at all, C. S. Peirce argues that what Descartes wants to do is impossible. And so it goes.

Not all the philosophers in this book have been involved in the same conversation, however. While this book focuses mainly on the Western tradition—the philosophical conversation that began in ancient Greece—other cultures have had their own philosophical conversations. Philosophy arose independently in India and China as well, and the conversations in South and East Asia have been as rich as those in the West. This book cannot hope to convey those conversations in their entirety, but it will introduce you to some key ideas in each of them. Examining early Indian and Chinese philosophy alongside Western philosophy helps illuminate both the commonalities among those traditions—the questions that human beings have wrestled with all over the globe—and the differences between them.

To emphasize the conversational and interactive aspect of philosophy, the footnotes in this book provide numerous cross-references, mainly within Western philosophy but also between Western and non-Western thinkers. Your understanding of an issue will be substantially enriched if you follow up on these. To appreciate the line one thinker is pushing, it is important to see what he is arguing against, where he thinks that others have made mistakes, and how other thinkers have approached the same problems. No philosopher simply makes pronouncements in the dark. There is always something that bugs each thinker, something she thinks is terribly wrong, something that needs correction. This irritant may be something current in the culture, or it may be what other philosophers have been saying. Using the cross-references to understand that background will help you to make sense of what is going on—and why. The index of names and terms at the back of this book will also help you.

Philosophers are noted for introducing novel terms or using familiar words in novel ways. They are not alone in this, of course; poets and scientists do the same. There is no reason to expect that our everyday language will be suited, just as it is, to express the truth of things, so you will have some vocabulary to master. You will find key words in boldface and a list of them at the end of each chapter. Use this list to help you review important concepts and arguments. Many of these boldfaced terms are defined in the Glossary at the back of the book.

The Issues

The search for wisdom—that is, philosophy—ranges far and wide. Who can say ahead of time what might be relevant to that search? Still, there are certain central problems that especially concern philosophers. In your study of this text, you can expect to find extensive discussions of these four issues in particular:

1. *Metaphysics*, the theory of reality. In our own day, Willard Quine has said that the basic question of metaphysics is very simple: *What is there?* The metaphysical question, of course, is not like, "Are there echidnas in Australia?" but "What kinds of things are there fundamentally?" Is the world through and through made of material stuff, or are there souls as well as bodies? Is there a God? If so, of what sort? Are there universal features to reality, or is everything just the particular thing that it is? Does everything happen necessarily or are fresh starts possible?

2. *Epistemology*, the theory of knowledge. We want to think not only about what there is, but also about *how we know* what there is—or, maybe, whether we can know anything at all! So we reflectively ask, What is it to know something anyway? How does that differ from just believing it? How is knowing something related to its being true? What is truth? How far can our knowledge reach? Are some things simply unknowable?

3. *Ethics*, the theory of right and wrong, good and bad. We aren't just knowers and believers. We are doers. The question then arises of what wisdom might say about how best to live our lives. Does the fact that something gives us pleasure make it the right thing to do? Do we need to think about how our actions affect others? If so, in what way? Are there really goods and bads, or does thinking so make it so? Do we have duties? If so, where do they come from? What is virtue and vice? What is justice? Is justice important?

4. *Human nature*—Socrates took as his motto a slogan that was inscribed in the temple of Apollo in Delphi: know thyself. But that has proved none too easy to do. What are we, anyway? Are we simply bits of matter caught up in the universal mechanism of the world, or do we have minds that escape this deterministic machine? What is it to have a mind? Is mind separate from body? How is it related to the brain? Do we have a free will? How important to my self-identity is my relationship to others? To what degree can I be responsible for the creation of myself?

Running through these issues is a fifth one that perhaps deserves special mention. It centers on the idea of *relativism*. The question is whether there is a way to get beyond the prejudices and assumptions peculiar to ourselves or our culture—or whether that's all there is. Are there *just* opinions, with no one opinion ultimately any better than any other? Are all views relative to time and place, to culture and position? Is there no *truth*—or, anyway, no truth that we can know to be true?

This problem, which entered all the great conversations early, has persisted to this day. Most of the Western philosophical tradition can be thought of as a series of attempts to kill such skepticism and relativism, but this phoenix will not die. Our own age has the distinction, perhaps, of being the first age ever in which the basic assumptions of most people, certainly of most educated people, are relativistic, so this theme will have a particular poignancy for us. We will want to understand how we came to this point and what it means to be here. We will also want to ask ourselves how adequate this relativistic outlook is.

What we are is what we have become, and what we have become has been shaped by our history. In this book, we look at that history, hoping to understand ourselves better and, thereby, gain some wisdom for living our lives.

Reading Philosophy

Reading philosophy is not like reading a novel, nor is it like reading a research report in biology or a history of the American South. Philosophers have their own aims and ways of proceeding, and it will pay to take note of them at the beginning. Philosophers aim at the truth about fundamental matters, and in doing so they offer arguments.

If you want to believe for good reasons, what you seek is an **argument**. An argument in philosophy is not a quarrel or a disagreement, but simply this business of offering reasons to believe. Every argument, in this sense, has a certain structure. There is some proposition the philosopher wants you to believe—or thinks every rational person ought to believe—and this is called the **conclusion**. And there are the reasons he or she offers to convince you of that conclusion; these are called the **premises**.

In reading philosophy, there are many things to look for—central concepts, presuppositions, overall view of things—but the main things to look for are the arguments. And the first thing to identify is the conclusion of the argument: What is it that the philosopher wants you to believe? Once you have identified the conclusion, you need to look for the reasons given for believing that

conclusion. Usually philosophers do not set out their arguments in a formal way, with premises listed first and the conclusion last. The argument will be embedded in the text, and you need to sniff it out. This is usually not so hard, but it does take careful attention.

Occasionally, especially if the argument is complex or obscure, we give you some help and list the premises and conclusion in a more formal way. You might right now want to look at a few examples. Socrates in prison argues that it would be wrong for him to escape; that is the conclusion, and we set out his argument for it on p. 144. Plato argues that being happy and being moral are the same thing; see an outline of his argument on p. 176. Anselm gives us a complex argument for the existence of God; see our summary on p. 314. And Descartes argues that we have souls that are distinct from and independent of our bodies; see p. 319.

Often, however, you will need to identify the argument buried in the prose for yourself. What is it that the philosopher is trying to get you to believe? And why does he think you should believe that? It will be helpful, and a test of your understanding, if you try to set the argument out for yourself in a more or less formal way; keep a small notebook, and list the main arguments chapter by chapter.

Your first aim should be to *understand* the argument. But that is not the only thing, because you will also want to discover how good the argument is. These very smart philosophers, to tell the truth, have given us lots of poor arguments; they're only human, after all. So you need to try to *evaluate* the arguments. In evaluating an argument, there are two things to look at: the truth or acceptability of the premises and whether the premises actually do support the conclusion.

For an argument to be a good one, the reasons given in support of the conclusion have to at least be plausible. Ideally the premises should be known to be *true*, but that is a hard standard to meet. If the reasons are either false or implausible, they can't lend truth or plausibility to the conclusion. If there are good reasons to doubt the premises, then the argument should not convince you.

It may be, however, that all the premises are true, or at least plausible, and yet the argument is a poor one. This can happen when the premises do not have the right kind of relation to the conclusion. Broadly speaking, there are two kinds of arguments: **deductive** and **inductive**. A good deductive argument is one in which the premises— if true—*guarantee* the truth of the conclusion. In other words, the conclusion couldn't possibly be false if the premises are true. When this condition is satisfied, we say that the argument is **valid**. Note that an argument may have validity even though the premises are not in fact true; it is enough that if the premises *were* true, then the conclusion *would have to be* true. When a deductive argument is both valid *and* has true premises, we say it is **sound**.

Inductive arguments have a looser relation between premises and conclusion. Here the premises give some support to the conclusion—the more support the better—but they fall short of guaranteeing the truth of the conclusion. Typically philosophers aim to give sound deductive arguments, and the methods of evaluating these arguments will be those of the preceding two paragraphs.

You will get some help in evaluating arguments because you will see philosophers evaluating the arguments of other philosophers. (Of course, these evaluative arguments themselves may be either good or bad.) This is what makes the story of philosophy so dramatic. Here are a few examples. Aristotle argues that Plato's arguments for eternal, unchanging realities (which Plato calls Forms) are completely unsound; see pp. 198–199. Augustine tries to undercut the arguments of the skeptics on pp. 267–268. And Hume criticizes the design argument for the existence of God on pp. 456-458.

Sometimes you will see a philosopher criticizing another philosopher's presuppositions (as Peirce criticizes Descartes' views about doubt, pp. 596–597) or directly disputing another's conclusion (as Hegel does with respect to Kant's claim that there is a single basic principle of morality, pp. 512–513). But even here, it is argument that is the heart of the matter.

In reading philosophy you can't just be a passive observer. It's no good trying to read for understanding while texting with your friends. You need to concentrate, focus, and be actively engaged in the process. Here are a few general rules:

1. Have an open mind as you read. Don't decide after the first few paragraphs that what a philosopher is saying is absurd or silly. Follow the argument, and you may change your mind about things of some importance.
2. Write out brief answers to the questions embedded in the chapters as you go along; check back in the text to see that you have got it right.
3. Use the key words to check your understanding of basic concepts.
4. Try to see how the arguments of the philosophers bear on your own current views of things. Bring them home; apply them to the way you now think of the world and your place in it.

Reading philosophy is not the easiest thing in the world, but it's not impossible either. If you make a good effort, you may find that it is even rather fun.

Web Resources

A website for this book is available at www.oup. com/us/melchert. Here you will find, for each chapter, the following aids:

> Essential Points (a brief list of crucial concepts
>   and ideas)
> Flashcards (definitions of basic concepts)
> Multiple-Choice Questions (practice tests)
> Web Resources (mostly original works
>   that are discussed in this text—e.g.,
>   Plato's *Meno* or Nietzsche's *Beyond Good*
>   *and Evil*—but also some secondary
>   treatments)

The web also has some general resources that you might find helpful:

> Stanford Encyclopedia of Philosophy: http://
>   plato.stanford.edu
> Internet Encyclopedia of Philosophy: http://
>   www.iep.utm.edu

Both these encyclopedias contain reliable in-depth discussions of the philosophers and topics we will be studying.

Philosophy Pages: http://www.philosophypages.com

A source containing a variety of things, most notably a Philosophical Dictionary.

Project Vox: http://www.projectvox.org

A source containing information about selected women philosophers of the early modern period, whose philosophical voices and contributions are being recovered and recognized by historians of philosophy.

YouTube contains numerous short interviews with and about philosophers, such as those at https://youtube/nG0EWNezFl4 and https://youtube/B2fLyvsHHaQ, as well as various series of short videos about philosophical concepts, such as those by Wireless Philosophy at https://www.youtube.com/user/WirelessPhilosophy

ACKNOWLEDGMENTS

We want to thank those readers of the seventh edition who thoughtfully provided us with ideas for improvement. We are grateful to Peter Adamson, Ludwig Maximilian University of Munich; Eric Boynton, Allegheny College; David Buchta, Brown University; Amit Chaturvedi, University of Hawai'i at Mānoa; Douglas Howie, North Lake College; Manyul Im, University of Bridgeport; Jon McGinnis, University of Missouri, St. Louis; Susan M. Mullican, University of Southern Mississippi – Gulf Coast Campus; Danny Muñoz-Hutchinson, St. Olaf College; Hagop Sarkissian, The City University of New York, Baruch College and Graduate Center; Stephanie Semler, Northern Virginia Community College; Nancy Shaffer, California University of Pennsylvania; Georgia Van Dam, Monterey Peninsula College; and Bryan William Van Norden, Yale-NUS College.

We are also grateful to the specialists in non-Western and Islamic philosophy who provided valuable feedback on the new chapters in this edition, including Peter Adamson, David Buchta, Amit Chaturvedi, Manyul Im, Jon McGinnis, and Hagop Sarkissian. All errors remain our own.

Finally, we would like to thank the editorial team at Oxford University Press, including Robert Miller, Alyssa Palazzo, Sydney Keen, and Marianne Paul.

Comments relating to this new edition may be sent to us at norm.mel@verizon.net or dmorrow2@gmu.edu.

I was aware that the reading of all good books is indeed like a conversation with the noblest men of past centuries who were the authors of them, nay a carefully studied conversation, in which they reveal to us none but the best of their thoughts.

—*René Descartes*

We—mankind—are a conversation.

—*Martin Heidegger*

In truth, there is no divorce between philosophy and life.

—*Simone de Beauvoir*

CHAPTER

1

BEFORE PHILOSOPHY

Myth in Hesiod and Homer

Everywhere and at all times, we humans have wondered at our own existence and at our place in the scheme of things. We have asked, in curiosity and amazement, "What's it all about?" "How are we to understand this life of ours?" "How is it best lived?" "Does it end at death?" "This world we find ourselves in—where does it come from?" "What is it, anyway?" "How is it related to us?"

These are some of the many philosophical questions we ask. Every culture offers answers, though not every culture has developed what we know as philosophy. Early answers to such questions universally take the form of stories, usually stories involving the gods—gigantic powers of a personal nature, engaged in tremendous feats of creation, frequently struggling with one another and intervening in human life for good or ill.

We call these stories *myths*. They are told and retold, taught to children as the plain facts, gaining authority by their age, by repetition, and by the apparent fact that within a given culture, virtually everyone accepts them. They shape a tradition, and traditions shape lives.

Philosophy, literally "love of wisdom," begins when individuals start to ask, "Why should we believe these stories?" "How do we know they are true?" When people try to give good reasons for believing (or not believing) these myths, they have begun to do philosophy. Philosophers look at myths with a critical eye, sometimes defending them and sometimes appreciating what myths try to do, but often attacking myths' claims to literal truth. So there is a tension between these stories and philosophy, a tension that occasionally breaks into open conflict.

This conflict is epitomized in the execution of the philosopher **Socrates** by his fellow Athenians in 399 B.C. The Athenians accused Socrates of corrupting the youth because he challenged the commonly accepted views and values of ancient Athens. But even though Socrates challenged those views, his own views were deeply influenced by them. He was part of a conversation, already centuries old among the Greeks, about how to understand the world and our place in it. That conversation continued after his death, right down to the present day, spreading far beyond Athens and winding its way through all of Western intellectual history.

If we want to understand this conversation, we need to understand where and how it began. We need to understand Socrates, and we need to understand where he came from. To do that, we need to understand the myths through which the ancient Greeks had tried to understand their world. Our aim is neither a comprehensive survey nor mere acquaintance with some of these stories. We will be trying to understand something of Greek religion and culture, of the intellectual and spiritual life of the people who told these stories. As a result, we should be able to grasp why Socrates believed what he did and why some of Socrates' contemporaries reacted to him as they did. With that in mind, we take a brief look at two of the great Greek poets: Hesiod and Homer.

Hesiod: War Among the Gods

The poet we know as **Hesiod** probably composed his poem *Theogony* toward the end of the eighth century B.C., but he drew on much older traditions and seems to have synthesized stories that are not always consistent. The term *theogony* means "origin or birth of the gods," and the stories contained in the poem concern the beginnings of all things. In this chapter, we look only at certain central events, as Hesiod relates them.

Hesiod claims to have written these lines under divine inspiration. (Suggestion: Read quotations aloud, especially poetry; you will find that they become more meaningful.)

> The Muses once taught Hesiod to sing
> Sweet songs, while he was shepherding his lambs
> On holy Helicon; the goddesses
> Olympian, daughters of Zeus who holds
> The aegis,* first addressed these words to me:
> "You rustic shepherds, shame: bellies you are,
> Not men! We know enough to make up lies
> Which are convincing, but we also have
> The skill, when we've a mind, to speak the truth."
> So spoke the fresh-voiced daughters of great Zeus
> And plucked and gave a staff to me, a shoot
> Of blooming laurel, wonderful to see,

And breathed a sacred voice into my mouth
With which to celebrate the things to come
And things which were before.
> —*Theogony*, 21–35[1]

The Muses, according to the tradition Hesiod is drawing on, are goddesses who inspired poets, artists, and writers. In this passage, Hesiod is telling us that the stories he narrates are not vulgar shepherds' lies but are backed by the authority of the gods and embody the remembrance of events long past. They thus represent the *truth*, Hesiod says, and are worthy of belief.

What have the Muses revealed?

> And sending out
> Unearthly music, first they celebrate
> The august race of first-born gods, whom Earth
> Bore to broad Heaven, then their progeny,
> Givers of good things. Next they sing of Zeus
> The father of gods and men, how high he is
> Above the other gods, how great in strength.
> —*Theogony*, 42–48

Note that the gods are *born*; their origin, like our own, is explicitly sexual. Their ancestors are Earth (Gaea, or Gaia) and Heaven (Ouranos).* And like people, the gods differ in status and power, with Zeus, king of the gods, being the most exalted.

There is confusion in the Greek stories about the very first things (no wonder), and there are contradictions among them. According to Hesiod, first there is *chaos*, apparently a formless mass of stuff, dark and without differentiation. Out of this chaos, Earth appears. (Don't ask how.) Earth then gives birth to starry Heaven,

> to be
> An equal to herself, to cover her
> All over, and to be a resting-place,
> Always secure, for all the blessed gods.
> —*Theogony*, 27–30

After lying with Heaven, Earth bears the first race of gods, the **Titans,** together with the

---

*The *aegis* is a symbol of authority.

*Some people nowadays speak of the Gaea hypothesis and urge us to think of Earth as a living organism. Here we have a self-conscious attempt to revive an ancient way of thinking about the planet we inhabit. Ideas of the Earth-mother and Mother Nature likewise echo such early myths.

Cyclops—three giants with but one round eye in the middle of each giant's forehead. Three other sons, "mighty and violent," are born to the pair, each with a hundred arms and fifty heads:

> And these most awful sons of Earth and Heaven
> Were hated by their father from the first.
> As soon as each was born, Ouranos hid
> The child in a secret hiding-place in Earth*
> And would not let it come to see the light,
> And he enjoyed this wickedness.
>
> —*Theogony*, 155–160

Earth, distressed and pained with this crowd hidden within her, forms a great sickle of hardest metal and urges her children to use it on their father for his shameful deeds. The boldest of the Titans, Kronos, takes the sickle and plots vengeance with his mother.

> Great Heaven came, and with him brought
>   the night.
> Longing for love, he lay around the Earth,
> Spreading out fully. But the hidden boy
> Stretched forth his left hand; in his right he took
> The great long jagged sickle; eagerly
> He harvested his father's genitals
> And threw them off behind.
>
> —*Theogony*, 176–182

Where Heaven's bloody drops fall on land, the Furies spring up—monstrous goddesses who hunt down and punish wrongdoers.†

In the Titans' vengeance for their father's wickedness, we see a characteristic theme in Greek thought, a theme repeated again and again in the great classical tragedies and also echoed in later philosophy: Violating the rule of **justice**—even in the service of justice—brings consequences.

The idea repeats itself in the Titan's story. Kronos, now ruler among the Titans, has children by Rhea, among them Hera, **Hades,** and **Poseidon.** Learning of a prophecy that he will be dethroned by one of these children, Kronos

seizes the newborns and swallows them.* When Rhea bears another son, however, she hides him away in a cave and gives Kronos a stone wrapped in swaddling clothes to swallow. The hidden son, of course, is **Zeus.**

When grown to full strength, Zeus disguises himself as a cupbearer and persuades Kronos to drink a potion. This causes Kronos to vomit up his brothers and sisters—together with the stone. (The stone, Hesiod tells us, is set up at Delphi, northwest of Athens, to mark the center of the earth.) Together with his brothers and their allies, Zeus makes war on the Titans. The war drags on for ten years until Zeus frees the Cyclops from their imprisonment in Tartarus. The Cyclops give Zeus a lightning bolt, supply Poseidon with a trident, and provide Hades with a helmet that makes him invisible. With these aids, the gods overthrow Kronos and the Titans and hurl them down into Tartarus. The three victorious brothers divide up the territory: Zeus rules the sky (he is called "cloudgatherer" and "storm-bringer"); Poseidon governs the sea; and Hades reigns in Tartarus. Earth is shared by all three. Again, the myths tell us that wickedness does not pay.

Thus, the gods set up a relatively stable order in the universe, an order both natural and moral. Although the gods quarrel among themselves and are not above lies, adultery, and favoritism, each guards something important and dear to humans. They also see to it that wickedness is punished and virtue is rewarded, just as was the case among themselves.

---

1. Why are philosophers dissatisfied with mythological accounts of reality?
2. What is the topic of Hesiod's *Theogony*?
3. Tell the story of how Zeus came to be king of the gods.
4. What moral runs through these early myths?

---

*This dank and gloomy place below the surface of the earth and sea is known as Tartarus.

†In contemporary literature, you can find these Furies represented in Jean-Paul Sartre's play *The Flies*.

*"Kronos" is closely related to the Greek word for time, "chronos." What might it mean that Kronos devours his children? And that they overthrow his rule to establish cities—communities of justice—that outlive their citizens?

Homer: Heroes, Gods, and Excellence

Xenophanes, a philosopher we will meet later,* tells us that "from the beginning all have learnt in accordance with **Homer.**"² As we have seen, poets were thought to write by divine inspiration, and for centuries Greeks listened to or read the works of Homer, much as people read the Bible or the Koran today. Homer, above all others, was the great teacher of the Greeks. To discover what was truly excellent in battle, governance, counsel, sport, the home, and human life in general, the Greeks looked to Homer's tales. These dramatic stories offered a picture of the world and people's place in it that molded the Greek mind and character. Western philosophy begins against the Homeric background, so we need to understand something of Homer.

Homer simply takes for granted the tradition of gods and heroes set down in Hesiod's *Theogony*. That sky-god tradition of Zeus, Athena, and Apollo celebrates clarity and order, mastery over chaos, intellect and beauty: fertile soil, one must think, for philosophy.

Homer's two great poems are *The Iliad* and *The Odyssey*. Here, we focus on *The Iliad*, a long poem about a brief period during the nine-year-long Trojan war.† This war came about when **Paris,** son of the Trojan king **Priam,** seduced **Helen,** the famously beautiful wife of the Spartan king **Menelaus.** Paris spirited Helen away to his home in **Troy,** across the Aegean Sea from her home in Achaea, in southern Greece (see Map 1). Menelaus's brother, **Agamemnon,** the king of Argos, led an army of Greeks to recover Helen, to avenge the wrong against his brother, and—not just incidentally—to gain honor, glory, and plunder.

---

*See "Xenophanes: The Gods as Fictions," in Chapter 2.

†The date of the war is uncertain; scholarly estimates tend to put it near the end of the thirteenth century B.C. The poems took form in song and were passed along in an oral tradition from generation to generation. They were written down some time in the eighth century B.C. Tradition ascribes them to a blind bard known as Homer, but the poems we now have may be the work of more than one poet.

Among Agamemnon's forces was **Achilles,** the greatest warrior of them all.

Here is how *The Iliad* begins.

> Rage—Goddess, sing the rage of Peleus'
>   son Achilles,
> murderous, doomed, that cost the Achaeans
>   countless losses,
> hurling down to the House of Death so many
>   sturdy souls,
> great fighters' souls, but made their bodies carrion,
>   feasts for the dogs and birds,
> and the will of Zeus was moving toward its end.
> Begin, Muse, when the two first broke and clashed,
> Agamemnon lord of men and brilliant Achilles.
> What god drove them to fight with such a fury?
> Apollo the son of Zeus and Leto. Incensed at
>   the king
> he swept a fatal plague through the army—men
>   were dying
> and all because Agamemnon had spurned
>   Apollo's priest.
>   —*The Iliad*, Book 1, 1–12³

The poet begins by announcing his theme: rage, specifically the excessive, irrational anger of Achilles—anger beyond all bounds that brings death and destruction to so many Greeks and almost costs them the war. So we might expect that the poem has a *moral* aspect. Moreover, in the sixth line we read that what happened was in accord with the will of Zeus, who sees to it that flagrant violations of good order do not go unpunished. In these first lines we also learn of **Apollo,** the son of Zeus, who has sent a plague on the Greek army because Agamemnon offended him. We can see, then, that Homer's world is one of kings and heroes, majestic but flawed, engaged in gargantuan projects against a background of gods who cannot safely be ignored.

The story Homer tells goes roughly like this. In a raid on a Trojan ally, the Greeks capture a beautiful girl who happens to be the daughter of a priest of Apollo. The army awards her to Agamemnon as part of his spoils. The priest comes to plead for her return, offering ransom, but he is rudely rebuffed. Agamemnon will not give back the girl. The priest appeals to Apollo, who, angered by the treatment his priest is receiving, sends a plague to Agamemnon's troops.

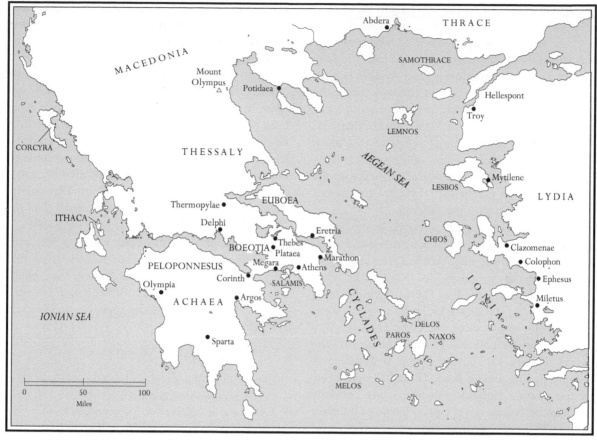

MAP 1 *The Greek Mainland*

The soldiers, wanting to know what is causing the plague, appeal to their seer, who explains the situation and suggests returning the girl. Agamemnon is furious. To forfeit his prize while the other warriors keep theirs goes against the honor due him as commander. He finally agrees to give up the girl but demands Achilles' prize, an exceptionally lovely woman, in exchange. The two heroes quarrel bitterly. Enraged, Achilles returns to his tent and refuses to fight anymore.

Because Achilles is the greatest of the Greek warriors, his anger has serious consequences. The war goes badly for the Greeks. The Trojans fight their way to the beach and begin to burn the ships. Patroclus, Achilles' dearest friend, pleads with him to relent, but he will not. If Achilles won't have pity on his comrades, Patroclus says, then at least let him take Achilles' armor and fight in his place. Achilles agrees, and the tactic has some success. The Greeks drive the Trojans back toward the city, but in the fighting Patroclus is killed by **Hector,** another son of Priam and the greatest of the Trojan warriors.

Achilles' rage now turns on Hector and the Trojans. He rejoins the war to wreak havoc among them. After slaughtering many, he comes face to face with Hector. Achilles kills him and drags his body back to camp behind his chariot—a profoundly disrespectful thing to do. As the poem ends, King Priam goes alone by night into the Greek camp to plead with Achilles for the body of his son. He and Achilles weep together, for Hector and for Patroclus, and Achilles gives up the body.

This summary emphasizes the human side of the story. From that point of view, *The Iliad* can be thought of as the story both of the tragedy that excess and pride lead to and of the humanization of Achilles. The main moral is the same as that expressed by a motto at the celebrated oracle at Delphi: "Nothing too much."* **Moderation** is what Achilles lacked, and his lack led to disaster. At the same time, the poem celebrates the "heroic virtues": *strength, courage, physical prowess,* and the kind of *wisdom* that consists in the ability to devise clever plans to achieve one's ends. For Homer and his audience, these characteristics, together with moderation, make up the model of human excellence. These are the virtues ancient Greeks taught their children.

The gods also appear throughout the story, looking on, hearing appeals, taking sides, and interfering. For instance, when Achilles is sulking about Agamemnon having taken "his" woman, he prays to his mother, the goddess Thetis. (Achilles has a mortal father.) Achilles asks Thetis to go to Zeus and beg him to give victory to—the Trojans!

Zeus frets that his wife Hera will be upset—she favors the Greeks—but he agrees. If Zeus grants an appeal, that will be done. (Recall the sixth line of the poem.) Homeric religion, while certainly not a monotheism, is not exactly a true polytheism either. The many powers that govern the world seem to be under the rule of one.† That rule gives a kind of order to the universe.

Moreover, this order is basically a just order, though it may not be designed altogether with human beings in mind. Zeus sees to it that certain customs are enforced: that oaths are kept, that suppliants are granted mercy, and that the rules governing guest and host are observed—the rules that Paris violated so grossly when he seduced Helen away from her husband, Menelaus. Homer suggests that the Greeks eventually win the war because Zeus punishes the violation of these customs. However, the Greeks are punished with great losses

before their eventual victory because Agamemnon had acted unjustly in taking Achilles' prize of war.

The Homeric idea of justice is not exactly the same as ours. The mortals and gods in Homer's world covet **honor** and glory above all else. Agamemnon is angry not primarily because "his" woman was taken back to her father but because his honor has been offended. Booty is valued not for its own sake so much as for the honor it conveys—the better the loot, the greater the honor. Achilles is overcome by rage because Agamemnon has humiliated him, thus depriving him of the honor due him. That is why Thetis begs Zeus to let the Trojans prevail until the Greeks restore to Achilles "the honor he deserves."

What is just in this social world is that each person receive the honor that is due, given that person's status and position. Nestor, wise counselor of the Greeks, tries to make peace between Agamemnon and Achilles by appealing to precisely this principle.

> "Don't seize the girl, Agamemnon, powerful as
>   you are—
> leave her, just as the sons of Achaea gave her,
> his prize from the very first.
> And you, Achilles, never hope to fight it out
> with your king, pitting force against his force:
> no one can match the honors dealt a king, you
>   know,
> a sceptered king to whom Zeus gives glory.
> Strong as you are—a goddess was your mother—
> he has more power because he rules more men."
>   —*The Iliad*, Book 1, 321–329

Nestor tries to reconcile them by pointing out what is just, what each man's honor requires. Unfortunately, neither one heeds his good advice.

The gods are also interested in honor. It has often been remarked that Homer's gods reflect the society that they allegedly govern; they are powerful, jealous of their prerogatives, quarrel among themselves, and are not above a certain deceitfulness, although some sorts of evil are simply beneath their dignity. The chief difference between human beings and the gods is that human beings are bound for death and the gods are not. Greeks often refer to the gods simply as "the immortals." Immortality makes possible a kind of blessedness among the gods that is impossible for human beings.

---

*This was one of several mottoes that had appeared mysteriously on the temple walls. No one could explain how they got there, and it was assumed that Apollo himself must have written them.

†We shall see philosophers wrestling with this problem of "the one and the many." In what sense, exactly, is this world *one* world?

As immortals, the gods are interested in the affairs of mortals, but only insofar as they are entertained or their honor is touched. They are spectators of the human comedy—or tragedy; they watch human affairs the way we watch soap operas and reality television. In a famous passage from the *Iliad*, Zeus decides to sit out the battle about to rage below and simply observe, saying,

> "These mortals do concern me, dying as they are.
> Still, here I stay on Olympus throned aloft,
> here in my steep mountain cleft, to feast my eyes
> and delight my heart."
> —*The Iliad*, Book 20, 26–29

The gods both deserve and demand honor, punishing humans who refuse to give it. We saw that Apollo sent a plague because Agamemnon refused the ransom offered by Apollo's priest. When humans dishonor the gods or do not respect their prerogatives, they are guilty of arrogance, or **hubris.** In this state, human beings in effect think of themselves as gods, forgetting their finitude, their limitations, their mortality. Hubris is punished by the gods, as hero after hero discovers to his dismay.

The gulf between Homeric gods and mortals—even those, like Achilles, who have one divine parent—is clear and impassable. In closing this brief survey of Greek myths, we want to emphasize a particular aspect of this gulf: Those whose thoughts were shaped by Homer neither believed in nor aspired to any immortality worth prizing. There is a kind of shadowy existence after death, but the typical attitude toward it is expressed by Achilles when Odysseus visits him in the underworld.

> "No winning words about death to me, shining
>   Odysseus!
> By god, I'd rather slave on earth for another
>   man—
> some dirt-poor tenant farmer who scrapes to keep
>   alive—
> than rule down here over all the breathless dead."
> —*The Odyssey*, Book 11, 555–558[4]

For these conquerors who glory in the strength of their bodies, nothing after death could compare to glory in this life. They know they are destined to die, believe that death is the end of any life worth living, and take the attitude expressed by Hector when faced with Achilles:

> "And now death, grim death is looming up beside
>   me,
> no longer far away. No way to escape it now. This,
> this was their pleasure after all, sealed long ago—
> Zeus and the son of Zeus, the distant deadly
>   Archer—
> though often before now they rushed to my
>   defense.
> So now I meet my doom. Well let me die—
> but not without struggle, not without glory, no,
> in some great clash of arms that even men to come
> will hear of down the years!"
> —*The Iliad*, Book 22, 354–362

Again, even at the end, the quest for honor is paramount.

1. Describe the main characters in Homer's poem *The Iliad*—for example, Agamemnon, Achilles, Apollo, Zeus, and Hector.
2. Retell the main outline of the story.
3. What is the theme of the poem, as expressed in the first lines?
4. How are honor and justice related in Homer's view of things?
5. What virtues are said to constitute human excellence?
6. Describe the relationship between humans and gods. In what ways are they similar, and how do they differ?
7. What is hubris, and what is its opposite?
8. Do Homer's heroes long for immortality? Explain.

FOR FURTHER THOUGHT

1. Gather examples of mythological thinking that are current today. What questions would a philosopher want to ask about them?

KEY WORDS

Socrates	Justice
Hesiod	Hades
Theogony	Poseidon
Titans	Zeus

Homer
Paris
Priam
Helen
Menelaus
Troy
Agamemnon

Achilles
Apollo
Hector
moderation
honor
hubris

NOTES

1. Hesiod, *Theogony*, trans. Dorothea Wender, in *Hesiod and Theognis* (New York: Penguin Books, 1973). All quotations are taken from this translation; numbers are line numbers.

2. Kathleen Freeman, *Ancilla to the Pre-Socratic Philosophers* (Cambridge, MA: Harvard University Press, 1948), 22.

3. Homer, *The Iliad*, trans. Robert Fagles (New York: Penguin Books, 1990). All quotations are taken from this translation; references are to book and line numbers.

4. Homer, *The Odyssey*, trans. Robert Fagles (New York: Penguin Books, 1996). References are to book and line numbers.

CHAPTER

2

PHILOSOPHY BEFORE SOCRATES

I f the great conversation of Western philosophy is rooted in the poetry of Hesiod and Homer, it first sprouted in the protoscientific thought of Ionia (see Map 1). A little more than a century before Socrates' birth, Greek thinkers on the eastern shore of the Aegean Sea began to challenge the traditional myths with attempts at more rational explanations of the world around them. Western philosophy was born in these attempts and in the conversation that it began. So, it is to these first Greek philosophers that we now turn.

It is seldom entirely clear why thinkers raised in a certain tradition become dissatisfied enough to try to establish a new one. The reason is even more obscure in the case of the earliest Greek philosophers because we have a scarcity of information about them. Although most of them wrote books, these writings are almost entirely lost, some surviving in small fragments, others known only by references to them and quotations or paraphrases by later writers. As a group, these thinkers are usually known as the "pre-Socratics." This name

testifies to the pivotal importance put on Socrates by his successors.*

For whatever reason, a tradition grew up in which questions about the nature of the world took center stage, a tradition that was not content with stories about the gods. For thinkers trying to *reason* their way to a view about reality, the Homeric tales and Hesiod's divine genealogy must have seemed impossibly crude. Still, the questions addressed by these myths were real questions: What is the true nature of reality? What is its origin? What is our place in it? How are we related to the powers that govern it? What is the best way to live? Philosophy is born when thinkers attempt to answer these questions more rationally than myth does.

In early Greek philosophical thought, certain issues took center stage. There is the problem of

---

*In this chapter, we look only at selected pre-Socratic thinkers. A more extensive and very readable treatment of others—including Anaximenes, Empedocles, and Anaxagoras—can be found in Merrill Ring, *Beginning with the Pre-Socratics* (Boston: McGraw-Hill, 1999).

the one and the many: If reality is in some sense one, what accounts for the many different individual things (and kinds of things) that we experience? Greek myth tends to answer this question in animistic or personal terms by referring either to birth or to spontaneous emergence. For instance, we find Hesiod simply asserting that "Chaos was first of all, but next appeared / Broad bosomed Earth" (*Theogony*, 116, 117). How, why, when, and by what means did it appear? On these questions the tradition is silent.

Then there is the problem of *reality and appearance*. True, things appear to change; they appear to be "out there," independent of us. But we all know that things are not always what they seem. Might reality in fact be very different from the way it appears in our experience? How could we know?

Of course, there is also the question about *human reality*: Who are we, and how are we related to the rest of what there is? These questions perplex our first philosophers and we shall see them struggling to frame ever more satisfactory answers to them.

Thales: The One as Water

Thales (c. 625–547 B.C.) of Miletus, a Greek seaport on the shore of Asia Minor (see Map 1), seems to have been one who was dissatisfied with the traditional stories. Aristotle, one of the most important philosophers in the Western tradition, calls Thales the founder of philosophy.* We know very little about Thales, and part of what we do know is arguably legendary. So, our consideration here is brief and somewhat speculative. He is said to have held (1) that the cause and element of all things is water and (2) that all things are filled with gods. What could these two rather obscure sayings mean?

Concerning the first, it is striking that Thales supposes there is some *one* thing that is both the origin and the underlying nature of all things. It is surely not obvious that wine and bread and stones and wind are really the same stuff despite all their differences. It is equally striking that Thales chooses one of the things that occur naturally in the world of our experience to play that role, rather

than one of the gods. Here we are clearly in a different thought-world from that of Homer. Thales' motto seems to be this: *Account for what you can see and touch in terms of things you can see and touch.* This idea is a radical departure from anything prior to it.

Why would Thales choose water to play the role of the primeval stuff? Aristotle speculates that Thales must have noticed that water is essential for the nourishment of all things and that without moisture, seeds will not develop into plants. We might add that Thales must have noticed that water is the only naturally occurring substance that can be seen to vary from solid to liquid to gas. The fact that the wet blue sea, the white crystalline snow, and the damp and muggy air seem to be the same thing despite their differences could well have suggested that water might take even more forms.

At first glance, the saying that all things are full of gods seems to go in a quite different direction. If we think a moment, however, we can see that it is consistent with the saying about water. What is the essential characteristic of the gods, according to the Greeks? Their immortality. To say that all things are full of gods, then, is to say in effect that *in* each thing—not outside it or in addition to it—is a principle that is immortal. But this suggests that the things of experience do not need explanations from outside themselves as to why they exist. Moreover, tradition appeals to the gods as a principle of action. Why did lightning strike just there? Because Zeus was angry with *that man*. But to say that all things are themselves full of gods may well mean that we do not have to appeal beyond them to explain why events happen. Things have the principles of their behavior within themselves.

Both sayings, then, point thought in a direction quite different from the tradition of Homer and Hesiod. They suggest that if we want to understand this world, then we should look to this world, not to another. Thales seems to have been the first to have tried to answer the question, Why do things happen as they do? in terms that are not immediately personal. In framing his answer this way, Thales is not only the first philosopher in the Greek tradition, but also the first scientist. It is almost impossible to overestimate the significance of this shift for the story of Western culture.

---

*We cover Aristotle in Chapter 9.

1. In what way are the two sayings attributed to Thales consistent?
2. Contrast the view suggested by Thales' sayings with that of Homer.

Anaximander: The One as the Boundless

Let's grant that Thales produced a significant shift in Western thought. What next? Although he may have done so, we have no evidence that Thales addresses the question of *how* water accounts for everything else. If everything is water, why does it seem as though so many things are *not* water, that water is just one kind of thing among many?

There is something else unsatisfactory about his suggestion: Even though water has those unusual properties of appearing in several different states, water itself is not unusual. It is, after all, just one of the many things that need to be explained. If we demand explanations of dirt and bone and gold, why should we not demand an explanation for water as well?

Ancient Greeks would have found a third puzzling feature in Thales' idea. They tended to think in terms of opposites: wet and dry, hot and cold. These pairs are opposites because they cancel each other out. Where you have the wet, you can't have the dry, and so on. Water is wet, yet the dry also exists. If the origin of all things were water, how could the dry have ever come into existence? It seems impossible.

Although again we are speculating, it is reasonable to suppose that problems such as these led to the next stage in our story. We can imagine **Anaximander,** a younger fellow citizen from Miletus born about 612 B.C., asking himself—or perhaps asking Thales—these questions. How does water produce the many things of our experience? What makes water so special? So the conversation develops.

Like Thales, Anaximander wants an account of origins that does not appeal to the gods of Homer and Hesiod, but as we'll see, he does not reject the divine altogether. We can reconstruct Anaximander's reasoning thus:

1. Given any state of things X, it had a beginning.
2. To explain its beginning, we must suppose a prior state of things W.
3. But W also must have had a beginning.
4. So we must suppose a still prior state V.
5. Can this go on forever? No.
6. So there must be something that itself has no beginning.
7. We can call this "the infinite" or "**the Boundless.**"

It is from this, then, that all things come.

We are ready now to appreciate a passage of Aristotle's, in which he looks back and reports the views of Anaximander.

> Everything either is a beginning or has a beginning. But there is no beginning of the infinite; for if there were one, it would limit it. Moreover, since it is a beginning, it is unbegotten and indestructible. . . . Hence, as we say, there is no source of this, but this appears to be the source of all the rest, and "encompasses all things" and "steers all things," as those assert who do not recognize other causes besides the infinite. . . . And this, they say, is the divine; for it is "deathless" and "imperishable" as Anaximander puts it, and most of the physicists agree with him. (DK 12 A 15, *IEGP*, 24)[1]

Only the Boundless, then, can be a beginning for all other things. It *is* a beginning, as Aristotle puts it; it does not *have* a beginning. Because it is infinite, moreover, it has no end either—otherwise it would have a limit and not be infinite.

It should be no surprise that the infinite is called "divine." Recall the main characteristic of the Greek gods: They are immortal; they cannot die. As Anaximander points out, this is a key feature of the Boundless.

Here we have the first appearance of a form of reasoning that we will meet again when later thinkers try to justify belief in a god (or God) conceived in a much richer way than Anaximander is committed to.* Yet even here some of the key features of later thought are already present. The Boundless "encompasses all things" and "steers all things." Those familiar with the New Testament will be

---

*For examples, see Thomas Aquinas' proofs of the existence of God (Chapter 15).

reminded of Paul's statement that in God "we live and move and have our being" (Acts 17:28).[2]

We have seen how Anaximander deals with one of the puzzles bequeathed to him by Thales. It is not water but the Boundless that is the source and element of all things. What about the other problem? By what process does the Boundless produce the many individual things of our experience?

Here we have to note that the Boundless is thought of as indefinite in character, neither clearly this nor that. If it had a clear nature of its own, it would already exclude everything else; it would be, for instance, water but not fire, so it would have limits and not be infinite. Therefore, it must contain all things, but in a "chaotic" mixture.* The hot, the cold, the dry, and the wet are all present in the Boundless, but without clear differentiation.

How, then, does the process of differentiation from the Boundless work? If Anaximander could show how these basic four elements (hot, cold, dry, and wet) separate out from the chaos, his basic problem would be solved. The *one* would generate *many* things. The question of how particular things are formed could be solved along similar lines. Note that at this early stage of thought, no clear distinction is made between heat as a property of a thing and the thing that is hot. There is just "the hot" and "the cold," what we might think of as hot stuff and cold stuff. In fact, these stuffs are virtually indistinguishable from earth (the cold), air (the dry), fire (the hot), and water (the wet). To the ancient Greeks, the universe as we experience it seems to be composed of various mixtures of these elemental stuffs.†

To solve his problem, Anaximander uses an analogy: Fill a circular pan with water; add some bits of limestone, granite, and lead (what you need is a variety of different weights); and then swirl the water around. You will find that the heavier bits move toward the middle and the lighter bits to the

outside. Like goes to like; what starts as a jumble, a chaos, begins to take on some order. Anaximander is apparently familiar with this simple experiment and makes use of it to explain the origin of the many.

If the Boundless were swirling in a **vortex motion,** like the water in the pan, then what was originally indistinguishable in it would become separated out according to its nature. You might ask, Why should we think that the Boundless engages in such a swirling, vortex motion? Anaximander would simply ask you to look up. Every day we see the heavenly bodies swirl around the earth: the sun, the moon, and even the stars. Did you ever lie on your back in a very dark, open spot (a golf course is a good place) for a long time and look at the stars? You can see them move, although it takes a long while to become conscious of their movement.*

Furthermore, it seems clear that the motions we observe around us exemplify the vortex principle that like goes to like. What is the lightest of the elements? Anyone who has stared at a campfire for a few moments will have no doubt about the answer. The sticks stay put, but the fire leaps up, away from the cold earth toward the sky—toward the immensely hot, fiery sun and the other bright but less hot heavenly bodies. In short, Anaxminader turns not to gods or myths to try to explain the nature of the world, but to reasoning and experience.

Of Anaximander's many other interesting ideas, one deserves special attention—an idea that connects him to Hesiod and Homer as surely as his reliance on reasoning and experience sets him apart. Anaximander tells us that existing things "make reparation to one another for their injustice according to the ordinance of time" (DK 12 B 1, *IEGP*, 34). Several questions arise here. What existing things? No doubt it is the opposites of hot and cold, wet and dry that Anaximander has in mind, but why does he speak of injustice? How can the hot and cold do each other injustice, and how can they "make reparation" to each other?

---

*Remember that Hesiod tells us that "Chaos was first of all."

†Much of Greek medicine was based on these same principles. A feverish person, for instance, has too much of the hot, a person with the sniffles too much of the wet, and so on. What is required is to reach a balance among the opposite elements.

---

*Copernicus, of course, turns this natural view inside out. The stars only *appear* to move; in actuality, Copernicus suggests, it is *we* who are moving. See pp. 353–354.

Much as Homer requires a certain moderation or balance in human behavior, assuming, for instance, that too much anger or pride will bring retribution, Anaximander presupposes a principle of balance in nature. The hot summer is hot at the expense of the cold; it requires a cold winter to right the balance. The rainy season comes at the expense of the dry; it requires the dry season to right the balance. Thus, each season encroaches on the "rights" due to the others and does them an injustice, but reparation is made in turn when each gets its due—and more. This keeps the cycle going.

Unlike in Hesiod and Homer, though, Anaximander's cosmic balance is not imposed on reality by the gods. Anaximander conceives it as immanent in the world process itself. In this he is faithful to the spirit of Thales, and in this both of them depart from the tradition of Homer. Anaximander's explanations are framed impersonally. It is true that the Boundless "steers all things," but the jealous and vengeful Homeric gods who intervene at will in the world have vanished. To explain particular facts in the world, no will, no purpose, no emotion, no intention is needed. The gods turn out to be superfluous.

You can see that a cultural crisis is on the way. Since the Homeric tradition was still alive and flourishing in the religious, artistic, political, and social life of Greek cities, what would happen when this new way of thinking began to take hold? Our next thinker begins to draw some conclusions.

---

1. What puzzling features of Thales' view seem to have stimulated Anaximander to revise it?
2. State Anaximander's argument for the Boundless.
3. How, according to Anaximander, does the Boundless produce the many distinct things of our experience?
4. What evidence do we have in our own experience for a vortex motion?
5. How is the injustice that Anaximander attributes to existing things related to the Homeric virtue of moderation?
6. What sort of crisis was brewing in Ionia? Why?

Xenophanes: The Gods as Fictions

Anaximander, as far as we know, only criticized the gods implicitly. He focused on solving his problems about the nature and origins of the world. Although his results were at odds with tradition, we have no record that he took explicit notice of this. But about forty miles north of Miletus, in the city of Colophon (see Map 1), another thinker named **Xenophanes** did notice. Like Thales and Anaximander, Xenophanes was an Ionian Greek living on the eastern shores of the Aegean Sea. We are told that he fled in 546 B.C., when Colophon fell to the Persians, and that he lived at least part of his life thereafter in Sicily. Xenophanes was a poet and apparently lived a long life of more than ninety-two years.

Xenophanes is important to our story because he seems to have been the first to state clearly the religious implications of the new nature philosophy. He explicitly criticizes the traditional conception of the gods on two grounds. First, the way Hesiod and Homer picture the gods is unworthy of our admiration or reverence:

> Homer and Hesiod have attributed to the gods all those things which in men are a matter for reproach and censure: stealing, adultery, and mutual deception. (DK Z1 B11, *IEGP*, 55)*

What he says is true, of course. It has often been remarked that Homer's gods are morally no better (and in some ways may be worse) than the

---

*When the Greeks talk about "men," they may not have been thinking about women. Women were not citizens, for example, in ancient Athens. It does not follow, of course, that what the Greeks say about "men" has no relevance for women of today. Here is a useful way to think about this. Aristotle formulated the Greek understanding of "man" in terms of *rational animal*, a concept that can apply to human beings generally. What the Greeks say about "man" may well apply to women, too, although one should be on guard lest they sneak masculinity too much into this generic "man." Their mistake (and not theirs alone!) was to have underestimated the rationality and humanity of women.

We will occasionally use the term "man" in this generic sense, but we will often paraphrase it with "human being" or some other substitute. Rather than the awkward "he or she," we will sometimes use "he" and sometimes "she," as seems appropriate.

band of ruthless warrior barons on whom they are so clearly modeled. They are magnificent in their own fashion, but flawed, like a large and brilliant diamond containing a vein of impurities. What matters about Xenophanes' statement is that he not only notices this but also clearly expresses his disapproval.* He thinks it is shameful to portray the gods as though they are no better than the kind of human beings whom good men regard with disgust. That Homer, to whom all Greeks of the time look for guidance in life, should give us this view of the divine seems intolerable to Xenophanes. This moral critique is further developed by Plato.† For both of them, such criticism is the negative side of a more exalted idea of the divine.

This kind of criticism makes sense only on the basis of a certain assumption: that Homer is not simply reporting the truth but is inventing stories. Several sayings of Xenophanes make this assumption clear.

> The Ethiopians make their gods snub-nosed and black; the Thracians make theirs gray-eyed and red-haired. (DK 21 B 16, *IEGP*, 52)
> And if oxen and horses and lions had hands, and could draw with their hands and do what man can do, horses would draw the gods in the shape of horses, and oxen in the shape of oxen, each giving the gods bodies similar to their own. (DK 21 B 15, *IEGP*, 52)

Here we have the first recorded version of the saying that god does not make man in his own image but that we make the gods in our image. Atheists and agnostics have often made this point since Xenophanes' time. Was Xenophanes, then, a disbeliever in the divine? No, not at all. No more than Anaximander, who says the infinite sees all and steers all. Xenophanes tells us there is

> one god, greatest among gods and men, in no way similar to mortals either in body or mind. (DK 21 B 23, *IEGP*, 53)

Several points in this brief statement stand out. There is only **one god.*** Xenophanes takes pains to stress how radically different this god is from anything in the Homeric tradition. It is "in no way similar to mortals." This point is brought out in some positive characterizations he gives of this god.

> He sees all over, thinks all over, hears all over. (DK 21 B 24, *IEGP*, 53)
> He remains always in the same place, without moving; nor is it fitting that he should come and go, first to one place and then to another. (DK 21 B 26, *IEGP*, 53)
> But without toil, he sets all things in motion by the thought of his mind. (DK 21 B 25, *IEGP*, 53)

By contrast, we humans see with our eyes, think with our brain, and hear with our ears. We seldom remain in the same place for more than a short time, and if we want to set anything besides ourselves in motion, just thinking about it or wishing for it isn't enough. Xenophanes' god is very different from human beings indeed.

Yet there is a similarity after all, and Xenophanes' "in no way similar" must be qualified. The one god sees and hears and thinks; so do we. He does not do it in the way we do it; the way the god does it is indeed "in no way similar." But god is intelligent, and so are we.

Here is a good place to comment on an assumption that seems to have been common among the Greeks. Where there is order, there is intelligence. Order, whether in our lives or in the world of nature, needs an explanation, and only intelligence can explain it. Though never argued for, this assumption lies in the background as something almost too obvious to comment on. We can find experiences to give it some support, and perhaps these are common enough to make it *seem* self-evident—but it is not. For example, consider the state of papers on your desk or tools in your workshop. If you are like us, you find that these things,

---

*For a contrary evaluation, see Nietzsche, p. 564.

†See *Euthyphro* 6a, for instance. This criticism is expanded in Plato's *Republic*, Book II, where Plato explicitly forbids the telling of Homeric and Hesiodic tales of the gods to children in his ideal state.

---

*It may seem that Xenophanes allows the existence of other gods in the very phrase he uses to praise this one god. Scholars disagree about the purity of his monotheism. In the context of other things he says, however, it seems best to understand this reference to "gods" as a reference to "what tradition takes to be gods."

PYTHAGORAS

Pythagoras (b. 570 B.C.), about whom we have as many legends as facts, lived most of his adult life in Croton in southern Italy (see Map 2 on page 23). He combined mathematics and religion in a way strange to us and was active in setting up a pattern for an ideal community. The Pythagorean influence on Plato is substantial.*

Pythagoras and his followers first developed geometry as an abstract discipline, rather than as a tool for practical applications. It was probably Pythagoras himself who discovered the "Pythagorean theorem" (the square of the hypotenuse of a triangle is equal to the sum of the squares of the other two sides).

He also discovered the mathematical ratios of musical intervals: the octave, the fifth, and the fourth. Because mathematics informs these intervals, the

*We cover the great Greek philosopher Plato in Chapter 8.

Pythagoreans held, somewhat obscurely, that *all things are numbers*. They also believed that the sun, the moon, and other heavenly bodies make a noise as they whirl about, producing a cosmic harmony, the "music of the spheres."

Pythagoras believed that the soul is a distinct and immortal entity, "entombed" for a while in the body. After death, the soul migrates into other bodies, sometimes the bodies of animals. To avoid both murder and cannibalism, the Pythagoreans were vegetarians. Xenophanes tells the story, probably apocryphal, that Pythagoras saw a puppy being beaten and cried out, "Do not beat it; I recognize the voice of a friend."

Mathematics was valued not just for itself but as a means to purify the soul, to disengage it from bodily concerns. In mathematical pursuits the soul lives a life akin to that of the gods.

It is said that Pythagoras was the first to call himself a philosopher, a *lover* of wisdom.

---

if left to their own devices, degenerate slowly into a state of chaos. Soon it is impossible to find what you want when you need it and it becomes impossible to work. What you need to do then is *deliberately* and with some *intelligent plan in mind* impose order on the chaos. Order is the result of intelligent action, it seems. It doesn't just happen.

Whether this assumption is correct is an interesting question, one about which modern physics and evolutionary biology say interesting things.* Modern mathematicians tell us that however chaotic the jumble of books and papers on your desk, there exists some mathematical function according to which they are in perfect order. But for these ancient Greeks, the existence of order always presupposes an ordering

---

*See p. 361 for an example. Here Descartes claims that a chaos of randomly distributed elements, if subject to the laws of physics, would by itself produce an order like that we find in the world. For more recent views, see the fascinating book by James Gleick, *Chaos: Making a New Science* (New York: Penguin Books, 1987). The dispute over "intelligent design" shows that this is still a live issue.

intelligence. We find this assumption at work in Anaximander's and Xenophanes' ideas of god.

Consider now a saying that shows how closely Xenophanes' critique of the traditional gods relates to the developing nature philosophy:

> She whom men call "Iris," too, is in reality a cloud, purple, red, and green to the sight. (DK 21 B 32, *IEGP*, 52)

In *The Iliad*, Iris is a minor goddess, a messenger for the other gods. After Hector has killed Patroclus, Iris is sent to Achilles to bid him arm in time to rescue Patroclus' body (Book 18, 192–210). She seems to have been identified with the rainbow, which many cultures have taken as a sign or message from the gods. (Compare its significance to Noah, for example, after the flood in Genesis 9:12–17.)

Xenophanes tells us that rainbows are simply natural phenomena that occur in natural circumstances and have natural explanations. A rainbow, he thinks, is just a peculiar sort of cloud. This idea suggests a theory of how gods are invented. Natural phenomena, especially those that are particularly striking or important to us, are personified and given lives that go beyond what is observable. Like the theory that the gods are invented, this theory has often been held. It may not be stretching things too far to regard Xenophanes as its originator.

It is clear that there is a kind of natural unity between nature philosophy and criticism of Homer's gods. They go together and mutually reinforce one another. Together they are more powerful than either could be alone. We will see that they come to pose a serious threat to the integrity of Greek cultural life.

There is one last theme in Xenophanes that we should address. Poets in classical times typically appealed to the Muses for inspiration and seemed often to think that what they spoke or wrote was not their own—that it was literally inspired, breathed into them, by these goddesses. Remember Hesiod's claim that he was taught to sing the truth by the Muses. Similarly, Homer begins *The Iliad* by inviting the goddess to sing through him the rage of Achilles.* No doubt this is more than a literary conceit; many writers have experiences of inspiration when they seem to be no more than a mouthpiece for powers greater and truer than themselves. Hesiod and Homer may well have had such experiences. Whether such experiences guarantee the *truth* of what the writer says in such ecstatic states is, of course, another question. Listen to Xenophanes:

> The gods have not revealed all things from the beginning to mortals; but, by seeking, men find out, in time, what is better. (DK 21 B 18, *IEGP*, 56)
>
> No man knows the truth, nor will there be a man who has knowledge about the gods and what I say about everything. For even if he were to hit by chance upon the whole truth, he himself would not be aware of having done so, but each forms his own opinion. (DK 21 B 38, *IEGP*, 56)
>
> Let these things, then, be taken as like the truth. (DK 21 B 35, *IEGP*, 56)

This is a very rich set of statements. Let us consider them in six points.

1. Xenophanes is explicitly denying our poets' claims of inspiration. The gods have *not* revealed

to us in this way "from the beginning" what is true, Xenophanes says. If we were to ask him why he is so sure about this, he would no doubt remind us of the unworthy picture of deity painted by the poets and of the natural explanations that can be given for phenomena they ascribe to the gods. Xenophanes' point is that a poet's claim of divine revelation is no guarantee of her poem's truth.

2. How, then, should we form our beliefs? By **"seeking,"** Xenophanes tells us. This idea is extremely vague. How, exactly, are we to seek? No doubt he has in mind the methods of the Ionian nature philosophers, but we don't have a very good idea of just what they were, so we don't get much help at this point.

Still, his remarks are not entirely without content. He envisages a process of moving toward the truth. If we want the truth, we should face not the past but the future. It is no good looking back to the tradition, to Homer and Hesiod, as though they had already said the last words. We must look to ourselves and to the results of our seeking. He is confident, perhaps because he values the results of the nature philosophers, that "in time"—not all at once—we will discover "what is better." We may not succeed in finding the truth, but our opinions will be "better," or more "like the truth."*

3. It may be that we know some **truth** already. Perhaps there is even someone who knows "the whole truth." But even if he did, that person could not be sure that it is the truth. To use a distinction Plato later emphasizes, Xenophanes is claiming that the person would not be able to distinguish his knowledge of the truth from mere opinion.† (Plato, as we'll see, does not agree.) There is, Xenophanes means to tell us, no such thing as *certainty* for limited beings such as ourselves. Here is a theme that later skeptics take up.‡

---

*In recent philosophy these themes have been taken up by the *fallibilists*. See C. S. Peirce (p. 601).

†See pp. 149–151.

‡See, for instance, the discussions by Sextus Empiricus (pp. 246–251) and Montaigne (pp. 350–353). Similar themes are found in Descartes' first *Meditation* and, in the Chinese tradition, in the work of Zhuangzi (pp. 83–87).

---

*Look again at these claims to divine inspiration on pp. 2 and 4.

4. This somewhat skeptical conclusion does not mean that all beliefs are equally good. Xenophanes is clear that although we may never be certain we have reached the truth, some beliefs are better or closer to the truth than others. Unfortunately, he does not tell us how we are to tell which are better. Again we have a problem that many later thinkers take up.

5. Until Xenophanes, Greek thought had basically been directed outward—to the gods, to the world of human beings, to nature. Xenophanes directs thought back on itself. His questioning questions itself. How much can we know? How can we know it? Can we reach the truth? Can we reach certainty about the truth? These are the central questions that define the branch of philosophy called **epistemology,** the theory of knowledge. Xenophanes, it seems, is its father.

"I was born not knowing and have only had a little time to change that here and there."

Richard Feynman (1918–1988)

---

6. If we ask, then, whether there is anyone who can know the truth *and* know that he knows it, what is the answer? Yes. The one god does, the one who "sees all over, thinks all over, hears all over." In this answer, Xenophanes carries forward Homer's emphasis on the gulf between humans and gods. The most important truth about humans is that they are not gods. Xenophanes' remarks about human knowledge drive that point home once and for all.

---

1. What are Xenophanes' criticisms of the Homeric gods?
2. What is his conception of the one god?
3. Can we know the truth about things, according to Xenophanes? If so, how?
4. Relate his sayings about knowing the truth to the idea of hubris and to claims made by Hesiod and Homer.

Heraclitus: Oneness in the *Logos*

Heraclitus is said to have been at his peak (probably corresponding to middle age) shortly before 500 B.C. A native of Ephesus (see Map 1), he was, like the others we have considered, an Ionian Greek living on the shores of Asia Minor. We know that he wrote a book, of which about one hundred fragments remain. He had a reputation for writing in riddles and was often referred to in Roman times as "Heraclitus the obscure." His favored style seems to have been the epigram, the short, pithy saying that condenses a lot of thought into a few words. Despite his reputation, most modern interpreters find that the fragments reveal a powerful and unified view of the world and man's place in it. Furthermore, Heraclitus is clearly an important influence on subsequent thinkers such as Plato and the Stoics.

One characteristic feature of his thought is that reality is a flux.

> All things come into being through opposition, and all are in flux, like a river. (DK 22 A 1, *IEGP*, 89)

There are two parts to this saying, one about **opposition** and one about flux. Let's begin with the latter and discuss the part about opposition later.

Plato ascribes to Heraclitus the view that "you cannot step twice into the same river." If you know anything at all about Heraclitus, it is probably in connection with this famous saying. What Heraclitus actually says, however, is slightly different.

> Upon those who step into the same rivers flow other and yet other waters. (DK 22 B 12, *IEGP*, 91)

You can, he says, step several times into the same river. Yet it is not the same, for the waters into which you step the second time are different waters. So, you both can and cannot.

This oneness of things that are different—even sometimes opposite—is a theme Heraclitus plays in many variations:

> The path traced by the pen is straight and crooked. (DK 22 B 59, *IEGP*, 93)
> Sea water is very pure and very impure; drinkable and healthful for fishes, but undrinkable and destructive to men. (DK 22 B 61, *IEGP*, 93)
> The way up and the way down are the same. (DK 22 B 60, *IEGP*, 94)

The road from Canterbury to Dover is the road from Dover to Canterbury. They are "the same," just as the same water is healthful and destructive, the same movement of the pen is crooked (when you consider the individual letters) but also straight (when you consider the line written).

Consider the river. It is the same river, although the water that makes it up is continually changing. A river is not identical with the water that makes it up but is a kind of structure or pattern that makes a unity of ever-changing elements. It is a *one* that holds together the *many*. So it is, Heraclitus tells us, with "all things." All things are in flux, like the river: ever changing, yet preserving an identity through the changes. The river is for that reason a fitting symbol for reality.

Another appropriate symbol for this flux is fire.

> This world-order, the same for all, no god made
> or any man, but it always was and is and will be an
> ever-lasting fire, kindling by measure and going out
> by measure. (DK 22 B 30, *IEGP*, 90)

Is Heraclitus here disagreeing with Thales? Is he telling us Thales is wrong in thinking that water is the source of all things—that it isn't water, but fire? Not exactly.

Remember that at this early stage of Greek thought the very language in which thoughts can be expressed is itself being formed. This means that thought is somewhat crude, as we observed earlier. Greek thinkers have not yet made a distinction between "hot-stuff" and "fire that is hot." Heraclitus is reaching for abstractions that he hasn't quite got and cannot quite express. What he wants to talk about is the "world-order." This is, we would say, not itself a thing but an abstract pattern or structure in which the things of the world are displayed. Heraclitus, though, hasn't quite got that degree of abstraction, so he uses the most ethereal, least solid thing he is acquainted with to represent this world-order: fire.

We can be certain, moreover, that Heraclitus does not have ordinary cooking fires primarily in mind. Anaximander believed that the outermost sphere of the universe, in which the sun and stars are located, is a ring of fire. If you have ever been to Greece on a particularly clear day, especially on or near the sea, you can see even through our polluted atmosphere that not only the sun but also the entire sky shines. The heavens are luminous, radiant. It is not too much to say the sky blazes. In this luminous *aether*, as it was called, the gods are supposed to live. Olympus is said to be their home because its peak is immersed in this fiery element. Notice the epithet Heraclitus gives to fire: He calls it ever-lasting. For the Greeks, only the divine deserves this accolade.

It is, then, the world-order itself that is immortal, divine. No god made *that*, of course, for the world-order is itself eternal and divine. Heraclitus represents it as fire, the most ethereal and least substantial of the elements.

This divine fire is both the substance of the world and its pattern. In its former aspect it is ever "kindling by measure and going out by measure." This thought is also expressed in the following fragments:

> The changes of fire: first sea, and of sea half is earth,
> half fiery thunderbolt. . . . (DK 22 B 31, *IEGP*, 91)
>   All things are an exchange for fire, and fire for
> all things; as goods are for gold, and gold for goods.
> (DK 22 B 90, *IEGP*, 91)

The sea, we learn, is a mixture, half earth and half fire. All things are in continuous exchange. Earth is washed into the sea and becomes moist; sea becomes air, which merges with the fiery heavens, from which rains fall and merge again with earth. If Heraclitus were able to use the distinction between things and patterns, he might say that *as substance* fire has no priority over other things. It is just one of the four elements engaged in the constant cycles of change. But *as pattern*, as world-order, it does have priority, for this pattern is eternal and divine. He does not, of course, say this; he can't. If he were able to, he might be less obscure to his successors.

Return now to the first part of our original fragment, where Heraclitus says that "all things come into being through opposition." What can this mean? Compare the following statements:

> War is the father and king of all. . . . (DK 22 B 53,
> *IEGP*, 93)
>   It is necessary to understand that war is universal and justice is strife, and that all things take place
> in accordance with strife and necessity. (DK 22 B
> 80, *IEGP*, 93)

Strife, opposition, war. Why elevate these into universal principles? To see what Heraclitus is saying, think about some examples. A lyre will produce music, but only if there is a tension on the strings.* The arms of the lyre pull in one direction, the strings in the opposite. Without this opposition, there is no music. Consider the river. What makes it a river? It is the force of the flowing water struggling with the opposing forces of the containing banks. Without the opposition between the banks and the water, there would be no river.

Here's another example, showing two of Heraclitus' themes: A bicycle wheel is *one* thing, though it is composed of *many* parts: hub, spokes, and rim. What makes these many items into one wheel? It is the tension that truing the wheel puts on the spokes, so that the hub and rim are pulling in opposite directions.

Now, if we think not about physical phenomena but about society, we see that the same is true. What is justice, Heraclitus asks, but the result of the conflict between the desires of the wealthy and the desires of the poor? Were either to get the upper hand absolutely, there would be no justice. Tension, opposition, and conflict, he tells us, are *necessary*. Without them the universe could not persist. If we look carefully at each of these examples, we see that each consists of a unity of diverse elements. The lyre, the river, the bicycle wheel, and justice are each a one composed in some sense of many. In every "one," "many" strive.

In *The Iliad*, Achilles laments the death of Patroclus, saying,

> "If only strife could die from the lives of gods and men."
>
> —*The Iliad*, Book 18, 126

To this cry, Heraclitus responds,

> He did not see that he was praying for the destruction of the whole; for if his prayers were heard, all things would pass away. (DK 22 A 22, *IEGP*, 93)

Strife, then, is necessary. It produces not chaos but the opposite; in fact, the divine world-order is the guarantee that a balance of forces is maintained. The result is this:

> To god all things are beautiful and good and just; but men suppose some things to be just and others unjust. (DK 22 B 102, *IEGP*, 92)

Again we see the Homeric contrast between gods and mortals, and again the contrast is to the disadvantage of mortals. God, the divine fire, the world-order, sees things as they are; and they are good. Strife is not opposed to the good; strife is its necessary presupposition. Mortals, such as Achilles, only "suppose," and what they suppose is false.

We are now ready to consider the most explicit version of Heraclitus' solution to the problem of the one and the many. To do that, we must introduce a term that we will usually leave untranslated. It is a term that has numerous meanings in Greek and has had a long and important history, stretching from Heraclitus to the Sophists, to Plato and Aristotle, into the writings of the New Testament and the Christian church fathers, and beyond. The term is *logos*.*

Logos is derived from a verb meaning "to speak" and refers first to the word or words that a speaker says. As in English, however, a term is easily stretched beyond its simple, literal meaning. As we can ask for the latest word about the economy, the Greek can ask for the *logos* about the economy, meaning something like "message" or "discourse." This meaning easily slides into the *thought* expressed in a discourse. Because such thought is typically backed up by reasons or has a rationale behind it, *logos* also comes to mean "rationale" or "argument." Arguments are composed of conclusions and the reasons offered for those conclusions. So, an argument has a typical pattern or structure to it, which is the job of *logic* to display. (Our term logic is derived from the Greek *logos*.) *Logos*, then, can also mean a structure or pattern, particularly if the pattern is a rational one.

---

*A lyre is an ancient Greek musical instrument similar to a small harp.

*Postmodern critics of the Western philosophic tradition often call it "logocentric," meaning that it privileges rationality and assumes that words—especially spoken discourse—can adequately mirror reality. See Jacques Derrida, p. 700.

You can see that *logos* is a very rich term, containing layers of related meanings: word, message, discourse, thought, rationale, argument, pattern, structure. When the word is used in Greek, it reverberates with all these associations. We have no precise equivalent in English, and for that reason we usually do not translate it.

As we have seen, Heraclitus claims that all things are in a process of continual change and that part of what makes them the things they are is a tension between opposite forces. This world of changes is not a chaos but is structured by a world-order that is divine in nature; in itself, therefore, it is good and beautiful. Unfortunately,

> the many do not understand such things.* (DK 22 B 17, *IEGP*, 94)
>
> Though the *logos* is as I have said, men always fail to comprehend it, both before they hear it and when they hear it for the first time. For though all things come into being in accordance with this *logos*, they seem like men without experience. (DK 22 B 1, *IEGP*, 94)

Now Heraclitus tells us that there is a *logos* by which "all things come into being." What else is this but the structure or pattern of the world-order that we have met before? But now the conception is deepened. The *logos* is not just accidentally what it is. There is a logic to it that can be seen to be reasonable and right. It is not understood, however, by "the many." As Socrates does later, Heraclitus contrasts the few who are wise, who listen to the *logos*, with the many who are foolish.

Why is it that the many do not understand the *logos*? Is it so strange and distant that only a few people ever have a chance to become acquainted with it? Not at all.

> Though they are in daily contact with the *logos* they are at variance with it, and what they meet appears alien to them. (DK 22 B 73, *IEGP*, 94)
>
> To those who are awake the world-order is one, common to all; but the sleeping turn aside each into a world of his own. (DK 22 B 89, *IEGP*, 95)

> We ought to follow what is common to all; but though the *logos* is common to all, the many live as though their thought were private to themselves. (DK 22 B 2, *IEGP*, 95)

All people are "in daily contact" with this *logos*. It is all around us, present in everything that happens. You can't do or say anything without being immersed in it. Yet we ignore it. We are like sleepers who live in private dreams rather than in awareness of this rational pattern of things that "is common to all." We each manufacture a little world of our own, distorted by our own interests, fears, and anxieties, which we take for reality.

In so doing, we miss the *logos* and become foolish rather than wise. What is it, after all, to be wise?

> Wisdom is one thing: to understand the thought which steers all things through all things. (DK 22 B 41, *IEGP*, 88)
>
> The one and only wisdom is willing and unwilling to be called Zeus. (DK 22 B 32, *IEGP*, 88)

To be wise is to understand the nature and structure of the world. To be wise is to see that all is and must be ever-changing, that strife and opposition are necessary and not evil, and that if appreciated apart from our narrowly construed interests, they are good and beautiful. To be wise is to grasp the *logos*, the "thought which steers all things."* To be wise is to participate in the perspective of Zeus.

Why is this **wisdom** both "willing and unwilling" to be called by the name of Zeus? We can assume it is willing because Zeus is the common name for the highest of the gods, for the divine; to have such wisdom makes one a participant in the divine. Acting according to the *logos* is manifesting in one's life the very principles that govern the universe. However, such wisdom refuses the name of Zeus as Homer pictures him: immoral, unworthy, and no better than one of the many who do not understand the *logos*. Heraclitus, then, agrees with Xenophanes' criticisms of traditional religion.

---

*His term "the many" usually applies to all the individual things of which the world is composed; here, of course, it means "most people."

*Compare Anaximander, p. 11. Heraclitus here identifies that which "steers all things" as a thought. The Stoics later develop this same theme. See p. 243.

Perhaps people are not to be too much blamed, however, for their lack of wisdom. For

Nature loves to hide. (DK 22 B 123, *IEGP*, 96)

and

The lord whose oracle is at Delphi neither speaks out nor conceals, but gives a sign. (DK 22 B 93, *IEGP*, 96)

Even though the *logos* is common to all, even though all our experience testifies to it, discerning this *logos* is difficult. It is rather like a riddle; the answer may be implicit, but it is still hard to make out. Solving the problem is like interpreting the ambiguous pronouncements of the famous oracle at Delphi, located north and west of Athens (see Map 1). People could go there and ask the oracle a question, as Croesus, king of the Lydians (see Map 1), once did. He wanted to know whether to go to war against the Persians. He was told that if he went to war a mighty empire would fall. Encouraged by this reply, he set forth, only to find the oracle's pronouncement validated by his own defeat.

How, then, is the riddle to be unraveled? How can we become wise, learning the secrets of the *logos*? This is a question that we have asked before. Xenophanes has told us that by "seeking" we can improve our opinions, but that is pretty uninformative.* Does Heraclitus advance our understanding? To some degree he does. Two fragments that seem to be in some tension with each other address this issue:

Those things of which there is sight, hearing, understanding, I esteem most. (DK 22 B 55, *IEGP*, 96)
Eyes and ears are bad witnesses to men if they have souls that do not understand their language. (DK 22 B 107, *IEGP*, 96)

We can come to understand the world-order, then, not by listening to poets, seers, or self-proclaimed wise men but by using our eyes and ears. Yet we must be careful, for the senses can deceive us, can be "bad witnesses." They must be used critically, and not everyone "understands their language." These few remarks do not, of course, take us very far. Later philosophers will fill in this picture.

Finally, Heraclitus draws from his view of the *logos* some significant conclusions for the way humans should live:

It is not good for men to get all they wish. (DK 22 B 110, *IEGP*, 97)
If happiness consisted in bodily pleasures we ought to call oxen happy who find vetch to eat. (DK 22 B 4, *IEGP*, 101)
It is hard to fight against impulse; for what it wants it buys at the expense of the soul. (DK 22 B 85, *IEGP*, 101)
Moderation is the greatest virtue, and wisdom is to speak the truth and to act according to nature, giving heed to it. (DK 22 B 112, *IEGP*, 101)

Why is it not good for men to get all they wish? If they did so, they would destroy the necessary tensions that make possible the very existence of both themselves and the things they want. They would overstep the bounds set by the *logos*, which allows the world to exist at all—a "many" unified by the "one." We must limit our desires, not for prudish or puritanical reasons, but because opposition is the very life of the world-order. Impulses, like Achilles' impulse to anger, are "hard to fight against." Why? Because indulging them at all strengthens them, and we cannot help indulging them to some degree. Indulging an impulse seems to diminish the resources of the soul to impose limits on that impulse. Such indulgence is bought "at the expense of the soul."*

That is why wisdom is difficult and why few achieve it. Most people, like cattle, seek to maximize their bodily pleasures. In doing so, they are "at variance" with the *logos*, which requires of every force that it be limited. That is why "moderation is the greatest virtue"—and why it is so rare.

Note that Heraclitus ties his ethics intimately to his vision of the nature of things. The *logos* within should reflect the *logos* without. Wisdom is "to speak the truth and to act according to nature." To speak the truth is to let one's words (one's *logos*) be responsive to the *logos* that is the world-order. To speak falsely is to be at variance with that *logos*. All one's actions should reflect that balance, the

---

*See p. 16.

*For a more recent semi-Heraclitean view of the need to be hard on oneself, see Nietzsche, p. 585.

moderation nature displays to all who understand its ways. In the plea for moderation, Heraclitus reflects the main moral tradition of the Greeks since Homer, but he sets it in a larger context and justifies it in terms of the very nature of the universe itself and its divine *logos*.

In his exaltation of the few over the many, Heraclitus also reflects Homeric values.

> One man is worth ten thousand to me, if only he be best. (DK 22 B 49, *IEGP*, 104)
>
> For the best men choose one thing above all the rest: everlasting fame among mortal men. But the many have glutted themselves like cattle. (DK 22 B 29, *IEGP*, 104)

The Homeric heroes seek their "everlasting fame" on the field of battle. Heraclitus, we feel, would seek it on the field of virtue.

In Heraclitus, then, we have a solution to the problem of the one and the many. We do live in one world, a *uni*-verse, despite the multitude of apparently different and often conflicting things we find in it. It is made one by the *logos*, the rational, divine, firelike pattern according to which things behave. Conflict does not destroy the unity of the world; unless it goes to extremes, such tension is a necessary condition of its very existence. And if we see and hear and think rightly, we can line up our own lives according to this same *logos*, live in a self-disciplined and moderate way, and participate in the divine wisdom.

---

1. What does Heraclitus mean when he says that all things are "in flux"? Give your own examples.
2. In what sense is the "world-order" fire? Why was it not made by any god?
3. Explain the saying "War is the father and king of all."
4. What is the *logos*?
5. How is it that we "fail to comprehend" the *logos*?
6. What is wisdom? Why is it "willing and unwilling" to be called Zeus?
7. Why is it not good for us to get all we wish? Why is it "hard to fight against impulse"? Why should we fight against it anyway?
8. Sum up Heraclitus' solution to the problem of the one and the many.

Parmenides: Only the One

Parmenides introduces the strangest thought so far. His view is hard for us to grasp. Once we see what he is saying, moreover, we find it hard to take seriously. So we need to make a special effort to understand. It helps to keep in mind that Parmenides' views arise in the course of the great pre-Socratic conversation. He constantly has in mind the views of his predecessors and contemporaries.

What makes the argument of Parmenides so alien to us is its conclusion; most people simply cannot believe it. The conclusion is that there is no "many"; only **"the One"** exists. We find this hard to believe because our experience is so obviously manifold. There is the desk, and here is the chair. They are two; the chair is not the desk and the desk is not the chair. So it seems. If Parmenides is to convince us otherwise, he has his work cut out for him. He is well aware of this situation and addresses the problem explicitly.

Parmenides was not an Ionian, as were Thales, Anaximander, Xenophanes, and Heraclitus. This fact is significant because, in a sense, geographical location is not intellectually neutral. Different places develop different traditions. Parmenides lived at the opposite edge of Greek civilization in what is now the southern part of Italy, where there were numerous Greek colonies. He came from a city called Elea (see Map 2), which, according to tradition, was well governed in part through Parmenides' efforts. Plato tells us that Parmenides once visited Athens in his old age and conversed with the young Socrates. If this is so, Parmenides must have been born about 515 B.C. and lived until at least the year 450 B.C.

Parmenides wrote a book, in verse, of which substantial parts have come down to us. In the prologue, he claims to have been driven by horse and chariot into the heavens and escorted into the presence of a goddess who spoke to him, saying,

> Welcome, youth, who come attended by immortal charioteers and mares which bear you on your journey to our dwelling. For it is no evil fate that has set you to travel on this road, far from the beaten paths of men, but right and justice. It is meet that you learn all things—both the unshakable heart of well-rounded truth and the opinions of mortals in which there is no true belief. (DK 28 B 1, *IEGP*, 108–109)

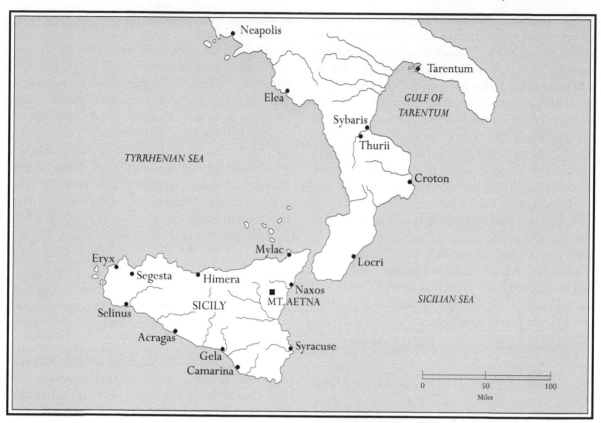

MAP 2 *Southern Italy and Sicily*

Such language might seem to be a throwback to the kinds of claims made by Hesiod.* Parmenides is telling us that the content of his poem has been revealed to him by divine powers. Is this philosophy? In fact, it is. The content of the revelation is an **argument,** and the goddess admonishes him to

> judge by reasoning the much-contested argument that I have spoken. (DK 28 B 7, *IEGP*, 111)

The claim that this argument was revealed to him by a goddess may reflect the fact that the argument came to him in an ecstatic or inspired state. Or it may just be a sign of how different from ordinary mortal thought the "well-rounded truth" really is. In either case, the claim that the poem is a

revelation is inessential. We are invited to *judge* it, not just to accept it; we are to judge it "by reasoning." This is the key feature of philosophy.*

Note that the goddess reveals to him two "ways": the truth and the "opinions of mortals," which deal not with truth but with **appearance.** His poem is in fact set up in two parts, "The Way of Truth" and "The Way of Opinion." Because it is the former that has been influential, we'll concentrate on it.

What, then, is this argument that yields Parmenides' strange conclusions? It begins with something Parmenides thought impossible to deny.

> Thinking and the thought that it is are the same; for you will not find thought apart from what is, in relation to which it is uttered. (DK 28 B 8, *IEGP*, 110)

---

*Look again at Hesiod's description of his inspiration by the Muses, p. 2.

*Socrates insists that when a statement is made, we must "examine" it. See pp. 95–97.

When you *think*, the content of your thinking is a *thought*. And every thought has the form: It *is* so and so. If you think, "This desk is brown," you are thinking what *is*, namely, the desk and its color. If you think "This desk is not brown," once more you are thinking of what *is*, namely, the desk. Suppose you say, "But I am thinking that it is *not brown*; so I am thinking of what is *not*." Parmenides will reply that "not brown" is just an unclear way of expressing the real thought, which is that the desk *is*, let us say, gray. If you are thinking of the desk, you are thinking of *it* with whatever color it has. Suppose you say, "But I am thinking of a unicorn, and there aren't any unicorns; so am I not thinking of what is not?" No, Parmenides might say, for what is a unicorn? A horse with a single horn, and horses and horns both *are*.* So once again we do not "find thought apart from what is." To think at all, he tells us, is to think that something *is*.

> For thought and being are the same. (DK 28 B 3, *IEGP*, 110)

They are "the same" in much the same way that for Heraclitus the way up and the way down are the same. If you have the one, you also have the other. The concept of "being" is just the concept of "what is," as opposed to "what is not." Whenever you think, you are thinking of what is. Thinking and being, then, are inseparable.

This is Parmenides' starting point. It seems rather abstract and without much content. How can the substantial conclusions we hinted at be derived from such premises? The way to do it is to derive a corollary of this point.

> It is necessary to speak and to think what is; for being is, but nothing is not. (DK 28 B 6, *IEGP*, 111)

You cannot think "nothing." Why not? Because nothing *is not*, and to think is (as we have seen) to think of what *is*. If you could think of nothing, it would (by the first premise) be *something*. But that

is contradictory. Nothing cannot be something! Nothing "is not."

That still does not seem very exciting. Yet from this point remarkable conclusions follow (or seem to follow; whether the argument is a sound one we will examine later).* In particular, all our beliefs about *the many* must be false. You believe, for example, that this book you are reading is one thing and the hand you are touching it with is another, so you believe that there are *many* things. If Parmenides' argument is correct, however, that belief is false. In reality there is no distinction between them. Parmenides describes ordinary mortals who do not grasp that fact in this way:

> Helplessness guides the wandering thought in their breasts; they are carried along deaf and blind alike, dazed, beasts without judgment, convinced that to be and not to be are the same and not the same, and that the road of all things is a backward-turning one. (DK 28 B 6, *IEGP*, 111)

This is harsh! The language he uses makes it clear that he has in mind not only common folks but also philosophers—Heraclitus in particular. It is Heraclitus who insists more rigorously than anyone else that "to be and not to be are the same" (to be straight, for instance, and not straight).† Whatever is, Heraclitus tells us, is only temporary; all is involved in the universal flux, coming into being and passing out of being. In that sense, "the road of all things" is indeed "a backward-turning one." You may be reminded of the phrase common in funeral services: "Ashes to ashes, dust to dust."

Parmenides tells us, however, that to think in this way is to be blind, deaf, helpless, dazed—no better than a beast. Things cannot be so. To say that something "comes into being" is to imply that it formerly *was not*. But this is something that you can neither imply, nor say, nor even think sensibly, for it involves the notion of **"not-being."** And we have already seen that not-being cannot be thought. It is inconceivable, for "thought and being are the same." So we are confused when we speak

---

*Actually, it is not entirely clear how Parmenides deals with thoughts that are apparently about nonexistent things. This is a puzzle that is not cleared up until the twentieth century by Bertrand Russell. See the brief treatment of his celebrated theory of definite descriptions on p. 619.

---

*See the critique by Democritus on pp. 29–30.

†See the remark on p. 17 about the path traced by the pen.

of something coming into being. We do not know what we are saying.

The same argument holds for passing away. The fundamental idea involved in passing away is that something leaves the realm of being (of what is) and moves into the realm of not-being (of what is not). A dog dies and *is no more*—or so it seems. But Parmenides argues that this is really inconceivable. Passing away would involve the notion of what is not, but *what is not* cannot be thought. If it cannot be thought, it cannot be. There is no "realm of not-being." There couldn't be.

Parmenides summarizes the argument:

> How could what is perish? How could it have come to be? For if it came into being, it is not; nor is it if ever it is going to be. Thus coming into being is extinguished, and destruction unknown. (DK 28 B 8, *IEGP*, 113)

But if there can be no coming into being and passing away, then there can be no Heraclitean flux. Indeed, the common experience that things do have beginnings and endings must be an illusion. **Change** is impossible!

> For never shall this prevail: that things that are not, are. But hold back your thought from this way of inquiry, nor let habit born of long experience force you to ply an aimless eye and droning ear along this road; but judge by reasoning the much-contested argument that I have spoken. (DK 28 B 7, *IEGP*, 111)

We have already examined the last part of this passage, but it is important to see what contrasts with the "reasoning" that Parmenides commends. We are urged not to let our thought be formed by "habit born of long experience." Parmenides acknowledges that experience is contrary to the conclusions he is urging on us. Of course the senses tell us that things change, that they begin and end, but Parmenides says not to rely on sensory experience. You must rely on reasoning alone. You must *go wherever the argument takes you,* even if it contradicts common sense and the persuasive evidence of the senses.*

In urging us to follow reason alone, Parmenides stands at the beginning of one of the major traditions in Western philosophy. Although we shouldn't take such "isms" too seriously, it is useful to give that tradition a name. It is called **rationalism.** Parmenides is rightly considered the first rationalist philosopher.

Notice the contrast to the Ionian nature philosophers. They all try to explain the nature of the things we observe; they start by assuming that the world is composed of many different things changing in many different ways, and it never occurs to them to question this assumption. Heraclitus, remember, says that he esteems most the things we can see and hear and understand.* Parmenides resolutely rejects this reliance on the senses.

He has not finished, however, deriving surprising conclusions from his principles. If we grant his premises, he tells us, we must also acknowledge that what exists

> is now, all at once, one and continuous. (DK 28 B 8, *IEGP*, 113)
>
> Nor is it divisible, since it is all alike; nor is there any more or less of it in one place which might prevent it from holding together, but all is full of what is. (DK 28 B 8, *IEGP*, 114)

What is must exist "all at once." This means that time itself must be unreal, an illusion. Why? Because the present can only be identified as the present by distinguishing it from the past (which is *no longer*) and from the future (which is *not yet*), and this shows that the notions of past and future both involve the unthinkable notion of "what is not." So "what is" must exist all at once in a continuous present. This thought is later exploited by St. Augustine in his notion of God.†

Moreover, *what is* must be indivisible; it cannot have parts. Why? Well, what could separate one thing from another? Only *what is not,* and what is

---

*We will see this theme repeated by Socrates; if it is true that as a young man Socrates conversed with Parmenides (as Plato tells us), it is likely that he learned this principle from him. For an example, see *Crito* 46b, p. 137.

---

*In the seventeenth and eighteenth centuries, such reliance on sensory data is called *empiricism* and is starkly contrasted to rationalism. For an example, see pp. 443–444.

†For Augustine, however, it is only God who enjoys this atemporal kind of eternity; time has a certain reality for Augustine—created and dependent, but not ultimate. See pp. 274–276.

not *cannot be*. You might be inclined to object at this point and say that one thing can be separated from another by some third thing. But the question repeats itself: What separates the first thing from the third? There can't be an infinite number of things between any two things, so at some point you will have to say that the only difference between them is that the one just *is not* the other. But, if Parmenides is right, that's impossible. So all is "full of what is."

It follows, of course, that there cannot be a vortex motion, as Anaximander thought, scattering stuff of different kinds to different places, because there cannot be things of different kinds. It is "all alike." There is not "any more or less of it in one place which might prevent it from holding together."* Why not? Because if there were "less" in some place, this could only be because it is mixed with some nonbeing. Because there is no nonbeing, there cannot be a **"many."** The problem of the one and the many should never have come up!

It also follows that being must be uncreated and imperishable, without beginning or end. If *what there is* had come into being, it must have come from not being—but this is impossible. To perish, it would have to pass away into nothingness—but nothingness is not. So being can neither begin nor end. "For never shall this prevail: that things that are not, are."

We can characterize *what is* in the following terms. It is one, eternal, indivisible, and unchanging. If experience tells you otherwise, Parmenides says, so much the worse for experience.

If you think about it for a moment, you can see that Parmenides has thrust to the fore one of the basic philosophical problems. It is called the problem of **appearance and reality.** Parmenides readily admits that the world *appears* to us to be many and to change continuously and that the things in it seem to move about. What he argues is that it is not so *in reality*. In reality, he holds, there is just the one.

Any convictions we have to the contrary are just "the opinions of mortals in which there is no true belief."

We are all familiar with things not really being what they appear to be. Sticks in water appear to be bent when they are not. Roads sometimes appear to be wet when there is no water on them, and so on. The distinction is one we can readily understand. What is radical and disturbing about Parmenides' position is that everything our senses acquaint us with is allocated to the appearance side of the dichotomy. Nowhere do we sense what really is. Can this be right? This problem puzzles many a successor to Parmenides—or at least *appears* to do so!

Because these views are so strange, so alien to the usual ways of thinking, it is worth noting the response of Parmenides' contemporaries and successors. Do they dismiss him as "that crazy Eleatic" who denies multiplicity and change? Do they think of him as a fool and charlatan? No, they take him very seriously. Plato, for example, always treats Parmenides with respect. Why? Because he, more successfully than anyone else up to his time, does what they are all trying to do: to follow reason wherever it leads. If his conclusions are uncongenial, that means only that his arguments must be examined carefully for any errors. Parmenides provides for the first time a coherent, connected argument—something you can really wrestle with. Succeeding Greek philosophers all try to come to terms with Parmenides in one way or another. Even though few accept his positive views, his influence is great, and his impact is still felt today.

---

1. What does Parmenides mean when he says that "thought and being are the same"?
2. What is the argument that there are not, in reality, *many* things?
3. If Parmenides is right, why must Heraclitus be wrong about all things being in flux?
4. Doesn't the testimony of our senses prove that there are many things? Why does Parmenides maintain that it does not?
5. How must reality (as opposed to appearance) be characterized?
6. In what sense is Parmenides a rationalist?

---

*Anaximenes, a nature philosopher we are not considering, holds that air, when compressed, becomes cloud, then water, then earth and stone. When more rarefied, it becomes fire. Parmenides argues that such an explanation for the many kinds of things we seem to experience is impossible, because such compression and rarefaction implicitly involve expelling or adding nonbeing.

Zeno: The Paradoxes of Common Sense

In response to Parmenides' strange argument, you may be tempted to slice an apple in two just to prove that there really are many things or wiggle your ears to show change actually happens. Of course, that won't do, because Parmenides has arguments to show that all this is merely appearance, not reality. Still, his conclusion is so at odds with common sense that we feel there must be something wrong with it.

But one of Parmenides' pupils, **Zeno**, claims to have arguments showing that common sense (and the natural science developing out of it) has its own problem: It generates logical contradictions. It is bad enough if a view conflicts with deeply held convictions, but it is even worse if those convictions turn out to be contradictory in themselves. So, Zeno holds, his arguments not only counter those who abuse his teacher, but also "pay them back with interest" (Plato, *Parmenides*, 128d).

Some of Zeno's arguments concern the many, but his most famous arguments concern change—in particular, the sort of change that we call "motion." Common sense assumes that motion is something real, but Zeno argues that these assumptions lead us into inconsistencies. Let us look at three of his arguments.

1. Suppose Achilles were to enter a race with a tortoise. Being honorable and generous, the great runner would offer the tortoise a head start. The tortoise would lumber laboriously along, and after a suitable interval Achilles would spring from the starting blocks. But surprise! He would be unable, despite his utmost efforts, to catch the tortoise. Why?

Consider this: when Achilles begins to run, the tortoise is already at some point down the race course; call it A. To catch him, Achilles must first reach point A. That seems obvious. By the time Achilles has reached A, however, the tortoise has moved on to some further point, B. That also seems obvious. So Achilles needs to race to point B. He does so. Of course, by the time Achilles has attained B, the tortoise is at C. Another effort, this time to get to C, and again the tortoise is beyond him—at D. You can see that no matter how long the race goes on, Achilles will not catch the tortoise. So much for all that training!

This looks like a perfectly fair deduction from commonsense principles. So common sense holds both that one runner can catch another (because we see it done) *and* that one runner cannot catch another (as the argument shows). This is self-contradictory.

2. Consider an arrow in flight. Common sense holds that the arrow moves. Where does it move? Once this question is asked, it looks as though there are just two possibilities. Either the arrow moves in the space where it is or it moves in some space where it is not—but neither is possible.

It obviously cannot move in a space it does not occupy, because it simply isn't there. Nor can it move in the space it occupies at any given moment, because at that moment it takes up the whole of that space, and there is no place left for it to move into. So the arrow cannot move at all. Once again, this seems a commonsense deduction; however, once again it is at odds with common sense itself, because nothing is more common than believing you can shoot an arrow at a target.

3. You no doubt believe that you can move from where you are now sitting to the door of the room. If you get a sudden yen for a pizza, you might just do it. Before you could get to the door, however, there is something else you would have to do first. You would have to get to the midpoint between where you are now and the door. That seems obvious—but consider: Before you could get to that point, there is something else you would have to do first. You would have to get to the midpoint between *that* point and where you are sitting. You can see how it goes. If you always have to get to one point before getting to another, you will not even be able to get out of your chair!

Once again we see common sense in conflict with itself. If our common belief in motion contains self-contradictions, it cannot possibly be true; therefore, it cannot describe reality. You can see why Zeno thought these arguments paid back Parmenides' opponents "with interest."

Let us pause a moment to reflect on what kind of argument Zeno is using here. Logicians call it a **reductio ad absurdum** argument, or a reduction to absurdity. It has a form like this. (Let's take the arrow case as an example.)

Assume the truth of a proposition.

1. The arrow can move.

Deduce consequences from that assumption.

2. a. It must move either where it is or where it is not.
   b. It can do neither.

Draw the conclusion.

3. The arrow cannot move.

Display the contradiction.

4. The arrow can move (by 1), and the arrow cannot move (by 3).

Draw the final conclusion.

5. Motion is impossible because assuming it yields a contradiction—in 4—and no contradiction can possibly be true.

Reductio arguments are **valid** arguments.* They are very powerful arguments. That is why Zeno's arguments are so disturbing, and that is why articles trying to resolve the **paradoxes** still appear today in philosophical and scientific journals.

These are serious paradoxes. Even if you cannot bring yourself to accept their conclusions, refuting Zeno's arguments requires us to reconsider the basic notions of space, time, and motion—a process still going on in contemporary physics. Furthermore, as an episode in the history of Western philosophy, Zeno's paradoxes present examples of rigorous argument that opponents had to imitate to refute—another push toward rationalism.

---

1. State Zeno's arguments against motion, and explain how they support Parmenides.
2. What is the pattern of a reductio ad absurdum argument?

---

*See the discussion of validity in the discussion of Aristotle's logic in Chapter 9 and the definition in the Glossary.

Atomism: The One and the Many Reconciled

Anaximander and other nature philosophers proceed on the assumption that the world is pretty much as it seems. We learn of it, as Heraclitus tells us, by sight, hearing, and understanding. We need only to set forth the elements of which it is made, its principles of organization, and why it changes. This might be difficult to do because the world is complex and human minds are limited, but there doesn't seem to be a shadow of suspicion that sight and hearing on the one hand (the senses) and understanding (reasoning) on the other hand might come into conflict. Yet that is precisely the outcome of Parmenidean logic. The world as revealed by our senses *cannot* be reality, and the force of that "cannot" is the force of reason itself. Parmenides has *proved* it. These arguments of Parmenides shake Ionian nature philosophy to its core.

Clearly, it is difficult simply to acquiesce in these results. It is not easy to say that our sensory convictions about the manyness of things, their changeableness, and their motion are all illusory. Several notable thinkers attempt to reconcile the arguments of Parmenides and his pupil Zeno with the testimony of the senses. Empedocles and Anaxagoras, in particular, struggle with these problems, but it is generally agreed that neither of them really resolves the issue. It is not until we come to the atomists that we find, in principle, a satisfactory solution.

Two figures are important in developing atomist thought: Leucippus and **Democritus.** About the former we know very little; two ancient authorities doubt even that he existed. Others, however, attribute to Leucippus the key idea that allows the Parmenidean argument to be met. About Democritus we know much more. He lived in Abdera, a city of Thrace in northern Greece (see Map 1), during the middle of the fifth century B.C. He wrote voluminously, perhaps as many as fifty-two books, of which well over two hundred fragments are preserved. He is also thoroughly discussed by later philosophers such as Aristotle, so we have a fairly complete notion of his teachings.

We need not try to sort out the separate contributions of Leucippus and Democritus. (We can't do so with certainty in any case.) They seem together to have developed the view known as **atomism,** to which we now turn.

THE KEY: AN AMBIGUITY

In a work titled *Of Generation and Corruption* (concerned with coming into being and passing away), Aristotle summarizes the Parmenidean arguments against these kinds of changes and then says,

> Leucippus, however, thought he had arguments which, while consistent with sense perception, would not destroy coming into being or passing away or the multiplicity of existing things. These he conceded to be appearances, while to those who upheld the "one" he conceded that there can be no motion without a void, that the void is not-being, and that not-being is no part of being; for what is, in the strict sense, is completely full. But there is not one such being but infinitely many, and they are invisible owing to the smallness of their bulk. They move in the void (for void exists) and, by coming together and separating, effect coming into being and passing away. (DK 67 A 7, *IEGP*, 196)

Notice that Aristotle does not say simply that Leucippus disagrees with Parmenides. To disagree with an opinion is easy—too easy. What is needed is a *reason* to think that other opinion is mistaken. Aristotle says that Leucippus has, or thinks he has, *arguments*. These arguments concede some things to the **monists** (the believers in the indivisible "one"), but they show that these concessions are not as damaging to common sense as the monists had thought. The acceptable parts of the monistic argument can be reconciled with sense perception, with beginning and ending, and with multiplicity. What are these arguments?

Surprisingly, a follower of Parmenides, Melissus, gives us a hint toward an adequate solution:

> If there were a many, they would have to be such as the one is. (DK 30 B 8, *IEGP*, 148)

Melissus does not accept that there is a many. He just tells us that *if* there were a many, each thing would have to have the characteristics Parmenides ascribes to the one. Each would have to be all-alike, indivisible, full, and eternal. What Leucippus does is to accept this principle and to say there are many such "ones." There are, in fact, an infinite number of them. Democritus was to call them "**atoms.**"

From all we have seen so far, however, this is mere assertion; we need an argument. It goes like this. We must grant to Parmenides that being and not-being are opposites, and of course not-being *is not*. It doesn't follow from these concessions, though, that there is no such thing as empty space. Space can be empty in precisely this sense: It contains no *things* or *bodies*. Nonetheless, space may have *being*. Empty space, which Democritus calls "**the void,**" is *not* the same as not-being. It only seems so if you do not distinguish *being* from *body*. Being a body or a thing may be just one *way* of being something. There may be others. Moreover, *what-does-not-contain-any-body* need not be the same as *what-is-not-at-all*.

Once that distinction is recognized, we can see that Parmenides' argument confuses the two. He argues that there can be only a "one" because if there were "many" they would have to be separated by *what is not*; and what is not *is not*. So there cannot be a many; what is must be all full and continuous. The atomists argue that there is an ambiguity here. Some of what is *can* be separated from other parts of what is—by the void. So there *can* be a many. The void does not lack being altogether. It only lacks the kind of being characteristic of *things*. Democritus also calls the void "no-thing"—not "nothing" (nothing at all), which he acknowledges *is not*. No-thing (the void) is a kind of being in which no body exists. He puts the point this way:

> No-thing exists just as much as thing. (DK 68 B 156, *IEGP*, 197)

A diagram may help to make this clear.

Parmenides

Being	Not-being
is	is not

Democritus

Being		Not-being
Thing	No-thing	Not-being
(Body)	(Void)	is not
is		

We noted earlier the struggle to develop a language adequate to describe reality. Language begins, as the language of children does, tied to the concrete. Only with great difficulty does it develop enough abstraction—enough distance, as it were, from concrete things—to allow for the necessary distinctions. The language of Parmenides simply lacks the concepts necessary to make these crucial distinctions. Leucippus and Democritus are in effect forging new linguistic tools for doing the job of describing the world. This is a real breakthrough: It makes possible a theory that does not deny the evidence of the senses and yet is rational (that is, does not lead to contradictions).

THE WORLD

Reality, then, consists of atoms and the void. Atoms are so tiny that they are mostly, perhaps entirely, invisible to us. Each of them is indivisible (the word "atom" comes from roots that mean "not cuttable").* Because they are indivisible, they are also indestructible; they exist eternally. Atoms are in constant motion, banging into each other and bouncing off, or maybe just vibrating like motes of dust in a stream of sunlight. Such motion is made possible by the existence of the void; the void provides a place into which a body can move. Their motion, moreover, is not something that must be imparted to them from outside. It is their nature to move.

These atoms are not all alike, although internally each is homogeneous, as Melissus argues it must be. Atoms differ from each other in three ways: in shape (including size), in arrangement, and in position. Aristotle gives us examples from the alphabet to illustrate these ways. *A* differs from *N* in shape, *AN* differs from *NA* in arrangement,

and *Z* differs from *N* in position. As the atoms move about, some of them hook into others, perhaps of the same kind, perhaps different. If enough get hitched together, they form bodies that are visible to us. In fact, such compounds or composites are what make up the world of our experience. Teacups and sparrow feathers differ from each other in the kinds of atoms that make them up and in the way the atoms are arranged. Light bodies differ from heavy bodies, for example, because the hooking together is looser and there is more void in them. Soft bodies differ from hard ones because the connections between the atoms are more flexible.

The atomists can explain coming into being and passing away as well. A thing comes into being when the atoms that make it up get hooked together in the appropriate ways. It passes away again when its parts disperse or fall apart.

These principles are obviously compatible with much of the older nature philosophy, and the atomists adopt or adapt a good bit of that tradition. The structure of the universe, for instance, is explained by a vortex motion or whirl that separates out the various kinds of compounds. Like tends to go to like, just as pebbles on a seashore tend to line up in rows according to their size. In this way, we get a picture of the world that is, in its broad features, not very different from that of Anaximander. There is, however, one crucial and very important difference.

Anaximander said that the Boundless "encompasses all things" and "steers all things." Xenophanes claims that the one god "sets all things in motion by the thought of his mind." Heraclitus identifies the principle of unity holding together the many changing things of the world as a divine *logos*, or thought. In contrast, Democritus' principles leave no room for this kind of intelligent direction to things. Remember: What exist are atoms and the void. Democritus boldly draws the conclusions from this premise. If we ask why the atoms combine to form a world or why they form some particular thing in this world, the only answer is that they *just do*. The only reason that can be given is that these atoms happened to be the sort, and to be in the vicinity of other atoms of a sort, to produce the kind of thing

---

*What we call "atoms" nowadays are not, as we well know, indivisible. We also know, since Einstein, that matter and energy are convertible. Nonetheless, physicists are still searching for the ultimate building blocks of nature. Perhaps they are what scientists call "quarks," "leptons," and "bosons." Whether that is so or not, however, the ancient atomists' assumption that there are such building blocks and that they are very tiny indeed is alive and well in the twenty-first century.

they did produce. There is no further reason, no intention or purpose behind it.*

> Nothing occurs at random, but everything occurs for a reason and by necessity. (DK 67 B 2, *IEGP*, 212)

By this, Democritus means that events don't just happen, but neither do they occur in order to reach some goal or because they were planned or designed to happen that way. If we are asked why so and so occurred, the proper answer will cite previously existing material causes. In one sense, this is the final destination of pre-Socratic speculation about nature. It begins by casting out the Homeric gods. It ends by casting out altogether intelligence and purpose from the governance of the world. Everything happens according to laws of motion that govern the wholly mechanical interactions of the atoms. In these happenings, mind has no place.

This account has—or seems to have—serious consequences for our view of human life. We normally think that we are pretty much in control of our lives, that we can make decisions to do one thing or another, go this way or that. It's up to us. If everything occurs "by necessity," however, as Democritus says, then each of these decisions is itself determined by mechanical laws that reach back to movements of atoms that long preceded our birth. It begins to look as if we are merely cogs in the gigantic machine of the world, no more really in control of our actions than the clouds are in control of (can choose) when it is going to rain. Supposing Democritus (or his modern followers) are right, what happens to our conviction that we have a free will? Democritus does not solve this problem, but he is the first to set out the parameters of the problem with some clarity.†

---

*Compare the nonpurposive character of evolutionary accounts of the origin of species with creationist accounts.

†Concerning free will, see the discussions by Epicurus (p. 238), the Stoics (p. 243), Augustine (pp. 281–282), Descartes (*Meditation IV*), Hume (pp. 453–455), Kant (pp. 482–483), Hegel (p. 513), Nietzsche (pp. 580–581), and de Beauvoir (pp. 687–688).

THE SOUL

If mind or intelligence cannot function as an explanation of the world-order, it is nonetheless obvious that it plays a role in human life. Democritus owes us an explanation of human intelligence that is compatible with his basic principles. His speculations are interesting and suggestive, though still quite crude. This problem is one we cannot claim to have solved completely even in our own day.

Atomistic accounts of **soul** and mind must, of course, be compatible with a general materialist view of reality: What exist are atoms and the void. According to Democritus, the soul is composed of exceedingly fine and spherical atoms; in this way, soul interpenetrates the whole of the body. Democritus holds that

> spherical atoms move because it is their nature never to be still, and that as they move they draw the whole body along with them, and set it in motion. (DK 68 A 104, *IEGP*, 222)

Soul-atoms are in this sense akin to fire-atoms, which are also small, spherical, and capable of penetrating solid bodies and (as Heraclitus has observed) are strikingly good examples of spontaneous motion. The soul or principle of life is, like everything else, *material*.

Living things, of course, have certain capacities that nonliving things do not: They experience sensations (tastes, smells, sights, sounds, pains). Some, at least, are capable of thought, and humans seem to have a capacity to know. Can Democritus explain these capacities using only atoms and the void?

Think first about sensations. Taste seems easy enough to explain. Sweet and sour, salty and bitter are just the results of differently shaped atoms in contact with the tongue. The sweet, Democritus says, consists of atoms that are "round and of a good size," the sour of "bulky, jagged, and many-angled" atoms, and so on (DK 68 A 129, *IEGP*, 200). These speculations are not grounded in anything like modern experimental method, but the kind of explanation is surely familiar to those who know something of modern chemistry.

Smells are explained along analogous lines, and sounds, too, are not difficult; Democritus explains them in terms of air being "broken up into bodies of like shape . . . rolled along with the fragments of the voice."[3] Vision is hardest to explain in terms of an atomistic view. Unlike touch, taste, and even hearing, it is a "distance receptor." With sight, it is as though we were able to reach out to the surfaces of things at some distance from us without any material means of doing so. In this respect, the eye seems quite different from the hand or the tongue.

Democritus, however, holds that sight is not really different. Like the other senses, it works by contact with its objects, only in this case the contact is more indirect than usual. The bodies made up of combined atoms are constantly giving off "images" of themselves, he tells us. These images are themselves material, composed of exceptionally fine atoms. These "effluences" strike the eye and stamp their shape in the soft and moist matter of the eye, whereupon it is registered in the smooth and round atoms of soul present throughout the body.

This kind of explanation is regarded by most of his Greek successors as very strange. Aristotle even calls it a great absurdity. It may not strike us as absurd. Indeed, it seems somewhere near the truth.

It does have a paradoxical consequence, though, which Democritus recognizes and is willing to accept. It means that our senses *do not give us direct and certain knowledge of the world.* Our experience of vision is the outcome of a complex set of interactions between the object seen, the intervening medium, and our sensory apparatus. Our experience when we look at a distant mountain is not a simple function of the characteristics of the mountain. That experience depends also on whether the air is clear or foggy, clean or polluted. It depends on whether it is dawn, dusk, or noon. Moreover, what we experience depends (we know now) on what kinds and proportions of rods and cones we have in our eyes, on complex sending mechanisms in the optic nerve, and the condition of the visual center in the brain.

Democritus cannot express his point in these contemporary terms, of course, but they underscore his point. Similar explanations also apply to the other senses. It was recognized in ancient times that honey, for example, can taste sweet to a healthy person and bitter to a sick one. Clearly, the difference depends on the state of the receptor organs. What is the character of the honey itself? Is it both sweet and bitter? That seems impossible. Democritus draws the conclusion that it is neither. Sweetness and bitterness, hot and cold, red and blue exist only in us, not in nature.

> Sweet exists by convention, bitter by convention, color by convention; but in reality atoms and the void alone exist. (DK 68 B 9, *IEGP*, 202)

To say that something exists by **convention** is to say that its existence depends on us.* In nature alone, it is not to be found. If our sense experience is conventional in this sense, then we cannot rely on it to tell us what the world is really like. In a way, Parmenides was right after all!†

> It is necessary to realize that by this principle man is cut off from the real. (DK 68 B 6, *IEGP*, 203)

We are "cut off from the real" because whatever impact the real has on us is in part a product of our own condition. This is true not only of the sick person but also of the well one. The sweetness of the honey to the well person depends on sensory receptors just as much as the bitterness to the sick one. Neither has a direct, unmediated avenue to what honey really is.

Later philosophers exploit these considerations in skeptical directions, doubting that we can have any reliable knowledge of the world at all. For Democritus, however, they do not lead to utter skepticism:

> There are two forms of knowledge: one legitimate, one bastard. To the bastard sort belong all the following: sight, hearing, smell, taste, touch. The legitimate is quite distinct from this. When the bastard form cannot see more minutely, nor hear nor smell nor taste nor perceive through the touch, then another, finer form must be employed. (DK 68 B 11, *IEGP*, 203–204)

---

*For a fuller discussion of the ancient Greek distinction between nature and convention, see "*Physis* and *Nomos*" in Chapter 4.

†See pp. 25–26.

He seems to be telling us that the senses can take us only so far, because they have a "bastard" parentage (that is, they are the products of both the objects perceived and the perceiving organs). But there is "another, finer" and "legitimate" form of knowledge available to the soul. This knowledge is no doubt based on reasoning. Its product is the knowledge that what really exist are atoms and the void. At this point, we would like reasoning itself to be explained in terms of the atomistic view, as the senses have been explained. Democritus offers no such explanation. This is not surprising; indeed, many think that a satisfactory account of reasoning on these materialistic principles is only now, after the invention of the computer, beginning to be constructed—but that, of course, is reaching far ahead of our story.*

HOW TO LIVE

Democritus wrote extensively on the question of the best life for a human being, but only fragments remain. Many of them are memorable, however, and we simply list without comment a number of his most lively aphorisms.

- Disease occurs in a household, or in a life, just as it does in a body. (DK 68 B 288, *IEGP*, 221)
- Medicine cures the diseases of the body; wisdom, on the other hand, relieves the soul of its sufferings. (DK 68 B 31, *IEGP*, 222)
- The needy animal knows how much it needs; but the needy man does not. (DK 68 B 198, *IEGP*, 223)
- It is hard to fight with desire; but to overcome it is the mark of a rational man. (DK 68 B 236, *IEGP*, 225)
- Moderation increases enjoyment, and makes pleasure even greater. (DK 68 B 211, *IEGP*, 223)
- It is childish, not manly, to have immoderate desires. (DK 68 B 70, *IEGP*, 225)
- The good things of life are produced by learning with hard work; the bad are reaped of their own accord, without hard work. (DK 68 B 182, *IEGP*, 226)

- The brave man is he who overcomes not only his enemies but his pleasures. There are some men who are masters of cities but slaves to women. (DK 68 B 214, *IEGP*, 228)
- In cattle excellence is displayed in strength of body; but in men it lies in strength of character. (DK 68 B 57, *IEGP*, 230)
- I would rather discover a single cause than become king of the Persians. (DK 68 B 118, *IEGP*, 229)

Many of the themes expressed here should be familiar by now. We will see them worked out more systematically in later Greek philosophy, particularly by Plato and Aristotle.

---

1. State as clearly as you can the argument by which the atomists defeat Parmenides and reconcile the one and the many.
2. How would atomists explain the difference between, say, chalk and cheese? How would they explain the making of cheese from milk?
3. On atomistic principles, what happens to the notion of a cosmic intelligence?
4. What is the atomist's account of soul?
5. What does it mean to say that sweet and bitter exist "by convention"?
6. Why does Democritus say that our senses cut us off from the real? Why are we not absolutely cut off?
7. What problem does atomism pose for the idea that we have a free will?

FOR FURTHER THOUGHT

1. Twentieth-century philosopher of science Karl Popper quotes Xenophanes approvingly and asserts that the development of thought we can trace in the pre-Socratics exemplifies perfectly the basic structure of scientific thinking. He calls it the "rational critical" method and says it works through a sequence of bold conjectures and incisive refutations. Can you identify such moves in the thinking of the philosophers we have studied so far? (See Popper's *Conjectures and Refutations: The Growth of Scientific Knowledge* [New York: Harper & Row, 1968].)

---

*But take a look at "The Matter of Minds" in Chapter 30, pp. 733–738.

2. What sort of defense could you mount against the attacks on common sense put forth by rationalists such as Parmenides and Zeno? Is there something you could do to show that the world of our sense experience is, after all, the real world? Why or why not?

3. Here is an argument to prove that a ham sandwich is better than perfect happiness: (1) A ham sandwich is better than nothing; (2) nothing is better than perfect happiness; therefore (3) a ham sandwich is better than perfect happiness. Will untangling this fallacy throw light on the atomists' critique of Parmenides?

4. If you know something about the physiology of the central nervous system, try to determine whether modern accounts of that system also "cut us off from the real."

KEY WORDS

Thales
Anaximander
the Boundless
vortex motion
Xenophanes
one god
seeking
truth
epistemology
Heraclitus
opposition
flux
logos
wisdom
Parmenides
the One
argument
appearance
not-being
change
rationalism
many
appearance/reality
Zeno
reductio ad absurdum
valid
paradox
Democritus
atomism
monists
atoms and the void
soul
convention

NOTES

1. Quotations from the pre-Socratic philosophers are in the translation by John Manley Robinson, *An Introduction to Early Greek Philosophy* (Boston: Houghton Mifflin, 1968). They are cited by the standard Diels/Kranz number, followed by *IEGP* and the page number in Robinson.

2. Biblical quotations in this text are taken from the Revised Standard Version, 1946/1971, National Council of Churches.

3. Quoted in G. S. Kirk and J. E. Raven, *The Presocratic Philosophers* (Cambridge: Cambridge University Press, 1960), 423.

CHAPTER

3

APPEARANCE AND REALITY IN ANCIENT INDIA

In Chapters 1 and 2, we examined how early Greek philosophy grew out of ancient myths and traditions. From these beginnings the conversation that is Western philosophy stretches down to the present. That tradition will remain our central focus in this book, but it is not the only great philosophical conversation. Interestingly, two other great philosophical traditions—the Indian and the Chinese—emerged at roughly the same time as Greek philosophy. As in Greece, these philosophical traditions grew out of the distinctive cultures of their native lands. Despite these very different starting points, all three traditions share certain ideas and concerns. Exploring the commonalities and differences between them illuminates all three traditions.

With that in mind, we turn now to some of the oldest philosophical traditions in India. Rather than attempt a comprehensive survey of the many schools of thought in ancient India, we will explore just a few, focusing on the themes of *the one and the many* and *appearance and reality*, along with the question of the *nature of the self*.

The Vedas and the Upaniṣads

Indian philosophy, like Greek philosophy, developed out of responses to mythical explanations of the origin and nature of the universe. Whereas we looked to the poets Hesiod and Homer to recount Greek myths, we find Indian myths recorded in an ancient set of religious hymns known as the **Vedas.** Composed during the second millennium B.C., the Vedas laid the foundation for Indian religion and philosophy.

Because the Vedic hymns were composed by so many authors over so many centuries, they offer many different accounts of the gods and the creation of the universe. The earliest hymns display a sort of nature worship. Somewhat later hymns introduce a panoply of gods and goddesses, including the mighty sky gods Varuṇa and Mitra; sun gods Sūrya and Savitṛ; Viṣṇu; the infinite and ineffable Aditi; the fire god Agni; Soma, god of inspiration; the mighty rain god Indra, and many more. At some times Varuṇa seems chief among them, giving way in later hymns to Indra, who later makes way for Prajāpati, lord of all creatures. These gods do not displace each other as part of a continuous narrative, as the Greek Zeus overthrows his father Kronos in Hesiod's telling. Rather, the hymns simply begin treating different gods as supreme, leaving others behind as Indian culture changes and develops. Later still, the hymns come to regard all these gods merely as aspects of a single deity. The *Ṛg Veda* (Rig Veda), says,

> They call it Indra, Mitra, Varuṇa, Fire (Agni); or it is the heavenly Sun-bird. That which is One . . . the seers speak of in various terms; they call it Fire, Yama, Matariśvan. (*Ṛg Veda* I.164.46)[1]

Eventually, this tentative monotheism broadens into a monistic view of the universe itself. Not only were the various gods really just aspects of a single supreme deity, but so was everything else: everything was but a manifestation of god; god was everything. This is an idea that appears in many traditions around the world.* In the Indian tradition, this all-encompassing deity eventually comes to be called **Brahman.**

Beginning in the first millennium B.C., other kinds of texts were composed to accompany the Vedas. The **Brāhmaṇas** set out the details of priestly rituals designed to influence worldly affairs. The **Upaniṣads** (Upanishads) contain philosophical reflections on the contents of the Vedas. Composed sometime around the seventh or sixth century B.C., the early Upaniṣads are "the mental background of the whole of the subsequent thought of the country."[2] In the Upaniṣads, we see early Indian thinkers grappling with many of the same philosophical problems that perplexed the earliest Greek thinkers: What is the world, and where does it come from? What are we, and how do we relate to the world? Unlike the Greek philosophers, however, the anonymous authors of the Upaniṣads did not reject the older myths, which by this time contained sophisticated ideas about the nature of reality. Instead, they built on those ideas and worked to fashion them into a rationally coherent doctrine,

expressed sometimes in verse, sometimes through direct explanation, and sometimes through stories and legends. Unlike Greek philosophy, then, Indian philosophy arises not from a rejection of myth but from an attempt to extend, explain, and rationalize it.

We will concentrate on just one key idea that crystallizes in the Upaniṣads: the idea of the self— *ātman,* as it is called in Sanskrit, the language in which the Vedas and the Upaniṣads were written. The *Chāndogya Upaniṣad* works out the nature of the self through a story in which the god Indra and the demon Virocana set out to learn about the self. They offer themselves as students to the god Prajāpati, who makes them wait thirty-two years before speaking to them. "Why have you lived here?" he asks. "What do you want?"

> They replied: "Sir, people report these words of yours: 'The self (*ātman*) that is free from evils, free from old age and death, free from sorrow, free from hunger and thirst; the self whose desires and intentions are real—that is the self that you should try to discover, that is the self that you should seek to perceive. When someone discovers that self and perceives it, he obtains all the worlds, and all his desires are fulfilled.'"
>
> "So, you have lived here seeking that self." Prajāpati then told them: "This person that one sees here in the eye—that is the self (*ātman*); that is the immortal; that is the one free from fear; that is *brahman*." (*Chāndogya Upaniṣad* 8.7.3–4)[3]

Indra and Virocana initially accept this explanation, that their self is their body. They leave satisfied, and Prajāpati remarks, "There they go, without learning about the self (*ātman*), without discovering the self!"

Virocana returns to the demons, announcing that the self is the body and that each person should care only for the body.

Indra, however, realizes his mistake. The body cannot be the true self, he reasons, because it is not "free from evils, free from old age and death." So he returns to Prajāpati, who makes him wait another thirty-two years before explaining that the true self is the self one encounters in a dream. Initially satisfied, Indra leaves again, only to realize that this self, too, can suffer sorrow and unpleasantness.

---

*In the West, the Stoics would adopt this view. See p. 243. See also the emanation theory of Plotinus (pp. 270–271).

After returning again and waiting another thirty-two years, Indra hears that the self is one who slumbers in a deep, dreamless sleep. Once again, he leaves satisfied, only to recognize his mistake later. In dreamless slumber, the self cannot recognize itself as a self; it is not what he seeks. Once more Indra returns to Prajāpati, who mercifully makes him wait only five more years before saying,

> This body . . . is mortal; it is in the grip of death. So, it is the abode of this immortal and non-bodily self. One who has a body is in the grip of joy and sorrow, and there is no freedom from joy and sorrow for one who has a body. Joy and sorrow, however, do not affect one who has no body. . . .
>
> Now, when this sight here gazes into space, that is the seeing person, the faculty of sight enables one to see. The one who is aware: "Let me smell this"—that is the self; the faculty of smell enables him to smell. The one who is aware: "Let me say this"—that is the self; the faculty of speech enables him to speak. The one who is aware: "Let me listen to this"—that is the self; the faculty of hearing enables him to hear. The one who is aware: "Let me think about this"—that is the self; the mind is his divine faculty of sight. This very self rejoices as it perceives with his mind, with that divine sight, these objects of desire found in the world of *brahman*. (*Chāndogya Upaniṣad* 8.12.1–5)

The self, then, is something immaterial and eternal that sees, smells, speaks, hears, and thinks on through the faculties of sight, smell, speech, hearing, and thought.

We cannot perceive the self directly, however. In the *Bṛhadāraṇyaka Upaniṣad*, the wise man Yājñavalkya discusses *ātman* with his wife Maitreyī, saying,

> By what means can one perceive him by means of whom one perceives this whole world?
>
> About this self (*ātman*), one can only say, "not ———, not ———." He is ungraspable, for he cannot be grasped. He is undecaying, for he is not subject to decay. He has nothing sticking to him, for he does not stick to anything. He is not bound; yet he neither trembles in fear nor suffers injury. (*Bṛhadāraṇyaka Upaniṣad* 4.5.15)

Just as your eye sees but cannot see itself, the self cannot perceive itself because it is the thing that does the perceiving. So we cannot say that it has any particular characteristics. We can, however, say what it is *not*—namely, it is not bodily or mortal or subject to fear or injury. It is beyond all of that.

The Upaniṣads introduce two other intriguing ideas about the self. The first is that after the death of the body, the self is reincarnated or reborn in a new body.* The god Kṛṣṇa (Krishna) expresses this idea quite dramatically in a later epic poem, the *Bhagavad Gītā*. Kṛṣṇa says,

> Just as a man casting off worn-out clothes takes up others that are new, so the embodied self, casting off its worn-out bodies, goes to other, new ones. (*Bhagavad Gītā* 2.22)
>
> Death is inevitable for those who are born; for those who are dead birth is just as certain. (*Bhagavad Gītā* 2.27)[4]

This cycle of birth, death, and **rebirth** is known as *saṃsāra*. With each turn of the wheel of *saṃsāra*, people leave their old bodies behind to be reborn into new ones. Furthermore, those who have lived good lives are reborn into good circumstances, whereas those who did not are reborn into bad circumstances—or even as lower animals. According to the *Chāndogya Upaniṣad*,

> Now, people whose behavior here is pleasant can expect to enter a pleasant womb [after death], like that of a woman of the Brahmin [priestly class], the Kṣatriya [warrior class], or the Vaiśya [trader and farmer] class. But people of foul behavior can expect to enter a foul womb, like that of a dog, a pig, or an outcaste woman. (*Chāndogya Upaniṣad* 5.10.7)

The idea that one's actions in this life can affect the circumstances of one's next life is part of the doctrine of **karma.** According to this doctrine, it is built into the very structure of the universe that every good action leads to good consequences for the actor, and every bad action leads to bad consequences for the actor. So, if you do something good for someone else, something good will one day happen to you in return. Some parts of the Indian tradition regard *karma* as the dispensation of the gods, while for others, *karma* is a law of nature in something like the way the law of gravity is a law of nature. (Note, though, that just as gravity

---

*Some Western thinkers, such as Pythagoras, endorsed this idea, too.

is but one cause that determines how things move, *karma* is only one cause that determines what happens to a person.) Crucially, the idea is not that good people *tend* to live good lives and bad people *tend* to suffer misfortune, but that performing each good deed *causes* good fortune and each bad deed *causes* misfortune for the one who performs it.

While the ideas of rebirth and *karma* are widely accepted throughout ancient India, another important Upaniṣadic idea about the self is endorsed only by some traditions and schools of thought. This is the idea that *ātman* is identical to Brahman, the supreme deity that comprises the whole world. As a famous passage puts it,

> This earth is the honey of all beings, and all beings are the honey of this earth. The radiant and immortal person in the earth and, in the case of the body (*ātman*), the radiant and immortal person residing in the physical body—they are both one's self (*ātman*). It is the immortal; it is *brahman*; it is the Whole. (*Bṛhadāraṇyaka Upaniṣad* 2.5.1)

Much as the various gods of the Vedas come to be seen merely as different aspects of a supreme deity, so the immaterial core of each person's being comes, in the Upaniṣads, to be seen merely an aspect of that same deity. In many ways, then, the appearance of many turns out to be an illusion; there is only the One.*

---

1. What is the relationship between the Upaniṣads and the Vedas?
2. What is *ātman*, according to the Upaniṣads?
3. What is *saṃsāra*? What is *karma*? How are the two connected?
4. In what sense is everything one in the Upaniṣads?

The Buddha

Sometime in the fifth century B.C., after the earliest Upaniṣads had already been written, a boy is born to a wealthy aristocratic family in northern India. His parents name him Siddhārtha Gautama. Siddhārtha grows up in the sheltering comforts of his father's palace. When he finally leaves its walls as a teenager, he discovers all the vicissitudes of life that his parents had concealed from him: old age, infirmity, disease, poverty, hunger, death—in a word, suffering. Shocked by what he sees, Siddhārtha eventually renounces his wealth and position to become a traveling ascetic. After several arduous years of the ascetic life, Siddhārtha seats himself beneath a tree and resolves to remain there until he has discerned the truth about how to live. According to legend, he remains there in meditation for forty-nine nights before achieving enlightenment by seeing the world for what it really is. Thereafter, he is known as the **Buddha,** which means "Awakened One." The views he developed during this time form the foundation of Buddhist philosophy. In time, a non-Vedic religion grew up around them, which we call Buddhism.

"All that is subject to arising is subject to cessation."
—THE BUDDHA

---

*Compare the views of Parmenides (p. 20).

THE FOUR NOBLE TRUTHS AND THE NOBLE EIGHTFOLD PATH

So what did the Buddha discover under that tree? As he eventually explained to his followers, he came to understand four fundamental ideas, which are called the **four Noble Truths.** They are as follows:

1. There is suffering (*duḥkha*).*
2. There is the origination of suffering.
3. There is the cessation of suffering.
4. There is a path to the cessation of suffering.

These claims form the basis of Buddhist philosophy, which became one of several early Indian philosophies to reject the authority of the Vedas and the Upaniṣads. If we can understand what the Buddha means by these four claims, we are well on our way to understanding the basics of Buddhist thought.

The first step to understanding the four Noble Truths is to understand what the Buddha means by "**suffering.**" He is not referring only to the things that shocked him when he ventured out of the palace—death, disease, and physical pain—though these are certainly forms of suffering. He also means to capture despair, frustration, fear, anxiety, lack of control, and a host of other ills. While we would not normally classify all these things as "suffering," they are all captured by the word *duḥkha*.

The observation that the world contains suffering would hardly seem like a fundamental insight, except perhaps to someone as sheltered as young Siddhārtha. But what the Buddha means is not simply that suffering occurs from time to time; he means that "all is suffering" or "everything suffers."

*Strictly speaking, the Buddha didn't use the Sanskrit word "*duḥkha*." The Buddha spoke a different language, called Pāli, and Buddhist philosophy was mostly written in Pāli for many centuries after his death. Much of the key terminology for Buddhist philosophy was therefore developed in Pali, but the terms tend to be very similar in sound and meaning. The Pāli equivalent of *duḥkha*, for instance, is *dukkha*, and the Pāli equivalent of *karma* is *kamma*. Because some of the Sanskrit terminology, such as *karma* and *nirvāṇa*, is more familiar to Western readers than their Pāli equivalents, we use the somewhat anachronistic Sanskrit terminology throughout this chapter.

Suffering, he claims, is a pervasive and fundamental feature of life. This may seem to go too far in the other direction. If the idea that suffering occurs seems trivial, the idea that "all is suffering" might seem obviously false. Life certainly has its bleak moments, but it also has moments of joy, of pleasure, of pride, and of satisfaction. Do even *those* moments involve suffering? Yes, says the Buddha, for even when we get what we want, we are constantly at risk of losing it. This threat looms over us, causing anxiety and concern. Furthermore, even for the most powerful among us, *whether* we get what we want—and how long we keep it— is never entirely under our control. All our plans remain forever hostage to fortune, which is a constant source of unease.

The Buddha's message is not as pessimistic as the first Noble Truth may make it seem. The second Noble Truth says that suffering has a cause; the third that it has an end; and the fourth that its end has a cause. These three truths point us down a path to the cessation of suffering. If we can understand the *cause* of suffering, we can discern the cause of its cessation. And if we can bring about that cause, we can bring suffering to an end.

So what is the cause of suffering, according to the Buddha? At a superficial level, the cause of suffering is craving or attachment. **Attachment** includes strong desires, including both desires for something and desires to avoid something. It is by pursuing what we desire and striving to avoid what we hate that we bring suffering on ourselves. But the Buddha also offers a deeper analysis of the cause of suffering: attachment itself is caused by delusion, by a false understanding of the way the world is. It is because we misunderstand the world that we feel greed and hatred.

With this in mind, the Buddha offers a path to the cessation of suffering, called the **Noble Eightfold Path.** This path, which lies at the foundation of the Buddha's ethical teachings, consists of the following:

1. Right view
2. Right intention
3. Right speech
4. Right conduct

5. Right livelihood
6. Right effort
7. Right mindfulness
8. Right concentration

It is worth noting that the Buddha lists "right view" first. While all eight aspects of the path are intertwined, such that we cannot really have one without the others, having the **right view**—that is, having the correct understanding of reality—plays a central role in achieving the others. This is because we will not have the right intentions, right speech, right conduct, and so on unless we dispel the delusions that cloud our understanding.

Before we consider exactly what those delusions are, let us say something about some of the other parts of the Eightfold Path. The ultimate goal of Buddhist ethics is the cessation of suffering, wherever it occurs. In this spirit, the Buddha encourages his followers to develop the **Four Divine Abidings:** lovingkindness, compassion, joy, and equanimity. **Lovingkindness** consists in wishing for others to be happy. **Compassion** consists in wishing for others to be free from suffering. **Joy,** in this context, involves being happy about others' happiness. **Equanimity** involves a calm, even-handed assessment of things as they are, without attachment or prejudice. Together with prohibitions of the kind found in most religious and philosophical traditions around the world, such as prohibitions on killing, theft, and lying, the cultivation of the Four Divine Abidings offers a path to right speech, right conduct, and so on. The Buddha places "right intention" before these other things, however, because it is one's intentions, more than anything else, that determine the quality of one's actions.

While actions performed from these noble intentions are clearly directed at easing suffering, the complete cessation of suffering requires something more. Even though he rejects the authority of the Vedas, the Buddha accepts the traditional doctrines of karma and rebirth. Given that all life involves suffering, the only way to escape suffering once and for all is to escape *saṃsāra* entirely. The Buddha claims that those who follow the Noble Eightfold Path can achieve a kind of liberation from *saṃsāra*

he calls *nirvāṇa*. The first stage of *nirvāṇa* occurs in this life, upon attaining enlightenment. In this state, an enlightened person still experiences many of the things that unenlightened people experience, including pleasant and unpleasant sensations, health and sickness, old age, infirmity, and ultimately death. But unlike the unenlightened person, the enlightened person does not respond to such experiences with strong desires or aversions.

Upon the death of the body, the enlightened person achieves the second, higher stage of *nirvāṇa*—**nirvāṇa without remainder.** The Buddha notoriously refuses to explain exactly what this involves. Instead, he explains *nirvāṇa* without remainder by invoking the common Buddhist metaphor of the self as a flame:

> The fire burned in dependence on its fuel of grass and sticks. When that is used up, if it does not get any more fuel, being without fuel, it is reckoned as extinguished. So too [after death, the enlightened being] has abandoned that material form by which one describing [the enlightened being] might describe him. . . . [He] is liberated . . . he is profound, immeasurable, hard to fathom like the ocean. (*MN* i.487)[5]

On the one hand, the comparison to a fire that has been extinguished suggests that the enlightened person simply ceases to exist after death. On the other hand, the claim that in *nirvāṇa* without remainder a person is "profound, immeasurable, hard to fathom like the ocean" suggests that the enlightened person does exist in some sense. How can something that does not exist at all be "hard to fathom like the ocean"? But when pressed for details, the Buddha rejects both the suggestion that the "liberated" person exists and the suggestion that he or she does not exist. For good measure, he also rejects the idea that the enlightened person neither exists nor doesn't exist and the suggestion that he or she both exists and does not exist, saying,

> "He reappears" does not apply; "he does not reappear" does not apply; "he both reappears and does not reappear" does not apply; "he neither reappears nor does not reappear" does not apply. (*MN* i.487)

It is hard to know what to make of these claims, and Buddhists have debated them ever since. We can at least say, though, that *nirvāṇa* without remainder involves an escape from *saṃsāra* and therefore the end of suffering.

---

1. What is suffering (*duḥkha*)? What do the four Noble Truths tell us about suffering?
2. What is the Noble Eightfold Path? Why is "right view" listed first?
3. What are the Four Divine Abidings and how do they relate to the ultimate goal of Buddhist ethics?
4. What is *nirvāṇa*? How does it compare to views of the afterlife in Western religions?

RIGHT VIEW

The first step toward *nirvāṇa*, we have seen, is having the right understanding of the world—the right view. But what view is that? What are the misunderstandings that condemn us to suffering and rebirth? Perhaps the most important delusion is the belief that objects we see around us are real, enduring entities. Although we seem to see people, animals, trees, stones, and so forth, all that really exists, according to the Buddha, are "heaps" or **aggregates** of momentary phenomena, which the Buddha called **skandhas.** Buddhists analyze reality into five kinds of skandhas: material form (or matter or body), affective sensations, perceptions, mental activity (or habitual mental tendencies), and consciousness. In early Buddhist thought, these skandhas are understood as something like momentary particles. Each form-*skandha* is something like an atom, the smallest possible particle of matter, though unlike the atoms of pre-Socratic Greek thought, each form-*skandha* comes into and blinks out of existence in a single moment.* The other types of skandhas are momentary mental phenomena, such as a particular momentary feeling of pain

or a perception of an object at a particular moment. A human being is nothing but a collection of these different kinds of skandhas.

The analysis of human beings into *skandhas* has profound implications in Buddhist thought. The most important is that it means the Upaniṣads (and perhaps common sense, as well) have foisted on us a deep misunderstanding of the nature of the self. Whereas the Upaniṣads identify the self with an enduring object, *ātman*, the Buddha advances the doctrine of **anātman,** which means "non-self." There is nothing, the Buddha asserts, that answers to the Vedic idea of the self as an eternal, unchanging entity that constitutes each person's essential core. Nor is the self to be identified with one's body or with anything else. One's body and mind consist of nothing more than a heap of momentary *skandhas*, each coming into being and passing away in every moment. In discussing this idea with his disciples, he considers each thing that might *seem* like it is or belongs to oneself. About each one, including the various kinds of mental *skandhas*, he advises his disciples to say,

> This is not mine, this I am not, this is not my self.
> (*MN* i.135)

This is a puzzling doctrine. It seems natural to ask, If none of these things are the self, is there a self at all? If so, what could it be? If not, *how* could that be? Different Buddhist philosophers have answered these questions in different ways over the centuries, and we will consider one of them later in this chapter. Here, however, we can at least ask why the Buddha would say such a thing.

One reason for rejecting the Upaniṣadic view of *ātman* is that clinging to the idea of a self breeds attachment. Addressing his disciples, the Buddha says,

> "You may well cling to that doctrine of self that would not arouse sorrow, lamentation, pain, grief, and despair in one who clings to it. But do you see any such doctrine of self . . . ?"—"No, venerable sir."—"Good. . . . I too do not see any doctrine of self that would not arouse sorrow, lamentation, pain, grief, and despair in one who clings to it."
> (*MN* i.138)

---

*This terminology can be confusing for those versed in classical Greek philosophy, in which entities are sometimes said to be composed of form and matter. (See Aristotle on form and matter, pp. 196–197.) In early Buddhist thought, *rūpa*, which is translated as "form," "material form," "material shape," or "corporeal form," just *is* matter, though they understand it rather differently than the Greeks do.

Your attachments, the Buddha is arguing, are ultimately bound up with the idea that there is some *self* that does or possesses the things you crave. Because there is no conception of an enduring self that avoids these pitfall, we can escape attachment—and therefore suffering—only by recognizing that the self is a delusion.

A second motivation for the doctrine of *anātman* lies in another fundamental Buddhist doctrine: *anitya* or **impermanence.** According to the Buddha, everything in the universe is in a constant state of flux, constantly coming into being and passing away.* Look around the room. The things you seem to see—this book, tables and chairs, your hands, and even yourself—are nothing more than streams of momentary skandhas. It follows, then, that there is no permanent, unchanging self—no *ātman* as the Upaniṣads understand it. Furthermore, all things and all events are fully caused by the conditions that preceded them—a view that would, with some modification, come to be called **dependent origination.** Each event, including events that would appear to be actions attributable to a self, is the outcome of events that preceded that self and of conditions that are clearly outside the self. Thus, even the idea of the self as the author of one's actions melts away.

Rejecting the Upaniṣadic view of the self creates a problem for the Buddhists. Recall that the Buddha accepts the ideas of rebirth and karma. In the Upaniṣads and the *Bhagavad Gītā*, however, it is the eternal, unchanging self—*ātman*—that is reborn again and again, shedding one body and accepting another like a change of clothes. But if there is no *ātman*, in what sense can we say that a particular person is the reincarnation of some other, deceased person? And perhaps more important, how can a person enjoy or suffer the karmic consequences generated by her past self if she has no self in the first place?

To understand the Buddhist reply to this question, let us consider a particular case—say, that of Emperor Aśoka, who converted to Buddhism after conquering most of the Indian subcontinent during the third century B.C. When Aśoka died, he was reborn, we will presume, as a human baby. On the Vedic view, what makes the baby a reincarnation of Aśoka, rather than a reincarnation of someone else, is that Aśoka and the baby share the same *ātman*. Furthermore, it is *because* that particular *ātman* did various good and bad deeds during its life as Aśoka that certain karmically caused consequences await it in this life. On the Buddhist view, however, this last step gets things exactly backward. It is *because* Aśoka's good and bad deeds carry karmic consequences for *this* baby, rather than for some other baby, that *this* baby counts as a reincarnation of Aśoka. Consider a parallel with the way that memory works on the Buddhist picture. Buddhists would say that it was because Aśoka saw the bloody battlefields of the Kaliṅga region that the bundle of *skandhas* we call Aśoka could later summon mental images of those battlefields; there is a certain kind of causal connection between one bundle of *skandhas* and another. A similar causal connection applies between the *skandhas* known as Aśoka and those making up some particular baby, except that this connection transmits not memories, but karmic consequences.

This illustrates the complicated relationship between the Vedic tradition and Buddhist thought. The Buddha accepts certain central ideas from the Vedas, such as the doctrines of rebirth and *karma* and the idea that the world we think we see is ultimately an illusion. But the Buddha turns many of those ideas on their heads: rebirth is understood in terms of *karma*, rather than vice versa, and whereas the Vedic tradition seeks an eternal, unchanging reality beneath the ever-changing surface of appearances, the Buddha claims that this constant flux *is* ultimate reality.

---

1. What are the five kinds of *skandhas*?
2. Explain the doctrine of *anātman*. How does it differ from the views of the authors of the Upaniṣads?
3. How is the doctrine of *anātman* supposed to help people advance along the Noble Eightfold Path?
4. Explain the Buddhist concepts of impermanence and dependent origination. What do those concepts have to do with the doctrine of *anātman*?
5. How do Buddhists reconcile the doctrine of *anātman* with the doctrine of *karma*?

---

*Compare to the views of Heraclitus (pp. 17–18).

Non-Self and Nāgasena

After the Buddha's death, his followers collect sayings attributed to him, along with stories about his life, into a text known as the Sūtra Piṭaka. (Since the Buddha did not write anything himself, the Sūtra Piṭaka is the source for the quotations we attributed to the Buddha in the previous section.) Over the next few centuries, other thinkers begin building on the Buddha's thought. Their efforts are compiled into two more texts, the Vinaya Piṭaka, which contains rules and instructions for Buddhist monks and nuns, and the **Abhidharma Piṭaka,** which constitutes an early attempt to develop a systematic interpretation of the theoretical aspects of the Buddha's teachings. The attempts to systematize, interpret, and develop the Buddha's ideas inevitably lead to controversies, debates, and disagreements. These, in turn, lead to the formation of distinct schools of Buddhist thought—eighteen in all, according to Buddhist tradition.

Many of the developments and controversies from this period are on display in a dialogue between a monk called Nāgasena and the brilliant and powerful King Milinda.* The record of their dialogue, *Milinda's Questions*, was probably written a few decades or centuries after Milinda's reign; its author is unknown. The book ranges over a wide range of theoretical controversies in Buddhist thought, but we will focus on just one: how to understand the doctrine of *anātman*.

The book opens with King Milinda seeking some wise man who could resolve his philosophical doubts. He visits various renowned sages but comes away disappointed each time. When Nāgasena arrives in Milinda's capital, Milinda summons five hundred servants, climbs into his royal chariot, and goes to pay the monk a visit.

---

*Milinda is believed to be another name for Menander, a Greek-speaking king of the second century B.C. whose domain stretched from modern-day Afghanistan into northwestern India. He was one of the "Indo-Greek" rulers whose kingdom was, in an indirect way, a remnant of Alexander the Great's conquest of central Asia in the fourth century B.C.

Milinda finds Nāgasena seated among a company of his fellow monks.

> Then King Milinda approached the venerable Nāgasena . . . and, having exchanged greetings of friendliness and courtesy, he sat down at a respectful distance. . . . Then King Milinda spoke thus to the venerable Nāgasena:
> "How is the revered one known? What is your name, revered sir?"
> "Sire, I am known as Nāgasena; fellow [monks] address me, sire, as Nāgasena. But though (my) parents gave (me) the name of Nāgasena . . . it is but a denotation, appellation, designation, a current usage, for Nāgasena is only a name since no person is got at here."
> Then King Milinda spoke thus: "Good sirs, let the five hundred [servants] and the eighty thousand monks hear me: This Nāgasena speaks thus: 'Since no person is got at here.' Now, is it suitable to approve of that?" And King Milinda spoke thus to the venerable Nāgasena:
> "If, revered Nāgasena, the person is not got at, who then is it that gives you the requisites of robe-material, almsfood, lodgings and medicines for the sick, who is it that makes use of them . . . ? (*MQ* II.25, pp. 34–35)[6]

We see here Nāgasena expressing the Buddhist doctrine of *anātman*: even though there is a convention of using the name "Nāgasena," there is no person—no self—who answers to that name. And we see Milinda respond with the disbelief and objections that one might expect. Milinda presses Nāgasena on just what the other monks mean when they use the name.

> "If you say: 'Fellow [monks] address me, sire, as Nāgasena,' what here is Nāgasena? Is it, revered sir, that the hairs of the head are Nāgasena?"
> "O no, sire."
> "That the hairs of the body are Nāgasena?"
> "O no, sire."
> "That the nails . . . the teeth, the skin, the flesh, the sinews, the bones, the marrow, the kidneys, the heart . . . or the brain in the head are (any of them) Nāgasena?"
> "O no, sire." (*MQ* II.1, pp. 35–36)

Finding that Nāgasena does not identify himself with his body or any of its parts, Milinda takes a different approach. He wonders if the name "Nāgasena" might refer to one of the five aggregates or *skandhas* that Buddhists take to be the fundamental constituents of reality. With this in mind, Milinda asks,

> Is Nāgasena material shape, revered sir?"
> "O no, sire."
> "Is Nāgasena feeling . . . perception . . . the habitual tendencies? Is Nāgasena consciousness?"
> "O no, sire."
> "But then, revered sir, is Nāgasena material shape and feeling and perception and habitual tendencies and consciousness?"
> "O no, sire."
> "But then, revered sir, is there Nāgasena apart from material shape, feeling, perception, the habitual tendencies and consciousness?"
> "O no, sire."
> "Though I, revered sir, am asking you repeatedly, I do not see this Nāgasena. Nāgasena is only a sound, revered sir. For who here is Nāgasena? You, revered sir, are speaking an untruth, a lying word. There is no Nāgasena." (*MQ* II.1, p. 36)

Having exhausted his options, Milinda finds no way to make sense of Nāgasena's claim about the name "Nāgasena." He concludes that if Nāgasena is not any of the things that he suggested, then Nāgasena must not exist at all. He states this conclusion dramatically by accusing Nāgasena of lying about his own existence.

Nāgasena responds with an analogy attributed to one of the Buddha's disciples, the nun Vajirā.

> Then the venerable Nāgasena spoke thus to King Milinda: "You, sire, are a noble delicately nurtured, exceedingly delicately nurtured. If you, sire, go on foot at noon-time on the scorching ground and hot sand, trampling on sharp grit and pebbles and sand, your feet hurt you, your body wearies, your thought is impaired, and tactile consciousness arises accompanied by anguish. Now, did you come on foot or in a conveyance?"
> "I, revered sir, did not come on foot, I came in a chariot."
> "If you, sire, came by chariot, show me the chariot. Is the pole the chariot, sire?"
> "O no, revered sir."
> "Is the axle the chariot?"
> "O no, revered sir."

"Are the wheels the chariot?"
"O no, revered sir."
"Is the body of the chariot the chariot . . . is the flag-staff of the chariot the chariot . . . is the yoke of the chariot the chariot . . . are the reins the chariot . . . is the goad the chariot?"
"O no, revered sir."
"But then, sire, is the chariot the pole, the axle, the wheels, the body of the chariot, the flag-staff of the chariot, the yoke, the reins, the goad?"
"O no, revered sir."
"But then, sire, is there a chariot apart from the pole, the axle, the wheels, the body of the chariot, the flag-staff of the chariot, the yoke, the reins, the goad?"
"O no, revered sir."
"Though I, sire, am asking you repeatedly, I do not see the chariot. Chariot is only a sound, sire. For what here is the chariot? You, sire, are speaking an untruth, a lying word. There is no chariot. (*MQ* II.1, pp. 36–37)

Let us see if we can make sense of this analogy between the self and the chariot. Nāgasena lays out three options: the chariot consists of some part of the chariot, it consists of all of them together, or it consists of something else entirely. It is clear why the chariot is not the same as any of its parts, such as its left wheel or its axle. And it might seem clear enough why Milinda would deny that the chariot is something *distinct* from all of its parts. After all, there is nothing there *in addition* to the parts of the chariot. But why does Milinda so readily deny that the chariot is *all* of its parts?

Neither Milinda nor Nāgasena elaborates on this point, but later commentators offer the following argument. Suppose the chariot were identical to all its parts, assembled in the proper way. If one thing is identical with another, then the first must have all the properties of the second and vice versa, but the chariot has properties that the parts do not. For instance, the chariot has the property of having carried Milinda to visit Nāgasena, whereas at least some of the parts, such as the flag-staff, clearly lack that property. More important, the chariot has the property of being *one* thing, whereas the parts are *many*. (There's the problem of the one and the many again!) Many non-Buddhist philosophers found this line of argument unconvincing, however, and the question of whether something can be identical to its parts remains a point of controversy in Indian philosophy for centuries.*

Whatever Nāgasena's reasons for denying all three options, we must be careful to understand the conclusion that he draws. As the fifth-century A.D. philosopher Buddhaghosa says, it remains true that

> when the component parts such as axles, wheels, frame poles, etc., are arranged in a certain way, there comes to be the mere term of common usage "chariot," yet *in the ultimate sense* when each part is examined, there is no chariot.[7]

Thus, Nāgasena is not advising Milinda to stop using the word "chariot" or to stop ordering his servants to bring him his chariot. He acknowledges that the word "chariot" serves a useful role: it is a convenient shorthand for chariot-parts assembled in a certain way. What Nāgasena denies, however, is that the word "chariot" names some enduring entity; in the final analysis, what *really* exists is simply a collection of chariot parts, assembled in a certain way.

Similarly, and more important, Milinda and the monks can use the name "Nāgasena" as a convenient shorthand, but there is ultimately no self that answers to it. This analogy raises an important question: if "chariot" is a convenient shorthand for the parts of the chariot, what is "Nāgasena" a shorthand *for*? Milinda came close to the answer to that question: the name "Nāgasena" is a shorthand for a particular collection of *skandhas*. To invoke another popular Buddhist metaphor—one that Nāgasena

himself uses later in his dialogue with Milinda— this collection of *skandhas* is a bit like the flame of a candle. We can explain the metaphor in modern, scientific terms: When a candle burns, molecules of the solid wax melt, vaporize, and then react with oxygen in the air. That reaction gives off heat and light. The resulting molecules drift away into the air, only to be replaced by other molecules of the wax. Those molecules react with other oxygen molecules precisely *because* of the heat given off by the molecules before them. Thus, the flame that exists in each moment is causally connected to the flame that existed in the moment before it, but it is also distinct from that flame.*

Nāgasena would happily agree that there is *some sense* in which we can say that there *is* a flame or a person there, as long as we acknowledge that there is no enduring *thing* behind the constant flow of *skandhas*. To acknowledge this, however, amounts to denying the Upaniṣadic view of the self, which is precisely what the Buddhists are concerned to deny.†

---

1. Explain the analogy between the self and the chariot. Why does Nāgasena think that the chariot is not just the sum of its parts?
2. Explain the analogy between the self and a flame. How does saying that the self is like a flame contradict the Upaniṣadic view of *ātman*?

The Brahmanical Schools

While Buddhist philosophers were busy systematizing the Buddha's teachings, other Indian thinkers began picking up ideas from the Vedas and Upaniṣads and developing them into philosophical systems. Six distinct schools of thought emerged from that process: Vaiśeṣika, Nyāya, Sāṃkhya, Yoga, Mīmāṃsā, and Vedānta. Because each of these intellectual traditions accepts the authority of

---

*Interestingly, Indian Buddhists never resorted to a kind of argument that the Greeks applied to problem of the one and the many: Imagine a ship made of wood. If we replace one piece of wood in the ship, it remains the same ship. But what if we replace *every* piece of wood, one by one, over many years? Is it still the same ship? If so, then the ship cannot be identical to its parts. If not, there is no non-arbitrary point at which it ceases to be the original ship, and its identity is a matter of convention. Applied to Milinda's chariot, this so-called Ship of Theseus problem could provide a further argument for the claim that the word "chariot" is simply a conventional term for a group of chariot parts. Perhaps Milinda would have said that although there are ship parts, there is no ship, except in a conventional sense.

---

*Buddhist philosophers have also used rivers as metaphors for *anātman*. Compare Heraclitus' use of both fire and a river as symbols for constant flux (p. 18).

†Compare to David Hume's theory of the self (pp. 451–453).

the Vedas, they are referred to as Vedic or **Brahmanical schools.*** Recall, though, that the Vedas and their accompanying writings are vast and complex. Thus, even though the schools all regard the Vedas as authoritative sources of knowledge, they focus on different parts and aspects of that tradition and come to incompatible conclusions. Some even reject apparently central teachings of the Vedas, such as the claim that all things are merely aspects of a single deity, Brahman. One thing they do share, however, is a belief in *ātman*.

Like the Buddhists, the Brahmanical schools first compiled their teachings into sets of aphorisms or *sūtras*. They also applied the term **sūtra** to the entire set of aphorisms that lays out the core teachings of a particular school. Modern scholars disagree about when these sūtras were composed and when they were first written down. Although traditional accounts attribute each sūtra to a particular person, we know very little about these **"sūtra-makers"** (*sutra-kāra*), including where and even when they lived. Scholars believe the sūtra-makers mostly lived between the second century B.C. and the second century A.D.

The sūtras themselves are often so brief and laconic that it is difficult or impossible to understand them without commentaries. At the time they were composed, these commentaries would have been transmitted orally from teacher to student through the generations. By the fifth century A.D., individual philosophers begin writing down commentaries on the sūtras—although, again, it is often hard to provide definite dates for many of these early commentators' lives. Coming to the sūtras some two millennia later, we generally depend on those written commentaries, which means that we often see the sūtras through the eyes of thinkers who lived centuries after the sūtras were originally written.

Given the breadth and depth of each of the six orthodox schools, we cannot hope to cover them all here. Instead, we focus here on two closely related schools, known as Vaiśeṣika and Nyāya, often with the help of later commentators.

VAIŚEṢIKA

The **Vaiśeṣika** (Vaisheshika) school, rooted in sūtras attributed to the sūtra-maker Kaṇāda, develops a realist understanding of the diversity of objects in the world. The sūtra-maker rejects the monism embraced by some of the Upaniṣads, arguing instead for the existence of independent material objects built out of the five elements attested elsewhere in the Upaniṣads: earth, water, fire, air, and ether. The first four elements consist of indivisible atoms, while the fifth—ether—is a single, all-pervading substance that serves as the medium for sound. The Vaiśeṣikas take all these elements to be real, enduring things that exist independent of any mind. Furthermore, the first four elements consist of innumerable indivisible atoms, which can combine to form new objects.* Those objects, in turn, are also understood as real, enduring wholes. The Vaiśeṣikas, then, would take a very different view of Milinda's chariot than the Buddhists do. Recall that Nāgasena laid out three options for the relation between the chariot and its parts, one of which was that the chariot is something distinct from its parts. While Nāgasena and Milinda reject that option out of hand, it is precisely what the Vaiśeṣikas take the chariot to be. When various atoms combine in the right way, something new comes into being—say, wood. And when wood is shaped and combined in the right way, a further thing comes into being: the chariot. On the Vaiśeṣika view, each of these things is a real object, distinct from its parts.

The key to understanding this idea is the concept of **inherence,** which plays a central and complex role in Vaiśeṣika metaphysics. One of its roles is to explain this relationship between a whole and its parts—between the one and the many. When the right kinds of parts are combined in the right way, a new object is said to inhere in those parts. This contrasts with what the Vaiśeṣika call the conjunction of different objects. When the pages of this book are bound together between two covers, you have a new object—a book, which is said to inhere in its parts. But when you place the book on

---

*The term Brahmanical comes from their ties to the priestly class known as the *brāhmaṇas*.

*Compare to the views of pre-Socratic atomists such as Democritus (pp. 29–30).

a table, you have not thereby created a new object; you have two distinct objects that are merely in conjunction with each other. An analogy with modern chemistry may help elucidate this point. At room temperature, hydrogen molecules—each composed of two hydrogen atoms—form an invisible gas. The same goes for oxygen molecules. But when you burn the two together, binding each hydrogen molecule to one oxygen atom, you get something quite different: water. Each molecule of water is said to inhere in its constituent atoms. The atoms still exist, of course, and each has properties that the water molecule lacks; but the water molecule is an object in its own right, with its own properties, and it will exist as long as its parts are combined in the right way. Similarly, Milinda's chariot inheres in its parts—the wheels, the axle, and so on—and those parts, in turn, inhere in the various atoms that make them up. The Buddhist view, according to the Vaiśeṣikas, fails to recognize the significance of this relation of inherence.

To understand the other roles that inherence plays in Vaiśeṣika thought, we must consider the other things that the Vaiśeṣikas take to exist. Atoms are said to be **substances,** which the Vaiśeṣikas understand as entities that have their own existence and in which things can inhere. The wholes that inhere in those atoms, such as wood and other objects of everyday experience, are also substances. The Vaiśeṣikas argue that such real, mind-independent substances must exist if we are to explain why our perceptions of the material world correlate with one another. When you see a piece of wood in front of you, you can also reach out and touch the wood. You can rap your knuckles on it and hear a certain sound. If the wood is freshly cut, it will have a certain odor. The best explanation for this correlation of perceptions, they argue, is that there exists some kind of substratum that causes all of those perceptions.

But atoms and the things that inhere in them are not the only kinds of substances. Besides atoms and the ether, there are four other kinds of substance in Vaiśeṣika thought: Time and space are considered substances, each real in themselves and irreducible to any of the other substances. So are selves (ātman) and minds, to which we will return shortly.

Substances, in turn, are but one of six **categories** in the Vaiśeṣika catalogue of existence. We will mention only three more of the categories. **Attributes,** such as redness or hardness, comprise the second category. Kaṇāda lists seventeen kinds of attributes, such as color, taste, and magnitude. The Vaiśeṣika commentator Praśastapāda adds seven more, to round out the traditional Vaiśeṣika list of twenty-four attributes. These attributes are said to inhere in substances. A red brick, for instance, has the attributes *red* and *hard* inhering in it.*

The second category to be mentioned here is *viśeṣa* or **particularity,** which is often regarded as a distinctive innovation of the Vaiśeṣikas.† Inhering in each individual substance—each fire-atom, for instance—is a unique identity, which differentiates it from all other substances, even those that are of the same kind and share all the same attributes. This identity has no attributes of its own; its only feature is that it is numerically distinct from all other particularities, so that by inhering in one particular substance, it marks that substance as numerically distinct from every other substance.‡ We can get a hint of what role particularity plays in Vaiśeṣika thought by recalling that the Upaniṣads declared that *ātman*, the self, lacked any defining characteristics. Some strands of Brahmanical thought inferred from this that there was only one *ātman*, since otherwise you would have two things that were utterly indistinguishable from one another. To resist the conclusion, the Vaiśeṣikas introduce the idea of particularities, which inhere in various selves, thereby distinguishing one *ātman* from another

---

*Compare this account of substances and attributes to Aristotle's account of substances and accidents (pp. 186–187, 194–196).

†In fact, the Vaiśeṣika school takes its name from this term.

‡This is a difficult concept to grasp. It may be useful to consider the name used for a similar idea, developed independently more than a thousand years after Kaṇāda by the medieval European philosopher Duns Scotus, who called this individuating property "thisness." Each thing has a "thisness" that distinguishes it from every other thing, just as, in Vaiśeṣika thought, each individual thing has a *viśeṣa* or particularity that distinguishes it from every other individual thing.

without attributing any particular characteristics to them.

The third category to be mentioned here are **universals,** which the Vaiśeṣikas understand as that which things of the same kind have in common. The Vaiśeṣikas take these to be eternal, independent entities that inhere in substances or attributes. The universal *fire* inheres in all fire-atoms, the universal *chariot* in all chariots, and the universal *redness* inheres in all instances of the attribute red (which, in turn, inhere in particular substances). On the Vaiśeṣika view, we perceive these universals whenever we perceive something in which they inhere.* It is on this basis that we recognize distinct fire-atoms, for instance, as belonging to the same kind.

Let us return now to the Vaiśeṣika view of two particularly important substances, self (*ātman*) and mind. The self, on the Vaiśeṣika view, is the substance that has knowledge. In opposition to the Buddhists and in keeping with the other Brahmanical schools, the Vaiśeṣika maintain that the self is a real, independent entity. In contrast to some of the other Brahmanical schools, however, the Vaiśeṣika insist that there are many selves—one for each person. This can be inferred, they argue, from the doctrine of rebirth, and so the Vedic passages on the unity of all selves are to be understood metaphorically. While the self cannot be perceived, except by the rare few who have advanced far enough in the practice of meditation, even the ordinary person is directly conscious of the existence of his or her self. The fact that each of us can, through inspection, come to recognize truths such as "I know" and "I am experiencing suffering" is taken to imply the existence of the self as something distinct from the atoms that make up one's body, since neither knowledge nor feeling can inhere in those atoms.†

That consciousness of one's self and one's attributes, however, occurs *through* an independent substance, mind, which is connected to but distinct from the self.* Your mind is regarded as something like a special internal sense organ or self-consciousness by which one becomes aware of your self, your body, and their attributes. The Vaiśeṣika argue that mind must be a separate substance from the self because the self is always present with the body, whereas consciousness is not; just as sight does not operate when your eyes are closed, so your inner awareness does not operate when your mind is not active.

On the whole, then, Vaiśeṣika ideas largely echo common sense. The world is much as it appears to be: the objects we perceive are real, independent things, as is the self. The problem of the one and the many is likewise resolved in favor of common sense: There are many things, including many selves, with each complex whole counting as one object that inheres in many parts for as long as those parts are joined together. Certain aspects of Vaiśeṣika thought go beyond common sense, of course, but this is only to be expected in any systematic attempt to make sense of the world around us.

Nyāya

A different Brahmanical school, the **Nyāya,** traces its roots to sūtras attributed to a somewhat later sūtra-maker called Akṣapāda Gautama.† Whereas the Vaiśeṣikas are best known for their development of a realist metaphysics, **Naiyāyikas**—as adherents of Nyāya are known—focus on logic and epistemology. Because they use their sophisticated logical theories to defend a broadly Vaiśeṣika metaphysics, Nyāya and Vaiśeṣika are regarded as natural allies among the Brahmanical schools.

Like the other Brahmanical schools, Nyāya builds its epistemology on the notion of a *pramāṇa*. A *pramāṇa*, or knowledge source, is a method of acquiring genuine knowledge. The Naiyāyikas

---

*The concept of universals plays a significant role in Greek philosophy beginning with Socrates, with Socrates' successors debating the proper way to understand universals and our knowledge of them. We will discuss these debates in detail in the coming chapters.

†Compare this to the views of Avicenna (p. 304) and Descartes (p. 369), who claim that we can know our selves through introspection and inference, respectively.

---

*Contrast this with the view of Descartes (pp. 369–372), who identifies the self with the mind, instead of regarding them as two separate entities.

†This Gautama is not to be confused with the Buddha, whose original name was Siddhārtha Gautama.

recognize four *pramāṇas*: perception, inference, analogy, and testimony.

About the *pramāṇa* called perception, the *Nyāya-sūtra* says,

> Perceptual knowledge arises from a connection of sense faculty and object, does not depend on language, is inerrant, and is definitive. (*NS* 1.1.4, p. 20)[8]

The first condition—that perceptual knowledge "arises from a connection of sense faculty and object"—is fairly straightforward: to gain knowledge through perception, some sensory organ must be connected to an object in the right way, as when your eyes see this book. Note that, according to the Naiyāyikas, your sense organs can connect not only with the atoms that comprise an object, but also with the object as a whole and even with the universals that inhere in that object. The second condition—that perception "does not depend on language"—is that acquiring perceptual knowledge does not require being able to put one's new knowledge into words. The third condition—that perception "is inerrant"—may seem surprising. After all, our eyes and ears often err; reality does not always match appearances. You think you see an old friend down the street, but as you get closer, you realize that it's a stranger. Gautama is not denying this; as the important Nyāya commentator Vātsyāyana (fl. c. 450 A.D.) explains, the point of the sūtra is that a particular instance of perception only counts as a *pramāṇa*—as a genuine source of knowledge—when the perceiver perceives things for what they really are. Similarly, Gautama includes the fourth condition—that perception is "definitive"—to exclude instances where someone perceives something indistinctly. When you see someone in the distance and cannot make out who it is, your perceptual experience is not definitive, and so it cannot count as a genuine *pramāṇa*.

After explaining perceptual knowledge, the *Nyāya-sūtra* continues:

> Next is inference, which depends on previous perception and is threefold: from something prior, from something later, and through experience of a common characteristic. (*NS* 1.1.5, p. 28)

A modern translator explains the threefold nature of inference with several examples:

> If we see a river swollen we infer that there has been rain, if we see the ants carrying off their eggs, we infer that there will be rain and if we hear a peacock scream, we infer that clouds are gathering.[9]

In the case of the swollen river, we see something and draw an inference about what happened earlier. In the case of the fleeing ants, we see something and draw an inference about what will happen later. In the case of the screaming peacock, we hear something and draw an inference about what is happening now. The things on which we base our inferences—the swollen river, the fleeing ants, and the peacock's scream—are called **inferential marks,** because they mark or indicate the presence of some other event or entity. As with perception, however, the sūtra-maker emphasizes that to count as a legitimate *pramāṇa*, our inferences must meet certain standards. In particular, we must base our inferences on the right inferential marks. For instance, if we mistake ants fleeing chaotically from a damaged nest for ants moving their eggs systematically before a storm, we cannot properly be said to be using inference in the strict sense. The Naiyāyika develop these ideas into a sophisticated theory of logic.

The third Nyāya *pramāṇa*, analogy, is generally regarded as the least important of the *pramāṇas*. It involves recognizing what something is based on its similarity to another thing.

As for the final *pramāṇa*, testimony, the *Nyāya-sūtra* describes it this way:

> Testimony is instruction by a trustworthy authority. (*NS* 1.1.7, p. 35)
> Such testimony is of two kinds, because it has two kinds of objects: that which is experienced (here in this world), and that which is not experienced (here in this world). (*NS* 1.1.8, p. 36)

Vātsyāyana explains:

> A trustworthy authority is someone who knows something directly, an instructor with the desire to communicate it faithfully as it is known. (*NS*, p. 35)

When it comes to "that which is experienced," testimony might come from an expert teacher explaining a topic she knows well or from a friend describing something he has just seen. But testimony's most important role in Nyāya thought is as the basis for accepting "that which is not experienced"—namely, the supernatural claims of the Vedas, which the Naiyāyikas count as the faithful communication of sages who could perceive that which ordinary mortals could not.

Equipped with this theory of knowledge the *Nyāya-sūtra* proceeds to develop a sophisticated account of philosophical method. A key concept in this method is *tarka,* which the sūtra-maker defines as follows:

> *Tarka* is reasoning that proceeds by considering what is consistent with knowledge sources [*pramāṇa*], in order to know the truth about something that is not [yet] definitely known. (*NS* 1.1.40, p. 44)

Vātsyāyana explains:

> Desire to know arises, in the first instance, when the truth about something is not known. . . . And the thing being considered has two contrary properties attributed to it, such that one wavers, thinking, "Maybe it is this way, maybe not." Granting that there is a means to establish one of the two properties, he holds that there is a *pramāṇa* that would settle which is possible. One side is possible, given the evidence of knowledge sources, and not the other.

The basic method of *tarka,* then, is to begin with a controversy between two mutually incompatible views and then refute one of those views by showing that it is inconsistent with something that is known through a recognized *pramāṇa.**

Vātsyāyana explains that this does not, in itself, produce definitive knowledge, since it only suggests that the remaining alternative is consistent with the truth. The next step in Nyāya philosophical method is to establish that alternative directly on the basis of one or more *pramāṇas.*

The Naiyāyikas deploy their methodology to defend a realist metaphysics very similar to that of the Vaiśeṣika. The *Nyāya-sūtra* begins by arguing for the reality of everyday objects. The sūtra-maker does this by voicing claims or arguments advanced by imaginary critics of realism. For instance, he imagines a critic saying,

> But when we examine things closely through cognition, we do not find true objects, just as we do not find a cloth when we distinguish the threads. (*NS* 4.2.26, p. 62)

The thought here is the same one that Nāgasena defends in his discussion with Milinda: when we consider a complex object, such as a cloth or a chariot, we find that there is nothing there but its parts, arranged in a particular way. Gautama responds to this view by noting that the *pramāṇa* of perception delivers knowledge of the whole that inheres in the parts—of the cloth that inheres in the threads, for instance—as well as knowledge of its attributes. You might see that a cloth is gray, for instance, even though each individual thread is either black or white. Since denying that the cloth exists or that it is gray is inconsistent with this perceptual *pramāṇa,* we can reject the view that wholes do not exist. This argument is an example of *tarka*: Gautama takes up a controversy about whether complex wholes exist and shows that one position in that controversy is inconsistent with knowledge gained through a particular *pramāṇa.*

The *Nyāya-sūtra* also considers some more radical possibilities. Suppose someone argued not just against the existence of wholes, but against the existence of anything at all. Vātsyāyana explains Gautama's characteristically terse response:

> And, accordingly, there is no possibility of the thesis, "Nothing exists." "Why?" It's wrong because of [what the *Nyāya-sūtra* calls] the possibility and impossibility of knowledge sources. If the thesis, "Nothing exists," were supported by a *pramāṇa,* then that *pramāṇa* would contradict the claim, "Nothing exists." But on the second option, if there were no *pramāṇa* in support, then how would the thesis, "Nothing exists," be proved? (*NS,* p. 64)*

But suppose, Gautama imagines someone saying, that our "conception of things known through

---

*Compare to Socrates' method of questioning (p. 95).

*Compare this to Descartes' famous *cogito* argument (pp. 369, 373).

knowledge sources is akin to conceptions of objects encountered in a dream" (*NS* 4.2.31, p. 65). That is, perhaps what we *think* are perceptions of real objects are just the creations of our minds, like the objects in a dream. Vātsyāyana explains the sūtra-maker's rebuttal in several steps. First, he demands a reason to believe this hypothesis that our perceptions are like perceptions in our dreams. Second, he points out that even if we did have a reason to think that our waking perceptions are like dream perceptions, the opponent has not actually argued that the objects we perceive in dreams are unreal. He then imagines the following exchange:

> Opponent: The reason is that upon awakening we no longer see them.
>
> Response [from Vātsyāyana]: On your view, one has no resources to deny the reality of dream objects by comparison with the objects of waking experience. If dream objects do not exist because they are not experienced upon awakening, then those very objects we find in waking life must exist, as they are in fact experienced. Your reasoning supports the opposite of what you claim. Non-experience of something can prove that it is absent only when positive experience of it can prove that it exists. But if nothing is true in either case, then not having an experience of something could not be evidence for its absence. . . . Here, determining an absence—the absence of visible objects—depends upon a presence, the presence of visible objects that do in fact exist. (*NS*, p. 66)

Let us see if we can piece together the Naiyāyika argument here. The opponent has suggested that our waking life is like a dream, meaning that nothing real corresponds to the images we have of things. But how, the sūtra-maker replies, do we identify dream images as unreal? By the fact that they disappear when we wake up, according to the opponent. So identifying something as a dream depends on a contrast, something that we take to be real. But if that is so, argues the sūtra-maker, then the "waking world" cannot be a mere dream. If it were, then we would have no experience of anything real at all. In that case, then there would be no way to contrast "visible objects" with the unreal

objects in a dream and so no basis for calling "visible objects" unreal. In other words, if our waking life were just a dream, we could have no reason to think that to be the case. Notice that this argument does not, by itself, prove that the objects we perceive while awake *are* real. It only shows that one specific argument fails to show that they are unreal.*

This brings us to the reality of the object that receives the most attention in Indian philosophy: the self. We have seen that the Buddhists deny the existence of a real, enduring self behind the various series of physical and mental events that we designate with names like Nāgasena and Gautama, whereas the Vaiśeṣika affirm the existence of such a self. The Naiyāyikas side with the Vaiśeṣika, and their argument for this view has the Buddhist alternative in mind. The *Nyāya-sūtra* says,

> Inferential marks for the self are desire, aversion, effort, pleasure, pain, and knowledge. (*NS* 1.1.10, p. 75)

Recall that in Nyāya epistemology, an inferential mark is something that indicates the presence of something else. This *sūtra*, then, claims that certain things, such as desire and aversion, indicate the presence of a real, enduring self. A person often comes to desire an object by recognizing it as being a kind of thing that has produced pleasure *for the person himself or herself* in the past. This implies a self that endures from one moment to the next—in other words, *ātman*. Similarly, aversion often arises from the recognition of an object as a past source of pain. The desire for knowledge functions slightly differently in the argument: a person desires to know something and therefore deliberates about it. Recognizing the desire to know and the deliberation as belonging to the same person, the person infers the existence of a self that endures across time.

A second Naiyāyika argument about *ātman* inverts the Vaiśeṣika argument for the existence of ordinary objects. Recall that the Vaiśeṣika argue

---

*Compare this to Descartes' treatment of the idea that the world we perceive might be like a dream (pp. 366–368).

that substances must be real, independent entities because our perceptions of them through different sense organs correlate with one another: you can both see the book in front of you and feel the smoothness of its pages. Turning this argument on its head, the *Nyāya-sūtra* says,

> Because one grasps the same object through sight and touch, there is a self that is distinct from the body and sense organs. (*NS* 3.1.1, p. 80)

Vātsyāyana explains:

> Some particular object is grasped by sight; the same object is also grasped by touch: "That very thing which I saw with my eyes I am now feeling through my sense of touch," and "That very thing which I felt through my sense of touch I am now seeing with my eyes." The two instances of mental content that are each directed towards one and the same object have—in being comprehended—a single subject. (*NS*, pp. 80–81)

Whereas the Vaiśeṣika would emphasize the use of "that very object" in both of the observations Vātsyāyana mentions, the Naiyāyikas emphasize the use of "I." The "I" who grasps something by both sight and touch is a unified subject; it is one and the same thing that perceives the object in front of it through various means. This unified subject cannot be the sense organs, Vātsyāyana argues, because each sense organ can only perceive things in one way; the eyes cannot perceive the object through touch, nor the fingers through sight. The "I" cannot be just a bundle of atoms, either, for conscious awareness cannot inhere in atoms. Thus, the self must be something other than the body. It must be an immaterial *ātman*, of the sort the Upaniṣads describe and the Buddhists deny.

A third Naiyāyika argument for the existence of *ātman* rests on the necessity of an enduring self to explain *karma*. The *Nyāya-sūtra* says,

> When a living body is harmed, no sin would be incurred (if there were no self). (*NS* 3.1.4, p. 84)

Vātsyāyana explains:

> One who (for example) burns a living body causes harm to the living being, committing a wicked act called sin. "No sin" means that (for those who deny

a permanent self) there would be no connection between the agent of sin and its results. . . . And so, this being the case, the living being . . . who causes harm would not be the one connected to the karmic fruits of harm, and the one who would be connected would not be the one who caused the harm. Thus, on the view that there are distinct beings (in a series, as opposed to a single enduring self), there results the unacceptable consequence of losing what one has done and acquiring what one has not done. (*NS*, p. 84)

The argument here rests on the uncontested assumption that actions have karmic consequences for the person who performs them. If that is true, the Naiyāyikas argue, then there must be an enduring self. Otherwise, the person who performs the actions will not bear the karmic consequences of that action, and the person who *does* bear those consequences will not be the person who performed them.

A fourth argument appeals to rebirth:

> Because happiness, fear, and unhappiness are experienced by a new-born appropriately, through connection with what was previously practiced and remembered (a self endures beyond death). (*NS* 3.1.18, p. 86)

Vātsyāyana explains:

> A new-born is a child who has not in this lifetime experienced things that cause happiness, fear, and unhappiness. These emotions are nevertheless experienced by the new-born, since the baby shows signs by which these feelings may be inferred. And such experiences come about only through connection with memories. Such connection with memory does not come about without prior practice and experience. And in the case of a new-born, the prior practice and experience can only be during a previous lifetime. In this way we establish that there is a state of the self afterwards too, because the self is different from the body. (*NS*, p. 86)*

Even if we cannot perceive *ātman*, then, we can infer its existence in many ways.

---

*Compare to Socrates' argument that the soul exists before the body on pp. 133–134.

1. What are complex objects made of, according to the Vaiśeṣikas?
2. What role(s) does the concept of inherence play in Vaiśeṣika thought?
3. How would the Vaiśeṣikas respond to Nāgasena's arguments about Milinda's chariot?
4. What are the six categories in Vaiśeṣika metaphysics? What role does particularity play in that system?
5. What is the relation between the body, the self, and the mind, according to the Vaiśeṣikas?
6. What is a *pramāṇa*? What *pramāṇas* do the Naiyāyikas acknowledge?
7. Explain the Nyāya account of perceptual knowledge. Why do they count perceptual knowledge as "inerrant"?
8. What is *tarka*? What role does it play in Naiyāyika philosophical method?
9. What arguments do the Naiyāyikas give for the reality of everyday objects?
10. What arguments do the Naiyāyikas give for the reality of *ātman*?

The Great Conversation in India

We have surveyed only the earliest beginnings of philosophy in India—and, indeed, only a few aspects of those early stages. There are entire schools of thought, both Brahmanical and non-Brahmanical, that have gone unmentioned here. From what little we have covered, however, we can see that a sophisticated philosophical conversation began in India around the same time as in Greece, though it seems to have developed more gradually.

This great Indian conversation accelerated and intensified sometime around the second century A.D. One major cause of this acceleration is that Buddhist philosophers began writing in Sanskrit rather than Pāli. This brought them more directly into contact with the Brahmanical philosophers, stimulating centuries of especially intense debate, clarification, elaboration, and philosophical innovation. The period following this change featured such famous Buddhist philosophers as Nāgārjuna and Vasubandhu and the rise of new Buddhist schools of thought, such as Madhyamaka and Yogācāra, as

well as the great commentators of the Brahmanical tradition, such as Vātsyāyana and Śaṅkara. It is one of the richest periods of philosophical debate in all human history.

Toward the end of the first millennium A.D., Buddhism began to decline socially, politically, and intellectually within India. By that time, it had already spread throughout east and southeast Asia, where it would thrive and develop to the present day. As the Buddhists faded from the scene in India, the Brahmanical schools turned inward, beginning a new period in the great Indian conversation. But just as European philosophy has been permanently shaped by the debates in ancient Greece, so Indian philosophy has been shaped by the early stages of the conversation that we have surveyed here.

KEY WORDS

Vedas	*skandhas* (aggregates)
Brahman	*anātman*
Upaniṣads	impermanence
ātman	dependent origination
rebirth	Abhidharma Piṭaka
saṃsāra	Brahmanical schools
karma	*sūtra*
Buddha	*sūtra*-maker
four Noble Truths	Vaiśeṣika
suffering (*duḥkha*)	inherence
attachment	substances
Noble Eightfold Path	categories
right view	attributes
Four Divine Abidings	particularity
lovingkindness	universals
compassion	Nyāya
joy	Naiyāyikas
equanimity	*pramāṇa*
nirvāṇa	inferential mark
nirvāṇa without remainder	*tarka*

FOR FURTHER THOUGHT

1. The Buddhists and the Vaiśeṣikas take themselves to be disagreeing about the nature of complex objects. Do you think that one

of them is right? Why? Is it necessary that one of them is wrong, or could these just be two ways of looking at the same thing? What about their disagreement about the nature of the self?

2. Keeping in mind the methods that Buddhists recommend for ending suffering, do you think the cessation of suffering is a worthy goal in life? Why or why not?

3. Write a paragraph in which you apply the doctrine of *anātman* to yourself (or "yourself").

4. Between the Vaiśeṣikas and Naiyāyikas and the Buddhists, whose arguments do you find more convincing as to the existence of an enduring self? Why?

5. Philosophers in every major tradition in the world have suggested, at least for the sake of argument, that our experiences might be nothing more than a dream. Do you find the Naiyāyikas' response to this suggestion persuasive? Why or why not?

6. In what sense are the Indian thinkers discussed in this chapter engaged in the same kind of enterprise as the Greek thinkers discussed in the previous chapter? That is, what justifies calling both activities "philosophy"?

7. Based on what you have read here, how do the early philosophical traditions of India and Greece overlap? How do they differ?

NOTES

1. Quotations from the *Ṛg Veda* are from Franklin Edgerton, *The Beginnings of Indian Philosophy: Selections from the Rig Veda, Atharva Veda, Upaniṣads, and Mahabharata* (Cambridge, MA: Harvard University Press, 1965).

2. S. Radhakrishnan, *Indian Philosophy*, 2nd ed. (New Delhi: Oxford University Press, 2008), 1:41.

3. Quotations from the Upaniṣads are from Patrick Olivelle, trans., *Upaniṣads* (Oxford: Oxford University Press, 1996).

4. W. J. Johnson, trans., *The Bhagavad Gita* (New York: Oxford University Press, 1994), 9.

5. Bhikkhu Ñanamoli and Bhikkhu Bodhi, trans., *The Middle-Length Discourses of the Buddha*, 4th ed. (Somerville, MA: Wisdom, 2015), 229–230. Quotations from this text are marked *MN* for *Majjima Nikaya* ("Middle-Length Discourses").

6. I. B. Horner, trans., *Milinda's Questions* (London: Luzac, 1964). Quotations from this text are marked *MQ.*

7. Quoted in Amber Carpenter, *Indian Buddhist Philosophy* (Abingdon: Routledge, 2014), 37.

8. Quotations from the *Nyāya-sūtra* and from Vātsyāyana's commentary, both marked *NS*, are from Matthew Dasti and Stephen Phillips, trans., *The Nyāya-sūtra: Selections with Early Commentaries* (Indianapolis, IN: Hackett, 2017).

9. Satīśa Chandra Vidyābhuṣana, trans., *The Nyāya Sūtras of Gotama* (Allahabad, India: The Panini Office, 1913), available at https://archive.org/details/TheNyayaSutrasOfGotama.

CHAPTER

4

THE SOPHISTS

Rhetoric and Relativism in Athens

When we think of "the glory that was Greece," we think inevitably of **Athens** (see Map 1). To this point, however, we have mentioned Athens scarcely at all. Greek culture, as we have seen, ranged from the southern parts of Italy and Sicily in the west to the Ionian settlements on the shores of Asia Minor and to Thrace in the north. In the fifth and fourth centuries B.C., however, Greek culture came more and more to center in one city: Athens. It is there that we find the next major developments in Greek thought. The story of how this came about is a fascinating tale recorded by the Greek historian Herodotus and pieced together by modern writers from his history and many other sources. To understand the context of our next set of philosophers, we need to understand several key elements of that story. What kind of city was Athens in that time, what was it like to live in Athens, and how was it different from other cities?[1]

Although we have used the terms "Greece" and "Greek culture," there was at the beginning of the fifth century (around 500 B.C.) nothing like a unified Greek state. Instead, Greek civilization comprised various independent city-states. A city-state (a *polis*) was an area—an island, perhaps, or an arable plain with natural boundaries of mountains and the sea—in which one city was dominant. The city was usually fortified and offered protection to those within and around its walls. The prominent city-states of that time were Thebes, Corinth, Argos, Sparta, and Athens, but there were many more. Among these city-states there were often rivalries, quarrels, shifting alliances, and wars.

Two things happened around the beginning of the fifth century that contributed to the preeminence of Athens among the city-states: the beginnings of **democracy** in government and the **Persian wars.**

Democracy

The common people of Athens first gained a voice in government when the statesman Solon reformed the city-state's constitution around 600 B.C. That reform divided government power among several bodies. Among them were the Council, which was composed of "the best men" (aristocrats), and the Assembly, to which all free men belonged. Important decisions were made by the Council, but the Assembly could veto measures that were excessively unpopular. This structure was modified over the years, but it took on the character of an ideal; again and again reforms of various kinds were justified as being a return to the constitution of Solon.*

During a large part of the sixth century, Athens was ruled by "tyrants." This word did not originally have all the negative connotations it now has. It simply meant "boss" or "chief" and was applied to a ruler who was not a hereditary king but had seized power some other way. Some of the tyrants of Athens more or less respected Solon's constitution, but at least one tyrant was killed to restore the democracy.

In 508 B.C., a quarrel arose concerning citizenship for a large influx of immigrants to the city. The aristocrats, fearful for their power, tried to purge the citizenship rolls, but the Assembly passed a proposal to extend citizenship to many of the new residents. After a three-day siege of the Acropolis by the people, the aristocrats—who had been backed by a king of Sparta and his soldiers—capitulated. Citizenship was broadened, though not so far as to include women and slaves, and the citizens gained control of major decisions. It was to be so for the next hundred years and, with a few exceptions, for some time after that.

The Persian Wars

Meanwhile, a different kind of power struggle was brewing across the Aegean Sea. The rising Persian Empire had been encroaching on the Greek colonies in Asia Minor. These Greek cities paid taxes to the Persians, but in 499 B.C. they rebelled. Athens sent twenty ships to aid the colonies, and in the fighting they burned the Persian city of Sardis. The Persian king Darius the Great put down the rebellion and, seeking vengeance, turned his attention to mainland Greece.*

In 490 B.C., the Persians came in force across the Aegean, conquered a coastal island, and landed at Marathon. In a famous battle on the plain twenty-six miles north and east of Athens, the Greeks defeated the Persians, killing 6,400 of them. The victory invigorated the democratic city of Athens, which had supplied most of the soldiers for the battle.

It was clear to the Athenians, however, that the Persians would not be stopped by the loss of one battle, no matter how decisive at the time. Herodotus represents the Darius' successor Xerxes as saying,

> I will bridge the Hellespont [see Map 1] and march an army through Europe into Greece, and punish the Athenians for the outrage they committed upon my father and upon us. As you saw, Darius himself was making his preparations for war against these men; but death prevented him from carrying out his purpose. I therefore on his behalf, and for the benefit of all my subjects, will not rest until I have taken Athens and burnt it to the ground, in revenge for the injury which the Athenians without provocation once did to me and my father [the burning of Sardis]. . . . If we crush the Athenians and their neighbours in the Peloponnese, we shall so extend the empire of Persia that its boundaries will be God's own sky, so that the sun will not look down upon any land beyond the boundaries of what is ours. (Histories 7.8)[2]

There was much debate in Athens about how to meet the danger. One party favored land-based defenses, citing the former victory at Marathon. The other party, led by Themistocles, favored building up the navy and a defense by sea. After much infighting, the Athenians decided on a large increase in fighting ships of the latest style—and just in time. In the year 480 B.C., Xerxes, lashing ships together to make a bridge, led an army of perhaps 200,000 men across the Hellespont (which separates Asia from Europe), subdued Thrace, and began to advance south toward Athens. Advice was

---

*For democracy in Athens, see https://en.wikipedia.org/wiki/Athenian_democracy.

*For the Greco-Persian Wars, see https://en.wikipedia.org/wiki/Greco-Persian_Wars.

sought, in time-honored fashion, from the Oracle at Delphi (see Map 1). The oracle was not favorable. A second plea brought this response:

That the wooden wall only shall not fall, but help you and your children. (*Histories* 7.141)

How should this opaque answer be interpreted? Some believed that wooden walls on the hill of the Acropolis would withstand the aggressor. Themistocles argued that the "wooden wall" referred to the ships that had been built and that they must abandon Athens and try to defeat the Persians at sea. Most of the Athenians followed Themistocles, though some did not.

First, however, it was necessary to stop the advance of the Persian army. Many saw it as a threat against Greece as a whole, not just against Athens. A force led by Spartan soldiers under the Spartan king Leonidas met the Persians at Thermopylae, eighty miles northwest of Athens (see Map 1). Greatly outnumbered, the Greeks fought valiantly, inflicting many deaths, but were defeated. Leonidas was killed.*

The Persians took Athens, overwhelmed the defenders on the Acropolis, and burned the temples. However, the main Athenian forces, in ships off the nearby island of Salamis, were still to be dealt with. On a day splendid in Greek history, Xerxes sat on a mountain above the bay of Salamis (see Map 1) and saw the Greeks tear apart his navy. Themistocles' strategy had worked. The next spring (479 B.C.), however, the Persians occupied Athens again. It took a great victory by the combined Athenian and Spartan armies at Plataea to expel the Persians for good.

These victories had several results. Athens, which had borne the brunt of the defense of Greece, became preeminent among the city-states. The city had displayed its courage and prowess for all to see and took the lead in forming a league for the future defense of the Greek lands. In time, the league turned into an Athenian empire. Other states paid tribute to Athens, which saw to their protection, and Athens became a great sea power.

Athens also became very wealthy. It was not only the tribute from the allies, although that was significant. With their control of the sea, Athenians engaged in trading far and wide. A wealthy merchant class developed, and Athens became the center of Greek cultural life. Under **Pericles,** the most influential leader of the democratic city in the middle of the fifth century B.C., the city built the magnificent temples on the Acropolis. Pericles encouraged Greek art and sculpture, supported the new learning, and was a close associate of certain philosophers. A speech of his, commemorating fallen soldiers in the first year of the tragic war with Sparta, gives a sense of what it meant to Athenians to be living in Athens at that time. Only part of it, as represented for us by the historian Thucydides, is quoted here. (Suggestion: Read it aloud.)

Let me say that our system of government does not copy the institutions of our neighbours. It is more a case of our being a model to others, than of our imitating anyone else. Our constitution is called a democracy because power is in the hands not of a minority but of the whole people. When it is a question of settling private disputes, everyone is equal before the law; when it is a question of putting one person before another in positions of public responsibility, what counts is not membership of a particular class, but the actual ability which the man possesses. No one, so long as he has it in him to be of service to the state, is kept in political obscurity because of poverty. And, just as our political life is free and open, so is our day-to-day life in our relations with each other. We do not get into a state with our next-door neighbour if he enjoys himself in his own way, nor do we give him the kind of black looks which, though they do no real harm, still do hurt people's feelings. We are free and tolerant in our private lives; but in public affairs we keep to the law. This is because it commands our deep respect.

We give our obedience to those whom we put in positions of authority, and we obey the laws themselves, especially those which are for the protection of the oppressed, and those unwritten laws which it is an acknowledged shame to break. . . .

Then there is a great difference between us and our opponents in our attitude towards military security. Here are some examples: Our city is open to

---

*This battle is celebrated in the movie *300*.

the world, and we have no periodical deportations in order to prevent people observing or finding out secrets which might be of military advantage to the enemy. This is because we rely, not on secret weapons, but on our own real courage and loyalty. . . .

Our love of what is beautiful does not lead to extravagance; our love of the things of the mind does not make us soft. We regard wealth as something to be properly used, rather than as something to boast about. As for poverty, no one need be ashamed to admit it: the real shame is in not taking practical measures to escape from it. Here each individual is interested not only in his own affairs but in the affairs of the state as well. . . . We do not say that a man who takes no interest in politics is a man who minds his own business; we say that he has no business here at all. . . .

Again, in questions of general good feeling there is a great contrast between us and most other people. We make friends by doing good to others, not by receiving good from them. . . . We are unique in this. When we do kindnesses to others, we do not do them out of any calculations of profit or loss: we do them without afterthought, relying on our free liberality. Taking everything together then, I declare that our city is an education to Greece, and I declare that in my opinion each single one of our citizens, in all the manifold aspects of life, is able to show himself the rightful lord and owner of his own person, and do this, moreover, with exceptional grace and exceptional versatility. . . . Mighty indeed are the marks and monuments of our empire which we have left. Future ages will wonder at us, as the present age wonders at us now. We do not need the praises of a Homer, or of anyone else whose words may delight us for the moment, but whose estimation of facts will fall short of what is really true. For our adventurous spirit has forced an entry into every sea and into every land; and everywhere we have left behind us everlasting memorials of good done to our friends or suffering inflicted on our enemies.[3]

Such was the spirit of the Golden Age of classical Athens: proud, confident, serenely convinced that the city was "an education to Greece"—and not without reason. Twenty-five hundred years later, we still are moved by their tragedies, laugh at their comedies, admire their sculpture, are awed by their architecture, revere their democracy, and study their philosophers.

1. How did Athens come to preeminence among Greek cities?
2. For what qualities does Pericles praise Athens?

The Sophists

The social situation in fifth-century B.C. Athens called for innovations in education. The "best men" in the old sense no longer commanded a natural leadership. What counted was ability, as Pericles said, so men sought to develop their abilities.

Aristocratic education centering on Homer was no longer adequate. Most citizens received an elementary education that made them literate and gave them basic skills. If a father wanted his son to succeed in democratic Athens, however, more was needed.

To supply this need, a class of teachers arose offering what we can call higher education. Many of these teachers traveled from city to city as the call for their services waxed and waned. They were professionals who charged for their instruction. Because there was a substantial demand for their services, the best of them became quite wealthy. We can get a sense of what they claimed to provide for their students and of the eagerness with which they were sought out from the beginning of Plato's dialogue *Protagoras*. As we'll see, Protagoras was one of the greatest of these teachers.* Socrates is the speaker.

> Last night, just before daybreak, Hippocrates, the son of Apollodorus and brother of Phason, began knocking very loudly on the door with his stick, and when someone opened it he came straight in in a great hurry, calling out loudly, "Socrates, are you awake or asleep?" I recognized his voice and said, "It's Hippocrates; no bad news, I hope?" "Nothing but good news," he said. "Splendid," I said; "what is it, then? What brings you here so early?" He came

---

*Protagoras was paid in the following way. Before the instruction, he and his pupil would go to the temple; there the student would vow to pay, when the course was finished, whatever he then thought Protagoras' instruction was worth. It is said that when he died, Protagoras was wealthier than five Phidiases. (Phidias was the most famous sculptor in Athens.)

and stood beside me; "Protagoras has come," he said. "He came the day before yesterday," I said; "have you only just heard?" "Yes, indeed," he said; "yesterday evening. . . . Late as it was, I immediately got up to come and tell you, but then I realized that it was far too late at night; but as soon as I had had a sleep and got rid of my tiredness, I got up straight away and came over here, as you see."

I knew him to be a spirited and excitable character, so I said, "What's all this to you? Protagoras hasn't done you any wrong, has he?"

He laughed. "By heavens, he has, Socrates. He is the only man who is wise, but he doesn't make me wise too."

"Oh yes, he will," I said; "If you give him money and use a little persuasion, he'll make you wise as well."

"I wish to God," he said, "that that was all there was to it. I'd use every penny of my own, and of my friends too. But it's just that that I've come to you about now, so that you can put in a word for me with him. First of all, I'm too young, and then I've never seen Protagoras." (*Protagoras* 310a–e)[4]

Note the eagerness expressed by Hippocrates—and for education, too! What could this education be that excited such desire? What did the **Sophists,** as these teachers were called, offer?

While they wait for day to dawn, Socrates tries in his questioning fashion to see whether Hippocrates really knows what he is getting into. Not surprisingly, it turns out that he doesn't. Undaunted, they set off and go to the home where Protagoras is staying. After some difficulty (the servant at the door is sick of Sophists and slams the door in their faces), they meet Protagoras, who is in the company of a number of other young men and fellow Sophists. Socrates makes his request:

Hippocrates here is anxious to become your pupil; so he says that he would be glad to know what benefit he will derive from associating with you. (*Protagoras* 318a)

Protagoras answers,

Young man, . . . if you associate with me, this is the benefit you will gain: the very day you become my pupil you will go home a better man, and the same the next day; and every day you will continue to make progress. (*Protagoras* 318a)

Socrates, of course, is not satisfied with this answer. If Hippocrates were to associate with a famous painter, then each day his painting might improve. If he studied with a flutist, his flute playing would get better. But in what respect, exactly, will associating with Protagoras make Hippocrates "a better man"?

You have put a good question, Socrates, and I like answering people who do that. . . . What I teach is the proper management of one's own affairs, how best to run one's household, and the management of public affairs, how to make the most effective contribution to the affairs of the city both by word and action. (*Protagoras* 318d–319a)

Here we have the key to the excitement of Hippocrates and to the demand for this instruction from the rising middle class of Athens. The Sophists claim to be able to teach the things that foster success, both personal and political, in this democratic city. Many of them also teach specialized subjects such as astronomy, geometry, arithmetic, and music. Nearly all are committed to the new learning developed by the nature philosophers. They are self-consciously "modern," believing they represent progress and enlightenment as opposed to ignorance and superstition.

However, it is their claim to teach "excellence" or "virtue" (the Greek word *areté* can be translated either way) both in mastering one's own affairs and in providing leadership in the city that makes them popular.* The excellences they claim to teach are the skills, abilities, and traits of character that make one competent, successful, admired, and perhaps even wealthy.

The term "sophist" has rather negative connotations for us. A *sophism*, for instance, is a fallacious argument that looks good but isn't, and *sophistry*

---

*The Greek *areté* (ahr-e-tay) can apply to horses and knives, to flutists and cobblers, as well as to human beings as such. It has to do with the excellence of something when it does well what it is supposed to do. So it goes beyond the sphere of morality but includes it. Though usually translated "virtue," this English word is really too narrow. We will often use the broader term "excellence," and especially "human excellence," when what is in question is not someone's excellence as a teacher or sailor but as a human being.

is verbally pulling the wool over someone's eyes. The term did not always have such connotations. "Sophist" comes from the Greek *sophos*, meaning wise. The term was applied in the fifth century to many earlier wise men, including Homer and Hesiod. Undoubtedly, the best of the Sophists, such as Protagoras, were neither charlatans nor fools. In connection with their teaching the young, they also made important contributions to the great conversation. They were philosophers who had to be taken seriously; for this reason, they are of interest to us.

RHETORIC

All of the Sophists taught **rhetoric,** the principles and practice of persuasive speaking. Some of the Sophists, Gorgias for example, claimed to teach nothing but that. Clearly, in democratic Athens this art would be very valuable. Suppose, for instance, that you are brought into court by a neighbor. If you hem and haw, utter only irrelevancies, and cannot present the evidence on your side in a coherent and persuasive way, you are likely to lose whether you are guilty or not. Or suppose you feel strongly about some issue that affects the welfare of the city; only if you can stand up in the Assembly of citizens and speak persuasively will you have any influence. You must be able to present your case, marshal your arguments, and appeal to the feelings of the audience. This is the art the Sophists developed and taught.

In one of his dialogues, Plato represents Gorgias as claiming to teach

> the ability to use the spoken word to persuade the jurors in the courts, the members of the Council, the citizens attending the Assembly—in short, to win over any and every form of public meeting. (*Gorgias* 452e)[5]
>
> A rhetorician is capable of speaking effectively against all comers, whatever the issue, and can consequently be more persuasive in front of crowds about . . . anything he likes. (*Gorgias* 457b)

We need to understand what rhetoric means to the Sophists because its philosophical consequences are deep. The central idea is that by using the principles of persuasive speaking, one can make a case for any position at all. It follows that if there

are, as we often say these days, two sides to every issue, someone skilled in rhetoric should be able to present a persuasive argument for each side. In fact, this idea was embodied in one of the main teaching tools of the Sophists.

A student was encouraged to construct and present arguments on both sides of some controversial issue. He was not judged to be proficient until he could present a case as persuasive on one side as on the other. This method, presumably, was designed to equip a student for any eventuality; one never knew on what side of some future issue one's interests would lie.

A humorous story about Protagoras illustrates this method. Protagoras agreed to teach a young man how to conduct cases in the courts. Because the young man was poor, it was agreed that he would not have to pay his teacher until he won his first case. Some time elapsed after the course of instruction was over, and the student did not enter into any cases. Finally Protagoras himself brought the student to court, prosecuting him for payment. The student argued thus: If I win this case, I shall not have to pay Protagoras, according to the judgment of the court; if I lose this case, I will not yet have won my first case, and so I will not have to pay Protagoras according to the terms of our agreement; since I will either win or lose, I shall not have to pay. Protagoras, not to be outdone by his student, argued as follows: If he loses this case, then by the judgment of the court he must pay me; if he wins it, he will have won his first case and therefore will have to pay me; so, in either case, he will have to pay me.

The story is probably apocryphal, and the arguments may be "sophistical" in the bad sense, but it is not easy to see what has gone wrong. The example is not far from the flavor of much of the Sophists' teaching.

The philosophical interest of this technique can be seen if we recall certain meanings of the term *logos*, which connotes speech, thought, argument, and discourse. The Sophists trained their students to present opposite *logoi*. There was the *logos* (what could be said) on one side, and there was the *logos* on the other. The presumption was that for every side of every issue a persuasive *logos* could be developed. Some Sophists seem to have written works consisting of just such opposed *logoi*, presumably as examples for their students.

In this connection, we must note a phrase that later became notorious. It seems to have expressed a boast made by Protagoras and some of the other Sophists. They claimed to teach others *how to make the weaker argument into the stronger*. Suppose you are in court with what looks like a very weak case. The principles of rhetoric, if cleverly applied, could turn your argument into the stronger one—in the sense that it would be victorious.

Such a technique has profoundly skeptical implications. Think back to Heraclitus.* He believes that there is one *logos* uniting the many changing things of the world into one world-order. This *logos* is "common to all." Although many deviate from the *logos*, it is there and available to everyone. The wise are those who "listen to the *logos*" and order their own lives in accord with the pattern of the world-order. Think of Parmenides, who acknowledges that there is such a thing as the way of opinion but holds that it is quite distinct from the way of truth, in which "thought and being are the same."†

The practice of the Sophists seems to show that thought and being are *not* the same. Thought and being fall apart; there is no necessary correlation at all. No matter what the reality is, thought can represent it or misrepresent it with equal ease. If a *logos* that will carry conviction can be constructed on any side of any issue, how is one to tell when one is in accord with Heraclitus' *logos* and when one is not? How is one to discriminate the truth from mere opinion?

The Sophists' answer is that one cannot. All we have—and all we ever can have—are opinions. Parmenides writes of two ways, the way of truth and the way of opinion. The former represents the way things *are*, whereas the latter sets forth the way things *appear*. The practice of rhetoric raises doubts about our ability to distinguish appearance from reality. For human beings, things are as they seem to be. No more can be said.

So the Sophists agree with Democritus that we are "cut off from the real" by the conventional nature of our sense experience.* But unlike Democritus, they hold that there is no other avenue to the truth. Democritus thinks that reasoning can reveal what the eyes and ears cannot—that reality is composed of atoms and the void. However, if the Sophists are right, then the appeal to reasoning cannot be sustained. For one can reason equally well for and against atoms and the void—or, indeed, anything else!

As you can see, the Sophists tend to be skeptical about their predecessors' claims to reveal the truth, skeptical of human ability to come to know truth at all. You should be able to see how this **skepticism** is intimately related to the way they conceive and teach rhetoric. If rhetoric can make a convincing case for absolutely anything, then what can one know?

Such skepticism does not reduce them to silence, however. A person can still talk intelligibly about how things seem, even if not about how they really are. No doubt many of the theories of the nature philosophers are understood in just this way; they are plausible stories that represent the way the world seems to be. These stories represent probabilities at best, not the truth; but probabilities are the most that human beings can hope to attain. Without trying to penetrate to the core of reality, the Sophists are content with appearances. Without insisting on certainty, they are content with plausibility. Without knowledge, they are content with opinion.

The skeptical attitude is displayed in a statement by Protagoras concerning the gods. He is reported to have said,

> Concerning the gods I am not in a position to know either that they are or that they are not, or what they are like in appearance; for there are many things that are preventing knowledge, the obscurity of the matter and the brevity of human life. (DK 80 B 4, *IEGP*, 269)[6]

This statement seems to have been the basis for an accusation that Protagoras was an atheist. We

---

*See especially p. 20.
†See pp. 23–24.

---

*See p. 32.

know that he was at one time banished from Athens and that certain of his books were burned; it is likely that such statements were among those that aroused the anger of the citizens. (We will see a parallel in the case of Socrates.) Protagoras does not, however, deny the existence of the gods. He says that in light of the difficulty of the question, we are prevented from knowing about the gods. His view is not that of the atheist, then, but that of the **agnostic.** The only reasonable thing to do, he says, is to suspend judgment on this issue. This is the view of the skeptic.

1. What do the Sophists claim to teach? How do they understand *areté*?
2. What is rhetoric? How was it taught?
3. How does the concept of a *logos* come into Sophist teaching?

RELATIVISM

The Sophists' point of view is best summed up in a famous saying by Protagoras.

> Of all things the measure is man: of existing things, that they exist; of non-existing things, that they do not exist. (DK 80 B 1, *IEGP*, 245)

A "measure" is a standard or criterion to appeal to when deciding what to believe. Protagoras' statement that man is the measure of all things means that there is no criterion, standard, or mark by which to judge, except ourselves. We cannot jump outside our skins to see how things look independent of how they appear to us. *As they appear to us, so they are.*

Clearly, he means, in the first instance at least, that things are as they appear to the individual. A common example is the wind. Suppose the wind feels cold to one person and warm to another. Can we ask whether the wind is cold or warm in itself— apart from how it seems? Protagoras concludes that this question has no answer. If the wind seems cold to the first one, then to that person it *is* cold; and if it seems warm to the second, then it *is* warm—to that person. About the warmth or coldness of the wind, no more than this can be said. Each person

is the final judge of how the wind seems. Since it is not possible to get beyond such seemings, each individual is the final judge of how things *are* (to that individual, of course).

This doctrine is the heart of a viewpoint known as **relativism.** Here is the first appearance of one of the focal points of this book. From this point on, we see the major figures in our tradition struggling with the problems raised by relativism and the skepticism about our knowledge that attends it. Most of them oppose it. Some make certain concessions to it. But it has never been banished for long, and in one way or another it reappears throughout our history. In our own time, many have adopted some form of it. The Sophists set out the question in the clearest of terms and force us to come to grips with it.

We have now its essence. We need yet to understand what recommends it and what its implications are.

One implication that must have been obvious is that well-meaning citizens, not clearly prejudiced by self-interest, could disagree about the course the city should take. Another is that a well-wrought speech on any side of an issue could in fact convince a court or assembly of citizens. If you put these two observations together, it is not hard to draw the conclusion that the *best logos* about an issue is simply the one that does the best job of convincing. How can one judge which of two opposing *logoi* is the best, if not in terms of success? (An independent "logic," in terms of which one might judge that a certain persuasive device was "fallacious," had not yet been developed.) However, if there is no way to tell which *logos* is best except by observing which one *seems* best, then knowledge cannot be distinguished from opinion.* The best opinion is simply that which is generally accepted. But that means it may differ from culture to culture, from time to time, and even from individual to individual. There is no truth independent of what people accept. What seems true to one person or at one time may not seem true to another person or at another time. These observations and arguments

----

*See "Knowledge and Opinion" in Chapter 8 to see how Plato struggles against this view.

were surely among those that motivated the Sophists to adopt their relativism.

❧

"Relativists tend to understate the amount of attunement, recognition, and overlap that actually obtains across cultures."

Martha Nussbaum (b. 1947)

There was another factor. Greeks in general, and Athenians in particular, had expanded their horizons. They continued to distinguish, as Greeks always had done, between themselves and "barbarians," whom they took to be inferior to themselves. But the more they traveled and learned about the customs and characters of other nations, the harder it became to dismiss them as stupid and uncivilized. This exposure to non-Greek ways of doing things exerted a pressure on thought. These ways came to be seen not as inferior but simply as different. There is a famous example given by the historian Herodotus, who was himself a great traveler and observer.

> Everyone without exception believes his own native customs, and the religion he was brought up in, to be the best. . . . There is abundant evidence that this is the universal feeling about the ancient customs of one's country. One might recall, in particular, an anecdote of Darius. When he was king of Persia, he summoned the Greeks who happened to be present at his court, and asked them what they would take to eat the dead bodies of their fathers. They replied that they would not do it for any money in the world. Later, in the presence of the Greeks, and through an interpreter, so they could understand what was said, he asked some Indians, of the tribe called Callatiae, who do in fact eat their parents' dead bodies, what they would take to burn them. They uttered a cry of horror and forbade him to mention such a dreadful thing. One can see by this what custom can do, and Pindar, in my opinion, was right when he called it "king of all."[7]

PHYSIS AND NOMOS

The Sophists developed this notion that custom was "king of all" in terms of a distinction between *physis* and *nomos*. The word **physis** is the term for what

the nature philosophers were studying. It is usually translated as "nature" and means the characteristics of the world, or things in general, independent of what human beings impose on it. It is the word from which our "physics" is derived.

Nomos is the word for custom or convention, for those things that are as they are because humans have decided they should be so. Americans drive on the right side of the road, the English on the left. Neither practice is "natural," or by *physis*. This is a clear example of convention. We drive on one side in America and on the other side in England simply because we have agreed to. In the case Herodotus refers to, it is not so clear that an explicit decision is responsible for how the Greeks and the Indians care for their dead. These are practices that probably go back into prehistory. Still, neither practice is "by nature." Herodotus assigns the difference to custom, which is certainly *nomos*, for it is possible that, difficult as it might be, Greeks and Indians alike might change their practices. The mark of what is true by *physis* is that it is not up to us to decide, nor can we change it if we want to. If by agreement we can change the order of certain things (for example, which side of the road to drive on), then these things exist by *nomos*, not by *physis*.

Let us talk in terms of "the way things are." The way things are may be due to *physis* or to *nomos*. If they are due to *physis*, then we cannot go against them. For instance, it is part of the way things are that taking an ounce of strychnine will, unless immediate remedies are taken, cause one to die. It is not possible to swallow an ounce of strychnine, take no remedy, and continue to live. The connection between taking strychnine and death is a matter of *physis*. It does not depend on our decisions.

It is also part of the way things are that poisoning another person is punished in some way. In some societies, the punishment is death, whereas in others, it is imprisonment or a fine. How poisoners are punished is up to people. A particular poisoner could even be pardoned. If the way things are can be changed, then they are established by *nomos* and not by *physis*. It is for this reason that in cases of *nomos* we are likely to talk in terms of what a person "ought" to do: what is "right" or "appropriate" or "good" to do. With respect to the laws of nature, we have no choice, so there is no question of appropriateness. But conventions, customs, or laws that exist by *nomos* have a "normative" character to them. They state what we should do but may fail to do. We should not, in England, drive on the right, but we can. Murderers should be punished, but they sometimes are not.

The distinction is an important one, and the credit for making it clearly must go to the Sophists. But how, you might ask, did they use it?

The question about the gods can be put clearly using this terminology. Do the gods exist by *physis* or by *nomos*? To answer that they exist by nature is to claim that their existence is independent of whatever humans believe about them. To say that the gods exist only by *nomos* amounts to saying that they are dependent on our belief; they have no reality independent of what we believe about them. The skeptical and relativistic nature of Sophist thought favors the latter alternative. Certain Sophists may have said that if it seems to you the gods exist, then they do exist—for you. But the agnosticism of Protagoras is probably more representative.

The distinction between *nomos* and *physis* is also applied to the virtues and, in particular, to justice. If a settled community like a city-state is to survive, then a certain degree of justice must prevail. Agreements must be kept, deceptions must be exceptions, and each individual must be able to count on others to keep up their end of things. So much is clear.* But is justice, which demands these things, something good by nature? Or is it merely a convention, foisted on individuals perhaps against their own best interest? Is justice a matter of *physis*, or is it entirely *nomos*? This question is important. The Sophists debated it extensively, as did Plato and his successors.

It is clear how the Sophists must answer this question. They can look back to the creation of democracy, which is obviously a change made by

human beings. They can see the process of laws being debated and set down. They observe decisions being made and sometimes reversed. Clearly, forms of government, laws, and customs are matters of *nomos*. They are made by and can be altered by human decisions.

From the Sophists' point of view, if you want to know what is right or just, consult the laws. Is it just to keep agreements made? It is if the laws say so. How much tax is owed? The laws will tell you. For matters not covered explicitly by law, you must look to the customs of the people. Where else can one look? Just as there is no sense in asking whether the wind in itself is either cold or warm (apart from the way it seems to those who feel it), so is there no sense in asking whether a given law is really just. If it seems just to the people of Athens, say, then it is just (for the Athenians).

For clarity's sake, let's call this sense of justice conventional justice. Conventional justice is defined as whatever the conventions (the *nomoi*) of a given society lay down as just.

We can contrast with this the idea of natural justice. Heraclitus, for instance, holds that

> all human laws are nourished by the one divine law. For it governs as far as it will, and is sufficient for all things, and outlasts them. (DK 22 B 114, *IEGP*, 103)

His idea is that human laws do not have their justification in themselves. They are "nourished," or get their sustenance, from a "divine law." This divine law, of course, is "common to all," the one *logos*. So human laws are not self-sufficient, in Heraclitus' view. Because people are often "at variance" with the *logos*, we can infer that human law, too, may diverge from the *logos*. It makes sense for Heraclitus to contrast conventional justice with real or natural justice. He believes not only that there is a court of appeal from a possibly unjust human law, but also that human beings can know what divine law requires.

An example of such an appeal is found in **Sophocles'** play *Antigone*. Following a civil war, Creon, king of Thebes, proclaims that the body of Polyneices, leader of the opposition, remain unburied. This was, in Greek tradition, a very bad thing; only if one's body was buried could the

---

*Justice in this context is clearly something more than the justice of Homeric heroes giving one another the honor due to each (see p. 6). What is needed in settled city-states is more extensive than what is needed by warrior bands. Some notion of fair play or evenhandedness seems to be involved. The nature of justice is a perennial problem, and we will return to it.

spirit depart for Hades. Polyneices' sister, **Antigone,** defies the decree and covers the body with dirt. Before the king, she acknowledges that she knew of the king's order and defends her action in these words.

> It was not Zeus who published this decree,
> Nor have the Powers who rule among the dead
> Imposed such laws as this upon mankind;
> Nor could I think that a decree of yours—
> A man—could override the laws of Heaven
> Unwritten and unchanging. Not of today
> Or yesterday is their authority;
> They are eternal; no man saw their birth.
> Was I to stand before the gods' tribunal
> For disobeying them, because I feared
> A man?[8]

Both Heraclitus and Antigone suggest that beyond conventional justice there is another justice. If the laws established by convention violate these higher laws, it may be permissible to violate the conventions.* For the Sophists, however, no such appeal is possible. One might not like a law and therefore work to change it, but there is no appeal to another kind of law to justify its violation. Their skepticism about any reality beyond appearances and their consequent relativism rule out any such appeal.

A certain conservatism seems to be a consequence of this way of looking at justice. Protagoras, for instance, in promising to make Hippocrates a "better man," one able to succeed in Athenian society, would scarcely teach him that Athens is profoundly mistaken in her ideas of justice. He certainly would not turn him into a rebel and malcontent or even into a reformer. That is no way to attain the admiration of one's fellow citizens; that is the way to earn their hostility and hatred. So it is likely that the Sophists taught their students to adapt to whatever society they found.

Some of the Sophists, though, draw different conclusions. They agree with Heraclitus that there is a natural justice, but they disagree completely about its content. Natural justice, they hold, is not the "nourisher" of conventional justice, but its enemy. A Sophist named **Antiphon** writes,

> Life and death are the concern of nature, and living creatures live by what is advantageous to them and die from what is not advantageous; and the advantages which accrue from law are chains upon nature, whereas those which accrue from nature are free. (DK 87 B 44, *IEGP*, 251)

Antiphon is telling us that if we only observe, we can see that a *natural* law governs the affairs of men and other living creatures: the law of self-preservation. Like all laws, it carries a punishment for those who violate it: death. Unlike conventional laws, this punishment necessarily follows the violation of the law. That is what makes it a natural law rather than a matter of convention. All creatures, he says, follow this law by seeking what is "advantageous" to themselves.

In contrast to *this* natural law, the restraints conventional justice places on human behavior are "chains upon nature." Antiphon goes as far as to claim that

> most of the things which are just by law [in the conventional sense] are hostile to nature. (DK 87 B 44, *IEGP*, 251)

It is natural, then, and therefore right or just (in the sense of *physis*) to pursue what is advantageous. Some of the time your advantage may coincide with the laws of the city. But because there is a tension between conventional law and your advantage, and because seeking your advantage is in accord with natural law, Antiphon gives us this remarkable piece of advice:

> A man will be just, then, in a way most advantageous to himself if, in the presence of witnesses, he holds the laws of the city in high esteem, and in the absence of witnesses, when he is alone, those of nature. For the laws of men are adventitious, but those of nature are necessary; and the laws of men are fixed by agreement, not by nature, whereas the laws of nature are natural and not fixed by agreement. He who breaks the rules, therefore, and escapes detection by those who have agreed to them, incurs no shame or penalty; if detected he does. (DK 87 B 44, *IEGP*, 250–251)

---

*Note that we have here a justification for civil disobedience. A more recent example is Martin Luther King Jr.'s 1963 "Letter from Birmingham Jail."

If you break conventional laws without getting caught, then you have not brought any disadvantage on yourself by doing so. Furthermore, the law of self-preservation takes precedence over the conventional laws because it is "necessary" and "natural." Only *its* prescriptions cannot be evaded. Antiphon drives the point home:

> If some benefit accrued to those who subscribed to the laws, while loss accrued to those who did not subscribe to them but opposed them, then obedience to the laws would not be without profit. But as things stand, it seems that legal justice is not strong enough to benefit those who subscribe to laws of this sort. For in the first place it permits the injured party to suffer injury and the man who inflicts it to inflict injury, and it does not prevent the injured party from suffering injury nor the man who does the injury from doing it. And if the case comes to trial, the injured party has no more of an advantage than the one who has done the injury; for he must convince his judges that he has been injured, and must be able, by his plea, to exact justice. And it is open to the one who has done the injury to deny it; for he can defend himself against the accusation, and he has the same opportunity to persuade his judges that his accuser has. For the victory goes to the best speaker. (DK 87 B 44, *IEGP*, 252–253)

"For the victory goes to the best speaker": We come around again to rhetoric. No matter which of the sophistic views of justice you take, rhetoric is of supreme importance. Whether you say that conventional justice is the only justice there is or hold that there is a natural justice of self-preservation, it is more important to *appear* just than to *be* just. According to the former view, appearances are all anyone can know; according to the latter, the way you appear to others determines whether you obtain what is most advantageous to yourself.

The Sophists produced a theory of the origins of conventional justice as well. It is not clear how widespread it was; there was no unified sophistic doctrine. But it is of great interest and was picked up in the nineteenth century by Friedrich Nietzsche, who made it a key point in his attempt

at a "revaluation of values."* It is represented for us by **Callicles** in Plato's *Gorgias*.

> In my opinion it's the weaklings who constitute the majority of the human race who make the rules. In making these rules, they look after themselves and their own interest, and that's also the criterion they use when they dispense praise and criticism. They try to cow the stronger ones—which is to say, the ones who are capable of increasing their share of things—and to stop them getting an increased share, by saying that to do so is wrong and contemptible and by defining injustice in precisely those terms, as the attempt to have more than others. In my opinion, it's because they're second-rate that they're happy for things to be distributed equally. Anyway, that's why convention states that the attempt to have a larger share than most people is immoral and contemptible; that's why people call it doing wrong. But I think we only have to look at nature to find evidence that it is *right* for better to have a greater share than worse, more capable than less capable. The evidence for this is widespread. Other creatures show, as do human communities and nations, that right has been determined as follows: the superior person shall dominate the inferior person and have more than him. By what right, for instance, did Xerxes make war on Greece or his father on Sythia, not to mention countless further cases of the same kind of behaviour? These people act, surely, in conformity with the natural essence of right and, yes, I'd even go so far as to say that they act in conformity with natural *law*, even though they presumably contravene our man-made laws.
>
> What do we do with the best and strongest among us? We capture them young, like lions, mould them, and turn them into slaves by chanting spells and incantations over them which insist that they have to be equal to others and that equality is admirable and right. But I'm sure that if a man is born in whom nature is strong enough, he'll shake off all these limitations, shatter them to pieces, and win his freedom; he'll trample all our regulations, charms, spells, and unnatural laws into the dust; this slave will rise up and reveal himself as our master; and then natural right will blaze forth. (*Gorgias* 483b–484a)

---

*See Chapter 24, especially pp. 580–581.

Callicles' basic idea is that we are by nature equipped with certain passions and desires. It is natural to try to satisfy these. Although the weak may try to fetter the strong by imposing a guilty conscience on them, the strong do nothing contrary to nature if they exert all their power and cleverness to satisfy whatever desires they have. Such behavior may be conventionally frowned upon, but it is not, in itself, unjust.

Note how dramatically this contrasts with the ethics of the Greek tradition. Compare it, for instance, to Heraclitus, who holds that it is not good for men to get all they wish, that "moderation is the greatest virtue."*

Callicles advocates satisfying one's desires to the fullest extent, not moderating them. The really happy man is the one who is strong enough to do this without fear of retaliation. Here we have the very opposite of the "nothing too much" doctrine at Delphi—a negation of the tradition of self-restraint.

The Sophists' views are bold and innovative, a response to the changing social and political situation, particularly in democratic Athens. But they are more than just reflections of a particular society at a given time. They constitute a serious critique of the beliefs of their predecessors and a challenge to those who come after them. These views force us to face the question: Why shouldn't we be Sophists too?

1. Explain Protagoras' saying, "Man is the measure of all things."
2. What in the Sophists' teaching tends toward relativism?
3. Contrast *physis* with *nomos*.
4. Contrast conventional justice with natural justice. What two different concepts of natural justice can be distinguished?
5. How could the *physis/nomos* distinction be turned toward an antisocial direction?
6. Would a Sophist say that it is more important to be just or to appear just? Why?

*See p. 21.

Athens and Sparta at War

In the context of the sophistic movement, we are philosophically prepared to understand Socrates and his disciple, Plato. But to understand why Socrates was brought to trial, we need to know something of the **Peloponnesian War,** as it was called by the historian Thucydides, who lived through it.* The Peloponnesus is the large peninsula at the southern tip of mainland Greece, connected by the narrow Isthmus of Corinth to Greece proper. It was named for a largely mythical ancestor, Pelops, supposedly the grandson of Zeus and the grandfather of Agamemnon and Menelaus of Trojan War fame. In the fifth century B.C., the dominant power on the peninsula was the city-state of Sparta (see Map 1).

Sparta was quite unlike Athens. The Spartans had taken an important role in the defeat of the Persians, but thereafter, unlike Athens, they had followed a more cautious and defensive policy. Sparta was primarily a land power; Athens ruled the seas. Although the Spartans had allies, mostly in the Peloponnesus, Athens had created an empire dominating most of the north of Greece and most of the islands in the Aegean. Sparta was not democratic. Rule in Sparta was in the hands of a relatively small portion of the population, in effect a warrior class. Their way of life was austere and, as we say, spartan—devoted not to wealth and enjoyment but to rigorous training and self-discipline. They were supported by a large slave population called Helots and by other subject peoples in the area.

Perhaps it was inevitable that two such formidable powers in close proximity and so different would clash. They cooperated well enough in repelling the Persian invasion, but when that danger was past, their interests diverged. As Thucydides tells us,

What made war inevitable was the growth of Athenian power and the fear which this caused in Sparta. (*HPW* 1.23)[9]

*For Peloponnesian War, see https://en.wikipedia.org/wiki/Peloponnesian_War.

War may have been inevitable, but its coming was tragic. In the end, it led to the defeat of Athens and to the weakening of Greece in general. It meant the beginning of the end of the Golden Age of Greece.

The war itself was long and drawn out, lasting from 431 to 404 B.C., with an interval of seven years of relative peace in the middle. It was immensely costly to both sides, in terms of both men lost and wealth squandered. We will not go into the details of the war; they can be found in Thucydides or any of a number of modern histories.* But war does things to a people, especially a long and inconclusive war fought with increasing desperation.

Athens encouraged the development of democracy in her allies and appealed to the people (as opposed to the aristocrats) in cities she hoped to bring into her empire. These moves were resisted by the aristocratic or oligarchical parties in these states, who were often supported by Sparta. Thucydides records the events in Corcyra (see Map 1) after the victory of the democratic side over the oligarchs.

> They seized upon all their enemies whom they could find and put them to death. They then dealt with those whom they had persuaded to go on board the ships, killing them as they landed. Next they went to the temple of Hera and persuaded about fifty of the suppliants there to submit to a trial. They condemned every one of them to death. Seeing what was happening, most of the other suppliants, who had refused to be tried, killed each other there in the temple; some hanged themselves on the trees, and others found various other means of committing suicide. During the seven days that Eurymedon [an Athenian naval commander] stayed there with his sixty ships, the Corcyreans continued to massacre those of their own citizens whom they considered to be their enemies. Their victims were accused of conspiring to overthrow the democracy, but in fact men were often killed on grounds of personal hatred or else by their debtors because of the money they owed. There was death in every shape and form. And, as usually happens in such situations, people went to every extreme and beyond it. There were fathers who killed their sons; men were dragged from the temples or butchered on the very

altars; some were actually walled up in the temple of Dionysus and died there. . . .

Later, of course, practically the whole of the Hellenic world was convulsed, with rival parties in every state—democratic leaders trying to bring in the Athenians, and oligarchs trying to bring in the Spartans. (*HPW* 3.81–3.83)

We can see here the disintegration of the traditional Greek ideal of moderation; people "went to every extreme and beyond it." Moreover, the arguments of the more extreme Sophists found a parallel in concrete political undertakings. Naked self-interest came more and more to play the major role in decisions no longer even cloaked in terms of justice. Perhaps worst of all, Thucydides says, the very meaning of the words for right and virtue changed. When that happens, confusion reigns while moral thought and criticism become impossible.

Pericles died in the early years of the war, leaving Athens without a natural leader. Leadership tended to flow to those who could speak persuasively before the Assembly. These leaders were called "demagogues," those who could lead (*agoge*) the *demos*. Policy was inconstant and sometimes reversed, depending on who was the most persuasive speaker of the day. Dissatisfaction with democracy began to grow, especially in quarters traditionally allied with the "best people." When Athens was finally defeated in 404, treachery on the part of these enemies of democracy was suspected but could not be proved.

According to the terms of the peace treaty imposed on Athens, she had to receive returning exiles (most of whom were antidemocratic), agree to have the same friends and enemies as Sparta, and accept provisional government by a Council that came to be known as **the Thirty.** A new constitution was promised, but naturally the Thirty were in no hurry to form a new government. Supported by Spartan men-at-arms, they purged "wrongdoers," executing criminals and those who had opposed surrender. They soon began to persecute dissidents, as well as people they just didn't like, expropriating their property to support the new system. They claimed, of course, to be enforcing virtue. In classic fashion, they tried to involve as

---

* See suggestions in Note 1, at the close of this chapter.

many Athenian citizens as possible in their adventures to prevent them from making accusations later. Socrates, as we learn, was one of five persons summoned to arrest a certain Leon of Salamis. (He refused.) The rule of the Thirty became, in short, a reign of terror. Ever after, Athenians could not hear the words "the Thirty" without a shudder.

This rule lasted less than a year. Exiles, joined by democratic forces within the city, attacked and defeated the forces backing the Thirty. Their leader **Critias** was killed in the fighting, the others were exiled, and democracy was restored. Though a bloodbath was resisted, bad feelings on all sides continued for many years.

Because of the war and its aftermath, Athenians lost confidence in their ability to control their own destiny. The satisfaction in their superiority expressed so well by Pericles disintegrated. Men seemed torn by forces beyond their ability to control in a world that was not well ordered, whether by the gods or by something like the Heraclitean *logos*. The world and human affairs seemed chaotic, beyond managing.

The Greeks had always believed, of course, that humans were not complete masters of their own fate. This belief was expressed in the ideas that the gods intervene in human affairs for their own ends and that none of us can escape our fate. We find such ideas in the works of Homer and in the tragedies of Aeschylus and Sophocles. But in the time of the war, these notions were tinged with a new sense of bitterness and despair.

The third of the great Greek tragedians, **Euripides,** expresses the new mood in his play, *Hippolytus*. The play opens with Aphrodite condemning Hippolytus for scorning love (and so, by extension, Aphrodite). By sparking a passionate desire for Hippolytus in his stepmother, Phaedra, Aphrodite sets off a chain of events that leads to both Phaedra's and Hippolytus' deaths. As Hippolytus dies, the goddess Artemis, to whom he had been devoted, vows to take vengeance against Aphrodite by killing whichever mortal she loves best. The impression left by the play is that humans are mere pawns in the hands of greater powers—powers that are in opposition to each other, that make no sense, and have no rhyme or

reason in some higher unity of purpose. Led this way or that by passions we cannot control, we are bound for destruction.

> The chorus laments near the end:
> The care of God for us is a great thing,
> if a man believe it at heart:
> it plucks the burden of sorrow from him.
> So I have a secret hope
> of someone, a God, who is wise and plans;
> but my hopes grow dim when I see
> the deeds of men and their destinies.
> For fortune is ever veering, and the currents of life
>   are shifting,
> shifting, wandering forever. [10]

We have the hope, the chorus says, that our lives are more than "sound and fury, signifying nothing."* We would like to believe that there is a wise plan to our lives, but if we look about us at the world—and, the Sophists would say, what else can we do?—we find no such reason to hope. Men's fortunes are "ever veering, and the currents of life are shifting, shifting, wandering forever."†

So things must have looked in the last decades of the fifth century B.C. in Athens.

Aristophanes and Reaction

Although the Sophists were popular in some circles, they were hated and feared in others. They were a phenomenon that both depended on and fostered the kind of democracy Athens practiced: direct democracy where decisions were made by whichever citizens were present in the Assembly on a given day. Political power rested directly with the people in this system, but the masses, of course, tended to be at the mercy of those who possessed the rhetorical skills to sway them in the direction of their own interests: the demagogues. The old families who could look back to the "good old days" when the "best people" ruled were never happy in this state of affairs. As we have seen, they tried, when they

---

*Shakespeare's *Macbeth*, act 5, scene 5.
†A somewhat altered version of the play is available in the movie *Phaedra*, starring Melina Mercouri and Anthony Perkins.

could, to reverse the situation—not always with better results!

Among those who were unhappy were certain intellectuals, including a writer of comedies named **Aristophanes.** One of his plays, ***The Clouds**,** satirizes the Sophists. It is worth a look not only because it gives us another point of view on the Sophists but also because Aristophanes makes Socrates a principal character in the play. In fact, Socrates appears in *The Clouds* as the leading Sophist, who runs a school called the "Thinkery" to which students come to learn—provided they pay. When we first see Socrates, he is hanging in the air, suspended in a basket.

> You see,
> only by being suspended aloft, by dangling
> my mind in the heavens and mingling my rare
>   thought
> with the ethereal air, could I ever achieve strict
> scientific accuracy in my survey of the vast
>   empyrean.
> Had I pursued my inquiries from down there on
>   the ground,
> my data would be worthless. The earth, you see,
>   pulls down
> the delicate essence of thought to its own gross
>   level.
>
> —*Clouds,* p. 33[11]

This is, of course, attractive nonsense. As we'll see, Socrates neither had a Thinkery, charged for instruction, nor was interested in speculations about the heavens and earth. Most important, although he shared the Sophists' interest in human affairs, Socrates was one of their most severe critics. Aristophanes' picture of Socrates is satire painted with a broad brush.

Socrates' students are represented as engaging in scientific studies to determine, for example, how far a flea can jump and out of which end a gnat tootles. But that is not the main interest of the play. Strepsiades, a man from the country who has married an extravagant city wife and has a son who loves horse racing, is worried about the debts they have piled up. In particular, several of his son's

debts are coming due and he hasn't the money to pay them. So he sends his son to the Thinkery to learn the new sophistic logic, which can make the weaker argument into the stronger. He thinks that by getting his son to learn these rhetorical tricks he may be able to avoid paying back the money.

Strepsiades is at first unable to persuade his son to go. So he becomes a student himself. He does not prove an apt pupil, however, and Socrates eventually kicks him out, but not before he has learned a thing or two. When he meets his son, Pheidippides, he again tries to force him to go to the school.

PHEIDIPPIDES: But Father,
    what's the matter with you? Are you out of your
    head?
    Almighty Zeus, you must be mad!
STREPSIADES: "Almighty Zeus!"
    What musty rubbish! Imagine, a boy your age still
    believing in Zeus!
P: What's so damn funny?
S: It tickles me when the heads of toddlers like you are
    still stuffed with such outdated notions.
    Now then,
    listen to me and I'll tell you a secret or two that
    might make an intelligent man of you yet. But re-
    member. You mustn't breathe a word of this.
P: A word of what?
S: Didn't you just swear by Zeus?
P: I did.
S: Now learn what Education can do for you: Pheidip-
    pides, there is no Zeus.
P: There is no Zeus?
S: No Zeus. Convection-Principle's in power now.
    Zeus has been banished.

            —*Clouds,* pp. 75–76

The "convection principle" is our old friend the vortex motion or cosmic whirl, by means of which the nature philosophers explain the structure of the world. In the form given this principle by the atomists, as we have seen, there is no need for—indeed, no room for—any intelligent purpose at all. Everything is caused to happen in a completely mechanical fashion. Zeus has indeed been "banished."

Aristophanes, far from conceding that this is progress, deplores the new thought. The old

---

*First performed in Athens in 423 B.C., the eighth year of the war.

methods of education are farcically confronted with the new by means of two characters, dressed in the masks of fighting cocks, called the just *logos* and the unjust *logos*. (In this translation, they are called "Philosophy" and "Sophistry," respectively.) After some preliminary sparring and insult trading, the just *logos* speaks first.

PHILOSOPHY: Gentlemen,
I propose to speak of the Old Education, as it flourished once
beneath my tutelage, when Homespun Honesty, Plainspeaking, and Truth
were still honored and practiced, and throughout the schools of Athens
the regime of the three D's—DISCIPLINE, DECORUM, and DUTY—
enjoyed unchallenged supremacy.
Our curriculum was Music and Gymnastics, enforced by that rigorous discipline summed up in the old adage:
BOYS SHOULD BE SEEN BUT NOT HEARD. . . .
SOPHISTRY: Ugh, what musty, antiquated rubbish. . . .
P: Nonetheless, these were the precepts on which I
bred a generation of heroes, the men who fought at Marathon. . . .
No, young man, by your courage I challenge you. Turn your back upon his blandishments of vice,
the rotten law courts and the cheap, corrupting softness of the baths.
Choose instead the Old, the Philosophical Education. Follow me
and from my lips acquire the virtues of a man:—
A sense of shame, that decency and innocence of mind that shrinks from doing wrong.
To feel the true man's blaze of anger when his honor is provoked.
Deference toward one's elders; respect for one's father and mother.

—*Clouds*, pp. 86–89

This speech is applauded roundly by the chorus, who say that the unjust *logos* will have to produce "some crushing *tour de force*, some master stroke" to counter these persuasive comments. The unjust *logos* is not at a loss.

SOPHISTRY: Now then, I freely admit
that among men of learning I am—somewhat pejoratively—dubbed
the Sophistic, or Immoral Logic. And why? Because I first
devised a Method for the Subversion of Established Social Beliefs
and the Undermining of Morality. Moreover, this little invention of mine,
this knack of taking what might appear to be the worse argument
and nonetheless winning my case, has, I might add, proved to be
an *extremely* lucrative source of income. . . .
—Young man,
I advise you to ponder this life of Virtue with scrupulous care,
all that it implies, and all the pleasures of which its daily practice
must inevitably deprive you. Specifically, I might mention these:
Sex. Gambling. Gluttony. Guzzling. Carousing. Etcet.
And what on earth's the point of living, if you leach your life
of all its little joys?
Very well then, consider your natural needs.
Suppose, as a scholar of Virtue, you commit
some minor peccadillo,
a little adultery, say, or seduction, and suddenly find yourself
caught in the act. What happens? You're ruined, you can't defend yourself
(since, of course, you haven't been taught). But follow me, my boy,
and obey your nature to the full; romp, play, and laugh
without a scruple in the world. Then if caught in flagrante,
you simply inform the poor cuckold that you're utterly innocent
and refer him to Zeus as your moral sanction. After all, didn't he,
a great and powerful god, succumb to the love of women?
Then how in the world can you, a man, an ordinary mortal,

be expected to surpass the greatest of gods in moral self-control?

Clearly, you can't be.

—*Clouds*, pp. 91–94

To his father's satisfaction, Pheidippides is persuaded to study with the Sophists. But the climax comes when the son turns what he has learned, not on the creditors, but on his father. After a quarrel, he begins to beat his father with a stick. This is not bad enough; he claims to be able to *prove* that he is right to do so!

PHEIDIPPIDES: Now then, answer my question: did you lick me when I was a little boy?

STREPSIADES: Of course I licked you.

For your own damn good. Because I loved you.

P: Then *ipso facto*,

since you yourself admit that loving and lickings are synonymous, it's only fair that I—for your own damn good,

you understand—whip you in return.

In any case by what right do you whip me but claim exemption for yourself?

What do you think I am? A slave?

Wasn't I born as free a man as you?

Well?

S: But . . .

P: But what?

Spare the Rod and Spoil the Child?

Is that your argument?

If so,

then I can be sententious too. *Old Men Are Boys Writ Big*,

as the saying goes.

A fortiori then, old men logically deserve to be beaten more, since at their age they have clearly less excuse for the mischief that they do.

S: But it's unnatural! It's . . . *illegal!*

Honor your father and mother.

That's the law.

Everywhere.

P: The *law*?

And who made the law?

An ordinary man. A man like you or me.

A man who lobbied for his bill until he persuaded the people to make it law.

By the same token, then, what prevents me now from proposing new legislation granting sons the power to

inflict corporal punishment upon wayward fathers? . . .

However, if you're still unconvinced, look to Nature for a sanction. Observe the roosters,

for instance, and what do you see?

A society

whose pecking order envisages a permanent state of open

warfare between fathers and sons. And how do roosters

differ from men, except for the trifling fact that human society is based upon law and rooster society isn't?

—*Clouds*, pp. 122–124

Strepsiades is forced by the "persuasive power" of this rhetoric to admit defeat: "The kids," he says, "have proved their point: naughty fathers should be flogged." But when Pheidippides adds that since "misery loves company" he has decided to flog his *mother*, too, and can prove "by Sokratic logic" the propriety of doing so, that's the last straw. Strepsiades cries out,

By god, if you prove *that*,
then for all I care, you heel,
you can take your stinking Logics
and your Thinkery as well
with Sokrates inside it
and damn well go to hell!

—*Clouds*, p. 126

Disillusioned by the promise of sophistry, Strepsiades admits he was wrong to try to cheat his son's creditors. Convinced that the new education is, as the just *logos* has put it, the "corrupter and destroyer" of the youth, he ends the play by burning down the Thinkery. The moral is drawn, as it typically is, by the chorus—in this case a chorus of Clouds representing the goddesses of the new thought:

This is what we are,
the insubstantial Clouds men build their hopes upon,
shining tempters formed of air, symbols of desire;
and so we act, beckoning, alluring foolish men
through their dishonest dreams of gain to overwhelming

ruin. There, schooled by suffering, they learn at last to fear the gods.

—*Clouds*, p. 127

The Clouds is surely not a fair and dispassionate appraisal of the sophistic movement. It is a caricature by a traditionalist deeply antagonistic to the changes Athenian society was going through. And yet it poses some serious questions. Is there a way to distinguish between *logoi* independent of their persuasiveness? If not, is argument just a contest that the most persuasive must win? And if Strepsiades can think of no logical rejoinder to his son's sophisms, what is the outcome? Are arson and violence the only answer? But if that is so, in what sense is that answer superior to the rhetoric that it opposes? Isn't it just employing another tool of force, less subtle than the verbal manipulations of the rhetorician?

What is put in question by the Sophists and Aristophanes' response to them is this: Is there any technique by which people can discuss and come to agree on matters important to them that does not reduce to a power struggle in the end? Is there something that can be identified as being reasonable, as opposed to being merely persuasive? Can human beings, by discussing matters together, come to know the truth? Or is it always just a question of who wins?

This is the question that interests Socrates.

---

1. What philosophical question is posed by Aristophanes' play *The Clouds*?

KEY WORDS

Athens	relativism
democracy	*physis*
Persian wars	*nomos*
Pericles	Sophocles
Sophists	Antigone
areté	Antiphon
rhetoric	Callicles
skepticism	Peloponnesian War
agnostic	The Thirty

Critias
Euripides
Hippolytus

Aristophanes
The Clouds

FOR FURTHER THOUGHT

1. Sophist/relativist views about the good or the true are often expressed by the question "Who's to say?" Is that a good question? If not, why not?
2. What do you think? Is it more important to *be* just or to *appear* just? Why?

NOTES

1. *The Pelican History of Greece* by A. R. Burn (New York: Penguin Books, 1984) is a lively treatment of these matters. A standard source is J. B. Bury, *A History of Greece* (London: Macmillan, 1951). The Greek historians Herodotus, Thucydides, and Xenophon are also quite readable.
2. Quotations from Herodotus, *The Histories* (New York: Penguin Books, 1972), are cited in the text by title, book number, and section number.
3. Thucydides, *History of the Peloponnesian War*, trans. Rex Warner (New York: Penguin Books, 1954), 2.35–41.
4. Quotations from Plato's *Protagoras*, trans, C. C. W. Taylor (Oxford: Oxford University Press, 1996), are cited in the text by title and section numbers.
5. Quotations from Plato's *Gorgias*, trans. Robin Waterfield (Oxford: Oxford University Press, 1994), are cited in the text by title and section number.
6. Quotations from John Manley Robinson's *An Introduction to Early Greek Philosophy* (Boston: Houghton Mifflin, 1968) are cited in the text using the standard Diels/Kranz numbers, followed by the page number in *IEGP*.
7. Herodotus, *The Histories* (Penguin Books, 1972), bk. 3, sec. 38.
8. Sophocles, *Antigone*, trans. H. D. F. Kitto, in *Sophocles: Three Tragedies* (London: Oxford University Press, 1962), ll. 440–450.
9. Quotations from Thucydides, *History of the Peloponnesian War*, trans. Rex Warner (New York: Penguin Books, 1954), are cited in the text using

the abbreviation *HPW*. References are to book and section numbers.

10. Euripides'*Hippolytus*, trans. David Grene, in *Euripides I*, ed. David Grene and Richmond Lattimore (Chicago: University of Chicago Press, 1965), ll. 1102–1110.

11. Quotations from Aristophanes' *Clouds*, trans. William Arrowsmith (New York: New American Library, 1962), are cited in the text by title and page numbers.

CHAPTER

5

REASON AND RELATIVISM IN CHINA

Social and political turmoil, it seems, makes fertile ground for philosophy. In the previous chapter, we considered how Greek philosophy flowered in Athens during the political turmoil of the fifth century B.C. In this chapter, we look to another society in turmoil to find a similar philosophical flowering: ancient China. From the sixth century B.C. until China's political reunification under the Qin dynasty in 221 B.C., Chinese thinkers developed a variety of philosophies, known as the **Hundred Schools of Thought.** Of these, six emerged as most important. In this chapter, we will focus on three of these schools that illustrate the development of logic and reason in ancient China: the Mohists, named after their founder Mozi; the School of Names, sometimes called the Logicians; and Daoism, especially as embodied in the work of Zhuangzi. As when we examined some early philosophical movements in India, we will not attempt a complete survey of these schools. Instead, we will consider specific aspects that throw the Chinese and Western traditions into sharper relief by bringing out the similarities and differences between them. For though

Western and Chinese philosophy had no interaction with each other until much later, we can learn a great deal about each of these great conversations by using one to see how differently the other might have turned out.

A Brief History of Ancient China

In recounting the earliest history of China, it is hard to know where legend ends and fact begins. That is because by the time our story begins, in about 551 B.C., the story of Chinese history was already more than two thousand years long. That story begins with the mythical founders of civilization, including Fuxi (who taught the people how to hunt and fish), Shen Nong (who taught them how to farm), and the **Yellow Emperor.** After a series of other famous rulers, there allegedly arose the three **sage kings:** Emperor Yao, whose morally perfect leadership culminated in his decision to pass the throne to a worthy successor rather than to his unworthy sons; Emperor

Shun, the able administrator to whom Yao passed the throne; and Emperor Yu, whom Shun chose as his own successor. These mythical figures would be remembered as model rulers and moral exemplars. Yu, it is said, founded the Xia dynasty, the first of three ancient dynasties in traditional accounts of Chinese history. It is unclear whether the Xia dynasty really existed. If it did, it may have been the same as the ancient Erlitou culture uncovered by archaeologists in what is now north-central China and believed to date from the eighteenth to the sixteenth centuries B.C., roughly consistent with the traditional histories that place the Xia dynasty in the first half of the second millennium B.C.

No later than the middle of the second millennium B.C., however, legend gives way to fact with the rise of the Shang dynasty, the first dynasty with a clear grounding in the historical and archaeological record. Founded by King Tang, the Shang developed a sophisticated Bronze Age society and pioneered the earliest form of Chinese writing. After nearly five centuries ruling what is now north-central China, they were conquered by the **Zhou dynasty** in 1046 B.C.

Building on the Shang culture, the Zhou dynasty established a complex society governed by a vast constellation of feudal states, all subordinate to the Zhou kings.* The Zhou kings claimed that they ruled with Heaven's blessing, which had passed to them from the Shang because of their moral superiority to the degenerate late Shang kings. This established the idea of the **Mandate of Heaven,** a divine right to rule based on moral goodness and beneficence toward the people. Although the dynasty's founding rulers, King Wen and his son, King Wu, were revered as models of good leadership, the strength and moral superiority of the Zhou kings dwindled as the centuries passed. By the eighth century B.C., various feudal lords seized power from the king, who remained in place as a figurehead.

Over the following centuries, these feudal lords fought among themselves for power and influence. And just as the lords had struggled to seize power from the Zhou king, the powerful families within their own states fought to seize power and influence for themselves. The result was a period of great conflict, in which ancient social and political structures were upended and everything seemed in flux. For three hundred years, various factions battled for supremacy in what is known as the **Spring and Autumn Period.** By the early fifth century B.C., seven large states had established themselves. They would continue fighting among themselves for nearly three hundred more years, in what is known as the **Warring States Period.** Throughout this chaotic age, the Chinese fondly recalled the way their ancient rulers had delivered peace and prosperity through virtuous government. It was in the context of this social chaos and the wistful recollection of a lost golden age that philosophy first emerged in China.

As with early Greek philosophy, early Chinese philosophy responded to the dominant myths of its time. Unlike the Greeks, however, the Chinese did not focus on myths about gods or the creation of the world. Indeed, while the Chinese did believe in an all-powerful but impersonal Heaven and in the existence of ghosts and spirits, they had no equivalent to the gods of Hesiod and Homer. Their myths were about mortals. What is more, these mortals were not the heroic warriors of Homeric legend, but wise and benevolent rulers—kings and ministers who improved the well-being of their people through competent administration and clever inventions rather than warfare and who embodied virtues like loyalty and benevolence rather than courage and martial skill. Unsurprisingly, then, early Chinese philosophy had a different focus and a different flavor than did early Greek philosophy.

Whereas the earliest Greek philosophers sought to offer rational *alternatives* to the mythical explanations of the world and its origins, the founding figure of Chinese philosophy, **Confucius,** sought to offer a rationally coherent *justification* of the particular moral and political ideals embodied in mythical accounts of Chinese history. We will set

---

*This is roughly around the time of the Trojan War, the reign of King David in Israel, and the middle of the Vedic period in India. See p. 4, p. 255, and pp. 35–36, respectively.

that justifications aside until a later chapter, instead skipping ahead a few generations to consider an important critical response to Confucius and the intellectual developments he sparked. Some of these developments resemble the pre-Socratic and Sophist contributions to Greek thought.

---

1. What role did the Yellow Emperor, the sage kings, and the early Zhou kings play in ancient Chinese thought? Are there people who played a similar role in ancient Greek thought? What about in modern thought?
2. In what ways were the Spring and Autumn Period and the Warring States Period socially and politically tumultuous? How does the turmoil during those periods compare to the social and political turmoil in Greece in the fifth century B.C.?
3. How did the dominant myths of ancient China differ from those of ancient Greece?

Mozi

Mozi, the man, is a mystery; we know remarkably little about him. He was probably born in Lu, one of the warring states in what is now Shandong province in China. He was probably born sometime between 500 B.C. and about 470 B.C., around the end of Confucius' lifetime, and probably survived until about the beginning of the fourth century B.C. (This makes him a contemporary of the Sophists and Socrates.) He may have been born to a lower-class family of artisans, but if so, he apparently rose to become a renowned military engineer and builder of fortifications, the well-educated founder of a flourishing philosophical school, and, for a time, a minister in the neighboring state of Song. His philosophy retains the indelible stamp of his engineering background: careful, methodical, rational, and practical. That philosophy is expounded in a book that, like many books in ancient China, was compiled over many generations but named after the famous philosopher on whose ideas it was based: the *Mozi*.

Among Mozi's philosophical innovations was the introduction of criteria by which to test the acceptability of a claim.

Master Mo Zi* spoke, saying: "In general, it is not permissible, when making a statement, to fail to establish a standard first and [then] speak. If you do not establish a standard first and [then] speak, it is like using the upper part of a potter's revolving wheel and trying to establish the direction of the sunrise and sunset with it. I think that, although there is a distinction between the sunrise and the sunset, you will, in the end, certainly never be able to find it and establish it. This is why, for a statement, there are three criteria. What are the three criteria? I say there is examining it, there is determining its origin, and there is putting it to use. How do you examine it? You examine the affairs of the first sages and great kings. How do you determine its origin? You look at the evidence from the ears and eyes of the multitude. How do you put it to use? You set it out and use it in governing the state, considering its effect on the ten thousand people. These are called the 'three criteria.' " (*Mozi* 37.1)[1]

The idea here is that the "first sages and great kings" were wise men who knew how to conduct their affairs. The fact that they accepted a certain doctrine is therefore taken as evidence of its acceptability. That people can see and hear evidence for something themselves is further evidence of its acceptability. And finally, an acceptable doctrine, according to Mozi, will produce benefits if it is put into practice, whereas an unacceptable one will bring harm. There is some ambiguity in the *Mozi* about whether these standards are supposed to bring us closer to the *truth* or simply lead us to beneficial opinions. Standing as he does near the very beginning of the philosophical tradition in China, Mozi may not have been able to clearly distinguish between these possibilities. At any rate, the benefit that Mozi takes to justify a belief is not necessarily a benefit for the believer himself or herself, as it is for the Sophists, but for the society as a whole.

We can see these three criteria at work in Mozi's arguments for the existence of ghosts and spirits:

Master Mo Zi spoke, saying: "Since the passing of the three sage kings of the Three Dynasties of

---

*The *zi* at the end of Mozi means "Master," making "Master Mo Zi" somewhat redundant. Many Chinese philosophers are known by such names, including Laozi, Zhuangzi, and Confucius, who is known in Chinese as Kongzi or "Master Kong." Mozi's full name was said to be Mo Di.

former times, the world has lost righteousness and the feudal lords use [military] force in governing [rather than virtue], so that those living now who are rulers and ministers, and superiors and inferiors, are without kindness or loyalty whilst fathers and sons, the younger and older brothers, are without compassion, filial conduct, respect, upright behavior and goodness. . . . Why have things come to this? It is because everyone is doubtful and suspicious on the question of whether ghosts and spirits exist or not, and do not clearly understand that ghosts and spirits are able to reward the worthy and punish the wicked. Now if all the people of the world could be brought to believe that ghosts and spirits are able to reward the worthy and punish the wicked, then how could the world be in disorder?" (*Mozi* 31.1)

Here we have Mozi bemoaning the chaotic and violent nature of his time and encouraging the belief in ghosts for the good consequences it would bring. He goes on to argue that

in bringing up the method of how [the people of the world] examine and know whether something exists or not, we must certainly take the ears and eyes of the multitude to be a standard on the matter of existence and non-existence. If someone has genuinely heard something or seen something, then we must take it as existing. . . . If this is the case, why not put the matter to the test by going into a district or a village and asking about it? If, from ancient times to the present, since people came into existence, there have been those who have seen ghost-like or spirit-like things, or have heard ghost-like or spirit-like sounds, then how can ghosts and spirits be said to be non-existent? (*Mozi* 31.3)*

To counter the objection that many of these people may be untrustworthy, Mozi relates five cases of kings or dukes who encountered ghosts, often in the company of others. Finally, he alludes to the practices of the sage kings.

Master Mo Zi said: "Suppose we accept that the evidence of the ears and eyes of the masses is not enough to trust and cannot be used to resolve doubt. Would we not accept that the sage kings of the Three Dynasties of former times—Yao, Shun,

Yu, Tang, Wen and Wu—are enough to be taken as standards? . . .

"When the sage kings bestowed their rewards, they invariably did so in the ancestral temple, and when they meted out [capital] punishment, they invariably did so at the altar of soil. Why did they bestow rewards in the ancestral temple? To announce [to the ghosts and spirits] that the apportionment was equitable. Why did they mete out [capital] punishment at the altar of soil? To announce [to the ghosts and spirits] that the judgment was fair. . . .

"In ancient times, the sage kings certainly took ghosts and spirits to exist and their service to the ghosts and spirits was profound. But they also feared that their descendants of later generations would not be able to know this, so they wrote it on bamboo and silk to transmit it and hand it down to them. . . . What is the reason for this? It is because the sage kings took it to be important. . . . To oppose what the sage kings took to be fundamental cannot be regarded as the Way of the gentleman." (*Mozi* 31.9–31.11)

We can also see some of these same criteria at work in the *Mozi*'s arguments for the foundation of his ethical and political philosophy: the doctrine of impartial concern or **mutual care,** according to which the guiding principle of life is to care for everyone equally.* This is the most famous of Mozi's doctrines, in part because it conflicted with the traditional Chinese view that people would *and should* prioritize their own family, friends, and associates over strangers.

Master Mo Zi spoke, saying: "The way in which the benevolent man conducts affairs must be to promote the world's benefit and eliminate the world's harm. It is in this way he conducts affairs." If this is so, then what is the world's benefit? What is the world's harm?

Master Mo Zi said: "Now if states attack each other, if houses usurp each other, if people harm each other, if there is not kindness and loyalty between rulers and ministers, if there is not love and filiality between fathers and sons, if there is not concord and harmony between older and younger brothers, then this is harmful to the world."

---

*Compare to what Heraclitus says about "eyes and ears" on p. 21.

*Compare with Jesus' instruction to love "your neighbor as yourself." See pp. 256–258.

If this is so, then how can we not examine from what this harm arises? Does it not arise through mutual love?* Master Mo Zi spoke, saying: "It arises through *lack* of mutual love. Nowadays, feudal lords know only to love their own states and not to love the states of others, so they have no qualms about mobilizing their own state to attack another's state. Nowadays, heads of houses know only to love their own house and not to love the houses of others, so they have no qualms about promoting their own house and usurping another's house. Nowadays, individual people know only to love their own person and not to love the persons of others, so they have no qualms about promoting their own person and injuring the persons of others. For this reason, since the feudal lords do not love each other, there must inevitably be savage battles; since heads of houses do not love each other, there must inevitably be mutual usurpation; and, since individuals do not love each other, there must inevitably be mutual injury. Since rulers and ministers do not love each other, there is not kindness and loyalty; since fathers and sons do not love each other, there is not compassion and filial conduct; and, since older and younger brothers do not love each other, there is not harmony and accord. When the people of the world do not all love each other, then the strong inevitably dominate the weak, the many inevitably plunder the few, the rich inevitably despise the poor, the noble inevitably scorn the lowly, and the cunning inevitably deceive the foolish. Within the world, in all cases, the reason why calamity, usurpation, resentment and hatred arise is because mutual love does not exist, which is why those who are benevolent condemn this state of affairs."

Since they already condemn it, how can it be changed? Master Mo Zi spoke, saying: "It can be changed by the methods of universal mutual love and the exchange of mutual benefit." In this case, then, what are the methods of universal mutual love and exchange of mutual benefit? Master Mo Zi said:

---

*The translator uses the term "mutual love" instead of "mutual care." Other translators have used the term "universal love" as well. This can be misleading because Mozi's concern is with how we *treat* one another, not with the emotions we feel toward one another; he is encouraging us to care *for* everyone equally, even if we do not *care about* everyone equally. It may not be possible to love everyone (in an emotional sense) in the way you love your own family, but that doesn't mean it's impossible to behave impartially.

"People would view others' states as they view their own states. People would view others' houses as they view their own houses. People would view other people as they view themselves. . . . If the people of the world all loved each other, the strong would not dominate the weak, the many would not plunder the few, the rich would not despise the poor, the noble would not scorn the lowly, and the cunning would not deceive the foolish. Within the world, in all cases, there would be nothing to cause calamity, usurpation, resentment and hatred to arise because of the existence of mutual love. This is why those who are benevolent praise it." (*Mozi* 15.1–15.3)

Here we have Mozi arguing for his doctrine of mutual care by pointing out the good consequences of people's practicing it and the bad consequences of people's rejecting it. Again, Mozi bemoans the state of society and prescribes a solution. (His insistence that people should be taught to believe in ghosts seems to have been, in part, a way of encouraging people to put the difficult doctrine of mutual care into practice.)

Mozi then turns to consider some objections to his solution, including the claim that

"If it [love] were universal, it would be good. However, this is something that cannot be done. It is comparable to lifting up [Mount Tai] and jumping over the Yellow River and the Qi Waters." Master Mo Zi said: "That is not a valid comparison. Lifting up [Mount Tai] and jumping over the Yellow River could be said to be a feat of extraordinary strength. From ancient times to the present, no-one has been able to do this. By comparison, universal mutual love and exchange of mutual benefit are quite different from this. The sage kings of ancient times practiced these things." (*Mozi* 15.8)

This last claim would surely have surprised many of Mozi's contemporaries, who took the sage kings' behavior as evidence for the rightness of prioritizing one's friends and family over strangers. Nonetheless, Mozi goes on to support his claim about the sage kings by listing the ways in which Emperor Yu, King Wen, and King Wu practiced mutual care through their diligent efforts to bring benefits to their people, concluding that

if [officers and gentlemen] wish the world to be well ordered and abhor its disorder, [they] should take as right universal mutual love and exchange of mutual benefit. These were the methods of the sage kings and the Way of order for the world, so it is impossible that they not be assiduously pursued. (*Mozi* 15.10)

Here we have Mozi applying the first criterion, which is examining the "affairs of the first sages and great kings." Thus, even in advocating for a radical revision in Chinese social practices, Mozi paints his proposals as in step with the practices of the great kings of old.

---

1. What three criteria does Mozi propose for determining the acceptability of a claim? What do you think of those criteria?
2. How does Mozi argue for the existence of ghosts? How do his arguments relate to his three criteria?
3. What is Mozi's doctrine of mutual care? What arguments does he give for it?

The School of Names

Whereas Mozi is famous for the practicality of his philosophical interests, other ancient Chinese philosophers are notorious for the supposed frivolity of their arguments. They delight in logical paradoxes, in drawing subtle distinctions, in using convoluted arguments to prove the opposite of whatever anyone else believed (which they called "**making the inadmissible admissible**"), and in pursuing what their contemporaries saw as pointless word games with the names of things. Because of this last tendency, later scholars would group these disparate thinkers together as the **School of Names.** They are often compared to the Sophists of ancient Greece, but in many ways, they are closer to the Eleatics like Parmenides and Zeno.* Just as the Eleatics pushed the limits of

---

*The thinker who most resembles the Sophists was a contemporary of Confucius and early forerunner of the School of Names called Deng Xi. It is said that he would, for a fee, argue either side of any case—and sometimes both sides—and, by twisting the letter of the law, prove whichever side he was hired to argue. According to legend, a frustrated ruler eventually executed him, thereby restoring peace and order to his land.

early Greek logic to explore key themes in Greek philosophy, such as appearance and reality, the philosophers of the School of Names explored key themes in early Chinese philosophy, such as sameness and difference.

The Eleatic tendencies of the School of Names appear most clearly in Hui Shi, whose life remains even more mysterious than Mozi's. He lived during the fourth century B.C. and is often described as a statesman, sometimes as talented and sometimes not. One account even depicts him as an expert in the sort of protoscience that motivated the Eleatics. He is best known, however, for a set of cryptic and sometimes paradoxical aphorisms known as the **Ten Theses:**

> The largest thing has nothing beyond it; it is called the One of largeness. The smallest thing has nothing within it; it is called the One of smallness.
>
> That which has no thickness cannot be piled up; yet it is a thousand *li* [about three hundred miles] in dimension.
>
> Heaven is as low as the earth; mountains and marshes are on the same level.
>
> The sun at noon is the sun setting. The thing born is the thing dying.
>
> Great similarities are different from little similarities; these are called the little similarities and differences. The ten thousand things all are similar and all are different; these are called the great similarities and differences.
>
> The southern region has no limit and yet has a limit.
>
> I set off for Yue today and came there yesterday.
>
> Linked rings can be separated.
>
> I know the center of the world: it is north of Yan [in the north] and south of Yue [in the south].
>
> Let love embrace the ten thousand things; Heaven and earth are a single body. (*Zhuangzi* 33)[2]

Although the original explanations of and arguments for these aphorisms have been lost, we can see several themes that we have already encountered among the pre-Socratics, such as the relativity of perspective and an interest in infinitely large and infinitesimally small measures of space or time. From today's perspective, a journey to Yue occurs today, but from tomorrow's perspective, it occurred yesterday. A line consists of infinitesimally thin points that have no thickness, but it can stretch over great distances. The world (allegedly) being infinitely large, anywhere that you can stand has the same (infinite) amount of space in all directions; everywhere is the center of the world. At the exact moment when the sun reaches its zenith, it is already beginning to decline. Elsewhere, Hui Shi even offers some paradoxes that seem to echo Zeno's paradoxes of motion:*

> No matter how swift the barbed arrow, there are times when it is neither moving nor at rest. . . .
>
> Take a pole one foot long, cut away half of it every day, and at the end of ten thousand generations, there will still be some left. (*Zhuangzi* 33)

Whereas we only know of Hui Shi's thought from others' brief reports, we have some complete writings from the other leading figure of the School of Names, Gongsun Long (c. 320–250 B.C.). Gongsun is most famous for a maddeningly cryptic dialogue about the classical problem of **"hardness and whiteness."** In ancient Chinese philosophy, the phrase "hardness and whiteness" stands for conceptually distinct but physically overlapping qualities or properties of an object, such as the hardness and whiteness of a white stone; you can *think* about the stone's color and firmness as distinct aspects of the stone, but you cannot remove one from the stone while leaving the other.

In the dialogue, Gongsun draws on this idea to argue that "a white horse is not a horse." While there are as many interpretations of this dialogue as there are interpreters, many interpretations take Gongsun to be intentionally twisting the meaning of phrases to "make the inadmissible admissible." His goal, on these interpretations, is not really to convince anyone that a white horse is not a horse, but to perplex, dazzle, and amuse his listeners with his cleverness. At the beginning of the dialogue, for instance, Gongsun argues as follows.

A. Is it correct to say that a white horse is not a horse?
B. It is.

---

* See p. 27.

A. Why?
B. Because "horse" denotes the form and "white" denotes the color. What denotes the color does not denote the form. Therefore we say that a white horse is not a horse.
A. There being a horse, one cannot say that there is no horse. If one cannot say that there is no horse, then isn't [it] a horse? Since there being a white horse means that there is a horse, why does being white make it not a horse?
B. Ask for a horse, and either a yellow or a black one may answer. Ask for a white horse, and neither the yellow horse nor the black one may answer. If a white horse were a horse, then what is asked in both cases would be the same. If what is asked is the same, then a white horse would be no different from a horse. If what is asked is no different, then why is it that yellow and black horses may yet answer in the one case but not in the other? Clearly the two cases are incompatible. Now the yellow horse and the black horse remain the same. And yet they answer to a horse but not to a white horse. Obviously a white horse is not a horse. . . . ("On the White Horse")[3]

While it is obvious that Gongsun's conclusion is false, it is not always obvious exactly how his argument has gone astray. And for every objection that his partner raises, Gongsun has a ready and witty reply. After many more iterations of this sort, one can imagine a frustrated courtier throwing up his hands, pointing at a horse, and shouting, "That thing! Right there! I don't care what you call it, just give it to me! I want to go riding!"

Neither Gongsun Long nor Hui Shi, nor any of the other members of the School of Names, is known to have explicitly endorsed relativism or skepticism. Instead, they used their newfound powers of reasoning to defend seemingly inadmissible claims. In this way they are more like the Eleatics than the Sophists. But their eagerness to "make the inadmissible admissible" and their facility in doing so instills exactly the kind of doubts about knowledge that the Sophists sowed in ancient Athens.

1. Pick one of Hui Shi's ten theses. What do you think it means?
2. How do you interpret Gongsun Long's argument that "a white horse is not a horse"?
3. How are the philosophers of the School of Names like the Eleatics in ancient Greek philosophy? How are they like the Sophists?

The Later Mohists

Confronted with the sophistry of the School of Names, Mozi's later followers set about the hard work of transforming logic from a source of paradoxes into a source of knowledge. Over the course of two centuries or so, these followers, known as **Mohists,** developed sophisticated views about a range of philosophical topics, including logic, metaphysics, epistemology, philosophy of language, and ethics. In doing so, they explicitly address many of the logical issues raised by the School of Names, such as sameness and difference, "hard and white," the endless and dimensionless, and the relation of names to objects. They also explored a range of other topics, including geometry, optics, engineering, and economics. The later sections of the *Mozi* record their work on all of these topics, sometimes in cryptic formulations. We will focus here on their development of logic.

In contrast to the School of Names, the Mohists explicitly reject the idea that a statement and its denial can both be admissible.

> The other is not admissible; two are not admissible.
> . . . Everything is either "ox" or "not-ox." It is like a hinge. There are two—there is no way to deny (this).
> Disputation is contending about "that" (the other). Winning in disputation depends on validity. . . . One says it is "ox," one says it is "not-ox"; this is contending about "that" (the other). In this case, both are not valid. Where both are not valid, of necessity, one is not valid. . . . (*Mozi* Canons & Explanations A74–75)

The first part of this passage says that a particular thing is either an ox or not an ox. It must be one or the other and it cannot be both an ox and a non-ox. The second part of the passage explains that in an argument, the winner is the one who gets the right answer; in an argument about whether some creature is an ox, it cannot be that both sides are correct. Thus, these passages express two central principles of logic, which Aristotle articulated at roughly the same time in Greece: the law of non-contradiction, which says that a statement and its denial cannot both be true, and the law of excluded middle, which says that either a statement or its denial is true.

Given that the "admissible" cannot also be "inadmissible," the Mohists concluded that Hui Shi's and Gongsun Long's paradoxical reasoning must contain mistakes. But it is easier to see *that* such reasoning is mistaken than to say exactly *how* it is mistaken. The Mohists set about explaining away such sophistry by aiming for ever greater logical precision in their concepts and definitions. For instance, they note that

> A beginning is a specific instant of time. . . . Time in some cases has duration and in some cases does not. A beginning is a specific instant of time without duration. (*Mozi* Canons & Explanations A44)

This careful definition of a beginning seems aimed at dispelling some of Hui Shi's paradoxes, such as the claim that the sun is simultaneously at its zenith and declining or that an arrow is simultaneously moving and at rest. Other Mohist claims seem similarly aimed at specific paradoxes associated with the School of Names. Those paradoxes, then, arose not from being too clever about logic, but from not being clever enough. Used correctly, the Mohists believed, logic could be a powerful tool for distinguishing true from false and right from wrong.

> Disputation is about making clear the distinction between right and wrong (true and false), and investigating the pattern of order and disorder. It is about clarifying instances of sameness and difference, examining the principles of name and entity, determining what is beneficial and harmful, and resolving what is doubtful and uncertain. With it, there is enquiry and investigation into how the ten thousand things are; there is discussion and analysis of the kinds of the many words. Names are the means of "picking out" entities; words are the means of expressing concepts; explanations are the means of bringing out causes. Through kinds (classes) choices are made; through kinds (classes) inferences are drawn. (*Mozi* Choosing the Lesser 45.1)

Picking out the correct entities and drawing correct inferences requires following acceptable patterns of reasoning and avoiding unacceptable ones.

> With respect to things (the following apply):
> Sometimes a thing is so if it is this.
> Sometimes a thing is not so if it is this.
> Sometimes a thing is so if it is not this.
> Sometimes a thing is general (in one case) but is not general (in another case).
> Sometimes a thing is so (in one case) but not so (in another case). (*Mozi* Choosing the Lesser 45.4)

These principles sound odd to us, but they relate to typical forms of disputation in which one argues that because a thing *x* is *y* and because something is true of *x* it must also be true of *y*. The *Mozi* points out that principles of reasoning like this are sometimes correct, but other times are not:

> A white horse is a horse. To ride a white horse is to ride a horse. A black horse is a horse. To ride a black horse is to ride a horse. *Huo* is a person. To love *Huo* is to love a person. *Zang* is a person. To love *Zang* is to love a person. These are examples of there being this and it is so. (*Mozi* Choosing the Lesser 45.5)

These examples illustrate the first principle in the list above. Because a particular entity—such as this white horse or this person—is of a particular kind, an action performed with that particular entity is an action performed with an entity of that particular kind. The obvious target here is Gongsun Long's infamous claim that a white horse is not a horse.

> Huo's parents are people. Huo's serving his parents is not serving people. His younger brother is a beautiful person. Loving a younger brother is not loving a beautiful person. A cart is wood. Riding a cart is not riding wood. A boat is wood. Boarding a boat is not boarding wood. A robber is a person. . . . Not being a robber isn't not being a person. How can this be made clear? . . . To wish there were no robbers is not to wish there were no people. (*Mozi* Choosing the Lesser 45.6)

The examples given here illustrate the second principle in the list above, which warns against various mistaken inferences that *appear* similar to the acceptable inferences endorsed by the first principle. For instance, although the name "people" applies to Huo's parents, we cannot infer from the fact that Huo loves his parents *as parents* that he loves them *as people*. Although a robber is a person, we cannot infer that someone who dislikes robbers or wishes there were no robbers dislikes people per se or wishes there were no people.

Other passages illustrate the third, fourth, and fifth principles, further distinguishing between patterns of interpretations or inference that differ in acceptability despite being grammatically similar. For instance, from the fact that an ox has yellow hairs, we may infer that it is a yellow ox; but from the fact that the ox has many hairs, we cannot infer that it is many oxen.

If the Mohists used their disagreements with the School of Names to sharpen their logical skills, they mainly deployed those skills against their primary philosophical rivals at the time, the Confucians. Much of the *Mozi* consists of detailed arguments for their own moral and political views as opposed to the Confucians'. They regarded argumentation and rational criticism as the primary means of demonstrating that their views were true and the Confucians' views were false. For much of the golden age of classical Chinese philosophy, it seems that their criticisms were taken seriously. Indeed, Mohism seems to have been the main competitor to Confucianism during this period. After the reunification of China in 221 B.C., however, Confucianism decisively eclipsed Mohism, which faded into obscurity.

---

1. How might the Mohists use the claim about starting points having no duration to refute some of Hui Shi's paradoxical claims?
2. How do the examples given above illustrate the Mohists' five principles of argumentation?
3. How does the Mohists' use of reasoning differ from that of the School of Names?

Zhuangzi

Whereas the Mohists responded to the School of Names by trying to set logic on a firmer foundation, another philosopher, Zhuangzi, responded very differently. He turned reason against itself, using it to argue for its uselessness in attaining genuine knowledge. And whereas the later Mohists left no trace of their personalities in their writings, the book named for Zhuangzi bursts with character, revealing an educated, eccentric, playful genius deeply at odds with the elite culture of his time. He lived sometime in the late fourth century B.C., but unlike the other great philosophers of his day, he neither sought nor held a position at court (except, perhaps, a minor post in his home state). Indeed, Zhuangzi disdained such positions, preferring the life of a hermit.

> Once, when Zhuangzi was fishing in the Pu River, the king of Chu sent two officials to go and announce to him: "I would like to trouble you with the administration of my realm."
>
> Zhuangzi held on to the fishing pole and, without turning his head, said, "I have heard that there is a sacred tortoise in Chu that has been dead for three thousand years. The king keeps it wrapped in cloth and boxed, and stores it in the ancestral temple. Now would this tortoise rather be dead and have its bones left behind and honored? Or would it rather be alive and dragging its tail in the mud?"
>
> "It would rather be alive and dragging its tail in the mud," said the two officials.
>
> Zhuangzi said, "Go away! I'll drag my tail in the mud!" (*Zhuangzi* 17)

It seems that Zhuangzi's one connection to the world of politics was through a friendship with Hui Shi of the School of Names, who was chief minister of the king of Wei. The stories about them depict the two as friendly intellectual sparring partners:

> Zhuangzi and Huizi were strolling along the dam of the Hao River when Zhuangzi said, "See how the minnows come out and dart around where they please! That's what fish really enjoy!"
>
> Huizi said, "You're not a fish—how do you know what fish enjoy?"
>
> Zhuangzi said, "You're not I, so how do you know I don't know what fish enjoy?"
>
> Huizi said, "I'm not you, so I certainly don't know what you know. On the other hand, you're certainly not a fish—so that still proves you don't know what fish enjoy!"
>
> Zhuangzi said, "Let's go back to your original question, please. You asked me *how* I know what

fish enjoy—so you already knew I knew it when you asked the question. I know it by standing here beside the Hao." (*Zhuangzi* 17)

Indeed, after Hui Shi's death, Zhuangzi is said to have remarked that

> Since you died, Master Hui, I have had no material to work on. There's no one I can talk to any more. (*Zhuangzi* 24)

It was not only in his alienation from public life that Zhuangzi defied the spirit of his times. He also took a radically different attitude toward death and mourning. He regarded the fear of death as folly. Even when his own wife died, Zhuangzi responded differently than most people would.

> Zhuangzi's wife died. When Huizi went to convey his condolences, he found Zhuangzi sitting with his legs sprawled out, pounding on a tub and singing. "You lived with her, she brought up your children and grew old," said Huizi. "It should be enough simply not to weep at her death. But pounding on a tub and singing—this is going too far, isn't it?"
>
> Zhuangzi said, "You're wrong. When she first died, do you think I didn't grieve like anyone else? But I looked back to her beginning and the time before she was born. Not only the time before she was born, but the time before she had a body. Not only the time before she had a body, but the time before she had a spirit. In the midst of the jumble of wonder and mystery a change took place and she had a spirit. Another change and she had a body. Another change and she was born. Now there's been another change and she's dead. It's just like the progression of the four seasons, spring, summer, fall, winter.
>
> "Now she's going to lie down peacefully in a vast room. If I were to follow after her bawling and sobbing, it would show that I don't understand anything about fate. So I stopped." (*Zhuangzi* 18)

These stories about Zhuangzi's life come from the *Zhuangzi*, a collection of writings compiled some six centuries after his death. Some of it probably includes Zhuangzi's own writing, but much of it, including the stories about his life, was written by others after Zhuangzi's death. By that time, the same historians who had grouped Hui Shi, Gongsun Long, and others into the School of Names had lumped Zhuangzi and an enigmatic character called

Laozi together as Daoists. **Daoism** came to be understood loosely as the school of thought descended from the *Zhuangzi* and the *Dàodéjīng*, both of which emphasize certain themes such as a skeptical bent, an admiration for nature, and an emphasis on spontaneous, effortless action.

The *Zhuangzi* blends stories, poetry, and clever argumentation—often in a single passage—producing a work quite unlike anything else in ancient Chinese philosophy. One striking aspect of the *Zhuangzi* is the way it uses reason to undermine confidence in reason's ability to deliver knowledge.

> Nie Que asked Wang Ni, "Do you know what all things agree in calling right?"
>
> "How would I know that?" said Wang Ni.
>
> "Do you know that you don't know it?"
>
> "How would I know that?"
>
> "Then do things know nothing?"
>
> "How would I know that? However, suppose I try saying something. What way do I have of knowing that if I say I know something I don't really not know it? Or what way do I have of knowing that if I say I don't know something I don't really in fact know it? Now let me ask *you* some questions. If a man sleeps in a damp place, his back aches and he ends up half paralyzed, but is this true of [a fish]? If he lives in a tree, he is terrified and shakes with fright, but is this true of a monkey? Of these three creatures, then, which one knows the proper place to live? Men eat the flesh of grass-fed and grain-fed animals, deer eat grass, centipedes find snakes tasty, and hawks and falcons relish mice. Of these four, which knows how food ought to taste? Monkeys pair with monkeys, deer go out with deer, and fish play around with fish. Men claim that Maoqiang and Lady Li were beautiful; but if fish saw them, they would dive to the bottom of the stream; if birds saw them, they would fly away; if deer saw them, they would break into a run. Of these four, which knows how to fix the standard of beauty for the world? The way I see it, the rules of benevolence and righteousness and the paths of right and wrong all are hopelessly snarled and jumbled. How could I know anything about such discriminations?" (*Zhuangzi* 2)

Here Zhuangzi has Wang Ni respond to a question about knowledge by asking for a criterion by which to determine whether he knows. When Nie Que presses Wang Ni to admit that he does *not* know,

Wang Ni refuses, asking for a criterion by which to know whether he knows whether he knows. Nie Que thinks he sees where this is going and suggests that Wang Ni is leading him down the path to skepticism. But Wang Ni sidesteps the accusation of skepticism by denying that he knows whether skepticism is true. He then resorts to a common skeptical tactic of pointing out the diversity of opinions about any given subject, though in his typically atypical fashion, he refers not to the diversity of opinions among different people, but to the diversity of opinions among different species.

Still, Zhuangzi is not quite a skeptic. He does not claim that we cannot know anything. Instead, he skillfully uses reason to shake our confidence in what we think we know, and especially in what we think we know through reason. In another passage, he writes,

> Suppose you and I have an argument. If you have beaten me instead of my beating you, then are you necessarily right, and am I necessarily wrong? If I have beaten you instead of your beating me, then am I necessarily right, and are you necessarily wrong? Is one of us right and the other wrong? Are both of us right, or are both of us wrong? If you and I don't know the answer, then other people are bound to be even more in the dark. Whom shall we get to decide what is right? Shall we get someone who agrees with you to decide? But if he already agrees with you, how can he fairly decide? Shall we get someone who agrees with me? But if he already agrees with me, how can he decide? Shall we get someone who disagrees with both of us? But if he already disagrees with both of us, how can he decide? Shall we get someone who agrees with both of us? But if he already agrees with both of us, how can he decide? Obviously, then, neither you nor I nor anyone else can know the answer. Shall we wait for still another person? (*Zhuangzi* 2)

Taking aim squarely at rational argument, Zhuangzi raises the classical epistemological problem of finding a criterion by which to determine what counts as knowledge.* Even having the better argument

---

* On the Western treatment of this "problem of the criterion," see pp. 248–249.

may not suffice, Zhuangzi suggests, for even the better of two arguments could be flawed. After working carefully through some possible ways to resolve the problem, Zhuangzi concludes that "neither you nor I nor anyone else can know the answer." But consider carefully what question it is that goes unanswered: it is the question of *whether the winner of the argument is necessarily right*. Once again, Zhuangzi is simply raising doubts, not denying that we know anything.

The problem for Zhuangzi is not that knowledge is impossible or that reasoning is useless. The problem is that words often lead us astray. One reason for this is that by naming something, we are adopting a particular perspective, which closes off other equally valid perspectives and other possibilities of thought.

> Everything has its "that," everything has its "this."* From the point of view of "that," you cannot see it; but through understanding, you can know it. . . . Therefore the sage does not proceed in such a way but illuminates all in the light of [Nature]. (*Zhuangzi* 2)

Zhuangzi offers a concrete example of words leading his friend Hui Shi astray:

> Huizi said to Zhuangzi, "The king of Wei gave me some seeds of a huge gourd. I planted them, and when they grew up, the fruit was big enough to hold five piculs.† I tried using it for a water container, but it was so heavy I couldn't lift it. I split it in half to make dippers, but they were so large and unwieldy that I couldn't dip them into anything. It's not that the gourds weren't fantastically big—but I decided they were no use and so I smashed them to pieces."
>
> Zhuangzi said, "You certainly are dense when it comes to using big things! In Song there was a man who was skilled at making a salve to prevent chapped hands, and generation after generation his family made a living by bleaching silk in water. A traveler

heard about the salve and offered to buy the prescription for a hundred measures of gold. The man called everyone to a family council. 'For generations we've been bleaching silk and we've never made more than a few measures of gold,' he said. 'Now, if we sell our secret, we can make a hundred measures in one morning. Let's let him have it!' The traveler got the salve and introduced it to the king of Wu, who was having trouble with the state of Yue. The king put the man in charge of his troops, and that winter they fought a naval battle with the men of Yue and gave them a bad beating [because the salve, by preventing the soldiers' hands from chapping, made it easier for them to handle their weapons]. A portion of the conquered territory was awarded to the man as a fief. The salve had the power to prevent chapped hands in either case; but one man used it to get a fief, while the other one never got beyond silk bleaching—because they used it in different ways. Now you had a gourd big enough to hold five piculs. Why didn't you think of making it into a great tub so you could go floating around the rivers and lakes, instead of worrying because it was too big and unwieldy to dip into things! Obviously you still have a lot of underbrush in your head!" (*Zhuangzi* 1)

To see the point of this story, imagine that Zhuangzi asked Hui Shi, "Is a gourd a boat?" Hui Shi, quite reasonably, would reply, "It's not." And so from the perspective of thinking of his giant gourds *as gourds*, Hui Shi deems it unallowable to call what he has a boat. But from another perspective, that is precisely what he has. Calling the thing a gourd has led Hui Shi astray by making it harder for him to see certain possibilities. So it is, Zhuangzi thinks, whenever we rely too heavily on words and the conventional meanings attached to them. Thus, he laments,

> Where can I find a man who has forgotten words so I can have a word with him? (*Zhuangzi* 26)

There is hope, however. For while words will lead us astray, a certain kind of knowledge is still possible. Zhuangzi delights in depicting knowledge and expertise in people his fellow philosophers would have disdained. Among the famous examples is his story of **Cook Ding.**

> Cook Ding was cutting up an ox for [King Hui of Wei]. At every touch of his hand, every heave of his shoulder, every move of his feet, every thrust

---

*The references to "this" and "that" are to an ancient Chinese style of argument in which one person asserts that a particular name applies to a particular entity—"This entity is *this* kind of thing, not *that* kind of thing"—and the other person either affirms or denies it.

†A picul is the amount of weight that someone could carry on his or her shoulder. It was probably equivalent to a little more than one hundred pounds.

of his knee—zip! zoop! He slithered the knife along with a zing, and all was in perfect rhythm, as though he were performing the dance of the Mulberry Grove or keeping time to the Jingshou music.

"Ah, this is marvelous!" said [the king.] "Imagine skill reaching such heights!"

Cook Ding laid down his knife and replied, "What I care about is the Way, which goes beyond skill. When I first began cutting up oxen, all I could see was the ox itself. After three years I no longer saw the whole ox. And now—now I go at it by spirit and don't look with my eyes. Perception and understanding have come to a stop and spirit moves where it wants. I go along with the natural makeup, strike in the big hollows, guide the knife through the big openings, and follow things as they are. So I never touch the smallest ligament or tendon, much less a joint.

"A good cook changes his knife once a year—because he cuts. A mediocre cook changes his knife once a month—because he hacks. I've had this knife for nineteen years and I've cut up thousands of oxen with it, and yet the blade is as good as though it had just come from the grindstone. There are spaces between the joints, and the blade of the knife really has no thickness. If you insert what has no thickness into such spaces, then there's plenty of room—more than enough for the blade to play about in. That's why after nineteen years the blade of my knife is still as good as when it first came from the grindstone.

"However, whenever I come to a complicated place, I size up the difficulties, tell myself to watch out and be careful, keep my eyes on what I'm doing, work very slowly, and move the knife with the greatest subtlety, until—flop! The whole thing comes apart like a clod of earth crumbling to the ground. I stand there holding the knife and look all around me, completely satisfied and reluctant to move on, and then I wipe off the knife and put it away."

"Excellent!" said [the king]. "I have heard the words of Cook Ding and learned how to care for life!" (*Zhuangzi* 3)

Cook Ding knows how to butcher an ox, but his knowledge surpasses anything he can put into words. He understands the world—or, at least, his small part of it—in a far more subtle, nuanced, and flexible way than words could ever capture.

Putting this knowledge into practice, Cook Ding embodies one of the Daoists' most famous ideas, *wúwéi*, meaning something like "nonpurposive action" or "acting without artificial interpretation." It is sometimes described as "acting without acting" or "achieving without acting." The idea is, roughly, that a person who is guided by nature and well-honed intuition—the person who turns nature and natural processes to his or her advantage rather than trying to force nature to comply with human desires—will achieve more than a person guided by deliberation or clunky linguistic conceptualizations of the situation before them. We can see this ourselves in especially gifted athletes. Watch Roger Federer or Rafael Nadal play tennis. They don't deliberate about how to respond to their opponent's shot. And yet fluidly, almost effortlessly, they are right where they need to be to hit the ball.

The story of Cook Ding suggests that Zhuangzi is not, ultimately, a skeptic. How so? Cook Ding keeps his cleaver sharp by carving his ox at the joints. This implies that the world *is* a particular way, independent of our beliefs about it. When Zhuangzi says that "what from somewhere is so from somewhere else is not so," he is not denying that the world has this objective reality; he is denying that our language—our *names* for the parts of the world—can capture the subtle variations in the world around us. Furthermore, trying to capture the world in language invariably highlights some ways of thinking of a thing while setting others aside. Thus, while there is an objective world and we can have some kind of genuine knowledge about it, this knowledge does not come from language or reasoning.

Zhuangzi expresses a corollary of this lesson in another story of an artisan.

Duke Huan was in his hall reading a book. The wheelwright Pian, who was in the yard below chiseling a wheel, laid down his mallet and chisel, stepped up into the hall, and said to Duke Huan, "This book Your Grace is reading—may I venture to ask whose words are in it?"

"The words of the sages," said the duke.

"Are the sages still alive?"

"Dead long ago," said the duke.

LAOZI

The other founding document of Daoism, besides the *Zhuangzi*, is a small book of eighty-one chapters, each containing a set of brief, aphoristic sayings, often obscure to the casual reader. This book is widely known as the *Dàodéjīng*, which means "Classic of the Way of Virtue," but it is also known as the *Laozi*, after its alleged author, Laozi.* Ancient tradition identifies this Laozi with the sixth-century B.C. thinker Lao Dan, but the book's true author—or, more likely, authors—probably lived in the fourth century B.C. and simply presented his own work as the wisdom of an ancient sage. Despite this mystery, we will use Laozi as a pseudonym for whoever actually wrote the text.

One of the central concepts in the *Dàodéjīng* is the **Dào**. The word literally means "the Way," as in a way or path that one might follow. Many ancient Chinese thinkers used the term to mean something like the correct way to live one's life.† Laozi understands the word in this way, too, but he also uses it to mean something much broader. The *Dàodéjīng*'s cryptic opening lines famously declare,

> A Way that can be followed is not a constant Way.
> A name that can be named is not a constant name.
> Nameless, it is the beginning of Heaven and Earth;
> Named, it is the mother of all myriad creatures. (*DDJ*, 1)

Laozi is telling us that the *Dào* is the source of all things, both because the entire universe emerges from it and because every creature is created by it.* But Laozi is also telling us that human language is not up to the task of describing or telling us what the *Dào* is or how to follow it.† In this respect, he shares Zhuangzi's views about the limits of language. So instead of trying to describe the *Dào*, Laozi often turns to metaphors. For instance, he compares the *Dào* to water, which moves effortlessly through the world, nourishing all things without distinction, and to unhewn wood, which has not yet been divided into distinct objects for human purposes.

Because the *Dào* is also the path for living properly, these metaphors for the *Dào* are also models for human life. Somewhat paradoxically, Laozi tells us we should try for effortlessness in our actions—here is the famous Daoist doctrine of *wúwéi* again—and unsophisticated simplicity in our desires.

> The greatest misfortune is not to know contentment.
> The worst calamity is the desire to acquire. (*DDJ*, 46)
> Your name or your body, which do you hold more dear?
> Your body or your property, which is of greater value?
> Gain or loss, which is the greater calamity?
> For this reason, deep affections give rise to great expenditures.
> Excessive hoarding results in great loss.
> Know contentment and avoid disgrace;
> Know when to stop and avoid danger;
> And you will long endure. (*DDJ*, 44)

Why do we endanger our health and our bodies, Laozi is asking us, to acquire more things? Why do we risk "danger" and "disgrace" to acquire one shiny

---

*It is also widely known in the West as the *Tao Te Ching*, following an older system for romanizing Chinese characters. In that system, *Dào* is spelled *Tao* and Laozi is spelled Lao Tzu.

†It is of interest to note that early Christianity was known simply as "the Way." And in his book *The Abolition of Man*, the Christian writer, C. S. Lewis, refers to the pattern of objective values in reality as "the *Tao*."

---

*Compare Plotinus on the emanation of all things from the One (pp. 270–271).

†Compare Maimonides (p. 309) and Aquinas (p. 325) on negative theology.

LAOZI

bauble after another? If we think these things will make us happy, we are wrong. So Laozi is telling us. If only we could "know when to stop," we could find contentment.*

The world has lost its way, Laozi believes, precisely because people lost sight of the natural simplicity of the *Dào*.† Whereas the waterlike *Dào* embraces and supports all things without distinction, humans carve the world into good and bad according to their own purposes: into the beautiful and the ugly, the strong and the weak, the rich and the poor; and then we prize the beautiful, strong, hard, and rich and set about contending with one another to acquire more and more of these things.

To try to manage the strife that accompanies this contention, people develop elaborate systems of law and etiquette, logic and disputation. All of this, Laozi argues, is futile. Only by returning to the natural simplicity of the *Dào* can we find virtue, contentment, peace, and security.‡ The *Dàodéjīng* closes with this paradox-laden warning:

> Words worthy of trust are not beautiful;
> Words that are beautiful are not worthy of trust.
> The good do not engage in disputations;

---

*Compare the Buddha on attachment (p. 39) and Epicurus on desire (pp. 239–240).

†Compare Heraclitus, who warns us against being "at variance with" the *logos*, from which all things are created (pp. 20).

‡Compare St. Paul in Romans 2:16: "By works of the law shall no one be justified."

Those who engage in disputation are not good.
Those who know are not full of knowledge;
Those full of knowledge do not know.*
Sages do not accumulate.
The more they do for others, the more they have;
The more they give to others, the more they possess.
The Way of Heaven is to benefit and not harm.
The Way of the sage is to act but not contend.
(*DDJ*, 81)

Social media is full of people trying to present themselves as beautiful, trustworthy, knowledgeable, wealthy, and powerful. Things were not so different in Laozi's day, even if they took different forms, and he is dismissing that preening as foolishness. He is advising us not to try to show off, accumulate wealth, or outdo other people. True happiness is not to be found there, but in the humble life of following the *Dào*.†

NOTE

There are many translations of the *Dàodéjīng*, and they differ considerably from one another. These quotations are from Philip J. Ivanhoe (trans.), *The Daodejing of Laozi* (Indianapolis, IN: Hackett, 2003). References are to chapter numbers.

---

*Compare Socrates' claim to ignorance (p. 97).

†Compare the Stoics on keeping our wills in harmony with nature (p. 243).

"In that case, what you are reading there is nothing but the chaff and dregs of the men of old!"

"Since when does a wheelwright have permission to comment on the books I read?" said Duke Huan. "If you have some explanation, well and good. If not, it's your life!"

Wheelwright Pian said, "I look at it from the point of view of my own work. When I chisel a wheel, if the blows of the mallet are too gentle, the chisel will slide and won't take hold. But if they're too hard, it will bite and won't budge. Not too gentle, not too hard—you can get it in your hand and feel it in your mind. You can't put it into words, and yet there's a knack to it somehow. I can't teach it to my son, and he can't learn it from me. So I've gone along for seventy years, and at my age I'm still chiseling wheels. When the men of old died, they took with them the things that couldn't be handed down. So what you are reading there must be nothing but the chaff and dregs of the men of old." (*Zhuangzi* 13)

Zhuangzi's writings have continued to be influential throughout Chinese history. During the Han dynasty, the so-called Neo-Daoists claimed that the Way of Confucius and the Way of Daoists were actually one. Roughly half a millennium later, after the fall of the Han dynasty, Zhuangzi's and Laozi's ideas fused with Buddhist ideas imported from India to create a distinctly East Asian style of Buddhism, known in China as Chan Buddhism and in Japan as Zen Buddhism. So it often happens in the great philosophical conversations of the world: An idea born in one tradition meets some other idea, perhaps drawn from some other great conversation, and the meeting kindles new insights and opens new directions for thought.

---

1. In what sense is Zhuangzi skeptical? In what ways is he not a skeptic?
2. Is Zhuangzi a relativist? Why or why not?
3. If the truth cannot be taught in words, why did Zhuangzi write a book?

KEY WORDS

Hundred Schools of Thought
Yellow Emperor
sage kings
Zhou dynasty
Mandate of Heaven
Spring and Autumn Period
Warring States Period
Confucius
mutual care
making the inadmissible admissible
School of Names
Ten Theses
hardness and whiteness
Mohism
Daoism
Cook Ding
wúwéi
Dào

NOTES

1. Quotations from Ian Johnston, trans., *Mozi* (New York: Columbia University Press, 2010) in this section are cited in the text by chapter name and section number.
2. Quotations labeled *Zhuangzi* are from Burton Watson, trans., *The Complete Works of Zhuangzi* (New York: Columbia University Press, 2013) and are cited by chapter number.
3. Wing-Tsit Chan, *A Source Book in Chinese Philosophy* (Princeton, NJ: Princeton University Press, 1963).

CHAPTER
6
SOCRATES

To Know Oneself

Some philosophers are important just for what they say or write. Others are important also for what they are—for their personality and character. No better example of the latter exists than **Socrates.**

Socrates wrote nothing, save some poetry written while awaiting execution; he is said to have written a hymn to Apollo and to have put the fables of Aesop into verse. But those have not survived. His impact on those who knew him, however, was extraordinary, and his influence to the present day has few parallels.

The fact that he wrote nothing poses a problem. We depend on other writers for our knowledge of him. Aristophanes is one source, but such farce cannot be taken at face value. Another source is **Xenophon,** who tells numerous stories involving Socrates but is philosophically rather unsophisticated.* Aristotle, too, discusses him. But our main source is Plato, a younger companion of Socrates and a devoted admirer.

Note: This is not Xenophanes, the pre-Socratic philosopher discussed in Chapter 2.

Plato didn't write a biography or a scholarly analysis of his master's thought. He left us a large number of dialogues, or conversations, in most of which Socrates is a participant, often the central figure. But these dialogues were all written after Socrates' death, many of them long after. And in the later dialogues, there can be no doubt that Plato is putting ideas of his own into the mouth of Socrates. We should not think there is anything dishonest about this practice. The ancient world would have accepted it as perfectly in order; Plato surely believed that his own ideas were a natural development from those of Socrates and that in this way he was honoring his master. But it does pose a problem if we want to discuss the historical Socrates rather than Plato's Socrates. No definitive solution to this problem may ever be found. Still, some things are reasonably certain.

For the most part, the dialogues of Plato can be sorted into three periods, as follows.

1. The early dialogues, such as *Euthyphro*, *Crito*, and the *Apology*, are thought to represent quite

accurately Socrates' own views and ways of proceeding. They seem to have been written soon after his death. In these dialogues, Socrates questions various individuals about the nature of piety, courage, justice, or virtue/excellence (*areté*).* The outcome of the conversation is usually negative in the sense that no agreed-on solution is reached. The participant, who at the dialogue's beginning claims to know the answer, is forced to admit ignorance. You might ask, Is there any point to such conversations? Well, the participants do learn something—that is, how little they really know. In this way the ground is cleared of at least some intellectual rubbish.

2. In the middle dialogues, such as *Meno*, *Phaedo*, *Symposium*, and the monumental *Republic*, Socrates is still the main protagonist. Here, however, we find positive doctrines aplenty, supported by many arguments. Here Plato is working out his own solutions to the problems that the Sophists posed and trying to go beyond the negative outcomes of Socratic questioning. What Plato is doing here will be the main subject of Chapter 8.

3. The late dialogues contain further developments and explore difficulties discovered in the doctrines of the middle period. Here Socrates' role diminishes; in the very late *Laws*, he disappears altogether.

In this chapter and the next, we discuss Socrates primarily as he appears in the early works of Plato, and we read in their entirety three short dialogues. Before reading those, however, we need to learn something about Socrates' character and person.

Character

Socrates was born in 470 or 469 B.C. His father was a stonemason and perhaps a minor sculptor. It is thought that Socrates pursued this same trade as a young man. He married Xanthippe, a woman with a reputation for shrewishness, and had three sons, apparently rather late in life.

His mother was a midwife, and Socrates calls himself a "midwife" in the realm of thought. A midwife does not give birth herself, of course. In a similar way, Socrates makes no claim to be able to give birth to true ideas but says he can help deliver the ideas of others and determine their truth. He does this by examining them and testing their consistency with other ideas expressed in the conversation. The question is always this: Do the answers to Socrates' questions fit together with the original claim that what was said is true? As we read the three dialogues, we will see numerous examples of his "midwifery."*

No one ever claimed that Socrates was good-looking, except in a joke. Xenophon reports on an impromptu "beauty contest" held at a banquet. The contestants are Critobulus, a good-looking young man, and Socrates. Socrates is challenged to prove that he is the more handsome.

SOCRATES: Do you think beauty exists in man alone, or in anything else?

CRITOBULUS: I believe it is found in horse and ox and many inanimate things. For instance, I recognize a beautiful shield, sword or spear.

S: And how can all these things be beautiful when they bear no resemblance to each other?

C: Why, if they are well made for the purposes for which we acquire them, or well adapted by nature to our needs, then in each case I call them beautiful.

S: Well then, what do we need eyes for?

C: To see with of course.

S: In that case my eyes are at once proved to be more beautiful than yours, because yours look only straight ahead, whereas mine project so that they can see sideways as well. . . .

C: All right, but which of our noses is the more beautiful?

S: Mine, I should say, if the gods gave us noses to smell with, for your nostrils point to earth, but mine are spread out widely to receive odours from every quarter.

---

*The meaning of this important word is discussed in Chapter 4, on p. 59.

*You might like to look at the actual words in which Socrates claims this role of midwife for himself. See Chapter 7, p. 134.

c: But how can a snub nose be more beautiful than a straight one?

s: Because it does not get in the way but allows the eyes to see what they will, whereas a high bridge walls them off as if to spite them.

c: As for the mouth, I give in, for if mouths are made for biting you could take a much larger bite than I.

s: And with my thick lips don't you think I could give a softer kiss?[1]

After this exchange, the banqueters take a secret ballot to determine who is the more handsome. Critobulus gets every vote, so Socrates exclaims that he must have bribed the judges! It must have been nearly impossible to resist caricaturing this odd-looking man who shuffled about Athens barefoot and peered sideways at you out of his bulging eyes when you spoke to him. Aristophanes was not the only writer of comedies to succumb to the temptation.

We see several things about Socrates in this little excerpt: (1) It was not for his physical attractiveness that Socrates was sought after as a companion; he was acknowledged on all sides to be extraordinarily ugly, though it seems to have been an interesting kind of ugliness; (2) we see something of Socrates' humor; here it is light and directed at himself, but it could also be sharp and biting; (3) we have our first glimpse of the typical Socratic method, which proceeds by question and answer, not by long speeches; and (4) we see that Socrates here identifies the good or the beautiful in terms of usefulness or advantage, and this is typical of his views on these questions of value.

He served in the army several times with courage and distinction. In Plato's *Symposium*, the story of an all-night banquet and drinking party, **Alcibiades,** a brilliant young man we shall hear more of, gives the following testimony:

Now, the first thing to point out is that there was no one better than him in the whole army at enduring hardship: it wasn't just me he showed up. Once, when we were cut off (as happens during a campaign), we had to do without food and no one else could cope at all. At the same time, when there *were* plenty of provisions, he was better than the rest of

"I do not even have any knowledge of what virtue itself is."

—Socrates

us at making the most of them, and especially when it came to drinking: he was reluctant to drink, but when pushed he proved more than a match for everyone. And the most remarkable thing of all is that no one has ever seen Socrates drunk. . . .

Once—and this was the most astonishing thing he did—the cold was so terribly bitter that everyone was either staying inside or, if they did venture out, they wore an incredible amount of clothing, put shoes on, and then wrapped pieces of felt and sheepskin around their feet. Socrates, however, went out in this weather wearing only the outdoor cloak he'd usually worn earlier in the campaign as well, and without anything on his feet; but he still made his way through the ice more easily than the rest of us with our covered feet. . . .

One morning, a puzzling problem occurred to him and he stayed standing where he was thinking about it. Even when it proved intractable, he didn't give up: he just stood there exploring it. By the time it was midday, people were beginning to notice him and were telling one another in amazement that Socrates had been standing there from early in the morning deep in thought. Eventually, after their evening meal, some men from the Ionian contingent took their pallets outside—it was summer at the time—so that they could simultaneously sleep outside where it was cool and watch out for whether he'd stand there all night as well. In fact, he stood there until after sunrise the following morning, and then he greeted the sun with a prayer and went on his way. (*Symposium* 219e–220d)[2]

Alcibiades goes on to tell how Socrates saved his life and in a retreat showed himself to be the coolest man around, so that

> anyone could tell, even from a distance, that here was a man who would resist an attack with considerable determination. And that's why he and Laches got out of there safely, because the enemy generally don't take on someone who can remain calm during combat. (*Symposium* 221b)

He sums up his view by saying that

> there's no human being, from times past or present, who can match him. . . .
>
> The first time a person lets himself listen to one of Socrates' arguments, it sounds really ridiculous. . . . He talks of pack-asses, metal-workers, shoe-makers, tanners; he seems to go on and on using the same arguments to make the same points, with the result that ignoramuses and fools are bound to find his arguments ridiculous. But if you could see them opened up, if you can get through to what's under the surface, what you'll find inside is that his arguments are the only ones in the world which make sense. And that's not all: under the surface, his arguments abound with divinity and effigies of goodness. They turn out to be extremely far-reaching, or rather they cover absolutely everything which needs to be taken into consideration on the path to true goodness. (*Symposium* 221c–222a)

It is somewhat ironic to hear Alcibiades talking of "true goodness" here. He was for a time a close associate of Socrates but in later life became

notorious for lechery and lust for power. Eventually he deserted and offered his services as a general to the Spartans! The common opinion was that Alcibiades was handsome and brilliant but also treacherous and despicable. Nonetheless, there is no reason to doubt the testimony to Socrates that Plato here puts into his mouth.

The party is invaded by a bunch of revelers, and everyone drinks a great deal. One by one, everyone but Socrates leaves or falls asleep. Shortly after dawn,

> Socrates went to the Lyceum for a wash, spent the day as he would any other, and then went home to sleep in the evening. (*Symposium* 223d)

He "spent the day as he would any other." How was that? Socrates' days seem to have been devoted mainly to conversations in the public places of Athens. He was not independently wealthy, as you might suspect. Xenophon tells us that

> he schooled his body and soul by following a system which . . . would make it easy to meet his expenses. For he was so frugal that it is hardly possible to imagine a man doing so little work as not to earn enough to satisfy the needs of Socrates. (*Memorabilia* 1.3.5)[3]

"That man is richest whose pleasures are the cheapest."

Henry David Thoreau (1817–1862)

He was temperate in his desires and possessed remarkable self-control with regard not only to food and drink but also to sex. He apparently refrained from the physical relationship that was a fairly common feature of friendships between older men and their young protégés in ancient Athens.* Although he used the language of "love" freely, he held that the proper aim of such friendships was to make the "beloved" more virtuous, self-controlled, and just. No doubt he believed that the young could not learn self-control from

---

*See, for example, the complaint of Alcibiades in *Symposium* 217a–219d.

someone who did not display it. By common consent the judgment of Alcibiades was correct: Socrates was unique.

Is Socrates a Sophist?

In *The Clouds*, Aristophanes presents Socrates as a Sophist. There are undeniable similarities between Socrates and the Sophists, but there are also important differences. We need to explore this a bit.

Socrates clearly moves in the same circles as the Sophists; he converses with them eagerly and often, and his interests are similar. His subject matter is human affairs, in particular *areté*—excellence or virtue. As we have seen, the Sophists set themselves up as teachers of such excellence. Socrates does not. He cannot do so, he might insist, because he does not rightly know what it is, and no one can teach what he doesn't understand. Nonetheless, he explores this very area, trying to clarify what human excellence consists in, whether it is one thing or many (for example, courage, moderation, wisdom, justice), and whether it is the kind of thing that can be taught at all.

We have noted that many of the Sophists also teach specialized subjects, including geometry, astronomy, and nature philosophy in general. Socrates apparently was interested in nature philosophy as a youth but gave it up because it could not answer the questions that really intrigue him, such as Why are we here? and What is the best kind of life? Human life is what fascinates him.

Young men associate themselves with Socrates, too, sometimes for considerable periods of time, and consider him their teacher. He does not, as we noted in connection with Aristophanes' "Thinkery," have a school. And he does not consider himself a teacher. In fact, we will hear his claim that he has never taught anyone anything. (This takes some explaining, which we will do later.) So he is unlike the Sophists in that regard, for they do consider that they have something to teach and are proud to teach it to others.

Socrates is unlike the Sophists in another regard. He takes no pay from those who associate themselves with him. This is, of course, perfectly consistent with his claim that he has nothing

to teach. Xenophon adds that Socrates "marvelled that anyone should make money by the profession of virtue, and should not reflect that his highest reward would be the gain of a good friend" (*Memorabilia* 1.2.7).

Like the Sophists, Socrates is interested in the arts of communication and argument, in techniques of persuasion. But it is at just this point that we find the deepest difference between them, the difference that perhaps allows us to deny that Socrates is a Sophist at all. For the Sophists, these arts (rhetoric) are like strategies and tactics in battle. The whole point is to enable their practitioner to win. Argument and persuasion are thought of as a kind of contest where, as Antiphon put it, "victory goes to the best speaker." The Sophists aim at *victory*, not *truth*. This is wholly consistent with their skepticism and relativism. If all you can get are opinions anyway, then you might as well try to make things appear to others in whatever way serves your self-interest. And rhetoric, as they conceive and teach it, is designed to do just that.*

For Socrates, on the other hand, the arts of communication, argument, and persuasion have a different goal. His practice of them is designed not to win a victory over his opponent but to advance toward the truth. He is convinced that there is a truth about human affairs and that we are capable of advancing toward it, of shaping our opinions so that they are more "like truth," to use that old phrase of Xenophanes.† Socrates could never agree that if a man *thinks* a certain action is just, then it *is* just—not even "for him." So he is neither a relativist nor a skeptic. Justice, Socrates believes, is something quite independent of our opinions about it. And what it is needs investigation.

Socrates' way of proceeding coheres well with this conviction about truth. He usually refrains from piling up fine phrases in lengthy speeches that might simply overwhelm his listeners; he does not want them to agree with his conclusions for reasons they do not themselves fully understand and agree to. So he asks questions. He is very insistent

---

*See the Antiphon quote on p. 66.

†Look again at the fragment from Xenophanes on p. 16.

that his listeners answer in a sincere way, that they say what they truly believe. Each person is to speak for himself. In the dialogue *Meno*, for instance, Socrates professes not to know what virtue is. Meno expresses surprise, for surely, he says, Socrates listened to Gorgias when he was in town. Yes, Socrates admits, but he does not altogether remember what Gorgias said; perhaps Meno remembers and agrees with him. When Meno admits that he does, Socrates says,

> Then let's leave him out of it; he's not here, after all. But in the name of the gods, Meno, please do tell me in your own words what you think excellence is. (*Meno* 71d)[4]

So Meno is put on the spot and has to speak for himself. Again and again Socrates admonishes his hearers not to give their assent to a proposition unless they really agree.

The course of Socrates' conversations generally goes like this. Someone, often Socrates himself, asks a question: "What is piety?" or "Can human excellence be taught?" Someone, usually someone other than Socrates, suggests a reply. Socrates then proposes they "examine" whether they agree or disagree with this proposition. The examination proceeds by further questioning, which leads the person questioned to realize that the first answer is not adequate. A second answer that seems to escape the difficulties of the first is put forward, and the pattern repeats itself. A good example is found in *Euthyphro*, to which we'll turn shortly. In the early, more authentically Socratic dialogues, we are usually left at the end with an inconsistent set of beliefs; it is clear that we cannot accept the whole set, but neither Socrates nor his partner knows which way to go. Thus the participant is brought to admit that he doesn't understand the topic at all—although he thought he did when the conversation began.

This technique of proposal–questions–difficulties–new proposal–questions is a technique that Plato calls **dialectic.** Socrates thinks of it as a way, the very best way, of improving our opinions and perhaps even coming to know the truth. What is the connection between dialectic and truth? The connection is this: So long as people sincerely say what they believe and are open to revising this on the basis of good reasons, people can *together* identify inadequate answers to important questions. There really can be no doubt that certain answers won't do. But if you can be sure that some opinions aren't right, what remains unrefuted may well be in the vicinity of the truth. It is important, however, to note that even in the best case this sort of examination cannot *guarantee* the truth of what is left standing at the end. Socrates apparently knows this; that's why he so often confesses his ignorance.

This dialectical procedure, then, is better at detecting error than identifying truth, and for it to do even that, certain conditions must be met. Each participant must say what he or she really believes, and no one must be determined to hang on to a belief "no matter what." In other words, the aim must be not victory over the other speaker, but progress toward the truth. Dialectic is the somewhat paradoxically cooperative enterprise in which each *assists* the others by *raising objections* to what the others say.

We should reflect a moment on how odd this seems. We usually think we are being helped when people agree with us, support us in our convictions, and defend us against attacks. Socrates, however, thinks the best help we can get—what we really need—is given by questions that make us think again, questions that make us uncomfortable and inclined to be defensive. Again like Xenophanes, Socrates does not think that truth is obvious. It is by "seeking" that we approach the truth, and that's neither easy nor comfortable. Socrates' technique for seeking the truth is this dialectic of question and answer.

That this is a cooperative enterprise and not merely a competition to see who wins is displayed in the fact that communication is not one way. Socrates does not deliver sermons; he does not lecture, at least not in the early dialogues. Also, anyone can ask the questions. In Plato's dialogues, it is usually Socrates who asks, but not always. Sometimes he gives his partner a choice of either asking or answering questions.

As you can imagine, this rather antagonistic procedure was not always understood or appreciated by Socrates' compatriots. It was certainly one of the factors that generated hostility toward him. In fact, you had to be a certain kind of person to enjoy talking with Socrates and to benefit from a conversation with him, as a passage from the *Gorgias* makes clear. Here the topic is rhetoric, or the art of persuasion. At issue is whether persuasion can lead to knowledge of truth or whether it is restricted to opinion. Socrates says to Gorgias, who teaches rhetoric,

> If you're the same kind of person as I am, I'd be glad to continue questioning you; otherwise, let's forget it. What kind of person am I? I'm happy to have a mistaken idea of mine proved wrong, and I'm happy to prove someone else's mistaken ideas wrong, I'm certainly not *less* happy if I'm proved wrong than if I've proved someone else wrong, because, as I see it, I've got the best of it: there's nothing worse than the state which I've been saved from, so that's better for me than saving someone else. You see, there's nothing worse for a person, in my opinion, than holding mistaken views about the matters we're discussing at the moment. (*Gorgias* 458a)[5]

This is a crucial passage for understanding Socrates' technique. He is in effect telling us that he will converse only with those who have a certain *character*. Progress in coming to understand the truth is as much a matter of character as intelligence. If you care more for your reputation, for wealth, for winning, or for convincing others that your opinion

is the right one, Socrates will leave you alone. Or, if you insist on talking with him, you are bound to leave feeling humiliated rather than enlightened; for your goals will not have been reached. To make progress, he says, you must be such a person as he himself claims to be. What sort of person is that? You must be just as happy to be shown wrong as to show someone else to be wrong. No—you must be even *happier*, for if you are weaned from a false opinion, you have escaped a great evil.

It is worth expanding on this point a bit. To profit from a conversation with Socrates, you must (1) be open and honest about what you really do believe; and (2) not be so wedded to any one of your beliefs that you consider an attack on it as an attack on yourself. In other words, you must have a certain objectivity with respect to your own opinions. You must be able to say, "Yes, that is indeed an opinion of mine, but I shall be glad to exchange it for another if there is good reason to do so." This outlook skirts two dangers: wishy-washiness and **dogmatism.** People with these Socratic virtues are not wishy-washy, because they really do have opinions. But neither are they dogmatic, because they are eager to improve their opinions.

This attitude does, in any case, seem to characterize Socrates. At this point, the character and aims of Socrates stand as a polar opposite to those of the Sophists. There could never have been a day on which Socrates taught his students "how to make the weaker argument into the stronger." To take that as one's aim is to show that one cares not for the truth but only for victory. To teach the techniques that provide victory is to betray one's character, to show that one is looking for the same thing oneself: fame, wealth, and the satisfaction of one's desires. That is why the Sophists taught for pay and grew wealthy. That is why Socrates refused pay and remained poor. And that is why the portrait Aristophanes gives us in *The Clouds* is only a caricature—not the real Socrates.

What Socrates "Knows"

Socrates' most characteristic claim concerns his ignorance. In his conversations, he claims not to know what human excellence, courage, or piety is.

He begs to be instructed. Of course, it is usually the instructors who get instructed, who learn that they don't know after all. How shall we understand Socrates' claim not to know?

In part, surely, he is being ironic, especially in begging his partner in the conversation to instruct him. Socrates is simply playing the role of ignorant inquirer. But there is more to it than that. With respect to those large questions about the nature of human excellence, it is fairly clear that Socrates never does get an answer that fully satisfies him. In the sense of "know" that implies you can't be wrong, Socrates does not claim to know these things. Even on points he might be quite confident about, he must allow that the next conversation could raise new difficulties—difficulties he cannot overcome. In this respect, his confession of ignorance is quite sincere.

❧

"The wisest man is he who does not fancy that he is so at all."

Nicolas Boilean Despreau (1636–1711)

Nonetheless, there are things that are *as good as known* for Socrates, things he is so confident about that he is even willing to die for them. When we read his defense before the jury, we will see him affirm a number of things—remarkable things—with the greatest confidence. He will say, for instance, that a good man cannot be harmed—something, we wager, that you don't believe. This combination of ignorance and conviction seems paradoxical. How can we understand it?

As Socrates examines his convictions and the beliefs of others, discarding what is clearly indefensible, certain affirmations survive all the scrutiny. These are claims that neither Socrates nor any of his conversational partners have been able to undermine; these claims have *stood fast*. You can imagine that as the years go by and his convictions come under attack from every conceivable quarter, those few principles that withstand every assault must come to look more and more "like the truth," to recall that phrase from Xenophanes, so much like the truth that it becomes almost

inconceivable that they should be upset in the future. These convictions Socrates is willing to bet on, even with his life.

Before we examine some of the early dialogues, it will be useful to identify several of them.*

WE OUGHT TO SEARCH FOR TRUTH

In his conversation with Meno, Socrates says that

> there's one proposition that I'd defend to the death, if I could, by argument and by action: that as long as we think we should search for what we don't know we'll be better people—less fainthearted and less lazy—than if we were to think that we had no chance of discovering what we don't know and that there's no point in even searching for it. (*Meno* 86b–c)

This remark occurs in the context of an argument we will examine later,† that the soul is directly acquainted with truth before it enters a human body. This argument has the practical consequence that we may hope to recover the knowledge we had before birth. Socrates says that although he is not certain about every detail of this argument, he is sure that we will be better persons if we do not give up hope of attaining the truth.

Again we can see the Sophists lurking in the background; for it is they who claim that knowledge of truth is not possible for human beings, each of us being the final "measure," or judge, of what seems so to us. Socrates believes that this doctrine (relativism) will make us worse persons, fainthearted and lazy. After all, if we can dismiss any criticism by saying, "Well, it's true for *me*," then our present beliefs are absolutely secure; so why should we undertake the difficult task of examining them? The Sophist point of view seems to Socrates like a prescription for intellectual idleness and cowardice. And he is certain that to be idle and cowardly is to be a worse person rather than a better one. So one thing that "stands fast" for Socrates is that we ought to search for the truth.

---

*Because in this section we make use of material from several of the middle dialogues, we cannot claim with certainty to be representing the historical Socrates.
†See pp. 133–134.

HUMAN EXCELLENCE IS KNOWLEDGE

Socrates seems to have held that human excellence consists in knowledge. No doubt this strikes us as slightly odd; it seems overintellectualized, somehow. Knowledge, we are apt to think, may be one facet of being an excellent human being, but how could it be the whole of it?

The oddness is dissipated somewhat when we note what sort of knowledge Socrates has in mind. He is constantly referring us to the craftsmen—to "metal-workers, shoe-makers, tanners," as Alcibiades said—and to such professions as horse training, doctoring, and piloting a ship. In each case, what distinguishes the expert from a mere novice is the possession of knowledge. Such knowledge is not just having abstract intellectual propositions in your head, however; it is knowledge of *what* to do and *how* to do it. The Greek word here is **techne**, from which our word "technology" comes. This *techne* is a kind of applied knowledge. What distinguishes the competent doctor, horse trainer, or metal-worker, then, is that he or she possesses a *techne*. The amateur or novice does not.

Socrates claims that human excellence is a *techne* in exactly this same sense. What does the doctor know? She knows the human body and what makes for its health—its physical excellence. What does the horse trainer know? He knows horses—their nature and the kind of training they need to become excellent beasts. In a quite parallel fashion, the expert in human excellence (or virtue)—if there is one—would have to know human nature, how it functions, and wherein its excellence consists.*

Just as the shoemaker must understand both his materials (leather, nails, thread) and the use to which shoes are put—the point of having shoes—so those who wish to live well must understand themselves and what the point of living is. And just as one who has mastered the craft of shoemaking will make fine shoes, Socrates thinks, so one who has mastered the craft of living will live well. Knowledge in this *techne* sense, Socrates holds, is

_____

*See Aristotle's development of just this point, pp. 210–211.

both a necessary condition for human excellence (without it you cannot be a good person) and a sufficient condition (when it is present, so are all the excellent qualities of human life).

In the *Meno* we find another argument that knowledge is necessary for living well. Socrates gets agreement that human excellence must be something beneficial. But, he argues, things that are generally beneficial need not always be so. For instance, whether wealth, health, and strength are an advantage to the possessor depends on whether they are used wisely or foolishly. And the same goes for what people generally call virtues.

S: Now, among these qualities, take those that you think aren't knowledge—those that are different from knowledge—and let me ask you whether they're sometimes harmful and sometimes beneficial. Take courage, for instance, when it isn't wisdom but is something like recklessness. Isn't it the case that unintelligent recklessness harms people, while intelligent boldness does them good?

M: Yes.

S: And does the same go for self-control and cleverness? Are intelligent learning and training beneficial, while unintelligent learning and training are harmful?

M: Most definitely.

S: In short, then, mental endeavour and persistence always end in happiness when they are guided by knowledge, but in the opposite if they are guided by ignorance.

(*Meno* 88b–c)

The conclusion that human excellence consists in knowledge faces a difficulty. If it is knowledge, then it should be teachable. Recall Socrates' conversation with Protagoras. He points out that if a father wanted his son to be a painter, he would send him to someone who knew painting. If he wanted him to learn the flute, he would send him to someone who was an expert in flute playing. But where are the teachers of human excellence? Socrates could not allow that the Sophists were such. And he disclaims any knowledge of what such excellence consists in, so he can't teach it. But if there are no teachers, perhaps it isn't knowledge after all.

Socrates is able to resist this conclusion by a device that we'll examine soon.* For now, it is enough to note that this is one thing that "stands fast" for him: that human excellence is wisdom or knowledge.†

ALL WRONGDOING IS DUE TO IGNORANCE

This thesis is a corollary to the claim that virtue is knowledge. If to know the right is to do the right, then failing to do the right must be due to not knowing it. Not to know something is to be ignorant of it. So whoever acts wrongly does so out of ignorance. If we knew better, we would do better.

Socrates holds that we always act out of a belief that what we are doing is good. At the least, we think that it will produce good in the long run. We never, Socrates thinks, intend to do what we *know* is wrong or bad or evil or wicked. So if we do things that are wrong, it must be that we are not well-informed. We believe to be good what is in fact evil—but that is to believe something false, and to believe the false is to be ignorant of the true. Here we have a strong argument for the importance of moral education for the young. They can be brought up to be excellent human beings if only they come to learn what is in fact good and right and true.

For a comparison, let us look again to Euripides' *Hippolytus*, where Phaedra (who is, you remember, in love with her stepson) struggles with her passion.

> We know the good, we apprehend it clearly. But
> we can't bring it to achievement. Some are be-
> trayed by their own laziness, and others value some
> other pleasure above virtue.[6]

Here Phaedra expresses the view that even when we "know the good," we sometimes fail to do it. Socrates does not agree; he believes it is not possible to apprehend the good clearly and not do it.

Neither laziness nor pleasure can stand in the way. For human excellence *is* knowledge.

This view is connected intimately to Socrates' practice. He is not a preacher exhorting his fellow men to live up to what they know to be good. He is an inquirer trying to discover exactly what human excellence is. All people, he assumes, do the best they know. If people can be brought to understand what human excellence is, an excellent life will follow.

This view has seemed mistaken to many people. Not only Euripides disagrees. Among others, so do Aristotle, Saint Paul, and Augustine.

THE MOST IMPORTANT THING OF ALL IS TO CARE FOR YOUR SOUL

There is a final cluster of things Socrates seems to "know." They all hang together and are represented in the dialogues we'll be reading, so I'll just mention several of them briefly here.

Among the striking and unusual propositions that Socrates embraces are that it is better to suffer injustice than to commit injustice and that a good person cannot be harmed in either life or death.

These claims have to do with the soul. The soul, Socrates believes, is the most important part of a human being; from convictions in the soul flow all those actions that reveal what a person really is. Indeed, Socrates even seems to identify himself with his soul.* For that reason, the most important task any person has is to care for the soul. And to that end nothing is more crucial than self-knowledge. Just as the shoemaker cannot make good shoes unless he understands his material, you cannot construct a good life unless you know yourself.

In the *Apology*, Socrates says that for a human being "the unexamined life is not worth living." In particular, we need to know what we *do* know and what we *do not* know so that we can act wisely, and not foolishly. For foolishness is behavior based on false opinions. As you can see, this concern with the soul animates Socrates' practice; it is in pursuit of such self-knowledge that he questions his

---

*See pp. 132–133.
†There is a kind of paradox here, as you may already suspect. Socrates claims (1) that human excellence is knowledge, (2) that he lacks this knowledge, and yet (3) that he is a good man. It seems impossible to assert all three consistently; to assert any two seems to require the denial of the third. Socrates, however, has a way out. In Chapter 7, we address this Socratic paradox. See p. 130.

---

*See the jest Socrates makes just before he drinks the hemlock in *Phaedo* 115c, p. 145.

contemporaries—both for their sake and for his. One of the two mottoes at the Delphic Oracle might be the motto for Socrates' own life and practice: "Know Thyself."

"Ful wys is he that can himselven knowe."
Geoffrey Chaucer (1343–1400)

1. Describe briefly the character of Socrates, as we know it from the testimony of his friends.
2. In what ways is Socrates like the Sophists?
3. In what ways is he different?
4. How does Socrates proceed in his "examination" of his fellow citizens?
5. What is the connection between dialectic and truth?
6. What kind of a person do you have to be to profit from a conversation with Socrates?
7. A number of things seem to have "stood fast" for Socrates in the course of all his examinations, things that in some sense we can say he "knows." What are they?

FOR FURTHER THOUGHT

Here are several convictions Socrates thinks have withstood all the criticisms to which they have been exposed:

- That the most important thing in life is to care for the well-being of the soul
- That a good person cannot be harmed by a worse person

- That it is better to suffer injustice than to commit it

Choose one to consider. If you agree, try to say why. If you disagree, try to come up with a critique that might get Socrates to change his mind.

KEY WORDS

Socrates	dialectic
Xenophon	dogmatism
Alcibiades	*techne*

NOTES

1. Xenophon, *Symposium V*, trans. W. K. C. Guthrie, in *Socrates*, 67–68.
2. Quotations from Plato's *Symposium*, trans. Robin Waterfield (Oxford: Oxford University Press, 1994), are cited in the text by title and section number.
3. Quotations from Xenophon, *Memorabilia*, in *Xenophon: Memorabilia and Oeconomicus*, ed. E. C. Marchant (London: Heinemann, 1923), are cited in the text by title and book and section number.
4. Quotations from Plato's *Meno*, trans. Robin Waterfield in *Meno and Other Dialogues* (Oxford: Oxford University Press, 2005), are cited in the text by title and section number.
5. Quotations from Plato's *Gorgias*, trans. Robin Waterfield (Oxford: Oxford University Press, 1994), are cited by title and section number.
6. Euripides, *Hippolytus*, trans. David Grene, in *Euripides I*, ed. David Grene and Richmond Lattimore (Chicago: University of Chicago Press, 1965), ll. 380–384.

THE TRIAL AND DEATH OF SOCRATES

We are now ready to read several of Plato's early dialogues. In each of them Socrates is the major figure. They must have been written soon after Socrates' death. Because many people witnessed the trial and would have known of his conduct while awaiting execution, scholars think they present as accurate a picture of the historical Socrates as we can find. We'll read *Euthyphro*, *Apology*, and *Crito* in their entirety and a selection from *Phaedo*.

This chapter is partitioned into two parts for each dialogue. The text of the dialogue is printed first; this is followed by a section of commentary and questions. Here is a suggestion for you. Begin by giving each dialogue in turn a quick reading (they are all quite short). Don't try to understand everything the first time through; just get a feel for it. It would be ideal to read them aloud with a friend, each taking a part. After you have done the quick read-through, go to the commentary and questions that follow. Using these as a guide, reread each dialogue section by section, trying this time to understand everything and answering the questions as you go along. A good plan is to write out brief answers. You will be amazed at how rich these brief works are.

References are to page numbers in a standard Greek text of Plato.[1] These numbers are printed in the margins and are divided into sections *a* through *e*.

EUTHYPHRO

Translator's Introduction

Euthyphro is surprised to meet Socrates near the king-archon's court, for Socrates is not the kind of man to have business with courts of justice. Socrates explains that he is under indictment by one Meletus for corrupting the young and for not believing in the gods in whom the city believes. After a brief discussion of this, Socrates inquires about Euthyphro's business at court and is told that he is prosecuting his own father for the murder of a laborer who is himself a murderer. His family and friends believe his course of action to be impious, but Euthyphro explains that in this they are mistaken and reveal their ignorance of the nature of piety. This naturally leads Socrates to ask, What is piety? and the rest of the dialogue is devoted to a search for a definition of piety, illustrating the Socratic search for universal definitions of ethical terms, to which a number of early Platonic dialogues are devoted. As usual, no definition is found that satisfies Socrates.

The Greek term hosion *means, in the first instance, the knowledge of the proper ritual in prayer and sacrifice and, of course, its performance (as Euthyphro himself defines it in 14b). But obviously Euthyphro uses it in the much wider sense of pious conduct generally (e.g., his own) and in that sense the word is practically equivalent to righteousness (the justice of the Republic), the transition being by way of conduct pleasing to the gods.*

Besides being an excellent example of the early, so-called Socratic dialogues, Euthyphro contains several passages with important philosophical implications. These include those in which Socrates speaks of the one Form, presented by all the actions that we call pious (5d), as well as the one in which we are told that the gods love what is pious because it is pious; it is not pious because the gods love it (10d). Another passage clarifies the difference between genus and species (11e). The implications are discussed in the notes on those passages.

The Dialogue

2 EUTHYPHRO:[1] What's new, Socrates, to make you leave your usual haunts in the Lyceum and spend your time here by the king-archon's court? Surely you are not prosecuting anyone before the king-archon as I am?

SOCRATES: The Athenians do not call this a prosecution but an indictment, Euthyphro.

b E: What is this you say? Someone must have indicted you, for you are not going to tell me that you have indicted someone else.

S: No indeed.

E: But someone else has indicted you?

S: Quite so.

E: Who is he?

S: I do not really know him myself, Euthyphro. He is apparently young and unknown. They call him Meletus, I believe. He belongs to the Pitthean deme, if you know anyone from that deme called Meletus, with long hair, not much of a beard, and a rather aquiline nose.

E: I don't know him, Socrates. What charge does he bring against you?

c S: What charge? A not ignoble one I think, for it is no small thing for a young man to have knowledge of such an important subject. He says he knows how our young men are corrupted and who corrupts them. He is likely to be wise, and when he sees my ignorance corrupting his contemporaries, he proceeds

d to accuse me to the city as to their mother. I think he is the only one of our public men to start out the right way, for it is right to care first that the young should be as good as possible, just as a good farmer is likely to take care of the young plants first, and of the others later. So, too, Meletus first gets rid of us who

3 corrupt the young shoots, as he says, and then afterwards he will obviously take care of the older ones and become a source of great

---

[1] We know nothing about Euthyphro except what we can gather from this dialogue. He is obviously a professional priest who considers himself an expert on ritual and on piety generally, and, it seems, is generally so considered.

One Euthyphro is mentioned in Plato's *Cratylus* (396d) who is given to *enthousiasmos*, inspiration or possession, but we cannot be sure that it is the same person.

blessings for the city, as seems likely to happen to one who started out this way.

E: I could wish this were true, Socrates, but I fear the opposite may happen. He seems to me to start out by harming the very heart of the city by attempting to wrong you. Tell me, what does he say you do to corrupt the young?

b S: Strange things, to hear him tell, for he says that I am a maker of gods, and on the ground that I create new gods while not believing in the old gods, he has indicted me for their sake, as he puts it.

E: I understand, Socrates. This is because you say that the divine sign keeps coming to you.[2] So he has written this indictment against you as one who makes innovations in religious matters, and he comes to court to slander you, knowing that such things are easily misrepre-

c sented to the crowd. The same is true in my case. Whenever I speak of divine matters in the assembly and foretell the future, they laugh me down as if I were crazy; and yet I have foretold nothing that did not happen. Nevertheless, they envy all of us who do this. One need not worry about them, but meet them head-on.

S: My dear Euthyphro, to be laughed at does not matter perhaps, for the Athenians do not mind anyone they think clever, as long as he does not teach his own wisdom, but if they think that he makes others to be like himself they get angry,

d whether through envy, as you say, or for some other reason.

E: I have certainly no desire to test their feelings towards me in this matter.

S: Perhaps you seem to make yourself but rarely available, and not to be willing to teach your own wisdom, but I'm afraid that my liking for people makes them think that I pour out to anybody anything I have to say, not only without charging a fee but even glad to reward anyone who is willing to listen. If then they were intending to laugh at me, as you say they laugh

e at you, there would be nothing unpleasant in

their spending their time in court laughing and jesting, but if they are going to be serious, the outcome is not clear except to you prophets.

E: Perhaps it will come to nothing, Socrates, and you will fight your case as you think best, as I think I will mine.

S: What is your case, Euthyphro? Are you the defendant or the prosecutor?

E: The prosecutor.

S: Whom do you prosecute?

4 E: One whom I am thought crazy to prosecute.

S: Are you pursuing someone who will easily escape you?

E: Far from it, for he is quite old.

S: Who is it?

E: My father.

S: My dear sir! Your own father?

E: Certainly.

S: What is the charge? What is the case about?

E: Murder, Socrates.

S: Good heavens! Certainly, Euthyphro, most

b men would not know how they could do this and be right. It is not the part of anyone to do this, but of one who is far advanced in wisdom.

E: Yes, by Zeus, Socrates, that is so.

S: Is then the man your father killed one of your relatives? Or is that obvious, for you would not prosecute your father for the murder of a stranger.

E: It is ridiculous, Socrates, for you to think that it makes any difference whether the victim is a stranger or a relative. One should only watch whether the killer acted justly or not; if he acted justly, let him go, but if not, one should

c prosecute, even if the killer shares your hearth and table. The pollution is the same if you knowingly keep company with such a man and do not cleanse yourself and him by bringing him to justice. The victim was a dependent of mine, and when we were farming in Naxos he was a servant of ours. He killed one of our household slaves in drunken anger, so my father bound him hand and foot and threw him in a ditch, then sent a man here to enquire from the priest what should be done. During

d that time he gave no thought or care to the bound man, as being a killer, and it was no matter if he died, which he did. Hunger and cold and his bonds caused his death before the messenger came back from the seer. Both my father and my other relatives are angry that I

---

[2]In Plato, Socrates always speaks of his divine sign or voice as intervening to prevent him from doing or saying something (e.g., *Apology* 31d), but never positively. The popular view was that it enabled him to foretell the future, and Euthyphro here represents that view. Note, however, that Socrates dissociates himself from "you prophets" (3e).

am prosecuting my father for murder on behalf
of a murderer when he hadn't even killed him,
they say, and even if he had, the dead man does
not deserve a thought, since he was a killer.

e   For, they say, it is impious for a son to prosecute his father for murder. But their ideas
of the divine attitude to piety and impiety are
wrong, Socrates.

s: Whereas, by Zeus, Euthyphro, you think that
your knowledge of the divine, and of piety and
impiety, is so accurate that, when those things
happened as you say, you have no fear of having
acted impiously in bringing your father to trial?

e: I should be of no use, Socrates, and Euthyphro
5   would not be superior to the majority of men,
if I did not have accurate knowledge of all such
things.

s: It is indeed most important, my admirable
Euthyphro, that I should become your pupil, and as regards this indictment challenge
Meletus about these very things and say to him:
that in the past too I considered knowledge
about the divine to be most important, and
that now that he says I am guilty of improvising
and innovating about the gods I have become
b   your pupil. I would say to him: "If, Meletus,
you agree that Euthyphro is wise in these matters, consider me, too, to have the right beliefs
and do not bring me to trial. If you do not
think so, then prosecute that teacher of mine,
not me, for corrupting the older men, me and
his own father, by teaching me and by exhorting and punishing him." If he is not convinced,
and does not discharge me or indict you instead of me, I shall repeat the same challenge
in court.

e: Yes, by Zeus, Socrates, and, if he should try to
indict me, I think I would find his weak spots
c   and the talk in court would be about him
rather than about me.

s: It is because I realize this that I am eager to
become your pupil, my dear friend. I know
that other people as well as this Meletus do not
even seem to notice you, whereas he sees me
so sharply and clearly that he indicts me for ungodliness. So tell me now, by Zeus, what you
just now maintained you clearly knew: what
d   kind of thing do you say that godliness and ungodliness are, both as regards murder and other
things; or is the pious not the same and alike
in every action, and the impious the opposite

of all that is pious and like itself, and everything that is to be impious presents us with one
form[3] or appearance in so far as it is impious?

e: Most certainly, Socrates.

s: Tell me then, what is the pious, and what the
impious, do you say?

e: I say that the pious is to do what I am doing
now, to prosecute the wrongdoer, be it about
murder or temple robbery or anything else,
e   whether the wrongdoer is your father or your
mother or anyone else; not to prosecute is
impious. And observe, Socrates, that I can
quote the law as a great proof that this is so.
I have already said to others that such actions
are right, not to favour the ungodly, whoever
they are. These people themselves believe
that Zeus is the best and most just of the
gods, yet
6   they agree that he bound his father because he
unjustly swallowed his sons, and that he in turn
castrated his father for similar reasons. But
they are angry with me because I am prosecuting my father for his wrongdoing. They contradict themselves in what they say about the gods
and about me.

s: Indeed, Euthyphro, this is the reason why I
am a defendant in the case, because I find it
hard to accept things like that being said about
the gods, and it is likely to be the reason why
I shall be told I do wrong. Now, however, if
you, who have full knowledge of such things,
b   share their opinions, then we must agree with
them too, it would seem. For what are we to
say, we who agree that we ourselves have no
knowledge of them? Tell me, by the god of
friendship, do you really believe these things
are true?

3This is the kind of passage that makes it easier for us to
follow the transition from Socrates' universal definitions to
the Platonic theory of separately existent eternal universal
Forms. The words *eidos* and *idea*, the technical terms for
the Platonic Forms, commonly mean physical stature or
bodily appearance. As we apply a common epithet, in this
case pious, to different actions or things, these must have a
common characteristic, present a common appearance or
form, to justify the use of the same term, but in the early
dialogues, as here, it seems to be thought of as immanent in
the particulars and without separate existence. The same is
true of 6d where the word "form" is also used.

E: Yes, Socrates, and so are even more surprising things, of which the majority has no knowledge.

S: And do you believe that there really is war among the gods, and terrible enmities and battles, and other such things as are told by the poets, and other sacred stories such as are embroidered by good writers and by representations of which the robe of the goddess is adorned when it is carried up to the Acropolis? Are we to say these things are true, Euthyphro?

E: Not only these, Socrates, but, as I was saying just now, I will, if you wish, relate many other things about the gods which I know will amaze you.

S: I should not be surprised, but you will tell me these at leisure some other time. For now, try to tell me more clearly what I was asking just now, for, my friend, you did not teach me adequately when I asked you what the pious was, but you told me that what you are doing now, prosecuting your father for murder, is pious.

E: And I told the truth, Socrates.

S: Perhaps. You agree, however, that there are many other pious actions.

E: There are.

S: Bear in mind then that I did not bid you tell me one or two of the many pious actions but that form itself that makes all pious actions pious, for you agreed that all impious actions are impious and all pious actions pious through one form, or don't you remember?

E: I do.

S: Tell me then what this form itself is, so that I may look upon it, and using it as a model, say that any action of yours or another's that is of that kind is pious, and if it is not that it is not.

E: If that is how you want it, Socrates, that is how I will tell you.

S: That is what I want.

7 E: Well then, what is dear to the gods is pious, what is not is impious.

S: Splendid, Euthyphro! You have now answered in the way I wanted. Whether your answer is true I do not know yet, but you will obviously show me that what you say is true.

E: Certainly.

S: Come then, let us examine what we mean. An action or a man dear to the gods is pious, but an action or a man hated by the gods is impious. They are not the same, but quite opposite, the pious and the impious. Is that not so?

E: It is indeed.

S: And that seems to be a good statement?

b E: I think so, Socrates.

S: We have also stated that the gods are in a state of discord, that they are at odds with each other, Euthyphro, and that they are at enmity with each other. Has that, too, been said?

E: It has.

S: What are the subjects of difference that cause hatred and anger? Let us look at it this way. If you and I were to differ about numbers as to which is the greater, would this difference make us enemies and angry with each other, or would we proceed to count and soon resolve our difference about this?

c E: We would certainly do so.

S: Again, if we differed about the larger and the smaller, we would turn to measurement and soon cease to differ.

E: That is so.

S: And about the heavier and the lighter, we would resort to weighing and be reconciled.

E: Of course.

S: What subject of difference would make us angry and hostile to each other if we were unable to come to a decision? Perhaps you do not

d have an answer ready, but examine as I tell you whether these subjects are the just and the unjust, the beautiful and the ugly, the good and the bad. Are these not the subjects of difference about which, when we are unable to come to a satisfactory decision, you and I and other men become hostile to each other whenever we do?

E: That is the difference, Socrates, about those subjects.

S: What about the gods, Euthyphro? If indeed they have differences, will it not be about these same subjects?

E: It certainly must be so.

e S: Then according to your argument, my good Euthyphro, different gods consider different things to be just, beautiful, ugly, good, and bad, for they would not be at odds with one another unless they differed about these subjects, would they?

E: You are right.

s: And they like what each of them considers beautiful, good, and just, and hate the opposites of these?

e: Certainly.

s: But you say that the same things are considered
8   just by some gods and unjust by others, and as they dispute about these things they are at odds and at war with each other. Is that not so?

e: It is.

s: The same things then are loved by the gods and hated by the gods, and would be both god-loved and god-hated.

e: It seems likely.

s: And the same things would be both pious and impious, according to this argument?

e: I'm afraid so.

s: So you did not answer my question, you surprising man. I did not ask you what same thing is both pious and impious, and it appears that
b   what is loved by the gods is also hated by them. So it is in no way surprising if your present action, namely punishing your father, may be pleasing to Zeus but displeasing to Kronos and Ouranos, pleasing to Hephaestus but displeasing to Hera, and so with any other gods who differ from each other on this subject.

e: I think, Socrates, that on this subject no gods would differ from one another, that whoever has killed anyone unjustly should pay the penalty.

c: s: Well now, Euthyphro, have you ever heard any man maintaining that one who has killed or done anything else unjustly should not pay the penalty?

e: They never cease to dispute on this subject, both elsewhere and in the courts, for when they have committed many wrongs they do and say anything to avoid the penalty.

s: Do they agree they have done wrong, Euthyphro, and in spite of so agreeing do they nevertheless say they should not be punished?

e: No, they do not agree on that point.

s: So they do not say or do anything. For they do not venture to say this, or dispute that they must not pay the penalty if they have done
d   wrong, but I think they deny doing wrong. Is that not so?

e: That is true.

s: Then they do not dispute that the wrongdoer must be punished, but they may disagree as to who the wrongdoer is, what he did and when.

e: You are right.

s: Do not the gods have the same experience, if indeed they are at odds with each other about the just and the unjust, as your argument maintains? Some assert that they wrong one another, while others deny it, but no one among gods or men ventures to say that the
e   wrongdoer must not be punished.

e: Yes, that is true, Socrates, as to the main point.

s: And those who disagree, whether men or gods, dispute about each action, if indeed the gods disagree. Some say it is done justly, others unjustly. Is that not so?

e: Yes, indeed.

9   s: Come, now, my dear Euthyphro, tell me, too, that I may become wiser, what proof you have that all the gods consider that man to have been killed unjustly who became a murderer while in your service, was bound by the master of his victim, and died in his bonds before the one who bound him found out from the seers what was to be done with him, and that it is right for a son to denounce and to prosecute his father on behalf of such a man. Come, try to show me a clear sign that all the gods definitely be-
b   lieve this action to be right. If you can give me adequate proof of this, I shall never cease to extol your wisdom.

e: This is perhaps no light task, Socrates, though I could show you very clearly.

s: I understand that you think me more dull-witted than the jury, as you will obviously show them that these actions were unjust and that all the gods hate such actions.

e: I will show it to them clearly, Socrates, if only they will listen to me.

c: s: They will listen if they think you show them well. But this thought came to me as you were speaking, and I am examining it, saying to myself: "If Euthyphro shows me conclusively that all the gods consider such a death unjust, to what greater extent have I learned from him the nature of piety and impiety? This action would then, it seems, be hated by the gods, but the pious and the impious were not thereby now defined, for what is hated by the gods has also been shown to be loved by them." So I will not insist on this point; let us assume, if you wish, that all the gods consider this unjust and that they all hate it. However, d is this the correction we are making in our discussion, that what all the gods hate is impious, and what they all love is pious, and that what some gods love and others hate is neither or both? Is that how you now wish us to define piety and impiety?

E: What prevents us from doing so, Socrates?

S: For my part nothing, Euthyphro, but you look whether on your part this proposal will enable you to teach me most easily what you promised.

e E: I would certainly say that the pious is what all the gods love, and the opposite, what all the gods hate, is the impious.

S: Then let us again examine whether that is a sound statement, or do we let it pass, and if one of us, or someone else, merely says that something is so, do we accept that it is so? Or should we examine what the speaker means?

E: We must examine it, but I certainly think that this is now a fine statement.

10 S: We shall soon know better whether it is. Consider this: Is the pious loved by the gods because it is pious, or is it pious because it is loved by the gods?

E: I don't know what you mean, Socrates.*

11 S: I'm afraid, Euthyphro, that when you were asked what piety is, you did not wish to make its nature clear to me, but you told me an affect or quality of it, that the pious has the quality of being loved by all the gods, but you

b have not yet told me what the pious is. Now, if you will, do not hide things from me but tell me again from the beginning what piety is, whether loved by the gods or having some other quality—we shall not quarrel about that—but be keen to tell me what the pious and the impious are.

E: But Socrates, I have no way of telling you what I have in mind, for whatever proposition we put forward goes around and refuses to stay put where we establish it.

S: Your statements, Euthyphro, seem to belong

c to my ancestor, Daedalus. If I were stating them and putting them forward, you would

perhaps be making fun of me and say that because of my kinship with him my conclusions in discussion run away and will not stay where one puts them. As these propositions are yours, however, we need some other jest, for they will not stay put for you, as you say yourself.

E: I think the same jest will do for our discussion, Socrates, for I am not the one who makes them go round and not remain in the same place; it

d is you who are the Daedalus; for as far as I am concerned they would remain as they were.

S: It looks as if I was cleverer than Daedalus in using my skill, my friend, in so far as he could only cause to move the things he made himself, but I can make other people's move as well as my own. And the smartest part of my skill is that I am clever without wanting to be, for I would rather have your statements to me

e remain unmoved than possess the wealth of Tantalus as well as the cleverness of Daedalus. But enough of this. Since I think you are making unnecessary difficulties, I am as eager as you are to find a way to teach me about piety, and do not give up before you do. See whether you think all that is pious is of necessity just.

E: I think so.

S: And is then all that is just pious? Or is all that

12 is pious just, but not all that is just pious, but some of it is and some is not?

E: I do not follow what you are saying, Socrates.

S: Yet you are younger than I by as much as you are wiser. As I say, you are making difficulties because of your wealth of wisdom. Pull yourself together, my dear sir, what I am saying is not difficult to grasp. I am saying the opposite of what the poet said who wrote:
You do not wish to name Zeus, who had

b done it, and who made all things grow, for where there is fear there is also shame.
I disagree with the poet. Shall I tell you why?

E: Please do.

S: I do not think that "where there is fear there is also shame," for I think that many people who fear disease and poverty and many other such things feel fear, but are not ashamed of the things they fear. Do you not think so?

E: I do indeed.

S: But where there is shame there is also fear. For is there anyone who, in feeling shame and

---

*From 10a to 11a, there appears a complex and rather confusing argument. We omit it here and supply a paraphrase in the commentary section that follows the dialogue.—N.M. & D.M.

c embarrassment at anything, does not also at the same time fear and dread a reputation for wickedness?

E: He is certainly afraid.

S: It is then not right to say "where there is fear there is also shame," but that where there is shame there is also fear, for fear covers a larger area than shame. Shame is a part of fear just as odd is a part of number, with the result that it is not true that where there is number there is also oddness, but that where there is oddness there is also number. Do you follow me now?

E: Surely.

S: This is the kind of thing I was asking before,
d whether where there is piety there is also justice, but where there is justice there is not always piety, for the pious is a part of justice. Shall we say that, or do you think otherwise?

E: No, but like that, for what you say appears to be right.

S: See what comes next: if the pious is a part of the just, we must, it seems, find out what part of the just it is. Now if you asked me something of what we mentioned just now, such as what part of number is the even, and what number that is, I would say it is the number that is divisible into two equal, not unequal, parts. Or do you not think so?

E: I do.

e S: Try in this way to tell me what part of the just the pious is, in order to tell Meletus not to wrong us any more and not to indict me for ungodliness, since I have learned from you sufficiently what is godly and pious and what is not.

E: I think, Socrates, that the godly and pious is the part of the just that is concerned with the care of the gods, while that concerned with the care of men is the remaining part of justice.

S: You seem to me to put that very well, but I
13 still need a bit of information. I do not know yet what you mean by care, for you do not mean the care of the gods in the same sense as the care of other things, as, for example, we say, don't we, that not everyone knows how to care for horses, but the horse breeder does.

E: Yes, I do mean it that way.

S: So horse breeding is the care of horses.

E: Yes.

S: Nor does everyone know how to care for dogs, but the hunter does.

E: That is so.

S: So hunting is the care of dogs.
b E: Yes.

S: And cattle raising is the care of cattle.

E: Quite so.

S: While piety and godliness is the care of the gods, Euthyphro. Is that what you mean?

E: It is.

S: Now care in each case has the same effect; it aims at the good and the benefit of the object cared for, as you can see that horses cared for by horse breeders are benefited and become better. Or do you not think so?

E: I do.

S: So dogs are benefited by dog breeding, cattle
c by cattle raising, and so with all the others. Or do you think that care aims to harm the object of its care?

E: By Zeus, no.

S: It aims to benefit the object of its care?

E: Of course.

S: Is piety then, which is the care of the gods, also to benefit the gods and make them better? Would you agree that when you do something pious you make some of the gods better?

E: By Zeus, no.

S: Nor do I think that this is what you mean—far from it—but that is why I asked you what you meant by the care of gods, because I did not
d believe you meant this kind of care.

E: Quite right, Socrates, that is not the kind of care I mean.

S: Very well, but what kind of care of the gods would piety be?

E: The kind of care, Socrates, that slaves take of their masters.

S: I understand. It is likely to be a kind of service of the gods.

E: Quite so.

S: Could you tell me to the achievement of what goal service to doctors tends? Is it not, do you think, to achieving health?

E: I think so.

e S: What about service to shipbuilders? To what achievement is it directed?

E: Clearly, Socrates, to the building of a ship.

S: And service to housebuilders to the building of a house?

E: Yes.

S: Tell me then, my good sir, to the achievement of what aim does service to the gods tend? You obviously know since you say that you, of all men, have the best knowledge of the divine.

E: And I am telling the truth, Socrates.

S: Tell me then, by Zeus, what is that excellent aim that the gods achieve, using us as their servants?

E: Many fine things, Socrates.

14 S: So do generals, my friend. Nevertheless you could easily tell me their main concern, which is to achieve victory in war, is it not?

E: Of course.

S: The farmers too, I think, achieve many fine things, but the main point of their efforts is to produce food from the earth.

E: Quite so.

S: Well then, how would you sum up the many fine things that the gods achieve?

E: I told you a short while ago, Socrates, that it b is a considerable task to acquire any precise knowledge of these things, but, to put it simply, I say that if a man knows how to say and do what is pleasing to the gods at prayer and sacrifice, those are pious actions such as preserve both private houses and public affairs of state. The opposite of these pleasing actions are impious and overturn and destroy everything.

S: You could tell me in far fewer words, if c you were willing, the sum of what I asked, Euthyphro, but you are not keen to teach me, that is clear. You were on the point of doing so, but you turned away. If you had given that answer, I should now have acquired from you sufficient knowledge of the nature of piety. As it is, the lover of inquiry must follow his beloved wherever it may lead him. Once more then, what do you say that piety and the pious are? Are they a knowledge of how to sacrifice and pray?

E: They are.

S: To sacrifice is to make a gift to the gods, whereas to pray is to beg from the gods?

E: Definitely, Socrates.

d S: It would follow from this statement that piety would be a knowledge of how to give to, and beg from, the gods.

E: You understood what I said very well, Socrates.

S: That is because I am so desirous of your wisdom, and I concentrate my mind on it, so that no word of yours may fall to the ground. But tell me, what is this service to the gods? You say it is to beg from them and to give to them?

E: I do.

S: And to beg correctly would be to ask from them things that we need?

E: What else?

e S: And to give correctly is to give them what they need from us, for it would not be skillful to bring gifts to anyone that are in no way needed.

E: True, Socrates.

S: Piety would then be a sort of trading skill between gods and men?

E: Trading yes, if you prefer to call it that.

S: I prefer nothing, unless it is true. But tell me, what benefit do the gods derive from the gifts they receive from us? What they give us is obvious to all. There is for us no good that we 15 do not receive from them, but how are they benefited by what they receive from us? Or do we have such an advantage over them in the trade that we receive all our blessings from them and they receive nothing from us?

E: Do you suppose, Socrates, that the gods are benefited by what they receive from us?

S: What could those gifts from us to the gods be, Euthyphro?

E: What else, do you think, than honour, reverence, and what I mentioned just now, gratitude?

b S: The pious is then, Euthyphro, pleasing to the gods, but not beneficial or dear to them?

E: I think it is of all things most dear to them.

S: So the pious is once again what is dear to the gods.

E: Most certainly.

S: When you say this, will you be surprised if your arguments seem to move about instead of staying put? And will you accuse me of being Daedalus who makes them move, though you are yourself much more skillful than Daedalus and make them go round in a circle? Or do you not realize that our argument has moved around and come again to the same place? You c surely remember that earlier the pious and the god-beloved were shown not to be the same but different from each other. Or do you not remember?

E: I do.

S: Do you then not realize now that you are saying that what is dear to the gods is the pious? Is this not the same as the god-beloved? Or is it not?

E: It certainly is.

S: Either we were wrong when we agreed before, or, if we were right then, we are wrong now.

E: That seems to be so.

S: So we must investigate again from the beginning what piety is, as I shall not willingly give up before I learn this. Do not think me

d unworthy, but concentrate your attention and tell the truth. For you know it, if any man does, and I must not let you go, like Proteus, before you tell me. If you had no clear knowledge of piety and impiety you would never have ventured to prosecute your old father for murder on behalf of a servant. For fear of the gods you would have been afraid to take the risk lest you should not be acting rightly, and would have been ashamed before men, but now I know well that you believe you have

e clear knowledge of piety and impiety. So tell me, my good Euthyphro, and do not hide what you think it is.

E: Some other time, Socrates, for I am in a hurry now, and it is time for me to go.

S: What a thing to do, my friend! By going you have cast me down from a great hope I had, that I would learn from you the nature of the

16 pious and the impious and so escape Meletus' indictment by showing him that I had acquired wisdom in divine matters from Euthyphro, and my ignorance would no longer cause me to be careless and inventive about such things, and that I would be better for the rest of my life.

COMMENTARY AND QUESTIONS

Read 2a–5a Note that **Euthyphro** is surprised to find Socrates at court, suggesting that Socrates is neither the sort who brings suit against his fellow citizens nor the sort one would expect to be prosecuted.

Q1. Why does Socrates say that **Meletus** is likely to be wise? (2c)

Q2. What sort of character does Socrates ascribe to Meletus here? Is Socrates sincere in his praise of Meletus?

Q3. There seem to be two charges against Socrates. Can you identify them? (2c, 3b)

Socrates famously claims to have a "**divine sign**" that comes to him from time to time. We hear of it again in the *Apology*. That the gods should speak to mortals in signs does not strike the ancient Greeks as a strange notion. Usually the gods speak through oracles, prophets, or seers. Euthyphro claims this ability for himself, saying that he "foretells the future." He assumes (mistakenly) that Socrates too claims this ability, and he concludes that it is out of envy for this talent that Meletus and the others are pressing charges. Moreover, Socrates' "sign" from the gods, Euthyphro thinks, would also explain the accusation that Socrates is introducing "new gods."

Does Socrates believe in the "old gods"? There can be little doubt that his view of the Olympians is much the same as that of Xenophanes or Heraclitus: The stories of Homer cannot be taken literally. (See *Euthyphro* 6a.) Yet he always speaks reverently of "god" or "the god" or "the gods" (these three terms being used pretty much interchangeably). And he feels free to use traditional language in speaking about the divine, so he writes that last hymn to Apollo and would probably have agreed with Heraclitus that the divine is "willing and unwilling to be called Zeus."*

Moreover, Xenophon tells us that Socrates behaves in accord with the advice given by the Priestess at Delphi when asked about sacrifice and ritual matters: "Follow the custom of the State: that is the way to act piously." Xenophon goes on to tell us,

> And again, when he prayed he asked simply for good gifts, "for the gods know best what things are good." Though his sacrifices were humble, according to his means, he thought himself not a whit inferior to those who made frequent and magnificent sacrifices out of great possessions. . . . No, the greater the piety of the giver, the greater (he thought) was the delight of the gods in the gift.[2]

There seems every reason to suppose that Socrates is pious in the conventional sense. Still, he would not have held back his beliefs if asked directly about the gods; as he says in 3d, his "liking for people" makes it seem that he pours out to anybody what he has to say. And traditionalists might well take exception to some of that.

---

*See p. 20.

What of the "sign"? Was that an introduction of new gods? Socrates does not seem to have thought of it as such. It seems to be analogous to what we would call the voice of conscience, though clearly it was much more vivid to him than to most of us. It never, he tells us, advises him positively to do something; it only prevents him, and it is clearly nothing like Euthyphro's future-telling. (Note that in 3e he separates himself from "you prophets.") But he clearly thinks of the sign as a voice of the divine.

Q4. Why is Euthyphro in court?
Q5. What does Euthyphro claim to know?

Read 5a–6e We now know what the topic of this conversation is to be. Socrates says he is "eager" to be Euthyphro's pupil.

Q6. Why does Socrates say he wants Euthyphro to instruct him? Do you think he really expects to be helped?
Q7. Do you think this is going to be a serious inquiry? Or is Socrates just having some sport with Euthyphro?

Notice in 5d the three requirements that must be met to satisfy Socrates. He wants to know what **the "pious"** or the "holy" or the "godly" is (all these words may translate the Greek term).

1. A satisfactory answer will pick out some feature that is the same in every pious action.
2. This feature will not be shared by any impious action.
3. It will be that feature (or the lack of it) that *makes* an action pious (or impious).

What Socrates is searching for, we can say, is a **definition** of piety or holiness.* He wants to know what it is so that it can be recognized when it

appears. It is like wanting to know what a crow is: We want to know what features all crows have that are not shared by eagles and hedgehogs, the possession of which ensure that this thing we see before us is indeed a crow.

Would knowing what piety is be useful if one were about to be tried for impiety? A Sophist might not think so at all. At that point, the typical Sophist would just dazzle the jury with rhetoric. But Socrates, as always, wants to know the truth. He wants to know the truth even more than he wants to be acquitted. We can think of this as one aspect of his persistent search to know himself. Who is he? Has he been guilty of impiety? Only an understanding of what piety truly is will tell.

Q8. What does Euthyphro say piety is?
Q9. What does Socrates focus on as the likely reason he is on trial?
Q10. What is Socrates' objection to the definition Euthyphro has proposed?

Note particularly the term **"form"** in 6d–e. It clearly does not mean "shape," except perhaps in a most abstract sense. The form of something is whatever makes it the kind of thing it is. The form may sometimes be shape, as the "form" of a square is to be an area bounded by equal straight lines and right angles, but it need not be. When we ask in this sense for the "form" of an elephant, we are asking for more than an outline drawing and for more than even a photograph can supply. What we want is what the biologist can give us; we are asking what an elephant is. Notice that the biologist can do this not only for elephants but also for mammals—and no one can draw the geometrical shape of a mammal. (True, you can draw a picture of *this* mammal or *that* mammal, but not a picture of a mammal *as such*. Yet it can be given a definition.) In the same way, it is perfectly in order to ask for the "form" of abstract qualities such as justice, courage, or piety.

Read 7a–9b Here we have Euthyphro's second attempt at answering Socrates' question.

---

*There are a number of different kinds of definition. For a critique of Socrates' kind, see Wittgenstein's notion of "family resemblances" in Chapter 26.

Q11. What is Euthyphro's second answer?

Q12. Why does Socrates exclaim, "Splendid!"?

Q13. What is the difference between answering "in the way" he wanted and giving a "true" answer?

Note Socrates' characteristic invitation in 7a: "Let us examine what we mean." How does this examination proceed? He reminds Euthyphro of something he admitted earlier—that there is "war among the gods" (6b)—and wonders whether that is *consistent* with the definition Euthyphro now proposes; do the two fit together, or do they clash?

Q14. How does Socrates derive the conclusion (8a) that "the same things then are loved by the gods and hated by the gods"? Is this a correct deduction from the statements Euthyphro previously agreed to?

Q15. What further conclusion follows? Why is that disturbing?

In 8b, Socrates drives the disturbing consequence home by applying it to Euthyphro's own case. Socrates is never one to leave things up in the air, unconnected to practical life. If this is a good understanding of piety, then it ought to illumine the matter at hand. But of course, Euthyphro cannot admit that his own prosecution is loved by some of the gods and hated by others—that it is both pious and impious. He protests that *none* of the gods would disagree that "whoever has killed anyone unjustly should pay the penalty."

Now, this is sneaky. Can you see why? It is a move that might slide past a lesser antagonist, but Socrates picks it up immediately.

Q16. What do people dispute about concerning wrongs and penalties? And what not?

So Socrates drives Euthyphro back to the issue: In light of the admission that the gods quarrel, what reason is there to think that prosecuting his father is an instance of what the gods love and thus an example of piety?

Q17. Do you believe that Socrates has put Euthyphro in an untenable position here?

Read 9c–11d   Socrates takes the lead here and proposes a modification to the earlier definition. Euthyphro embraces the suggestion with enthusiasm in 9e. Be sure you are clear about the new definition. Write it down.

Again we get the invitation to examine this new attempt. In 9e, Socrates backs it up with this question: "Or do we let it pass, and if one of us, or someone else, merely says that something is so, do we accept that it is so?" Are there reasons why this should not be accepted? The mere fact that someone—anyone—says it is so does not make it so. Do you agree with Socrates here?

In 10a, we get an important question, one that reverberates through later Christian theology and has a bearing on whether there can be an **ethics** independent of what God or the gods approve. Suppose we agree that in normal circumstances it is wrong to lie (allowing that a lie may be justified, for example, if it is the only way to save a life). And suppose, for the sake of the argument, we also agree that God or the gods hate lying (in those normal circumstances). What is it, we still might ask, that *makes* lying wrong? Is it the fact that it is hated by the divine power(s)? Or is there something about lying itself that makes it wrong—and that is why the gods hate it? To ask these questions is a way of asking for the "form" of wrongness. (Look again at the three requirements for a satisfactory definition in 5d and on page 112; it is the third requirement that is at issue.)

Suppose we agree, Socrates says, that what all the gods love is pious and what they all hate is impious; the question remains whether it is this love that explains the piety of the pious. Suppose it is. Then a behavior is pious *simply because* that behavior pleases the gods. It follows that if the gods loved lying, stealing, or adultery, that would make it right to lie, steal, or sleep with your neighbor's spouse. In this case, ethics is tied intrinsically to religion.

The alternative is that there is something about these actions that makes them wrong—and that is why the gods hate them. If this alternative is correct, then a secular ethics, independent of God, is possible. If we could identify what it is about lying that makes it wrong, we would have a reason not to lie whether we believe in the gods or not. Those who think that God's command (or love) is what *makes* lying wrong will be likely to say, if they lose faith in God, that "everything is permitted."* But on the alternative to divine command theory, this radical consequence does not follow. The question Socrates raises is an important one.

Assuming that the alternatives are clear, which one should we prefer? There is no doubt about Socrates' answer: the pious is pious *not* because the gods love it; rather, the gods love what is pious because of what it is. In the omitted section (10a–11a), Socrates piles up analogies to explain this. Let's try to simplify. Suppose that Henry, a gardener, loves his roses. The roses are loved, then, because Henry loves them. But he doesn't love them because they are loved by him! That would be absurd. He loves them because of something in the roses, something that makes them worthy of his love—their fragrance, perhaps, or their beauty.

In the same way, Socrates argues, if the gods love piety in humans, it must be because there is something lovable about it. Socrates wants to understand what it is. That is why he complains in 11a that Euthyphro has not answered his question. He says that Euthyphro has told him only "an affect or quality" of the pious—namely, that it is loved by the gods. But, he claims, Euthyphro has not yet made its "nature" or "form" clear. To be told only that the pious is what all the gods love is to learn only about how it is regarded by them. Euthyphro has spoken only of something external; he has not revealed what it really is!

_____
*This formula, "Everything is permitted," is that of Ivan Karamazov, the atheist in Dostoyevsky's novel, *The Brothers Karamazov.* The servant of the family, Smerdyakov, is persuaded that this is so, and on these grounds he murders the brothers' father.

Q18. Is this a good argument? Suppose, in response to the question, "Why do the gods love the pious?" one were to reply, "They just do!" Is Socrates assuming that there must be a reason? Is he assuming what he needs to prove?

Socrates probably calls Daedalus (in 11c) his "ancestor" because Daedalus was the mythical "patron saint" of stonemasons and sculptors. He was reputed to be such a cunning artisan that his sculptures took life and ran away.

Q19. Why is Socrates reminded of Daedalus here?

Read 11e–end Again Socrates makes a suggestion, this time that piety and justice are related somehow. It seems a promising idea, but some clarifications are needed. Are they identical? Or is one a part of the other? And if the latter, which is part of which?

Q20. What answer do the two settle on? Why?
Q21. In what way are the fear/shame and odd/number distinctions analogous?
Q22. What are the two kinds of "care" that are distinguished? (13a–c and 13d–e)
Q23. Which one is the relevant one? Why?

In 14c we reach a crucial turning point in the dialogue. Note that Socrates here says they were on the verge of solving the problem, but Euthyphro "turned away." If only he had answered a certain question, Socrates says, he "should now have acquired . . . sufficient knowledge of the nature of piety." But Euthyphro didn't answer it.

Apparently Socrates feels that they were on the right track. Let us review. Piety is part of justice. It is that part consisting in **care of the gods.** The kind of care at issue is the kind that slaves offer their masters. Such service on the part of slaves is always directed to some fine end (for example, health, ships, houses). The question arises, To what fine end is service to the gods devoted? To put it another way, what is the point of piety? What is it *for*? What is "that excellent aim that the gods achieve, using us as their servants?" Remember that for Socrates the good is always something useful or advantageous. He is here asking—on the tacit assumption that piety is something good—what advantage piety produces. We can identify the good things produced by service to doctors. What good things are produced by service to the gods? If one could answer this question, the nature of piety might finally be clarified.

Unfortunately, all Euthyphro can say is that piety produces "many fine things." When pressed harder, he in effect changes the subject, although he probably doesn't realize he is doing so. He says in 14b that "to put it simply," piety is knowing "how to say and do what is pleasing to the gods at prayer and sacrifice." This certainly does not answer the question of what aim the gods achieve through our service!

Let us, however, briefly consider Euthyphro's statement. First, it does go some way toward answering the question of what we should do to be pious. Euthyphro's answer is in fact the traditional answer common to most religions: pray and offer sacrifice. That answer would have been the standard one in Athens, and it is a little surprising that it comes out so late in the dialogue. It corresponds to the advice of the Delphic Oracle to "follow the custom of the state."

Second, Euthyphro's statement mentions some advantages to being pious in this way: preserving "both private houses and public affairs of state." But this is puzzling. Why does Socrates not accept this as an answer to the question about the aim we seek to achieve by being pious in just this way?

No answer is given in the dialogue; perhaps it must just remain puzzling. But here is a suggestion. Socrates, at the end of the Peloponnesian War, may simply be unable to believe this is true. No doubt Athens had offered many prayers and had made all the required sacrifices during the war. Athens had prayed for victory, just as Sparta must have prayed for victory. Yet Athens not only lost; she also did irreparable damage to

herself. Such piety, it seemed, did *not* preserve private houses and public affairs. If the promised advantages do not materialize, Socrates would conclude, this kind of piety is not after all a good thing. Perhaps the exasperation evident in 14c expresses Socrates' view that by this time in history it is all too clear piety can't be that. It can't be a kind of "trading skill" between gods and mortals. And on the assumption that piety is a good thing, it must be something quite different from Euthyphro's version of it.

This is rather speculative but not, we think, implausible. As we'll see, Jesus and the Christians have an answer about what piety is for. We find it clearly, for instance, in St. Augustine.* It is an answer that Socrates is close to but does not quite grasp. It demands that we rethink the nature of God and the relations of man to God altogether. But that is a story for later.

Socrates, regretfully, feels it is necessary to follow his "teacher" and once more takes up his questioning in 14c. There is a fairly simple argument running through these exchanges, but it is

*See p. 283.

not easy to pick it out. Let us try to identify the steps; check the text to see that we are getting it right.

1. Piety is prayer and sacrifice. (This is Euthyphro's latest definition, now up for examination.)
2. Prayer and sacrifice are begging from the gods and giving to the gods.
3. The giving must, to be "skillful," be giving what they need.
4. To give what they need would be to benefit them.
5. But we cannot benefit the gods.
6. If our giving does not benefit the gods, the only alternative is that this giving "pleases" them.
7. But that is just to say that they like it, it is dear to them—it is what they love.
8. And that returns us to the earlier definition: that piety is what all the gods love. (And we already know that this is not satisfactory. So we are going in a circle.)

The crux of the argument is, no doubt, Premise 5. It is expressed by Euthyphro in a surprised question in 15a and accepted by Socrates. Why can't we benefit the gods? No reasons are given here, but they are not hard to find. The gods, recall, are the immortals, the happy ones. To think of them as having needs that mere mortals could supply would have seemed to many Greeks as impious in the extreme. We receive all our benefits from them. To think that we could benefit them would be arrogance and hubris of the first rank.

Q24. Do you agree with this view? What do you think of this argument? Has the discussion really come full circle?

Q25. What characteristic of Socrates do you think Plato means to impress on us in Socrates' next-to-last speech?

Q26. Has Euthyphro learned anything in the course of this discussion?

Q27. Have you? If so, what?

At the end of the dialogue, Euthyphro escapes, leaving us without an answer to the question examined. Socrates must go to his trial still ignorant of the nature of piety.

APOLOGY

Translator's Introduction

The Apology[1] professes to be a record of the actual speech that Socrates delivered in his own defence at the trial. This makes the question of its historicity more acute than in the

dialogues in which the conversations themselves are mostly fictional and the question of historicity is concerned only with how far the theories that Socrates is represented as expressing were those of the historical Socrates. Here, however, we are dealing with a speech that Socrates made as a matter of history. How far is Plato's account accurate? We should always remember that the ancients did not expect historical accuracy in the way we do. On the other hand, Plato makes it clear

---

[1]The word *apology* is a transliteration, not a translation, of the Greek *apologia*, which means defense. There is certainly nothing apologetic about the speech.

that he was present at the trial (34a, 38b). Moreover, if, as is generally believed, the Apology was written not long after the event, many Athenians would remember the actual speech, and it would be a poor way to vindicate the Master, which is the obvious intent, to put a completely different speech into his mouth. Some liberties could no doubt be allowed, but the main arguments and the general tone of the defence must surely be faithful to the original. The beauty of language and style is certainly Plato's, but the serene spiritual and moral beauty of character belongs to Socrates. It is a powerful combination.

Athenian juries were very large, in this case 501, and they combined the duties of jury and judge as we know them by both convicting and sentencing. Obviously, it would have been virtually impossible for so large a body to discuss various penalties and decide on one. The problem was resolved rather neatly, however, by having the prosecutor, after conviction, assess the penalty he thought appropriate, followed by a counter-assessment by the defendant. The jury would then decide between the two. This procedure generally made for moderation on both sides.

Thus the Apology is in three parts. The first and major part is the main speech (17a–35a), followed by the counter-assessment (35a–38c), and finally, last words to the jury (38c–42a), both to those who voted for the death sentence and those who voted for acquittal.

The Dialogue

17 I do not know, men of Athens, how my accusers affected you; as for me, I was almost carried away in spite of myself, so persuasively did they speak. And yet, hardly anything of what they said is true. Of the many lies they told, one in particular surprised me, namely that you should be careful not to be deceived by an accomplished speaker like **b** me. That they were not ashamed to be immediately proved wrong by the facts, when I show myself not to be an accomplished speaker at all, that I thought was most shameless on their part—unless indeed they call an accomplished speaker the man who speaks the truth. If they mean that, I would agree that I am an orator, but not after their manner, for indeed, as I say, practically nothing **c** they said was true. From me you will hear the whole truth, though not, by Zeus, gentlemen, expressed in embroidered and stylized phrases like theirs, but things spoken at random and expressed in the first words that come to mind, for I put my trust in the justice of what I say, and let none of

you expect anything else. It would not be fitting at my age, as it might be for a young man, to toy with words when I appear before you.

One thing I do ask and beg of you gentlemen: if you hear me making my defence in the same kind of language as I am accustomed to use in the market place by the bankers' tables,[2] where many of you have heard me, and elsewhere, do not be surprised or create a disturbance on that account. **d** The position is this: this is my first appearance in a law-court, at the age of seventy; I am therefore simply a stranger to the manner of speaking here. Just as if I were really a stranger, you would certainly excuse me if I spoke in that dialect and **18** manner in which I had been brought up, so too my present request seems a just one, for you to pay no attention to my manner of speech—be it better or worse—but to concentrate your attention on whether what I say is just or not, for the excellence of a judge lies in this, as that of a speaker lies in telling the truth.

It is right for me, gentlemen, to defend myself first against the first lying accusations made against me and my first accusers, and then against the later accusations and the later accusers. There have **b** been many who have accused me to you for many years now, and none of their accusations are true. These I fear much more than I fear Anytus and his friends, though they too are formidable. These earlier ones, however, are more so, gentlemen; they got hold of most of you from childhood, persuaded you and accused me quite falsely, saying that there is a man called Socrates, a wise man, a student of all things in the sky and below the earth, who **c** makes the worse argument the stronger. Those who spread that rumour, gentlemen, are my dangerous accusers, for their hearers believe that those who study these things do not even believe in the gods. Moreover, these accusers are numerous, and have been at it a long time; also, they spoke to you at an age when you would most readily believe them, some of you being children and adolescents, and they won their case by default, as there was no defence.

What is most absurd in all this is that one cannot even know or mention their names unless one

---

[2]The bankers or money-changers had their counters in the market place. It seems that this was a favourite place for gossip.

of them is a writer of comedies.[3] Those who maliciously and slanderously persuaded you—who also, when persuaded themselves then persuaded others—all those are most difficult to deal with: one cannot bring one of them into court or refute him; one must simply fight with shadows, as it were, in making one's defence, and cross-examine when no one answers. I want you to realize too that my accusers are of two kinds: those who have accused me recently, and the old ones I mention; and to think that I must first defend myself against the latter, for you have also heard their accusations

e   first, and to a much greater extent than the more recent.

Very well then. I must surely defend myself and

19   attempt to uproot from your minds in so short a time the slander that has resided there so long. I wish this may happen, if it is in any way better for you and me, and that my defence may be successful, but I think this is very difficult and I am fully aware of how difficult it is. Even so, let the matter proceed as the god may wish, but I must obey the law and make my defence.

Let us then take up the case from its beginning.

b   What is the accusation from which arose the slander in which Meletus trusted when he wrote out the charge against me? What did they say when they slandered me? I must, as if they were my actual prosecutors, read the affidavit they would have sworn. It goes something like this: Socrates is guilty of wrongdoing in that he busies himself studying things in the sky and below the earth; he makes the worse into the stronger argument, and he teaches these same things to others. You have seen

c   this yourselves in the comedy of Aristophanes, a Socrates swinging about there, saying he was walking on air and talking a lot of other nonsense about things of which I know nothing at all. I do not speak in contempt of such knowledge, if someone is wise in these things—lest Meletus bring more cases against me—but, gentlemen, I have no part in it, and on this point I call upon the majority of you as witnesses. I think it right that all those of you who have heard me conversing, and many of you

d   have, should tell each other if anyone of you have ever heard me discussing such subjects to any extent

at all. From this you will learn that the other things said about me by the majority are of the same kind.

Not one of them is true. And if you have heard from anyone that I undertake to teach people and

e   charge a fee for it, that is not true either. Yet I think it a fine thing to be able to teach people as Gorgias of Leontini does, and Prodicus of Ceos, and Hippias of Elis.[4] Each of these men can go to any city and persuade the young, who can keep company with anyone of their own fellow-citizens

20   they want without paying, to leave the company of these, to join with themselves, pay them a fee, and be grateful to them besides. Indeed, I learned that there is another wise man from Paros who is visiting us, for I met a man who has spent more money on Sophists than everybody else put together, Callias, the son of Hipponicus. So I asked him—he has two sons—"Callias," I said, "if your sons were colts or calves, we could find and engage a supervisor for them who would make them excel

b   in their proper qualities, some horse breeder or farmer. Now since they are men, whom do you have in mind to supervise them? Who is an expert in this kind of excellence, the human and social kind? I think you must have given thought to this since you have sons. Is there such a person," I asked, "or is there not?" "Certainly there is," he said. "Who is he?" I asked, "What is his name, where is he from? and what is his fee?" "His name, Socrates, is Evenus, he comes from Paros, and his

c   fee is five minas." I thought Evenus a happy man, if he really possesses this art, and teaches for so moderate a fee. Certainly I would pride and preen myself if I had this knowledge, but I do not have it, gentlemen.

One of you might perhaps interrupt me and say: "But Socrates, what is your occupation? From where have these slanders come? For surely if you did not busy yourself with something out of the common, all these rumours and talk would not

---

[3]This refers in particular to Aristophanes, whose comedy, *The Clouds*, produced in 423 B.C., ridiculed the (imaginary) school of Socrates.

[4]These were all well-known Sophists. Gorgias, after whom Plato named one of his dialogues, was a celebrated rhetorician and teacher of rhetoric. He came to Athens in 427 B.C., and his rhetorical tricks took the city by storm. Two dialogues, the authenticity of which has been doubted, are named after Hippias, whose knowledge was encyclopedic. Prodicus was known for his insistence on the precise meaning of words. Both he and Hippias are characters in the *Protagoras* (named after another famous Sophist).

have arisen unless you did something other than most people. Tell us what it is, that we may not

d speak inadvisedly about you." Anyone who says that seems to be right, and I will try to show you what has caused this reputation and slander. Listen then. Perhaps some of you will think I am jesting, but be sure that all that I shall say is true. What has caused my reputation is none other than a certain kind of wisdom. What kind of wisdom? Human wisdom, perhaps. It may be that I really possess this, while those whom I mentioned just now are

e wise with a wisdom more than human; else I cannot explain it, for I certainly do not possess it, and whoever says I do is lying and speaks to slander me. Do not create a disturbance, gentlemen, even if you think I am boasting, for the story I shall tell does not originate with me, but I will refer you to a trustworthy source. I shall call upon the god at Delphi as witness to the existence and nature of my wis-

21 dom, if it be such. You know Chairephon. He was my friend from youth, and the friend of most of you, as he shared your exile and your return. You surely know the kind of man he was, how impulsive in any course of action. He went to Delphi at one time and ventured to ask the oracle—as I say, gentlemen, do not create a disturbance—he asked if any man was wiser than I, and the Pythian replied that no one was wiser. Chairephon is dead, but his brother will testify to you about this.

b Consider that I tell you this because I would inform you about the origin of the slander. When I heard of this reply I asked myself: "Whatever does the god mean? What is his riddle? I am very conscious that I am not wise at all; what then does he mean by saying that I am the wisest? For surely he does not lie; it is not legitimate for him to do so." For a long time I was at a loss as to his meaning; then I very reluctantly turned to some such investigation as this: I went to one of those reputed

c wise, thinking that there, if anywhere, I could refute the oracle and say to it: "This man is wiser than I, but you said I was." Then, when I examined this man—there is no need for me to tell you his name, he was one of our public men—my experience was something like this: I thought that he appeared wise to many people and especially to himself, but he was not. I then tried to show him

d that he thought himself wise, but that he was not. As a result he came to dislike me, and so did many of the bystanders. So I withdrew and thought to myself: "I am wiser than this man; it is likely that

neither of us knows anything worthwhile, but he thinks he knows something when he does not, whereas when I do not know, neither do I think I know; so I am likely to be wiser than he to this small extent, that I do not think I know what I do not know." After this I approached another man,

e one of those thought to be wiser than he, and I thought the same thing, and so I came to be disliked both by him and by many others.

After that I proceeded systematically. I realized, to my sorrow and alarm, that I was getting unpopular, but I thought that I must attach the greatest importance to the god's oracle, so I must go to all those who had any reputation for knowledge to examine its meaning. And by the dog,[5] gentlemen

22 of the jury—for I must tell you the truth—I experienced something like this: in my investigation in the service of the god I found that those who had the highest reputation were nearly the most deficient, while those who were thought to be inferior were more knowledgeable. I must give you an account of my journeyings as if they were labours I had undertaken to prove the oracle irrefutable. After the politicians, I went to the poets, the writers

b of tragedies and dithyrambs and the others, intending in their case to catch myself being more ignorant than they. So I took up those poems with which they seemed to have taken most trouble and asked them what they meant, in order that I might at the same time learn something from them. I am ashamed to tell you the truth, gentlemen, but I must. Almost all the bystanders might have explained the poems better than their authors could.

c I soon realized that poets do not compose their poems with knowledge, but by some inborn talent and by inspiration, like seers and prophets who also say many fine things without any understanding of what they say. The poets seemed to me to have had a similar experience. At the same time I saw that, because of their poetry, they thought themselves very wise men in other respects, which they were not. So there again I withdrew, thinking that I had the same advantage over them as I had over the politicians.

Finally I went to the craftsmen, for I was con-

d scious of knowing practically nothing, and I knew that I would find that they had knowledge of many

[5]A curious oath, occasionally used by Socrates, it appears in a longer form in the *Gorgias* (482b) as "by the dog, the god of the Egyptians."

fine things. In this I was not mistaken; they knew things I did not know, and to that extent they were wiser than I. But, gentlemen of the jury, the good craftsmen seemed to me to have the same fault as the poets: each of them, because of his success at his craft, thought himself very wise in other most important pursuits, and this error of

e theirs overshadowed the wisdom they had, so that I asked myself, on behalf of the oracle, whether I should prefer to be as I am, with neither their wisdom nor their ignorance, or to have both. The answer I gave myself and the oracle was that it was to my advantage to be as I am.

As a result of this investigation, gentlemen of

23 the jury, I acquired much unpopularity, of a kind that is hard to deal with and is a heavy burden; many slanders came from these people and a reputation for wisdom, for in each case the bystanders thought that I myself possessed the wisdom that I proved that my interlocutor did not have. What is probable, gentlemen, is that in fact the god is wise and that his oracular response meant that human wisdom is worth little or nothing, and that when

b he says this man, Socrates, he is using my name as an example, as if he said: "This man among you, mortals, is wisest who, like Socrates, understands that his wisdom is worthless." So even now I continue this investigation as the god bade me—and I go around seeking out anyone, citizen or stranger, whom I think wise. Then if I do not think he is, I come to the assistance of the god and show him that he is not wise. Because of this occupation, I do not have the leisure to engage in public affairs to any extent, nor indeed to look after my own, but I live in great poverty because of my service to the god.

c Furthermore, the young men who follow me around of their own free will, those who have most leisure, the sons of the very rich, take pleasure in hearing people questioned; they themselves often imitate me and try to question others. I think they find an abundance of men who believe they have some knowledge but know little or nothing. The result is that those whom they question are angry,

d not with themselves but with me. They say: "That man Socrates is a pestilential fellow who corrupts the young." If one asks them what he does and what he teaches to corrupt them, they are silent, as they do not know, but, so as not to appear at a loss, they mention those accusations that are available against all philosophers, about "things in the sky and things below the earth," about "not

believing in the gods" and "making the worse the stronger argument"; they would not want to tell the truth, I'm sure, that they have been proved to lay claim to knowledge when they know nothing. These people are ambitious, violent and numer-

e ous; they are continually and convincingly talking about me; they have been filling your ears for a long time with vehement slanders against me. From them Meletus attacked me, and Anytus and Lycon, Meletus being vexed on behalf of the poets, Anytus on behalf of the craftsmen and the politicians, Lycon on behalf of the orators, so that, as

24 I started out by saying, I should be surprised if I could rid you of so much slander in so short a time. That, gentlemen of the jury, is the truth for you. I have hidden or disguised nothing. I know well enough that this very conduct makes me unpopular, and this is proof that what I say is true, that such is the slander against me, and that such

b are its causes. If you look into this either now or later, this is what you will find.

Let this suffice as a defence against the charges of my earlier accusers. After this I shall try to defend myself against Meletus, that good and patriotic man, as he says he is, and my later accusers. As these are a different lot of accusers, let us again take up their sworn deposition. It goes something like this: Socrates is guilty of corrupting the young and of not believing in the gods in whom the city believes, but in other new divinities. Such is their

c charge. Let us examine it point by point.

He says that I am guilty of corrupting the young, but I say that Meletus is guilty of dealing frivolously with serious matters, of irresponsibly bringing people into court, and of professing to be seriously concerned with things about none of which he has ever cared, and I shall try to prove that this is so. Come here and tell me, Meletus.

d Surely you consider it of the greatest importance that our young men be as good as possible?[6] — Indeed I do.

Come then, tell the jury who improves them. You obviously know, in view of your concern. You say you have discovered the one who corrupts them, namely me, and you bring me here and accuse me to the jury. Come, inform the jury and

---

[6]Socrates here drops into his usual method of discussion by question and answer. This, no doubt, is what Plato had in mind, at least in part, when he made him ask the indulgence of the jury if he spoke "in his usual manner."

tell them who it is. You see, Meletus, that you are silent and know not what to say. Does this not seem shameful to you and a sufficient proof of what I say, that you have not been concerned with any of this? Tell me, my good sir, who improves

e our young men? —The laws.

That is not what I am asking, but what person who has knowledge of the laws to begin with? —These jurymen, Socrates.

How do you mean, Meletus? Are these able to educate the young and improve them? —Certainly.

All of them, or some but not others? —All of them.

Very good, by Hera. You mention a great

25 abundance of benefactors. But what about the audience? Do they improve the young or not? —They do, too.

What about the members of Council? —The Councillors, also.

But, Meletus, what about the assembly? Do members of the assembly corrupt the young, or do they all improve them? —They improve them.

All the Athenians, it seems, make the young into fine good men, except me, and I alone corrupt them. Is that what you mean? —That is most definitely what I mean.

b You condemn me to a great misfortune. Tell me: does this also apply to horses do you think? That all men improve them and one individual corrupts them? Or is quite the contrary true, one individual is able to improve them, or very few, namely the horse breeders, whereas the majority, if they have horses and use them, corrupt them? Is that not the case, Meletus, both with horses and all other animals? Of course it is, whether you and Anytus say so or not. It would be a very happy state of affairs if only one person corrupted our youth, while the others improved them.

c You have made it sufficiently obvious, Meletus, that you have never had any concern for our youth; you show your indifference clearly; that you have given no thought to the subjects about which you bring me to trial.

And by Zeus, Meletus, tell us also whether it is better for a man to live among good or wicked fellow-citizens. Answer, my good man, for I am not asking a difficult question. Do not the wicked do some harm to those who are ever closest to them, whereas good people benefit them? —Certainly.

d And does the man exist who would rather be harmed than benefited by his associates? Answer, my good sir, for the law orders you to answer. Is there any man who wants to be harmed? —Of course not.

Come now, do you accuse me here of corrupting the young and making them worse deliberately or unwillingly? —Deliberately.

What follows, Meletus? Are you so much wiser at your age than I am at mine that you understand that wicked people always do some harm to their

e closest neighbours while good people do them good, but I have reached such a pitch of ignorance that I do not realize this, namely that if I make one of my associates wicked I run the risk of being harmed by him so that I do such a great evil deliberately, as you say? I do not believe you, Meletus, and I do not think anyone else will. Either I do not

26 corrupt the young or, if I do, it is unwillingly, and you are lying in either case. Now if I corrupt them unwillingly, the law does not require you to bring people to court for such unwilling wrongdoings, but to get hold of them privately, to instruct them and exhort them; for clearly, if I learn better, I shall cease to do what I am doing unwillingly. You, however, have avoided my company and were unwilling to instruct me, but you bring me here, where the law requires one to bring those who are in need of punishment, not of instruction.

And so, gentlemen of the jury, what I said is clearly true: Meletus has never been at all con-

b cerned with these matters. Nonetheless tell us, Meletus, how you say that I corrupt the young; or is it obvious from your deposition that it is by teaching them not to believe in the gods in whom the city believes but in other new divinities? Is this not what you say I teach and so corrupt them? —That is most certainly what I do say.

Then by those very gods about whom we are talking, Meletus, make this clearer to me and to

c the jury: I cannot be sure whether you mean that I teach the belief that there are some gods—and therefore I myself believe that there are gods and am not altogether an atheist, nor am I guilty of that—not, however, the gods in whom the city believes, but others, and that this is the charge against me, that they are others. Or whether you mean that I do not believe in gods at all, and that this is what I teach to others. —This is what I mean, that you do not believe in gods at all.

d   You are a strange fellow, Meletus. Why do you say this? Do I not believe, as other men do, that the sun and the moon are gods? —No, by Zeus, jurymen, for he says that the sun is stone, and the moon earth.

My dear Meletus, do you think you are prosecuting Anaxagoras? Are you so contemptuous of the jury and think them so ignorant of letters as not to know that the books of Anaxagoras[7] of Clazomenae are full of those theories, and further, that the young men learn from me what they can

e   buy from time to time for a drachma, at most, in the bookshops, and ridicule Socrates if he pretends that these theories are his own, especially as they are so absurd? Is that, by Zeus, what you think of me, Meletus, that I do not believe that there are any gods? —That is what I say, that you do not believe in the gods at all.

You cannot be believed, Meletus, even, I think, by yourself. The man appears to me, gentlemen of the jury, highly insolent and uncontrolled. He seems to have made this deposition out of inso-

27 lence, violence and youthful zeal. He is like one who composed a riddle and is trying it out: "Will the wise Socrates realize that I am jesting and contradicting myself, or shall I deceive him and others?" I think he contradicts himself in the affidavit, as if he said: "Socrates is guilty of not believing in gods but believing in gods," and surely that is the part of a jester!

Examine with me, gentlemen, how he appears

b   to contradict himself, and you, Meletus, answer us. Remember, gentlemen, what I asked you when I began, not to create a disturbance if I proceed in my usual manner.

Does any man, Meletus, believe in human affairs who does not believe in human beings? Make him answer, and not again and again create a disturbance. Does any man who does not believe in horses believe in equine affairs? Or in flute music but not in flute-players? No, my good sir, no man could. If you are not willing to answer, I will tell

c   you and the jury. Answer the next question, however. Does any man believe in divine activities who does not believe in divinities? —No one.

---

[7]Anaxagoras of Clazomenae, born about the beginning of the fifth century B.C., came to Athens as a young man and spent his time in the pursuit of natural philosophy. He claimed that the universe was directed by Nous (Mind) and that matter was indestructible but always combining in various ways. He left Athens after being prosecuted for impiety.

Thank you for answering, if reluctantly, when the jury made you. Now you say that I believe in divine activities and teach about them, whether new or old, but at any rate divine activities according to what you say, and to this you have sworn in your deposition. But if I believe in divine activities I must quite inevitably believe in divine beings. Is that not so? It is indeed. I shall assume that you

d   agree, as you do not answer. Do we not believe divine beings to be either gods or the children of gods? Yes or no? —Of course.

Then since I do believe in divine beings, as you admit, if divine beings are gods, this is what I mean when I say you speak in riddles and in jest, as you state that I do not believe in gods and then again that I do, since I believe in divine beings. If on the other hand the divine beings are children of the gods, bastard children of the gods by nymphs or some other mothers, as they are said to be, what man would believe children of the gods to exist, but not gods? That would be just as absurd as

e   to believe the young of horses and asses, namely mules, to exist, but not to believe in the existence of horses and asses. You must have made this deposition, Meletus, either to test us or because you were at a loss to find any true wrongdoing of what to accuse me. There is no way in which you could persuade anyone of even small intelligence that it is not the part of one and the same man to be-

28 lieve in the activities of divine beings and gods, and then again the part of one and the same man not to believe in the existence of divinities and gods and heroes.

I do not think, gentlemen of the jury, that it requires a prolonged defence to prove that I am not guilty of the charges in Meletus' deposition, but this is sufficient. On the other hand, you know that what I said earlier is true, that I am very unpopular with many people. This will be my undoing, if I am undone, not Meletus or Anytus but the slanders and envy of many people. This has destroyed many

b   other good men and will, I think, continue to do so. There is no danger that it will stop at me.

Someone might say: "Are you not ashamed, Socrates, to have followed the kind of occupation that has led to your being now in danger of death?" However, I should be right to reply to him: "You are wrong, sir, if you think that a man who is any good at all should take into account the risk of life or death; he should look to this only in his actions, whether what he does is right or wrong, whether c he is acting like a good or a bad man." According to your view, all the heroes who died at Troy were inferior people, especially the son of Thetis who was so contemptuous of danger compared with disgrace.[8] When he was eager to kill Hector, his goddess mother warned him, as I believe, in some such words as these: "My child, if you avenge the death of your comrade, Patroclus, and you kill Hector, you will die yourself, for your death is to follow immediately after Hector's." Hearing this, he despised death and danger and was much more afraid to live a coward who did not avenge his

d friends. "Let me die at once," he said, "when once I have given the wrongdoer his deserts, rather than remain here, a laughingstock by the curved ships, a burden upon the earth." Do you think he gave thought to death and danger?

This is the truth of the matter, gentlemen of the jury: wherever a man has taken a position that he believes to be best, or has been placed by his commander, there he must I think remain and face danger, without a thought for death or anything

e else, rather than disgrace. It would have been a dreadful way to behave, gentlemen of the jury, if, at Potidaea, Amphipolis and Delium, I had, at the risk of death, like anyone else, remained at my post where those you had elected to command had ordered me, and then, when the god ordered me, as I thought and believed, to live the life of a philosopher, to examine myself and others, I had aban-

29 doned my post for fear of death or anything else. That would have been a dreadful thing, and then I might truly have justly been brought here for not believing that there are gods, disobeying the oracle, fearing death, and thinking I was wise when I was not. To fear death, gentlemen, is no other than to think oneself wise when one is not, to think one knows what one does not know. No one knows whether death may not be the greatest of all blessings for a man, yet men fear it as if they knew that it is the greatest of evils. And surely it is

b the most blameworthy ignorance to believe that one knows what one does not know. It is perhaps on this point and in this respect, gentlemen, that I differ from the majority of men, and if I were to claim that I am wiser than anyone in anything, it would be in this, that, as I have no adequate knowledge of things in the underworld, so I do not

think I have. I do know, however, that it is wicked and shameful to do wrong, to disobey one's superior, be he god or man. I shall never fear or avoid things of which I do not know, whether they may not be good rather than things that I know

c to be bad. Even if you acquitted me now and did not believe Anytus, who said to you that either I should not have been brought here in the first place, or that now I am here, you cannot avoid executing me, for if I should be acquitted, your sons would practise the teachings of Socrates and all be thoroughly corrupted; if you said to me in this regard: "Socrates, we do not believe Anytus now; we acquit you, but only on condition that you spend no more time on this investigation and do not practise philosophy, and if you are caught

d doing so you will die," if, as I say, you were to acquit me on those terms, I would say to you: "Gentlemen of the jury, I am grateful and I am your friend, but I will obey the god rather than you, and as long as I draw breath and am able, I shall not cease to practise philosophy, to exhort you and in my usual way to point out to any one of you whom I happen to meet: Good Sir, you are an Athenian, a citizen of the greatest city with the greatest reputation for both wisdom and power;

e are you not ashamed of your eagerness to possess as much wealth, reputation and honours as possible, while you do not care for nor give thought to wisdom or truth, or the best possible state of your soul?" Then, if one of you disputes this and says he does care, I shall not let him go at once or leave him, but I shall question him, examine him and test him, and if I do not think he has attained the goodness that he says he has, I shall reproach him because he attaches little importance to the

30 most important things and greater importance to inferior things, I shall treat in this way anyone I happen to meet, young and old, citizen and stranger, and more so the citizens because you are more kindred to me. Be sure that this is what the god orders me to do, and I think there is no greater blessing for the city than my service to the god. For I go around doing nothing but persuading both young and old among you not to care for

b your body or your wealth in preference to or as strongly as for the best possible state of your soul as I say to you: "Wealth does not bring about excellence, but excellence brings about wealth and all other public and private blessings for men."

---

[8]The scene between Thetis and Achilles is from *The Iliad* (18, 94ff.).

Now if by saying this I corrupt the young, this advice must be harmful, but if anyone says that I give different advice, he is talking nonsense. On this point I would say to you, gentlemen of the jury: "Whether you believe Anytus or not, whether you acquit me or not, do so on the understanding

c that this is my course of action, even if I am to face death many times." Do not create a disturbance, gentlemen, but abide by my request not to cry out at what I say but to listen, for I think it will be to your advantage to listen, and I am about to say other things at which you will perhaps cry out. By no means do this. Be sure that if you kill the sort of man I say I am, you will not harm me more than yourselves. Neither Meletus nor Anytus can harm me in any way; he could not harm me, for I do not

d think it is permitted that a better man be harmed by a worse; certainly he might kill me, or perhaps banish or disfranchise me, which he and maybe others think to be great harm, but I do not think so. I think he is doing himself much greater harm doing what he is doing now, attempting to have a man executed unjustly. Indeed, gentlemen of the jury, I am far from making a defence now on my own behalf, as might be thought, but on yours, to prevent you from wrongdoing by mistreating the

e god's gift to you by condemning me; for if you kill me you will not easily find another like me. I was attached to this city by the god—though it seems a ridiculous thing to say—as upon a great and noble horse which was somewhat sluggish because of its size and needed to be stirred up by a kind of gadfly. It is to fulfill some such function that I believe the god has placed me in the city. I never cease to rouse each and every one of you, to persuade and reproach you all day long and every-

31 where I find myself in your company.

Another such man will not easily come to be among you, gentlemen, and if you believe me you will spare me. You might easily be annoyed with me as people are when they are aroused from a doze, and strike out at me; if convinced by Anytus you could easily kill me, and then you could sleep on for the rest of your days, unless the god, in his care for you, sent you someone else. That I am the kind of person to be a gift of the god to the city you might realize from the fact that it does not seem

b like human nature for me to have neglected all my own affairs and to have tolerated this neglect now for so many years while I was always concerned with you, approaching each one of you like a father

or an elder brother to persuade you to care for virtue. Now if I profited from this by charging a fee for my advice, there would be some sense to it, but you can see for yourselves that, for all their shameless accusations, my accusers have not been

c able in their impudence to bring forward a witness to say that I have ever received a fee or ever asked for one. I, on the other hand, have a convincing witness that I speak for truth, my poverty.

It may seem strange that while I go around and give this advice privately and interfere in private affairs, I do not venture to go to the assembly and there advise the city. You have heard me give the reason for this in many places. I have a divine sign

d from the god which Meletus has ridiculed in his deposition. This began when I was a child. It is a voice, and whenever it speaks it turns me away from something I am about to do, but it never encourages me to do anything. This is what has prevented me from taking part in public affairs, and I think it was quite right to prevent me. Be sure, gentlemen of the jury, that if I had long ago attempted to take part in politics, I should have died

e long ago, and benefited neither you nor myself. Do not be angry with me for speaking the truth; no man will survive who genuinely opposes you or any other crowd and prevents the occurrence of many

32 unjust and illegal happenings in the city. A man who really fights for justice must lead a private, not a public, life if he is to survive for even a short time.

I shall give you great proofs of this, not words but what you esteem, deeds. Listen to what happened to me, that you may know that I will not yield to any man contrary to what is right, for fear of death, even if I should die at once for not yielding. The things I shall tell you are commonplace and smack of the lawcourts, but they are true. I

b have never held any other office in the city, but I served as a member of the Council, and our tribe Antiochis was presiding at the time when you wanted to try as a body the ten generals who had failed to pick up the survivors of the naval battle.[9]

---

[9] This was the battle of Arginusae (south of Lesbos) in 406 B.C., the last Athenian victory of the war. A violent storm prevented the Athenian generals from rescuing their survivors. For this they were tried in Athens and sentenced to death by the Assembly. They were tried in a body, and it is this to which Socrates objected in the Council's presiding committee which prepared the business of the Assembly. He obstinately persisted in his opposition, in which he stood alone, and was overruled by the majority. Six generals who were in Athens were executed.

This was illegal, as you all recognized later. I was the only member of the presiding committee to oppose your doing something contrary to the laws, and I voted against it. The orators were ready to prosecute me and take me away, and your shouts were egging them on, but I thought I should run

c any risk on the side of law and justice rather than join you, for fear of prison or death, when you were engaged in an unjust course.

This happened when the city was still a democracy. When the oligarchy was established, the Thirty10 summoned me to the Hall, along with four others, and ordered us to bring Leon from Salamis, that he might be executed. They gave many such orders to many people, in order to

d implicate as many as possible in their guilt. Then I showed again, not in words but in action, that, if it were not rather vulgar to say so, death is something I couldn't care less about, but that my whole concern is not to do anything unjust or impious. That government, powerful as it was, did not frighten me into any wrongdoing. When we left the Hall, the other four went to Salamis and brought in Leon, but I went home. I might have been put to death for this, had not the government fallen

e shortly afterwards. There are many who will witness to these events.

Do you think I would have survived all these years if I were engaged in public affairs and, acting as a good man must, came to the help of justice and considered this the most important thing? Far from it, gentlemen of the jury, nor would any other

33 man. Throughout my life, in any public activity I may have engaged in, I am the same man as I am in private life. I have never come to an agreement with anyone to act unjustly, neither with anyone else nor with any one of those who they slanderously say are my pupils. I have never been anyone's teacher. If anyone, young or old, desires to listen to me when I am talking and dealing with my own concerns, I have never begrudged this to anyone, but I do not converse when I receive a fee and not

b when I do not. I am equally ready to question the rich and the poor if anyone is willing to answer my questions and listen to what I say. And I cannot justly be held responsible for the good or bad

conduct of these people, as I never promised to teach them anything and have not done so. If anyone says that he has learned anything from me, or that he heard anything privately that the others did not hear, be assured that he is not telling the truth.

Why then do some people enjoy spending con-
c siderable time in my company? You have heard why, gentlemen of the jury, I have told you the whole truth. They enjoy hearing those being questioned who think they are wise, but are not. And this is not unpleasant. To do this has, as I say, been enjoined upon me by the god, by means of oracles and dreams, and in every other way that a divine manifestation has ever ordered a man to do anything. This is true, gentlemen, and can easily be established.

d If I corrupt some young men and have corrupted others, then surely some of them who have grown older and realized that I gave them bad advice when they were young should now themselves come up here to accuse me and avenge themselves. If they are unwilling to do so themselves, then some of their kindred, their fathers or brothers or other relations should recall it now if their family had been harmed by me. I see many of these present here, first Crito, my contempo-
e rary and fellow demesman, the father of Critoboulos here; next Lysanias of Sphettus, the father of Aeschines here; also Antiphon the Cephisian, the father of Epigenes; and others whose brothers spent their time in this way; Nicostratus, the son of Theozotides, brother of Theodotus, and Theodotus has died so he could not influence him; Paralios

34 here, son of Demodocus, whose brother was Theages; there is Adeimantus, son of Ariston, brother of Plato here; Acantidorus, brother of Apollodorus here.

I could mention many others, some one of whom surely Meletus should have brought in as witness in his own speech. If he forgot to do so, then let him do it now; I will yield time if he has anything of the kind to say. You will find quite the contrary, gentlemen. These men are all ready to come to the help of the corruptor, the man who
b has harmed their kindred, as Meletus and Anytus say. Now those who were corrupted might well have reason to help me, but the uncorrupted, their kindred who are older men, have no reason to help me except the right and proper one, that they know that Meletus is lying and that I am telling the truth.

10This was the harsh oligarchy that was set up after the final defeat of Athens in 404 B.C. and that ruled Athens for some nine months in 404–3 before the democracy was restored.

Very well, gentlemen of the jury. This, and maybe other similar things, is what I have to say in my defence. Perhaps one of you might be angry as he recalls that when he himself stood trial on a less dangerous charge, he begged and implored the jury with many tears, that he brought his children and many of his friends and family into court to arouse as much pity as he could, but that I do none of these things, even though I may seem to be running the ultimate risk. Thinking of this, he might feel resentful toward me and, angry about this, cast his vote in anger. If there is such a one among you—I do not deem there is, but if there is—I think it would be right to say in reply: My good sir, I too have a household and, in Homer's phrase, I am not born "from oak or rock" but from men, so that I have a family, indeed three sons, gentlemen of the jury, of whom one is an adolescent while two are children. Nevertheless, I will not beg you to acquit me by bringing them here. Why do I do none of these things? Not through arrogance, gentlemen, nor through lack of respect for you. Whether I am brave in the face of death is another matter, but with regard to my reputation and yours and that of the whole city, it does not seem right to me to do these things, especially at my age and with my reputation. For it is generally believed, whether it be true or false, that in certain respects Socrates is superior to the majority of men. Now if those of you who are considered superior, be it in wisdom or courage or whatever other virtue makes them so, are seen behaving like that, it would be a disgrace. Yet I have often seen them do this sort of thing when standing trial, men who are thought to be somebody, doing amazing things as if they thought it a terrible thing to die, and as if they were to be immortal if you did not execute them. I think these men bring shame upon the city so that a stranger, too, would assume that those who are outstanding in virtue among the Athenians, whom they themselves select from themselves to fill offices of state and receive other honours, are in no way better than women. You should not act like that, gentlemen of the jury, those of you who have any reputation at all, and if we do, you should not allow it. You should make it very clear that you will more readily convict a man who performs these pitiful dramatics in court and so makes the city a laughing-stock, than a man who keeps quiet.

Quite apart from the question of reputation, gentlemen, I do not think it right to supplicate the jury and to be acquitted because of this, but to teach and persuade them. It is not the purpose of a juryman's office to give justice as a favour to whoever seems good to him, but to judge according to law, and this he has sworn to do. We should not accustom you to perjure yourselves, nor should you make a habit of it. This is irreverent conduct for either of us.

Do not deem it right for me, gentlemen of the jury, that I should act towards you in a way that I do not consider to be good or just or pious, especially, by Zeus, as I am being prosecuted by Meletus here for impiety; clearly, if I convinced you by my supplication to do violence to your oath of office, I would be teaching you not to believe that there are gods, and my defence would convict me of not believing in them. This is far from being the case, gentlemen, for I do believe in them as none of my accusers do. I leave it to you and the god to judge me in the way that will be best for me and for you.

[The jury now gives its verdict of guilty, and Meletus asks for the penalty of death.]

There are many other reasons for my not being angry with you for convicting me, gentlemen of the jury, and what happened was not unexpected. I am much more surprised at the number of votes cast on each side, for I did not think the decision would be by so few votes but by a great many. As it is, a switch of only thirty votes would have acquitted me. I think myself that I have been cleared on Meletus' charges, and not only this, but it is clear to all that, if Anytus and Lycon had not joined him in accusing me, he would have been fined a thousand drachmas for not receiving a fifth of the votes.

He assesses the penalty at death. So be it. What counter-assessment should I propose to you, gentlemen of the jury? Clearly it should be a penalty I deserve, and what do I deserve to suffer or to pay because I have deliberately not led a quiet life but have neglected what occupies most people: wealth, household affairs, the position of general or public orator or the other offices, the political clubs and factions that exist in the city? I thought myself too honest to survive if I occupied myself with those things. I did not follow that path that would have made me of no use either to you or to myself, but I went to each of you privately and conferred upon him what I say is the greatest benefit, by trying to persuade him not to care for any of his belongings before caring that he himself should be as good and as wise as possible, not to care for the city's possessions more than for the city itself, and to care

d for other things in the same way. What do I deserve for being such a man? Some good, gentlemen of the jury, if I must truly make an assessment according to my deserts, and something suitable. What is suitable for a poor benefactor who needs leisure to exhort you? Nothing is more suitable, gentlemen, than for such a man to be fed in the Prytaneum,[11] much more suitable for him than for any of you who has won a victory at Olympia with a pair or a team of horses. The Olympian victor

e makes you think yourself happy; I make you be happy. Besides, he does not need food, but I do. So if I must make a just assessment of what I deserve,

37 I assess it at this: free meals in the Prytaneum.

When I say this you may think, as when I spoke of appeals to pity and entreaties, that I speak arrogantly, but that is not the case, gentlemen of the jury; rather it is like this: I am convinced that I never willingly wrong anyone, but I am not convincing you of this, for we have talked together but a short time. If it were the law with us, as it is

b elsewhere, that a trial for life should not last one but many days, you would be convinced, but now it is not easy to dispel great slanders in a short time. Since I am convinced that I wrong no one, I am not likely to wrong myself, to say that I deserve some evil and to make some such assessment against myself. What should I fear? That I should suffer the penalty Meletus has assessed against me, of which I say I do not know whether it is good or bad? Am I then to choose in preference to this something that I know very well to be an evil

c and assess the penalty at that? Imprisonment? Why should I live in prison, always subjected to the ruling magistrates? A fine, and imprisonment until I pay it? That would be the same thing for me, as I have no money. Exile? for perhaps you might accept that assessment.

I should have to be inordinately fond of life, gentlemen of the jury, to be so unreasonable as to suppose that other men will easily tolerate my company and conversation when you, my fellow

d citizens, have been unable to endure them, but found them a burden and resented them so that

you are now seeking to get rid of them. Far from it, gentlemen. It would be a fine life at my age to be driven out of one city after another, for I know very well that wherever I go the young men will

e listen to my talk as they do here. If I drive them away, they will themselves persuade their elders to drive me out; if I do not drive them away, their fathers and relations will drive me out on their behalf.

Perhaps someone might say: But Socrates, if you leave us will you not be able to live quietly, without talking? Now this is the most difficult point on which to convince some of you. If I say

38 that it is impossible for me to keep quiet because that means disobeying the god, you will not believe me and will think I am being ironical. On the other hand, if I say that it is the greatest good for a man to discuss virtue every day and those other things about which you hear me conversing and testing myself and others, for the unexamined life is not worth living for man, you will believe me even less.

What I say is true, gentlemen, but it is not easy

b to convince you. At the same time, I am not accustomed to think that I deserve any penalty. If I had money, I would assess the penalty at the amount I could pay, for that would not hurt me, but I have none, unless you are willing to set the penalty at the amount I can pay, and perhaps I could pay you one mina of silver.[12] So that is my assessment.

Plato here, gentlemen of the jury, and Crito and Critobulus and Apollodorus bid me put the penalty at thirty minae, and they will stand surety for the money. Well then, that is my assessment, and they will be sufficient guarantee of payment.

[The jury now votes again and sentences Socrates to death.]

c It is for the sake of a short time, gentlemen of the jury, that you will acquire the reputation and the guilt, in the eyes of those who want to denigrate the city, of having killed Socrates, a wise man, for they who want to revile you will say that I am wise even if I am not. If you had waited but a little while, this would have happened of its own accord. You see my age, that I am already advanced in years and close to death. I am saying this not

_____

[11]The Prytaneum was the magistrates' hall or town hall of Athens in which public entertainments were given, particularly to Olympian victors on their return home.

_____

[12]One mina was 100 drachmas, equivalent to, say, twenty-five dollars, though in purchasing power probably five times greater. In any case, a ridiculously small sum under the circumstances.

d to all of you but to those who condemned me to death, and to these same jurors I say: Perhaps you think that I was convicted for lack of such words as might have convinced you, if I thought I should say or do all I could to avoid my sentence. Far from it. I was convicted because I lacked not words but boldness and shamelessness and the willingness to say to you what you would most gladly have heard from me, lamentations and tears and

e my saying and doing many things that I say are unworthy of me but that you are accustomed to hear from others. I did not think then that the danger I ran should make me do anything mean, nor do I now regret the nature of my defence. I would much rather die after this kind of defence than live after making the other kind. Neither I nor any

39 other man should, on trial or in war, contrive to avoid death at any cost. Indeed it is often obvious in battle that one could escape death by throwing away one's weapons and turning to supplicate one's pursuers, and there are many ways to avoid death in every kind of danger if one will venture to do or say anything to avoid it. It is not difficult to avoid death, gentlemen of the jury, it is much more dif-

b ficult to avoid wickedness, for it runs faster than death. Slow and elderly as I am, I have been caught by the slower pursuer, whereas my accusers, being clever and sharp, have been caught by the quicker, wickedness. I leave you now, condemned to death by you, but they are condemned by truth to wickedness and injustice. So I maintain my assessment, and they maintain theirs. This perhaps had to happen, and I think it is as it should be.

c Now I want to prophesy to those who convicted me, for I am at the point when men prophesy most, when they are about to die. I say gentlemen, to those who voted to kill me, that vengeance will come upon you immediately after my death, a vengeance much harder to bear than that which you took in killing me. You did this in the belief that you would avoid giving an account of your life, but I maintain that quite the opposite will happen to you. There will be more people to test you, whom I now held back, but you did not notice it.

d They will be more difficult to deal with as they will be younger and you will resent them more. You are wrong if you believe that by killing people you will prevent anyone from reproaching you for not living in the right way. To escape such tests is neither possible nor good, but it is best and easiest not

to discredit others but to prepare oneself to be as good as possible. With this prophecy to you who convicted me, I part from you.

e I should be glad to discuss what has happened with those who voted for my acquittal during the time that the officers of the court are busy and I do not yet have to depart to my death. So, gentlemen, stay with me awhile, for nothing prevents us from talking to each other while it is allowed. To

40 you, as being my friends, I want to show the meaning of what has occurred. A surprising thing has happened to me, judges—you I would rightly call judges. At all previous times my usual mantic sign frequently opposed me, even in small matters, when I was about to do something wrong, but now that, as you can see for yourselves, I was faced with what one might think, and what is generally thought to be, the worst of evils, my divine sign has not opposed me, either when I left home

b at dawn, or when I came into court, or at any time that I was about to say something during my speech. Yet in other talks it often held me back in the middle of my speaking, but now it has opposed no word or deed of mine. What do I think is the reason for this? I will tell you. What has happened to me may well be a good thing, and those of us who believe death to be an evil are certainly mis-

c taken. I have convincing proof of this, for it is impossible that my customary sign did not oppose me if I was not about to do what was right.

Let us reflect in this way, too, that there is good hope that death is a blessing, for it is one of two things: either the dead are nothing and have no perception of anything, or it is, as we are told, a change and a relocating for the soul from here to another place. If it is complete lack of percep-

d tion, like a dreamless sleep, then death would be a great advantage. For I think that if one had to pick out that night during which a man slept soundly and did not dream, put beside it the other nights and days of his life, and then see how many days and nights had been better and more pleasant than that night, not only a private person but the great king would find them easy to count com-

e pared with the other days and nights. If death is like this I say it is an advantage, for all eternity would then seem to be no more than a single night. If, on the other hand, death is a change from here to another place, and what we are told is true and all who have died are there, what greater

41 blessing could there be, gentlemen of the jury? If anyone arriving in Hades will have escaped from those who call themselves judges here, and will find those true judges who are said to sit in judgement there, Minos and Radamanthus and Aeacus and Triptolemus and the other demi-gods who have been upright in their own life, would that be a poor kind of change? Again, what would one of you give to keep company with Orpheus and Musaeus, Hesiod and Homer? I am willing to die many times if that is true. It would be a won-
b derful way for me to spend my time whenever I met Palamedes and Ajax, the son of Telamon, and any other of the men of old who died through an unjust conviction, to compare my experience with theirs. I think it would be pleasant. Most important, I could spend my time testing and examining people there, as I do here, as to who among them is wise, and who thinks he is, but is not.

What would one not give, gentlemen of the jury, for the opportunity to examine the man who led the great expedition against Troy, or Odys-
c seus, or Sisyphus, and innumerable other men and women one could mention. It would be an extraordinary happiness to talk with them, to keep company with them and examine them. In any case, they would certainly not put one to death for doing so. They are happier there than we are here in other respects, and for the rest of time they are deathless, if indeed what we are told is true.

You too must be of good hope as regards death, gentlemen of the jury, and keep this one truth in mind, that a good man cannot be harmed either
d in life or in death, and that his affairs are not neglected by the gods. What has happened to me now has not happened of itself, but it is clear to me that it was better for me to die now and to escape from trouble. That is why my divine sign did not oppose me at any point. So I am certainly not angry with those who convicted me, or with my accusers. Of course that was not their purpose when they accused and convicted me, but they
e thought they were hurting me, and for this they deserve blame. This much I ask from them: when my sons grow up, avenge yourselves by causing them the same kind of grief that I caused you, if you think they care for money or anything else more than they care for virtue, or if they think they are somebody when they are nobody.

Reproach them as I reproach you, that they do not care for the right things and think they are worthy
42 when they are not worthy of anything. If you do this, I shall have been justly treated by you, and my sons also.

Now the hour to part has come. I go to die, you go to live. Which of us goes to the better lot is known to no one, except the god.

COMMENTARY AND QUESTIONS

As we delve into the character of Socrates as Plato portrays it in this dialogue, we should be struck by his single-mindedness. If it should turn out that death is a "change from here to another place," how would Socrates spend his time there? He would continue precisely the activities that had occupied him in this life; he would "examine" all the famous heroes to see which of them is wise. And why does he think such examination is so important, a "service to the god"? No doubt because it undermines hubris, that arrogance of thinking one possesses "a wisdom more than human."

Read 17a–18a   In this short introductory section, Socrates contrasts himself with his accusers, characterizes the kind of man he is, and reminds the jury of its duty.

Q1. What is the function of Socrates' contrast between **persuasion** and **truth**? List the terms in which each is described.
Q2. What kind of man does Socrates say that he is?
Q3. What is his challenge to the jury?

"As scarce as truth is, the supply has always been in excess of the demand."
Josh Billings (1818–1885)

Read 18b–19a   *Socrates distinguishes between two sets of accusers.*

Q4. Identify the **earlier accusers** and the later accusers. How do they differ?

Q5. Why is it going to be very difficult for Socrates to defend himself against the earlier accusers?

Read 19b–24b   Here we have Socrates' defense against the "earlier accusers." He tries to show how his "unpopularity" arises from his practice of questioning. He describes the origins of this occupation of his and discusses the sort of wisdom to which he lays claim.

Q6. What are the three points made against him in the older accusations?
Q7. What does Socrates say about each of these accusations?
Q8. How does Socrates distinguish himself from the Sophists here?

We have mentioned the **Oracle at Delphi** before. One could go there and, after appropriate sacrifices, pose a question. The "Pythian" (21a) was a priestess of Apollo who would, in the name of the god, reply to the questions posed. We have noted that the Oracle characteristically replied in a riddle, so it is not perverse for Socrates to wonder what the answer to Chairephon's question means. What sort of wisdom is this in which no one can surpass him? He devises his questioning technique to clarify the meaning of the answer.

Note that several times during his speech Socrates asks the jury not to create a disturbance (20e, 27b, 30c). We can imagine that he is interrupted at those points by hoots, catcalls, or their ancient Greek equivalents.

Q9. Which three classes of people did Socrates question? What, in each case, was the result?
Q10. What conclusion does Socrates draw from his investigations?

Here we can address that paradox noted earlier (page 100) arising out of Socrates' simultaneous profession of ignorance, his identification of virtue with knowledge, and the claim (obvious at many points in the *Apology*) that he is both a wise

and a good man. In light of his confessed ignorance and the identification of knowledge with virtue, it seems he should conclude that he *isn't* virtuous. But it is the distinction drawn in 22e–23b between a wisdom appropriate for "the god" on the one hand and **"human wisdom"** on the other that resolves this paradox. The god, Socrates assumes, actually knows the forms of piety, justice, *areté*, and the other excellences proper to a human being. Humans, by contrast, do not; and this is proved, Socrates thinks, by the god's declaration that there is no man wiser than he—who knows that he doesn't know!

"Knowledge is proud that he has learned so much; Wisdom is humble that he knows no more."

William Cowper (1731–1800)

Because humans do not know what makes for virtue and a good life, the best they can do is subject themselves to constant dialectical examination. This searching critique will tend to rid us of false opinions and will also cure us of the hubris of thinking that we have a wisdom appropriate only to the god. The outcome of such examination, acknowledging our ignorance, Socrates calls "human wisdom," which by comparison with divine wisdom is "worth little or nothing." Still, it is the sort of wisdom, Socrates believes, that is appropriate to creatures like us. And that is why "the unexamined life is not worth living" for a human being (38a). And that is why there is "no greater blessing for the city" than Socrates' never-ending examination of its citizens (30a). Such self-examination is the way for us to become as wise and good as it is possible for human beings to be.

Read 24b–28a   At this point, Socrates begins to address the **"later accusers."** He does so in his usual question-and-answer fashion. Apparently, three persons submitted the charge to the court: Meletus, Anytus, and Lycon. Meletus seems to have been the primary sponsor of the charge, seconded by the other two. So Socrates calls Meletus forward and questions him. As in the *Euthyphro*, two charges are mentioned. Be sure you are clear about what they are.

In 24c Socrates tells the jury his purpose in cross-examining Meletus. He wants to demonstrate that Meletus is someone who ought not to be taken seriously, that he has not thought through the meaning of the charge, and that he doesn't even care about these matters.* In short, Socrates is about to demonstrate to the jury not only what sort of man Meletus is, and that he is not wise, but also what sort of man Socrates is. It is the truth, remember, that Socrates is after; if the jury is going to decide whether Socrates is impious and a corrupter of youth, they should have the very best evidence about what sort of man they are judging. Socrates is going to oblige them by giving them a personal demonstration.

He begins by taking up the charge of corrupting the youth. If Meletus claims that Socrates corrupts the youth, he must understand what corrupting is. To understand what it is to corrupt, one must also understand what it is to improve the youth. And so Socrates asks him, "Who improves them?"

Q11. Does Meletus have a ready answer? What conclusion does Socrates draw from this? (24d)

When Meletus does answer, Socrates' questions provoke him to say that all the other citizens improve the youth and only Socrates corrupts them!

Q12. How does Socrates use the analogy of the horse breeders to cast doubt on Meletus' concern for these matters?

Starting in 25c, Socrates presents Meletus with a **dilemma.** The form of a *dilemma* is this: Two

alternatives are presented between which it seems necessary to choose, but each alternative has consequences that are unwelcome, usually for different reasons. The two alternatives are called the "horns" of a dilemma, and there are three ways to deal with them. One can grasp one of the horns (that is, embrace that alternative with its consequences); one can grasp the other horn; or one can (sometimes, but not always) "go between the horns" by finding a third alternative that has not been considered.

Q13. What are the horns of the dilemma that Socrates presents to Meletus?
Q14. How does Meletus respond?
Q15. How does Socrates refute this response?
Q16. Supposing that this refutation is correct and that one cannot "pass through" the horns, what is the consequence of embracing the other horn? How does Socrates use the distinction between punishment and instruction?

Again Socrates drives home the conclusion that Meletus has "never been at all concerned with these matters." If he had been, he surely would have thought these things through. As it is, he cannot be taken seriously.

At 26b, the topic switches to the other charge. As the examination proceeds, we can see Meletus becoming angrier and angrier, less and less willing to cooperate in what he clearly sees is his own destruction. No doubt this is an example—produced right there for the jury to see—of the typical response to Socrates' questioning. We might think Socrates is not being prudent here in angering Meletus and his supporters in the jury. But again, it is for Socrates a matter of the truth; this is the kind of man he is. And the jury should see it if they are going to judge truly.

Q17. Socrates claims that Meletus contradicts himself. In what way?
Q18. What "divine activities" must the jury have understood him to be referring to? (27d–e)

---

*Compare *Apology* 24c, 25c, 26a,b with *Euthyphro* 2c–d, 3a.

Q19. What does Socrates claim will be his undoing, if he is undone?

___

Read 28b–35d Socrates is now finished with Meletus, satisfied that he has shown him to be thoughtless and unreliable. He even claims to have proved that he is "not guilty" of the charges Meletus has brought against him. No doubt Socrates believes that one cannot be rightly convicted on charges that are as vague and undefined as these have proved to be. Do you think this suffices for a defense?

Socrates then turns to more general matters relevant to his defense. He first imagines someone saying that the very fact that he is on trial for his life is shameful. How could he have behaved in such a manner as to bring himself to this?

___

Q20. On what principle does Socrates base his response? Do you agree with this principle?

Q21. To whom does Socrates compare himself? Is the comparison apt? How do you think this would have struck an Athenian jury?

Q22. Socrates refers to his military service; in what respects does he say his life as a philosopher is like that?

Q23. Why does he say that to fear death is to think oneself wise when one is not? Do you agree with this? If not, why not?

___

In 29c–d Socrates imagines that the jury might offer him a "deal," sparing his life if only he ceased practicing philosophy. Xenophon tells us that during the reign of the Thirty, Critias and another man, Charicles, demanded that Socrates cease conversing with the young. If this story is accurate, it may be that Socrates has this demand in mind. Or it may be that there had been talk of such a "deal" before the trial.

___

Q24. What does Socrates say his response would be? (Compare Acts 5:29 in the Bible.)

Q25. Why does he say that "there is no greater blessing for the city" than his service to the god? What are "the most important things"? Do you agree?

___

In the section that begins in 30b, Socrates makes some quite astonishing claims:

- If they kill him, they will harm themselves more than they harm him.
- A better man cannot be harmed by a worse man.
- He is defending himself not for his own sake but for theirs.

These claims seem to turn the usual ways of thinking about such matters completely upside down. Indeed, to our natural common sense, they seem incredible. They must have seemed so to the jury as well. We usually think that others can harm us. Socrates tells us, however, that this natural conviction of ours is false. It's not that we cannot be harmed at all, however. Indeed, we can be harmed—but only if we do it to ourselves! How can we harm ourselves? By making ourselves into worse persons than we otherwise would be. We harm ourselves by acting unjustly. That is why Socrates says that if his fellow citizens kill him they will harm themselves more than they will harm him. They will be doing injustice, thereby corrupting their souls; and the most important thing is care for the soul.

___

Q26. Socrates claims throughout to be concerned for the souls of the jury members. Show how this is consistent with his daily practice in the streets of Athens.

Q27. What use does Socrates make of the image of the "gadfly"?

___

Socrates feels a need to explain why, if he is so wise, he has not entered politics. There are two reasons, one being the nature of his "wisdom." He focuses here on the other reason: his "sign" prevented it. If it had not, he says, there is little doubt that he would "have died long ago" and could not have been a "blessing to the city" for all these years.

He cites two incidents as evidence of this, one occurring when the city was democratic, one under the rule of the Thirty. He is trying to convince the jury that he is truly apolitical because he was capable of resisting both sorts of government. In both cases, he resisted alone because the others were doing something contrary to law, and in both cases he was in some danger. Why should he feel the need to establish his political neutrality? Surely because there was a political aspect to the trial—not explicit, but in the background.

In 33a, he gets to what many people feel is the heart of the matter. Let us ask: Why was Socrates brought to trial at all? There was his reputation as a Sophist, of course—all those accusations of the "earlier accusers." There was the general hostility that his questioning generated. There was his "divine sign." But it is doubtful that these alone would have sufficed to bring him to court. What probably tipped the balance was the despicable political career of some who had once been closely associated with him, in particular Critias, leader of the Thirty, and Alcibiades, the brilliant and dashing young traitor. This kind of "guilt by association" is very common and very hard to defend against. If these men had spent so much time with Socrates, why hadn't they turned out better? Socrates must be responsible for their crimes! This could not be mentioned in the official charge because it would have violated the amnesty proclaimed by the democracy after the Thirty were overthrown. But it is hard not to believe that it is lurking in the background.

In defending himself against this charge, Socrates makes another remarkable claim. He has *never*, he says, "been anyone's teacher." For that reason, he cannot "be held responsible for the good or bad conduct of these people, as I never promised to teach them anything and have not done so." This requires some explaining.

In the dialogue *Meno*, Socrates calls over a slave boy who has never studied geometry. He draws a square on the ground and divides it equally by bisecting the sides vertically and horizontally. (Draw

such a square yourself.) He then asks the boy to construct another square with an area twice the original area. Clearly, if the original area is four, we want a square with an area of eight. But how can we get it? (Before you go on, think a minute and see if you can solve it.)

Socrates proceeds by asking the boy questions. The first, rather natural suggestion is to double the length of the sides. But on reflection, the boy can see (as you can, too) that this gives a square of sixteen. Wanting something between four and sixteen, the boy tries making the sides of the new square one and a half times the original. But this gives a square of nine, not eight. Finally, at a suggestion from Socrates, the boy sees that taking the diagonal of the original square as one side of a new square solves the problem. (Do you see why?)*

How does this illuminate Socrates' claim never to have been anyone's teacher? The crucial point is that the boy can just "see" that the first two solutions are wrong. And when the correct solution is presented, he "recognizes" it as correct. But he has never been taught geometry! Moreover, his certainty about the correct solution does not now rest on Socrates' authority, but on his own recognition of the truth. So Socrates doesn't teach him this truth!

This leaves us with another puzzle. How could the boy have recognized the true solution as the true one? Consider this analogy. You are walking down the street and see someone approaching. At first she is too far away to identify, but as she gets nearer you say, "Why, that's Joan!" Now, what must be the case for you to "recognize" Joan truly? You must already have been acquainted with Joan in some way. That alone is the condition under which recognition is possible.

Socrates thinks the slave boy's case must be similar. He must already have been acquainted with this truth; otherwise, it is not possible to explain how he recognizes it when it is present before him.

---

*A fuller explanation with a diagram of the square can be found on p. 151.

But when? Clearly not in this life. Socrates draws what seems to be the only possible conclusion: that he was acquainted with this truth before birth and that it was always within him. (This is taken as evidence that the soul exists before the body, but that is not our present concern.) Coming to know is just recognizing what, in some implicit sense, one has within oneself all along. Socrates simply asks the right questions or presents the appropriate stimuli. But he doesn't "implant" knowledge; he doesn't teach.

In the dialogue *Theatetus*, Plato represents Socrates as using a striking image:

> I am so far like the midwife that I cannot myself give birth to wisdom, and the common reproach is true, that, though I question others, I can myself bring nothing to light because there is no wisdom in me. . . . The many admirable truths they bring to birth have been discovered by themselves from within. But the delivery is heaven's work and mine. (*Theatetus* 150c–d)[3]

Here, then, is the background for the claim that Socrates has never taught anyone anything. His role is not that of teacher or imparter of knowledge but that of "midwife," assisting at the birth of ideas which are within the "learner" all along and helping to identify those that are "illegitimate." This is why he says that he cannot be held responsible for the behavior of men like Critias and Alcibiades.

Q28. What additional arguments does Socrates use in 33d–34b?
Q29. Why does he refuse to use the traditional "appeal to pity"? See particularly 35c.

Read 35e–38b The verdict has been given, and now, according to custom, both the prosecution and the defense may propose appropriate penalties. Meletus, of course, asks for death.

Q30. What penalty does Socrates first suggest? Why?

Along the way, Socrates says something interesting. "The Olympian victor makes you think yourself happy; I make you be happy." What could this mean? Compare health. Is it possible to feel healthy, think yourself healthy, while actually being unhealthy? Of course. A beginning cancer hurts not at all; in that condition, one can feel perfectly all right. No one, however, would say that a person in whom a cancer is growing is healthy. In the same way, Socrates suggests that feeling happy is not the same thing as actually being happy. Think of a city the night after its major league team wins the championship. People are dancing in the streets, hugging each other, laughing and celebrating. They are feeling happy. Are these happy people? Not necessarily. When the euphoria wears off, they may well return to miserable lives. Happiness, Socrates suggests, is a condition or state of the soul, not a matter of how you feel.* This condition, he claims, is what his questioning about virtue can produce.

Q31. Why does Socrates resist exile as a penalty?
Q32. What does he say is "the greatest good" for a man? Why?
Q33. What penalty does he finally offer?

Read 38c–end After being sentenced to death, Socrates addresses first those who voted to condemn him and then his friends. To both, he declares himself satisfied. He has presented himself for what he is; he has not betrayed himself by saying what they wanted to hear to avoid death.

Q34. What does Socrates say is more difficult to avoid than death? And who has not avoided it?
Q35. What does he "prophesy"?
Q36. What "surprising thing" does he point out to his friends? What does he take it to mean?
Q37. What two possibilities does Socrates consider death may hold? Are there any he misses?
Q38. What is the "one truth" that Socrates wishes his friends to keep in mind? How does he try to comfort them?

*If Socrates is right, our contemporary, endless fascination with how we feel about things—including ourselves—is a mistake.

CRITO

Translator's Introduction

About the time of Socrates' trial, a state galley had set out on an annual religious mission to Delos, and while it was away no execution was allowed to take place. So it was that Socrates was kept in prison for a month after the trial. The ship has now arrived at Cape Sunium in Attica and is thus expected at the Piraeus momentarily. So Socrates' old and faithful friend, Crito, makes one last effort to persuade him to escape into exile, and all arrangements for this plan have been made. It is this conversation between the two old friends that Plato professes to report in this dialogue. It is, as Crito plainly tells him, his last chance, but Socrates will not take it, and he gives his reasons for his refusal. Whether this conversation took place at this particular time is not important, for there is every reason to believe that Socrates' friends tried to plan his escape, and that he refused. Plato more than hints that the authorities would not have minded much, as long as he left the country.

The Dialogue

43 SOCRATES: Why have you come so early, Crito? Or is it not still early?

CRITO: It certainly is.

S: How early?

C: Early dawn.

S: I am surprised that the warder was willing to listen to you.

C: He is quite friendly to me by now, Socrates. I have been here often and I have given him something.

S: Have you just come, or have you been here for some time?

C: A fair time.

b S: Then why did you not wake me right away but sit there in silence?

C: By Zeus no, Socrates. I would not myself want to be in distress and awake so long. I have been surprised to see you so peacefully asleep. It was on purpose that I did not wake you, so that you should spend your time most agreeably. Often in the past throughout my life, I have considered the way you live happy, and especially so now that you bear your present misfortune so easily and lightly.

S: It would not be fitting at my age to resent the fact that I must die now.

c C: Other men of your age are caught in such misfortunes, but their age does not prevent them resenting their fate.

S: That is so. Why have you come so early?

C: I bring bad news, Socrates, not for you, apparently, but for me and all your friends the news is bad and hard to bear. Indeed, I would count it among the hardest.

d S: What is it? Or has the ship arrived from Delos, at the arrival of which I must die?

C: It has not arrived yet, but it will, I believe, arrive today, according to a message brought by some men from Sunium, where they left it. This makes it obvious that it will come today, and that your life must end tomorrow.

S: May it be for the best. If it so please the gods, so be it. However, I do not think it will arrive today.

C: What indication have you of this?

44 S: I will tell you. I must die the day after the ship arrives.

C: That is what those in authority say.

S: Then I do not think it will arrive on this coming day, but on the next. I take to witness of this a dream I had a little earlier during this night. It looks as if it was the right time for you not to wake me.

C: What was your dream?

S: I thought that a beautiful and comely woman dressed in white approached me. She called me and said: "Socrates, may you arrive at fer-

b tile Phthia[1] on the third day."

---

[1] A quotation from the ninth book of *The Iliad* (363). Achilles has rejected all the presents of Agamemnon for him to return to the battle and threatens to go home. He says his ships will sail in the morning, and with good weather he might arrive on the third day "in fertile Phthia" (which is his home). The dream means, obviously, that on the third day Socrates' soul, after death, will find its home. As always, counting the first member of a series, the third day is the day after tomorrow.

c: A strange dream, Socrates.

s: But it seems clear enough to me, Crito.

c: Too clear it seems, my dear Socrates, but listen to me even now and be saved. If you die, it will not be a single misfortune for me. Not only will I be deprived of a friend, the like of whom I shall never find again, but many people who do not know you or me very well will think that I could have saved you if I were willing to spend money, but that I did not care

c to do so. Surely there can be no worse reputation than to be thought to value money more highly than one's friends, for the majority will not believe that you yourself were not willing to leave prison while we were eager for you to do so.

s: My good Crito, why should we care so much for what the majority think? The most reasonable people, to whom one should pay more attention, will believe that things were done as they were done.

d c: You see, Socrates, that one must also pay attention to the opinion of the majority. Your present situation makes clear that the majority can inflict not the least but pretty well the greatest evils if one is slandered among them.

s: Would that the majority could inflict the greatest evils, for they would then be capable of the greatest good, and that would be fine, but now they cannot do either. They cannot make a man either wise or foolish, but they inflict things haphazardly.

e c: That may be so. But tell me this, Socrates, are you anticipating that I and your other friends would have trouble with the informers if you escape from here, as having stolen you away, and that we should be compelled to lose all our property or pay heavy fines and suffer other

45 punishment besides? If you have any such fear, forget it. We would be justified in running this risk to save you, and worse, if necessary. Do follow my advice, and do not act differently.

s: I do have these things in mind, Crito, and also many others.

c: Have no such fear. It is not much money that some people require to save you and get you out of here. Further, do you not see that those informers are cheap, and that not much money would be needed to deal with them? My

money is available and is, I think, sufficient. If, because of your affection for me, you feel you

b should not spend any of mine, there are those strangers here ready to spend money. One of them, Simmias the Theban, has brought enough for this very purpose. Cebes, too, and a good many others. So, as I say, do not let this fear make you hesitate to save yourself, nor let what you said in court trouble you, that you would not know what to do with yourself if you left Athens, for you would be welcomed

c in many places to which you might go. If you want to go to Thessaly, I have friends there who will greatly appreciate you and keep you safe, so that no one in Thessaly will harm you. Besides, Socrates, I do not think that what you are doing is right, to give up your life when you can save it, and to hasten your fate as your enemies would hasten it, and indeed have hastened it in their wish to destroy you. Moreover, I think you are betraying your sons

d by going away and leaving them, when you could bring them up and educate them. You thus show no concern for what their fate may be. They will probably have the usual fate of orphans. Either one should not have children, or one should share with them to the end the toil of upbringing and education. You seem to me to choose the easiest path, whereas one should choose the path a good and courageous man would choose, particularly when one claims throughout one's life to care for virtue.

e I feel ashamed on your behalf and on behalf of us, your friends, lest all that has happened to you be thought due to cowardice on our part: the fact that your trial came to court when it need not have done so, the handling of the trial itself, and now this absurd ending which will be thought to have got beyond our control through some cowardice and unmanliness

46 on our part, since we did not save you, or you save yourself, when it was possible and could be done if we had been of the slightest use. Consider, Socrates, whether this is not only evil, but shameful, both for you and for us. Take counsel with yourself, or rather the

time for counsel is past and the decision should have been taken, and there is no further opportunity, for this whole business must be ended tonight. If we delay now, then it will no longer be possible, it will be too late. Let me persuade you on every count, Socrates, and do not act otherwise.

s: My dear Crito, your eagerness is worth much
b if it should have some right aim; if not, then the greater your keenness the more difficult it is to deal with. We must therefore examine whether we should act in this way or not, as not only now but at all times I am the kind of man who listens only to the argument that on reflection seems best to me. I cannot, now that this fate has come upon me, discard the arguments I used; they seem to me much the same. I value and respect the same principles
c as before, and if we have no better arguments to bring up at this moment, be sure that I shall not agree with you, not even if the power of the majority were to frighten us with more bogeys, as if we were children, with threats of incarcerations and executions and confiscation of property. How should we examine this matter most reasonably? Would it be by taking up first your argument about the opinions of men, whether it is sound in every case that one should pay attention to some opinions,
d but not to others? Or was that well-spoken before the necessity to die came upon me, but now it is clear that this was said in vain for the sake of argument, that it was in truth play and nonsense? I am eager to examine together with you, Crito, whether this argument will appear in any way different to me in my present circumstances, or whether it remains the same, whether we are to abandon it or believe it. It was said on every occasion by those who
e thought they were speaking sensibly, as I have just now been speaking, that one should greatly value some people's opinions, but not others. Does that seem to you a sound statement?

You, as far as a human being can tell, are exempt from the likelihood of dying tomorrow, so the present misfortune is not likely to lead
47 you astray. Consider then, do you not think it a sound statement that one must not value all the opinions of men, but some and not others,

nor the opinions of all men, but those of some and not of others? What do you say? Is this not well said?

c: It is.

s: One should value the good opinions, and not the bad ones?

c: Yes.

s: The good opinions are those of wise men, the bad ones those of foolish men?

c: Of course.

s: Come then, what of statements such as this:
b Should a man professionally engaged in physical training pay attention to the praise and blame and opinion of any man, or to those of one man only, namely a doctor or trainer?

c: To those of one only.

s: He should therefore fear the blame and welcome the praise of that one man, and not those of the many?

c: Obviously.

s: He must then act and exercise, eat and drink in the way the one, the trainer and the one who knows, thinks right, not all the others?

c: That is so.

c s: Very well. And if he disobeys the one, disregards his opinion and his praises while valuing those of the many who have no knowledge, will he not suffer harm?

c: Of course.

s: What is that harm, where does it tend, and what part of the man who disobeys does it affect?

c: Obviously the harm is to his body, which it ruins.

s: Well said. So with other matters, not to enumerate them all, and certainly with actions just and unjust, shameful and beautiful, good and bad, about which we are now deliberat-
d ing, should we follow the opinion of the many and fear it; or that of the one, if there is one who has knowledge of these things and before whom we feel fear and shame more than before all the others. If we do not follow his directions, we shall harm and corrupt that part of ourselves that is improved by just actions and destroyed by unjust actions. Or is there nothing in this?

c: I think there certainly is, Socrates.

s: Come now, if we ruin that which is improved by health and corrupted by disease by not following the opinions of those who know, is life e   worth living for us when that is ruined? And that is the body, is it not?

c: Yes.

s: And is life worth living with a body that is corrupted and in bad condition?

c: In no way.

s: And is life worth living for us with that part of us corrupted that unjust action harms and just action benefits? Or do we think that part of us, whatever it is, that is concerned with justice and injustice, is inferior to the body?

48   c: Not at all.

s: It is more valuable?

c: Much more.

s: We should not then think so much of what the majority will say about us, but what he will say who understands justice and injustice, the one, that is, and the truth itself. So that, in the first place, you were wrong to believe that we should care for the opinion of the many about what is just, beautiful, good, and their opposites. "But," someone might say "the many are able to put us to death."

b   c: That too is obvious, Socrates, and someone might well say so.

s: And, my admirable friend, that argument that we have gone through remains, I think, as before. Examine the following statement in turn as to whether it stays the same or not, that the most important thing is not life, but the good life.

c: It stays the same.

s: And that the good life, the beautiful life, and the just life are the same; does that still hold, or not?

c: It does hold.

s: As we have agreed so far, we must examine

c   next whether it is right for me to try to get out of here when the Athenians have not acquitted me. If it is seen to be right, we will try to do so; if it is not, we will abandon the idea. As for those questions you raise about money, reputation, the upbringing of children, Crito, those considerations in truth belong to those people who easily put men to death and would bring them to life again if they could, without thinking; I mean the majority of men. For us, however, since our argument leads to this, the only valid consideration, as we were saying just now, is whether we should be acting rightly in giving money and gratitude to those who will

d   lead me out of here, and ourselves helping with the escape, or whether in truth we shall do wrong in doing all this. If it appears that we shall be acting unjustly, then we have no need at all to take into account whether we shall have to die if we stay here and keep quiet, or suffer in another way, rather than do wrong.

c: I think you put that beautifully, Socrates, but see what we should do.

e   s: Let us examine the question together, my dear friend, and if you can make any objection while I am speaking, make it and I will listen to you, but if you have no objection to make, my dear Crito, then stop now from saying the same thing so often, that I must leave here against the will of the Athenians. I think it important to persuade you before I act, and not to act against your wishes. See whether the

49   start of our enquiry is adequately stated, and try to answer what I ask you in the way you think best.

c: I shall try.

s: Do we say that one must never in any way do wrong willingly, or must one do wrong in one way and not in another? Is to do wrong never good or admirable, as we have agreed in the past, or have all these former agreements been washed out during the last few days? Have we

b   at our age failed to notice for some time that in our serious discussions we were no different from children? Above all, is the truth such as we used to say it was, whether the majority agree or not, and whether we must still suffer worse things than we do now, or will be treated more gently, that nonetheless, wrongdoing is in every way harmful and shameful to the wrongdoer? Do we say so or not?

c: We do.

s: So one must never do wrong.

c: Certainly not.

s: Nor must one, when wronged, inflict wrong in return, as the majority believe, since one must never do wrong.

c   c: That seems to be the case.

s: Come now, should one injure anyone or not, Crito?

c: One must never do so.

s: Well then, if one is oneself injured, is it right, as the majority say, to inflict an injury in return, or is it not?

c: It is never right.

s: Injuring people is no different from wrong-doing.

c: That is true.

s: One should never do wrong in return, nor injure any man, whatever injury one has suffered at his hands. And Crito, see that you do

d   not agree to this, contrary to your belief. For I know that only a few people hold this view or will hold it, and there is no common ground between those who hold this view and those who do not, but they inevitably despise each other's views. So then consider very carefully whether we have this view in common, and whether you agree, and let this be the basis of our deliberation, that neither to do wrong or to return a wrong is ever right, not even to injure in return for an injury received. Or do you disagree and do not share this view as a

e   basis for discussion? I have held it for a long time and still hold it now, but if you think otherwise, tell me now. If, however, you stick to our former opinion, then listen to the next point.

c: I stick to it and agree with you. So say on.

s: Then I state the next point, or rather I ask you: when one has come to an agreement that is just with someone, should one fulfill it or cheat on it?

c: One should fulfill it.

s: See what follows from this: if we leave here

50   without the city's permission, are we injuring people whom we should least injure? And are we sticking to a just agreement, or not?

c: I cannot answer your question, Socrates. I do not know.

s: Look at it this way. If, as we were planning to run away from here, or whatever one should call it, the laws and the state came and confronted us and asked: "Tell me, Socrates, what are you intending to do? Do you not by this action you are attempting intend to

b   destroy us, the laws, and indeed the whole city, as far as you are concerned? Or do you think it possible for a city not to be destroyed if the verdicts of its courts have no force but are nullified and set at naught by private individuals?" What shall we answer to this and other such arguments? For many things could be said, especially by an orator on behalf of this law we are destroying, which orders that

c   the judgments of the courts shall be carried out. Shall we say in answer, "The city wronged me, and its decision was not right." Shall we say that, or what?

c: Yes, by Zeus, Socrates, that is our answer.

s: Then what if the laws said: "Was that the agreement between us, Socrates, or was it to respect the judgments that the city came to?" And if we wondered at their words, they would perhaps add: "Socrates, do not wonder at what we say but answer, since you are accustomed to proceed by question and answer.

d   Come now, what accusation do you bring against us and the city, that you should try to destroy us? Did we not, first, bring you to birth, and was it not through us that your father married your mother and begat you? Tell us, do you find anything to criticize in those of us who are concerned with marriage?" And I would say that I do not criticize them. "Or in those of us concerned with the nurture of babies and the education that you too received? Were those assigned to that subject not right to instruct your father to educate you in the arts and in physical culture?" And I would say that they were right. "Very well," they would continue, "and after you were born and nurtured and educated, could you, in the first

e   place, deny that you are our offspring and servant, both you and your forefathers? If that is so, do you think that we are on an equal footing as regards the right, and that whatever we do to you it is right for you to do to us? You were not on an equal footing with your father as regards the right, nor with your master if

51   you had one, so as to retaliate for anything they did to you, to revile them if they reviled you, to beat them if they beat you, and so with many other things. Do you think you have this right to retaliation against your country and its laws? That if we undertake to destroy you and think it right to do so, you can undertake to destroy us, as far as you can, in return? And will you say that you are right to do so, you who truly care for virtue? Is your wisdom such as not to realize that your country is to be honoured more than your mother, your father and

b

c

all your ancestors, that it is more to be revered and more sacred, and that it counts for more among the gods and sensible men, that you must worship it, yield to it and placate its anger more than your father's? You must either persuade it or obey its orders, and endure in silence whatever it instructs you to endure, whether blows or bonds, and if it leads you into war to be wounded or killed, you must obey. To do so is right, and one must not give way or retreat or leave one's post, but both in war and in courts and everywhere else, one must obey the commands of one's city and country, or persuade it as to the nature of justice. It is impious to bring violence to bear against your mother or father, it is much more so to use it against your country." What shall we say in reply, Crito, that the laws speak the truth, or not?

c: I think they do.

s: "Reflect now, Socrates," the laws might say "that if what we say is true, you are not treating us rightly by planning to do what you are planning. We have given you birth, nurtured you, educated you, we have given you and all

d

other citizens a share of all the good things we could. Even so, by giving every Athenian the opportunity, after he has reached manhood and observed the affairs of the city and us the laws, we proclaim that if we do not please him, he can take his possessions and go wherever he pleases. Not one of our laws raises any obstacle or forbids him, if he is not satisfied with us or the city, if one of you wants to go and live in a colony or wants to go anywhere else, and keep his property. We say, however, that whoever

e

of you remains, when he sees how we conduct our trials and manage the city in other ways, has in fact come to an agreement with us to obey our instructions. We say that the one who disobeys does wrong in three ways, first because in us he disobeys his parents, also those who brought him up, and because, in spite of his agreement, he neither obeys us nor, if we do something wrong, does he try to persuade

52

us to be better. Yet we only propose things, we do not issue savage commands to do whatever we order; we give two alternatives, either to persuade us or to do what we say. He does

b

c

d

e

neither. We do say that you too, Socrates, are open to those charges if you do what you have in mind; you would be among, not the least, but the most guilty of the Athenians." And if I should say "Why so?" they might well be right to upbraid me and say that I am among the Athenians who most definitely came to that agreement with them. They might well say: "Socrates, we have convincing proofs that we and the city were congenial to you. You would not have dwelt here most consistently of all the Athenians if the city had not been exceedingly pleasing to you. You have never left the city, even to see a festival, nor for any other reason except military service; you have never gone to stay in any other city, as people do; you have had no desire to know another city or other

laws; we and our city satisfied you. "So decisively did you choose us and agree to be a citizen under us. Also, you have had children in this city, thus showing that it was congenial to you. Then at your trial you could have assessed your penalty at exile if you wished, and you are now attempting to do against the city's wishes what you could then have done with her consent. Then you prided yourself that you did not resent death, but you chose, as you said, death in preference to exile. Now, however, those words do not make you ashamed, and you pay no heed to us, the laws, as you plan to destroy us, and you act like the meanest type of slave by trying to run away, contrary to your undertakings and your agreement to live as a citizen under us. First then, answer us on this very point, whether we speak the truth when we say that you agreed, not only in words but by your deeds, to live in accordance with us." What are we to say to that, Crito? Must we not agree?

c: We must, Socrates.

s: "Surely," they might say, "you are breaking the undertakings and agreements that you made with us without compulsion or deceit, and under no pressure of time for deliberation. You have had seventy years during which you could have gone away if you did not like us, and if you thought our agreements unjust. You did not choose to go to Sparta or to Crete, which you are always saying are well governed, nor to any other city, Greek or foreign. You

53

have been away from Athens less than the lame or the blind or other handicapped people. It is clear that the city has been outstandingly more congenial to you than to other Athenians, and so have we, the laws, for what city can please without laws? Will you then not now stick to our agreements? You will, Socrates, if we can persuade you, and not make yourself a laughingstock by leaving the city.

"For consider what good you will do yourself or your friends by breaking our agreements and committing such a wrong? It is pretty obvious that your friends will themselves be in danger of exile, disfranchisement

b and loss of property. As for yourself, if you go to one of the nearby cities—Thebes or Megara, both are well governed—you will arrive as an enemy to their government; all who care for their city will look on you with suspicion, as a destroyer of the laws. You will also strengthen the conviction of the jury that

c they passed the right sentence on you, for anyone who destroys the laws could easily be thought to corrupt the young and the ignorant. Or will you avoid cities that are well governed and men who are civilized? If you do this, will your life be worth living? Will you have social intercourse with them and not be ashamed to talk to them? And what will you say? The same as you did here, that virtue and justice are man's most precious possession, along with lawful behaviour and the laws? Do you not

d think that Socrates would appear to be an unseemly kind of person? One must think so. Or will you leave those places and go to Crito's friends in Thessaly? There you will find the greatest license and disorder, and they may enjoy hearing from you how absurdly you escaped from prison in some disguise, in a leather jerkin or some other things in which escapees wrap themselves, thus altering your appearance. Will there be no one to say that you, likely to live but a short time more, were

e so greedy for life that you transgressed the most important laws? Possibly, Socrates, if you do not annoy anyone, but if you do, many disgraceful things will be said about you. "You will spend your time ingratiating yourself with all men, and be at their beck and call. What will you do in Thessaly but feast, as if

you had gone to a banquet in Thessaly? As for those conversations of yours about justice and the rest of virtue, where will they be? You

54 say you want to live for the sake of your children, that you may bring them up and educate them. How so? Will you bring them up and educate them by taking them to Thessaly and making strangers of them, that they may enjoy that too? Or not so, but they will be better brought up and educated here, while you are alive, though absent? Yes, your friends will look after them. Will they look after them if you go and live in Thessaly, but not if you go away to the underworld? If those who profess themselves your friends are any good at all,

b one must assume that they will. "Be persuaded by us who have brought you up, Socrates. Do not value either your children or your life or anything else more than goodness, in order that when you arrive in Hades you may have all this as your defence before the rulers there. If you do this deed, you will not think it better or more just or more pious here, nor will any one of your friends, nor will it be better for you when you arrive yonder. As it is, you depart, if you depart, after being wronged not by us, the laws, but by men;

c but if you depart after shamefully returning wrong for wrong and injury for injury, after breaking your agreement and contract with us, after injuring those you should injure least— yourself, your friends, your country and us— we shall be angry with you while you are still alive, and our brothers, the laws of the underworld, will not receive you kindly, knowing that you tried to destroy us as far as you could. Do not let Crito persuade you, rather than us,

d to do what he says."

Crito, my dear friend, be assured that these are the words I seem to hear, as the Corybants seem to hear the music of their flutes, and the echo of these words resounds in me, and makes it impossible for me to hear anything else. As far as my present beliefs go, if you speak in opposition to them, you will speak in vain. However, if you think you can accomplish anything, speak.

c: I have nothing to say, Socrates.

s: Let it be then, Crito, and let us act in this way, since this is the way the god is leading us.

COMMENTARY AND QUESTIONS[4]

Read 43a–44b Plato opens the dialogue with a scene designed to reiterate how different Socrates is from most men. The time is approaching for his execution, yet he sleeps peacefully—as though he had not a care in the world. His dream confirms what he had concluded at the end of the trial: Death is not an evil to be feared but is more like the soul coming home again after many hardships.

Read 44b–46a **Crito** piles reason upon reason to persuade Socrates to escape.

Q1. List at least seven reasons Crito urges upon Socrates for making his escape.

Most of these reasons are prudential in nature, not moral. The one that does appeal to "what is right" seems to come right out of the Sophist's playbook: What is right, Crito says, is to preserve one's own life whenever one can.* Several of the reasons appeal to "what people will think" if Socrates does not take this opportunity. This leads Socrates to ask why one should pay any attention at all to what the majority of people say.

Q2. What does Crito say in response to this question, and what is Socrates' reply?

Q3. What does Socrates indicate is "the greatest good"?

Read 46b–49a Characteristically, Socrates says they must "examine" whether to act in this way.

Q4. What kind of man does Socrates here say that he is?

Socrates reminds Crito that he has always maintained that one should pay attention only to the opinions of the "most reasonable" people. He invites Crito to reexamine this conviction in the

light of his imminent death. Does it "stand fast" even now?

The examination is conducted, as so often, in terms of an analogy; Socrates draws a comparison between the health of the body and the health of the soul. He points out that you don't listen to just anybody when it comes to matters of bodily health. The same must also be true when it is a matter of the soul's well-being. You want to listen to those who are wise, not to the opinions of the many. So what most people might think if Socrates escapes or does not escape is, strictly speaking, irrelevant. It should be set aside. Reluctantly perhaps, Crito agrees.

Socrates adds that life is really not worth living when the body is corrupted by disease and ruined; the important thing is "not life, but the good life." The same must then be true of the soul.

Q5. What corrupts and ruins the soul, according to Socrates? What benefits it?

Q6. Which, body or soul, is most valuable? Why do you think he says that?

Q7. Socrates says that three kinds of life are "the same": The good life, the beautiful life, and the just life. Think about the lives you are familiar with. Do you agree? Is it really the just people whose lives are beautiful and good?

They agree, then, that the right thing to do is the only thing they should have in mind when making the decision. The question is simply this: Is it just or unjust to escape? Will escaping bring benefit or harm to the soul?

Read 49a–50a The next principle Socrates brings up for reexamination is this: that one should never willingly do wrong. Why not? Because doing wrong is "harmful and shameful to the wrongdoer." Again we see Socrates emphasizing that we harm ourselves by harming our souls, and we harm our souls by doing wrong, which makes us into worse people than we otherwise would be.

Q8. What corollary to this "never do wrong" principle does Socrates draw out in 49b–d?

---

*See the quotations from Antiphon, pp. 65–66.

Q9. Socrates says this is not something the majority of people believe. Do you believe it?

Note that injuring is not the same as inflicting harm. Remember, Socrates was a soldier, and a good one. He even cited his military experience with pride in his defense before the jury. But soldiers inflict damage on other soldiers, perhaps even kill them. Moreover, Athens is about to execute Socrates, but he says nothing to suggest that capital punishment is wrongdoing or injury. It may, then, be justifiable—in war or according to law—to inflict harm. Still, we must never injure each other. Injury is *unjust* harming of another.

What is wrong, Socrates says, is doing injustice in return for an injustice done to you. Wrong done to you never justifies your doing wrong. The reason is simply that doing injustice is *always* wrong, always a corruption of the soul. When you consider how to act, according to Socrates, you should never think about revenge. Revenge looks to the past, to what has happened to you, and you should look only to actions that will promote excellence—in your soul and in others. That is the way to care for your soul.

Socrates says they should examine next whether one should always keep agreements made, providing they are just agreements (49e). Crito agrees immediately, so we come to the major part of the argument.

Read 50a–54d In this section, we have a dramatic piece of rhetoric. Plato gives us a dialogue within the dialogue in the form of an imaginary "examination" of Socrates by the laws of Athens. It is rhetoric all right; but, like Parmenides' poem, it contains an argument. Socrates will look to this argument, this *logos*, in making his decision. Remember that Socrates says he is the kind of man who listens only to the best *logos*. So it is the argument that we must try to discern.

Socrates indicates the conclusion of the argument right off: that escaping will constitute an attempt to injure the laws, and indeed the whole city. It is this proposition that the laws have to prove. If they can do so, it will follow immediately that Socrates must not escape, because

that would amount to doing injury. It will also be no good for Socrates to reply, "Well, the laws injured me by convicting me unjustly!" because we have already agreed that one must not return injury for injury.

How will escaping injure the laws of Athens? This part of the argument begins with the laws claiming that they are to be honored more than mother, father, or all one's ancestors.

Q10. What reasons are offered by the laws for this claim?
Q11. What alternatives does Athens offer its citizens if they do not agree with or like the laws?
Q12. Could Socrates have left Athens at any time if he was not pleased with the laws?
Q13. What conclusion follows from the fact that Socrates stayed?

So the situation is this: In virtue of his long residence in Athens, Socrates has agreed to be a citizen under the laws, to accept their benefits and "live in accordance" with them. This agreement was made without any compulsion and in full knowledge of what was involved. There can be no doubt that it is a just agreement. Further, Socrates and Crito have already agreed that just agreements must be kept. But it is not yet clear how breaking this agreement will injure the laws and the city of Athens.

A clue is found in 54b, where the laws say that Socrates was wronged not by them, but by men. No legal order can exist without application and enforcement, courts and punishments, and part of voluntarily accepting citizenship is agreeing to abide by decisions of the legally constituted courts. There can be no doubt that the court that convicted Socrates was a legal court. It should also be noted that Socrates does not criticize the Athenian law against impiety on which he was tried. If the jury made a mistake and decided the case unjustly, that cannot be laid at the door of the laws. So the laws did Socrates no injustice. (Though even if they had, that would not, on Socrates' principles, justify his doing wrong in return.)

The situation then is this: To escape would be tantamount to an attack on the authority of this court to decide as it did. If *this* court lacks authority over its citizens, what court has such authority? To attack the authority of the courts is to attempt, insofar as it is possible for one man, to destroy the legal system, and the city, as a whole. "Or do you think it is possible for a city not to be destroyed if the verdicts of its courts have no force but are nullified and set at naught by private individuals?" (50b)

The argument is complex, and it may be useful to set it out in skeleton form.

1. One must never do wrong.
   a. Because to do wrong is "in every way harmful and shameful to the wrongdoer." (49b)
   b. Because doing wrong harms the part of ourselves that is "more valuable." (48a)
2. One must never return wrong for wrong done. (This follows directly from 1.)
3. To injure others (treat them unjustly) is to do wrong.
4. One must never injure others. (This follows from 1 and 3.)
5. To violate a just agreement is to do injury.
6. To escape would be to violate a just agreement with the laws. (Here we have the argument presented in the dialogue between Socrates and the laws.)
7. To escape would be an injury to the laws. (This follows from 5 and 6.)
8. To escape would be wrong. (This follows from 3 and 7.)
9. Socrates must not escape. (This follows from 1 and 8.)

This *logos* is one that Socrates finds convincing, and Crito has nothing to say against it. So it is the one Socrates will be content to live—and die—by. Once again, it is better to *suffer* injustice than to *do* it, even if that means losing one's life to avoid committing an unjust act.

There remains the task of countering the considerations Crito has put forward in favor of escape. In 53a–54a, the laws address these arguments point by point.

Q14. Go back to your list in Q1 and state the rebuttal offered by the laws. Who is more persuasive— Crito or the laws?

Read 54d–e *Corybants* are priests of Earth and the fertility goddess Cybele, who express their devotion in ecstatic dances, oblivious to what is going on around them. The dialogue ends with Plato once again emphasizing the very real piety of Socrates. He quietly accepts the verdict of the *logos* as guidance from the god. The voice of reason, as far as it can be discerned, is the voice of the divine.*

---

* Remember that human reason, for Socrates, is not the same as divine wisdom. We are not gods. That is why continual examination of ourselves is in order; and that is why his "voice" is significant; it supplies something human *logoi* could not. Compare what Heraclitus says about wisdom, the *logos*, and the divine, p. 20.

PHAEDO (DEATH SCENE)

Translator's Introduction

In the Phaedo, a number of Socrates' friends have come to visit him in prison on the last day of his life, as he will drink the hemlock at sundown. The main topic of their conversation is the nature of the soul and the arguments for its immortality.

This takes up most of the dialogue. Then Socrates tells a rather elaborate myth on the shape of the earth in a hollow of which we live, and of which we know nothing of the splendours of its surface, the purer air and brighter heavens. The myth then deals with the dwelling places of various kinds of souls after death. The following passage immediately follows the conclusion of the myth.

The Dialogue (Selection)

No sensible man would insist that these things are as I have described them, but I think it

114d is fitting for a man to risk the belief—for the risk is a noble one—that this, or something like this, is true about our souls and their dwelling places, since the soul is evidently immortal, and a man should repeat this to himself as if it were an incantation, which is why I have been prolonging my tale. That is the reason why a man should be of good cheer about his own soul, if during life he has ignored the pleasures

e of the body and its ornamentation as of no concern to him and doing him more harm than good, but has seriously concerned himself with the pleasures of learning, and adorned his soul not with alien but with its own ornaments, namely moderation, righteousness, courage,

115 freedom, and truth, and in that state awaits his journey to the underworld.

Now you, Simmias, Cebes, and the rest of you, Socrates continued, will each take that journey at some other time but my fated day calls me now, as a tragic character might say, and it is about time for me to have my bath, for I think it better to have it before I drink the poison and save the women the trouble of washing the corpse.

When Socrates had said this Crito spoke:

b Very well, Socrates, what are your instructions to me and the others about your children or anything else? What can we do that would please you most? —Nothing new, Crito, said Socrates, but what I am always saying, that you will please me and mine and yourselves, by taking good care of your own selves in whatever you do, even if you do not agree with me now, but if you neglect your own selves, and are un-

c willing to live following the tracks, as it were, of what we have said now and on previous occasions, you will achieve nothing even if you strongly agree with me at this moment.

We shall be eager to follow your advice, said Crito, but how shall we bury you?

In any way you like, said Socrates, if you can catch me and I do not escape you. And

laughing quietly, looking at us, he said: I do not convince Crito that I am this Socrates talking to you here

d and ordering all I say, but he thinks that I am the thing which he will soon be looking at as a corpse, and so he asks how he shall bury me. I have been saying for some time and at some length that after I have drunk the poison I shall no longer be with you but will leave you to go and enjoy some good fortunes of the blessed, but it seems that I have said all this to him in vain in an attempt to reassure you and myself too. Give a pledge to Crito on my behalf, he said, the opposite pledge to that he gave to the jury. He pledged that I would stay, you must

e pledge that I will not stay after I die, but that I shall go away, so that Crito will bear it more easily when he sees my body being burned or buried and will not be angry on my behalf, as if I were suffering terribly, and so that he should not say at the funeral that he is laying out, or carrying out, or burying Socrates. For know you well, my dear Crito, that to express oneself badly is not only faulty as far as the language goes, but does some harm to the soul. You must be of good cheer, and say you are burying my body, and bury it in any way you like and think

116 most customary.

After saying this he got up and went to another room to take his bath, and Crito followed him and he told us to wait for him. So we stayed, talking among ourselves, questioning what had been said, and then again talking of the great misfortune that had befallen us. We all felt as if we had lost a father and would be

b orphaned for the rest of our lives. When he had washed, his children were brought to him—two of his sons were small and one was older—and the women of his household came to him. He spoke to them before Crito and gave them what instructions he wanted. Then he sent the women and children away, and he himself joined us. It was now close to sunset, for he had stayed inside for some time. He came and sat down after his bath and conversed for a short

c while, when the officer of the Eleven came and stood by him and said: "I shall not reproach you as I do the others, Socrates. They are angry with me and curse me when, obeying the orders of my superiors, I tell them to drink the poison. During the time you have been here I have come to know you in other ways as the noblest, the gentlest, and the best man who has ever come here. So now too I know that you will not make trouble for me; you know who is responsible and you will direct your anger against them. You know what message I bring. Fare you well, and try to endure what you must as easily as possible." The officer was

d weeping as he turned away and went out. Socrates looked up at him and said: "Fare you well also, we shall do as you bid us." And turning to us he said: How pleasant the man is! During the whole time I have been here he has come in and conversed with me from time to time, a most agreeable man. And how genuinely he now weeps for me. Come, Crito, let us obey him. Let someone bring the poison if it is ready; if not, let the man prepare it.

e But Socrates, said Crito, I think the sun still shines upon the hills and has not yet set. I know that others drink the poison quite a long time after they have received the order, eating and drinking quite a bit, and some of them enjoy intimacy with their loved ones. Do not hurry; there is still some time.

It is natural, Crito, for them to do so, said **117** Socrates, for they think they derive some benefit from doing this, but it is not fitting for me. I do not expect any benefit from drinking the poison a little later, except to become ridiculous in my own eyes for clinging to life, and be sparing of it when there is none left. So do as I ask and do not refuse me.

Hearing this, Crito nodded to the slave who was standing near him; the slave went out and after a time came back with the man who was to administer the poison, carrying it made ready in a cup. When Socrates saw him he said: Well, my good man, you are an expert in this, what must one do? —"Just drink it and walk **b** around until your legs feel heavy, and then lie down and it will act of itself." And he offered the cup to Socrates who took it quite cheerfully, . . . without a tremor or any change of feature or colour, but looking at the man from under his eyebrows as was his wont, asked: "What do you say about pouring a libation from this drink? Is it allowed?" —"We only mix as much as we believe will suffice," said the man.

c I understand, Socrates said, but one is allowed, indeed one must, utter a prayer to the

gods that the journey from here to yonder may be fortunate. This is my prayer and may it be so.

And while he was saying this, he was holding the cup, and then drained it calmly and easily. Most of us had been able to hold back our tears reasonably well up till then, but when we saw him drinking it and after he drank it, we could hold them back no longer; my own tears came in floods against my will. So I covered my face. I was weeping for myself—not for him, but for my misfortune in being deprived of such a com-**d** rade. Even before me, Crito was unable to restrain his tears and got up. Apollodorus had not ceased from weeping before, and at this moment his noisy tears and anger made everybody present break down, except Socrates. "What is this," he said, "you strange fellows. It is mainly for this reason that I sent the women away, to **e** avoid such unseemliness, for I am told one should die in good omened silence. So keep quiet and control yourselves."

His words made us ashamed, and we checked our tears. He walked around, and when he said his legs were heavy he lay on his back as he had been told to do, and the man who had given him the poison touched his body, and after a **118** while tested his feet and legs, pressed hard upon his foot and asked him if he felt this, and Socrates said no. Then he pressed his calves, and made his way up his body and showed us that it was cold and stiff. He felt it himself and said that when the cold reached his heart he would be gone. As his belly was getting cold Socrates uncovered his head—he had covered it—and said—these were his last words—"Crito, we owe a cock to Asclepius;[1] make this offering to him and do not forget." —"It shall be done," said Crito, "tell us if there is anything else," but there was no answer. Shortly afterwards Socrates made a movement; the man uncovered him and his eyes were fixed. Seeing this Crito closed his mouth and his eyes.

Such was the end of our comrade, . . . a man who, we would say, was of all those we have known the best, and also the wisest and the most upright.

---

[1]A cock was sacrificed to Asclepius by the sick people who slept in his temples, hoping for a cure. Socrates obviously means that death is a cure for the ills of life.

COMMENTARY AND QUESTIONS

Read 114d–115e About fifteen people were present for this last conversation. Plato, it is said, was absent because he was ill. By this point, they have agreed that the soul is immortal and that the souls of the just and pious, especially if they have devoted themselves to wisdom, dwell after death in a beautiful place.

Q1. What are said to be the "ornaments" of the soul?
Q2. What harm, do you think, can it do the soul to "express oneself badly"?

Read 116–end Socrates seems to have kept his calm and courage to the end—and his humor. There is a little joke about burial at 115c. Xenophon, too, records this:

> A man named Apollodorus, who was there with him, a very ardent disciple of Socrates, but otherwise simple, exclaimed, "But Socrates, what I find it hardest to bear is that I see you being put to death unjustly!" The other, stroking Apollodorus' head, is said to have replied, "My beloved Apollodorus, was it your preference to see me put to death justly?" and smiled as he asked the question.[5]

The simple majesty of the final tribute is, perhaps, unmatched anywhere.

FOR FURTHER THOUGHT

1. Socrates believes that acts of injustice cannot be wrong simply because the gods disapprove of them. There must be something about such acts themselves, he claims, that makes them wrong. If you agree, try to say what that is. If you disagree, argue for that conclusion.

2. Imagine that you are a member of the Athenian jury hearing the case of Socrates. How would you vote? Why?
3. How might constant resort to the F-word harm the soul?
4. Should Socrates have accepted Crito's offer of escape? Construct a *logos* that supports your answer.

KEY WORDS

Euthyphro	persuasion
Meletus	truth
divine sign	earlier accusers
the pious	Oracle at Delphi
definition	human wisdom
form	later accusers
ethics	dilemma
care of the gods	Crito

NOTES

1. The dialogues and translator's introductions in this chapter are from Plato, *The Trial and Death of Socrates*, 2nd ed., trans. G. M. A. Grube (Indianapolis, IN: Hackett, 1975).
2. Xenophon, *Memorabilia*, trans. E. C. Marchant, in *Xenophon IV*, ed. E. C. Marchant and O. J. Todd (Cambridge, MA: Harvard University Press, 1979), bk. 1, 3, 2–3.
3. Plato, *Theatetus*, in *The Collected Dialogues of Plato*, ed. E. Hamilton and H. Cairns (Princeton, NJ: Princeton University Press, 1961).
4. We are indebted to R. E. Allen's interpretation of the *Crito* in his *Socrates and Legal Obligation* (Minneapolis: University of Minnesota Press, 1980).
5. Xenophon, *Apology 28*, trans. O. J. Todd, in *Xenophon IV*, ed. E. C. Marchant and O. J. Todd (Cambridge, MA: Harvard University Press, 1979).

CHAPTER
8

PLATO

Knowing the Real and the Good

When Socrates died in 399 B.C., his friend and admirer Plato was just thirty years old. He lived fifty-two more years. That long life was devoted to the creation of a philosophy that would justify and vindicate his master, "the best, and also the wisest" man he had ever known (*Phaedo* 118).[1] It is a philosophy whose influence has been incalculable in the West. Together with that of Plato's pupil Aristotle, it forms one of the two foundation stones for nearly all that is to follow; even those who want to disagree first have to pay attention. In a rather loose sense, everyone in the Western philosophical tradition is either a Platonist or an Aristotelian.

❖

"The safest general characterization of the European philosophical tradition is that it consists of a series of footnotes to Plato."

Alfred North Whitehead (1861–1947)

In Raphael's remarkable painting *The School of Athens* (see the cover of this book), all the sight lines draw the eye toward the two central figures. Plato is the one on the left, pointing upward. Aristotle is on the right with a hand stretched out horizontally. We will not be ready to appreciate the symbolism of these gestures until we know something of both, but that these two occupy center stage is entirely appropriate.

Plato apparently left Athens after Socrates' death and traveled widely. About 387 B.C., he returned to Athens and established a school near a grove called "Academus," from which comes our word "academy." There he inquired, taught, and wrote the dialogues.

Let us briefly review the situation leading up to Socrates' death. An ugly, drawn-out war with Sparta ends in humiliation for Athens, accompanied by internal strife between democrats and oligarchs, culminating in the tyranny of the Thirty, civil war, and their overthrow. The Sophists have been teaching doctrines that seem to undermine all the traditions and cast doubt on everything people hold sacred. The intellectual situation in general, though it will look active and fruitful from a future vantage point, surely looks chaotic and unsettled from close up. It is a war of ideas no one has definitely won. You have Parmenides' One versus Heraclitus' flux, Democritus' atomism versus the skepticism of the Sophists, and the controversy over *physis* and *nomos*. Some urge conformity to the laws of the city; others hold that such human justice is inferior to the pursuit of self-interest, which can rightly override such "mere" conventions. In this maelstrom appears Socrates—ugly to look at, fascinating in character, incredibly honest, doggedly persistent, passionately committed to a search for the truth, and convinced that *none* of his contemporaries know what they are talking about. Ultimately, he pays for that passion with his life.

After Socrates' execution, Plato takes up his teacher's tenacious search for the truth. He sets for himself the goal of refuting skepticism and relativism. He intends to *demonstrate*, contrary to the Sophists, that there is a truth about reality and that it can be known. And he intends to show, contrary to Democritus, that this reality is not indifferent to moral and religious values.

His basic goal, and in this he is typically Greek, is to establish the pattern for a good state.* If you were to ask him, "Plato, exactly what do you mean by 'a good state'?" he would have a ready answer. He would say that a good state is one in which a good person can live a good life. And if you pressed him about what kind of person was a good person, he would acknowledge that here was a hard question, one needing examination. But he would at least be ready with an example. And by now you know who the example would be. It follows that Athens as it existed in 399 B.C. was not, despite its virtues, a good state, for it had executed Socrates.

To reach this goal of setting forth the pattern of a good state, Plato has to show that there is such a thing as goodness—and not just by convention. It couldn't be that if Athens *thought* it was a good thing to execute Socrates then it *was* a good thing to execute Socrates. Plato knew in his heart that was wrong. But now he has to *show* it was wrong.

_____

*His *Republic* is an attempt to define an ideal state. The *Laws*, perhaps his last work, is a long and detailed discussion trying to frame a realistic constitution for a state that might actually exist.

Mere assertion was never enough for Socrates, and it won't do for Plato, either. He will construct a *logos*, a *dialectic*, to show us the goodness that exists in *physis*, not just in the opinions of people or the conventions of society. And he will show us how we can come to know what this goodness is and become truly wise. These, at least, are his ambitions.

Knowledge and Opinion

People commonly contrast what they *know* with what they merely *believe*. This contrast between mere belief, or opinion, and knowledge is important for Plato. Indeed, he uses it to critique sophistic relativism and skepticism and to derive surprising conclusions—conclusions that make up the heart of his philosophy.

The Sophists argue that if someone thinks the wind is cold, then it is cold—for that person.* And they generalize this claim. "Of *all* things, the measure is man," asserts Protagoras. In effect, all we can have are opinions or beliefs. If a certain belief is satisfactory to a certain person, then no more can be said. We are thus restricted to appearance; knowledge of reality is beyond our powers.

Plato tries to meet this challenge in three steps. First, he has to clarify the distinction between opinion and knowledge. Second, he has to show that we do have knowledge. Third, he needs to explain the nature of the objects that we can be said to know. As we will see, Plato's **epistemology** (his theory of knowledge) and his **metaphysics** (his theory of reality) are knit together in his unique solution to these problems.

MAKING THE DISTINCTION

What is the difference between **knowing** something and just **believing** it? The key seems to be this: You can believe falsely, but you can't know falsely. Suppose that on Monday you claim to know that John is Kate's husband. On Friday, you learn that John is unmarried and has never been anyone's husband. What will you then say about your Monday self? Will you say, "Well, I used to know (on Monday) that John was married, but now I

_____

*See p. 62.

know he is not"? This would be saying, "I did know (falsely) that John was married, but now I know (truly) that he is not." Or will you say, "Well, on Monday I *thought* I knew that John was married, but I *didn't* know it after all"? Surely you will say the latter. If we claim to know something but then learn it is false, we retract our claim. We can put this in the form of a principle: Knowledge involves truth.

Believing or having opinions is quite the opposite. If on Monday you *believe* that John is married to Kate and you later find out he isn't, you won't retract the claim that you did believe that on Monday. You will simply say, "Yes, I did believe that; but now I believe (or know) it isn't so." It is quite possible to believe something false; it happens all the time. Believing does not necessarily involve truth.

We can, of course, believe truly. But even so, belief and knowledge are not the same thing. In the *Meno*, Plato has Socrates say,

> As long as they stay put, true beliefs too constitute a thing of beauty and do nothing but good. The problem is that they tend not to stay for long; they escape from the human soul and this reduces their value, unless they're anchored by working out the reason. . . . When true beliefs are anchored, they become pieces of knowledge and they become stable. That's why knowledge is more valuable than true belief, and the difference between the two is that knowledge has been anchored. (*Meno* 98a)[2]

In the *Republic*, Plato compares people who have only true opinions to blind people who yet follow the right road (*R* 506c).[3] Imagine a blind woman who wanders along, turning this way and that. It just happens that each of her turnings corresponds to a bend in the road, but her correct turnings are merely a lucky accident. By contrast, those who can see the road have a reason why they turn as they do, for they can see where the road bends. They know that they must turn left here precisely because they can give an account of why they turn as they do—namely, to stay on the road.

We can connect this contrast between true belief and knowledge with the practice of Socrates. It is his habit, as we have seen, to examine others about their beliefs. And we can now say that surviving such examination is a necessary condition for any belief to count as knowledge. It is only a

negative condition, however, because such survival doesn't guarantee truth; perhaps we simply have not yet come across the devastating counterexample. But Plato wants more than survival. In addition to surviving criticism, he wants to supply positive reasons for holding on to a belief. What he hopes to supply is a *logos* that gives *the reason why*.

We have here a second and a third point of distinction between knowledge and belief (even true belief). Knowledge, unlike (true) belief, "stays put" because it involves the reason why.

> And this leads to a final difference. In the *Timaeus*, Plato tells us that the one [knowledge] is implanted in us by instruction, the other [belief] by persuasion; . . . the one cannot be overcome by persuasion, but the other can. (*Timaeus* 51e)[4]

The instruction in question will be an explanation of the reason why. But what is persuasion? Plato seems to have in mind here all the tricks and techniques of rhetoric. If you *know* something, he is saying, you will understand why it is so. And that understanding will protect you from clever fellows (advertisers, politicians, public relations experts) who use their art to "make the weaker argument appear the stronger." Opinion or mere belief, by contrast, is at the mercy of every persuasive talker that comes along. If you believe something but don't clearly understand the reason why it is so, your belief will easily be "overcome" by persuasion. Compare yourself, for instance, to the blind woman on the the road. She might easily be persuaded to go straight ahead, for she lacks a reason for turning where she does.

As you can see, Plato draws a sharp line between opinion and knowledge. We can summarize the distinction in a table.

Opinion	*Knowledge*
is changeable	endures or stays put
may be true or false	is always true
is not backed up by reasons	is backed up by reasons
is the result of persuasion	is the result of instruction

So far even Sophists need not quarrel; they could agree that such a distinction can be made. But they would claim that all we ever have are opinions. We can perhaps understand what it would be to have knowledge, but it doesn't follow that we actually have any. So Plato has to move to his second task; he has to demonstrate that we actually know certain things.

WE DO KNOW CERTAIN TRUTHS

Plato's clearest examples are the truths of mathematics and geometry. Think back to the slave boy and the problem of doubling the area of a square.* The correct solution is to take the diagonal of the original square as a side of the square to be constructed. That solution can be seen to be correct because an "account" or explanation can be given: the reason why. Now look at the following diagram.

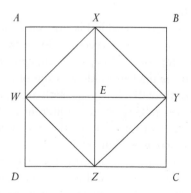

The reason why the square *WXYZ* is double the original square *WEZD* is that it is made up of four equal triangles, each of which is the same size as one-half the original. Because four halves make two wholes, we have a square twice the size of *WEZD*. This *logos* gives the reason why this is the correct solution. Once you (or the slave boy) understand this rationale, you cannot be persuaded to believe otherwise. What we have here, then, is an opinion that is true, will stay put, is backed up by reason, and is the result of instruction. In other words, we have not just opinion—we have knowledge.

"Knowledge, in truth, is the great sun in the Firmament. Life and power are scattered with all its beams."

Daniel Webster (1782–1852)

This example (and innumerable others of the same kind can be constructed) is absolutely convincing to Plato. There can be no doubt, he thinks, that this solution is not just a matter of how it seems to one person or another. About these matters cultures do not differ.* There is no sense in which man is the "measure" of this truth. It is not conventional or up to us to decide; we *recognize* it. Relativism, at least as a general theory, is mistaken. Skepticism is wrong. We do have knowledge of the truth.

But two important questions are still unsettled. First, what exactly do we have knowledge about when we know that this is the correct solution to the problem? Socrates probably drew the squares in the sand. Are we to suppose that he drew so accurately that the square made on the diagonal was really twice the area of the original? Not likely. The truth the slave boy came to know, then, is not a truth about that sand drawing. What is it about, then? Here is a puzzle. And Plato's solution to this puzzle is the key to understanding his whole philosophy.

The second question is whether this kind of knowledge can be extended to values and morality.

---

*See p. 133.

*Compare Socrates on what the gods do not quarrel about (*Euthyphro* 7b,c).

Can we know that deception is unjust with the same certainty as that a square on the diagonal is twice the size of an original square? We address the first of these questions now and come back to the second later.

---

1. What are Plato's goals? What does he aim to do?
2. Distinguish knowledge from opinion.

THE OBJECTS OF KNOWLEDGE

Plato would say that Socrates' sand drawing is not the object of the slave boy's knowledge. Let's make sure we see Plato's point here.

The slave boy's knowledge, being about something far more exact than Socrates' drawing, is not about that drawing, nor can it be derived from the drawing itself. In fact, we could never even know that any square we could draw or make or see or touch is exactly square. The senses (sight, hearing, and the rest) never get it right, Plato tells us; they are not clear or accurate. We grasp the truth only through reasoning—through a *logos*.

Here Plato agrees with Parmenides, who admonishes us not to trust our senses but to follow reasoning alone.* In this sense, Plato too is a rationalist. You should be able to see, from the example we have considered, why he thinks this is the only way to proceed if we want genuine knowledge.

You should also be able to see that Plato agrees with Heraclitus about the world revealed to us through the senses.† Consider the drawing of the square again. Suppose Socrates had drawn the two squares to exactly the right size. What is to prevent them, once drawn correctly, from turning incorrect in the very next moment? Suppose a breeze blows some sand out of place in one moment and back into place the next? It seems like a continual flux. And that is just what Heraclitus thinks it is. But our solution doesn't shift in and out of truth that way. It "stays put." Once again, the truth we know cannot be about

"So the philosopher, who consorts with what is divine and ordered, himself becomes godlike and ordered as far as a man can see...."

—PLATO

the world disclosed to our senses. Nothing in that world "stays put."

Interestingly, Plato holds that both Parmenides and Heraclitus are correct. They aren't in fact contradicting each other, even though one holds that reality is unchangeable and the other that reality is continually changing. Both are correct because each is talking about a different reality. The one is revealed to us through the senses, the other through reasoning. You are familiar with the reality of Heraclitus; it is just the everyday world we see, hear, smell, taste, and touch. The other world is not so ordinary, and we must say more about it.

We need to go back to the question, what is our truth about the square *true of*? If it is not about

---

*You might like to review briefly what Parmenides says; see p. 25.

†See p. 17–19.

any square you could see or touch, what then? Plato's answer is that it is a truth about the Square Itself. This is an object that can be apprehended only by the intellect, by thinking and reasoning. Still, it is an object, a reality; why should we suppose that the senses are our only avenue to what there is? It is, moreover, a public object, for you and I (and indeed anyone) can know the same truths about it. In fact, it is more public than sense objects. The square I see as red you may see as green, but everyone agrees that a square may be doubled by taking its diagonal as the base of another square.

Here is another feature of the Square Itself. It is not some particular square or other. It is not, for instance, one with an area of 4 rather than 6 or 10 or 19⅝. The doubling principle works for *any* square. So if our truth is a truth about the Square Itself, this must be a very unusual object! It must be an object that in some sense is *shared* by all the particular squares that ever have been or ever will be.

Here we are reminded of what Socrates is looking for. Remember that when Socrates questions Euthyphro, he isn't satisfied when presented with an *example* of piety. What he wants is something common to all pious actions, present in no impious actions, and which accounts for the fact that the pious actions are pious. He wants, he says, the "form" of piety.* Plato takes up the term **Form** and uses it as the general term for the objects of knowledge. In our example, what we know is something about the Form of the Square. We may use the terms "Form of the Square" and "the Square Itself" interchangeably. What we can know, then, are Forms (the Square Itself, the Triangle Itself) and how they are related to each other.

About the world of the senses, Plato tells us, no knowledge in the strict sense is possible. Here there are only opinions. Because the Square Itself does not fluctuate like visible and tangible squares, it can qualify as an object of knowledge.

Up to this point we have traced Plato's reasoning about the Forms on the basis of the assumption that we do have some knowledge. Let us recapitulate the major steps.

- Knowledge is enduring, true, rational belief based on instruction.
- We do have knowledge.
- This knowledge cannot be about the world revealed through the senses.
- It must be about another world, one that endures.
- This is the world of Forms.

Let us call this the **Epistemological Argument** for the Forms. Epistemology, you may recall, is the fancy term for the theory of knowledge—what knowledge is and what it is about.* And Plato has here concluded from a theory of what knowledge is that its objects must be realities quite different from those presented by the senses. These are realities that, like Parmenides' One, are eternal and unchanging, each one forever exactly what it is.

This very statement, however, reveals that Parmenides was not wholly right. For there is not just one Form. There is the Square Itself, the Triangle Itself, the Equal Itself, and, as we shall see, the Just Itself, the Good Itself, and the Form of the Beautiful as well. The reality that is eternal is not a blank One but an intricate, immensely complex pattern of Forms. This pattern is reflected partly in our mathematical knowledge. It is what mathematics is about.

This Epistemological Argument is one leg supporting the theory of Forms, but it is not the only one. Before we consider further the nature of Forms and their function in Plato's thought, let us look briefly at two more reasons why Plato believes in their reality.

In a late dialogue where Socrates is no longer the central figure, Plato has Parmenides say,

> I imagine your ground for believing in a single form in each case is this. When it seems to you that a number of things are large, there seems, I suppose, to be a certain single character which is the same when you look at them all; hence you think that largeness is a single thing. (*Parmenides* 132a)

---

*See *Euthyphro* 6d–e.

*See "A Word to Students."

Socrates agrees. What we might call the **Metaphysical Argument*** for the Forms goes like this. Consider two things that are alike. Perhaps they are both large or white or just. Think of two large elephants, Huey and Gertrude. They have a certain "character" in common. Each is large. Now, what they have in common (largeness) cannot be the same as either one; largeness is not the same as Huey and it is not the same as Gertrude. Nor is it identical with the two of them together, since their cousin Rumble is also large. What they share, then, must be a reality distinct from them. Let us call it the Large Itself. Alternatively, we could call it the Form of the Large.

This argument starts not from the nature of knowledge, but from the nature of *things*. That is why we can call it a "metaphysical" argument. A similarity among things indicates that they have something in common. What they have in common cannot be just another thing of the same sort as they are. Gertrude, for example, is not something that other pairs of things could share in the way they can share largeness; each of two other things can be large, but it is nonsense to suppose that each can be Gertrude. What Gertrude and Huey have in common must be something of another sort altogether. It is, Plato holds, a Form.

Finally, let us look at a **Semantic Argument** for the Forms. Semantics is a discipline that deals with words, in particular with the meanings of words and how words are related to what they are about. In the *Republic* we read that

> any given plurality of things which have a single name constitutes a specific type [Form]. (*R* 596a)

The interesting phrase here is "have a single name." What Plato has in mind here is the fact that we have names of several different kinds. The word "Gertrude" names a specific elephant. The word "elephant" is also a name, but it picks out every elephant that ever has been or ever will be. Why do we use a single name for all of those creatures? Because, Plato suggests, we are assuming that one Form is common to them all. Just as the name

"Gertrude" names some particular elephant, the name "elephant" names the Form Elephant—what all elephants have in common. Whenever we give the same name to a plurality of things, Plato tells us, it is legitimate to assume that we are naming a Form.

What we have in Plato's philosophy is a single answer to three problems that any philosophy striving for completeness must address. Let us summarize.

- *Problem One.* Assuming that we do have some knowledge, what is our knowledge about? What are the objects of knowledge? Plato's answer is that what we know are the Forms of things.
- *Problem Two.* The particular things that we are acquainted with can be grouped into kinds on the basis of what they have in common. How are we to explain these common features? Plato tells us that what they have in common is a Form.
- *Problem Three.* Some of our words apply not to particular things but to all things of a certain kind. How are we to understand the meaning of these general words? Plato's theory is that these general terms are themselves names and that what they name is not a particular sensible thing but a Form.

THE REALITY OF THE FORMS

We have, then, a number of lines of investigation—epistemological, metaphysical, and semantic—all of which seem to point in the same direction: In addition to the world of sense so familiar to us, there is another world, the world of Forms. The Forms are not anything we can smell, taste, touch, or see, but that is not to say they are unreal or imaginary. To suppose that they must be unreal if our senses do perceive them is just a prejudice; we could call it the Bias toward the Senses. But Plato believes he has already exposed this as a mere bias.*

Consider again the problem of doubling the size of a square. In the *Republic* Socrates imagines that he is questioning someone who only has opinion but thinks it is knowledge:

> "But can you tell us please, whether someone with knowledge knows something or nothing?" You'd better answer my questions for him.

---

*For an explanation of the term "metaphysics," see "A Word to Students."

*Here again Plato agrees with Parmenides. For Parmenides' critique of the senses, see pp. 23–25.

My answer will be that he knows something. . . .

Something real or something unreal?

Real. How could something unreal be known? (*R* 476e)

You can't know what *isn't*, Plato tells us, for the simple reason that in that case there isn't anything there to know. You can only know what *is*.* In other words, if you do know something, there must be something in reality for you to know. In the case of doubling the square, what you know concerns a set of Forms and their relations to each other. So there must be Forms; they cannot be merely unreal and imaginary.

There is a further and more radical conclusion. The Forms are not only real; they are also more real than anything you can see or hear or touch. What is Plato's argument for this surprising conclusion? The Forms, Plato argues, are more real than anything you can experience by means of your senses because, unlike sensible things, they are unchangeably what they are—forever. Even if every square thing ceased to exist, the Square Itself would remain. In comparison to the Forms, Helen and Gertrude—and just and pious actions, too—are only partly real. They have some reality; they are not nothing. But they are less real than the Forms, for they do not endure. For that reason we can have no knowledge of them, only opinion. They don't "stay put" long enough to be known. As Plato charmingly puts it, these things "mill around somewhere between unreality and perfect reality" (*R* 479d).

Plato thinks that in a sense there are two worlds. There is the world of the Forms, which can be known, but only by reasoning, by the intellect. This is the most real world. And there is the world of the many particular, ever-changing things that make up the flux of our lives. These can be sensed; about them we may have opinions, but they cannot

be known. This world is real, but less real than the world of the Forms.

If we grant that Plato is right to this point (and let us grant it provisionally), we now must insist on an answer to a further question: How are the two worlds related? With this question we arrive at the most interesting part of Plato's answer to sophistic skepticism and relativism.

---

1. In what way does Plato agree with Parmenides? With Heraclitus?
2. Be sure you can sketch the three lines of argument for the reality of the Forms: epistemological, metaphysical, and semantic.
3. If the objects of knowledge are the Forms, what are the objects of opinion?
4. Why does Plato think the Form of Bicycle is *more real* than the bicycle I ride to work?

The World and the Forms

If Plato is right, reality is not what it seems to be. What we usually take as reality is only partly real; reality itself is quite different. For convenience's sake, let us use the term "the world" to refer to this flux of things about us that appear to our senses: rivers, trees, desks, elephants, men and women, runnings, promisings, sleepings, customs, laws, and so on. This corresponds closely enough to the usual use of that term; however, the world must now be understood as less than the whole of reality and none of it entirely real. We can then put Plato's point in this way: In addition to the world, there are also the Forms, and they are what is truly real. This much, he would add, we already know. For we have given an account (a *logos*) of the reason why we must believe in the reality of the Forms.

HOW FORMS ARE RELATED TO THE WORLD

We must now examine the relationship between the two realities. Let us begin by thinking about shadows. We could equally well consider photographs, mirror images, and reflections in a pool of water.

---

*This is a narrower version of the Parmenidean principle that thought and being always go together (see p. 24). Plato accepts that *thought* might diverge from being, but the thought that meets the tests of *knowledge* will not. That is why we value it.

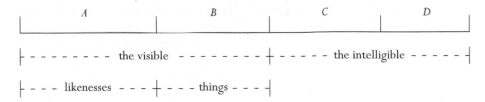

A shadow is in a certain sense less real than the thing that casts it. It is less real because it doesn't have any independent existence; its shape depends wholly on the thing that it is a shadow of (and of course the light source). Think about the shadow shapes you can make on a wall by positioning your hands in various ways in front of a strong lamp. Shaping your hands one way produces the shape of a rabbit; another way, an owl. What the shadow is depends on the shape of your hands. The shape of your hands does *not*, note well, depend on the shape of the shadow. If you turn off the lamp, your hands and their shape still exist, but the shadows vanish. This is the sense in which shadows are less real; your hands have an independent existence, but the shadows do not.

Both shadows and hands are parts of the world. So there are different degrees of reality *within* the world, too. Could we use the relationship between shadows and hands to illuminate the relationship between world and Forms? This is in fact what Plato does in a famous diagram called the **Divided Line.** Plato here calls the world **"the visible"** and the Forms **"the intelligible,"** according to how we are acquainted with them.

> Well, picture them as a line cut into two unequal sections and, following the same proportions, subdivide both the section of the visible realm and that of the intelligible realm. Now you can compare the sections in terms of clarity and unclarity. The first section in the visible realm consists of likenesses, by which I mean a number of things: shadows, reflections . . . and so on.
>
> And you should count the other section of the visible realm as consisting of the things whose likenesses are found in the first section: all the flora and fauna there are in the world, and every kind of artefact, too. (*R* 509e–510a)

Let us draw Plato's line, labeling as much of it as he has so far explained (p. 128).

It is important for the symbolism that the lengths of the various sections are *not equal*. These lengths are related to each other by a certain ratio or proportion: As B is related to A, and D to C, so is $(C + D)$ related to $(A + B)$. Plato intends this proportionality between the line segments to represent the fact that the intelligible world of the Forms is related to the entire visible world in exactly the same way as things within the visible world are related to their likenesses. (Note that the actual length of the sections is irrelevant. All that counts is how they are related to each other.)

Let's construct a more realistic example than shadows of hands. Imagine that we live at the bottom of a canyon. Our society has a very strong taboo against looking up, which has been handed down by our earliest ancestors from generation to generation. We do not look up to the rim of the canyon and the sky beyond. The sun shines down into the canyon during the middle part of each day, and we can see the shadows of the canyon walls move across the canyon floor from west to east. Eagles live high up in the canyon wall, but they never come down to the canyon floor, preferring to forage for their food in the richly supplied plains above. We have never seen an eagle, nor are we likely to.

We do see the shadows of eagles as they glide from one wall of the canyon to the other. Sometimes the eagles perch directly on the edge of the canyon wall and cast shadows of a very different shape, of many different shapes, in fact; sometimes they perch facing west, sometimes north, and so on. We do not know that these are eagle shadows, of course, for we are not acquainted with eagles. All we know are the shadows.

Could we have any reliable beliefs about eagles? We could. If we collected all the shadow shapes that we had seen, we could get a pretty good idea of what an eagle looks like and at least some idea of its behaviors. We might even get a kind of science of eagles on this basis; from certain shadows we might be able to make predictions about the shapes of others, and these predictions might often turn out to be true. The concept "eagle" would be merely a construct for us, of course; it would be equivalent to "that (whatever it is) which accounts for shadows of this sort." We would think of eagles as the things that explain such shadows, the things making the shadow-patterns intelligible. But we would never have any direct contact with eagles.

One day, an eagle is injured in a fight and comes fluttering helplessly down to the canyon floor. This has never happened before. We catch the injured bird and nurse it back to health. While we have it in our care, we examine it carefully. We come to realize that this is the creature responsible for the shadows we have been observing with interest all these generations. We already know a good bit about it, but now our concept of "eagle" is no longer just a construct. Now we have the *thing* in our sight, and we can see just what features of an eagle account for that shadow science we have constructed. We can say that this creature explains the shadows we were familiar with; it makes it intelligible that our experience of those shadows was what it was; now we understand why those shadows had just the shapes they did have and no others.

We can also say that this great bird is what produces these shadows; we now see that the shadows are caused by creatures like this; birds of this kind are responsible for the existence of those shadows. So we are attributing two kinds of relations between eagles themselves and their shadows, which we'll call the relations of **Making Intelligible** and of **Producing.**

Remember now that our example has been framed entirely within the sphere of the world, what Plato calls "the visible." So we have been discussing what falls only within the *A* and *B* portions of the Divided Line. Now we need to apply the relations between *A* and *B* to the relations between (*A* + *B*) and (*C* + *D*). In other words, we need now to talk about the relationship between the world and the Forms, between "the visible" and "the intelligible."

Let us return to our example. While we have the eagle in our care, we examine it carefully, take measurements and X rays, do behavioral testing, and come to understand the bird quite thoroughly. What do we learn? We learn a lot, of course, about this particular eagle (we have named him "Charlie"), but we are also learning about the *kind* of creature that produces and makes intelligible the shadows we have long observed. So we are learning about eagles in general. It is true that if we generalize from this one case only, we may make some mistakes. Charlie may in some respects not be a typical eagle, but we can ignore this complication for the moment.

If we are learning about eagles, not just about Charlie, then we could put it this way: We are getting acquainted with what makes an eagle an eagle (as opposed to an owl or an egret). This is very much like, we might reflect, coming to understand what makes pious actions pious. Socrates says that he wants to know not just which actions are pious, you remember, but what it is that *makes* them pious rather than impious. He wants to understand the Form of the Pious. So we can say that we are coming to know the Form of the Eagle. This Form is what explains or makes intelligible the fact that this particular bird is an eagle. We might go as far as to say that it is what makes Charlie an eagle; his having this Form rather than some other is responsible for the fact that Charlie is an eagle.

It may be that Charlie is not a perfect eagle. And further acquaintance with eagles would doubtless improve our understanding of what makes an eagle an eagle, of those characteristics that constitute "eaglehood." If we were to improve our understanding of the Eagle Itself, we might well reach the same conclusion we reached about squares: that no visible eagle is a perfect example of the type or Form. Still, any particular eagle must have the defining characteristics of the species; it must, Plato says, *participate* in the Form Eagle, or it wouldn't be an eagle at all.

What is this "participation" in a Form? We can now say that it is strictly analogous to the relationship between eagle shadows and actual eagles. Actual eagles participate in the Form Eagle in this sense: The Form makes the actual eagle intelligible and accounts for its existence as an eagle. So again there are two kinds of relationships, this time between the Form Eagle and particular eagles: the relationships of Making Intelligible and of Producing. The relationship on the Divided Line between $(A + B)$ and $(C + D)$ is indeed analogous to the relationship between A and B.

We should remind ourselves, too, that Forms have a kind of independence actual eagles lack. Should an ecological tragedy kill all the eagles in the world, the Form Eagle would not be affected. We might never again see an eagle, but we could still think about eagles; we could, for instance, regret their passing and recall what magnificent birds they were. The intelligible has this kind of superiority to the visible: it endures. And this, Plato would conclude, is a sign that the Form (the object of thought) is more real than those things (the objects of sight) that participate in it. In Forms we have the proper objects of knowledge, which must itself endure.

LOWER AND HIGHER FORMS

Let us return to the Divided Line. We need to note that the section of the Line representing the Forms is itself divided. There are, it seems, two kinds of Forms, just as there are two kinds of things in the visible world (likenesses and things). We need to understand why Plato thinks so and why he thinks this distinction is important.

He takes an example from mathematics to explain the leftward portion of the intelligible section of the line (C).

> I'm sure you're aware that practitioners of geometry, arithmetic, and so on take for granted things like numerical oddness and evenness, the geometrical figures, the three kinds of angle, and any other things of that sort which are relevant to a given subject. They act as if they know about these things, treat them as basic, and don't feel any further need to explain them either to themselves or to anyone else, on the grounds that there is nothing unclear about them. They make them the starting points for their investigations. (R 510c, d)

The important idea here is "taking for granted." When we thought about doubling the square, we took the ideas of Square, Triangle, Double, and Equal for granted. Operating in section C of the divided line, we used these Forms as "starting points" for thinking about the square Socrates drew in the sand.

Actually, the movements go like this: Beginning with the sand square, we hypothetically posit Forms to account for it. That is, we move *rightward* on the line from the visible to the intelligible. Then, taking these Forms for granted, we produce an explanation of the visible phenomenon. Explanation moves *leftward*. But we can now see that the Forms we posit as hypotheses—the Square, the Triangle, etc.—themselves need to be explained. And so we need to move rightward again, this time into the highest section of the line. Think about the Square again. The Square is *explained and produced* by Forms like Plane, Line, Straight, Angle, and Equal. (A square is a plane figure bounded by four equal straight lines joined by right angles.) In this kind of reasoning, reasoning that explains a Form, there is no reliance on sensory input. In moving to section D we move from Forms to more basic Forms based on intellect alone.

So the Forms in D make intelligible the Forms in C. Again, explanation goes right to left. But there must come a point where this pattern of explanation cannot be used anymore, where making intelligible can't operate by appealing to something still more basic. When you get to the end of the Divided Line, whatever is there will serve as the explanation for everything to the left of it. But that must be intelligible in itself.

Plato calls the construction of lower Forms "science." The scientist examines the actual things in the visible world (Charlie or the sand square) and posits explanations of them in terms of hypothetical Forms. Things that explain shadows are now treated by the scientist just as the shadows were—as likenesses of something still more real, to be explained by appeal to Forms. A Form loses its merely hypothetical character when it is explained in terms of higher Forms. We then understand why that Form must be as it is. And this purely conceptual process of moving from Forms to higher Forms, and eventually to the highest

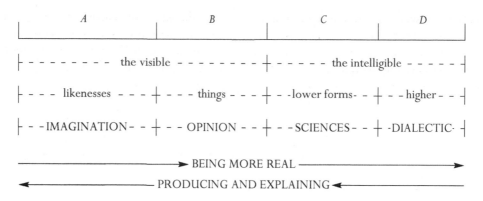

Form—the First Principle—Plato calls "dialectic" (see *R* 511b,c).*

Dialectic, then, is a purely intellectual discipline, no longer relying on the world of sense at all. It is a search for the ultimate presuppositions of all our hypothetical explanations and proceeds solely through awareness of Forms. If by such dialectical reasoning we should come to an ultimate presupposition, we will, Plato assures us, have discovered "the starting point for everything" (*R* 511b).

We obviously need to explore what Plato has to say about this Starting Point. But first let us amplify our understanding of the Divided Line (see the following chart) by adding some further characterizations. Notice the difference in labels given to the sections of the line on the second and third levels down. The second level characterizes reality in terms of what it is. These labels are *metaphysical* in nature. The third level (written in capital letters) characterizes reality in terms of how it is apprehended, so these labels have an *epistemological* flavor to them. (The first level is also epistemological, but less fine-grained than the third.) Here we see how intimately Plato's theory of knowledge is related to his theory of reality. We add two directional indicators to show that things get more real as you progress along the line from *A* to *D* and that items to the right are responsible for the existence of items to the left and explain them.

*Note that the term "dialectic" is used in a narrower sense here than that discussed in connection with Socratic question-and-answer method. For a comparison, see pp. 96–97.

The sciences, we can now say, are only stages on the way to true and final understanding. They are not yet "that place which, once reached, is traveller's rest and journey's end" (*R* 532e). The sciences do grasp reality to some extent; but because they do not themselves lead us to the Starting Point, Plato thinks scientists still live in a kind of dream world. "There's no chance of their having a conscious glimpse of reality as long as they refuse to disturb the things they take for granted and remain incapable of explaining them" (*R* 533c).

> It is for dialectic to give this reasoned account of first things. Its quest for certainty causes it to uproot the things it takes for granted in the course of its journey, which takes it towards an actual starting-point. When the mind's eye is literally buried deep in mud, far from home, dialectic gently extracts it and guides it upwards. (*R* 533c–d)

Let us note that dialectic, in leading us to the Starting Point, is supposed to give us certainty. This is very important to Plato; indeed, the quest for certainty is a crucial theme in most of Western philosophy. Why should Plato suppose that acquaintance with the Starting Point will be accompanied by certainty, by "traveller's rest and journey's end"? Because it is no longer hypothetical. The truth of the Starting Point need no longer be supported by principles beyond itself. It does not cry out for explanation; it does not beckon us on beyond itself. Its truth is evident. To see it—with "the mind's eye"—is to understand. Here we need no longer anxiously ask, "But is this really true?" Here we know we are not just dreaming. Here the soul can "rest."*

THE FORM OF THE GOOD

The examples we have considered recently—doubling the square, Charlie, and the Forms they participate in—are examples from mathematics and natural science. But we should not forget that there are other Forms as well: Piety, Morality, Beauty, and the Good. We'll soon explore the dialectic showing that the Form of Morality participates in the Form of the Good and say something about Beauty. But if we want to illuminate Plato's Starting Point, we shall have to look directly to the Form of the Good.

Let us begin by asking why Plato should think of Goodness Itself as that Form to which dialectic will lead us. As we consider this, we should remember that in moving higher and higher on the Divided Line we are always gaining clearer, less questionable explanations of why something is the way it is.

In the dialogue *Phaedo*, Plato relates a conversation that Socrates had with his friends on the day of his death. At one point Socrates says,

> When I was young . . . I was remarkably keen on the kind of wisdom known as natural science; it seemed to me splendid to know the reasons for each thing, why each thing comes to be, why it perishes, and why it exists. (*Phaedo* 96a)

He relates that he was unable to make much progress toward discovering those causes and became discouraged until hearing one day someone read from a book of Anaxagoras.† Socrates heard that Mind directs and is the cause of everything.

> Now this was a reason that pleased me; it seemed to me, somehow, to be a good thing that intelligence should be the reason for everything. And I thought that, if that's the case, then intelligence in ordering all things must order them and place each individual thing in the best way possible; so if anyone wanted

to find out the reason why each thing comes to be or perishes or exists, this is what he must find out about it: how is it best for that thing to exist, or to act or be acted upon in any way? (*Phaedo* 97c–d)

Socrates procured the books of Anaxagoras and read them eagerly. But he was disappointed. For when it came down to cases, Anaxagoras cited as causes the standard elements of Greek nature philosophy—air and water and such.

> In fact, he seemed to me to be in exactly the position of someone who said that all Socrates' actions were performed with his intelligence, and who then tried to give the reasons for each of my actions by saying, first, that the reason why I'm now sitting here is that my body consists of bones and sinews, and the bones are hard and separated from each other by joints, whereas the sinews, which can be tightened and relaxed, surround the bones, together with the flesh and the skin that holds them together; so that when the bones are turned in their sockets, the sinews by stretching and tensing enable me somehow to bend my limbs at this moment, and that's the reason why I'm sitting here bent this way. (*Phaedo* 98c–d)

Are these facts about his body the true explanation of why Socrates is sitting there in prison? It does not seem to Socrates to even be the right kind of explanation. These considerations do not even mention

> the true reasons: that Athenians judged it better to condemn me, and therefore I in my turn have judged it better to sit here, and thought it more just to stay behind and submit to such penalty as they may ordain. . . . Fancy being unable to distinguish two different things: the reason proper, and that without which the reason could never be a reason! (*Phaedo* 98e–99b)

Why is Socrates sitting in prison? The true explanation is that the Athenians decided it was better to condemn him and that Socrates has decided that not escaping was for the best. The behaviors of the various bodily parts are not irrelevant, but they are not the "true reason." They are just conditions necessary for that real reason to have its effect. We do not get a satisfactory explanation until we reach one that mentions what is *good*, or *better*, or *best*.

---

*Compare Heraclitus on how the many who do not recognize the *logos* live as though they were asleep, lost in a dream-world of their own making. See p. 20.

†A pre-Socratic nature philosopher. You may recall that Socrates mentions him in the speech at his trial: *Apology* 26d.

This suggests that explanations in which we can "rest" must be framed in terms of what is good. Because explanations proceed by citing Forms, the ultimate explanation of everything must be in terms of the **Form of the Good.** The Form of the Good, then, must play the part of the Starting Point. In the final analysis, to understand why anything is as it is, we must see that it is so because it participates in this Form, because it is good for it to be so.

That is why Plato thinks the Form of the Good is the Starting Point. But what is it? To call this Starting Point the Form of the Good is not very illuminating. It doesn't tell us any more than Socrates knows about the pious at the beginning of his examination of Euthyphro. Socrates knows that he is looking for the Form of the Pious, but he also knows that he doesn't know what that is. In just this sense, we might now ask Plato, "What is this Form which plays such a crucial role? Explain it to us."

At this point, Plato disappoints us; he tells us plainly that he cannot give such an explanation.* He says that "our knowledge of goodness is inadequate" (R 505a). When Socrates is pressed to discuss it, he says, "I'm afraid it'll be more than I can manage" (R 506d). But he does agree to describe "something which seems to me to be the child of goodness and to bear a very strong resemblance to it" (R 506e).

Consider sight, Plato suggests. What makes sight possible? Well, the eyes, for one thing. But eyes alone see nothing; there must also be the various colored objects to be seen. Even this is not enough, for eyes do not see colors in the dark. To eyes and objects we must add light. Where does light come from? From the sun. It is the sun, then, that is

> the child of goodness I was talking about. . . . It is a counterpart to its father, goodness. As goodness stands in the intelligible realm to intelligence and the things we know, so in the visible realm the sun stands to sight and the things we see. . . .

---

*This reticence on Plato's part contrasts dramatically with the confidence many have since displayed in giving us their accounts of what is good. These accounts, of course, do not all agree with one another.

What I'm saying is that it's goodness which gives the things we know their truth and makes it possible for people to have knowledge. It is responsible for knowledge and truth, and you should think of it as being within the intelligible realm, but you shouldn't identify it with knowledge and truth, otherwise you'll be wrong: for all their value, it is even more valuable. (R 508b–509a)

Knowledge, truth, and beauty are all good things. For Plato this means that they participate in the Form of the Good. This Form alone makes it intelligible that there should be such good things. You might ask in wonderment, why is there such a thing as knowledge at all? What accounts for that? If Plato is right here, you will not find a satisfactory answer to your question until you discover why it is for the best that knowledge should exist; and discovering that is equivalent to seeing its participation in the Form of Goodness Itself.

However, although knowledge is a good thing, Plato cautions us that it must not be thought of as identical with Goodness. The Form of the Good surpasses all the other Forms as well as the visible world in beauty and honor. If we think again about the Divided Line, we can now say that the Form of the Good is at the point farthest to the right of that Line, at the very end of section *D*. It makes intelligible everything to the left of it.

This ultimate Form not only makes everything else intelligible, but also is responsible for the very existence of everything else.

> I think you'll agree that the ability to be seen is not the only gift the sun gives to the things we see. It is also the source of their generation, growth, and nourishment. . . .
> And it isn't only the known-ness of the things we know which is conferred upon them by goodness, but also their reality and their being, although goodness isn't actually the state of being, but surpasses being in majesty and might. (R 509b)

Just as the is responsible for the world of sight, is actually its cause, so the Form of the Good is the cause of the reality of everything else; it both *produces* and *makes intelligible* everything that is.

Let us pause here and see what Plato takes himself to have accomplished. He has refuted the skeptics, he believes, by proving that we do have knowledge. He has unified Parmenides' and Heraclitus' conflicting views by showing that, while the sensory world is in constant flux, there is another world, the world of the Forms, that is eternal and unchanging. And he has refuted the atomists' view of the world as a purposeless, mechanical swirl of atoms amid the void by showing that the Forms transcend the material world and, through their participation in the Form of the Good, give the world purpose and value. Science, pursued to its basic presuppositions, reveals a world with a moral and religious dimension, albeit of a far more rationalistic kind than that depicted by Homer.

Coming to understand and appreciate all of this, however, is no easy feat, as Plato illustrates in his most famous story, the **Myth of the Cave.**

---

1. Draw Plato's Divided Line and explain what each of its parts represents. (Close the book, then try to draw and label it.)
2. What two relationships exist between a Form and some visible thing that "participates" in it?
3. What is the distinction Plato draws between "science" and "dialectic," and how does this relate to the distinction between hypotheses and first principles?
4. What is the argument that purports to show that the Starting Point—the rightmost point on the Divided Line—is the Form of the Good?
5. How do Plato's arguments up to this point help him achieve his aims?

The Love of Wisdom

There is a progress in the soul that corresponds to the degrees of reality in things. This idea is indicated in the various sections of the Divided Line. Contemplating the images of worldly things is analogous to the use of *imagination*; indeed, mental images are quite like shadows and mirror images in their dependence on things. About things and events in the world we can have probable beliefs or *opinions*. When we reason about them we are hypothesizing Forms; here is the domain of *science*. Finally, we reach *understanding* through the process of dialectic, which takes us upward to the highest Forms on which all the others depend.

We can think of this progress as progress toward **wisdom.**

What Wisdom Is

A wise person would understand everything in the light of the Forms, particularly the Form of the Good. To produce such wise individuals is the aim of education. Plato illustrates the progress toward wisdom in a dramatic myth told in the seventh book of the *Republic*. As you read it, keep the Divided Line and the analogy of the sun in mind.

"Imagine people living in a cavernous cell down under the ground; at the far end of the cave, a long way off, there's an entrance open to the outside world. They've been there since childhood, with their legs and necks tied up in a way which keeps them in one place and allows them to look only straight ahead, but not to turn their heads. There's firelight burning a long way further up the cave behind them, and up the slope between the fire and the prisoners there's a road, beside which you should imagine a low wall has been built—like the partition which conjurors place between themselves and their audience and above which they show their tricks."

"All right," he said.

"Imagine also that there are people on the other side of this wall who are carrying all sorts of artefacts, human statuettes, and animal models carved in stone and wood and all kinds of materials stick out over the wall; and as you'd expect, some of the people talk as they carry these objects along, while others are silent."

"This is a strange picture you're painting," he said, "with strange prisoners."

"They're no different from us," I said. "I mean, in the first place, do you think they'd see anything of themselves and one another except the shadows cast by the fire on to the cave wall directly opposite them?"

"Of course not," he said. "They're forced to spend their lives without moving their heads."

"And what about the objects which were being carried along? Won't they only see their shadows as well?"

"Naturally."

"Now, suppose they were able to talk to one another: don't you think they'd assume that their words applied to what they saw passing by in front of them?"

"They couldn't think otherwise."

"And what if sound echoed off the prison wall opposite them? When any of the passers-by spoke, don't you think they'd be bound to assume that the sound came from a passing shadow?"

"I'm absolutely certain of it," he said.

"All in all, then," I said, "the shadows of artefacts would constitute the only reality people in this situation would recognize."

"That's absolutely inevitable," he agreed.

"What do you think would happen, then," I asked, "if they were set free from their bonds and cured of their inanity? What would it be like if they found that happening to them? Imagine that one of them has been set free and is suddenly made to stand up, to turn his head and walk, and to look towards the firelight. It hurts him to do all this and he's too dazzled to be capable of making out the objects whose shadows he'd formerly been looking at. And suppose someone tells him that what he's been seeing all this time has no substance, and that he's now closer to reality and is seeing more accurately, because of the greater reality of the things in front of his eyes—what do you imagine his reaction would be? And what do you think he'd say if he were shown any of the passing objects and had to respond to being asked what it was? Don't you think he'd be bewildered, and would think that there was more reality in what he'd been seeing before than in what he was being shown now?"

"Far more," he said.

"And if he were forced to look at the actual firelight, don't you think it would hurt his eyes? Don't you think he'd turn away and run back to the things he could make out, and would take the truth of the matter to be that these things are clearer than what he was being shown?"

"Yes," he agreed.

"And imagine him being dragged forcibly away from there up the rough, steep slope," I went on, "without being released until he's been pulled out into the sunlight. Wouldn't this treatment cause him pain and distress? And once he's reached the sunlight, he wouldn't be able to see a single one of the things which are currently taken to be real, would he, because his eyes would be overwhelmed by the sun's beams?"

"No, he wouldn't," he answered, "not straight away."

"He wouldn't be able to see things up on the surface of the earth, I suppose, until he'd got used to his situation. At first, it would be shadows that he could most easily make out, then he'd move on to the reflections of people and so on in water, and later he'd be able to see the actual things themselves. Next he'd feast his eyes on the heavenly bodies and the heavens themselves, which would be easier at night: he'd look at the light of the stars and the moon, rather than at the sun and sunlight during the daytime."

"Of course."

"And at last, I imagine, he'd be able to discern and feast his eyes on the sun—not the displaced image of the sun in water or elsewhere, but the sun on its own, in its proper place."

"Yes, he'd inevitably come to that," he said.

"After that, he'd start to think about the sun and he'd deduce that it is the source of the seasons and the yearly cycle, that the whole of the visible realm is its domain, and that in a sense everything which he and his peers used to see is its responsibility."

"Yes, that would obviously be the next point he'd come to," he agreed.

"Now, if he recalled the cell where he'd originally lived and what passed for knowledge there and his former fellow prisoners, don't you think he'd feel happy about his own altered circumstances, and sorry for them?"

"Definitely."

"Suppose that the prisoners used to assign prestige and credit to one another, in the sense that they rewarded speed at recognizing the shadows as they passed, and the ability to remember which ones normally come earlier and later and at the same time as which other ones, and expertise at using this as a basis for guessing which ones would arrive next. Do you think our former prisoner would covet these honours and would envy the people who had status and power there, or would he much prefer, as Homer describes it, 'being a slave labouring for someone else—someone without property,' and would put up with anything at all, in fact, rather than share their beliefs and their life?"

"Yes, I think he'd go through anything rather than live that way," he said.

"Here's something else I'd like your opinion about," I said. "If he went back underground and sat down again in the same spot, wouldn't the sudden transition from the sunlight mean that his eyes would be overwhelmed by darkness?"

"Certainly."

"Now, the process of adjustment would be quite long this time, and suppose that before his eyes had settled down and while he wasn't seeing well, he had once again to compete against those same old prisoners at identifying those shadows. Wouldn't he make a fool of himself? Wouldn't they say that he'd come back from his upward journey with his eyes ruined, and that it wasn't even worth trying to go up there? And wouldn't they—if they could—grab hold of anyone who tried to set them free and take them up there, and kill him?"

"They certainly would," he said. (*R* 514a–517a)

Any such myth is subject to multiple interpretations. But let us see if we can, in light of what we know of Plato so far, identify the various stages of the ascent to wisdom. The people fettered in the cave, seeing only the shadows of things, are like those who gain their understanding of things from the poets, from Homer and Hesiod. Or, in our day, they are like those who get their impressions of the world by paying attention to the media— to movies, to the soaps, to headlines shared on social media. They see only images of reality— reflections, interpretations.

Those who climb up to the wall, on which are carried various items casting the shadows, are like those who can look directly on things in the visible world. The fire, I think, represents the physical sun, lighting up these perceptible realities so they can be apprehended. Looking on them directly reveals how fuzzy and indistinct the shadows of them on the wall actually were.

But to really understand these things it is necessary to climb higher, out of the cave altogether. This move is like the transition on the Divided Line between the visible world and the intelligible world; it is the transition from things to Forms. The sun outside the cave represents the Form of

The Divided Line

| | A | | B | | C | | D | |

the Good, just as it does in the **Analogy of the Sun.** First our adventurer can only see the lower Forms, reflections of the "Sun." But gradually, through dialectic, he can come to see the Form of the Good itself.

And what would happen if our adventurer returned to cave to tell the captives what he had seen? What would happen if someone who saw things as they really were and understood their participation in Goodness tried to tell those who had not ventured beyond the sensible world? Such a person would be mocked and maybe even killed. (Can there be any doubt that Plato is thinking of Socrates here?)

To love wisdom is to be motivated to leave the Cave. At each stage, Plato emphasizes how difficult, even painful, the struggle for enlightenment is. It is much easier, much more comfortable, to remain a prisoner in relative darkness and occupy oneself with what are, in reality, only shadows—content to be entertained by the passing show of images.

Indeed, the prisoners in the cave are not happy to hear that they suffer from an illusion. They are comfortable in the cave, enjoying its pleasures. What could motivate them to turn their souls toward reality and engage in a struggle that Plato warns is both difficult and dangerous? We need now to talk about the **love of wisdom.**

LOVE AND WISDOM

The theme of Plato's dialogue *Symposium*, from which Alcibiades' tribute to the character of Socrates was taken,* is love. After dinner each guest is obliged to make a speech in praise of love. When Socrates' turn comes, he protests that he cannot make such a flattering speech as the others have made, but he can, if they like, tell the truth about love.† They urge him to do so.

---

*Review pp. 93–95.

†This should remind you of the contrast Socrates draws between rhetoric and his own plain speaking at the very beginning of the *Apology*. About love, it must be noted that the Greeks had distinct words for several different kinds of love; in this their language was more discriminating than ours. The kind of love Socrates is here discussing is *eros*, from which our term "erotic" is drawn.

Socrates claims to have learned about love from a wise woman named **Diotima,** who instructed him by the same question-and-answer method he now uses on others.* We'll abbreviate the speech in which Socrates relates her instruction, keeping the question-and-answer mode. This very rich discussion of love is found in *Symposium* 198a–212b.

Q: Is love the love of something or not?

A: Of something.

Q: Does love long for what it loves?

A: Certainly.

Q: Is this something that love has, or something love lacks?

A: It must be what love lacks, for no one longs for what he or she has.

Q: What does love love?

A: Beauty.

Q: Then love must lack beauty?

A: Apparently so.

Q: Is love ugly, then?

A: Not necessarily. For just as opinion is a middle term between ignorance and knowledge, so love may be between beauty and ugliness.

Q: Is love a god?

A: No. For the gods lack nothing in the way of beauty or happiness. For that reason, the gods do not love beauty or happiness either. Nor do the gods love wisdom, for they are wise and do not lack it.

Q: What is love, then?

A: Midway between mortals and the gods, love is a spirit that connects the earthly and the heavenly. [Think of the world and the Forms.]

Q: What is the origin of love?

---

*Plato is known to have taught at least two women students, and he depicts two women as philosophers in his Socratic dialogues. Diotima is one of them. While the fact that no other mention of her survives from her own time has led some people to believe that she is a purely fictional character, other scholars argue that she was a historical person, like most of the other characters in Plato's dialogues. See Mary Ellen Waithe, "Diotima of Mantinea," in *A History of Women Philosophers*, vol. 1, ed. Mary Ellen Waithe (Dordrecht: Martinus Nijhoff, 1987), 83–116. On the role of women in ancient Greek philosophy, see Kathleen Wider, "Women Philosophers in the Ancient Greek World: Donning the Mantle," *Hypatia* 1, no. 1 (Spring 1986).

A: Love is the child of Need and Resourcefulness (the son of Craft). It is a combination of longing for what one does not have and ingenuity in seeking it.

Q: But what, more exactly, is it that love seeks?

A: Love seeks the beautiful. And the good.

Q: To what end?

A: To make them its own.

Q: And what will the lover gain by making the beautiful and the good his own?

A: Happiness.

Q: Does everyone seek happiness?

A: Of course.

Q: Then is everyone always in love?

A: Yes and no. We tend to give the name of love to only one sort of love. Actually, love "includes every kind of longing for happiness and the good." So those who long for the good in every field— business, athletics, philosophy—are also lovers.

Q: For how long does a lover want to possess that good that he or she longs for?

A: Certainly not for a limited time only. To think so would be equivalent to wanting to be happy for only a short time. So the lover must want the good to be his or hers forever.

Q: How could a mortal attain this?

A: By becoming immortal.

Q: So a mortal creature does all it can "to put on immortality"?

A: Evidently.

Q: Could this be why lovers are interested not just in beauty but in procreation by means of such beauty?

A: Yes. It is by breeding another individual as like itself as possible that mortal creatures like animals and humans attain as much of immortality as is possible for them. Such a creature cannot, like the gods, remain the same throughout eternity; it can only leave behind new life to fill the vacancy that is left in its species by its death.

Q: Is there any other way to approach immortality?

A: Yes, by attaining the "endless fame" that heroes and great benefactors of humankind attain. Think, for example, of Achilles and Homer and Solon.

Q: So some lovers beget children and raise a family, and others "bear things of the spirit . . . wisdom and all her sister virtues," especially those relevant to "the ordering of society, . . . justice and moderation"?

A: Yes. And the latter will be especially concerned to share these goods with friends and, with them, to educate each other in wisdom.

Q: Is there a natural progression of love?

A: Yes.

At this point, we need to hear Plato's words themselves. Diotima is speaking as if someone were to be initiated into a cult devoted to love.

> Well then, she began, the candidate for this initiation cannot, if his efforts are to be rewarded, begin too early to devote himself to the beauties of the body. First of all, if his preceptor instructs him as he should, he will fall in love with the beauty of one individual body, so that his passion may give life to noble discourse. Next he must consider how nearly related the beauty of any one body is to the beauty of any other, when he will see that if he is to devote himself to loveliness of form it will be absurd to deny that the beauty of each and every body is the same. Having reached this point, he must set himself to be the lover of every lovely body, and bring his passion for the one into due proportion by deeming it of little or of no importance.
>
> Next he must grasp that the beauties of the body are as nothing to the beauties of the soul, so that wherever he meets with spiritual loveliness, even in the husk of an unlovely body, he will find it beautiful enough to fall in love with and to cherish—and beautiful enough to quicken in his heart a longing for such discourse as tends toward the building of a noble nature. And from this he will be led to contemplate the beauty of laws and institutions. And when he discovers how nearly every kind of beauty is akin to every other he will conclude that the beauty of the body is not, after all, of so great moment.
>
> And next, his attention should be diverted from institutions to the sciences, so that he may know the beauty of every kind of knowledge. . . . And, turning his eyes toward the open sea of beauty, he will find in such contemplation the seed of the most fruitful discourse and the loftiest thought, and reap a golden harvest of philosophy, until, confirmed and strengthened, he will come upon one single form of knowledge, the knowledge of the beauty I am about to speak of.
>
> And here, she said, you must follow me as closely as you can.
>
> Whoever has been initiated so far in the mysteries of Love and has viewed all these aspects of the

beautiful in due succession, is at last drawing near the final revelation. And now, Socrates, there bursts upon him that wondrous vision which is the very soul of the beauty he has toiled so long for. It is an everlasting loveliness which neither comes nor goes, which neither flowers nor fades, for such beauty is the same on every hand, the same then as now, here as there, this way as that way, the same to every worshiper as it is to every other. (*Symposium* 210a–211a)

These are the steps, Plato tells us, that a resourceful lover takes. It is important to recognize that he sees these as making up a natural progression; there is nothing arbitrary about this series. In discussing these stages, let us remember that one can love in ways other than sexual. A lover, then, is someone who lacks that which will make him or her happy. What will make the lover happy is to possess the beautiful and the good—forever. For that the lover yearns. It is the lover's resourcefulness, propelled by longing, that moves the lover up the **ladder of love.** At each rung the lover is only partially satisfied and is therefore powerfully motivated to discover whether there might be something still more satisfying.

Being in the world, the lover naturally begins in the world. His or her first object is some beautiful body. But he or she will soon discover that the beauty in this body is not unique to that individual. It is shared by every beautiful body. What shall the lover do then? Although Plato does not say so explicitly, we might conjecture that at this point it is easy for the lover to go wrong by trying to possess each of these bodies in the same way as he or she longed to possess the first one—like Don Juan. We might think of it like this. Don Juan (with 1,003 "conquests" in Spain alone) has moved beyond the first stage of devotion to just one lovely body. He now tries to devote to many the same love that he devoted to the one. This is bound to be unsatisfying; if a single one does not satisfy, there is no reason to think that many will satisfy.

How does Plato describe the correct step at this point? The lover of "every lovely body" must "bring his passion for the one into due proportion by deeming it of little or of no importance." Rather than trying to multiply the same passion many times, the discovery of beauty in many bodies must

occasion what we might call a "sublimation" of the original passion. It must be transferred to a more appropriate kind of object. Indeed, it is at this point that the lover first becomes dimly aware of the Form of Beauty.* The resourcefulness of love makes it clear that only this sort of object is going to satisfy; only this sort of object endures.

The lover, moreover, discovers that a beautiful soul is even more lovely than a beautiful body, finding it so much more satisfying that he or she will "fall in love with" and "cherish" a beautiful soul even though it is found "in the husk of an unlovely body." (Could Plato here be thinking of the physical ugliness of Socrates?) The lover will then come to love *all* beautiful souls.

The next step is to "contemplate the beauty of laws and institutions." Presumably the transition from lovely individual souls to a pleasing social order is a small one. What explains the existence of lovely souls? They must have been well brought up. And that can happen only in a moderate, harmonious, and just social order. The beauty of a good state comes into view, and we move one more step away from the original passion for an individual beautiful body; when this stage is reached, the lover "concludes that beauty of the body is not, after all, of so great moment."

Once in the sphere of "spiritual loveliness," the lover comes to long for knowledge. Why? It is not difficult to see why if you keep the Divided Line in mind. What is it that makes intelligible and produces good social institutions? Surely they must be founded not on opinion, but on knowledge. Plato speaks movingly here of "the beauty of every kind of knowledge" and supposes that the lover—not yet satisfied—will explore all the sciences. Here the lover will find an "open sea of beauty," in contemplation of which he or she will be able to bring forth "the most fruitful discourse and the loftiest thought, and reap a golden harvest of philosophy."

---

*Recall the doctrine of learning by recollection (p. 134). The beautiful individual is the "occasion" for recollecting what the soul previously knew, Beauty Itself. Only by a prior acquaintance with this Form can the lover recognize the beloved as beautiful.

But even this is not the last stage. And we must note that Diotima cautions Socrates at this point to "follow . . . as closely as you can." The final stage, then, must be difficult to grasp. Indeed, those who have not attained it might well be unable to appreciate it fully. It is, in fact, a kind of mystical vision of the Form of Beauty Itself.* Note the rapturously emotional language Plato uses here. Presumably he is describing an experience that he himself had, one to which he ascribes a supreme value.

It is called a "wondrous vision," an "everlasting loveliness." Like all the Forms, the Form of Beauty is eternal. The religious character of the vision is indicated by the term "worshiper," which Plato applies to the lover who attains this "final revelation."

❧

> "Beauty crowds me till I die.
>   Beauty mercy have on me
> But if I expire today
>   Let it be in sight of thee—"
>   *Emily Dickinson (1830–1886)*

We began this discussion of love to find an answer to a question. Why, we wondered, would anyone be motivated to leave the Cave and make the difficult ascent to the sunlight, leaving behind the easy pleasures of worldly life? We now have Plato's answer. It is because we are all lovers.† We all want to be happy, to possess the beautiful and the good, forever. This is what we lack and long for. And to the extent of our resourcefulness, we will come to see that this passion cannot be satisfied by one beautiful body or even of many. We will be drawn out of the Cave toward the sun, toward the beautiful and the good in themselves, by the very nature of love. Plato is convinced that within each

of us there is motivation that, if followed, will lead us beyond shadows to the Forms.

In Plato's discussion of the love of wisdom we have an example of dialectic at work—the very dialectic that occupies the fourth section on the Divided Line. We see Plato exploring the nature of *eros*, teasing out of the Form of Love its intimate connections with the Forms of Knowledge and Beauty. In one sense we all know beauty when we see it. But if we truly understand *eros*, Plato tells us, we will see that its combination of need and resource must lead us beyond its immediate objects to the highest levels of intellectual activity and spirituality.

Wisdom, which for Plato is equivalent to seeing everything in the light of the Forms, particularly in the light of the highest Forms of Beauty and Goodness, is something we all need, lack, and want. Wisdom alone will satisfy. Only wisdom, where the soul actually participates in the eternality of the Forms, will in the end bring us as close to immortality as mortals can possibly get.

But this conclusion is not yet quite accurate. As stated, it assumes the Homeric picture of human beings as mortal through and through. This is not Plato's considered view, and we need now to inquire into his theory of the soul.

1. Relate the Myth of the Cave.
2. What is love (*eros*)?
3. Why would a lover of beauty ultimately seek wisdom?

The Soul

Plato thought about his central problems throughout a long life. And it is apparent, particularly in his doctrine of the **soul**, that his thought developed complexities unimagined early on. Scholars dispute whether Plato's later thought on this is in conflict with his earlier thought, but there is clearly at least a tension between the earlier and the later views. In this introductory treatment we will ignore these problems, presenting a picture of the soul that will be oversimplified and less than complete but true in essentials to Plato's views on the subject.[5]

---

*The language Plato uses to describe this experience is remarkably similar to the language of Christian mystics describing the "beatific vision" of God.

†Actually, this is not quite Plato's view. He thinks there are distinctly different sorts of people, and only some of them are lovers of wisdom. But we take here the more democratic view and give everyone the benefit of the doubt!

The Immortality of the Soul

At the end of his defense before the jury, Socrates concludes that "there is good hope that death is a blessing." He thinks one of two things must be true: Either death is a dreamless sleep, or we survive the death of the body and can converse with those who died before. But he does not try to decide between them.*

Plato offers arguments to demonstrate that the latter is the true possibility—that the soul is immortal. We find such an argument in the story of Socrates and the slave boy.† According to Socrates, the boy is able to recognize the truth when it is before him because he is remembering or recollecting what he was earlier acquainted with. But if that is so, then he—or rather his soul—must have existed before he was born and in such a state that he was familiar with the Forms. Similarly, in judging two numbers to be equal we are using a concept that we could not have gained from experience, for no two worldly things are ever exactly equal. Plato concludes that

> it must, surely, have been before we began to see and hear and use the other senses that we got knowledge of the equal itself, of what it is, if we were going to refer the equals from our sense-perceptions to it, supposing that all things are doing their best to be like it, but are inferior to it. (*Phaedo* 75b)

If we had knowledge of the Equal "before we began to see and hear and use the other senses," then we must have been acquainted with this Form before our birth.

We may have doubts about the adequacy of this argument for the preexistence of the soul; if we could give another explanation of how we come to know the truth or of how we develop ideal concepts such as "equal," it might be seriously undermined. But even if it were a sound argument, it would not yet prove that the soul is immortal. For even if our souls do antedate the beginnings of our bodies, it is still possible that they dissipate when our bodies do (or some time after). In that case, the soul would still be mortal.

---

*See *Apology* 40a–41c.
†In *Meno* 82b–86b.

Plato considers this possibility, but he has other arguments. Recall Socrates in his prison cell. Why is he there? As we have seen, it is not because his body has made certain movements rather than others—or at least this is a very superficial explanation. Socrates is still in prison because he has thought the matter through (with Crito) and as a result has decided not to escape.

Now Plato contrasts two kinds of things: those that move only when something else moves them and those that move themselves. To which class does the body belong? It must, Plato argues, belong to the first class; for a corpse is a body, but it doesn't move itself. The difference between living and nonliving bodies is that the former possess a principle of activity and motion within themselves. Such a principle of energy, capable of self-motion, is exactly what we call a soul. So a soul is essentially a self-mover, a source of activity and motion. It is because Socrates is "besouled," capable of moving himself, that he remains in prison. No explanation that does not involve Socrates' soul can be adequate. Therefore, his remaining in prison cannot be explained by talking only about his body, for the body is moved by something other than itself.

It is precisely because the body is not a self-mover that it can die. The body must be moved either by a soul or by some other body. But if the soul is a self-mover, if it is inherently a source of energy and life, if it does not depend on something outside itself to galvanize it into action—then the soul cannot die.

> All soul is immortal, for that which is ever in motion is immortal. But that which while imparting motion is itself moved by something else can cease to be in motion, and therefore can cease to live; it is only that which moves itself that never intermits its motion, inasmuch as it cannot abandon its own nature; moreover this self-mover is the source and first principle of motion for all other things that are moved. (*Phaedrus* 245c)

The argument seems to be that life—a principle of self-motion—is the very essence of the soul. Because nothing can "abandon its own nature," the soul cannot die.

If the soul is a source of energy distinct from the body, if it survives the body's decay, and if the soul is the essential self, then Socrates was right in not being dismayed at death. But Plato goes further. It must be the task of those who love wisdom to maximize this separation of soul from body even in this life. As we have seen, it is not through the body that we can come to know the reality of the Forms. The body confuses and distracts us. Only the intellect can lead us through the sciences, via dialectic, to our goal: the Beautiful and the Good. And intellect is a capacity of the soul.

It follows that those who seek to be wise should aim at

> the parting of the soul from the body as far as possible, and the habituating of it to assemble and gather itself together, away from every part of the body, alone by itself, and to live, so far as it can, both in the present and in the hereafter, released from the body, as from fetters. (*Phaedo* 67c–d)

If we understand by "the world" what we indicated previously, then it is accurate to say that Plato's philosophy contains a drive toward otherworldliness. Raphael was thus right to paint Plato pointing upward. Our true home is not in this world but in another. The love of wisdom, as he understands it, propels us out and away from the visible, the changeable, the bodily—out and away from the world. It is true that one who has climbed out of the Cave into the sunlight of the Forms may return to the darkness below, but only for the purpose of encouraging others to turn their souls, too, toward the eternal realities.

Yet this is not a philosophy of pure escape from the world. The otherworldly tendency is balanced by an emphasis on the practical, this-worldly usefulness of acquaintance with the Forms. To see this practical side of Plato at work, we must talk about the internal structure of the soul.

THE STRUCTURE OF THE SOUL

When a subject is both difficult and important, Plato often constructs an analogy or a myth. The analogy of the sun presented the Form of the Good. The struggle toward wisdom is the subject of the

Myth of the Cave. And to help us comprehend the soul, Plato tells the **Myth of the Charioteer.***

> As to soul's immortality then we have said enough, but as to its nature there is this that must be said. What manner of thing it is would be a long tale to tell, and most assuredly a god alone could tell it, but what it resembles, that a man might tell in briefer compass. Let this therefore be our manner of discourse. Let it be likened to the union of powers in a team of winged steeds and their winged charioteer. Now all the gods' steeds and all their charioteers are good, and of good stock, but with other beings it is not wholly so. With us men, in the first place, it is a pair of steeds that the charioteer controls; moreover, one of them is noble and good, and of good stock, while the other has the opposite character, and his stock is opposite. Hence the task of our charioteer is difficult and troublesome. (*Phaedrus* 246a–b)

We are presented with a picture of the soul in three parts, two of which contribute to the motion of the whole and one whose function is to guide the ensemble. The soul is not only internally complex, however; it is beset by internal conflict. The two horses are of very different sorts and struggle against each other to determine the direction the soul is to go. For this reason, "the task of our charioteer is difficult and troublesome."

In the *Republic*, Plato tells a story to illustrate one type of possible conflict in the soul.

> Leontius the son of Aglaeon was coming up from the Piraeus, outside the North Wall but close to it, when he saw some corpses with the public executioner standing near by. On the one hand, he experienced the desire to see them, but at the same time he felt disgust and averted his gaze. For a while, he struggled and kept his hands over his eyes, but finally he was overcome by the desire; he opened his eyes wide, ran up to the corpses, and said, "There you are, you wretches! What a lovely sight! I hope you feel satisfied!"
>
> Now what it suggests . . . is that it's possible for anger to be at odds with the desires, as if they were different things. (*R* 439e–440a)

This story also gives us a clue to further identification of the two horses in the Myth of the

---

*The image Plato uses here may well have been suggested by chariot racing in the Olympic games.

Charioteer. The ignoble, unruly steed is desire, or appetite. Leontius *wants* to look at the corpses. Though he struggles against it, he is finally "overcome by the desire."

This desire is opposed by what Plato calls the "spirited" part of the soul, which corresponds to the noble horse. When we call someone "animated" (in the sense this has in ordinary speech), we are calling attention to the predominance of "spirit" in that person. Children "are full of spirit from birth," Plato tells us. Spirit puts sparkle in the eyes and joy in the heart. Spirit makes us angry at injustice; it drives the athlete to victory and the soldier to battle. It is, Plato tells us, "an auxiliary of the rational part, unless it is corrupted by bad upbringing" (*R* 440e–441a).

The two horses, then, represent desire and spirit. What of the charioteer? Remember that the function of the charioteer is to guide the soul. What else could perform this guiding function, from Plato's point of view, but the rational part of the soul? Think of a desperately thirsty man in the desert. He sees a pool of water and approaches it with all the eagerness that deprivation can create. But when he reaches the pool, he sees a sign: "Danger: Do not drink. Polluted." He experiences conflict within. His *desire* urges him to drink. But *reason* tells him that such signs usually indicate the truth, that polluted water will make him very ill and may kill him, and that if he drinks he will probably be worse off than if he doesn't. He decides not to drink. In this case, it is the rational part of him that opposes his desire. His reason guides him away from the water and tries to enlist the help of spirit to make that decision effective.

Desire, spirit, and reason, then, make up the soul. Desire *motivates*, spirit *animates*, and reason *guides*. In the gods, these parts are in perfect harmony. The charioteer in a god's soul has no difficulty in guiding the chariot. In humans, though, there is often conflict, and the job of the rational charioteer is hard.*

---

*Recall the saying by Democritus, the atomist: "It is hard to fight with desire; but to overcome it is the mark of a rational man." See p. 33.

🔶

"Where id was, there shall ego be."
Sigmund Freud (1856–1939)

Plato supposes that any one of these parts may be dominant in a given person. This allows for a rough division of people into three sorts, according to what people take pleasure in:

> We found that one part is the intellectual part of a person, another is the passionate [spirited] part, and the third has so many manifestations that we couldn't give it a single label which applied to it and it alone, so we named it after its most prevalent and powerful aspect: we called it the desirous part, because of the intensity of our desires for food, drink, sex, and so on, and we also referred to it as the mercenary part, because desires of this kind invariably need money for their fulfilment. . . .
>
> Now, sometimes this intellectual part is the motivating aspect of one's mind; sometimes—as circumstances dictate—it's one of the other two. . . .
>
> Which is why we're also claiming that there are three basic human types—the philosophical, the competitive, and the avaricious. (*R* 580d–581c)

Plato uses the idea of three kinds of human beings in his plan for an ideal state, as we'll see. But first we need to examine his views on how the various parts of the soul *should* be related. This will allow us to see the practical use to which Plato thinks the Forms can be put.

---

1. What argument is offered for the soul's immortality?
2. Why does Plato advocate a separation of the soul and the body, even in life?
3. What are the parts of the soul? What are their functions?

Morality

Plato believes that he has met the challenge of skepticism. We do have knowledge; knowing how to double the square is only one example of innumerable other things we either know or can come to know. Relativism is also a mistake, he thinks; for the objects of such knowledge are public and available to all. It is by introducing the Forms that he has solved these problems. They are the public, enduring objects about which we can learn through reasoning and instruction. They are the realities that make intelligible all else and give even the fluctuating things of the world such stability as they do have.

We might not be satisfied yet, however. We might say, "That's all very well in the sphere of geometry and the like, but what about ethics and politics? Is there knowledge here, too?" And we might remind Plato of Socrates reminding Euthyphro that even the gods dispute with each other—not about numbers, lengths, and weights, but about "the just and the unjust, the beautiful and the ugly, the good and the bad" (*Euthyphro* 7d). If we are to meet the challenge of skepticism and relativism, we must do it in this sphere, too. Can we *know*, for instance, that justice is good rather than bad? Are there public objects in this sphere, too, about which rational persons can come to agreement? Or, in this aspect of human life, is custom "king of all"?* Is it true here, as the Sophists argue, that *nomos* rules entirely, that morality, for example, is merely conventional? Unless this challenge can be met, Plato has not succeeded. Skepticism and relativism, ruled out of the theoretical sphere, will reappear with renewed vigor in our practical life. And Plato will neither be able to prove that Athens was wrong to have executed Socrates nor be convincing about the structure of a good state.

Plato makes the problem of morality one of the main themes in the *Republic*. He is asking the Socratic question: What is morality? For Plato, this is equivalent to asking about the Form of Morality. The particular question is this: Is the **Form of the Moral** related to the Form of the Good? And if so, how? To put it in more familiar terms, is morality something good or not?† Remembering that

for Socrates the good is always some sort of *advantage*, we can ask: Will I be *better off* being moral than being immoral? Again Plato takes us up the Divided Line, this time with a dialectic designed to show us that the answer is yes, that being moral is indeed something good—and good by nature, not by convention.

As we have seen, Antiphon argues that conventional morality, which forbids deception, stealing, and breaking contracts, may not be in the interest of the individual. When it is not to his advantage, he says, there is nothing wrong with violating the conventional rules, following the law of self-preservation, and being (in the conventional sense) immoral. If you can deceive someone and get away with it when it is to your advantage, that is what you should do.

Plato always tries to present his opponents' views in a strong way, and in the *Republic* we find **Thrasymachus,** another Sophist, arguing the case. Because, he claims, the rules of morality are purely conventional and are made by those with the power to make them, it will seldom be to the advantage of an individual to be moral.* Thrasymachus addresses Socrates:

> In any and every situation, a moral person is worse off than an immoral one. Suppose, for instance, that they're doing some business together, which involves one of them entering into association with the other: by the time the association is dissolved, you'll never find the moral person up on the immoral one—he'll be worse off. Or again, in civic matters, if there's a tax on property, then a moral person pays more tax than an immoral one even when they're both equally well off; and if there's a hand-out, then the one gets nothing, while the other makes a lot. And when each of them holds political office, even if a moral person loses out financially in no other way, his personal affairs deteriorate through neglect, while his morality stops him making any profit from public funds, and moreover his family and friends fall out with him over his refusal to help them out in unfair ways; in all these

---

*Quoted by Herodotus from Pindar, after he tells the story of the Greeks and Indians before Darius (p. 63). Review the *nomos/physis* controversy that follows.

†This is Nietzsche's question, too. But unlike Plato, he answers no. See pp. 578–581.

---

*This principle is sometimes humorously called "The Golden Rule: He who has the gold, makes the rule." Another version of it is the principle that might makes right.

respects, however, an immoral person's experience is the opposite. . . .

So you see, Socrates, immorality—if practised on a large enough scale—has more power, licence, and authority than morality. (R 343d–344c)

From Thrasymachus' point of view, being moral is "sheer simplicity," whereas being immoral is "sound judgment" (R 348c–d). When the question is, "How anyone can live his life in the most rewarding manner?" (R 344e), Thrasymachus answers: Be immoral!

Now Plato accepts this as the right question, but he thinks Thrasymachus gives the wrong answer. Which life is the most worthwhile? Which kind of life is advantageous to the one who lives it? That is indeed the question. But how shall we answer it?

Here is a clue. As we saw in our discussion of love, everyone desires to be happy. No one doubts that what makes you truly happy (enduringly happy) is good. So it looks like **happiness** is one thing that everyone admits is good by nature (*physis*); it isn't just by convention (*nomos*) that we agree on that. This suggests a strategy that could counter the argument of Thrasymachus. If Plato could show that being moral is in your long-term interest because it is the only way to be truly happy, Thrasymachus would be defeated.

But is the moral person the happy person? That question is posed in a radical way by another participant in the dialogue of the *Republic*, **Glaucon,** who tells the following story. It is about an ancestor of **Gyges.**

He was a shepherd in the service of the Lydian ruler of the time, when a heavy rainstorm occurred and an earthquake cracked open the land to a certain extent, and a chasm appeared in the region where he was pasturing his flocks. He was fascinated by the sight, and went down into the chasm and saw there, as the story goes, among other artefacts, a bronze horse, which was hollow and had windows set in it; he stopped and looked in through the windows and saw a corpse inside, which seemed to be that of a giant. The corpse was naked, but had a golden ring on one finger; he took the ring off the finger and left. Now, the shepherds used to meet once a month to keep the king informed about his flocks, and our protagonist came to the meeting wearing the ring. He was sitting down among the others,

and happened to twist the ring's bezel in the direction of his body, towards the inner part of his hand. When he did this, he became invisible to his neighbours, and to his astonishment they talked about him as if he'd left. While he was fiddling about with the ring again, he turned the bezel outwards, and became visible. He thought about this and experimented to see if it was the ring which had this power; in this way he eventually found that turning the bezel inwards made him invisible, and turning it outwards made him visible. As soon as he realized this, he arranged to be one of the delegates to the king; once he was inside the palace, he seduced the king's wife and with her help assaulted and killed the king, and so took possession of the throne. (R 359d–360b)

Would you want a ring like this? How would you use it? You are invited to imagine a situation in which you could avoid any nasty consequences for behaving unjustly; all you have to do is use the ring. You could behave as badly as you like while invisible and no one could pin it on you. You would never be caught or punished. If you took a fancy to something, you could just take it. If you wanted to do something, nothing would prevent you. In a situation like this, what would be the best thing to do? What use of the ring would bring the greatest advantage?

On the one hand, if being moral is worthwhile only because of its consequences, then removing the consequences would diminish the worth of being a moral person; you might as well be unjust and satisfy your desires. On the other hand, if being moral is the true good, good in itself, then it would be better to refrain from unjust actions; it would be more advantageous not to steal, kill, or commit adultery, even if you could get away with it. Your life would be better being moral, even though you would have to do without some of the things that would please you.

Glaucon challenges Socrates to prove that being a moral person is something good in itself, not good just because it usually brings good consequences in its wake. He imagines two extreme cases:

Our immoral person must be a true expert. . . . [He] must get away with any crimes he undertakes in the proper fashion, if he is to be outstandingly immoral; getting caught must be taken to be a sign of incompetence, since the acme of immorality is to give an impression of morality while actually being immoral. So we must attribute consummate immorality to our consummate criminal, and . . . we should have him equipped with a colossal reputation for morality even though he is a colossal criminal. He should be capable of correcting any mistakes he makes. He must have the ability to argue plausibly, in case any of his crimes are ever found out, and to use force wherever necessary, by making use of his courage and strength and by drawing on his fund of friends and his financial resources.

Now that we've come up with this sketch of an immoral person, we must conceive of a moral person to stand beside him—someone who is straightforward and principled, and who . . . wants genuine goodness rather than merely an aura of goodness. So we must deprive him of any such aura, since if others think him moral, this reputation will gain him privileges and rewards, and it will become unclear whether it is morality or the rewards and privileges which might be motivating him to be what he is. We should strip him of everything except morality, then, and our portrait should be of someone in the opposite situation to the one we imagined before. I mean, even though he does no wrong at all, he must have a colossal reputation for immorality, so that his morality can be tested by seeing whether or not he is impervious to a bad reputation and its consequences; he must unswervingly follow his path until he dies—a saint with a lifelong reputation as a sinner. When they can both go no further in morality and immorality respectively, we can decide which of them is the happier. (R 361a–d)

Perhaps the just man languishes in prison, dirty, cold, and half-starved; all he has is justice. The unjust man, meanwhile, revels in luxuries and the admiration of all. The challenge is to show that the one who does right is, despite all, the happier of the two—the one who has the best life. If Plato can demonstrate this, he will have shown that morality, not immorality, participates in the Form of the Good. It is this bit of dialectic we now want to understand.

We should note at this point, however, that we have so far been discussing whether morality has the advantage over immorality without being very clear about the nature of morality. So we now have to address this Socratic question directly: What is it to be moral?

To answer this question, Plato draws on his description of the soul. As we have seen, there are three parts to the soul: reason, spirit, and appetite. Each has a characteristic function. In accord with its function, each has a peculiar excellence. Just as the function of a knife is to cut, the best knife is the one that cuts smoothly and easily; so the excellence of anything is the best performance of its function. What are the functions of the various parts of the soul?

The function of appetite or desire is to motivate a person. It is, if you like, the engine driving the whole mechanism forward. If you never *wanted* anything, it is doubtful that you would ever *do* anything. So appetite is performing its function and doing it well when it motivates you strongly to achievement.

Spirit's function is to animate life, so that it amounts to more than satisfying wants. Without spirit, life would perhaps go on, but it wouldn't be enjoyable; it might not even be worth living. Spirit is "doing its thing" if it puts sparkle into your life, determination into your actions, and courage into your heart. It supplies the pride and satisfaction that accompany the judgment that you have done well, and it is the source of indignation and anger when you judge that something has been done badly.

It is the task of the rational part of the soul to pursue wisdom and to make judgments backed by reasons. It performs this task with excellence when it judges in accord with knowledge. The rational part of the soul, then, works out by reasoning the best course of action. Its function is to guide or rule the other two parts. Desire, one could say, is blind; reason gives it sight. Spirit may be capricious; reason gives it sense.

Just as the body is in excellent shape when each of its parts is performing its function properly—heart, lungs, digestive system, muscles, nerves, and so on—so the whole soul is excellent when desire, spirit, and reason are all functioning well. The excellent human being is one who is strongly motivated, emotionally vivacious, and rational. Such a person, Plato believes, will also be happy.

For what is the source of unhappiness? Isn't it precisely a lack of harmony among the various parts of the soul? Desire wants what reason says it may not have. Spirit rejoices at what reason advises against. These are cases in which the parts of the soul are not content to perform their proper function. One wants to usurp the function of another. When, for example, you want what reason says is not good for you, it may be that your desire is so great that it overrides the advice given. In that case, desire takes over the guiding function that properly belongs to reason. But then you will do something unwise; and if it is unwise, you will suffer for it. And that is no way to be happy.

On the assumption that we all want to be happy and that being happy is what is good, the good life for human beings must be one in which each part of the soul performs its functions excellently—where reason makes the decisions, supported by spirit, and desire is channeled in appropriate directions. The good and happy person is the one who is internally harmonious. Though we do not all realize it, this internal harmony among the parts of the soul is what we all most want; for that is the only way to be happy.

But what does this have to do with morality? We can answer this question if we think again of an unharmonious soul. Suppose that desire, for instance, overrides reason. It wrongs reason, displacing it from its rightful place as a guide. It is not too much to say that it does reason an *injustice*. So there is a kind of justice and injustice in the individual soul, having to do with the way its parts relate to each other. Let us then speak of *justice in the soul*. In a just soul desire, spirit, and reason all do their thing without overreaching their proper bounds.

Given what we have just said about happiness, it is clear that justice in the soul correlates with happiness and injustice (internal conflict) with unhappiness. Insofar as we are internally just, we will be happy. Now happiness, we said, is something good by nature; everyone naturally desires to be happy. It follows that justice in the soul is also something good by nature. If we were wise, we would seek our happiness by trying to keep our souls harmonious, by promoting justice in the soul.

What Thrasymachus claims, of course, is not that injustice in the soul is a good thing but that our lives will be better if we are unjust in the community. He no doubt thinks that you can be internally happy and externally immoral. What Plato needs to

demonstrate is that this combination won't work, that there is a strict correlation between *justice in the soul* and *morality in the community*. Will the internally just person also be externally just? Will a just soul naturally express itself by keeping promises, refraining from stealing and deception, respecting the rights of others? That's the question. To put it another way, Will the person who behaves immorally in the community find it impossible to be just (and therefore happy) within herself?

Near the end of the *Republic* Plato has Socrates construct an imaginary model of the mind to address this question.

"Make a model, then, of a creature with a single—if varied and many-headed—form, arrayed all around with the heads of both wild and tame animals, and possessing the ability to change over to a different set of heads and to generate all these new bits from its own body."

"That would take some skilful modelling," he remarked, "but since words are a more plastic material than wax and so on, you may consider the model constructed."

"A lion and a man are the next two models to make, then. The first of the models, however, is to be by far the largest, and the second the second largest."

"That's an easier job," he said. "It's done."

"Now join the three of them together until they become one, as it were."

"All right," he said.

"And for the final coat, give them the external appearance of a single entity. Make them look like a person, so that anyone incapable of seeing what's inside, who can see only the external husk, will see a single creature, a human being."

"It's done," he said.

"Now, we'd better respond to the idea that this person gains from doing wrong, and loses from doing right, by pointing out to its proponent that this is tantamount to saying that we're rewarded if we indulge and strengthen the many-sided beast and the lion with all its aspects, but starve and weaken the man, until he's subject to the whims of the others, and can't promote familiarity and compatibility between the other two, but lets them bite each other, fight, and try to eat each other."

"Yes, that's undoubtedly what a supporter of immorality would have to say," he agreed.

"So the alternative position, that morality is profitable, is equivalent to saying that our words and behaviour should be designed to maximize the control the inner man has within us, and should enable him to secure the help of the leonine quality and then tend to the many-headed beast as a farmer tends to his crops—by nurturing and cultivating its tame aspects, and by stopping the wild ones growing. Then he can ensure that they're all compatible with one another, and with himself, and can look after them all equally, without favouritism."

"Yes, that's exactly what a supporter of morality has to say," he agreed. (R 588b–589b)

Plato uses this image to show the *identity* of the harmonious, internally just person and the moral person who does what is right. To do wrong to others is to allow the beast within to rule, to allow it to overwhelm the man within (who represents reason). But that means that the internal parts of the soul are no longer fulfilling their respective roles, but struggling for dominance. Harmony, and therefore happiness, is destroyed and the good is lost.*

The internally just person, in contrast, fostering the excellent functioning of each part of the soul in inner harmony, allows the man within to master the beast and tame the lion. The various parts are "compatible with one another." The external result of this inner harmony is a moral life, for the beast will not wildly demand what reason says it is not proper to want.

> Can there be any profit in the immoral acquisition of money, if this entails the enslavement of the best part of oneself to the worst part? . . . [And] do you think the reason for the traditional condemnation of licentiousness is the same—because it allows that fiend, that huge and many-faceted creature, greater freedom than it should have? . . .
>
> And aren't obstinacy and bad temper considered bad because they distend and invigorate our leonine . . . side to a disproportionate extent? . . .
>
> Whereas a spoilt, soft way of life is considered bad because it makes this part of us so slack and loose that it's incapable of facing hardship? (R 589da–590b)

---

*Compare this to Heraclitus' aphorism on p. 21, where he says that what impulse wants it buys "at the expense of the soul." Giving in to impulse is—in terms of Plato's image—feeding the beast. The beast grows strong at the expense of the lion and the man.

You can go through a list of the vices and show, Plato believes, that in each case they result from feeding the monster or from letting the lion run amok. The moral virtues, however, are exactly the opposite.

> "It is with our passions, as it is with fire and water, they are good servants but bad masters."
>
> *Aesop (620–560 B.C.)*

Here, then, is Plato's answer to Thrasymachus and to the challenge posed by Glaucon. The immoral man does not have the advantage after all. If we reason carefully about it, Plato says, we can see that it is more profitable to be moral because immorality entangles one's soul in disharmony. And disharmony in the soul is unhappiness. And a life of unhappiness is not the good life.

Justice in the soul, then, is correlated with a moral life. When each part of the soul is justly "doing its thing"—reason making the decisions, supported by the lion of the spirit and a domesticated appetite—a person's external actions will be morally acceptable actions. As we have seen, justice in the soul is happiness, and happiness is a natural good—good by *physis*, not just by *nomos*. So an attempt to understand the Form of Morality takes us necessarily to the Form of the Good. It is best to be moral, even though we suffer for it. And Plato can think he has given us a *logos* that supports Socrates' claim that it is worse to *do* injustice than to *suffer* it. Socrates believed this with full conviction; Plato thinks we can know it is true. The advantage lies with the moral person.

The argument is complex, but the heart of it is straightforward. Let us set down the key notions in this bit of dialectic.

1. Moral actions flow from a soul in harmony.
2. A harmonious soul is a happy soul.
3. Happiness is a natural good.
4. So morality is itself a natural good. (This follows from 1, 2, and 3.)
5. So acting morally is not good simply for its consequences, but is something good in itself.

Plato claims that by such dialectical reasoning we can have knowledge in the sphere of practice as well as in the theoretical sphere. Such dialectic, he believes, has defeated the skepticism and relativism of the Sophists and vindicated the practice of his master, who went around "doing nothing but persuading both young and old among you not to care for your body or your wealth in preference to or as strongly as for the best possible state of your soul" (*Apology* 30b).

---

1. What question does the Ring of Gyges story pose?
2. What is happiness? Unhappiness?
3. What is the psychology of the just person? Of the unjust person?
4. How is justice in the soul related to moral behavior in the community? Relate this to the image of the man, the lion, and the monster.

The State

We will not discuss Plato's views of the ideal state in any detail, but we must note several political implications of doctrines we have already canvassed. Like his views on the soul, his views on an ideal community developed throughout his lifetime, and his later thought manifests some deep changes in attitude and outlook. We will simplify by focusing on several famous doctrines of the middle-period *Republic*.

Plato sees a parallel between the internal structure of a soul and the structure of a community. Just as the parts of the soul have distinctive functions, individual men and women differ in their capacities and abilities. They can be grouped into three classes: (1) Some will be best fitted to be laborers, carpenters, stonemasons, merchants, or farmers; these can be thought of as the *productive* part of the community; they correspond to the part of the soul called "appetite." (2) Others, who are adventurous, strong, and brave, will be suited to serve in the army and navy; these form the *protective* part of the state, and they correspond to spirit in the soul. (3) The few who are intelligent, rational, self-controlled, and in love with wisdom will be suited to make decisions for the community; these are the *governing* part; their parallel in the soul is reason.

To this point, we have more or less been taking for granted that the search for wisdom is open to everyone. But this is not Plato's view. Like Socrates, Plato contrasts the few who know with the many who do not. A basic principle for Plato's ideal state is that there are only a few who are fit to rule. Obviously, Plato is consciously and explicitly rejecting the foundations of Athenian democracy as it existed in his day, where judges were selected by lot rather than by ability and where laws could be passed by a majority of the citizens who happened to show up in the Assembly on any given day. It is *not* the case, Plato urges, that everyone is equally fit to govern. Where democracy is the rule, rhetoric and persuasion carry the day, not reason and wisdom.

He is not in favor of tyranny or despotism, either; we can think of these as forms of government where the strong rule through power alone. Nor does he favor oligarchy, or rule by the wealthy. Who, then, are these "few" who are fit to be rulers? Consider again the harmonious, internally just soul. In such a soul, reason rules. So in the state,

> Unless communities have philosophers as kings, . . . or the people who are currently called kings and rulers practise philosophy with enough integrity . . . there can be no end to political troubles, . . . or even to human troubles in general, I'd say. (*R* 473c–d)

The **philosopher kings** will be those who love wisdom and are possessed of the ability to pursue it, those who have the ability to *know*. Because, as we have seen, knowledge is always knowledge of the Forms, philosopher kings will be those who have attained such knowledge, especially knowledge of the Forms of Justice and Morality and the Form of the Good. For how can one rule wisely unless one knows what is good for the community and what is right?

This is supported by an analogy, some form of which Plato uses again and again:

> Imagine the following situation on a fleet of ships, or on a single ship. The owner has the edge over everyone else on board by virtue of his size and strength, but he's rather deaf and short-sighted, and his knowledge of naval matters is just as limited. The sailors are wrangling with one another because each of them thinks that he ought to be the

captain, despite the fact that he's never learnt how, and can't name his teacher or specify the period of his apprenticeship. In any case, they all maintain that it isn't something that can be taught, and are ready to butcher anyone who says it is. They're for ever crowding closely around the owner, pleading with him and stopping at nothing to get him to entrust the rudder to them. Sometimes, if their pleas are unsuccessful, but others get the job, they kill those others or throw them off the ship, subdue their worthy owner by drugging him or getting him drunk or something, take control of the ship, help themselves to its cargo, and have the kind of drunken and indulgent voyage you'd expect from people like that. And that's not all: they think highly of anyone who contributes towards their gaining power by showing skill at winning over or subduing the owner, and describe him as an accomplished seaman, a true captain, a naval expert; but they criticize anyone different as useless. They completely fail to understand that any genuine sea-captain has to study the yearly cycle, the seasons, the heavens, the stars and winds, and everything relevant to the job, if he's to be properly equipped to hold a position of authority in a ship. . . . When this is what's happening on board ships, don't you think that the crew of ships in this state would think of any true captain as nothing but a windbag with his head in the clouds, of no use to them at all?

. . . I'm sure you don't need an analysis of the analogy to see that it's a metaphor for the attitude of society towards true philosophers. (*R* 488a–489a)

We need to make explicit something that Plato takes for granted here. This analogy assumes that there is a body of knowledge available to the statesman similar to that utilized by the navigator. It assumes that this can be taught and learned and that it involves some theory that can be applied by the skilled practitioner. Clearly, the knowledge of statecraft involves acquaintance with the Forms.

In a similar way, Plato compares the statesman to a doctor (*Gorgias* 463a–465e). We would never entrust the health of our bodies to just anybody. We rely on those who have been trained in that craft by skilled teachers. Furthermore, just as not everyone is by nature qualified to be a doctor, not everyone is fit to rule. Because the education

necessary to reach the higher level of the Forms is rigorous and demanding, only a few will be able to do it. And for that reason, government in the best state will be by the few: the few who are wise.

We still need, however, to ask about the many. If only the few will ever make it to wisdom, what are the many to do? If they cannot *know* the good, how can they be depended on to *do* the good? And if they do not do the good, won't the state fall apart in anarchy and chaos?

The state can be saved from this fate by the principle that, for purposes of action, right opinion is as effective as knowledge. If you merely believe that the cliff is directly ahead and as a result turn left, you will avoid falling over just as surely as if you knew that it was. The problem, then, is to ensure that the large majority has correct beliefs. They may not be able to follow the complicated dialectical reasoning demonstrating the goodness of morality, but they should be firmly persuaded that it pays to be moral.

Such right opinion is inculcated in the young by education, which is directed by the guardians or rulers, who know what is best. There are detailed discussions in the *Republic* about what sort of stories the young should be told and what sort of music should be allowed. Music and stories should both encourage the belief—which Plato thinks can be demonstrated dialectically to the few—that the best and happiest life is a life of moderation and rational self-control, a moral life.

There is in Plato's state, then, a distinct difference between the few and the many. The latter are brought up on a carefully censored educational regime; it would not be unfair to call the diet offered to the many propaganda, for it is persuasive rather than rational. The few, of course, are those who know what is best, for they have attained knowledge of the Forms. They arrange the education of the others so that they will attain as much goodness as they are capable of.

"But who is to guard the guards themselves?"

Juvenal (late first, early second century)

Those who find these antidemocratic consequences disturbing have reason to go back to their presuppositions. We will find subsequent philosophers raising serious questions both about the Forms and about Plato's view that some—but not all—of us are capable of knowing them.

---

1. Who should rule in the state? And why?
2. Explain the analogy of the navigator.
3. How will "the many" be "educated" in Plato's ideal republic?

Problems with the Forms

Plato offers a complete vision of reality, including an account of how knowledge is possible, an ethics that guides our practical lives, and a picture of an ideal community. As we have seen, all these aspects of reality involve the Forms. The Forms are the most real of all the things there are. They serve as the stable and enduring objects of our knowledge. They guide our goals, our behaviors, and our creative drives. And knowledge of them is the foundation for a good state.

But are there such realities? It is not only the political consequences that lead people to raise this question. It is raised in Plato's own school, and serious objections are explored—and not satisfactorily answered—by Plato himself in a late dialogue, the *Parmenides*. Here the leading character is made out to be Parmenides himself, the champion of the One, from whom Plato undoubtedly derives his inspiration in devising the doctrine of the eternal and unchanging Forms.

Parmenides examines the young Socrates:

I imagine your ground for believing in a single form in each case is this. When it seems to you that a number of things are large, there seems, I suppose, to be a certain single character which is the same when you look at them all; hence you think that largeness is a single thing.

True, he replied.

But now take largeness itself and the other things which are large. Suppose you look at all these in the same way in your mind's eye, will not yet another unity make its appearance—a largeness by virtue of which they all appear large?

So it would seem.

If so, a second form of largeness will present itself, over and above largeness itself and the things that share in it, and again, covering all these, yet another, which will make all of them large. So each of your forms will no longer be one, but an indefinite many. (*Parmenides* 131e–132b)

The argument begins with a statement we used before when the Forms were introduced.* But then an unacceptable conclusion is derived. Let us see if we can follow the argument.

Think again about Gertrude and Huey, the two elephants. Both are large. Let the small letters g and h represent Gertrude and Huey. Let the capital letter L represent the property they share of being large.† Then we have

$$Lg \qquad Lh$$

According to Plato's view of the Forms, this common feature means that Gertrude and Huey "participate" in a Form—the Large. Let's represent this Form by F. So we add the following to our diagram:

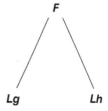

It is the Form F that *makes* the two elephants large and makes it intelligible that they are just what they are—that is, large.

Now Plato also regularly thinks of the Forms as *possessing* the very character that they engender in the particulars. Or, to put it the other way around, he says that individual things "copy" or "imitate" the Form. When writing about the Form of Beauty, for example, Plato says that it is in itself beautiful, that

---

*See p. 153.

†We here use a convention of modern logicians, for whom small letters symbolize individuals and large letters represent properties or features. The property symbols are written to the left of the individual symbols.

it exemplifies "the very soul of the beauty he has toiled for so long," that it possesses "an everlasting loveliness."* Particular individuals are beautiful just to the extent that they actually have that Beauty which belongs in preeminent fashion to the Form.

If that is right, then Largeness must itself be large. So we have to add this feature to our representation:

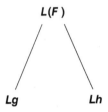

But now a problem stares us in the face: Now the Form and the two elephants all have something in common—Largeness. And according to the very principle Plato uses to generate the *F* in the first place, there will now have to be a *second F* to explain what the first *F* shares with the individuals! And that, of course, will also be Large. So we will have to put down:

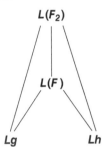

And now you can probably see how this is going to go. There will have to be a third *F*, a fourth, a fifth, and so on and on and on. We will no longer have just one Largeness, but two, three, four. . . . As Plato acknowledges through the character of Parmenides, each Form "will no longer be one, but an indefinite many." We are on the escalator of an *infinite regress*.

Moreover, at any stage of the regress what is real is supposed to depend on there already being a level above it, which explains the features at that stage. So this is what philosophers call a *vicious*

infinite regress. For any stage to exist, there must actually be an infinite number of stages in reality, on which its existence depends. We thought we were explaining something about Gertrude and Huey. But this explanation now dissipates itself in the requirement for a never-ending series of explanations—and all of exactly the same sort. This is bad news for Plato's theory of Forms.

Still further, this argument can be applied to any characteristic whatever. It is traditionally formulated in terms of the Form of Man. Heraclitus and Socrates are both men; so there must be a Form of Man to explain this similarity. If that Form is itself a man, you have a third man. In this guise the argument has a name. It is called the **Third Man Argument.**

The Forms are posited to explain the fact of knowledge, the meaning of general terms, and the common features of individuals.* But the Third Man Argument shows that—on principles accepted by Plato himself, at least in his middle period—the Forms do *not* explain what they are supposed to explain.

Like all such paradoxes, this indicates that something is wrong. But it does not itself tell us *what* is wrong. Some solution to the problem is needed. As we will see, Aristotle offers a solution.

---

1. Explain the threat posed to Plato's philosophy by the Third Man Argument.

FOR FURTHER THOUGHT

1. How persuaded are you by Plato's arguments for the reality of intelligible Forms? If you are not convinced, try to formulate your objections to these arguments in such a way that Plato would have to pay attention.
2. Consider someone you know whom you regard as an exceptionally good person. How much does this person resemble Plato's portrait of the just person? How is he or she different?

---

*See p. 167.

*Review pp. 153–154.

3. Would you characterize Plato's views about a good state as elitist or just realist? Justify your answer with a bit of dialectical reasoning.

KEY WORDS

epistemology	Myth of the Cave
metaphysics	wisdom
knowing	Analogy of the Sun
believing	love of wisdom
Form	Diotima
Epistemological Argument	ladder of love
	soul
Metaphysical Argument	Myth of the Charioteer
Semantic Argument	Form of the Moral
Divided Line	Thrasymachus
the visible	happiness
the intelligible	Glaucon
Making Intelligible	Gyges
Producing	philosopher kings
dialectic (Plato's)	Third Man Argument
Form of the Good	

NOTES

1. Quotations from Plato's *Phaedo*, trans. David Gallop (Oxford: Oxford University Press, 1993), are cited in the text by title and section numbers.

2. Plato, *Meno*, trans. Robin Waterfield, in *Meno and Other Dialogues* (Oxford: Oxford University Press, 2005).

3. Quotations from Plato's *Republic*, trans. Robin Waterfield (Oxford: Oxford University Press, 1993), are cited in the text using the abbreviation *R*. References are to section numbers.

4. Quotations from Plato's *Timaeus*, *Parmenides*, *Symposium*, and *Phaedrus*, in *The Collected Dialogues of Plato*, ed. E. Hamilton and H. Cairns (Princeton, NJ: Princeton University Press, 1961), are cited in the text by title and section numbers.

5. A discussion of these problems may be found in W. K. C. Guthrie, "Plato's Views on the Nature of the Soul," in *Plato II: A Collection of Critical Essays*, ed. Gregory Vlastos (Notre Dame, IN: University of Notre Dame Press, 1978), 230–243.

CHAPTER

9

ARISTOTLE

The Reality of the World

The year was 384 B.C. Socrates had been dead for fifteen years; Plato had begun his Academy three years earlier. In northern Thrace, not far from the border of what Athenians called civilization, a child was born to a physician in the royal court of Macedonia. This child, named Aristotle, was destined to become the second father of Western philosophy.

At the age of eighteen Aristotle went to Athens, where bright young men from all over desired to study, and enrolled in the Academy. He stayed there for twenty years, as a student, researcher, and teacher, until the death of Plato in 347 B.C. He then spent some time traveling around the Greek islands, studying what we would call marine biology. He returned briefly to Macedonia, where he tutored the young prince Alexander, later called "The Great" for completing his father's ambition of conquering and unifying the known world, including the Greek city-states.

By 335, Aristotle was back in Athens, where he founded a school of his own, the Lyceum. When Alexander died in 323, Aristotle fled—lest, he said, the Athenians "should sin twice against philosophy."[1] He died the following year at the age of sixty-three.

Aristotle and Plato

Let us begin by comparing Aristotle and his teacher, Plato.[2] First, Plato was born into an aristocratic family with a long history of participation in Athenian political life. Aristotle's father was a doctor in the Macedonian court. These backgrounds symbolize their different interests and outlook. The influence of Plato on Aristotle's thought is marked; still, Aristotle is a quite different person with distinct concerns, and his philosophy in some respects takes quite a different turn. That Aristotle's hand is stretched out horizontally in Raphael's painting symbolizes perfectly the contrast with Plato. Here are some comparisons.

In general, Plato tends toward otherworldliness in a way that Aristotle does not. Plato yearns to transcend the Heraclitean flux of the material world and reach the unchanging, eternal, genuinely real world of the Forms. To philosophize, for Plato, is to die away from sense and desire.

Aristotle regards the concrete particulars of the world as real and worthy of our attention, studying snails and octopuses alongside metaphysics and ethics. Philosophy, for Aristotle, offers not an escape from the world but an understanding of it.

Relatedly, Plato locates a person's true self in the soul, not the body, which is merely a temporary vessel for the soul to inhabit. Our souls possess knowledge of the Forms before we are born, and with determination, intelligence, and virtue, we can enjoy a blessed communion with the Forms after death. Aristotle's view of human beings is more complicated, though his main theme is simple. Man is a "rational animal," with a physical body that is an integral part of the self. Humans have a soul in some sense, for Aristotle, but the soul is not some ghostly entity that can exist separate from the body; it is, as we shall see, the "form" of the body. What we get in Aristotle is a (basically) this-worldly account of the soul.*

The two thinkers focus on different objects of knowledge. True knowledge, for Plato, is knowledge of the Forms, which can be attained only through reason—and, when you get far enough up the hierarchy of the Forms, through a somewhat mystical direct intellectual perception. This, perhaps, is why Plato offers us in crucial places his memorable myths and analogies to point us in a direction where we might be able to see for ourselves what language cannot describe. Aristotle, more down to earth, believes that language is capable of expressing the truth of things and that the senses, although not sufficient by themselves, are reliable avenues along which to pursue knowledge of the changing world about us.

Plato fixates on the Forms because they provide his solution to the problem of Protagorean relativism and skepticism. He is convinced that it was the Sophists who had really killed Socrates, not the particular members of the jury, for sophistic relativism had led the jurors to decide as they did. The Forms, the dialectic about morality, the subordination of everything else to the Form of the Good, and his outline of an ideal state offered a cure for this civic sickness. In a sense, refuting the Sophists is Plato's *one* problem, which drives everything else. To that problem Aristotle seems almost oblivious. Perhaps he believes Plato has succeeded, leaving him free to confront other problems. But there is probably more to it. As a biologist, he knows that not every opinion about crayfish, for example, is equally good, so he isn't overwhelmed by the arguments of the skeptics. The only problem, philosophically speaking, is to analyze the processes by which we attain knowledge of the world and to set out the basic features of the realities disclosed.

This difference carries over into the two thinkers' approaches to ethics. Plato wants and thinks we can, through knowledge of the Forms, get the same kind of certainty in rules of behavior that we have in mathematics.

Characteristically, Aristotle is less inclined to make such grandiose claims. In matters of practical

"It is those who act rightly who get the rewards and the good things in life."

—ARISTOTLE

---

*There is a complication here that should be noted. See the discussion of *nous* later in this chapter.

decision, he thinks, we are not likely to get the same certainty we can get in mathematics, but we can still discuss particular virtues and the conditions under which it is reasonable to hold people responsible for the exercise of these virtues, without ever appealing to the Form of the Good.

The Greek poet Archilochus had written in the seventh century,

> The fox knoweth many things, the hedgehog one great thing.[3]

Two quite different intellectual styles are exemplified by Plato and Aristotle. Plato is a man with one big problem, one passion, one concern; everything he touches is transformed by that concern. Aristotle has many smaller problems. These are not unrelated to each other, and there is a pattern in his treatment of them all. But he is interested in each for its own sake, not just in terms of how they relate to some grand scheme. Plato is a hedgehog. Aristotle is a fox.

It is easy to overdraw this contrast, however. There is an important respect in which Aristotle is a "Platonist" from beginning to end. Despite his interest in the changeable sensory world, Aristotle agrees with his teacher without qualification that knowledge—to be knowledge—must be certain and enduring. For both Plato and Aristotle, knowledge is knowledge of unchanging, eternal forms.* But they understand the forms differently—and thereon hangs the tale to come.

Logic and Knowledge

The Sophists' claim to teach their pupils "to make the weaker argument appear the stronger" has been satirized by Aristophanes, scorned by Socrates, and repudiated by Plato. But until Aristotle does his work in logic, no one gives a good answer to the question, Just what makes an argument weaker or stronger anyway? An answer to this question is essential for appraising the success of either the

Sophists or those who criticize them.* Unless you have clear criteria for discriminating weak from strong arguments, bad arguments from good, the whole dispute remains in the air. Are there standards by which we can divide arguments into good ones and bad ones? Aristotle answers this question.

He does not, of course, answer it once and for all—though for two thousand years many people will think he very nearly has. Since the revolution in logic of the past hundred years, we can now say that Aristotle's contribution is not the last word. But it is the first word, and his achievement remains a part of the much expanded science of logic today.

It is undoubtedly due in part to Aristotle's ability to produce criteria distinguishing sound arguments from unsound ones that he can take the sophistic challenge as lightly as he does. To Aristotle, the Sophists can be dismissed as the perpetrators of "sophisms," of bad arguments dressed up to look good. They are not such a threat as they seem, because their arguments can now be *shown* to be bad ones.

But it is not mainly as an unmasker of fraudulent reasoning that Aristotle values logic.† Aristotle thinks of logic as a *tool* to be used in every intellectual endeavor, allowing the construction of valid "accounts" and the criticism of invalid ones. As his universal intellectual tool, logic is of such importance that we need to understand at least the rudiments of Aristotle's treatment of the subject.

It will be useful, however, to work toward the logic from more general considerations. We need to think again about *wisdom*.

Aristotle begins the work we know as *Metaphysics* with these memorable words:

> All men by nature desire to have knowledge. An indication of this is the delight that we take in the senses; quite apart from the use that we make of them, we take delight in them for their own sake,

---

*Note that "form" is here uncapitalized. We will use the capitalized version, Form, only when referring to Plato's independent, eternal reality. For Aristotle's forms, an uncapitalized version of the word will do.

*Compare the later Mohists' work in logic and epistemology as a response to the sophistry of the School of Names in ancient China. See pp. 82–83.

†Aristotle does not himself use the term "logic," which is of a later origin. What we now call "logic" is termed by his successors the "organon," or "instrument" for attaining knowledge.

and more than of any other this is true of the sense of sight. . . . The reason for this is that, more than any other sense, it enables us to get to know things, and it reveals a number of differences between things. (*M* 1.1)[4]

This delight is characteristic even of the lower animals, Aristotle tells us, though their capacities for knowledge are more limited than ours. They are curious and take delight in the senses and in such knowledge as they are capable of. Some of the lower animals, though not all, seem to have *memory*, so that the deliverances of their senses are not immediately lost. Memory produces *experience*, in the sense that one can learn from experience. Some of the animals are quite good at learning from experience. Humans, however, are best of all at this; in humans, *universal judgments* can be framed in *language* on the basis of this experience. We not only see numerous black crows and remember them but also form the judgment that all crows are black and use this statement together with others to build up a knowledge of that species of bird.

We regard those among us as wisest, Aristotle says, who know not only that crows are black but also why they are so. Those who are wise, then, have knowledge of the *causes* of things, which allows them to use various arts for practical purposes (as the doctor is able to cure the sick because she knows the causes of their diseases). Knowing the causes, moreover, allows the wise person to teach others how and why things are the way they are.

Wisdom, then, either is or at least involves knowledge. And knowledge involves both *statements* (*that* something is so) and *reasons* (statements *why* something is so). Furthermore, for the possession of such statements to qualify as wisdom, they must be true. As Plato has pointed out, falsehoods cannot constitute knowledge.

Aristotle intends to clarify all this, to sort it out, put it in order, and show how it works. So he has to do several things. He has to (1) explain the nature of *statements*—how, for instance, they are put together out of simpler units called *terms*; (2) explain how statements can be *related* to each other so that some can give "the reason why" for others; and (3) give an account of what makes statements *true* or *false*. These tasks make up the logic.

TERMS AND STATEMENTS

When Aristotle discusses **terms,** the basic elements that combine to form **statements,** he is also discussing the world. In his view, the terms we use can be classified according to the kinds of things they pick out. He insists that things in the world can *be* in a number of different ways.* Correlated with the different kinds of things there are—or different ways things can be—are different kinds of terms. These kinds, called **categories,** are set out this way:

> Every uncombined term indicates substance or quantity or quality or relationship to something or place or time or posture or state or the doing of something or the undergoing of something. (*C* 4)

Aristotle gives some examples:

- substance—man or horse
- quantity—two feet long, three feet high
- quality—white or literate
- relationship—double, half, or greater
- place—in the Lyceum, in the marketplace
- time—yesterday or last year
- posture—reclining at table, sitting down
- state—having shoes on, being in armor
- doing something—cutting, burning
- undergoing something—being cut, being burned

He does not insist that this is a complete and correct list. But you can see that categories are very general concepts, expressing the various *ways* in which being is manifested. Such distinctions exist and must be observed.

> None of these terms is used on its own in any statement, but it is through their combination with one another that a statement comes into being. For every statement is held to be either true or false, whereas no uncombined term—such as "man," "white," "runs," or "conquers"—is either of these. (*C* 4)

Neither "black" nor "crow" is true or false. But "That crow is black" must be one or the other. Terms combine to make statements. For example,

---

*One of the mistakes made by Parmenides and others, he claims, is failing to recognize that being comes in kinds.

we might combine terms from the preceding list to make statements such as these:

- A man is in the Lyceum.
- A white horse was in the marketplace yesterday.
- That man reclining at a table was burning rubbish last year.

Terms can be combined in a wide variety of ways, but there are, Aristotle believes, certain standard and basic forms of combination to which all other combinations can be reduced. This means there are a limited number of basic forms that statements can take.

The clue to discovering these basic forms is noting that every statement is either true or false. Not every *sentence* we utter, of course, is either true or false. "Close the door, please" is neither. It may be appropriate or inappropriate, wise or foolish, but it isn't the right kind of thing to be true or false. It is not, Aristotle would say, a *statement*. Aristotle's own example is a prayer; it is, he says, "a sentence, but it is neither true nor false" (*I* 4).

Statements (the kinds of things that can be true or false) *state* something. And they state something *about* something. We can then analyze statements in two parts: there is the part indicating what we are talking about, and there is the part indicating what we are saying about it. Call the first part the *subject* and the second part the *predicate*. Every statement, Aristotle believes, can be formulated to display a pattern in which some term plays the role of subject and another term the role of predicate. It will be convenient to abbreviate these parts as *S* and *P*, respectively.

Not every term, however, can play both roles. This fact is of great importance for Aristotle, for it allows him to draw a fundamental distinction on which his whole view of reality is based.

> What is most properly, primarily, and most strictly spoken of as a substance is what is neither asserted of nor present in a subject—a particular man, for instance, or a particular horse. (*C* 5)

Look back to the list of terms on page 185. There is one kind of term that stands out from the rest: **substance.** Although there are several kinds of substance (as we shall see), the kind that is "properly, primarily, and most strictly" called substance

is distinguishable by the kind of role the term for it can play in statements—or rather, the kind of role it *cannot* play. Terms designating such substances can play the role only of subject, never of predicate. They can take only the *S* role in statements, not the *P* role.

Consider the term "Socrates." This term indicates one particular man, namely Socrates himself. And it cannot take the *P* place in a statement; we can say things about Socrates—that he is wise, or snub-nosed—but we cannot use the term "Socrates" to say something about a subject. We cannot, for example, say "Snub-nosed is Socrates," except as a poetic expression for "Socrates is snub-nosed." In both expressions, "Socrates" is in the *S* place and "is snub-nosed" is in the *P* position. In both, "is snub-nosed" is used to say something about Socrates. It is not *spatial* position in the sentence that counts, then, but what we could call *logical* position. In a similar way, it is clear that Socrates cannot be "present in" a subject, in the way the color blue can be present in the water of the Aegean Sea or knowledge of Spanish can be present in those who know the language.

Things *are*, Aristotle holds, in all these different ways. Some things have being as qualities, some as relations, some as places, and so on. But among all these, there is one *basic* way in which a thing can be: being an individual substance, a thing, such as Socrates. All the other ways of being are parasitic on this. They are all characteristics of these basic substances; our terms for them express things we can say *about* these primary substances. For example, we can say that Socrates is five feet tall (Quantity), that he is ugly (Quality), that he is twice as heavy as Crito (Relationship), that he is in prison (Place), and so on. But that about which we say all these things, of which they all are (or may be) true, is some particular individual. And that Aristotle calls **primary substance.**

> The reason why primary substances are said to be more fully substances than anything else is that they are subjects to everything else and that all other things are either asserted of them or are present in them. (*C* 5)

It is clear that Aristotle will reject the Platonic Forms. We shall explore what he says about the

Forms more fully later, but here he says that those things which are "more fully substances than anything else" are particular, individual entities such as this man, this horse, this tree, this snail. These are not shadows of more real things, as Plato held; they are the most real things there are. Everything else is real only in relation to them.

For now, however, we want to concentrate not on this metaphysical line of reasoning, but on the logical. Let us review. The wise person is the one who knows—both what is and why it is. Such knowledge is expressed in statements. Statements consist of terms put together in certain ways. All of them either are already or can be reformulated to be subject–predicate statements, in which something is said about something. And the ultimate subjects of statements are primary substances.

Before we leave this topic, we need to note a complication. We can say, "Socrates is a *man*." This conforms to our *S–P* pattern. But we can also say, "*Man* is an animal." This seems puzzling. How could "man" play the role of both *P* (in the first statement) and *S* (in the second)? If primary substances (individual things) are the ultimate subjects of predication, shouldn't we rule out "Man is an animal" as improper? Yet it is a common kind of thing to say; indeed, biology is chock full of such statements!

Aristotle solves this problem by distinguishing two senses of "substance."

> But people speak, too, of secondary substances, to which, as species, belong what are spoken of as the primary substances, and to which, as genera, the species themselves belong. For instance, a particular man belongs to the species "man," and the genus to which the species belongs is "animal." So it is these things, like "man" and "animal," that are spoken of as secondary substances. (*C* 5)

Individual humans, he notes, belong to a *species*: the species man. And each man, each human, is a kind of animal. So "animal" is a *genus*, under which there are many species: humans, lions, whales, and so on. In a sense, then, species and genera are substances, too. They are substances by virtue of expressing the essential nature of primary substances (the individual people, lions, whales). A genus or species, Aristotle holds, has no reality apart from the particular things that make it up, but we can

think of it as a derivative kind of substance about which we can say many interesting things. Terms for **secondary substances,** then, can also play the *S* role in a statement.

---

1. What is logic *for*?
2. What is a "category"? Give some examples.
3. What makes a statement different from a term?
4. What two roles can terms play in statements?
5. What distinguishes primary substance from all the other categories?
6. What kind of thing is *most real* for Aristotle? Contrast with Plato.

TRUTH

So far Aristotle has been dealing with issues of *meaning*. We turn now to what he has to say about **truth.** In one of the most elegant formulations in all philosophy, using only words any four-year-old can understand, Aristotle defines truth.

> To say that what is is not, or that what is not is, is false and to say that what is is, or that what is not is not, is true. (*M* 4.7)

Note that truth pertains to what we say. Grass is green. To say of it that it is green is to say something true about it. To say that it is not green— red or blue, perhaps—is to say something false. Contrariwise, Socrates was not beautiful. If we say that he was not beautiful, we speak truthfully, whereas if we say that he was beautiful, we speak falsely. Truth represents things as they are. Falsehood says of them that they are other than they are. This view of truth is not the only possible one.* We should, therefore, have a name for it. Let us call it the **correspondence** theory of truth, because it holds that a statement is true just when it "corresponds" to the reality it is about. We can also call it the classical view of truth.

---

*For other views of truth, see Hegel's claim that the truth is not to be found in isolated statements, but is only the *whole* of a completed system of knowledge ("Reason and Reality: The Theory of Idealism," in Chapter 21), and the pragmatist view that truth consists of all that a community of investigators would agree on if they inquired sufficiently long (Chapter 25, pp. 599–601).

❧

"Truth is truth to the end of reckoning."
William Shakespeare, Measure for Measure,
act 5, scene 1

Reasons Why: The Syllogism

We can now say that the wise person is able to make true statements about whatever subject she discusses. But she is able to do more than that; she is able to "give an account" of *why* what she says is true. In Aristotle's terminology, she is able to specify the *causes* of things.

With this we come to logic proper, the study of *reason-giving*. In saying why a certain statement is true, the wise person offers other statements. Will these constitute good reasons for what she claims to know or not? If she is truly wise, they presumably will; but to discover whether someone is wise, we may have to decide (1) whether what she says is true and (2) whether the reasons she offers for what she says actually support her claim. Giving a reason is giving an **argument:** offering premises for a conclusion. Perhaps it will be only a weak argument, perhaps a strong one. How can we tell? Aristotle insists that we cannot determine the strength of an argument based on how far it convinces us, or even most people. To Aristotle, the Sophist's reliance on persuasiveness as the key to goodness in argument must seem like Euthyphro's third answer to Socrates' questions about piety— that it gives at best a property of good arguments, not the essence of the matter. Aristotle is trying to find what it is about an argument that explains why people should—or should not—be convinced.

Remember that for Aristotle all statements have an *S–P* form; they say something about something. Such statements may either affirm that something is the case ("Grass is green") or deny it ("Socrates was not beautiful"). Call the former affirmative statements and the latter negative statements.

Moreover, *S–P* statements about secondary substances may be about every instance of a kind ("All whales are mammals") or only about *some* instances ("Some dogs are vicious"). The former statements can be called *universal*, because they predicate

something of each and every item talked about; each and every whale, for instance, is said to be a mammal. The latter statements can be called *particular*; our example does not say something about each and every dog, only about one or more dogs. These distinctions give us a fourfold classification of statements. It will be useful to draw a chart, with some examples of each.

	Affirmative	Negative
Universal	All men are mortal. (All *S* is *P*)	No men are mortal. (No *S* is *P*)
Particular	Some men are mortal. (Some *S* is *P*)	Some men are not mortal. (Some *S* is not *P*)

There are some interesting logical relationships among these statement forms. For example, a universal affirmative statement is the *contradictory* of a particular negative statement. To say that these are contradictories is to say that if either of them is true, the other must be false; and if either is false, the other must be true. (Look at the following chart and check whether this is so.) Universal negatives and particular affirmatives are likewise contradictories. The two statements at the top of the Square of Opposition (universal affirmative and negative) cannot be true together, but they can both be false. Analogously, the two statements at the bottom (particular affirmative and negative) can be true together, but they cannot both be false. For ease of reference, each of the statement forms is assigned a letter: *A, E, I,* or *O*.

Inferences in this square are called "immediate" inferences because they go from one statement directly or immediately to another. There are also "mediate" inferences, and to these we must now turn. Such inferences constitute arguments in which reasons are given to support a conclusion. For instance, suppose that someone claiming to be

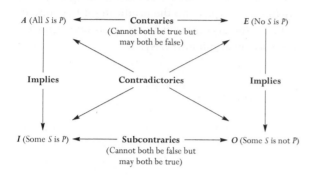

SQUARE OF OPPOSITION
(assuming at least one *S* exists)

A (All *S* is *P*) ◄——— **Contraries** ———► *E* (No *S* is *P*)
(Cannot both be true but
may both be false)

Implies **Contradictories** **Implies**

I (Some *S* is *P*) ◄——— **Subcontraries** ———► *O* (Some *S* is not *P*)
(Cannot both be false but
may both be true)

wise asserts, "All men are mortal." Remembering that wisdom includes not only knowing truths but also knowing their causes or reasons, we ask her why this is so. In response, she says, "Because all animals are mortal, and all men are animals." She has given us an argument.

All animals are mortal.
All men are animals.
Therefore: All men are mortal.

Aristotle calls this kind of argument a **syllogism.** Every syllogism is made up of three statements. In the three statements are three terms (here the terms are "man," "animal," and "mortal"), two terms in each statement. Two of the statements, called the **premises,** function as reasons for the third, called the **conclusion.**

Consider the terms that occur in the conclusion; each of these occurs also in just one of the premises. And the third term, which Aristotle calls the **middle term,** occurs once in each of the premises. It is the middle term that links the two terms in the conclusion. The fact that the middle term is related to each of the others in a certain specific way is supposed to be the *cause* or the *reason why* the conclusion is true.

One of Aristotle's greatest achievements is the realization that what makes a syllogism good or bad not only has nothing to do with its persuasiveness, but also has nothing to do with its subject matter. Its goodness or badness as a piece of reason-giving is completely independent of what it is about. It is not because it is about men and animals rather than gods and spirits that it either is or is not successful.

Its success is wholly a matter of its form.* In evaluating a syllogism, we might as well use letters of the alphabet in place of meaningful terms. In fact, this is what Aristotle does. How good an argument is, then, depends only on how terms are related to each other, not on what they are about.

We can represent the relevant structure or form of this example in the following way, using *S* for the subject of the conclusion, *P* for its predicate, and *M* for the middle term that is supposed to link these together.

All *M* is *P*.
All *S* is *M*.
Therefore: All *S* is *P*.

Remember, all that matters is how the terms are related to each other, not what the terms mean. If our original argument was a good one, any other argument that has this same form will also be a good one. What counts is form, not content.

But what is it for *any* argument to be good? Let us remind ourselves of the purpose of giving arguments in the first place. The point is to answer *why*. Any good argument, then, must satisfy two conditions: (1) The reasons offered (the premises) must be *true*; and (2) the *relation* between the premises and the conclusion must be such that *if* the premises are true, the conclusion can't possibly be false.† When an argument satisfies the second condition (if the premises are true, the conclusion *must* be true) it is **valid.** Note that an argument may have that part of logical goodness we call validity even though its premises are false. A poor argument fails to satisfy at least one of these conditions: Either (1) the premises are *not true* or (2) the relation between premises and conclusion is not such as to *guarantee* the truth of the conclusion when the premises are true.

---

*Form is here contrasted with content, or subject matter; it is not the Platonic contrast between the ultimate reality and the world of the senses.

† Note that we are talking about *deductive* arguments here. There are also *inductive* arguments, in which the tie between the premises and the conclusion is a looser one; the premises in an inductive argument give some reason to believe the conclusion, but they fall short of guaranteeing its truth.

Now we can ask, is the syllogism above a good argument? It should be obvious that it is. (Not all syllogisms are so obviously either bad or good; Aristotle uses obviously good ones like this as axioms to prove the goodness of less obvious ones.) If it is not obvious, it can easily be made so. Remembering that correctness is a matter of *form*, not content, let us take the terms as names for shapes. Then we can represent the argument in the following way:

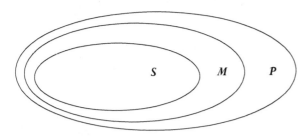

By looking at these shapes, we can now see that if all of *S* is included in *M*, and all of *M* is included in *P*, then all of *S* must be included in *P*. It couldn't be any other way. But that is exactly what a good argument is supposed to do: to show you that, given the truth of the premises, the conclusion must also be true. It gives you a reason why the conclusion is true. So this argument form is a valid one. Since our original argument (1) is an instance of this valid form and (2) has true premises, it is a good argument.

Let us consider another syllogism:

No sparrows are mammals.
No mammals are plants.
Therefore: No sparrows are plants.

Each of these statements is true. But is this a *valid* argument? Do the reasons offered *make true* the conclusion? No. It has this form:

No *S* is *M*.
No *M* is *P*.
Therefore: No *S* is *P*.

If that is a valid argument form, then any other argument having that form must be correct. This suggests a method of testing for goodness in arguments. Try to find another argument that has the same form as this one but that has true premises and a false conclusion. If you can, you have shown

that these reasons do *not* guarantee the truth of the conclusion. The middle term is not doing its job of linking the subject and the predicate of the conclusion. So the argument is not a good one. Can we find such an argument? Easy.

No Toyotas are Ferraris.
No Ferraris are inexpensive.
Therefore: No Toyotas are inexpensive.

You can see (check to be sure you do) that this argument has the same form as the argument about sparrows. But here, although the premises are both true, the conclusion is false. In a valid argument, however, the conclusion *must* be true if the premises are true. So this argument is not valid. The reasons offered do not give us the *reason why* the conclusion is true (since it *isn't* true). Since it is form that accounts for goodness in arguments, then if this argument is no good, neither is the one about sparrows—even though the conclusion in that example happens to be true. That is the problem; it just *happens* to be true; it is not true *because* the premises are true. So the argument doesn't do the job that arguments are supposed to do. It doesn't give the *reason why*.

On the basis of fairly simple examples such as these, Aristotle develops a complex system of logic. He tries to set out all the correct and all the incorrect forms of reasoning.* The result is a powerful tool both for testing arguments and for constructing arguments that tell us the cause or reason why things are as they are. In its latter use, logic is called *demonstration*. What can be demonstrated, we can know.

KNOWING FIRST PRINCIPLES

Can everything knowable be demonstrated? Can we give reasons for everything? Aristotle's answer is no:

For it is altogether impossible for there to be proofs of everything; if there were, one would go on to

---

*Aristotle is mistaken in thinking that syllogisms of this sort exhaust the forms of correct reasoning; we now know that there are many more correct forms. He also neglects, or gives an inadequate picture of, so-called inductive reasoning. But his achievement is impressive nonetheless.

infinity, so that even so one would end up without a proof. (*M* 4.4)

Giving a proof for a statement, as we have seen, means constructing a syllogism; that means finding premises from which the statement logically follows. But we can ask whether there is also a proof for these premises. If so, other syllogisms can be constructed with these premises as their conclusions. But then, what about the premises of these syllogisms? This kind of questioning, like the child's "why?" can go on indefinitely. And so we will continue to be unsatisfied about the truth of the statement we were originally seeking reasons to believe. But this means, as Aristotle says, that "it is impossible for there to be proofs for everything."

The chain of demonstrations must come to an end if we are to have knowledge. But where can it end? Socrates has an answer to this question.* If, as he thinks, our souls existed before we were born and had lived in the presence of the truth, then we might be able to "recollect" the truth when we were reminded of it, recognizing it immediately rather than learning it through demonstration. But Aristotle cannot use this Socratic solution. As we'll discover, he sees no reason to believe that our souls existed before we were born, nor does he think there are independently existing Forms we could have been acquainted with.

So Aristotle is faced with this problem: Since not everything can be known by demonstration, how do we come to know that which cannot be demonstrated? To avoid an infinite regression, we need starting points for our proofs.

> The starting point of demonstration is an immediate premise, which means that there is no other premise prior to it. (*PA* 1.2)

We can call these immediate premises **first principles.** Since all knowledge must rest on these starting points, we must be more certain of them than of anything else.

> Since we know and believe through the first, or ultimate, principles, we know them better and believe in them more, since it is only through them that we

know what is posterior to them. . . . This is because true, absolute knowledge cannot be shaken. (*PA* 1.2)

This means that we must be more certain about what makes something an animal than about what makes something a monkey; in geometry, we must know the definition of line with greater clarity than that of isosceles triangle.

But how are such principles to be known? We can't just start from nothing and—by a leap—get to knowledge. In this respect Socrates was right.

> All instruction and all learning through discussion proceed from what is known already. (*PA* 1.1)

This seems paradoxical. It is as though we were required to know *something* prior to our coming to know *anything*. But this is impossible.

The key to resolving the paradox, Aristotle holds, is the recognition that things may be "known" in several senses. What Aristotle does is to show how knowledge of these first principles *develops*. This is a characteristically Aristotelian tactic. Instead of saying that we either know or we don't know, Aristotle shows us how knowledge develops from implicit to more and more explicit forms. What is presupposed is not full-blown, explicit, and certain knowledge, but a series of stages, beginning in a *capacity* of a certain sort—namely, perceiving.

Aristotle agrees with Plato that perceiving something is not the same as knowing it. The object of perception is always an individual thing, but knowledge is of the universal; perception can be mistaken, but knowledge cannot. But these facts don't lead Aristotle, as they lead Plato, to disparage the senses, to cut them off from reality, and to install knowledge in another realm altogether. Perception is not knowledge, but it is where knowledge begins. (It is surely of crucial importance to note here that when Plato thinks of knowledge, his first thought is of mathematics; when Aristotle thinks of knowledge, his first thought is of biology.)

We noted earlier that some animals have memory in addition to their faculties of sense perception. Thus they can retain traces of what they perceive. These traces build up into what Aristotle calls "experience." And experience is the source of

---

*Discussed on pp. 133–134.

a *universal*, a sense of the unity of the many things encountered.

> Clearly it must be by induction that we acquire knowledge of the primary premises, because this is also the way in which sense-perception provides us with universals.[5]

How do we come to know the first principles, from which demonstrations may then proceed? By **induction,** Aristotle tells us. Imagine the biologist observing creatures in a tidal pool. At first, she can distinguish only a few kinds, those very different from each other. As she keeps watching closely, new differences (as well as new similarities) become apparent. She begins to group these creatures according to their similarities, bringing the Many under a variety of Ones. Then all these Ones are united under further universal principles, until finally all are classified under the One heading of "animals." "Is this like the one I saw a moment ago? Yes. So there is that kind; and that is different from this kind. Still, they are alike in a certain respect, so they may be species of the same genus." Eventually, the biologist comes to group the creatures according to characteristics they do and do not share with each other. Her perception provides her with "universals" under which she groups or organizes the various kinds of things that she has been observing.

These universals provide something like definitions of the natural kinds of things that exist. The wider one's experience of a certain field, the more firmly these inductive definitions are grounded. The first principles of any field are arrived at in this way. Thus we can come to know what a plant is, what an animal is, what a living being is. And these definitions can serve as the starting points, the ultimate principles of any science.

Not everything, as we have seen, can be known by demonstration. What cannot be demonstrated must be grasped some other way. That way is induction from sense perceptions. But what is there in us that is capable of such a grasp? On the one hand, it is clearly not the senses, or memory, or even experience. On the other hand, it is not our reasoning ability, for the capacity in question has nothing to do with proof. Aristotle uses a term for this capacity of ours that has no very adequate English counterpart: **nous.** It is sometimes translated as "mind" and sometimes as "intuition"; the English term "mind" seems too broad and "intuition" too vague. *Nous* is the name for that ability we have to grasp first principles by abstracting what is essential from many particular instances present to our senses.*

---

1. What is truth?
2. What is an argument? A syllogism? A middle term?
3. What is required in a good argument?
4. What is a first principle? Why are first principles needed? How are they known?
5. Do Aristotle's reflections on first principles do anything to resolve the puzzle about the slave boy and the preexistence of the soul? Explain.

The World

Aristotle discusses his predecessors often and in detail.† He believes that something can be learned from all of them and that by showing where they go wrong we can avoid their mistakes and take a better path. Such a dialectical examination of the older philosophers does not amount to knowledge, for it is neither demonstration of a truth nor insight into first principles. But it clears the ground for both and is therefore of considerable importance.

His fundamental conviction about the work of his predecessors is that they go wrong by not *observing* closely enough. With the possible exception of Socrates and some of the Sophists, they had all been searching for explanations that would make the world intelligible. But these explanations either are

---

*Do we really have such a faculty? Can we get certainty about premises from which the rest of our knowledge can be logically derived? Modern philosophy from the seventeenth century on will be preoccupied with these questions. What if we can't? Are we thrown back again into that sophistic skepticism and relativism from which both Plato and Aristotle thought us they had delivered us? See, for example, Montaigne, who thinks we are ("Skeptical Thoughts Revived," in Chapter 16), and Descartes, who is certain we are not (*Meditations*).

†In, for example, *Physics* I and *Metaphysics* I. The book you are now reading is itself an example of the Aristotelian conviction expressed in the next sentence.

excessively general (Thales' water, Anaximander's Boundless, and the rather different *logos* of Heraclitus) or seem to conclude that there is no intelligibility in the world at all (Parmenides condemns the world to the status of mere appearance, and Plato believes only the Forms are completely intelligible). Even Democritus, who was from a theoretical point of view superior to all but Plato, misses the intelligibility in the observable world and tries to find it in the unobservable atoms.

Aristotle, drawing on his own careful observations, is convinced that the things that make up the world have principles of intelligibility *within* them.* To explain their nature, their existence, and the changes they regularly undergo, it is necessary only to pay close attention to *them*. The world as it offers itself to our perception is not an unintelligible, chaotic flux from which we must flee to find knowledge. It is made up of things—the primary substances—that are ordered; the principles of their order are internal to them, and these principles, through perception, can be known.

NATURE

What Aristotle calls "**nature**" is narrower than what we have been calling "the world." Within the world there are two classes of things: *artifacts*, which are things made for various purposes by people (and by some animals), and *nature-facts*. There are beds, and there are boulders. These two classes differ in important respects. The basic science concerned with the world (what Aristotle calls "physics") deals with boulders, but only in a derivative sense with beds. Aristotle draws the distinction in the following way:

> Of the things that exist, some exist by nature, others through other causes. Those that exist by nature include animals and their parts, plants, and simple bodies like earth, fire, air, and water—for of these and suchlike things we do say that they exist by nature. All these obviously differ from things that have not come together by nature; for each of

them has in itself a source of movement and rest. This movement is in some cases movement from place to place, in others it takes the forms of growth and decay, in still others of qualitative change. But a bed or a garment or any other such kind of thing has no natural impulse for change—at least, not insofar as it belongs to its own peculiar category and is the product of art. (*PH* 2.1)

Of course, beds and garments change, too. But they change not because they are beds and garments but because they are made of natural things such as wood and wool. It is by virtue of being wood that the bedstead develops cracks and splinters, not by virtue of being a bedstead. The sword rusts not because it is a sword but because it is made of iron.

Nature, then, is distinguished from art and the products of art because it "has in itself a source of movement and rest." We should note that Aristotle understands "movement" here in a broad sense: there is (1) movement from place to place, also called local motion; (2) growth and decay; and (3) change in qualities. (We usually call only the first of these "movement.") Natural things, then, change in these ways because of what they are. An artifact like a bed may move from place to place, but only if someone moves it; it does not grow or decay; and any change in its qualities is due either to some external activity (someone paint his bed red) or to a property of the natural substance it is made of (the wood in the bedstead fades from dark to light brown). By contrast, a beaver moves about from place to place on its own, is born, matures, becomes wiser with age, and dies because this is the *nature* of beavers.

Nature, then, is the locus of change. Aristotle is convinced that if we observe closely enough, we can understand the principles governing these changes. Nature is composed of primary substances that are the *subjects* of change. They change in two ways: (1) they come into being and pass away again; (2) while in existence, they vary in quality, quantity, relation, place, and so on. About natural substances we can have knowledge. And because Aristotle agrees with his teacher Plato that knowledge is always knowledge of the real, it follows that nature is as real as anything could be!

---

*In this regard, Aristotle is carrying on the tradition begun by Thales but improving on it by making explanations more specific and detailed. See the discussion of Thales' remark, "All things are full of gods," p. 10.

THE FOUR "BECAUSES"

The wise person, as we have seen, knows not only what things are but also why. Aristotle sees that all his predecessors are asking why things are the way they are and giving these answers: because of water, because of the Boundless, because of opposition and the *logos*, because of atoms and the void, because of the Forms. What none of them sees is that this is not one question but four distinct questions.

> Some people regard the nature and substance of things that exist by nature as being in each case the proximate element inherent in the thing, this being itself unshaped; thus, the nature of a bed, for instance, would be wood, and that of a statue bronze. (*PH* 2.1)

People who think this way identify the substance of a thing—its nature—with the element or elements it is made of. Thales, for instance, thinks that the nature of all things is water; everything else is nonessential, just accidental ways in which the underlying substance happens, for a time, to be arranged. The underlying substratum, however, is eternal; that is the real stuff!

Those who think this way are taking the why-question in one very specific sense. They answer, "Because it is made of such and such stuff." Aristotle does not want to deny that this is one very proper answer to the why-question. Why is this statue what it is? Because it is made of bronze. The answer points to the *matter* from which it is made. Let us call this kind of answer to the why-question the **material cause.** Material causes, then, are one type of causation.

But citing a material cause does not give a complete answer to the why-question. That should be obvious enough; lots of bronze is not formed into statues. Consider some wood that has not been made into a bed. We could call such wood a "potential bed," but it is not yet a *bed*. It is the same, he says,

> with things that come together by nature; what is potentially flesh or bone does not yet have its own nature until it acquires the form that accords with the formula, by means of which we define flesh and bone; nor can it be said at this stage to exist by nature. So in another way, nature is the shape and

form of things that have a principle of movement in themselves—the form being only theoretically separable from the object in question. (*PH* 2.1)

Bone is what accords with "the formula" for bone—the definition that sets out the essential characteristics of bone. The elements of which bone is composed are not yet themselves bone; they are at best potential bone and may be formed into bone. In the case of bronze, there is no statue until it takes the shape of a statue. So here is another reason why a thing is the thing it is: It satisfies the requirements for being that sort of thing.

Aristotle here uses the term "form" both for the shape of something simple like a statue and for the definition of more complex things like bone. This is in accord with the usage for the term that comes down from Socrates and Plato. However, Aristotle adds this qualification: "the form being only theoretically separable from the object in question." He means that we can consider just the form of some substance independent of the material stuff that makes it up; but we must not suppose on that account that the form really is separable from the thing. Aristotle's forms are not Plato's Forms. The form of a thing is not an independent object, but just its-having-the-characteristics-that-make-it-the-thing-that-it-is.

So we can answer the why-question in a second way by citing the form. Why is this bit of stuff bone? Because it has the characteristics mentioned in the definition of bone. Aristotle calls this the **formal cause.**

But there must be something else, particularly in cases where a substance such as a mouse or a man comes into being. There is the material stuff out of which mice and men are made, and each has its proper form. But what explains the fact of their *coming to be?*

> Thus, the answer to the question "why?" is to be given by referring to the matter, to the essence, and to the proximate mover. In cases of coming-to-be it is mostly in this last way that people examine the causes; they ask what comes to be after what, what was the immediate thing that acted or was acted upon, and so on in order. (*PH 2.7*)

Here is a third answer to the why-question. This answer names whatever triggered the beginning of the thing in question, what Aristotle calls the "proximate mover." This sense of cause comes closest to our modern understanding of causes. For Aristotle, though, such causes are always themselves substances ("man generates man"), whereas for us causes tend to be conditions, events, or happenings. This cause is often called the **efficient cause.**

There is one more sense in which the why-question can be asked. We might be interested in the "what for" of something, particularly in the case of artifacts. Suppose we ask, "Why are there houses?" One answer is that cement and bricks and lumber and wallboard exist. Without them (or something analogous to them) there wouldn't be any houses. This answer cites the material cause. Another answer is that there are things that satisfy the definition for a house, an answer naming the formal cause. A third answer cites the fact that there are house builders—the efficient cause. But even if we had all these answers, we might want to know why there are houses in the sense of what purpose they serve, what ends they satisfy.

Why are there houses? To provide shelter from the elements for human beings. It is because they serve this purpose that they exist; the materials for houses might exist, but they would not have come together in the sort of form that makes a house a

house. When we answer the why-question in this way, Aristotle says we are giving the **final cause.***

> It is clear, then, that there are causes, and that they are as many in number as we say; for they correspond to the different ways in which we can answer the question "why?" The ultimate answer to that question can be reduced to saying what the thing is . . . or to saying what the first mover was . . . or to naming the purpose . . . or, in the case of things that come into being, to naming the matter. . . . Since there are these four causes, it is the business of the natural scientist to know about them all, and he will give his answer to the question "why?" in the manner of a natural scientist if he refers what he is being asked about to them all—to the matter, the form, the mover, and the purpose. (*PH 2.7*)

IS THERE PURPOSE IN NATURE?

The last "because" is the most controversial. We say there is a purpose for artifacts (houses, for example), but only because human beings have purposes. We need, want, desire shelter; so we form an intention to make shelters. We think, plan, and draw up a blueprint, then gather the materials together and assemble a house. But the crucial thing here is the intention—without that, no houses. To say that there are final causes in nature seems like imputing intentions to nature. We might be able to answer the question, What is a sheep dog for? because sheep dogs serve our purposes. But does it even make sense to ask what *dogs* are for?[6]

Yet Aristotle holds seriously that the question about final causes applies to nature-facts just as much as to artifacts. There may be some things that are accidental byproducts (two-headed calves and such), and they may not have a purpose. Such accidents, he says, occur merely from "necessity." But accidents apart, he thinks nature-facts are inherently purposive.

Aristotle does not think that there are *intentions* resident in all things; intentions are formed after deliberation, and only rational animals can deliberate. But that does not mean that nature in general

---

*Compare Socrates' answer to the question about why he is in prison, pp. 160–161.

is devoid of *purposes*, for the concept of purpose is broader than that of intention.

> Things that serve a purpose include everything that might have been done intentionally, and everything that proceeds from nature. When such things come to be accidentally, we say that they are as they are by chance. (*PH* 2.5)

But why couldn't everything in nature happen by chance, without purpose? This is what Democritus thinks the world is like—the accidental product of the necessary hooking up of atoms.* Why is that a mistake?

Aristotle has two arguments. (1) He draws on his close observations of nature to conclude that

> all natural objects either always or usually come into being in a given way, and that is not the case with anything that comes to be by chance. (*PH* 2.8)

Chance or accident makes sense only against a background of regularity, of what happens "either always or usually." Roses come from roses and not from grains of wheat; therefore, a rose coming from a rose is no accident. But since everything must occur either by chance or for a purpose, it must happen for some purpose. (2) Art (meaning something like the art of the physician or house builder) either completes nature or "imitates nature." But there is purpose in art, so there must be purpose in nature as well.†

TELEOLOGY

The idea that natural substances are *for* something is called **teleology,** from the Greek word *telos*, meaning end or goal. We can get a better feel for this by thinking about a concrete example. Consider a frog. Let it be a common leopard frog such as children like to catch by the lake in the summertime. We can consider the frog from two points of view: (1) at a given time we can examine a kind of cross section of its history, and (2) we can follow its development through time.

At the moment when he is caught by little Johnny, the frog has certain characteristics. Johnny might list them as spottedness, four-leggedness, and hoppiness. A biologist would give us a better list. This "what-it-is" the frog shares with all other frogs; it is what makes it a frog rather than a toad or a salamander. This is what Aristotle calls its form.

But of course it is one particular frog, the one Johnny caught this morning. It is not "frog in general" or "all the frog there is." What makes it the particular individual that it is? Surely it is the matter composing it; this frog is different from the one Sally caught, because even though they share the same form, each is made up of different bits of matter.

So in a cross section it is possible to distinguish form from matter. But now let us look at the history of the frog. Every frog develops from a fertilized egg into a tadpole and then into an adult frog. At each of these temporal stages, moreover, one can distinguish form and matter. The egg is matter that satisfies the definition for eggs; the tadpole has the form for tadpoles; the frog satisfies the formula for frogs. These stages are related in a regular, orderly way. As Aristotle puts it, this development is something that happens "always or usually." There is a determinate pattern in this history. And it is always the same.

In the egg, Aristotle will say, there is a potentiality to become a frog. It won't become a toad. It has, so to speak, a direction programmed into it. There is a goal or end *in* the egg, which is what determines the direction of development. The term for this indwelling of the goal is **entelechy.** The goal, or *telos*, is present in the egg. The goal (being a frog) is not present in actuality, of course—otherwise, the egg would not be an egg but already a frog. The egg has *actually* the form for an egg, but the form frog is there *potentially*. If it were not, Aristotle would say, the egg might turn into anything! (Note that the final cause toward which the egg and tadpole develop is itself a form; the goal is to actualize the form of a frog.)

This indwelling of the end, entelechy, is what Aristotle means by the purpose that is in natural things. Such things have purpose in the sense that there is a standard direction of development for them; they move toward an end. Earlier forms of a substance are already potentially what they will

---

*See pp. 30–31.

†Are these sound arguments? A key move in the development of modern science is their rejection. See pp. 355–356.

actually become only later. The tadpole is the potentiality of there being an actual frog. The frog is the actuality the tadpole tends toward.

Science, Aristotle says, can grasp not only the nature of static and eternal things, but also the natural laws of development. These laws are universals, too. Knowledge is always of the universal, of forms; in this Plato was right. But the forms are not outside the natural world; they are within it, guiding and making intelligible the changes that natural substances undergo either always or usually. The concepts of the four causes, plus actuality and potentiality, are the tools by which science can understand the natural world.

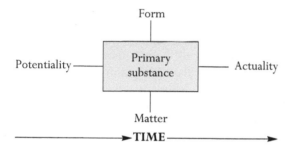

Once again we see a philosopher forging linguistic tools to make intelligible what seemed unintelligible to earlier thinkers. Parmenides, working only with concepts of being and not being, argued that change was impossible.* Aristotle uses the concepts of potentiality and actuality to discern universal laws governing orderly and intelligible change. Philosophy is argument and reason-giving. But it is also creation and invention, requiring the imagination to envision new conceptual possibilities.

---

1. How do nature-facts differ from artifacts? In what ways are they similar?
2. Explain each of the four causes.
3. How are Aristotle's forms both like and unlike Plato's Forms?
4. Describe how Aristotle uses the concepts of form/matter and actuality/potentiality to gain an understanding of the natural world, for example, of a frog.

---

*See p. 25.

First Philosophy

> It is from a feeling of wonder that men start now, and did start in the earliest times, to practice philosophy. (*M* 1.2)

Practicing philosophy, Aristotle makes clear, is not the basic activity of human beings. They must first see to the necessities of life, and only when these are reasonably secure will they have the leisure to pursue wisdom.

Whereas some kinds of knowledge have practical benefits, Aristotle believes that the pursuit of knowledge "for its own sake" is "more than human, since human nature is in many respects enslaved" (*M* 1.2). So much of our activity is devoted to the necessities of just staying alive that we are enslaved to the needs of our own nature. The knowledge that does nothing more than satisfy wonder, in contrast, is more than human because it would be free from this bondage. It is akin to the knowledge god would have. In our quest for such "divine" knowledge, we would have as our main concern those things that are "first" or "primary" or independent of everything else. We could call such a search **"first philosophy."**

Familiar as we are with the world of nature, we wonder now whether that is all there is.

> If there is no other substance apart from those that have come together by nature, natural science will be the first science. But if there is a substance that is immovable, the science that studies it is prior to natural science and is the first philosophy. . . . It is the business of this science to study being qua being, and to find out what it is and what are its attributes qua being. (*M* 6.1)

Biology, we might say, studies *being qua* (as) *living being*; or to put it another way, the biologist is interested in *what there is* just insofar as it is *alive*. There are many sciences, theoretical and practical, each of which cuts out a certain area of what there is—of being—for study. Each science brings its subject matter together under some unifying first principles. And this question must inevitably arise: Is there some still higher unity to what there is? Is being *one*? Is it unified by some principles that are true of it throughout?

If so, this too must be an area of knowledge, and the wise person's wonder will not be satisfied until it is canvassed and understood. This science would be concerned with the characteristics or attributes of being in an unqualified sense: of being qua being. If there is such a science, it is "first" in the sense that it would examine the principles taken for granted by all the special sciences. It would ask about the ultimate causes of all things. If, says Aristotle, natural substances are the only ones there are, then natural science will be this first science or philosophy. But if there are other substances—ones not subject to change—then the science that studies those will be first philosophy.* So first philosophy, also called **metaphysics,** looks for the ultimate principles and causes of all things. What are they?

Not Plato's Forms

Aristotle rejects Plato's answer to this question, which is that the Forms are the cause of all things. Not only are the Forms subject to the Third Man problem, but also they present many other difficulties.† Let us briefly explore some of them.

1. The things of this world are supposed to derive their reality from their "participation" in the Forms. But nowhere does Plato explain just what this "participation" amounts to. Without such an account, however, all we have are "empty phrases" and "poetic metaphors" (*M* 1.9).

2. The Forms are themselves supposed to be substantial realities—indeed, the most real of all the things there are. Aristotle comments,

> In seeking to find the causes of the things that are around us, they have introduced another lot of objects equal in number to them. It is as if someone who wanted to count thought that he would not be able to do so while the objects in question were

relatively few, and then proceeded to do so when he had made them more numerous. (*M* 1.9)

To say that the Form Human is the cause of humans is simply to multiply the entities needing explanation. If it is difficult to explain the existence and nature of human beings, it is certainly no easier to explain the existence and nature of humans-plus-the-Form-Human.

3. The Forms are supposed to be what many individuals of the same kind have in common. Yet they are also supposed to be individual realities in their own right. But, says Aristotle, these requirements conflict. If, on the one hand, the Forms are indeed individual substances, it makes no sense to think of them being shared out among other individual substances.* If, on the other hand, they are universal in character (nonindividual), there is no sense in thinking of them as things that exist separately from particulars. Being-a-man, Aristotle holds, is realized not in a substantial Form independent of all men, but precisely and only in *each individual man*. Because the "friends of the Forms" are unable to explain how such substances are both individual and universal,

> they make them the same in form as perishable things (since we know them), talking of "the man himself" and "the horse itself," just adding the word "self" to the names of sensible objects. (*M* 7.16)

But this is useless as an explanation.

4. Finally, there is no way to understand how the Forms, eternally unchanging, account for changes. They are supposed to be the first principles and causes of whatever happens in the world. But

> one is most of all bewildered to know what contribution the forms make either to the sensible things that are eternal or to those that come into being and perish; for they are not the cause of their movement or of any change in them. (*M* 1.9)

By "the sensible things that are eternal," Aristotle means the things in the natural world whose movement is (as he thought) regular and everlasting: the sun, moon, and the fixed stars. How can eternally

---

*Aristotle seems to be assuming here that the cause that accounts for the entire world of changing substances cannot itself just be a changing substance; if it were, it would itself need accounting for. So it must be—if it exists—something unchanging. If nature is defined as the sphere of those things that change because of a source of movement or change within them, an ultimate, unchanging cause of natural things would be beyond nature.

†Review the Third Man Argument on pp. 179–180.

*Review the discussion of substance on pp. 186–187.

stable Forms explain change either in these things or in the even more unstable items on earth?

Aristotle's critical appraisal of his master's metaphysics leads to a thoroughgoing rejection of the Forms. The fundamental things that exist have to be *individual* things and exist *independent* of other things. Plato's Forms do not satisfy either requirement. The Forms are supposed to be the common features of things that are individual, but such features, Aristotle believes, have no independent being; they depend for such being as they have on individual substances (of which they are the qualities, relations, and so on). The sensible things of nature, humans and beavers, surely exist; but being mortal and having a broad, flat tail are qualities existing only as modifications of these. Whether anything beyond these individual entities exists is still an open question. But if it does, it too will be substantial, individual, and capable of independent existence. It will not be a "common feature" of individual things.*

What of Mathematics?

The most convincing arguments for the Forms seem to be mathematical in nature. Socrates is not talking about his sand figure, so Plato concludes that Socrates is talking about the Square Itself, the Triangle Itself, and the Equal. Aristotle wishes to avoid drawing this conclusion. So how does he deal with mathematics?

The natural scientist, in studying changeable things, deals with subjects like the shape of the moon and the sphericity of the earth.

> Such attributes as these are studied by mathematicians as well as by natural scientists, but not by virtue of their being limits of natural bodies. The mathematician is not interested in them as attributes of whatever they are attributes of, and so he separates them. For these attributes can be conceptually separated from movement, without this separation making any difference or involving any false statement. (*PH* 2.2)

---

*We can think of these reflections as a critique of Plato's Metaphysical Argument for the Forms (see p. 154). In the following section, Aristotle examines the Epistemological Argument.

The crucial point is that we can "conceptually" separate attributes of things and consider them on their own, without supposing that they must be independent things. To use one of Aristotle's favorite examples, consider a snub nose. As a natural thing, a nose is a compound made up of form and matter; as such, it is of interest to the natural scientist but not to the mathematician. What makes it "snub," though, is its being curved in a certain way. And we can consider the curve alone, abstracting away from the matter in the nose. When we do this, we are taking up the mathematician's point of view. But the fact that we can adopt this viewpoint does not mean that Curvedness exists independent of noses. There need be no Form of the Curve to make mathematics intelligible.

There is no argument, Aristotle holds, from knowledge in mathematics to the reality of Platonic Forms independent of the world of nature. Mathematics is a science that, like natural science, has the world of nature as its only object. But it does not study it *as nature*; it studies only certain abstractions from natural things, without supposing that such abstractions are themselves things.

Substance and Form

When we considered Aristotle's categories, it was already apparent that certain terms were more basic than others.* These terms picked out substances and could play only the subject role in a statement. Now Aristotle reinforces this conclusion, looking more directly at things themselves.

> There are many ways in which the term "being" is used, corresponding to the distinctions we drew earlier, when we showed in how many ways terms are used. On the one hand, it indicates what a thing is and that it is this particular thing; on the other, it indicates a thing's quality or size, or whatever else is asserted of it in this way. Although "being" is used in all these ways, clearly the primary kind of being is what a thing is; for it is this alone that indicates substance. . . . All other things are said to be only insofar as they are quantities, qualities, affections, or something else of this kind belonging to what is in this primary sense. (*M* 7.1)

---

*See pp. 185–186.

We can ask many different questions about any given thing: How old is it? How large is it? What color is it? What shape is it? Is it alive? Does it think? Answers to each of these questions tell us something about the thing in question, describing a way the thing *is*, saying something about its *being*. But one question, Aristotle argues, is basic, namely, *What is it?* We may learn that it is thirty years old, six feet tall, white, fat, and thinking of Philadelphia, but until we learn that it is a *man* all these answers hang in the air. Aristotle puts it this way: that answer gives us the "substance." And substance is *what is*, in the basic, fundamental, primary sense.

This is the first answer to the metaphysical question about being qua being. For something to be, in the primary sense, is for it to be a substance. Whatever exists is dependent on substance. But more must be said. What is it that makes a given object a substance?

If we think back to the discussion of nature, we recall that natural things are composed of matter and form (the latter being expressed in a formula or definition). Could it be the matter that makes an object a substance? No. Matter, considered apart from form, is merely potentially something. If you strip off all form, you are tempted to say that what is left is sheer, undifferentiated, characterless something. But even that would be wrong, because every "something" has some character or form that differentiates it from something else. This "prime matter" can't be anything at all, on its own. It cannot have an independent existence; it exists only *as formed*. So matter cannot be what accounts for, or what makes or causes, something to be a substance. For what accounts for something being a substance must be at least as substantial as the substances it produces.

What of the other alternative? Could it be form that makes a portion of being into a substance? In a series of complex arguments, Aristotle argues that this is in fact the case. But not just any form makes the substance *what it is*. The form responsible for the substantiality of substances he calls the **essence** of the thing. *Essences* are expressed by definitions telling us *what things are*.

Johnny's frog may weigh five ounces, but weighing five ounces is not part of the essence of that frog. The proof is that if the frog eats well and gains weight, it does not cease to be a frog. What makes it a frog remains the same whether it weighs five, six, or seven ounces. The definition of frog allows a variation in many of the qualities and quantities Johnny's frog might have. But not in all. It could not cease to be amphibious and still be a frog. Amphibiousness is part of the essence of what it is to be a frog. All natural things (and artifacts, too), Aristotle holds, have an essence: a set of characteristics without which they would not be the things they are.

> Why, for instance, are these materials a house? Because of the presence of the essence of house. One might also ask, "Why is this, or the body containing this, a man?" So what one is really looking for is the cause—that is, the form—of the matter being whatever it is; and this in fact is the substance. (*M* 7.17)

We are, remember, looking for first principles and causes. We want to know what it is that makes a bit of matter what it is. We know that natural things are substances; they can exist independently and individually. But what makes this bunch of bricks a house, this mass of protoplasm a human? The answer is that each satisfies the definition of the essence of that thing. The presence of the essence house in the one case and the essence human in the other is the *cause* of each one being what it is.

So here we come to a second answer. Even more basic than substances composed of form and matter is the form itself. The cause of something could not be less real than the thing itself. So we find Aristotle asserting that this form—essence—is the very substance of substance itself.

In a way, this should be no surprise. Thinking back to the account Aristotle gives of natural substances, we can see how prominent form is. There are four causes, four explanations of why something is the particular substance it is. The material cause cannot be fundamental, as we have seen. But think about the other three: the form or essence of the thing; the final cause or goal, which is itself a form; and the efficient cause. Even this latter must involve a form, for it must be something actual, and actualities always embody form; as Aristotle likes to say, "man begets man." From all three points of view, then, form is the principal cause of the substantiality of things.

Aristotle gives us a simple example. Consider a syllable, *ba*. What makes this a syllable? There is the "matter" that makes it up: the elements *b* and *a*. But it is not the matter that makes these into the syllable *ba*, for these elements might also compose *ab*. So it must be the form. Moreover, the form cannot itself be an element, or we would need to explain how it is related to the *b* and the *a* (that is, we would have the Third Man problem). So the form must be something else.

> But this "something else," although it seems to be something, seems not to be an element; it seems in fact to be the cause of . . . that [the *b* and the *a*] being a syllable . . . ; in each case it is the thing's substance, since that is the ultimate cause of a thing's being. (*M* 7.17)

So form is the substance of things. But substance is what can exist independently and as an individual entity. This raises a very interesting possibility. Might there be substances that are not compounds of matter and form? Might there be substances that are *pure forms*?

All of nature is made up of material substances in which matter is made into something definite by the presence of form within it. But might there be something more fundamental than nature itself, in just the way that form is more basic than the compounds it forms? If there were any such substances, knowledge of them might be what the wise person seeks. Wisdom is knowing the being and causes of things. If there were substances of pure form, they would be less dependent and more basic than the things of nature, since even natural things depend on form for their substantiality. Knowledge of such "pure" substances would therefore be the knowledge most worth having, the most divine knowledge. We need now to explore this possibility.

Pure Actualities

If there are such purely formal substances, without any matter, they would be pure *actualities* as well. They couldn't involve any "might bes," for the principle of potentiality is matter and they would have no matter. Nor could such substances admit of any change, for every change is a movement from something potential to something actual (for example, from tadpole into frog). But then it would be *eternal* as well.

These would therefore be the *best* things. Why? Think again about natural things, for example, the frog that Johnny caught. When is that frog at its very best? Surely when it is most froggy—hopping around, catching flies, doing all the things frogs most typically do. It is not at its best when it has a broken leg, nor when it is feeling listless, nor when it is a mere tadpole. In Aristotle's terms, the frog is best when the form that makes it a frog (the essence) is most fully actualized in the matter—when it most fully is *what it is*. If there are substances lacking matter and potency altogether, substances that are fully actual, then they must be the best substances. For they cannot fail to display all the perfection of their form.

But are there any such substances—perfect, immaterial, and eternal—pure actualities without the possibility of change? If so, what are they like?

God

In the world of nature, the best things would be those that come closest to these ideals. Aristotle believes these are the heavenly bodies that move eternally in great circles. They change their positions constantly, but in a perfectly regular way, without beginning or ending.* But even such eternal motion is not self-explanatory.

> There is something that is always being moved in an incessant movement, and this movement is circular . . . : and so the first heaven will be eternal. There must, then, be something that moves it. But since that which is moved, as well as moving

---

*His reasons for thinking so are complex, involving a theory of the nature of time; we will not discuss that theory here. It can be found in *Physics* IV, 10–14. His theory was combined with the astronomy of the second-century Alexandrian, Ptolemy, and was to dominate scientific thinking until the beginnings of modern science in the sixteenth century. For a fuller discussion of this Aristotelian/Ptolemaic theory of the universe, see "The Celestial Spheres" in Chapter 14 (p. 299) and "The World God Made for Us" in Chapter 16.

things, is intermediate, there must be something that moves things without being moved; this will be something eternal, it will be a substance, and it will be an actuality. (*M* 12.7)

Think about baseball. A bat may impart movement to a ball, but only if put into movement by a batter. The bat is what Aristotle calls an "intermediate" mover; it moves the ball and is moved by the batter. The batter himself is moved to swing the bat by his desire to make a hit. Aristotle would put it this way: Making a hit is the final cause (the goal) that moves him to swing as he does. So the batter himself is only an "intermediate" mover. He moves as he does for the sake of making a hit. The goal of making a hit in turn exists for the sake of winning the game, which has as *its* goal the league championship. In the world of baseball, the ultimate final cause putting the whole season in motion is the goal of winning the World Series. Each batter is striving to embody the form: Member of a Team That Wins the World Series.

Let's return to the world of nature, containing the eternal movements of the heavenly bodies. Is there any ultimate mover here? There must be, Aristotle argues; otherwise we could not account for the movement of anything at all. Not all movers can be "intermediate" movers. If they were, that series would go on to infinity, but there cannot be any actually existing collection of infinitely many things. There must, then, be "something that moves things without being moved."*

Moreover, we can know certain facts about it. It must itself be eternal because it must account for the eternal movement of the heavenly bodies and so cannot be less extensive than they are. It must be a substance, for what other substances depend on cannot be less basic than they are. And, of course, it must be fully actual; otherwise, its being what it is would cry out for further explanation—for a mover for it.

What kind of cause could this **unmoved mover** be? Let's review the four causes. It clearly couldn't be a material cause, since that is purely potential. It couldn't be an efficient cause, for the eternal movement of the heavens does not need a temporal trigger. It is not the formal cause of a compound of form and matter because it contains no matter. It could only be a final cause. This conclusion is driven home by an analogy.

> Now, the object of desire and the object of thought move things in this way: they move things without being moved. (*M* 12.7)

Our baseball example already indicated this. What sets the whole baseball world in motion is a goal, namely, winning the World Series. Within the world of baseball, there is no further purpose. It moves the players, managers, umpires, and owners, but without being moved itself.* It is "the object of desire and thought" and functions that way as a final cause. It is what they all "love."

> The final cause then moves things because it is loved, whereas all other things move because they are themselves moved. . . . The first mover, then, must exist; and insofar as he exists of necessity, his existence must be good; and thus he must be a first principle. . . .
>
> It is upon a principle of this kind, then, that the heavens and nature depend. (*M* 12.7)

The ultimate cause of all things is a final cause; it is what all other things love. Their love for it puts them in motion, just as the sheer existence of a bicycle stimulates a boy or girl into activity, delivering papers, mowing lawns, and saving to buy it. As the object of desire and love, this first mover must be something good. Can we say anything more about the nature of this unmoved mover?

> Its life is like the best that we can enjoy—and we can enjoy it for only a short time. It is always in this state (which we cannot be), since its actuality is also pleasure. . . . If, then, God is always in the good state which we are sometimes in, that is something to wonder at; and if he is in a better state than we are ever in, that is to be wondered at even more.

---

*This is a form of argument that looks back to Anaximander (see p. 11) and forward to Saint Thomas Aquinas (see his first and second arguments for the existence of God, pp. 320–322).

---

*You may object that there are further goals: fame, money, and so on. And you are right. But that just shows that the "world" of baseball is not a self-contained world; it is not *the* world, but has a place in a wider setting.

This is in fact the case, however. Life belongs to him, too; for life is the actuality of mind, and God is that actuality; and his independent actuality is the best life and eternal life. We assert, then, that God is an eternal and most excellent living being, so that continuous and eternal life and duration belong to him. For that is what God is. (*M* 12.7)

There must be such an actuality, Aristotle argues, to explain the existence and nature of changing things. As the final cause and the object of the "desire" in all things, it must be the best. What is the best we know? The life of the mind.* So God must enjoy this life in the highest degree.

God, then, is an eternally existing, living being who lives a life of perfect thought. But this raises a further problem. What does God think about? Aristotle's answer to this question is reasonable, but puzzling, too.

Plainly, it thinks of what is most divine and most valuable, and plainly it does not change; for change would be for the worse. . . . The mind, then, must think of itself if it is the best of things, and its thought will be thought about thought. (*M* 12.9)

It would not be appropriate for the best thought to be about ordinary things, Aristotle argues. It must have only the best and most valuable object. But that is itself! So God will think only of himself. He will not, in Aristotle's view, have any concern or thought for the world. He will engage eternally in a contemplation of his own life—which is a life of contemplation. His relation to the world is not that of *creator* (the world being everlasting needs no efficient cause), but of *ideal*, inspiring each thing in the world to be its very best in imitation of the divine perfection. God is not the origin of the world, but its goal. Yet he is and must be an actually existing, individual substance, devoid of matter, and the best in every way.

God, then, is to *the* world as winning the World Series is to the "world" of baseball. He functions as the unifying principle of reality, that cause to which all other final causes must ultimately be referred. There is no multitude of ultimate principles, no

polytheism. The world is one world. As Aristotle puts it,

The world does not wish to be governed badly. As Homer says: "To have many kings is not good; let there be one." (*M* 12.10)

---

1. What is "first" philosophy? Is there another name for it?
2. List four criticisms of Plato's doctrine that the Forms are the most real of all things.
3. How does Aristotle's understanding of mathematics tend to undermine Plato's epistemological argument for the Forms?
4. In what way is substance the primary category of being?
5. What is an essence?
6. In what ways is form the most basic thing in substances?
7. What is God like? What kind of cause is God?

The Soul

Plato locates the essence of a person in the soul, an entity distinct from the body. Souls exist before their "imprisonment" in a body and survive the death of the body. The wise person tries to dissociate himself as much as possible from the harmful influences of the body. The practice of philosophy is a kind of purification making a soul fit for blessedness after death.

Aristotle rejects the otherworldliness implicit in such views. One of the causes of such otherworldliness, Aristotle holds, is a too-narrow focus.

Till now, those who have discussed and inquired about the soul seem to have considered only the human soul; but we must take care not to forget the question of whether one single definition can be given of soul in the way that it can of animal, or whether there is a different one in each case—for horse, dog, man, and god, for instance. (*PS* 1.1)

The term "soul" is the English translation of the Greek *psyche.* And that is the general word applied to life. So, things with *psyche*—ensouled things— are living things. But not only humans are alive. Aristotle is raising the question whether soul or life or *psyche* is something shared in common among

---

*This is discussed in more detail later in this chapter. See "The Highest Good."

all living things. If you think only about the life characteristic of humans, you might well think of soul as something quite other than nature; but if you observe the broader context, you may end up with a very different account of soul. Again we see Aristotle the biologist at work, trying to organize and classify all living things, humans being just one species among many.

LEVELS OF SOUL

There is "one definition of soul in the same way that there is one definition of shape" (*PS* 2.3). Just as there are plane figures and solid figures, and among the latter there are spheres and cubes, so souls come in a variety of kinds.

> We must, then, inquire, species by species, what is the soul of each living thing—what is the soul of a plant, for instance, or what is that of a man or a beast. (*PS* 2.3)

The general definition of soul involves life: "that which distinguishes what has a soul from what has not is life" (*PS* 2.2). But souls differ from one another in their complexity, with more complex kinds of souls building on simpler kinds. Aristotle distinguishes three general levels of soul: that of plants, that of beasts, and that of humans.

> The most fundamental of these forms is that of the plants, for clearly they have within themselves a faculty and principle such that through it they can grow or decay in opposite directions. For they do not just grow upwards without growing downwards; they grow in both directions alike, and indeed in every direction . . . for as long as they can receive nourishment. This nutritive faculty can be separated from the other faculties, but the other faculties cannot exist apart from it in mortal creatures. This is clear in the case of plants, since they have none of the other faculties of the soul. (*PS* 2.2)

Nutritive soul, the capacity to take in nourishment and convert it to life, is basic to all living things. Plants, however, do not share the higher levels of soul. They live and reproduce and so have a kind of soul, but without the capacities of movement, sensation, and thought.

We should pause a moment to consider reproduction. Why do plants (as well as animals) reproduce? We know that for Aristotle the answer is incomplete if it makes no mention of the final cause. What is the final cause for reproduction?

> The most natural function of any living being that is complete, is not deformed, and is not born spontaneously is to produce another being like itself . . . so that it may share, as far as it can, in eternity and divinity; that is what they all desire, and it is the purpose of all their natural activities. (*PS* 2.4)

This is an application of the principle uncovered in first philosophy. There is an eternal unmoved mover—the final cause of whatever else exists—and the fact that living things reproduce can be explained by their "desire" to share, as far as possible, the eternity and divinity that caps off the universe. Each thing imitates God in the way possible for it, striving to come as close as mortal beings can come to a kind of eternity.*

More complex forms of soul are built on the nutritive soul and are never found in nature without it. The next level can be called the level of **sensitive soul;** it belongs to the animals.

> Plants possess only the nutritive faculty, but other beings possess both it and the sensitive faculty; and if they possess the sensitive faculty, they must also possess the appetitive; for appetite consists of desire, anger, and will. All animals possess at least one sense, that of touch; anything that has a sense is acquainted with pleasure and pain, with what is pleasant and what is painful; and anything that is acquainted with these has desire, since desire is an appetite for the pleasant. (*PS* 2.3)

Animals, then, have sensations and desires in addition to the faculties of nutrition and reproduction.

Finally, there is **rational soul,** soul that has the capacity to think. Among naturally existing species, it seems to be characteristic only of human beings.

In general, then, there are three kinds or levels of soul: nutritive, sensitive, and rational. They correspond to three great classes of living things: plants, animals, and human beings. They are related in such a way that higher kinds of soul incorporate the lower, but the lower can exist without the higher.

---

*Compare Plato's discussion of love, pp. 165–168.

SOUL AND BODY

How are souls related to bodies? Can we give the same sort of answer for each of the kinds of soul? Plato, concentrating on human beings, holds that souls are completely distinct entities, capable of existence on their own. That is not so plausible in the case of plant and animal souls. What does Aristotle say?

Actually, Aristotle gives two answers, and that fact has generated much subsequent debate. There is a general answer and an answer that pertains specifically to the rational form of soul. Let's look first at the general answer.

> It is probably better to say not that the soul feels pity or learns or thinks, but that man does these things with his soul; for we should not suppose that the movement is actually in the soul, but that in some cases it penetrates as far as the soul, in others it starts from it; sensation, for instance, starts from the particular objects, whereas recollection starts from the soul and proceeds to the movements or their residues in the sense organs. (*PS* 1.4)

This view of soul is one that firmly embeds soul in the body and makes us unitary beings. It is not the case that certain operations can be assigned to the soul and certain others to the body. It is not the soul that feels or learns or thinks while the body eats and walks; it is the *person* who does all these things. It would be no more sensible, Aristotle holds, to say that the soul is angry than that the body weaves or builds. Neither souls nor bodies do these things; human beings do them all. Sensation is not something the soul accomplishes; it cannot occur at all without a body, sense organs, and objects to which those sense organs are sensitive. Recollection has its effects in bodily movements (remembering an appointment makes you run to catch the bus). A person is *one being* with *one essence*.

But what exactly is a soul, and how is it related to a body? We must remind ourselves of the results of Aristotle's investigations of being qua being. The basic things that exist are substances, and in natural substances there is a material substratum that is actualized—made into the substance it is—by a form.

> The soul, then, must be a substance inasmuch as it is the form of a natural body that potentially possesses life; and such substance is in fact realization, so that the soul is the realization of a body of this kind. (*PS* 2.1)

Remember that "form" does not stand for shape (except in very simple cases) but for the essence, the definition, the satisfaction of which makes a thing the substance it is. Remember also that form is the principle of actualization or realization; it is what makes a bit of matter into an actual thing. And remember that form is itself substance: the very substance of substances.

Now you can understand Aristotle's view of soul as "the form of a natural body that potentially possesses life" and as the "realization of a body of this kind." An ensouled body is capable of performing all the activities that are appropriate to that kind of being; it feeds itself and perhaps sees, desires, and thinks. And its being capable of those activities is the *same* as its having certain essential characteristics, which is the same as its having a form of a certain kind.

Think of the body of Frankenstein's monster before it was jolted into life. It was initially a mosaic of body parts—matter of the right *kind* to carry out the activities of a living thing, but not actually living. What the tragic doctor provided for the body was a soul. But what is that? He didn't plug a new thing into that body; he just actualized certain potentialities the body already had. The doctor made it able to walk and eat, to see and talk, to think. Having a soul is just being able to do those kinds of things. A soul, then, is just a form for a primary substance, not a separate entity in itself.

It should be no surprise, then, to hear Aristotle say, rather offhandedly,

> We do not, therefore, have to inquire whether the soul and body are one, just as we do not have to inquire whether the wax and its shape, or in general the matter of any given thing and that of which it is the matter, are one. (*PS* 2.1)

This problem, which so occupies Plato and for which he constructs so many proofs, is simply one that we do not have to inquire into! The answer is *obvious*, as obvious as the answer to the question whether the shape of a wax seal can exist independent of the wax.

Aristotle briefly indicates how this view works in practice. Consider anger. Some people define anger as a disposition to strike out or retaliate in response to some perceived wrong. Its definition therefore involves beliefs, desires, and emotions—all mental states of one sort or another. Others say that anger is just a bodily state involving heightened blood pressure, tensing of muscles, the flow of adrenaline, and so on. Nothing mental needs to be brought into its explanation. What would Aristotle say? He contrasts the viewpoint of the natural scientist with that of the "logician," by which he means one who seeks the definition of such states.

> The natural scientist and the logician would define all these affections in different ways; if they were asked what anger is, the one would say that it was a desire to hurt someone in return, or something like that, the other that it was a boiling of the blood and the heat around the heart. Of these, one is describing the matter, the other the form and the definition; for the latter is indeed the definition of the thing, but it must be in matter of a particular kind if the thing is going to exist. (*PS* 1.1)

If Aristotle is right, psychology and physiology in fact study the same thing. The former studies the form, and the latter the matter. From one point of view anger is a mental state, from the other a physical state. There need be no quarrel between the psychologist and the physiologist. Certain kinds of physical bodies have capacities for certain kinds of activities, and the exercise of those activities is their actuality and form; it is their life—their soul.*

This, then, is Aristotle's general account of the relation of soul and body. Souls are the forms (the essential characteristics) of certain kinds of bodies, and as such they do not exist independent of bodies. This means, of course, that a soul cannot survive the death of the body to which it gives form any more than sight can survive the destruction of the eyes.

This general account, however, stands in tension with his account of the rational soul, or perhaps just a part of the rational soul, to which we now turn.

Nous

For the most part, Aristotle's account of the soul is thoroughly "naturalistic." Soul is just how naturally existing, living bodies of a certain kind function; it is not an additional part separable from such bodies. In this regard, things with souls are thoroughly embedded in the world of nature. But can this naturalistic form-of-the-body account be the *complete* story about soul? Or could it be that a part of some souls—of rational souls—has an independent existence after all?

Sensation is passive, simply registering the characteristics of the environment, but thinking seems to be more active; otherwise mirrors and calm pools would be thinking about what they reflect. Consider, for example, using induction to grasp the first principles of natural kinds.* We aren't simply absorbing what comes in through the senses, but actively observing, noting, classifying things. Thinking is *doing* something. Aristotle's word for this active capacity of ours is *nous*. And the question is whether *nous* (translated below as "mind") can be adequately understood as nothing more than one aspect of the human form.

> There is the mind that is such as we have just described by virtue of the fact that it becomes everything; then, there is another mind, which is what it is by virtue of the fact that it makes everything; it is a sort of condition like light. For in a way light makes what are potentially colors become colors in actuality. This second mind is separable, incapable of being acted upon, mixed with nothing, and in essence an actuality. (*PS* 3.5)

Here Aristotle distinguishes between two aspects of *nous* itself. There is the side of *nous* that "becomes everything." What he means by this is that the mind can adapt to receive the form of just about anything; it is flexible, malleable, open to being written on. But there is also the side of *nous* that "makes everything." Mind lights things up, makes them stand out clearly. Here is an example that may help. Think of daydreaming. Your eyes are open, and there is in your consciousness

---

*This paragraph has a very contemporary ring to it. It expresses a view called "functionalism," the dominant theory of mind in recent cognitive science. See pp. 735–738.

*Review the discussion of induction on pp. 191–192.

a kind of registration of everything in your visual field, but you aren't paying it any heed. Your mind is "elsewhere," and you don't *know* what is before you. Suddenly, however, your attention shifts and what has been present all along is noted. Actively paying attention makes what was just potentially knowable into something actually known—just as light makes colors visible, although the colors were there all along before they were lighted up.

According to Aristotle's principles, only an actuality can turn something that is potentially *X* into something actually *X*. So active *nous* must be an actual power to produce knowledge from the mere registrations of passive *nous*. In fact, Aristotle concludes that the active and passive powers of *nous* are distinct and separable. Sometimes he goes so far as to speak not just of two powers, but of two minds.

The second mind, he says, is "mixed with nothing" and "separable" from the first. To say it is mixed with nothing must mean that it is a pure form unmixed with matter. If you think a moment, you should be able to see that it must be a pure form if it can actualize *everything*; if it were mixed with matter, it would be some definite thing and would lack the required plasticity. The eye, for instance, is a definite material organ. As such, its sensitivity is strictly limited; it can detect light, but not sounds or tastes. The ear is tuned to sounds alone and the tongue restricted to tastes. If *nous* is not limited in this way, it seems that it cannot be material. If it is not material, it cannot be a part of the body. And if it is not part of the body, it must be a separable entity.

There is another reason Aristotle believes that active *nous* must be an actuality separate from the body. He cannot find any "organ" or bodily location for this activity. Sight is located in the eyes, hearing in the ears, and so on. But where could the faculty of knowing be? Reflecting on his general view of the soul, Aristotle writes,

> Clearly, then, the soul is not separable from the body; or, if it is divisible into parts, some of the parts are not separable, for in some cases the realization is just the realization of the parts. However, there is nothing to prevent some parts being separated, insofar as they are not realizations of any body. (*PS* 2.1)

Sight is the "realization" of the eye. But what part of the body could have as its function something as infinitely complex as thinking and knowing? The seat of sensation and emotions, Aristotle thinks, is the heart. When we are afraid or excited we can feel our heart beating fast. The brain he considers an organ for cooling the body. (This is wrong, but not implausible; one of the best ways to keep warm on a cold day is to wear a hat.) Without knowledge of the microstructure of the brain, it must have seemed to him that there is nothing available in the body to serve as the organ of thought, so the active part of *nous* must be separable from the body.

It is not only separable, Aristotle holds; it is also

> immortal and eternal; we do not remember this because, although this mind is incapable of being acted upon, the other kind of mind, which is capable of being acted upon, is perishable. But without this kind of mind nothing thinks. (*PS* 3.5)

Why should active *nous* be eternal? Because it is not material; it is not the form of a material substance (i.e., of part of the body). It is rather one of those substantial forms that can exist separately. Lacking matter, it also lacks potentiality for change and is fully and everlastingly what it is. If *nous* is eternal and immortal, it must, like the soul of Socrates and Plato, have existed prior to our birth. But, Aristotle insists, we do not *remember* anything we know before birth—because there is nothing there to remember. Active *nous*, remember, is like the light. It lights up what the senses receive, making actual what is so far only a potentiality for knowledge. But it is not itself knowledge; it only produces knowledge from material delivered by the senses.* And before birth there were no senses or sense organs to produce

---

*Immanuel Kant's view of the relation between concepts and percepts is very similar to this account of *nous*. Like *nous*, concepts alone cannot give us any knowledge; they structure, or interpret, or "light up" the deliverances of the senses; knowledge is a product of the interplay of "spontaneous" conceptualization and "receptive" sensation. (See pp. 476–479.) It is also interesting to compare this discussion of *nous* with Heidegger's view of the "clearing" in which things become present. See "Modes of Disclosure" in Chapter 27.

this material. Aristotle cannot accept the Socratic and Platonic doctrine of recollection as an explanation of knowing.

For similar reasons, it does not seem that *nous* can be anything like personal immortality, in which an individual human being survives death and remembers his life. Active *nous*, in fact, seems impersonal.

A number of questions arise, but Aristotle does not give us answers. Is *nous* numerically the same thing in all individuals, or is there a distinct *nous* for each person? What is the relation between *nous* and God, to which it bears some striking resemblances? How, if *nous* is independent and separable, does it come to be associated with human souls at all?

These questions give rise to a long debate, partly about what Aristotle means, partly about what truth there is to all this. In the Middle Ages, for instance, Jewish, Muslim, and Christian thinkers, trying to incorporate Aristotle into a broader theological context, wrestled determinedly with these problems. But for our purposes it is enough to register his conviction that there is something about human beings, and particularly about them as knowers, that cannot be accounted for in purely naturalistic terms. There is a part of the soul that is, after all, otherworldly.

---

1. What is Aristotle's objection to Plato's account of the soul?
2. Characterize the three levels of soul.
3. Why do living things reproduce? (Compare Plato on love.)
4. How is a soul related to a body? Be sure you understand the concepts of "substratum," "realization," and "formal substance."
5. Why does Aristotle think there is something (*nous*) about human souls that is eternal?

The Good Life

Aristotle's views on the good life for human beings, like his views of knowledge, reality, and human nature, resemble Plato's views in some ways and differ from them in others. While they agree on many substantive points, such as the importance

of traditional virtues like moderation, justice, and courage, they approach ethics in very different ways. Whereas Plato seeks a science of ethics based on the Form of the Good, Aristotle sees ethics as more of an art than a science. It requires a different sort of wisdom—wisdom about choice, character, and action—that pertains to particulars rather than unchanging universal truths. Given this emphasis, Aristotle insists that ethics will never attain the precision or certainty available in theoretical knowledge:

> Our treatment will be adequate if we make it as precise as the subject matter allows. The same degree of accuracy should not be demanded in all inquiries any more than in all the products of craftsmen. Virtue and justice—the subject matter of politics—admit of plenty of differences and uncertainty. . . .
>
> Then, since our discussion is about, and proceeds from, matters of this sort, we must be content with indicating the truth in broad, general outline. . . . The educated man looks for as much precision in each subject as the nature of the subject allows. (*NE* 1.3)

The point of studying ethics and politics, then, is not knowledge in the strict sense, for like Plato, Aristotle believes that genuine knowledge requires certainty. Instead, studying ethics has a more practical payoff.

> We are not studying in order to know what virtue is, but to become good, for otherwise there would be no profit in it. (*NE* 2.2)

What is it, then, to "become good," and how can we do so?

HAPPINESS

Aristotle begins his main treatise on ethics, the *Nicomachean Ethics*, with these words:

> Every skill and every inquiry, and similarly, every action and choice of action, is thought to have some good as its object. This is why the good has rightly been defined as the object of all endeavor. (*NE* 1.1)

Whenever we do something, we have some end in view. If we exercise, our end is health; if we study, our end is knowledge or a profession. And we consider that end to be good; no one strives for what he or she considers bad.*

> Now, if there is some object of activities that we want for its own sake (and others only because of that), and if it is not true that everything is chosen for something else—in which case there will be an infinite regress, that will nullify all our striving—it is plain that this must be the good, the highest good. Would not knowing it have a great influence on our way of living? Would we not be better at doing what we should, like archers with a target to aim at? (*NE* 1.2)

We often do one thing for the sake of another. But this cannot go on forever, or there will be no point to anything we do. What we want to find is some end that we want, but not for the sake of anything else: something we prize "for its own sake." That would be the highest good, since there is nothing else we want that *for*. If we can identify something like that and keep it clearly before our eyes, as an archer looks at the target while shooting, we will be more likely to attain what is truly good.

Is there anything like that?

> What is the highest good in all matters of action? As to the name, there is almost complete agreement; for uneducated and educated alike call it happiness, and make happiness identical with the good life and successful living. They disagree, however, about the meaning of happiness. (*NE* 1.4)

Aristotle's term for happiness is *eudaemonia*. Whether "happiness" is the best English translation for this term is unclear. A better alternative might be "well-being," and some speak of human "flourishing." In any case, it is clear that *eudaemonia* is not merely a matter of *feeling* happy; Aristotle, as much as Socrates, wants to distinguish being happy

from just feeling happy.* In this book, we will follow the major tradition, however, and speak of what all of us desire as happiness.

Everyone wants to be happy. And the question, "Why do you want to be happy—for what?" seems to be senseless. This is the end, the final goal. Money we want for security, but happiness for its own sake. Yet, for us as well as for Aristotle, there is something unsatisfying about this answer, something hollow. For we immediately want to ask: "What is happiness, anyway?"

Many people, Aristotle notes, think that happiness is pleasure and live as though that were so. But that cannot be correct. For the good of every creature must be appropriate to that creature's nature; it couldn't be right that the good life for human beings is the same as "the kind of life lived by cattle" (*NE* 1.4). It is true that "amusements" are pleasant and that they are chosen for their own sake. Within limits, there is nothing wrong with that. But

> it would be absurd if the end were amusement and if trouble and hardship throughout life would be all for the sake of amusing oneself. . . . It would be stupid and childish to work hard and sweat just for childish amusement. (*NE* 10.6)†

Other people think that happiness is a matter of fame and honor. Again, there is something to be said for that; it is more characteristically human than mere pleasure. Aristotle does not want to deny that honor is something we can seek for its own sake; still

> it seems to be more superficial than what we are looking for, since it rests in the man who gives the honor rather than in him who receives it, whereas our thought is that the good is something proper to the person, and cannot be taken away from him. (*NE* 1.5)

Here Aristotle is surely drawing on the tradition of Socrates, who believes that "the many" could neither bestow the greatest blessings nor

---

*This is true in general. Both Socrates and Plato, however, hold it is universally true. For that reason, they hold that if we know what is good, we will do what is good. But Aristotle believes there are exceptions when people can act contrary to what they themselves consider their best judgment. Euripides expresses this Aristotelian view in Hippolytus, and Saint Paul and Augustine both agree with Aristotle that such inner conflict is possible. See pp. 260 and 277–282.

*See Socrates making this distinction in his trial speech, *Apology* 36e, and p. 134.

†Contemporary American culture sometimes makes one think that we are making this Aristotelian mistake on a massive scale.

inflict the greatest harms.* The highest good, happiness, must be something "proper to the person" that "cannot be taken away." The problem with honor and fame—or popularity—is that you are not in control of them; whether they are bestowed or withdrawn depends on others. If what you most want is to be popular, you are saying to others: "Here, take my happiness; I put it into your hands." This seems unsatisfactory to Aristotle.

"Popularity? It is glory's small change."
Victor Hugo (1802–1885)

How, then, shall we discover what happiness is?

> We might achieve this by ascertaining the specific function of man. In the case of flute players, sculptors, and all craftsmen—indeed all who have some function and activity—"good" and "excellent" reside in their function. Now, the same will be true of man, if he has a peculiar function to himself. Do builders and cobblers have functions and activities, but man not, being by nature idle? Or, just as the eye, hand, foot, and every part of the body has a function, similarly, is one to attribute a function to man over and above these? In that case, what will it be? (*NE* 1.7)

The eye is defined by its **function.** It is a thing for seeing with; an eye is a good one if it performs that function well—gives clear and accurate images. A woman is a flutist by virtue of performing a certain function: playing the flute. A good flutist is one who plays the flute excellently, and that is in fact what each flutist aims at. Again we see that the good of a thing is relative to its proper function. Moreover—and this will be important— the flutist is *happy* when she plays excellently.

This suggests to Aristotle that if human beings had a function—not as flutists or cobblers, but just in virtue of being human—we might be able to identify the good appropriate to them. He thinks we can discover such a function.

> The function of man is activity of soul in accordance with reason, or at least not without reason. (*NE* 1.7)

Let's examine this statement. Aristotle is claiming that there is something in human beings analogous to the function of a flutist or cobbler: "activity of soul in accordance with reason."* What does that mean? And why does he pick on that, exactly?

If we are interested in the function of a human being, we must focus on what makes a human being human: the soul. As we have seen, soul is the realization of a certain kind of body; it is its life and the source of its actuality as an individual substance. It is the *essence* of a living thing. A dog is being a dog when it is doing essentially doglike things. And human beings are being human when they are acting in essentially human ways. Now what is peculiarly characteristic of humans? We already know Aristotle's answer to that: Humans are different from plants and the other animals because they have the *rational* level of soul. So the function of a human being is living according to reason, or at least, Aristotle adds, "not without reason." This addition is not insignificant. It means that although an excellent human life is a rational one, it is not limited to purely intellectual pursuits. There are excellences (virtues) that pertain to the physical and social aspects of our lives as well. The latter he calls the *moral virtues*.

Furthermore, although the function of the cobbler is simply to make shoes, the best cobbler is the one who makes excellent shoes. As Aristotle says, "Function comes first, and superiority in excellence is superadded." If that is so, then

> the good for man proves to be activity of soul in conformity with excellence; and if there is more than one excellence, it will be the best and most complete of these. (*NE* 1.7)

Doing what is characteristic of humans to do, living in accord with reason, and in the most excellent kind of way, is the good for humans. And if

---

*See *Apology* 30d, *Crito* 44d.

*In one important respect, Aristotle is Plato's faithful pupil. Look again at the functions of the soul for Plato (pp. 170–171). Which one is dominant?

that is the human being's good, then it also constitutes human happiness. One of us used to have a big black Newfoundland dog named Shadow, a wonderful dog. When was Shadow happiest? When he was doing the things that Newfoundlands characteristically do—running along between the canal and the river, retrieving sticks thrown far out into the water. He loved that, he was *good* at it, and you could see it made him happy. It is the same with human beings, except that humans have capacities that Shadow didn't have.

> It seems as though everything that people look for in connection with happiness resides in our definition. Some think it to be excellence or virtue; others wisdom; others special skill; whereas still others think it all these, or some of these together with pleasure, or at least not without pleasure. Others incorporate external goods as well. (*NE* 1.8)

Happiness is not possible without excellence or virtue (*areté*), any more than a flutist is happy over a poor performance. It surely includes wisdom, for excellent use of one's rational powers is part of being an excellent human being. Special skills are almost certainly included, for there are many necessary and useful things to be done in a human life, from house building to poetry writing. And it will include pleasure, not because pleasure is itself the good—we have seen it cannot be that—but because the life of those who live rationally with excellence is in itself pleasant.

The things thought pleasant by the vast majority of people are always in conflict with one another, because it is not by nature that they are pleasant; but those who love goodness take pleasure in what is by nature pleasant. This is the characteristic of actions in conformity with virtue, so that they are in themselves pleasant to those who love goodness. Their life has no extra need of pleasure as a kind of wrapper; it contains pleasure in itself. (*NE* 1.8)

❦

> "In the long run men hit only what they aim at."
> *Henry David Thoreau (1817–1862)*

Does a happy life "incorporate external goods as well," as some say? Aristotle's answer is, yes—at least in a moderate degree.

> It is impossible (or at least not easy) to do fine acts without a supply of "goods." Many acts are done through friends, or by means of wealth and political power, which are all, as it were, instruments. When people are without some of these, that ruins their blessed condition—for example, noble birth, fine children, or beauty. The man who is quite hideous to look at or ignoble or a hermit or childless cannot be entirely happy. Perhaps this is even more so if a man has really vicious children or friends or if they are good but have died. So, as we have said, happiness does seem to require this external bounty. (*NE* 1.8)

A certain amount of good fortune is a necessary condition for happiness. One would not expect the Elephant Man, for example, to be entirely happy, or a person whose children have become thoroughly wicked. This means, of course, that your happiness is not entirely in your own control. To be self-sufficient in happiness may be a kind of ideal, but in this world it is not likely to be entirely realized.

One point needs special emphasis. The happy life, which is one and the same with the good life, is a life of *activity*. Happiness is not something that happens to you. It is not passive. Think about the following analogy:

> At the Olympic games, it is not the handsomest and strongest who are crowned, but actual competitors,

some of whom are the winners. Similarly, it is those who act rightly who get the rewards and the good things in life. (*NE* 1.8)

Happiness is an *activity* of soul in accord with excellence.

And finally, Aristotle adds, "in a complete life." Just as one swallow does not make a summer, so "a short time does not make a man blessed or happy" (*NE* 1.7). There is a certain unavoidable fragility to human happiness.

> There are many changes and all kinds of chances throughout a lifetime, and it is possible for a man who is really flourishing to meet with great disaster in old age, like Priam of Troy. No one gives the name happy to a man who meets with misfortune like that and dies miserably. (*NE* 1.9)

---

1. Why does Aristotle say that ethics cannot be an exact science?
2. Why does Aristotle think happiness is the highest good?
3. Why cannot pleasure be the essence of happiness? Why not honor or fame?
4. How does the idea of function help in determining the nature of happiness?
5. What is the function of human beings? What is their good?
6. How does pleasure come into the good life?

Virtue or Excellence (*Areté*)

The good for human beings, then, is happiness, and happiness is the full development and exercise of our human capacities "in conformity with excellence." But what kind of thing is this excellence? How is it attained? Is there just one excellence which is appropriate to human beings, or are there many? We often speak of the "virtues" in the plural—courage, moderation, justice, temperance, and so on; are these independent of one another, or can you be an excellent human being only if you have them all? These are the questions we now address. (We shall speak in terms of "**virtues**" for the time being and postpone the question about their unity.)

1. In considering what kind of thing a virtue is, Aristotle notes that it is for our virtues and vices

that we are praised and blamed. A virtue, then, cannot be a simple emotion or feeling, for two reasons: (1) we are blamed not for being angry, but for giving in to our anger, for nursing our anger, or for being unreasonably angry, and those things are in our control; and (2) we feel fear and anger without choosing to, but the virtues "are a sort of choice, or at least not possible without choice" (*NE* 2.5). Nor can the virtues be mere capacities; again, we are called good or bad not because we are *capable* of feeling angry or *capable* of reasoning, but because of the ways we use these capacities.

But if the virtues are not emotions or capacities, what can they be? Aristotle's answer is that they are *dispositions* or **habits.** To be courageous is to be disposed to do brave things. To be temperate is to have a tendency toward moderation in one's pleasures. These dispositions have intimate connections with choice and action. People who never do the brave thing when they have the opportunity are not brave, no matter how brave they happen to feel. And the person who just happens to do a brave thing, in a quite accidental way, is not brave either. The brave person acts bravely whenever the occasion calls for it; and the more the person is truly possessed of that virtue, the more easily and naturally courageous actions come. There is no need to engage in fierce internal struggles to screw up the courage to act rightly.

So this is the answer to the first question. To have a virtue of a certain kind is to have developed a habit of choosing and behaving in ways appropriate to that virtue.

2. How are the virtues attained? They are not innate in us, though we have a natural capacity for them. They are, Aristotle tells us, learned. And they are learned as all habits are learned, by practice.

> Where doing or making is dependent on knowing how, we acquire the know-how by actually doing. For example, people become builders by actually building, and the same applies to lyre players. In the same way, we become just by doing just acts; and similarly with "temperate" and "brave." (*NE* 2.1)

This leads, moreover, to a kind of "virtuous circle."

We become moderate through abstaining from pleasure, and when we are moderate we are best able to abstain. The same is true of bravery. Through being trained to despise and accept danger, we become brave; we shall be best able to accept danger once we are brave. (*NE* 2.2)

So we learn these excellences by practicing behavior that eventually becomes habitual in us. And if they can be learned, they can be taught. Socrates seems forever unsure whether human excellence is something that can be taught.* Aristotle is certain that it can be and tells us how.

The point is that moral virtue is concerned with pleasures and pains. We do bad actions because of the pleasure going with them, and abstain from good actions because they are hard and painful. Therefore, there should be some direction from a very early age, as Plato says, with a view to taking pleasure in, and being pained by, the right things. (*NE* 2.3)

A child can be taught virtue—moderation, courage, generosity, and justice—by associating pleasures with them and pains with their violation—by rewarding and punishing. A child needs to be taught to find pleasure in virtuous behavior and shame in vice. If we can teach a person to build well or to play the lyre well in this way, we can also teach the more specifically human excellences. Why should we teach these virtues to our children? Aristotle has a clear answer: If they find pleasure in the most excellent exercise of their human nature, they will be happier people. Such happy people are also the virtuous and good, for the good person is the one who takes pleasure in the right things.

3. Our third question is whether virtue is one or many. Can a person be partly good and partly bad, or is goodness all or nothing? Plato and Socrates are both convinced that goodness is one. For Plato, knowledge of the Form of the Good is the only secure foundation for virtue; and that Form is *one*. Whoever grasped it fully would be good through and through. We might expect Aristotle to be more pluralistic. In fact, he

says that Socrates and Plato are in one sense right and in one sense wrong. There are indeed many virtues, and they can perhaps even exist in some independence of each other. Often, a brave man is not particularly moderate in choosing his pleasures; James Bond would be an example. But in their perfection, Aristotle holds, you can't have one virtue without having them all. What will the brave man without moderation do, for example, when he is pulled in one direction by his bravery and in another by some tempting pleasure? Won't his lack of moderation hamper the exercise of his courage?

The unity of human excellence in its perfection is a function of the exercise of reason. If you follow reason, you will not be able to develop only one of these virtues to the exclusion of others. This use of reason Aristotle calls *practical sense* or **practical wisdom.** "Once the single virtue, practical sense, is present, all the virtues will be present" (*NE* 6.13).

To this "single virtue," which provides the foundation and unity of all the rest, we now turn.

The Role of Reason

Happiness is living the life of an excellent human being; you can't be an excellent human being unless you use your rational powers. But how, exactly, does Aristotle think that rationality helps in living an excellent life?

Let us consider this first: it is in the nature of things for the virtues to be destroyed by excess and deficiency, as we see in the case of health and strength—a good example, for we must use clear cases when discussing abstruse matters. Excessive or insufficient training destroys strength, just as too much or too little food and drink ruins health. The right amount, however, brings health and preserves it. So this applies to moderation, bravery, and the other virtues. The man who runs away from everything in fear, and faces up to nothing, becomes a coward; the man who is absolutely fearless, and will walk into anything, becomes rash. It is the same with the man who gets enjoyment from all the pleasures, abstaining from none: he is immoderate; whereas he who avoids all pleasures, like a boor, is a man of no sensitivity.

*See *Meno* and pp. 99 and 133.

Moderation and bravery are destroyed by excess and deficiency, but are kept flourishing by the mean. (*NE* 2.2)

We can think of an emotion or an action tendency as laid out on a line, the extremes of which are labeled "too much" and "too little." Somewhere between these extremes is a point that is "just right." This point Aristotle calls **"the mean."** It is at this "just right" point that human excellence or virtue flourishes. To possess a virtue, then, is to have a habit that keeps impulse and emotion from leading action astray.

In feeling fear, confidence, desire, anger, pity, and in general pleasure and pain, one can feel too much or too little; and both extremes are wrong. The mean and good is feeling at the right time, about the right things, in relation to the right people, and for the right reason; and the mean and the good are the task of virtue. (*NE* 2.6)

Think about bravery, surely one of the virtues. Aristotle's analysis says that bravery lies on a mean between extremes of fear and confidence. If we feel too much fear and too little confidence, we are paralyzed and cannot act rightly; we are cowards. If we feel too little fear and are overconfident, we act foolishly, recklessly. At each extreme, then, there is a vice, and the virtue lies in a mean between these extremes. But it doesn't lie exactly in the middle. What is courageous in any given circumstance depends on the facts.

Consider this example. You are walking down a dark and lonely street, and you feel a pointed object pressed into your back and hear the words, "Your money or your life." What would be the brave thing for you to do? Turn and try to disarm the thug? Try to outrun him? If you are like most people, either action would be foolhardy, rash, stupid. There would be no taint of cowardice in you if you meekly handed over your wallet, especially because it is not worth risking your life over the money in your wallet. If you happen to be a Green Beret or a Navy Seal in a similar situation, someone superbly trained in hand-to-hand combat, however, then disarming your attacker would not be rash or reckless. What counts as extreme will depend, then, on facts about who is facing danger, what kind of danger he or she is facing, what he or she is seeking to protect by facing danger, and so on. These facts will differ from case to case, and so what is courageous will differ from case to case.

X: the mean for me
Y: the mean for a Navy Seal

Or let's think about being angry; again, it is a matter of degree. You can have too much anger (like Achilles) or too little (simply being a doormat for everyone to walk over). Each of these is a vice, wrathfulness at the one extreme and subservience at the other. The virtue (which, in this case, may not have a clear name) lies at the mean between these extremes. Aristotle doesn't intend to say that we should always get only moderately angry. About certain things, in relation to a given person, and for some specific reason, it might be the right thing to be very angry indeed. But in relation to other times, occasions, persons, and reasons, that degree of anger may be excessive. We should always seek the mean, but what that is depends on the situation in which we find ourselves. All of the virtues, Aristotle says, can be given this sort of analysis.

Notice that this is not a doctrine of *relativism* in the Sophist's sense. It is clearly not the case that if Jones thinks in certain circumstances that it's right to get angry to a certain degree, then it *is* (therefore) right—not even for Jones. Jones can be mistaken in his judgment. True, there is a certain relativity involved in judgments about the right; and without careful thought, this might be confusing. But it is an *objective* relativity; what is right depends on objective facts—on actual facts about the situation in which Jones finds himself. It is those facts that determine where the mean lies, not what Jones thinks or feels about them.

"The fact that a good and virtuous decision is context-sensitive does not imply that it is right only *relative* to, or *inside*, a limited context, any more than the fact that a good navigational judgment is sensitive to particular weather conditions shows that it is correct only in a local or relational sense. It is right absolutely, objectively, from anywhere in the human world, to attend to the particular features of one's context; and the person who so attends and who chooses accordingly is making . . . the humanly correct decision, period."

Martha Nussbaum (b. 1947)

Finding the mean in the situation is the practical role of *reason* in ethics. The virtuous or excellent person is the one who is good at rationally discovering the mean relative to us with regard to our emotions, our habits, and our actions. How much, for instance, shall we give to charity? About these things we deliberate and choose. Because these are matters of degree and because the right degree depends on our appreciation of subtle differences in situations, being truly virtuous is difficult. As Aristotle says,

> going wrong happens in many ways, . . . whereas doing right happens in one way only. That is why one is easy, the other difficult: missing the target is easy, but hitting it is hard. (*NE* 2.6)

> This is why it is a hard job to be good. It is hard to get to the mean in each thing. It is the expert, not just anybody, who finds the center of the circle. In the same way, having a fit of temper is easy for anyone; so is giving money and spending it. But this is not so when it comes to questions of "for whom?" "how much?" "when?" "why?" and "how?" This is why goodness is rare, and is praiseworthy and fine. (*NE* 2.9)

"Wickedness is always easier than virtue; for it takes the shortcut to everything."

Samuel Johnson (1709–1784)

If you are good at using your reason to find the mean, you have *practical wisdom*. (The Greek word is *phronesis*.) Because virtue or excellence lies in the mean, and the mean is determined by reasoning, we can now also say that virtue is "disposition *accompanied* by right reason. Right reason, in connection with such matters is practical sense" (*NE* 6.13).

Aristotle does not give a formula or an algorithm to use in making choices. He apparently thinks that no such formula is possible in practical matters pertaining to particular choices. If a formula were possible, ethics could be a science rather than an art.* Nonetheless, there is a kind of standard for judging whether the right thing is being done. That standard is the virtuous and good person.

Protagoras holds that "man is the measure of all things." We have seen how this leads to a kind of relativism; if Jones thinks something is good, then it is good—to Jones. Aristotle disagrees and argues in this way: We do not take the word of someone who is color-blind about the color of a tie; in the same way, not everyone is adept at judging the goodness of things. Protagorean relativism is a mistake because it is not everyone, but only the good person, who is the "measure of each thing." In every situation, virtuous and good actions are defined by the mean. The mean is discovered by "right reason" or practical wisdom. So the "measure" of virtue and goodness will be the person who judges according to practical wisdom.

You might still want to ask, But how do we recognize these practically wise persons? To this question Aristotle has no very clear answer.† Again, there is no formula for recognizing such persons. But that need not mean we cannot in general tell who they are. They tend to be those persons, we might suggest, to whom you would turn for advice.

---

*We will see that some later writers on ethics, the utilitarians, for example, try to supply such a formula (p. 547). Kant also tries to find a single principle from which the right thing to do can be derived. See p. 489.

†Compare Augustine, who does have a clear answer to this question, pp. 283–284.

RESPONSIBILITY

The virtues, as we have seen, are dispositions to choose and behave in certain ways, according to right reason or practical wisdom. If we have these dispositions, we are called good; if we lack them, we are called bad. It is for our virtues and vices that we are praised and blamed. But under certain conditions, praise or blame are inappropriate. Let's call these "excusing conditions."

Aristotle is the first to canvass excusing conditions systematically and so to define when persons should not be held responsible for their actions. This is an important topic in its own right, useful "for those who are laying down laws about rewards and punishments" (*NE* 3.1). It has, moreover, been discussed in a variety of ways by subsequent philosophers. So we must look briefly at the way Aristotle begins this conversation.

> Praise and blame are accorded to voluntary acts; but involuntary acts are accorded pardon, and at times pity. (*NE* 3.1)

Aristotle assumes that in the normal course of events most of our actions are voluntary. Occasionally, however, we do something involuntarily, and then we are pardoned or pitied. What conditions qualify an action as involuntary? He identifies two excusing conditions: compulsion and ignorance. Let us briefly discuss each one.

When someone acts under compulsion we mean, says Aristotle, that

> the principle of action is external, and that the doer . . . contributes nothing of his own—as when the wind carries one off somewhere, or other human beings who have power over one do this. (*NE* 3.1)

Now, having your ship driven somewhere by a storm or being tied up and carried somewhere are particularly clear cases. If something bad should happen as a result of either of these, no one would blame you for it, for "the principle of action is external."

There are more debatable cases. For example, we would normally blame a ship's captain who lost his cargo by throwing it overboard. But if he threw it overboard during a storm to save his ship, we might excuse him, saying that the storm forced him to do it. Yet we can't say that he contributed "nothing of his own." He did make the decision; in that respect, the action was voluntary. Still, because this is what "all people of sense" would do in those circumstances, the captain is pardoned. Aristotle concludes that though such actions are voluntary if considered as particular acts, they are involuntary when considered in context—for no one would ordinarily choose them. And that is the ground on which we excuse the captain from blame.

Again Aristotle insists that we not try to find a precise formula for deciding such cases. He stresses how difficult such decisions may be.

> There are times when it is hard to decide what should be chosen at what price, and what endured in return for what reward. Perhaps it is still harder to stick to the decision.
>
> It is not easy to say if one course should be chosen rather than another, since there is great variation in particular circumstances. (*NE* 3.1)

Only by applying practical wisdom can we discern whether something was done by compulsion.

Let us consider the second condition. What sort of ignorance excuses us from responsibility? It is not, Aristotle says, ignorance of what is right. Those who do not know what is right are not ignorant, but wicked! We do not excuse people for being wicked. (Here is the source of the adage that ignorance of the law is no excuse.)

If ignorance of the right does not excuse, neither does ignorance of what everybody ought to know. But

> ignorance in particular circumstances does—that is, ignorance of the sphere and scope of the action. . . . A man may be ignorant of *what* he is doing: e.g., when people say that it "slipped out in the course of a conversation"; or that they did not know these things were secret . . . or like the man with the catapult, who wanted "only to demonstrate it," but fired it instead. Someone, as Merope does, might think his son an enemy; or mistake a sharp spear for one with a button. . . . One might give a man something to drink, with a view to saving his life, and kill him instead. (*NE* 3.1)

It is ignorance about particular circumstances that makes an action involuntary and leads us to excuse the agent from responsibility. In such cases, a person can say, If I had only known, I would have done differently. The mark of whether that is true, Aristotle suggests, is regret. If someone does something bad through ignorance and later regrets doing it, that is a sign that she is not wicked. It shows that she would indeed have done otherwise if she had known. And in that case she can truly be said to have acted involuntarily and deserve pardon.

Again, there are difficult cases. What about the person who acts in ignorance because he is drunk and is not in a condition to recognize the facts of the case? Here Aristotle suggests that it is not appropriate to excuse him, because he was responsible for getting himself into that state. The same is true for someone ignorant through carelessness; that person should have taken care. Here is, perhaps, a harder case.

> But perhaps the man's character is such that he cannot take care. Well, people themselves are responsible for getting like that, through living disorderly lives: they are responsible for being unjust or profligate, the former through evildoing, the latter through spending their time drinking, and so on. Activity in a certain thing gives a man that character; this is clear from those who are practicing for any contest or action, since that is what they spend their time doing. Not knowing that dispositions are attained through actually doing things is the sign of a complete ignoramus. (*NE* 3.5)

No one, Aristotle suggests, can be that ignorant.

This provides the main outlines of Aristotle's views on **responsibility.** We can see that he assumes people must normally be held responsible for what they do, that compulsion and ignorance may be excusing conditions, and that he is rather severe in his estimation of when these conditions may hold. Although Aristotle does not explicitly say so, it is a fair inference that he considers the acceptance of responsibility and the sparing use of excuses to be a part of the good life. By our choices and actions we create the habits that become our character. And so we are ourselves very largely responsible for our own happiness or lack thereof.

❧

> "Oh well," said Mr. Hennessy, "We are as th' Lord made us." "No," said Mr. Dooley, "lave us be fair. Lave us take some iv the blame ourselves."
>
> *Finley Peter Dunne (1876–1936)*

THE HIGHEST GOOD

When Aristotle defines the good for human beings as "activity of soul in conformity with excellence," he adds that "if there is more than one excellence, it will be the best and most complete of these." We need now to examine what the "best and most complete" excellence is.

The best activity of soul must be the one that activates whatever is best in us. And what is that? Think back to Aristotle's discussion of the human soul. It incorporates the levels of nutrition and reproduction, sensation, and reason. At the very peak is *nous*, or mind: the nonpassive, purely active source of knowledge and wisdom that is the most divine element in us.

Thus, the best activity is the activity of *nous*. And such activity should be not only the highest good but also the greatest happiness for a human being. The activity of *nous*—discovering and keeping in mind the first principles of things—Aristotle calls "**contemplation.**" The life of contemplation is said to be the very best life partly because it is the exercise of the "best" part of us and partly because we can engage in it "continuously." But this life is also the most pleasant and the most self-sufficient. For these reasons it is the happiest life.

> We think it essential that pleasure should be mixed in with happiness, and the most pleasant of activities in accordance with virtue is admittedly activity in accordance with wisdom. Philosophy has pleasures that are marvelous for their purity and permanence. Besides, it is likely that those who have knowledge have a more pleasant life than those who are seeking it. Sufficiency, as people call it, will be associated above all with contemplation. The wise man, the just, and all the rest of them need the necessities of life; further, once there is an adequate supply of these, the just man needs people with and towards

whom he may perform just acts; and the same applies to the temperate man, the brave man, and so on. But the wise man is able to contemplate, even when he is on his own; and the more so, the wiser he is. It is better, perhaps, when he has people working with him; but still he is the most self-sufficient of all. (*NE* 10.7)

Aristotle dismisses honor as a candidate for the good, you will recall, on the grounds that it is too dependent on others. What is truly good, it seems, must be more "proper to the person, and cannot be taken away." The same point is here used to recommend the life of contemplation as the very best life, for it is more "self-sufficient" than any other, less dependent on other people. The other virtues need the presence of other people for their exercise, while the wise man can engage in contemplation "even when he is on his own." And to Aristotle this seems to recommend such a life as the very best.*

Aristotle does not deny that there are good human lives that are noncontemplative. Ordinary men and women, not devoting themselves to science and philosophy, can also be excellent human beings—and therefore happy. But only those fortunate enough to be able to devote themselves to intellectual pursuits will experience the very best life—that pinnacle of human happiness which is most like the happiness of God. We see clearly that Aristotle's ethics (and classical Greek ethics in general) is an ethics of self-perfection, or self-realization. There is not much in it that recommends caring for others for *their* sakes.†

This attitude underlies the rational justification for being virtuous in both Plato and Aristotle. They try to show that we should be just and moderate because, to put it crudely, it *pays*. True, neither argues that the consequences of virtue will necessarily be pleasing. Glaucon's picture of the perfectly moral and perfectly immoral men had ruled out that sort of appeal. Happiness is not related to virtue as a paycheck is related to a week's work. The relation for both Plato and Aristotle is internal; the just and virtuous life is recommended because it is in *itself* the happiest life (though they also believe that in *general* its consequences will be good). Although Aristotle always thinks of the good of a person as essentially involving the good of some community, and especially as involving friends, it remains true nonetheless that individuals are primarily interested in their own happiness. This may, we might grant, be a stimulus to achievement, but there is not much compassion in it.

1. What *kind* of a thing is a virtue? Can virtue be taught? How?
2. Is virtue just one? Or are there many virtues?
3. Explain Aristotle's doctrine of the mean.
4. Why is it "a hard job to be good"?
5. What is practical wisdom?
6. What is "the measure of all things," so far as goodness goes?
7. What conditions, according to Aristotle, excuse a person from responsibility? Explain each.
8. Does having a bad character excuse a person? Explain.
9. What is the very best life?

FOR FURTHER THOUGHT

1. In your view, does Aristotle's logic do anything to undercut the relativism spawned by the Sophists' teaching of rhetoric? Explain your answer.
2. Keeping in mind Aristotle's doctrine of how soul and body are related, try to construct an Aristotelian account of *fear*. (Hint: You will have to consider both mental and physical factors and how they are related.)
3. Write a short paragraph giving an Aristotelian account of the virtue of moderation.
4. We read that young people attracted to gang life are seeking "respect." Write an Aristotelian critique of this motivation.

---

*Contemplation, for Aristotle, is not what is often called "meditation" these days. It is not an attempt to empty the mind, but an active life of study to uncover the wonder and the whys of things.

†Such compassion, or caring, under the names of "love" and "charity" (*agape*, not *eros*) comes into our story with the Christians. See pp. 257 and 260.

KEY WORDS

terms	efficient cause
statements	final cause
categories	teleology
substance	entelechy
primary substance	first philosophy
secondary substances	metaphysics
truth	essence
correspondence	unmoved mover
argument	God
syllogism	nutritive soul
premises	sensitive soul
conclusion	rational soul
middle term	*eudaemonia*
valid	function
first principles	virtues
induction	habits
nous	practical wisdom
nature	the mean
material cause	responsibility
formal cause	contemplation

NOTES

1. Quoted from Ps. Ammonius, *Aristotelis Vita*, in W. D. Ross, *Aristotle* (New York: Meridian Books, 1959), 14.
2. We are indebted here to Marjorie Grene's excellent little book, *A Portrait of Aristotle* (Chicago: University of Chicago Press, 1963), 38–65.
3. Quoted in J. M. Edmonds, *Elegy and Iambus with the Anacreontea II* (New York: G. P. Putnam's Sons, 1931), 175.
4. All quotations from Aristotle's works are from *The Philosophy of Aristotle*, ed. Renford Bambrough (New York: New American Library, 1963), unless noted otherwise. Within this text, references to specific works will be as follows (numerical references are to book and section numbers).
   C: *Categories*
   I: *On Interpretation*
   M: *Metaphysics*
   PA: *Posterior Analytics*
   PH: *Physics*
   PS: *Psychology*
   NE: *Nicomachean Ethics*
5. As quoted in Grene, *Portrait of Aristotle*, 105.
6. We owe this example to J. L. Ackrill, *Aristotle the Philosopher* (Oxford: Oxford University Press, 1981), 42.

10

CONFUCIUS, MENCIUS, AND XUNZI

Virtue in Ancient China

In the West, the story of ancient philosophy revolves around three central characters: Socrates, Plato, and Aristotle. In China, the story of ancient Confucian philosophy features another famous trio: Confucius, Mencius, and Xunzi. There were other influential philosophers in each tradition, such as the Stoics in the West and Hanfeizi and Zhuangzi in China, but these philosophers exerted an especially profound influence on the course of Western and Chinese civilization, respectively.

In this chapter, we survey the central ideas of Confucius and their development by Mencius and Xunzi, all of whom focused primarily on moral and political concerns. The Confucians, like Socrates, Plato, and Aristotle, understand morality in terms of virtue. But while their understanding of virtue resembles the Greeks' in some ways, it differs markedly in others.

Confucius

Confucius was born in 552 or 551 B.C. under circumstances that gave no hint of how profoundly he would shape Chinese civilization. Some traditional accounts credit him with royal ancestors in the state of Song, but by the time of his great grandfather, the family had moved to the small state of Lu in what is now eastern China. The family settled near the city of Qufu, where it fell into poverty. Ancient sources say that he grew up impoverished and, as a young man, supported himself with various menial jobs.

Despite such humble beginnings, Confucius acquired a deep knowledge of genteel traditions that were already ancient by the time he was born. These included the rituals and stories of the Zhou dynasty and of the earlier sage kings.* According to Confucius, this first stage of his development took fifteen years:

> At fifteen, I set my mind upon learning; at thirty, I took my place in society; at forty, I became free from doubts; at fifty, I understood Heaven's Mandate; at sixty, my ear was attuned; and at seventy, I could follow my heart's desires without overstepping the bounds of propriety. (*Analects* 2.4)[1]

---

*For background on the Zhou dynasty and the sage kings, see pp. 75–76.

"The gentleman cherishes virtue, whereas the petty person cherishes physical possessions."

—CONFUCIUS

When, upon completing his initial education, he "took his place in society," Confucius established himself as a person of some repute in his native state of Lu. He became part of a rising social class of scholar-officials known as *shi*, who advised various hereditary rulers during the later Zhou dynasty. Confucius held a government position in Lu at some point, but political chaos there forced him to travel from state to state struggling to find a ruler who would put his ideas into practice. By 484 B.C., having failed to convince any ruler to follow his philosophy, Confucius returned to Lu, where he spent the rest of his days teaching and (according to tradition) editing or compiling books that later became the Confucian classics. His disciples came to call him Kongzi, which means "Master Kong." He died in 479 B.C., a decade before Socrates was born, presumably unaware that his life's work would transform China forever.

THE WAY OF CONFUCIUS

After Confucius died, his students compiled his sayings, along with various anecdotes about him, into a collection known as the **Analects.** One rarely finds in the *Analects* the sort of dialectical or discursive reasoning so common in Greek philosophy. In this respect, the *Analects* resembles Heraclitus' aphorisms more than it resembles Plato's dialogues or Aristotle's treatises. Each

passage presents one or more ideas—sometimes clearly, sometimes cryptically—but understanding those ideas and the reasoning behind them requires reading different passages together. Taken together, the *Analects* provide the first expression in China of a rational, systematic set of answers to distinctively philosophical questions—in this case, questions about how to live and how to organize society. Works more paradigmatically philosophical in style appear soon afterward in China, both reacting to and building on the views laid out in the *Analects.*

Given Confucius' long quest to find rulers to put his teachings into practice, you might expect the *Analects* to focus on practical questions of government. So it might surprise you to discover that the book focuses mainly on being a good person, on the finer points of rituals and etiquette, and on the various social relationships that people occupy. For Confucius, however, these topics lie at the very heart of good government.

The most fundamental thing a ruler needs to do, according to Confucius, is to be virtuous. The central virtue in Confucius' thought is called *rén,* which is a notoriously difficult word to translate into English. In the centuries before Confucius, the word referred to the ideal demeanor and behavior of a Chinese aristocrat; it meant something like "manliness" or "nobility." Confucius elevates it to an overarching virtue and transforms it into something grander than it had been. Some translators have rendered it as "humaneness" or "human-heartedness," others as "authoritative conduct" or "comprehensive virtue," and still others simply as "Goodness." We will adopt this last translation, since loving, cultivating, and manifesting *rén* is what it takes, according to Confucius, to be a good person.

Cultivating and manifesting genuine Goodness involves cultivating and manifesting various subsidiary virtues, such as dutifulness, understanding, righteousness or integrity, benevolence, trustworthiness, filial piety, and ritual propriety. We cultivate these virtues, according to Confucius, through a lifelong process of assiduous **moral self-cultivation** that requires learning, reflection, and deliberate effort to put

Confucian teachings into practice.* One of Confucius' prominent disciples explains his own process this way:

> Master Zeng said, "Every day I examine myself on three counts: in my dealings with others, have I failed in any way failed to be dutiful? In my interactions with friends and associates, have I in any way failed to be trustworthy? Finally, have I in any way failed to repeatedly put into practice what I teach?" (*Analects* 1.4)

Another disciple cites one of the **Odes** as inspiration. The *Odes* is a set of ancient Chinese poems that Confucians regard as a storehouse of wisdom.

> Zigong says, "An ode says,
>   'As if cut, as if polished;
>   As if carved, as if ground.'
> Is this not what you have mind?"
> The Master said, "Zigong, you are precisely the kind of person with whom one can begin to discuss the *Odes*. Informed as to what has gone before, you know what is to come." (*Analects* 1.15)

Zigong's point is that cultivating virtue is a slow process requiring patience and diligence, like polishing ivory or cutting and grinding stone. Confucius makes the point himself in his statement that it took until the age of seventy before he could "follow [his] heart's desires without overstepping the bounds of propriety."

⬦

"There's only one corner of the universe you can be certain of improving, and that's your own self."

Aldous Huxley (1894–1963)

The Confucian virtues are not an assorted grab bag of admirable character traits, to be cultivated one by one. They are aspects of a systematic view about how to live. Confucius explains to his disciple Zeng Shen:

> "Master Zeng! All that I teach can be strung together on a single thread."
> "Yes, sir," Master Zeng responded.
> After the Master left, the disciples asked, "What did he mean by that?"
> Master Zeng said, "All that the Master teaches amounts to dutifulness tempered by understanding." (*Analects* 4.15)

And what, for Confucius, is dutifulness? We find an answer to this question in a discussion about Ziwen, a famous government official from the seventh century B.C.

> Zizhang said, "Prime Minister Ziwen was given three times the post of prime minister, and yet he never showed a sign of pleasure; he was removed from this office three times, and yet never showed a sign of resentment. When the incoming prime minister took over, he invariably provided him with a complete account of the official state of affairs. What do you make of Prime Minister Ziwen?"
> The Master said, "He certainly was dutiful."
> "Was he not Good?"
> "I do not know about that—what makes you think he deserves to be called Good?" (*Analects* 5.19)

Dutifulness, we learn, involves doing one's best to carry out one's responsibilities, whatever they may be. We also see in this passage that while dutifulness is central to comprehensive virtue, it alone is not sufficient to be Good.

What of understanding? Consider Confucius' response to a question from his disciple Zigong:

> Zigong asked, "Is there one word that can serve as a guide for one's entire life?"
> The Master answered, "Is it not 'understanding'? Do not impose upon others what you yourself do not desire." (*Analects* 15.24)

Understanding, then, is the ability to understand how you yourself would feel in another's situation and so refrain from doing to others what you would not want done to you.* Thus, while dutifulness requires carrying out one's responsibilities conscientiously, "tempering" that dutifulness

---

*Compare Socrates on virtue as knowledge (pp. 99–100) and Aristotle on the development of virtue as the formation of habits (pp. 212–213).

---

*Compare to Jesus' proclamation that loving your neighbor means that "as you wish that men would do to you, do so to them." See pp. 257.

with understanding means carrying them out in ways that account for particular circumstances and individuals.

A person's responsibilities, for Confucius, arise from the particular social relationships they occupy, most of which Confucius understands to be hierarchical and asymmetrical, so that each person in the relationship has different responsibilities. Among the most important of these relationships is that between children and parents. A person's responsibilities toward his or her parents are embodied in the important virtue of **filial piety,** which involves respect, obedience, and care. Confucius explains filial piety in various ways.

> Meng Yizi asked about filial piety. The Master replied, "Do not disobey." (*Analects* 2.5)
>
> The Master said, "In serving your parents you may gently remonstrate with them. However, once it becomes apparent that they have not taken your criticism to heart you should be respectful and not oppose them, and follow their lead diligently without resentment." (*Analects* 4.18)
>
> Meng Wubo asked about filial piety. The Master replied, "Give your parents no cause for anxiety other than the possibility that they might fall ill." (*Analects* 2.6)
>
> Ziyou asked about filial piety. The Master said, "Nowadays, 'filial' means simply being able to provide one's parents with nourishment. But even dogs and horses are provided with nourishment. If you are not respectful, wherein lies the difference?" (*Analects* 2.7)
>
> Zixia asked about filial piety. The Master said, "It is the demeanor that is difficult. . . . When wine and food are served, elders are given precedence, but surely filial piety consists of more than this." (*Analects* 2.8)

These passages introduce another key Confucian idea. In insisting that filial piety requires more than carrying out your responsibilities toward your parents, Confucius highlights that manifesting the virtue of filial piety requires carrying out those responsibilities with a certain demeanor and having a certain attitude. It requires fulfilling your responsibilities sincerely and out of respect for your parents, rather than just out of a sense of duty. This idea pervades Confucian thought on virtue: being virtuous is about more than going through the motions—it is more than just doing the things that virtuous people do.*

Taken together, these passages suggest a certain picture of the virtuous person: A virtuous person has carefully cultivated the tendency to fulfill his or her responsibilities to others conscientiously, with the right attitude, and with sympathetic understanding for other people.

RITUAL PROPRIETY

Confucius also gives another explanation of the path to Goodness—an explanation that seems, at first, to be at odds with his claim that dutifulness tempered by understanding is the "single thread" on which all his moral teachings can be strung.

> Yan Hui asked about Goodness.
>
> The Master said, "Restraining yourself and returning to the rites constitutes Goodness. If for one day you managed to restrain yourself and return to the rites, in this way you could lead the entire world back to Goodness. The key to achieving Goodness lies within yourself—how could it come from others?"
>
> Yan Hui asked, "May I inquire into the specifics?"
>
> The Master said, "Do not look unless it is in accordance with ritual; do not listen unless it is in accordance with ritual; do not speak unless it is in accordance with ritual; do not move unless it is in accordance with ritual."
>
> Yan Hui asked, "Although I am not quick to understand, I ask permission to devote myself to this teaching." (*Analects* 12.1)

Here we have another distinctively Confucian idea—adherence to the **rites** or rituals. Painting a complete picture of Confucian Goodness requires understanding how this idea fits together with his basic picture of virtue. The basic idea of ritual is familiar enough in Western culture. Certain kinds of activities are to be done in certain ways: religious ceremonies follow set conventional patterns; so do funeral services, weddings, graduations, and birthdays; and even many of our

---

*Compare Aristotle on choosing virtuous actions for the right reason and doing them in the right way. See pp. 213–215.

daily interactions, such as greetings, goodbyes, meals, and conversations, are guided by conventions that specify right and wrong ways of doing things. In the West, however, we usually think of the rules for daily interactions as a matter of etiquette more than a question of morality. We say that someone who follows these rules has "good manners." Furthermore, we usually separate the rules of etiquette from the conventions for things like funerals and religious ceremonies. Confucius, however, lumps the rules for formal ceremonies and the rules for everyday behaviors together in the single category of ritual.

Confucius sees the proper performance of ritual as central to Goodness partly because the rites offer specific ways of carrying out your responsibilities to other people. Consider some contemporary Western examples: Bringing a small gift to a dinner party, such as a dessert or a bottle of wine, demonstrates your appreciation of your host's hospitality. Starting an email to a person you have never met with "Yo, what's up?" can convey a lack of respect. Dressing appropriately for a funeral signals your sorrow and your sympathy for the deceased's loved ones; wearing a Hawaiian shirt and cracking jokes during the funeral would normally signal a lack of those things.

Furthermore, the proper performance of ritual helps you cultivate virtue by restraining unvirtuous tendencies, channeling your efforts at virtue in the right direction, and making social interactions run more smoothly.

> The Master said, "If you are respectful but lack ritual you will become exasperating; if you are careful but lack ritual you will become timid; if you are courageous but lack ritual you will become unruly; and if you are upright but lack ritual you will become inflexible." (*Analects* 8.1)

As with the virtues, the proper performance of ritual requires having the right attitude.

> The Master said, "Someone who lacks magnanimity when occupying high office, who is not respectful when performing ritual, and who remains unmoved by sorrow when overseeing mourning rites—how could I bear to look upon such a person?" (*Analects* 3.26)

"Sacrifice as if they were present" means that, when sacrificing to the spirits, you should comport yourself as if the spirits were present.

> The Master said, "If I am not fully present at the sacrifice, it is as if I did not sacrifice at all." (*Analects* 3.12)

Furthermore, the proper performance of ritual involves intelligent, flexible behavior that flows from a sincere appreciation for and understanding of the rites. Thus, even though Confucius believes that the rules for carrying out your responsibilities were laid down long before he was born, there is some room for deviation as the circumstances require.

> The Master said, "A ceremonial cap made of linen is prescribed by the rites, but these days people use silk. This is frugal, and I follow the majority. To bow before ascending the stairs is what is prescribed by the rites, but these days people bow after ascending. This is arrogant, and—though it goes against the majority—I continue to bow before ascending." (*Analects* 9.3)

The correct performance of the rites depends ultimately on a sincere expression of the emotions and virtues that each specific rite is intended to convey or cultivate. Only when you understand the "roots" of each ritual can you know which deviations from the standard rules are acceptable.

> Lin Fang asked about the roots of ritual.
> The Master exclaimed, "What a noble question! When it comes to ritual, it is better to be spare than extravagant. When it comes to [rituals related to] mourning, it is better to be excessively sorrowful than fastidious." (*Analects* 3.4)

The proper performance of ritual, then, requires conscientious application of the rules of ritual, all while appreciating the purpose of the rules and adjusting one's behavior to the circumstances as necessary. Thus, even this "key to achieving Goodness" can be seen as a matter of dutifulness tempered by understanding.

GOOD GOVERNMENT

We are now in a position to see why Confucius, who spent his life trying to promote good government, devoted so much of his teaching to the cultivation of personal virtue. A genuinely Good person would conscientiously and intelligently carry out his or her responsibilities based on a sympathetic understanding of others' situations and a deep appreciation of the proper way to do things. If rulers and their ministers behaved this way, Confucius believed, then the common people would prosper and be virtuous themselves. Social harmony would prevail. Thus, for Confucius, virtue turns out to be the solution to the most vexing problem of his time: the social and political chaos of the later Zhou dynasty.*

Yet, when asked what he would do first if given a position in government, Confucius offers a surprising answer.

> Zilu asked, "If the Duke of Wei were to employ you to serve in the government of his state, what would be your first priority?"
>
> The Master answered, "It would, of course, be the rectification of names."†
>
> Zilu said, "Could you, Master, really be so far off the mark? Why worry about rectifying names?"
>
> The Master replied, "How boorish you are, Zilu! When it comes to matters that he does not understand, the gentleman should remain silent. If names are not rectified, speech will not accord with reality; when speech does not accord with reality, things will not be successfully accomplished. When things are not successfully accomplished, ritual practice and music will fail to flourish; when ritual and music fail to flourish, punishments and penalties will miss the mark. And when punishment and penalties miss the mark, the common people will be at a loss as to what to do with themselves. This is why the gentleman only applies names that can be properly spoken and assures that what he says can be properly put into action. The gentleman simply guards against arbitrariness in his speech. That is all there is to it." (*Analects* 13.3)

We might wonder, with Zilu, why the **rectification of names** is of paramount importance

in government. The answer lies in understanding another surprising passage from the *Analects*:

> Confucius said of the Ji Family, "They have eight rows of dancers performing in their courtyard. If they can condone this, what are they *not* capable of?"

How could Confucius be so incensed about how many rows of dancers someone had in their courtyard? It is because by having eight rows of dancers, the Ji family was violating the rites. The Ji family controlled Confucius' home state of Lu, but the head of the Ji family was not a king; he was merely a minister to the duke of Lu, who was himself subordinate to the reigning Zhou dynasty king. The rites dictate that only a king can have eight rows of dancers. For the head of the Ji family to have eight rows of dancers, then, is for him to act as if he were king. If he acts as if he were king, then he will not be fulfilling his responsibilities toward either his immediate ruler, the duke of Lu, or the Zhou king; in turn, neither the duke nor the king could fulfill his responsibilities toward his subjects. This makes social harmony impossible.

Rectifying names, then, means ensuring that everyone is carrying out their respective roles properly. Someone who bears the title of "minister" in the king's government should act like a minister; whoever bears the title of "king" should act like a king; whoever is called a "father" should act like a father, and so on. And since a "true king" will carry out his responsibilities conscientiously and virtuously, in accordance with the rites, once names are rectified, everyone will be acting virtuously.

Furthermore, Confucius believes that this process can begin at the top, as it were, with the rulers and ministers themselves. Their virtue will act as an inspiration and example for the common people, who will follow suit, ushering in an era of peace, stability, and prosperity. When kings and ministers rule virtuously, Confucius believes, they will have no need for coercion and harsh punishments. Thus, when asked about governing, Confucius offers the following advice:

> Ji Kangzi asked, "How can I cause the common people to be respectful, dutiful, and industrious?"
>
> The Master said, "Oversee them with dignity, and the people will be respectful; oversee them

---

*On the political situation in Confucius' time, see Chapter 5 (pp. 76).

†The term that is translated as "rectification of names" literally means something like "making names correct." As we saw in Chapter 5, the topic of "names" fascinated ancient Chinese philosophers. See pp. 80–81.

with filiality and kindness, and the people will be dutiful; oversee them by raising up the accomplished and instructing those who are unable, and the people will be industrious." (*Analects* 2.20)

Duke Ai asked, "What can I do to induce the common people to be obedient?"

Confucius replied, "Raise up the straight and apply them to the crooked, and the people will submit to you. If you raise up the crooked and apply them to the straight, the people will never submit." (*Analects* 2.19)

Ji Kangzi asked Confucius about governing, saying, "If I were to execute those who lacked the Way in order to advance those who possessed the Way, how would that be?"

Confucius responded, "In your governing, Sir, what need is there for executions? If you desire goodness, then the common people will be good. The Virtue of a gentleman is like the wind, and the Virtue of a petty person is like the grass—when the wind moves over the grass, the grass is sure to bend." (*Analects* 12.19)

The "Virtue" of this last passage is more than virtue in the ordinary sense. The word "Virtue" here translates a Chinese word *dé,* which signifies a special sort of charisma radiating from a morally good leader— a quality so powerful that, according to Confucius,

One who rules through the power of Virtue [*dé*] is analogous to the Pole Star: it simply remains in its place and receives the homage of the myriad lesser stars. (*Analects* 2.1)

The *Analects*, then, offers a systematic view of what it would take to restore the lost Golden Age: If rulers become Good by cultivating the virtues, including dutifulness, understanding, and the proper performance of ritual, their example and their actions will bring their ministers and the common people into harmony with one another.

1. How is the virtue of filial piety related to Goodness, according to Confucius?
2. What are the rites? What role do they play in Confucius' theory of virtue?
3. What does Confucius mean by the "rectification of names"? Why is that the first thing that Confucius would pursue if given a position in government?
4. Why, according to Confucius, is it important for rulers to be virtuous?

Mencius

While Plato studied directly with Socrates, the connection between Confucius and the next great Confucian thinker, Mencius, is less direct. Confucius' disciples took it on themselves to transmit the Master's teachings to the next generation, and their disciples continued that tradition. Roughly a century after Confucius' death, Confucius' grandson or one of his grandson's disciples took on a pupil named Meng Ke, who would eventually come to be known as Mengzi or "Master Meng." We do not know exactly when Mencius lived, but he was probably born in the early fourth century B.C. and lived a long life, making him a contemporary of Plato and Aristotle. Mencius spent his life trying to convince rulers of the chaotic Warring States period to adopt the Confucian way, much as Confucius had done generations earlier. Mencius' thought is recorded in a book called the *Mengzi*. Like the *Analects*, it consists of a loosely organized collection of sayings and anecdotes. Many of these are considerably longer than the passages in the *Analects* and offer more systematic, discursive reasoning than we find in Confucius. Like Confucius, Mencius is mainly interested in virtue and good governance, and his views on these topics resemble Confucius' own. By Mencius' day, however, the great conversation of Chinese philosophy had developed considerably, and so he devotes significant effort to defending the Confucian outlook against more recent competitors. Mencius also takes a keen interest in another philosophical innovation that would become a hallmark of Chinese thought: the question of human nature.

DIFFERENTIATED LOVE

Mencius identifies two rival schools of thought as particularly pernicious and sets himself the task of arguing against them. The first school is that of Mozi, who famously advocated a doctrine of "mutual care" or "impartial concern," according to which each person ought to show equal and impartial concern for everyone.* The second consists of

―――――――――――

*See pp. 78–80.

"Benevolence is simply being human. The Way is simply to harmonize with benevolence and put it into words."

—MENCIUS

followers of a fourth-century philosopher named Yang Zhu, who seems to have taught that each person should strive to protect his or her own person and that, at least in the chaos of the Warring States period, this meant withdrawing from public life. Mencius complains that

> the doctrines of Yang Zhu and Mozi fill the world. If a doctrine does not lean toward Yang Zhu, then it leans toward Mozi. Yang Zhu is "for oneself." This is to not have a ruler. Mozi is "impartial caring." This is to not have a father. . . .
>
> If the Ways of Yang Zhu and Mozi do not cease, and the way of Kongzi [Confucius] is not made evident, then evil doctrines will dupe the people and obstruct benevolence and righteousness. If benevolence and righteousness are obstructed, that leads animals to devour people, and then people will begin to devour one another. Because I fear this, I preserve the Way of the former sages, fend off Yang

Zhu and Mozi, and get rid of specious words, so that evil doctrines will be unable to arise. (*Mengzi* 3B9)[2]

> Mengzi said, "Yang Zhu favored being 'for oneself.' If plucking out one hair from his body would have benefited the world, he would not do it. Mozi favored 'impartial caring.' If scraping himself bare from head to heels would benefit the whole world, he would do it." (*Mengzi* 7A26)

Yang Zhu errs, according to Mencius, in attaching too much weight to one's own interests. Mencius takes Yang Zhu to be selfish. Those who follow Yang Zhu's advice will not fulfill their responsibilities to their superiors.

Mozi errs, according to Mencius, by going to the opposite extreme. Rather than focusing too narrowly on one's own interests, Mozi demands that we give *everyone's* interests equal weight. Mencius regards this as both unrealistic and immoral. It is unrealistic because, as Mencius scoffs at a Mohist rival, it is implausible to think that "one's affection for one's own nephew is like one's affection for a neighbor's baby" (*Mengzi* 3A5). It is immoral because the truly virtuous person demonstrates different levels of concern and love for different people. On the Confucian view, one's love and concern ought to radiate out from oneself like ripples in a pond, strongest near the center and weakening gradually as one moves away.

> Mengzi said, "Gentlemen, in relation to animals, are sparing of them but are not benevolent toward them. In relation to the people [in their society], they are benevolent toward them but do not treat them as kin. They treat their kin as kin, and then are benevolent toward the people. They are benevolent toward the people, and then are sparing of animals." (*Mengzi* 7A45)

The correct view, then, is somewhere between Yang Zhu's and Mozi's. But as Mencius says after condemning Yang Zhu's and Mozi's extreme position, adhering slavishly to the mean between selfishness and selflessness is not good enough.

> Zimo [unlike Yang Zhu and Mozi] held to the middle. Holding to the middle is close to [the Way]. But if one holds to the middle without discretion, that is the same as holding to one extreme. What I

dislike about those who hold to one extreme is that they detract from the Way. They elevate one thing and leave aside a hundred others. (*Mengzi* 7A26)*

The sort of "discretion" that Mencius has in mind comes through in a parable that Mencius relates about Emperor Shun, an ancient sage renowned for his filial piety. Shun's younger brother, Xiang, was "consummately lacking in benevolence," not to mention respect for his elder brother, whom he repeatedly tried to kill. But whereas Shun executed other ministers and rulers for lacking benevolence, he made Xiang the ruler of a territory called Youbi. This, Mencius explains, is because

> benevolent people do not store up anger nor do they dwell in bitterness against their younger brothers. They simply love and treat them as kin. Treating them as kin, they desire them to have rank. Loving them, they desire them to have wealth. [Shun] gave [Xiang] Youbi to administer to give him wealth and rank. If he himself was the [emperor], and his young brother was a common fellow, could this be called loving and treating as kin? (*Mengzi* 5A3)

Thus, whereas Mencius accepts Shun's decision to execute unbenevolent ministers, he takes Shun's familial relationship with Xiang to justify not only a stay of execution but also an elevation to power and wealth. Still, it would not have been right for Shun to elevate familial responsibilities and leave aside his other responsibilities. So, Shun arranged it so that

> Xiang did not have effective power in his state. [Shun] instructed officials to administer the state and collect tribute and taxes. . . . So could Xiang have succeeded in being cruel to his subjects? Nonetheless, Shun desired to see him often. Hence, Xiang came to court as constantly as a flowing spring. (*Mengzi* 5A3)

By keeping Xiang away from Youbi and restricting his actual powers there, Shun balanced his duties to his younger brother with his royal responsibilities to the common people of Youbi. This nicely illustrates the Confucian doctrine of

___

*Compare with Aristotle's view on using practical reason to correctly identify the mean with respect to each virtue. See pp. 213–215.

differentiated love: in contrast to the self-interested Yangists and the impartial Mohists, Confucians will give preferential treatment to those closest to them, especially their own family members, but they will still extend some degree of love and concern to everyone.

> "Then, too, there are a great many degrees of closeness or remoteness in human society. To proceed beyond the universal bond of our common humanity, there is the closer one of belonging to the same people, tribe, and tongue . . . but a still closer social union exists between kindred."
>
> *Cicero (106–43 B.C.)*

HUMAN NATURE IS GOOD

Mencius also wades into another debate that had arisen since Confucius' time: the goodness or badness of human nature. By the fourth century B.C., a number of positions on this matter had been staked out. For instance, a philosopher named Gaozi held that human nature is neither good nor bad.

> Mengzi debated Gaozi, who said, "Human nature is like a willow tree; righteousness is like cups and bowls. To make human nature benevolent and righteous is like making a willow tree into cups and bowls." (*Mengzi* 6A1)

Gaozi means that just as being a cup or a bowl is not part of a willow tree's nature, so benevolence and righteousness are not part of human nature. But just as people can, through deliberate effort, shape the branches of a willow tree into cups or bowls, so they can, through deliberate effort, shape themselves to become benevolent and righteous. But there is nothing in human nature, according to Gaozi, that inclines it toward virtue.

> Gaozi said, "Human nature is like swirling water. Make an opening for it on the eastern side, then it flows east. Make an opening for it on the western side, then it flows west. Human nature not

distinguishing between good and not good is like water not distinguishing between eastern and western." (*Mengzi* 6A2)

Other philosophers had held that "human nature can become good, and it can become not good" and still others that there "are [human] natures that are good, and there are natures that are not good" (*Mengzi* 6A6). Mencius disagrees with all of these positions. In replying to Gaozi's comparison with swirling water, he says,

> Water surely does not distinguish between east and west. But doesn't it distinguish between upward and downward? Human nature being good is like water tending downward. There is no human who does not tend toward goodness. There is no water that does not tend downward.
>
> Now, by striking water and making it leap up, you can cause it to go past your forehead. If you guide it by damming it, you can cause it to remain on a mountaintop. But is this the nature of water? It is only that way because of the circumstances. When humans are caused to not be good, it is only because their nature is the same way. (*Mengzi* 6A2)

To make sense of Mencius' position, we need to answer three questions. What does Mencius mean by "**human nature**"? In what sense is there "no human who does not tend toward goodness"? And if all humans naturally tend toward goodness, how do we explain the fact that many people are not virtuous?

With respect to the first question, Mencius means that all humans intrinsically have certain emotions that, under favorable circumstances, will lead them toward goodness and that when someone does not develop into a good person, this is because of unfavorable circumstances, not some fault in their nature. Each person's innate tendencies toward goodness, then, are like water's tendency to flow downward. It is not inevitable that people will become good or that water will flow downward. Furthermore, when people become bad, it is no more because their natures have become bad than that water's natural tendencies change when it is dammed atop a mountain.

To put this in terms of Mencius' favorite metaphor for human nature, all people are born with emotional tendencies that are like newly sprouted plants. Given an appropriate environment, with good soil and adequate water and sun, sprouts will naturally grow into healthy plants. Likewise, given an appropriate environment, with economic security and a loving family living in a stable, flourishing society, people will naturally grow into good people.* These inborn emotional capacities and their natural course of development, then, are what Mencius means by human nature.

What of the second question? Now that we understand what Mencius means by human nature, what is he saying when he says that it is good? He means that our inborn tendencies direct us toward certain virtues.

> Humans all have the feeling of compassion. Humans all have the feelings of disdain. Humans all have the feeling of respect. Humans all have the feeling of approval and disapproval. The feeling of compassion is benevolence. The feeling of disdain is righteousness. The feeling of respect is propriety. The feeling of approval and disapproval is wisdom. Benevolence, righteousness, propriety, and wisdom are not welded to us externally. We inherently have them. (*Mengzi* 6A6)

Mencius takes four virtues—benevolence, righteousness, propriety, and wisdom—to be of the first importance. To have them is to be a good person. Thus, the "**four sprouts**" of compassion, disdain, respect, and approval or disapproval are the roots of virtue and goodness. If they are cultivated and given an appropriate setting in which to develop, people will naturally grow into virtue.

Why, then, do so many people fail to be virtuous? Mencius explains this through the allegory of **Ox Mountain.**

> Mengzi said, "The trees of Ox Mountain were once beautiful. But because it bordered on a large state, hatchets and axes besieged it. Could it remain verdant? Due to the respite it got during the day or night, and the moisture of rain and dew, there were sprouts and shoots growing there. But oxen and sheep came and grazed on them. Hence, it was as if it were barren. Seeing it barren, people believed that there had never been any timber there. But could this be the nature of the mountain?

---

*Compare Aristotle on nature, entelechy, and potentiality (pp. 196–197, 199–200).

"When we consider what is present in people, could they truly lack the hearts of benevolence and righteousness? The way that they discard their genuine hearts is like the hatchets and axes in relation to the trees. With them besieging it day by day, can it remain beautiful? With the respite it gets during the day or night . . . their likes and dislikes are sometimes close to those of others. But then what they do during the day again fetters and destroys it. If the fettering is repeated . . . then one is not far from an animal. Others see that he is an animal, and think that there was never any capacity there. But is this what a human is like inherently?

"Hence, if it merely gets nourishment, there is nothing that will not grow. If it merely loses its nourishment, there is nothing that will not vanish." (*Mengzi* 6A8)

Bad people are bad, then, not because of their nature, but because outside influences prevent their "sprouts" from developing properly or because they have failed to cultivate their natural tendencies in the proper way.

What reason do we have to believe Mencius' view, aside perhaps from a desire to take an optimistic view of ourselves and the people around us? Mencius argues that we can see our natural tendencies toward goodness in certain actions and impulses. His arguments focus mainly on benevolence, which he takes to be the most important of the four cardinal virtues. (In fact, the word we have been translating as "benevolence" in discussing Mencius is *rén*, which Confucius uses to mean "Goodness" or "comprehensive virtue." While Mencius understands *rén* much more narrowly in terms of helping others achieve what is good in life and avoid what is bad, he shares Confucius' view that the person who manifests *rén* will also manifest all of the virtues.*)

Mencius asks us to imagine a small child who is about to fall into a well. Anyone who sees this, he claims,

would have a feeling of alarm and compassion—not because one sought to get in good with the child's parents, not because one wanted fame among one's

neighbors and friends, and not because one would dislike the sound of the child's cries.

From this we can see that if one is without the feeling of compassion, one is not human. . . . The feeling of compassion is the sprout of benevolence. (*Mengzi* 2A6)

Mencius also tells a story about a ruler named King Xuan. The king witnessed an ox that was about to be sacrificed. Feeling compassion for it, the king ordered that it be spared, but allowed for a sheep to be sacrificed instead. Mencius explains to the king that his feeling sorry for the ox proves that he has a natural tendency to feel compassion. If only he could extend that compassion, not only to the sheep—which the king could sacrifice because he had not seen it—but also to his people, then he would be truly benevolent. Actions like this, Mencius is suggesting, reveal our inner capacity for goodness, and it is through the cultivation of and reflection on those feelings that we grow into virtue.

---

1. What is the Confucian doctrine of "differentiated love?" Why, according to Mencius, is it better than the doctrines of Mozi and Yang Zhu?
2. What does Mencius mean by "human nature?" In what sense is human nature good, according to Mencius?
3. What point is Mencius making with the allegory of Ox Mountain?
4. In your own words, restate Mencius' arguments for his claim that human nature is good.

Xunzi

The third great Confucian in ancient China was Xunzi, who takes a very different view of human nature from most of his predecessors. Whereas Gaozi argued that human nature has no tendency toward either good or evil and Mencius argued that human nature is good, Xunzi declares that "human nature is bad." The book that records Xunzi's ideas, the *Xunzi*, says,

People's nature is bad. Their goodness is a matter of deliberate effort. Now people's nature is such that they are born with a fondness for profit in them. If they follow along with this, then struggle and

---

*Compare Aristotle's view on the unity of the virtues. See p. 213.

contention will arise, and yielding and deference will perish therein. They are born with feelings of hate and dislike in them. If they follow along with these, then cruelty and villainy will arise, and loyalty and trustworthiness will perish therein. They are born with desires of the eyes and ears, a fondness for beautiful sights and sounds. If they follow along with these, then lasciviousness and chaos will arise, and ritual and *yi* [righteousness], proper form and order, will perish therein. Thus, if people follow along with their inborn dispositions and obey their nature, they are sure to come to struggle and contention, turn to disrupting social divisions and order, and end up becoming violent. (*Xunzi* 23)[3]

People's bad nature not only leads them away from virtue and righteousness, but also undermines the stability and prosperity of society.

> Humans are born having desires. When they have desires but do not get the objects of their desire, then they cannot but seek some means of satisfaction. If there is no measure or limit to their seeking, then they cannot help but struggle with each other. If they struggle with each other then there will be chaos, and if there is chaos then they will be impoverished.* (*Xunzi* 19)

Fortunately, people are not irredeemably bad. Anyone can become good, says Xunzi, through proper training by good teachers and "deliberate effort" at moral self-cultivation. In fact, he claims that

> among all people, no one fails to follow that which they approve and to abandon that which they do not approve. For a person to know that there is nothing as great as the Way and yet not follow the Way—there are no such cases.† (*Xunzi* 22)

Thus, proper training and deliberate effort are both necessary and sufficient for becoming good. In this way, his view differs not only from Mencius', but also from Gaozi's view that people are morally directionless by nature and other ancient Chinese thinkers' view that some people are good by nature and others bad.

Before we turn to consider what kind of training Xunzi recommends, it is worth noting an important way in which Xunzi's view is not as diametrically opposed to Mencius' as it might appear. Mencius conceived of human nature as including that which develops naturally from certain inborn emotional tendencies. Thus, when someone learns to be good by extending their natural feelings of compassion, shame, and so on, this reveals the inherent goodness of their nature, according to Mencius. But Xunzi conceives of human nature more narrowly as including only the dispositions, desires, and abilities that people have at birth. As we saw, these include "a fondness for profit," "feelings of hate and dislike," and "desires of the eyes and ears" for "beautiful sights and sounds." Xunzi does not count anything that people have to learn or work at as part of their nature.

We might be tempted to say that Mencius and Xunzi are simply talking past each other—that they are only disagreeing about the meaning of the term "human nature" rather than about human nature itself. Xunzi does not see it this way. He takes their disagreement to be important because of his views about language, which he develops in response to the philosophical innovations of the School of Names and Zhuangzi.* He accepts Zhuangzi's insight that the meaning of a word is a matter of convention. In keeping with his knack for turning his rivals' ideas against them, however, Xunzi argued that the existing conventions had been established long ago by the sage kings and that deviating from these conventions leads to misunderstandings and chaos. He cites the chicanery of the School of Names as an example and uses his sophisticated philosophy of language to resolve the paradoxes they raised.† Within his own Confucian tradition, Xunzi alleged that Mencius had misused the term "human nature" and that this leads him to misguided prescriptions about how to cultivate virtue. In other words, it is because he misunderstands the term "human nature" that Mencius misunderstands how people become good. By attending carefully

---

*Compare to Thomas Hobbes' view of human nature and its connection to a state of nature in which life is "solitary, poor, nasty, brutish, and short." See pp. 410–413.

†Compare to Socrates' view that anyone who knows the right thing to do will do the right thing. See pp. 99–100.

---

*See pp. 80–81 and 83–86.

†See pp. 80–81.

to the proper use of words—by "rectifying names," as Confucius puts it—we can avoid such mistakes.

There is a further reason why Mencius and Xunzi are not merely talking at cross purposes when they argue over whether "human nature is good" or "human nature is bad." Recall that, for Mencius, part of what it means to say that "human nature is good" is that we have innate, virtuous dispositions that merely need to be given the right environment to naturally reach their full potential. In contrast, Xunzi describes our innate dispositions as almost exclusively self-interested.

If he rejects Mencius' proposal to simply give people a healthy environment in which their moral sprouts can grow into genuine virtue, what does Xunzi propose instead? Xunzi argues that we need to transform our nature through deliberate effort. Whereas Mencius looks to nature and agriculture for metaphors for self-cultivation, Xunzi looks to crafts and industry.

> Through steaming and bending, you can make wood as straight as an ink-line into a wheel. And after its curve conforms to the compass, even when parched under the sun it will not become straight again, because the steaming and bending have made it a certain way. (*Xunzi* 1)

We cannot do this on our own, according to Xunzi. Instead, we need to make use of the wisdom that people have accumulated over generations of deliberate effort.

> I once spent the whole day pondering, but it was not as good as a moment's worth of learning. I once stood on my toes to look far away, but it was not as good as the broad view from a high place. . . . One who makes use of a chariot and horses has not thereby improved his feet, but he can now go a thousand [miles]. One who makes use of a boat and oars has not thereby become able to swim, but he can now cross rivers and streams. The gentleman is exceptional not by birth, but rather by being good at making use of things. (*Xunzi* 1)

The way to learn this accumulated wisdom and develop one's ability to put it into practice is to find good teachers and carefully adhere to the rites, which the sages of old established as the proper conventions for guiding personal conduct.

Indeed, the earliest sage kings created order out of social chaos by developing rites that would tame and correct people's desires and dispositions. After explaining how people's bad nature once created chaos and poverty, Xunzi says,

> The former kings hated such chaos, and so they established rituals and *yi* in order to divide things among people, to nurture their desires, and to satisfy their seeking. They caused desires never to exhaust material goods, and material goods never to be depleted by desires, so that the two support each other and prosper. This is how ritual arose.* (*Xunzi* 19)

Ritual, according to Xunzi, accomplishes four main things. First, as Confucius taught, ritual cultivates proper desires and dispositions in people who follow it. It does this both by inculcating new dispositions and by restraining our ignoble, natural ones. For instance, ritual propriety demands that people defer to their elders and serve them, even when doing so goes against their inborn dispositions. Observing this aspect of ritual cultivates attitudes of respect and deference and restrains selfish impulses. In this way, ritual makes people virtuous.

Second, ritual regulates and guides people's emotions in the moment, in addition to helping them develop the right attitudes over the long run. Xunzi gives a detailed example in which he explains how Confucian funerary practices elicit the proper emotions of sadness and respect for a deceased parent or ruler.

> The standard practice of funeral rites is that one changes the appearance of the corpse by gradually adding more ornamentation, one moves the corpse gradually further away [during the long period of lying in state before burial], and over a long time one gradually returns to one's regular routine. Thus, the way that death works is that if one does not ornament the dead, then one will come to feel disgust at them, and if one feels disgust, then one will not feel sad. If one keeps them close, then one will become casual with them, and if one becomes casual with them, then one will grow tired of them. If one grows tired of them, then one will forget one's place, and if one forgets one's place, then one will not be respectful. (*Xunzi* 19)

---

*Compare to Hobbes' account of how people escape from the chaotic state of nature. See pp. 413–415.

Third, ritual gives people appropriate and publicly recognized ways of expressing their emotions and attitudes. Having publicly recognized ways of conveying these things is important to ensure proper communication between persons, and it is part of being virtuous. Thus, observing the existing conventions, as laid down by the kings of old, is as important to Xunzi as observing the conventions they established for the use of words.

"You can't be truly rude until you understand good manners."

Rita Mae Brown (b. 1944)

Last but not least, because ritual demands different things of people in different social roles, it establishes and clarifies social distinctions. Society can only function smoothly, on Xunzi's view, when each person knows his or her place and fulfills the responsibilities that come with his or her social role. Thus, by reinforcing those roles and directing people in carrying out their responsibilities, ritual promotes social stability. In this way, ritual makes society more secure and prosperous.

Thus, ritual plays an essential role in achieving the twin goals of Confucian philosophy: virtuous people and a harmonious society. Neither Mencius nor Confucius would disagree with this, even if they would not always agree with Xunzi's reasoning. In the end, despite their sharp disagreements, Mencius and Xunzi both represent developments of a single Confucian intellectual tradition—a tradition that would soon emerge as the dominant voice in the great conversation in Chinese culture.

1. In what sense does Xunzi think that "human nature is bad"?
2. How does Xunzi's idea of human nature differ from Mencius'?
3. How do people become good, according to Xunzi?
4. What role(s) does ritual play in Xunzi's ethical and political philosophy?

The Confucians' Legacy

The Warring States period in which Mencius and Xunzi lived saw vigorous debate between rival intellectual schools. The period came to a climactic close in 221 B.C., in part through the influence of a school we have not yet discussed. This school, known as **legalism,** shared Xunzi's view that human nature is bad. Two of the most famous proponents of legalist thought, Li Si and Han Fei, are even said to have studied with Xunzi. But unlike Xunzi, legalists thought that human nature could not be reformed; people were irredeemably self-interested. Rather than place their hopes in the appearance of some virtuous ruler who could reform the people, they argued that the only recipe for social stability was a strong state with a powerful army that governed the populace under a strict, impersonal rule of law. The state of Qin adopted legalist policies during the fourth century B.C. In the late third century, when Li Si was serving as its prime minister, Qin conquered all of China, reunifying the empire for the first time in centuries. In 221 B.C., the king of Qin founded the Qin dynasty and declared himself emperor. Li Si became prime minister and extended his legalist philosophy across all of China. Thus, at the end of the Warring States period, it may have seemed that legalism had emerged triumphant.

It would not last. The Qin dynasty collapsed after just fifteen years, toppled by a popular revolt against its harsh rule. In its place rose the Han dynasty. To distance themselves from their Qin predecessors, the Han emperors repudiated legalism and adopted a version of Confucianism that combined the ideas of many different schools of thought. Over four centuries of Han rule, Confucianism became even more deeply embedded in Chinese culture. From China, it would spread to other parts of East Asia, especially Korea and Japan. Mohism virtually disappeared with the end of the Warring States period. Philosophical Daoism diminished in prominence for centuries, though a religious strand of Daoist thinking remained popular. So, despite legalism's brief ascendancy, Confucianism would ultimately triumph in the competition among the Hundred Schools.

Even centuries later, with Daoism resurgent and Buddhism gaining a foothold in China,* Confucian ethical and political views continued to thrive. During the Song dynasty (A.D. 960–1279), a resurgence in Confucian thought, known as neo-Confucianism, ushered in another great era of philosophical activity. The great neo-Confucian philosopher Zhu Xi established a set of four Confucian classics as the canon of Chinese philosophical thought. Two come from the ancient *Book of Rites*. The other two are the *Analects* and the *Mengzi*. Right up until the end of the imperial age in China, in 1912, anyone aspiring to political office in China had to master these texts. It is therefore hard to exaggerate the influence that the Confucians had over the development of Chinese thought and culture. It may even exceed the influence of Socrates, Plato, and Aristotle in the West.

FOR FURTHER THOUGHT

1. What are some examples of rituals, in the Confucian sense, that you think are important in your culture today? Do you think adhering to those rituals is an important part of being a good person? Why or why not?

---

*On Buddhism and its legacy in China, see pp. 38–45 and 53.

2. What do you think about the Confucian doctrine of differentiated love? Is it an accurate account of how people actually behave? Is it a good account of how they should behave?

3. Do you agree more with Mencius or Xunzi about human nature? Why?

KEY WORDS

Analects	*dé*
rén	differentiated love
moral self-cultivation	human nature
Odes	four sprouts
filial piety	Ox Mountain
rites	legalism
rectification of names	

NOTES

1. Quotations from Confucius, *Analects: With Selections from Traditional Commentaries*, trans. Edward Slingerland (Indianapolis, IN: Hackett, 2003). References are to book and chapter numbers.

2. Quotations from Mencius, *Mengzi: With Selections from Traditional Commentaries*, trans. Bryan W. van Norden (Indianapolis, IN: Hackett, 2008). References are to book and chapters numbers.

3. Quotations from Eric L. Hutton, *Xunzi: The Complete Text* (Princeton, NJ: Princeton University Press, 2014).

11

EPICUREANS, STOICS, AND SKEPTICS

Happiness for the Many

It is customary to discuss the development of ancient philosophy after Aristotle in terms of three schools, or movements of thought. We will follow this practice, looking at a few central tenets of these schools to see how they addressed some new problems facing people of those times.

These new problems arose from changes in the social and religious climate of the ancient Mediterranean world. The era of the city-state was fading. After the war between Athens and Sparta, the regions of Greece engaged in a long series of struggles to achieve dominance, and some, Thebes and Macedonia, for instance, managed it for a time (see Map 1). The constant warfare eroded the belief that a city could be an arena for living a good life. People lost confidence in it, retreating into smaller units and leaving the politics of cities to be settled by rather crude military types. (The Epicureans, as we'll see, are prominent among those who seek their happiness not as citizens but as members of a smaller voluntary community.) Under Philip of Macedon and his son Alexander, vast territories were conquered and unified politically.* And finally Rome established her dominance over the entire Mediterranean basin, bringing a kind of stability and enforced peace to the region. The Romans were good administrators and warriors and contributed much in the sphere of law but not much original philosophy.

With the loss of confidence in the cities went a loss of faith in the gods of the cities. In the era of empires, Athena seemed too restricted even for Athens. The Olympians had apparently failed, and their authority waned. It is true that the Romans took over the Greek pantheon and gave the old gods new names (Jove, Juno, Venus), but the vigor of the religion was gone. This didn't mean, however, that religion was dead or dying—far from it. The old religions of the earth (religions of fertility, ancestor worship, and ecstasy), suppressed for a time by the Homeric gods of the sky, had never disappeared. Now they flourished with new vigor. To

*For Alexander, see http://en.wikipedia.org/wiki/Alexander_the_Great.

this was added a flood of religious cults and ideas from the East, all seeming to promise what the new age demanded. There was a proliferation of initiations into sacred and secret mysteries, of mediators and saviors, and of claims to esoteric knowledge.

Politicians, of course, turned religion to their own ends, accepting (and encouraging) the accolades of divinity people laid on them. Alexander was proclaimed a god; his successors liked the status it gave them and continued the practice.

The world seemed hostile and society brutal. People had lost control and grasped desperately at almost any promise to reestablish it. Fortune and chance themselves came to seem divine and were worshiped and feared. Astrology, never a force in the Golden Age of Greece, "fell upon the Hellenistic mind," Gilbert Murray says, "as a new disease falls upon some remote island people."[1] The stars were thought to be gods, the planets living beings (or controlled by living beings).* Their positions in the heavens were consulted as signs of things happening and to happen on earth. The heavens were thought to be populated by myriads of spirits, powers, principalities, demons, and gods, and one never knew when they would cause some fresh disaster.

The tradition established by Thales and his successors, never widespread, was impotent to stop all this. Rational criticism had not completely disappeared, but it must have seemed to many thinkers that they were in a new dark age. People were anxious and afraid.

What could those who wished to carry on the enterprise of the nature philosophers, of Socrates, Plato, and Aristotle, do to stem the tide? Let us look first at Epicurus.

The Epicureans

It is not possible for one to rid himself of his fears about the most important things if he does not

understand the nature of the universe but dreads some of the things he has learned in the myths. Therefore, it is not possible to gain unmixed happiness without natural science. (*PD* 12.143)[2]

This passage strikes the key notes in the philosophy of **Epicurus** (341–270 B.C.). The aim of life is happiness. Happiness depends above all on ridding oneself of fears. And the basis for the removal of fear is science. We want to examine what fears Epicurus thinks stand in the way of happiness, what he thinks happiness is, why an understanding of the universe will help, and what kind of science will give us this understanding.

According to Epicurus,

pleasure is the beginning and end of the blessed life. We recognize pleasure as the first and natural good; starting from pleasure we accept or reject; and we return to this as we judge every good thing, trusting this feeling of pleasure as our guide. (*LM* 129a)

The Greek word translated as pleasure is *hedone*, and the viewpoint expressed in the preceding passage is therefore called **hedonism.** As we have seen, Aristotle considers the view that pleasure is the good and rejects it.* He argues that something we share with the lower animals could not be the distinctively human good. But Epicurus is unmoved. Just look about you, he seems to be saying. Every living thing takes pleasure as a natural good; it is clearly one thing that is good not by convention but by *physis*. It is the ground of what we accept and reject, of what we pursue and avoid. And if we want to judge the goodness of some course of action, we ask whether there is more pleasure than pain involved in pursuing it.

He does not claim that this is the way it should be but that this is how it is. Good and evil are measured by this standard of pleasure and pain. It is no use, Epicurus might say, to complain that this is unworthy of human beings; this is the way we are made—all of us. This fact levels things out and defeats the elitism of the philosophers. Perhaps only a few are capable of the tortuous dialectic that leads to the vision of the Form of the Good. Not many can live the life of divine contemplation that

---

*The philosophers were, perhaps, not altogether blameless in this. It was common to ascribe greater perfection to the heavenly bodies in their eternal course than to the changeable world we live in. And more than one philosopher spoke of them as divine. In Plato's later political thought, the supreme object of worship for the masses was to be the sun.

*See p. 209.

Aristotle recommends as the highest good. But a pleasant life is available to all.

It is in terms of pleasure and pain, then, that we must understand happiness.* The happy life is the pleasant life. And philosophy, Epicurus holds, is the study of what makes for happiness—nothing more, nothing less.

> Let no young man delay the study of philosophy, and let no old man become weary of it; for it is never too early nor too late to care for the well-being of the soul. The man who says that the season for this study has not yet come or is already past is like the man who says it is too early or too late for happiness. (*LM* 122)

But what, exactly, can philosophy do for us to make us happy? Contrary to Aristotle's view, the pursuit of philosophy is not in itself the recipe for the happy life. Philosophy is basically a tool for Epicurus. Though philosophical discussion with a group of friends is one of the great pleasures in life, Epicurus recommends only those parts of philosophy that serve the end of happiness. As he says,

> do not think that knowledge about the things above the earth, whether treated as part of a philosophical system or by itself, has any other purpose than peace of mind and confidence. This is also true of the other studies. (*LP* 85b)

Epicurus' single-minded practicality brushes to one side all that does not serve his goal. So we should not expect much from him in the way of new developments in science, logic, or epistemology; indeed, his contributions in these areas are mostly secondhand, as we will see. But in ethics he has some originality and has had some influence.

The study of philosophy can do two things for us. It can free us from certain fears and anxieties that spoil our happiness, and it can provide directions for maximizing pleasure in life. Let us look at each of these in turn.

Some pains and displeasures are natural and cannot always be avoided, such as illness and separation from loved ones because of death. Such pains, Epicurus says, must be endured, but the intense pains typically do not last very long, and those that last a long time are usually not very intense (*PD* 4; *VS* 4). Other pains are due to certain *beliefs* we hold, and for these there is a sure remedy: change these beliefs. Philosophy can help with this because the beliefs that cause us distress are *false*. So we can rid ourselves of these pains by a true apprehension of *the way things are.**

What are these false beliefs that distress us? In the main, they are beliefs about **the gods** and beliefs about **death.** About the gods, people are misled by the "myths," as Epicurus calls them, which permeate the cults of popular religion. The heart of such myths is that the gods take an interest in human affairs, meddling in the universe to make things happen according to their whims, and so need to be appeased if things are not to go badly with us. Such beliefs fill us with dread, Epicurus believes, because we never know when some god or demon is going to crush us—perhaps for no reason we can discern at all. So we anxiously inquire of the prophets, soothsayers, astrologers, and priests about what went wrong or whether this is a good time to do so-and-so and, if not, whether we can do something to make it a good time. (Usually, of course, we can, to the benefit of the "sage" in question.) Fear of the gods, then, is one of the most potent spoilers of contentment.

The other fear concerns death. It is the same anxiety that pulls Hamlet up short and prevents him from taking his own life:

> To die, to sleep;
> To sleep: perchance to dream: ay, there's the rub;
> For in that sleep of death what dreams may come
> When we have shuffled off this mortal coil,
> Must give us pause.[3]

Tradition was full of dreadful stories of the fates of the dead. Lucretius lists some of them: Tantalus, frozen in terror, fears the massive rock balanced above him; Tityos is food for the vultures; Sisyphus

---

*This theme is taken up in the nineteenth century by the utilitarians. See Chapter 23.

**In the first century B.C., the Roman poet Lucretius wrote a long poem popularizing the views of Epicurus. Its title in Latin is *De Rerum Natura* ("on nature"). We borrow the phrase "the way things are" from Rolfe Humphries' version of that title in his very readable translation (Bloomington: Indiana University Press, 1969).

must forever roll his rock up the hill, only to see it crash down again; and so on (*WTA*, pp. 114–115).[4]

The good news Epicurus proclaims is that none of this is true. As Lucretius put it,

> Our terrors and our darknesses of mind
> Must be dispelled, not by the sunshine's rays,
> Not by those shining arrows of the light,
> But by insight into nature, and a scheme
> Of systematic contemplation.
>
> —*WTA*, p. 24

What wonderful "insight into nature" will dispel such terrors? It is nothing new; we are already familiar with it, but not exactly in this guise. What the Epicureans have in mind is the **atomism** of Leucippus and Democritus.* Why do they choose atomism as the philosophy that tells us "the way things are"? They never make that very clear. One suspects that Epicurus and Lucretius see atomism as particularly serviceable in the role of terror dispeller.

Let us remind ourselves of a few of the main points of atomism:

- Atoms and the void alone exist.
- The common things of the world, including living things, are temporary hookings together of atoms.
- The soul is material, made of very fine atoms, and is therefore mortal.
- Whatever happens is mechanistically determined to happen according to the laws by which atoms combine and fall apart again.

Epicurus accepts atomism as an account of the way things are, except for a slight but crucial modification to the fourth point. The universal determinism envisaged by Democritus is modified so that our free will to act can be salvaged.† After all, if we were not free, how could we follow the prescriptions for happiness Epicurus sets out? Although the atoms mostly follow strictly determined mechanistic paths, *sometimes*, he holds, they

"swerve" unaccountably. Lucretius presents the argument:

> If cause forever follows after cause
> In infinite, undeviating sequence
> And a new motion always has to come
> Out of an old one, by fixed law; if atoms
> Do not, by swerving, cause new moves which break
>   break
> The laws of fate; if cause forever follows,
> In infinite sequence, cause—where would we get
> This free will that we have, wrested from fate,
> By which we go ahead, each one of us,
> Wherever our pleasures urge? Don't we also swerve
>   swerve
> At no fixed time or place, but as our purpose
> Directs us?
>
> —*WTA*, p. 59

With this alteration, the rest of atomist metaphysics is acceptable to Epicurus. How, exactly, does this "insight into nature" dispel the terrors of religious myths?

The gods exist, Epicurus maintains, but being immortal and eternally blessed, they take no interest in human affairs.

> That which is blessed and immortal is not troubled itself, nor does it cause trouble to another. As a result, it is not affected by anger or favor, for these belong to weakness. (*PD* 1)

How, after all, could the gods be blessed if they had to worry about what Jones is going to do tomorrow? Furthermore, to poke around in the world, changing this and adjusting that, would jeopardize the gods' immortality, for they could not help but be affected by their interventions; the gods, like everything else, consist of atoms, and such bumps and bruises are what shake the atoms loose and lead to disintegration and death.

The heavenly bodies, moreover, are not demons or divinities that rule our destinies. Sun and moon, planets and stars are composed of atoms and the void just like everything else. Their behavior can be explained in exactly the same kinds of ways we explain familiar phenomena on earth. So it is inappropriate—ignorant—to look to the heavens for signs and portents, to go to astrologers for predictions, and try to read the riddle of the future

---

*You may find it helpful to review that philosophy, looking especially at pp. 28–33.

†Look again at p. 31 to see what problem atomism poses for free will.

in the stars. After summarizing some of the traditional stories of the gods, Lucretius says,

> All this, all this is wonderfully told,
> A marvel of tradition, and yet far
> From the real truth. Reject it—for the gods
> Must, by their nature, take delight in peace,
> Forever calm, serene, forever far
> From our affairs, beyond all pain, beyond
> All danger, in their own resources strong,
> Having no need of us at all, above
> Wrath or propitiation.
>
> —*WTA*, p. 70

So much, then, for fear of the gods. What of death? If atomism is correct, soul and body dissipate together in the event we call death. So there is no future life to look forward to. In what is probably Epicurus' best known saying, he draws the moral.

> Accustom yourself to the belief that death is of no concern to us, since all good and evil lie in sensation and sensation ends with death. . . . Death, the most dreaded of evils, is therefore of no concern to us; for while we exist death is not present, and when death is present we no longer exist. It is therefore nothing either to the living or to the dead since it is not present to the living, and the dead no longer are. (*LM* 124b–125)

Good and evil, of course, are pleasure and pain. These are the sources of happiness and unhappiness. Fear of death is predicated on the assumption that we will experience these sensations after death and perhaps be wretchedly unhappy. But that makes no sense at all, for when we are, death is not, and when death is, we are not. What, then, is there to fear? Death "is of no concern to us." Epicurus adds that it is also foolish to quake in *anticipation* of death. For what isn't painful when it is present should cause no pain when it is anticipated.

🌑

"After the game, the king and the pawn go into the same box."

Italian proverb

Such "insight into nature" can remove at least certain virulent strains of unhappiness from our lives. This is the negative benefit philosophy can confer, but it is not yet enough for happiness. We need also to know how to *live well*. And here too Epicurus gives guidance. The key point is clearly put in the following passage:

> For the very reason that pleasure is the chief and the natural good, we do not choose every pleasure, but there are times when we pass by pleasures if they are outweighed by the hardships that follow; and many pains we think better than pleasures when a greater pleasure will come to us once we have undergone the long-continued pains. . . . By measuring and by looking at advantages and disadvantages, it is proper to decide all these things; for under certain circumstances we treat the good as evil, and again, the evil as good. (*LM* 129b–130a)

The terms "Epicurean" or "hedonist" nowadays suggest someone who is a glutton for pleasures of every kind and indulges to excess in the satisfaction of every desire. This is a complete distortion of the philosophy of Epicurus; in his view, there is no better way to secure for yourself a life of misery than such sensual indulgence. If what you want is pleasure—the most pleasure—then you must be prudent in your pursuit of it.

> When we say that pleasure is the end, we do not mean the pleasure of the profligate or that which depends on physical enjoyment . . . but by pleasure we mean the state wherein the body is free from pain and the mind from anxiety. Neither continual drinking and dancing, nor sexual love, nor the enjoyment of fish and whatever else the luxurious table offers brings about the pleasant life; rather it is produced by the reason which is sober, which examines the motive for every choice and rejection, and which drives away all those opinions through which the greatest tumult lays hold of the mind. (*LM* 131b–132a)

To implement these principles, we must distinguish different sorts of **desire.**

> You must consider that of the desires some are natural, some are vain, and of those that are natural, some are necessary, others only natural. Of the necessary desires, some are necessary for happiness, some for the ease of the body, some for life itself. (*LM* 127b)

The classification of desires, then, looks like this:

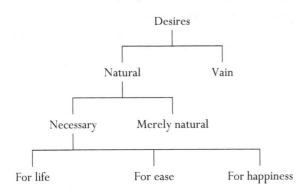

Let us fill in each of these categories with some plausible examples:

- vain desires: luxuries, designer clothing, being thin, keeping up with the Joneses
- merely natural desires: sexual desire (natural but not necessary)
- necessary for life: food, drink, shelter
- necessary for ease: a bed
- necessary for happiness: friendship

Philosophy makes clear that not all desires are on a par and that satisfying some of them costs more than it is worth. That is surely the case, Epicurus believes, with vain desires. It is likely to be the case with the merely natural desires; at least it is clear that following every sexual passion is a sure prescription for unhappiness. The point is that if we want to be happy, the crucial step is to control and limit our desires—if possible to those which are necessary. Epicurus recommends the simple life, as the following sayings make clear:

> Natural wealth is limited and easily obtained; the wealth defined by vain fancies is always beyond reach. (*PD* 15.144)
>
> Nothing satisfies him to whom what is enough is little. (*VS* 68)
>
> To be accustomed to simple and plain living is conducive to health and makes a man ready for the necessary tasks of life. It also makes us more ready for the enjoyment of luxury if at intervals we chance to meet with it, and it renders us fearless against fortune. (*LM* 131a)

> "A human being has a natural desire to have more of a good thing than he needs."
>
> *Mark Twain (1835–1910)*

So this hedonist, who finds pleasure to be the only natural good, values the old Greek virtue of moderation after all. Now, however, it is recommended on the grounds that it will give us the pleasantest life possible. What of the other **virtues,** of justice, for instance? Justice is not something good in itself, Epicurus argues, taking the view that Glaucon and Adeimantus urge against Socrates (*PD* 31–38).* Justice arises when people make a "compact" together not to injure one another, and it is reasonable to be just as long as that compact pays off—in increased pleasure, of course. Justice, then, is wholly a matter of *nomos* for the Epicureans. It is true that justice and the other virtues are praised, but only as means to a happy life for the individual.

The virtue of **friendship,** by contrast, is held in the highest esteem among the Epicureans. They are famous for it. Epicurus established in Athens a "garden" in which his followers lived, sharing work, study, and conversation. In this garden and in similar communities across the ancient world, men—including at least some women and slaves—cultivated this virtue. Friendship, they believed, is the key to the highest blessings this life holds. As Epicurus says,

> Friendship dances through the world bidding us all to waken to the recognition of happiness. (*VS* 52)

This blessing, Epicurus assumes, is open to all who pursue their pleasures with prudence and moderation. So, he assures us, happiness is not restricted to the few. The many, too, may participate.

1. Why does Epicurus fasten on pleasure as the good?
2. For what kinds of pain is there a remedy? What is it?
3. What, according to the Epicureans, are the false beliefs about the gods, and how do these false beliefs distress us?

---

*See *Republic*, Book II, and pp. 173–174.

4. What false beliefs about death distress us, according to the Epicureans?
5. How is atomism "corrected"?
6. How does the wise person sort out and deal with desires?
7. What is the Epicurean view of moderation? Of justice? Of friendship?

The Stoics

Although in many respects the Stoics are consciously opposed to the main principles of the Epicureans, the two schools share one core belief: that philosophy is to serve the aim of promoting the best and happiest life a human being could live. In the service of that goal, the Stoics not only developed an important approach to ethics, but also made original contributions to logic, set forth a detailed theory of knowledge, and spent considerable effort on theories of the nature of the universe. We'll touch on those other contributions, but we will concentrate on the Stoics' views about the good life.

Stoicism began with Zeno of Citium, a city in Cyprus.* Like several other important figures in this tradition, he was not a native Greek, though he came to Athens as a young man (in about 320 B.C.), studied there, and taught there until his death, about 260 B.C. The fact that Stoic teachers came from areas that Plato and Aristotle would have regarded as barbarian is a sign that times had changed for philosophy. Stoic doctrines from the first had a universality about them that reached beyond the parochial concerns of any city or nation; in this way, they were both a reflection of the enlarged political situation and an influence on it. Socrates had thought of himself as a citizen of Athens. The Stoics considered themselves citizens of the world.

The universality of Stoicism appears in another way. It appealed to members of all social classes. Its leading figures include a freed slave, Epictetus (c. A.D. 51–135), and the Roman emperor Marcus Aurelius (A.D. 121–180).

Let us begin with some reflections on happiness. Stoic ideas of **happiness** owe much to Socrates, Plato, and Aristotle, all of whom argue that what makes for a truly good life cannot depend on anything outside ourselves.* Stoics carry this ideal of self-sufficiency to the extreme by claiming that absolutely nothing that happens to the wise can disturb their calm happiness. This may seem a startling suggestion.†

How can this be? Epictetus puts his finger on the crux of the matter:

> What upsets people is not things themselves but their judgments about the things. For example, death is nothing dreadful (or else it would have appeared dreadful to Socrates), but instead the judgment about death that it is dreadful—*that* is what is dreadful. So when we are upset or distressed, let us never blame someone else but rather ourselves, that is, our own judgments. (*E* 5)[5]

What makes you unhappy? Suppose you learn that someone you trusted has been spreading nasty lies about you. Friends abandon you and acquaintances begin to avoid you. Would this make you unhappy? Most of us would probably say yes.

But, the Stoic urges, think more carefully. It can't really be these events as so far described that make you unhappy. What if you didn't care about such things? Then they wouldn't make you unhappy.

This kind of thought experiment, the Stoic believes, proves that what happens to you can never *make* you unhappy. What makes you unhappy is "the judgment" you make on what happens to you: that this is important, terrible, and distressing. If that is so, then your happiness is not beyond your control. Nothing can make you unhappy unless you allow it to do so. Your happiness is entirely up to you.

---

*Note that this is not the Zeno of the paradoxes, the associate of Parmenides.

*Socrates holds that a good person cannot be harmed (*Apology* 41c–d) and Plato argues that happiness is a condition of the harmonious soul. Aristotle claims that "the good is something proper to the person and cannot be taken away from him" (see p. 209).

†Compare Aristotle, p. 211. As you study Stoicism, ask yourself: Is this an improvement on Aristotle, who holds that there is nonetheless some element of fortune in our happiness?

To understand this in depth, we need to appreciate a crucial distinction:

> Some things are up to us and some are not up to us. Our opinions are up to us, and our impulses, desires, aversions—in short, whatever is our own doing. Our bodies are not up to us, nor are our possessions, our reputations, or our public offices, or, that is, whatever is not our own doing. The things that are up to us are by nature free, unhindered, and unimpeded; the things that are not up to us are weak, enslaved, hindered, not our own. So remember, if you think that things naturally enslaved are free or that things not your own are your own, you will be thwarted, miserable, and upset, and will blame both gods and men. But if you think that only what is yours is yours, and that what is not your own is, just as it is, not your own, then no one will ever coerce you, no one will hinder you, you will blame no one, you will not accuse anyone, you will not do a single thing unwillingly, you will have no enemies, and no one will harm you, because you will not be harmed at all. (*E* 1)[6]

This distinction between what is and what is not within our power makes possible the remarkable claims of the Stoic. When are we happy? When we get what we desire. Suppose now that we set our heart on the things that are beyond our power—a beautiful body, fame, wealth, professional success. Reflection will surely convince you that these things are at best only partly in our power; circumstances must cooperate if they are to be ours. If these are what we really want, disappointment is sure to follow. If we don't get them, we will be unhappy. If we do get them, we will be anxious lest we lose them. And neither disappointment nor anxiety is part of a happy life.

What, then, is within our control? "Your way of dealing with appearances" (*E* 6), Epictetus answers. What appears in the world is not in our control, but how we deal with it is. How we view appearances, our opinions about them, whether we desire or fear them—all this is within our power. This is our proper area of concern. Of anything beyond this sphere, we should be prepared to say, "You are nothing in relation to me" (*E* 1).

> "The last of the human freedoms is to choose one's attitudes."
>
> *Victor Frankl (1905–1997)*

What this means in practice can be gathered from several examples.

> A little oil is spilled, a little wine is stolen: say, "This is the price of tranquility; this is the price of not being upset." Nothing comes for free. When you call the slave boy, keep in mind that he is capable of not paying attention, and even if he does pay attention he is capable of not doing any of the things that you want him to. But he is not in such a good position that your being upset or not depends on him. (*E* 12)
>
> A person's master is someone who has power over what he wants or does not want, either to obtain it or take it away. Whoever wants to be free, therefore, let him not want or avoid anything that is up to others. Otherwise he will necessarily be a slave. (*E* 14)
>
> It is possible to learn the will of nature from the things in which we do not differ from each other. For example, when someone else's little slave boy breaks his cup we are ready to say, "It's one of those things that just happen." Certainly, then, when your own cup is broken you should be just the way you were when the other person's was broken. Transfer the same idea to larger matters. Someone else's child is dead, or his wife. There is no one who would not say, "It's the lot of a human being." But when one's own dies, immediately it is, "Alas! Poor me!" But we should have remembered how we feel when we hear of the same thing about others. (*E* 26)

Suppose now that we have, through long practice (for this is what it would take), gotten to the point where we always make the distinction. We never set our hearts on the things that are not in our power to control. It seems we have gotten ourselves into a serious difficulty. Having enough food to eat (to take just one example) is not something entirely within our control. Are we not to desire food? And if not, how are we to live? Or should we simply starve, virtuous to the end? Is there a way they can solve this problem?

The solution lies in the Stoics' positive advice: *to keep our wills in harmony with nature* (*E* 4, 6, 13, 30; and *M* 2.9). To understand this, we have to explore what the Stoics mean by "**nature.**" We need not go into the details of their nature philosophy, but the central idea is crucial.

Whatever exists, according to the Stoics, is material or corporeal. Our only certainties come from sense experience, and sense experience always reveals the material. But like Heraclitus, they hold that the material world is ordered by a rational principle, a *logos*.* This principle, which (like Heraclitus) they sometimes call the fiery element, is not just a passive pattern in things; it is the ordering of the world by and for a reason.† As the ordering principle of the world, it is appropriately called divine.

Thus **God,** for the Stoics, is not like the distant, indifferent gods of the Epicureans. Nor is the Stoic God like the unmoved mover of Aristotle, independent and self-sufficient, related to the world only as an ideal that the world tries to emulate. The Stoics conceive of God (whom, again like Heraclitus, they are willing to call Zeus) as *immanent* in the world.‡ Every material being has a divine element within it. So the Stoics are committed to a version of **pantheism** (God is all and all is God), though the term "God" emphasizes the *ordering* and the term "nature" the *ordered* aspects of things.

This commits the Stoics to believing in Destiny or Fate. Whatever happens happens of necessity. But this is not a cause for despair, since Destiny is the same as Divine Providence. Whatever happens is determined by the divine reason, and so it must happen for the best.§

Although "whatever will be, will be," it does not follow that we can simply drift. Your attitude toward what happens makes an enormous difference, for on that your happiness or unhappiness depends.

---

*See pp. 19–20.
†See p. 20.
‡See p. 20.
§Compare Heraclitus again, p. 20.

Do not seek to have events happen as you want them to, but instead want them to happen as they do happen, and your life will go well. (*E* 8)

If we are to be happy, then, we must keep our wills in harmony with nature. And we now can see that this is identical with keeping our wills in harmony with both reason and God, for nature is the sphere of events governed by the benevolent purpose of a rational deity.

"Never does nature say one thing and wisdom another."

Juvenal (late first, early second centuries)

Now we can see how the Stoics address the problem raised earlier. Everything in nature contains its own ordering principle in harmony with the great order of the whole. In living things there is a natural tendency toward certain ends—self-preservation in particular, together with all that serves that end. This is part of the Divine Providence. Denying these *natural* tendencies, then, would certainly not keep one's will in harmony with nature!

So the Stoics eat when hungry, drink when thirsty, and do what is necessary to preserve themselves from the weather. But, and this point is crucial, they pursue these natural goals with **equanimity,** not being disturbed if their quest for them is frustrated. Thus, Epictetus advises that

you must behave as you do at a banquet. Something is passed around and comes to you: reach out your hand politely and take it. It goes by: do not hold it back (*E* 15).

In regard to what is natural to a living being, the Stoics distinguish what is *preferred*, what is *shunned*, and what is *indifferent*. We humans "prefer" not only food and shelter, but also skills, knowledge, health, reputation, and wealth. We "shun" their opposites, and we find many things "indifferent"; about them we simply don't care. The natural tendencies in human beings determine what falls in one class or another.

So there is nothing wrong with pursuing what is preferred. Where people go wrong, however, is in

MARCUS AURELIUS

Marcus Aurelius (A.D. 121–180) was emperor of Rome for nineteen years. Late in life, while leading an army in the far north, he recorded his most intimate thoughts in a journal. The journal has come down to us as a small volume called *Meditations*, divided into twelve books, each made up of numbered paragraphs, often in no direct relation to each other. Marcus died in the army camp of an infectious disease. Here are a few samples of Stoic thought as filtered through the mind of an emperor.

A little flesh, a little breath, and a Reason to rule all—that is myself. (2,2)

Hour by hour resolve firmly, like a Roman and a man, to do what comes to hand with correct and natural dignity, and with humanity, independence, and justice. Allow your mind freedom from all other considerations. (2,5)

Remembering always what the World-Nature is, and what my own nature is, and how the one stands in respect to the other—so small a fraction of so vast a Whole—bear in mind that no man can hinder you from conforming each word and deed to the Nature of which you are a part. (2,9)

If the power of thought is universal among mankind, so likewise is the possession of reason, making us rational creatures. It follows, therefore, that this reason speaks no less universally to us all with its "thou shalt" or "thou shalt not." So then there is a world-law; which in turn means that we are all fellow-citizens and share a common citizenship, and that the world is a single city. (4,4)

What does not corrupt a man himself cannot corrupt his life, nor do him any damage either outwardly or inwardly. (4,8)

Your mind will be like its habitual thoughts; for the soul becomes dyed with the colour of its thoughts. (4,16)

My own nature is a rational and civic one; I have a city, and I have a country; as Marcus I have Rome, and as a human being I have the universe; and consequently, what is beneficial to these communities is the sole good for me. (6,44)

All things are interwoven with one another; a sacred bond unites them; there is scarcely one thing that is isolated from another. Everything is coordinated, everything works together in giving form to the one universe. The world-order is a unity made up of multiplicity: God is one, pervading all things; all being is one, all law is one (namely, the common reason which all thinking creatures possess) and all truth is one—if, as we believe, there can be but one path to perfection for beings that are alike in kind and reason. (7,9)

Do not indulge in dreams of having what you have not, but reckon up the chief of the blessings you do possess, and then thankfully remember how you would crave for them if they were not yours. At the same time, however, beware lest delight in them leads you to cherish them so dearly that their loss would destroy your peace of mind. (7,27)

Universal Nature's impulse was to create an orderly world. It follows, then, that everything now happening must follow a logical sequence; if it were not so, the prime purpose towards which the impulses of the World-Reason are directed would be an irrational one. Remembrance of this will help you to face many things more calmly. (7,75)

Nothing can be good for a man unless it helps to make him just, self-disciplined, courageous, and independent; and nothing bad unless it has the contrary effect. (8,1)

Despise not death; smile, rather, at its coming; it is among the things that Nature wills. (9,3)

The sinner sins against himself; the wrongdoer wrongs himself, becoming the worse by his own action. (9,4)

Quotations are from *Meditations*, Maxwell Staniforth, trans. (Middlesex, England: Penguin Books, 1964); numbers are to book and paragraph.

attributing some *absolute value* to these things. And the mark of this wrong turn is their reaction when they do not get what they want: distress, resentment, and unhappiness. The wise person, by contrast, "uses such things without requiring them."[7] This attitude enables the equanimity of the Stoics, in which nothing that happens can destroy their calm. The Stoic attaches absolute value to only one thing: the harmony of the will with nature. In comparison with that, even the things "preferred" seem only indifferent.

This means that the only true good is **virtue:** a life in harmony with nature, reason, and God. Stoics and Epicureans carry on a running battle over just this point. The Epicureans, of course, hold that the only good is pleasure, and everything else (including virtue) is good only in relation to that. Stoics typically respond in an extreme fashion, denying not only that pleasure is the one true good, but also that it is even in the realm of the "preferred." Pleasure, according to the Stoics, is *never* to be pursued; it is not an appropriate end at all.

The Epicureans argue, as we have seen, that pleasure is the root of all our choosing. The Stoics reply that our natural tendencies are for the acquisition of certain *things*, such as food, which is necessary for self-preservation. They do not deny that eating when hungry is pleasurable, but the pleasure is an *accompaniment* to the eating, not the end sought. Pleasure on its own won't keep you alive! People go wrong exactly here, in seeking the byproduct instead of the end—a sure recipe, the Stoics think, for disaster. A virtuous person will in fact lead a pleasant life. But if she makes the pleasant life her object, she will miss both virtue *and* the pleasure that accompanies it!

There are two corollaries to the view that only virtue is the good. First, the only thing that counts in estimating the goodness of an action is the **intention** of the agent. An action is an attempt to change the world in some way; whether the action succeeds depends on circumstances beyond the actor's control; and so the goodness or badness of the *person* or the *action* cannot depend on the action's outcome. But this means that a judgment on the agent must be a judgment on the agent's intention. Cleanthes gives the example of two slaves sent out to find someone. One slave searches diligently but

fails to find him. The other loafs about and runs into him by accident. Which is the better man (*SES* 264)? The Stoic has no doubt about the answer and takes it to show that results are to be considered indifferent. What counts is the state of your will; that is in your control, and that is what is absolutely good or bad. So the entire concentration of life must be put into the effort to set your will in harmony with nature. The outcome must be nothing to you.

This leads us to the second corollary. The important thing is to do one's **duty.** The notion of "duty" has not played a large role to this point. We hardly find it in Socrates or Plato, or Aristotle, or Epicurus. These philosophers are asking, What is the best life for a human being to live? They never imagine that it might be a duty or an obligation to lead such a life. It is just a question of what the prudent or wise person would do. Why, we might wonder, does the notion of duty suddenly come to prominence in Stoic thought?

❧

"Happiness and moral duty are inseparably connected."

George Washington (1732–1799)

It has a natural home here because of the connection between the divine, rational principle that providentially guides the course of the world and the notion of *law*. It is law that shows us our duties. The principles governing the world are not only descriptions of how the world inevitably *does* go; they express how things, according to their natures, *should* go. So they take on for us the aspect of law reflected in civil law: they prescribe to us our duties and obligations. This notion of **natural law** (a concept we owe largely to the Stoics) is obviously a development of Heraclitean ideas about the *logos*. If we behave in certain ways, consequences—determined by the ordering principles of the world—necessarily follow. For example, if you smoke cigarettes for a while, you will become addicted. Since addictions are bad—they hand control of your life over to something "not your own"—understanding the order of the world is also understanding that you have a duty not to smoke.

The Stoics devote considerable attention to duties, distinguishing several classes of duties and examining particular cases. We need not explore the details, but we should note the one duty that is clear and always overriding: the duty to harmonize our intentions with the law of nature. This is the duty to be virtuous or to perfect ourselves. And this means that we must concern ourselves above all with the things in our power—with our beliefs, attitudes, and desires. Everything else must be, as Epictetus says, nothing to us in comparison. We began the discussion of Stoic thought by considering happiness. But now we can see that if we devote ourselves to virtue, to doing our duty, our happiness will take care of itself.*

---

1. On what distinction does Stoicism rest? Explain how making this distinction is the key, for the Stoic, to both happiness and freedom.
2. How are God and nature related? What of evil?
3. What does it mean to keep one's will in line with nature?
4. Why doesn't a Stoic starve to death?
5. What is virtue, according to the Stoics?
6. Explain the Stoic critique of Epicurean philosophy.
7. Why does the Stoic believe intention is more important than results in evaluating the worth of a person?
8. What is it about the Stoic view of nature that makes duty an important notion?

The Skeptics

What has **skepticism** to do with happiness? We are apt to suppose that someone who doesn't know, or at least thinks he doesn't know, must on that account be *unhappy*. Aristotle, who holds that all men by nature desire to know, would surely think so. Moreover, we are almost all brought up as believers in something or other. Belief is as natural to us as breathing. What sense could it make to suspend all our beliefs, to get rid of that habit?

---

*Compare this thought with what Jesus says in the Sermon on the Mount: "Seek first the Kingdom of God and his righteousness, and all these things will be added to you as well" (Matt. 6:33).

And how could that make us happy? The ancient skeptics give some surprising answers to these perplexing questions.

Again we shall simplify, this time by focusing on the most radical group of skeptics, named after a shadowy fourth-century figure **Pyrrho**.* From what little we know of him, it seems that Pyrrho is interested only in the practical question of how best to live. He exhibits a principled disinterest in speculative or scientific philosophy. His pupil Timon reportedly said that the nature of things is **"indeterminable,"** meaning that we cannot determine that things are more like this than they are like that.[8] But why not? Let us review a little of the story we have been telling.

Since Parmenides, Greek thinkers had distinguished between things as they appear to us and things as they are in themselves. Appearances, after all, may deceive us: The straight oar in water looks bent; square towers in the distance look round; honey tastes bitter to a sick person; and so on. Many thinkers turned to reason or intelligence to discern reality, with varying results. Parmenides concludes that reality is the One. Democritus argues that it is atoms and the void. For Plato, the independent world of eternally unchanging Forms constitutes the really real. And for Aristotle, reality consists of individual substances that are composites of matter and form.

It is partly this diversity of answers that motivates the Pyrrhonists, who like to gather examples of disagreement among the philosophers. But sheer disagreement does not prove that nothing can be

---

*One fascinating biographical tidbit is that Pyrrho allegedly accompanied Alexander the Great on his forays into northwestern India. There, it is said, Pyrrho encountered Indian philosophers and adopted some of their ideas. Although it is possible that Greek intellectuals had some exposure to Indian philosophical ideas before this, Pyrrho appears to represent the earliest case of direct causal influence of Indian thought on Greek thought. See Christopher I. Beckwith, *Greek Buddha: Pyrrho's Encounter with Early Buddhism in Central Asia* (Princeton, NJ: Princeton University Press, 2017). On the more general question of Indian influence on ancient Greek thought, listen to Peter Adamson and Jonardon Ganeri, "Looking East: Indian Influence on Greek Thought," *History of Philosophy in India*, February 4, 2018, https://historyofphilosophy.net/india-greece.

known about reality; some one of these views may well be correct and the others mistaken; or perhaps none of them is correct, but some future development of them might be. And we might come to know that. To support the claim that the nature of things is "indeterminable," we must say more.

The later Pyrrhonists systematize the arguments in favor of skeptical conclusions in a number of types or *modes* of reasoning. Our best source for these is a Greek physician, **Sextus Empiricus,** who lived in the second century A.D. Let us survey several of these modes.

The first mode stresses that the sense organs of animals differ from species to species. His arguments are rather primitive, since not much was known about the details of animal sense organs until recent times. But we can think of the registration of the world in the many-faceted eye of a fly, in the echolocation of a bat, and in what the frog's eye tells the frog's brain.[9] Cats see much better in the dark than we do, and dogs smell many things that escape our senses. In terms like these, we can understand what Sextus says:

> But if the same things appear different owing to the variety in animals, we shall, indeed, be able to state our own impressions of the real object, but as to its essential nature we shall suspend judgment. For we cannot ourselves judge between our own impressions and those of the other animals, since we ourselves are involved in the dispute and are, therefore, rather in need of a judge than competent to pass judgment ourselves. . . . If, then, owing to the variety in animals their sense-impressions differ, and it is impossible to judge between them, we must necessarily suspend judgment regarding the external underlying objects.[10] (*OP* 1.59–61)

Here we have some of the key notions of skepticism. Because objects appear differently to creatures with different sense organs, we cannot confidently judge that these objects really are as they appear to us. If they appear one way to us and another way to the bat or fly or frog, it would be arbitrary to pick one of those ways rather than another and say that is how the "external underlying objects" are. The result is that we must **"suspend judgment."**

The second mode concerns differences among human beings, especially concerning objects of choice. He quotes poets and dramatists who exclaim about the variations in human preferences and adds,

> Seeing, then, that choice and avoidance depend on pleasure and displeasure, while pleasure and displeasure depend on sensation and sense-impression, whenever some men choose the very things which are avoided by others, it is logical for us to conclude that they are also differently affected by the same things, since otherwise they would all alike have chosen or avoided the same things. But if the same objects affect men differently owing to the differences in the men, then, on this ground also, we shall reasonably be led to suspension of judgment. For while we are, no doubt, able to state what each of the underlying objects appears to be, relatively to each difference, we are incapable of explaining what it is in reality. For we shall have to believe either all men or some. But if we believe all, we shall be attempting the impossible and accepting contradictories; and if some, let us be told whose opinions we are to endorse. (*OP* 1.87–88)

The message is the same; we must suspend judgment. What does that mean? It means that we do not say either yes or no; we do not affirm or deny any proposition about the real nature of the underlying objects.

Note carefully that we *can* state what the object *appears* to be. We just refrain from making any further judgments. In terms of the appearance/reality distinction, the skeptic restricts himself to appearance. He is forced to this by the considerations in the "modes," of which we have examined only two. Some of the others concern the differences among our own organs of sense, the dependence of appearances on differing circumstances, and the differences in customs and laws.

There are also more formal modes, standard ways of criticizing the arguments of the philosophers. A skeptic considers someone who affirms what is not evident *dogmatic*; and any claim about how things *really* are, independent of their appearance to our senses, is a claim about the nonevident. To be **dogmatic,** in this sense, is to claim to know something for which you have no evidence. So all the other schools of philosophy, with their theories about the reality beyond the appearances, are classified as dogmatic by the skeptics.

One of these more formal modes is based on an "infinite regress" argument and another on the charge of "circular reasoning." Suppose claim *A* is supported by claim *B*. The skeptic will ask what supports *B*. If *B* is supported by *C*, and *C* by *D*, and so on forever, we have an **infinite regress.** If *B* is supported by *C* and *C* by *A*, we have **circular reasoning,** for the argument leads back to where we began. In neither case can we claim to know that *A* is true.

Here is an example of Sextus using these modes. Suppose some "dogmatic" philosopher (a Platonist, perhaps, or a Stoic) has made some claim about the real nature of an object.

> The matter proposed is either a sense-object or a thought-object, but whichever it is, it is an object of controversy; for some say that only sensibles are true, others only intelligibles, others that some sensibles and some intelligible objects are true. Will they then assert that the controversy can or cannot be decided? If they say it cannot, we have it granted that we must suspend judgement. . . . But if they say that it can be decided, we ask by what is it to be decided? For example, in the case of the sense-object . . . is it to be decided by a sense-object or a thought-object? For if they say by a sense-object, since we are inquiring about sensibles that object itself also will require another to confirm it; and if that too is to be a sense-object, it likewise will require another for its confirmation, and so on ad infinitum. And if the sense-object shall have to be decided by a thought-object, then, since thought-objects also are controverted, this being an object of thought will need examination and confirmation. Whence then will it gain confirmation? If from an intelligible object, it will suffer a similar regress ad infinitum; and if from a sensible object, since an intelligible was adduced to establish the sensible and a sensible to establish the intelligible, the Mode of circular reasoning is brought in. (*OP* 1.170–72)

The key question here is, "By what is it to be decided?" To use Protagoras' term, what is the "measure" we are to judge by? These modes attempt to show that the question cannot be satisfactorily answered, for the answer either will itself be subject to that same question (infinite regress) or will assume what is to be proved (circular reasoning). The moral is the same: We must suspend judgment.

All the various modes circle around a central point, which can be called the problem of the **criterion.** Claims to knowledge are a dime a dozen; the Hellenistic world, as we have seen, is filled with them (just as ours is). The problem we face is how to decide among them. By what mark or standard or criterion are we to decide where truth and knowledge really lie? Different philosophers, as we have seen, offer different solutions, but the skeptics argue that this is an insoluble problem: *No* satisfactory criterion is to be found. In a chapter called "Does a Criterion of Truth Really Exist?" Sextus Empiricus writes,

> Of those, then, who have treated of the criterion some have declared that a criterion exists—the Stoics, for example, and certain others—while by some its existence is denied, as by . . . Xenophanes of Colophon, who say—"Over all things opinion bears sway";* while we have adopted suspension of judgement as to whether it does or does not exist. This dispute, then, they will declare to be either capable or incapable of decision; and if they shall say it is incapable of decision they will be granting on the spot the propriety of suspension of judgement, while if they say it admits of decision, let them tell us whereby it is to be decided, since we have no accepted criterion, and do not even know, but are still inquiring, whether any criterion exists. Besides, in order to decide the dispute which has arisen about the criterion, we must possess an accepted criterion by which we shall be able to judge the dispute; and in order to possess an accepted criterion, the dispute about the criterion must first be decided. And when the argument thus reduces itself to a form of circular reasoning, the discovery of the criterion becomes impracticable, since we do not allow them to adopt a criterion by assumption, while if they offer to judge the criterion by a criterion we force them to a regress ad infinitum. And furthermore, since demonstration requires a demonstrated criterion, while the criterion requires an approved demonstration, they are forced into circular reasoning. (*OP* 2.18–20)

Let us note several points in this passage. First, any claim that some principle is a criterion for truth itself needs to be supported. We shall need

---

a criterion to decide whether that support is successful. And any attempt to provide such a criterion will either be forced into the infinite regress of criteria by which to decide criteria by which to decide . . . or be circular, begging the question in favor of some assumed criterion. We can represent the argument by a flow chart. (See the figure on page 250.)

No matter which alternatives we choose, the result is the same. And if we suspend judgment about a criterion, it follows that judgment is suspended about each and every claim to knowledge; for each claim to know depends on there being a criterion by which it is singled out as true knowledge. So if we cannot solve the problem of the criterion, we must suspend judgment generally.

❧

> "I was gratified to be able to answer promptly. I said, 'I don't know.'"
>
> *Mark Twain (1835–1910)*

Second, note that Sextus does *not* claim there is no criterion of truth; about that very question—is there or is there not a criterion?—the Pyrrhonian skeptic suspends judgment. There is a kind of skeptic who claims that nothing can be known. This kind is subject to a devastating counter: He can be asked how he knows *that*. But Sextus is careful not to make any such claim. He does not know whether anything can be known. If he is pushed back a step and asked whether he knows that he does not know, he will presumably confess that he doesn't. His attitude throughout is one of *noncommitment* to any knowledge claims that concern how things really are.

The argument about the criterion seems like a very powerful argument indeed. It sweeps the board clean.*

But this leads to a pressing question: How then can we live? If we make no judgments about the world we are in, won't we be paralyzed? To eat bread rather than a stone seems to depend on a

judgment that bread will nourish you and a stone will not. *Can* we suspend judgments like that?

Remember that skeptics do not deny **appearances.** Skeptics claim that we can live, and live well, by restricting ourselves to how things seem. Though there may not be a criterion to distinguish reality from appearance, there is a criterion for life and action. Sextus tells us that this practical criterion

> denotes the standard of action by conforming to which in the conduct of life we perform some actions and abstain from others. . . . The criterion, then, of the Skeptic School is, we say, the appearance, giving this name to what is virtually the sense-presentation. For since this lies in feeling and involuntary affection, it is not open to question. . . .
>
> Adhering, then, to appearances we live in accordance with the normal rules of life, undogmatically, seeing that we cannot remain wholly inactive. (*OP* 1.21–23)

Sextus was a physician, a member of a school of medicine that followed similar principles. These doctors were unwilling to speculate about the "real" nature of diseases. They restricted themselves to what they observed, to appearances. If they observed that certain symptoms responded to certain medicines, they noted and remembered this. If they observed that diet positively affected the outcome of a certain disease, they prescribed that diet for that disease. It was, we might say, empirical medicine rather than speculative. If medicine can be done in this way, then why can't life be lived according to the same principles?*

So skeptics can eat what experience has shown to be connected with health and behave in ways correlated with positive outcomes. We do not pronounce things to be truly good or truly bad, for about such claims we suspend judgment. But it is beyond question that bread *appears* to nourish us and scarcely less so that obedience to the law *appears* to be profitable. In the matter of behavior,

---

*Compare Montaigne, pp. 350–353.

*One might question, of course, how successfully medicine can be done on such a restricted empirical base. Modern medicine does not restrict itself to what is observable but makes use of the theoretical constructions of modern science. Does the same hold for principles of living?

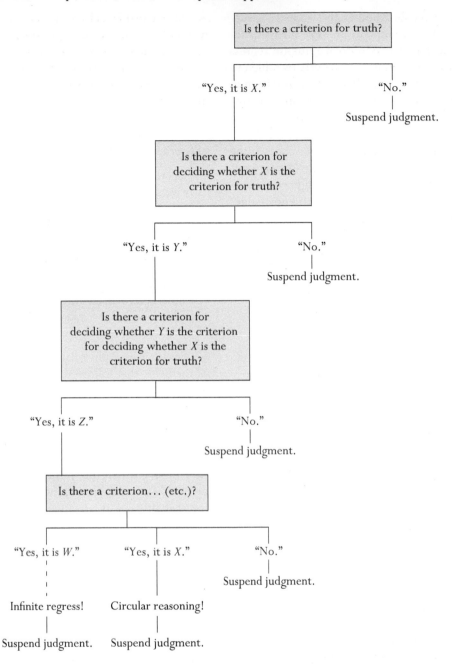

we conform to the customs of the land in which we live, for these customs express what appears to our fellow citizens to be good. We live "in accordance with the normal rules of life," but "undogmatically," not claiming that this is somehow the absolutely best or right thing to do.

Thus, the relativism against which Plato struggles and which Aristotle thinks he has overcome is reborn. It is not reborn as a doctrine claiming to be the truth about matters, for no such claims are made. But since things may appear differently to different people or cultures, a *practical relativism* is the result.

On what grounds could skeptics recommend their views? There are two. One amounts to the argument that there really is no alternative. Every nonskeptical view founders in one way or another on the problem of the criterion. The other brings us back to the connection between skepticism and happiness. As long as we seek certainty about the true nature of things, we will be in doubt; as long as we are in doubt, we will be perturbed; as long as we are perturbed, we will be unhappy. So the key to quietude and happiness is to give up the search for certainty. We must cease to be dogmatists and become skeptics.

> For the man who opines that anything is by nature good or bad is for ever being disquieted; when he is without the things which he deems good he believes himself to be tormented by things naturally bad and he pursues after the things which are, as he thinks, good; which when he has obtained he keeps falling into still more perturbations because of his irrational and immoderate elation, and in his dread of a change of fortune he uses every endeavor to avoid losing the things which he deems good. On the other hand, the man who determines nothing as to what is naturally good or bad neither shuns nor pursues anything eagerly; and in consequence, he is unperturbed. (*OP* 1.27–28)

This quietude, or tranquility of soul, is what the skeptic means by happiness. Or, if happiness is more than this, it is at least a necessary condition for happiness; without it no one can be happy. Though no one can escape trouble entirely, most people are doubly troubled, once by the pain or suffering and once by two further beliefs: that this is something bad or evil they are undergoing and that either they do not (in some absolute sense) deserve it or—worse yet—that they do. The skeptic at least does not suffer these further agonies. So the skeptics recommend the suspension of judgment about all claims to truth on the grounds that doing so provides a basis on which a happy life can be built.

These may seem rather minimal claims and their kind of happiness rather a pale one. It seems to be a retreat of some magnitude from the "high" view of happiness expressed, for instance, by Aristotle: activity of soul in accord with excellence. But perhaps the times did not realistically allow for more—for most people. Furthermore, the problem of the criterion remains; unless this can be solved, maybe no more can reasonably be expected. This is a very real problem with which numerous future philosophers struggle.*

---

1. What should we conclude from an examination of (a) differences in sense organs among animals; and (b) differences in taste among humans?
2. About what kind of thing does the skeptic "suspend judgment"? What does that term mean?
3. What is it to be "dogmatic"?
4. How does the skeptic use infinite regress and circular reasoning arguments?
5. What is the problem of the criterion? (Study the flow chart carefully.)
6. By what practical criterion does the skeptic live?
7. Why does the skeptic recommend suspending judgment as a key to happiness?

FOR FURTHER THOUGHT

1. Evaluate Epicurus' reasons for thinking that pleasure is the good for human beings in the light of (a) Aristotle's reasons for thinking that this could not possibly be correct and (b) the Stoic critique of this claim. Who do you think has the best of the argument here? Why?
2. Apply the problem of the criterion (with its considerations of infinite regress and circular reasoning) to Aristotle's theory of knowledge in terms of deduction, induction, and first principles. Can Aristotle survive such a critique? If you think he can, try to say how. If not, why not?
3. If you consider the popular culture of our day, would you say it is Platonistic, Aristotelian, Epicurean, Stoic, or skeptical? Or is it just in large measure unwise?

---

*See, for example, Augustine (pp. 267–269) and particularly René Descartes (*Meditation III*) and Hegel (pp. 498–502).

KEY WORDS

Epicurus	virtue
hedonism	intention
the gods	duty
death	natural law
atomism	skepticism
desire	Pyrrho
virtues	indeterminable
friendship	Sextus Empiricus
Stoicism	suspend judgment
happiness	dogmatic
nature	infinite regress
logos	circular reasoning
God	criterion
pantheism	appearances
equanimity	

NOTES

1. Gilbert Murray, *Five Stages of Greek Religion* (New York: Doubleday, Anchor Books, 1955), 139. We are indebted to this source for numerous points in this section.

2. All quotations from Epicurus' works are from *Letters, Principal Doctrines, and Vatican Sayings*, trans. Russel M. Geer (Indianapolis, IN: Library of Liberal Arts, 1964). Within this text, references to specific works will be as follows: *PD, Principal Doctrines; LM, Letter to Menoeceus; LP, Letter to Pythocles;* and *VS, Vatican Sayings.*

3. William Shakespeare, *Hamlet*, act 3, scene 1, lines 64–68.

4. Quotations from Lucretius, *The Way Things Are*, trans. Rolfe Humphries (Bloomington: Indiana University Press, 1969), are cited in the text using the abbreviation *WTA*. References are to page numbers of this edition.

5. Quotations from *The Handbook of Epictetus*, trans. Nicholas P. White (Indianapolis, IN: Hackett, 1983), are cited in the text using the abbreviation *E*.

6. See also Marcus Aurelius, *Meditations*, trans. Maxwell Staniforth (New York: Penguin Books, 1964), 6.41. Quotations from this work are hereafter cited in the text using the abbreviation *M*.

7. Attributed to Chrysippus by Eduard Zeller in *Stoics, Epicureans, and Skeptics* (New York: Russell & Russell, 1962), 284–285. Subsequent quotations from this work are cited in the text using the abbreviation *SES*.

8. Charlotte L. Stough, *Greek Scepticism* (Berkeley: University of California Press, 1969), 17.

9. There is a well-known study of interest in this connection: "What the Frog's Eye Tells the Frog's Brain," by J. Y. Lettvin, H. R. Maturana, W. S. McCulloch, and W. H. Pitts, *Proceedings of the Institute of Radio Engineers* 47 (1959): 1940–1951.

10. Quotations from Sextus Empiricus, *Outlines of Pyrrhonism* (Cambridge, MA: Harvard University Press, 1955), are cited in the text using the abbreviation *OP*.

CHAPTER

12

JEWS AND CHRISTIANS

Sin, Salvation, and Love

In Chapter 1 we sketched the religious and cultural traditions of the ancient Greeks. This was not philosophy, but the ground from which Greek philosophy grew. We noted then that we would need to examine another prephilosophical tradition if we are to understand medieval and later Western philosophy. In this short chapter, we look at the early Judeo-Christian tradition.

Background

Jesus, whom the Christians call "Christ" or "Messiah" (meaning "the anointed one"), was a Jew. So were his first followers; Christianity is a modification of the Jewish heritage. Thus, to understand the Christians, we must sketch something of the history in terms of which they understood themselves. Their history is the history of the Hebrew people. Let us outline, then, certain central convictions that grow out of that history and that the Christians take for granted.

Of the very first importance is the conviction that there is *one* **God.** We may be able to trace some development of this concept—from a kind of tribal deity, to a God superior to the gods of their neighbors, to one having the exclusive claim to worship—but by the time of the great prophets from the eighth to the sixth centuries B.C., it was already clear to the Hebrews that all other "gods" were mere pretenders, "idols" that it was sinful to reverence.*

> Thus says the Lord, the King of Israel
> and his Redeemer, the Lord of hosts:
> "I am the first and I am the last;
> besides me there is no god. . . .
> "To whom will you liken me and make me equal,
> and compare me, that we may be alike?
> Those who lavish gold from the purse,
> and weigh out silver in the scales,
> hire a goldsmith, and he makes it into a god;
> then they fall down and worship!
> They lift it upon their shoulders, they carry it,
> they set it in its place, and it stands there;
> it cannot move from its place.
> If one cries to it, it does not answer
> or save him from his trouble."
>
> —Isa. 44:6, 46:5–7[1]

---

*Compare Xenophanes, pp. 13–14, who is writing at about this same time.

The one true god differs from idols in all these respects. He is not made by men; he cannot be seen or touched; he is not restricted to any one place; he responds when you cry to him. As "the first and the last," he is eternal. He alone is worthy of worship and reverence.

God is the creator of the entire visible universe. The world is not eternal, as Aristotle thinks; nor is it God or an aspect of God, as the Stoics believed. God precedes and transcends the world, which is, however, wholly dependent on his power. The first words in the Hebrew scriptures are

In the beginning God created the heavens and the earth. (Gen. 1:1)

Moreover, God is entirely good, righteous, just, and holy. And this goodness is transmitted to the **creation;** on each of the "days" of creation, after God made light, the heavens, dry land, vegetation, animals, and human beings, we read that "God saw that it was good." Finding the world to be good, the Hebrews have a positive attitude toward it; the world is not something to escape from; it is not some shadowy image of true reality, as it is for Plato. It is in this world that we have a home; it is here that God has put us; it is here that our tasks and purposes are to be accomplished and our happiness achieved. The shadowy existence in the underworld after death is not anything to desire.*

But this task and happiness are complicated by the fact of sin. In the well-known story of the first man and woman, we read that human beings have succumbed to the temptation to "be like God, knowing good and evil" (Gen. 3:5). Not content with their status, wanting to play God themselves, humans have made themselves corrupt. Of the first pair of brothers, one murders the other. And so it has been ever since.

The rest of the Hebrew scriptures concerns a series of attempts to remedy this situation. They tell the story of how God, sometimes directly and sometimes through representatives, acts to reestablish his rule in a community of righteousness and justice. It is often understood in terms of the concept of the "**Kingdom of God.**" This story expresses the self-understanding of Jews and Christians alike.

A central episode in this story comes when God calls a certain man, Abram (later called **Abraham**), to leave his home, his culture, his nation, and to venture to a new land.

Now the Lord said to Abram, "Go from your country and your kindred and your father's house to the land that I will show you. And I will make of you a great nation, and I will bless you, and make your name great, so that you will be a blessing." (Gen. 12:1–2)

The Hebrew people identify themselves in terms of this promise and burden. They trace their heritage back to Abraham and believe that they play a special role in the history of the world: It is their privilege—and responsibility—to be agents for the reestablishment of God's kingdom on earth. They consider that they have a covenant with God, the terms of which are to reverence him, obeying him only, establishing justice among themselves, and so be a blessing to the rest of corrupt mankind—who can learn from them the blessings of righteousness.

A second crux is the **Exodus.** After some generations, the children of Abraham, faced with famine in Palestine, move to Egypt. Eventually they are enslaved there and spend "four hundred years" suffering considerable oppression. Against all odds, they leave Egypt under the guidance of **Moses** and reestablish themselves in the land promised to Abraham. This event, which leaves an indelible mark on the national character, is the sign and seal of their mission.

During the Exodus, the Hebrews receive **the Law** ("Torah") at Mount Sinai. What has distinguished the Jews to this day is the continuous possession of that Law, which begins with these words:

I am the Lord your God, who brought you out of the land of Egypt, out of the house of bondage. You shall have no other gods before me.
—Exod. 20:2–3

---

*See, for instance, Psalms 39:3 and 88:3–5, 10–12. Compare also Homer's Achilles on p. 7. Belief in a "resurrection of the body" grew among Jews in the several centuries before Jesus, however. In Jesus' time, one party, the Sadducees, held out against the belief. See Mark 12:18–27.

The Law goes on to forbid misusing God's name, killing, adultery, theft, false witness, and covetousness and to require keeping a Sabbath day holy and honoring one's parents. These statutes are well known as the Ten Commandments. But the Law also states in great detail how the people of God are to live, specifying dietary and health rules, principles of reparation for wrongs done, and regulations for religious observances.

The life of the Hebrew people remains precarious after their return from Egypt. They achieve some years of security and prosperity in the time of David and Solomon.* But thereafter it is a struggle to keep the community together. Surrounded by hostile nations, dominated for a time by the powerful Assyrians, exiled to Babylon, conquered by Alexander's armies, and finally made a province of the Roman Empire, they fight tenaciously for their heritage. They are constantly falling away from the Abrahamic covenant and the Law, if we are to judge by the succession of prophets who condemn their waywardness and call them back again to God. Still, despite the people's "hardness of heart," as the prophets call it, there is truth in the boast of Josephus, the first-century A.D. Jewish historian:

> Throughout our history we have kept the same laws, to which we are eternally faithful.[2]

During the period of foreign domination there grows up an expectation that God will send someone to establish God's kingdom of righteousness among men. This agent of God is sometimes conceived in terms of a political liberator who will expel the oppressors and restore the ancient kingdom of David; sometimes he is conceived in more cosmic and apocalyptic terms, as one who will rescue the faithful few and destroy the wicked. This hoped-for figure is given a variety of titles: Son of David, Son of Man, Messiah.

It is into this context that Jesus is born. Jesus is called by all these titles and often calls himself "Son of Man." Christians will look back particularly to Isaiah's prophecy about a "Suffering Servant" who will create the kingdom not by might, but by bearing the burdens of the people.

> He was despised and rejected by men;
> a man of sorrows and acquainted with grief;
> and as one from whom men hide their faces
> he was despised, and we esteemed him not.
> Surely he has borne our griefs
> and carried our sorrows;
> yet we esteemed him stricken,
> smitten by God, and afflicted.
> But he was wounded for our transgressions,
> he was bruised for our iniquities;
> upon him was the chastisement that made us
> whole;
> and with his stripes we are healed.
> All we like sheep have gone astray;
> we have turned every one to his own way;
> and the Lord has laid on him the iniquity of us all.
> —Isa. 53:3–6

These words are applied to the life, and particularly to the death, of Jesus. We now turn to Jesus himself to see what leads so many to think of him in these terms.

---

1. How do prophets differ from philosophers?
2. What are the characteristics of God, according to the Judeo–Christian tradition?
3. What is the significance of God's call to Abraham? Of the Exodus?

Jesus

In the earliest Gospel* Mark introduces **Jesus,** after his baptism by John, with these words:

> Now after John was arrested, Jesus came into Galilee, preaching the gospel of God, and saying, "The time is fulfilled, and the kingdom of God is at hand; repent and believe in the gospel." (Mark 1:14–15)

---

*This apex of the nation's power corresponds roughly to the time of the Trojan War.

*The word "gospel" means "good news." The four accounts we have of the life of Jesus (Matthew, Mark, Luke, and John) are called Gospels because they present the good news that God has fulfilled his promises to Abraham in the life and death of Jesus. It should be noted that each of these accounts is written by someone who believes that Jesus is Lord, Savior, and the expected Messiah. We have no hostile or even neutral accounts of his life.

That which the prophets foretold is now "at hand." The "kingdom of God" is about to be established, and Jesus sees himself as the one to do it.

That the kingdom is indeed at hand is manifest in the healing miracles of Jesus. According to the gospel writers, Jesus cures leprosy, gives sight to the blind and hearing to the deaf, casts out demons, and even brings the dead back to life. These miracles are signs of God's presence and power.

The attitude and behavior of Jesus bear out his sense of a new beginning. He is without any class consciousness, associating with poor and rich, learned and ignorant, righteous and sinner alike. A common complaint among those who carefully observe the Law is that he associates with undesirables. He does not do so, of course, to sanction their sin, but to lead them to righteousness, as the following parable illustrates.

> Now the tax collectors and sinners were all drawing near to hear him. And the Pharisees and the scribes murmured, saying, "This man receives sinners and eats with them."
>
> So he told them this parable: "What man of you, having a hundred sheep, if he lost one of them, does not leave the ninety-nine in the wilderness, and go after the one which is lost, until he finds it? And when he has found it, he lays it on his shoulders, rejoicing. And when he comes home, he calls together his friends and his neighbors, saying to them, 'Rejoice with me, for I have found my sheep which was lost.' Just so, I tell you, there will be more joy in heaven over one sinner who repents than over ninety-nine righteous persons who need no repentance." (Luke 15:1–7)

Absolute indifference to wealth and worldly goods is characteristic of both his life and his teaching. Of himself he says,

> Foxes have holes, and birds of the air have nests; but the Son of man has nowhere to lay his head. (Luke 9:58)

And he emphasizes repeatedly that attachment to riches will keep one out of the kingdom.* A wealthy man asks him what he must do to inherit eternal life. Jesus replies that he must keep the commandments. The man says he has done so all his life. Then,

> Jesus looking upon him loved him, and said to him, "You lack one thing; go, sell what you have, and give to the poor, and you will have treasure in heaven; and come, follow me." At that saying his countenance fell, and he went away sorrowful; for he had great possessions.
>
> And Jesus looked around and said to his disciples, "How hard it will be for those who have riches to enter the kingdom of God!" (Mark 10:21–23)

There are many sayings to the same effect. To be part of the kingdom of God requires absolute singleness of mind; care for possessions distracts one from that intensity.

> And he said to him, "Take heed, and beware of all covetousness; for a man's life does not consist in the abundance of his possessions." (Luke 12:15)

> No one can serve two masters; for either he will hate the one and love the other, or he will be devoted to the one and despise the other. You cannot serve God and mammon [riches].

> "Therefore I tell you, do not be anxious about your life, what you shall eat or what you shall drink, nor about your body, what you shall put on. Is not life more than food, and the body more than clothing? Look at the birds of the air: they neither sow nor reap nor gather into barns, and yet your heavenly Father feeds them. Are you not of more value than they? And which of you by being anxious can add one cubit to his span of life? . . . Therefore do not be anxious, saying, 'What shall we eat?' or 'What shall we drink?' or 'What shall we wear?' For the Gentiles seek all these things; and your heavenly Father knows that you need them all. But seek first his kingdom and his righteousness, and all these things shall be yours as well." (Matt. 6:24–33)

What kind of righteousness does Jesus have in mind? When a lawyer asks him what to do to inherit eternal life, Jesus answers,

> "What is written in the law? How do you read?" And he answered, "You shall love the Lord your God with all your heart, and with all your soul, and with all your strength, and with all your mind; and your neighbor as yourself." And he said to him,

---

*Compare Socrates' voluntary poverty and the way he describes his divine mission in *Apology* 29d–30b.

"You have answered right; do this, and you will live." (Luke 10:26–28)

The key to the righteousness of the kingdom is **love.** But "love," of course, is a word with many meanings.* What does it mean here? With reference to God, it means a kind of undivided and absolute devotion; it is the appropriate response to the creator who provides for us. This devotion to God has a corollary: that we love our "neighbors" as ourselves. No better explanation of this requirement can be given than the one Jesus gives to the lawyer who asks, "Who is my **neighbor**?"

> "A man was going down from Jerusalem to Jericho, and he fell among robbers, who stripped him and beat him, and departed, leaving him half dead. Now by chance a priest was going down that road; and when he saw him he passed by on the other side. So likewise a Levite, when he came to the place and saw him, passed by on the other side. But a Samaritan, as he journeyed, came to where he was; and when he saw him, he had compassion, and went to him and bound up his wounds, pouring on oil and wine; then he set him on his own beast and brought him to an inn, and took care of him. And the next day he took out two denarii and gave them to the innkeeper, saying, 'Take care of him; and whatever more you spend, I will repay you when I come back.' Which of these three, do you think, proved neighbor to the man who fell among the robbers?" He said, "The one who showed mercy on him." And Jesus said to him, "Go and do likewise." (Luke 10:30–37)†

Several things in this famous parable of the good Samaritan merit comment. First, note that Jesus does not exactly answer the question he is asked, "Who is my neighbor?" Rather, he answers the question, "What is it to *act* as a neighbor?" The lawyer's reaction to the story shows that he knows enough about *how to be a neighbor* that putting off action until he

has clarified the concept of *what a neighbor is* just constitutes rationalization and evasion of responsibility.* So the closing line directs the lawyer's attention to himself: Do likewise—see that *you* act as a neighbor. This redirecting of attention from externals to the condition of one's own heart is quite characteristic of Jesus.

Second, note that the key word here is "compassion." Jesus is explaining the second part of the Law. To love your neighbor as yourself is to have compassion, to "feel with" your fellow human being, and to act in accord with that feeling. Just as we feel our own desires, anxieties, pains, and joys, so are we to "feel with" the desires, anxieties, pains and joys of others. And as we act to fulfill the intentions that grow out of these self-directed passions, so, like the Samaritan, must we act to satisfy the needs of others.

> And as you wish that men would do to you, do so to them. (Luke 6:31)

Love, understood in this way, strikes a new note in the story of Western philosophy. It is a conception quite foreign to the Greek philosophers. For them the basic human problem focuses on the control of the passions; by and large, they ascribe the locus of control to reason. Plato sees it as a struggle to subjugate the beast within, Aristotle as a matter of channeling the passions by means of virtuous habits. The Stoics almost recommend the elimination of feelings altogether.† For all of them, the goal is finding the best possible way to live. And though the Platonic wise man will return to the cave to try to enlighten those still in bondage, none of them would say that the best way to live necessarily involves feeling for others just as we feel for ourselves. What Jesus recommends is not the control or extinction of passion, but its *extension*; it is in

---

*See the discussion of love in Plato's *Symposium* (pp. 165–166). The word the New Testament writers use for love is *agape*. It is interesting to compare the *eros* that Socrates extols with the *agape* that, Jesus holds, is the key to the kingdom of God.

†Note the three types and their response to the injured man. The priest represents the religious leadership; Levites were lay assistants to the priests; and Samaritans were foreigners who were despised by the Jews.

---

*Compare Augustine on the priority of will over intellect, p. 289.

†The Stoics, for example, oppose pity. In considering what behavior is appropriate when someone is weeping, Epictetus advises us not to be overcome; we should remember that his weeping has its source not in what has happened but in the view he takes of it. We may, perhaps, go as far as to moan with him, but Epictetus says, "Be careful not to moan inwardly" (*The Handbook of Epictetus* 16).

universal compassion that we will find the kingdom of God. And though the Stoics do think of all men as brothers, not even they would say this:

> Love your enemies, do good to those who hate you, bless those who curse you, pray for those who abuse you. (Luke 6:27)

We do seem to have something genuinely new here.*

A corollary to this love is a new virtue: humility. **Humility** is conspicuously lacking from the Greek lists of virtues, but it is nearly the very essence of perfection according to Jesus. For humility is the opposite of pride, and **pride** is the very root of sin. It is pride—wanting to be like God—that leads to the sin of Adam. Pride sets human beings against each other; the proud man, glorying in his superiority, cannot consider his neighbor equal in importance to himself and so cannot love as Jesus requires.

Pride, particularly pride in one's righteousness, is the attitude most at variance with the kingdom of God.

> He also told this parable to some who trusted in themselves that they were righteous and despised others: "Two men went up into the temple to pray, one a Pharisee and the other a tax collector. The Pharisee stood and prayed thus with himself, 'God, I thank thee that I am not like other men, extortioners, unjust, adulterers, or even like this tax collector. I fast twice a week, I give tithes of all that I get.' But the tax collector, standing far off, would not even lift up his eyes to heaven, but beat his breast, saying, 'God, be merciful to me a sinner!' I tell you, this man went down to his house justified rather than the other; for every one who exalts himself will be humbled, but he who humbles himself will be exalted." (Luke 18:9–14)†

---

*It seems new, at least, to the Western tradition. Compare Jesus' teachings on this point to the Four Divine Abidings in Buddhist thought (p. 40), the "impartial concern" of the Mohists (pp. 78–80), and the importance of understanding others in the Confucian tradition (p. 222).

†The Pharisees claimed that they observed all the details of the Law. Tax collectors, working for the Roman occupiers, were generally despised; and it is true that many of them were corrupt. A "tithe" is one-tenth of one's income, which is what the Law required to be given for religious and charitable purposes.

Jesus denounces those—usually the wealthy and powerful—who consider themselves righteous but do not act as neighbors should act. Like Socrates, he thereby incurs hostility among those in a position to do him harm. Unlike Socrates, of course, he does not do so by asking questions. Like the prophets of old, Jesus thunders out condemnation; and it is not a claim to know that he tries to undermine, but pretensions to righteousness.* Here is an example.

> Woe to you, scribes and Pharisees, hypocrites! for you are like whitewashed tombs, which outwardly appear beautiful, but within they are full of dead men's bones and all uncleanness. So you also outwardly appear righteous to men, but within you are full of hypocrisy and iniquity. (Matt. 23:27–28)

His antagonism to mere outward observance leads him to internalize the Law. About the Law he speaks with authority, contrasting the *words* of the Law, which can be kept simply by behaving in certain ways, with the *spirit* of the Law, which requires an attitude of love. For example,

> You have heard that it was said to the men of old, "You shall not kill; and whoever kills shall be liable to judgment." But I say to you that every one who is angry with his brother shall be liable to judgment. (Matt. 5:21–22)
>
> You have heard that it was said, "You shall not commit adultery." But I say to you that every one who looks at a woman lustfully has already committed adultery with her in his heart. (Matt. 5:27–28)

This attitude toward the Law brings him into conflict with the authorities. He seems to them to take the Law lightly; on several occasions, for example, they clash with him on the details of Sabbath observance. He is, moreover, popular among the common people and must seem to be undermining the authority of the Jewish leaders. They determine to put him to death.

Because of Roman law, they cannot execute Jesus themselves. So after a trial in the religious

---

*This difference, while significant, may be diminished by the observation that for Socrates virtue is knowledge. So one who claims to know what piety is, for example, would also—in Socrates' eyes—be claiming to be pious.

court in which he is convicted for blasphemy (putting himself in the place of God), the Jewish leaders bring him before the Roman governor, Pilate. Here he is accused of treason, of setting himself up as king of the Jews (a charge of blasphemy would not have impressed this cosmopolitan Roman). Pilate reluctantly accedes to their demands, and Jesus is crucified.

Each of the four Gospels ends with an account of the discovery, on the third day after Jesus' death, of an empty tomb and of numerous appearances of Jesus to his disciples. His followers come to believe that he has risen from the dead. And they take this as a sign that he is indeed God's anointed, the suffering servant who takes upon himself the sins of the world, thereby bringing in the kingdom of God in an unexpectedly spiritual way. Their response is to set about making disciples of all nations.

---

1. How, according to Jesus, are we to love God? Our neighbor?
2. Do the Christians present new virtues?
3. Christians accept as a fact that Jesus rose from the dead. What do they think that means for us?

The Meaning of Jesus

We have noted that the Gospels are written by believers; they are shot through with the significance his followers attribute to Jesus after their experience of his resurrection. But it will be useful to discuss more explicitly how his life and death are interpreted. For this purpose, we will look particularly at the Gospel of John and at some letters written by the greatest of the early missionaries, Paul.

John begins his Gospel with a majestic prologue.

In the beginning was the Word, and the Word was with God, and the Word was God. He was in the beginning with God; all things were made through him, and without him was not anything made that was made. . . .

And the Word became flesh and dwelt among us, full of grace and truth; we have beheld his glory, glory as of the only Son from the Father. . . . And from his fullness have we all received, grace upon grace. For the law was given through Moses; grace

and truth came through Jesus Christ. No one has ever seen God; the only Son, who is in the bosom of the Father, he has made him known. (John 1:1–3, 14–18)

Notice the exalted conception of Jesus we have here. John identifies Jesus with the **Word** itself—the *logos*, the wisdom through which all things are made. This *logos* was "in the beginning" with God (a phrase meant to recall the first line of Genesis). Though this Word exists beyond the world, it enters the world through Jesus, enlightening all and bringing those who are willing into the family of God.

John reports Jesus expressing these ideas in various ways. Jesus says, "He who has seen me has seen the Father" (John 14:9). He says, "I and the Father are one" (John 10:30). He calls himself "the light of the world" (John 8:12), "the bread of life" (John 6:48), and "the good shepherd" who "lays down his life for the sheep" (John 10:11).

If Jesus is the manifestation of God in the world, what do we learn of God from him?

For God so loved the world that he gave his only Son, that whoever believes in him should not perish but have eternal life. For God sent the Son into the world, not to condemn the world, but that the world might be saved through him. (John 3:16–17)

The God whom Jesus reveals is not Aristotle's unmoved mover, thinking true thoughts about himself. Nor is he akin to the indifferent gods of the Epicureans. The message is that God is Love, that he cares for us and will save us from our sinfulness through his Son Jesus, who took our sin upon himself in his death. The life and death of the Christ manifest the extremity of that Love and serve, in turn, as a model for life in the kingdom of God.

What is required is a "new birth," not of flesh and the will of man, but "of God."* And this new life—this is the gospel—is now available to all by trust in Jesus, the Christ.

Paul was a Jew who at first vigorously opposed the new "sect" of Christians. While engaged in persecuting them, he saw a vision of Jesus and

---

*See Jesus' conversation with the Jewish leader Nicodemus in John 3:1–15.

was converted, after which he devoted his life to spreading the gospel. He traveled extensively, establishing churches all over Asia Minor and Greece. He visited Athens and argued there with both the Jews and the philosophers, appalled by the "idolatry" he found there and preaching the one creator God and Jesus who rose from the dead.*

> "The whole of history is incomprehensible without the Christ."
>
> *Ernest Renan (1823–1892)*

Paul comes to believe it is hopeless to try to attain the righteousness of the kingdom of God by observing the Law; no doubt this reflects in part his own zealous efforts before his conversion. All men, Paul holds, are inextricably caught in the web of sinfulness and cannot by their own (sinful) efforts "justify" themselves before the righteous judge. But what we cannot do for ourselves God has graciously done for us through Jesus.

> For no human being will be justified in his sight by works of the law, since through the law comes knowledge of sin.
> But now the righteousness of God has been manifested apart from the law, although the law and the prophets bear witness to it, the righteousness of God through faith in Jesus Christ for all who believe. (Rom. 3:20–22)

> There is therefore now no condemnation for those who are in Christ Jesus. For the law of the Spirit of life in Christ Jesus has set me free from the law of sin and death. (Rom. 8:1–2)

Having been freed from the burden of the Law and no longer needing to prove ourselves righteous, says Paul, allows us to participate in the Spirit of Christ, loving our neighbors and serving their needs. It really is Jesus, then, who has brought in the kingdom of God. All who believe in him be raised to a blessed life with him.

We close our consideration of Christian teaching with these words from another author.

We know that we have passed out of death into life, because we love the brethren. He who does not love remains in death. Any one who hates his brother is a murderer, and you know that no murderer has eternal life abiding in him. By this we know love, that he laid down his life for us; and we ought to lay down our lives for the brethren. But if anyone has the world's goods and sees his brother in need, yet closes his heart against him, how does God's love abide in him? Little children, let us not love in word or speech but in deed and in truth. (1 John 3:14–18)

1. What does it mean when John calls Jesus "the *logos*"? Relate this to Heraclitean and Stoic views.
2. How, according to Paul, can we be "justified" before God, the judge?
3. *Why* should we love our neighbors as ourselves?

FOR FURTHER THOUGHT

You should now have a fairly clear understanding of how Plato, Aristotle, Epicurus, and the Stoics envision the good life. Choose one of these philosophies and work out a comparison (both similarities and differences) between it and the Christian view of the good life.

KEY WORDS

God	Jesus
creation	love
Kingdom of God	neighbor
Abraham	humility
Exodus	pride
Moses	Word
the Law	

NOTES

1. Biblical quotations in this text are taken from the Revised Standard Version.
2. Josephus, *Against Apion* 200:20; quoted in C. K. Barrett, ed., *The New Testament Background: Selected Documents* (London: S.P.C.K., 1956), 202.

*See Acts 17:16–34.

CHAPTER

13

AUGUSTINE

God and the Soul

Our story has reached a crucial turning point: on the cusp of the early medieval period, the philosopher and theologian Augustine (A.D. 354–430) melded the heritage of the Greek philosophers with early Christian thought. Both of these traditions are given a unique stamp by Augustine's penchant for introspection, his passionate search for happiness, and the impress of his undeniably powerful mind. He would himself say that if he had contributed anything of value, it was due entirely to the grace of God. This would not be merely an expression of modesty; Augustine believes it to be the literal truth. Whether we agree with that or not, we can fairly say that no one else did as much to shape the intellectual course of the next thousand years of European thought.

Augustine's thought is so entangled with his life experiences that we need to understand something of his life.[1] There is no better introduction to his early years than his own *Confessions*, in which he reflects—before God but also before us all—on his youthful waywardness. By the time he wrote this reflective look at his life (in 397), he was

forty-three years old and had been a Christian for eleven years, a priest for eight years, and a bishop for two. We cannot hope here to imitate the richness of these meditations but will try just to get a feel for how he saw his life from the point of view he had reached.

Augustine was born in northern Africa, which had been Roman for many generations but was always precariously perched between the sea and the barbarian interior. Christianity had taken root there but, despite its legitimation by the emperor Constantine in 325, was still in competition with the old pagan beliefs and ways. Augustine was the child of a Christian mother, Monica, and a pagan father who converted to Christianity before he died. Monica was the stronger influence, convinced all her life that her son would be "saved." But it was Patricius, his father, who resolutely determined that Augustine should be educated; he studied literature and rhetoric and, for a while, the law. His education was intense but narrow, concentrating on the masters of Latin style and consisting of enormous amounts of memorization of, for example, Virgil's *Aeneid*. He read very little philosophy.

Meanwhile, he lived the life of pleasure. The bishop he became, looking back on those days, puts it this way:

> I cared for nothing but to love and be loved. But my love went beyond the affection of one mind for another, beyond the arc of the bright beam of friendship. Bodily desire, like a morass, and adolescent sex welling up within me exuded mists which clouded over and obscured my heart, so that I could not distinguish the clear light of true love from the murk of lust. Love and lust together seethed within me. In my tender youth they swept me away over the precipice of my body's appetites and plunged me in the whirlpool of sin. (*C* 2.2)²

His "whirlpool of sin" involved more than just sex. He is almost more perplexed over a single act that comes to represent for him the puzzling nature of human wickedness. He, together with some companions, had shaken down an enormous quantity of pears from a neighbor's tree and had stolen them away. And why did they steal the pears? Did they need them? No. Did they eat them? No. They threw them to the pigs.

Why, then, did they steal the pears? This is what puzzles Augustine. In a judicial inquiry, he notes, no one is satisfied until the motive has been produced: a desire of gaining some good or of avoiding some evil. But what was the good gained here? What evil was avoided? He concludes: "our real pleasure consisted in doing something that was forbidden" (*C* 2.4). But why was that a pleasure? Augustine's reflective answer is that the act was, in a perverse sort of way, an imitation of God; it was an attempt to exercise a liberty that belongs to God alone: that of being unconstrained by anything outside himself (*C* 1.6). No one, Augustine felt, was going to make rules for *him* to live by. We come, then, even in this simple teenage prank, to Augustine's analysis of the root of the human predicament: **pride.**

He also notes that he surely would not have stolen the pears on his own.

> It was not the takings that attracted me but the raid itself, and yet to do it by myself would have been no fun and I should not have done it. This was friendship of a most unfriendly sort, bewitching my mind in an inexplicable way. For the sake of a laugh, a little sport, I was glad to do harm and anxious to damage another; and that without a thought of profit for myself or retaliation for injuries received! And all because we are ashamed to hold back when others say "Come on! Let's do it!" (*C* 2.9)

This power of the group to incite to evil deeds is expressed also in the following passage, in which Augustine sets out a very common experience of the young.

> I was so blind to the truth that among my companions I was ashamed to be less dissolute than they were. For I heard them bragging of their depravity, and the greater the sin the more they gloried in it, so that I took pleasure in the same vices not only for the enjoyment of what I did, but also for the applause I won.
>
> Nothing deserves to be despised more than vice; yet I gave in more and more to vice simply in order not to be despised. If I had not sinned enough to rival other sinners, I used to pretend that I had done things I had not done at all, because I was afraid that innocence would be taken for cowardice and chastity for weakness. (*C* 2.3)

It is clear that the Christian bishop at age forty-three does not take lightly the peccadilloes of his youth. It is not prudishness that accounts for this, however; it is a considered judgment that pursuing such desires is a sure way to miss true happiness. But the young Augustine had a long way to go before he would see things this way.

He took a mistress, to whom he was apparently faithful for many years. They had a son. Augustine completed his education and became a teacher of rhetoric and literature, first in the provincial north African town of Thagaste and then in Carthage, the great city of Roman Africa. He was an able teacher and earned a reputation, for which he was most eager.

But he was eager for something else as well. At nineteen, he read a (now lost) work by Cicero,

❧

"Perverseness is one of the primitive impulses of the human heart."

Edgar Allan Poe (1809–1849)

the great orator, which contains an exhortation to study philosophy. Augustine was carried away:

> The only thing that pleased me in Cicero's book was his advice not simply to admire one or another of the schools of philosophy, but to love wisdom itself, whatever it might be, and to search for it, pursue it, hold it, and embrace it firmly. (*C* 4.4)

The young Augustine embraced this love of wisdom with a "blaze of enthusiasm." But where to look? He knew very little of classical philosophy, which is what Cicero surely had in mind. In Augustine's circle in late fourth-century Africa, it was Christ who was portrayed as "the wisdom of God"; so Augustine turned to the Bible. But he was greatly disappointed. Not only did it seem to lack the polish of the best Roman poets, but also its conceptions seemed crude and naive to him. In Genesis, after Adam and Eve had disobeyed God, we read that they "heard the sound of the Lord God walking in the cool of the day." What a way to think of God!

Moreover, Christianity seemed unable to solve a great puzzle, which was to perplex Augustine for many years. Christians proclaimed God to be both almighty and perfectly good. But if this is so, where does evil come from? If the answer is the devil, the question can be repeated: Where does the devil come from? If from God, then God is the source of evil. And if God is almighty, where else could the devil come from? But God is good; so how could he be the source of evil?

It may be useful to set the problem out in a more formal way.

1. If God is omnipotent (all powerful), omniscient (all knowing), and perfectly good, then there can be no evil, because
   a. being all-powerful, he *could do* something about any existing evil,
   b. being all-knowing, he *would know* about any existing evil, and
   c. being perfectly good, he *would want to eliminate* any existing evil.
2. But there is evil.
3. Therefore God is either
   a. not all-powerful (He *can't* do anything about the evil), or

   b. not all-knowing (He could do something if only he *knew* about it), or
   c. not perfectly good (He does know and could do something, but He *doesn't care*)—or
   d. some combination of a, b, and c.

Augustine could not see that the Christians had any satisfactory answer to this puzzle, traditionally called "the **Problem of Evil.**" You should be able to see that it is quite a formidable problem. The argument looks valid; that is, if its premises are true, it looks as though the conclusion will have to be true. So that leads us to ask whether the premises are true. Obviously, there are two main possibilities here. We could argue that premise 1 is false; or we could argue that premise 2 is false. Roughly speaking, Augustine tries out each of these possibilities.

The first possibility was represented for him by a popular movement in his day called "**Manicheanism.**" Augustine was a "hearer" (more than an outsider, but less than a full member) among the Manichees for nine years.

Manicheanism was a sect founded by the Babylonian Mani in the third century. Mani synthesized themes from the Persian religion of Zoroastrianism and Christianity. Manicheanism is often thought of as one of the many "heresies" prevalent during the first centuries of the Christian era, as the church tried to sort out an orthodox view of revealed truth. Religious authorities executed Mani in A.D. 277, which only helped spread the sect more widely.

The complex doctrines of the sect combine astrology, half-digested bits of natural science, and borrowings from traditional religions. But the key beliefs are simple and provide a solution of sorts to the problem of evil. The reason there is evil in the world, say the Manichees, is that there is *no omnipotent good power*. Rather, there are two equal and opposed powers, one good and one evil. It has always been this way, they say, and will always be so. So you can see that the Manichees deny the antecedent in the first premise.

This opposition, moreover, is not just "out there" in the world. It resides in each of us, since we are ourselves a battleground between good and evil. That may not sound very profound; but the

Manichees explain this dichotomy in a particular way. The good part of ourselves is the soul (composed of the light), and the bad part is the body (composed of the dark earth). A human being is literally part divine and part demonic.

> I have known my soul and the body that lies upon it,
> That they have been enemies since the creation of
> the worlds. (*MP*, p. 49)[3]

In fact, the entire earth is the province of the evil power, since evil resides in matter as such. We are, however, essentially *souls*; and as souls we experience ourselves to be under the domination of a foreign power—matter, the body, the world. The "gospel" of the Manichees is that we can be saved from the domination of the evil power—matter—if we come to *know who we are*.

Manicheanism, then, claims to solve the *theoretical* problem of evil by the postulation of the two powers—denying the infinite perfection of God—and the *practical* problem of evil by the doctrine that the soul is essentially good, untouched by the evil of the body. If only you can come to identify yourself with your soul, you will experience "salvation" from the evil. Augustine apparently felt that this solution freed him from his theoretical perplexities and allowed him to think of himself as "essentially good." This, then, was the first "wisdom" that he embraced in his enthusiasm for the truth.

He noticed, however, that some of the doctrines were obscure and that others seemed to conflict with the best astronomical knowledge of the day. When one of the Manichean "Elect," a certain Faustus, came to Carthage, Augustine determined to inquire about these things. On examination it became obvious that Faustus was not wise.* So Augustine was disappointed a second time; neither Christianity nor Manicheanism seemed to offer the wisdom he was seeking.

Moreover, he found Manichean views unhelpful in a practical sense. Their key to salvation lay in knowledge, in a recognition of the true nature of the self as good. But this didn't seem to help one change one's life. It was too passive. (It may have

been his experience as a Manichee that led to his later view that the root of sin lies not in the intellect but in the *will*.) The bishop he became reflects on his experience:

> I still thought that it is not we who sin but some other nature that sins within us. It flattered my pride to think that I incurred no guilt and, when I did wrong, not to confess it so that you [God] might bring healing to a soul that had sinned against you. (Psalm 41:4) I preferred to excuse myself and blame this unknown thing which was in me but was not part of me. The truth, of course, was that it was all my own self, and my own impiety had divided me against myself. My sin was all the more incurable because I did not think myself a sinner. (*C* 5.10)

Eventually, Augustine drifted away from the Manichees, but these notions of pride, guilt, and a divided self remained with him.

He began to read the philosophers and found himself attracted to skepticism. He left Africa and went to Rome, where again he taught rhetoric and literature. He was recommended to the more attractive post of professor of rhetoric in Milan, where he was joined by his widowed mother; with her, he attended Christian services conducted by the bishop of Milan, Ambrose. **Ambrose** was an immensely learned man, far more learned in the traditions of the Greek church fathers and Greek philosophy than Augustine (whose Greek skills were always imperfect). Through Ambrose, Augustine began to discover the possibility of a Christianity that was not naive and crude but that could bear comparison with the best thought of the day.

What made the Christianity of Ambrose a revelation to Augustine, who had, in a sense, been familiar with Christianity since his childhood? There seem to have been three things. (1) There was the idea of God and the soul as *immaterial* realities. Augustine had found great difficulty in thinking of either as other than some sort of *body*, even if very ethereal bodies. (Recall that the Manichees thought of God and the soul as light.) But if God is a body, God cannot be everywhere present (and this idea fits with the Manichean dualism of two equal and opposite realities). If God is an immaterial spirit, however, then he is not excluded by the material world and he can be omnipresent. (2) Ambrose

---

*Compare Socrates asking questions in Athens: *Apology* 21b–22c.

"I was in love with beauty of a lower order and it was dragging me down."

—St. Augustine

Yet he hesitated. What would happen if he became a Christian? In Augustine's view, this was a serious matter. His life would have to change drastically, for he was still preoccupied with worldly things: his career, his reputation, and sex. His mistress had returned to Africa, and marriage with an heiress was being arranged. Would he have to give all this up? Augustine was never one for half measures, and it seemed to him that he would. But could he? He procrastinated. The bishop he had become expresses the agony of that time in the following way:

> I was held fast, not in fetters clamped upon me by another, but by my own will, which had the strength of iron chains. The enemy held my will in his power and from it he had made a chain and shackled me. For my will was perverse and lust had grown from it, and when I gave in to lust habit was born, and when I did not resist the habit it became a necessity. These were the links which together formed what I have called my chain, and it held me fast in the duress of servitude. But the new will which had come to life in me and made me wish to serve you freely and enjoy you, my God, who are our only certain joy, was not yet strong enough to overcome the old, hardened as it was by the passage of time. So these two wills within me, one old, one new, one the servant of the flesh, the other of the spirit, were in conflict and between them they tore my soul apart. (*C* 8.5)

The *perversity of the will*, which leads to *lust*, which leads to *habit*, which becomes a virtual *necessity*, forms a chain that will play a crucial role in Augustine's analysis of what is wrong with human beings and how it can be cured.

"Nothing is stronger than habit."

Ovid (43 B.C.–A.D. 17)

In a dramatic experience, which Augustine relates in the *Confessions*, the chain of necessity was broken. After hearing from a traveler the stories of several others who had renounced the world and devoted themselves to God, Augustine rushed into a garden in a tumult. "My inner self," he says,

was not afraid to plunder the Greek philosophical tradition, which had often emphasized immaterial reality, for help in making Christianity intelligible. (3) Ambrose offered allegorical interpretations to Scripture, particularly to the Old Testament. Taken allegorically rather than literally, many passages ceased to offend and took on the aspect of conveying deep spiritual truths.

Augustine began to study the Bible seriously for the first time and to read philosophy. The Bible spoke of the Wisdom of God, and philosophers loved wisdom. Could Christianity contain the truth the philosophers were seeking? He began to suspect so. He grew more sure of it and then became virtually certain.

"was a house divided against itself." "I was my own contestant."

> I felt that I was still the captive of my sins, and in my misery I kept crying, "How long shall I go on saying 'tomorrow, tomorrow'? Why not now? Why not make an end of my ugly sins at this moment?"
>
> I was asking myself these questions, weeping all the while with the most bitter sorrow in my heart, when all at once I heard the sing-song voice of a child in a nearby house. Whether it was the voice of a boy or a girl I cannot say, but again and again it repeated the refrain "Take it and read, take it and read." At this I looked up, thinking hard whether there was any kind of game in which children used to chant words like these, but I could not remember ever hearing them before. I stemmed my flood of tears and stood up, telling myself that this could only be a divine command to open my book of Scripture and read the first passage on which my eyes should fall. . . .
>
> So I hurried back to the place where Alypius was sitting, for when I stood up to move away I had put down the book containing Paul's Epistles. I seized it and opened it, and in silence I read the first passage on which my eyes fell: Not in reveling and drunkenness, not in lust and wantonness, not in quarrels and rivalries. Rather, arm yourselves with the Lord Jesus Christ; spend no more thought on nature and nature's appetites. (Romans 13:13, 14) I had no wish to read more and no need to do so. For in an instant, as I came to the end of the sentence, it was as though the light of confidence flooded into my heart and all the darkness of doubt was dispelled. (C 8.12)

Augustine had found the **wisdom** he had been searching for.

He gave up his career and his prospects for marriage. He retired for some months with some friends and his mother to a retreat where he studied and wrote. On Easter Day in 387, he was baptized by Ambrose, thus making his break with "the world" public. Not long thereafter, his mother having died, he returned to Africa, was made a priest (somewhat against his will), and in 391 was ordained bishop of Hippo, a city on the Mediterranean coast of Africa.

Thereafter he was engaged in practical affairs of the church: in serving as a judge (one of the tasks of a bishop in those days), in controversies to define

and defend the faith, and in much writing. There are, of course, the sermons. But there are also letters and pamphlets and book after book in which Augustine explores the meaning of the faith he had adopted. In these the theme is—again and again—to try to *understand* what he has *believed*. For Augustine, faith must come first; understanding may follow (though on some difficult topics, such as the Trinity, even understanding will be only partial).* This order of things may seem strange to some of us. We may think that unless we understand first, we will not know what it is that we are believing. But it is a reflection of Augustine's conviction that will is more fundamental than intellect and that only if the will is first directed by faith to the right end will the intellect be able to do its job rightly.†

With this point we are ready to leave the life of Augustine and focus on his philosophy. It is characteristic of Augustine's thought that we cannot do so without at the same time discussing his theology, or doctrine of God. For wisdom, Augustine is convinced, is *one*. And that means that philosophy and theology, understanding and faith, science and religion are inextricably bound together. What the lover of wisdom wants is the truth. And the truth is God. And God is most fully known by faith in Christ. We will not do full justice to this unity, but in selecting out certain themes that are of particular philosophical interest, we will try to keep in mind the whole context in which they play their part for Augustine. Part of Augustine's legacy is just this unity of thought. It sets the intellectual tone in the West for a thousand years.

---

*Here is an analogy to Augustine's motto, *faith seeking understanding*. Suppose you are unable to solve a certain mathematical problem. Then you are given the answer. *Believing* that this is the correct answer, you are now able to work back and *understand* why it is correct.

†Think about Socrates. We said that to benefit from a conversation with Socrates, you had to be a person of a certain *character*. The arrogant, the proud, the self-satisfied would only be humiliated. (See pp. 96–97.) Augustine agrees that character is more fundamental than intellect. But whereas Socrates thinks of virtue or character as a matter of knowledge, for Augustine it is a matter of faith, or commitment.

1. Explain what Augustine thinks we should learn from the adventure of the pears.
2. What advice of Cicero's shaped Augustine's life?
3. What problem made Augustine dissatisfied with Christianity?
4. How did the Manichees explain evil? Where is evil located? Where is good located?
5. For what reasons did Augustine become dissatisfied with the Manichees?
6. Describe the links in the chain leading to the bondage of the will.
7. What, according to Augustine, is the relation between belief and understanding?

Wisdom, Happiness, and God

Augustine takes for granted that philosophy, the pursuit of wisdom, has just one aim: happiness. This was the common assumption in late antiquity, shared by the Epicureans, the Stoics, and the skeptics. Augustine had little interest in nature philosophy and eventually turned away from it as Socrates had done.* It could not make one happy.

What does interest Augustine intensely is the soul, for happiness and unhappiness are clearly conditions of the soul. How does Augustine understand **happiness**? That soul is happy which possesses what it most desires, *provided* that it most desires what wisdom approves.

> Just as it is agreed that we all wish to be happy, so it is agreed that we all wish to be wise, since no one without wisdom is happy. No man is happy except through the highest good, which is to be found and included in that truth which we call wisdom. (*FCW* 2.9.102–103)

You cannot be happy unless you have what you desire; yet having what you desire does not guarantee happiness, for you must desire the right things. Certain things, if they are desired and attained, will produce misery rather than happiness. Augustine knows this from bitter experience.

Moreover, the appropriate objects of desire must be things that cannot be taken away from us

against our will, and they must be enduring.† If they could be taken away from us, we could not be secure in the enjoyment of them; and if they could fade or disappear on their own, we would fear their prospective loss even if we had them. What makes for happiness must *last*. These are among the truths that wisdom teaches.

But again we need to backtrack a bit. For, as we have seen, some philosophers—the skeptics—doubt whether any such truths can be known. Augustine himself had been attracted to **skepticism** for a time and saw that he had to refute it for anything else to stand firm. So we must take another logical step backward.

Can the skeptical objections be met? Augustine believes they can be met, and decisively so. Although we can be deceived by the senses and can make purely intellectual mistakes, there are three things we know with absolute certainty:

> The certainty that I exist, that I know it, and that I am glad of it, is independent of any imaginary and deceptive fantasies.
>
> In respect of these truths I have no fear of the arguments of the Academics.* They say, "Suppose you are mistaken?" I reply, "If I am mistaken, I exist." A non-existent being cannot be mistaken; therefore I must exist, if I am mistaken. Then since my being mistaken proves that I exist, how can I be mistaken in thinking that I exist, seeing that my mistake establishes my existence? Since therefore I must exist in order to be mistaken, then even if I am mistaken, there can be no doubt that I am not mistaken in my knowledge that I exist. It follows that I am not mistaken in knowing that I know. For just as I know that I exist, I also know that I know. And when I am glad of those two facts, I can add the fact of that gladness to the things I know, as a fact of equal worth. For I am not mistaken about the fact of my gladness, since I am not mistaken about the things which I love. Even if they were illusory, it would still be a fact that I love the illusions. (*CG* 11.27)

Knowledge and certainty are possible; skepticism is mistaken. Truth is available to us, at least to this

---

*See *Apology* 19c–d and p. 160.

†This is by now a familiar point. See, for instance, pp. 209–210.

*The Academics were members of the Academy after Plato who turned to skepticism.

small extent. And notice what this truth is about: his own existence, his thought, and his feelings. In short, the first thing we know for certain concerns ourselves and, in particular, the soul.*

The next question is whether we can know *more* than this. Like the Platonic philosophers, Augustine turns to mathematics. Imagine a circle, from the center of which two radii are drawn to the circumference. Let the points at which the radii meet the circle be as close together as you like; it will still be the case that these two lines meet only at that point which is the center. You cannot draw it to look this way (try!), but it is true nonetheless.† Furthermore, we know that between any two such lines, no matter how close together they are, innumerable other lines—or even another circle—can be drawn. This is true, and we know it to be true (*SO* 20.35). And this truth is not something private to any one of us. It is knowledge common to all.

> Whatever I may experience with my bodily senses, such as this air and earth and whatever corporeal matter they contain, I cannot know how long it will endure. But seven and three are ten, not only now, but forever. There has never been a time when seven and three were not ten, nor will there ever be a time when they are not ten. Therefore, I have said that the truth of number is incorruptible and common to all who think. (*FCW* 2.7.82–83)

Augustine concludes that mathematical truth exists and we can know it.

Perhaps, however, we grant that there is mathematical truth but doubt that there is such a thing as practical truth—truth about how to be happy, about the highest good. But, Augustine asks,

> Will you deny that the incorrupt is better than the corrupt, the eternal better than the temporal, the inviolable better than the violable? (*FCW* 2.10.114)

Here is a truth that seems as secure to Augustine as the truths of mathematics. How, for example, could the beauty of a flower that lasts for a day be as good as an equivalent beauty that lasts for two days? And how could that be as good as the same beauty lasting forever? But this, notice, is a truth about what is "better," and so it has direct practical implications. Whatever is the highest good, whatever will actually fulfill the desire for happiness, must be the best of all possible things—incorruptible, eternal, inviolable. Otherwise, even if we possessed it, it could be taken away from us without our consent. To settle for less than such a good is to resign ourselves to unhappiness.

But if this is *true*, then this **truth** is itself eternal—as unchanging a truth as seven plus three makes ten. And it is a truth common to and knowable by all. Furthermore, their existence does not depend on either me or you. We do not *decide* their truth; we *acknowledge* it as something beyond and superior to ourselves.

> When a man says that the eternal is more powerful than the temporal, and that seven plus three are ten, he does not say that it ought to be so; he knows it is this way, and does not correct it as an examiner would, but he rejoices as if he has made a discovery.
>
> If truth were equal to our minds, it would be subject to change. Our minds sometimes see more and sometimes less, and because of this we acknowledge that they are mutable. Truth, remaining in itself, does not gain anything when we see it, or lose anything when we do not see it. It is whole and uncorrupted. With its light, truth gives joy to the men who turn to it, and punishes with blindness those who turn away from it. (*FCW* 2.12.134–35)

Let us review. We want to be happy, and to find happiness we desire to be wise. Wisdom will tell us what the highest good is. Possession of this good will make us happy. Such a good must be eternal, available to all, and superior to ourselves. But we have now found something with precisely those characteristics: truth itself.*

> We possess in the truth, therefore, what we all may enjoy, equally and in common; in it are no defects or limitations. For truth receives all its lovers without arousing their envy. It is open to all, yet it is always chaste. No one says to the other, "Get back!

---

*At the beginning of modern philosophy in the seventeenth century, this theme will be picked up by René Descartes. See *Meditation II*.

†Compare discussion of Socrates' sand drawings on pp. 152–153.

---

*The common, public nature of truth is stressed also by Plato. See pp. 151–152.

Let me approach too! Hands off! Let me also embrace it!" All men cling to the truth and touch it. The food of truth can never be stolen. (*FCW* 2.14.145)

Truth is something we cannot lose against our will. And since it is superior to our minds, it is a candidate for being the highest good and the source of our happiness.

Now we can *understand* (not just believe) why God must be brought into the picture. Think back to what Augustine claims to know: he exists, he lives, and he knows and feels. These facts are ordered in a kind of hierarchy. The latter facts presuppose the former; you cannot live unless you exist, and you cannot know and feel unless you are alive. Moreover, this is a hierarchy of value, for it is better to be alive than just to exist, and it is better to know and feel than just to live. These are the reasons we judge plants superior to rocks, animals to plants, and ourselves to all. At the top of this hierarchy is our own rational nature, by which we judge the rest and guide our own behavior. This is best of all among the things of experience. But what if there were something superior even to this? Would it not be right to acknowledge that as *God*, particularly if it were shown to be eternal and immutable?

But this is just what Augustine claims already to have shown! Truth itself exists. It is immutable and eternal. And it is superior to our reason. By definition, **God** is "that to whom no one is superior" (*FCW* 2.6.54).* So we can now say that, on the assumption that there is nothing superior to the truth, the truth itself is God. If there should exist something superior to the truth, then that is God. On either hypothesis, God exists! As Augustine puts it in a dialogue with a friend,

You granted . . . that if I showed you something higher than our minds, you would admit, assuming that nothing existed which was still higher, that God exists. I accepted your condition and said that it was enough to show this. For if there is something more excellent than truth, this is God. If there is not, then truth itself is God. Whether or not truth

is God, you cannot deny that God exists, and this was the question with which we agreed to deal. (*FCW* 2.15. 153–154)

> "Truth—is as old as God—
>   His Twin Identity
> And will endure as long as He
>   A Co-Eternity—"
>
> *Emily Dickinson (1830–1886)*

Again let's set out the structure of the argument:

1. God is (by definition) that to whom there is nothing superior.
2. Truth exists and is superior to us.
3. If nothing is superior to truth, then God = truth and God exists.
4. If there is something superior even to truth, then God is that thing, and God exists.
5. Either 3 or 4.
6. So God exists.

To this demonstration his friend, Evodius, exclaims,

I can scarcely find words for the unbelievable joy that fills me. I accept these arguments, crying out that they are most certain. And my inner voice shouts, for truth itself to hear, that I cling to this: not only does good exist, but indeed the highest good—and this is the source of happiness. (*FCW* 2.15.156)

Since his experience in the garden Augustine has believed this, and now he also understands it in a way that satisfies his reason. But one's reason is not unaffected by one's will and desires; without a will to truth, even the best rational demonstration may fail to convince. As we'll see, in a certain sense Augustine holds that *will* is basic.

1. How are wisdom and happiness related?
2. What is Augustine's argument against the Skeptics?
3. What shows that truth is superior to ourselves?
4. What is Augustine's argument for the existence of God?
5. What is the essence of God?

---

*This idea is the root from which a much more sophisticated and complex proof will be drawn by Anselm of Canterbury. See Chapter 15.

God and the World

Augustine has come to believe in the God of the Christians. Here, he is convinced, is wisdom and the path to happiness. But he needs also to understand what he has come to believe. He has discovered a rational proof that God exists. Could reason, employed in support of faith, also understand how this world is related to God?

Here too Augustine draws extensively but critically from the wisdom of the philosophers, especially from the Platonists. For as Augustine reads them, they express in a perfectly rational way, without relying on the authority of revelation, ideas that mesh remarkably well with the Scriptures. To see how, it will be useful to take a detour to the views of Plotinus (A.D. 204–270), the main source for **Neoplatonism.** This tradition, within which Augustine himself must be counted a distinguished figure, lasted well into the eighteenth century.

THE GREAT CHAIN OF BEING

Plotinus blends mystical insight and rational elaboration, the latter largely dependent on Plato. Mystical experience, which Plotinus is clearly familiar with, has certain characteristics that reappear in all ages and cultures. It is an experience of a particularly powerful and persuasive sort in which the focus is an absolute unity. The multiplicity of things disappears; one is no longer able even to distinguish oneself from other objects. Mystics talk of this experience in terms of identity of the self with "the All," with "the One," or with "God." It is accompanied by an absolutely untroubled bliss.

Plotinus knows such experience firsthand, so he is certain that there is another, better reality than the one we ordinarily experience. When he tries to express this reality, he speaks in terms of **the One.** About this One, Plotinus holds, we can literally say nothing, for to predicate any properties of it would be to imply some multiplicity in it, some division. It is "ineffable." We cannot even say that it *is.* It resides in a majesty *beyond being.** Plotinus allows

that it can be given names, but none of these should be understood literally; they are at best hints that point in a certain direction. Some of these names are "Unity," "the Transcendent," "the Absolute," "the Good," and "the Source."*

Like Plato's Form of the Good, the One is the source of whatever else exists. But at this point, we must ask: why should anything else exist? The One is absolutely self-sufficient; it needs nothing. But this is precisely the key. To make it clear, Plotinus uses a pair of analogies.

> Picture a spring that has no further origin, that pours itself into all rivers without becoming exhausted of what it yields, and remains what it is, undisturbed. The streams that issue from it, before flowing away each in its own direction, mingle together for a time, but each knows already where it will take its flood. Or think of the life that circulates in a great tree. The originating principle of this life remains at rest and does not spread through the tree because it has, as it were, its seat in the root. The principle gives to the plant all its life in its multiplicity but remains itself at rest. Not a plurality, it is the source of plurality. (*EP*, p. 173)[4]

The One is like the spring that, being itself full and lacking nothing, gives of itself without ever diminishing itself; or like the originating principle of life in a great tree that remains at rest in the root, though the whole tree pulses with life. Plotinus thinks of all reality as an **emanation** from the One. To use another analogy, it is like the light that streams from the candle, while the light of the flame remains undiminished.

Note that this is the old problem of the one and the many: whence this plurality of beings, this multiplicity all about us? The answer is, they originate in the One.† If we ask why there are so *many*, the

---

*Compare Plato on the Form of the Good (p. 160), various Indian philosophies in Chapter 3, and Laozi's understanding of the Dào (p. 88–89).

---

*Compare the terminology in the *Star Wars* movies.

†See the earlier discussion of this same problem by Heraclitus (pp. 19–20), Parmenides (p. 22), and Plato (p. 155ff.). At the very beginning of the process of emanation, Plotinus holds, the One produces an image of itself in which it knows itself. He calls this reflective image "Intelligence." Intelligence in turn produces "Soul," the principle of life. Augustine reads this as a pagan version of the Christian Trinity: the One = the Father, the Creator; the Intelligence = the Word, Wisdom, the Christ; and the Soul = the Holy Spirit.

answer is that there must be as many as possible, for the One is ungrudging in its giving.

> Every nature must produce its next, for each thing must unfold, seedlike, from indivisible principle into a visible effect. Principle continues unaltered in its proper place; what unfolds from it is the product of the inexpressible power that resides in it. It must not stay this power and, as though jealous, limit its effects. It must proceed continuously until all things, to the very last, have within the limits of possibility come forth. All is the result of this immense power giving its gifts to the universe, unable to let any part remain without its share.
> (*EP*, p. 68)

Just as there are all possible degrees of brightness in the emanation of light from a candle, until it vanishes at last in the darkness, so there will be found all degrees of being, intelligibility, and life in the world. Reality is partitioned in graded steps, which are, however, infinitely close to each other. No degree can be lacking; every possible level of being is represented, from the complete self-sufficiency of the One to vanishingly small realities near absolute nothingness. In the world as we see it, being and nothingness are mixed in all degrees.

We get the picture of a **Great Chain of Being,** an image that is to be enormously influential for centuries.* How does Augustine make use of these ideas in trying to understand what he has come to believe about God and the world?

First we must note that, as a Christian, Augustine rejects one aspect of Plotinus' thought. A Christian believes the world was *created*, and creation is distinct from emanation. Creation is a free act, voluntarily chosen; there is no necessity in it. Emanation, by contrast, is a necessary and continuous process. In the emanation picture, moreover, the *substance* of the world is not distinct from its source; the one flows indiscernibly into the other. Everything partakes of divinity. But in a creation scenario, there is discontinuity; what is created does *not* have the same substance as the creator has. Augustine agrees with Plotinus that the world

is not a self-sufficient reality, that it depends for both its being and its character on a deeper reality. But the nature of that dependence is altogether different.

How are we to understand the creation of the world? It could not be like the creation of buildings by stonemasons or of sculptures by artists. For in these cases people merely give new shape and form to existing realities, rather than creating new realities. That is exactly what we discover in Genesis 1:3, where we read, "God said, 'Let there be light,' and there was light."

> You did not work as a human craftsman does, making one thing out of something else as his mind directs. . . . Nor did you have in your hand any matter from which you could make heaven and earth, for where could you have obtained matter which you had not yet created, in order to use it as material for making something else? Does anything exist by any other cause than that you exist?
> It must therefore be that you spoke and they were made. (Ps. 33:9) In your Word alone you created them. (*C* 11.5)

Other than God himself, there is nothing but what he has made—again a rejection of Manicheanism, according to which the powers of light and darkness, good and evil, are equally eternal and uncreated. God "spoke" and the heavens and the earth *were*. Remember that in this context "your Word" represents not a spoken word but the *logos*, the Wisdom of God, the second person of the Trinity, who is "with God" and "is God," as John's Gospel tells us. It is through this rational, intelligent, and ultimately loving Word that God makes all things **ex nihilo,** or *out of nothing*. The world, then, is entirely, without any exception, dependent on God.

Because the world is created through Wisdom (compare Plotinus' Intelligence, Plato's Forms), the world is a rational and well-ordered whole. Here again the philosophers confirm the biblical tradition. In the Genesis story we read that God looked at what he had made and "saw that it was good." How could it be otherwise, since God himself is good? For Augustine, as for Plotinus and Plato, there is a direct correlation between being and goodness. The more being something has

---

*For a fascinating study of the history of this idea, see Arthur Lovejoy, *The Great Chain of Being: A Study of the History of an Idea* (Cambridge, MA: Harvard University Press, 1936).

The Great Chain of Being

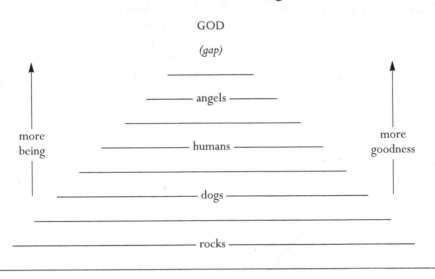

(which means, of course, the more self-sufficient and eternal it is), the better it is. God, being completely self-sufficient and eternal, is completely good. The created world is less good than God. But still it is *good*. From the premise that the world is less good than God, one cannot conclude that it is therefore *bad*.

Here again Augustine parts company from the Manicheans. The source of evil is not to be found in body or matter, for these are creations of God and so are good. Not everything created is equally good, of course. As we have already seen, life is better than mere existence and intellect better than mere life. In fact, Augustine follows Plotinus here and urges that there is a continuous gradation of goodness in things. The Great Chain of Being reaches from the most insignificant bits of inanimate matter through primitive life forms, to rational creatures like ourselves, and beyond to the angels. That this is a chain of *being* can be seen from the following examples.

A dog does not have language, but you do. So, compared to you, there is something lacking in the dog. You have an ability, the power to utter truths and falsehoods, which the dog just does not have. So there is *more to you* than there is to the dog; you have more of being, and the dog has less.

Or imagine a professor standing at a chalkboard, eraser in hand. Suddenly, she wheels about and hurls the eraser at the board. You are surprised—perhaps puzzled. But you don't think any the less of her or her character because of it. Then she says, "Imagine now that instead of an eraser in my hand it had been a kitten. . ." The situation would be altogether different, and her character would drop precipitously in your estimation. Why? Because a kitten is higher on the Chain of Being than an eraser? Perhaps you, too, believe in the great chain.

The second example makes clear that the chain is not only a chain of being, but also a hierarchy of value. So value and being correlate: the more being, the more goodness. And the great ladder reaches from sheer nothingness at the bottom (no being, no value) to God at the top (supreme being, supreme value). Even the lowest degree of existence, however, has its correlative degree of goodness. Nothing God has made is to be despised.

HYPATIA OF ALEXANDRIA

While Augustine is now the best known of the fourth-century Neoplatonists, in his own day that honor belonged to a woman named Hypatia of Alexandria (c. 350–415). Alexandria was the intellectual capital of the Western world at the time, and Hypatia was among its most famous minds. Her main intellectual contributions were in mathematics and astronomy, but she was also widely known as a great teacher of Platonic and Aristotelian philosophy. Toward the end of her life, tensions between Christians and pagans roiled the city. In A.D. 415, a mob of Christian zealots pulled the pagan philosopher from her carriage and beat her to death.

EVIL

Having abandoned Manicheism, Augustine once again faces the problem of evil. If God is good and the material world is good, where does evil come from?

He tackles the problem in two parts by distinguishing **moral evil,** which depends on the free choices of rational agents, and **natural evil,** such as illness or any other bad thing that does not depend on rational agents' free choices. We will postpone consideration of moral evil until we have a better understanding of Augustine's views on human nature. But we can state Augustine's view of natural evil quite simply: Natural evil does not exist! You can see that Augustine now proposes to solve the problem as we stated it on page 263 by denying the *second* premise. This allows him to continue to assert the first premise and to deny the conclusion.

Augustine does not wish to deny that we experience some things as evil. He denies only that evil is a *reality*. If you were to make a list of all the things there *are*—solar systems, chairs, lobsters,

volcanoes, enchiladas—evil would appear nowhere on that list. Nor would anything on the list be evil—insofar as it is. Being, remember, is goodness. Insofar as something *is*, then, it is *good*. What we *call* evil is just a *lack* of the being that something should have. Evil is the *privation of good*.

> For as, in the bodies of animate beings, to be affected by diseases and wounds is the same thing as to be deprived of health, . . . so also of minds, whatever defects there are are privations of natural good qualities, and the healing of these defects is not their transference elsewhere, but that the defects which did exist in the mind will have no place to exist, inasmuch as there will be no room for them in that healthiness. (*AE* 2.10–25)

There is a kind of primitive magic that "cures" by moving the disease or wound out of the body and into, for example, a tree. From Augustine's perspective, this misconceives the nature of the problem. For a disease or wound is not a "thing," having some reality of its own, nor is healing "removing" that thing. Disease is just the privation of healthiness, and healing is restoring the body to that condition of health (of being and goodness) in which there will be nothing lacking, leaving "no room" for the defect.

Augustine is again making use of Plotinus here. For if we equate goodness and being, we must also equate evil and nothingness. And, as Parmenides already taught us, nothing *is not*. So ignorance is not a reality, but just the lack of knowledge; it is knowledge that is the reality and, therefore, good. Nor is weakness a reality, but simply the absence of strength; strength—that good thing—is the reality.

Since all created things are arranged in degrees of reality, they all participate to some degree in nothingness. Does this mean that they are all evil to some degree? True, they do not have the full degree of being and goodness that belongs only to God, but we ought not to call them "evil" on that score. It is irrational to complain that created things are not as good as God; to do so is tantamount to wishing that only God should exist and that there should be no created world at all! Created being is necessarily finite, inevitably limited. There is always much that any created thing *is not*. If it were not so, it would itself be God! For what makes the world distinct from God is precisely its admixture of nonbeing. The very *being* of created things, remember, is good to some degree; and isn't it better that the created world exist rather than not? It adds to the sum total of being and goodness in reality.

If, by contrast, you complain not that some created thing could have been perfectly good, but that it could have been better than it is, your complaint is equally irrational. For there is already in existence something better than that; and to wish the thing you complain about to be better is to wish it not to be what it is, but to be that other thing (see *FCW* 2.5).

The conclusion is that evil can exist only where there is good. To put it another way, evil depends on good. Whatever is, insofar as it is, is good; and if there is evil in it, the reason is only that it—like all things less than God—has some part in nothingness as well as being. But no aspect of its nature can be evil per se.

TIME

The world's temporality also puzzles Augustine. How does the changeable, impermanent creation come from an eternal, unchangeable God? There is an additional sting in the problem of time for Augustine because the Manichees target time as an irrational element in the orthodox notion of creation. They ask the Christians what they take to be an unanswerable question: What was God doing before he made the world? Without an answer, there seems to be something irrational about believing in creation, as opposed to Manichean belief in the *eternal* conflict of light and darkness.

Apparently there was a snappy answer in circulation.

> My answer to those who ask "What was God doing before he made heaven and earth?" is not "He was preparing Hell for people who pry into mysteries." This frivolous retort has been made before now, so we are told, in order to evade the point of the question. But it is one thing to make fun of the questioner and another to find the answer. So I shall refrain from giving this reply. (*C* 11.12)

Augustine's answer is, rather, a long and famous meditation on the nature of time and eternity. In it he establishes his view of God and God's relation to the created world. Let us see if we can follow his reasoning.

The first point is that God's **eternity** is not to be understood as everlastingness. God is not eternal in that he outlasts all other things; he is eternal in that he is not located in time at all. Those who imagine that God was idle through countless ages before engaging in the work of creation should think again.

> How could those countless ages have elapsed when you, the Creator, in whom all ages have their origin, had not yet created them? What time could there have been that was not created by you? How could time elapse if it never was?
>
> You are the Maker of all time. If, then, there was any time before you made heaven and earth, how can anyone say that you were idle? You must have made that time, for time could not elapse before you made it.

But if there was no time before heaven and earth were created, how can anyone ask what you were doing "then"? If there was no time, there was no "then."

Furthermore, although you are before time, it is not in time that you precede it. If this were so, you would not be before all time. It is in eternity, which is supreme over time because it is a never-ending present, that you are at once before all past time and after all future time. . . . You made all time; you are before all time; and the "time," if such we may call it, when there was no time was not time at all. (*C* 11.13)

So time was created along with the world. God did not create the world at a given time, since before the creation, time itself did not exist.

What, then, is time? It is something we are all intimately familiar with. But in a much-quoted sentence, Augustine says,

I know well enough what it is, provided that nobody asks me; but if I am asked what it is and try to explain, I am baffled. (*C* 11.14)

We can divide time into the **past,** the **present,** and the **future.** Since the past no longer exists and the future does not yet exist, the only aspect of time that actually exists is the present. This seems simple enough, but it creates profound puzzles.

Consider what we call a "long time." It seems evident that only what exists can be long. What does not exist cannot be either long or short, any more than it can be sweet or smell of roses. A "long time," then, cannot include the past or present, since neither of those exists. A long time must exist entirely in the present.

Let us, Augustine says, "see if our human wits can tell us whether present time can be long" (*C* 11.15). A century is surely a long time. Can that exist in the present? Suppose we are in the first year of the century; then ninety-nine years are still in the future—and these *are not yet*. Perhaps only a year, then, can be in the present. But suppose it is April. Three months have passed, and eight are yet to come; so most of the year either *is no more* or *is not yet*. Most of the year does not exist, and what does not exist cannot be long.

This thought experiment can be repeated, as you can readily see, for months, days, hours, minutes, seconds, until this conclusion is forced on us:

The only time that can be called present is an instant, if we can conceive of such, that cannot be divided even into the most minute fractions, and a point of time as small as this passes so rapidly from the future to the past that its duration is without length. For if its duration were prolonged, it could be divided into past and future. When it is present it has no duration. (*C* 11.15)

The present is just that knife edge where *what is not yet* becomes *what is no longer*, where the future turns into the past. The present itself "has no duration." So the present could not possibly be long. Where, then, does the time we call "long" exist? It cannot exist in the past or in the future, as we have seen. But now we see that it cannot exist in the present either. You can see why Augustine is baffled.

"Where is it, this present? It has melted in our grasp, fled ere we could touch it, gone in the instant of becoming."

William James (1842–1910)

Nonetheless, with prayers to God for help, Augustine presses on. It is evident that we are aware of different periods of time; and we can compare them in length to each other. How do we do this? We can see only what exists. We may predict the future and make inferences about the past, but since only the present exists, it is only the present we can be aware of. How, then, are we aware of times that do not exist? Augustine again looks into his soul.

When we describe the past correctly, it is not past facts which are drawn out of our memories but only words based on our memory-pictures of those facts, because when they happened they left an impression on our minds, by means of sense-perception. My own childhood, which no longer exists, is in past time, which also no longer exists. But when I remember those days and describe them, it is in the present that I picture them to myself, because their picture is still present in my memory. (*C* 11.18)

Augustine concludes that though there are three times, they are not—strictly speaking—past, present, and future. If we speak accurately, we should speak of a *present of things past* (the memory), a *present of things present* (direct awareness), and a *present of things future* (which he calls expectation). These times exist in the mind, nowhere else.

> It is in my own mind, then, that I measure time. I must not allow my mind to insist that time is something objective. . . . I say that I measure time in my mind. For everything which happens leaves an impression on it, and this impression remains after the thing itself has ceased to be. It is the impression that I measure, since it is still present, not the thing itself, which makes the impression as it passes and then moves into the past. When I measure time it is this impression that I measure. . . .
>
> It can only be that the mind, which regulates this process, performs three functions, those of expectation, attention, and memory. The future, which it expects, passes through the present, to which it attends, into the past, which it remembers. (*C* 11.27–28)

This clinches the argument. Time has no meaning apart from the mind, so it must have come into being along with creation. Our minds are not eternal; they are part of creation. In possessing these powers of expectation, attention, and memory, our minds are the locale where time realizes itself. Our minds are in this respect a faint image of the mind of God, which also sees past, present, and future. But unlike us, God, who lives in that "never-ending present," sees all time "at once."

> If there were a mind endowed with such great power of knowing and foreknowing that all the past and all the future were known to it as clearly as I know a familiar psalm, that mind would be wonderful beyond belief. We should hold back from it in awe at the thought that nothing in all the history of the past and nothing in all the ages yet to come was hidden from it. It would know all this as surely as, when I sing the psalm, I know what I have already sung and what I have still to sing, how far I am from the beginning and how far from the end. But it is unthinkable that you, Creator of the universe,

> Creator of souls and bodies, should know all the past and all the future merely in this way. Your knowledge is far more wonderful, far more mysterious than this. It is not like the knowledge of a man who sings words well known to him or listens to another singing a familiar psalm. While he does this his feelings vary and his senses are divided, because he is partly anticipating words still to come and partly remembering words already sung. It is far otherwise with you, for you are eternally without change, the truly eternal Creator of minds. (*C* 11.31; see also *CG* 11.21)

Time is indeed puzzling, and Augustine expresses the perplexities as well as anyone ever has. The puzzle matters deeply to Augustine because it concerns the relation between God and the Soul, the two foci of wisdom that bear on human happiness. Augustine's meditations on time reaffirm the sharp line of distinction between creation—even including its highest part, the mind—and God who created it. We are not divine or parts of the divine.* We, together with the whole temporal order, are absolutely dependent on God for our very being. Still, our relation to time is part of the image of God within us. Unlike God, we are in time; yet, like God to some degree, we are above it. God sees all time in a single moment. We cannot do that, but we do measure time and are aware of past, present, and future.

You should be able to see a correlation between being more like God in relation to time and our place on the Great Chain of Being. A stone, we think, has no temporal horizon at all; a honey bee is somewhat more open to past, present, and future; and a dog still more so, but less than we. (Wittgenstein once remarked that a dog can expect his master, but can he expect him *next week*?) Moreover, our relation to time, and particularly to our future, is the foundation for our free will, our responsibility, and our hope of happiness.

---

1. What are the characteristics of mystical experience?
2. What does Plotinus mean by "emanation"?

---

*Here Augustine agrees with Homer and disagrees with both the Manichees and more respectable philosophies such as Stoicism (see p. 243).

3. What is the Great Chain of Being? How are being and goodness related?
4. Explain what is meant by "creation *ex nihilo*."
5. How does Augustine solve the problem of natural evil?
6. In what sense is God eternal, according to Augustine?
7. What is puzzling about past, present, and future?
8. How does Augustine resolve the puzzles about time?

Human Nature and Its Corruption

What is man? He is a creature of God, like all other creatures. If we look to the biblical story of creation, we are told that God "formed man of dust from the ground, and breathed into his nostrils the breath of life" (Gen. 2:7). It seems that human beings are here conceived as material beings— living bodies. Perhaps it is possible to understand the "breath of life" as the creation of an immaterial soul, but this seems strained. The Platonistic tradition, however, is unequivocal: A person is an immaterial soul, who may for a time inhabit a body.

Augustine's thought about human nature is thus pulled in two directions as he tries to reconcile these traditions. In trying to remain true to the biblical tradition, he emphasizes that a human being is a unitary being: one thing. God did not create a soul when he took up the dust of the earth; he created *man*. But Augustine also believes in the soul and accepts Platonic arguments about its immateriality and its distinctness from the body. But if man is one thing, how can he be composed of two things? Aristotle solves this problem by considering the soul to be the form of a certain kind of living body; in the thirteenth century Thomas Aquinas will adapt this solution in his Christian Aristotelianism. But Augustine, drawing on the Platonic tradition, cannot take this line. The result is an uneasy compromise. Man is one being, created by God, but he is composed of both body and soul, each a distinct created being.

How, then, are soul and body related to each other? Augustine tries to answer this question in the very definition of a soul.

But if you want a definition of the soul, and so ask me—what is the soul? I have a ready answer. It seems to me to be a special substance, endowed with reason, adapted to rule the body. (*GS* 13)

So a soul is, by its very nature, suited to "rule the body" by virtue of possessing reason. Clearly, the soul and its powers are superior to the body. This fact is crucial to Augustine's view of the human predicament—of what stands in the way of our happiness and how we may after all attain it.

We are created by God and so, by nature, are something good. Yet on all sides we find ourselves involved in evil. We are created in the image of God's justice, yet we act unjustly. We are created for happiness, but we find ourselves miserable. Why? The biblical answer is that we have sinned. This seems precisely the right answer to Augustine. But, again, he wants to understand what that means. Augustine's analysis of sin and the way to blessedness draws on his own experience. But to understand that experience he needs to come to terms with freedom and responsibility, with God's grace and foreknowledge, and above all with the nature of the will. These are perhaps the most original and penetrating parts of Augustine's philosophy.

Augustine takes the biblical story of Adam and Eve's sin quite literally. Though they were created good and lived happily in the Garden, the serpent tempts them to disobey God, and they do. God punishes them by driving them from the Garden, making them subject to death and struggle. Their descendants inherit this status, called **original sin,** from the moment of their birth. Its characteristics are ignorance (i.e., lack of wisdom) and what Augustine calls "concupiscence," or wrong desire. If Augustine is right, we are in trouble from the very start of our lives. Look, he says, at infants.

It can hardly be right for a child, even at that age, to cry for everything, including things which would harm him; to work himself into a tantrum against people older than himself and not required to obey him; and to try his best to strike and hurt others who know better than he does, including his own parents, when they do not give in to him and refuse to pander to whims which would only do him harm.

This shows that, if babies are innocent, it is not for lack of will to do harm, but for lack of strength.

I have myself seen jealousy in a baby and know what it means. He was not old enough to talk, but whenever he saw his foster-brother at the breast, he would grow pale with envy. . . . it surely cannot be called innocence, when the milk flows in such abundance from its source, to object to a rival desperately in need and depending for his life on this one form of nourishment. (C 1.7)

Innocence and guilt, it should be noticed, are to be found not in outward actions but in desires, in such things as jealousy and the "will to do harm." It is this condition of the heart, much more than the actions that flow from it, that is the essence of **sin.** Babies may be "innocent" in a shallow sense, but only because they lack the ability to do what they very much want to do. As Augustine allows, babies tend to grow out of crying and throwing tantrums. But this does not mean that their desires change; it may only mean that their concupiscence takes on more sophisticated and socially acceptable forms.

❧

> "In Adam's fall
> We sinned all."
>
> *The New England Primer*

To understand how sin originated in a world that was created good, we must understand its elements. Sin clearly has something to do with the motivation for action. Whatever we do, Augustine says, is done from a desire for something. These desires Augustine calls **"loves."** We seek to delight in possessing the object of our love. If we think that wealth will make us happy, we love riches, and so we are moved by this love to acquire wealth.

Remember that reality is ordered in a Great Chain of Being, reaching from God down to the merest speck of existence. Things higher up the chain, having greater value, should be loved more than those lower on the chain. If our loves were rightly ordered, they would match the order of value in things themselves. This means that God, who is perfect being and goodness, should be

loved most of all and all the rest of creation in appropriate degrees corresponding to their goodness. In fact, the injunction of Jesus to love God absolutely, "with all your heart, and with all your soul, and with all your strength, and with all your mind," corresponds to the absolute value to be found in God. The rule to love our neighbors as ourselves also fits this ordering rule, for each of us has the same degree of value. Those who are perfectly virtuous—that is, righteous—have their loves rightly ordered. They love all things appropriately, in accord with their worthiness to be loved.

Sin, we can now say, is **disordered love.** It is loving things inappropriately, loving more what is of lower value and loving less what is of higher or highest value. Since our loves move us to action, these sinful desires produce wicked acts: murder, theft, adultery, deception, and so on. For example, Jane loves money and is willing to kill her aged aunt to get it. What this means is that she loves money (which is less valuable) more than she loves the person who has it (who is more valuable). Her desires are not ordered correctly, and the result is wickedness.

We have not yet plumbed the depths of sin, however. Two errors must be avoided. First, we may think that sin is just a *mistake*—a failure to recognize the true ordering of value in the world. This is akin to the view of Socrates, who holds that virtue is knowledge and vice ignorance.* The person who acts wrongly, according to this view, simply doesn't *know* what is right. Augustine agrees that there is a kind of ignorance involved in sin. But it is not *simple* ignorance, for he holds that the light of Wisdom has "enlightened every man,"† and the rules of righteousness are written in the human heart. So if we are ignorant, we are *willingly* ignorant. We don't *want* to see the truth. Sin, then, is not just ignorance. Socrates and Plato are on that score too optimistic; education alone will not solve the problem. Instead, overcoming sin requires *conversion*. And that concerns the **will.**

---

*See pp. 99–100.
†John 1:9.

The second error is to suppose that sin might be something that just *happens* to us. Our wickedness and disordered loves may be just bad luck—the luck of a bad upbringing, for example—and for luck no one is to blame. A key aspect of the notion of sin, however, is that we are to blame for it. For our sins we are punished, and justly so. Therefore something must be missing in this analysis.

We need to bring in the aspect of *will*. Augustine does this by offering an analysis of four basic emotions: desire, joy, fear, and grief.

> The important factor in those emotions is the character of a man's will. If the will is wrongly directed, the emotions will be wrong; if the will is right, the emotions will be not only blameless, but praiseworthy. The will is engaged in all of them; in fact they are all essentially acts of will. (*CG* 14.6)

To desire something is not just to have a tendency to acquire it. To desire is to *consent* to that tendency, to give in to it, to say yes to it—in short, to *will* it. In a similar way, to fear something is not just to be disposed to avoid something, perhaps with a feeling of panic added. To be afraid is to "disagree" that something should happen, and that disagreement is an act of will. What are joy and grief? They, too, are acts of will, joy being consent in the attainment of something desired and grief disagreement in the possession of something feared. In general, Augustine says that

> as a man's will is attracted or repelled in accordance with the varied character of different objects which are pursued or shunned, so it changes and turns into feelings of various kinds. (*CG* 14.6)

We noticed at various points the prominence that Augustine gives to the concept of will. Here we see why. It is the character of the human will that accounts for emotions and actions alike. We may be motivated by our loves, but in the last analysis, these loves come down to will. And for what we will we are responsible. The will is *free*.

Sin, then, for which we are properly held responsible, is a matter of the will having gone wrong. As Augustine puts it,

> When an evil choice happens in any being, then what happens is dependent on the will of that being;

the failure is voluntary, not necessary, and the punishment that follows is just. (*CG* 12.8)

Note that this account does not locate sin in the body, as the Manichees do, but in the soul—precisely in that superior part of the human being that mirrors most clearly the image of God. The soul, which by means of reason is "fit to rule the body," consents instead to be the body's slave, preferring what is less good to what is better.

But now we must face the question, How can this happen in a world created by a good God? Here we discover the second part of Augustine's solution to the problem of evil. The first part, you will remember, consisted in arguing that natural evil is not a reality but simply the privation of goodness. Whatever exists is good, simply in virtue of its *being*. How, then, can we explain moral evil, where it looks as though the bad will is itself a positive reality?

The first thing to be established is that the will is itself a good thing. This is easily done, not only from the principle that all created things are good, but also from the reflection that without free will no one can live rightly. To live rightly is to choose to live rightly; no one can choose rightly without a free will; and since living rightly is acknowledged to be a good, the necessary condition for that good must itself be good (*FCW* 2.18.188–190).

There are, Augustine tells us, three classes of goods. There are great goods, such as justice, the mere possession of which guarantees a righteous life. There are lesser goods, such as wealth and physical beauty, which, though good, are not essential to the highest goods of happiness and a virtuous life. And then there are intermediate goods. Of these intermediate goods we can say that their possession does not guarantee either virtue or happiness, yet without them no one can be virtuous or happy. Such an intermediate good is free will. Whether it leads to happiness depends on what we do with it; and that is up to us.

Augustine thinks it obvious that the human race has misused its free will; prizing lesser goods over greater, we have sought our happiness where it is not to be found. How are we to understand that?

The will . . . commits sin when it turns away from immutable and common goods, towards its private good, either something external to itself or lower than itself. It turns to its own private good when it desires to be its own master; it turns to external goods when it busies itself with the private affairs of others or with whatever is none of its concern; it turns to goods lower than itself when it loves the pleasures of the body. Thus a man becomes proud, meddlesome, and lustful; he is caught up in another life which, when compared to the higher one, is death. (*FCW* 2.19.199–200)

The result of such "turning away" from the higher goods and "turning toward" the lower is *pride*, *meddlesomeness*, and *lust*. When we value most highly the goods we can all have in common—such as justice, love, and truth—peace reigns in our community. When our loves are fastened on lower goods—such as money, power, and fine possessions—the result is discord and strife, for if you have something of this sort, I do not have it—and often enough, I want it. Proud, meddlesome, and greedy individuals will never be at peace with one another.*

Pride, however, is more than the result of sin. It is the very root of sin itself.† Why did the first couple disobey God's command? Augustine emphasizes that it was not because the command was difficult to obey; in fact, nothing was easier. They simply had to refrain from eating the fruit of one of the many bountiful trees in the Garden. In no way did they *need* to eat that piece of fruit. Why, then, did they disobey? The words of the serpent that tempted them suggest the answer. He said, "God knows that when you eat of it your eyes will be opened, and you will be like God, knowing good and evil" (Gen. 3:5). This is the key. They wanted to be "like God." It is only because their wills had

already "turned away" from a determination to be obedient to the truth that the temptation had any power over them.

It was in secret that the first human beings began to be evil; and the result was that they slipped into open disobedience. For they would not have arrived at the evil act if an evil will had not preceded it. Now, could anything but pride have been the start of the evil will? For "pride is the start of every kind of sin." (Ecclesiasticus 10:13) And what is pride except a longing for a perverse kind of exaltation? For it is a perverse kind of exaltation to abandon the basis on which the mind should be firmly fixed, and to become, as it were, based on oneself, and so remain. This happens when a man is too pleased with himself: and a man is self-complacent when he deserts that changeless Good in which, rather than in himself, he ought to have found his satisfaction. . . .

This then is the original evil: man regards himself as his own light, and turns away from that light which would make man himself a light if he would set his heart on it. (*CG* 14.13)

Pride, then, caused man's fall. Trying to lift ourselves above the place proper to us in the Chain of Being, we seek to become "like God." But in trying to rise above our place, we fall into anxiety and concern for our own well-being, which we ourselves now have to guarantee. Not content with the true goods that are available to all, we find ourselves engaged in ruthless competition with others for the lower goods. Our loves settle on the things of this world, and greed, lust, and covetousness reign among our desires. No longer are our wills ordered according to the worthiness of goods to be desired.

The sin of pride shows itself also in the fact that the first couple, when confronted with their disobedience, make excuses:

The woman said, "The serpent led me astray, and I ate," and the man said, "The woman whom you gave me as a companion, she gave me fruit from the tree, and I ate." There is not a whisper anywhere here of a plea for pardon, nor of any entreaty for healing. (*CG* 14.14)

One of the manifestations of sin is a refusal to admit that it is sin. Neither of the first humans would admit to sin; each tried to pin it on someone else.

---

*Compare this to Thomas Hobbes' account of the origins of strife on pp. 410–412.

†Note that in attacking pride Augustine is not recommending obsequiousness, or slavishness, or a groveling, fawning, or cringing attitude. There is a proper self-respect that each of us both needs and deserves. We are all creatures of God with a place on the Chain of Being; so each of us has an intrinsic value, and it is as bad to deny that as to claim more than is our due. Compare Augustine's pride to the Greek *hubris*, the sort of arrogance that puts oneself in the place of God. (See p. 7.)

The root of sin, then, is pride—setting ourselves up as the highest good when the highest good is rather something we should acknowledge as above us. Pride is the sixteen-year-old Augustine posing as the arbiter of right and wrong when stealing and trashing his neighbor's pears. Pride is the will turning away from God and to itself, resulting in a set of disordered loves.

Suppose we ask, What causes that? Why does that happen? God, after all, created us good. We have free will, to be sure, but why do we use our freedom in that way?

> If you try to find the efficient cause of this evil choice, there is none to be found. For nothing causes an evil will, since it is the evil will itself which causes the evil act; and that means that the evil choice is the efficient cause of an evil act, whereas there is no efficient cause of an evil choice. . . . It is not a matter of efficiency, but of deficiency; the evil will itself is not effective but defective. For to defect from him who is the Supreme Existence, to something of less reality, this is to begin to have an evil will. To try to discover the causes of such defection . . . is like trying to see darkness or to hear silence. . . .
>
> No one therefore must try to get to know from me what I know that I do not know. (*CG* 12.6–7)

We can understand Augustine's argument in this way. Suppose that there were an answer to the question, Why do we sin? Suppose that we could find some *X* that is the cause of the will's turning away from the highest good. Then that *X* would—since it has being—be something good. But something good cannot cause something evil. So there cannot be such a cause in being.

Yet we must remember that created wills, living in time and subject to change, are a mixture of being and nonbeing. If the will, like God's will, were unmixed with nothingness, then it could not fall. So there is a "cause" for sin in the sense that the incomplete being of the will is a *necessary condition* for sin. This is what Augustine calls a "deficient" cause and compares to darkness or silence, which are merely the absence of light and sound, respectively. A deficient cause is the absence of the fullness of being that would make sin impossible. The presence of such a deficient cause does not guarantee

that the will turns away from God; it just makes that turning possible. So if we ask, then, what does cause the turning away of the evil will, the answer, literally, is *nothing*. The act is voluntary. For Augustine, this means that it cannot have an efficient cause. If it had an efficient cause it would occur necessarily and not be subject to just punishment.* Again, Augustine relies on the Neoplatonic idea of the Chain of Being to solve this problem.

He has not yet solved it completely, however. Recall his doctrine of God. God exists "all at once" in a timeless eternity and "sees all things in a single moment." But that means that God knew—or foreknew—even before man was created that man would sin. So it was true that Adam was going to sin even before he chose to sin. And if that is so, did he really have any choice? Doesn't God's foreknowledge take away man's free will?

Clearly Augustine needs to affirm both; free will is necessary for responsibility, and God's foreknowledge is a necessary consequence of his perfection. Can Augustine have it both ways? "It does not follow," he says,

> that there is nothing in our will because God foreknew what was going to be in our will; for if he foreknew this, it was not nothing that he foreknew. Further, if, in foreknowing what would be in our will, he foreknew something, and not nonentity, it follows immediately that there is something in our will, even if God foreknows it. Hence we are in no way compelled either to preserve God's prescience by abolishing our free will, or to safeguard our free will by denying (blasphemously) the divine foreknowledge. We embrace both truths, and acknowledge them in faith and sincerity, the one for a right belief, the other for a right life. . . . The fact that God foreknew that a man would sin does not make a man sin; on the contrary, it cannot be doubted that it is the man himself who sins just because he whose prescience cannot be mistaken has foreseen that

---

*Here we meet for the first time a theme that will puzzle philosophers down to the present day: Does responsibility require exemption from the causal order of the world? Augustine thought the answer was an obvious yes. For other views, see Aristotle (pp. 216–217), David Hume ("Rescuing Human Freedom," in Chapter 19), and Immanuel Kant (pp. 492–494).

the man himself would sin. A man does not sin unless he wills to sin; and if he had not willed to sin, then God would have foreseen that refusal. (*CG* 5.10)

If God foresees that I am going to freely will something, then I will undoubtedly will that thing freely. But it would be a crazy mistake, Augustine thinks, to conclude that this somehow robs me of my free will. How could it not be my will if what God infallibly foresees is that I am going to exercise my will? So Augustine does not see that there is any conflict between God's omniscience and individual freedom.

Augustine's analysis of the human predicament, then, reveals us to be in a pretty sorry state. We are proud, determined to be masters of our own destiny, turned away from the highest goods and anxiously devoted to the lower; our desires are not ordered by the order of objective value in things. Furthermore, we are continually turning away from the source of our being. And we cannot escape responsibility for this descent into evil, with all its consequences, both personal and social.

Is there any way out of this desperate plight?

---

1. How, for Augustine, are soul and body related?
2. What is "original" sin? We often say babies are "innocent." What does Augustine think?
3. What is "sin"? How is the will involved in it?
4. If the will is a good thing, why does it go bad?
5. In what way is pride the root of sin?
6. How does Augustine reconcile free will with God's foreknowledge?

Human Nature and Its Restoration

Sin diminishes the very being of human beings; they become smaller—more ignorant, weaker, and less in control of themselves. It divides their very will. With one part of the mind they continue to acknowledge the truth of God and the righteousness of his law (since they cannot entirely put out the light that enlightens everyone); but with another

part they love what is of lesser value. This was Augustine's own experience before his conversion. He often quotes a passage from Saint Paul to the same effect.

I do not understand my own actions. For I do not do what I want, but I do the very thing I hate. . . . I can will what is right, but I cannot do it. For I do not do the good I want, but the evil I do not want is what I do. Now if I do what I do not want, it is no longer I that do it, but sin which dwells within me. (Rom. 7:15, 18–20)

Augustine is convinced that this condition is so desperate that none of us can rescue ourselves from it.*

For by the evil use of free choice man has destroyed both himself and it. For as one who kills himself, certainly by being alive kills himself, but by killing himself ceases to live, and can have no power to restore himself to life after the killing; so when sin was committed by free choice, sin became victor and free choice was lost. (*AE* 9.30)

Here, however, is the point where the distinctive "gospel" of Christianity comes into its own. What we cannot do for ourselves, God has done for us through his Son Jesus, who took on himself the sins of the world. All that is required is to trust, by faith, that God has forgiven and received us, despite our turning away, and we will be healed.

This may seem simple enough. But once again there are problems in trying to understand it. We cannot save ourselves from our disordered loves, precisely because our loves are disordered. It would be as impossible as trying to lift ourselves off the ground by wrapping our arms around our own chests and lifting. The restoration of human nature—its re-creation—is no more possible for us than its original creation. So God has to do it. And he has in fact done it in Christ. All we need is to accept it by faith.

But is faith itself within our power? Saying yes to God's offer of forgiveness and healing seems like an act of will. Yet we have seen that our wills are divided against themselves. How then can

---

*See again Augustine's theory of the "chain" that sin forms, by which the soul becomes enslaved and loses its ability to do even what it truly wants to do (pp. 265–266).

we wholeheartedly will to have faith? It seems impossible.

Our salvation (a life of ordered love) must then depend entirely on God's grace; it is not something we can do on our own. And yet accepting God's offer of salvation must be entirely up to us, for without our freely turning to the grace that is offered, it is also impossible. In a section of the *Confessions* where Augustine records his continuing struggles to get his loves in order, he says over and over,

> Give me the grace to do as you command, and command me to do what you will! (*C* 10.29, 31, 37)

This phrase perfectly expresses that paradoxical combination of reliance on God's grace and determination to will the right that Augustine discovers when he tries to *understand* what he has come to *believe* in becoming a Christian. Our salvation—happiness, blessedness—is up to us. Yet it is wholly a product of God's grace; we have nothing that we have not received.

Let us say a bit more about the life in which Augustine claims to have found both wisdom and happiness. What is it like to live as a Christian? As we have seen, Augustine's theory of motivation holds that we are moved by our various "loves." Our loves are expressions of the will as we desire a variety of presumed goods. Since it is the interior life that really counts, the quality of our lives will be determined by the nature of our loves.

As we have seen, things in the world are ordered in value according to their place in the Great Chain of Being. And the degree of value a thing possesses determines its worthiness to be loved. Happiness and virtue (which coincide as surely for Augustine as they do for Plato or the Stoics) consist in **"ordered love,"** where our loves are apportioned according to the worth of their objects.

> He lives in justice and sanctity who is an unprejudiced assessor of the intrinsic value of things. He is a man who has an ordinate love: he neither loves what should not be loved nor fails to love what should be loved; he neither loves more what should be loved less, loves equally what should be loved less or more, nor loves less or more what should be loved equally. (*OCD* 1.27)

But we can now add two further distinctions.

Here is the first one. Some things are to be **used,** whereas others are to be **enjoyed.** And some may be both used and enjoyed.

> To enjoy something is to cling to it with love for its own sake. To use something, however, is to employ it in obtaining that which you love, provided that it is worthy of love. For an illicit use should be called rather a waste or an abuse. (*OCD* 1.4)

What is appropriately loved *for its own sake?* For Augustine there can be just one answer: God. In loving the eternal truth, wisdom, and goodness of God we find blessedness. Here alone we can *rest,* content at last; for there exists no higher good to be enjoyed than the creator and restorer of our human nature. As Augustine says in a famous phrase,

> You made us for yourself and our hearts find no peace until they rest in you. (*C* 1.1)*

The enjoyment we seek is a never-ending delight in the object of our love, which nothing but the highest and eternal good will provide. All other things are to be used in the service of that end so that we may find the blessedness of that enjoyment. Even other humans, though we are to love them as we love ourselves, are not to be loved *for their own sake.* To do so would be a kind of idolatry, an attempt to find our end, our "rest" in them rather than in the source of all good. Delight in friends and neighbors—or in our own talents and excellences—must be a delight that always turns to gratitude by being referred to the One who provides it all.

We can see now that Augustinian Christianity is totally different from that "trading skill" piety Socrates rejects in the *Euthyphro* (see 13a–15b and p. 115). Like much religious practice in our day, Euthyphro seeks to *use* the gods to attain what he *enjoys.* And he "turns away" from the question that Socrates says is the crucial one: What is that good *X* the gods accomplish through our service to them? Augustine absolutely rejects the notion that we can "use" what is highest for our own ends or "trade" our sacrifice and prayer for blessings from on high.

---

*Compare Plato on "traveller's rest and journey's end," pp. 159–160.

Whatever good we have is a gift from God; we have nothing to trade with! God is to be sought not for the sake of some worldly advantage, but for his own sake. We don't treat God as a means to some further end. In God we "rest." God is to be *enjoyed*. And you can see that Augustine has an answer to Socrates' question. The good *X* in question is the *transformation of our desire-structure* so that our ordered loves enjoy and use each thing appropriately. The point of piety is not to get what we want from God, but to allow God to change us so that we don't want the same things anymore.

The second distinction corresponds to that between enjoyment and use. Augustine divides love into two kinds: charity and cupidity.

> I call "charity" the motion of the soul toward the enjoyment of God for his own sake, and the enjoyment of one's self and of one's neighbor for the sake of God; but "cupidity" is a motion of the soul toward the enjoyment of one's self, one's neighbor, or any corporeal thing for the sake of something other than God. (*OCD* 3.10)

From cupidity comes both **vice** (by which Augustine means whatever corrupts one's own soul) and **crime** (which harms someone else). We try to enjoy what should only be used and destroy both ourselves and others. Greed, avarice, lust, and gluttony are all forms of cupidity. **Cupidity** is disordered love.

Charity, by contrast, is ordered love, directed toward enjoying God and all other things only in God. If charity is the motivation for one's life, all will be well. "Love, and do what you will," Augustine tells us.[5] You can do whatever you want, provided that your motivation is charity. Charity will motivate us to behave appropriately to all things (i.e., in accord with their actual value). From charity will flow all the virtues: temperance, prudence, fortitude, and justice.*

We must never assume, however, that what motivates us is pure charity. Augustine's own self-examination revealed the cupidity that remained in his life even as a Christian bishop. The Christian may be "on the way" toward the blessedness of truly ordered loves but cannot expect to find it entire until the resurrection of the dead.

---

1. Why, according to Augustine, can we not save ourselves?
2. What is virtue? How is it related to grace?
3. What can we properly enjoy? What can we properly use?
4. Contrast Augustine's notion of piety with the piety described in *Euthyphro* 13a–15b.
5. What are the two kinds of love?

Augustine on Relativism

As we have seen, Augustine argues against skepticism. And everything we have seen so far should lead us to conclude that he is completely opposed to relativism as well. No believer in God could accept Protagoras' saying that *man* is the measure of all things. There is indeed a "measure," a standard by which to judge. But it could not be any created thing, much less a human being whose valuations are determined by a set of disordered loves.† Moreover, if the doctrine of relativism is that (1) Jones can judge some particular action to be right, (2) Smith can judge that very same action to be wrong, and (3) both Jones and Smith are correct, then Augustine is certainly not a relativist.

Nonetheless, there is a sense in which Augustine can admit a good deal of what the relativist wishes to urge. Part of what makes relativism plausible are the differences in customs among the nations.‡

---

*Compare Aristotle on the unity of the virtues, p. 213. There is much similarity between his view and that of Augustine. But there is one great difference: For Augustine, charity (the source of the virtues) is a result of God's grace, not something we have in our control.

†Again, a comparison with Aristotle is instructive. Aristotle also disagrees with Protagoras; for him the "measure" is the good man (see p. 215), not just *any* man. Augustine might not disagree with this in principle, but he would ask, Where is this good man to be found? Among men, he would say, there is but one without sin—the Christ, the incarnation of the Wisdom of God, the *logos*. He can be the "measure." Aristotle's "good man" might have many virtues, but from Augustine's point of view, he is puffed up with pride—which undermines them all.

‡Recall the example of the Greeks before Darius cited by Herodotus (see p. 63) and the judgment that custom is king over all.

Another part of its plausibility is the conviction (which most people share) that it is usually wrong to lie, or steal, but not always. Augustine does justice to both these intuitions by recognizing that particular actions are always done out of particular *motivations* and in particular *circumstances*, which must both be taken into account when judging the act. Remember Augustine's rule: Love and do what you will. One crucial fact in the evaluation of all actions concerns the way they are motivated: Is the motivation charity or cupidity? A second crucial fact is an appraisal of what the circumstances require.

These principles give Augustine great flexibility with regard to outward behavior while rigorously constraining judgment about motives. Externally considered, one and the same act may be right in one circumstance and wrong in another. Think about a lie that consists simply in replying yes to a question. This may be wrong if it is said to gain an unfair advantage for oneself, but right if it is the only way to save a life. Without a full knowledge of both motivation and circumstances, we should be very cautious about pronouncing judgment. As we shall see in the next section, there is even one sense in which such judgment is reserved to God.

In pointing to these two factors, Augustine makes a significant contribution to the debate about **relativism.** While allowing considerable relativity to moral judgments, Augustine is saved from a complete relativism by (1) the Neoplatonic conviction that reality itself is ordered in value, corresponding to the degrees of being, and (2) the thesis about motivation. It is not merely by a conventional agreement that eternal things are of more value than temporal things. Nor is it just *nomos* to praise charity and condemn lust, greed, and hatred. Here we reach values that cannot be relativized. The command of Jesus to love God without reserve and our neighbors as ourselves is *absolute*. Augustine goes as far as to say, "Scripture teaches nothing but charity, nor condemns anything except cupidity, and in this way shapes the minds of men" (*OCD* 3.10).

Similar considerations apply to justice. Some men, he says,

> misled by the variety of innumerable customs, thought that there was no such thing as absolute justice but that every people regarded its own way

of life as just. . . . They have not understood, to cite only one instance, that "what you do not wish to have done to yourself, do not do to another"* cannot be varied on account of any diversity of peoples. When this idea is applied to the love of God, all vices perish; when it is applied to the love of one's neighbor, all crimes disappear. For no one wishes his own dwelling corrupted, so that he should not therefore wish to see God's dwelling, which he is himself, corrupted. And since no one wishes to be harmed by another, he should not harm others. (*OCD* 3.14)

In effect, then, Augustine makes two moves: (1) he breaks up the question about whether values are relative by saying that some are and some are not; and (2) he locates those that are not in the realm of motivation. Augustine is certainly not a relativist, but neither is he a simple absolutist. The subtlety of his analyses of the interior life serve him in good stead in advancing the conversation at this point.

---

1. How can one and the same behavior be sometimes right and sometimes wrong?
2. Contrast Augustine's view of relativism with that of Protagoras.

The Two Cities

There is an old joke that there are just two kinds of people in the world: those who think that there are just two kinds of people and those who don't. Augustine is emphatically a member of the first group. The two kinds are the saved and the damned, those destined for eternal blessedness in heaven and those to be punished for their sins in hell.

But, as you might expect, Augustine's view is more sophisticated and subtle than that bare statement suggests. It is set forth in a book of more than a thousand pages that presents us with an entire philosophy of history. In *The City of God* he brings together all he has learned in the forty and more years since first dedicating himself to the search for wisdom. Here he provides a unified interpretation of human history from creation to the end of the world.

The occasion for writing this magnum opus was the sack of Rome by a Gothic army under the

---

*Luke 6:31 and Matt. 7:12. See pp. 256–257.

leadership of Alaric in August of A.D. 410. The late Roman Empire had been harried by barbarians from the north and east for some time, but for a barbarian army to take Rome, the "eternal city," was a profound shock to every Roman citizen, Christian and pagan alike. People asked: "How could this happen?" Jerome, who had translated the Bible into Latin, wrote, "If Rome can perish, what can be safe?"[6]

Augustine's answer distinguishes "two cities," an **earthly city** and a **heavenly city.** The goal of each city is the same: peace. Members of the earthly city seek peace (harmony and order) in this life: such a peace is a necessary condition for happiness, the ultimate end of all men. For this reason states and empires are established, the noblest of them all (in Augustine's view) being the Roman Empire. It is noblest in this respect: It succeeded in guaranteeing the earthly peace of its citizens better and for a longer time than any other state known to Augustine.

Yet see to what a pass it had come! Why? To answer this question Augustine reaches back into his theory of motivation and applies its insights to Roman history. What motivated the founders of Rome and all its greatest statesmen? Like Homer's heroes, they wanted *glory*.*

> They were passionately devoted to glory; it was for this that they desired to live, for this they did not hesitate to die. This unbounded passion for glory, above all else, checked their other appetites. They felt it shameful for their country to be enslaved, but glorious for her to have dominion and empire; and so they set their hearts first on making her free, and then on making her sovereign. (*CG* 5.12)

The best among the Romans directed this quest for glory into the "right path"; it "checked their other appetites," and they were exemplars of virtue, "good men in their way," as Augustine puts it (*CG* 5.12). Those virtues (personal moderation and devotion to the good of their country) led to Rome's greatness. The passion for glory can yield magnificent results, as Augustine acknowledges:

> By such immaculate conduct they laboured towards honours, power and glory, by what they took to be

the true way. And they were honoured in almost all nations; they imposed their laws on many peoples; and today they enjoy renown in the history and literature of nearly all races. (*CG* 5.15)

And, Augustine adds (quoting from Matt. 6:2), "they have received their reward."

The passion for glory, however, is a peculiarly unstable motivation; it can lead as easily to vice and crime as to virtue. Since the glory sought is the praise and honor of others, what happens when the others honor wealth and domination more than moderation and justice? The result is obvious. In fact, the earthly city is always a mix of virtue and vice—precisely because it is an *earthly* city. The aim of its citizens is to *enjoy* what they should only *use*: earthly peace, possessions, and bodily well-being. Since these are exclusive goods (if I possess an estate, you necessarily do not possess it), any earthly city is bound to generate envy and conflict and to tend toward its own destruction.*

> We see then that the two cities were created by two kinds of love: the earthly city was created by self-love reaching the point of contempt for God, the Heavenly City by the love of God carried as far as contempt of self. In fact, the earthly city glories in itself, the Heavenly City glories in the Lord. The former looks for glory from men, the latter finds its highest glory in God, the witness of a good conscience. The earthly lifts up its head in its own glory, the Heavenly City says to its God: "My glory; you lift up my head." In the former, the lust for domination lords it over its princes as over the nations it subjugates; in the other both those put in authority and those subject to them serve one another in love, the rulers by their counsel, the subjects by obedience. The one city loves its own strength shown in its powerful leaders; the other says to its God, "I will love you, my Lord, my strength." (*CG* 14.28)

Pursuing earthly goods for their own sake is self-destructive, for it leads to competition, conflict, and

---

*See pp. 6–7.

*It is the hope of Karl Marx and the communists that such envy and conflict can be overcome in *this* world; the key, they believe, is overcoming private property, so that the ground of envy is undercut. See Chapter 22. Augustine would have considered this naive.

disaster. That is why Rome fell. Rome was not, as some Christians held, particularly wicked; in fact, its empire was a magnificent achievement, characterized by the real, though flawed, provision of peace and order for its citizens. But it reaped the inevitable consequence of earthly cities that cherish earthly glory.

Members of the heavenly city realize that here in this world they have no continuing home; they look for the fulfillment of their hopes in the life to come. Here they have a taste of blessedness, and through God's grace a beginning of true virtue can begin to grow on the ground of charity. But the culmination of these hopes lies beyond.

Nonetheless, citizens of the heavenly city duly appreciate the relative peace provided by the earthly city and contribute to it as they can. While on earth they consider themselves resident aliens and follow the laws and customs of the society they are dwelling in, to the extent that doing so is consistent with their true citizenship. They *use* the arrangements of their society, but they do not settle down to *enjoy* them.

> However, it would be incorrect to say that the goods which [the earthly] city desires are not goods, since even that city is better, in its own human way, by their possession. . . . These things are goods and undoubtedly they are gifts of God. (*CG* 15.4)

So, with respect to laws that establish "a kind of compromise between human wills about the things relevant to mortal life," there is "a harmony" between members of the two cities. It is only when the earthly city tries to impose laws at variance with the laws of God that citizens of the heavenly city must dissent (*CG* 19.17).

There are, then, two kinds of people, distinguished by their loves. But this very fact—that it is motivation that makes the difference—removes the possibility that anyone can with certainty sort people into one class or the other. We might think Augustine would be tempted to equate membership in the church with citizenship in the heavenly city, but he does not. The church is, collectively, the custodian of the truth about God; individuals are another matter. We can tell who is on the church rolls, but we cannot tell for certain who is a member of the City of God. Only God can judge that.

Among the professed enemies of the City of God, Augustine tells us,

> are hidden future citizens; and when confronted with them she must not think it a fruitless task to bear with their hostility until she finds them confessing the faith. In the same way, while the City of God is on pilgrimage in this world, she has in her midst some who are united with her in participation in the sacraments, but who will not join with her in the eternal destiny of the saints. . . .
>
> In truth, these two cities are interwoven and intermixed in this era, and await separation at the last judgment. (*CG* 1.35)

This epistemological obscurity concerning the saints (for us, though not for God) is a direct consequence of the fact that people's motivations and desires that make the difference. Behavior is always ambiguous; once more it is the will that tells.

We shall not pursue the details of Augustine's interpretation of history in these terms. It is enough to say that *The City of God* understands human history as *meaningful*. It is not, as a distinguished historian once said, "just one damn thing after another." It has a narrative unity; there is plan and purpose in it; and the story found in the Christian Scriptures provides the key.* History is about God's calling citizens of a heavenly city out of the sinful world. These will eventually enjoy blessedness in perfect peace with one another and rest in enjoyment of the one eternal good. For Augustine, all of history must be seen in relation to that end.

---

1. What distinguishes the two cities from one another?
2. Why are we unable to tell with certainty who belongs to each city?

Augustine and the Philosophers

Augustine melds two traditions, the classical and the Christian. Tensions show up at various points in Augustine's work, but the degree of success he achieves makes him a peculiarly important figure

---

*Review the major "chapters" in this story by looking again at Chapter 12.

and one of the most influential contributors to the conversation still to come.

He is convinced that truth is one and that both philosophers and prophets have made important contributions to our understanding of it. But there is never any doubt which tradition has priority when there is a conflict: Augustine is first, last, and always a Christian, convinced that the one and only wisdom is most fully revealed in the Christ. He has put us in a good position to sketch some broad contrasts between classical and Christian philosophy.

Reason and Authority

Augustine is no despiser of reason. Not for him the *credo quia absurdum est* of some church fathers.* He wants to understand what he believes and thinks this can, to a large extent, be done through reason.

Nevertheless, belief has the priority. It must have, for rational understanding could never by itself discover the truth about the Word becoming flesh or about the Trinity. These things must be believed on the **authority** of the prophets and apostles who bear testimony to them. This authority is founded on eyewitnesses and is handed on in the church. The key that unlocks the mystery of life is *revealed*, not *discovered*. As Augustine never tires of saying, unless you believe, you will not understand.

The following example may make this relation of belief and understanding clearer to you. Imagine a young woman who has listened only to rock music. Now put her in a concert hall where Beethoven's violin concerto is being performed. She is not likely to get much out of it, but should she believe that there is something of great value going on in that hall? At that point she could accept that this is superb music only by relying on authority. But there is such authority—that of musicians, music critics, and music lovers over nearly two centuries. Augustine would say that it is reasonable for her to believe this on the basis of such authority. This belief not only

is reasonable, but also may lead her to listen to the concerto again and again, until she eventually comes to the point where she understands for herself how magnificent it is.[7] Belief, Augustine holds, often properly precedes understanding.

Greek philosophy, by contrast, takes the opposite point of view: Unless I understand, the philosopher says, I will not believe. The extreme case is, of course, the skeptic, who, applying this exact principle, suspends judgment about virtually everything. But Xenophanes already set the pattern:*

> The gods have not revealed all things from the beginning to mortals; but, by seeking, men find out, in time, what is better.[8]

Having shaken themselves loose from their own tradition, from Homeric authority, philosophers on the whole are convinced that there is no alternative to trying to achieve wisdom on our own. And part of this pattern is the value they put on human excellence in the search for truth, on self-sufficiency, and on pride in one's attainments.

Here we have one of the great watersheds in the quest for wisdom: Is wisdom something we can *achieve*, or is it something we must *receive*? Augustine is convinced that we must receive it because of the absolute distinction between God and humans (we are too limited to discover truth on our own), sin (we are too corrupted to do it), grace (God provides it for us), and gratitude and humility (the appropriate responses to the situation).

Intellect and Will

Greek philosophers tend to see human problems and their solution in terms of ignorance and knowledge. This is particularly clear in Socrates, for whom virtue or excellence *is* knowledge. But the pattern is very broad, reflected in the importance of education for Plato's guardians, of practical wisdom and contemplation for Aristotle, and of knowledge of reality (in their different theories) by Epicureans and Stoics. Roughly, the pattern takes

---

*"I believe because it is absurd." This formula is attributed to Tertullian, a Christian writer of the second century.

*Review the discussion of the whole passage from which these words are taken, pp. 16-17.

this form: Inform the intellect and the rest of life will take care of itself.*

Augustine, expressing both the Christian tradition and his own experience, disagrees. Intellect may well be impotent—or worse—unless the will is straightened out. The basic features of human life are desire and love, which are matters of the will. What is needed is not (at first) education, but *conversion*; not inquiry, but *faith*.

Again we have a watershed, which correlates fairly well with the first one. The Christian philosopher believes that we cannot rely on reason alone; its use depends on the condition of the will, and the will is corrupted. On this view, our predicament is a deep one; we are not in a position to help ourselves out of it, but—this is crucial—help is available. From the point of view of the Greek philosophers, the human predicament may be serious, but well-intentioned intellectual work will lead us out of it. Reason can master desire.

There is a sense, then, in which Christian thinkers are more pessimistic about humanity than the Greek philosophers.

EPICUREANS AND STOICS

We can cap this contrast by noting Augustine's criticisms of several pagan philosophies that may be serious rivals to Christianity's claim to wisdom. Platonism is the one Augustine thinks nearest the truth, but the Platonists go wrong in allowing worship of powers greater than human beings but inferior to God. Augustine concedes that there are such powers (whether called angels, demons, or gods) but insists that devotion, prayer, and worship belong only to God.

Augustine's interest in Epicurean and Stoic philosophers is sharpened because Saint Paul is alleged to have debated with them in Athens (see Acts 17:18). Moreover, between them they seem to cover neatly the this-worldly possibilities for happiness, the Epicureans seeking it in the pleasures of a material world and the Stoics in the virtues of the soul.

Recall that Epicurus and Lucretius hold that there is no sense in which we survive our physical death; the soul is as physical as the body and disperses when the body disintegrates. Augustine combines this view with their hedonism and concludes that they recommend nothing but the pursuit of bodily pleasures.* He ascribes to them the slogan, "Let us eat and drink, for tomorrow we shall die," which expresses a hedonist's determination to experience as much bodily pleasure as possible before death extinguishes all sensation.

This doctrine, Augustine says, is "more fitting for swine than for men." Even worse, it is a doctrine that will inevitably lead to injustice and the oppression of the poor (*SS* 150). And the reason is by now a familiar one: They are trying to enjoy what should only be used and as a result are dominated by their disordered loves. Epicureanism in this life makes sense only if they are right about consciousness ending in the grave, and of course Augustine is convinced that cannot be right.

The Stoics, who locate happiness in the virtues of the soul, are considered more worthy opponents. Augustine cannot help admiring their courage and steadfastness. But Augustine is convinced that the Stoics have not found the key to blessedness. The Stoics' aim is to live in harmony with nature.† Recall the advice of Epictetus: "Do not seek to have events happen as you want them to, but instead want them to happen as they do happen, and your life will go well." Augustine caustically asks,

> Now is this man happy, just because he is patient in his misery? Of course not! (*CG* 14.25)

It is real happiness that we are interested in, not just contentment with what the world happens to dish out; the Stoic version of happiness is just a makeshift second best. True happiness is delight in the possession of the highest good, to which only the Christian has the key.

---

*The contrast, put this baldly, is overdrawn. For Plato's view of education, the *love* of the good is a crucial factor, and this isn't just a matter of intellect. Still, there is something essentially right about it.

---

*Is this justified? Compare Epicurus on pp. 239–240.
†This concept is discussed on pp. 243–245.

But, Augustine suggests, what else could you expect? The Stoic, like the Epicurean, "puts his hope in himself" (*SS* 150). This is simply another display of pride, which is the root of human trouble in the first place. From Augustine's point of view, even the virtues of the pagans are but "splendid vices."

Thus Augustine, though a great admirer of pagan learning, is also one of its most severe critics. He brings to the fore a number of "choice points" in which the Christian tradition differs from non-Christian rational philosophy. These traditions differ in their conceptions of God and of God's relation to the world; they differ about appeal to authority, about the priority of will or intellect in human nature, about whether pride is a virtue or a vice; and they differ in their conceptions of love. The general pattern on these issues that Augustine sets will dominate Western philosophy for a thousand years.

---

1. What tension exists between reason and authority? Between intellect and will?
2. What is Augustine's critique of the Epicureans? Of the Stoics?

FOR FURTHER THOUGHT

1. Compare Socrates' view that no one ever knowingly does wrong with Augustine's contrary conviction. Which do you think is nearer the truth? Why?
2. State as clearly as you can Augustine's charge that the philosophers are guilty of pride. Then try to defend philosophy against that charge. Which position do you think has the stronger arguments?

KEY WORDS

pride	wisdom
Problem of Evil	happiness
Manicheanism	skepticism
Ambrose	truth
God	loves
Neoplatonism	disordered love
Plotinus	will
the One	ordered love
emanation	use
Great Chain of Being	enjoyment
ex nihilo	vice
moral evil	crime
natural evil	cupidity
eternity	charity
past	relativism
present	earthly city
future	heavenly city
original sin	authority
sin	

NOTES

1. An excellent and readable biography is *Augustine of Hippo* by Peter Brown (London: Faber and Faber, 1967). A classic discussion of his philosophy is Etienne Gilson, *The Christian Philosophy of St. Augustine* (London: Victor Gollanz, 1961).
2. References to the works of Augustine are as follows:

    C: *Confessions*, trans. R. S. Pine-Coffin (Harmondsworth, Middlesex, England: Penguin Books, 1961).

    FCW: *On Free Choice of the Will*, trans. Benjamin G. Hackstaff (New York: Macmillan, 1964).

    CG: *The City of God*, trans. Henry Bettenson (Harmondsworth, Middlesex, England: Penguin Books, 1972).

    OCD: *On Christian Doctrine*, trans. D. W. Robertson Jr. (New York: Macmillan, 1958).

    SO: *The Soliloquies of St. Augustine*, trans. Rose Elizabeth Cleveland (London: Williams and Norgate, 1910).

    T: *The Teacher*, and *GS*, *The Greatness of the Soul*, in *Ancient Christian Writers*, ed. Johannes Quasten and Joseph C. Plumpe (Westminster, MD: Newman Press, 1964).

    AE: *Saint Augustine's Enchiridion*, trans. Ernest Evans (London: S.P.C.K., 1953).

    SL: *The Spirit and the Letter*, trans. John Burnaby, vol. 8 of *The Library of Christian Classics* (London: SCM Press, 1955).

    SS: *Selected Sermons of St. Augustine*, ed. Quincy Howe Jr. (London: Victor Gollanz, 1967).

3. Quotations from a *Manichean Psalmbook* in Brown, *Augustine of Hippo*, are cited in the text using the abbreviation *MP*. References are to page numbers.

4. Quotations from *The Essential Plotinus*, ed. Elmer O'Brien (Indianapolis, IN: Hackett, 1980), are cited in the text using the abbreviation *EP*. References are to page numbers.

5. Quoted in Gilson, *Christian Philosophy of St. Augustine*, 140.

6. Quoted in Brown, *Augustine of Hippo*, 289.

7. The example is adapted from Jerry P. King, *The Art of Mathematics* (New York: Plenum Press, 1992), 138.

8. Quoted in John Manley Robinson, *An Introduction to Early Greek Philosophy* (Boston: Houghton Mifflin, 1968), 56.

14

PHILOSOPHY IN THE ISLAMIC WORLD

The Great Conversation Spreads Out

What distinguishes a conversation from a series of speeches is that participants in a conversation respond to one another. What makes Western philosophy a single conversation and what distinguishes it from other philosophical conversations is that the philosophers involved are responding, in one way or another, to a particular tradition of thought that first arose in ancient Greece.[1] Up to this point in our story, everyone participating in that conversation has been part of the Greco-Roman world. In the centuries after Augustine's death, however, the conversation that first arose in the Greek colonies of Asia Minor would migrate to new lands—including lands that are not typically considered part of the West. Thinkers in Italy and then northern Europe would eventually reengage with it, but not before it had been transformed by the philosophers who carried it through the intervening centuries. While these post-Augustinian thinkers continue to explore classical philosophical topics, such as the problem of the one and the many, they also apply the tools of Greek philosophy to more characteristically medieval themes: the relationship

between reason and revealed religion, the nature and origin of the universe, and the nature of the soul. In this chapter, we will explore those themes mainly through the thought of four great Muslim philosophers: al-Kindī, al-Fārābī, Avicenna (Ibn Sīnā), and al-Ghazālī.

A Sea Change in the Mediterranean Basin

To understand the next part of the great conversation, we need to understand the historic cultural and political shift that occurred in the Mediterranean and Middle East between the fifth and eighth centuries. By the time of Augustine's death in A.D. 430, the Roman Empire had converted to Christianity and fractured into two parts. The Western Roman Empire, with its capital in Rome, finally collapsed in A.D. 476. The glory of Rome faded as the early Middle Ages settled over western Europe. But the Eastern Roman Empire—often known as the **Byzantine Empire** because its capital, Constantinople, had once been called

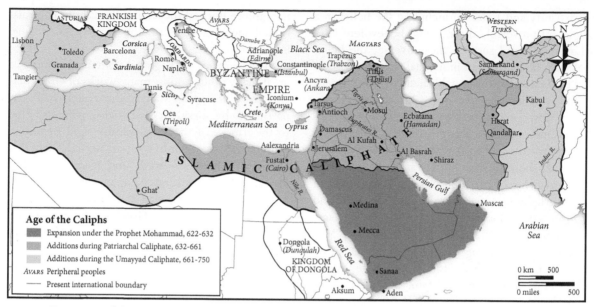

MAP 3 *Expansion of the Caliphate*

Byzantium—survived for another thousand years or so. The Greek language predominated there, making it easy for the Byzantines to carry on the study of Western philosophy. Working primarily in Alexandria and Athens, prominent Neoplatonists like the pagan **Simplicius** (c. 490–c. 560) and the Christian **John Philoponus** (c. 490–c. 570) taught and wrote commentaries on ancient texts, including many of Aristotle's works. By the early seventh century, however, this tradition faltered and began to disappear. The great conversation had all but died out in its native land.

Just as the philosophical traditions of Greece were vanishing from the Byzantine Empire, however, a new intellectual and political force arose in the deserts of the Arabian Peninsula. A new religion, **Islam,** emerged when, according to Muslim belief, God revealed the Qur'ān to his final prophet, **Muhammad** (c. 570–632). Muslims regard the **Qur'ān,** the holy scripture of Islam, as the direct word of God, transmitted through Muhammad in a series of revelations between about 610 and 632. During that time, Muhammad unified the Arab tribes and established political control over most of the Arabian Peninsula. In the decades after his death, a series of four **caliphs**—literally,

the "successors" of Muhammad who served as both religious and political leaders—quickly conquered much of the Middle East, subduing the Persian Empire and capturing Syria, Egypt, and other lands from the Byzantines. The Umayyad family seized control in 661 and continued the Arab expansion. By the middle of the eighth century, the Umayyad caliphs had assembled the largest empire the world had yet seen, stretching from the Atlantic coasts of North Africa and Europe all the way to the Indian subcontinent. In 750, the Umayyads were overthrown by another Arab family, the Abbasids, who established Baghdad as their capital. This multiethnic, polyglot empire, known as the Abbasid **caliphate,** united people of many different cultures and religions under a single ruler. Although real power would soon devolve from the caliphs to a constellation of regional rulers, this initial unification would spur a flowering of arts, science, and philosophy.

Given the importance of Islam to this part of our story, it is worth saying something about its main tenets. According to Muslim belief, Muhammad is the last of a long line of prophets that included Jesus and the Hebrew prophets of the Torah. Accordingly, Islam shares many beliefs with

Christianity and Judaism, including the belief in a single, all-powerful, all-knowing, benevolent God who created and sustains the universe; the belief that each human has an individual, immortal soul; and the belief that God established laws for humans to follow. Islam departs from Christianity and Judaism, however, on several crucial points of doctrine. One important example is that Muslims do not regard any of the prophets as divine. Whereas Christians believe that Jesus was God incarnate, Muslims believe that Muhammad, Jesus, and the other prophets were mortals who received and transmitted God's word. As the Muslim declaration of faith says, "There is no god but God. Muhammad is the messenger of God." More generally, the principle of *tawḥīd*—that God is One, an absolute unity—is central to Islam. Jews and Christians also believe in just one God, of course, but Muslims have often accused Christians of straying from this belief by embracing the idea of the Holy Trinity, according to which God is mysteriously complex, comprising three aspects or "persons": Father, Son, and Holy Spirit. Because of this sharp contrast between Islam and Christianity, the principle of *tawḥīd* would figure prominently in early Islamic philosophy.

---

1. What are main tenets of Islam? How do they resemble those of Christianity and Judaism? How do they differ?
2. What is the principle of *tawḥīd*? Why do Muslims understand it as contrasting with Christian doctrine?

Al-Kindī, the "Philosopher of the Arabs"

As the Arab conquests swept through the Mediterranean and Middle East in the seventh and eighth centuries, the caliphs began amassing libraries of books written in the many languages spoken throughout their empire as well as books collected from even farther afield in India and China. By the early ninth century, the Abbasid caliphs had established Baghdad as an important cultural and intellectual center. Many of the greatest minds of the empire flocked there, and the caliphs commissioned them to translate the world's knowledge into Arabic.

The libraries of Baghdad contained, among a great many other books, many works of Greek science and philosophy. Many of these books had been preserved by dissident Christians, who had fled to the fringes of the theologically rigid Byzantine Empire and beyond into western Persia. These dissidents continued to study and teach Aristotle's logical works and various Neoplatonic commentaries on Aristotle. Christian and Muslim translators rendered these and other Greek works into Arabic, where they came to the attention of Abu Yūsuf Ya'qūb **al-Kindī** (c. 800–c. 870).

As the brilliant scion of a prominent Arab family, al-Kindī was well positioned to serve as an ambassador for Greek thought in the Muslim world. He produced important and original philosophy, earning himself the nickname "the philosopher of the Arabs." But his most important contribution to the great conversation was getting the Muslim world to take Greek philosophy seriously. He famously wrote,

> We must not be ashamed to admire the truth or to acquire it, from wherever it comes. Even if it should come from far-flung nations and foreign peoples, there is for the student of truth nothing more important than the truth, nor is the truth demeaned or diminished by the one who states or conveys it; no one is demeaned by the truth, rather all are ennobled by it. (*On First Philosophy* I.4)[2]

To claim that the ancient Greeks had indeed conveyed "the truth," al-Kindī had to show that Greek philosophy did not conflict with the revealed truth of Islam. So, like many of his Christian predecessors in Alexandria and Athens and his eventual successors in medieval Europe, al-Kindī set out to reconcile philosophy with religion—and, indeed, to show that philosophy provided additional avenues for knowing and understanding what religion had already revealed.

One of his priorities is to substantiate the Islamic doctrine that God is the eternal, unitary creator of the universe. In his greatest work, *On First Philosophy*, he goes about this in a rigorous but roundabout way by taking up the old Greek problem of the one and the many.

> Let us now discuss the number of ways that "one" is said. We say that "one" is said of everything united, but also of anything that is not said to be "many." It is thus said in many ways, including genus, form, individual, difference, proper accident, and common accident. (*On First Philosophy* XI.1)

Each of these things is sometimes called "one," as when we regard giraffes as a single genus, but al-Kindī argues that they are all, in fact, many. Each genus contains many species—if not actually, then potentially. (Notice how much Greek metaphysical terminology al-Kindī adopts.) Each species contains many individuals. Even individuals are only one "by convention," since they too could be divided into parts. Accidental properties of objects, such as the purple of a giraffe's tongue, are many because they occur in many individuals. And yet, it is not simply a mistake to call each of these "one" thing, for they cannot plausibly be conceived as "multiplicity without unity." Al-Kindī summarizes a series of dense arguments for this claim as follows:

> Hence it has been shown that it is impossible even that some things are only multiplicity, because it is impossible that anything be only multiplicity. For, either it is something or not. If it is something then it is one [thing] . . . so it is a multiplicity and not a multiplicity, and this is an impossible contradiction. So it is impossible that some things are only multiplicity without unity. (*On First Philosophy* XIV.11)

The idea here is that for anything that seems to be multiple, we can find some term that collects it together into one thing. Thus, nothing can exist *only* as a multiplicity. Nor is it tenable to think that our world consists only in a unity, as Parmenides did.* Following his favorite tactic of arguing by *reductio ad absurdum*,† al-Kindī begins by assuming that there is no multiplicity.

We say that, if there is only unity without multiplicity, there is no contrariety. For the contrary has something other than it as its contrary. But otherness occurs in at least two things, and two is a multiplicity. If there is no multiplicity there is then no contrariety, but if there is contrariety then there is multiplicity. But contrariety does exist, so multiplicity does as well. But we have supposed that it does not . . . and this is an impossible contradiction. So it is impossible that there is no multiplicity. (*On First Philosophy* XV.1)

The argument is dense, but let us consider it step by step to see if we can follow al-Kindī's reasoning.

1. There is no multiplicity. (starting assumption)
2. If there is no multiplicity, there is no contrariety because
   a. something can only be contrary to something *other* than itself, and
   b. this requires the existence of two things, and
   c. if there are at least two things, then there is multiplicity.
3. Contrariety does exist. (assumption)
4. There is multiplicity. (from 2 and 3)
5. There is multiplicity and there is no multiplicity. (from 1 and 4)
6. So premise 1 cannot be true. (by 5 and the principle of *reductio ad absurdum*)
7. So there is multiplicity.

Notice that in this argument al-Kindī simply takes it for granted that the contrariety that appears all around us is real. As we have seen, the Eleatic philosophers of ancient Greece denied this.* They might have been more easily moved by the series of similarly dense arguments by which al-Kindī claims to show that nothing can be unity without multiplicity if it has a beginning, middle, and end; if it is describable by geometry; or if it moves or changes in terms of any of the Aristotelian categories. These arguments, too, take the form of *reductio ad absurdum*. Al-Kindī seems to have developed

---

*See p. 22.

†See pp. 27–28 for a discussion of this form of argument, which begins by assuming the opposite of what it wants to prove and proceeds to derive a contradiction from that assumption.

---

*In particular, Parmenides and his student Zeno argued that only the One exists (pp. 22–28). Al-Kindī would not have had access to their writings, though he may have known their ideas through Aristotle's *Physics*.

his fondness for this tactic by reading an Arabic translation of Euclid's geometrical treatise, the *Elements*. Like many Western philosophers before and after him, al-Kindī's passion for philosophy seems to have grown from an interest in geometry and mathematics.

The one and the many, al-Kindī concludes, underpin all physical things. This leaves him with a problem, however, for it seems to conflict with the fundamental principle of *tawḥīd*—the absolute Oneness of God. The solution to this problem lies in the fact that al-Kindī's arguments against unity without multiplicity all rely on features of the various terms of Aristotelian logic, such as genus, species, and the categories. Working backward, then, al-Kindī argues that none of those terms applies to the "true One."

> Therefore, the true One possesses neither matter, form, quantity, quality, nor relation. Nor is it described by any of the other terms [of Aristotle's logic]: it has no genus, no specific difference, no individual, no proper accident, and no common accident. It does not move, and is not described through anything that is denied to be one in truth. It is therefore pure unity alone, I mean nothing other than unity. (*On First Philosophy* XX.2)

In other words, one cannot apply any of the terms of Aristotelian logic to God. By this circuitous route, al-Kindī arrives at a deeply Neoplatonic view of God* that supports the central Islamic teaching that God is One.

From these ideas about the one and the many, it is a short step for al-Kindī to show that God created and sustains all things. Each thing that exists has an element of unity in it. That is what makes it a single thing. And anything that has unity must receive that unity from something that is essentially unitary—that is, God. For good measure, al-Kindī also proves that the universe has not always existed and thus that it, too, was created. He offers several distinct arguments for this claim, the clearest of which begins from an argument that time had a beginning.

Now let us make clear in another way that time cannot be actually infinite, either past or future. We say that before every segment of time there is [another] segment, until we reach a segment of time before which there is no other segment. . . . It cannot be otherwise. For, if it could be otherwise, every segment of time would be followed by another segment, to infinity. In that case we could never reach a specified time, because from infinitely long ago up until this given time is a duration equal to the duration from this given time, all the way back in time to infinity. If [the duration] from infinity to a determined time were known, then [the duration] from this known time back along an infinity of time would [also] be known. Then the infinite would be finite, and this is an impossible contradiction.

Also, if one does not reach the determined time, such that one reaches a prior time, and a time prior to that, and a time prior to that, and likewise to infinity, and if the [whole] distance of infinite cannot be traversed, nor its end reached, then infinite time cannot be traversed at all so as to reach a determined time [such as the present]. But a determined time is in fact reached. So necessarily the [given] time is not preceded by infinity, but rather by the finite. There cannot, however, be a body without duration. So the being of the body is not infinite; rather, the being of the body is finite, and it is impossible that there be a body that has always existed (*On First Philosophy* VIII.1–2)

Since what has not always existed is originated—that is, brought-to-be—and being-brought-to-be occurs through what has unity in its essence, the entire universe was brought-to-be by God, the true One. Thus, al-Kindī uses the tools of Aristotelian philosophy to argue against Aristotle, who affirms the eternity of the world, and in favor of Islam, which denies it.

One more feature of al-Kindī's philosophical thought deserves special mention: his ideas about how we come to grasp universals. Aristotle believed that the rational part of the soul possessed a special power to abstract universals from the sensible objects that it perceived. It is through this power that the soul comes to understand abstract ideas of, say, a genus or a species.* Al-Kindī broadly

---

*Plotinus argued that we cannot say anything about the One, since to do so would imply that it is not truly One. See p. 270.

---

*See the discussion of Aristotle's views on induction (p. 192) and *nous* (p. 206–208).

shares this view, with one important modification: Those abstract ideas are already being thought about by a separate and purely immaterial intellect, called the **Active Intellect.** This intellect is distinct both from God and from human souls, but al-Kindī never illuminates us as to its exact nature. He extracts the idea of the Active Intellect from an obscure passage in Aristotle and gives it a prominent role in human thought. According to al-Kindī, a human soul comes to understand an abstract idea only when it receives that idea from the Active Intellect. Al-Kindī does not explain how this happens, but he maintains that once it does happen, the human soul stores the idea in itself to be recalled as needed. Appropriately enough, al-Kindī's interpretation of the Active Intellect would pass into Islamic intellectual consciousness, to be recalled later and elaborated on by many of his successors. To understand it more deeply, we must turn to the next great philosopher in the Islamic tradition.

---

1. What is al-Kindī's argument that Muslims should study the works of Greek philosophy?
2. How does al-Kindī defend the doctrine of *tawḥīd*?
3. In your own words, explain al-Kindī's argument that the world is created rather than eternal.

Al-Fārābi, the "Second Master"

While al-Kindī laid the foundation for philosophy in the Muslim world, the first great systematic philosopher of the Islamic Golden Age was Abū Naṣr **al-Fārābi** (c. 870–c. 950), whose logical acumen and reputation among his successors earned him the moniker of "the Second Master." (The first "master" was Aristotle.) For someone of such enduring fame, we know surprisingly little about his life. He hailed from central Asia, of either Turkic or Persian ancestry, but spent his professional life mainly in Baghdad, the Byzantine Empire, Egypt, and Damascus. His voluminous writing ranged over nearly every area of philosophy, including logic, the history of philosophy, philosophy of religion, philosophy of language, epistemology, metaphysics, ethics, and political philosophy; and he also took a keen interest in music, composing an important treatise called the *Great Book of Music.*

RELIGION AS SUBORDINATE TO PHILOSOPHY

Like al-Kindī, al-Fārābi takes a keen interest in the relationship between philosophy and revealed religion. Unlike al-Kindī, al-Fārābi sets philosophy above religion. According to al-Fārābi,

> Religion is opinions and actions, determined and restricted with stipulations and prescribed for a community by their first ruler, who seeks to obtain through their practicing it a specific purpose with respect to them or by means of them. (*Book of Religion* §1)[3]

In the case of Islam, the "first ruler" is Muhammad, who determines the opinions and actions of his followers through revelation.

> If the first ruler is virtuous and his rulership truly virtuous, then in what he prescribes he seeks only to obtain, for himself and for everyone under his rulership, the ultimate happiness that is truly happiness; and that religion will be virtuous religion. (*Book of Religion* §1)

The "ultimate happiness" at which the virtuous ruler aims cannot "come to be in this life, but rather in a life after this one, which is the next life" (*Enumeration of the Sciences* 5.1). The opinions the ruler teaches to lead his followers to that happiness concern two things.

> Some of the opinions in virtuous religion are about theoretical things and some about voluntary things.
> Among the theoretical are those that describe God, may He be exalted. Then there are some that describe the spiritual beings, their ranks in themselves, their stations in relation to God, may He be exalted, and what each one of them does. Then there are some about the coming into being of the world, as well as some that describe the world, its parts, and the ranks of its parts . . . how the things the world encompasses are linked together and organized and that whatever occurs with respect to them is just and has no injustice; and how each one of them is related to God, may he be exalted, and to the spiritual beings. Then there are some about the coming into

being of the human being and the soul occurring in him, as well as about the intellect. . . . Then there are some that describe what prophecy is and what revelation is like and how it comes into being. Then there are some that describe death and the afterlife and, with respect to the afterlife, the happiness to which the most virtuous and the righteous proceed and the misery to which the most depraved and the profligate proceed. (*Book of Religion* §2)

In addition to teaching correct opinions about the nature of the cosmos, virtuous religion correctly specifies the actions that people should perform, such as the way to worship God and praise the prophets, the way to act toward other human beings, and so on. So far, there is nothing unusual in this account of religion: A prophet receives a revelation from God about the nature of the cosmos and humanity's place in it and communicates that revelation to others.

However, al-Fārābī insists that these "two parts of which religion consists are subordinate to philosophy" because only philosophy offers genuine *knowledge* of them. Religion's role—and especially the role of the theologians and jurists who defend, explain, and apply it through dialectic and rhetoric—is to ensure that everyone can believe and act rightly, even if they lack the philosophical training to achieve genuine knowledge of the nature of the universe and right action. Thus,

> most people who are taught the opinions of religion and instructed in them and brought to accept its actions are not of such a station [as to understand what is spoken about only in a philosophic manner]—and that is either due to [their] nature or because they are occupied with other things. Yet they are not people who fail to understand generally accepted or persuasive things. For that reason, both dialectic and rhetoric are of major value for verifying the opinions of religion for the citizens and for defending, supporting, and establishing those opinions in their souls, as well as for defending those opinions when someone appears who desires to deceive the followers of the religion by means of argument, lead them into error, and contend against the religion. (*Book of Religion* §6)

Thus, the purpose of religion, according to al-Fārābī, is to enable people who are incapable of

philosophy to enter heaven and avoid hell by ensuring that they have right opinions about God, the universe, and the proper way to live. Furthermore, this is necessary because most people cannot follow the philosophical demonstrations by which one can achieve genuine knowledge of these things. The implication is that virtuous religion and true philosophy cannot conflict, for they are merely different ways of reaching the same truths.

To understand why al-Fārābī thinks that only philosophy can produce genuine knowledge, we need to understand his theory of knowledge. But to understand his theory of knowledge, we first need to understand his cosmology.

EMANATION AND THE ACTIVE INTELLECT

In explaining the structure and origin of the universe, al-Fārābī blends Neoplatonic ideas with Islamic doctrine. God is an absolute unity, just as Plotinus says of the One. God created all things, as Islam affirms. But whereas the Qur'ān depicts an act of voluntary creation, al-Fārābī follows the Neoplatonists in describing creation as a process of emanation from the One.* God, al-Fārābī says, is an immaterial thinking being. Indeed, he is "thought thinking itself," as Aristotle says. From God emanates a second immaterial entity—another pure intellect, which thinks about both itself and God. From this intellect arises a third immaterial intellect, from the third a fourth, and so on until we come to the tenth intellect. Each of these intellects is an immaterial, thinking being. Each of the last eight, al-Fārābī believed, was associated with (but distinct from) a specific heavenly body: the tenth with the moon, the rest with the planets, the sun, and the so-called sphere of fixed stars. From the tenth intellect comes the material world, which unlike the immaterial intellects, is subject to change, growth, generation, and decay. Here lies all matter and so all material things, including humans.

The tenth intellect in this series of emanations occupies a special place in al-Fārābī's philosophy.

---

*See p. 270.

THE CELESTIAL SPHERES

Philosophical books were not the only Greek works translated into Arabic. Scholars also translated Greek mathematics, medicine, astronomy, and more, and the Islamic golden age witnessed important advances in all those fields. We can better appreciate al-Fārābī's vision of the cosmos by understanding how Greek, Roman, and Islamic astronomers understood the physical structure of the universe.

By Aristotle's day, the Greeks had already understood that earth was a sphere. One of Plato's other students, Eudoxus, had developed an elaborate model of the universe in which earth sat, unmoving, at the center of the universe, surrounded by layers of concentric **celestial spheres** in which the moon, the sun, the planets, and the fixed stars were embedded like jewels in a series of hollow crystal balls. The moon, for instance, resides in a crystalline sphere that surrounds earth, which is in turn surrounded by a second sphere for Mercury, and so on. The fixed stars sit in the outermost sphere.

Later astronomers developed similar but more complex theories. Recognizing, for instance, that the planets sometimes appear to reverse their course across the sky, they postulated more complex mechanisms involving dozens of spheres. For instance, they proposed that Mercury is not actually embedded in the second sphere; it is embedded in a smaller sphere that is *connected* to the second sphere, but rotates independent of it to account for Mercury's occasional retrograde motion. In the second century A.D., the great Egyptian astronomer **Ptolemy** built on these ideas to devise a model of the cosmos that was good enough to make accurate predictions of eclipses and of the movements of celestial bodies.*

Muslim thinkers adopted this **Ptolemaic model** of the universe and refined it still further, while retaining the basic picture of a stationary earth at the center of a layered, spherical universe. Thus, when al-Fārābī writes of "higher" and "lower" intellects associated with the various planets, he has in mind spheres that are literally higher or lower in relation to earth.

---

*For helpful animations of the Ptolemaic model, see Dennis Duke, "Almagest Planetary Model Animations," n.d., available online at https://people.sc.fsu.edu/~dduke/models.htm.

This is the Active Intellect. Like al-Kindī, al-Fārābī takes the Active Intellect to play an essential role in human thought. The Active Intellect understands and contains within it all Aristotelian forms, both the forms of the higher intellects and the forms of all things that are or could be in the material world. The human intellect comes to grasp these forms only when the Active Intellect illuminates it. Until then, the rational part of the human soul remains merely a "potential intellect." Al-Fārābī compares this process to the process by which the sun makes objects visible to the eye. In the darkness, the eye has the potential to see, but vision becomes actual only when the sun illuminates the objects before it. Similarly, the human intellect has the potential to grasp forms, but that intellectual capacity becomes actual only through the agency of the Active Intellect.*

CERTITUDE, ABSOLUTE CERTITUDE, AND OPINION

With the idea of the Active Intellect in mind, we are ready to consider al-Fārābī's epistemology. For al-Fārābī, only certain kinds of beliefs can count as knowledge, and then only if they are acquired in a particular way. He calls the highest form of knowledge "absolute certitude." We can achieve absolute

---

*Compare to Plato's analogy between the sun and the Form of the Good (p. 161) and Aristotle's description of *nous* as a light that makes colors visible (p. 206).

certitude only about statements that are essentially, necessarily, and permanently true. Furthermore, we can only know such a statement if we *know* that it is essentially necessarily and permanently true. This is a high standard for knowledge. Ordinary humans can only meet that standard by learning something through logical demonstrations. (Prophets, as we'll see, are a different story.) Thus, for al-Fārābī as for Plato and Aristotle, the highest form of knowledge involves scientific demonstrations of truths about abstract universals, not about the changeable, contingent features of the world.* This is where the Active Intellect comes in. We acquire our understanding of universals from the Active Intellect, and so it is only through the Active Intellect that we can have genuine knowledge of anything at all.

What of prophets? Al-Fārābī does not pretend that Muhammad or the other prophets acquired their beliefs through logical demonstration, but he does want to claim that they know things. How is this possible? To answer that question, we must delve into al-Fārābī's metaphysics and cosmology.

Al-Fārābī also appeals to the Active Intellect to explain the knowledge of the prophets. All human souls, according to al-Fārābī, have an imaginative faculty, which is intermediate between the sensitive and the rational parts of the soul. The Active Intellect can illuminate the imaginative faculty, too, which is what al-Fārābī takes to be happening when people dream. Some humans, however, have an especially keen imaginative faculty. The Active Intellect imparts visions to such humans that give them a special kind of knowledge, including knowledge of God. These are the prophets, who come to know God not through the rational demonstrations of philosophy, but through the revelatory visions of the imagination. They use the symbolic images from these visions as a way to communicate what they know to others. Through them, the masses can acquire right opinions and learn right actions.

Still, because ordinary humans do not have direct access to the prophet's imaginative insights, but can only learn from the prophet's words and deeds,

beliefs acquired by religious teaching cannot rise to the level of absolute certitude: When we accept something on the basis of religious teaching, we have not demonstrated its necessity, and so cannot know it in the strictest sense. For ordinary humans, genuine knowledge comes only through careful reasoning.

---

1. What is the relationship between philosophy and religion, according to al-Fārābī?
2. What does al-Fārābī say is the purpose of religion?
3. What is the Active Intellect? Where does it come from?
4. What is required for a belief to count as knowledge, according to al-Fārābī?

Avicenna, the "Preeminent Master"

No one in the history of the world, perhaps, had yet come as close to achieving al-Fārābī's philosophical ideal as the man who would pass into history as the "Preeminent Master," Abū 'Alī al-Husayn **ibn Sīnā**, more commonly known in English as **Avicenna** (980–1037). Avicenna achieved such philosophical heights in part because of his early skill as a medical doctor, which earned him an invitation to the royal palace in Bukhara to treat the emir of the Sāmānid Empire. (During Avicenna's youth, the Sāmānid Empire controlled the eastern part of the Islamic world, even though nominal authority still remained with the Abbasid caliphs in Baghdad. Their capital, Bukhara, is in central Asia, in what is now Uzbekistan.) The grateful emir rewarded sixteen-year-old Avicenna with access to the royal library, which contained room after room, each devoted to a particular science. Amid the chests of books, stacked atop one another, Avicenna completed his philosophical education on his own. In addition to Islamic treatises on astronomy, mathematics, philosophy, and so on, he pored over the works of Aristotle, rewriting each argument in strict syllogistic form.* In this way, he came to a deep and thorough understanding of

---

*For Plato's views on these matters, see pp. 152–153. For Aristotle's, see pp. 190–192.

*On syllogistic arguments, see pp. 188–190.

Aristotelian philosophy. On the basis of this understanding, Avicenna constructed his own highly original philosophical system that is deeply indebted to Aristotle but infused with Neoplatonic and Islamic elements. His greatest work, *The Healing*, expresses this comprehensive system in its entirety, including logic, physics, mathematics, and metaphysics.

EXISTENCE AND ESSENCE

Because Avicenna's metaphysical views are so heavily influenced by Aristotle, it is worth reviewing some of the main features of Aristotelian metaphysics.*

We can remind ourselves of these features by considering an example. Think of a horse. Avicenna and Aristotle both say that a horse is a *substance*—that is, a complex item composed of form and matter. The *form* accounts for its being a horse rather than something else, and the *matter* makes it the particular horse it is. The form of the horse does not have any being outside of or beyond horses, as Plato had thought, but exists only in actual tangible, sensible horses. Its form as a horse is its *essence*—what it is, its defining characteristics. It is horses and the like—substances—that make up reality. This view is sometimes called **hylomorphism,** from the Greek words for matter (*hyle*) and form (*morphe*).

Such a substance does not, however, have only essential properties—its "horsiness," so to speak. A horse can be white or black, fast or slow, in the barn or out at pasture. The medievals call these properties "accidents" or "incidental properties," to distinguish them from a horse's essential properties. Aristotle refers to incidental properties in terms of categories such as quantity, quality, relation, position, and so on. Such properties can change without changing the essential nature of the horse they qualify. As a horse ages, it may grow grayer, thinner, and slower. If, by contrast, a horse should lose its essential properties, it would no longer be a horse. Like essential properties, accidental properties have their being only in some

substance. No such thing as *white* exists on its own, though there are *white horses*.*

We can address the question of why horses and other substances are the way they are in terms of Aristotle's four causes: (1) the *formal cause* or the formula that makes it the kind of thing it is; (2) the *material cause*—the stuff making it up; (3) its *efficient cause*, or the trigger that brought it into being at a given time; and (4) the final cause, the end or goal it is driving toward. In addition, we can explain change in substantial entities in terms of the principles of *potentiality* and *actuality*. Any change is a shift from potentially being so-and-so to actually being so-and-so.

Matter is the principle of potentiality in the horse and form is the principle of actuality. For instance, the fertilized egg of a mare is not yet a horse, but, Aristotle would say, it is matter for becoming a horse. It is actually an egg (embodies the form of an egg), but it is also potentially a horse. That bit of matter has within it a *telos*—a dynamism that, if all goes normally, will result in its coming to embody the form of a horse in actuality.

Avicenna shares all these metaphysical principles with Aristotle. You then might ask, Why should we pay any separate attention to Avicenna? Why not be content with the metaphysics of the ancient philosopher? Because Avicenna sees, or thinks he sees, that Aristotle misses something—something fundamental, far-reaching, and extremely important. Strange as it may seem at first, what Aristotle overlooks is *existence*.

"A wise man's question contains half the answer."

Solomon Ibn Gabirol (c. 1021–c. 1058)

Perhaps it would be better to say that Aristotle takes existence for granted. Remember that when he is pursuing what he calls "first" philosophy, he

---

*We do this briefly here. A more extended look back at pp. 192–203 might be helpful.

---

*In his book on the *Categories*, Aristotle himself uses the example of a horse to explain these ideas and lists whiteness as an example of an accident. This is an interesting coincidence in light of the classic sophistical paradox in Chinese philosophy that "a white horse is not a horse." See p. 81.

notes that form is prior to substances; it is form that makes a substance real. Form is what *actualizes*, what transforms a potentiality into some existing, substantial thing. For that reason he calls form the substance of substance itself. Form brings existence along with it.

When Aristotle asks about how a particular substance comes into being, his answer is in terms of efficient causation by a prior actuality, an earlier substance, itself made what it is by form. Aristotle's god is a cause of motion, not existence. And we don't have to ask whether this god exists; that he is form without matter settles the question.

Individual things within the world—this or that horse, for instance—require an efficient cause for their beginning to be at a certain time; but as a whole, no efficient cause is required for the world. It has its being eternally. It's just there. Why? Because of form. Existence (actuality) and essence (form) simply make a package. It follows from this, and from the fact that whatever exists has some form or other, that there could be no further question about existence.

Avicenna, however, detects a problem here. When we think about something, such as humans or horses, we are thinking of the thing's essence. This is true even when we think about things that do not exist, such as centaurs, the mythical half-horse–half-human creatures of Greek legend. After hearing someone describe a centaur, a child might grasp the form or essence of a centaur and then come to wonder whether centaurs really exist. What the child wants to know is not whether the *form* of the centaur exists. She knows it does, for she has it in her mind. Instead, she wants to know whether that form has combined with matter anywhere out there in the world to create a living, breathing centaur. This perfectly reasonable question only makes sense, however, if essence and existence are distinct. Existence, then, is not something to be taken for granted. Nor is it an automatic consequence of form. Existence, wherever we find it in the natural world, is *something added*.*

---

*Following Avicenna, the great Catholic theologian Thomas Aquinas will pick up this distinction between essence and existence and use it in similar ways.

THE NECESSARY EXISTENT, GOD

Having distinguished essence from existence, Avicenna turns to the possibility that there could be something whose existence is part of its essence. Because it would be inconceivable for such a thing not to exist, it would exist *necessarily*—and not because some other necessary thing necessarily caused it to exist, but rather because it is **necessary in itself.** If there is no absurdity in supposing that some thing exists or does not exist, then Avicenna calls it "possibly existent." Most things are like this: you, this book, centaurs, and even Avicenna himself. In fact, we might wonder whether *everything* is only possibly existent. Avicenna thinks not. He thinks he has a proof that there is a **necessary existent,** a thing that is necessary in itself. Furthermore, he thinks he can prove that this necessary existent is God.

> Undoubtedly there is existence, and all existence is either necessary or possible. If it is necessary, then in fact there is a necessarily existent being, which is what is sought. If it is possible, then we will show that the existence of the possible terminates in a necessarily existent being. (*The Salvation*, Metaphysics II.12)[4]

Consider, Avicenna says, the totality of all things that are merely possible, rather than necessary. To say that something's existence is possible in itself, as opposed to necessary in itself, is to say that its essence does not require its existence. Its existence must therefore be added to it by something else; it must be caused to exist. Thus,

> if the totality is something existing possibly in itself, then the totality needs for existence something that provides existence, which will be either external or internal to the totality.
>
> If it is something internal to it, then one of its members is something existing necessarily, but each one of them exists possibly—so this is a contradiction. Or it is something existing possibly and so is a cause of the totality's existence, but a cause of the totality is primarily a cause of the existence of its members, of which it is one. Thus, it would be a cause of its own existence, which is impossible. . . .
>
> The remaining option is that [what gives existence to the totality] is external to it, but it cannot

be a possible cause, since we included every cause existing possibly in this totality. So since [the cause] is external to it, it also is something existing necessarily in itself. Thus, things existing possibly terminate in a cause existing necessarily. (*The Salvation*, Metaphysics II.12)

Although the argument, as Avicenna lays it out here, is complex, the basic idea is this: Consider the set of all possible things. Since those things are (merely) possible in themselves, they each need something to cause them to exist. Could that cause be something in the set itself? No. For if it were, the set would cause itself. Inconceivable! So it must be outside the set. But if it is something outside the set of all (merely) possible things, then it must be necessary in itself. Thus, from the fact that things exist, we can infer that there is *something* that is necessary in itself.

This marks a clear departure from Aristotle. In saying that the necessary existent, whatever it is, causes the world to exist, Avicenna is saying that the world itself has an efficient cause, which Aristotle rejected. To a Muslim—or a Christian, for that matter—that efficient cause is clearly God.

Avicenna still has a long way to go to *prove* that the necessary existent is the God of the Qur'ān. So far he has proven only that there is *at least one* necessary existent and that if there are any things whose existence is only possible in themselves, this existent is the cause of at least some of those things. To complete his proof of God's existence, Avicenna sets out to establish each of God's attributes, one by one: The necessary existent is unique, perfect, immaterial, and unitary, that it caused the universe to exist, and so on. We need not concern ourselves with the details of these proofs here. Suffice it to say that Avicenna believes he can derive, from the very idea of a necessary existent, all of God's essential attributes, as described in the Qur'ān.

One implication of this view is that everything that exists, exists necessarily. God is the cause of all things, and everything about God is necessary. Thus, for each thing that he caused to exist, he caused it necessarily. So we were mistaken, in a sense, to suggest that you, this book, and Avicenna might not have existed. This book is not necessary *in itself*, of course, but it is what Avicenna calls

necessary through a cause or necessary through another. Everything that exists, except for the necessary existent, God, is like that: necessary through another.

God's necessity has other, more dangerously unorthodox implications, too. Avicenna endorses the Qur'ānic view that God is the cause of the world. But because Avicenna, like Aristotle, conceives of God as unchanging, he insists that God cannot cause the world in the way that, say, a spark causes fire. That is, God cannot create the universe *at a moment in time*, for this would entail that at some moment, God changes from having not created the world to having created it. The universe must, therefore, be eternal. This puts Avicenna in an awkward position. Muslim theologians and philosophers had long fretted about Aristotle's arguments for the eternity of the universe precisely because it seems that if the universe is eternal, then it cannot have been created. Muslim philosophers had considered the view that time is created along with the universe,* but Avicenna rejects that option in favor of a system very much like al-Fārābī's, which allows him to maintain that the universe is both eternal and created. On this view, the universe, complete with celestial spheres, emanates necessarily from God. This cascade of emanations does not happen in time, and yet God is still the cause of it all. Avicenna compares this to a hand turning a key: Even though the turning of the hand and the turning of the key occur simultaneously, the first causes the second.

Avicenna draws one more controversial conclusion from the idea that God is unchanging. Consider the fact that a particular Newfoundland dog, Shadow, used to live with one of the authors of this book. When you learned this fact, you changed in one tiny way: You changed from not knowing that fact to knowing it. God, however, does not change, and so it might seem that God cannot know such facts about particular things. Rather, God can only know eternal truths about universals. How can we reconcile this with the Qur'ānic view that God knows everything and that "not even the

---

*Compare this to Augustine's view on the matter (pp. 274–276). Augustine's works were unknown in the medieval Islamic world.

weight of a dust speck, whether in the heavens or on Earth, escape His notice"? Avicenna admits that this "is one of those wonders that requires a subtle genius to understand" (*The Salvation*, Metaphysics, II.18.5). The explanation, in unsubtle form, is that God knows everything about the material world because of his perfect knowledge of universals. Avicenna compares this to the way someone might deduce an eclipse from a perfect knowledge of the heavenly bodies and their motions. Since these are eternal and unchanging, on Avicenna's view, it is possible to know eternally that a particular eclipse will occur at a particular time. All of God's knowledge of events in the material world is like that.

THE SOUL AND ITS FACULTIES

Avicenna relies on his "subtle genius" to resolve another tension between his Neoplatonist-inflected Aristotelian metaphysics and his Muslim faith. This tension relates to the human soul. Following Aristotle, Avicenna understands the soul as the form of a living thing. And like Aristotle, Avicenna maintains that the soul has three parts: the vegetative, animal, and rational.* But like al-Fārābī, Avicenna takes forms, including the form of a human, to reside in the Active Intellect. An individual thing, such as a person, comes to exist when appropriately prepared matter receives a form from the Active Intellect. Only then does the individual person acquire his or her form, which is his or her soul. Notice, however, that the Active Intellect has only a single, universal form for all humans; it does not contain a separate form for each person who is born. And since the form *is* the soul, this means that separate souls do not exist prior to the form's union with a particular bit of matter. Each person's soul, in other words, only comes into existence when the person is born; it does not exist eternally.

This is not in itself a problem, from a Muslim perspective. The worry arises when we ask what happens when the body dies. Aristotle maintained that while most of the soul ceases to exist upon the death of the body, a certain part of the rational soul survives. Indeed, Aristotle maintained that

this part of the soul, *nous*, is immortal and eternal, existing before the body is born and remaining after it dies. For Aristotle, however, the survival of *nous* does not seem to secure any sort of personal immortality or afterlife.* Avicenna has already rejected the idea that any part of the individual soul exists before birth, but he believes that it does survive after death. Furthermore, he needs the soul to maintain its individuality in the afterlife.

To do this, Avicenna elaborates on and extends Aristotle's idea of *nous* in various ways. First, he argues that the rational part of the soul is an immaterial substance, rather than something imprinted in matter, as the vegetative and animal parts of the soul are. He offers various arguments for this. Some are based on the fact that the rational part of the soul can understand universals, which matter cannot do. His most famous argument, however, is one that he describes as

> a pointer that serves [both] as an alert and reminder by hitting the mark with anyone who is at all capable of catching sight of the truth on his own. . . . So we say that it has to be imagined as though one of us were created whole in an instant but his sight is veiled from directly observing the things of the external world. He is created as though floating in air or in a void but without the air supporting him in such a way that he would have to feel it, and the limbs of his body are stretched out and away from one another, so they do not come into contact or touch. Then he considers whether he can assert the existence of his self. He has no doubts about asserting his self as something that exists without also [having to] assert the existence of any of his exterior or interior parts, his heart, his brain, or anything external. He will, in fact, be asserting the existence of his self without asserting that it has length, breadth, or depth, and, if it were even possible for him in such a state to imagine a hand or some other extremity, he would not imagine it as a part of his self or as a necessary condition of his self. . . . Thus, what [the reader] has been alerted to is a way to be made alert to the existence of the soul as something that is not the body—nor in fact *any* body—to recognize it and be aware of it. (*Healing*, "The Soul," I.7.7)

---

*On Aristotle's view of the soul, see pp. 203–204.

*See pp. 206–208.

This hypothetical person, whom modern scholars dubbed the **Flying Man,** would grasp the fact of his own existence based solely on his experience of self-awareness. Moreover, he would recognize the existence of his own soul as something distinct from and independent of the existence of his body.* Since this part of his soul can exist independent of his body, it can survive the death of his body.

This still leaves Avicenna with the problem of showing that individual souls retain their individuality after the death of the body. If their union with the body is what initially distinguished them from other souls, how can they remain distinct when separated from the body? The answer, according to Avicenna, is that once a soul has acquired its individuality through union with matter, it always retains its awareness of itself as a distinct entity. It will always be *this* soul, the one that was conjoined to *that* body and had *those* experiences and thoughts. This makes it distinct from all other souls, dissolving the worry that it will merge back into a universal form in the Active Intellect.

Avicenna also extends Aristotle's theory of soul in other ways, especially in terms of the faculties of the soul. In addition to positing various inner senses, such as the imagination, Avicenna develops a detailed account of the theoretical intellect, which is for understanding what is true or false. (He contrasts this with the practical intellect, which is for understanding what is good or evil.) It is through the theoretical intellect that we come to have knowledge of the world.

As an Aristotelian, Avicenna maintains that genuine knowledge rests on philosophical demonstrations using syllogisms. We build up our knowledge by reasoning from things we know to things we did not yet know. Such a process must begin somewhere. Avicenna identifies various starting points. Some universals, such as existence and necessity,

are acquired as soon as the soul becomes conscious of itself, even if we may sometimes need someone to bring them to our attention. We grasp the concept of existence, for instance, when we reflect on our own existence when imagining the Flying Man. Some statements are self-evident and graspable without any demonstration. Avicenna's examples are "our belief that the whole is greater than the part and that things equal to one thing are equal to one another" (*The Healing,* "The Soul," I.5.15).

Other starting points we must acquire from experience. Here, too, Avicenna extends Aristotle's theory. He recognizes Aristotelian induction as a source of our foundational beliefs, but he regards it as importantly limited.* When we perceive many instances of the same type, our mind extracts the universal form that they share in common, on the basis of which we come to accept various statements about that type of thing. Avicenna gives the example of seeing different people and extracting from our various perceptions of them the universal form of *personhood.* Although we all form beliefs on this basis, it cannot provide genuine knowledge. Genuine knowledge, for Avicenna as for Aristotle, is knowledge of necessary truths. But when we perceive particular members of a species, we perceive both their essential features (such as their rationality, in the case of humans) and their nonessential features (such as their skin color), and unless we already grasp the universal form of the species, we have no way to distinguish between them. Thus, even if by happenstance we did extract only the essential features from our perceptions, we could not know that we had done so. Induction, Avicenna concludes, cannot provide the foundations for genuine knowledge.

To overcome this problem, Avicenna introduces the more rigorous notion of **methodic experience,** which somewhat resembles scientific experimentation. Methodic experience is experience of one thing following another over many repetitions, either always or with few (and hopefully explicable) exceptions. Avicenna's examples are that magnets attract iron and that ingesting the scammony plant

---

*The Flying Man argument is often compared to Descartes' famous *cogito* (pp. 373), but this comparison is misleading. Although they share some superficial similarities, the two arguments serve very different purposes. Avicenna is considering the relationship between the mind and the body, whereas Descartes is looking for an indubitable starting point to overcome skepticism.

---

*See p. 192.

rids the body of excess bile.* Doctors had observed this effect of scammony over many cases, finding few, if any, exceptions. If the connection between ingesting scammony and purging bile were accidental, rather than somehow connected to the essential nature of scammony, then we would not expect to find such a firm connection between the two. This is not foolproof, of course. And it can deliver nothing more than "conditional universal knowledge," since methodic experience can show only that the connection exists in the conditions in which it was observed. Avicenna acknowledges, for instance, that his knowledge of scammony's medicinal powers extends only to "the scammony in [his] country" (*The Healing*, "Book of Demonstration," I.9.11). Thus, Avicenna concludes,

> the difference between what is acquired by perception and what is acquired by induction and methodic experience is that what is acquired by perception in no way provides a universal concept, whereas the latter two might. The difference between what is acquired by induction and what is acquired by methodic experience is that what is acquired by induction does not ensure a universal, whether conditional or not, but produces probable belief, unless it leads to methodic experience; and what is acquired by methodic experience ensures a universal with the aforementioned condition. (*The Healing*, "Book of Demonstration," I.9.21)

These methods, then, provide the main foundations for human knowledge. Building new knowledge on those foundations, in turn, requires figuring out the connection between our existing knowledge and some new conclusion. In strict syllogistic form, grasping this connection means grasping a "middle term" that connects the conclusion's subject to its predicate.† We recognize which universals can provide appropriate connections, according to Avicenna, through a capacity called **intuition.** Some people have a keener intuition than others, enabling them to figure things out for themselves more quickly or more thoroughly.

---

*The scammony plant is a type of climbing, flowering vine that grows in the eastern Mediterranean basin. Its roots react with bile in the intestines to produce a kind of laxative.
†See p. 189.

The prophets, according to Avicenna, have the keenest intuition of all, and so can grasp all knowledge in a flash of intellectual insight. As a result, the prophets' knowledge, like the philosopher's, is ultimately based on philosophical demonstration. The difference is that whereas Avicenna labored for years in the royal library at Bukhara to acquire his knowledge, Muhammad's keener intuition enabled him to receive his knowledge directly from the Active Intellect.

---

1. What basic phenomenon does Avicenna think Aristotle overlooked?
2. How does the distinction between essence and existence help Avicenna prove the existence of God?
3. What conclusions does Avicenna draw from the fact that God has all of his attributes necessarily?
4. What is the Flying Man argument supposed to show?
5. What is the difference between induction and methodic experience?

Al-Ghazālī

Avicenna's reworking of Aristotle transformed philosophy in the Islamic world. For those who came before him, studying philosophy meant studying Aristotle. For most who came after him, studying philosophy meant studying Avicenna. That earned him lavish praise, but it also attracted plenty of critics. Despite Avicenna's attempts to reconcile his Greek metaphysics with Islam, not everyone who read his works thought he had succeeded. Among his most vocal critics was Abu Hamid Muhammad **al-Ghazālī** (1058–1111), a distinguished religious scholar and teacher from what is now northeastern Iran.

After a pair of spiritual crises in about 1090, al-Ghazālī set for himself a daunting task. Seeking knowledge of the true nature of things, he aspired to understand the true nature of knowledge. Certain knowledge, he surmised, requires a thing to be made "so manifest that no doubt clings to it, nor is it accompanied by the possibility of error and deception."[5] Resolving to cast aside all of his beliefs that did not meet this high standard, al-Ghazālī initially finds himself left with but two things: his sensory perceptions and self-evident truths, such as the truth that ten is more than three. But he comes to realize that even these are suspect. His senses, for instance, sometimes deceive him: When he looks at a shadow, it appears not to move, but when he sees it in another position an hour later, he reasons that it must have been moving all along. As for self-evident truths, he muses that if reason can overturn his sensory perceptions, he cannot be sure that some higher authority may not overturn his own reasoning. He may one day awaken to some higher state and recognize that everything he believed was an illusion, just as the dreamer awakens to recognize that he has merely been dreaming. (Avicenna himself had suggested that we may recognize new truths once our souls escape the distorting confines of our bodies.) Thus, no matter how self-evident some truth seems to be, he cannot rule out the possibility that he has made some kind of error.*

Trapped in this skeptical quagmire, al-Ghazālī concluded that no philosophical demonstrations would suffice to escape. For any demonstration would require him to affirm its premises and to recognize that those premises entailed its conclusion. But his skeptical thoughts had foreclosed certainty about both those things. He escaped this brooding skepticism, he says, only because God cast a light into his heart that revealed the truth to him and restored his belief in his senses and intellect.

Having escaped from skepticism, al-Ghazālī began an earnest study of various ways of attaining knowledge. He studied two kinds of Islamic theologians, including those whom al-Fārābī had disdained. He also studied the mystical traditions of Sufism. The Sufis were Muslims who pursued knowledge of God through practices designed to achieve a higher state of consciousness. Like many Christian mystics, early Sufis practiced a rigorous asceticism, rejecting worldly things and looking inward to find God. Following a twelve-year foray into Sufi asceticism, al-Ghazālī concludes that through sufficiently rigorous mystical practice, humans can, in fact, achieve an immediate

experience of nearness to God and that, through this experience, we can learn things that cannot be expressed in words.*

In addition, al-Ghazālī studied the philosophers, from ancient Greece down to Avicenna. While he allows that some of what they say is correct, especially concerning mathematics and logic, he condemns them all for being "infidels and irreligious men." Mentioning al-Fārābī and Avicenna by name, he argues that they do not count as Muslims because they deny basic tenets of the faith: the resurrection of the body, the createdness of the universe, and God's knowledge of particulars. Furthermore, he insists that they often fall short of the demonstrative certainty to which they aspire. He concludes that even by their own standards, and even setting aside the skeptical worries that had plagued him earlier, the philosophers cannot deliver the knowledge that al-Ghazālī sought.

During the course of this study, al-Ghazālī sets out to refute "the philosophers" in a book known as *The Incoherence of the Philosophers*. In practice, his target is almost invariably Avicenna. Having absorbed the philosophers' methods, he argues skillfully against twenty propositions, including the three mentioned above as disqualifying Avicenna from being a true Muslim. In some of these discussions, he aims to prove "the philosophers" wrong. In others, he aims only to prove that their arguments fail and so cannot provide the genuine knowledge at which philosophy aims. They need revelation after all.

A particularly interesting example will serve to illustrate al-Ghazālī's approach. Avicenna holds that causes produce their effects necessarily. Taking this as an affront to God's unlimited power, al-Ghazālī writes,

> The connection between what is habitually believed to be a cause and what is habitually believed to be an effect is not necessary, according to us. But [with] any two things, where "this" is not "that" and "that" is not "this" and where neither the affirmation of the one entails the affirmation of the other nor the

---

*Compare al-Ghazālī's skeptical reasoning to Descartes' in the first *Meditation*.

*Compare to the epistemological claims of the Vedic and Buddhist philosophers in Chapter 3.

negation of the one entails negation of the other, it is not a necessity of the existence of the one that the other should exist, and it is not a necessity of the nonexistence of the one that the other should not exist—for example, the quenching of thirst and drinking, satiety and eating, burning and contact with fire, light and the appearance of the sun, death and decapitation . . . and so on to [include] all [that is] observable among connected things in medicine, astronomy, arts, and crafts. Their connection is due to the prior decree of God, who creates them side by side, not to its being necessary in itself, incapable of separation. On the contrary, it is within [divine] power to create satiety without eating, to create death without decapitation, to continue life after decapitation, and so on to all connected things. (*IP* 17.1)[6]

Al-Ghazālī considers two main arguments for this view. The first is that the philosophers' claims that one thing causes another—much less that it does so *necessarily*—are simply unsupported. Although we observe, say, cotton burning when exposed to flame, such observation does not prove that it is the flame that causes the cotton to burn, rather than something else, such as God. The second argument targets philosophers who acknowledge a divine role in causation but insist that a cause has its effects necessarily. Whenever a proper set of circumstances arises, on this view, divine influence necessarily produces the appropriate effect. But this, al-Ghazālī argues, is an unacceptable limitation on God's freedom and power. For surely, he contends, it is possible for God to choose to create one thing without the other at a particular moment in time, even if, in practice, God rarely chooses to do so. As a result of God's regularity in creating both together,

> the continuous habit of their occurrence repeatedly, one time after another, fixes unshakably in our minds the belief in their occurrence according to past habit.* (*IP* 17.15)

At stake here is an understanding of God's perfection and omnipotence. Avicenna counts it as part of God's perfection that both his attributes

and his actions are necessary. On this view, we do not deny his omnipotence when we say that God could not have done otherwise, for in saying that, we are simply saying that God could not fail to be perfect. Al-Ghazālī, by contrast, counts it as part of God's perfection that he has ultimate freedom and power. To understand his omnipotence in such a limited way as to think that he could not stop a flame from burning cotton is to deny him perfect freedom and power.

It is worth noting that al-Ghazālī does not take a definite position here about how causation works. His argument is consistent with the view that, say, flames *normally* cause cotton to burn without God's assistance, but that God can intervene to prevent this from happening in particular cases. But it is also consistent with the view that God actively intervenes in every instance, voluntarily creating the burned cotton every time cotton comes into contact with flame. This reflects al-Ghazālī's larger project in his *Incoherence of the Philosophers*: He aims to undermine the philosophers' pretensions to knowledge, not to provide philosophical demonstrations of his own. While he sketches some striking philosophical positions along the way, his is primarily a critical undertaking.

Ironically, however, his mission of undermining Avicenna may have backfired. Al-Ghazālī presents the *Incoherence* as a critique of philosophy as a whole. In practice, he offers a critique of certain parts of Avicenna's thought. The implicit suggestion is that Avicenna embodies the whole of philosophy—or, at least, the best that it has to offer. In the eastern reaches of the Muslim world, future generations seem to take this implicit suggestion more seriously than they take al-Ghazālī's critique. In the end, then, al-Ghazālī may have further cemented Avicenna's position as the "preeminent master" of philosophy in the Islamic world.

---

1. What argument does al-Ghazālī give for doubting the things he learns by reasoning?
2. What is al-Ghazālī's argument against Avicenna's claim that everything happens by necessity?

---

*Compare to David Hume's view of causation (pp. 445–451).

MAIMONIDES (MOSES BEN MAIMON)

This formative period for Islamic philosophy also boasted its share of Jewish philosophers, such as Saadia Gaon and Solomon ibn Gabirol. The most important of these was **Maimonides** (1135–1204), who was born in the territory of **al-Andalus**, which covered modern-day Spain and Portugal. Al-Andalus was home to a thriving philosophical and intellectual community, but Maimonides does not get to remain there for long. In 1148, a new dynasty, the Almohads, captures his hometown of Córdoba as part of their gradual conquest of al-Andalus. The Almohads reject the established custom of allowing non-Muslims to practice their own faiths, and so Maimonides' family flees to Morocco rather than be forcibly converted to Islam. Maimonides eventually moves to Cairo, where he serves as physician to the vizier of Saladin, ruler of Egypt. He writes extensively on medicine and Jewish law, but his most influential philosophical work is the *Guide for the Perplexed*.

The *Guide* is addressed to those intellectuals who are in perplexity over apparent contradictions between Scripture and the best science and philosophy of the day. The latter he takes to be represented by Aristotle, especially as understood by his Muslim interpreters. He agrees with Avicenna that being and essence are separable, but holds that the celestial spheres and the Intelligences governing them are created by God *ex nihilo*, not emanations from the very substance of God himself. This allows him to deny that everything happens necessarily in this world, thus making room for free will, evil, and miracles.

As to whether the universe is eternal, he holds that this cannot be proved either way, but that on either assumption the existence of God can be demonstrated. We know God exists, but we know of his nature only what we can learn from his works. So the study of these works by way of natural science yields such knowledge as we can have of the divine nature. However, because all language is derived from our experience of the natural world, he holds that none of our words can apply literally to God, who infinitely exceeds his creation. We can, then, say what God is *not*, but never positively what God *is*. Thus Maimonides is one of the principal sources for the tradition of *negative theology*.

Maimonides believes that the highest perfection possible for a human being is to know God and to love him. Because we know God only through his works, the pursuit of science and metaphysics is, as Aristotle said, the best and happiest life. It also provides as much of immortality as is possible for us, since what will be preserved after death is the knowledge we have acquired. In the greatest human beings, however, this theoretical life can be combined with practical influence in the community, as is proved by the greatest of the prophets, Moses.

The Great Conversation in the Islamic World

The Muslim thinkers of the ninth through the twelfth century would extend and shape the influence of Greek thought over a large part of the globe. Philosophy continued to thrive throughout the Islamic world long after this period, with Avicenna's thought dominating philosophical work for centuries. If we define Western philosophy as philosophy that grows out of the thought of ancient Greece, then the responses to Avicenna constitute a distinct branch of Western philosophy—a rich, post-Avicennan conversation involving hundreds of philosophers spanning many generations, carried on more or less separate from the one that would dominate Europe from the late medieval period on.

FOR FURTHER THOUGHT

1. The philosophers discussed in this chapter offer different views about the relationship between reason and revealed religion. Do you think any of them is correct? Why or why not?

2. Do you think Avicenna's proof of the existence of God is faulty? If so, what is wrong with it?

3. Do you find Avicenna's conception of God's omnipotence more compelling than al-Ghazālī's or vice versa? Why?

KEY WORDS

Byzantine Empire
Simplicius
John Philoponus
Islam
Muhammad
Qu'rān
caliph
caliphate
tawḥīd
al-Kindī
Active Intellect
al-Fārābī
celestial spheres

Ptolemy
Ptolemaic model
Avicenna (ibn Sīnā)
hylomorphism
necessary in itself
necessary existent
Flying Man
methodic experience
intuition
al-Ghazālī
Maimonides
al-Andalus

NOTES

1. For a discussion of this way of determining what counts as Western philosophy, see Peter Adamson, "Out of Europe," *Philosophy Now* 116 (2016), https://philosophynow.org/issues/116/Out_of_Europe.

2. Quotations from Peter Adamson and Peter E. Pormann, *The Philosophical Works of al-Kindī* (Karachi: Oxford University Press, 2012).

3. Quotations from al-Fārābi's *Book of Religion* and *Enumeration of the Sciences* are from Al-Fārābi, *Alfarabi: The Political Writings*, trans. Charles E. Butterworth (Ithaca, NY: Cornell University Press, 2001).

4. Quotations from Jon McGinnis and David C. Reisman, eds., *Classical Arabic Philosophy: An Anthology of Sources* (Indianapolis, IN: Hackett, 2007).

5. Al-Ghazālī, *Freedom and Fulfillment*, trans. Richard J. McCarthy (Boston: Twayne, 1980), 7.

6. Quotations marked *IP* are from Al-Ghazālī, *The Incoherence of the Philosophers*, trans. Michael E. Marmura (Provo, UT: Brigham Young University Press, 2000).

ANSELM AND AQUINAS

Existence and Essence in God and the World

Augustine's influence in Western philosophy and theology was so great that when Peter Lombard, about A.D. 1150, collected notable sayings of the church fathers in the *Book of Sentences*, 90 percent of the quotations were from Augustine's writings.[1]

After the fall of Rome, intellectual work in Latin-speaking Europe was carried on largely within the church. It was churchmen who preserved libraries, copied manuscripts, and wrote books. Over most of this work presided the Augustinian spirit, with its convictions that Wisdom is one, that Scripture and Reason are essentially in harmony, and that the interesting and important topics are God and the soul. For more than five hundred years, the churchmen carried out their work with limited access to ancient Greek thought and in isolation from the philosophers in the Islamic world.

Later medieval European philosophy, from the eleventh to the fifteenth centuries, is exceedingly rich and inventive, in part because of the translation of Greek and Islamic learning into

Latin during the eleventh and twelfth centuries. For the purposes of this selective introduction, however, we focus on two examples: a famous argument put forward by Anselm of Canterbury and—at considerably more length—the Christian Aristotelianism of Thomas Aquinas. Anselm and Aquinas, both made saints of the church after their deaths, exemplify some of the best, though by no means the only, European philosophy of this period. The chapter closes by considering some doubts that were raised about the confident claim that reason and faith are harmonious, doubts that look forward to the birth of self-conscious modern philosophy.

Anselm: On That, Than Which No Greater Can Be Conceived

In about three pages, **Anselm** (A.D. 1033–1109) sets forth an argument concluding not only that God exists but also that he exists "so truly" that we cannot even *conceive* that he doesn't. This apparently simple, yet deeply perplexing argument is known to history as the **ontological argument.***

Anselm, who eventually rose to become archbishop of Canterbury, was obviously a man of deep faith. But as someone steeped in the Augustinian tradition, he wanted not only to believe, but also to understand.† As a young Benedictine monk in Normandy, he set out to determine how far reason alone, independent of Scripture, could substantiate the central doctrines of Christianity. He took himself to have proven many—but not all—of those doctrines in a book called the *Monologium*, but since it involved such complex reasoning, he began to wonder

> whether there might be found a single argument which would require no other for its proof than itself alone; and alone would suffice to demonstrate that God truly exists. (*Proslogium* preface, p. 1)²

Anselm concluded that there is such an argument, and he set it out in a book with the title *Faith Seeking Understanding*.‡

The argument begins with an abstractly stated expression of the *idea* of God, a definition, if you like, of what we have in mind when we use the word "God." **God,** says Anselm, is *that, than which*

*no greater can be conceived.** Why does he use this strangely convoluted phrase, *that, than which no greater can be conceived?* Why not just say that God is the greatest being we can conceive? For one thing, Anselm doesn't want the idea of God to be limited by what *we* may be able to conceive. Furthermore, he doesn't want to suggest that a positive conception of God may be entirely comprehensible to us. The strange phrase pushes us out beyond everything familiar by forcing us to ask again and again, Can something greater than this be conceived?

Suppose you imagine or conceive a certain being. Now ask yourself the question, Can I conceive of something that is in some way "greater" than this? If you can, then it is not yet God that you have conceived. Think, for instance, of an oak tree. Some oak trees are great, but it is not very hard to think of something "greater" than any oak tree—something, perhaps, that can move and think. It follows that God is not an oak tree.

What if we think of a human being? Is a human being something than which no greater can be conceived? Hardly. For one thing, human beings are mortal. Surely any being not subject to death would be greater than a human. And humans have many other limitations besides mortality; we can surely conceive a being that knows more than any human knows, is more powerful than any human, is not so dependent on other things, and is not subject to the moral failures of human beings. So when we think of God, we are not thinking of a human being, but of something much greater.

Until we reach the conception of *that, than which no greater can be conceived*, we have not yet thought of God. That is what we mean when we use the word "God."

Notice, also, that Anselm frames his idea of God in terms of the Great Chain of Being.† This Augustinian notion is so much a part of Anselm's outlook that it is simply taken for granted. That the world is ordered by the degrees of being and value (greatness) in its various parts must seem to Anselm so obvious that it is beyond question. If you

---

*The term "ontological" comes from the Greek word for *being*. The argument in question was given this name in the eighteenth century by one of its critics, Immanuel Kant, because (unlike the arguments of Aquinas) it does not begin from facts about the world, but goes straight from the idea of God to a conclusion about his being. Many thinkers find it important to distinguish two, or even more, distinct arguments because at least one form of the argument is clearly invalid. Anselm himself does not do so, and we will interpret it as one argument. We will try to formulate this argument in its strongest form, while remaining fairly colloquial in manner. (Discussions of the soundness of this argument often bristle with technical-logical apparatus.)

†In light of this goal, it is important not to take Anselm's search for a proof of God's existence as evidence of doubt. Anselm wishes to understand what it is that he so firmly believes. Furthermore, Anselm seeks a proof that is valid quite independent of any Christian assumptions. He thinks that a good proof should convince *anyone* who reads it, including *you*, regardless of his or her faith.

‡It was later titled *Proslogium*, or *A Discourse*. This is the title under which it is now known.

*Compare Augustine's formulation, p. 269.
†Review this Neoplatonic notion on pp. 271–272.

run up and down the chain, you find it easy to conceive of beings both lesser and greater; and your mind is inevitably carried to the idea of something that is not only actually greater than other existing things, but something than which you cannot even conceive a greater. And that, Anselm says, is what we mean by God.

But now the question arises: Is there a being answering to that conception? There really are oak trees and wolves and human beings. Is there a being than which nothing greater can be conceived?

To see how Anselm gets from this idea of God to God's reality, consider Psalm 14:1, which says, "The fool says in his heart, 'There is no God.'" If this "fool" truly understands what he is saying—if the idea of God that he has in his head is the one Anselm describes—then he is saying, "That, than which no greater can be conceived does not exist." And to say this, Anselm argues, is to fall into error.

For suppose the fool were right. Then *that, than which no greater can be conceived* would exist only in his understanding and not in reality. It would exist in the same way, Anselm says, as a painting exists in the mind of a painter who changes his mind before putting brush to canvas. The painter has the painting "in his understanding," as Anselm puts it; but it does not exist also in reality.

It is easy to see how this might be the case with the painting. But can it be the case that *that, than which no greater can be conceived* exists only in the understanding? No, argues Anselm, because something that exists only in someone's understanding is not after all *that, than which no greater can be conceived*. For you can conceive of something just like it except that it exists both in the understanding and in reality.

Such a being will be "greater" in the sense that it has more powers and is less dependent on other things; it occupies a higher place on the Great Chain of Being. So it couldn't be true that *that, than which no greater can be conceived* exists only in our minds. God must exist in reality.

In fact, Anselm adds, this being exists so truly "that it cannot be conceived not to exist" (*Proslogium* 3). Most beings—trees and humans, for example—you can imagine as never having existed. Could *that, than which no greater can be*

conceived be like these beings? Could it be the sort of thing that we can conceive as not existing? Again let us suppose that it were; then it would depend on the cooperation or goodwill of other things for its existence—or maybe on sheer good luck!

But then it wouldn't be *that, than which no greater can be conceived*, for we can surely conceive a greater being than that. We can conceive of a being that is not so dependent on other things. In fact, we can conceive of a being that we cannot even *conceive* as not existing.

> Hence, if that, than which nothing greater can be conceived, can be conceived not to exist, it is not that, than which nothing greater can be conceived. But this is an irreconcilable contradiction. (*Proslogium* 3)

You cannot even conceive that God does not exist. You can, of course, say the words, "There is no God"; but, Anselm says, you cannot clearly think what they mean without falling into contradiction. What is contradictory cannot possibly be true. So what the fool says is necessarily false. It follows not only that God does exist but also that it is impossible that he does not.

Here is an analogy. You can *say* that one plus one equals three, but you cannot *conceive* that it is true. If you understand what one is and what three is, and if you understand the concepts of addition and equality, then you cannot possibly believe or even understand that one plus one equals three. To try to do so would be like trying to believe that three both *is* three and also *is not* three (but two). But that is impossible, a contradiction. It is necessarily false that three both is and is not three. Just so, it is necessarily false that *that, than which no greater can be conceived* does not exist. To try to believe it is like trying to believe that *that, than which no greater can be conceived* both does exist (since it *is* that, than which no greater can be conceived) and does not exist. But you can't believe both. So, you must believe that it does exist. You cannot even truly conceive that God does not exist. That God should not exist is as impossible as that one plus one should equal three.

Why, then, does the fool say in his heart, "There is no God"? It is either because he does not truly understand what he says or because he is a dim-witted fool who believes contradictions! The nonexistence of God is something that cannot be rationally thought.

It is little wonder that Anselm exclaims,

> I thank thee, gracious Lord, I thank thee; because what I formerly believed by thy bounty, I now so understand by thine illumination, that if I were unwilling to believe that thou dost exist, I should not be able not to understand this to be true.
> (*Proslogium* 4)

Even if Anselm *wanted* to disbelieve in God, he couldn't manage it. It would now be clear to him that the very sentence in which he expressed his disbelief is necessarily false, like the sentence "One plus one equals three."

Anselm's argument can be formulated in a variety of ways. Here is one way. See whether you can follow the steps, then see whether you can pick out a flaw in the argument. (Note that it is in form a **reductio ad absurdum;** look again at the discussion of this kind of argument in the section on Zeno, p. 28.)

1. God does not exist. (assumption)
2. By "God," I mean *that, than which no greater can be conceived (NGC)*.
3. So *NGC* does not exist. (from 1 and 2)
4. So *NGC* has being only in my understanding, not also in reality. (from 2 and 3)
5. If *NGC* were to exist in reality, as well as in my understanding, it would be greater. (from the meaning of "greater")
6. But then, *NGC* is not *NGC*. (from 4 and 5)
7. So *NGC* cannot exist only in my understanding. (from 6)
8. So *NGC* must exist also in reality. (from 5 and 7)
9. So God exists. (from 2 and 8)
10. So God does not exist and God exists. (from 1 and 9)
11. So premise 1 cannot be true. (by 1 through 10 and the principle of reductio ad absurdum)
12. So God exists. (from 11)

Note that this is an argument that moves from the **essence** of God to God's **existence.** That is, it moves from our grasp of *what* God is—the

NGC—to the fact *that* God is. In a certain sense, the argument is a claim that the existence of God is *self-evident.* What that means is that it is enough to understand the conception of God to know that God must exist. Nothing else is required. God's essence *entails* God's existence. In this regard, if the argument is correct, knowing that God exists is like knowing that all bachelors are unmarried. Knowing what bachelors are (their essence) is sufficient for knowing that they are unmarried. That's entailed by the definition of "bachelor." You don't have to add anything else to get that conclusion. It's not like knowing (supposing this is true) that all bachelors are melancholy—a proposition for which we would need *evidence* about the way the world is. If Anselm is right, thinking clearly about the implications of the *NGC* concept is enough to guarantee the conclusion that there is a God. Just as it is necessarily false that there are married bachelors, so it is necessarily false that there is no God. As befits an argument following in the Platonistic tradition of Augustine, Anselm's argument draws a conclusion about what is eternally, genuinely, and necessarily real by looking inward at our own ideas.

Is Anselm's argument a sound one? Should we be convinced by it? Discussion since the eleventh century has been intense, beginning with Gaunilo of Marmoutiers, a monk who was Anselm's contemporary. Gaunilo, writing "in behalf of the fool," notes that he can conceive of a lost island filled with riches and delicacies, an island more excellent than any other island. This island exists in his understanding. If we follow the principle of Anselm's argument, however, the island would be still more excellent if it were in reality as well. So, the island must exist. Otherwise, any actually existing island would be more excellent than it, and it wouldn't be the island more excellent than any other. But that is absurd.

Anselm replies to this criticism by acknowledging that it would indeed be absurd to infer the actual existence of such an island from the mere conception of it. But what holds for islands doesn't hold for the singular case of *that, than which no greater can be conceived.* You can't prove the existence of a perfect island, or of Zeus or Apollo either, from the concepts that designate them. But this concept, the

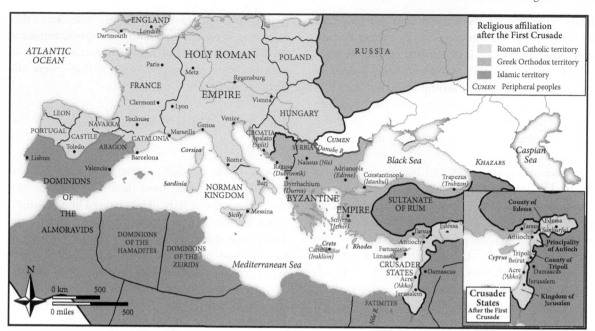

MAP 4 *The Mediterranean and Europe (c. 1100)*

NGC, is unique, pointing us out beyond any finite thing. If the argument works, it works only in this one case, only for that being described by this odd phrase, *that, than which no greater can be conceived.* Neither Zeus nor perfect islands exist *necessarily.* But God does—or so Anselm means to convince us.

The argument has had both defenders and critics down to the present day. It is not only the conclusion that attracts attention, but also the difficult notions of existence, conceivability, possibility, and necessity. And these are notions that run deep in our conception of reality—whatever it might be like.

We will meet the argument again.*

---

1. What phrase does Anselm use to designate God? Why?
2. Study carefully the steps in Anselm's argument. Write down questions you have about its correctness.
3. What is Gaunilo's objection to the argument? How does Anselm reply?

---

*See Descartes (*Meditation V*, Chapter 17) and Kant ("The Ontological Argument," Chapter 20).

The Transfer of Learning

Anselm lived in the Abbey of Our Lady of Bec, which then was an important center of learning by European standards. In the grander scheme of things, though, it was something of a backwater, nestled in a valley in Normandy, across the English Channel from Britain. Many of the works of the Greek philosophers had been lost to Catholic Europe, having been preserved only by the Arabs and Byzantines. Furthermore, from Augustine's time until Anselm's, most philosophy and science was done elsewhere and in other languages, especially Arabic, Sanskrit, and Chinese. The Latin-speaking scholars of eleventh-century Europe therefore knew relatively little of the Greek tradition and had very little access to the vast stores of new knowledge others had accumulated in the past several centuries.

A series of military conquests in the late eleventh century brought those vast stores of knowledge within reach of the Latin West. Norman invaders seized Sicily from a Muslim emir and gradually wrested control of southern Italy from the Byzantine Empire. These lands were eventually unified into the kingdom of Sicily. The Spanish kings of León and Castile were waging war against Muslim princes in what is now Spain. In 1085, they captured Toledo, a far greater center of learning than the abbey at Bec. At the end of the century, the First Crusade brought parts of the eastern Mediterranean under Catholic control for the first time in over four centuries.*

Translations of Greek and Islamic texts began to trickle into Latin-speaking Europe. One of the first translators, **Constantine the African** (c. 1020–c. 1098), arrived from his native Tunisia in about 1065, carrying Arabic medical texts. He soon converted to Christianity and settled at an important Benedictine monastery north of Naples called Monte Cassino, where he translated those medical texts into Latin. The texts spread far and wide through Europe, helping whet Catholics' appetite for foreign knowledge. The kingdom of Sicily soon became a thriving center of translation, from both Arabic and Greek into Latin. Further west, Muslim, Jewish, and Christian scholars set to work translating Arabic manuscripts from the vast library of Toledo. These translators rendered many works of Islamic and Jewish philosophy and science into Latin for the first time. These scholars are sometimes referred to collectively as the **Toledo School of Translators.** By the end of the twelfth century, efforts in Toledo, Sicily, and elsewhere had translated a large part of the lost Greek tradition and the new Arabic science, medicine, and philosophy.

♦

Our books have informed us that the pre-eminence in chivalry and learning once belonged to Greece. Then chivalry passed to Rome, together with that highest learning which has now come to France.

Chrétien de Troyes (1135–1190)

It is through the efforts of these translators that the Latin West came to know the great minds of the Islamic world and many forgotten works of ancient Greek philosophy. Among these were the works of Aristotle.

Thomas Aquinas: Rethinking Aristotle

In A.D. 1225, Landulf, count of Aquino, and his wife Theodora welcomed their seventh son in a castle in southern Italy. They named him Thomas. When he was five years old, they sent him to the nearby monastery at Monte Cassino, where Constantine had begun the great translation project over a century earlier. His parents hoped that he would rise to a position of power and influence. In a sense, he exceeded their wildest expectations, though not in the way they had planned.

After nine years of schooling at Monte Cassino, young **Thomas Aquinas** relocated to Naples, where he soon entered the newly founded university. There he encountered the works of Aristotle, freshly rendered into Latin. He also encountered the newly founded Dominican order of friars. Friars were very different from settled, respectable, and often wealthy monks. Friars were itinerant preachers, going from town to town, begging for a living. They took literally Jesus' directions to his disciples in Mark 6:8, to take nothing with them except their walking sticks—"no bread, no bag, no money in their belts; but to wear sandals and not put on two tunics." So when Aquinas decided, at the age of nineteen or twenty, to become a Dominican friar, his dismayed family kidnapped him and spirited him away to their castle.

They held Aquinas there for a year, but when his family could not induce him to change his mind, they finally released him. He studied for some years in Cologne, Germany, with a man of vast learning and Aristotelian persuasions, Albert the Great. Aquinas was rotund, a large man of slow movements, unusually quiet and calm. His fellow students began to call him "the dumb ox." His brilliance occasionally showed through, however, and on one such occasion, Albert is reported to have said, "This dumb ox will fill the whole world with his bellowing."

---

*Compare Map 4 with Map 3 on p. 293 to see which territories changed hands.

AVERROËS, THE COMMENTATOR

Aquinas and many of his Christian contemporaries read Aristotle side by side with the commentaries of a Muslim philosopher named Abū al-Walīd Muhammad **ibn Rushd** (1126–1198), better known in English as **Averroës.** Born into a distinguished family in Córdoba in al-Andalus, Averroës resists Avicenna's transformative influence on Islamic philosophy. Instead, he writes voluminous commentaries on Aristotle, defending him against the criticisms of al-Ghazālī and the alleged misunderstandings of Avicenna. He is largely ignored in the Islamic world, but he exerts a significant influence on medieval Christian thinkers, who refer to him simply as "the Commentator."

In the Latin-speaking world, Averroës was famous for—and attacked because of—the doctrine of **"double truth,"** the idea that truths from Qu'rānic revelation could contradict what philosophical reason could demonstrate and yet both be true. It is puzzling how this view came to be attributed to him, since he explicitly denies it. He holds that the Qu'rān was revealed so that even the humblest could participate in the truth, though in its purity that truth is available only to the philosopher. When such apparent conflicts appear, he suggests that Scripture must be interpreted metaphorically.

Not everything in Averroës' thought is easily reconciled with revealed religion, however. One of the points on which he is suspected of holding the "double truth" pertains to personal immortality. The human soul is, as Aristotle says, the form of a human body and its active intellect (*nous*) is indeed a substance; but what makes me an individual person (distinct from other humans) is not this form but the particular matter it "informs." As form, this Intelligence is identical in all humans. When my body dies, then, *nous* continues on, but not as *mine*. Thus there is a kind of immortality, but it is strictly impersonal.

Aquinas became a priest and studied to become a master in theology. He lectured on the Bible for several years and began to write. Meanwhile, he participated in regular **disputations,** as they were called. These were debates that took a more or less standard form. A question was announced for discussion—for instance, Is truth primarily in the mind or in things? Conflicting opinions were stated, often citing some authority. These opinions would then be critically evaluated, arguments for and against each opinion being put forward. Finally, a judgment would be given by a master or a professor. Much of what Aquinas wrote is structured in a similar way. This form of presentation, which came to be known (later, with scorn) as "scholastic," had certain advantages. It made for comprehensiveness and careful attention to detail. It depended absolutely on the ability of writers and readers to distinguish good arguments from bad. But it required enormous patience, and in the

hands of lesser intellectuals than Aquinas it often degenerated into pedantry.

Aquinas spent time not only in Paris, but also in several places in Italy—and all the time, he wrote, or rather, he dictated to a secretary, and often to more than one. It is said that like a grand master at chess who can play numerous games at once, Aquinas could keep four secretaries busy writing separate texts. His collected works are enormous and touch every philosophical and theological topic.

In December 1273, while saying Mass, Aquinas seems to have had a mystical vision. He wrote no more. When urged to return to his writing, he said that he could not, that everything he had written to that point now seemed "like straw." He died in 1274 at the age of forty-nine. Although there was continuing suspicion of Aquinas' reliance on Aristotle—that pagan thinker—and several of his theses were condemned by ecclesiastical authorities, on July 21, 1323, the pope declared Aquinas a saint. Because few miracles had been attributed to him, the pope is reputed to have said, "There are as many miracles as there are articles of the *Summa*."*

PHILOSOPHY AND THEOLOGY

Aquinas does not think of himself as a philosopher. When he talks about philosophers, he usually has in mind the ancients (Plato, Aristotle, and so on), but sometimes the more recent Muslim thinkers, such as Avicenna and Averroës. Philosophers are lovers of wisdom, Aquinas thinks, who lack the fullness of wisdom as it is revealed in Christ. Yet he has great respect for these philosophers, especially for Aristotle, whom he sometimes quotes as simply "the philosopher." He writes about the same topics as they do, discusses them frequently, borrows arguments from them, and happily acknowledges his debt to them. Yet he never uses them uncritically. Aquinas agrees with Augustine that (1) truth is one, (2) all men have been enlightened by the word or the wisdom of God, and (3) humans, in pride, have turned away from God and from the truth. He concludes that the light of reason in sinful minds may be obscured, but it has not been wiped out. And intellect on its own can do a great deal.

In particular, Aquinas regards Aristotle as having discovered a great deal through reason alone. Of all the philosophers, it is Aristotle whom Aquinas regards as having the best arguments and the soundest overall vision. He wrote a number of careful commentaries on works by Aristotle, and when he speaks on his own behalf, Aquinas often sounds like a recording of Aristotle. As Augustine draws on the Platonists, Aquinas draws from and builds on the Aristotelians, including Muslim Aristotelians such as Avicenna and Averroës.†

"As sacred doctrine is based on the light of faith, so is philosophy founded on the natural light of reason."
—THOMAS AQUINAS

Revelation, then, does not displace reason, but it does build on it. Aquinas carefully distinguishes what natural human reason can do from what must be learned from Scripture. You can compare the situation, as Aquinas sees it, to a three-story house. On the bottom floor, reason and natural experience do their work without the need of any supernatural aid. On the second floor, we find things that are both revealed to us by God and demonstrable by reason. Among the truths that overlap in this way are the existence of God and the immortality of the human soul.

---

*The *Summa Theologica* (*Summary of Theology*) is the major work of Aquinas' maturity.

†Given how heavily Aquinas leans on Aristotle's metaphysics, in particular, you may find it helpful to review Aristotle's ideas, either in our brief review of them in the

previous chapter (p. 301) or in our longer discussion on pp. 192–203.

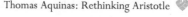

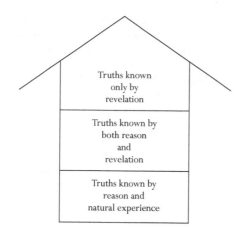

Truths known
only by
revelation

Truths known by
both reason
and
revelation

Truths known by
reason and
natural experience

It is good, Aquinas thinks, that God has revealed such truths, even though reason can access them on its own,

> for otherwise they would have been arrived at only by a few, and after a long period, and then mixed with errors; more especially when we consider that man's entire salvation, which is God, depends on such knowledge. (*ST* 1a.i.1; *PT*, p. 32)[3]

The third floor contains truths that are beyond the capacity of natural intellect to discover, such as the internal nature of God as triune—as Father, Son, and Holy Spirit—and the historical fact of God's becoming incarnate in Jesus of Nazareth.

Though Aquinas always writes as a theologian, we can set out his contributions to the philosophical conversation by focusing our attention on the first and second stories of this house. We do, however, need to keep in mind his view that human beings have a supernatural end. He says,

> The happiness of human beings is twofold. There is an imperfect happiness in this life of which Aristotle is speaking, consisting in the contemplation of immaterial substances to which wisdom disposes us, an imperfect contemplation such as is possible in this life, which does not know what such substances are. The other happiness is the perfect happiness of the next life, when we will see the very substance of God himself and the other immaterial substances. But what brings that happiness won't be any theoretical science, but the light of glory. (*DT*, question 6; *SPW*, p. 50)

---

1. How does Aquinas understand the relationship between human reason and divine revelation?

FROM CREATION TO GOD

Can we know, through reason and experience alone, that God exists? And can we know anything about what God is, about his essence? We have seen that Anselm answered both questions at once with his conception of God as *that, than which no greater can be conceived*. If we understand what God is, he argued, we must know that God is. Aquinas is, of course, familiar with this famous argument, but unlike Anselm, he does not think we should be convinced by it.

> A self-evident proposition, though always self-evident in itself, is sometimes self-evident to us and sometimes not. For a proposition is self-evident when the predicate forms part of what the subject means: thus it is self-evident that human beings are animals, since being an animal is part of what being human means. . . . But if there are people to whom the meanings of subject and predicate are not evident, then the proposition, though self-evident in itself, will not be so to such people. . . .
>
> I maintain then that the proposition *God exists* is self-evident in itself, since its subject and predicate are identical: God, I shall argue later, is his own existence. But because what it is to be God is not evident to us the proposition is not self-evident to us. It needs to be made evident by things less evident in themselves but more evident to us, namely, God's effects. (*ST* 1a.2.1; *SPW*, pp. 196–197)

Here, Aquinas is telling us that we cannot *start* where Anselm starts in his argument. Maybe we will end up in the same place, but we have to get there by another way. This is partly because Aquinas accepts the Aristotelian view of how humans acquire knowledge.* It may be appropriate for a Platonist such as Augustine or Anselm to think that we have direct insight into the essences of things (an immediate grasp of the Platonic Forms, if you will). For Aristotle and Aquinas, however, human beings are animals, and the knowledge animals have *begins* with sensation. So if we are to prove God's

---

*Human knowledge is discussed in more detail in the subsequent section, "Humans: Their Knowledge."

existence, we must begin with things we perceive using our senses.

Aquinas says that there are two kinds of arguments dealing with causes and effects. One begins from causes and shows why things are as they are. The other begins from effects and shows what must have been the case to bring these effects into existence. It is the latter kind of argument that we can use to prove the existence of God.

> Now any effect that is better known to us than its cause can demonstrate that its cause exists: for effects are dependent on their causes and can only occur if their causes already exist. From effects evident to us, therefore, we can demonstrate something that is not self-evident to us, namely, that God exists. (*ST* 1a.22; *SPW*, p. 198)

Now Aquinas holds that the existence of God can be proved in five ways. Like Anselm's argument, these "five ways" have been subjected to exhaustive logical scrutiny, often in a forbidding forest of technical symbols. I present Aquinas' arguments in his own words and then add some interpretive remarks. In these remarks I try to present the argument in as strong and sympathetic a way as I can. You may be inclined to try to criticize these arguments, but it is important that you first understand them.

The Argument from Change

The first and most obvious way is based on change. For certainly some things are changing: this we plainly see. Now anything changing is being changed by something else. (This is so because what makes things changeable is unrealized potentiality, but what makes them cause change is their already realized state: causing change brings into being what was previously only able to be, and can only be done by something which already is. For example, the actual heat of fire causes wood, able to be hot, to become actually hot, and so causes change in the wood; now what is actually hot can't at the same time be potentially hot but only potentially cold, can't at the same time be actual and potential in the same respect but only in different respects; so that what is changing can't be the very thing that is causing the same change, can't be changing itself, but must be being changed by something else.) Again this something else, if itself changing, must be being changed by yet another thing; and this last

by another. But this can't go on for ever, since then there would be no first cause of the change, and as a result no subsequent causes. (Only when acted on by a first cause do intermediate causes produce a change; unless a hand moves the stick, the stick won't move anything else.) So we are forced eventually to come to a first cause of change not itself being changed by anything, and this is what everyone understands by *God*. (*ST* 1a.3; *SPW*, p. 200)

Change is understood to be an alteration in something, by which it becomes *actually* what it was only *potentially* until then. If the sun heats the sidewalk so that you can't stand on it with bare feet, this is a change from being actually cool (but potentially hot) to being actually hot. The world is full of such changes.

The next point is that each of these changes is brought about by something that is, in the appropriate way, *actual*. The ball thrown by the pitcher has the potential of being over the fence, but it cannot realize that potentiality by itself. It takes an actual batter swinging an actual bat and actually hitting the ball to get it actually over the fence. In the same way, wood does not actualize its potentiality for being hot on its own; it takes something actually hot to make the wood hot, too. Because nothing can be both actual and potential in the same respect, the wood cannot be at the same time merely potentially hot and actually hot, so it cannot make itself hot.

So, Aquinas tells us, nothing can change itself. Everything that is changed must be changed by another thing. But here you can see a question: What accounts for this second thing that actually brings the change about? If it is actualized by some third thing, the question repeats itself, until we come to what Aquinas calls a "first cause of change"; it changes the thing in question without itself being actualized by another.

Could this series of changes go on to infinity? Might it be that there is no first cause of change at all, nothing that is the source of change without itself being changed by some other thing? Could it be that *everything* is changed by something else, which thing in turn is itself changed by something else? This is a tricky question, on which the proof probably rests.

Aquinas answers no. He reasons that if this were true there would be no first cause of change. But if there were no first, then there would not be any secondary changers either, since each of them causes change only insofar as it is itself actualized by some prior cause. And, of course, if there were no secondary changers, there would be no change at all. But that is obviously false. We do see home runs hit and campfires started, so the series cannot go on to infinity. There must be a point where change originates. This must be something that is not merely potential, but is fully and entirely actual. Otherwise, it would need something outside itself to actualize its possibilities.

"Something deeply hidden had to be behind things."

Albert Einstein (1879–1955)

It is important to guard against a misinterpretation here. Aquinas is not thinking of a first thing in a temporal series. His argument is not that one change precedes another, a second precedes that, and so on to the beginning of the world in time. Rather, his argument concerns a nested set of necessary conditions, not a temporal series of changes. (This matters to Aquinas because he does not think reason alone can prove that the world has a beginning in time.) A necessary condition for the actualization of something is the reality of something that is not merely potential. Unless there were already something actual, no actualization of any potentiality could occur. The set of conditions cannot be infinite, so there must be some condition that is itself *sufficient* to account for the rest. There must be something, then, that exists on its own, without requiring something else to bring it into existence. This would be a completely actual first cause of change. And that, says Aquinas, is what "everyone understands by *God*."

The Argument from Efficient Causality

In the observable world causes are found ordered in series: we never observe, nor ever could, something causing itself, for this would mean it preceded

itself, and this is not possible. But a series of causes can't go on for ever, for in any such series an earlier member causes an intermediate and the intermediate a last (whether the intermediate be one or many). Now eliminating a cause eliminates its effects, and unless there's a first cause there won't be a last or an intermediate. But if a series of causes goes on for ever it will have no first cause, and so no intermediate causes and no last effect, which is clearly false. So we are forced to postulate some first agent cause, to which everyone gives the name *God*. (*ST* 1a.3; *SPW*, pp. 200–201)

An efficient (or agent) cause, you will recall, is the trigger that sets a process going, such as the spark that produces the explosion or the wind that blows down the fence. We perceive that these efficient causes are ordered in series. We never find that something is the efficient cause of itself. The spark may cause the explosion, but it cannot be the cause of the spark. To be its own cause, it would have to preexist itself, and that is absurd. It cannot exist before it exists! The spark itself requires another efficient cause, perhaps a hammer striking a rock.

Another obvious fact is that if you take away the cause, you take away the effect: no hammer, no spark (or at least not this particular spark); no spark, no explosion (this particular explosion). What we find in the world, then, is that one cause depends on another for its existence. Again, this order need not be a temporal one. Aquinas is not trying to prove that there was a temporally first event in the world's history. Even if the world is eternal, everything in it needs an efficient cause for its very existence. We can think of this as a hierarchically ordered set of dependencies, rather than a temporally ordered series of successive events.*

Again the question arises, Could this series of dependencies be infinite? Aquinas again says no. For if the series were infinite, there would be no cause that is "first." A "first" cause would be one on

---

*If you want an example of a causal relation of the efficient sort that is not temporally ordered, think of the depression of the sofa cushion, which is simultaneous with your sitting on it. Your sitting is the efficient cause of the depression in the cushion, but they happen precisely together.

which the whole causal order depended, while it depended on nothing beyond itself. If there were no such cause, Aquinas says, there would be no intermediate causes and no ultimate effects. But there are causes and effects, so there must be a first cause. And that is what "everyone gives the name *God*."

One commentator gives a helpful analogy.[4] Suppose you are in your car, stopped at a red light, and are hit from behind. You want to know the cause of this unfortunate event. So you get out and see that the car that hit you had itself been stopped but was hit from behind. As you look at the car behind that one, you notice that it, too, was hit from behind, and so on. Who caused your accident? *Someone* clearly did, since the pileup actually happened, and the chain of cars does not go on forever. It must be the driver of some car that hit another car, but was not himself hit, who caused each of the other cars to cause an accident, ending in yours. He produced the whole series of causes. He is the "first" cause.

The Argument from Possibility and Necessity

Some of the things we come across can be but need not be, for we find them being generated and destroyed, thus sometimes in being and sometimes not. Now everything cannot be like this, for a thing that need not be was once not; and if everything need not be, once upon a time there was nothing. But if that were true there would be nothing even now, because something that does not exist can only begin to exist through something that already exists. If nothing was in being nothing could begin to be, and nothing would be in being now, which is clearly false. Not everything then is the sort that need not be; some things must be, and these may or may not owe this necessity to something else. But just as we proved that a series of agent causes can't go on for ever, so also a series of things which must be and owe this to other things. So we are forced to postulate something which of itself must be, owing this to nothing outside itself, but being itself the cause that other things must be. (*ST* 1a.3; *SPW*, p. 201)

This argument proceeds in two stages. To understand each stage, we must be clear about what Aquinas means by things that "need not be" and things that "must be." Both terms are applied to

entities of various sorts, and he thinks we have examples of both sorts in our experience.

A thing that need not be can be generated (can come into being) and can be destroyed again (can pass away). The plants and animals of our experience are such beings. Mountains and rivers, too, are things that need not be. There was a time when the Rockies did not exist, and eventually erosion will wear them away. The mighty Mississippi, relatively stable though it has been for eons, will disappear someday. Such beings, Aquinas would say, can suffer *essential* changes, meaning that they can come to be what they are and they can cease being that again.

Given that account, we can consider the first stage of the argument. Aquinas argues that at one time, whatever need not be was not (did not exist). This is true of the Rockies and the Mississippi. He asks us to suppose that everything were like that. Then there would have been a time when nothing existed. But if there ever had been such a time, there would be nothing now. Why? Because from nothing you get nothing. But as we can see, something does exist. So there could never have been a time when there was nothing at all. But that means that there must be things that don't just have possible being; there must be some things that have necessary being, things that *must* be.

This, then, is the first stage of the argument. Not everything can have merely possible being, or nothing at all would exist. Some beings simply must be.

In the second stage, Aquinas admits that some of these necessary beings may owe their necessity to another necessary being. But, using the same reasoning as he used for agent causation, he argues that this series of necessary dependencies could not go on forever. So there exists something that simply *must be* (period!)—something necessarily existing that doesn't owe its necessity to another, but is the cause of whatever is necessary in other beings. This being is in itself eternal and necessary in the most proper sense of the word.* And this being, "all men speak of as *God*."

---

*Compare to Avicenna's proof of the existence of God on pp. 302–303.

The Argument from Grades of Goodness in Things

Some things are found to be better, truer, more excellent than others. Such comparative terms describe varying degrees of approximation to a superlative; for example, things are hotter the nearer they approach what is hottest. So there is something which is the truest and best and most excellent of things, and hence the most fully in being; for Aristotle says that the truest things are the things most fully in being. Now *when many things possess a property in common, the one most fully possessing it causes it in the others: fire*, as Aristotle says, *the hottest of all things, causes all other things to be hot*. So there is something that causes in all other things their being, their goodness, and whatever other perfections they have. And this is what we call *God*. (*ST* 1a.3; *SPW*, p. 201)

This proof begins with the observation that the things we experience do not all have the same value. Some are better than others, some truer, some more excellent. All these comparative judgments, however, make sense only if we assume that in each case there is something that exemplifies those characteristics to a superlative degree.

Aquinas borrows the example of hot things from Aristotle: things are judged more or less hot as they more or less resemble the hotness of fire. (*We* know there are many things hotter than ordinary fire, but that just means we have a longer scale by which to make such comparative judgments; perhaps we would judge heat in comparison with the temperature of atomic fusion in stars and cold in comparison with absolute zero.) Something is better than another thing, then, to the extent that it more closely resembles the best. Something is truer if it is more like the truth, and so on.

But that is not the only point on which this argument rests. It is not just that the comparative degrees in such things are measured by the superlative; their very being depends on a superlative. As Aquinas says, fire is the cause of all hot things; and this must be actually existing fire. Again this is a *causal* proof. Aquinas is claiming that if there were not in existence a superlative degree of goodness, truth, and being, the existence of any lesser degree would be inexplicable. So there must be a maximum best, noblest, truest, and so on.

But since the lower degrees actually exist, the maximum must also really exist. This maximum is what explains the fact that we observe all these degrees of goodness in things: It is their cause. This maximum "best" of all things, Aquinas says, "we call *God*."

The Argument from the Guidedness of Nature

Goal-directed behaviour is observed in all bodies in nature, even those lacking awareness; for we see their behaviour hardly ever varying and practically always turning out well, which shows they truly tend to goals and do not merely hit them by accident. But nothing lacking awareness can tend to a goal except it be directed by someone with awareness and understanding: arrows by archers, for example. So everything in nature is directed to its goal by someone with understanding, and this we call *God*. (*ST* 1a.3; *SPW*, pp. 201–202)

This proof is often called "the argument from design." It is probably the one that turns up most often in popular "proofs" of the existence of God, and it has a famous history.* The key idea is that intelligent beings act purposefully, arranging means suitable to achieve ends they have in mind. We plant and harvest and store, for example, so that we will have food in the winter when we know there will be none to gather. We can look ahead to a situation that does not now exist and take steps to meet it satisfactorily.

This capacity is none too surprising in intelligent beings; perhaps it is even the main thing that constitutes intelligence. But when we look at the nonrational part of the world, we see the same thing. And this *is* surprising. We can hardly suppose that shaggy dogs, such as Newfoundlands, grow a thick coat in the fall and shed it in the spring because they foresee that otherwise they would be uncomfortable! Yet it is just as if they had planned that rationally.

---

*See particularly the discussion by David Hume ("Is It Reasonable to Believe in God?" in Chapter 19). Many people think that Darwinian modes of explanation tend to undermine the argument. A recent version of the argument, written with Darwinian evolution in mind, appears in *Darwin's Black Box* by biochemist Michael Behe.

We see the same apparently rational planning wherever we look. Moths are camouflaged to escape predators. Early-blooming snowdrop flowers have downward-facing blossoms, as if to shield themselves from snow. And so on. Things appear as if aiming to achieve certain goals. But we cannot believe that moths and flowers are doing that planning. Someone else must be doing it for them.

"Earth, with her thousand voices, praises God."

Samuel Taylor Coleridge (1772–1834)

Here is an analogy: People sometimes wonder whether computers are intelligent. Computers can certainly do some remarkable things: solve problems, rotate images in three dimensions on a screen, guide spacecraft. A standard reply is that though computers may look intelligent, the intelligence they display is not their own, but that of their designers and programmers. They have a "borrowed" intelligence.

Aquinas is claiming something similar for naturally existing beings. They do remarkable things, things that seem inexplicable in the absence of intelligence. We see their behavior "practically always turning out well." We cannot believe that they are themselves intelligent. So they must be directed to their goals "by someone with understanding."* This being, Aquinas says once more, "we call *God*."

Aquinas thinks, then, that by such reasoning from effects to causes we can prove the existence of God. In fact these five ways do not quite do that; they do not prove that there is one unique being who has all these traits: first cause of change, first efficient cause, a necessary being, a best being, and the intelligent designer of all the rest. But Aquinas thinks this is something reason can also prove. Such proofs provide a foundation on which Aquinas thinks all reasonable people should agree. If we think about the matter carefully, he contends, we should agree that atheism is irrational. This does

not necessarily mean that every rational person will be a Christian, for some of the truths recognized in Christian faith cannot be rationally demonstrated. But the message of the Bible and the doctrines of the church can rest on this foundation.

THE NATURE OF GOD

Suppose we are convinced. We know *that* God exists. How much do we know about *what* God is? Here Aquinas is quite cautious. This is representative:

> In this life we cannot see God's substance but know him only from creatures: as their non-creaturely and transcendent cause. So this is where our words for God come from: from creatures. Such words, however, will not express the substance of God as he is in himself, in the way words like *human being* express the substance of what human beings are in themselves. (*ST* 1a.13.1; *SPW*, p. 215)

Our finite minds cannot adequately grasp what God is. Still, we are not entirely ignorant. We know that God is the cause of all the features of the world we live in, and we know that God is the source of the very existence of anything at all. So what can we say about God on that basis?

The first and most important truth we know about God is that God *is*. If we ask, "Is what?" the most fundamental answer is that God is existence, being, itself. Like Augustine, Aquinas harks back to God's answer to Moses before the burning bush, when Moses asks who is sending him back into Egypt. God there says (Exodus 3:14), "I AM WHO I AM. . . . Say to the people of Israel, 'I AM has sent me to you.'" But Aquinas thinks philosophical reason also must reach this conclusion. (Here we have something on the second floor of our house!)

> God's existing doesn't differ from his substance. To be clear about this, note that when several causes producing different effects have also, besides those differing effects, one effect in common, then they must produce that common effect in virtue of some higher cause to which it properly belongs. For the effect properly belonging to a cause is determined by the cause's own proper nature and form; so that effects properly belonging to causes of diverse nature and form must differ, and any effect produced in common must properly belong not to any

---

*Note the persistence of the Greek assumption that where there is order there is intelligence. See pp. 14–15.

one of them but to a higher cause in virtue of which they act. . . . Now all created causes, distinguished by the effects that properly belong to each of them, have also one effect in common, namely existence: heat, for example, causes things to be—or exist as—hot, and builders cause there to be—or exist— houses. So they agree in causing things to exist, but differ in this: that heat causes heat and builders houses. So there must be some cause higher than all of them in virtue of which they all cause existence, a cause of which existence is the proper effect. And this cause is God. Now the proper effect of any cause issues from it by reproducing its nature. So existing must be God's substance or nature.
(*DPG* 7.2; *SPW*, pp. 205–206)

Because existence is (as we saw earlier) something added to essence, it cannot be just by virtue of their essence that fires or house builders produce their effects. True, their effects differ because of the kinds of things they are. But that they both bring into being something that actually exists cannot be ascribed to those kinds. That is something separate and requires a separate explanation. It must be that, in addition to being the kinds of things they are, they participate in being—which is not identical with either of them. This being, this existing, this energy or source of the existence of finite things cannot itself just be another finite thing. It is being itself. And that, Aquinas says, is the very substance of God. That's what God is—a great, unlimited, activity of existing. So Anselm is right after all: God's essence *is* his existence. But now we know that in a way appropriate to the kind of mind human beings have: as the cause of effects we are aware of through our senses.

Contrast this with Aristotle's conception of God. Aristotle thought of God as a pure form existing in isolated splendor, contemplating its own contemplation. Aquinas thinks of God as an efficient cause, an agent continually bringing into existence all the many things that do exist. This is a God who is involved in the creation, a God who might well (though this has not been proved) know the number of hairs on a man's head and be aware of the fall of every sparrow, a God who might love human beings with a love beyond all comparing. Whether we can go that far or not, this is clearly a God on whose creative activity we absolutely

depend; if for one moment God turned away from the creation, everything would disappear back into nothingness. Existence, remember, is something added to essence. And now we know that it is added by God, whose very essence is existence.

As for what else we might know about God, Aquinas says, first, that we can know a great deal about what God is not. Drawing on a long tradition of "negative theology," Aquinas says that God is not, for instance, finite, material, potential, a tree or star, bad, and so on. We can pile on negatives, and this is useful. But no list of negative terms, no matter how long, will tell us what God *is*.

A second truth about God derives from the way we know of God at all: as the cause of effects in creatures. In the world around us, we observe many good things; in their fullness, we could call them "perfections." Life is such a perfection, for example, or wisdom, or power. All of these derive their being from the source of all being. But we don't merely want to say, Aquinas reminds us, that God is the *cause of life or wisdom or goodness*.* We want to be able to say that in some sense, this great act of existing is itself alive and wise and good. How can we do that?

We have to acknowledge that what we mean by these terms is not derived from a direct acquaintance with God. We learn what "wise" means by experience with human or animal wisdom in this finite creaturely world, but we are also familiar with extensions of a word's meaning. For instance, "healthy" is a term that belongs to people in its primary application, but because of cause-and-effect relations with other things, the term is extended. We call certain foods "healthy" because they contribute to health in humans. Or we call urine or blood healthy because they are a symptom or sign of health. Aquinas thinks something of the same sort is true of the words we use about God.

So creatures having any perfection represent and resemble him . . . as effects partially resemble a cause

---

*Note that an atheistic materialist might want to acknowledge a cause for life or wisdom; she would, however, point to matter or the evolutionary process as that cause. What she would want to deny is that the cause is itself alive or wise.

of a higher kind though falling short of reproducing its form. . . . So the sort of words we are considering express God's substance, but do it imperfectly just as creatures represent him imperfectly.

So when we say *God is good* we mean neither *God causes goodness* nor *God is not bad*, but *What in creatures we call goodness pre-exists in a higher way in God*. Thus God is not good because he causes goodness; rather because he is good, goodness spreads through things. (*ST* 1a.13.2; *SPW*, p. 218)

Because the words we use of God get their original meaning from our experience in this world, they cannot mean exactly the same thing when they are applied to God. For instance, Socrates is wise and Socrates exists, but Socrates' wisdom is not the same thing as his existence. So

words expressing creaturely perfections express them as distinct from one another: *wise* for example, used of a human being expresses a perfection distinct from his nature, his powers, his existence, and so on; but when we use it of God we don't want to express anything distinct from his substance, powers, and existence. So the word *wise* used of human beings somehow contains and delimits what is meant; when used of God, however, it doesn't, but leaves what it means uncontained and going beyond what the word can express. Clearly then the word *wise* isn't used in the same sense of God and man, and the same is true of all the other words. No word, then, is said of God and creatures univocally. (*ST* 1a.13.5; *SPW*, p. 224)

A word is *univocal* when it is used with just one meaning. Aquinas denies that a word applied to both creatures and creator is used univocally. But it isn't used *equivocally*, either; that is, it's not the case that there is no connection between the meanings in the two cases, as there is between "bank" when used as a place to keep your money and "bank" as a place on which to stand while fishing. Rather,

these words apply to God and creatures by **analogy** or proportion. . . .

And this way of sharing a word lies somewhere between pure equivocation and straightforward univocalness. . . .

Whenever words are used analogically of several things, it is because they are all related to some one thing; so that one thing must help define the others. . . . In the same way then all words used

metaphorically of God apply first to creatures and then to God, since said of God they only express some likeness to creatures. Just as talking of a *smiling* meadow expresses a proportion: that flowers adorn a meadow like a smile on a man's face, so talking of God as a *lion* expresses this proportion: that God is powerful in his doings like lions in theirs. And so clearly we can't define what such words mean when used of God unless we refer to what they mean used of creatures. . . .

But, as we have seen, such names don't simply express God's causality, but his substance, for calling God *good* or *wise* doesn't only mean that he causes wisdom or goodness, but that these perfections pre-exist in him in a more excellent way. (*ST* 1a.13.5,6; *SPW*, pp. 224–227)

In this way Aquinas explains how we can talk intelligibly of God, while carefully preserving the ultimate mystery of God's being to creatures such as ourselves.

---

1. Why does Aquinas not accept Anselm's ontological argument for God?
2. According to Aquinas, from what basis must we argue if we are to prove God's existence?
3. Be sure to grasp the main points in each of the "five ways."
4. What is God's essence? How do we know?
5. How does analogy work in understanding God's nature?

Humans: Their Souls

Aquinas takes for granted the basic concepts involved in the Great Chain of Being idea, but he elaborates the higher reaches of the chain more than Augustine did.* God, as perfect being and goodness, is at the very top of the chain, separated from the highest of created creatures by an unbridgeable gap.

Below this gap are the **angels,** purely spiritual beings defined by a form or essence, but lacking any material substratum. Lacking any matter, angels also lack what individuates material things.

---

*Review Plotinus and Augustine's development of the idea of the Great Chain of Being, pp. 271–272.

(Remember that what makes this frog distinct from that frog is not its form, but the fact that it is composed of different matter.) Still, an angel is not, like God, a simple existence whose essence just is its existence. Like all created beings, angels are composite; they are made up of a form or essence plus existence. This lack of material stuff in spiritual intelligences means that there cannot be more than one angel of a given kind. To put it another way, each angel is an entire species in itself, every one differing from every other in essence—differing not as this dog differs from that dog, but as dogs differ from horses.

Human beings exist on the border between such pure intelligences and the material world, sharing something with beings both above and below them on the chain. This participation in higher and lower levels of being is already summed up, Aquinas thinks, in Aristotle's formula for humans: They are *animals* (material beings) whose distinctive characteristic is *rationality* (or intelligence).

Aquinas agrees substantially with Aristotle about soul and body. Because soul is the principle of life in things, there are various levels of soul. Plants have a kind of soul, which enables them to nourish themselves, grow, and reproduce. In addition to these powers, animals have sentient (sensitive) soul—that is, abilities to see and hear and so on, together with instincts and inclinations that draw them toward and move them away from things. Humans have rational soul, adding the abilities to abstract universals, think logically, and plan future actions in the light of goals. In all these ways, **soul** is the form of a body of a particular sort.

Aquinas adamantly insists that there are *not* three souls in a human being—vegetative, sensitive, and rational—as though we were composite beings made up of three substances.

> If we hold that the soul is united to the body as its substantial form, then the co-existence of several essentially different souls in the same body cannot be entertained. To begin with, an animal having several souls would not compose an essential unity, for nothing is simply one except by one form. Form gives being and unity. Were man alive by one form, namely by vegetable soul, and animal by another, namely by sensitive soul, and human by a third,

namely by rational soul, he would not be one thing simply speaking. (*ST* 1a.76.3; *PT*, pp. 204–205)

But a human being *is* one thing, and the rational soul incorporates and governs all the rest. This kind of holism means that features we in some way share with the lower animals—emotion and desire, for instance—are transformed into *human* emotion and desire. In us, emotion and desire involve conceptualizations impossible for a nonrational creature. We can, but a cat cannot, fear damage to our reputation or hope to meet someone we admire. Everything in us, even our bodily state, is affected by our dominant form, the rational form of a human soul.

We could put this point another way. The human body is not, in a living human being, a substance. Some philosophers—Plato comes to mind—have thought so and have thought of a human being as a kind of dual creature: a body conjoined for a time to a substantial soul. Aquinas will have none of this. Death is not one of the substances in a human being (the soul) departing the other (the body). A dead body is not, properly speaking, a human being, but something else entirely: a corpse. We may call it human by extension or by analogy, but because the corpse has lost the form of a human being, it is no longer literally correct to call the corpse human. A human body is not a thing on its own, but *material* for a human being, made into one substance by the human soul, which is its form.

> So the human soul is the form of the human body. Further, if soul inhabited body like a sailor his ship, it wouldn't give body or its parts their specific nature; yet clearly it does since when it leaves the body the various parts lose the names they first had, or keep them in a different sense; for a dead man's eyes are eyes only in the sense that eyes in a picture or a statue are, and the same goes for the other parts of the body. Moreover, if soul inhabited body like a sailor his ship the union of body and soul would be accidental, and when death separated them it wouldn't be decomposition of a substance, which it clearly is.* (*PDS* art. 1; *SPW*, p. 188)

---

*Descartes, in the seventeenth century, uses this same figure, also denying that the soul is like a sailor in a ship. But he has an even harder time than Aquinas in making it stick, since he thinks the soul is a separate substance in its entirety. See pp. 395 and 399.

Despite this insistence on the unity of a human being, however, Aquinas also agrees with Aristotle that a rational soul is not *just* the form of a human body, the way the soul of a lobster is just the form of life in a lobster. There is something substantial about a human soul after all, something akin to angelic intelligences.* He agrees, moreover, for essentially the same reason: Reasoning souls

> cannot share that special activity of theirs with any bodily organ, in the sense of having a bodily organ for thinking as an eye is the bodily organ for seeing. And so the life principle of a thing with understanding has to act on its own, with an activity peculiar to itself not shared with the body. And because activity flows from actuality, the understanding soul must possess an existence in and of itself, not dependent on the body. (*PDS* art. 1; *SPW*, pp. 187–188)

You can see Aquinas, like Augustine, struggling to unify two strands of thought that are not easy to harmonize. On the one hand, a man or woman is one substance, and the soul is its form. On the other hand, a human soul, by virtue of its capacity to abstract universals and reason with them, its ability to know virtually anything, is an intellectual substance in its own right, able to subsist even when the body is destroyed.†

On the one hand, a soul becomes a determinate, individual soul only by virtue of its intimate relation to the body because whatever is in a soul is conveyed there by the specific bodily sense experience of some individual human. On the other hand, it is the soul's possible subsistence without the body that gives it immortality. Although Aquinas has rational arguments for each part of this view, in the end it may be a matter of faith that these demands can be reconciled. He calls on the Christian doctrine of the resurrection of the body to do the job.

> Firstly, if we deny the resurrection of the body it isn't easy—indeed it becomes very difficult—to defend the immortality of the soul. The union of body and soul is certainly a natural one, and any

separation of soul from body goes against its nature and is imposed upon it. So if soul is deprived of body it will exist imperfectly as long as that situation lasts. . . . Secondly, what human beings desire by nature is their own well-being. But soul is not the whole human being, only part of one; my soul is not me. So that even if soul achieves well-being in another life, that doesn't mean I do or any other human being does. (*CC* 15:17–19; *SPW*, pp. 192–193)

"My soul is not me." This definitive rejection of Platonism means that even if my soul is a substance capable of existing after my body dies, *I* may not survive. For *my* survival, that soul must be the form of a body—my body. And to buttress this hope of immortality, Aquinas looks not to reason, but to the resurrection of Christ. Just as Christ's body was transformed into a heavenly body, so, Aquinas believes, will our bodies be also.

HUMANS: THEIR KNOWLEDGE

We have seen how humans can know something of God by (1) reasoning from effects to causes and (2) using analogies from common experience to partially describe this cause of existing things. But how do we come to have knowledge of those effects in the first place? As we have noted, knowing begins with sensing. How does sensing work? Take the eye, for example. An eye has the power to receive images of external things—their shape, color, texture, motion. These images are the sensible forms of the things we perceive.

Imagine you are stroking a cat that is purring contentedly on your lap. You see the cat stretch with pleasure, feel the softness of its fur, and hear the purr. Each of these sensible forms is received by the appropriate sense. Yet it is not three experiences you are having, but one. So these images must be united in what Aquinas (following Aristotle) calls your "common root sensitivity." The unified complex image formed in you is a particular item that mirrors a determinate, particular substance outside you: contented Tabby at a certain moment in time. When the cat jumps off your lap, your current sensory experience changes, but something is left behind in you. The proof is that you can later remember that experience, bring its images back

---

*See Aristotle on *nous*, pp. 206–208.
†See the fuller discussion in the following section, "Humans: Their Knowledge."

into consciousness, and, as it were, run the experience again. So images are stored in you somewhere; Aquinas (again following Aristotle) calls this storehouse *the imagination*.

Thus far described, our minds do not differ much from the minds of the higher animals, which also have sensitivity, imagination, and (limited) memory. But we have an additional capacity called **intellect.** Using intellect, we can form *ideas* from the images stored in imagination. And ideas are not just more images, not copies of images, but what the medievals called "universals."* **Universals** are features of things that can be expressed in language and formulated in definitions. So while our senses can take in the sensible form of Tabby and the imagination can store that image, it is the intellect that can abstract the universal features of this cat and all other cats and formulate the *idea* of a *cat*.

> The senses are bodily powers and know singular objects tied down by matter, whereas mind [intellect] is free from matter and knows universals, which are abstract from matter and contain limitless instances. (*ST* 1a.2ae. 2.6; *PT*, p. 231)

When this happens we have the form of the cat actually resident in the intellect itself. That's what a concept or idea of a cat is: the actual presence in the intellect of the very *form* that makes a cat a cat—only without making the intellect into a cat because the usual *material* for cats (flesh, bone, fur) is missing.

There might be a problem here. If our intellect deals in universals such as "small domestic feline" or "rational animal," which are true of limitless individuals, how is it possible for us to know particular things—Tabby or Socrates—that aren't pure forms? It is, after all the *matter* composing this cat or this human that make them the particular things that they are. But matter as such is unknowable; matter is what the intellect abstracts *from*. Aquinas solves this problem by noting that sensory images have two uses. They are the originals from which knowledge starts, but they are also needed when we think about particular things. We may be

able to know a lot about cats-as-such in terms of forms or universals, but if we want to direct our thought to Tabby in particular, we need to recall an image of Tabby to tie our thought down to her. The image, remember, is as particular as the individual that produced it and will ensure that we are indeed thinking about that specific cat. Knowledge of particulars, then, is possible; it will involve both universals and images, as when we say that Tabby is gray or that Socrates is wise.

Intellect has two distinguishable operations. In the first of these the intellect enjoys a simple apprehension of some object; it grasps, more or less adequately, the *whatness* of the object, its *nature*, or what Aquinas calls its **quiddity** (from the Latin for "what it is"). So a child learns to identify a cat and distinguish it from a dog. The child's idea of a cat is not false to the reality, but it is incomplete. An adult's idea is more adequate and a biologist's concept more adequate still. Our idea of what a cat is can expand and improve; typically, it does improve with continued experience of cats. In such a simple grasp of a nature, there is, properly speaking, no truth or falsity. It's just there in the intellect. (Compare Aristotle on truth not being applicable to *terms*, but only to *statements*, p. 185.)

In the second operation, which Aquinas calls "making connections and disconnections," the intellect unites ideas to make judgments about the things apprehended. Such judgments may be affirmative or negative. So we say, "All cats meow," or "Socrates is not stupid." With respect to judgments the concept of **truth** is in place.

> For the meaning of true consists in a matching of thing and understanding, and matching presupposes diversity, not identity. So the notion of truth is first found in understanding when understanding first starts to have something of its own which the external thing doesn't have, yet which corresponds to the thing and can be expected to match it. Now when articulating what things are, understanding possesses only a likeness of the external thing, just as the senses do when they take in the appearance of what they sense. But when understanding starts to make judgements about the thing it has taken in, then those are the understanding's own judgements not found in the thing outside, yet called true judgements in so far as they match what is outside. Now

---

*Contrast David Hume, who thinks ideas just are faint copies of images. See pp. 443–444.

understanding makes judgements about the thing it takes in when it says something about how it is or is not, and that we call understanding making connections and disconnections. . . . So that is why truth is found first in understanding making connections and disconnections. (*PDT* 1.2; *SPW*, p. 59)

Truth, then, just as in Aristotle, is a matter of correspondence or matching between judgments made by the intellect and the thing being judged. To say "Socrates is wise" is true, provided Socrates is wise. Otherwise, the statement is false.*

There also seem to be two powers in the intellect: an active power and a receptive power. The former does the abstracting; the latter stores the abstract ideas, functioning for the active intellect as imagination does for the senses. There must be such a passive power, Aquinas argues, because we can bring back into active consideration ideas that have not been present to the conscious mind for some time; these ideas have not completely disappeared but are potentially present, ready once again to play a role in current thinking. It is the active power of intellect that Aquinas believes is not and cannot be tied down to any bodily organ. It is to this agent intellect that he looks when he searches for a proof of the immortality of the soul. But the receptive intellect is equally important, lest our minds be restricted solely to awareness of the present moment.

It is very important to note that although intellect gets its material from the images stored in imagination, it is not those images that we know (at least not in the first instance). What we know are those hylomorphic objects that produced the images—the cat, the chair, the person sitting in the chair holding the cat.† We know them by virtue of, or by means of, these images. But the images are not the primary objects of knowledge.‡ True, we can reflect on our own mental operations, draw back and pay attention to the image as such. In general, however, what we know is not limited to

the contents of our minds. We know Tabby and Socrates and the fact that fire causes water to boil. None of these is a mental phenomenon.

This, then, is the account Aquinas gives of our knowledge of the material world. All our knowledge begins with what our senses reveal about it. This explains how we can know that the premises of his arguments for the existence of God are true. We begin from simple facts about the world—that things change, that one thing causes another, and so on. Starting there, Aquinas believes we can work back to that cause, which is its own existence, and the cause of whatever else there is.

---

1. On Aquinas' view, in what sense is the Psalmist right when he says we were created "a little lower than the angels"? (Ps. 8:5)
2. How does Aquinas explain the fact that a human being is one, unified thing?
3. Is the soul (agent intellect) immortal? Why?
4. What are universals? Give some examples.
5. How does the intellect acquire universals?

HUMANS: THEIR GOOD

Following Aristotle again, Aquinas holds that every finite substance tends naturally toward its perfection, toward realizing its potential. Actualization of a thing's potential is in fact the *good* for that thing. This natural teleology of final causes is present even in the inanimate world, but it is strikingly apparent in animals; they are always seeking something. This is especially true of human beings, who can scarcely sit still an hour without planning what to do next. We regard what we seek—rightly or wrongly—as good, as contributing to our perfection. We want dinner, or a movie, or exercise. These things are goals that move us to action, so we go to the kitchen or head toward the theater or change into our running shoes. We choose such actions as means to reach the goal, and we wouldn't engage in them if the goal didn't seem good to us.

This much seems mere common sense. But Aquinas pushes these thoughts in two directions. First, suppose we ask why we want exercise. We might answer, for the sake of health, which also

---

*See Aristotle's definition of truth, p. 187.

†On hylomorphism, see p. 301.

‡Contrast this "realism" about knowledge with the "empiricism" of John Locke, who says that the mind has "no other immediate object but its own ideas," p. 422.

seems good to us. Why do we want health? It must be for the sake of some further good. That such questions can be repeated leads us to ask, Is there any goal that we want simply for itself, not for the sake of something beyond it? Like Aristotle, Aquinas says that there is and identifies the goal as happiness (*eudaemonia*) or beatitude.* Whatever else seems good to us does so because it seems either to be a part of happiness or to contribute to our happiness. That it is good to be happy or blissful is beyond proving, but also beyond question.

Second, humans differ from other animals in being able to frame ideas in terms of universal concepts. We want dinner, but that concept can be filled out in a great many ways. Do we want steak, or chicken, or vegetables? Something simple or something fancy? Dinner is good, but that rather empty concept cries out for a multitude of decisions. A sheep that is hungry and is put in a green pasture faces no such quandaries; it simply starts eating the nearest grass. The sheep's actions are fairly closely determined by what its senses reveal in its immediate environment. Human action is unlike that because our universalizing intellect presents possibilities to us. Among these possibilities we must choose. And if you think "dinner" is a concept that can be filled out in numerous ways, consider "happiness."

We all want to be happy, then—to flourish, to fare well. This is a desire implanted in us by nature; whether that *should* be our goal is not up to us. (Though we have each asked many students, neither of us has ever found a single one who confessed to having as a goal being unhappy in life!) Happiness is a natural good.† We don't consider whether to take happiness as a goal, but only how to achieve that goal. This thinking eventuates in acts of will that produce actions.

> There is a desire for good in everything: good, the philosophers tell us, is what all desire. In things

*Note that happiness is no more just the *feeling* of happiness for Aquinas than it was for Socrates, Plato, or Aristotle. It is a condition of the person. Compare pp. 134, 175, and 209.

†Compare Plato's argument for morality in the *Republic*, which depends on precisely this premise. See p. 175.

without awareness this desire is called natural desire: the attraction a stone has for downwards, for instance. In things with sense-awareness it is called animal desire, and divides into capabilities of affective and aggressive feeling. In things with understanding it is called intellectual or rational desire: will. So created intellectual substances have wills. (*SCG* 2.47; *SPW*, p. 169)

Will, then, is a species of desire. It is differentiated from desire in general by being rational desire, desire that is informed by intellectual knowledge and reason. We, like sheep, may simply be attracted to food that is before us. But unlike sheep, we can also apply universal concepts in reasoning about food; we can say, "That's filled with saturated fats, and though I'm sure I would like it, I will not eat it." Such a decision, made in the light of rational knowledge, in the light of some goal that reason approves (such as health), is an act of will. Humans, by virtue of their intellectual nature, have wills.

What that means is that human beings are not at the mercy of their desires. They can choose which desires to satisfy and which to leave unsatisfied—and that means the will is free.

> Things lack freedom to decide either because they lack all judgement, like stones and plants which lack awareness, or because their judgements are fixed by nature, like nonreasoning animals. . . . But wherever judgement of what to do is not fixed by nature, there is freedom to decide. And all creatures with understanding are of this sort. For understanding takes in not only this or that good but the notion of good as such. . . . So all things with understanding have freedom of will deriving from understanding's judgement, and that is freedom of decision, which is defined as free judgement of reason. (*SCG* 2.48; *SPW*, pp. 170–171)

Aquinas means that we can evaluate particular goods (such as this rich, dark, sweet, chocolate cake) in the light of "good as such" and decide in the light of our more general good whether *this* good is one that should be chosen. The fact that we can do this means we are responsible for our actions. We are not simply determined to act by our immediate surroundings.

Aquinas distinguishes between *acts of a human* and *human acts*. A man does, in a sense, grow a beard every night. But whether he shaves it off in the morning or lets it grow is a matter for decision and the exercise of his will. Only the latter is properly called a *human act*. Why? Because only that is under the control of the form that makes him human: his rational nature. Suppose someone really would like to have a beard but his wife just hates beards. Then he must decide between incompatible goods—having a beard or pleasing his wife. He is free to decide either way. Whichever he does will be voluntary. What he decides will be willed in the light of intellectual reflection on overall goodness, and that will be not only something he is responsible for, but also a revelation of his character.

Before we discuss character (virtue and vice), however, we should ask, What makes an individual action good or bad?

> We should judge actions good and bad in the same way we do things, since what things do reflects what they are. Now a thing's goodness is measured by how fully it exists; for . . . good and existent are interchangeable terms. . . .* Full human being, for example, demands a complex of soul and body endowed with every ability and organ needed for knowledge and movement, and if an individual lacks any of this he would not exist fully. As existing he would be good, but as not fully existing he would lack goodness and be called bad: thus for blind men it is good to be alive, but bad to be without sight. . . .
>
> In a similar way then actions must be called good in so far as they exist, but in so far as they exist less fully than human actions should they will lack goodness and be called bad: if, for example, we don't do as much as we reasonably should, or do something out of place or the like. (*ST* 1a2e.18.1; *SPW*, pp. 343–344)

What actions would "exist less fully than human actions should"? Clearly, actions would not exist as fully human if they were not under the control of our intellectual, rational faculties—because those faculties are what make us distinctively human. Those actions, then, would lack goodness and would be called bad. Good actions are actions that flow from our nature, fulfilling and perfecting that nature.

---

*This is, you will recall, one of the principles of the Great Chain of Being idea.

This principle allows Aquinas to formulate the notion of a **natural law.** Everything in the created world, of course, expresses the divine reason, according to which it was designed. God's reason can be called an **eternal law,** and nothing can happen that is not permitted to happen by God's eternal law. In creating the world, God brought substances into being that have natures or essences of their own, and these natures incorporate within themselves something of the eternal law. A stone, for instance, naturally falls to earth. Sheep or wolves naturally act out their nature. Sheep eat grass, and wolves eat sheep; they have no choice. Human beings also have a given nature. But, as we have seen, our nature includes the capacity to formulate universals and to think about what to do in terms of them. This provides us with a freedom of action that stones and sheep and wolves lack. Unlike sheep and wolves, we can act in ways that are contrary to our nature, detrimental to it.

But we also have the capacity to know what the law of our nature is, together with a partial ability (even apart from the special grace of God) to act in accordance with it. How do we know what the natural law says? Its first principle, Aquinas tells us, is this: "Good should be done and evil avoided." Now this is not something that can be proved from more general principles, or it wouldn't be first. It is a practical parallel to that principle of intellectual life in general, the principle of noncontradiction, which says that two contradictory propositions cannot both be true. Though it cannot be proved, there does seem to be something incoherent in its denial. Since I always act for the sake of some good, for me to say, "Let me do evil," is equivalent to saying, "Let evil be good."*

Beyond this self-evident principle, we know natural law by observing the natural inclinations of things. For example, all human beings experience

---

*Notice that the first natural law does *not* say, "What I think is good should be done and what I take to be evil should be avoided." Aquinas does think that we have no alternative but to do the best we know, so if, after reflection, our conscience tells us to do something that is in fact wrong, that is what we should do. But that doesn't mean we are doing the right thing.

the drive to continue in existence. Our reason apprehends this universal drive as good. It is good to continue to live—so murder is wrong. And it is part of our nature to eat when hungry—so feeding the hungry is good. Humans have a natural tendency to mate and care for their children—so marriage, intended to provide a safe and lasting environment to meet these goals, is a good thing. In general, law is what reason declares to be fitting in the light of the nature of something. By using our intellect, reflecting on the nature of human beings and other essences, we can discern the image of God's eternal law that is resident in the things he has created. Aquinas believes that in addition to murder and adultery, reason tells us that drunkenness, gluttony, suicide, lying, homosexuality, and the breaking of promises are contrary to nature. The argument is that all of these, in one way or another, violate the natural inclinations of a being with a nature like ours.

> Now since everything subjected to God's providence is measured by the standards of his eternal law, as we have said, everything shares in some way in the eternal law, bearing its imprint in the form of a natural tendency to pursue the behaviour and goals appropriate to it. Reasoning creatures are subject to God's providence in a special, more profound way than others, by themselves sharing the planning, making plans both for themselves and for others; thus sharing in the eternal reasoning itself that is imprinting them with their natural tendencies to appropriate behaviour and goals. And it is this distinctive sharing in the eternal law by reasoning creatures that we call the law we have in us by nature. (ST 1a2ae.91.2; SPW, p. 418)

In addition to the eternal law, which is part of the nature of God, and the natural law, which is resident in our own natures, Aquinas distinguishes two further kinds of law. The third kind is **human law.** This is law that is devised and promulgated by an authority in a community for the good of that community—or, at least, that is its essence. When human law is in accord with that goal, it mirrors the eternal and natural law. But, as humans are subject to sin—rulers no less than the rest of us—human law may deviate from natural goodness and often does. Where human law deviates from natural law,

Aquinas says, it is not truly law at all, but lawlessness. Why? Because it is not in accord with reason, which is the source of all law.

Human law, then, must meet four conditions to be true law: (1) It must issue from a legitimate authority that has responsibility for a community; (2) it must be promulgated publicly so that people can know what is and is not acceptable; (3) it must further the good of that community; and (4) it must be in conformity with reason. In terms of these criteria, Aquinas distances himself from any notion of law as simply what the sovereign declares or whatever is customarily accepted.*

Finally, there is **divine law.** This is law that is beyond our natural capacities to discover but is revealed to us in the Scriptures. An example might be the New Testament commandment to believe in the Lord Jesus Christ in order to be saved. Reason cannot figure this out for itself; but, Aquinas holds, it is necessary to enable us to reach our final bliss. Here we have something on the third floor of the house.

We can now return to the issue of character. Like Aristotle, Aquinas holds that we shape our characters by developing habits or dispositions to act in certain ways. And we build such habits by acting in those ways. These habits of character are virtues and vices. *Virtues* incline us to act in ways that reason approves of; when you have a virtue, it is easy to do what otherwise is difficult. *Vices* are contrary habits, which incline us to ignore or neglect the discernment of good by our reason.

Virtues are important to us. The reason is that, though we are naturally oriented toward bliss or happiness, it is not so clear what contributes to that blessed state. Our rational faculties have (in addition to the task of finding truth) the practical role of choosing actions suitable to promoting our blessedness. But we are not, as the angels are, pure intellectual beings. We also feel the attractions of

---

*Aquinas thereby aligns himself with those who claim that there is a criterion for judging human laws, from Heraclitus and Antigone through Plato, Aristotle, and the Stoics. He sets himself against Sophist understandings of law and justice as wholly conventional and against notions of law as simply what the ruler declares. Compare Hobbes, p. 415.

the senses and the pleasures of the body, and these animal propensities have some independence of our intellect. Thus, they need to be habituated to the good—trained, if you like, to obey their rightful master, reason. That's just what a **virtue** is: a habit of choosing wisely in light of the ultimate end of blessedness. Aquinas, again following Aristotle, says that the soul rules the body like a tyrant. He means that if I will to raise my arm, my arm (other things being equal) simply obeys and goes up. But our desires and emotions are different; they

> don't obey my reason's slightest signal, but have their own ways of acting, which are sometimes at odds with reason: reason rules my affections and my aggressions, Aristotle goes on to say, *democratically*, like free people are ruled, who have their own will in certain areas. (*ST* 1a2ae.56.4; *SPW*, p. 406)

As we see in this quote, Aquinas divides our desires and emotions into two large classes: the *affective* and the *aggressive*.*

> The object of our affective ability [is] anything sensed as straightforwardly good or bad, pleasurable or painful. But sometimes the animal has a hard struggle attaining such good or avoiding such bad things, because they are not within its immediate power, and then good or bad, seen as challenging or requiring effort, becomes an object of our aggressive ability. . . .
>   . . . the function of aggressive feelings in animals is to remove obstacles preventing affective feelings from pursuing their objective, obstacles that make good difficult to attain or bad difficult to avoid. So all aggressive feelings end up in affective feeling, so that even aggressive feelings *are accompanied by* the affective feelings of *joy or sadness.* (*ST* 1a2ae.23; *SPW*, pp. 163–164)

One function of virtue is to order these emotions and desires toward the good—that is, toward blessedness. So we have, Aquinas says, a virtue specific to the affective emotions, those that are immediately attracted by pleasure and repelled by pain. This virtue is **temperance,** which brings the impulse to pursue the pleasant and avoid the

painful under the tutelage of practical reason. Temperance prevents us from indulging too much in pleasures, keeping us on an even keel and aimed at the blessed state.

With respect to the aggressive feelings, we have a second virtue: **fortitude** or *courage*. Fortitude makes us tenacious in pursuing what our reason determines to be truly good, so that we don't give up easily in the face of obstacles. It is firmness or resolve when temptations arise to distract us from our ultimate good by promising some minor gain. Fortitude is being steadfast rather than wimpy, determined rather than reckless. It keeps us from being overpowered by fear on the one hand or being rashly bold on the other hand.

In addition to these two virtues governing our emotional life, there is **justice,** which ensures that we are not inclined to take more than our share of goods. Distributive justice does not apply so much to what we feel as to what we do. It has an intrinsic reference to others. To be just is to be fair and equitable in allotting to each person what is due to him or her. A just person, for instance, will not even be tempted to steal money lying in plain sight on someone's desk; to a just person, the possibility of stealing simply doesn't appear in the list of options for action. To truly have the virtue of justice is for it to be *easy* to leave the money there.

Finally, there is **prudence,** a virtue that pertains more directly to the intellect than do the others. Prudence involves habits that lead us to think again when we are being hasty and keep in mind the overall good when we are deliberating.*

These four (temperance, fortitude, justice, and prudence) do not exhaust all the virtues there are, but Aquinas calls them the **cardinal virtues,** the most important of them. If human beings were simply animal beings, with no hope of immortality, these would be sufficient to produce whatever degree of happiness is attainable in this life. If we were restricted to the first two floors of the house, there would be nothing to add. But if it is rational to believe that our good is not exhausted by such

---

*The traditional terms for these are the *concupiscible* and the *irascible* desires and feelings.

*Compare Aristotle on "practical wisdom," pp. 213–214.

bliss as this life offers, blessedness also requires the **theological virtues** of faith, hope, and love.

Here Aquinas self-consciously goes beyond Aristotle. He says that Aristotle understands perfectly well what we require for *eudaemonia* (happiness). But then, confined to this world, he resigns himself to making do with less. Happiness, Aristotle says, is activity of soul, in accord with reason, over an entire lifetime, which cannot be taken away from us, together with modest external goods—the most satisfying activity being that of intellectual contemplation. But Aristotle realizes that happiness in this world is fragile, as his reference to Priam makes clear.* In this life, we are ever subject to fortune, and though he rightly says our highest happiness is in contemplation, he acknowledges that even this cannot be continuously engaged in. So if this life is all there is, we can at best approximate the goal that we all have.

What would true happiness consist in, then? It would have to be total immersion in absolute goodness forever—in the presence of and being suffused by that original energy or existence that *is* goodness and is the source of all good. That's what we all want, though we don't usually realize it. That's the goal of all our desiring. But we are talking of the mystical vision of God. Philosophy can perhaps point to that bliss, but philosophy cannot supply it. That's a gift reserved for God's grace.

Because we are not self-sufficient in our existence, Aquinas writes, we have a "twofold ultimate goal." We are aiming at an internal perfection, which can only come when we deeply and wholeheartedly love God above all else and love our neighbors as ourselves. And we are aiming at unity with God, the source of all goodness and so also of that very perfection within.

> Bliss then, the ultimate human goal, will be twofold: one within, the ultimate perfection human beings can attain, a created bliss; and one without, union with which causes that bliss within, and this is God himself, an uncreated bliss. (*CPLS* Bk. 4, 49; *SPW*, p. 328)
>
> Now the activity of seeing God, which we hold human bliss to be, cannot be measured by time:

neither in itself, since it has no before and after, nor on the side of the seer or the seen, since both exist outside change, . . . for seeing God transcends the native power of all creatures and is something no creature can attain by nature. What properly measures it is eternity itself; and the seeing of God, bliss itself, is thus eternal life. (*CPLS* Bk. 4, 49; *SPW*, p. 332)

---

1. What is the good for humans?
2. In what way does a human being have a will, rather than just a set of desires, like the lower animals?
3. Is the human will free? Why?
4. What distinguishes an act of a human being from a human act?
5. What does Aquinas mean by the natural law? How can we know what the natural law is?
6. Why are the virtues important to us?
7. Explain each of the four cardinal virtues. What does each put in order? And to what end?
8. What is the final source of blessedness for human beings?

Ockham and Skeptical Doubts—Again

Since Augustine rebutted skepticism in the late fourth century, there had been a broad consensus in the West that human minds were capable of knowing the truth, even if they sometimes disagreed about what constituted the truth.* God had created the world, and he created human beings in his own image. It would not have been suitable for God to mismatch reality and the mind. And Christian thinkers held that it was through Wisdom, the logos, the second person of the Trinity, that everything was created. So it was natural to suppose that the patterns in reality could be reproduced in the mind.

It is true that our minds are finite and limited. We cannot discover the whole truth on our own. But God has graciously come to our aid; he has revealed to us the truths necessary for our salvation, which are beyond our finite grasp. These revealed truths, which Catholic philosophers accepted on the authority of the Scriptures and the church, are

---

*See p. 212.

*Review Augustine's arguments on pp. 267–269.

not in conflict with the truths we can discover on our own. How could they be, since both come ultimately from the same God? Revealed truth supplements our rational knowledge, completes it, and provides an overall framework within which all correct believing and knowing are carried on.

We must add two further notes to this happy picture.

1. Knowledge is understood in that very strong classical sense delineated by Plato when he distinguishes it from opinion.* In medieval philosophy, the requirement that knowledge "stays put" or "endures" is understood to mean that it involves *absolute certainty*. If you *know* something, you are certain of it. As with Plato, this feature is correlated with the fact that knowledge is something for which reasons can be given. The reasons are sometimes based on logic, sometimes on experience, and sometimes on the Scriptures—often on a combination of them. But there is always "an account" that can be given.

2. Knowledge, and the certainty that goes with it, is crucially important. Your eternal salvation depends on getting it right. That is why **heresy**—erroneous belief—is so terrifying. The difference between correct, or orthodox, belief and heresy is the difference between *heaven* and *hell*. So it is not just an attempt to satisfy Aristotelian "wonder" that motivates the medieval theologians and philosophers.† Getting it right has an intensely personal and practical aspect.

All this is common ground in the thirteenth century. On these foundations Thomas Aquinas builds a remarkably comprehensive system of thought. The kind of confidence in the intellect that Aquinas expresses has perhaps not been seen since the time of Aristotle himself.

But this systematic synthesis, so marvelous in its way, was already under threat in the fourteenth century. Doubts raise their ugly heads once again: doubts not about some detail, but about the very foundation that has been taken for granted in the

centuries since Augustine. It is even more surprising to learn that these doubts have their source not, as you might suspect, among some atheist or agnostic folks who can't accept the claims about revealed truth, but among theologians whose orthodoxy (at least on central issues) is beyond question.[5]

"I believe in one God, the Father Almighty," begins the Nicene Creed. What does this mean? During the medieval period, God's **omnipotence** is understood to mean that he can do anything that is not self-contradictory. He cannot make a cube with only five sides, since by definition a cube has six sides. Nor can he make something that did happen not happen; for in this case it would be true of some event x that x both happened and did not happen—and that is contradictory. But since contradictory expressions do not describe real possibilities, this is no limitation on God's power. God can do anything that is possible. For any state of affairs that can be given a consistent description, then, God can realize that state of affairs. This doctrine is important partly because it protects the possibility of miracles.

Among those who derive some surprising consequences from this doctrine is **William of Ockham** (born in the 1280s and died about 1349). Ockham was English, taught at Oxford, and was embroiled in some nasty confrontations between his Franciscan order and the pope. Like all the major philosophers of the period, he thinks of himself first and foremost as a theologian. He is also a very acute logician, and any adequate treatment of Ockham's thought would have to include his logic. But we will concentrate on what he says about the omnipotence of God—specifically, on the impact this doctrine has on views of the world and our knowledge of it.

Consider the following case. You are sitting at a table, in good light, looking directly at a tangerine about three feet in front of your eyes. You are wide awake, not under the influence of any drugs, and are paying attention to what is before you. This seems to be the most favorable sort of case we can imagine for knowing something. We would ordinarily say that you know that there is a tangerine on the table.

---

*See pp. 149–151.
†See Aristotle on wonder, p. 197.

But what does your knowledge consist in? It is clearly some state of yourself—what Ockham calls an "intuitive cognition." In standard cases, we think, this state is caused in part by the tangerine and in part by your sense organs and intellect. The first part of the cause is a matter of how the world is—that there happens to be a tangerine on the table. The second part is a matter of how you are—where you are, whether your eyes are open, whether you have learned what a tangerine is, and so on. In the standard case, your "intuitive cognition" of the tangerine depends both on the actual existence of a tangerine on the table and on a suitable state within you. Ockham accepts this.

But now consider the impact that the doctrine of God's omnipotence has on this case. God, remember, can do anything that is not self-contradictory. This means that he can cause to happen anything that does not have an inconsistent description. God has created a world that operates as we have described in the foregoing standard case. But could God *directly* cause you to have that "intuitive cognition" of the tangerine? In the standard case, your experience is caused by the presence of the tangerine, but could God cause this experience without the mediation of the actual piece of fruit?

He certainly could, since it is not self-contradictory to imagine him doing so. The presence of that piece of fruit on the table neither entails nor is entailed by your "intuitive cognition" of it. Either, so far as logic goes, could exist without the other. So, God could cause you to have such an experience even in the absence of the tangerine.

Evidently, then, our conviction that we *know* that the tangerine exists—even in this most favorable case—is mistaken. For knowledge, remember, involves absolute certainty that could not possibly be mistaken. But if God can produce in us the internal state that is usually caused by the tangerine even in the absence of the tangerine, there is a possibility that our "intuitive cognition" is mistaken.

At best, our belief that there is a tangerine in front of us is merely *probable* belief. It amounts to no more than what Plato calls "opinion." But since all our knowledge of the world rests ultimately on such favorable cases of "intuitive cognition," the claim to know is seriously undermined.

Ockham does not draw the completely skeptical conclusion that knowledge is impossible for us. But these reflections deal a serious blow to confidence in our ability to find such absolute knowledge. And, as you can see, the blow comes from a consideration of God's omnipotence.

A similar conclusion follows about the causality we claim to find in the world. A piece of cloth is brought near a flame and starts to burn. How are we to explain the burning? It might be possible for God to cause it directly, so that our usual account in terms of the causal efficacy of the fire would be mistaken.* Again, we can give only probable explanations of why things happen in the world. It seems that our explanations might always be mistaken. And if that isn't skepticism itself, it moves us toward skeptical doubts, especially if one insists that knowledge must involve absolute certainty.

This produces an interesting situation. For a thousand years thinkers assumed that reason and revelation are compatible, that reason can supply foundations—with certainty—for revelation to build on. Philosophy, the pursuit of wisdom by our human wits, has been treated as the "handmaiden" of theology, which in turn is the "queen" of the sciences. And suddenly the suspicion arises that perhaps natural reason and experience are not well suited for this task!

Let us ask what effect this has on attempts to prove the existence of God. Ockham himself thinks that a certain form of proof is still possible, but let us consider some propositions put forward in the late fourteenth century by Pierre d'Ailly, a cardinal of the church. He is discussing Aristotle's argument for a first mover (which was adapted by Aquinas in his "first way").† And he considers what a "captious debater" could say.

---

*We have here an anticipation of one of the most influential of all treatments of causality, that by David Hume in the eighteenth century. Hume does not depend on the doctrine of God's omnipotence; and the skeptical consequences are more determinedly drawn. See "Causation: The Very Idea," in Chapter 19.

†See again pp. 320–321.

1. It is not unqualifiedly evident that something is moved; movement may be only apparent. . . .
2. Even if we grant that an object is in motion, we do not have to grant that it comes from some other object.
3. Granted that all motion originates in another thing and granting that there is no infinite series of movers, we cannot infer a first unmoved mover, for the first mover might be unmoved for the present but not absolutely unmovable.
4. We cannot exclude the possibility that there is a circularity of causes and effects, i.e., A causes B, B causes C, and C causes A.
5. We cannot be sure that there is no infinity of essentially ordered causes. For God by His absolute power could create such an infinite series.
6. It is not evident that if something exists anew, it was produced.
7. It is very difficult to explain what it means for one thing to be effected or produced by another thing.[6]

This piling up of alternative possibilities that have not been definitively excluded seriously undermines our confidence in the "proof." At the very least, it shows us that a defender of the argument will have to do a lot more work if the argument is to succeed.

It is important to note that d'Ailly does not intend to call the existence of God into question. Far from it. We know God exists on the authority of the Scriptures and the church. Rather, such reflections serve to undermine confidence in our natural ability to substantiate such truths apart from authority—at least with the certainty necessary for faith. (The cardinal allows that a *probable* argument for God's existence can be constructed.) Skepticism such as this, then, casts us more firmly than ever into the arms of the church, which has such truths in its care. The moral is this: Aristotle and those who, like him, rely on our natural reason should be approached with caution.

It seems then that the late Middle Ages is busily undoing the grand synthesis of classical and Christian thought of the earlier Middle Ages. When several more ingredients are added to this mix—namely, the scientific revolution, the humanism of the Renaissance, and the impact of the Reformation on the church—the modern era in philosophy will begin.

---

1. What assumptions about knowledge do thinkers in the late Middle Ages commonly make?
2. What Aristotelian views were condemned as heretical?
3. What effect did this condemnation have?
4. What impact does Ockham's reflection on God's omnipotence have on our claim to know something?
5. What impact does it seem to have on proofs for the existence of God?

FOR FURTHER THOUGHT

1. If you think Anselm's argument is faulty, write a brief explanation of what, exactly, is wrong with it.
2. What do you think about the prospects for proving that there is a God? (Don't just react. Give a reasoned explanation for your answer.)
3. Can God make a stone so heavy that he can't lift it? If he can't, does that mean his power is limited?
4. If our life is limited to this world, does that mean true happiness is impossible?

KEY WORDS

Anselm	soul
ontological argument	intellect
God	universals
reductio ad absurdum	quiddity
essence	truth
existence	will
Constantine the African	natural law
Toledo School of	eternal law
Translators	human law
Thomas Aquinas	divine law
disputations	virtue
Averroës (ibn Rushd)	temperance
double truth	fortitude
analogy	justice
angels	prudence

cardinal virtues
theological virtues
heresy

omnipotence
William of Ockham

NOTES

1. Jasper Hopkins, *A Companion to the Study of St. Anselm* (Minneapolis: University of Minnesota Press, 1972), 17.

2. Quotations from Anselm's *Proslogium*, in *St. Anselm: Basic Writings*, trans. S. N. Deane (La Salle, IL: Open Court, 1962), are cited in the text by chapter number.

3. Quotations from Thomas Aquinas are from one of the following:

   St. Thomas Aquinas: Philosophical Texts, trans. Thomas Gilby (London: Oxford University Press, 1951), abbreviated as *PT*, or

   Aquinas: Selected Philosophical Writings, trans. Timothy McDermott (New York: Oxford University Press, 1993), abbreviated as *SPW*.

References are first to the source in Aquinas, then to page numbers in these collections. References to the works of Aquinas are as follows:

ST: Summa Theologica
DT: Commentary on Boethius' De Trinitate
DPG: Disputations on the Power of God
PDS: Public Disputations on the Soul
CC: Commentary on St. Paul's First Letter to the Corinthians
PDT: Public Disputations on Truth
CPLS: Commentary on Peter Lombard's Sentences
SCG: Summa Contra Gentiles

4. Patterson Brown, "Infinite Causal Regression," in *Aquinas: A Collection of Critical Essays*, ed. Anthony Kenny (London: Macmillan, 1969), 234–235.

5. We are especially indebted in this section to Julius R. Weinberg's *Short History of Medieval Philosophy* (Princeton, NJ: Princeton University Press, 1964).

6. Cited in Weinberg, *Short History of Medieval Philosophy*, 287–288.

CHAPTER

16

FROM MEDIEVAL TO MODERN EUROPE

It is not clear just when the modern era begins. But it cannot be denied that something of immense significance happens in Europe in the sixteenth and seventeenth centuries that changes life and thought startlingly. This turning point changes the kinds of questions that Western philosophers ask and the methods they use to answer them. To understand these later philosophers, we need to step back a bit and look at the broader changes in Europe. Though we are interested primarily in the era's intellectual ferment, we cannot help but note some of the social, political, and economic factors that make this an age of change. It is useful to start with a review of the medieval picture of the world.

The World God Made for Us

Europeans in the late Middle Ages largely shared the same picture of the world, though they differed about details.[1] The universe, they thought, is a harmonious and coherent whole, created by an infinite and good God as an appropriate home for human beings, for whose sake it was made. Furthermore, humans have secure access to knowledge of this world and their place in it, both through divine revelation and through philosophical proof. For the Christian faithful in Latin Europe, the Catholic Church is the supreme guardian of that knowledge and Aristotle's philosophy is accepted as almost gospel truth. It is difficult for us now to put ourselves in the place of medieval men and women and to see the world as they saw it. But let us try.

It will help if we set aside all we have learned in school about the structure of the universe and attempt to recapture a more direct and naive interpretation of our experience. Consider the sky as you see it on a clear day or night. If you look *at* it, rather than *through* it, you will almost certainly conclude that it has a certain shape. It is *something*, and it has roughly the shape of an upside-down bowl. It is the roof of the earth, the "firmament" of Genesis 1 that God created to separate the primeval waters and make a place for dry land and living creatures. This view of the heavens is very common among primitive people and among children, too. We have to *learn* that the sky is not a thing.

Medieval Europeans had already progressed considerably beyond this simplistic view of the sky, though they continued to see it as a thing whose nature is defined in relation to earth. For one thing, they had inherited the Ptolemaic model of the universe developed by the Greeks and refined in the Islamic world, according to which earth sat, unmoving, at the center of the universe, surrounded by a set of concentric spheres containing the various heavenly bodies.* Thus, for medieval Europeans, the universe literally revolves around the earth and its inhabitants.

Adding to the Ptolemaic model, medieval Christians believed that beyond the fixed stars lay a realm called the **Empyrean,** the place of perfect fire or light; it is the dwelling place of God and the destination of saved souls. (Note that heaven, in this view, has a physical location. From any place on earth, it is *up*.) By contrast, Aristotle had denied that there was anything beyond the fixed stars—no matter, no space, not even a void.

In this universe, everything has its natural place. The earth is the center toward which heavy objects naturally fall. The heavy elements, earth and water, find their natural place as near this center as they can. The lighter elements, air and fire, have a natural home between the earth and the sphere of the moon. But these four elements are continually being mixed up with one another and suffer constant change.

This change is explained by the motions of the heavens.† Aristotle supplies a mechanism to explain such change. The outermost celestial sphere rotates at great speed, as it must to return to the same position in only twenty-four hours. (Compare the speed at the inside of a merry-go-round with that at its edge.) This motion drags the sphere of Saturn (just inside it) along by friction; and this process is repeated all the way to the spheres of the sun and moon. These then produce changes in the air and on the earth: the tides, the winds, and the seasons, for example, and the generation of plants and animals. On this basis, medievals believed that signs in the heavens—comets and

eclipses, for instance—are omens that need interpretation. Virtually every astronomer is also an astrologer; as late as the seventeenth century, Kepler, recognized to possess unusually accurate astronomical data, is consulted for horoscopes, and reference to astrological phenomena is common in the work of Dante and Chaucer. Everything in the heavens is significant because it all exists for the sake of humankind.

Here we come to the heart of the medieval worldview. Earth is not only the physical center of the universe; it is also the religious center. For on this stationary globe lives the human race, made in the image of God himself, the summit of his creative work. The universe revolves around human beings figuratively as well as literally. Earth is the stage whereon humans act out the great drama of salvation and damnation. It is on Earth that humans fall from grace. It is to Earth that God's Son comes to redeem fallen men and women and lead them to that heavenly realm in which they can forever enjoy blessedness in light eternal.

The eleventh-century German philosopher **Hildegard of Bingen** (1098–1179) articulates this worldview in the course of explaining a mystical vision she claimed to experience late in her life. She describes the vision itself as a series of concentric circles, with humanity at the center:

Then a wheel of marvelous appearance became visible. . . . At the top of the wheel . . . there appeared a circle of *luminous fire*, and under it there was another circle of *black fire*. . . . Under the black circle appeared another circle as of *pure ether*. . . . Under this ether circle was a circle of *watery air*. . . . Beneath this circle of watery air appeared another circle of *sheer white clear air*. . . . Under this sheer white clear air, finally, there appeared still another *thin stratum of air*. . . . In addition, in the middle of the sphere of thin air was seen a sphere, which was equally distant all around from the sheer white and luminous air. . . . In the middle of the giant wheel appeared a human figure. . . . Above the head of this human figure the seven planets were sharply delineated from each other. Three were in the circle of luminous fire, one was in the sphere of black fire beneath it, while another three were farther below in the circle of pure ether. (*BDW* II.1)[2]

*Review the description on p. 299 for a more detailed picture of the Ptolemaic model of the cosmos.

†See the pre-Socratic speculations about the vortex, p. 12.

Along with the vision, Hildegard heard a "voice from the sky," which said,

> God has composed the world out of its elements for the glory of God's name. God has strengthened it with the winds, bound and illuminated it with the stars, and filled it with the other creatures. On this world God has surrounded and strengthened human beings with all these things and steeped them in very great power so that all creation supports the human race in all things. (*BDW* II.2)

Hildegard earned her fame as a theologian—among many other things—in no small part by interpreting such mystical experiences to support and explain Catholic doctrine. Her interpretations combine Christian and Aristotelian themes. For instance, the concentric circles of Hildegard's vision represent the medieval Christian understanding of the physical universe, but in Aristotelian fashion, she explains that the "circle of luminous fire at the top . . . indicates that fire, as the first element, is at the top because it is light" (*BDW* II.4). And most important,

> Humanity stands in the midst of the structure of the world. For it is more important than all other creatures which remain dependent on that world. Although small in stature, humanity is powerful in the power of its soul. . . . Thus persons who are believers have their existence in the knowledge of God and strive for God in their spiritual and worldly endeavors. . . . It is God whom human beings know in every creature. For they know that he is the Creator of the whole world. (*BDW* II.15)

God created the universe for humanity, Hildegard is saying, and in return, human beings live to seek and exalt God.

Over two centuries later, the Italian poet Dante would express the moral implications of this view of the universe.* His great poem, *Divine Comedy*, recounts Dante's imaginary journey across the universe, led first by Virgil and later by Beatrice. As we follow that journey we learn both physical and religious truths, inextricably linked. Let us trace the outline of that journey.

---

*Dante's *Divine Comedy* was written in the first decades of the fourteenth century.

Dante begins his poem by telling us that he had lost his way and could not find it again. (Suggestion: read the poetry aloud.)

> Midway life's journey I was made aware
> That I had strayed into a dark forest,
> And the right path appeared not anywhere.
> Ah, tongue cannot describe how it oppressed,
> This wood, so harsh, dismal and wild, that fear
> At thought of it strikes now into my breast.
> —*Inferno* 1.1–6[3]

The ancient poet **Virgil** appears and offers to lead him down through hell and up through purgatory as far as the gates of heaven. There Virgil will be supplanted by another guide, as the pagan poet is not allowed into paradise. A vision of these moral and religious realities, embedded as they are in the very nature of things, should resolve Dante's crisis and show both Dante and his readers the right path forward.

We can read this complex allegory with an eye only to the values it expresses, but there is little doubt that Dante means its cosmology to be taken with equal seriousness. The point we need to see is that, for medieval thinkers like Hildegard and Dante, the cosmos is not an indifferent and valueless place; every detail speaks of its creator, who inscribed the "right path" in its very structure.

We can do no more than sketch that structure. There are three books in the poem—*Inferno*, *Purgatorio*, and *Paradiso*—each of which explores a specific part of the physical and moral/religious universe. To begin their journey into hell (the inferno), Virgil leads Dante *down*—deep into the earth. Hell is a complex place of many layers. After an antechamber in which the indifferent reside (offensive both to God and to Satan), Dante and Virgil cross the river Acheron and find hell set up as a series of circles, descending ever deeper into the earth. As they descend through these circles, Dante finds souls that have committed ever more serious sins and suffer ever more terrible punishment amid ever more revolting conditions. The first circle is limbo, in which are found the virtuous pagans, including Homer and Aristotle; this is Virgil's own home. Here there is no overt punishment; only the lack of hope for blessedness.

Descending from limbo, they find the damned in circles of increasingly awful punishments, corresponding to their sins:

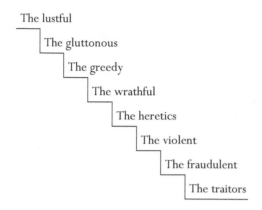

These last are frozen up to their necks in ice at the very center of the earth, guarded by Satan—the arch traitor—in whose three mouths are the mangled bodies of Judas, Brutus, and Cassius.

From that deepest circle of hell, Virgil and Dante climb up through a passage in the earth until they come out on the opposite side from which they began. There they find themselves facing a mountain that rises to the sky. This is the mountain of purgatory, where those who will ultimately be saved are purified of their remaining faults. Here there are seven levels (corresponding to the "seven deadly sins"), each populated by persons whose loves are not yet rightly ordered.* These people have repented and will be saved, but they still love earthly things too much, not enough, or in the wrong way. From the lower levels to the higher, the unpurged sins are ranked from more to less serious, those highest on the mountain being farthest from hell and closest to heaven. Let us list them in that "geographical" order, so that we can imagine Virgil and Dante mounting from the bottom of the list to the top:

---

* For the concept of a proper ordering of one's loves, see Augustine, p. 283.

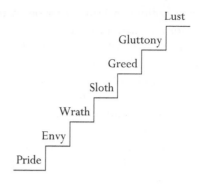

Those who dwell at each level are purging their predominant passion by suffering penances of an appropriate kind. The proud, for example, are bowed down by carrying heavy stones, so that they can neither look arrogantly about nor look down on their fellows. It is worth noting that the "spiritual" sins of pride, envy, and anger are judged to be more serious (farther from heaven) than the "fleshly" sins of gluttony and lust; this ranking roughly corresponds to the evaluations of church fathers such as Augustine, for whom pride is the root of all sin.*

At the top of the purgatorial mountain, Virgil disappears, and **Beatrice,** who represents Christian love, takes his place. She transports Dante to the lowest celestial sphere, that of the moon. She answers Dante's question about why the moon seems to have shadows on it and in the process gives a fine description of the celestial realm:

> The glory of Him who moveth all that is
> Pervades the universe, and glows more bright
> In the one region, and in another less. . . .
> "All things, whatever their abode, [*Beatrice says*]
> Have order among themselves; this Form it is
> That makes the universe like unto God.
> Here the high beings see the imprint of His
> Eternal power, which is the goal divine
> Whereto the rule, aforesaid testifies.
> In the order I speak of, all natures incline
> Either more near or less near to their source
> According as their diverse lots assign.
> To diverse harbors thus they move perforce
> O'er the great ocean of being, and each one
> With instinct given it to maintain its course."
>
> —*Paradiso* 1.1–3, 103–114

---

*For Augustine on pride, see pp. 280–281.

The key notions in Dante's vision of the universe are order, harmony, justice, and, finally, love. The poem ends with Dante trying to describe, inadequately, he admits, the vision of God. This vision is both intelligible and emotional. Its object both explains the universe and draws Dante's soul toward itself. In the end, imagination fails to communicate the glory.

Such is the world for late medieval Catholics: harmonious, ordered, finite, displaying the glories of its creator. Physics, astronomy, and theology are one in a marvelous integration of life and knowledge. Everything in the universe embodies a goal and purpose set within it by the divine love, which governs all. To understand it is to understand this purpose, to gain guidance for life, and to see that absolutely everything depends on and leads to God.

---

1. Describe the medieval European picture of the physical universe.
2. Why, given that picture of the universe, is it appropriate for Virgil and Beatrice to take Dante on a tour of the world to show him "the right path"?
3. What do the levels in hell and purgatory show us about medieval views of virtue and vice?

Reforming the Church

The worldview Dante expresses in his great poem was institutionalized in the church, the keeper and protector of Christian truths and the harbor of salvation for those at sea in sin. But the institutional church had strayed far from the precepts of humility and love enjoined by Jesus. It had become a means of securing worldly prestige, power, and wealth for those clever and ruthless enough to bend it to their will.

The church in the West was dominated by the papacy in Rome, whose occupants had, through the centuries, brought a great variety of incomes, privileges, and powers under their control. More than one pope during this period exceeded in influence, wealth, and power any secular prince, king, or emperor. His court was more splendid, his staff more extensive, and his will more feared than theirs. A king could torture and kill the body; but the pope

had the power to cast the soul into hell. A king who displeased the pope might find his entire land under a papal "interdict," which meant that no masses and no sacraments could be celebrated there—a dire threat indeed for those who depended on them for their eternal salvation.

No one doubts—and few doubted even then—that the church had grown corrupt. Dante had set several popes, bishops, friars, and priests in the Inferno. There had been numerous attempts at reform. Saint Francis and Saint Dominic had tried to recapture the purity of Christian life by establishing monastic orders that renounced wealth and power. Unfortunately, their very success ensured the acquisition of wealth and power, with all the inevitable outcomes.

Unless they could be assimilated into the structure of the church, as the monastic orders were, reformers were harshly dealt with, often on the pretense of stamping out heresy. The church regarded heresy as "the greatest of all sins because it was an affront to the greatest of persons, God; worse than treason against a king because it was directed against the heavenly sovereign; worse than counterfeiting money because it counterfeited the truth of salvation; worse than patricide and matricide, which destroy only the body." If a heretic recanted under torture, he "might be granted the mercy of being strangled before being burned at the stake."[4] The followers of John Wycliffe in England (the Lollards) were sent to the stake in 1401. Jan (John) Hus of Bohemia was burned in 1415. Savonarola of Florence was hanged and then burned in 1498.

Meanwhile the church, clutching its pomp and privileges, went from corruption to corruption. Here are a few examples. Pope Alexander VI (1431–1503) had four illegitimate children (including Cesare and Lucrezia Borgia), though clerical celibacy was the rule. His successor, Pope Julius II, led his own troops in armor to regain certain papal territories. When Julius died, the church selected a scion of the Medici family as his successor, whereupon the new pope supposedly exclaimed, "The papacy is ours. Let us enjoy it."[5]

Albert of Brandenburg (1490–1545), already bishop of two districts, aspired to be also archbishop of Mainz, which would make him the top cleric in Germany. The price demanded by the pope was high—ten thousand ducats. Because his parishes could not supply that fee, he paid it himself, borrowing the money at 20 percent interest from the banking house of Fugger. It was agreed that "indulgences" (more about these later) would be sold in his territories; half of the income he could use to repay the loan and half would go to Rome to help build Saint Peter's Cathedral.

Affronts such as these called forth a steady stream of critical responses. In the eyes of many, they discredited the claim of the church to be the repository of truth about God and man. But it was not until the protests of **Martin Luther** (1483–1546) that the situation was ripe for such moral objections to make a real difference. Luther's appeal for reform coincided with a new assertion of the rights of nations against domination by the church. Princes heard not only the cry for religious reform but also an opportunity to stop wealth and power from flowing interminably to Rome.*

Luther was a monk troubled about his sins and in mortal terror of God's justice. His sins did not in fact seem so terrible in the eyes of the world, for he was a monk of a most sincere and strict kind. But he had early seen the point that God looks not at externals, but at motivations; and he could not be sure that his motives were pure.† No matter how much he confessed, he was never confident that he had searched out every tinge of selfishness, greed, lust, and pride. And these sins the righteous God would judge. Luther did rigorous penances, going so far as to scourge himself. But he suffered agonies of doubt and self-accusation: Had he done enough to make himself worthy of salvation?

> Though I lived as a monk without reproach, I felt that I was a sinner before God with an extremely disturbed conscience. I could not believe that he was placated by my satisfaction. I did not love, yes,

I hated the righteous God who punishes sinners, and secretly, if not blasphemously, certainly murmuring greatly, I was angry with God.[6]

He was assigned by his superior to study the Bible and become a professor of theology. As he wrestled with the text of the Psalms and the letters of Saint Paul, it gradually dawned on him that his anxieties about sin were misplaced. He was, to be sure, a sinner. But the righteous God, whom Luther had so much feared, had sent Jesus, his Son, the Christ, precisely to win forgiveness for such sinners. This was an undeserved gift of **grace** and needed only to be believed to be effective. Even though one was not just, God "justified" the unjust person by means of the cross and resurrection of Christ, who had taken upon himself the sins of the world. Salvation did not have to be *earned*! It was a *gift*!

> I began to understand that the righteousness of God is that by which the righteous lives by a gift of God, namely by faith. And this is the meaning: the righteousness of God is revealed by the gospel, namely, the passive righteousness with which merciful God justifies us by faith, as it is written, "He who through faith is righteous shall live." Here I felt that I was altogether born again and had entered paradise itself through open gates. . . .
>
> Thus that place in Paul was for me truly the gate to paradise. Later I read Augustine's *The Spirit and the Letter*, where contrary to hope I found that he, too, interpreted God's righteousness in a similar way, as the righteousness with which God clothes us when he justifies us.[7]

With this insight, the Reformation was born. The power of this idea was first demonstrated in relation to the indulgences being sold under the authority of the pope and Archbishop Albert of Mainz. An **indulgence** was a piece of paper assuring the purchaser of the remission of certain penalties—perhaps in this life, perhaps in purgatory, and perhaps escape from hell itself. The practice of promising such spiritual benefits in return for worldly goods can be traced back to the Crusades. Popes offered heavenly blessings in return for military service in the Holy Land against the Turks. But for those who could not serve or were reluctant to go, a payment in cash to support the effort was accepted instead. This practice had

---

*For the Reformation, see "Reformation," Wikipedia, https://en.wikipedia.org/wiki/Reformation.

†See the discussion of Jesus on pp. 257–260 and the similar point made by Augustine on pp. 277–278 and 283. It is perhaps significant that Luther was a monk of the Augustinian order.

proved so lucrative that, as we have seen, it was extended for other purposes—including the repayment of loans for the purchase of an archbishopric!

The set of indulgences sponsored by Albert were peddled in 1517 by a Dominican monk named Tetzel, who advertised his wares with a jingle:

> As soon as the coin in the coffer rings,
> The soul from purgatory springs.[8]

Although prohibited in Wittenberg, where Luther was both parish priest and teacher of theology, indulgences were sold near enough that his parishioners traveled to buy them. They came back boasting that they could now do what they liked, for they were guaranteed heaven. Luther was troubled. Was this Christianity—to buy salvation for a few gold coins? Didn't this make a mockery of repentance and the attempt to reform one's life? Indeed, didn't it make a mockery of God's grace, which was sold for worldly gain like any other commodity? On the eve of All Saints' Day 1517, Luther posted **ninety-five theses** on the door of the Castle Church. He had drafted them quickly and meant them only to form the substance of a scholarly debate among theologians. But they caused a sensation, escaped his control, and were published and disseminated widely. Among the theses were these:

> 27. There is no divine authority for preaching that the soul flies out of purgatory immediately the money clinks in the bottom of the chest.
>
> . . .
>
> 36. Any Christian whatsoever, who is truly repentant enjoys plenary remission from penalty and guilt, and this is given him without letters of indulgence.
>
> . . .
>
> 43. Christians should be taught that one who gives to the poor, or lends to the needy, does a better action than if he purchases indulgences.[9]

Let us think about thesis 27 for a moment. Here Luther says there is no "divine authority" for Tetzel's rhyme. What does he mean by this? There clearly was ecclesiastical authority for it, in the sense that the pope and an archbishop supported the sale of indulgences. But for Luther, who had spent five years trying to understand the Bible and

who knew well the works of the early church fathers, particularly Augustine, this does not settle the matter at all. Popes and councils of the church had often disagreed with one another and with the words of Scripture. So the fact that the highest church authority of the day supported the sale of indulgences does not, in Luther's eyes, make the practice *right*. Only a *divine* authority can determine that.*

What does Luther mean by "divine authority"? Above all, he means the words and deeds of Christ. But secondarily, he means the testimony of the apostles who had known Jesus or of those (like Paul) to whom Christ had specially revealed himself. So Luther appeals to the Bible, that collection of the earliest records we have of the life and impact of Jesus. This was Luther's authority, against which even the words of popes had to be measured.

It is precisely here that his conflict with the established church is sharpest. In a certain sense, the church does not deny that Scripture is the ultimate authority; however, Scripture needs to be interpreted. And the proper interpretation of Scripture, according to the church, is that given by the church itself in the *tradition* that reaches back in a long, unbroken historical sequence to the apostles. Ultimately the authority to interpret Scripture resides in the pope, the successor of the apostle Peter, of whom Jesus had said, "You are Peter, and on this rock I will build my church" (Matt. 16:18).

In a great debate at Leipzig in 1519, Luther went as far as to say,

> A simple layman armed with Scripture is to be believed above a pope or a council without it.

His opponent in the debate replied,

> When Brother Luther says that this is the true meaning of the text, the pope and councils say, "No, the brother has not understood it correctly." Then I will take the council and let the brother go. Otherwise all the heresies will be renewed. They have all appealed to Scripture and have believed

---

*Compare the speech in which Antigone defends her action defying the king's command, p. 65.

their interpretation to be correct, and have claimed that the popes and the councils were mistaken, as Luther now does.[10]

This exchange gives the tenor of the arguments that continued for about four years while the church was trying to decide what to do about the rebel. Luther appeals to the Scriptures against the pope and the ecclesiastical establishment. They in turn point out the damaging consequences—heresy and the destruction of the unity of Christendom—if Luther is allowed to be right.

In 1521, Pope Leo X formally excommunicated Luther from the church, making the split between "Protestants" and "Roman Catholics" official. There is much more to this story, but we have enough before us to draw some lessons relevant to our philosophical conversation.

For more than a thousand years there had been a basic agreement in the West about how to settle questions of truth. Some questions could be settled by reason and experience; the great authority on these matters for the past few centuries had been Aristotle, whom Aquinas had called simply "the philosopher." But above these questions were others—the key questions about God and the soul and the meaning of life—which were answered by *authority*, not reason. And the authority had been that of the church, as embedded in the decision-making powers of its clergy, focused ultimately in the papacy.

When Luther challenges this authority, he attacks the very root of a whole culture. It is no wonder that he faced such opposition. His appeal to the authority of Scripture offers a different standard for settling those higher questions. And we can now see that the crisis Luther precipitates is a form of the old skeptical *problem of the criterion*, one of the deepest and most radical problems in our intellectual life.* By what criterion or standard are we going to tell when we know the truth? If a criterion is proposed, how do we know that it is the right one? Is there a criterion for choosing the criterion?

---

*For a discussion of the problem about the criterion, see pp. 248–250.

"By humbly raising the questions he had in 1517, and then by responding to the attacks that followed as truthfully as carefully as he could, Luther ended up cracking the great edifice of medieval Christendom in twain. And for good and for ill both, out of the opening the future itself seemed to fly."

Eric Metaxas (b. 1963)

In the religious disputes of the following century, each side busies itself in demolishing the claims of the other side. On the one hand, Protestants show that if we accept the Catholic criterion, we can be sure of nothing because—as Luther points out—popes and councils disagree with one another. If there are contradictions in the criterion itself, how can we choose which of the contradictory propositions to accept?

Catholics, on the other hand, argue that reliance on one's individual conscience after reading Scripture could not produce certainty, for the conscience of one person may not agree with the conscience of another. Indeed, it is not long before the Protestants are as divided among themselves as they are united in opposing the Catholics.

The consequence is that each side appeals to a criterion that is not accepted by the other side, but neither can find a criterion to decide which of these criteria is the correct one!

This quarrel is political as much as it is intellectual and religious. A series of savage and bloody quasi-religious wars ensues, in which princes try not only to secure territories, but also to determine the religion of the people residing in them.* Indeed, one outcome of these wars is that southern Germany is to this day overwhelmingly Catholic, whereas northern Germany is largely Protestant.

---

* Here you may be reminded of Socrates' point in *Euthyphro* 7b–d: The gods do not quarrel about length and weight and such matters, but about good and justice. Where there are accepted criteria (rules of measurement, for instance) for settling disputes, wars are unlikely. But where there are apparently irresolvable disagreements, involving appeal to differing standards, might may seem like the only thing that *can* make right.

What the Reformation does, philosophically speaking, is to unsettle the very foundations of medieval European culture. Though the reformers only intend to call an erring church back to its true and historical foundations, the consequences are lasting divisiveness, with those on each side certain of their own correctness and of the blindness (or wickedness) of their opponents.

---

1. In what ways had the church grown corrupt?
2. What does Luther find in the New Testament that leads to his objection to indulgences?
3. To what authority does Luther appeal?
4. How did the challenge posed by the Reformation raise again the problem of the criterion?

Revolutions

Like the great cathedrals of Europe, the comforting, coherent medieval view of the universe had been built up slowly over many generations. Just as the Reformation was shaking the foundations of that worldview, new intellectual currents began to erode them. These included humanism, skepticism, and a new scientific approach to the world. By the end of the sixteenth century, these currents would leave behind a vastly different intellectual landscape.

HUMANISM

That magnificent flowering of arts and letters we call the **Renaissance** is greatly influenced by the rediscovery of classical literature—poetry, histories, essays, and other writings—that followed the recovery of Aristotelian philosophy and science.* These Greek and Roman works breathe a spirit quite different from the extreme otherworldliness of monk's vows, on the one hand, and the arid disputations of scholastic theologians on the other. They present a model of style, both in language and in life, that resonates in the city-states of fourteenth- and fifteenth-century Italy. In time,

a rather diffuse movement called **humanism** spreads northward into the rest of Europe.

Some of the humanists are churchmen, but many are not. They belong to that aristocratic stratum of society that has leisure to cultivate the arts, paint, compose, or write. They all tend to see a profound harmony between Christianity and the classics, just as Augustine and Aquinas did. But those theologians regard pagan philosophy as subordinate to Christian understanding. Even in Dante, the greatest of the pagans reside in hell, albeit in the tamest circle. Many humanists, however, equate faith with virtue and move toward a kind of universalism: The virtuous sage is blessed, whether he knows of Christ as savior or not.

In a dialogue called "The Godly Feast," printed in 1522, **Erasmus** (the "prince of humanists") has one of the characters say,

> Whatever is devout and contributes to good morals should not be called profane. Sacred Scripture is of course the basic authority in everything; yet I sometimes run across ancient sayings or pagan writings—even the poets—so purely and reverently and admirably expressed that I can't help believing their authors' hearts were moved by some divine power. And perhaps the spirit of Christ is more widespread than we understand, and the company of saints includes many not in our calendar.[11]

One of his partners in the conversation, on being reminded of Socrates' attitude at his death, exclaims,*

> An admirable spirit, surely, in one who had not known Christ and the Sacred Scriptures. And so, when I read such things of such men, I can hardly help exclaiming, "Saint Socrates, pray for us!"[12]

In another dialogue, "The Epicurean," Erasmus argues that those who spend their lives pursuing fine food, sex, wealth, fame, and power in a quest for pleasure actually miss the greatest pleasures: those of righteousness, moderation, an active mind, and a calm conscience. It is Epicurus, of course, who

---

* For the Renaissance, see "Renaissance," Wikipedia, http://en.wikipedia.org/wiki/Renaissance.

*Contrast this with Dante's vision two hundred years earlier, in which virtuous pagans are consigned—at best—to limbo. See *Inferno*, canto IV. For the last moments of Socrates' life, see *Phaedo* 114c–118a.

holds that pleasure is the one true good.* It follows that the *successful* Epicurean—the one who gets the most pleasure out of life—will live righteously and moderately, preferring the approval of God to the satisfaction of bodily appetites. But these are precisely the virtues cultivated by the Christian!

> If people who live agreeably are Epicureans, none are more truly Epicurean than the righteous and godly. And if it's names that bother us, no one better deserves the name of Epicurean than the revered founder and head of the Christian philosophy [Christ], for in Greek *epikouros* means "helper." He alone, when the law of Nature was all but blotted out by sins, when the law of Moses incited to lusts rather than cured them, when Satan ruled in the world unchallenged, brought timely aid to perishing humanity. Completely mistaken, therefore, are those who talk in their foolish fashion about Christ's having been sad and gloomy in character and calling upon us to follow a dismal mode of life. On the contrary, he alone shows the most enjoyable life of all and the one most full of true pleasure.[13]

This gives us an insight into why these thinkers are called humanists.† Their concern is the development of a full and rich human life—the best life for a human being to live. Their quest is stimulated by the works of classical antiquity, which they read, edit, translate, and imitate with eagerness. They live, of course, in a culture dominated by Christianity and express that quest in basically Christian terms, but their interests focus on the human. To that end they recommend and propagandize for what they call "humane studies": an education centering on the Greek and Latin classics, on languages, grammar, and rhetoric. They are convinced that "the classics represent the highest level of human development."[14] The ideal is a person who can embody all the excellences a human being is capable of: music, art, poetry, science, soldiery, courtesy, virtue, and piety.

In 1486, a twenty-three-year-old Italian wrote a preface to nine hundred theses that he submitted for public debate. As it turned out, the debate was never held, but the *Oration on the Dignity of Man* by Giovanni **Pico della Mirandola** has seldom been equaled as a rhetorical tribute to the glory of being human. We could say it is the apotheosis of humanism. Pico finds the unique dignity of man in the fact that human beings alone have no "archetype" they are predetermined to exemplify. Everything else has a determinate nature, but it is man's privilege to be able to *choose* his own nature. He imagines God creating the world. All is complete, from the intelligences above the heavens to the lowest reaches of earth.

> But, when the work was finished, the Craftsman kept wishing that there were someone to ponder the plan of so great a work, to love its beauty, and to wonder at its vastness. Therefore, when everything was done. . . . He finally took thought concerning the creation of man. But there was not among His archetypes that from which He could fashion a new offspring, nor was there in His treasurehouses anything which He might bestow on His new son as an inheritance, nor was there in the seats of all the world a place where the latter might sit to contemplate the universe. All was now complete. . . .
> At last the best of artisans ordained that that creature to whom He had been able to give nothing proper to himself should have joint possession of whatever had been peculiar to each of the different kinds of being. He therefore took man as a creature of indeterminate nature and, assigning him a place in the middle of the world, addressed him thus: "Neither a fixed abode nor a form that is thine alone nor any function peculiar to thyself have we given thee, Adam, to the end that according to thy longing and according to thy judgment thou mayest have and possess what abode, what form and what functions thou thyself shalt desire. The nature of all other beings is limited and constrained within the bounds of laws prescribed by Us. Thou, constrained by no limits, in accordance with thine own free will, in whose hand We have placed thee, shalt ordain for thyself the limits of thy nature. We have set thee at the world's center that thou mayest from thence more easily observe whatever is in the world. We have made thee neither of heaven nor

---

*See pp. 236–237.

†Note that Erasmus here follows the lead of much Greek thought, from Homer to Epicurus. Pursuit of virtue is recommended on the basis of *self-interest*. Why be moral? Because you will be happier that way.

of earth, neither mortal nor immortal, so that with freedom of choice and with honor, as though the maker and molder of thyself, thou mayest fashion thyself in whatever shape thou shalt prefer. Thou shalt have the power to degenerate into the lower forms of life, which are brutish. Thou shalt have the power, out of thy soul's judgment, to be reborn into the higher forms, which are divine."

O supreme generosity of God the Father,
O highest and most marvelous felicity of man!
To him it is granted to have whatever he chooses,
to be whatever he wills.[15]

Man is "maker and molder" of himself, able "to have whatever he chooses, to be whatever he wills." * Pico exclaims, "Who would not admire this our chameleon?"[16] With such possibilities open to them, it is no wonder that human beings should develop in so many different ways. Along with the theme of an essential unity that runs through humanity, the diversity of individuals comes to be valued more and more. **Individualism,** the idea that there is value to sheer uniqueness, begins to counter the uniformity of Christian schemes of salvation. Portrait painters strive to capture the unique character of each of their subjects, and variety and invention flourish in music and literature.

Some of the humanists, both men and women, also begin to question traditional views about women and their role in society. In the medieval period, women were largely excluded from public and intellectual life. They could participate in the great conversation only by entering a convent, as Hildegard did. Beginning in the fourteenth century, women outside the church began publishing books on a range of topics, often anonymously. **Christine di Pizan**'s *The Book of the City of Ladies*, published in 1405, offers a prominent early example. Through an allegory about a "City of Ladies" inhabited by famous women from history, di Pizan defends women against the negative depictions so common in medieval society, argues for education for women, and advocates for an expanded role for women in European society. In works like di Pizan's, the humanists begin the centuries-long

labor of freeing women from the constraints that society had imposed on them.

Finally, the humanists recapture some of the confidence that had characterized Athenians of the Golden Age. Human failings are more apt to be caricatured as foolishness (as Erasmus satirically did in *Praise of Folly*) than to be condemned as sins. And this reveals a quite different attitude and spirit. Though the humanists do not deny sin and God's grace, they tend to focus on our capability to achieve great things. As often happens in such cases, they thereby help to make great things happen.

---

1. What rediscoveries stimulate the movement we know as Renaissance humanism?
2. Describe the ideal human life, as pictured by the humanists.
3. In what feature of human beings does Pico della Mirandola find their "dignity"?

SKEPTICAL THOUGHTS REVIVED

Just as the recovery of Greek and Roman poetry, histories, and essays inspired Renaissance humanism, another rediscovery revived a different ancient tradition.[17] In 1562 the first Latin edition of a work by Sextus Empiricus is published, and within seven years all his writings are available.* Sextus called his views "Pyrrhonism," after one of the earliest Greek skeptics, Pyrrho. In this period of intellectual upheaval, Pyrrhonism strikes a responsive chord in more than one thinker who considers that an impasse has been reached, but we will focus on just one man: Michel de Montaigne.

Montaigne (1533–1592) was a Frenchman of noble birth who, after spending some years in public service as a magistrate, retired at the age of thirty-eight to think and write. His essays are one of the glories of French literature. We are interested not in his style, however, but in his ideas—ideas that a great many people begin to find attractive in the late sixteenth and early seventeenth centuries.

---

*Compare with the existentialism of Simone de Beauvoir and Jean-Paul Sartre in Chapter 28.

*For a discussion of the skeptical philosophy of Sextus, see Chapter 11.

His point of view comes out most clearly in a remarkable essay called *Apology for* **Raymond Sebond**. Sebond had been a theologian of the fifteenth century who had exceeded the claims of Augustine, Anselm, and Aquinas by claiming not only that the existence and nature of God could be proved by reason, but also that rational proofs could be given for *all* the distinctive doctrines of Christianity. This is an astonishing claim; if true, it would mean that clear thinking alone would suffice to convince us all (Jews, Muslims, and pagans alike) that we should be Christians. No one had ever gone so far before. As you can imagine, Sebond attracted critics like clover attracts bees.

Montaigne's book appears to defend Sebond against his critics. ("Apology" here means "defense," as it does in the title of Plato's account of Socrates' trial.) It is an unusual defense, however; and Sebond, had he been alive, might well have exclaimed that he needed no enemies with friends like this!

Montaigne's strategy is to demonstrate that Sebond's "proofs" of Christian beliefs are not in the slightest inferior to reasons offered for any other conclusion whatsoever. He claims that Sebond's arguments will

> be found as solid and as firm as any others of the same type that may be opposed to them. . . .
>
> Some say that his arguments are weak and unfit to prove what he proposes, and undertake to shatter them with ease. These must be shaken up a little more roughly. . . .
>
> Let us see then if man has within his power other reasons more powerful than those of Sebond, or indeed if it is in him to arrive at any certainty by argument and reason. (*ARS*, 327–328)[18]

Montaigne, then, is going to "defend" Sebond's claim to prove the doctrines of the faith by showing that his arguments are as good as those of his critics—because *none* of them is any good at all!

The essay is a long and rambling one, but with a method in its madness. It examines every reason that has been given for trusting our conclusions and undermines each with satire and skeptical arguments. Are we capable of knowing the truth because of our superiority to the animals? In example after example, Montaigne causes us to wonder whether we are superior at all. Have the wise given us insight into the truth? He collects a long list of the different conceptions of God held by the philosophers and then exclaims,

> Now trust to your philosophy . . . when you consider the clatter of so many philosophical brains! (*ARS*, 383)

He adds,

> Man is certainly crazy. He could not make a mite, and he makes gods by the dozen. (*ARS*, 395)

Can we not at least rely on Aristotle, the "master of those who know"? But why pick out Aristotle as our authority? There are numerous alternatives.

> The god of scholastic knowledge is Aristotle. . . . His doctrine serves us as magisterial law, when it is peradventure as false as another. (*ARS*, 403)

Surely, however, we can depend on our senses to reveal the truth about the world.

> That things do not lodge in us in their own form and essence, or make their entry into us by their own power and authority, we see clearly enough. Because, if that were so, we should receive them in the same way: wine would be the same in the mouth of a sick man as in the mouth of a healthy man; he who has chapped or numb fingers would find the same hardness in the wood or iron he handles as does another. . . .
>
> We should remember, whatever we receive into our understanding, that we often receive false things there, and by these same tools that are often contradictory and deceived. (*ARS*, 422–424)

Well, maybe the world around us just isn't the kind of thing we can know. But surely reason can demonstrate truth about right and wrong?

> Truth must have one face, the same and universal. If man knew any rectitude and justice that had body and real existence, he would not tie it down to the condition of this country or that. It would not be from the fancy of the Persians or the Indians that virtue would take its form. . . .
>
> But they are funny when, to give some certainty to the laws, they say that there are some which are firm, perpetual and immutable, which they call natural, which are imprinted on the human race by the

condition of their very being. And of those one man says the number is three, one man four, one more, one less: a sign that the mark of them is as doubtful as the rest. . . .

It is credible that there are natural laws, as may be seen in other creatures; but in us they are lost; that fine human reason butts in everywhere, domineering and commanding, muddling and confusing the face of things in accordance with its vanity and inconsistency. . . . *

See how reason provides plausibility to different actions. It is a two-handled pot, that can be grasped by the left or the right. (*ARS*, 436–438)

Finally Montaigne gives us a summary of the chief points of skeptical philosophy. Whenever we try to justify some claim of ours, we are involved either in a *circle* or in an *infinite regress* of reason giving. In neither case can we reach a satisfactory conclusion.

To judge the appearances we receive of objects, we would need a judicatory instrument; to verify this instrument, we need a demonstration; to verify the demonstration, an instrument: there we are in a circle!

Since the senses cannot decide our dispute, being themselves full of uncertainty, it must be reason that does so. No reason can be established without another reason; there we go retreating back to infinity. . . .†

Finally, there is no existence that is constant, either of our being or of that of objects. And we, and our judgment, and all mortal things go on flowing and rolling unceasingly. Thus nothing certain can be established about one thing by another, both the judging and the judged being in continual change and motion. (*ARS*, 454)

Montaigne remarks that if the senses do not simply record external realities (as Aristotle assumes,

using the image of a seal impressing its form on the wax), then our ideas may not correspond at all to those realities. Even worse, we are never in a position to find out whether they do or not. We may be in the position of having only pictures, without ever being able to compare these pictures to what they are pictures of. Here is that depressing and familiar image of the mind as a prisoner within its own walls, constantly receiving messages but forever unable to determine which of them to trust and utterly incapable of understanding what is really going on. This image plagues many modern thinkers.

Like all radical skeptics, Montaigne is faced with the question of how to manage the business of living. To live, one must choose, and to choose is to prefer one course as better than another. But this seems to require precisely those beliefs (in both facts and values) that skeptical reflections undermine. Montaigne accepts the solution of Protagoras and Sextus Empiricus before him of simply adapting himself to the prevailing opinions. We see, he says, how reason goes astray—especially when it meddles with divine things. We see how

when it strays however little from the beaten path and deviates or wanders from the way traced and trodden by the Church, immediately, it is lost, it grows embarrassed and entangled, whirling round and floating in that vast, troubled, and undulating sea of human opinions, unbridled and aimless. As soon as it loses that great common highroad it breaks up and disperses onto a thousand different roads. (*ARS*, 387)

. . . since I am not capable of choosing, I accept other people's choice and stay in the position where God put me. Otherwise I could not keep myself from rolling about incessantly. Thus I have, by the grace of God, kept myself intact, without agitation or disturbance of conscience, in the ancient beliefs of our religion, in the midst of so many sects and divisions that our century has produced. (*ARS*, 428)

You can see that skepticism is here being used as a defense of the status quo. Montaigne was born and brought up a Catholic. No one can bring forward reasons for deserting Catholic Christianity that are any better than Raymond Sebond's

---

*Note that Montaigne is making essentially the same point as Pico (p. 349). There are no determinate laws for human nature. But whereas Pico takes this to be the *glory* of man, Montaigne draws from it a *despairing* conclusion: The truth is unavailable to us.

†Here we have a statement of that problem of the criterion that was identified by Sextus. For a more extensive discussion of it, see pp. 248–250. In the Chinese tradition, Zhuangzi articulates a similar argument. See pp. 85–86.

reasons for supporting Catholic Christianity. So to keep from "rolling about incessantly," the sensible course is to stick with the customs in which one has been brought up.* In one of his sharpest aphorisms, Montaigne exclaims,

> The plague of man is the opinion of knowledge. That is why ignorance is so recommended by our religion as a quality suitable to belief and obedience. (*ARS*, 360)

It is not knowledge, note well, that Montaigne decries as a plague, but the opinion that one possesses it. If you are reminded of Socrates, it is no coincidence.† He was known to his admirers as "the French Socrates."

Such is Montaigne's "defense" of the rational theology of Raymond Sebond. In an age of social and intellectual tumult and disagreement, the view has a certain attractiveness. While despairing and pessimistic in one way, it seems at least to promote tolerance. Someone who is a Catholic in Montaigne's sense is unlikely to have any incentive to burn someone who differs. This is no doubt one, but only one, of the reasons for the spread of Pyrrhonism among intellectuals and even among some members of the clergy.

---

1. What is Montaigne's strategy in "defending" Raymond Sebond?
2. What does Montaigne have to say about depending on authority? Our senses? Science? Reason?
3. How does Montaigne try to show that we are involved either in a circle or in an infinite regress?
4. How does he recommend we live?

---

*Note how different this religiosity is from both that of the Catholic Dante (for whom the "indifferent" are rejected by both God and Satan) and that of the reformer Luther (for whom commitment and certainty are essential to Christianity). Can it count as being religious at all? What do you think?

†For the claim that Socrates is the wisest of men because he knows that he doesn't know, see Plato's *Apology*, 20e–23b. Socrates, however, is not a Pyrrhonian skeptic; he does not doubt that knowledge is possible; he just confesses that (with some possible few exceptions), he does not possess it.

COPERNICUS TO KEPLER TO GALILEO: THE GREAT TRIPLE PLAY*

While humanism transformed Europeans' view of how to live, another development ushered in a new view of the universe and humanity's place in it. This development decisively overturns the entire medieval worldview and undermines forever the authority of its philosophical bulwark, Aristotle. It is traditionally called the **Copernican revolution.** Though there were anticipations of it before **Copernicus,** and the revolution was carried to completion only in the time of Newton over a century later, it is the name of Copernicus we honor. For his work is the turning point. The key feature of that work is the displacement of the earth from the center of the universe.

We saw earlier how the centrality of the earth had been embedded in the accepted astronomical and physical theories. A stationary earth, moreover, had intimate links with the entire medieval Christian view of the significance of man, of his origins and destiny, and of God's relation to his creation. If the earth is displaced and becomes just one more planet whirling about in infinite space, we can expect consequences to be profound. And so they are, though the more radical consequences are not immediately perceived.

> "It [the scientific revolution] outshines everything since the rise of Christianity and reduces the Renaissance and Reformation to the rank of mere episodes, mere internal displacements within the system of medieval Christendom."
>
> *Herbert Butterfield (1900–1979)*

The earth-centered, multisphere Ptolemaic model of the universe had dominated astronomy and cosmology for eighteen hundred years. With a complex system of epicycles to account for the

---

*When your team is in the field, a triple play is a great success.

"wanderings" of the planets, it was an impressive mathematical achievement, and its accuracy in prediction was not bad. But it never quite worked. And Copernicus (1473–1543) tells us that this fact led him to examine the works of previous astronomers to see whether some other system might improve accuracy. He discovered that certain ancient thinkers had held that the earth moved.

> Taking advantage of this I too began to think of the mobility of the Earth; and though the opinion seemed absurd, yet knowing now that others before me had been granted freedom to imagine such circles as they chose to explain the phenomena of the stars, I considered that I also might easily be allowed to try whether, by assuming some motion of the Earth, sounder explanations than theirs for the revolution of the celestial spheres might so be discovered.[19]

It is important to recognize that the heart of Copernicus' achievement is in the mathematics of his system—in the geometry and the calculations that filled most of his 1543 book, *De Revolutionibus*. As he himself puts it, "Mathematics are for mathematicians."[20] He expects fellow astronomers to be the ones to appreciate his results; from nonmathematicians he expects trouble.

We cannot go into the mathematical details. But we should know in general what Copernicus does—and does not—do. He does not entirely abolish the Ptolemaic reliance on epicycles centered on circles to account for apparent motion. His computations are scarcely simpler than those of Ptolemy. He retains the notion that all celestial bodies move in circles; indeed, the notion of celestial spheres is no less important for Copernicus than for the Ptolemaic tradition. And he accepts the idea that the universe is finite—though considerably larger than had been thought. Even the sun is not located clearly in the center, as most popular accounts of his system state.[21]

But his treatment of the apparently irregular motions of the planets is a breakthrough. The planets appear to move, against the sphere of the fixed stars, slowly eastward. But at times they reverse course and move back westward. This **retrograde motion** remains a real puzzle as long as it is ascribed to the planets themselves. But Copernicus

treats it as merely an *apparent* motion, the appearance being caused by the *actual* motion of the observers on an earth that is not itself stationary. And this works; at least, it works as well as the traditional assumptions in accounting for the observed phenomena. Moreover, it is aesthetically pleasing, unlike the inexplicable reversals of earlier theory. Copernicus' view, though not less complex and scarcely more accurate in prediction, allows for a kind of unity and harmony throughout the universe that the renegade planets had previously spoiled. Until the availability of better naked-eye data and the invention of the telescope (about fifty years later), these "harmonies" are what chiefly recommend the Copernican system to his astronomical successors.

At first some of them simply use his mathematics without committing themselves to the truth of this new picture of the universe. Indeed, in a preface to Copernicus' major work, a Lutheran theologian, Osiander, urges this path. Copernicus' calculations are useful, but to give up the traditional picture of the universe would mean an overhaul of basic beliefs and attitudes that most are not ready for. So if one could treat the system merely as a calculating device, without any claims to truth, one could reconcile the best of the new science with the best of ancient traditions.*

Johannes **Kepler** (1571–1630), however, is not content with this restricted view of the theory. A lifelong Copernican, he supplies the next major advance in the system by taking the sun more and more seriously as the true center. Oddly enough, his predilection for the sun as the center has its roots not so much in observation, or even in mathematics, as in a kind of mystical Neoplatonism, which takes the sun to be "the most excellent" body in the universe.† Its essence, Kepler says,

---

*Here is foreshadowed one of the intense debates in current philosophy of science: Should we understand terms in explanatory theories in a "realistic" way or take such terms as mere "instruments" for calculation and prediction?

†In *Republic* 506d–509b, Plato uses the sun as a visible image of the Form of the Good (see p. 161). And in his later work *Laws*, he recommends a kind of sun worship as the heart of a state-sponsored religion.

is nothing else than the purest light, than which there is no greater star; which singly and alone is the producer, conserver, and warmer of all things; it is a fountain of light, rich in fruitful heat, most fair, limpid, and pure to the sight, the source of vision, portrayer of all colours, though himself empty of colour, called king of the planets for his motion, heart of the world for his power, its eye for his beauty, and which alone we should judge worthy of the Most High God, should he be pleased with a material domicile and choose a place in which to dwell with the blessed angels.[22]

It may be somewhat disconcerting to hear this sort of rhetoric from one we honor as a founder of the modern scientific tradition; but it is neither the first nor the last time that religious or philosophical views function as a source of insights later confirmed by more exact and pedestrian methods.

Part of Kepler's quasi-religious conviction is that God's creation is governed by mathematically simple laws. This view can be traced back through Plato to the Pythagoreans, who hold (rather obscurely) that all things are numbers. In the work of Kepler and his successors, this conviction gains an unprecedented confirmation. This mathematical approach to the natural world would become a hallmark of the new science.

Drawing on more accurate data compiled by the great observer of the heavens, Tycho Brahe, Kepler makes trial after trial of circular hypotheses, always within the Copernican framework. None of them exactly fits the data. For the greater part of ten years he works on the orbit of Mars. At last, he notices certain regularities suggesting that the path of a planet might be that of an ellipse, with the sun at one of the two foci that define it. And that works; the data and the mathematical theory fit precisely.

The significance of Kepler's work is that for the first time we have a simple and elegant mathematical account of the heavens that matches the data. For the first time we have a really powerful alternative to the medieval picture of the world. Its ramifications are many, however, and will take time to draw out. Part of this development is the task of Galileo.

In 1609, **Galileo** Galilei (1564–1642) turns the newly invented telescope toward the heavens. The result was a multitude of indirect but persuasive evidences for the Copernican view of the universe. New stars in prodigious numbers were observed. The moon's cratered topography was charted, cutting against the distinction between terrestrial imperfection and celestial perfection. Sun spots were observed; it was not perfect either! And it rotated—it was not immutable! The moons of Jupiter provided an observable model of the solar system itself. The phases of Venus indicated that it moved in a sun-centered orbit.

Encouraged by the successful application of mathematics to celestial bodies, Galileo sets himself to use these same powerful tools for the description and explanation of terrestrial motion. Previous thinkers, influenced by Aristotle, had asked primarily *why* bodies move. *Why* does a rock fall to earth when unsupported? Aristotelians answered that it is *seeking its natural place*. The earth, at the center of the celestial spheres, is the **place** for heavy things. Note three things: (1) this is an explanation by appeal to a *final cause* or purpose; (2) a place has certain *essential qualities*; and (3) such an explanation gives no insight as to *how* the rock falls—no laws explaining its speed or acceleration.

The new science substitutes the concept of **space** for that of place. Space is an infinitely extended *neutral* container with a purely mathematical description. Galileo's theory of motion supplies laws that apply to *all* motion, terrestrial and celestial alike. Explanation and prediction of the rock's fall are possible for the first time. And final causes are banished. For Galileo, as for Copernicus and Kepler, the great book of nature is written in mathematical language. And we, by using that language, can understand it.

Let us set down some of the consequences of the new science. First, our sense of the size of the universe changes. Eventually it will be thought to be infinitely extended in space. This means it has *no center* because in an infinite universe every point has an equal right to be considered the center; from each point, the universe extends infinitely in every direction. As a result, it becomes more difficult to think of human beings as the main attraction in this extravaganza, where quite probably there are planets similar to earth circling other suns in other galaxies. The universe no longer seems a cozy home in which everything exists for our sake. Blaise Pascal, himself a great mathematician and contributor to the new science, would exclaim a hundred years after Copernicus, "The eternal silence of those infinite spaces strikes me with terror."[23]

Second, our beliefs about the nature of the things in the universe change. Celestial bodies seem be made of the same lowly stuff as we find on the earth, so that the heavens are no longer eternal, immutable, and akin to the divine. Furthermore, matter seems to be peculiarly *quantitative*. For Aristotle and medieval science alike, mathematics had been just one of the ways in which substances could be described. Quantity was only one of the ten categories, which together supplied the basic concepts for describing and explaining reality. Substances were fundamentally qualitative in nature, and science had the job of tracing their qualitative development in terms of changes from potentiality to actuality.*

But now mathematics promises a privileged way to describe and explain things. Mathematicians solved the puzzle of the heavens; it is mathematics that can describe and predict the fall of rocks and the trajectory of a cannonball. Mathematics, it seems, can tell us what *really* is. The result is a strong push toward thinking of the universe in purely quantitative terms, as a set of objects with purely quantitative characteristics (size, shape, motion) that interact with each other according to fixed laws. It is no surprise that the implications of the new science move its inventors in the direction of atomism or, as they call it, "**corpuscularism.**"† (A "corpuscle" was thought to be a tiny particle, similar to an atom in the ancient sense.)

In the third place, the new science does away with teleological explanations, or final causes. Explanations are framed in terms of mathematical laws that account for *how* it behaves. Why does it

behave in a certain way? Because it is a thing of just this precise quantity in exactly these conditions, and things of that quantity in those conditions necessarily behave in accordance with a given law. It is no longer good enough to explain change in terms of a desire to reach a body's natural resting place.*

This way of viewing the universe puts values in a highly questionable position. If we assume that the valuable is somehow a goal, something desirable—and this is the common assumption of virtually all Western philosophers and theologians up to this time—where is there room for such goals in a universe like this? A goal seems precisely to be a final cause. But if everything simply happens as it must in the giant machine that is the universe, how can there be values, aspirations, goals?

It looks as though knowledge and value, science and religion are being pulled apart again after two thousand years of harmony. Plato, and Aristotle after him, opposes the atomism of Democritus to construct a vision of reality in which the ultimate facts are not indifferent to goodness and beauty. Christian thinkers take over these schemes and link them intimately to God. But all this, which Dante expresses so movingly, seems to be in the process of coming unstuck.

One more consequence of the new science will prove to be perhaps the most perplexing of all. Galileo sees that the quantitative, corpuscular universe throws the qualities of experience into question. If reality is captured by mathematics and geometry, then the real properties of things are just their size, shape, velocity, acceleration, direction, weight: those characteristics treatable by numbers, points, and lines. But what becomes of those fuzzy, intimate, and lovable characteristics, such as warmth, yellow–orange, or sweetness? It is in terms of such properties that we make contact with the world beyond us; it is they that delight or terrify us, attract or repel us. But what is their relation to those purely quantitative things revealed by Galilean science as the real stuff of the universe?

---

*See Aristotle's development of these ideas on pp. 194–197. For Aristotle's categories, see pp. 185–186.

†The key notions of ancient atomism are discussed on pp. 28–33.

---

*Compare the teleological explanations of Aristotle (pp. 194–197).

Our instinctive habit is to consider the apple red, the oatmeal hot, cookies sweet, and roses fragrant. But is this correct? Do apples and other such things really have these properties? Here is Galileo's answer:

> that external bodies, to excite in us these tastes, these odours, and these sounds, demand other than size, figure, number, and slow or rapid motion, I do not believe; and I judge that, if the ears, the tongue, and the nostrils were taken away, the figure, the numbers, and the motions would indeed remain, but not the odours nor the tastes nor the sounds, which, without the living animal, I do not believe are anything else than names, just as tickling is precisely nothing but a name if the armpit and the nasal membrane be removed; . . . having now seen that many affections which are reputed to be qualities residing in the external object, have truly no other existence than in us, and without us are nothing else than names; I say that I am inclined sufficiently to believe that heat is of this kind, and that the thing that produces heat in us and makes us perceive it, which we call by the general name fire, is a multitude of minute corpuscles thus and thus figured, moved with such and such a velocity; . . . But that besides their figure, number, motion, penetration, and touch, there is in fire another quality, that is heat—that I do not believe otherwise than I have indicated, and I judge that it is so much due to us that if the animate and sensitive body were removed, heat would remain nothing more than a simple word.[24]

Galileo is here sketching a distinction between two different kinds of qualities: those that can be attributed to things themselves and those that cannot. The former are often called **primary qualities** and the latter **secondary qualities.** Primary qualities are those that Galilean mathematical science can handle: size, figure, number, and motion. These qualities are now thought to characterize the world—or what we might better call the *objective* world—exhaustively. All other qualities exist only *subjectively*—in us. They are caused to exist in us by the primary (quantitative) qualities of things.

Heat, for example, experienced in the presence of a fire, no more exists in the fire than a tickle exists in the feather brushing my nose. If we try to use the term "heat" for something out there in the world, it turns into "nothing but a name"—that is, it does not describe any reality, since the reality is just the motion of "a multitude of minute corpuscles." The tickle exists only in us; and if the term "heat" (or for that matter "red" or "sweet" or "pungent") is to be descriptive, then what it describes is also only in us. Take away the eye, the tongue, the nostrils, and all that remains is figure and motion.

Democritus, the ancient atomist, draws the same conclusion. He remarks in a poignant phrase, "By this man is cut off from the real."* The problem that Galileo's distinction between primary and secondary qualities bequeaths to subsequent philosophers is this: If, to understand the world, we must strip it of its experienced qualities, where do those experienced qualities exist? If they exist only in *us*, what then are *we*? If they are mental, or subjective, what is the *mind*? And how is the mind related to the corpuscular world of the new science? Suppose we agree, for the sake of the mastery of the universe given us by these new conceptions, to kick experienced qualities "inside." Then how is this "inside" related to the "outside"? Galileo, concerned as he is with the objective world, can simply relegate secondary qualities to some otherwise specified subjective realm. But the question will not go away.

It is a new world, indeed. The impact of all these changes on a sensitive observer is registered in a poem by John Donne in 1611.

> And new philosophy calls all in doubt,
> The element of fire is quite put out;
> The sun is lost, and th' earth, and no man's wit
> Can well direct him where to look for it.
> And freely men confess that this world's spent,
> When in the planets, and the firmament
> They seek so many new; they see that this
> Is crumbled out again to his atomies.
> 'Tis all in pieces, all coherence gone;
> All just supply, and all relation:
> Prince, subject, father, son, are things forgot,
> For every man alone thinks he hath got
> To be a phoenix, and that then can be
> None of that kind, of which he is, but he.
> This is the world's condition now.[25]

---

* See p. 32.

Here is a lament founded on the new developments. Point after point recalls the detail we have just surveyed: Pyrrhonism, secondary qualities (why is the sun, source of light, heat, and color "lost"?), the moving earth, the expanding universe, corpuscularism, and in the last few lines, the new individualism, which seems to undermine all traditional authority. The medieval world has vanished: "'tis all in pieces, all coherence gone."

If we wanted to sum up, we could say that the new science bequeaths to philosophers four deep and perplexing problems:

1. What is the place of mind in this world of matter?
2. What is the place of value in this world of fact?
3. What is the place of freedom in this world of mechanism?
4. Is there any room left for God at all?

Responding to these questions is perhaps the major preoccupation of philosophers in the modern era.

---

1. How does Copernicus resolve the puzzle about the apparent irregularity in the motions of the planets?
2. What is the impact of a moving earth on Dante's picture of the world?
3. What does Kepler add to the Copernican picture?
4. Contrast Aristotelian explanations of motion with those of Galileo.
5. What impact does giving up final causes have on values?
6. What happens to the qualities we think we experience in objects? Explain the difference between primary and secondary qualities.
7. What questions does the new science pose to the philosophical quest for wisdom?

THE COUNTER-REFORMATION

The Catholic Church does not sit idly by while these changes wash over Europe. Various streams of reform come together by the mid-sixteenth century, capped by a major assembly of Catholic luminaries at the Council of Trent in 1545. The council, meeting intermittently until 1563, both reaffirms Catholic doctrine and institutes a diverse set of reforms aimed at shoring up the intellectual foundations and social position of the church. These efforts become known as the **Counter-Reformation.**

While we cannot survey every aspect of Catholic reform, we can consider one example that illustrates how the church adapts to the changing intellectual climate. The first is the foundation of a new religious order, the Society of Jesus, better known as the **Jesuits.** Established in 1540 by **Ignatius Loyola**, the Jesuits describe themselves as "soldiers of God" dedicated to "the progress of souls in the Christian life and doctrine and for the propagation of the faith."[26] Ignatius composes a book, entitled *Spiritual Exercises*, which walks the reader through a series of reflections meant to guide the reader toward a deeper faith and a better life—reflections that, according to the Jesuits' critics, place too much emphasis on the individual reader's direct relationship with God and not enough on the role of the church. What most distinguishes the Jesuits, however, is that they open highly respected schools throughout Europe—and beyond—in which members of the order teach students both the new science and the classical literature that underpins European humanism. Through their teaching, the Jesuits immerse themselves and their students in the new learning of their age.[27]

By the end of the sixteenth century, then, even the Catholic Church has entered the early modern era. Medieval Europe has vanished, swept away by an irresistible tide of intellectual and social change. Medieval Western philosophy, focused on reconciling ancient Greek philosophy with Christianity, would disappear with it, to be replaced by a new set of philosophical problems.

FOR FURTHER THOUGHT

Imagine that you are a philosopher living in the early seventeenth century. You are acquainted with the writings of the humanists, with Luther's reforming views of Christianity, with Montaigne's skeptical arguments, and with the new science. A friend asks you, "What should I live for? What is the point of life?" How do you reply?

KEY WORDS

Empyrean
Hildegard of Bingen
Virgil
Beatrice
Martin Luther
grace
indulgence
ninety-five theses
Renaissance
humanism
Erasmus
Pico della Mirandola
individualism
Christine di Pizan
Montaigne

Raymond Sebond
Copernican revolution
Copernicus
retrograde motion
Kepler
Galileo
place
space
corpuscularism
primary qualities
secondary qualities
Counter-Reformation
Jesuits
Ignatius Loyola

NOTES

1. We are indebted for much in this chapter to the excellent book by Thomas Kuhn, *The Copernican Revolution* (Cambridge, MA: Harvard University Press, 1957).

2. Quotations from Matthew Fox, trans., *Hildegard of Bingen's Book of Divine Works* (Santa Fe, NM: Bear, 1987) are cited in the text using the abbreviation *BDW*. References are to the chapters (listed as "Visions") and paragraph number.

3. Quotations from Dante, *The Divine Comedy*, in *The Portable Dante*, ed. Paolo Milano (New York: Penguin Books, 1947), are cited in the text by canto and line numbers.

4. Roland H. Bainton, *Christendom: A Short History of Christianity and Its Impact on Western Civilization* (New York: Harper and Row, 1964), 1:218.

5. Bainton, *Christendom*, 1:249.

6. Quoted in John Dillenberger, "Preface to the Complete Edition of Luther's Latin Writings," in *Martin Luther* (New York: Anchor Books, 1962), 11.

7. Quoted in Dillenberger, *Martin Luther*, 11–12.

8. Quoted in Roland H. Bainton, *Here I Stand: A Life of Martin Luther* (London: Hodder and Staughton, 1951), 78.

9. Martin Luther, "The Ninety-Five Theses," in Dillenberger, *Martin Luther*, 493–494.

10. Quoted in Bainton, *Here I Stand*, 117.

11. Erasmus, "The Godly Feast," in *The Colloquies of Erasmus*, trans. Craig R. Thompson (Chicago: University of Chicago Press, 1965), 65.

12. Erasmus, "Godly Feast," 68.

13. Erasmus, "The Epicurean," in *Colloquies*, 549.

14. Ernst Cassirer, Paul Oskar Kristeller, and John Herman Randall Jr., *The Renaissance Philosophy of Man* (Chicago: University of Chicago Press, 1948), 4.

15. Giovanni Pico della Mirandola, *Oration on the Dignity of Man*, in Cassirer, Kristeller, and Randall, *Renaissance Philosophy of Man*, 224–225.

16. Pico, *Oration*, 225.

17. We rely here on Richard H. Popkin's *History of Scepticism from Erasmus to Descartes* (Assen, Netherlands: Van Gorcum, 1960).

18. Quotations from Michel de Montaigne, *Apology for Raymond Sebond*, in *The Complete Works of Montaigne*, trans. Donald M. Frame (Palo Alto, CA: Stanford University Press, 1958), are cited in the text using the abbreviation *ARS*. References are to page numbers.

19. Quoted from Copernicus, *De Revolutionibus*, in Kuhn, *Copernican Revolution*, 141.

20. Quoted in Kuhn, *Copernican Revolution*, 142.

21. Kuhn, *Copernican Revolution*, 164–170.

22. Quoted in Edwin Arthur Burtt, *The Metaphysical Foundations of Modern Physical Science* (London: Routledge and Kegan Paul, 1924), 48.

23. Kuhn, *Copernican Revolution*, 86.

24. Blaise Pascal, *The Pensées*, trans. J. M. Cohen (New York: Penguin Books, 1961), sec. 91, p. 57.

25. Quoted in Burtt, *Metaphysical Foundations*, 78.

26. John Donne, "An Anatomy of the World," in *John Donne: The Complete English Poems* (New York: Penguin Books, 1971), 276.

27. "Regimini militantis Ecclesiae," Boston College Institute for Advanced Jesuit Studies, n.d., http://jesuitportal.bc.edu/research/documents/1540_Formula/

28. John W. O'Malley, *The Jesuits* (Lanham, MD: Rowman and Littlefield, 2014): 1–26.

When he is just twenty-three years old, René **Descartes** (1596–1650) experiences a vision in a dream. He writes down,

10, November 1619; I discovered the foundations of a marvellous science.[1]

The "marvellous science" that he built on this foundation was analytic geometry.* The nocturnal insight that enabled it was that things describable by geometry could also be described algebraically. When we understand why such an insight would excite Descartes so much, we will be in a position to understand why he is often credited as the "father of modern philosophy."

Descartes had received a good Jesuit education, from which he had expected to obtain "a clear and certain knowledge . . . of all that is useful in life." Instead, he tells us,

I found myself beset by so many doubts and errors that I came to think I had gained nothing from my

attempts to become educated but increasing recognition of my ignorance. (*DM* 1.4, p. 113)[2]

Dissatisfied, Descartes made a bold move in his bid to "learn to distinguish the true from the false" (*DM* 1.10, p. 115).

I entirely abandoned the study of letters. Resolving to seek no knowledge other than that which could be found in myself or else in the great book of the world, I spent the rest of my youth travelling, visiting courts and armies, mixing with people of diverse temperaments and ranks, gathering various experiences, testing myself in the situations which fortune offered me, and at all times reflecting upon whatever came my way so as to derive some profit from it. (*DM* 1.9, p. 115)

In turning away from "letters"—from what others had written—and striking out to discover the truth for himself, Descartes reflects the spirit of his age. During his stint as a military engineer, he encountered a Dutchman who encouraged him to pursue mathematical solutions to problems in the new physics. Having long admired mathematics for "the certainty of its demonstrations and the evidence

---

*So-called Cartesian coordinates are, of course, named for Descartes.

of its reasoning," Descartes takes up this challenge eagerly. This is why his discovery of analytic geometry excites him: Since the natural world can be geometrically represented in terms of the size, figure, volume, and spatial relations of natural things, analytic geometry promises an algebraic treatment of all of nature.* Descartes realizes he has found a new way to read the "great book of the world."

For the rest of his life Descartes works, in constant communication with the best minds in Europe, to understand the world through the lens of mathematics. He applies his new understanding of the world to a wide variety of topics: the sun, moon, and the stars; comets; metals; fire; glass; the magnet; and the human body, particularly the heart and the nervous system (for which he gathers observations from animal bodies at a local slaughterhouse). He formulates several "laws of nature." Here are two influential ones:

> that each thing as far as in it lies, continues always in the same state; and that which is once moved always continues to move.
>
> . . . that all motion is of itself in a straight line; and thus things which move in a circle always tend to recede from the centre of the circle that they describe. (*PP* 2.37–39, p. 267)[3]

Newton will later adopt both, and so they pass into the foundations of classical physics; but they were revolutionary in Descartes' day. Both laws contradict Aristotelian assumptions built into the worldview of medieval science. It had been thought that rest (at or near the center of the universe) is the natural state of terrestrial things, while the heavenly spheres revolve naturally in perfect circles. To say that rest is not more "natural" than motion and that motion is "naturally" in a straight line is radical indeed.

Descartes applies these principles to a world that he takes to be geometrical in essence. For Descartes, bodies are sheer extended volumes. They interact according to mechanical principles that can be mathematically formulated. The paths and positions of interacting bodies can therefore be plotted and predicted. Since extension is the essence of body, there can be no vacuum or void. (If bodies are just extended volumes, the idea of such a volume containing *no body* is self-contradictory.) So the universe is full, and motion takes place by a continual recirculation of bodies, each displacing another. Bodies near the earth fall because they are pressed down by others in the air, which in turn are being pressed down by others out to the edges of the solar system. This system forms a huge vortex bound in by the vortices of other systems, which force the moving bodies in it to deviate from otherwise straight paths into the roughly circular paths traced by the planets.*

The key idea here is that everything in the material world can be treated in a purely geometrical and mathematical fashion. Descartes vigorously promotes the new "corpuscularism."† Though he departs from the ancient atomists in important respects, he enthusiastically adopts their mechanistic picture of the natural world.‡ He states explicitly that "the laws of mechanics . . . are identical with the laws of Nature" (*DM* 5.54, p. 139).

The radical nature of this conception can be appreciated by noting a thought experiment Descartes recommends. Imagine, he says, that God creates a space with matter to fill it and shakes it up until there is thorough chaos. If God then decreed that this matter should behave according to the laws of Nature, Descartes argues, it would eventually settle into just the sort of universe we see around us. Descartes is quick to add that he does not infer from this thought experiment that the world was actually formed in that way, only that it could have been. Careful about charges of heresy, he says it is "much more probable" that God made it just as it now is. Still, the daring conception of a universe

---

*In light of the overarching narrative of this book, it is worth noting that Descartes' insight rests on a synthesis of Greek geometry, Middle Eastern algebra, and European physics.

---

*The notion of a cosmic vortex, a huge, swirling mass of matter, is already found in the speculations of Anaximander; see p. 12. Compare also Parmenides' arguments against the existence of a void, pp. 24–25.

†See p. 356.

‡For the views of the atomists, see Chapter 2. Descartes' criticisms may be found in Part IV, CCII, of *The Principles of Philosophy*.

evolving itself in purely mechanistic ways has been enormously influential; and we haven't yet finished exploring its ramifications.

This part of Descartes' work reveals the influence of the new sciences on early modern philosophy: By positing a universe where neither final causes nor God's will plays a direct role in the day-to-day operations of the universe, Descartes displaces Aristotelian and Christian metaphysics in favor of a mechanistic, corpuscular one.

The Method

While working on these physical problems, and feeling confident in his progress, Descartes asks himself why more progress hadn't been made in the past. The problem, he concludes, is not that his predecessors were less intelligent than he and his contemporaries, but that they lacked a sound *method*. They did not proceed in as careful and principled a way as they might have, leaving them mired in obscure ideas, unjustified conclusions, avoidable disagreements, and general intellectual chaos.

Descartes sets himself to draw up some rules for the direction of the intellect. These **rules of method** formulate what Descartes takes himself to be doing in his scientific work. In particular, they are indebted to his experience as a mathematician. They are not picked arbitrarily, then, but express procedures that actually seem to be producing results. If only other thinkers could be persuaded to follow these four rules, he thinks, what progress might be made!

> The first was never to accept anything as true if I did not have evident knowledge of its truth: that is, carefully to avoid precipitate conclusions and preconceptions, and to include nothing more in my judgments than what presented itself to my mind so clearly and distinctly that I had no occasion to doubt it.
>
> The second, to divide each of the difficulties I examined into as many parts as possible and as may be required in order to resolve them better.
>
> The third, to direct my thoughts in an orderly manner, by beginning with the simplest and most easily known objects in order to ascend little by little, step by step, to knowledge of the most complex, and by supposing some order even among objects that have no natural order of precedence.

> And the last, throughout to make enumerations so complete, and reviews so comprehensive, that I could be sure of leaving nothing out. (*DM* 2.18–19, p. 120)

He says of these four rules that he thought they would be "sufficient, provided that I made a strong and unswerving resolution never to fail to observe them" (*DM* 2.18, p. 120). They are difficult to put into practice, as any attempt to do so will convince you immediately. But let us explore their content more carefully.

The first one has to do with a condition for accepting something as true. In placing stringent demands on knowledge, it reflects the resurgent skepticism of the early modern period. Descartes warns us to avoid two things: "precipitate conclusions" (hastiness) and "preconceptions" (categorizing something before you have good warrant to do so). How do you do this? By accepting only those things that are *so clear and distinct* that you have no occasion to doubt them. Descartes obviously has in mind such propositions as "three plus five equals eight" and "the interior angles of a triangle are equal to two right angles." Once you understand these, you really cannot bring yourself to doubt that they are true.

What do the key words "clear" and "distinct" mean? In *The Principles of Philosophy* (*PP* 1.45, p. 237) Descartes explains them as follows. Something is "clear" when it is "present and apparent to an attentive mind, in the same way as we assert that we see objects clearly when, being present to the regarding eye, they operate upon it with sufficient strength." Seeing an apple in your hand in good light would be an example. We are not to accept any belief unless it is as clear as that.

By "distinct" he means "so precise and different from all other objects that it contains within itself nothing but what is clear." An idea not only must be clear in itself but also impossible to confuse with any other idea. There must be no ambiguity in its meaning. Ideas must be as distinct as the idea of a triangle is from the idea of a square.

How many of *your* beliefs are clear and distinct in this way? Descartes is under no illusions about the high standard he sets for belief. In the first of his *Meditations, he stresses just* how many of our everyday beliefs his standard excludes.

"It is much easier to have some vague notion about any subject, no matter what, than to arrive at the real truth about a single question."

—René Descartes

The second rule recommends **analysis.** Solving complex problems requires breaking them into smaller problems. Anyone who has tried to program a computer will have an excellent feel for this rule. Often more than half the battle is to discover smaller problems we already have the resources to solve, so that by combining the solutions to these more elementary problems we can solve the big problem. We move, by analysis, not only from the complex to the simple, but also from the obscure to the clear and distinct, and so we follow the first rule as well.

The third rule recognizes that items for consideration may be more or less simple. It recommends beginning with the simpler ones and proceeding to the more complex. Here is a mathematical example. If we compare a straight line to a curve, we can see that there is a clear sense in which the straight line is simple and the curve is not; no straight line is more or less straight than another, but curves come in all degrees. But it is possible to analyze a curve

into a series of straight lines at various angles to each other, thus "constructing" the more complex curve from the simple straights.

For Descartes, this serves as a model of all good intellectual work. There are two basic procedures: a kind of **insight** or *intuition* of simple natures (which must be clear and distinct) and then **deduction** of complex phenomena from perceived relations among the simples. A deduction, too, is in fact just an insight: insight into the connections holding among simples. Geometry, again, provides examples. We deduce theorems from the axioms and postulates, which are simply "seen" to be true; for example, through two points in a plane, one and only one straight line can be drawn. The same kind of "seeing" is required to recognize that each step in a proof is correct.

Deductions, of course, can be very long and complex, even though each of the steps is clear and distinct. That is the reason for the fourth rule: to set out all the steps completely (we all know how easily mistakes creep in when we take something for granted) and to make comprehensive reviews.

Descartes believes that by following this method we can achieve certainty about "all the things that can fall under human knowledge" (*DM* 2.19, p. 120). We will see this optimism at work when Descartes tackles knotty problems such as the existence of God and the relation between soul and body. But first we need to ask, Why does Descartes feel a need to address these *philosophical* problems at all? Why doesn't he just stick to mathematical physics?

For one thing, he is confident that his method will allow him to succeed where so many have failed. But a deeper reason is that he needs to show that his physics is more than a fairy tale, that it is actually true of something real, that it correctly describes the world. He is quite aware of the skeptical doubts of the Pyrrhonists, of the way they undermine the testimony of the senses and cast doubt on our reasoning. In particular, he is aware of the problem of the criterion.* Unless this can be solved, no certainty is possible.

---

*For a discussion of this problem by the ancient Greek skeptics, see pp. 248–250. For the impact of skepticism nearer to Descartes' time, see pp. 350–353.

Descartes thinks he has found a way to solve this problem of problems. He will outdo the Pyrrhonists at their own game; when it comes to doubting, he will be the champion doubter of all time. The first rule of his method already gives him the means to wipe the slate clean—unless, perhaps, there remains something that is *so clear and distinct that it cannot possibly be doubted*. If there were something like that (and, as we shall see, Descartes thinks that there is), the rest of the method could gain a foothold, and deductions could lead us to further truths. We could, perhaps, claw our way from the depths of doubting despair to the bliss of certainty.

This is Descartes' strategy. And it is this attempt to justify his physics that makes Descartes not just a great scientist, but a great philosopher as well. We are now ready to turn to this philosophy as expressed in the *Meditations*.

Meditations on First Philosophy

Meditations, first published in 1641, is Descartes' most famous work. We focus our attention on the text itself, as we did earlier with certain dialogues of Plato. It is a remarkably rich work, and if you come to understand it, you will have mastered many of the concepts and distinctions that philosophers use to this day. We cannot emphasize too much that in this section you must wrestle with the *text*, the words of Descartes himself. It is he who is your partner in this conversation, and you must make him speak to you and—as far as possible—answer your questions. What we do is offer some commentary on particularly difficult aspects, fill in some background, and ask some questions.

Though it is usually known just as the *Meditations*, the full title of the work is *Meditations on First Philosophy, In Which the Existence of God and the Distinction of the Soul from the Body Are Demonstrated*. The title gives you some idea what to expect. But as you will see, Descartes' experience as a mathematician and physicist is everywhere present.

Although not represented in our text, Descartes prefaces the *Meditations* with a letter to "the Wisest and Most Distinguished Men, the Dean and Doctors of the Faculty of Theology in Paris."

The motivation behind this letter is fairly transparent. It had been just eight years since the condemnation of Galileo, whose basic outlook Descartes shares. Since the Faculty of Theology in Paris had been an illustrious one for some centuries, securing their approval would shield Descartes from Galileo's fate. The *Meditations* was examined carefully by one of the theologians, who expressed his approval, but twenty-two years later it was placed on the *Index Librorum Prohibitorum* of books dangerous to read.*

Descartes had also asked one of his close friends, the priest and scientist Mersenne, to circulate the text to some distinguished philosophers, who were then invited to write criticisms of it. These criticisms, including some from his English contemporary Thomas Hobbes, were printed along with Descartes' replies at the end of the volume.†

In the letter to the theologians, Descartes refers to "believers like ourselves." He professes to be absolutely convinced that it is sufficient in these matters to rely on Scripture. But there is a problem. On the one hand, God's existence, he says, is to be believed because it is taught in Scripture. Scripture, on the other hand, is to be believed because God is its source. It is fairly easy to see that there is a rather tight circle here. It comes down to believing that God exists because you believe that God exists.

To break into the circle, Descartes thinks it necessary to *prove rationally* that God exists and that the soul is distinct from the body. His claim that reason should be able to do this is no innovation; Augustine, Avicenna, Maimonides, Anselm, Aquinas, and many others had said as much before. Descartes, however, claims to have proofs superior to any offered by these philosophers.

He refers to some thinkers who hold that it is rational to believe the soul perishes with the body. Aristotle seems in the main to think so (though he

---

*The *Index* was created in 1571 by Pope Pius V, after approval by the Council of Trent. See p. 358.

†We discuss the views of Hobbes in the next chapter. For his criticisms of the *Meditations*, see the "Third Set of Objections" in Haldane and Ross, *The Philosophical Works of Descartes*, vol. 2.

waffles).* Christian Aristotelians like Thomas Aquinas labor mightily, but inconclusively, to reconcile this view with the tradition of an immortal soul. Descartes thinks he has a proof of the soul that is direct, simple, and conclusive.† He claims, in fact, that his proofs will "surpass in certitude and obviousness the demonstrations of geometry." A strong claim indeed! You will have to decide whether you agree.

These are meditations on **first philosophy.** This is a term derived from Aristotle, who means by it a search for the first principles of things. First philosophy is also called *metaphysics.* Descartes uses a memorable image.

> Thus the whole of philosophy is like a tree; the roots are metaphysics, the trunk is physics, and the branches that issue from the trunk are all the other sciences.[4]

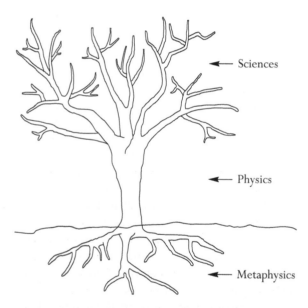

Metaphysics, then, is thought to be more fundamental even than physics. Physics and the other sciences give us detailed knowledge of material things; first philosophy inquires whether material things are the only things there are. What Descartes is seeking is a set of concepts that will give us an inventory of the *basic kinds of being.** As it turns out, his inventory of what exists looks fairly simple. We can diagram it this way:

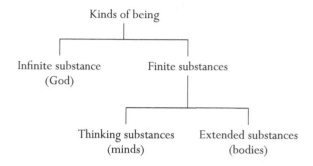

By itself this chart isn't very informative. It is time to turn to the *Meditations* themselves, to see how Descartes fills in this schema and why it turns out just that way.

The full text of Descartes' *Meditations* is represented here.[5] After each of the six sections, you will find commentary and questions. Read through each meditation quickly. (They aren't very long.) Then go to the discussion, moving back to the text to check your understanding. Write out brief answers to the questions. Descartes is a careful and clear writer and says exactly what he means. If you proceed in this way, you will not only learn some philosophy but also gain skill in reading a text of some difficulty—a valuable ability.

It may be helpful to have a preview of this dramatic little work. We offer an outline that sketches the progression from the first *meditation* to the last.

Meditation I. The Problem:
   Can anything be known?
Meditations II–VI. The Solution: I can know . . .
   II.   that I exist.
   III.   that God exists.
   IV.   why we make mistakes and how to avoid them.
   V.   that material things *might* exist; and again, that God exists.
   VI.   that material things *do* exist and are distinct from souls.

---

*For Aristotle's view of the soul as "the form of a living human body" see pp. 205–206.

†Descartes tends to use the terms "soul," "mind," and "spirit" interchangeably. They are all terms for "the thing that thinks." Some philosophers and theologians make distinctions among them.

---

*Aristotle calls such fundamental concepts "categories." See p. 185. It is interesting to note that in 1641 all the sciences are still counted as parts of philosophy, the love of wisdom.

Meditation I: On What Can Be Called into Doubt

For several years now, I've been aware that I accepted many falsehoods as true in my youth, that what I built on the foundation of those falsehoods was dubious, and accordingly that once in my life I would need to tear down everything and begin anew from the foundations if I wanted to establish any stable and lasting knowledge. But the task seemed enormous, and I waited until I was so old that no better time for undertaking it would be likely to follow. I have thus delayed so long that it would be wrong for me to waste in indecision the time left for action. Today, then, having rid myself of worries and having arranged for some peace and quiet, I withdraw alone, free at last earnestly and wholeheartedly to overthrow all my beliefs.

To do this, I don't need to show each of them to be false; I may never be able to do that. But, since reason now convinces me that I ought to withhold my assent just as carefully from what isn't obviously certain and indubitable as from what's obviously false, I can justify the rejection of all my beliefs if in each I can find some ground for doubt. And, to do this, I need not run through my beliefs one by one, which would be an endless task. Since a building collapses when its foundation is cut out from under it, I will go straight to the principles on which all my former beliefs rested.

Of course, whatever I have so far accepted as supremely true I have learned either from the senses or through the senses. But I have occasionally caught the senses deceiving me, and it's prudent never completely to trust those who have cheated us even once.

But, while my senses may deceive me about what is small or far away, there may still be other things that I take in by the senses but that I cannot possibly doubt—like that I am here, sitting before the fire, wearing a dressing gown, touching this paper. And on what grounds might I deny that my hands and the other parts of my body exist?—unless perhaps I liken myself to madmen whose brains are so rattled by the persistent vapors of melancholy that they are sure that they're kings when in fact they are paupers, or that they wear purple robes when in fact they're naked, or that their heads are clay, or that they are gourds, or made of glass. But these people are insane, and I would seem just as crazy if I were to apply what I say about them to myself.

This would be perfectly obvious—if I weren't a man accustomed to sleeping at night whose experiences while asleep are at least as far-fetched as those that madmen have while awake. How often, at night, I've been convinced that I was here, sitting before the fire, wearing my dressing gown, when in fact I was undressed and between the covers of my bed! But now I am looking at this piece of paper with my eyes wide open; the head that I am shaking has not been lulled to sleep; I put my hand out consciously and deliberately and feel. None of this would be as distinct if I were asleep. As if I can't remember having been tricked by similar thoughts while asleep! When I think very carefully about this, I see so plainly that there are no reliable signs by which I can distinguish sleeping from waking that I am stupefied—and my stupor itself suggests that I am asleep!

Suppose, then that I am dreaming. Suppose, in particular, that my eyes are not open, that my head is not moving, and that I have not put out my hand. Suppose that I do not have hands, or even a body. I must still admit that the things I see in sleep are like painted images which must have been patterned after real things and, hence, that things like eyes, heads, hands, and bodies are real rather than imaginary. For, even when painters try to give bizarre shapes to sirens and satyrs, they are unable to give them completely new natures; they only jumble together the parts of various animals. And, even if they were to come up with something so novel that no one had ever seen anything like it before, something entirely fictitious and unreal, at least there must be real colors from which they composed it. Similarly, while things like eyes, heads, and hands may be imaginary, it must be granted that some simpler and more universal things are real—the "real colors" from which the true and false images in our thoughts are formed.

Things of this sort seem to include general bodily nature and its extension, the shape of extended things, their quantity (that is, their size and number), the place in which they exist, the time through which they endure, and so on.

Perhaps we can correctly infer that, while physics, astronomy, medicine, and other disciplines that require the study of composites are dubious, disciplines like arithmetic and geometry, which deal only with completely simple and universal things without regard to whether they exist in the world, are somehow certain and indubitable. For, whether we are awake or asleep, two plus three is always five, and the square never has more than four sides. It seems impossible even to suspect such obvious truths of falsity.

Nevertheless, the traditional view is fixed in my mind that there is a God who can do anything and by whom I have been made to be as I am. How do I know that He hasn't brought it about that, while there is in fact no earth, no sky, no extended thing, no shape, no magnitude, and no place, all of these things seem to me to exist, just as they do now? I think that other people sometimes err in what they believe themselves to know perfectly well. Mightn't I be deceived when I add two and three, or count the sides of a square, or do even simpler things, if we can even suppose that there is anything simpler? Maybe it will be denied that God deceives me, since He is said to be supremely good. But, if God's being good is incompatible with His having created me so that I am deceived always, it seems just as out of line with His being good that He permits me to be deceived sometimes—as he undeniably does.

Maybe some would rather deny that there is an omnipotent God than believe that everything else is uncertain. Rather than arguing with them, I will grant everything I have said about God to be fiction. But, however these people think I came to be as I now am—whether they say it is by fate, or by accident, or by a continuous series of events, or in some other way—it seems that he who errs and is deceived is somehow imperfect. Hence, the less power that is attributed to my original creator, the more likely it is that I am always deceived. To these arguments, I have no reply. I'm forced to admit that nothing that I used to believe is beyond legitimate doubt—not because I have been careless or playful, but because I have valid and well-considered grounds for doubt. Hence, I must withhold my assent from my former beliefs as carefully as from obvious falsehoods if I want to arrive at something certain.

But it's not enough to have noticed this: I must also take care to bear it in mind. For my habitual views constantly return to my mind and take control of what I believe as if our long-standing, intimate relationship has given them the right to do so, even against my will. I'll never break the habit of trusting and giving in to these views while I see them for what they are—things somewhat dubious (as I have just shown) but nonetheless probable, things that I have much more reason to believe than to deny. That's why I think it will be good deliberately to turn my will around, to allow myself to be deceived, and to suppose that all my previous beliefs are false and illusory. Eventually, when I have counterbalanced the weight of my prejudices, my bad habits will no longer distort my grasp of things. I know that there is no danger of error here and that I won't overindulge in skepticism, since I'm now concerned, not with action, but only with gaining knowledge.

I will suppose, then, not that there is a supremely good God who is the source of all truth, but that there is an evil demon, supremely powerful and cunning, who works as hard as he can to deceive me. I will say that sky, air, earth, color, shape, sound, and other external things are just dreamed illusions that the demon uses to ensnare my judgment. I will regard myself as not having hands, eyes, flesh, blood, and senses—but as having the false belief that I have all these things. I will obstinately concentrate on this meditation and will thus ensure by mental resolution that, if I do not really have the ability to know the truth, I will at least withhold assent from what is false and from what a deceiver may try to put over on me, however powerful and cunning he may be. But this plan requires effort, and laziness brings me back to my ordinary life. I am like a prisoner who happens to enjoy the illusion of freedom in his dreams, begins to suspect that he is asleep, fears being awakened, and deliberately lets the enticing illusions slip by unchallenged. Thus, I slide back into my old views, afraid to awaken and to find that after my peaceful rest I must toil, not in the light, but in the confusing darkness of the problems just raised.

Commentary and Questions

Note the personal, meditative character of the writing. Descartes is inviting us to join him in thinking certain things through, asking us to mull them over and see whether we agree. He is not making authoritative pronouncements. Just as he reserves the right to be the judge of what *he* should believe, so he puts you on the spot. You will have to be continually asking yourself, Do I agree with this or not? If not, why not? This familiar first-person style is quite different from most of medieval philosophy; it resembles Counter-Reformation texts such as Ignatius Loyola's *Spiritual Exercises* and Teresa of Ávila's popular meditation *The Interior Castle** and harks back even further to Augustine's *Confessions* in the late fourth century. Descartes is, as it were, having a conversation with himself, so the structure of *Meditation I* is dialectical: proposal, objection, reply, objection, reply. . . Try to distinguish the various "voices" in this internal dialogue.

Note that there are three stages in the "tearing down" of opinions and one principle running throughout. The principle is that we ought to withhold assent from anything uncertain, just as much as from what we see clearly to be false. This is simply a restatement of the first rule of his method but is of the greatest importance.† The three stages concern (1) the **senses,** (2) **dreams,** and (3) the **evil demon** hypothesis.

---

*Some scholars argue that Teresa's text, which was widely read throughout Europe in Descartes' youth, may have influenced both the form and the content of Descartes' own *Meditations*.

†A brief look back at the four rules of the method will be of use at this point. See p. 362. Following Aristotle, Aquinas had also noted that big mistakes come from small beginnings. Once, when a friend stumbled on an unusually high first step of a staircase, one of us formulated what came jokingly to be known as Norman's first law: Watch that first step; it's a big one—good advice for appraising philosophical systems. For an alternative to Descartes' view, see the critique by C. S. Peirce on pp. 596–597.

Q1. Aren't you strongly inclined to think, just like Descartes by the fire, that you can't deny that you are now reading this book, which is "right there" in your hands? Should you doubt it anyway?

Q2. What do you think of Descartes' rule that we shouldn't completely trust those who have cheated us even once? Does this rule apply to the senses?

Q3. Could you be dreaming right now? Explain.

Q4. What is the argument that even in dreams some things—for example, the truths of mathematics—are not illusory?

Q5. How does the thought of God, at *this* stage, seem to reinforce skeptical conclusions—even about arithmetic?*

---

*"All that we see or seem
Is but a dream within a dream."*

Edgar Allan Poe (1809–1849)

Here Descartes avails himself of the techniques of the Pyrrhonists, who set argument against plausible argument until they find themselves no more inclined to judge one way than another. But he acknowledges that this equilibrium or suspension of judgment is difficult to achieve. "Habit" strongly inclines him to believe some of these things as "probable." Like Descartes, you almost certainly take it as *very* probable that you are now looking at a piece of paper, which is located a certain distance before your eyes, that you have eyes, and that two plus three really does equal five. And you almost certainly find it very hard *not* to believe these things. You probably find yourself so committed to them that you almost *can't* doubt them. But if Descartes is right so far, we know that we *should* doubt them. How can we overcome these habits? As a remedy against these habitual believings, Descartes determines *deliberately* (as an act of will) to suppose that all his prior beliefs are false.

---

*Review the consequences William of Ockham draws from the doctrine of God's omnipotence (pp. 336–337).

Q6. How does the hypothesis of the evil demon help?

Descartes now thinks that he has canvassed every possible reason for doubting. We cannot rely on our senses; we cannot even rely on our rational faculties for the simplest truths of mathematics, geometry, or logic. All our beliefs, it seems, are dissolved in the acid of skeptical doubt.

Q7. Before going on to *Meditation II*, ask yourself the question, Is there anything at all that I am *so certain* of that I could not *possibly* doubt it? (Meditate on this question awhile.)

Meditation II: On the Nature of the Human Mind, Which Is Better Known Than the Body

Yesterday's meditation has hurled me into doubts so great that I can neither ignore them nor think my way out of them. I am in turmoil, as if I have accidentally fallen into a whirlpool and can neither touch bottom nor swim to the safety of the surface. I will struggle, however, and try to follow the path that I started on yesterday. I will reject whatever is open to the slightest doubt just as though I have found it to be entirely false, and I will continue until I find something certain—or at least until I know for certain that nothing is certain. Archimedes required only one fixed and immovable point to move the whole earth from its place, and I too can hope for great things if I can find even one small thing that is certain and unshakeable.

I will suppose, then, that everything I see is unreal. I will believe that my memory is unreliable and that none of what it presents to me ever happened. I have no senses. Body, shape, extension, motion, and place are fantasies. What then is true? Perhaps just that nothing is certain.

But how do I know that there isn't something different from the things just listed that I do not have the slightest reason to doubt? Isn't there a God, or something like one, who puts my thoughts into me? But why should I say so when I may be the author of those thoughts? Well, isn't it at least the case that I am something? But I now am denying that I have senses and a body. But I stop here. For what follows from these denials? Am I so bound to my body and to my senses that I cannot exist without them? I have convinced myself that there is nothing in the world—no sky, no earth, no minds, no bodies. Doesn't it follow that I don't exist? No, surely I must exist if it's me who is convinced of something. But there is a deceiver, supremely powerful and cunning whose aim is to see that I am always deceived. But surely I exist, if I am deceived. Let him deceive me all he can, he will never make it the case that I am nothing while I think that I am something. Thus having fully weighed every consideration, I must finally conclude that the statement "I am, I exist" must be true whenever I state it or mentally consider it.

But I do not yet fully understand what this "I" is that must exist. I must guard against inadvertently taking myself to be something other than I am, thereby going wrong even in the knowledge that I put forward as supremely certain and evident. Hence, I will think once again about what I believed myself to be before beginning these meditations. From this conception, I will subtract everything challenged by the reasons for doubt that I produced earlier, until nothing remains except what is certain and indubitable.

What, then, did I formerly take myself to be? A man, of course. But what is a man? Should I say a rational animal? No, because then I would need to ask what an animal is and what it is to be rational. Thus, starting from a single question, I would sink into many that are more difficult, and I do not have the time to waste on such subtleties. Instead, I will look here at the thoughts that occurred to me spontaneously and naturally when I reflected on what I was. This first thought to occur to me was that I have a face, hands, arms, and all the other equipment (also found in corpses) which I call a body. The next thought to occur to me was that I take nourishment, move myself around, sense, and think—that I do things which I trace back to my soul. Either I didn't stop to think about what this soul was, or I imagined it to be a rarified air, or fire, or ether permeating the denser parts of my body. But, about physical objects, I didn't have any doubts whatever: I thought that I distinctly knew their nature. If I had tried to describe my conception of this nature, I might have said this: "When I call something a physical object, I mean that it is capable of being bounded by a shape and limited to a place; that it can fill a space so as to exclude other objects from it; that it can be perceived by touch, sight, hearing, taste, and smell; that it can be moved in various ways, not by itself, but by something else in contact with it." I judged that the powers of self-movement, of sensing, and of thinking did not belong to the nature of physical objects, and, in fact, I marveled that there were some physical objects in which these powers could be found.

But what should I think now, while supposing that a supremely powerful and "evil" deceiver completely devotes himself to deceiving me? Can I say that I have any of the things that I have attributed to the nature of physical objects? I concentrate, think, reconsider—but nothing comes to me; I grow tired of the pointless repetition. But what about the things that I have assigned to soul? Nutrition and self-movement? Since I have no body, these are merely illusions. Sensing? But I cannot sense without a body, and in sleep I've seemed to sense many things that I later realized I had not really sensed. Thinking? It comes down to this: Thought and thought alone cannot be taken away from me. I am, I exist. That much is certain. But for how long? As long as I think—for it may be that, if I completely stopped thinking, I would completely cease to exist. I am not now admitting anything unless it must be true, and I am therefore not admitting that I am anything at all other than a thinking thing— that is, a mind, soul, understanding, or reason (terms whose meaning I did not previously know). I know that I am a real, existing thing, but what kind of thing? As I have said, a thing that thinks.

What else? I will draw up mental images. I'm not the collection of organs called a human body. Nor am I some rarified gas permeating these organs, or air, or fire, or vapor, or breath—for I have supposed that none of these things exist. Still, I am something. But couldn't it be that these things, which I do not yet know about and which I am therefore supposing to be nonexistent, really aren't distinct from the "I" that I know to exist? I don't know, and I'm not going to argue about it now. I can only form judgments on what I do know.

I know that I exist, and I ask what the "I" is that I know to exist. It's obvious that this conception of myself doesn't depend on anything that I do not yet know to exist and, therefore, that it does not depend on anything of which I can draw up a mental image. And the words "draw up" point to my mistake. I would truly be creative if I were to have a mental image of what I am, since to have a mental image is just to contemplate the shape or image of a physical object. I now know with certainty that I exist and at the same time that all images—and, more generally, all things associated with the nature of physical objects—may just be dreams. When I keep this in mind, it seems just as absurd to say "I use mental images to help me understand what I am" as it would to say "Now, while awake, I see something true—but, since I don't yet see it clearly enough, I'll go to sleep and let my dreams present it to me more clearly and truly." Thus I know that none of the things that I can comprehend with the aid of mental images bear on my knowledge of myself. And I must carefully draw my mind away from such things if it is to see its own nature distinctly.

But what then am I? A thinking thing. And what is that? Something that doubts, understands, affirms, denies, wills, refuses, and also senses and has mental images.

That's quite a lot, if I really do all of these things. But don't I? Isn't it me who now doubts nearly everything, understands one thing, affirms this thing, refuses to affirm other things, wants to know much more, refuses to be deceived, has mental images (sometimes involuntarily), and is aware of many things "through his senses"? Even if I am always dreaming, and even if my creator does what he can to deceive me, isn't it just as true that I do all these things as that I exist? Are any of these things distinct from my thought? Can any be said to be separate from me? That it's me who doubts, understands, and wills is so obvious that I don't see how it could be more evident. And it's also me who has mental images. While it may be, as I am supposing, that absolutely nothing of which I have a mental image really exists, the ability to have mental images really does exist and is a part of my thought. Finally, it's me who senses—or who seems to gain awareness of physical objects through the senses. For example, I am now seeing light, hearing a noise, and feeling heat. These things are unreal, since I am dreaming. But it is still certain that I seem to see, to hear, and to feel. This seeming cannot be unreal, and it is what is properly called sensing. Strictly speaking, sensing is just thinking.

From this, I begin to learn a little about what I am. But I still can't stop thinking that I apprehend physical objects, which I picture in mental images and examine with my senses, much more distinctly than I know this unfamiliar "I," of which I cannot form a mental image. I think this, even though it would be astounding if I comprehended things which I've found to be doubtful, unknown, and alien to me more distinctly than the one which I know to be real: my self. But I see what's happening. My mind enjoys wandering, and it won't confine itself to the truth. I will therefore loosen the reigns on my mind for now so that later, when the time is right, I will be able to control it more easily.

Let's consider the things commonly taken to be the most distinctly comprehended: physical objects that we see and touch. Let's not consider physical objects in general, since general conceptions are very often confused. Rather, let's consider one, particular object. Take, for example, this piece of wax. It has just been taken from the honeycomb; it hasn't yet completely lost the taste of honey; it still smells of the flowers from which it was gathered; its color, shape, and size are obvious; it is hard, cold, and easy to touch; it makes a sound when rapped. In short, everything seems to be present in the wax that is required for me to know it as distinctly as possible. But, as I speak, I move the wax toward the fire; it loses what was left of its taste; it gives up its smell; it changes color; it loses its shape; it gets bigger; it melts; it heats up; it becomes difficult to touch; it no longer makes a sound when struck. Is it still the same piece of wax? We must say that it is: not one denies it or thinks otherwise. Then what was there in the wax that I comprehended so distinctly? Certainly nothing that I reached with my senses—for, while everything having to do with taste, smell, sight, touch, and hearing has changed, the same piece of wax remains.

Perhaps what I distinctly knew was neither the sweetness of honey, nor the fragrance of flowers, nor a sound, but a physical object that once appeared to me one way and now appears differently. But what exactly is it of which I now have a mental image? Let's pay careful attention, remove everything that doesn't belong to the wax, and see what's left. Nothing is left except an extended, flexible, and changeable thing. But what is it for this thing to be flexible and changeable? Is it just that the wax can go from round to square and then to triangular, as I have mentally pictured? Of course not. Since I understand that the wax's shape can change in innumerable ways, and since I can't run through all the changes in my imagination, my comprehension of the wax's flexibility and changeability cannot have been produced by my ability to have mental images. And what about the thing that is extended? Are we also ignorant of its extension? Since the extension of the wax increases when the wax melts, increases again when the wax boils, and increases still more when the wax gets hotter, I will be mistaken about what the wax is unless I believe that it can undergo more changes in extension than I can ever encompass with mental images. I must therefore admit that I do not have an image of what the wax is—that I grasp what it is with only my mind. (While I am saying this about a particular piece of wax, it is even more clearly true about wax in general.) What then is this piece of wax that I grasp only with my mind? It is something that I see, feel, and mentally picture—exactly what I believed it to be at the outset. But it must be noted that, despite the appearances, my grasp of the wax is not visual, tactile, or pictorial. Rather, my grasp of the wax is the result of a purely mental inspection, which can be imperfect and confused, as it was once, or clear and distinct, as it is now, depending on how much attention I pay to the things of which the wax consists.

I'm surprised by how prone my mind is to error. Even when I think to myself non-verbally, language stands in my way, and common usage comes close to deceiving me. For, when the wax is present, we say that we see the wax itself, not that we infer its presence from its color and shape.

I'm inclined to leap from this fact about language to the conclusion that I learn about the wax by eyesight rather than by purely mental inspection. But, if I happen to look out my window and see men walking in the street, I naturally say that I see the men just as I say that I see the wax. What do I really see, however, but hats and coats that could be covering robots? I *judge* that there are men. Thus I comprehend with my judgment, which is in my mind, objects that I once believed myself to see with my eyes.

One who aspires to wisdom above that of the common man disgraces himself by deriving doubt from common ways of speaking. Let's go on, then, to ask when I most clearly and perfectly grasped what the wax is. Was it when I first looked at the wax and believed my knowledge of it to come from the external senses—or at any rate from the so-called "common sense," the power of having mental images? Or is it now, after I have carefully studied what the wax is and how I come to know it? Doubt would be silly here. For what was distinct in my original conception of the wax? How did that conception differ from that had by animals? When I distinguish the wax from its external forms—when I "undress" it and view it "naked"—there may still be errors in my judgments about it, but I couldn't possibly grasp the wax in this way without a human mind.

What should I say about this mind—or, in other words, about myself? (I am not now admitting that there is anything to me but a mind.) What is this "I" that seems to grasp the wax so distinctly? Don't I know myself much more truly and certainly, and also much more distinctly and plainly, than I know the wax? For, if I base my judgment that the wax exists on the fact that I see it, my seeing it much more obviously implies that I exist. It's possible that what I see is not really wax, and it's even possible that I don't have eyes with which to see—but it clearly is not possible that, when I see (or, what now amounts to the same thing, when I think I see), the "I" that thinks is not a real thing. Similarly, if I base my judgment that the wax exists on the fact that I feel it, the same fact makes it obvious that I exist. If I base my judgment that the wax exists on the fact that I have a mental image of it or on some other fact of this sort, the same thing can obviously be said. And what I've said about the wax applies to everything else that is outside me. Moreover, if I seem to grasp the wax more distinctly when I detect it with several senses than when I detect it with just sight or touch, I must know myself even more distinctly—for every consideration that contributes to my grasp of the piece of wax or to my grasp of any other physical object serves better to reveal the nature of my mind. Besides, the mind has so much in it by which it can make its conception of itself distinct that what comes to it from physical objects hardly seems to matter.

And now I have brought myself back to where I wanted to be. I now know that physical objects are grasped, not by the senses or the power of having mental images, but by understanding alone. And, since I grasp physical objects in virtue of their being understandable rather than in virtue of their being tangible or visible, I know that I can't grasp anything more easily or plainly than my mind. But, since it takes time to break old habits of thought, I should pause here to allow the length of my contemplation to impress the new thoughts more deeply into my memory.

Commentary and Questions

Descartes seems to have gotten nowhere by doubting. What to do? He resolves to press on, suspecting that the terrors of skepticism can be overcome only by enduring them to the end. The particular horror, of course, is that all our beliefs might be false—that nowhere would they connect at all with reality. If Descartes has carried us with him to this point, we know that we have lots of ideas and beliefs, but whether any one of them represents something that really *exists* seems quite uncertain. Perhaps they are just webs of illusion, like those spun by a master magician—or the evil demon.

Descartes here presents a pattern of thought that deserves a name. Let us call it the representational theory of knowledge and perception, or the **representational theory** for short. The basic ideas of this theory are very widely shared in modern philosophy. We can distinguish five points:

1. We have no immediate or direct access to things in the world, only to the world of our ideas.*
2. "Ideas" must be understood broadly to include all the contents of the mind, including perceptions, images, memories, concepts, beliefs, intentions, and decisions.
3. These ideas serve as *representations* of things other than themselves.
4. Much of what these ideas represent they represent as "out there," or "external" to the mind containing them.
5. It is in principle possible for ideas to represent these things correctly, but they may also be false and misleading.

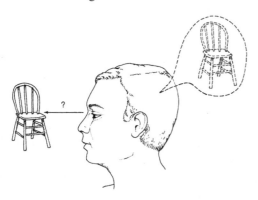

In *Meditation I*, Descartes draws a certain consequence of the representational theory. It seems that mind and world could be disconnected in a perplexing way, that even the most solid ideas might represent things all wrong—or maybe even not represent anything at all! This possibility, foreshadowed by the ancient skeptics and by William of Ockham in his reflections on God's omnipotence, provokes thinkers to try to find a remedy. What we need is a bridge across the chasm between mind and world, and it is clear that it will have to be built by inference and argument. We want *good reasons* to believe that our ideas represent the "external" world truly. But the good reasons must be of a peculiar sort. We have to start this construction project while isolated on one side, restricted in our choice of materials to those available there. It is from the vantage point of the mind that we try to stretch the girders of our argument across the gulf to the world.

We will examine Descartes' effort to build such a rational bridge. The difficulty of that task is emphasized in the dramatic rehearsal of skeptical worries about knowledge in *Meditation I*. And we can now see that these worries hover around the representational theory. The gulf between mind and external reality seems immense.* We might remember Archimedes, who says, "Give me a lever long enough, and a place on which to rest it, and I can move the earth." Descartes thinks that if he can find just one certainty, he might, like Archimedes, do marvels.

Q8. To what certainty does Descartes' methodical doubt lead? Is he right about that?†

The principle "I think, therefore I am" is often referred to as the **cogito,** from the Latin "I think," and we will use that shorthand expression from time to time. It is worth emphasizing that in the *cogito* Descartes has an example of *knowledge*, of knowledge about *reality*, and so of *metaphysical* knowledge. He has thrown the first plank of his bridge across the chasm.‡

Note that Descartes rejects the standard, long-accepted way of answering the question, What am I? (p. 369). According to a tradition stretching back to Socrates (and codified by Aristotle), the

---

*The American philosopher John Searle calls this view that we only perceive our *ideas* of objects "the greatest single disaster in the history of philosophy over the past four centuries." In *Mind: A Brief Introduction* (Oxford: Oxford University Press, 2004), 23.

*Other thinkers after Descartes also wrestle with this problem. Locke recognizes the gulf but papers it over, Berkeley settles down on one side of it, Hume despairs of a solution, Kant redefines the problem so as to make the gulf (partially) disappear, Hegel denies there is a gulf at all, and Kierkegaard opens it up again. The problem is not dead today.

†Descartes' central idea here is anticipated by Augustine in his refutation of the skeptics. See pp. 267–268.

‡Compare Descartes' *cogito* to Avicenna's "Flying Man" argument (p. 304). Contrast both Descartes' and Avicenna's arguments with the Buddhist arguments for the principle of *anātman* (pp. 41–45).

way to answer such a question is to give a *definition*. The traditional way to define something will tell you (a) what *genus* it belongs to and (b) the *difference* between it and other things in that genus. Not surprisingly, this is called *definition* by **genus and difference**. A human being is said to belong to the genus *animal*; and the difference between a human and other animals is that a human is *rational*. Human beings, Aristotle says, are *rational animals*.

Descartes objects to such a definition because it simply calls for more definitions; you need next a definition of *animal* and a definition for *rational*. Then, presumably, you will require definitions for the terms used to define *them*. And so on.

This whole process has to come to ground somewhere. There must be some terms, Descartes thinks, that do not need definition of this sort, but whose meaning can just be "seen." These will be the *simple* terms, from which more complex terms can be built up. We see in Descartes' rejection of the traditional definition procedure an application of the second and third rules of his method. He is searching for something so simple, clear, and distinct that it just presents itself without any need for definition. He is looking for something **self-evident.** If that can be found, he can use it as a foundation on which to build more complex truths.

Q9. What, then, does Descartes conclude that he is?

Note that Descartes briefly considers the view that he may after all *be* a body, or some such thing, even though he does not *know* he is (p. 370).* But he does not try to refute it here; that proof comes in *Meditation VI*. Here he is interested in what he knows that he *is*—not in what he can infer that he *is not*.

Q10. Why does Descartes rule out the use of the imagination in answering the question, What am I?

Q11. What is included in "thinking," as Descartes understands the term? (See p. 370.) Note how broad the term is for him.

———

*This is the view that Thomas Hobbes urges against Descartes. See "Minds and Motives" in Chapter 18.

Q12. Suppose you feel certain that you see a cat on the mat. Is it certain that there is a cat on the mat? What, in this situation, *can* you be certain of?

———

How difficult it is to stay within the bounds of what we know for certain! As Descartes says, his "mind enjoys wandering." And so it is with us. We, too, keep slipping back into the error of thinking that we know *sensible* things best—this desk, this computer keyboard, this hand. (Do you find that too?)

It is to cure this inclination to rely on the senses that Descartes considers the bit of wax. Read that passage once more (pp. 371–372). All the sensible qualities by means of which we recognize the wax can change. But we still judge that it is the same wax. What does that mean?

The distinction between *ordinary perception* and *judgment* is crucial for Descartes. It is illustrated by the hats and coats we see through the window. We say that we *see* men passing, but this is inaccurate, for they may be just robots dressed like men. What is actually happening in ordinary perception is that our intellect is drawing an *inference* on the basis of certain *data* (supplied by the senses) and issuing a judgment. Judging is an activity of the mind—indeed, as we'll see in *Meditation IV*, of the will.

Perceiving, then, is not a purely passive registration by the senses. Implicit in all perception is judgment, or *giving assent*. In ordinary perception, these judgments are apt to be obscure, confused, and just plain wrong. But fortunately they can be corrected by the application of ideas that are clear and distinct. (These points will be crucial in *Meditation IV*, where Descartes explains how it is possible for us to err.)

With respect to the bit of wax, the moral is that it is "grasped, not by the senses or the power of having mental images, but by the understanding alone." When based wholly on sense, our perception is "imperfect and confused." When directed, however, to "the things of which the wax consists" (the mathematically determinable simples of extension, figure, and motion), knowledge of the wax can be *clear and distinct*.

Both inferences seem to be correct. What reason is there to prefer Bridget's formulation?

Now we can understand why Descartes introduces the wax example. If even here knowledge cannot be found in sensation, but only in a "purely mental inspection," then we should recognize that knowledge of *what we are* must also be approached in this way. Our tendency to think of ourselves as what we can *sense* of ourselves—these hands, this head, these eyes—is considerably undermined. Indeed, I must know myself "much more truly and certainly" even than the wax.

There follows a remarkable conclusion: "I can't grasp anything more easily or plainly than my mind." (What would Freud have said to that?)

Q13. What qualities, then, belong to the wax essentially? (Look again at the basic principles of Descartes' physics on pp. 361–362.)

Q14. Why is our imagination incapable of grasping these qualities of the wax? By what faculty do we grasp it?

Q15. How does the wax example help to cure our habitual inclination to trust the senses?

Q16. How does our language tend to mislead us?

Meditation III: On God's Existence

I will now close my eyes, plug my ears, and withdraw all my senses. I will rid my thoughts of the images of physical objects—or, since that's beyond me, I'll write those images off as empty illusions. Talking with myself and looking more deeply into myself, I'll try gradually to come to know myself better. I am a thinking thing—a thing that doubts, affirms, denies, understands a few things, is ignorant of many things, wills, and refuses. I also sense and have mental images. For, as I've noted, even though the things of which I have sensations or mental images may not exist outside me, I'm certain that the modifications of thought called sensations and mental images exist in me insofar as they are just modifications of thought.

That's a summary of all that I really know—or, at any rate, of all that I've so far noticed that I know. I now will examine more carefully whether there are other things in me that I have not yet discovered. I'm certain that I am a thinking thing. Then don't I know what's needed for me to be certain of other things? In this first knowledge, there is nothing but a clear and distinct grasp of what I affirm, and this grasp surely would not suffice to make me certain if it could ever happen that something I grasped so clearly and distinctly was false. Accordingly, I seem to be able to establish the general rule that whatever I clearly and distinctly grasp is true.

But, in the past, I've accepted as completely obvious and certain many thoughts that I later found to be dubious. What were these thoughts about? The earth, the sky, the stars, and other objects of sense. But what did I clearly grasp about these objects? Only that ideas or thoughts of them appeared in my mind. Even now, I don't deny that these ideas occur in me. But there was something else that I used to affirm—something that I used to believe myself to grasp clearly but did not really grasp at all: I affirmed that there were things besides me, that the ideas in me came from these things, and that the ideas perfectly resembled these things. Either I erred here, or I reached a true judgment that wasn't justified by the strength of my understanding.

But what follows? When I considered very simple and easy points of arithmetic or geometry—such as that two and three together make five—didn't I see them clearly enough to affirm their truth? My only reason for judging that I ought to doubt these things was the thought that my God-given nature might deceive me even about what seems most obvious. Whenever I conceive of an all-powerful God, I'm compelled to admit that, if He wants, He can make it the case that I err even about what I take my mind's eye to see most clearly. But, when I turn to the things that I believe myself to grasp very clearly, I'm so convinced by them that I spontaneously burst forth saying, "Whoever may deceive me, he will never bring it about that I am nothing while I think that I am something, or that I have never been when it is now true that I am, or that two plus three is either more or less than five, or that something else in which I recognize an obvious inconsistency is true." And, since I have no reason for thinking that God is a deceiver—indeed since I don't yet know whether God exists—the grounds for doubt that rest on the supposition that God deceives are very weak and "metaphysical." Still, to rid myself of these grounds, I ought to ask as soon as possible whether there is a God and, if so, whether He can be a deceiver. For it seems that, until I know these two things, I can never be completely certain of anything else.

The structure of my project seems to require, however, that I first categorize my thoughts and ask in which of them truth and falsity really reside. Some of my thoughts are like images of things, and only these can properly be called ideas. I have an idea, for example, when I think of a man, of a chimera, of heaven, of an angel, or of God. But other thoughts have other properties: while I always apprehend something as the object of my thought when I will, fear, affirm, or deny, these thoughts also include a component in addition to the likeness of that thing. Some of these components are called volitions or emotions; others, judgments.

Now, viewed in themselves and without regard to other things, ideas cannot really be false. If I imagine a chimera and a goat, it is just as true that I imagine the chimera as that I imagine the goat. And I needn't worry about falsehoods in volitions or emotions. If I have a perverse desire for something, or if I want something that doesn't exist, it's still true that I want that thing. All that remains, then, are my judgments; it's here that I must be careful not to err. And the first and foremost of the errors that I find in my judgments is that of assuming that the ideas in me have a similarity or conformity to things outside me. For, if I were to regard ideas merely as modifications of thought, they could not really provide me with any opportunity for error.

Of my ideas, some seem to me to be innate, others acquired, and others produced by me. The ideas by which I understand reality, truth, and thought seem to have come from my own nature. Those ideas by which I hear a noise, see the sun, or feel the fire I formerly judged to come from things outside me. And the ideas of sirens, hippogriffs, and so on I have formed in myself. Or maybe I can take all of my ideas to be acquired, all innate, or all created by me: I do not yet clearly see where my ideas come from.

For the moment, the central question is about the ideas that I view as derived from objects existing outside me. What reason is there for thinking that these ideas resemble the objects? I seem to have been taught this by nature. Besides, I find that these ideas are independent of my will and hence of me—for they often appear when I do not want them to do so. For example, I now feel heat whether I want to or not, and I therefore take the idea or sensation of heat to come from something distinct from me: the heat of the fire by which I am now sitting. And the obvious thing to think is that a thing sends me its own likeness, not something else.

I will now see whether these reasons are good enough. When I say that nature teaches me something, I mean just that I have a spontaneous impulse to believe it, not that the light of nature reveals the thing's truth to me. There is an important difference. When the light of nature reveals something to me (such as that my thinking implies my existing) that thing is completely beyond doubt, since there is no faculty as reliable as the light of nature by means of which I could learn that the thing is not true. But, as for my natural impulses, I have often judged them to have led me astray in choices about what's good, and I don't see why I should regard them as any more reliable on matters concerning truth and falsehood.

Next, while my sensory ideas may not depend on my will, it doesn't follow that they come from outside me. While the natural impulses of which I just spoke are in me, they seem to conflict with my will. Similarly, I may have in me an as yet undiscovered ability to produce the ideas that seem to come from outside me—in the way that I used to think that ideas came to me in dreams.

Finally, even if some of my ideas do come from things distinct from me, it doesn't follow that they are likenesses of these things. Indeed, it often seems to me that an idea differs greatly from its cause. For example, I find in myself two different ideas of the sun. One, which I "take in" through the senses and which I ought therefore to view as a typical acquired idea, makes the sun look very small to me. The other, which I derive from astronomical reasoning (that is, which I make, perhaps by composing it from innate ideas), pictures the sun as many times larger than the earth. It clearly cannot be that both of these are accurate likenesses of a sun that exists outside me, and reason convinces me that the one least like the sun is the one that seems to arise most directly from it.

All that I've said shows that, until now, my belief that there are things outside me that send their ideas or images to me (perhaps through my senses) has rested on blind impulse rather than certain judgment.

Still, it seems to me that there may be a way of telling whether my ideas come from things that exist outside me. Insofar as the ideas of things are just modifications of thought, I find no inequality among them; all seem to arise from me in the same way. But, insofar as different ideas present different things to me, there obviously are great differences among them. The ideas of substances are unquestionably greater—or have more "subjective reality"—than those of modifications or accidents. Similarly, the idea by which I understand the supreme God—eternal, infinite, omniscient, omnipotent, and creator of all things other than Himself—has more subjective reality in it than the ideas of finite substances.

Now, the light of nature reveals that there is at least as much in a complete efficient cause as in its effect. For where could an effect get its reality if not from its cause? And how could a cause give something unless it had it? It follows both that

something cannot come from nothing and that what is more perfect—that is, has more reality in it—cannot come from what is less perfect or has less reality. This obviously holds, not just for those effects whose reality is actual or formal, but also for ideas, whose reality we regard as merely subjective. For example, it's impossible for a nonexistent stone to come into existence unless it's produced by something containing, either formally or eminently, everything in the stone. Similarly, heat can only be induced in something that's not already hot by something having at least the same degree of perfection as heat. Also, it's impossible for the *idea* of heat or of stone to be in me unless it's been put there by a cause having at least as much reality as I conceive of in the heat or the stone. For, although the cause doesn't transmit any of its actual or formal reality to the idea, we shouldn't infer that it can be less real than the idea; all that we can infer is that by its nature the idea doesn't require any formal reality except what it derives from my thought, of which it is a modification. Yet, as the idea contains one particular subjective reality rather than another, it must get this reality from a cause having at least as much formal reality as the idea has subjective reality. For, if we suppose that an idea has something in it that wasn't in its cause, we must suppose that it got this thing from nothing. However imperfect the existence of something that exists subjectively in the understanding through an idea, it obviously is something, and it therefore cannot come from nothing.

And, although the reality that I'm considering in my ideas is just subjective, I ought not to suspect that it can fail to be in an idea's cause formally—that it's enough for it to be there subjectively. For, just as the subjective existence of my ideas belongs to the ideas in virtue of their nature, the formal existence of the ideas' causes belongs to those causes—or, at least, to the first and foremost of them—in virtue of the causes' nature. Although one idea may arise from another, this can't go back to infinity; we must eventually arrive at a primary idea whose cause is an "archetype" containing formally all the reality that the idea contains subjectively. Hence, the light of nature makes it clear to me that the ideas in me are like images that may well fall short of the things from which they derive, but cannot contain anything greater or more perfect.

The more time and care I take in studying this, the more clearly and distinctly I know it to be true. But what follows from it? If I can be sure that the subjective reality of one of my ideas is so great that it isn't in me either formally or eminently and hence that I cannot be the cause of that idea, I can infer that I am not alone in the world—that there exists something else that is the cause of the idea. But, if I can find no such idea in me, I will have no argument at all for the existence of anything other than me—for, having diligently searched for such an argument, I have yet to find one.

Of my ideas—besides my idea of myself, about which there can be no problem here—one presents God, others inanimate physical objects, others angels, others animals, and still others men like me.

As to my idea of other men, of animals, and of angels, it's easy to see that—even if the world contained no men but me, no animals, and no angels—I could have composed these ideas from those that I have of myself, of physical objects, and of God.

And, as to my ideas of physical objects, it seems that nothing in them is so great that it couldn't have come from me. For, if I analyze my ideas of physical objects carefully, taking them one by one as I did yesterday when examining my idea of the piece of wax, I notice that there is very little in them that I grasp clearly and distinctly. What I do grasp clearly and distinctly in these ideas is size (which is extension in length, breadth, and depth), shape (which arises from extension's limits), position (which the differently shaped things have relative to one another), and motion (which is just change of position). To these I can add substance, duration, and number. But my thoughts of other things in physical objects (such as light and color, sound, odor, taste, heat and cold, and tactile qualities) are so confused and obscure that I can't say whether they are true or false—whether my ideas of these things are of something or of nothing. Although, as I noted earlier, that which is properly called falsehood—namely, *formal* falsehood—can only be found in judgments, we can still find falsehood of another sort—namely, *material* falsehood—in an idea when it presents what is not a thing as though

it were a thing. For example, the ideas that I have of coldness and heat are so unclear and indistinct that I can't tell from them whether coldness is just the absence of heat, or heat just the absence of coldness, or both are real qualities, or neither is. And, since every idea is "of something," the idea that presents coldness to me as something real and positive could justifiably be called false if coldness were just the absence of heat. And the same holds true for other ideas of this sort.

For such ideas, I need not posit a creator distinct from me. I know by the light of nature that, if one of these ideas is false—that is, if it doesn't present a real thing—it comes from nothing—that is, the only cause of its being in me is a deficiency of my nature, which clearly is imperfect. If one of these ideas is true, however, I still see no reason why I couldn't have produced it myself—for these ideas present so little reality to me that I can't even distinguish it from nothing.

Of the things that are clear and distinct in my ideas of physical objects, it seems that I may have borrowed some—such as substance, duration, and number—from my idea of myself. I think of the stone as a substance—that is, as something that can exist on its own—just as I think of myself as a substance. Although I conceive of myself as a thinking and unextended thing and of the stone as an extended and unthinking thing so that the two conceptions are quite different, they are the same in that they both seem to be of substances. And, when I grasp that I exist now while remembering that I existed in the past, or when I count my various thoughts, I get the idea of duration or number, which I can then apply to other things. The other components of my ideas of physical objects—extension, shape, place, and motion—can't be in me formally, since I'm just a thinking thing. But, as these things are just modes of substance, and as I am a substance, it seems that they may be in me eminently.

All that's left is my idea of God. Is there something in this idea of God that couldn't have come from me? By "God" I mean a substance that's infinite, independent, supremely intelligent, and supremely powerful—the thing from which I and everything else that may exist derive our existence.

The more I consider these attributes, the less it seems that they could have come from me alone. So I must conclude that God necessarily exists.

While I may have the idea of substance in me by virtue of my being a substance, I who am finite would not have the idea of infinite substance in me unless it came from a substance that really was infinite.

And I shouldn't think that, rather than having a true idea of infinity, I grasp it merely as the absence of limits—in the way that I grasp rest as the absence of motion and darkness as the absence of light. On the contrary, it's clear to me that there is more reality in an infinite than in a finite substance and hence that my grasp of the infinite must somehow be prior to my grasp of the finite—my understanding of God prior to my understanding of myself. For how could I understand that I doubt and desire, that I am deficient and imperfect, if I didn't have the idea of something more perfect to use as a standard of comparison?

And, unlike the ideas of hot and cold which I just discussed, the idea of God cannot be said to be materially false and hence to come from nothing. On the contrary, since the idea of God is completely clear and distinct and contains more subjective reality than any other idea, no idea is truer *per se* and none less open to the suspicion of falsity. The idea of a supremely perfect and infinite entity is, I maintain, completely true. For, while I may be able to suppose that there is no such entity, I can't even suppose (as I did about the idea of coldness) that my idea of God fails to show me something real. This idea is maximally clear and distinct, for it contains everything that I grasp clearly and distinctly, everything real and true, everything with any perfection. It doesn't matter that I can't fully comprehend the infinite—that there are innumerable things in God which I can't comprehend fully or even reach with thought. Because of the nature of the infinite, I who am finite cannot comprehend it. It's enough that I think about the infinite and judge that, if I grasp something clearly and distinctly and know it to have some perfection, it's present either formally or eminently—perhaps along with innumerable other things of which I am ignorant—in God. If I do this, then of all my ideas the idea of God will be most true and most clear and distinct.

But maybe I am greater than I have assumed; maybe all the perfections that I attributed to God are in me potentially, still unreal and unactualized. I have already seen my knowledge gradually increase, and I don't see anything to prevent its becoming greater and greater to infinity. Nor do I see why, by means of such increased knowledge, I couldn't get all the rest of God's perfections. Finally, if the potential for these perfections is in me, I don't see why that potential couldn't account for the production of the ideas of these perfections in me.

None of this is possible. First, while it's true that my knowledge gradually increases and that I have many as yet unactualized potentialities, none of this fits with my idea of God, in whom absolutely nothing is potential; indeed, the gradual increase in my knowledge shows that I am *imperfect*. Besides, I see that, even if my knowledge were continually to become greater and greater, it would never become actually infinite, since it would never become so great as to be unable to increase. But I judge God to be actually infinite so that nothing can be added to his perfection. Finally, I see that an idea's subjective being must be produced, not by mere potentiality (which, strictly speaking, is nothing), but by what is actual or formal.

When I pay attention to these things, the light of nature makes all of them obvious. But, when I attend less carefully and the images of sensible things blind my mind's eye, it's not easy for me to remember why the idea of an entity more perfect than I am must come from an entity that really is more perfect. That's why I'll go on to ask whether I, who have the idea of a perfect entity, could exist if no such entity existed.

From what might I derive my existence if not from God? Either from myself, or from my parents, or from something else less perfect than God—for nothing more perfect than God, or even as perfect as Him, can be thought of or imagined.

But, if I derived my existence from myself, I wouldn't doubt, or want, or lack anything. I would have given myself every perfection of which I have an idea, and thus I myself would be God. And I shouldn't think that it might be harder to give myself what I lack than what I already have. On the contrary, it would obviously be much harder for me, a thinking thing or substance, to emerge from nothing than for me to give myself knowledge of the many things of which I am ignorant, which is just an attribute of substance. But surely, if I had given myself that which is harder to get, I wouldn't have denied myself complete knowledge, which would have been easier to get. Indeed, I wouldn't have denied myself *any* of the perfections that I grasp in the idea of God. None of these perfections seems harder to get than existence. But, if I had given myself everything that I now have, these perfections would have seemed harder to get than existence if they were harder to get—for in creating myself I would have discovered the limits of my power.

I can't avoid the force of this argument by supposing that, since I've always existed as I do now, there's no point in looking for my creator. Since my lifetime can be divided into innumerable parts each of which is independent of the others, the fact that I existed a little while ago does not entail that I exist now, unless a cause "recreates" me—or, in other words, preserves me—at this moment. For, when we attend to the nature of time, it's obvious that exactly the same power and action are required to preserve a thing at each moment through which it endures as would be required to create it anew if it had never existed. Hence, one of the things revealed by the light of nature is that preservation and creation differ only in the way we think of them.

I ought to ask myself, then, whether I have the power to ensure that I, who now am, will exist in a little while. Since I am nothing but a thinking thing—or, at any rate, since I am now focusing on the part of me that thinks—I would surely be aware of this power if it were in me. But I find no such power. And from this I clearly see that there is an entity distinct from me on whom I depend.

But maybe this entity isn't God. Maybe I am the product of my parents or of some other cause less perfect than God. No. As I've said, there must be at least as much in a cause as in its effect. Hence, since I am a thinking thing with the idea of God in me, my cause, whatever it may be, must be a thinking thing having in it the idea of every perfection that I attribute to God. And we can go on to

ask whether this thing gets its existence from itself or from something else. If it gets its existence from itself, it's obvious from what I've said that it must be God—for it would have the power to exist on its own and hence the power actually to give itself every perfection of which it has an idea, including every perfection that I conceive of in God. But, if my cause gets its existence from some other thing, we can go on to ask whether this other thing gets its existence from itself or from something else. Eventually, we will come to the ultimate cause, which will be God.

It's clear enough that there can't be an infinite regress here—especially since I am concerned, not so much with the cause that originally produced me, as with the one that preserves me at the present moment.

And I can't suppose that several partial causes combined to make me or that I get the ideas of the various perfections that I attribute to God from different causes so that, while each of these perfections can be found somewhere in the universe, there is no God in whom they all come together. On the contrary, one of the chief perfections that I understand God to have is unity, simplicity, inseparability from everything in Him. Surely the idea of the unity of all God's perfections can only have been put in me by a cause that gives me the ideas of all the other perfections—for nothing could make me aware of the unbreakable connection of God's perfections unless it made me aware of what those perfections are.

Finally, even if everything that I used to believe about my parents is true, it's clear that they don't preserve me. Insofar as I am a thinking thing, they did not even take part in creating me. They simply formed the matter in which I used to think that I (that is, my mind, which is all I am now taking myself to be) resided. There can therefore be no problem about my parents. And I am driven to this conclusion: The fact that I exist and have an idea in me of a perfect entity—that is, God—conclusively entails that God does in fact exist.

All that's left is to explain how I have gotten my idea of God from Him. I have not taken it in through my senses; it has never come to me unexpectedly as the ideas of sensible things do when those things affect (or seem to affect) my external organs of sense. Nor have I made the idea myself; I can't subtract from it or add to it. The only other possibility is that the idea is innate in me, like my idea of myself.

It's not at all surprising that in creating me God put this idea into me, impressing it on His work like a craftsman's mark (which needn't be distinct from the work itself). The very fact that it was God who created me confirms that I have somehow been made in His image or likeness and that I grasp this likeness, which contains the idea of God, in the same way that I grasp myself. Thus, when I turn my mind's eye on myself, I understand, not just that I am an incomplete and dependent thing which constantly strives for bigger and better things, but also that He on whom I depend has all these things in Himself as infinite reality rather than just as vague potentiality and hence that He must be God. The whole argument comes down to this: I know that I could not exist with my present nature—that is, that I could not exist with the idea of God in me—unless there really were a God. This must be the very God whose idea is in me, the thing having all of the perfections that I can't fully comprehend but can somehow reach with thought, who clearly cannot have any defects. From this, it's obvious that He can't deceive—for, as the natural light reveals, fraud and deception arise from defect.

But before examining this more carefully and investigating its consequences, I want to dwell for a moment in the contemplation of God, to ponder His attributes, to see and admire and adore the beauty of His boundless light, insofar as my clouded insight allows. As I have faith that the supreme happiness of the next life consists wholly of the contemplation of divine greatness, I now find that contemplation of the same sort, though less perfect, affords the greatest joy available in this life.

Commentary and Questions

In the first paragraphs, Descartes resolves to explore more carefully his own mind. But then what alternative does he have, now that he has resolved to consider everything else "as empty illusions"?

A momentous step is taken: He *solves* (or at least he thinks he solves) the problem of the criterion! Here are the steps.

1. He is certain that he exists as a **thinking thing.**
2. He asks himself, What is it about this proposition that accounts for my certainty that it is true?
3. He answers, The fact that I grasp it so clearly and distinctly that I perceive it could not possibly be false.
4. He concludes, Let this then be a general principle (a *criterion*): Whatever I grasp with *like clarity and distinctness* must also be true.

He then reviews (yet again) the things he had at one time thought were true and reminds himself that no matter how sure he feels about them, he can't be absolutely certain.

Q17. Why does he feel a need to inquire about the existence and nature of God?

Descartes now tries to make clear a crucial distinction between **ideas** on the one hand and **volitions, emotions,** and **judgments** on the other (pp. 376–377). This distinction is embedded in an inventory of the varied contents of the mind (which is all that we can so far be certain of). You will find a schematic representation of that inventory in the following diagram.

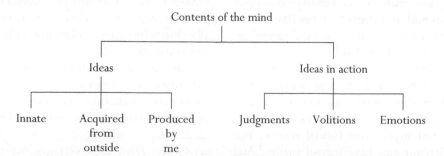

Q18. What is the key difference between ideas and judgments?

Q19. What is the key difference between judgments on the one hand and volitions and emotions on the other?

Q20. What question arises with respect to the ideas that seem to be acquired from outside myself?

Q21. What (provisional) examples does Descartes give of each class of ideas?

We need to comment on the notion of **innate ideas.** In calling them "innate," Descartes does not mean to imply that they are to be found in babies and mentally defective adults, as some of his critics suppose. He merely means that there are some ideas we would have even if nothing existed but ourselves. These ideas do not require external causes for their existence in us; every developed rational mind will possess them from its own resources. Thus, the idea of a *thing* can originate with the *cogito*, which gives me the certainty that I exist as a thing that thinks—even if nothing else exists. Perhaps my idea of an antelope is caused in me only by seeing antelopes in a zoo (though this remains to be proved). But we would have the ideas of thing, thought, and truth in any case.

Q22. Why do you think Descartes believes that the ideas of truth and thought are innate?

Q23. Why is he inclined to believe that some ideas do originate from objects outside himself? He gives two reasons (p. 377).

Q24. Are these two reasons conclusive?

Q25. What is the difference between being taught "by nature" and being taught "by the light of nature"? (See p. 376.) What is the **light of nature**?

We come now to a point of terminology. Descartes distinguishes **subjective reality** on the one hand from **formal** and **eminent reality** on the other. If we are going to understand Descartes' argument, we must be clear about how he uses these terms and keep his use firmly in mind.

It is easier to begin with formal reality. Something has formal reality if it is, in our terms, actual or existing. If there really are giraffes and angels, then giraffes and angels have formal reality. You also, because you exist, have formal reality. And when you form an image of a giraffe in your mind, that image also has formal reality—that is, it actually exists as *an image* in your mind. So any idea actually present in a mind is formally real. This means that (if there are giraffes) both the idea of a giraffe (when being thought) and the giraffe you are thinking of are formally real. They are distinct realities, but related: The one *represents* the other.

What you are thinking about when you entertain an idea has subjective reality, reality "for you." Thus, when you think about giraffes and angels, they have both formal and subjective reality. The objects of some ideas, though, have *only* subjective reality: the tooth fairy, for instance, or unicorns. These, of course, are examples of ideas "produced by us." But if we look carefully, we can see that they have not been invented out of nothing. The idea of a unicorn comes from the ideas of a horse and a single horn. And (though Descartes has not proved it yet) it may be that horses and horns are formally real. Already he remarks (p. 377) that although one idea may be derived from others, this cannot go on to infinity: There must eventually be a cause for these ideas; and the reality of that cause must be more than "merely subjective." If this were not so, we would have gotten something "from nothing." And the light of nature assures us that this is impossible. There is an old Latin saying: *ex nihilo nihil fit,* or "from nothing, nothing comes."

Descartes does not, of course, make these distinctions for their own sake. There is a problem he is trying to solve: Given that I can be certain that I exist (together with all my ideas), can I be certain of the *formal* existence of anything else? Although thoroughgoing skepticism may have been refuted (we do know something in the *cogito*), *we have not got beyond solipsism.* **Solipsism** is a view that each of you (if there is anyone out there!) must state for yourself in this way: "I am the only thing that actually (formally) exists; everything else is only subjectively real."

Another step in solving that problem is to note that there are *degrees of reality*: some things have more reality than others. This is the cardinal principle of the Great Chain of Being.* Descartes gives

---

*See pp. 271–272.

two examples, framed in terms of subjective reality (p. 377), though the same is true for formal reality as well.

Q26. Why does the idea of *substance* contain more subjective reality than that of *modification* or *accident*? (Think of a fender and the dent in it.)*

Q27. Why does the idea of infinite substance have more subjective reality than that of finite substance?

On the basis of these distinctions, Descartes formulates a *causal principle*: There must be at least as much reality in the cause as there is in the effect. A cause is said to be *formally real* when it has the same degree of reality as the effect it produces; it is said to be *eminently real* when it has even more reality than its effect.

Q28. What examples does Descartes offer to illustrate this causal principle?

Once more Descartes canvases the various kinds of ideas he finds in himself as a thinking thing. He is looking for some idea of which he himself could not possibly be the cause. Such an idea must have a cause (since nothing comes from nothing). If (1) he is not the cause and (2) there is a cause, then (3) he knows that he is not alone in the universe. Something else exists!

Descartes thinks his meditations to this point give him the materials with which to prove that God exists. Let us see what the argument looks like:

1. I have an idea of an infinitely perfect substance.
2. Such an idea must have a cause.
3. *Ex nihilo nihil fit.*
4. So the cause of an idea must have at least as much *formal* reality as there is *subjective* reality in the idea.
5. Though I am a substance, I am not infinitely perfect.
6. So I could not be the cause of this idea.

---

*We owe this nice example to Ronald Rubin, the translator of these *Meditations*.

7. So there must be a formal reality that is an infinitely perfect substance.
8. So God exists.

Q29. Is this argument valid?

Q30. Are there premises in the argument that are less than certainly true?

Meditation III contains two separate arguments for God's existence. The first one, which we have now examined, begins with the fact that each of us has an *idea* of God. The second one begins (on p. 379) with the fact that I exist. The argument then addresses whether I could exist if God does not. It is an argument by exclusion; it considers the other plausible candidates for the cause of my existence and shows in each case that it won't do. Note that both arguments are *causal* arguments. The first inquires about the cause of my *idea* of God and the second about the cause of my *existence*. Both make use of the causal principle Descartes has formulated.

Let us sketch the principal steps in this argument.

1. I exist.
2. There must be a cause for my existence.
3. The cause must be one of the following: (a) myself, (b) my always having existed, (c) my parents, (d) something else less perfect than God, or (e) God.
4. Not (a), or I would have given myself perfections I now lack—because creating the properties of a substance is not as hard as creating the substance itself.
5. Not (b), because my existing now does not *follow from* my having existed in the past.
6. Not (c), for this leads to an infinite regress.
7. Not (d), for this couldn't account for the unity of the idea of God that I have.
8. So (e), and God exists.

Q31. Is there a weak point in this argument? Is there more than one?

Q32. Why does Descartes think his idea of God must be innate?

Q33. Explain why Descartes says we cannot "comprehend" God but can "reach" him in thought. (Compare touching an elephant and wrapping your arms around it.)*

At the end of the third *meditation*, Descartes feels he has achieved his aim. He now knows that he is not alone. In addition to himself, there is at least one other being—a substance infinite in intelligence and power and perfect in every way. This latter fact will prove to be of very great significance, for Descartes will use it to defeat the hypothesis of the evil demon; a perfect being could not be a deceiver. Thus he thinks he can overcome the deepest ground for skepticism about knowledge of the external world. But that is a line of argument pursued in the remaining meditations.

Meditation IV: On Truth and Falsity

In the last few days, I've gotten used to drawing my mind away from my senses. I've carefully noted that I really grasp very little about physical objects, that I know much more about the human mind, and that I know even more about God. Thus, I no longer find it hard to turn my thoughts away from things of which I can have mental images and toward things completely separate from matter, which I can only understand. Indeed, I have a much more distinct idea of the human mind, insofar as it is just a thinking thing that isn't extended in length, breadth, or depth and doesn't share anything else with physical objects, than I have of physical objects. And, when I note that I doubt or that I am incomplete and dependent, I have a clear and distinct idea of a complete and independent entity: God. From the fact that this idea is in me and that I who have the idea exist, I can clearly infer both that God exists and that I am completely dependent on Him for my existence from moment to moment. This is so obvious that I'm sure that people can't know anything more evidently or certainly. And it now seems to me that, from the contemplation of the true God in whom are hidden all treasures of knowledge and wisdom, there is a way to derive knowledge of other things.

* Compare the similar thought by Aquinas, p. 324.

In the first place, I know that it's impossible for Him ever to deceive me. Wherever there is fraud and deception, there is imperfection, and, while the ability to deceive may seem a sign of cunning or power, the desire to deceive reveals malice or weakness and hence is inconsistent with God's nature.

Next, I find in myself an ability to judge which, like everything else in me, I've gotten from God. Since He doesn't want to deceive me, He certainly hasn't given me an ability which will lead me wrong when properly used.

There can be no doubt about this—except that it may seem to imply that I don't err at all. For, if I've gotten everything in me from God and He hasn't given me the ability to err, it doesn't seem possible for me ever to err. Thus, as long as I think only of God and devote all my attention to Him, I can't find any cause for error and falsity. When I turn my attention back to myself, however, I find that I can make innumerable errors. In looking for the cause of these errors, I find before me, not just the real and positive idea of God, but also the negative idea of "nothingness"—the idea of that which is completely devoid of perfection. I find that I am "intermediate" between God and nothingness, between the supreme entity and nonentity. Insofar as I am the creation of the supreme entity, there's nothing in me to account for my being deceived or led into error, but, insofar as I somehow participate in nothingness or the nonentity—that is, insofar as I am distinct from the supreme entity itself and lack many things—it's not surprising that I go wrong. I thus understand that, in itself, error is a lack, rather than a real thing dependent on God. Hence, I understand that I can err without God's having given me a special ability to do so. Rather, I fall into error because my God-given ability to judge the truth is not infinite.

But there's still something to be explained. Error is not just an absence, but a deprivation—the lack of knowledge that somehow ought to be in me. But, when I attend to God's nature, it seems impossible that He's given me an ability that is an imperfect thing of its kind—an ability lacking a perfection that it ought to have. The greater the craftsman's skill, the more perfect his product.

Then how can the supreme creator of all things have made something that isn't absolutely perfect? There's no doubt that God could have made me so that I never err and that He always wants what's best. Then is it better for me to err than not to err?

When I pay more careful attention, I realize that I shouldn't be surprised at God's doing things that I can't explain. I shouldn't doubt His existence just because I find that I sometimes can't understand why or how He has made something. I know that my nature is weak and limited and that God's is limitless, incomprehensible, and infinite, and, from this, I can infer that He can do innumerable things whose reasons are unknown to me. On this ground alone, I regard the common practice of explaining things in terms of their purposes to be useless in physics: it would be foolhardy of me to think that I can discover God's purposes.

It also seems to me that, when asking whether God's works are perfect, I ought to look at all of them together, not at one in isolation. For something that seems imperfect when viewed alone might seem completely perfect when regarded as having a place in the world. Of course, since calling everything into doubt, I haven't established that anything exists besides me and God. But, when I consider God's immense power, I can't deny that He has made—or, in any case, that He could have made—many other things, and I must therefore view myself as having a place in a universe.

Next, turning to myself and investigating the nature of my errors (which are all that show me to be imperfect), I notice that these errors depend on two concurrent causes: my ability to know and my ability to choose freely—that is, my understanding and my will. But, with my understanding, I just grasp the ideas about which I form judgments, and error therefore cannot properly be said to arise from the understanding itself. While there may be innumerable things of which I have no idea, I can't say that I am deprived of these ideas, but only that I happen to lack them—for I don't have any reason to think that God ought to have given me a greater ability to know than He has. And, while I understand God to be a supremely skilled craftsman, I don't go on to think that He ought to endow each of his works with all the perfections that He can put in the others.

Nor can I complain about the scope or perfection of my God-given freedom of will—for I find that my will doesn't seem to me to be restricted in any way. Indeed, it seems well worth noting that nothing in me other than my will is so great and perfect that it couldn't conceivably be bigger or better. If I think about my ability to understand, for example, I realize that it is very small and restricted and I immediately form the idea of something much greater—indeed, of something supremely perfect and infinite. And, from the fact that I can form the idea of this thing, I infer that it is present in God's nature. Similarly, if I consider my other abilities, like the abilities to remember and to imagine, I clearly see that they all are weak and limited in me, but boundless in God. My will or freedom of choice is the only thing I find to be so great in me that I can't conceive of anything greater. In fact, it's largely for this reason that I regard myself as an image or likeness of God. God's will is incomparably greater than mine, of course, in virtue of the associated knowledge and power that make it stronger and more effective, and also in virtue of all its greater range of objects. Yet, viewed in itself as a will, God's will seems no greater than mine. For having a will just amounts to being able either to do or not to do (affirm or deny, seek or avoid)—or, better, to being inclined to affirm or deny, seek or shun what the understanding offers, without any sense of being driven by external forces. To be free, I don't need to be inclined towards both alternatives. On the contrary, the more I lean towards one alternative—either because I understand the truth or goodness in it, or because God has so arranged my deepest thoughts—the more freely I choose it. Neither divine grace nor knowledge of nature ever diminishes my freedom; they increase and strengthen it. But the indifference that I experience when no consideration impels me towards one alternative over another is freedom of the lowest sort, whose presence reveals a defect or an absence of knowledge rather than a perfection. For, if I always knew what was good or true, I wouldn't ever deliberate about what to do or choose, and thus, though completely free, I would never be indifferent.

From this I see that my God-given ability to will is not itself the cause of my errors—for my will is great, a perfect thing of its kind. Neither is my power of understanding the cause of my errors; whenever I understand something, I understand it correctly and without the possibility of error, since my understanding comes from God. What then is the source of my errors? It is just that, while my will has a broader scope than my understanding, I don't keep it within the same bounds, but extend it to that which I don't understand. Being indifferent to these things, my will is easily led away from truth and goodness, and thus I am led into error and sin.

For example, I've asked for the last few days whether anything exists in the world, and I've noted that, from the fact that I ask this, it follows that I exist. I couldn't fail to judge that which I so clearly understood to be true. This wasn't because a force outside me compelled me to believe, but because an intense light in my understanding produced a strong inclination of my will. And, to the extent that I wasn't indifferent, I believed spontaneously and freely. However, while I now know that I exist insofar as I am a thinking thing, I notice in myself an idea of what it is to be a physical object and I come to wonder whether the thinking nature that's in me—or, rather, that is me—differs from this bodily nature or is identical to it. Nothing occurs to my reason (I am supposing) to convince me of one alternative rather than the other. Accordingly, I am completely indifferent to affirming either view, to denying either view, and even to suspending judgment.

And indifference of this sort is not limited to things of which the understanding is completely ignorant. It extends to everything about which the will deliberates in the absence of a sufficiently clear understanding. For, however strong the force with which plausible conjectures draw me towards one alternative, the knowledge that they are conjectures rather than assertions backed by certain and indubitable arguments is enough to push my assent the other way. The past few days have provided me with ample experience of this—for I am now supposing each of my former beliefs to be false just because I've found a way to call them into doubt.

If I suspend judgment when I don't clearly and distinctly grasp what's true, I obviously do

right and am not deceived. But, if I either affirm or deny in a case of this sort, I misuse my freedom of choice. If I affirm what is false, I clearly err, and, if I stumble onto the truth, I'm still blameworthy since the light of nature reveals that a perception of the understanding should always precede a decision of the will. In these misuses of freedom of choice lies the deprivation that accounts for error. And this deprivation, I maintain, lies in the working of the will insofar as it comes from me—not in my God-given ability to will, or even in the will's operation insofar as it derives from Him.

I have no reason to complain that God hasn't given me a more perfect understanding or a greater natural light than He has. It's in the nature of a finite understanding that there are many things it can't understand, and it's in the nature of created understanding that it's finite. Indeed, I ought to be grateful to Him who owes me absolutely nothing for what He has bestowed, rather than taking myself to be deprived or robbed of what God hasn't given me.

And I have no reason to complain about God's having given me a will whose scope is greater than my understanding's. The will is like a unity made of inseparable parts; its nature apparently will not allow anything to be taken away from it. And, really, the wider the scope of my will, the more grateful I ought to be to Him who gave it to me.

Finally, I ought not to complain that God concurs in bringing about the acts of will and judgment in which I err. Insofar as these acts derive from God, they are completely true and good, and I am more perfect with the ability to perform these acts than I would be without it. And, the deprivation that is the real ground of falsity and error doesn't need God's concurrence, since it's not a thing. When we regard God as its cause, we should say that it is an absence rather than a deprivation. For it clearly is no imperfection in God that He has given me the freedom to assent or not to assent to things of which He hasn't given me a clear and distinct grasp. Rather, it is undoubtedly an imperfection in me that I misuse this freedom by passing judgment on things that I don't properly understand. I see, of course, that God could easily have brought it about that, while I remain free and limited in knowledge, I never err: He could have implanted in me a clear and distinct understanding of everything about which I was ever going to make a choice, or He could have indelibly impressed on my memory that I must never pass judgment on something that I don't clearly and distinctly understand. And I also understand that, regarded in isolation from everything else, I would have been more perfect if God had made me so that I never err. But I can't deny that, because some things are immune to error while others are not, the universe is more perfect than it would have been if all its parts were alike. And I have no right to complain about God's wanting me to hold a place in the world other than the greatest and most perfect.

Besides, if I can't avoid error by having a clear grasp of every matter on which I make a choice, I can avoid it in the other way, which only requires remembering that I must not pass judgment on matters whose truth isn't apparent. For, although I find myself too weak to fix my attention permanently on this single thought, I can—by careful and frequent meditation—ensure that I call it to mind whenever it's needed and thus that I acquire the habit of avoiding error.

Since the first and foremost perfection of man lies in avoiding error, I've profited from today's meditation, in which I've investigated the cause of error and falsity. Clearly, the only possible cause of error is the one I have described. When I limit my will's range of judgment to the things presented clearly and distinctly to my understanding, I obviously cannot err—for everything that I clearly and distinctly grasp is something and hence must come, not from nothing, but from God—God, I say, who is supremely perfect and who cannot possibly deceive. Therefore, what I clearly and distinctly grasp is unquestionably true. Today, then, I have learned what to avoid in order not to err and also what to do to reach the truth. I surely will reach the truth if I just attend to the things that I understand perfectly and distinguish them from those that I grasp more obscurely and confusedly. And that's what I'll take care to do from now on.

Commentary and Questions

Note the transitional character of the first paragraph. Descartes sums up the argument so far, expresses his confidence that God's existence is more certain than anything else (except the *cogito*), and looks forward to further progress.

Q34. Is Descartes' assertion (p. 384) that deception is an evidence of weakness rather than power plausible? Explain your answer.

Before God's existence was proved, it was unclear whether any of our beliefs were true. Now there is a new puzzle: How can any of them be false? (Do you see why this puzzle arises?) So Descartes has to provide an explanation of the obvious fact that we can and do make mistakes.

For the basic framework he depends again on the idea of the Great Chain of Being. He finds that he is an "intermediate" between God and nothingness, having less reality than God, whose perfection excludes error, but more reality than sheer nonbeing. Error, in any case, is not a positive reality; it is only a defect, as weakness is only the absence of strength and cold the absence of heat. So it should not be too surprising that Descartes, and we, too, should be susceptible to error.

Two points he makes in passing are worth noting.

1. Why did God create me so that I could make mistakes? I don't know, he says, but if I could see the world as God sees it, it is quite possible that I would judge it to be for the best.*

Q35. How does recognizing that you are only a part of a larger whole help answer this question?

---

* Here is one expression of that attitude expressed in Leibniz and other later writers to the effect that "this is the best of all possible worlds." It is this optimism that Voltaire caricatures so savagely in *Candide*. These reflections of Descartes form part of a project known as *theodicy*—the justification of the ways of God to man. For another attempt at theodicy, see Hegel (pp. 516–519). You might also review the Stoic notion that evil does not exist in the world, only in our perception of it (p. 243).

2. Among the many things we do not know are God's purposes. It follows that Aristotelian final causes—the *what for*—are not appropriate in the explanations given by physics. Thus Descartes buttresses the mechanistic character of his (and the modern world's) scientific work. We can come to know *how* things happen, but not *why*.

A more detailed analysis of error can be given. It depends on the distinction between entertaining a belief, or having it in mind (which is the function of the **understanding**), and assenting to that belief, or accepting it (which is the function of the **will**).

Q36. How does this distinction between *understanding* and *will* explain the possibility of error?
Q37. In what way is the will more perfect than the understanding?
Q38. Can God be blamed for our errors?
Q39. How can we avoid error?

Meditation V: On the Essence of Material Objects and More on God's Existence

Many questions remain about God's attributes and the nature of my self or mind. I may return to these questions later. But now, having found what to do and what to avoid in order to attain truth, I regard nothing as more pressing than to work my way out of the doubts that I raised the other day and to see whether I can find anything certain about material objects.

But, before asking whether any such objects exist outside me, I ought to consider the ideas of these objects as they exist in my thoughts and see which are clear and which confused.

I have a distinct mental image of the quantity that philosophers commonly call continuous. That is, I have a distinct mental image of the extension of this quantity—or rather of the quantified thing—in length, breadth, and depth. I can distinguish various parts of this thing. I can ascribe various sizes, shapes, places, and motions to these parts and various durations to the motions.

In addition to having a thorough knowledge of extension in general, I grasp innumerable particulars about things like shape, number, and motion, when I pay careful attention. The truth of these particulars is so obvious and so consonant with my nature that, when I first think of one of these things, I seem not so much to be learning something novel as to be remembering something that I already knew—or noticing for the first time something that had long been in me without my having turned my mind's eye toward it.

What's important here, I think, is that I find in myself innumerable ideas of things which, though they may not exist outside me, can't be said to be nothing. While I have some control over my thoughts of these things, I do not make the things up: they have their own real and immutable natures. Suppose, for example, that I have a mental image of a triangle. While it may be that no figure of this sort does exist or ever has existed outside my thought, the figure has a fixed nature (essence or form), immutable and eternal, which hasn't been produced by me and isn't dependent on my mind. The proof is that I can demonstrate various propositions about the triangle, such as that its angles equal two right angles and that its greatest side subtends its greatest angle. Even though I didn't think of these propositions at all when I first imagined the triangle, I now clearly see their truth whether I want to or not, and it follows that I didn't make them up.

It isn't relevant that, having seen triangular physical objects, I may have gotten the idea of the triangle from external objects through my organs of sense. For I can think of innumerable other figures whose ideas I could not conceivably have gotten through my senses, and I can demonstrate facts about these other figures just as I can about the triangle. Since I know these facts clearly, they must be true, and they therefore must be something rather than nothing. For it's obvious that everything true is something, and, as I have shown, everything that I know clearly and distinctly is true. But, even if I hadn't shown this, the nature of my mind would have made it impossible for me to withhold my assent from these things, at least when I clearly and distinctly grasped them. As I recall, even when I clung most tightly to objects of sense, I regarded truths about shape and number—truths of arithmetic, geometry, and pure mathematics—as more certain than any others.

But, if anything whose idea I can draw from my thought must in fact have everything that I clearly and distinctly grasp it to have, can't I derive from this a proof of God's existence? Surely, I find the idea of God, a supremely perfect being, in me no less clearly than I find the ideas of figures and numbers. And I understand as clearly and distinctly that eternal existence belongs to His nature as that the things which I demonstrate of a figure or number belong to the nature of the figure or number. Accordingly, even if what I have thought up in the past few days hasn't been entirely true, I ought to be at least as certain of God's existence as I used to be of the truths of pure mathematics.

At first, this reasoning may seem unclear and fallacious. Since I'm accustomed to distinguishing existence from essence in other cases, I find it easy to convince myself that I can separate God's existence from His essence and hence that I can think of God as nonexistent. But, when I pay more careful attention, it's clear that I can no more separate God's existence from His essence than a triangle's angles equaling two right angles from the essence of the triangle, or the idea of a valley from the idea of a mountain. It's no less impossible to think that God (the supremely perfect being) lacks existence (a perfection) than to think that a mountain lacks a valley.

Well, suppose that I can't think of God without existence, just as I can't think of a mountain without a valley. From the fact that I can think of a mountain with a valley, it doesn't follow that a mountain exists in the world. Similarly, from the fact that I can think of God as existing, it doesn't seem to follow that He exists. For my thought doesn't impose any necessity on things. It may be that, just as I can imagine a winged horse when no such horse exists, I can ascribe existence to God when no God exists.

No, there is a fallacy here. From the fact that I can't think of a mountain without a valley it follows, not that the mountain and valley exist, but only that whether they exist or not they can't be separated from one another. But, from the fact that I can't think of God without existence, it follows that existence is inseparable from Him and hence that He really exists. It's not that my thoughts make it so or impose a necessity on things. On the contrary, it's the fact that God does exist that necessitates my thinking of Him as I do. For I am not free to think of God without existence—of the supremely perfect being without supreme perfection—as I am free to think of a horse with or without wings.

Now someone might say this: "If I take God to have all perfections, and if I take existence to be a perfection, I must take God to exist, but I needn't accept the premise that God has all perfections. Similarly, if I accept the premise that every quadrilateral can be inscribed in a circle, I'm forced to the patently false view that every rhombus can be inscribed in a circle, but I need not accept the premise." But this should not be said. For, while it's not necessary that the idea of God occurs to me, it is necessary that, whenever I think of the primary and supreme entity and bring the idea of Him out of my mind's "treasury," I attribute all perfections to Him, even if I don't enumerate them or consider them individually. And this necessity ensures that, when I do notice that existence is a perfection, I can rightly conclude that the primary and supreme being exists. Similarly, while it's not necessary that I ever imagine a triangle, it is necessary that, when I do choose to consider a rectilinear figure having exactly three angles, I attribute to it properties from which I can rightly infer that its angles are no more than two right angles, perhaps without noticing that I am doing so. But, when I consider which shapes can be inscribed in the circle, there's absolutely no necessity for my thinking that all quadrilaterals are among them. Indeed, I can't even think that all quadrilaterals are among them, since I've resolved to accept only what I clearly and distinctly understand. Thus my false suppositions differ greatly from the true ideas implanted in me, the first and foremost of which is my idea of God. In many ways, I see that this idea is not a figment of my thought, but the image of a real and immutable nature. For one thing, God is the only thing that I can think of whose existence belongs to its essence.

For another thing, I can't conceive of there being two or more such Gods, and, having supposed that one God now exists, I see that He has necessarily existed from all eternity and will continue to exist into eternity. And I also perceive many other things in God that I can't diminish or alter.

But, whatever proof I offer, it always comes back to the fact that I am only convinced of what I grasp clearly and distinctly. Of the things that I grasp in this way, some are obvious to everyone. Some are discovered only by those who examine things more closely and search more carefully, but, once these things have been discovered, they are regarded as no less certain than the others. That the square on the hypotenuse of a right triangle equals the sum of the squares on the other sides is not as readily apparent as that the hypotenuse subtends the greatest angle, but, once it has been seen, it is believed just as firmly. And, when I'm not overwhelmed by prejudices and my thoughts aren't besieged by images of sensible things, there surely is nothing that I know earlier or more easily than facts about God. For what is more self-evident than there is a supreme entity—that God, the only thing whose existence belongs to His essence, exists?

While I need to pay careful attention in order to grasp this, I'm now as certain of it as of anything that seems most certain. In addition, I now see that the certainty of everything else so depends on it that, if I weren't certain of it, I couldn't know anything perfectly.

Of course, my nature is such that, when I grasp something clearly and distinctly, I can't fail to believe it. But my nature is also such that I can't permanently fix my attention on a single thing so as always to grasp it clearly, and memories of previous judgments often come to me when I am no longer attending to the grounds on which I originally made them. Accordingly, if I were ignorant of God, arguments could be produced that would easily overthrow my opinions, and I therefore would have unstable and changing opinions rather than true and certain knowledge. For example, when I consider the nature of the triangle, it seems plain to me—steeped as I am in the principles of geometry—that its three angles equal two right angles: I can't fail to believe this as long as I pay attention to its demonstration. But, if I were ignorant of God, I might come to doubt its truth as soon as my mind's eye turned away from its demonstration, even if I recalled having once grasped it clearly. For I could convince myself that I've been so constructed by nature that I sometimes err about what I believe myself to grasp most plainly—especially if I remember that, having taken many things to be true and certain, I had later found grounds on which to judge them false.

But now I grasp that God exists, and I understand both that everything else depends on Him and that He's not a deceiver. From this, I infer that everything I clearly and distinctly grasp must be true. Even if I no longer pay attention to the grounds on which I judged God to exist, my recollection that I once clearly and distinctly knew Him to exist ensures that no contrary ground can be produced to push me towards doubt. About God's existence, I have true and certain knowledge. And I have such knowledge, not just about this one thing, but about everything else that I remember having proven, like the theorems of geometry. For what can now be said against my believing these things? That I am so constructed that I always err? But I now know that I can't err about what I clearly understand. That much of what I took to be true and certain I later found to be false? But I didn't grasp any of these things clearly and distinctly; ignorant of the true standard of truth, I based my belief on grounds that I later found to be unsound. Then what can be said? What about the objection (which I recently used against myself) that I may be dreaming and that the things I'm now experiencing may be as unreal as those that occur to me in sleep? No, even this is irrelevant. For, even if I am dreaming, everything that is evident to my understanding must be true.

Thus I plainly see that the certainty and truth of all my knowledge derives from one thing: my thought of the true God. Before I knew Him, I couldn't know anything else perfectly. But now I can plainly and certainly know innumerable things, not only about God and other mental beings, but also about the nature of physical objects, insofar as it is the subject-matter of pure mathematics.

Commentary and Questions

This brief meditation is a transition to the more important sixth meditation. Though Descartes says at the beginning that he wants to investigate whether we can know anything about material things (so far, only God and the soul are known), he doesn't solve that problem here. But he does take a significant step toward its solution. Along the way, he discovers a third proof that God exists.

Again we find the typical Cartesian strategy at work. He wants to know whether **material things** exist independent of himself. How can he proceed? He can't just look to see because he has put the testimony of the senses in doubt. So he must consider more carefully the *idea* of material things, which is all that is available to him. And again he finds that some of these ideas are confused and obscure, while others are clear and distinct. The latter are those of extension, duration, and movement—the qualities that can be treated geometrically or mathematically. Material things, if there are any, are essentially extended volumes.* Once we are clear about their *essence*, it makes sense to inquire about their *existence*; and that is the subject of *Meditation VI*.

Note that these mathematical ideas are not just imaginary inventions. You cannot put them together any way you like, as you can construct fantastic creatures by combining heads, bodies, and hides at will. You may not yet know whether there are any triangular things outside yourself, but the idea of a triangle "can't be said to be nothing" (p. 388). It has a *nature* that is "immutable and eternal." This nature does not depend on me.

The point can be put in this way. Suppose you imagine a creature with wings covered with scales, a long furry tail, six legs, and an elephantlike nose covered with spikes. Then someone asks you, does this creature have claws? You will have to *invent* the answer. You cannot discover it. But if you imagine a triangle and someone asks you whether the interior angles equal two right angles, you do not have to invent an answer. You could investigate and discover that the answer is yes. With respect to these geometrical properties, there are *truths*.* And these, remember, are the very properties that determine the essence of material things.

Since the idea of a material thing is the idea of something extended, and since extended things can be treated geometrically, it follows that the *idea* of a material thing is clear and distinct. Material substances have an essence or nature that would make a *science* of them a possibility—if only we could be assured that they exist. And we know that such a science is a possibility merely from an examination of their ideas. So, provided we can discover a proof that some *formal* reality corresponds to the *subjective* reality of our ideas of material things, we can have a science of material things. In this way, then, he hopes to give a metaphysical foundation to his mechanistic physics.

The discovery that certain ideas have a nature or essence of their own, quite independent of our inventions, also supplies Descartes with material for a third proof of God's existence.† If we simply pay close attention to what is necessarily involved in our idea of *what* God is (his essence or nature), we can discover, Descartes argues, *that* God is (that he exists). God's existence is included in his essence. Notice that, unlike the first two arguments, this is not a *causal* proof. In its bare essentials, it looks like this:

1. God, by definition, is a being of infinite perfection.
2. Existence is a perfection (that is, no being could be perfect that lacked it).
3. So God exists.

---

*Review the discussion of the bit of wax in *Meditation II* and on p. 375.

*Socrates thinks that we can never be taught anything other than what we in some sense already know; what we call "learning" is in fact just remembering. (See p. 169.) Descartes alludes to this doctrine here; in discovering the properties of a triangle you are "noticing for the first time something that had long been in [you] without [your] having turned [your] mind's eye towards it." Descartes is not, however, committed to the Socratic doctrine of the preexistence of the soul as an explanation of this phenomenon, since he thinks God's creation of a soul possessing certain innate ideas will suffice.

†This proof is a version of the ontological argument first worked out by Anselm of Canterbury in the eleventh century. See Chapter 15.

Q40. Is the argument valid?

Q41. Can the premises be questioned?

This last proof of God's existence allows Descartes to lay to rest a final worry that has been tormenting him. You really cannot help believing, he suggests, that your clear and distinct thoughts are true—while you are thinking them. But later you may not be so sure! You may then think you were dreaming what earlier seemed so certain. But now this worry can be dealt with. And *Meditation V* closes on a note of reassurance.

Q42. How are the dream and demon worries finally disposed of?

Q43. Can an atheist do science? (See the last paragraph.)

Meditation VI: On the Existence of Material Objects and the Real Distinction of Mind from Body

It remains for me to examine whether material objects exist. Insofar as they are the subject of pure mathematics, I now know at least that they can exist, because I grasp them clearly and distinctly. For God can undoubtedly make whatever I can grasp in this way, and I never judge that something is impossible for Him to make unless there would be a contradiction in my grasping the thing distinctly. Also, the fact that I find myself having mental images when I turn my attention to physical objects seems to imply that these objects really do exist. For, when I pay careful attention to what it is to have a mental image, it seems to me that it's just the application of my power of thought to a certain body which is immediately present to it and which must therefore exist.

To clarify this, I'll examine the difference between having a mental image and having a pure understanding. When I have a mental image of a triangle, for example, I don't just understand that it is a figure bounded by three lines; I also "look at" the lines as though they were present to my mind's eye. And this is what I call having a mental image.

When I want to think of a chiliagon, I understand that it is a figure with a thousand sides as well as I understand that a triangle is a figure with three, but I can't imagine its sides or "look" at them as though they were present. Being accustomed to using images when I think about physical objects, I may confusedly picture some figure to myself, but this figure obviously is not a chiliagon—for it in no way differs from what I present to myself when thinking about a myriagon or any other many sided figure, and it doesn't help me to discern the properties that distinguish chiliagons from other polygons. If it's a pentagon that is in question, I can understand its shape, as I can that of the chiliagon, without the aid of mental images. But I can also get a mental image of the pentagon by directing my mind's eye to its five lines and to the area that they bound. And it's obvious to me that getting this mental image requires a special mental effort different from that needed for understanding—a special effort which clearly reveals the difference between having a mental image and having a pure understanding.

It also seems to me that my power of having mental images, being distinct from my power of understanding, is not essential to my self or, in other words, to my mind—for, if I were to lose this ability, I would surely remain the same thing that I now am. And it seems to follow that this ability depends on something distinct from me. If we suppose that there is a body so associated with my mind that the mind can "look into" it at will, it's easy to understand how my mind might get mental images of physical objects by means of my body. If there were such a body, the mode of thinking that we call imagination would differ from pure understanding in only one way: when the mind understood something, it would turn "inward" and view an idea that it found in itself, but, when it had mental images, it would turn to the body and look at something there which resembled an idea that it had understood by itself or had grasped by sense. As I've said, then, it's easy to see how I get mental images, if we supposed that my body exists. And, since I don't have in mind any other equally plausible explanation of my ability to have mental images, I conjecture that physical objects probably do exist. But this conjecture is only probable. Despite my careful and thorough investigation, the distinct idea of bodily nature that I get from mental images does not seem to have anything in it from which the conclusion that physical objects exist validly follows.

Besides having a mental image of the bodily nature that is the subject-matter of pure mathematics, I have mental images of things which are not so distinct—things like colors, sounds, flavors, and pains. But I seem to grasp these things better by sense, from which they seem to come (with the aid of memory) to the understanding. Thus, to deal with these things more fully, I must examine the senses and see whether there is anything in the mode of awareness that I call sensation from which I can draw a conclusive argument for the existence of physical objects.

First, I'll remind myself of the things that I believed really to be as I perceived them and of the grounds for my belief. Next, I'll set out the grounds on which I later called this belief into doubt. And, finally, I'll consider what I ought to think now.

To begin with, I sensed that I had a head, hands, feet, and the other members that make up a human body. I viewed this body as part, or maybe even as all, of me. I sensed that it was influenced by other physical objects whose effects could be either beneficial or harmful. I judged these effects to be beneficial to the extent that I felt pleasant sensations and harmful to the extent that I felt pain. And, in addition to sensations of pain and pleasure, I sensed hunger, thirst, and other such desires— and also bodily inclinations towards cheerfulness, sadness, and other emotions. Outside me, I sensed, not just extension, shape, and motion, but also hardness, hotness, and other qualities detected by touch. I also sensed light, color, odor, taste, and sound—qualities by whose variation I distinguished such things as the sky, earth, and sea from one another.

In view of these ideas of qualities (which presented themselves to my thought and were all that I really sensed directly), I had some reason for believing that I sensed objects distinct from my thought—physical objects from which the ideas came. For I found that these ideas came to me independently of my desires so that, however much I tried, I couldn't sense an object when it wasn't present to an organ of sense or fail to sense one when it was present. And, since the ideas that I grasped by sense were much livelier, more explicit, and (in their own way) more distinct than those I deliberately created or found impressed in my memory, it seemed that these ideas could not have come from me and thus that they came from something else. Having no conception of these things other than that suggested by my sensory ideas, I could only think that the things resembled the ideas. Indeed, since I remembered using my senses before my reason, since I found the ideas that I created in myself to be less explicit than those grasped by sense, and since I found the ideas that I created to be composed largely of those that I had grasped by sense, I easily convinced myself that I didn't understand anything at all unless I had first sensed it.

I also had some reason for supposing that a certain physical object, which I viewed as belonging to me in a special way, was related to me more closely than any other. I couldn't be separated from it as I could from other physical objects; I felt all of my emotions and desires in it and because of it; and I was aware of pains and pleasant feelings in it but in nothing else. I didn't know why sadness goes with the sensation of pain or why joy goes with sensory stimulation. I didn't know why the stomach twitchings that I call hunger warn me that I need to eat or why dryness in my throat warns me that I need to drink. Seeing no connection between stomach twitchings and the desire to eat or between the sensation of a pain-producing thing and the consequent awareness of sadness, I could only say that I had been taught the connection by nature. And nature seems also to have taught me everything else that I knew about the objects of sensation— for I convinced myself that the sensations came to me in a certain way before having found grounds on which to prove that they did.

But, since then, many experiences have shaken my faith in the senses. Towers that seemed round from a distance sometimes looked square from close up, and huge statues on pediments sometimes didn't look big when seen from the ground. In innumerable such cases, I found the judgments of the external senses to be wrong. And the same holds for the internal senses. What is felt more inwardly than pain? Yet I had heard that people with amputated arms and legs sometimes seem to feel pain in the missing limb, and it therefore didn't seem perfectly certain to me that the limb in which I feel a pain is always the one that hurts. And, to these grounds for doubt, I've recently added two that are very general: First, since I didn't believe myself to sense anything while awake that I couldn't also take myself to sense in a dream, and since I didn't believe that what I sense in sleep comes from objects outside me, I didn't see why I should believe what I sense while awake comes from such objects. Second, since I didn't yet know my creator (or, rather, since I supposed that I didn't know Him), I saw nothing to rule out my having been so designed by nature that I'm deceived even in what seems most obviously true to me.

And I could easily refute the reasoning by which I convinced myself of the reality of sensible things. Since my nature seemed to impel me toward many things that my reason rejected, I didn't believe that I ought to have much faith in nature's teachings. And, while my will didn't control my sense perceptions, I didn't believe it to follow that these perceptions came from outside me, since I thought that the ability to produce these ideas might be in me without my being aware of it.

Now that I've begun to know myself and my creator better, I still believe that I oughtn't blindly to accept everything that I seem to get from the senses. Yet I no longer believe that I ought to call it all into doubt.

In the first place, I know that everything that I clearly and distinctly understand can be made by God to be exactly as I understand it. The fact that I can clearly and distinctly understand one thing apart from another is therefore enough to make me certain that it is distinct from the other, since the things could be separated by God if not by something else. (I judge the things to be distinct regardless of the power needed to make them exist

separately.) Accordingly, from the fact that I have gained knowledge of my existence without noticing anything about my nature or essence except that I am a thinking thing, I can rightly conclude that my essence consists solely in the fact that I am a thinking thing. It's possible (or, as I will say later, it's certain) that I have a body which is very tightly bound to me. But, on the one hand, I have a clear and distinct idea of myself insofar as I am just a thinking and unextended thing, and, on the other hand, I have a distinct idea of my body insofar as it is just an extended and unthinking thing. It's certain, then, that I am really distinct from my body and can exist without it.

In addition, I find in myself abilities for special modes of awareness, like the abilities to have mental images and to sense. I can clearly and distinctly conceive of my whole self as something that lacks these abilities, but I can't conceive of the abilities' existing without me, or without an understanding substance in which to reside. Since the conception of these abilities includes the conception of something that understands, I see that these abilities are distinct from me in the way that a thing's properties are distinct from the thing itself.

I recognize other abilities in me, like the ability to move around and to assume various postures. These abilities can't be understood to exist apart from a substance in which they reside any more than the abilities to imagine and sense, and they therefore cannot exist without such a substance. But it's obvious that, if these abilities do exist, the substance in which they reside must be a body or extended substance rather than an understanding one—for the clear and distinct conceptions of these abilities contain extension but not understanding.

There is also in me, however, a passive ability to sense—to receive and recognize ideas of sensible things. But, I wouldn't be able to put this ability to use if there weren't, either in me or in something else, an active power to produce or make sensory ideas. Since this active power doesn't presuppose understanding, and since it often produces ideas in me without my cooperation and even against my will, it cannot exist in me. Therefore, this power must exist in a substance distinct from me. And, for reasons that I've noted, this substance must contain, either formally or eminently, all the reality that is contained subjectively in the ideas that the power produces. Either this substance is a physical object (a thing of bodily nature that contains formally the reality that the idea contains subjectively), or it is God or one of His creations that is higher than a physical object (something that contains this reality eminently). But, since God isn't a deceiver, it's completely obvious that He doesn't send these ideas to me directly or by means of a creation that contains their reality eminently rather than formally. For, since He has not given me any ability to recognize that these ideas are sent by Him or by creations other than physical objects, and since He has given me a strong inclination to believe that the ideas come from physical objects, I see no way to avoid the conclusion that He deceives me if the ideas are sent to me by anything other than physical objects. It follows that physical objects exist. These objects may not exist exactly as I comprehend them by sense; in many ways, sensory comprehension is obscure and confused. But these objects must at least have in them everything that I clearly and distinctly understand them to have— every general property within the scope of pure mathematics.

But what about particular properties, such as the size and shape of the sun? And what about things that I understand less clearly than mathematical properties, like light, sound, and pain? These are open to doubt. But, since God isn't a deceiver, and since I therefore have the God-given ability to correct any falsity that may be in my beliefs, I have high hopes of finding the truth about even these things. There is undoubtedly some truth in everything I have been taught by nature— for, when I use the term "nature" in its general sense, I refer to God Himself or to the order that He has established in the created world, and, when I apply the term specifically to *my* nature, I refer to the collection of everything that God has given *me*.

Nature teaches me nothing more explicitly, however, than that I have a body which is hurt when I feel pain, which needs food or drink when I experience hunger or thirst, and so on. Accordingly, I ought not to doubt that there is some truth to this.

Through sensations like pain, hunger, and thirst, nature also teaches me that I am not present in my body in the way that a sailor is present in his ship. Rather, I am very tightly bound to my body and so "mixed up" with it that we form a single thing. If this weren't so, I—who am just a thinking thing—wouldn't feel pain when my body was injured; I would perceive the injury by pure understanding in the way that a sailor sees the leaks in his ship with his eyes. And, when my body needed food or drink, I would explicitly understand that the need existed without having the confused sensations of hunger and thirst. For the sensations of thirst, hunger, and pain are just confused modifications of thought arising from the union and "mixture" of mind and body.

Also, nature teaches me that there are other physical objects around my body—some that I ought to seek and others that I ought to avoid. From the fact that I sense things like colors, sound, odors, flavors, temperatures, and hardnesses, I correctly infer that sense perceptions come from physical objects that vary as widely (though perhaps not in the same way) as the perceptions do. And, from the fact that some of these perceptions are pleasant while others are unpleasant, I infer with certainty that my body—or, rather, my whole self which consists of a body and a mind—can be benefited and harmed by the physical objects around it.

There are many other things that I seem to have been taught by nature but that I have really accepted out of a habit of thoughtless judgment. These things may well be false. Among them are the judgments that a space is empty if nothing in it happens to affect my senses; that a hot physical object has something in it resembling my idea of heat; that a white or green thing has in it the same whiteness or greenness that I sense; that a bitter or sweet thing has in it the same flavor that I taste; that stars, towers, and other physical objects have the same size and shape that they present to my senses; and so on.

If I am to avoid accepting what is indistinct in these cases, I must more carefully explain my use of the phrase "taught by nature." In particular, I should say that I am now using the term "nature" in a narrower sense than when I took it to refer to the whole complex of what God has given me. This complex includes much having to do with my mind alone (such as my grasp of the fact that what is done cannot be undone and of the rest of what I know by the light of nature) which does not bear on what I am now saying. And the complex also includes much having to do with my body alone (such as its tendency to go downward) with which I am not dealing now. I'm now using the term "nature" to refer only to what God has given me insofar as I am a composite of mind and body. It is this nature that teaches me to avoid that which occasions painful sensations, to seek that which occasions pleasant sensations, and so on. But this nature seems not to teach me to draw conclusions about external objects from sense perceptions without first having examined the matter with my understanding—for true knowledge of external things seems to belong to the mind alone, not to the composite of mind and body.

Thus, while a star has no more effect on my eye than a flame, this does not really produce a positive inclination to believe that the star is as small as the flame; for my youthful judgment about the size of the flame, I had no real grounds. And, while I feel heat when I approach a fire and pain when I draw nearer, I have absolutely no reason for believing that something in the fire resembles the heat, just as I have no reason for believing that something in the fire resembles the pain; I only have reason for believing that there is something or other in the fire that produces the feelings of heat and pain. And, although there may be nothing in a given region of space that affects my senses, it doesn't follow that there aren't any physical objects in that space. Rather I now see that, on these matters and others, I used to pervert the natural order of things. For, while nature has given sense perceptions to my mind for the sole purpose of indicating what is beneficial and what harmful to the composite of which my mind is a part, and while the perceptions are sufficiently clear and distinct for that purpose, I used these perceptions as standards for identifying the essence of physical objects—an essence which they only reveal obscurely and confusedly.

I've already explained how it can be that, despite God's goodness, my judgments can be false. But a new difficulty arises here—one having to do with the things that nature presents to me as desirable or undesirable and also with the errors that I seem to have found in my internal sensations. One of these errors seems to be committed, for example, when a man is fooled by some food's pleasant taste into eating poison hidden in that food. But surely, in this case, what the man's nature impels him to eat is the good tasting food, not the poison of which he knows nothing. We can draw no conclusion except that his nature isn't omniscient, and this conclusion isn't surprising. Since a man is a limited thing, he can only have limited perfections.

Still, we often err in cases in which nature does impel us. This happens, for example, when sick people want food or drink that would quickly harm them. To say that these people err as a result of the corruption of their nature does not solve the problem—for a sick man is no less a creation of God than a well one, and it seems as absurd to suppose that God has given him a deceptive nature. A clock made of wheels and weights follows the natural laws just as precisely when it is poorly made and inaccurate as when it does everything that its maker wants. Thus, if I regard a human body as a machine made up of bones, nerves, muscles, veins, blood, and skin such that even without a mind it would do just what it does now (except for things that require a mind because they are controlled by the will), it's easy to see that what happens to a sick man is no less "natural" than what happens to a well one. For instance, if a body suffers from dropsy, it has a dry throat of the sort that regularly brings the sensation of thirst to the mind, the dryness disposes the nerves and other organs to drink, and the drinking makes the illness worse. But this is just as natural as when a similar dryness of throat moves a person who is perfectly healthy to take a drink that is beneficial. Bearing in mind my conception of a clock's use, I might say that an inaccurate clock departs from its nature, and, similarly, viewing the machine of the human body as designed for its usual motions, I can say that it drifts away from its nature if it has a dry throat when drinking will not help to maintain it. I should note, however, that the sense in which I am now using the term "nature" differs from that in which I used it before. For, as I have just used the term "nature," the nature of a man (or clock) is something that depends on my thinking of the difference between a sick and a well man (or of the difference between a poorly made and a well-made clock)—something regarded as extrinsic to the things. But, when I used "nature" before, I referred to something which is in things and which therefore has some reality.

It may be that we just offer an extrinsic description of a body suffering from dropsy when, noting that it has a dry throat but doesn't need to drink, we say that its nature is corrupted. Still, the description is not purely extrinsic when we say that a composite or union of mind and body has a corrupted nature. There is a real fault in the composite's nature, for it is thirsty when drinking would be harmful. It therefore remains to be asked why God's goodness doesn't prevent *this* nature's being deceptive.

To begin the answer, I'll note that mind differs importantly from body in that body is by its nature divisible while mind is indivisible. When I think about my mind—or, in other words, about myself insofar as I am just a thinking thing—I can't distinguish any parts in me; I understand myself to be a single, unified thing. Although my whole mind seems united to my whole body, I know that cutting off a foot, arm, or other limb would not take anything away from my mind. The abilities to will, sense, understand, and so on can't be called parts, since it's one and the same mind that wills, senses, and understands. On the other hand, whenever I think of a physical or extended thing, I can mentally divide it, and I therefore understand that the object is divisible. This single fact would be enough to teach me that my mind and body are distinct, if I hadn't already learned that in another way.

Next, I notice that the mind isn't directly affected by all parts of the body, but only by the brain—or maybe just by the small part of the brain containing the so-called "common sense." Whenever this part of the brain is in a given state,

it presents the same thing to the mind, regardless of what is happening in the rest of the body (as is shown by innumerable experiments that I need not review here).

In addition, I notice that the nature of body is such that, if a first part can be moved by a second that is far away, the first part can be moved in exactly the same way by something between the first and second without the second part's being affected. For example, if A, B, C, and D are points on a cord, and if the first point (A) can be moved in a certain way by a pull on the last point (D), then A can be moved in the same way by a pull on one of the middle points (B or C) without D's being moved. Similarly, science teaches me that, when my foot hurts, the sensation of pain is produced by nerves distributed throughout the foot which extend like cords from there to the brain. When pulled in the foot, these nerves pull the central parts of the brain to which they are attached, moving those parts in ways designated by nature to present the mind with the sensation of a pain "in the foot." But, since these nerves pass through the shins, thighs, hips, back, and neck on their way from foot to brain, it can happen that their being touched in the middle, rather than at the end of the foot, produces the same motion in the brain as when the foot is hurt and, hence, that the mind feels the same pain "in the foot." And the point holds for other sensations as well.

Finally, I notice that, since only one sensation can be produced by a given motion of the part of the brain that directly affects the mind, the best conceivable sensation for it to produce is the one that is most often useful for the maintenance of the healthy man. Experience teaches that all the sensations put in us by nature are of this sort and therefore that everything in our sensations testifies to God's power and goodness. For example, when the nerves in the foot are moved with unusual violence, the motion is communicated through the middle of the spine to the center of the brain, where it signals the mind to sense a pain "in the foot." This urges the mind to view the pain's cause as harmful to the foot and to do what it can to remove that cause. Of course, God could have so designed man's nature that the same motion of the brain presented something else to the mind, like the motion in the brain, or the motion in the foot, or a motion somewhere between the brain and foot. But no alternative to the way things are would be as conducive to the maintenance of the body. Similarly, when we need drink, the throat becomes dry, the dryness moves the nerves of the throat thereby moving the center of the brain, and the brain's movements cause the sensation of thirst in the mind. It's the sensation of thirst that is produced, because no information about our condition is more useful to us than that we need to get something to drink in order to remain healthy. And the same is true in other cases.

This makes it completely obvious that, despite God's immense goodness, the nature of man (whom we now view as a composite of mind and body) cannot fail to be deceptive. For, if something produces the movement usually associated with an injured foot in the nerve running from foot to brain or in the brain itself rather than in the foot, a pain is felt as if "in the foot." Here the senses are deceived by their nature. Since this motion in the brain must always bring the same sensation to mind, and since the motion's cause is something hurting the foot more often than something elsewhere, it's in accordance with reason that the motion always presents the mind a pain in the foot rather than elsewhere. And, if dryness of the throat arises, not (as usual) from drink's being conducive to the body's health, but (as happens in dropsy) from some other cause, it's much better that we are deceived on this occasion than that we are generally deceived when our bodies are sound. And the same holds for other cases.

In addition to helping me to be aware of the errors to which my nature is subject, these reflections help me readily to correct or avoid these errors. I know that sensory indications of what is good for my body are more often true than false; I can almost always examine a given thing with several senses; and I can also use my memory (which connects the present to the past) and my understanding (which has now examined all the causes of error). Hence, I need no longer fear that

what the senses daily show me is unreal. I should reject the exaggerated doubts of the past few days as ridiculous. This is especially true of the chief ground for these doubts—namely, my inability to distinguish dreaming from being awake. For I now notice that dreaming and being awake are importantly different: the events in dreams are not linked by memory to the rest of my life like those that happen while I am awake. If, while I'm awake, someone were suddenly to appear and then immediately to disappear without my seeing where he came from or went to (as happens in dreams), I would justifiably judge that he was not a real man but a ghost—or, better an apparition created in my brain. But, if I distinctly observe something's source, its place, and the time at which I learn about it, and if I grasp an unbroken connection between it and the rest of my life, I'm quite sure that it is something in my waking life rather than in a dream. And I ought not to have the slightest doubt about the reality of such things if I have examined them with all my senses, my memory, and my understanding without finding any conflicting evidence. For, from the fact that God is not a deceiver, it follows that I am not deceived in any case of this sort. Since the need to act does not always allow time for such a careful examination, however, we must admit the likelihood of men's erring about particular things and acknowledge the weakness of our nature.

Commentary and Questions

We now know what the essence of material things is: To be such a thing is to be extended in space in three dimensions, to have shape and size, to endure, and to be movable and changeable in these dimensions. This is what a material thing would be—if there were any. At last we face the haunting question: Are there any?

The first thing to note is that they *can* exist.

Q44. What is Descartes' reason for thinking this?

If, moreover, we examine our *images* of material things, it seems that the imagination produces these images by turning "to the body" and looking "at something there" (p. 392). It is as though a representation of a triangle were physically stored in the body (or brain); and imagination is looking not at a real triangular thing, but at that stored representation. Because we can undoubtedly form mental images, it certainly seems as though some material things exist—namely, our bodies.

But to make this clearer, Descartes draws a sharp distinction between **imagining** something and **conceiving** it.

Q45. How does the example comparing the triangle with the chiliagon help to clarify this distinction? (See p. 392.)

We still have no proof, of course, that there are any bodies. But again, progress has been made; for we now have an account of how one of the faculties of the mind works—on the assumption that there really are bodies. If we can find a proof of this assumption, it will "fit" with what we know about our mental capacities.

Descartes now turns from imagining to sensing. On pages 393–394, he reviews again his reasons for confidence in the senses and then his reasons for doubt.* At the end of this review he concludes again that what he is taught "by nature" does not deserve much credence.

However, the situation is now very different from that of the first *meditation*. For now he knows that God exists and is not a deceiver. And in short order Descartes offers proofs that the soul is distinct from the body and that material things exist. Both of these depend on clear ideas of the essence

of material things, which he arrived at in the fifth *meditation*.

Here, in outline, is his proof for the distinctness of soul from body.

1. God can create anything that I can clearly and distinctly conceive—there being no impossibility in it.
2. If God can create one thing independent of another, the first thing is distinct from the second.
3. I have a clear and distinct idea of my essence as a thinking thing.
4. So God can create a thinking thing (a soul) independent of a body.
5. I also have a clear and distinct idea of my body as an extended thing—its essence.
6. So God can create a body independent of a soul.
7. So my soul is a reality distinct from my body.
8. So I, as a thinking thing (soul), can exist without my body.

Q46. How sound is this argument? What are the weak points, if any?
Q47. Is there a tension between the conclusion of this argument and Descartes' assertion (p. 395) that you are not in your body the way a sailor is in his ship?*

Descartes' proof for the reality of material things goes roughly like this:

1. I have a "strong inclination" to believe in the reality of the material (extended) things that I seem to sense. (To put it another way, their independent reality seems to be one of the things I am "taught by nature.")
2. God must have created me with this inclination.
3. If material things do not exist independently, then God is a deceiver.
4. But God is not a deceiver.
5. So material things exist with those properties I conceive to be essential to them.

Q48. Evaluate the soundness of this argument.

*In the course of this review he paraphrases one of the basic principles of Thomas Aquinas, who derives it from Aristotle: There is no idea in the intellect, which was not previously in the senses. This is, for instance, the foundation for Aquinas's rejection of the ontological argument (see p. 319). Descartes allows that this principle is superficially plausible, but in the light of his skeptical doubts he considers it naive. Not only do we know that we have ideas before we know we have senses, we know that some of these ideas must be innate—that is, they could not plausibly be derived from sensible experience. Such are the ideas of thing, thought, truth, and God.

*Compare the use that Aquinas makes of this same image, p. 327.

At this point, Descartes has, he thinks, defeated both skepticism and solipsism. He has delineated the basic structure of reality: God, souls, and material things. Reality, then, is composed of infinite substance and two kinds of finite substances—thinking and extended. The bridge has been built. Knowledge has been shown to be possible. Physics has been supplied with a foundation in metaphysics. And all this with a certainty that rivals that of geometry!

The rest of *Meditation VI* attends to a few details that are left.

Q49. Compare what Descartes says on p. 395 with Galileo's view of "secondary qualities" (pp. 356–357).

Q50. If the senses present external things in such an inadequate way, what use are they?

Q51. How are we to account for certain errors the senses seem to lead us to—such as the pain in an amputated limb or the desire of a person with dropsy (edema) to drink?

Q52. What is the final disposition of the problem arising from dreams?

What Has Descartes Done?

It is possible to argue whether Descartes is the last of the medievals or the first of the moderns. Like most such arguments about transitional figures, there is truth on both sides. But that both philosophy and our general view of the world have been different ever since is indisputable. Descartes develops a philosophy that reflects the newly developing sciences and, in turn, gives them a legitimacy they otherwise lack. A measure of his lasting influence is the fact that a significant part of philosophy since World War I has been devoted to showing that he was crucially wrong about some basic things (which would not be worth doing unless his influence was still powerfully felt).* Descartes is *our* ancestor.

---

*Among the critics are C. S. Peirce, Martin Heidegger, Ludwig Wittgenstein, Willard Quine, Richard Rorty, and Daniel Dennett. See the chapters on their philosophies.

Let us sum up several key features of his thought and then indicate where certain problems crop up.

A New Ideal for Knowledge

One commentator says of the Cartesian revolution that it "stands for the substitution of free inquiry for submission to authority, for the rejection of Faith without reason for faith *in* reason, and the replacement of Faith by Demonstration."[6] Though Descartes is far from trying to reject religious belief (indeed, he thinks he can rationally justify its two most important parts, God and the soul), in the end everything comes down to what the rational mind finds clear and distinct enough to be indubitable. Nothing else will be accepted, regardless of its antiquity or traditional claims to authority. We each contain within ourselves the criterion for truth and knowledge. This radical individualism is qualified only by the conviction that rationality is the same for every individual (just as mathematics is the same for all). No longer can we put the responsibility for deciding what to believe on someone else, whether priest, pope, or king. It lies squarely on each of us.

Moreover, the ideal for such belief is the clarity and certainty of mathematics. Probability or plausibility is not enough. Being vaguely right is not enough. The habits of thought developed in us by nature are not enough. By analysis we can resolve problems into their simple elements; by intuition we can see their truth; and by demonstration we can move to necessary consequences. Knowledge has the structure of an axiomatic system. All this is possible. Anything less is unacceptable. To be faithful to this ideal is to free oneself from error and to attain truth.

In all this Descartes deserves his reputation as Prince of the Rationalists.* The ultimate court of appeal is reason—the light of nature. We ought to rely on intellect rather than sense, on intuition and deduction rather than imagination; "for true

---

*Though (almost) all philosophers try to reach their conclusions rationally, a rationalist is one who emphasizes the exclusive role of reason in the formation of knowledge. For one of Descartes' most distinguished predecessors in this tradition, see the discussion of the pre-Socratic thinker, Parmenides, in Chapter 2.

knowledge of external things seems to belong to the mind alone, not the composite of mind and body" (p. 396).

A NEW VISION OF REALITY

Descartes' metaphysics completes the worldview that was emerging already in the work of Copernicus, Kepler, and Galileo. Our world is a giant mechanism, not unlike a clock (see Descartes' analogy on p. 396). It was created by God, but now it runs on the principles of mechanics, and our science is mechanistic in principle. The entire material universe, including the human body, is just a complex machine. The world has become a *secular* world. What happens can be explained and predicted without reference to any purposes or intentions of the creator. We are, we might say, worlds away from the intrinsically purposive, inherently value-laden, God-directed world of the medievals. Dante now begins to look like a fairy tale or, at best, a moral allegory with no literal truth value at all. It is, perhaps, no great surprise that the *Meditations* ends up on the index of forbidden books.

There are, to be sure, human minds or souls, and they are not caught up in the mechanism of the material world. They are, in fact, radically free. Even God does not have more freedom than a soul (see *Meditation IV*). But as we'll see, this disparity between soul and body is not so much the solution to a problem as it is a problem in itself.

PROBLEMS

Great as Descartes' achievement is, he bequeaths to his successors a legacy of unsolved problems. There are those who refuse to accept his radical beginning point and remain true to a more traditional approach, usually Aristotelian. But his methodological doubt has been powerfully persuasive to many, and the continued progress of physics seems to be evidence that his basic view of the world is correct. For the next 150 years, Cartesianism, together with its variants, will be the dominating philosophy on the European continent. As we'll see, different assumptions are at work in Britain, but even here the Cartesian spirit of independence is pervasive. Still, there are nagging worries. Let us note three of them.

The Place of Humans in the World of Nature

Descartes is intent on legitimizing the new science. But what place is there for *us* in the universe of the new physics? Could we, too, be mere cogs in this universal machine? We assume that we have purposes and act to realize certain values. But where is there room for purposes and values in this mechanistic world? Is our assumption just an illusion? We assume that we can make a difference in the outcome of physical processes. But if the world is a closed mechanism, how can this be? We experience ourselves as conscious beings, aware of ourselves and the world around us. But can a machine be conscious? These are very contemporary questions, the sort cognitive science aims to sort out and solve.

All these questions force themselves on us once we take Descartes' vision of the universe seriously. Descartes is not unaware of them. His basic strategy for dealing with them consists in the radical split that he makes between mind and body. Bodies, he holds, are parts of the mechanical universe; minds are not. Physics can deal with the body, but not with the mind. We know that we are not merely automata because (1) we can use language, and (2) we are flexible and adaptable in a way no machine could be; reason, Descartes says, "is a universal instrument which can be used in all kinds of situations." It is quite possible, he says, that we could construct a machine that utters words—even one that utters words corresponding to movements of its body. But it is not possible, he thinks, for a machine to "give an appropriately meaningful answer to whatever is said in its presence, as the dullest of men can do" (*DM* 6.56–57, p. 120).*

But merely dividing mind from body does not completely solve the problem. The question arises, How are they related?

The Mind and the Body

Descartes concludes that the mind and the body are distinct substances, so independent of each other that either could exist without the other. They are,

---

*This, of course, is precisely the aim of research on artificial intelligence. Will it be successful? Descartes bets not.

moreover, of a radically different character. Still, he says, mind and body are so intimately related as to form "a single unified thing" (p. 397). But how can you be two things and yet one single thing? Descartes gives no explanation.

❦

"What is matter?—Never mind.
What is mind?—No matter."

Punch

Furthermore, the mind must be able to affect the body. When you decide to eat an ice cream cone, your body obeys its commands. But as some of Descartes' contemporaries pointed out to him, it is at best unclear how this is possible on his view, since he posits an immaterial mind that is completely distinct from the mechanistic world of extended things. The diplomat and philosopher Princess Elisabeth of Bohemia puts the problem pointedly in a letter to Descartes. She cannot comprehend, she writes,

> the idea through which we must judge how the soul (nonextended and immaterial) can move the body; nor why [we should sooner believe] that a body can be pushed by some immaterial thing, than the demonstration of a contrary truth (which [Descartes] promises in [his] physics) should confirm us in the opinion of its impossibility. . . . I nevertheless have never been able to conceive of such an immaterial thing as anything other than a negation of matter which cannot have any communication with it.[7]

Not only has Descartes failed to explain this obvious phenomenon, Elisabeth suggests, but also his views seem to imply that the phenomenon is impossible.

The problem runs the other way, too. For just as the mind can move the body, so events affecting the body can affect the mind, as when you stub your toe or light reflects from this book into your eye, leading you to perceive the words on the page. How can an alteration in the shape or position of certain material particles cause us to feel pain or think of Cleveland? Descartes seems to have no clear answer to these questions.

The view that the mind and body have a two-way causal interaction is known as **interactionism,** and one of Descartes' lasting legacies is a philosophical puzzle about how it is possible. But it is safe to say that a philosophy that does not solve the mind–body problem cannot be considered entirely acceptable.

God and the Problem of Skepticism

As we have seen, Descartes takes skepticism very seriously. He pushes skeptical arguments about as far as they can be pushed, and he thinks that in the *cogito* he has found the key to overcoming skepticism. But even if we grant that each of us knows, by virtue of the *cogito*, that we exist, knowledge of the *world* depends on the fact that God is not a deceiver. And that depends on the proofs for the existence of God.

What if those proofs are faulty? Then I am back again in solipsism, without a guarantee that anything exists beyond myself. Are the proofs—or at least one of them—satisfactory? Descartes is quite clear that everything depends on that question; "the certainty and truth of all my knowledge derives from one thing: my thought of the true God" (p. 390). He is sure that the proofs are as secure as the theorems of geometry. But is he right about that?

THE PREEMINENCE OF EPISTEMOLOGY

In earlier philosophies there are many problems—the one and the many, the nature of reality, explaining change, the soul, the existence of God—and the problem of knowledge is just one among the rest. Descartes' radical skepticism changes that. After Descartes and until very recent times, most philosophers have regarded epistemological problems as foundational. Among these problems of knowledge, the problem about knowing the external world is the sharpest and most dangerous. Can we know anything at all beyond the contents of our minds? Unless this skeptical question can be satisfactorily answered, nothing else can be done. Epistemology is, for better or worse, the heart of philosophy for the next several hundred years.

These are problems that Descartes' successors wrestle with, as we'll see. Next, however, we want to look at a figure who is often neglected in the history of modern philosophy: Thomas Hobbes. Hobbes is more interesting to us than to previous generations, perhaps, because he presents an alternative response to the new science. Some recent thought about the mind—that associated with artificial intelligence—can be regarded as a struggle to replace the paradigm of Descartes with that of Hobbes.

FOR FURTHER THOUGHT

Descartes argues that there is no way you could tell that your ideas about the external world were correct unless there were a nondeceptive God to guarantee their basic rightness. Can you think of any way you might be able to know there is a world corresponding to your ideas? Try to construct a view that provides this reassurance without depending on God.

KEY WORDS

rules of method	self-evident
clear and distinct	thinking thing
analysis	ideas
insight	volitions
deduction	emotions
first philosophy	judgments
senses	innate ideas
dreams	light of nature
evil demon	subjective reality
representational theory	formal reality
cogito	eminent reality
ex nihilo nihil fit	material things
solipsism	imagining
understanding	conceiving
will	interactionism

NOTES

1. Quoted in S. V. Keeling, *Descartes* (London: Oxford University Press, 1968).
2. Quotations from René Descartes' *Discourse on the Method of Rightly Conducting One's Reason and Seeking the Truth in the Sciences*, in *The Philosophical Writings of Descartes*, ed. John Cottingham, Robert Stoothoff, and Dugald Murdoch (Cambridge: Cambridge University Press, 1985), are cited in the text using the abbreviation *DM*. References are to part numbers and page numbers in the classic French edition, followed by page numbers in this edition.
3. Quotations from René Descartes, *The Principles of Philosophy*, in *The Philosophical Works of Descartes*, vol. 1, ed. Elisabeth S. Haldane and G. R. T. Ross (n.p.: Dover, 1955), are cited in the text using the abbreviation *PP*. References are to the classic French edition, followed by the page numbers in this edition.
4. Quoted by Martin Heidegger in *The Way Back into the Ground of Metaphysics*, reprinted in *Existentialism from Dostoevsky to Sartre*, ed. Walter Kaufmann (New York: Merchant Books, 1957).
5. Trans. Ronald Rubin, *Meditations on First Philosophy* (Claremont, CA: Areté Press, 1986).
6. Keeling, *Descartes*, 252.
7. Trans. Lisa Shapiro, *The Correspondence between Princess Elisabeth of Bohemia and René Descartes* (Chicago: University of Chicago Press, 2007), 68.

CHAPTER

18

HOBBES, LOCKE, AND BERKELEY

Materialism and the Beginnings of Empiricism

Descartes offered a dramatic new beginning in philosophy. Besides sweeping away old rubbish and legitimating the new science, Descartes' work seemed a breath of fresh air in its clarity and apparent simplicity. But—there were those nagging problems. If mind and body are as distinct as Descartes claims, how do they communicate? Does the will really escape the causal net? Do we really have all those innate ideas? Are Descartes' proofs for God's existence really *proofs*? And if not, can we escape skepticism about the external world?

Across the English Channel, British thinkers read Descartes with interest, but they were not entirely convinced. In this chapter, we look at three of these philosophers, examining their response to the challenges of Cartesian thought: Thomas Hobbes, who refuses to exclude human beings from the new scientific principles; John Locke, who is determined to trace all our ideas to their source in experience; and George Berkeley, who tries to apply empiricist principles more consistently than Locke does. A consideration of these three will prepare us for that most radical of empiricists in the next chapter: David Hume.

Thomas Hobbes: Catching Persons in the Net of the New Science

For various reasons, Descartes stops short of supposing that his geometrical mechanics can account for everything. The most obvious exceptions are mental activities: thinking, imagining, doubting, feeling, and willing. Because Descartes believes it is beyond question that each of us is first and foremost a thinking thing—and as free in our decisions as God himself—there can be no Cartesian physics of human beings. As thinkers, we escape the web of mechanical causality.*

---

*For Descartes' reasons, see his argument for the distinctness of mind and body in *Meditation VI*. He is also convinced that our minds, being rational, are *infinitely adaptable*. This, he thinks, distinguishes us from any conceivable automaton, no matter how cleverly designed. See p. 401.

But are Descartes' reasons for thinking so really conclusive? What would happen if we tried to understand human beings as systems of matter in motion, completely enclosed in the natural world described by mechanical physics? Thomas Hobbes (1588–1679) makes the experiment. We will not survey the whole of Hobbes' philosophy, but it will prove useful to bring into our sense of the great conversation what he has to say about human beings—our place in the world and our life together. So we focus our attention on his views about mind and morals.

Hobbes accepts without reservation the new physics of the nonhuman world. Let us review some of the salient features of this new science and contrast them with the older, Aristotelian view.

- Whereas for Aristotle and his medieval disciples, motion is development toward some fulfilling goal (a change from potentiality to actuality), for the new science, motion is simply a body's change of place in a neutral geometrical space.
- Galileo substitutes the distinction between accelerated motion and constant motion for the Aristotelian distinction between motion and rest. For Galileo, rest is simply a limiting case of motion. In no sense is rest the culmination or fulfillment or goal of a motion.
- Motion is the normal state of things; it does not require explanation, as in the medieval view. Only changes in motion (in direction or rate) need to be explained, and they are explained in terms of other motions.
- Therefore, there is no natural center to the universe where things "rest." Since something in motion continues in a straight line to infinity unless interfered with, the universe is conceived to be infinite rather than finite, and there are no privileged places in it.
- Scientific explanation can no longer mention the final causes of things—those essences toward which development has been thought to strive. In the geometrical world of Galileo and Descartes, all explanation is in terms of *contact*, of some prior impetus or push. It is as if the rich Aristotelian world with its four causes is stripped down to only the "efficient cause."

Purposiveness is eliminated from the physical world.*

In his comments on the *Meditations*, Hobbes claims to be unconvinced by Descartes' arguments concerning the independence of the mind from the body. For all Descartes has said, Hobbes thinks, the thing that thinks may just as well be a physical body! Indeed, Hobbes is convinced that "the subject of all activities can be conceived only after a corporeal fashion."[1] If so, then the mind cannot be thought of as a thing independent of the body. It becomes just one of the ways that bodies of a certain sort function.† Can this claim be plausible?

METHOD

Hobbes is as convinced as Descartes that method is the key to progress. He calls his method—which he claims to have learned from Galileo and his friend William Harvey (who discovered the circulation of the blood)—the method of **resolution and composition.** The first stage, resolution, consists in the analysis of complex wholes into simple elements. It resembles Descartes' second rule.‡ In the second stage, the elements are reassembled, or composed again into a whole. This is analogous to Descartes' third rule. When we have both resolved and composed the complex whole we began with, we understand it better than we did before we applied the method. Both Galileo and Harvey offer impressive examples of successes attained by this

---

*Compare Hobbes in this respect to the Greek atomists ("The World," in Chapter 2). You might also like to remind yourself of Plato's critique of this kind of nonpurposive explanation, pp. 160–161.

†Hobbes, like nearly all the moderns, is a great opponent of Aristotle. And yet this conclusion is basically Aristotelian. (See p. 206.) Likewise, his account of how we gain knowledge about the world is Aristotelian in spirit, if not in detail. In more than one way, Hobbes must be counted a "critical Aristotelian." Descartes, by contrast, clearly stands in the Plato–Augustine tradition. The principal difference between Hobbes and Aristotle is the former's repudiation of final causes, of potentiality, and of the essences that make them work. This difference transforms everything it touches.

‡See p. 362.

method. Galileo uses it to understand and predict the trajectory of cannonballs and other projectiles. Harvey uses it to understand and explain the circulation of blood in the human body.

We will see Hobbes trying to use these methods to understand both mind and society. His aim is to analyze human beings into their simplest elements—which he takes to be bits of matter in motion—and then understand a community of persons in terms of the way these elements interact. Hobbes aspires to be the Galileo or the Harvey of the human world. He is convinced that a scientific understanding of human nature will be both a contribution to knowledge and a practical benefit. If we could but organize society on the basis of truths about ourselves, rather than on the basis of ignorance and superstition, we could avoid conflict and live together in peace.

Minds and Motives

Life, says Hobbes,

> is but a motion of limbs, the beginning whereof is in some principle part within; why may we not say, that all *automata* (engines that move themselves by springs and wheels as doth a watch) have an artificial life? For what is the heart, but a spring; and the nerves, but so many strings, and the joints, but so many wheels, giving motion to the whole body, such as was intended by the artificer? (*L*, 129)[2]

The distinction, in other words, between living and nonliving things is not to be found in a soul, or a life principle, or in anything nonmaterial. Living things are just those things that *move* because they have a source of motion *within* them. They are not in principle different from automata or robots that we ourselves might make. In fact, we could say that robots are alive, too; their life is *artificially created*, but it is life nonetheless. The internal motions causing the movements of automata are, in principle, no different from the heart, nerves, and joints of the human body. Living things, whether natural or artificial, are just matter in motion.

In a way, Descartes does not yet disagree. For he thinks that animals are just "machines"; and animals are undoubtedly alive. But what about the life of the mind? What of thought and feeling? What of desire, imagination, and memory? Can these too

be plausibly considered just matter in motion? We have seen Descartes' negative answer. Can Hobbes make a positive answer plausible?

Let us begin with thinking. What are thoughts?

> They are everyone a *representation* or *appearance*, of some quality or other accident of a body without us, which is commonly called an *object*. (*L*, 131)

Note that Hobbes expresses no doubt that there are indeed bodies—objects—independent of ourselves. He seems simply not to take the Cartesian reasons for doubting seriously.* Descartes, notoriously, thinks there is a serious problem here—that all our experience might be just as it is while *nothing at all* corresponds to it in the world beyond our minds. That there are bodies, Descartes holds, is something that needs to be proved. Hobbes offers no proofs. It is as though he thinks it beyond question. *Of course* our thoughts represent bodies. *Of course* bodies really exist. To be sure, we are sometimes mistaken about them, but these mistakes give us no reason to withhold belief in external things altogether. In fact, if it were not for those objects, we would not have any thoughts at all!

> The original of them all is that which we call *sense*, for there is no conception in a man's mind which hath not first, totally or by parts, been begotten upon the organs of sense. The rest are derived from that original. (*L*, 131)

The source of all our thoughts is to be found in sensation.† And **sensation** is an effect in us of the action of those external bodies on our eyes, ears, nose, skin, and tongue. Motions are communicated to our sense organs from these bodies; these motions set up other motions in the sense organs; and these motions are in turn propagated by the nerves "inwards to the brain and heart." We take the

---

*Here again Hobbes stands to Descartes as Aristotle to Plato. See p. 183.

†For all Hobbes' tirades against Aristotle, this is a very Aristotelian view. It is the dead opposite of Descartes' belief in innate ideas (see p. 382). It means that he can have no tolerance for Descartes' first proof for the existence of God. Compare Thomas Aquinas' rejection of the ontological argument of Saint Anselm on essentially similar Aristotelian grounds (see p. 319).

MARGARET CAVENDISH

While women were generally excluded from formal education in early modern Europe, some educated themselves and published their own works of philosophy. Some, such as Anne Conway and Mary Astell, published their works anonymously. The poet, playwright, and scientist **Margaret Cavendish** (1623–1673) was one of the few who published under her own name, producing philosophical treatises, a book of philosophical letters, and a philosophically significant science fiction novel. She personally knew Descartes, Hobbes, and other intellectual luminaries of her time.

Cavendish shares Hobbes' commitment to materialism, writing,

> Nature is material, or corporeal, and so are all her Creatures, and whatsoever is not material is no part of Nature, neither doth it belong any ways to Nature.[3]

But, setting herself against Hobbes and the dominant Western tradition as a whole, she offers a novel way to navigate between Cartesian dualism and the Hobbesian view of the world as a purely mechanistic assemblage of atoms. She argues that all material things are composed of three types of matter—inanimate, sensitive, and rational—blended together in every particle of the natural world. Inanimate matter cannot move itself, but is moved by self-moving sensitive matter; sensitive matter, in turn, takes direction from rational matter. Such a view is superior to Descartes', she thinks, because his dualistic view cannot explain how immaterial mind moves material bodies. It is superior to Hobbes', she thinks, because it avoids the unsavory and, to many, implausible implication that mind is nothing more than a particularly complicated mechanism composed of lifeless atoms.

On this basis, Cavendish also develops alternative theories of causation and perception. Bodies do not cause other bodies to move by imparting motion to them. Rather, self-moving matter *perceives* the motions of bodies around it and at least usually responds to those motions in particular ways. For instance, when you throw a ball, the animate matter in the ball perceives the motion of your hand and responds by *moving itself* in the direction that your hand is traveling. Perception works similarly: as the ball flies through the air, the sensitive matter in the air perceives its motion and communicates a pattern to the sensitive matter in your eyes, which moves itself to form a sensory impression of the ball.

Cavendish's philosophical work was mostly ignored in the seventeenth century, but she anticipates positions and arguments developed by other early modern philosophers and discusses issues relevant to twentieth- and twenty-first-century philosophy of mind. Her unusual brand of materialism demonstrates that Hobbes' mechanistic view of the world was not the only way to respond to the rise of the new science.

---

disturbance inside us to be a representation of the object from which the motions originated. Here, then, are the origins of our experiences of colors, sounds, tastes, smells, hardness and softness, and so on. These experiences we call sensations, or, to use Hobbes' seventeenth-century term, "fancy."

But what of these experiences themselves? Can the smell of a rose really be "resolved" into motions? Here is what Hobbes says. In the objects that cause them, these qualities are

> but so many several motions of the matter, by which it presseth our organs diversely. Neither in us that are pressed, are they anything else but divers motions; for motion produceth nothing but motion. But their appearance to us is fancy. (*L*, 131)

It will pay us to consider this passage carefully, for it contains a crucial ambiguity. On the one hand, Hobbes says that sensations are themselves nothing but motion; "for motion produceth nothing but motion." If we take that seriously, then Hobbes is what we call a **materialist.** The entire life of the mind is nothing more than matter in motion. For sensations are motions, and all the rest is built up out of sensations. There are no distinctive mental

"The light of human minds is perspicuous words . . .; reason is the pace, increase of science, the way and the benefit of mankind, the end."

—THOMAS HOBBES

qualities at all. Mind is just matter that is moved in distinctive ways.

On the other hand, Hobbes says of these motions that "their appearance to us is fancy." Now if it is not the motions themselves that constitute the sensations, but their *appearance* to us, then the sensations must be distinct from the motions. Under this interpretation Hobbes is not a materialist at all; he is what we call an **epiphenomenalist.** An epiphenomenalist thinks there are unique mental qualities, that they are causally dependent on physical states, but that they do not in turn affect the physical world. They more or less ride piggyback on the physical, but they have no physical effects.

Is Hobbes a materialist or an epiphenomenalist about the mind? It is probably impossible to decide. He talks both ways, perhaps because he is simply unaware of the distinction. His intentions, however, are fairly clear. He wants to be a materialist, to resolve everything—including all aspects of mental life—into matter in motion. Let us consider him, therefore, to be a materialist about the mind. In this way, he stands in dramatic opposition to Descartes, for whom mind is a radically different kind of substance from body. Descartes, then, is a metaphysical **dualist,** and Hobbes is a **monist.** For Hobbes, there is only one kind of finite substance.

Sensations, the "original" of thought, are motions. But this poses a problem. Paraphrasing Galileo's laws of inertia, Hobbes admits that "when a body is once in motion, it moveth, unless something else hinder it, eternally" (*L*, 133). Why is it, then, that sensations do not remain with us? The answer is that in a way they do—but in a diminished way only. For new sensations are ever pouring in on us; and by these succeeding motions the previous ones are weakened. This "*decaying sense,*" as Hobbes calls it (*L*, 133), is **imagination** and **memory.**

When an image (the decayed motion left by a sensation) is combined with a sign, he says, we have **understanding.** And this is common to both humans and the higher animals. For instance, a dog who comes when his master whistles gives evidence that he understands what is wanted of him. The whistle is a sign connected in this case to tendencies to act. Hobbes, unlike Descartes, is quite content to speak of a dog as thinking this or that. The difference between the dog and ourselves is not absolute (that we have a soul, which the dog completely lacks) but is a matter of degree.

Because all thinking originates in sensation, we cannot think of something we have not experienced. We can combine sense elements in novel ways to produce purely imaginative thoughts of unicorns or centaurs. But things that are neither sensed nor invented on the basis of sensations are *inconceivable.* This has an important consequence: We can have, Hobbes says, no positive thought of **God.** "Whatsoever we imagine," he says, "is finite. Therefore there is no idea or conception of anything we call *infinite*" (*L*, 140). We do, of course, have *words* for God; we can call him a "being of infinite perfection"—as Descartes does. But these terms do not really function to describe God; rather, says Hobbes, they are signs of our intention to honor him.

Hobbes groups our thoughts into two classes: *unregulated* (as when we daydream) and *regulated* thoughts. The first kind may seem to follow each other in a wholly random way, but on careful observation, Hobbes tells us, we can see that their order mirrors a prior order of sense experiences. The appearance of randomness comes from the variety of our experiences. If at one time we *see* Mary with John and then again with Peter, the *thought* of Mary may be accompanied by either that of John or that of Peter. But it will be associated in some way dependent on earlier experiences. In trying to find a pattern to unregulated thoughts, Hobbes is making a suggestion that will be developed into the doctrine of the *association of ideas.**

More interesting, however, are **regulated thoughts.** These do not even have an appearance of randomness but exhibit a definite order. One thing Hobbes has in mind is the kind of thinking that looks for means to attain some goal, as when a student considers which classes take to complete her degree. Another kind of regulated thought consists in inquiry about the consequences of taking a certain action, as when a student considers what her life will be like if she changes her curriculum from history to engineering. In regulated thought about the world, we are always searching for either causes or effects.

Such a hunt for causes is usually carried out in *words*, which are useful both as aids to memory and as signs representing our thoughts to others. Hobbes recognizes the benefits we derive from having such objective signs of our inner thoughts, but he also warns us about the errors into which they can easily trap us.

> Seeing then the truth consisteth in the right ordering of names in our affirmations, a man that seeketh precise truth had need to remember what every name he uses stands for, and to place it accordingly, or else he will find himself entangled in words, as a bird in lime twigs, the more he struggles the more belimed. (*L*, 142)

The cure for these evils of confusion is to be found in *definition*, to which Hobbes attributes the success of geometry, "the only science that it hath pleased God hitherto to bestow on mankind" (*L*, 142). Words need to be carefully defined, lest we

find ourselves "entangled" in them like the bird in the lime twigs.* In an often quoted phrase, Hobbes tells us that

> words are wise men's counters, they do but reckon by them; but they are the money of fools, that value them by the authority of an Aristotle, a Cicero, or a Thomas. (*L*, 143)

Only a "fool" thinks that we can buy truth with the words of some authority. A "wise man" realizes that they are only *signs* that, if properly used to "reckon" with, may possibly yield us a science.

"When ideas fail, words come in very handy."
Johann Wolfgang von Goethe (1749–1832)

We use words to *reason*, to think rationally about some matter. What is **reasoning**? Hobbes has a view of reasoning that some artificial intelligence researchers these days look back to as prophetic. Reasoning, he tells us, is "nothing but *reckoning*, that is adding and subtracting, of the consequences of general names agreed upon for the marking and signifying of our thoughts" (*L*, 133–134). As the cognitive scientist nowadays says, reasoning is computation.

Whether we reason about the theoretical consequences of some geometrical axiom, about means to attain a certain end, or about the practical consequences of some course of action, these regulated thoughts are governed by *desire*. We wouldn't bother if we didn't want to find out the answer. So the motivation behind all our rational thinking is passion. Hobbes must now ask, Can these desires and wants, these likes and dislikes, themselves be accounted for in terms of the metaphysics of motion?†

---

*Compare to the Confucian doctrine of the rectification of names (p. 225).

†What is at stake here is whether *purpose* and *intention* can be given a mechanistic explanation. We have seen that Plato and, following him, Aristotle, think not. For this reason, Aristotle believes we need to ask about final causes in addition to the other three kinds. This question is still hotly debated.

---

*See the use to which David Hume puts this notion, Chapter 19.

We have seen that living things are distinguished from nonliving things by having the origins of some of their motions within them. Hobbes must now give a more careful account of this. He distinguishes two sorts of motions peculiar to animals: vital and voluntary motions. **Vital motions** are such things as the circulation of the blood, the pumping of the heart, breathing, and digestion. **Voluntary motions,** by contrast, are those for which the cause is to be found in some imagination. John imagines how pleasant it would be to go with Jane to the movies; he walks out of his way in the hope that their paths will cross. It is clear that if imagination itself is nothing but the diminished motions of sense, voluntary motions such as walking in a certain direction have their origin in internal motions.

These small, perhaps infinitesimally small beginnings of motion Hobbes calls **endeavor.** Endeavor can either be toward something (in which case it is called **desire**) or away from something (which is called **aversion**). In desire and aversion we find the sources of all human action.

Desire and aversion allow Hobbes to introduce certain value notions. What we desire, he says, we call **good;** what we wish to avoid we call **evil.** And these value distinctions are invariably founded on pleasure and pain, respectively: What gives us pleasure we call good; what causes pain we call evil.* It is important to realize that good and evil are not thought to attach absolutely to things. They are not properties that things have independent of our relation to them. The words "good" and "evil," Hobbes tells us,

> are ever used with relation to the person that useth them; there being nothing simply and absolutely so; nor any common rule of good and evil to be taken from the nature of the objects themselves; but from the person of the man, where there is no commonwealth; or, in a commonwealth, from the person that representeth it; or from an arbitrator or judge, whom men disagreeing shall by consent set up, and make his sentence the rule thereof. (*L*, 150)

The idea that in a "commonwealth," or state, good and evil are not relative to *individuals* is one we will explore shortly. But in what Hobbes calls a **"state of nature,"** where there is no government, good and evil strictly depend on the individual. If an individual desires *X*, she judges *X* to be good; if he dislikes *Y*, he considers *Y* evil. And from those judgments there is (in the state of nature) no appeal.*

This analysis is an important step in Hobbes' materialistic program. Goodness is not a Platonic Form or an unanalyzable property that some things have. Everything is just body and motion. But some (living) bodies are related in certain ways to other bodies in such a way that the former bodies utter the words "That is good" about those latter bodies. They do so when the latter produce motions in the former that are pleasurable.

What is pleasure? **Pleasure,** Hobbes tells us, is just "a corroboration of vital motion, and a help thereunto," while **pains** are a "hindering and troubling [of] the motion vital" (*L*, 150). Feeling good, in other words, is just having all our normal bodily processes working smoothly; the more active and untroubled they are, the better we feel—and what we all want is to feel good.

"Pleasure is Nature's test, her sign of approval."
Oscar Wilde (1854–1900)

It seems, then, that regulated thoughts are regulated by desire, that desire is always for the good, and that "good" is our name for whatever produces pleasure. The end point of a train of regulated thoughts is some action on our part—an action we think will gain us some good. These actions, when caused by thoughtful desires in this way, are called "voluntary."

At this point, Hobbes meets a natural objection. It is not, someone might claim, *desire* that causes voluntary action; it is *will*. And willpower

---

*It is clear that Hobbes is a hedonist. See Epicurus, p. 236.

*Compare the doctrine of Protagoras, the Sophist, who said, "Of all things, the measure is man" (p. 62).

can override our desires. I desperately want another slice of that dark, rich chocolate cake, but I exercise my will and say, "Thank you, but no." Can Hobbes deal with this common experience?

He does so by asking what we mean by "will." It cannot be anything else, he thinks, than *the last appetite in deliberating*" (*L*, 154). **Will,** then, *is* a desire. I do desire that slice of cake, but I also have desires that run counter to that desire: I want not to look piggish; I want not to gain too much weight. On this occasion, these latter desires outweigh the former; they dictate my action, and so they are what we *call* my will. Will is nothing but *effective desire*. Since we have already seen that Hobbes believes desire and aversion can be given an analysis in terms of matter in motion, there is no need (as Descartes thinks) to bring in nonmaterial factors to explain the origin of voluntary actions.*

Our voluntary actions, then, are governed in the last analysis by passion—by our desires and aversions, our loves and hates. And since the good we seek and the evil we try to avoid are rooted in our own pleasures and pains, action is always egoistic. It is my own good that I seek, if Hobbes is right—not yours. As Hobbes puts it, "of the voluntary acts of every man, the object is some *good to himself*" (*L*, 165).

Moreover, we seek such good *continually*. It is not enough to act once for our own pleasure; the next moment demands other acts that have the same end. Happiness—or **felicity,** as Hobbes calls it—is just a life filled with the satisfaction of our desires.

Continual success in obtaining those things which a man from time to time desireth, that is to say,

continual prospering, is that men call *felicity*; I mean the felicity of this life. For there is no such thing as perpetual tranquility of mind, while we live here; because life itself is but motion, and can never be without desire, nor without fear, no more than without sense. (*L*, 155)

In this life there can be no resting, no "tranquility." No sooner has one desire been fulfilled than another takes its place. The reason Hobbes gives for this is that life itself is nothing but motion. So there is a perpetual striving for the satisfaction of desires; when this is successful over some period of time, we say that during that period a person is happy.*

All of us desire this felicity, Hobbes says. But it is easy to see that if we are not to be mere pawns of fortune, we must also control access to it; that is, we must be guaranteed the *power* to satisfy whatever desires we may happen to have.

I put for a general inclination of all mankind, a perpetual and restless desire of power after power, that ceaseth only in death. And the cause of this, is not always that a man hopes for a more intensive delight, than he has already attained to; or that he cannot be content with a moderate power: but because he cannot assure the power and means to live well, which he hath present, without the acquisition of more. (*L*, 158–159)

This kind of power is, of course, a relative matter. In a world of limited resources, if I gain more power to guarantee the satisfaction of *my* desires, I often diminish *your* power to satisfy your desires. In seeking to assure my own felicity, I threaten yours. So we are naturally competitors. I seek my good. You seek yours. And we each seek to increase our own power to ensure that we at least do not lose those goods we now have.†

---

*It is clear that Hobbes is a **determinist**—that is, one who thinks that for every event, including all human actions, there is a set of sufficient conditions guaranteeing its occurrence. All actions are caused; and the causes of these causes themselves have causes. This poses a problem, of course: the problem of freedom of the will. We saw that Descartes, who is not a materialist, can hold that our decisions escape this universal determinism that holds for the material world; even God, Descartes says, is not more free than we are. Hobbes cannot think so. He has a solution to this problem, but because the same solution is more elegantly set out by Hume, we consider it in the next chapter. If you want a preview, see "Rescuing Human Freedom" in Chapter 19.

---

*Contrast this notion of happiness to the rather different hedonistic doctrine of the Epicureans (pp. 236–240).

†If this seems unrealistic to you as a model of relations among individuals, consider political and economic rivalries among nations. As we will see, Hobbes has an explanation of how we have gotten beyond this competitive situation on the individual level. It is instructive to compare this picture of restless competitiveness to Augustine's two cities, pp. 286–287.

FRANCIS BACON

Although Francis Bacon (1561–1626) was both a jurist and a statesman (rising as high as lord high chancellor in the England of James I), he was most passionately interested in reforming intellectual life and creating a new kind of science. His principal philosophical works are *The Advancement of Learning* (1605) and *Novum Organum* (1620).

Bacon believed that old habits had to change; it was a bad mistake to look to the authorities of the past because nearly everything about the natural world remained to be discovered. Traditional philosophers, he said, are like spiders, spinning out intricate conceptions from their own insides. Alchemists and other early investigators were like ants, scurrying about collecting facts without any organized method. We should rather follow the example of the bees; let scientists cooperate in acquiring data, offering interpretations, conducting experiments, and drawing judicious conclusions.

Bacon identified four "idols" that, he said, have hindered the advance of knowledge: (1) idols of the tribe—tendencies resident in human nature itself, such as imagining that the senses give us a direct picture of their objects or imagining there is more order in experience than we actually find; (2) idols of the den—people's inclination to interpret experiences according to their private dispositions or favorite theories; (3) idols of the marketplace—language that subverts communication through ambiguities in words or in names that are assumed to name something but actually do not; and (4) idols of the theater—the dogmas of traditional philosophy, which portray the universe no more accurately than stage plays portray everyday life.

How can we counter these tendencies to revere the past and idolize the wrong things? Bacon recommended a method of careful experimentation and induction. Supporting a theory by simple enumeration of positive instances, however, is not good enough. We must look particularly, he said, for negative instances—especially if the theory is one we are fond of—and for variations in the degrees of presence and absence of factors so that we can find correlations between them.

Nature, Bacon told us, can be commanded only by obeying her; by submitting to nature's own ways through carefully designed experiments, we can gain knowledge. Knowledge, he said, is power. And the result of a reformed science will be mastery of nature, leading to a higher quality of human life.

Although there are natural differences in our power, we are equal enough in natural gifts that each of us has reason to fear the other. As Hobbes says, even "the weakest has strength enough to kill the strongest" (*L*, 159), whether by force, stealth, or collusion with others. Because of this equality, the egoistic desire for happiness—plus the need to be assured of it by a continual increase of power—leads human beings to be enemies. So our *natural* condition (i.e., before any artificial arrangements or agreements among us) is one of *war* of "every man against every man." Even when we are not actually fighting one another, the threat of conflict always looms over us. In such a condition, Hobbes argues,

> there is no place for industry, because the fruit
> thereof is uncertain; and consequently no culture of

the earth; no navigation, nor use of the commodities that may be imported by sea; no commodious building; no instruments of moving and removing, such things as require much force; no knowledge of the face of the earth; no account of time; no arts; no letters; no society; and which is worst of all, continual fear, and danger of violent death; and the life of man, solitary, poor, nasty, brutish, and short. (*L*, 161)

Solitary, poor, nasty, brutish—and short! Such is our life in a state of nature.*

Let us remind ourselves of what Hobbes claims to be doing here. He is trying to use the same method on human nature and society that

---

*Compare to Xunzl's views about the result of our natural desires, untamed by social rules. See pp. 230–231.

Galileo and Harvey use on the nonhuman world. He resolves human beings into their component elements—the motions characteristic of living things—and finds this competitive and restless striving to be the result.

This analysis is supported, he believes, by observation. Hobbes lived during extremely troubled times in England.* There was a long struggle between king and Parliament over the right to make laws and to collect taxes. This struggle reflected a broader quarrel between the old nobility and the established Church of England on the one hand and the rising middle classes and religious dissenters of a more radical Protestant sort on the other. Those on each side, in Hobbes' view, were trying to preserve against the other side the means of their own happiness.

The outcome was a protracted and bloody civil war, the execution of King Charles I, a period of government without a king under the protectorate of Oliver Cromwell, and finally the Restoration of the monarchy under Charles II (to whom Hobbes had been a tutor in mathematics). The "state of nature" into which Hobbes resolves human society was very nearly the actual state of affairs in England during a good part of Hobbes' life. Hobbes did not conjure the war of all against all from nowhere; he saw it—or something like it—with his own eyes.

Still, Hobbes does not intend his account of the state of nature to describe society at all times and places. Nor is it supposed to describe society at some time in the distant past. It is intended to picture the results of an analytical decomposition of human society into its elements. Left to their own devices, the theory says, individuals will always act egoistically for their own good, and the inevitable consequence is a state of war—each of us fearing our neighbor and striving to extend our sphere of control at our neighbor's expense. This is the result of the *resolution phase* of Hobbes' method.

We now need to look at the *composition phase*, where the elements are put back together again. And here we focus primarily on Hobbes' view of the ethical consequences.

---

*For the English Civil War, see "English Civil War," *Wikipedia*, https://en.wikipedia.org/wiki/English_Civil_War.

The Natural Foundation of Moral Rules

Hobbes has "resolved" human society into its elements. Let us see how he thinks it can be "composed" back again into a whole. If Hobbes succeeds in this stage, we will have an explanation of the human world, including its ethical and political aspect, in purely mechanistic terms.

In the state of nature, human beings are governed by their egoistic passions, their endeavor to ensure their own happiness. This leads to the "war of everyone against everyone," a deadly competition for the power to guarantee for each person what he considers good. How can this "state of nature" be overcome? Partly, Hobbes says, by passion itself and partly by reason.

One of the strongest passions is the *fear of death*. It is this fear, together with the desire for happiness, that motivates us to find a way to end the state of nature. We must remember that in the state of nature there are no rights and wrongs, no goods and bads, except where an individual thinks there are. We each take as much as we have power to take and keep. An individual's liberty extends as far as his power. But if a person in this state of nature realizes how unsatisfactory this condition is, he will see that

> it is a precept, or general rule of reason, that every man ought to endeavor peace, as far as he has hope of obtaining it; and when he cannot obtain it, that he may seek and use all helps and advantages of war. The first branch of which rule containeth the first and fundamental law of nature; which is, to seek peace and follow it. The second, the sum of the right of nature; which is, by all means we can, to defend ourselves. (*L*, 163)

Hobbes speaks here of a *right* of nature and of a *law* of nature. What can he mean? In a universe composed merely of matter in motion, how can there be rights and laws *in nature*? Hasn't Hobbes already denied that there is any right or wrong in this condition?

If we interpret Hobbes sympathetically, it seems that a law of nature must simply be an expression of the way things go. Jones, who by nature seeks his own happiness and fears death, is worried about his future. This is just how it is. In reasoning about his situation, Jones sees that replacing war with peace would relieve his fear of death; and if he didn't have to be so afraid of his neighbors, he could more satisfactorily fill his own life with "felicity." The rule to "seek peace" is a rule that an egoistic but rational creature such as Jones will inevitably—naturally—come upon. He will reason that if he is going to have any chance of a good life, he has to get beyond this state of war. A **law of nature** for Hobbes is simply a rule of prudence that results from the shrewd calculation of a scared human being.

A **right of nature** must have a similar foundation. In the state of nature there are no "rights" in the usual sense. If, in a state of nature, someone injures me, I cannot complain that my "rights" have been infringed. But precisely because there are no rules, I am *at liberty* to use whatever means I can muster to preserve my life and happiness. Hobbes uses the term "right" to refer to this liberty everyone has in the state of nature. So Jones having the "right" to defend himself is simply the fact that there are no rules that curtail his tendency to preserve his life and happiness. If, however, Jones (and everyone else) exercises this liberty without limit, the results will be a war of all against all.

This suggests to the rational person that some of the liberty we have in the state of nature must be given up. To give it up entirely, however, would make no sense at all; if Jones gave up the liberty of defending himself altogether, he would become the prey of everyone—and an egoistic agent could not rationally allow that. So this "right" of self-defense remains something that Jones will always retain.

We have, then, one right and one law, which Hobbes uses as the foundation for a series of deductions. Once we have these, others "follow" in almost geometrical fashion. For instance, the second law, Hobbes tells us, is

> that a man be willing, when others are so too, as far forth as peace and defense of himself he shall think it necessary, to lay down this right to all things; and be contented with so much liberty against other men, as he would allow other men against himself. (*L*, 163–164)

Each of us, according to this second law, should be content with as much liberty with respect to others as we are willing to allow with respect to ourselves. There should be—to end the state of war—a mutual limiting of rights, as far as this is of mutual benefit to each. (Note that Hobbes does not suppose that anyone would do this altruistically or out of sheer goodwill. The motivation throughout is hedonistic and egoistic.)

This agreement to limit one's claims has the flavor of a contract. And, indeed, Hobbes' view is one version of a **social contract** theory,* but you can see that there is a difficulty at this point. Suppose Jones and Smith, in a state of nature, each agree to limit their own liberty to the extent that the other does as well. What reason does each one have to trust the other to keep his promise? Is there anything to keep Smith from violating the contract if he thinks it is in his interest to do so and calculates that he can get away with it? It seems not. Hence, in a state of nature, contracts and promises are useless. They are just words! This is a serious problem. It looks as if you cannot get here from there—that is, to a moral community from a state of nature. Can Hobbes solve this problem?

What is necessary to make the contract operative, Hobbes says, is "a common power set over them both, with right and force sufficient to compel performance" (*L*, 167). Only when punishment threatens can Jones trust Smith to keep her promise. For only then will it clearly be in Smith's self-interest not to break it. There is, then, a necessity for

> some coercive power, to compel men equally to the performance of their covenants . . . and such power there is none before the erection of a commonwealth. (*L*, 168)

---

*The idea of a contract or agreement as the basis for society is taken up by a number of other political thinkers: Spinoza, Rousseau, and—most important for the founding of the American Republic—John Locke (see the following section). They differ about the powers such a contract bestows on a government, about whether such a contract could or could not be revoked, and about the grounds on which a citizen might withdraw allegiance. Nonetheless, social contract theories generally stress both the rights of individuals and the necessity of consent as the basis of legitimate government. Thus, they are both a reflection of and an influence on the individualism of the times.

This is the rationale for that "great *Leviathan*," that "artificial man," that "mortal god," the state. It is the state, together with the power of enforcement that we agree to give it, that gets us beyond the state of nature. Only in such a community can moral and legal rules exist and structure our lives.

The great danger in any community, Hobbes believes, is that it might fall back again into the state of nature, where everyone thinks he or she has the right to be judge of everything. So a state cannot allow individuals to follow their own consciences, to decide for themselves what is good and evil. The **sovereign** established by the contract, whether king or governing assembly, must be absolute; its word must be law. The sovereign declares what is good, what is evil—and even what those terms shall mean. Lacking this absolute power in the sovereign, we stare chaos and civil war in the face again.

In setting up a government for the purpose of escaping the dangers of the state of nature, then, we are bound to treat its actions as our own. So once a sovereign power is established, there can be no right of rebellion against it, for it cannot be right to rebel against ourselves. Nor can any subject claim that the sovereign power has acted unjustly, no matter what it does, for whatever it does is done by the citizens themselves who established it. Moreover, because the sovereign is not a party to the contract, but is established by it, it follows that the sovereign cannot violate the contract. A government may do bad things, Hobbes allows, but it can never be accused of injustice.

Because the aim of government is to secure a condition of peace among the citizens, it must have all the powers that are necessary to this end. And because individual actions are governed by opinions, the sovereign must have the power to determine which opinions and doctrines may be taught in the state. Finally, the sovereign power must be one and undivided. Hobbes thought one lesson of the civil war was that power divided between king and Parliament made conflict inevitable. So a unified sovereign must have the power to make the law, to judge cases according to the law, and to administer the application of law. Otherwise, the whole point of establishing a government by limiting individual natural rights would be lost.

You might think that this is a rather extreme position, but remember that Hobbes' analysis of human beings leads to a rather extreme view of the problem: the war of all against all. For extreme situations, extreme solutions may be required. In any case, we have here an example of a worldview built on the foundations of the new science, a view that *includes* human beings, together with their mental and moral life. Let us summarize a few of the main points:

- Sensation, thought, motivation, and voluntary action are all analyzed in terms of matter in motion.
- All events, including human actions, are subject to the same laws of motion that Galileo has discovered.
- Only egoistic desires are recognized as motivators, so all actions are performed for the welfare of the agent.
- If you peel off the veneer of civilization, you are left with individuals in conflict.
- This conflict can be resolved on the basis of the very passions that produce it, provided people reason well about their individual long-term interest.
- Morality and law are simply the best means available, the *only* means to stave off imminent death and the possible loss of felicity. Being moral and law-abiding is no more than a smart strategy for self-preservation.
- Unless these rules are enforced by a powerful ruler, everything will collapse again into the state of nature.

It is a stark vision that Hobbes gives us. He thinks that acceptance of modern science forces that view upon us. Is that correct, or are there less forbidding alternatives?

---

1. Contrast the world-picture we get from the Galileo–Descartes–Hobbes gang with that of Aristotle and his medieval followers with respect to

   - a description of the universe;
   - what needs explaining;
   - kinds of explanation desired; and
   - the place of values in the world.

2. How does Hobbes try to explain thinking? Compare his views, if you can, with recent work in artificial intelligence.

3. How are good and evil explained by Hobbes? Compare with the view of Augustine (e.g., pp. 270–274.).

4. How do Hobbes and Descartes differ on the nature of the will? Relate this to the metaphysics of each one.

5. Describe what Hobbes calls "the state of nature," and explain why it has the character it does have.

6. How does Hobbes think we can have gotten, or can get, beyond the state of nature?

7. What makes Hobbes think that a "social contract" will require the "coercive power" of a state?

John Locke: Looking to Experience

Although a clear implication of Cartesian method is that "first" philosophy is really epistemology, Descartes' own meditations are still in the metaphysical mode. Hobbes, too, is primarily a metaphysician—the metaphysician of matter in motion, in contrast to Descartes' dualism. The credit (or blame) for taking seriously the idea that theory-of-knowledge issues must come first in philosophical thought belongs to the English philosopher John Locke (1632–1704). With Locke the lesson is drawn: Unless we are clear about our capacities for gaining knowledge, we are likely to waste our time in controversies over matters that are beyond our grasp and end in confusion. Understanding how our kind of mind works and whence its contents come has to be the first order of business. So he writes, over a period of years, the famous *Essay Concerning Human Understanding*. This long and complex treatise, in four books, is usually thought to mark the proper beginning of **empiricism** in philosophy.* Locke begins the *Essay* with these words:

> Since it is the *understanding* that sets man above the rest of sensible beings, and gives him all the advantage and dominion which he has over them; it is

"It is ambition enough to be employed as an under-labourer in clearing the ground a little, and removing some of the rubbish which lies in the way to knowledge."
—JOHN LOCKE

certainly a subject, even for its nobleness, worth our labour to inquire into. . . .

If by this inquiry into the nature of the understanding, I can discover the powers thereof; how far they reach; to what things they are in any degree proportionate; and where they fail us, I suppose it may be of use to prevail with the busy mind of man to be more cautious in meddling with things exceeding its comprehension; to stop when it is at the utmost extent of its tether; and to sit down in a quiet ignorance of those things which, upon examination, are found to be beyond the reach of our capacities. (*Essay*, Intro, 1, 3; vol. 1, pp. 25–28)[4]

You can see that Locke intends to recommend a certain modesty with respect to our capacity for knowledge. Moreover, he thinks that circumscribing the scope of our understanding will be a very *useful* thing to do; he is not writing just to satisfy curiosity on this score, but to mitigate the quarrels—religious, political, or what have you—leading even to wars, that arise when men believe they have certainty about things that are actually beyond our powers to know.

---

*There are, of course, forerunners of the empirical trend. Francis Bacon is a distinguished empiricist (see the Sketch on p. 412) and Hobbes also, to some extent. There is an immense amount of detail in Locke's long and rambling *Essay*, much of it having only historical interest. We will focus our attention on those parts that have made a lasting impact on the great conversation.

How shall he proceed? He states his purpose more precisely in these words:

> to inquire into the original, certainty, and extent of *human knowledge*. (*Essay*, Intro, 2; vol. 1, p. 26)

He says that he will use a "historical, plain method" in this investigation. By this, he means that he will try to trace our ideas to their origin, using no more esoteric technique than directing our attention to what should be obvious to any careful inquirer. So we find him again and again asking us to look and see whether we agree with what he finds.

He notes in the introduction that he will use the word "**idea**" in a very broad sense: for "whatsoever is the *object* of the understanding when a man thinks" (*Essay*, Intro, 8; vol. 1, p. 32). He means to include everything from sensations of red and warm, through the contents of memory and imagination, to abstract ideas of a circle or an animal species, and even to our idea of God. That there are such ideas in our minds, Locke says, we all admit. The first question is this: How do they get there?

ORIGIN OF IDEAS

Book I of the *Essay* is devoted to destroying one possible answer: that ideas, any or all of them, are innate. Locke's argument is that if there are **innate ideas,** they must be universally held in all minds. Perhaps the most plausible cases are trivialities such as "Whatever is, is." But Locke argues that (1) not even such ideas are universal (e.g., they are not present in the minds of children or idiots), and (2) universality would prove innateness only if there were no other way such ideas could be acquired.* Locke is convinced that there is another way, and to that he turns in Book II, the longest and most influential book of the *Essay*.

If the mind is not innately supplied with ideas, where do they come from?

> Let us then suppose the mind to be, as we say, white paper, void of all characters, without any

ideas: —How comes it to be furnished? Whence comes it by that vast store which the busy and boundless fancy of man has painted on it with an almost endless variety? Whence has it all the *materials* of reason and knowledge? To this I answer, in one word, from EXPERIENCE. In that all our knowledge is founded; and from that it ultimately derives itself. (*Essay*, II, I, 2; vol. 1, pp. 121–122)

There are two sources of such **experience.** On the one hand, there is the experience of external objects via our senses; this is the first and greatest source of ideas. Locke calls this source **sensation.** Here we get the ideas of yellow, hot, cold, hard, soft, bitter, sweet, and so on. On the other hand, we can reflect internally on how our minds work, garnering ideas of mental operations. Locke calls this source **reflection.** From reflection we get the ideas of perceiving, thinking, doubting, believing, reasoning, knowing, willing, and so on. These two sources supply the raw materials for all our knowledge.

> The understanding seems to me not to have the least glimmering of any ideas which it doth not receive from one of these two. *External objects* furnish the mind with the ideas of sensible qualities, which are all those different perceptions they produce in us; and *the mind* furnishes the understanding with ideas of its own operations. (*Essay*, II, I, 5; vol. 1, p. 124)

It is worth noting that Locke takes for granted, as Hobbes also does but Descartes does not, that there *are* "external objects" supplying us with ideas of themselves.* This supposition sits uneasily with other parts of Locke's view, and Berkeley (later in this chapter) and Hume (Chapter 19) exploit this tension.

Ideas can be classified as either simple or complex. A **simple idea** is one that, "being in itself uncompounded, contains in it nothing but *one uniform appearance, or conception in the mind*" (*Essay*, II, II, 1; vol. 1, p. 145). What might seem to be a

---

*Locke is attacking a very crude version of innate ideas; it is not clear that it applies to Descartes' version of innateness as an idea that a thinking being would possess even if nothing else but that being existed. See p. 382.

*Locke does offer some arguments on behalf of this assumption much later in the *Essay* (see Book IV, Chapter XI), but they seem to be no stronger than the arguments Descartes destroys in *Meditation I*.

single experience may be composed of several simple ideas; touching a piece of ice, for instance, produces not one idea but the two distinguishable ideas of cold and hard. Simple ideas are the *elements* of all our thinking.

> When the understanding is once stored with these simple ideas, it has the power to repeat, compare, and unite them, even to an almost infinite variety, and so can make at pleasure new complex ideas. But it is not in the power of the most exalted wit, or enlarged understanding, by any quickness or variety of thought, to *invent* or *frame* one new simple idea in the mind, not taken in by the ways before mentioned. (*Essay*, II, II, 2; vol. 1, p. 145)

🔹

"Nothing ever becomes real till it is experienced."

John Keats (1795–1821)

Even with respect to simple ideas, however, the mind carries on certain operations. For instance, (1) we can *distinguish* one clearly from another; (2) we can *compare* them, noting their likenesses and differences; (3) we can *put them together* in various ways; (4) we can *name* them; and most important, (5) we can *frame abstract ideas*. How do we do that? Locke gives this example. Seeing the same color today, in chalk or snow, which we yesterday observed in milk, we consider that appearance alone (disregarding the crumbly nature, the coldness, or the liquidity it is associated with) and give it the name *whiteness*. We *abstract* the color from the other qualities by paying selective attention to it, neglecting its surroundings. That is the way, Locke says, "universals, whether ideas or terms, are made" (*Essay*, II, XI, 9; vol. 1, p. 207). It is this power to abstract that distinguishes us from the other animals. All of these powers are known to us by reflection on the operations of our own minds.

We come now to **complex ideas,** which can be classified under three heads, Locke tells us: modes, relations, and substances. There is a long and complicated chapter on our ideas of *modes* (what the medievals called "accidents" or "incidental properties"). These do not exist on their own,

but only as modifications of a substance. Locke strives to show that our ideas of space, time, and infinity are modes, built by adding simple ideas to simple ideas.

Relations are of many kinds and are very important in our knowledge. Examples are knowing that one thing occurs before another, that this is next to that, that *a* causes *b*, that *x* is identical with *y*, and that two numbers added make a third number. But because Locke's discussion of the general nature of relations is both complex and confused, we pass it by—though we will examine what he says about certain relations, such as are involved in our idea of personal identity and in our knowledge of things external to us.

Of more lasting significance is what Locke has to say about *substances*. The notion of substance, as we have seen, plays a significant role in philosophical thought from the time of Aristotle onward. In that tradition, a substance is a composite of *form* (making it the kind of thing it is) and *matter* (which makes it the particular instance of that kind of thing). Substances have properties, some of which are essential to its nature—the properties that make it what it is—and some are incidental. But in trying to trace our idea of substance back to simple ideas, Locke finds nothing, either in sensation or in reflection, that answers to this Aristotelian notion of substance. Instead, he says, we find only the properties of the substance—its color, for instance, or its shape and hardness. We simply posit the existence of the **substance** as the substratum in which those properties inhere, as the thing that has these properties. And we name particular substances, such as gold, for the distinctive collection of properties it has: yellowness, hardness, malleability, and so on.

Not all of those properties, Locke says, are of the same kind.

> For, to speak truly, yellowness is not actually in gold, but is a power in gold to produce that idea in us by our eyes, when placed in a due light: and the heat, which we cannot leave out of our ideas of the sun, is no more really in the sun, than the white colour it introduces into wax. These are both equally powers in the sun, operating, by the motion and figure of its sensible parts, so on a man, as to

make him have the idea of heat; and so on wax, as to make it capable to produce in a man the idea of white. (*Essay*, II, XXIII, 10; vol. 1, pp. 400–401)

From this, we see that Locke accepts that division of qualities into primary and secondary that we first met in Galileo.* The properties that are actually in gold are its extension, shape, motion, and impenetrability. These are gold's **primary qualities,** the qualities it really has.

Properly speaking, however, gold is not yellow; that color is not one of its primary qualities, does not belong to it as it is—apart from us. Gold does have a **secondary quality:** the power to produce yellow sensations in creatures such as ourselves. The idea is that the primary qualities of gold, when joined with the primary qualities of light, of the eye, and of the nervous system of a human being, bring about (somehow) an experience of color. But we would be mistaken to read that sensation back into the substance itself.

IDEA OF THE SOUL

Substances, then, can be known to exist as the *causes* of the ideas they produce in us. But this means, Locke holds, that we have just as good an idea of spiritual substance as of material. Just as we frame the idea of a material substance from the ideas of sensation, so from ideas of reflection,

> we are able to frame the *complex idea of an immaterial spirit.* And thus . . . we have as clear a perception and notion of immaterial substances as we have of material. . . . The one is as clear and distinct an idea as the other. . . . For whilst I know, by seeing or hearing &c., that there is some corporeal being without me, the object of that sensation, I do more certainly know, that there is some spiritual being within me that sees and hears. (*Essay*, II, XXIII, 15; vol. 1, pp. 406–407)

What applies in the one case applies in the other, however. In neither case do we have any knowledge of what such a substance is in itself. We know only that there must be such a substance to serve as the substratum for physical properties in the one case and mental properties in the other.

So Locke comes to agree with Descartes—and to disagree with Hobbes—in believing that there are minds *and* bodies and that they are radically different kinds of things.

In sum, although we have clear ideas of some of the primary qualities of both bodies and souls (for instance, solidity on the one hand and thinking on the other), the substance of each is unknown to us—and is bound to remain so.

> For whensoever we would proceed beyond these simple ideas we have from sensation and reflection, and dive further into the nature of things, we fall presently into darkness and obscurity, perplexedness and difficulties, and can discover nothing further but our own blindness and ignorance. (*Essay*, II, XXIII, 32; vol. 1, p. 418)

IDEA OF PERSONAL IDENTITY

Still, Locke holds that there are such immaterial substances as souls. But if we know substances, including souls, through their properties, can we count a thing as the *same* thing if its properties change? This question becomes more pressing when we apply it to our selves. I, in my maturity, possess very different qualities from those I had at ten years old. What is it that makes me the same person throughout? Is this the rule: same person, same soul? That had been the traditional answer, at least in the West, but Locke gives a different answer, which has had great influence.

Locke argues that it turns out to be completely irrelevant whether the soul substance present in me at age ten is the same soul substance I now have. In keeping with his determination to trace all our ideas to experience, Locke asks, What is it that gives me the *idea of myself* at all? and he answers, **consciousness.**

> For, since consciousness always accompanies thinking, and it is that which makes every one to be what he calls self, . . . as far as this consciousness can be extended backwards to any past action or thought, so far reaches the identity of that person. (*Essay*, II, XXVII, 11; vol. 1, p. 449)

If I were not conscious of myself, I would be no more a self than a stone is. Then if I ask what makes the self I now am identical with the self I was

---

*See pp. 357–358.

yesterday, the answer has to be in conformity with this. I must be conscious of that self—remember having the experiences of yesterday's self.

Personal identity, then, cannot consist in sameness of substance. For all we know, it might be that a succession of soul substances could constitute a self, provided each were connected to the last by memories of what was thought and done in it.* To take the contrary view, if a single substance were "wholly stripped of all consciousness of its past existence . . . beyond the power of ever retrieving it again," that would constitute the end of one person and the beginning of another (*Essay*, II, XXVII, 14; vol. 1, p. 455).

In the movie *All of Me*, Lily Tomlin wakes up in the body of Steve Martin. In fact, she shares that body with him. What is it that accounts for Tomlin still being Tomlin, for her continued identity—even in a new body? Is it that her substantial soul has moved over? Locke says we could not know that, and it is irrelevant in any case. What makes her remain herself is the memory of her past life and the continuity of her interests, passions, and goals—in short, her consciousness.

Locke gives us this example. Consider your little finger and suppose that it gets cut off.

> Upon separation of this little finger, should this consciousness go along with the little finger, and leave the rest of the body, it is evident the little finger would be the person, the same person; and self would then have nothing to do with the rest of the body. (*Essay*, II, XXVII, 17; vol. 1, p. 459)

Locke remarks that "person" is a *forensic* term, the sort of term that appears in courts of law. It has to do with what we can be held responsible for, praised and blamed for, rewarded and punished for. If Locke is right about personal identity, my person

> extends itself beyond present existence to what is past, only by consciousness,—whereby it becomes concerned and accountable; owns and imputes to itself past actions, just upon the same ground and for the same reason as it does the present. (*Essay*, II, XXVII, 26; vol. 1, p. 467)

We own up to our present actions as ours because we are conscious of doing them. We own up to having done past actions on exactly the same grounds. Locke thinks it is "probable" that one and the same consciousness is always attached to the same soul, but personal identity has a psychological rather than a metaphysical basis.*

LANGUAGE AND ESSENCE

Book III of the *Essay* has to do with words.† It is in words, by and large, that we express our knowledge, so an examination of the "origins, extent, and certainty" of our knowledge ought to clarify how language works. According to Locke, words are necessary for "sociable" creatures such as ourselves, language being "the great instrument and common tie of society" (*Essay*, III, I, 1; vol. 2, p. 3). Their principal function is to stand as signs for ideas.

> The comfort and advantage of society not being to be had without communication of thoughts, it was necessary that man should find out some external sensible signs, whereof those invisible ideas, which his thoughts are made up of, might be made known to others. . . . The use, then, of words, is to be sensible marks of ideas; and the ideas they stand for are their proper and immediate signification. (*Essay*, III, II, 1; vol. 2, pp. 8–9)

Words, then, "in their primary or immediate signification, stand for nothing but *the ideas in the mind of him that uses them*" (*Essay*, III, II, 2; vol. 2, p. 9). And the aim of speaking is to make hearers understand these ideas by awakening similar ideas in them. The connection between a word and the idea it stands for is arbitrary. The word "black" no more resembles my idea of black than the word

---

*In recent decades the concept of personal identity has been given extended consideration, often in terms of science fiction examples. The work of Bernard Williams, Derek Parfit, and Peter Unger makes clear the philosophers' debt to Locke. You might look at the delightful little book by John Perry, *A Dialogue on Immortality and Personal Identity* (Indianapolis, IN: Hackett, 1978).

†Here is another way in which Locke is a forerunner of things to come; much twentieth-century philosophy was preoccupied with linguistic matters. See, for instance, Chapter 26, on the thought of Ludwig Wittgenstein.

---

*Compare this line of thought to the Buddhist doctrine of *anātman* (pp. 41–45).

"schwarz" does. But if hearing one of these words brings an idea into my mind that is similar to the idea in the speaker's mind, the word has done its job. Locke takes pains to deny that words stand directly for things in the world. It is not entirely wrong to think this, he says, but *precisely put*, words represent such things only indirectly, by representing ideas, which in turn stand for these things.

Again we pass by much of the detail in Locke's discussion. Let us look, though, at what Locke has to say about words for essences. As we have seen, knowledge in the Aristotelian tradition is knowledge of substance and principally of the form of a substance that is its essence. Such knowledge tells us what it is to be a thing of a certain kind. Essences determine kinds of things: horses, clouds, tides, memories, thefts, and so on.

Now our ideas for kinds of things are, as Locke has told us, formed by abstraction, and we understand how that works. We consider a theft, say, and ignore everything that makes it this *particular* theft; we are then left with the general idea of theft. And general words represent general ideas. Most of our words—proper names aside—are general in this sense and represent abstract ideas.

But where in the world do we find essences or universals?

> It is plain, by what has been said, that *general* and *universal* belong not to the real existence of things; but are the inventions and creatures of the understanding, made by it for its own use, and concern only signs, whether words or ideas. Words are general . . . when used for signs of general ideas, and so are applicable indifferently to many particular things; and ideas are general when they are set up as the representatives of many particular things. (*Essay*, III, III, 11; vol. 2, pp. 21–22)

This is a conclusion of considerable importance. If Locke is right, the whole tradition stemming from Plato and Aristotle has been mistaken in thinking of universality as a feature of reality—whether in the Platonic heaven of Forms or in Aristotelian real essences embedded in things. Everything is particular. Universality is to be found only in the way certain particular things (mental ideas and words) *function*. Ideas and words are universal in their use, but not in their nature. My idea

of a raven is as particular a thing as any individual raven. The way it differs is this: I *use* it to represent this raven and that raven—and indeed all the ravens there are or could be.

It is true that nature produces things that are similar to each other: ravens, for example. And it is even true, Locke admits, that a particular raven has a **real essence,** meaning by that those elements that are the ultimate foundation of the qualities we are aware of through our senses. But such real essences of things are completely unknown to us. Whatever it is in a given substance that causes our simple ideas of black, feathered, and winged is forever beyond our ken.

Moreover, though the things we call ravens are undeniably similar to each other, there is nothing that all ravens have that forces this similarity: no form or essence that *determines* the existence or coexistence of those qualities. Locke cites natural variations in individuals as evidence of this. Nature produces "monsters" of various kinds, deformed individuals without what we normally take to be properties essential to a kind. If we just pay attention to our experience, it seems clear that *any* property of a thing, no matter how "essential" we deem it, may, in a given instance, be lacking. How could that happen if nature were arranged in species where each particular instance of the species were determined to be the kind of thing it is by a universal form?

We do, of course, have abstract ideas and words, and they do present essences to us. But these are what Locke calls **nominal essences.** As the word suggests, nominal essences are attached to names. Nominal essences, while not entirely arbitrary, are our own creations; they are not read off directly from nature itself. We do not consider the ultimate constitution of things in forming our ideas of essences because we cannot. Nor do we consider substantial forms, since those are mere inventions of the philosophers. What we do consider are the sensible qualities of things—those clusters of qualities that seem to hang together with some regularity and get a name.

> And if this be so, it is plain that *our distinct species* are *nothing but distinct complex ideas, with distinct names annexed to them.* It is true every substance that exists

has its peculiar constitution, whereon depend those sensible qualities and powers we observe in it; but the ranking of things into species (which is nothing but sorting them under several titles) is done by us according to the ideas that *we* have of them: which, though sufficient to distinguish them by names, . . . yet if we suppose it to be done by their real internal constitutions, . . . by real essences, . . . we shall be liable to great mistakes. (*Essay*, III, VI, 13; vol. 2, p. 69)

Nominal essences, then, are not "copied from precise boundaries set by nature," but are "made by man with some liberty" (*Essay*, III, VI, 27; vol. 2, p. 77). They may be more or less carefully constructed, given our experience of things. And, no doubt, they can be improved by more careful observation. But they are one and all creatures of their creator, not a simple mirror of reality.

This, then, in short, is the case: Nature makes many *particular things*, which do agree one with another in many sensible qualities, and probably too in their internal frame and constitution: but it is not this real essence that distinguishes them into species; it is men who, taking occasion from the qualities they find united in them . . . range them into sorts, in order to their naming, for the convenience of comprehensive signs. (*Essay*, III, VI, 36; vol. 2, p. 86)

It is, then, Locke says, "evident that *men* make sorts of things" (*Essay*, III, VI, 35; vol. 2, p. 85). Nature produces particular beings in great abundance; many of them resemble each other. But "it is nevertheless true, that the boundaries of the species, whereby men sort them, are made by men" (*Essay*, III, VI, 37; vol. 2, p. 87). That science of the real essences of things that Aristotle and his followers dreamed of is not possible.

THE EXTENT OF KNOWLEDGE

Locke told us in the beginning of the *Essay* that his purpose was to determine the origins, the certainty, and the extent of our knowledge. His method has been to examine our understanding, getting clear about the materials it has to work with and how it operates with them. Now, in the fourth book of the *Essay*, he is at last ready to address the questions about knowledge directly. It begins this way:

Since the mind, in all its thoughts and reasonings, hath no other immediate object but its own ideas, which it alone does or can contemplate, it is evident that our knowledge is only conversant about them.

Knowledge then seems to me to be nothing but *the perception of the connexion of and agreement, or disagreement and repugnancy of any of our ideas.* In this alone it consists. (*Essay*, IV, I, 1; vol. 2, p. 167)

We can have knowledge no further than we have *ideas*. (*Essay*, IV, III, 1; vol. 2, p. 190)*

This might not seem to be a very promising beginning. Surely, you want to say, we want to know more than how our ideas are related to *each other*. We want to know about reality, the world—what there actually is! In fact, Locke himself states such an objection, but he thinks he can meet it. Let us see how.

First we should note that he accepts that view of knowledge common in the tradition from Plato to Descartes—when we know, we have certainty. "The highest probability amounts not to certainty, without which there can be no true knowledge," Locke says (*Essay*, IV, III, 14; vol. 2, p. 203). This, of course, sets the standard very high.† The higher you set the standard, the fewer propositions will pass muster, so we mustn't be surprised when Locke again and again laments the small extent of our knowledge.

By the agreement and disagreement of ideas, he means the way ideas are put together in propositions. There are many distinct ways this happens, but let us focus on only one, that concerning *real existence*. He has said that we can have no knowledge beyond our ideas, but here, apparently without realizing it, he strikes a new note. He explains this kind of knowledge as "of *actual real existence* agreeing to any idea" (*Essay*, IV, I, 7; vol. 2, p. 171). Now the existence of something that "agrees to" one of our ideas cannot just be a matter of the relations *among* ideas. Yet it is only with this

---

*See again the remark about "disaster" by John Searle, footnote, p. 373.

†For a critique of this demand for certainty, see C. S. Peirce, p. 597. See also Ludwig Wittgenstein, pp. 645–649.

sort of agreement that Locke can meet that natural objection to his principles that we noted previously.

What then can we know to "really" exist? Like Descartes, Avicenna, and Augustine before him, Locke believes we have a clear *intuitive* knowledge of our own existence. This "we perceive . . . so plainly and so certainly, that it neither needs nor is capable of any proof. For nothing can be more evident to us than our own existence" (*Essay*, IV, IX, 3; vol. 2, pp. 304–305). We can know *demonstratively* that God exists. Locke rejects Descartes' first proof of God, which depends on an innate idea of God in us, but he offers an argument based on our own existence and the *ex nihilo nihil fit* principle: From nothing, you get nothing.

The knowledge of other things we have by *sensation*. Other than ourselves and God, we can know of the existence of any other thing

> only when, by actual operating upon [us], it makes itself perceived by [us]. For the having the idea of anything in our mind, no more proves the existence of that thing, than the picture of a man evidences his being in the world, or the visions of a dream make thereby a true history.
>
> It is therefore the *actual receiving* of ideas from without that gives us notice of the existence of other things, and makes us know, that something doth exist at that time without us, which causes that idea in us. . . . And of this, the greatest assurance I can possibly have . . . is the testimony of my eyes, . . . whose testimony . . . I can no more doubt, whilst I write this, that I see white and black, and that something really exists that causes that sensation in me, than that I write or move my hand. . . .
>
> The notice we have by our senses of the existing of things without us, though it be not altogether so certain as our intuitive knowledge, or the deductions of our reason employed about the clear abstract ideas of our own minds; yet it is an assurance that deserves the name of *knowledge*. (*Essay*, IV, XI, 1–3; vol. 2, pp. 325–327)

Several questions press themselves on us: (1) If our knowledge does not reach further than our ideas, as Locke insists, how do we know these ideas are being received from something outside ourselves? (2) Isn't his confidence in the testimony of the senses simply naive, given Descartes' first

meditation? (3) Locke has told us that knowledge requires certainty, but now he says that though it is not as certain as intuition or demonstration, the assurance of the senses amounts to knowledge anyway. We will see other philosophers exploring these problems.*

It is clear that Locke has accepted the main themes in the *representational theory of perception and knowledge*.† The mind is a storehouse of ideas. These ideas are the immediate or direct objects of our knowledge. We suppose them to be representations or signs of things beyond themselves. They are such, we think, by virtue of their being produced in the mind by the causal powers of those external things. So we can know "real existence" indirectly, by virtue of the "correspondence" of our ideas with those really existing items in the world beyond the mind. This is a pattern of thought that ever totters on the brink of skepticism—How do you check the correspondence?—and we see Locke struggling against drawing the skeptical conclusion.‡ He piles reason on inconclusive reason for resisting the plunge, but it is not clear that anything will rescue him.

---

1. What is Locke's aim in the *Essay Concerning Human Understanding*?
2. What are Locke's arguments against innate ideas?
3. What are the two sources of our ideas?
4. How do we get abstract ideas?
5. How do we come to have the idea of substance?
6. What can we know of substance?
7. What is the idea of a soul? How does it arise?
8. What is, and what is not, the origin of our idea of personal identity?
9. Contrast real essences with nominal essences. Why is it important to Locke to make this distinction?
10. How do we know real things existing outside our minds?

---

*See especially Berkeley and David Hume, pp. 431 and 463.

†Review the discussion of these themes in the chapter on Descartes, pp. 372–373.

‡Compare the view of Aquinas, who does not make ideas the objects of our mental acts, p. 330.

OF REPRESENTATIVE GOVERNMENT

Locke's influence extends far beyond his epistemology. In fact, he may be best known in America for his political thought, which had a decisive impact on Thomas Jefferson and the other founders of the United States. Though trained as a physician, Locke was near the centers of power in late seventeenth-century England, serving in several official posts himself and being a close friend and associate of Lord Shaftesbury, who rose to be Lord Chancellor. Because of the intrigues of the time, he left England on several occasions for his safety and lived for some years in France and in Holland. He lived through the "Glorious Revolution" of 1688, which brought William and Mary to the English throne and established the rights of an independent Parliament. So he had reason to be interested in political matters.

Like Hobbes, Locke begins his theory of government with speculations about a state of nature. But unlike Hobbes, he doesn't end up justifying an absolute sovereign. Locke follows Thomas Aquinas in thinking that even before government is instituted, human beings, through their reason, have access to the **natural law.*** So he does not see men in a state of nature as mere calculating desire machines, the way Hobbes does. In a natural state, humans have a sense for justice and injustice, right and wrong, independent of any law declared by a sovereign. And this makes a difference.

Locke does not discuss the contents of this natural law to any great extent. It seems to be more or less coextensive with the Golden Rule: Do unto others as you would have them do unto you.

> The state of Nature has a law of Nature to govern it, which obliges every one, and reason, which is that law, teaches all mankind who will but consult it, that being all equal and independent, no one ought to harm another in his life, health, liberty, or possessions; for men being all the workmanship of one omnipotent and infinitely wise Maker; . . . they are made to last during His, not one another's pleasure. . . . Every one as he is bound to preserve himself, . . . so by the like reason, when his own preservation comes not in competition, ought he

as much as he can to preserve the rest of mankind. (*Gov't*, II, II, 6; pp. 119–120)

Locke realizes, of course, that not everyone will conform to this natural law, even though it is present in their reason. So, like law under government, it needs to be enforced. But who will do it where there is no government? The answer is—everyone.

> And that all men may be restrained from invading others' rights, and from doing hurt to one another, and the law of Nature be observed, which willeth the peace and preservation of all mankind, the execution of the law of Nature is in that state put into every man's hands, whereby every one has a right to punish the transgressors of that law to such a degree as may hinder its violation. (*Gov't*, II, II, 6; p. 120)

Violations of the natural law, together with this universal right to punish violations of it, produce the "inconveniences" men hope a government will save them from. For in the state of nature, there is no avoiding the situation where men will be judges in their own cause; and we know that in such cases,

> self-love will make men partial to themselves and their friends; and, on the other side, ill-nature, passion, and revenge will carry them too far in punishing others, and hence nothing but confusion and disorder will follow. (*Gov't*, II, II, 13; p. 123)

It is to restrain the "partiality and violence of men" that God instituted **government,** Locke says.

"No man is good enough to govern another man without that other's consent."

Abraham Lincoln (1809–1865)

Obviously, however, there is a problem here. For absolute rulers are men, too. What is there in absolute sovereignty to restrain *their* partiality and violence? So Hobbes' solution won't work; it won't solve the problem of partiality and violence but, at best, will locate it at one very powerful point in a community. What would work? Because men are

> by nature all free, equal, and independent, no one can be put out of this estate and subjected to the political power of another without his own consent,

---

*See the fuller discussion of natural law in the chapter on Aquinas, pp. 332–333.

which is done by agreeing with other men, to join and unite into a community for their comfortable, safe, and peaceable living, one amongst another, in a secure enjoyment of their properties. . . . When any number of men have so consented to make one community or government, they are thereby presently incorporated, and make one body politic, wherein the majority have a right to act and conclude the rest. (*Gov't*, II, VIII, 95; pp. 164–165)

🍂

> "Man's capacity for justice makes democracy possible, but man's inclination to injustice makes democracy necessary."
>
> *Reinhold Niebuhr (1892–1971)*

Like Hobbes, Locke envisages a "contract" as the basis for government. But Locke's contract is not made between the people with a sovereign; it is a contract people make with each other. Each agrees to give up the right to punish violations of the natural law, provided the others do so too. And each agrees to abide by majority rule. So they institute a government with political power, which Locke defines as

> a right of making laws, with penalties of death, and consequently all less penalties for the regulating and preserving of property, and of employing the force of the community in the execution of such laws, and in the defence of the commonwealth from foreign injury, and all this only for the public good. (*Gov't*, II, I, 3; p. 118)

Note that Locke assumes that there is such a thing as **property** before there is a government; in fact, one of the chief functions of a government is to guarantee persons security in the enjoyment of their property.* But property entails rights; for something to be your property means that you have a right to its use and others do not. How could there be such rights without government?

Locke imagines that in a state of nature the fruit on the trees, the water in the streams, and the animals in the forest are common to all. What could make part of that mine rather than yours? Locke gives some examples. If you fill a bucket with water from the common source and take it to your dwelling, and if someone else then takes that water rather than fetch some for himself or herself, that person has injured you and have done you an injustice. Why? Because you have mixed your labor with this water; and your labor belongs to you. Anyone can fish in the ocean and bring back a catch, but the catch then belongs to the one who fishes, and whoever takes it away without permission does wrong.

> He that is nourished by the acorns he picked up under an oak, or the apples he gathered from the trees in the wood, has certainly appropriated them to himself. Nobody can deny but the nourishment is his. I ask, then, when did they begin to be his? when he digested? or when he ate? or when he boiled? or when he brought them home? or when he picked them up? And it is plain, if the first gathering made them not his, nothing else could. That labour put a distinction between them and common. That added something to them more than Nature, the common mother of all, had done, and so they became his private right. (*Gov't*, II, V, 27; p. 130)

Private property, then, antedates the institution of government; it is not created by positive law, but secured by it.*

What sort of government is it, then, that can best protect life, health, liberty, and possessions? To avoid the dangers of anarchy at the one extreme and tyranny at the other, it must be a government of limited powers. And to ensure that it resists the temptation to make itself an exception to the laws it passes for others, it must be responsible to the people who established it. So Locke envisions a representative government with two powers: the legislative, to enact laws for the good of the whole, and

---

*It should be noted that Locke uses "property" in a broad sense to include life and liberty, as well as possessions (see *Gov't* II, IX, 123; p. 180), but he definitely does mean to include possessions as things to which we have a natural right.

---

*This "labor theory of value" was adopted by the political economist Adam Smith and used by Karl Marx in his critique of capitalism. Marx, of course, does not agree that private property is a natural right. See pp. 540–541.

the executive, to enforce the laws and protect the commonwealth against external enemies. It is most important, however, not to think of these powers as having the ultimate or supreme authority in a community. They are established by the people for certain ends, so they exist by the will of the people—and only for so long as they serve those ends.

The legislative power, Locke says,

> being only a fiduciary power to act for certain ends, there remains still in the people a supreme power to remove or alter the legislative, when they find the legislative act contrary to the trust reposed in them. For all power given with trust for the attaining an end being limited by that end, whenever that end is manifestly neglected or opposed, the trust must necessarily be forfeited, and the power devolve into the hands of those who gave it, who may place it anew where they shall think best for their safety and security. And thus the community perpetually retains a supreme power of saving themselves from the attempts and designs of anybody, even of their legislators, whenever they shall be so foolish or so wicked as to lay and carry on designs against the liberties and properties of the subject. (*Gov't*, II, XIII, 149; p. 192)

It was thoughts like these that inspired the American revolutionaries in the late eighteenth century and laid the foundations for the Constitution of the United States of America.

OF TOLERATION

We conclude our brief consideration of Locke's thinking with a look at another influential view of his, concerning religious toleration. In Locke's day, political struggles were entangled with religious quarrels. If the king was Roman Catholic, he sought to enact privileges for Catholics and restrictions on Anglicans. If Parliament was dominated by the Church of England, it decreed penalties on dissenters—Baptists, Presbyterians, and Quakers. Wars were fought over such issues. So while in exile in Holland, Locke wrote *A Letter Concerning Toleration*, which did more to change that situation than anything else ever did.

He draws a distinction between the civil **commonwealth** and a church. The commonwealth is

> a Society of Men constituted only for the procuring, preserving, and advancing of their own *Civil Interests*.
>
> *Civil Interests* I call Life, Liberty, Health, and Indolency of Body; and the Possession of outward things, such as Money, Lands, Houses, Furniture, and the like.
>
> It is the Duty of the Civil Magistrate, by the impartial Execution of equal Laws, to secure unto the People in general, and to every one of his Subjects in particular, the just Possession of these things belonging to this Life. (*Toleration*, p. 26)

A **church,** on the other hand, is

> a voluntary Society of Men, joining themselves together of their own accord, in order to the publick worshipping of God, in such a manner as they judge acceptable to him, and effectual to the Salvation of their Souls. (*Toleration*, p. 28)

Locke argues that it is not the business of the civil authorities to prescribe the way in which God is to be worshipped; they have no wisdom in this sphere. Nor is it appropriate for ecclesiastical authorities to try to gain worldly power. For this reason the civil power is obliged to tolerate differences in the ways men seek to relate to God and organize their worship.

Locke piles up a variety of arguments in favor of religious toleration by the state. Here is an influential one. It is said that religious dissenters from the established church are dangerous to civil order, that they breed sedition and rebellion. Historically, there was truth to this. But, Locke asks, why is this? It is *because* they are adversely discriminated against by the civil authority that they are a threat to that authority. Take away their oppression, and they will be as loyal as any other subjects.

> It is not the diversity of Opinions, (which cannot be avoided) but the refusal of Toleration to those that are of different Opinions, (which might have been granted) that has produced all the Bustles and Wars, that have been in the Christian World, upon account of Religion. (*Toleration*, p. 55)

If we in the West now take such toleration and religious liberty pretty much for granted, we owe a debt of gratitude to Locke as much as to anyone else.

1. How does Locke's notion of a state of nature differ from Hobbes' notion?
2. What are the "inconveniences" in a state of nature that lead to the formation of a government?
3. Why can't Locke adopt Hobbes' view of an absolute sovereignty as the solution for these problems?
4. What is the origin of private property, according to Locke?
5. What sort of government does Locke recommend?
6. How does Locke distinguish the two spheres of church and state?
7. Why should governments be tolerant of religious differences?

George Berkeley: Ideas into Things

Born near Kilkenny, Ireland, George Berkeley (1685–1753) became a cleric and later a bishop. At the youthful age of fifteen, he entered Trinity College, Dublin, where he became acquainted with the latest science of the day, including the work of Isaac Newton, and with Locke's *Essay Concerning Human Understanding*. He had a decidedly negative reaction to much in the *Essay*. He came to think that the doctrines Locke taught were mistaken in their fundamentals and pernicious in their effects. In short, Berkeley thought Locke's views led directly to the errors of *skepticism* and the evils of *atheism*. By his mid-twenties he had worked out a view that he believed would save us from these two errors. It is a view, moreover, that allows Berkeley to present himself as a determined defender of *common sense* against the meaningless jargon of the philosophers and the unnecessary materialism of the scientists.*

Perhaps the best place to begin is with a characterization of **common sense,** as Berkeley understands it. Two principles characterize what we might call *commonsense realism* about the world.[5]

---

*Not everyone agrees that Berkeley's views are harmonious with commonsense views of the world. In some respects they obviously are; in others, perhaps they are not. You will have to make up your own mind. His philosophy is set forth mainly in two small, clearly written books: *The Principles of Human Knowledge* (1710) and the charming *Three Dialogues between Hylas and Philonous* (1713).

"What do we perceive besides our own ideas or sensations?"
—GEORGE BERKELEY

1. Things exist independent of our perceiving that they do.
2. Things have the qualities they seem to have: The rose we see is really red, the sugar on our tongue is really sweet, and the fire we approach is really hot.

Surely he is right that before we study philosophy, this is what we do think. Berkeley wants to defend our natural belief in both these claims.

Let us try to get a sense for why he thinks they need defending. According to Locke, material substances do exist independent of our perception of them. Moreover, they have qualities of their own—the primary qualities of extension, figure, solidity, and motion. However, Locke insists that the true nature of substance is unknowable. Berkeley asks, How does this differ from skepticism?

Furthermore, we have seen that Galileo, Descartes, and Locke deny the second principle and hold that color, taste, and feeling are not in things at all! They exist only in us, as a result of the action of material things on our senses. According to them, the rose is not literally red; in reality, it is an uncolored extended substance with a power to produce a sensation of red in us.

But this means that the accepted philosophical view denies one of these two commonsense claims and flirts with skepticism about the other. Furthermore, Berkeley thinks the arguments for that view are a tissue of confusions. With respect to views such as Locke's, Berkeley comments, "We have first raised a dust and then complain we cannot see" (*Principles*, Intro, p. 8).[6]

Berkeley, then, sets himself to defend common sense. But you will be surprised at the way he does it.

ABSTRACT IDEAS

At the root of the confusion into which Berkeley believes modern philosophy has fallen is what he calls "Abuse of Language." In particular, philosophers have not understood how general terms work. That we have words general in their meaning is beyond doubt; *most* words are like that—tiger, snow, woman, rainbow, planet, wood, word, and so on. But in what does their universality consist?

Locke tells us that general words function as *names for* **abstract ideas.** So the word "tiger" stands not for this tiger or that one, or for the idea of this or that particular tiger, but for the abstract idea of a tiger. And we get the abstract idea of a tiger by selective attention, focusing on only those features of a thing that make it a tiger, or by noting what particular tigers have in common.

To Berkeley, this is just nonsense. A "chief part in rendering speculation intricate and perplexed," producing "innumerable errors and difficulties in almost all parts of knowledge," is

> the opinion that the mind hath a power of framing *abstract ideas* or notions of things. (*Principles*, Intro, 6; p. 9)

We are supposed to be able to look at Peter, James, and John and abstract from them *the idea of man*. But then, Berkeley notes, in this idea

> there is included colour, because there is no man but has some colour, but then it can be neither white, nor black, nor any particular colour, because

there is no one particular colour wherein all men partake. So likewise there is included stature, but then it is neither tall stature, nor low stature, nor yet middle stature, but something abstracted from all three. (*Principles*, Intro, 9; p. 10)

What kind of idea can this be—with a color that is no particular color and a height that is no specific height? It seems to embody a contradiction. Berkeley is certain he has no such ideas and asks us to examine and see whether we do.*

Moreover, once you allow abstract ideas, where do you stop? The idea of a material substance is clearly an abstract idea. It is constructed to play the role of substratum for qualities that need such support. Because such qualities are of widely different kinds—inanimate, animal, and human, for instance—the idea of a substance has to be the idea of something neither animate nor inanimate, neither human nor nonhuman—and yet all these at once. Is it even *possible* that there should be such ideas? Berkeley thinks not.

The idea of existence, too, is supposed to be an abstract idea. So we think we have an idea that substances exist, even though substances lie beyond all possible experiencing. We also suppose that we have abstract ideas of the extension, motion, and solidity of those substances. But these would have to be ideas of an object having some size, but no determinate size; moving at some speed, but no specific speed; and so on. Do we have—*could* we have—such ideas?

Berkeley actually quotes a passage from Locke to illustrate his point that abstract ideas are impossible. Locke says,

---

*In asking ourselves this question, we must keep in mind that Berkeley agrees with Locke that the origin of all our ideas is in sensation or reflection. Whatever other ideas we have are derived from that source as pale copies or images of sensation. So we are being asked whether we have an *image* of something colored, but without any particular color. You probably have to confess that you do not. Whether such images exhaust what we can properly mean by "ideas," however, is an important question. If they do not, perhaps abstract ideas are not in such disrepute as Berkeley claims. See Kant on the distinction between *intuitions* and *concepts*, pp. 473–474.

when we nicely reflect upon them, we shall find that *general ideas* are fictions and contrivances of the mind, that carry difficulty with them, and do not so easily offer themselves as we are apt to imagine. For example, does it not require some pains and skill to form the general idea of a triangle, . . . for it must be neither oblique nor rectangle, neither equilateral, equicrural, nor scalenon; but all and none of these at once. In effect, it is something imperfect, that cannot exist; an idea wherein some parts of several different and inconsistent ideas are put together. (*Essay*, IV, VII, 9; vol. 2, p. 274)

Berkeley could only wonder why Locke himself did not jettison such a monster.

Berkeley does not, of course, deny that we have general words. We may even have general ideas, Berkeley says. But these are not *abstract* general ideas. Their generality lies in the way we *use* them, not in their intrinsic nature. He gives an example. Suppose a math teacher is showing you how to bisect a line using intersecting arcs. She draws a line on the chalkboard. Then she takes a piece of string with chalk attached to one end of it and cuts two arcs, the first with the fixed point at one end of the line and the second with the fixed point at the other end. Then she takes a straightedge and connects the points of intersection in the arcs. Notice that what you have in your perception of this performance is completely particular. It is an image of one specific line and two arcs. But the point is completely general: This method will work for lines of *any* length.

Suppose you ask, How do we know that the method will work for lines of other lengths, since you have only demonstrated it for a line of this given length? Berkeley replies that we know it will work for other lines because there is nothing in the demonstration that depends on the length of this line. The length is arbitrarily chosen, so it doesn't matter what it is. So it will work for any line at all.

The example shows how universality works in our words and ideas. Nowhere do we need to appeal to abstract ideas. Every word and every idea can be as particular as that line.

It is, I know, a point much insisted on, that all knowledge and demonstration are about universal notions, to which I fully agree: but then it does

not appear to me that those notions are formed by *abstraction* in the manner premised—*universality*, so far as I can comprehend, not consisting in the absolute, positive nature or conception of anything, but in the relation it bears to the particulars signified or represented by it; by virtue whereof it is that things, names, or notions, being in their own nature *particular*, are rendered *universal*. (*Principles*, Intro, 15; pp. 15–16)

The word "tiger," then, has a universal significance not because it stands for an abstract idea of a tiger (there is no such idea), but because we use those letters or sounds to refer indifferently to any tiger at all. It is an abuse of language to think that all words have to be *names*, like "Socrates," and that they must name ideas that are abstract. To think so is just part of that dust we raise that makes it hard for us to see.

Another part of the dust, closely connected to abstract ideas, is Locke's view that the sole function of language is to communicate ideas from my mind to yours—that it is a kind of code for transporting ideas across an otherwise incommunicable gap. Berkeley says there are two things wrong with that. First, even where words *are* names that stand for ideas, it is not necessary that these ideas be brought to mind on every occasion of their use.

Second, it is a mistake to think that language is restricted to the function of communicating ideas.

There are other ends, as the raising of some passion, the exciting to or deterring from an action, the putting the mind in some particular disposition. . . . Even proper names themselves do not seem always spoken with a design to bring into our view the ideas of those individuals that are supposed to be marked by them. For example, when a schoolman tells me *Aristotle hath said it*, all I conceive he means by it is to dispose me to embrace his opinion with the deference and submission which custom has annexed to that name. (*Principles*, Intro, 20; pp. 19–20)

Language has multiple functions, then, the communicating of ideas being just one. And even when that is what I intend to do, I cannot communicate to you my *abstract* ideas because there aren't any. Words for them—including "material substance"—are just meaningless noise.

He that knows he has no other than particular ideas, will not puzzle himself in vain to find out and conceive the abstract idea annexed to any name. And he that knows names do not always stand for ideas will spare himself the labour of looking for ideas where there are none to be had. (*Principles*, Intro, 24; p. 22)

In these reflections, Berkeley sounds quite contemporary, playing notes that help constitute familiar melodies in twentieth-century philosophy of language.*

IDEAS AND THINGS

If the problem is abuse of words, the solution must be a careful use of words. If the notion of abstract ideas has led philosophers astray, we must adhere strictly to *non*abstract ideas. Berkeley does not see this as jettisoning Locke's whole approach. He endorses Locke's empiricism, but thinks that Locke did not stick to it rigorously enough. Berkeley is determined to be more consistent.†

It is evident to anyone who takes a survey of the objects of human knowledge, that they are either ideas actually imprinted on the senses; or else such as are perceived by attending to the passions and operations of the mind; or lastly, ideas formed by help of memory and imagination. (*Principles*, I, 1; p. 24)

Here we have Locke's simple ideas of sensation and reflection, together with complex ideas we put together as we like. Note that Berkeley also agrees with Locke that these ideas are the *objects* of our knowledge.

In addition to these ideas, however,

there is likewise something which knows or perceives them; and exercises divers operations, as willing, imagining, remembering, about them. This perceiving, active being is what I call *mind, spirit, soul,* or *myself.* By which words I do not denote any one of my ideas, but a thing entirely distinct

from them, wherein they exist, or, which is the same thing, whereby they are perceived—for the existence of an idea consists in its being perceived. (*Principles*, I, 2; p. 24)

Here we have Locke's spiritual substance. Note that Berkeley says we do not, strictly speaking, have an *idea* of it, yet the mind or spirit or soul is so evident to us at every moment that it cannot be doubted. If ideas are what we have, spirit is what has them. Berkeley sometimes says that though we do not have an idea of it, we do have a *notion* of spirit.

So far, then, we have two kinds of items in our inventory of reality: spirits and their ideas. Berkeley boldly claims that *that's all there is.* Whatever exists is either a mind or an idea in such a mind. And Berkeley thinks he can show us that anything else is strictly *inconceivable*—that is, involves a contradiction.

But ask yourself: Is that what you commonsensically believe? We doubt it! Surely this violates principle 1 (mentioned earlier) which says that things exist *independent* of our minds. So it looks like Berkeley violates common sense as clearly as Locke does. If we are to understand Berkeley, we have to solve this puzzle. We need to answer three questions: (1) How is Berkeley's view consistent with common sense? (2) How does it defeat skepticism? and (3) How does it kill atheism?

The first point to note is that Berkeley insists that ideas exist only *as perceived.* He thinks that this will be evident to us if we just pay attention to what we mean when we say something *exists.*

The table I write on I say exists, that is, I see and feel it; and if I were out of my study I should say it existed—meaning thereby that if I was in my study I might perceive it, or that some other spirit actually does perceive it. There was an odour, that is, it was smelt; there was a sound, that is, it was heard; a colour or figure, and it was perceived by sight or touch. This is all I can understand by these and the like expressions. For as to what is said of the absolute existence of unthinking things without any relation to their being perceived, that is to me perfectly unintelligible. Their *esse* is *percipi,* nor is it possible they should have any existence out of the minds or thinking things which perceive them. (*Principles,* I, 3; p. 25)

---

*See the discussion regarding analytic and ordinary language philosophy in Chapter 26. See also the aims of phenomenology in Chapter 27, pp. 655–657.

†It is traditional to see Locke, Berkeley, and Hume as three philosophers who more and more thoroughly apply empiricist principles in philosophy. This is a bit too schematic to be wholly correct, but there is a lot of truth in it.

This is an extremely important set of claims for Berkeley. Let us make sure we understand what he is saying. The first claim is that there is no abstract idea of existence, such as might be applied to things beyond our experience like Locke's material substances. The existence (*esse*) of things *consists in* their being perceived (*percipi*). For ideas, including simple sensations, to be *is* to be perceived. To exist is to be experienced. (Actually, Berkeley should say, and sometimes does say, that to be is *either* to be an idea perceived *or* to be a perceiver of ideas—a spirit.) The supposition that ideas might exist on their own, apart from a knower, Berkeley claims to be "unintelligible."

The second thing to note is that Berkeley talks about "the table I write on." Now a table, we usually think, is a thing, not an idea. But its inclusion here is not, as you might suspect, a slip on his part. For Berkeley, the table is also an idea—or rather, a complex of ideas presented to the various senses, sight and touch predominantly. So the table as experienced has its being only in being perceived. We will examine Berkeley's argument for this claim subsequently.

Third, note that Berkeley says of the table, when it is not in my presence, that its existence consists in its being either *actually* perceived by another spirit or in a *hypothetical* condition such as this: *If* you were in your study, *then* you would perceive it. In fact, Berkeley thinks both halves of this disjunction are the case. If your table actually exists in your absence, then it *is* being perceived by another spirit, *and* it is true that if you were there in your study, you would perceive it. (This will become clearer in a moment.)

But a table is a **thing,** we say. What can we make of Berkeley's claim that it is an idea? Here is the argument:

> It is indeed an opinion strangely prevailing amongst men that houses, rivers, and in a word all sensible objects, have an existence, natural or real, distinct from their being perceived by the understanding. But, with how great an assurance and acquiescence soever this principle may be entertained in the world, yet whoever shall find it in his heart to call it in question may, if I mistake not, perceive it to involve a manifest contradiction. For, what are the forementioned objects but the things we perceive

by sense? and what do we perceive besides our own ideas or sensations? and is it not plainly repugnant that any one of these, or any combination of them, should exist unperceived? (*Principles*, I, 4; p. 25)

What is the contradiction in thinking that sensible things exist unperceived? Let us set out the argument, using the table as an example.

1. A table is a sensible thing.
2. Sensible things are perceived by sense.
3. Whatever is perceived by sense is a sensation.
4. No sensation can exist unperceived.
5. So, no table can exist unperceived.
6. So, to say that a table exists even when not perceived is to say, This table, which exists only as perceived, exists unperceived.

And 6 is self-contradictory. Berkeley holds that it is only because of the confused doctrine of abstract ideas that we can separate existence from appearance in our experience.

You may still not be convinced. In particular, you may balk at proposition 3 in the preceding argument. You may say that you do perceive tables by means of your senses, but what you perceive that way is *not* a sensation—it is a thing. And Berkeley would want to reply that you are partly right and partly wrong. True, he says, it is indeed a thing you sense. That part is right. But you are wrong if you assume that a thing exists independent of perception. For what do we mean by the term "thing"? If this is to be a meaningful term, it must be filled out in terms of experience. And what do we experience the table *as*?

Well, for one thing, we experience a table as colored. But the philosophers have demonstrated that neither color nor any other secondary quality can exist independent of us. It is too variable, too dependent on the light, the condition of the eyes, and the proper functioning of the nervous system to be a property of the thing. Berkeley presents a well-known experiment in his dialogue. Hylas has been arguing that heat is really present in fire, and Philonous (who usually speaks for Berkeley) replies,*

---

*The name "Hylas" comes from the Greek word for matter, *hyle*. And "Philonous" obviously means *lover of mind or spirit*. So Berkeley gives us in the dialogue a conversation between a would-be materialist and a champion of the spirit.

PHIL.: Can any doctrine be true that necessarily leads a man into an absurdity?

HYL.: Without doubt it cannot.

PHIL.: Is it not an absurdity to think that the same thing should be at the same time both cold and warm?

HYL.: It is.

PHIL.: Suppose now one of your hands hot, and the other cold, and that they are both at once put into the same vessel of water, in an intermediate state; will not the water seem cold to one hand, and warm to the other?

HYL.: It will.

PHIL.: Ought we not therefore, by our principles, to conclude it is really both cold and warm at the same time, that is, according to your own concession, to believe an absurdity?

HYL.: I confess it seems so.

PHIL.: Consequently, the principles themselves are false, since you have granted that no true principle leads to an absurdity.

—*Dialogues*, pp. 115–116

The principle proved false by this experiment is that secondary qualities have an existence outside the mind that perceives them. The same goes for all such qualities, including the color of the table. For secondary qualities, then, the tradition has it right: To be is to be perceived.

But you, having learned of the distinction between secondary qualities and primary qualities, now say, "That may be true of the color of the table, but its size, its extension, its solidity—these qualities it *really has*. These qualities may be *represented* by ideas in my mind, but their *existence* is not *percipi*." But Berkeley and his alter ego, Philonous, argue that whatever goes for odors, tastes, colors, sounds, and textures goes also for the primary qualities of extension, solidity, and motion. Let's take the argument concerning extension as illustrative. Take a piece of paper and lay it on the desk before you. Then move around it, looking at it from this angle, now that. Move away from it, then close. Then very, very close. Pay careful attention to your experience of what we call "the paper." Is there anything in that experience that remains constant from one moment to the next? No, the ideas or sensations you are provided with

vary continuously in both size and shape. Wherever did you get the idea that the size of the paper was something constant and unchanging, a given absolute property of the paper? Not from any experience you ever had. All you know of the paper is supplied by your experience; and nothing in that experience testifies to such a permanent and immutable property. It must be that the idea you *think* you have of the paper's extension is an *abstract* idea. But there are no abstract ideas, so you don't really have a proper idea of that at all! To talk about an objective, mind-independent, absolute property of extension is just meaningless jargon, an empty abuse of words.

In this way Berkeley argues that the distinction between secondary and primary qualities breaks down. What is true of the former is true also of the latter: They too have their being only in being perceived. But now we may begin to feel dizzy. What has happened to our familiar world? It looks as though all the everyday, stable, commonsense, dependable things we thought we were dealing with have been dissolved into a giddy whirl, where nothing remains the same from moment to moment—a chaos of changes. It looks as though *the world* has been lost, and all we are left with is a flux of ever-shifting sensations.

But at this point, Berkeley, the defender of common sense, comes back and says,

I do not argue against the existence of any one thing that we can apprehend either by sense or reflection. That the things I see with my eyes and touch with my hand do exist, really exist, I make not the least question. The only thing whose existence we deny is that which philosophers call matter or corporeal substance. And in doing of this there is no damage done to the rest of mankind, who, I dare say, will never miss it.

. . .

If any man thinks this detracts from the existence or reality of things, he is very far from understanding what hath been premised in the plainest terms I could think of.

. . .

. . . if the word *substance* be taken in the vulgar sense—for a combination of sensible qualities, such as extension, solidity, weight, and the like—this we cannot be accused of taking away; but if it be taken in a philosophic sense, for the support of accidents or qualities without the mind, then indeed I acknowledge that we take it away, if one may be said to take away that which never had any existence, not even in the imagination. (*Principles*, I, 35, 36, 37; pp. 38–39)

Does the paper on your desk really exist? Yes, says Berkeley. Of course. In fact, it exists with all those qualities that it *seems* to have—just that whiteness, that combination of shapes, that coolness to the touch, that flexibility, and so on that you perceive it to have. The piece of paper is not a mysterious something behind or beyond our experience of it but is itself just a *combination* of the qualities we attribute to it. We *call* such a combination that is regularly ordered by the laws of nature "a thing," or "a substance," and that's the only sense the term "thing" could meaningfully have for us. This is the way Berkeley defends the second principle of common sense: that things have just the properties they appear to have.

Still, we may have an uneasy feeling, expressed clearly by a question Hylas asks in the dialogues: "Can anything be plainer than that you are for changing all things into ideas?" (*Dialogues*, III, p. 188). But to this Philonous replies,

> You mistake me. I am not for changing things into ideas, but rather ideas into things; since those immediate objects of perception, which, according to you, are only appearances of things, I take to be the real things themselves. . . . In short, you do not trust your senses, I do. (*Dialogues*, III, p. 188)

But we still may not be satisfied. How can Berkeley avoid the charge that he destroys the independent existence of things, making them wholly relative to our perceiving of them? That is, can he show that principle 1 (cited at the outset of this section) is also true on his account—that things *do* exist independent of our perceiving them? He makes several points.

1. He echoes Descartes, Locke, and others in observing that while I can, in my imagination, arrange ideas pretty much as I like, I cannot do that with my senses. What I see when I open my eyes is not in my control. I cannot decide not to feel heat

when I put my hand near a fire. With respect to my sensations (which are, remember, the origin of all my ideas) I am *passive*.

2. Moreover, ideas are *inert*. That is, they are causally inactive. It is never the case that one idea *causes* another idea to appear. What Berkeley has in mind here is this: The *sensation* of water boiling is not caused by the *sensation* of the kettle on the fire. True, the one follows the other with regularity, according to the laws of nature. But this just shows that the laws of nature are not *causal* laws. They don't tell us that *x causes y*; they just describe the uniformities in our experience: Kettles left on a fire long enough are followed by water boiling.

> The connexion of ideas does not imply the relation of *cause* and *effect*, but only of a mark or *sign* with the thing *signified*. The fire which I see is not the cause of the pain I suffer upon my approaching it, but the mark that forewarns me of it. In like manner the noise that I hear is not the effect of this or that motion or collision of the ambient bodies, but the sign thereof. (*Principles*, I, 65; p. 52)

Sensations and ideas, then, do not *act*. (Berkeley takes this as an additional proof that a secondary quality such as color could not be *caused* in us by primary qualities such as extension and motion; *no* such qualities are causes!)

3. Do we have any experience, then, of something with causal power? Yes, virtually every moment of our lives. I stand, I sit, I raise my arm, I walk, I write. In all these ways activity is evident— the activity of the **will.** We have been thinking almost exclusively of ideas or things (things being just ideas that are connected in the right ways). And the constant theme has been that *their being* consists in their being perceived. But we must now turn our attention to the perceivers of these ideas. **Spirits** are not merely passive receivers of sensations; they also have control over some of their ideas—and even over some sensations. Not only can I decide to recall the capital of Ohio and (usually) do so, but also I can also decide to move my finger and (usually) my finger moves. The finger—that combination of ideas we call "a finger"—does not itself contain any powers or causal energies; Berkeley takes it that he has proved that. But my will does. True, I cannot

decide what I will see when I open my eyes, but I decide when to open them. Here, in spirit or mind, which we know not by sense but by reflection, we discover causal power. Philonous says,

> How often must I repeat, that I know or am conscious of my own being; and that I myself am not my ideas, but something else, a thinking, active principle that perceives, knows, wills, and operates about ideas? I know that I, one and the same self, perceive both colours and sounds: that a colour cannot perceive a sound, nor a sound a colour: that I am therefore one individual principle, distinct from colour and sound; and for the same reason, from all other sensible things and inert ideas. (*Dialogues*, III, p. 176)
>
> I have no notion of any action distinct from volition, neither can I conceive volition to be anywhere but in a spirit; therefore, when I speak of an active being, I am obliged to mean a spirit. (*Dialogues*, III, pp. 182–183)

And now we are near the point where Berkeley thinks that his way of looking at things refutes atheism. What makes **atheism** both possible and attractive, Berkeley holds, is the hypothesis of matter or corporeal substance as the bearer of real existence. We do need to explain the regular, uniform course that our sensations take, and matter seems to provide an explanation. The reason we see what we see, hear what we hear, and touch what we touch is that there is an objectively existing, material world out there affecting us, producing these sensations in our minds. But if it is matter that is doing it, who needs God?

But we have seen that Berkeley has argued that the abstract idea of a material substance independent of mind is a grotesque construction, full of contradiction. And in any case, the qualities we are acquainted with in sensation are none of them causes. So materialism is broken-backed as an explanation for the course of our experience. It cannot do the job it is supposed to do.

GOD

We do, however, need an account of why our experience is as regular and well-ordered as it is. For a sensation to *be* is for it to be *perceived*—but not

necessarily by us. Since we are not in control of the course of those ideas we call the world, and yet they must exist in a spirit, it follows that there must be a spirit in which these ideas exist and which produces them in us. So, Berkeley thinks, if we get our epistemology and metaphysics straight, we are presented with a new and extremely simple proof for the existence of **God.**

You know your own existence as a spirit by a kind of immediate intuition. You know your friends' existence only indirectly. That is, you observe in the course of your experience certain conjunctions of sensations, which act as a *sign* of the presence of other finite spirits like yourself; to put it colloquially, some of what you observe you take to be *behavior* expressing other minds.

> But, though there be some things which convince us *human* agents are concerned in producing them, yet it is evident to every one that those things which are called the Works of Nature—that is, the far greater part of the ideas or sensations perceived by us—are not produced by, or dependent on, the wills of men. There is therefore some other Spirit that causes them; since it is repugnant that they should subsist by themselves. . . . But, if we attentively consider the constant regularity, order, and concatenation of natural things, the surprising magnificence, beauty and perfection of the larger, and the exquisite contrivance of the smaller parts of the creation, together with the exact harmony and correspondence of the whole . . . and at the same time attend to the meaning and import of the attributes One, Eternal, Infinitely Wise, Good, and Perfect, we shall clearly perceive that they belong to the aforesaid Spirit, "who works all in all," and "by whom all things consist." (*Principles*, I, 146, pp. 139–140)

So we see how Berkeley means to support commonsense principle 1 as well as 2. Principle 1 says that things have a reality independent of our perceiving them—and so they do. Theirs is not the reality of material substance, however, but the reality of ideas perceived by an infinite Spirit. Given the difficulties attaching to the idea of matter, together with the apparent impossibility of explaining how matter can cause ideas in us, this might seem like a good trade. After all, we do have a clear notion,

Berkeley assures us, of an active mind or self, and we do need an account of the regular course of nature. The providential guidance of an Almighty Spirit is near at hand to supply it.

We can perhaps sum up Berkeley's argument in this way:

1. The regular succession of changes in ideas must be caused by either
   a. the ideas themselves;
   b. material substances;
   c. some other finite Spirit, such as yourself; or
   d. God.
2. Not *a*, for ideas, unlike spirits, are inert and have no causal power.
3. Not *b*, since material substances are (necessarily) nonexistent.
4. Not *c*, because you and all other finite spirits are largely passive with respect to this succession.
5. So *d*, and this succession is caused to be what it is because it is perceived by an infinitely powerful Spirit, which (as Aquinas might say) we all call *God*.

Thus we have an answer to an obvious question: If to be is to be perceived, what happens to my desk when I'm not perceiving it? Does it jump in and out of existence when I open and close my eyes? No, of course not. It continues to exist in both of those senses we distinguished earlier: the hypothetical sense (*If* I were to open my eyes, *then* I would perceive it) and the absolute sense (It is all the while being perceived by God).

This feature of Berkeley's thought has been memorialized in a pair of limericks.[7]

> There was a young man who said, "God
> Must think it exceedingly odd
>   If he finds that this tree
>   Continues to be
> When there's no one about in the Quad."

> Dear Sir:
>   Your astonishment's odd;
> *I* am always about in the Quad.
>   And that's why the tree
>   Will continue to be,
> Since observed by
>   *Yours faithfully*,
>   God.

You have probably noticed something that Hylas also remarks about near the end of his dialogue with Philonous. All along, it has been Philonous who has been trotting out arguments characteristic of the skeptics, showing again and again how anything we perceive is relative to the perception of it—how it has no objective, absolute existence at all. Then at the end, like a judo master, he turns the tables, using the strength of the skeptical arguments against themselves to show that what, on traditional principles, was merely appearance is in fact the reality itself!

Skepticism, then, is refuted in virtue of the fact that the things of our experience are actually just as we perceive them to be. And atheism is refuted in virtue of these things having a necessary dependence on God. Common sense is vindicated, Berkeley believes, in both its main tenets. And he considers himself to be altogether successful in dispelling the dust that previous philosophers' thoughts had raised, leaving us with a clear and coherent vision of things.

---

1. What two principles of common sense does Berkeley hope to defend?
2. How does the distinction between primary and secondary qualities undermine common sense?
3. Why does Berkeley think that abstract ideas are impossible?
4. How, according to Berkeley, do general words and ideas work?
5. What's wrong with the notion that language is for the communication of ideas?
6. In what basic way does Berkeley agree with Locke, despite his criticisms?
7. Explain the slogan that "*esse* is *percipi*."
8. What does it mean, for Berkeley, that your bicycle exists even when neither you nor any other person is observing it?
9. What does he say we must mean when we use the word "thing"?
10. What is the argument that shows that the existence of primary qualities is *percipi* just as truly as is the existence of secondary qualities?
11. What does it mean to say ideas are "inert"?
12. Where do we experience causal power?
13. Why does God need to be brought into the picture?

14. How is skepticism defeated?
15. How is atheism defeated?
16. Sketch the argument by which Berkeley would claim to be a defender of common sense.

FOR FURTHER THOUGHT

1. Write a dialogue in which Descartes and Hobbes (who were contemporaries and met at least once) debate about the nature of human beings.
2. Imagine that your soul left your body and went to heaven, but your consciousness (including your memories and your basic character traits) remained here on earth in your body. Where would *you* be? Why? (Or couldn't you imagine that? Why not?)
3. Berkeley says that a *thing*—your left running shoe, for instance—is just a combination of ideas. We doubt that you believe this. Try to construct a critique of this claim that doesn't allow Berkeley an immediate comeback.

KEY WORDS

Hobbes

resolution and
  composition
sensation
materialist
epiphenomenalist
dualist
monist
imagination
memory
understanding
God
regulated thoughts
reasoning
vital motions
voluntary motions
endeavor

desire
aversion
good
evil
state of nature
pleasure
pains
will
determinist
felicity
law of nature
right of nature
social contract
Leviathan
sovereign

Locke

empiricism
idea

innate ideas
experience

sensation
reflection
simple idea
complex ideas
substance
primary qualities
secondary quality
consciousness

personal identity
real essence
nominal essences
natural law
government
property
commonwealth
church

Berkeley

common sense
abstract ideas
esse
percipi
thing

will
spirits
atheism
God

NOTES

1. Quoted in *Objections III with Replies* in *The Philosophical Works of Descartes*, vol. 2, ed. Elisabeth S. Haldane and G. R. T. Ross (n.p.: Dover, 1955), 62.
2. Quotations from Thomas Hobbes, *Leviathan, or The Matter, Form, and Power of a Commonwealth, Ecclesiastical and Civil*, in *The English Philosophers from Bacon to Mill*, ed. Edwin A. Burtt (New York: Modern Library, 1939), are cited in the text using the abbreviation *L*. References are to page numbers.
3. Margaret Cavendish, *Philosophical Letters, or Modest Reflections upon Some Opinions in Natural Philosophy Maintained by Several Famous and Learned Authors of this Age, Expressed by Way of Letters* (London: s.n., 1664), 320–321. Available online at http://name.umdl.umich.edu/A53058.0001.001.
4. Quotations from Locke are cited as follows:
   Essay: An Essay Concerning Human Understanding, ed. Alexander Campbell Fraser (New York: Dover, 1959), by book, chapter, and section number, followed by the volume and page number in this edition.
   Gov't: Of Civil Government, Two Treatises (London: J. M. Dent and Sons, 1924), cited by book, chapter, and section number, followed by the page number in this edition.
   Toleration: A Letter Concerning Toleration (Indianapolis, IN: Hackett, 1983).
5. We are indebted to A. C. Grayling, who frames the puzzle of Berkeley's commonsense claims in

this way in his book *Berkeley: The Central Arguments* (London: Duckworth, 1986).

6. Quotations from Berkeley are from *George Berkeley: Principles of Human Knowledge and Three Dialogues*, ed. Howard Robinson (Oxford: Oxford University Press, 1996), cited as follows:

Principles, by book and section number, followed by the page number in this edition

Dialogues, by page number in this edition

7. In Bertrand Russell's *History of Western Philosophy* (London: Allen and Unwin, 1946), 623; Russell attributes it, or at least the first stanza, to Ronald Knox.

DAVID HUME

Unmasking the Pretensions of Reason

The eighteenth century is often called the age of enlightenment. Those who lived through this period in Europe and some of its colonies felt they were making rapid progress toward overthrowing superstition and arbitrary authority, replacing ignorance with knowledge and blind obedience with freedom. It is an age of optimism. One of the clearest expressions of this attitude is found in a brief essay by Immanuel Kant (the subject of our next chapter). Writing in 1784, Kant defines what the age understands by **"enlightenment."**

> *Enlightenment is man's emergence from his self-imposed immaturity. Immaturity* is the inability to use one's understanding without guidance from another. This immaturity is *self-imposed* when its cause lies not in lack of understanding, but in lack of resolve and courage to use it without guidance from another. *Sapere Aude!* "Have courage to use your own understanding!"—that is the motto of enlightenment.[1]

This call to think for oneself, to have the courage to rely on one's own abilities, is quite characteristic of European thinkers of the age. For Kant, the lack of courage is "self-imposed." Working oneself out of this immaturity is difficult, Kant says, but not impossible—as had been clearly shown in the triumphs of the scientific revolution from Copernicus to that most admired of thinkers, Isaac Newton (1642–1727). Newton's unified explanatory scheme for understanding both terrestrial and celestial movements symbolized what human efforts could achieve—if only they could be freed from the dead hand of the past. And thinkers throughout the eighteenth century busy themselves applying Newton's methods to other subjects: to the mind, to ethics, to religion, and to the state of society.

Yet none of them would claim to have arrived at the goal. Here again is Kant:

> If it is now asked, "Do we presently live in an *enlightened* age?" the answer is, "No, but we do live in an age of *enlightenment*."[2]

The key word is "progress." Newton showed that progress is really possible. And the conviction spreads that this progress can be extended indefinitely if only we can muster the courage to do what Newton had done in physics and astronomy. We were not yet mature, but we were becoming mature.

How Newton Did It

It is almost impossible to exaggerate Newton's impact on the imagination of the eighteenth century. As a towering symbol of scientific achievement, he can be compared only to Einstein in the twentieth century. The astonished admiration his work evoked is expressed in a couplet by Alexander Pope.

> Nature and Nature's laws lay hid in night;
>   God said, Let Newton be, and all was light.*

Everyone has some idea of Newton's accomplishment, of how his theory of universal gravitation provides a mathematically accurate and powerful tool for understanding not only the motions of heavenly bodies but also such puzzling phenomena as the tides. We don't go into the details of this theory here, but every science is developed on the basis of certain methods and presuppositions that may properly be called philosophical. It is these philosophical underpinnings that we must take note of, for they are crucially important to the development of thought in the eighteenth century—not least to the philosophy of David Hume.

How had **Newton** been able to pull it off? His methods are not greatly different from those of Galileo and Hobbes. There are two stages (like Hobbes' resolution and composition), which he calls **analysis** and **synthesis.** But there is a particular insistence in some of his pronouncements that strikes a new note.

> I frame no hypotheses; for whatever is not deduced from the phenomena is to be called an hypothesis; and hypotheses, whether metaphysical or physical, whether of occult qualities or mechanical, have no place in experimental philosophy.[3]

The key to doing science, he believes, is to stay close to the phenomena rather than to **frame hypotheses.** Newton's long and persistent series of experiments with the prism exemplifies this maxim. The fact that white light is not a simple phenomenon (as it seems to naive sight) is disclosed only by an immensely detailed series of investigations, which reveal its composition out of the many simpler hues of the rainbow.

The explanations of his experiments are to be "deduced from the phenomena." This emphasis on paying attention to the facts of experience is Aristotelian in character, but in the modern era, we can trace it back through John Locke to Francis Bacon. In Newton its fruitfulness pays off in a way that had never been seen before. Newton expresses a deep suspicion of principles not derived from a close experimental examination of the sensible facts. We cannot *begin* with what *seems* right to us. Hypotheses not arrived at by way of careful analysis of the sensible facts are arbitrary—no matter how intuitively convincing they may seem. And Newton's success is, to the eighteenth-century thinker, proof that his methods are sound.

Note how different this is from the rationalism of Descartes. Always the mathematician, Descartes seeks to find starting points for science and philosophy that are intuitively certain, axioms that are "so clear and distinct" that they cannot possibly be doubted. He is confident that reason, the "light of nature," will certify some principles as both knowable and known. So the structure of wisdom, for Descartes, is the structure of an axiomatic, geometrical system. Intuitive insight and deduction from first principles will get you where you want to go.

But for eighteenth-century thinkers inspired by Newton, this smells too much of arbitrariness. One man's intuitive certainty, they suspect, is another man's absurdity.* The only cure is to stick closely to the facts. The *rationalism* of Descartes is supplanted by the *empiricism* of Locke, Berkeley, and David Hume.

---

* Epitaph intended for Sir Isaac Newton. John Bartlett, *Familiar Quotations*, 14th ed. (Boston: Little, Brown, 1968).

---

* They feel confirmed in this suspicion by the example of rationalist philosophy after Descartes. First-rate intellects such as Malebranche, Spinoza, and Leibniz developed remarkably different philosophical systems on the basis of supposedly "self-evident" truths.

ÉMILIE DU CHÂTELET

Born into an aristocratic French family, **Émilie du Châtelet** (1706–1749) juggled many identities during her short life: She was a learned natural philosopher, a courtier in the palace of King Louis XV, a member of Parisian high society, and the wife of an ambitious nobleman. She was also an active participant in the **Republic of Letters**, early modern Europe's intellectual elite, who shared and debated their ideas through correspondence and publications. Despite the demands her social role placed on her, she embodied the advice she set forth in her *Discourse on Happiness* "to be resolute about what one wants to be and about what one wants to do" (*DH*, 355).[4] After studying philosophy, physics, analytic geometry, and the newly invented calculus, she published a number of philosophical treatises and translated Newton's *Principia Mathematica* into French. Her *Foundations of Physics* synthesizes Newtonian mechanics with the ideas of the great German philosopher Leibniz to set Newtonian science on firmer metaphysical foundations.

Du Châtelet grounds all human knowledge on two basic principles. The first is Aristotle's principle of noncontradiction, which says that something cannot be both true and false at the same time. Something is impossible, du Châtelet says, just in case it implies a contradiction. She warns that many things that *seem* possible, such as

the largest prime number, are in fact impossible on careful consideration and that many philosophers have blundered into mistakes by supposing that they have a clear idea of something that turns out to be impossible. The second principle is Leibniz's principle of sufficient reason, which says that there must be a sufficient reason to explain why things are as they are.* According to du Châtelet, the principle of noncontradiction explains all *necessary* truths, because denying them leads to contradiction, but if we want to establish some contingent truth, we need to identify a sufficient reason that enables us to understand why things are as they are and not some other way. Furthermore, these reasons must actually improve our understanding of the phenomenon. Otherwise, it is just a meaningless way of claiming that there is *some* reason.

Acquiring knowledge of contingent facts, du Châtelet argues, often requires framing hypotheses.

> When certain things are used to explain what has been observed, and though the truth of what has been supposed is impossible to demonstrate, one is making a hypothesis. (*FP*, 148)

Especially at the beginning of an inquiry, there is often no way to proceed except by framing hypotheses. Doing science well, du Châtelet says, involves testing those hypotheses against observations and accepting hypotheses as probable only when they have been confirmed repeatedly and explain a wide range of observations. This is how astronomy advanced from a primitive understanding of the skies to Ptolemy's system to Copernicus and Kepler's. Since it is on the basis of Kepler's system that Newton showed that the laws of motion apply to the heavens, du Châtelet argues, even Newton himself depended on others' framing and testing of hypotheses. She objects that whereas natural philosophers in Descartes' day had embraced unfounded hypotheses without testing them, building whole systems on "fables" or "fictions," thinkers in her own time had swung too

Le Jour in l'Heure : Marianne Loir, c. 1715-ap. 1769, Émilie du Châtelet 1706-1749, Bordeaux, inv. 28 novembre 2015, 6605.1.

ÉMILIE DU CHÂTELET

far in the other direction by trying to do without hypotheses altogether. Those who refuse to entertain hypotheses at all, she cautions, will seldom reach the truth.

> The true causes of natural effects and of the phenomena we observe are often so far from the principles on which we can rely and the experiments we can make that one is obliged to be content with probable reasons to explain them. Thus, probabilities are not to be rejected in the sciences, not only because they are often of great practical use, but also because they clear the path that leads to the truth. (*FP*, 147)

———

* On Leibniz, see p. 478.

To Be the Newton of Human Nature

David Hume (1711–1776) aspires to do for human nature what Isaac Newton did for nonhuman nature: to provide principles of explanation both simple and comprehensive.[5] There seem to be two motivations. First, Hume shares with many other Enlightenment intellectuals the project of debunking what they call "popular superstition." By this they usually mean the deliverances of religious enthusiasm, together with the conviction of certainty that typically accompanies them.* (The era of religious wars based on such certainties is still fresh in their memory.) But they also mean whatever cannot be demonstrated on a basis of reason and experience common to human beings. Hume's prose betrays his passion on this score. Remarking on the obscurity, uncertainty, and error in most philosophies, he pinpoints the cause:

> They are not properly a science; but arise either from the fruitless efforts of human vanity, which would penetrate into subjects utterly inaccessible to the understanding, or from the craft of popular superstitions, which, being unable to defend themselves on fair ground, raise these entangling brambles to cover and protect their weakness. Chased

from the open country, these robbers fly into the forest, and lie in wait to break in upon every unguarded avenue of the mind, and overwhelm it with religious fears and prejudices. The stoutest antagonist, if he remit his watch a moment, is oppressed. And many, through cowardice and folly, open the gates to the enemies, and willingly receive them with reverence and submission, as their legal sovereigns.

> But is this a sufficient reason, why philosophers should desist from such researches, and leave superstition still in possession of her retreat? Is it not proper to draw an opposite conclusion, and perceive the necessity of carrying the war into the most secret recesses of the enemy? (*HU*, 91–92)[6]

The basic strategy in this war is to show what the human understanding is (and is not) capable of. And this is what a science of human nature should give us. If we can show that "superstition" claims to know what no one can possibly know, then we undermine it in the most radical way.

———

> "Superstition is the religion of feeble minds."
> *Edmund Burke (1729–1797)*

———

Hume's second motivation is his conviction that a science of human nature is, in a certain way, fundamental. Because all our intellectual endeavors are *products* of human understanding, an examination of that understanding should illumine them

———

*"Enthusiasm" is the word eighteenth-century thinkers use to describe ecstatic forms of religion involving the claim that one is receiving revelations, visions, or "words" directly from God. This form of religion is far from dead.

all, even mathematics, natural philosophy, and religion. Such an inquiry will reveal how the mind works, what materials it has to operate on, and how knowledge in any area at all can be constructed.

Hume is aware that others before him have formulated theories of the mind (or human understanding), but they have not satisfactorily settled matters.

> There is nothing which is not the subject of debate, and in which men of learning are not of contrary opinions. . . . Disputes are multiplied, as if every thing was uncertain; and these disputes are managed with the greatest warmth, as if every thing was certain. (*T*, Intro. p. 3)

Consider the wide disagreement between Descartes and Hobbes, for instance. Descartes, as we have seen, believes that the freedom and rationality of our minds exempts them from the kind of causal explanation provided for material bodies. A mind, he concludes, is a thing completely distinct from a body. Hobbes, however, includes the mind and all its ideas and activities within the scope of a materialistic and deterministic science. "Mind," for Hobbes, is just a name for certain ways a human body operates. Who is right here?

From Hume's point of view, neither one prevails. Hobbes simply *assumes* that our thoughts represent objects independent of our minds and that whatever principles explain these objects will also explain the mind. But surely Descartes has shown us that this is something we should not assume. Whatever our experience "tells" us about reality, things could actually be different. That is the lesson of Descartes' doubt. Hobbes' assumption that sensations and thoughts generally represent realities accurately is nothing but a "hypothesis." And, Hume says (following Newton), we must avoid framing hypotheses. Similarly, Descartes' positive doctrine of a separate mind-substance is just as "hypothetical" as that of Hobbes. It is derived from principles that may *seem* intuitively obvious but have not been "deduced from the phenomena."

We do not have, Hume thinks, any insight into the "essence" of either material bodies or minds, as Hobbes and Descartes seem to assume. We have made progress in understanding the physical world

"As the science of man is the only solid foundation for the other sciences, so the only solid foundation we can give to this science itself must be laid on experience and observation."

—DAVID HUME

only by sticking close to the experimental facts; we can hope to progress in understanding the mind only if we do the same.

> For to me it seems evident, that the essence of the mind being equally unknown to us with that of external bodies, it must be equally impossible to form any notion of its powers and qualities otherwise than from careful and exact experiments, and the observation of those particular effects, which result from its different circumstances and situations. And tho' we must endeavour to render all our principles as universal as possible, by tracing up our experiments to the utmost, and explaining all effects from the simplest and fewest causes, 'tis still certain we cannot go beyond experience; and any hypothesis, that pretends to discover the ultimate original qualities of human nature, ought at first to be rejected as presumptuous and chimerical. (*T*, Intro, p. 5)

The Newtonian tone is unmistakable. What, then, are the *data* that scientists of human nature must "observe" and from which they may draw principles "as universal as possible"? Hume calls them **"perceptions,"** by which he means all the contents of our minds when we are awake and alert.* Among perceptions are all the ideas of the sciences, as well as ideas arbitrary and superstitious. Hume aims to draw a line between legitimate ideas and ideas that are confused, unfounded, and nonsensical. The first thing to do is to inquire about the *origin* of our ideas.

The Theory of Ideas

A science of human nature must concentrate on what is peculiarly human. A person's height, weight, and shape are characteristics of a human being, but these are properties shared with the non-human objects Newtonian science explains so well. It is human ideas, feelings, and actions that require special treatment. Ideas are particularly important because they are involved in nearly all the activities that are characteristically human. What are ideas, and how do we come to have them?

Perceptions, Hume claims, can be divided into two major classes: **impressions** and **ideas.**

> The difference betwixt these consists in the degrees of force and liveliness with which they strike upon the mind, and make their way into our thought or consciousness. Those perceptions, which enter with most force and violence, we may name *impressions*; and under this name I comprehend all our sensations, passions and emotions, as they make their first appearance in the soul. By *ideas* I mean the faint images of these in thinking and reasoning. (*T*, I, 1, 1 p. 7)

You can get a vivid illustration of the difference between the two classes if you slap the table smartly with your hand (the sound you hear is an impression) and then, a few seconds later, recall that sound (the content of your memory is an idea).

Hume thinks that we are all familiar with this difference. There may be borderline cases such as a terrifying dream, in which the ideas are very nearly as lively as the actual impressions would be. But on the whole, the distinction is familiar and clear. One other important distinction must be observed: that between *simple* and *complex* perceptions. The impression you have when you slap the table is simple; the impression you have when you hear a melody is complex. Complex impressions and ideas are built up from simple ones.

The next thing Hume notices is "the great resemblance betwixt our impressions and ideas" (*T*, I, 1, 1, p. 8). It seems as though "all the perceptions of the mind are double, and appear both as impressions and ideas" (*T*, I, 1, 1, p. 8). No, he adds, this is not quite correct. For you have the idea of a unicorn, but you have never experienced a unicorn impression. (Ah, you say; but I have seen a *picture* of a unicorn! True enough, but your experience on that occasion did not constitute an impression of a unicorn, but that of a unicorn picture. Your idea of a unicorn is not the idea of a picture.) So you do have an idea that does not correspond to any impression; so not all our perceptions are "double."

But a closer look, Hume thinks, will convince us that although this principle does not hold for **complex ideas,** it does hold for all **simple ideas.** We need not analyze the idea of a unicorn very far to notice that it is made up of two simpler ideas: that of a horse and that of a single horn. Impressions do correspond to these simpler ideas, for we have all seen horses and horns. So the revised principle is that to every *simple idea* corresponds a *simple impression* that resembles it.

If impressions and simple ideas come in pairs like this, so that there is a "constant conjunction" between them, the next question is, Which comes first? Hume again notes that in his *experience*, it is always the impression that appears first; the idea comes later.

> To give a child an idea of scarlet or orange, of sweet or bitter, I present the objects, or in other words, convey to him these impressions; but proceed not so absurdly, as to endeavour to produce the impressions by exciting the ideas. . . . We cannot form

---

*Here Hume shows that he, like Descartes (and Locke and Berkeley, too), is committed to the basic principle of the representational theory (pp. 372–373)—that what we know first and best are our ideas. Unlike Descartes, as we will see, Hume believes there are no legitimate inferences from ideas to things.

to ourselves a just idea of the taste of a pine-apple, without having actually tasted it. (*T*, I, 1, 1, p. 9)

This suggests that there is a relation of *dependence* between them; Hume concludes that every simple idea has some simple impression as a causal antecedent. Every simple idea, in fact, is a *copy* of a preceding impression.* What is the origin of all our ideas? The impressions of experience. The rule is this: *no impression, no idea.*

This is an apparently simple principle, but Hume warns us that taking it seriously will have far-reaching consequences. It is, in fact, a rule of procedure that Hume makes devastating use of.

> All ideas, especially abstract ones, are naturally faint and obscure: The mind has but a slender hold of them: They are apt to be confounded with other resembling ideas; and when we have often employed any term, though without a distinct meaning, we are apt to imagine it has a determinate idea, annexed to it. On the contrary, all impressions, that is, all sensations, either outward or inward, are strong and vivid: The limits between them are more exactly determined: Nor is it easy to fall into any error or mistake with regard to them. When we entertain, therefore, any suspicion, that a philosophical term is employed without any meaning or idea (as is but too frequent), we need but enquire, *from what impression is that supposed idea derived?* And if it be impossible to assign any, this will serve to confirm our suspicion. (*HU*, 99)

Every meaningful term (word), Hume tells us, is associated with an idea. Some terms, however, have no clear idea connected with them. We get used to them and think they mean something, but we are deceived. Hume in fact thinks this happens all too frequently! How can we discover whether a term really means something? Try to trace the associated *idea* back to an *impression.* If you can, it is a meaningful word that expresses a real idea.

If you try and fail, then all you have are meaningless noises or nonsensical marks on paper.

Hume has here a powerful critical tool. It seems innocent enough, but Hume makes radical use of it. The rule is a corollary to Hume's Newtonian analysis of phenomena. It is a result of the theory of ideas.

The Association of Ideas

The results so far constitute the stage of analysis. What we find, on paying close attention to the contents of the human mind, are impressions and ideas, the latter in complete dependence on the former. Hume now proceeds to the stage of synthesis: What are the principles that bind these elements together to produce the rich mental life characteristic of humans? Like Newton, he finds that the great variety of phenomena can be explained by a few principles, surprisingly simple in nature. These are principles of **association,** and they correspond in the science of human nature to universal gravitation in the purely physical realm.

> It is evident that there is a principle of connexion between the different thoughts or ideas of the mind, and that, in their appearance to the memory or imagination, they introduce each other with a certain degree of method and regularity. . . . Were the loosest and freest conversation to be transcribed, there would immediately be observed something, which connected it in all its transitions. Or where this is wanting, the person, who broke the thread of discourse, might still inform you, that there had secretly resolved in his mind a succession of thought, which had gradually led him from the subject of conversation. (*HU*, 101)

You should be able to test whether this observation is correct by observing your own trains of thought or noting how one topic follows another in a conversation you are party to.

If Hume is right here, the next question is, What are these principles of association?

> To me, there appear to be only three principles of connexion among ideas, namely *Resemblance, Contiguity* in time or place, and *Cause* or *Effect.*
>
> That these principles serve to connect ideas will not, I believe, be much doubted. A picture naturally

---

*Compare Hobbes, p. 406, and Locke, p. 417. Hume's theory of the origin of ideas is similar, but without Hobbes' mechanistic explanation and without the assumption that external objects are the cause of our impressions. Hume considers both these claims merely "hypotheses." The perceptions of the mind are our data; beyond them we may not safely go.

leads our thoughts to the original [Resemblance]: The mention of one apartment in a building naturally introduces an enquiry or discourse concerning the others [Contiguity]: And if we think of a wound, we can scarcely forbear reflecting on the pain which follows it [Cause and Effect]. (*HU*, 101–102)

There is some question about whether this list of three principles is complete; Hume thinks it probably is and invites you to try to find more if you think otherwise. The world of ideas, then, is governed by the "gentle force" of association. He likens it to "a kind of ATTRACTION, which in the mental world will be found to have as extraordinary effects as in the natural, and to shew itself in as many and as various forms" (*T*, I, 1, 4, pp. 12, 14).

It is important to note that this "gentle force" operates entirely without our consent, will, or even consciousness of it. It is not something in our control, any more than we can control the force of gravity. If Hume is right, it just happens that this is how the mind works. He does not think it possible to go on to explain *why* the mind works the way it does; explanation has to stop somewhere, and, like Newton, he does not "frame hypotheses." But these principles, he thinks, can be "deduced from the phenomena."

---

1. Using the quotation from Immanuel Kant as a cue, explain the notion of *enlightenment*.
2. Contrast rationalism, materialism, and empiricism and relate each to Newton's rule about not framing hypotheses.
3. How does Hume explain the origin of our ideas? (Distinguish complex from simple ideas.)
4. What principles govern transitions from one idea or impression to another?

Causation: The Very Idea

We now have the fundamental principles of Hume's science of human nature: an analysis into the elements of the mind (impressions and ideas), the relation between them (dependence), and the principles that explain how ideas interact (association). We are now ready for the exciting part: What happens when this science is applied?

One more distinction will set the stage.

All the objects of human reason or enquiry may naturally be divided into two kinds, to wit, **Relations of Ideas**, and **Matters of Fact**. Of the first kind are the sciences of Geometry, Algebra, and Arithmetic; and in short, every affirmation, which is either intuitively or demonstratively certain. *That the square of the hypothenuse is equal to the square of the two sides*, is a proposition, which expresses a relation between these figures. *That three times five is equal to the half of thirty*, expresses a relation between these numbers. Propositions of this kind are discoverable by the mere operation of thought, without dependence on what is anywhere existent in the universe. Though there never were a circle or triangle in nature, the truths, demonstrated by Euclid, would forever retain their certainty and evidence.

Matters of fact, which are the second objects of human reason, are not ascertained in the same manner; nor is our evidence of their truth, however great, of a like nature with the foregoing. The contrary of every matter of fact is still possible; because it can never imply a contradiction, and is conceived by the mind with the same facility and distinctness, as if ever so conformable to reality. *That the sun will not rise to-morrow* is no less intelligible a proposition, and implies no more contradiction, than the affirmation, *that it will rise*. We should in vain, therefore, attempt to demonstrate its falsehood. Were it demonstratively false, it would imply a contradiction, and could never be distinctly conceived by the mind. (*HU*, 108)

The contrast drawn in these paragraphs is an important one. Let's be sure we understand it. Suppose that yesterday you had uttered two statements:

A: Two plus three is not five.
B: The sun will not rise tomorrow.

The sun did rise this morning.* Thus, both statements are false. But what Hume draws our attention to is that they are *false in different ways*. *A* is false simply because of the way in which the ideas "two," "plus," "three," "five," and "equals" are related to each other. To put them together as *A* does

---

*We feel safe saying this because if the sun had not risen this morning, you almost certainly would not be reading this.

is not just to make a false statement; it is to utter a *contradiction*, to say something that cannot even be clearly conceived. As Hume puts it, we can know it is false "by the mere operation of thought." We do not have to make any experiments or look to our experience. The opposite of *A* can in turn be known to be true, no matter what is "anywhere existent in the universe."

However, we can clearly conceive *B* even though it turned out to be false. It is not false because the ideas in it are related the way they are; given the way they are related, it might have been true. We can clearly conceive what that would have been like: You woke up to total and continuing darkness. Whether *B* is true or false depends on the *facts*, on what actually happened in nature. And to determine its truth or falsity you needed to do more than just think about it. You needed to consult your experience. The falsity of *B*, Hume says, cannot be *demonstrated*. Reason alone will not suffice to convince us of matters of fact; here only experience will do.

And he suggests one further difference between them: About relations of ideas like *A* we can be certain, but with respect to propositions stating matters of fact, our evidence is never great enough to amount to certainty.*

We need to remind ourselves once again that Hume is committed to sticking to the phenomena: the perceptions of the mind, its impressions, and its ideas. These are the data that need explaining in a science of human nature. But now it is obvious that a question forces itself on us. Is that all we can know about?

---

*Hume is here suggesting a revolutionary understanding of the kind of knowledge we have in mathematics. A contrast with Plato will be instructive. For Plato (see pp. 152–153), mathematics is the clearest case of knowledge we have. Not only is it certain and enduring, but also it is also the best avenue into acquaintance with absolute reality, for its *objects* are independent of the world of sensory experience—eternal and unchanging Forms. Hume, however, suggests that mathematics is certain not because it introduces us to such realities, but simply because of how it relates *ideas* to one another. Mathematics *has no objects*. This suggestion undermines the entire Platonic picture of reality. It is further developed in the twentieth century by Ludwig Wittgenstein and the logical positivists. See pp. 626–627 and 634–635.

We don't usually think so. We talk confidently of things beyond the reach of our senses and memory—of what's going on in the next room or on the moon, of what happened long before we were born, of a whole world of objects that exist (we think) quite independent of our minds, and many of us think it sensible to talk of God and the soul. All this is common sense, and yet it goes far beyond the narrow bounds of Hume's data. What can we make of this? Or rather, what can Hume make of it? He considers some examples:

- A man believes that his friend is in France. Why? Because he has received a letter from his friend.
- You find a watch on a desert island and conclude that some human being had been there before you.
- You hear a voice in the dark and conclude there is another person in the room.

In each of these cases, where someone claims to know something not present in his perceptions, you will find that a connection is being made by the relation of *cause and effect*. In each case a present impression (reading the letter, seeing the watch, hearing the voice) is *associated* with an idea (of the friend's being in France, of a person's dropping the watch, of someone speaking). The way we get beliefs about matters of fact beyond the present testimony of our senses and memory is by relying on our sense of causal relations. The letter is an *effect* of our friend's having sent it; the watch was *caused* to be there on the beach by another person; and voices are *produced* by human beings. Or so we believe. It is causation that allows us to reach out beyond the limits of present sensation and memories.

> All reasonings concerning matter of fact seem to be founded on the relation of *Cause and Effect*. By means of that relation alone we can go beyond the evidence of our memory and senses. (*HU*, 109)

This seems like progress, though it is hardly very new. Descartes, you will recall, escapes solipsism by a causal argument for the existence of God. But Hume now presses these investigations in a novel direction. How, he asks, do we arrive at the knowledge of cause and effect?

The first part of his answer to this question is a purely negative point. We do not, and cannot, arrive at such knowledge independent of experience, or **a priori:** Our knowledge of causality is not a matter of the *relations of ideas.*

Consider two events that are related as cause and effect. To use a typical eighteenth-century example, think about two balls on a billiard table: the cue ball strikes the eight ball, causing the eight ball to move. Suppose we know all about the cue ball— its weight, its direction, its momentum—but have never had any experience whatsoever of one thing striking another. Could we predict what would happen when the two balls meet? Not at all. For all we would know, the cue ball might simply stop, reverse its direction, pop straight up in the air, go straight through, or turn into a chicken. Our belief that the effect will be a movement of the second ball is completely dependent on our having observed that sort of thing on prior occasions. Without that experience, we would be at a total loss.

> No object ever discovers, by the qualities which appear to the senses, either the causes which produced it, or the effects which will arise from it; nor can our reason, unassisted by experience, ever draw any inference concerning real existence and matter of fact. . . . *causes and effects are discoverable, not by reason, but by experience.* (HU, 110)

My expectation that the second ball will move when struck is based entirely on past experience. I have seen that sort of thing happen before. This seems entirely reasonable: I make a prediction on the basis of past experience. But if that prediction is reasonable, we ought to be able to set out the reason for it. Reasons can be given in arguments. Let us try to make the argument explicit.

1. I have seen one ball strike another many times.
2. Each time, the ball that was struck has moved. Therefore,
3. The struck ball will move this time.

If we look at the matter this way, however, it is easy to see that proposition 3 does not *follow* from propositions 1 and 2. It seems *possible* that this time, something else could happen. To be sure, none of us believes that anything else will happen, but it is precisely this belief, the belief that the first one *causes* the second to move, that needs explanation.

Hume is searching for what, if anything, makes this a *rational* thing to believe. Because this time could be very different from all those past times, the argument is invalid and does not give us a *good reason* to believe that the second ball will move. Can we patch up the argument?

Suppose we add a premise to the argument.

1a. The future will (in the relevant respect) be like the past.

Now the argument looks valid. Propositions 1a, 1, and 2 do indeed entail proposition 3. If we know that 1a is true, then, in the light of our experience summed up in 1 and 2, it is rational to believe that the second billiard ball will move when struck by the first one. We could call proposition 1a the principle of *the uniformity of nature.*

But how do you know that proposition 1a is true? Think about that a minute. How *do* you know that the future will be like the past? It is surely not *contradictory* to suppose that the way events hang together might suddenly change; putting the kettle on the fire after today *could* produce ice. So 1a is not true because of the relation of the ideas in it.* Whether 1a is true or false must surely be a *matter of fact.* So if we know it, we must know it on the basis of experience. What experience? If we look back, we can see that the futures we were (at various points) looking forward to always resembled the pasts we were (at those points) recalling. This suggests an argument to support 1a.

1b. I have experienced many pairs of events that have been constantly conjoined in the past.
1c. Each time I found that similar pairs of events were conjoined in the future. Therefore,
1a. The future will (in these respects) be like the past.

But it is clear that this argument is no better than the first one; we are trying to justify our general principle 1a in *exactly* the same way as we tried to justify the expectation that the struck billiard ball would move (proposition 3). If it didn't work the first time, it surely won't work now. The fact

---

*You should review the discussion of the distinction between relations of ideas and matters of fact, pp. 445–446.

that past futures resembled past pasts is simply no good reason to think that future futures will resemble their relevant pasts.

Yet we all think that is so, don't we? Our practical behavior surely testifies to that belief; we simply have no hesitation in walking about on the third floor of a building, believing that it will support us now just as it always has in the past. We all believe in the uniformity of nature. But why? For what *reason*?

Let us review. Hume is inquiring into the foundation of ideas about things that go beyond the contents of our present consciousness. These ideas all depend on relations of cause and effect: They are effects caused in us by impressions of some kind. But what is the foundation of these causal inferences? It can only be experience. But now we see that *neither experience nor the relations of idea can supply a good reason* for believing that my friend is in France, for that belief rests on the assumption that the future will resemble the past, which cannot itself be justified by appealing to experience or to the relations of ideas.

And so we have the first part of Hume's answer to the question about what justifies us in believing in so many things independent of our present experience: *not any reason!*

We must be careful here. Hume is not advising us to give up such beliefs; he thinks we could not, even if we wanted to. "Nature will always maintain her rights," he says, "and prevail in the end over any abstract reasoning whatsoever" (*HU*, 120). The fact that these beliefs do not rest on any rational foundation is an important result in his science of human nature, and, as we'll see, its philosophical consequences are dramatic. But he acknowledges that we cannot really do without these beliefs. Our survival depends on them.

If we allow that these beliefs about the world are not rationally based, the next obvious question is this: What *is* their foundation? Hume suggests a thought experiment.

> Suppose a person, though endowed with the strongest faculties of reason and reflection, to be brought on a sudden into this world; he would, indeed, immediately observe a continual succession of objects, and one event following another; but he would not

be able to discover any thing farther. He would not, at first, by any reasoning, be able to reach the idea of cause and effect; since the particular powers, by which all natural operations are performed, never appear to the senses; nor is it reasonable to conclude, merely because one event, in one instance precedes another, that therefore the one is the cause, the other the effect. Their conjunction may be arbitrary and casual. . . .

> Suppose again, that he has acquired more experience, and has lived so long in the world as to have observed similar objects or events to be constantly conjoined together; what is the consequence of this experience? He immediately infers the existence of one object from the appearance of the other. (*HU*, 120–121)

This seems plausible. But what is the difference between the first and the second supposition? The only difference is that in the first case the man lacks sufficient experience to notice which events are "constantly conjoined" with each other. But what difference does this difference make? What allows him in the second case to make inferences and have expectations, when he cannot do that in the first case? If it is not a matter of reasoning, then there must be

> some other principle, which determines him to form such a conclusion. This principle is CUSTOM or HABIT. (*HU*, 121)

Note carefully what Hume is saying. Our belief that events are related by cause and effect is a completely *nonrational* belief. We have no good reason to think this. We cannot help but believe in causation, but we believe in it by a kind of instinct built into human nature: When we experience the **constant conjunction** of events, we form a habit of expecting the second when we observe the first, and we believe the first causes the second.*

> Custom, then, is the great guide of human life. It is that principle alone, which renders our experience useful to us, and makes us expect, for the future, a similar train of events with those which

---

*Compare this to al-Ghazālī theory about causation (pp. 307–308).

have appeared in the past. Without the influence of custom, we should be entirely ignorant of every matter of fact, beyond what is immediately present to the memory and senses. (*HU*, 122)

Hume is here turning upside down the major theme of nearly all philosophy before him. Almost everyone in the philosophical tradition has agreed that a person has a right to believe something only if a good reason can be given for it. This goes back at least to Plato.* The major arguments among the philosophers concern what can (and what cannot) be adequately supported by reason. This commitment to the rationality of belief is most prominent, of course, in a rationalist such as Descartes, who determines to doubt everything that cannot be certified by the "light of reason." The skeptics, on these same grounds, argue that virtually no belief in matters of fact can be known because virtually nothing can be shown to be reasonable. Hume seems to agree that virtually no belief in matters of fact can be shown to be reasonable; is he, then, a skeptic? We return to this question later in this chapter.

For now, let us note his conclusion that almost none of our most important beliefs (all of which depend on the relation between cause and effect) can be shown to be rational. We hold them simply out of habit. Our tendency to form beliefs about the external world is just a *fact* about us; this is the way human nature works. Hume does not try to explain *why* human nature functions this way—it just does. We should not frame hypotheses!

There is a corollary, which Hume is quick to draw. Sometimes a certain event is *always* conjoined with another event. But in other cases, one event follows another only in *some* or *most* cases. Water always boils when put on a hot fire, but it only sometimes rains when it is cloudy. These facts are the foundation of *probabilistic* expectations. Our degree of belief corresponds to the degree of connection that our experience reveals between the two events. The more constant the conjunction

between event *A* and event *B*, the more probable we think it that a new experience of *A* will be followed by *B*. Again, note that for Hume this is not the result of a rational calculation. We do not *decide* to believe with a particular degree of assurance. It just happens. That is how we are made.*

This might seem unsatisfactory, for the idea of constant conjunction does not seem to exhaust the notion of causality. When we say that *X* causes *Y*, we don't just mean that whenever *X* occurs *Y* also occurs. We mean that if *X* occurs, *Y* *must* occur, that *X* produces *Y*, that *X* has a certain *power* to bring *Y* into being. In short, we think that in some sense the connection between *X* and *Y* is a **necessary connection.** This is part of what we mean by the idea of a cause. We could express this idea in a formula:

CAUSE = CONSTANT CONJUNCTION + NECESSARY CONNECTION

Hume now owes us an account of this latter aspect of the idea.

How can he proceed? The idea of cause is one of those metaphysical ideas we are all familiar with, but whose exact meaning is obscure. Hume has already given us a rule to deal with these cases: Try to trace the idea back to an impression. What happens if we try to do that?

Think again about the billiard balls on the table. Try to describe with great care your exact experience when seeing the one strike the other. Isn't it your impression that the cue ball moves across the table, it touches the eight ball, and the eight ball moves? Is there anything else you observe? In particular, do you observe the *force* that *makes* the second ball move? Do you observe the *necessary connection* between the two events? Hume is convinced that you do not.

---

*Review Plato's distinction of knowledge from opinion in terms of the former being "backed up by reasons" (pp. 150–151).

*A qualification needs to be made here. While our degree of confidence in our beliefs is usually governed by this principle, there are exceptions. We can be misled by thinking that certain ideas have meaning when they do not. Or we can generalize too soon on the basis of limited information. These mistakes lead to what Hume calls "superstition." Most superstitions are erroneous beliefs about causes and effects. Think about the bad luck supposedly associated with breaking a mirror or walking under a ladder.

We are never able, in a single instance, to discover any power or necessary connexion; any quality which binds the effect to the cause, and renders the one an infallible consequence of the other. We only find, that the one does actually, in fact, follow the other. . . . Consequently, there is not, in any single, particular instance of cause and effect, any thing which can suggest the idea of power or necessary connexion. (*HU*, 136)

Mental phenomena are no different. If you will to move your hand, your hand moves. If you try to picture your best friend's face, you can do it. But no matter how closely you inspect these operations, all you can observe is one thing being followed by another. You never get an impression of the *connection* between them. All relations of cause and effect must be learned from experience; and experience can show us only "the frequent CONJUNCTION of objects, without being ever able to comprehend any thing like CONNEXION between them" (*HU*, 141).

Where then do we get this second part of our idea of cause? Is it one of those ideas that is simply meaningless? Should we discard it or try to do without it? That seems hardly possible. Yet a close inspection of all the data seems to confirm Hume's conclusion:

Upon the whole, there appears not, throughout all nature, any one instance of connexion, which is conceivable by us. All events seem entirely loose and separate. One event follows another; but we can never observe any tie between them. They seem *conjoined*, but never *connected*. And as we can have no idea of any thing, which never appeared to our outward sense or inward sentiment, the necessary conclusion *seems* to be, that we have no idea of connexion or power at all, and that these words are absolutely without any meaning, when employed either in philosophical reasonings, or common life. (*HU*, 144)

"All events seem entirely loose and separate." And the conclusion *seems* to be that we have no idea of cause at all—because there is no corresponding impression of necessary connections. But then it is really puzzling why this idea should be so natural, so pervasive, and so useful. It is an idea we all have, and one we can hardly do without.

This puzzle, Hume thinks, can be solved. To solve it, we have to go back to the fact that exposure to constant conjunctions builds up an associationistic *habit* of expecting one event on the appearance of the other. This habit is the key to understanding the full concept of a cause.

After a repetition of similar instances, the mind is carried by habit, upon the appearance of one event, to expect its usual attendant, and to believe that it will exist. This connexion, therefore, which we *feel* in the mind, this customary transition of the imagination from one object to its usual attendant, is the sentiment or impression, from which we form the idea of power or necessary connexion. (*HU*, 145)

As we have seen, there are two things that go into the concept of a cause. One component is a constant conjunction of events. Of that we have experience, and on that basis Hume offers the following definition of a **cause:**

an object, followed by another, and where all the objects, similar to the first, are followed by objects similar to the second. (*HU*, 146)

Notice that this is a reduced, cautious definition of "cause." It is not a definition of the *full* notion of cause, which includes the idea of a necessary connection between events. We cannot, Hume says, "point out that circumstance in the cause, which gives it a connexion with its effect. We have no idea of this connection" (*HU*, 146).

But we do experience something relevant to our *belief* in necessary connection. We cannot help but *feel* that there is a connection. It is on the basis of this kind of **subjective** experience that we *project* a necessary connection into the relation between objective events. And Hume gives us a second definition of cause:

an object followed by another, and whose appearance always conveys the thought to that other. (*HU*, 146)

Hume has done two things. (1) He has provided an account of the basis on which we have the idea of cause at all—the observed constant conjunctions between kinds of events. (2) He has given an explanation of why we attribute a necessary connection to those pairs of events—even though such necessary connections are never experienced. The full concept of a cause is a kind of fiction.* Necessary connections do not appear anywhere in our experience, but we cannot help applying that notion to observed events.

Remembering that we rely on cause and effect for all our inferences to realities beyond present consciousness, we now see that all such beliefs are simply based on habit. We have *no reason* for belief in an external world, in the reality of other persons, or even in past events. If knowledge is based on reason, as the philosophical tradition has held, there is precious little we can claim to know!

---

1. Contrast relations of ideas with matters of fact. Give some examples of your own.
2. What is Hume's argument for the conclusion that causes and effects are discoverable not by reason but by experience?
3. If our beliefs about causation are dependent on experience, what experiences are of the relevant kind?
4. How does Hume explain our judgments of probability?
5. Granted that the idea of *necessary connection* is an important part of our idea of a cause, how does Hume account for that?
6. What part of our idea of causation is a fiction, according to Hume? What part is not?

The Disappearing Self

Most philosophers in the Western tradition, along with many in the Indian tradition, have taken human beings to have an enduring self that is somehow distinct from the body. Plato argues that a person is really a *soul*. Aristotle holds (with qualifications) that the soul is a functional aspect of a living body.

The Brahmanical philosophers in India identify the self with *ātman*. Avicenna imagines that his Flying Man could recognize the existence of his self.* In modern times, Descartes follows Plato's lead, maintaining that the soul or mind is an immaterial and immortal substance, Locke posits spiritual substances, and Berkeley argues that spirits and their ideas make up the whole of reality.

Hume can hardly avoid dealing with this question, since he claims to be constructing a science of human nature. The first thing we need to do, to the extent possible, is to clarify the meaning of the central term. What Plato called "soul" and Descartes the "mind," Hume names the "self." A **self** is supposedly a substance or thing, simple (not composed of parts), and invariably the same through time. It is the "home" for all our mental states and activities, the "place" where these characteristics are "located." (The terms in quotes are used metaphorically.) Your self is what is supposed to account for the fact that you are one and the same person today as you were at the age of four, even though nearly all your characteristics have changed over the years. You are larger, stronger, and smarter; you have different hopes and fears, different thoughts and memories; your interests and activities are remarkably different. Yet you are the *same self*. Or so the story goes.†

It is clear what Hume will ask here. Remember his rule: If a term is in any way obscure, or a subject of much controversy, try to trace it back to an impression.

> From what impression cou'd this idea be derived? This question 'tis impossible to answer without a manifest contradiction and absurdity; and yet 'tis a question, which must necessarily be answer'd, if we wou'd have the idea of self pass for clear and intelligible. It must be some one impression, that gives rise to every real idea. But self or person is

---

*Hume does not apply the term "fiction" to his account of causality; but he does use it when talking of (1) the identity of objects through time, (2) the existence of objects independent of experience, and (3) personal identity in a continuing self. Since the pattern of analysis is similar in all these cases, we think it is justified to use the term here. We are indebted to Matthew McKeon for additional clarity on this topic.

---

*For Plato's views, see p. pp. 168–170. For Aristotle's, see pp. 203–206. On *ātman*, see pp. 36–37. For Avicenna's views, see pp. 304–305.

†It would be helpful at this point to review what Locke says about personal identity (pp. 419–420). Note that he argues that my identity cannot *consist* in sameness of soul or self, though he doesn't find those terms meaningless.

not any one impression, but that to which our several impressions and ideas are suppos'd to have a reference. If any impression gives rise to the idea of self, that impression must continue invariably the same, thro' the whole course of our lives; since self is suppos'd to exist after that manner. But there is no impression constant and invariable. (*T*, I, 4, 6, p. 164)

Let us be clear about the argument here. The term "self" is supposed to represent an idea of something that continues unchanged throughout a person's life. Since the idea is supposed to be a simple one, there must be a simple impression that is its "double." But there is no such impression, Hume claims, "constant and invariable" through life. It follows, according to Hume's rule, that *we have no such idea*! The term is one of those meaningless noises that we wrongly suppose to mean something, when it really doesn't.

This is a most radical way of undermining belief in the soul or self. Some philosophers claim to have such an idea and to be able to prove the self really exists. Others claim to be able to prove that it doesn't exist. But Hume undercuts both sides; they are just arguing about words, he holds, because neither side really knows what it is talking about. Literally! There simply is no such idea as the (supposed) idea of the self, so it doesn't make sense to affirm it *or* to deny it.

This claim, of course, rests on the theory of ideas. It is only as strong as that theory is good. Is that a good theory? This is an important question; in later chapters, we meet other philosophers who investigate this question.* But for now, let us explore in a bit more depth why Hume thinks there is no impression that corresponds to the (supposed) idea of the self. In a much-quoted passage, Hume says,

For my part, when I enter most intimately into what I call *myself*, I always stumble on some particular perception or other, of heat or cold, light

or shade, love or hatred, pain or pleasure. I never can catch *myself* at any time without a perception, and never can observe any thing but the perception. When my perceptions are remov'd for any time, as by a sound sleep; so long am I insensible of *myself*, and may truly be said not to exist. And were all my perceptions remov'd by death, and cou'd I neither think, nor feel, nor see, nor love, nor hate after the dissolution of my body, I shou'd be entirely annihilated, nor do I conceive what is farther requisite to make me a perfect non-entity. If any one upon serious and unprejudic'd reflexion, thinks he has a different notion of *himself*, I must confess I can reason no longer with him. All I can allow him is, that he may be in the right as well as I, and that we are essentially different in this particular. (*T*, I, 4, 6, p. 165)

Again, Hume tries to pay close attention to the phenomena and tries not to frame hypotheses. If we look inside ourselves, do we find an impression of something simple, unchanging, and continuing? He confesses that *he* can find no such impression, and his suggestion that maybe *you* can, that maybe *you* are "essentially different" in this regard, is surely ironic. His claim is that none of us ever finds more in ourselves than fleeting perceptions—ideas, sensations, feelings, and emotions.

"Since our inner experiences consist of reproductions and combinations of sensory impressions, the concept of a soul without a body seems to me to be empty and devoid of meaning."

Albert Einstein (1879–1955)

So we have no reason to suppose that we are selves, or minds, or souls, if we understand those terms to refer to some simple substance that underlies all our particular perceptions. But what, then, are we?

I may venture to affirm of the rest of mankind, that they are nothing but a bundle or collection of different perceptions, which succeed each other with an inconceivable rapidity, and are in a perpetual flux and movement. . . . The mind is a kind of theatre,

---

*Kant, for instance, denies a key premise of the theory of ideas: that all our ideas (Kant calls them "concepts") arise from impressions. Some of our concepts, Kant claims, do not *arise* out of experience, though they may *apply* to experience. See pp. 473–474.

where several perceptions successively make their appearance; pass, re-pass, glide away, and mingle in an infinite variety of postures and situations. There is properly no *simplicity* in it at any one time, nor *identity* in different; whatever natural propensity we may have to imagine that simplicity and identity. The comparison of the theatre must not mislead us. They are the successive perceptions only, that constitute the mind; nor have we the most distant notion of the place, where these scenes are represented, or of the materials, of which it is compos'd. (*T*, I, 4, 6, p. 165)

Like the idea of cause, the idea of the self is a fiction. As selves or minds, we are nothing but a "bundle" of perceptions. Anything further is sheer, unsupported hypothesis. We have not only no reason to believe in a world of "external" things independent of our minds, but also no reason to believe in mind as a thing.*

In thinking of ourselves, Hume suggests, the analogy of a theater is appropriate. In this theater, an amazingly intricate play is being performed. The players are just all those varied perceptions that succeed each other, as Hume says, with "inconceivable rapidity." But if we are to understand the analogy correctly, we must think away the walls of the theater, think away the stage, think away the seats and even the audience. What is left is just the performance of the play. Such a performance each of us *is*.

How does this bundle theory of the self bear on Descartes' *cogito*, "I think, therefore I am"? Descartes takes this as something each of us knows with certainty. And in answer to the question, "What, then, am I?" he says, "I am a thing (a substance) that thinks." Hume is in effect saying that Descartes is going beyond what the phenomena reveal. A twentieth-century Humean, Bertrand Russell, puts it this way: The most that Descartes is entitled to claim is that there is thinking going on. To claim that there is a mind or self—a thing—doing the

thinking is to frame a hypothesis, to go beyond the evidence available.[7] If this criticism is correct, it undermines Descartes' dualistic metaphysics; we cannot know that the mind is a substance distinct from the body because we cannot know it is a substance at all! All we have is acquaintance with that bundle of perceptions.

Rescuing Human Freedom

A science of human nature must also address whether human actions are in some sense *free*. The mechanistic physical theories of Galileo and Newton give this question new urgency. As long as the entire world is conceived in Aristotelian terms, where a key mode of explanation is teleological,* the question of freedom is not pressing. If *everything* acts for the sake of some end, pursuing its good in whatever way its nature allows, human actions would fit the general pattern neatly. Humans have more alternatives available than do petunias and snails, and they make choices among the available goods. But the pattern of explanation would be common to all things.

Early modern science, however, has banished explanation in terms of ends or goals; explanation by prior causes is "in." The model of the universe is mechanical; the world is compared to a gigantic clock. Stones do not fall *in order to* reach a goal, and oak trees do not grow because of a *striving* to realize the potentiality in them. Everything happens as it *must happen*, according to laws that make no reference to any end, goal, or good.

Are human actions like this, as strictly determined by law and circumstance as the fall of the stone? The view that human actions constitute no exception to the universal rule of causal law is known as **determinism.** The successes of modern science give it plausibility. But it seems to clash with a deeply held conviction that sometimes we are *free* to choose, will, and act.

---

*Compare the Buddhist doctrine of *anātman* or non-self (pp. 41–45). The psychologist and philosopher Alison Gopnik speculates that Hume might have learned about Buddhist philosophy through the Jesuit missionary Charles Francois Dolu while both were living in La Flèche, France, in the 1730s.

---

*An explanation is *teleological* if it makes essential reference to the realization of a goal or end state. Aristotle's discussion of "final causes" provides a good case study (see pp. 195–197).

Descartes shows us one way to deal with this problem: Make an exception for human beings! Mechanical principles might govern material bodies, but they can have no leverage on a non-material mind. The will, Descartes says, is completely free. And by "free" he means "not governed by causal laws."

But Hume cannot take this way, for he is convinced we have no idea of a substantial self, so we can have no reason to think such a nonmaterial mind or soul exists. Hume's solution to this puzzle is quite different from Descartes', and it is justly famous. Its basic pattern is defended by numerous philosophers (but not all) even today.

He begins by asserting that "all mankind" is of the same opinion about this matter. Any controversy is simply due to "ambiguous expressions" used to frame the problem. In other words, if we can get our terms straight, we should be able to settle the matter to everyone's satisfaction. What we need is a set of *definitions* for what Hume calls **"necessity"** on the one hand and **"liberty"** on the other.

> I hope, therefore, to make it appear, that all men have ever agreed in the doctrine both of necessity and of liberty, according to any reasonable sense, which can be put on these terms; and that the whole controversy has hitherto turned merely upon words. (*HU*, 149)

We already know what Hume says about *necessity*. The idea of necessity is part of our idea of a cause but is a kind of fiction. It arises not from impressions, but from that habit our minds develop when confronted with regular conjunctions between events. All we ever observe, when we believe that one event causes another, is the constant conjunction of events of the first kind with events of the second.

Are human actions caused? If we understand this in what Hume thinks is the only possible way, we are simply asking whether there are *regularities* detectable in human behavior.* And he thinks we

all must admit that there are. He gives some examples (*HU*, 150, 151):

- Motives are regularly conjoined to actions: Greed regularly leads to stealing, ambition to the quest for power.
- If a foreigner acts in unexpected ways, there is always a cause—some condition (education, perhaps) that regularly produces this behavior.
- Where we are surprised by someone's action, a careful examination always turns up some unknown condition that allows it to be fit again into a regular pattern.

If all that we can possibly mean by "caused" is that events are regularly connected, we should all agree that human behavior is caused. Why do some of us resist this conclusion? Because, Hume says,

> men still entertain a strong propensity to believe, that they penetrate farther into the powers of nature, and perceive something like a necessary connexion between the cause and the effect. When again they turn their reflections towards the operations of their own minds, and *feel* no such connexion of the motive and the action; they are thence apt to suppose, that there is a difference between the effects, which result from material force, and those which arise from thought and intelligence. (*HU*, 156, 157)

But this is just a confusion! Causality on the side of the objects observed is just regularity, and on the side of the observer it is the generation of a habit based on regularities. In neither case, material or intelligent, is there any necessity observed. Human actions are "caused" in exactly the same sense as events in the material world.

What then of freedom or liberty?

> It will not require many words to prove, that all mankind have ever agreed in the doctrine of liberty as well as in that of necessity, and that the whole dispute, in this respect also, has been hitherto merely verbal. For what is meant by liberty, when applied to voluntary actions? We cannot surely mean, that actions have so little connexion with motives, inclinations, and circumstances, that one does not follow with a certain degree of uniformity from the other, and that one affords no inference by which we can conclude the existence of the other. . . . By liberty, then, we can only mean a

---

*Look again at Hume's two definitions of "cause" on p. 450.

power of acting or not acting, according to the determinations of the will; that is, if we choose to remain at rest, we may; if we choose to move, we also may. Now this hypothetical liberty is universally allowed to belong to everyone, who is not a prisoner and in chains. (*HU*, 158–159)

Perhaps the most accessible way to understand Hume's point is to think of cases where a person is said to be *unfree*. Hume's example is that of a man in chains. Isn't such a man unfree precisely because he cannot do what he *wants* to do? Even if he *yearns* to walk away, *wills* to walk away, *tries* to walk away, he will be *unable* to walk away. He is unfree because his actions are *constrained*—against his will, as we say.

Suppose we remove his chains. Then he is free, at liberty to do what he wants. And isn't this the very essence of freedom: to be able to do whatever it is that you want or choose to do? We could put this more formally in the following way:

A person *P* is *free* when the following condition is satisfied: *If P chooses to do action A, then P does A.*

If this condition were *not* satisfied (if *P* should choose to do *A* but be *unable* to do it), then *P* would *not be at liberty* with respect to *A*.

Hume wants to *reconcile* our belief in causality with our belief in human freedom. We do not have to choose between them. We can have both modern science and human freedom. Newtonian science and freedom would clash only if freedom entailed exemption from causality. But causes are simply regularities; and freedom is not an absence of regularity, but the "hypothetical" power to do something *if* we choose to do it. It is, in fact, a certain kind of regularity. It is the regularity of having the actions we choose to do follow regularly upon our choosing to do them.

There is no reason, then, in human liberty, to deny that a science of human nature—a causal science of a Newtonian kind—is possible. And Newtonian, mechanistic science is no reason to deny or doubt human freedom or to postulate a Cartesian mind that eludes the basic laws of the universe. Hume's **compatibilism,** as it is sometimes called, is an important part of a kind of **naturalism,** a view that takes the human being to be a natural fact, without remainder.

1. What does Hume fail to find when—as he says—he enters most intimately into what he calls *himself*?
2. What conclusions does Hume draw about the nature of a "self"?
3. Explain how Hume thinks the necessity of actions (i.e., that they have causes) is compatible with the fact of liberty in actions (i.e., that sometimes we act freely).

Is It Reasonable to Believe in God?

After doubting everything doubtable, Descartes finds himself locked into solipsism—unless he can demonstrate that he is not the only thing that exists. The way he does this, you recall, is to try to demonstrate the existence of God. He looks, in other words, for a good reason to believe that something other than his own mind exists. If he can prove that God exists, he knows he is not alone; and, God being what God is, he will have good reason to trust at least what is clear and distinct about other things as well. Thus everything hangs, for Descartes, on whether it is reasonable to believe that there is a God.*

What does Hume say about this quest to show that belief in God is more reasonable than disbelief? We review briefly two of the arguments Descartes presents, together with a Humean response to each, and then we look at a rather different argument that was proving very popular in the atmosphere after Newton.

Descartes first argues that we can infer God's existence from the mere fact that we have an idea of an infinite and perfect being. Claiming that he himself cannot be the source of such an idea, Descartes concludes that God himself must be its cause.† Hume counters that

---

*Earlier thinkers, too, from Aristotle on, think they can give good reasons for concluding that some ultimate perfection exists and is in one way or another responsible for all other things. Review the proofs given by Augustine (p. 269), Anselm (pp. 312–314), Avicenna (p. 323), and Aquinas (pp. 302–304). The arguments of Descartes are in *Meditations III* and *V*.

†See Descartes' argument in *Meditations III*, pp. 378–379.

the idea of God, as meaning an infinitely intelligent, wise, and good Being, arises from reflecting on the operations of our own mind, and augmenting, without limit, those qualities of goodness and wisdom. (*HU*, 97–98)

By extrapolating from our internal impressions of intelligence, goodness, and wisdom, we can get the idea of a being that is perfectly intelligent and completely good. And this is the idea of God.* This undercuts Descartes' argument.

Descartes' third argument is, roughly, that because the idea of God as nonexistent is as absurd as the idea of a mountain without a valley or a triangle with more than three sides, the mere fact that we have the idea of God means that God exists.† But this, Hume objects, is to illegitimately infer a *matter of fact* from a mere *relation of ideas*. Perhaps thinking of God entails *thinking* that he exists; but that concerns only how those *ideas* are related to each other, not whether God *in fact* exists. That is a question that can only be settled by reference to experience.

The most popular argument for God during the Enlightenment, among common folk and intellectuals alike, does begin from experience. It can be called the **argument from design.**‡ Newton set the idea that the universe is a magnificently ordered arrangement on a firm scientific footing. The image of a great machine, or clockwork, dominates eighteenth-century thought about the nature of the world. And it suggests a powerful analogy. Just as machines are the effects of intelligent design and workmanship, so the universe is the work of a master craftsman, supremely intelligent and wonderfully skilled. Machines don't just happen and neither does the world.

In a set of dialogues that Hume did not venture to publish during his lifetime, one of the participants sets out this argument:

Look round the world: Contemplate the whole and every part of it: You will find it to be nothing but one great machine, subdivided into an infinite number of lesser machines, which again admit of subdivisions to a degree beyond what human senses and faculties can trace and explain. All these various machines, and even their most minute parts, are adjusted to each other with an accuracy which ravishes into admiration all men who have ever contemplated them. The curious adapting of means to ends, throughout all nature, resembles exactly, though it much exceeds, the productions of human contrivance; of human design, thought, wisdom, and intelligence. Since therefore the effects resemble each other, we are led to infer, by all the rules of analogy, that the causes also resemble, and that the Author of Nature is somewhat similar to the mind of man, though possessed of much larger faculties, proportioned to the grandeur of the work which he has executed. By this argument *a posteriori*, and by this argument alone, do we prove at once the existence of a Deity and his similarity to human mind and intelligence. (*D*, II, 45)

Let us note several points about this argument. It is an argument, Hume says, **a posteriori;** that is, it depends in an essential way on experience. Our experience of the world as an ordered and harmonious whole provides one crucial premise; our experience of how machines come into being provides another. Note also that it is an argument *by analogy*. Its structure looks like this (*M* = a machine; *I* = intelligence; *W* = the world):

1. *M* is the effect of *I*.
2. *W* is like *M*. Therefore,
3. *W* is the effect of something like *I*.

Finally, you should recognize that this, like Descartes' first two arguments, is a *causal* argument. Both the first premise and the conclusion deal with causal relations.

Hume says many interesting things about this argument, partly through his spokesmen in the dialogue. Here we are brief, simply listing a number of the points he makes.

1. No argument from experience ever can establish a certainty. The most that experience can yield is probability (since experience is always limited and cannot testify to what is beyond its limits).

---

*Descartes foresees this line of argument and tries to block it. Go back to *Meditation III*, p. 378–379, to see if you think he is successful.

†See Descartes' argument in *Meditation V* (p. 389) and our discussion on pp. 391–392.

‡Compare the fifth way of Thomas Aquinas, pp. 323–324. See also Berkeley, pp. 434–435.

So even if the argument is a good one (of its kind), it does not give us more than a probability that the "Author of Nature" is analogous to a human designer.

2. There is a sound principle to be observed in all causal arguments: that "the cause must be proportioned to the effect."

> A body of ten ounces raised in any scale may serve as a proof, that the counterbalancing weight exceeds ten ounces; but can never afford a reason that it exceeds a hundred. . . . If the cause be known only by the effect, we never ought to ascribe to it any qualities, beyond what are precisely requisite to produce the effect. (*HU*, 190)

If we look around at the world, can we say that it is perfectly good? That is hard to believe. If we think of this proof as an attempt to demonstrate the existence of God as he is traditionally conceived—infinite in wisdom and goodness—it surely falls short. For the proportion of goodness we are *justified* in ascribing to the cause (God) cannot far exceed the proportion of goodness (in the world) that needs to be explained.

3. The analogy is supposed to exist between the productions of intelligent human beings and the world as an effect of a supremely intelligent designer. But a number of consequences follow if we take the analogy seriously.

- Many people cooperate to make a machine; by analogy, the world may have been created through the cooperation of many gods.
- Wicked and mischievous people may create technological marvels; by analogy, the creator(s) of the world may be wicked and mischievous.
- Machines are made by mortals; by analogy, may not the gods be mortal?
- The best clocks are a result of a long history of slow improvements; by analogy,

Many worlds might have been botched and bungled, throughout an eternity, ere this system was struck out; much labor lost; many fruitless trials made; and a slow but continued improvement carried on during infinite ages in the art of world-making. (*D*, 36)

The point here is not that any of these possibilities is likely but that analogies always have resemblances in certain respects and differences in others. How do we know which are the similarities in this case and which are the differences? Unless we have some principled way to make this distinction, any one of these conclusions is as justified as the one theists wish to draw.

4. Finally, we have to ask what we can learn from a single case. Here Hume applies his analysis of the idea of causality to the case of the cause of the world.

> It is only when two *species* of objects are found to be constantly conjoined, that we can infer the one from the other; and were an effect presented, which was entirely singular, and could not be comprehended under any known *species*, I do not see, that we could form any conjecture or inference at all concerning its cause. (*HU*, 198)

There is one respect in which this universe is entirely *unlike* the clocks and automobiles and iPhones of our experience: It is, in our experience, "entirely singular." We can infer that the cause of a new computer is some intelligent human because we have had past experience of the constant conjunction of computers and intelligent designers. We experience *both* the effects *and* the causes. To apply this kind of analogical reasoning to the universe, we would need past experience of the making of worlds; and in each instance there would have to have been a conjoined experience of an intelligent being. On the basis of such a constant conjunction, we could infer justly that this world, too, is the effect of intelligence. But since the universe is, in our experience, "entirely singular," we can make no such inference. These, and more, are the difficulties Hume finds in the design argument.

"I myself believe that the evidence for God lies primarily in inner personal experiences."
William James (1842–1910)

According to Hume's principles, *any* causal argument for God is subject to this last criticism. But now we are in a position to see that our situation is much worse than we ever imagined.

These reflections not only undercut causal arguments for God's existence, but also undermine causal arguments for the existence of *anything at all* beyond our own impressions!* For causal judgments are always founded on the constant conjunction of pairs of events *within our experience*. To judge that some extramental object is the cause of a perception, we would need to be able to observe a constant conjunction of that perception with its extramental cause. But to do that we would need to jump out of our own skins, observe the perception from outside, and compare it with the external thing correlated with it. And that we cannot do.

If Hume is right about the origin of the concept of causality *within* experience, we could never have the evidence required to validate any claim about external objects. All we can do is relate perceptions to perceptions. And if Descartes is right that without *good reason* to believe in God we are caught within the web of our own ideas, then solipsism seems (rationally) inescapable†—a dismal and melancholy conclusion.

After reviewing these attempts to make belief in God reasonable, it seems that we have so far not found good reason to believe in God. Now we must add that neither have we found good reason to believe in the existence of a material world independent of our perceptions. We can think of this as a radical consequence of the representational theory (p. 372). Hume shows us that if we begin from ideas in the mind, there is no way to build that bridge to the world beyond.

This is not, however, Hume's last word on the subject of religion. In a passage that has puzzled many commentators, one of Hume's characters goes on to say,

A person, seasoned with a just sense of the imperfections of natural reason, will fly to revealed truth with the greatest avidity: While the haughty dogmatist, persuaded that he can erect a complete system of theology by the mere help of philosophy, disdains any further aid and rejects this adventitious

instructor. To be a philosophical skeptic is, in a man of letters, the first and most essential step towards being a sound, believing *Christian*. (D, XII, 130)

What can we make of this? Is Hume serious here? Or, more important, is this a serious possibility, this combination of religious faith and philosophical skepticism? What would this be like?*

---

1. How, according to Hume, does the idea of God originate? Compare Hume's view to Descartes' view.
2. How does Hume use the notion of relations of ideas to block the ontological arguments of Anselm (pp. 312–314) and Descartes (*Meditation V*)?
3. State clearly the argument from design and sketch several of Hume's criticisms.

Understanding Morality

We often find ourselves making judgments like this: "That was a bad thing Jones did," "Smith is a good person," "Telling the truth is the right thing to do," and "Justice is a virtue." You see twenty dollars in an unattended backpack in the library; no one is around, and you could pick it up; you say to yourself, "That would be wrong," and walk away. Such moral judgments are very important to us, both as evaluations of the actions of others and as guides to our own behavior. They are no less important to society. A science of human nature ought to have something to say about this feature of human life, so Hume tries to understand our propensity to make judgments of this kind. As we might anticipate by now, he puts his question this way: Are these judgments founded in some way on reason, or do they have some other origin?

REASON IS NOT A MOTIVATOR

Nothing is more usual in philosophy, and even in common life, than to talk of the combat of passion and reason, to give the preference to reason,

---

*Here we see how—accepting the starting points of Locke and Berkeley—Hume presses their empiricist principles to radical and (apparently) skeptical conclusions.

†Solipsism is explained on p. 382.

Fideism, as this view is sometimes called, is explored in the work of Søren Kierkegaard. See "The Religious," in Chapter 22.

and to assert that men are only so far virtuous as they conform themselves to its dictates. Every rational creature, 'tis said, is oblig'd to regulate his actions by reason; and if any other motive or principle challenge the direction of his conduct, he ought to oppose it, 'til it be entirely subdu'd, or at least brought to a conformity with that superior principle. . . . In order to shew the fallacy of all this philosophy, I shall endeavour to prove first, that reason alone can never be a motive to any action of the will; and *secondly*, that it can never oppose passion in the direction of the will. (*T*, II, 3, 3, p. 265)

Hume's claim that "reason alone" can never motivate any action has clear moral implications, for moral considerations can be motivators. We sometimes refrain from doing something simply because we judge that it would be *wrong*. If reason alone cannot motivate an action, it seems to follow that morality cannot be a matter of reason alone.

But what does this mean, that **reason** alone can neither motivate an action nor oppose **passion** (e.g., desire or inclination)? Recall Hume's claim that "all the objects of human reason or enquiry may naturally be divided into two kinds, to wit, *Relations of Ideas* and *Matters of Fact*" (*HU*, 108). If reason is going to motivate action, it must do so in one of these two ways. Let us examine each possibility.

Consider adding up a sum, which Hume takes to be a matter of the relations of ideas. Suppose you are totaling up what you owe to my dentist, Dr. Payne. Will this reasoning lead to any action? Not by itself, says Hume. If you *want* to pay Payne what you owe her, this reasoning will guide what you do: you will pay her the total and not some other amount. But in the absence of that (or another) want, the reasoning alone will not produce an action. The motivator is the want; and a want is what Hume calls a *passion*.

Consider next these examples:

Ask a man *why he uses exercise*; he will answer *because he desires to keep his health*. If you then enquire *why he desires health*, he will readily reply *because sickness is painful*. If you push your enquiries further and desire a reason *why he hates pain*, it is impossible he can ever give any. This is an ultimate end, and is never referred to any object.

Perhaps to your second question, *why he desires health*, he may also reply that *it is necessary for the exercise of his calling*. If you ask *why he is anxious on that head*, he will answer, *because he desires to get money*. If you demand why? *It is the instrument of pleasure*, says he. And beyond this it is an absurdity to ask for a reason. It is impossible there can be a progress in infinitum; and that one thing can always be a reason why another is desired. Something must be desirable on its own account, and because of its immediate accord or agreement with human sentiment and affection. (*PM*, 163)

Here we have reasoning about matters of fact; it is a fact that exercise is conducive to health, that health is required to pursue a profession successfully, and so on. But mere knowledge of these matters of fact will not motivate action unless one cares about the end to which they lead. And this caring is not itself a matter of reason. It is a matter of *sentiment* or *passion*. Hume draws this conclusion:

It appears evident that the ultimate ends of human actions can never, in any case, be accounted for by *reason*, but recommend themselves entirely to the sentiments and affections of mankind, without any dependence on the intellectual faculties. (*PM*, 162–163)

So reason alone can never motivate us to action. But Hume goes even further; he claims that reason can never oppose passion; only a passion can oppose another passion. For example, as you contemplate a roller coaster ride, fear fights with the desire for thrills. Likewise, one rational proposition can be opposed to another when they are contradictory. But for reason to oppose passion, it would have to be a motivator in itself, and Hume argues that it is not. Reason, we might say, is *inert*.

We speak not strictly and philosophically when we talk of the combat of passion and of reason. Reason is, and ought only to be the slave of the passions, and can never pretend to any other office than to serve and obey them. (*T*, II, 3, 3, 266)

Reason can instruct us how to satisfy our desires, but it cannot tell us what desires to have.*

---

*You might think there is an obvious exception: Suppose you had a desire to smoke cigarettes. Couldn't reason tell you that it would be better for you if you didn't have that desire? And wouldn't this be a case of reason opposing a desire you have? What would Hume say?

Reason can only be the "slave" of the passions. In a few dramatic sentences, Hume drives this point home.

> Where a passion is neither founded on false suppositions, nor chuses means insufficient for the end, the understanding can neither justify nor condemn it. 'Tis not contrary to reason to prefer the destruction of the whole world to the scratching of my finger. (*T*, II, 3, 3, 267)

Reason is motivationally impotent; it cannot rule. Its role is that of a slave! The master says, "I want that," and it is the job of the slave to figure out how it can be got. The slave deals with *means*. Reason has an important place in action, since if we calculate wrong or make a mistake about the facts, we will be likely to miss our ends. But those ends are dictated by the nonrational part of our nature, the wants and desires, the passions and sentiments, that are simply given with that nature. If you truly prefer the destruction of the world to the scratching of my finger, there is nothing *irrational* about that.

The Origins of Moral Judgment

What, then, of morality? If moral judgments are to have any effect on actions, they cannot be purely rational judgments. They must be the expression of passions of some sort. This is just what Hume claims.

Let us again consider the two classes of things subject to reason. Could morality be simply a matter of the relations between ideas? There is a conceptual relation between the ideas of murder and wrongness: All murder is wrong—because what "murder" means is "wrongful killing." But this can hardly be all that is involved in morality because morality is supposed to be applied to the facts. Just pointing out that murder involves the idea of wrongful killing is no help at all when we are asking of a certain action, Is this murder? So morality, if it is going to have any practical effects, cannot be merely a matter of the relations between ideas.

Can morality be a matter of fact (the second province of reason)?

Take any action allow'd to be vicious: Wilful murder, for instance. Examine it in all lights, and see if you can find that matter of fact, or real existence, which you call *vice*. In whichever way you take it, you find only certain passions, motives, volitions and thoughts. There is no other matter of fact in the case. The vice entirely escapes you, as long as you consider the object. You can never find it, till you turn your reflexion into your own breast, and find a sentiment of disapprobation, which arises in you, towards this action. Here is a matter of fact; but 'tis the object of feeling, not of reason. It lies in yourself, not in the object. So that when you pronounce any action or character to be vicious, you mean nothing, but that from the constitution of your nature you have a feeling or sentiment of blame from the contemplation of it. Vice and virtue, therefore, may be compar'd to sounds, colours, heat and cold, which, according to modern philosophy, are not qualities in objects, but perceptions in the mind. (*T*, II, 3, 1, 301)

Compare this analysis to Hume's discussion of causation. When we observe carefully any instance of a causal relation, we never observe the causing itself. We attribute a causal connection between two things because long habit of seeing them together creates a *feeling* in our minds of a necessary connection between them. Moral judgments, Hume is saying, resemble judgments of causality. Here, too, we project onto the facts an idea with an origin that is simply a feeling in the mind. In this case, the feelings are those of approval and disapproval, which we express in terms of the concepts "right/good" and "wrong/bad." No matter how closely you examine the facts of any action, you will never discover in them its goodness or badness. The moral quality of the action is a matter of how the author of the moral judgment *feels* about them.

In a famous passage that widely influences subsequent moral philosophy, Hume marks out clearly the distinction between *the facts* on the one hand (expressible in purely descriptive language) and *the value qualities of the facts* on the other (expressible in evaluations).

> In every system of morality, which I have hitherto met with, I have always remark'd, that the author

proceeds for some time in the ordinary way of reasoning, and establishes the being of a God, or makes observations about human affairs; when of a sudden I am surpriz'd to find, that instead of the usual copulations of propositions, *is*, and *is not*, I meet with no proposition that is not connected with an *ought*, or *ought not*. This change is imperceptible; but is, however, of the last consequence. For as this *ought* or *ought not*, expresses some new relation or affirmation, 'tis necessary that it shou'd be observ'd and explain'd; and at the same time that a reason should be given, for what seems altogether inconceivable, how this new relation can be a deduction from others, which are entirely different from it. But as authors do not commonly use this precaution, I shall presume to recommend it to the readers; and am persuaded, that this small attention wou'd subvert all the vulgar [i.e., common] systems of morality, and let us see, that the distinction of vice and virtue is not founded merely on the relations of objects, nor is perceiv'd by reason. (*T*, II, 3, 1, 302)

Hume is here pointing to what is often called the **fact/value gap,** or the **is/ought problem.*** Reason can tell us what the facts are, but it cannot tell us how to value them. And from premises that mention only the facts, no conclusions about value may be derived.

A contrast with Augustine may help clarify Hume's claim. For Augustine and other believers in the Great Chain of Being, everything that exists has a value. Some things—those nearer to God and farther from nothingness—have more value than others.† That's just a fact, Augustine believes. There is value *in* things, and it is incumbent on us to adjust our desires to the degree of value that

things *in fact* have. It would be wrong—objectively wrong—to treat a child and a rock the same way.

For Hume there are no value-facts. Value has its origin in *valuing*—in feelings of desire, aversion, love, hate, and so on. Values are **projections** onto the facts, all of which have the same value—that is, none. This is not to say that we should stop making value judgments. As with causal judgments, Hume admits we neither could nor should try to make our way through life without them, even though he takes his science of human nature to show that neither is founded on reason.

The foundation of morality is to be found, rather, in **sentiment**—in feelings of approval and disapproval. A scientific examination of morality ought to do more than discover these foundations, however. It ought also to reveal what *kinds of things* we approve and disapprove and why. Hume has many interesting things to say about this matter, but we'll be brief.

Hume claims that we tend to approve of those things which are either **agreeable** or **useful,** either to *ourselves* or to *others*. Agreeable things, such as white sand on a warm beach, naturally elicit our immediate approval. Useful things, such as a visit to Dr. Payne, are means to some agreeable end. Hume believes that we often feel a kind of approval for things agreeable to others, as well as to ourselves. If Hume is right, an egoistic account of human motivation (such as that of Hobbes) is inadequate.* A Hobbesian might claim, of course, that when we approve of another's enjoyment we do so because such approval is a *means* to our own pleasure. But Hume argues that this can't be right. The pleasure or satisfaction we feel on viewing another's enjoyment *is* our approval of it, so it could not possibly be that for the sake of which we approve. Furthermore, we make moral judgments about figures in past history, where there is no possible impact on our present or future interests. These judgments, Hume concludes, are caused not by self-interest but by **sympathy,** which he

---

*Reflection should tell you that this problem, too, is a consequence of the change produced by the development and acceptance of modern science. Dante's world contained no such gap; he could find the "right way" by discovering the facts about the universe. In general, where final causes are an intrinsic part of the *way things are*, no such gap exists. For the ends of things are part of their very being. When final causes are cast out, however, values lose their rootedness in the way things are.

†Take another look at the diagram of the Great Chain on p. 272.

---

*Compare Hobbesian egoism, pp. 411–413.

understands as the tendency for the perception of another's situation to excite feelings similar to those the other person is feeling. This is why perceiving another person's agreeable experience elicits feelings of approval in our own minds.

We will not follow the development of Hume's ideas about the particular virtues, but we should note one aspect. His insistence that morality is not founded on reason would seem to catapult him directly into moral relativism because feelings seem so personal. What I approve, we may think, might be quite different from what you approve. But the insistence on sympathy as an original passion in human nature—within every individual—works toward a commonality in the moral sense of us all. It does not make moral disagreements between cultures or individuals impossible, but it is a pressure built into us all that explains the large agreement in moral judgment we in fact find.

---

1. Explain what Hume means when he says that reason is the slave of the passions.
2. How does Hume explain our judgment that a certain action is bad or wrong or vicious? In what do we find the viciousness of a vicious action?
3. What keeps Hume from complete moral relativism?

Is Hume a Skeptic?

On topic after topic, Hume sets himself against the majority tradition in the West. But just as Galilean and Newtonian science had overthrown traditional views about the nonhuman world, it should be no surprise that applying the same methods to human nature should have the same result. Aristotle had defined man as a rational animal; ever since, the emphasis had been on the "rational" aspect. In deciding what to believe, what to do, how to live, and how to judge, philosophers had looked to reason. The prerogatives of reason had lately been exalted in an extreme way by Descartes, who held that we shouldn't accept *anything* unless it was attested by rational insight or rational deduction. What Hume thinks he has shown is that *if this is the right rule*, then there is *virtually nothing* we should accept.

Let us review:

- The principles governing the way ideas succeed each other are nonrational principles—those of sheer mechanical association, analogous in their function to the principle of gravitation.
- All knowledge of anything beyond our perceptions depends on the relation of cause and effect, but our idea of causality is rooted in nonrational habits.
- We have no reason to believe in a substantial self; any such belief is a fiction foisted on us by detectable mistakes.
- We have no reason to believe in God.
- Our actions are governed by nonrational passions.
- Our liberty in action is not a matter of reason freeing us from the causal order, but simply a matter of nothing standing in the way of following our passions.
- Moral judgments, too, are founded on nonrational sentiments that are simply a given part of human nature.

In every area, Hume discovers the limits of reason. There is no good reason to believe in an objective causal order, in the existence of a material world independent of our perceptions, in God, in a soul or self, or in objective moral values. These certainly seem to be skeptical themes. Is Hume, then, a skeptic?

He makes distinctions among several kinds of skepticism. Let us examine two. There is Descartes' type, which Hume calls **"antecedent skepticism"** because it is supposed to come *before* any beliefs are deemed acceptable. Against this sort, he makes two points. First, you cannot *really* bring yourself to doubt everything. You find yourself believing in the reality of the world whether you want to or not. Second, if you could doubt everything, there would be no way back to rational belief; to get back, you would have to use your reasoning faculties, the competence of which is one of the things you are doubting.* So Hume dismisses

---

*Hume seems to be saying that we must be content with the things we are "taught by nature," as Descartes would say. See *Meditation III*. Is this criticism of Descartes correct? Compare also the critique of Descartes by C. S. Peirce, p. 597.

Cartesian "antecedent" skepticism as both unworkable and barren.

There is another kind of skepticism, however, which Hume thinks is quite useful. This is not an attempt to doubt everything in the futile hope of gaining something impossible to doubt, but an attempt to keep in mind "the strange infirmities of human understanding."

> The greater part of mankind are naturally apt to be affirmative and dogmatical in their opinions. . . . But could such dogmatical reasoners become sensible of the strange infirmities of human understanding, even in its most perfect state, and when most accurate and cautious in its determinations; such a reflection would naturally inspire them with more modesty and reserve, and diminish their fond opinion of themselves, and their prejudice against antagonists. . . . In general there is a degree of doubt, and caution, and modesty, which, in all kinds of scrutiny and decision, ought for ever to accompany a just reasoner. (*HU*, 207–208)

This **mitigated skepticism,** Hume says, makes for modesty and caution; it will "abate [the] pride" (*HU*, 208) of those who are haughty and obstinate. It will teach us the limitations of our human capacities and encourage us to devote our understanding, not to abstruse problems of metaphysics and theology, but to the problems of common life.

In sponsoring such modesty about our intellectual attainments, Hume reflects Enlightenment worries about the consequences of dogmatic attachments to creeds that have only private backing. And if reason is really as broken-backed as Hume says, then dogmatic attachment to what appears rational is just as worrisome. One of the virtues of his examination of human nature, he feels, is that it makes such dogmatism impossible.

There might be an opposite worry, however. Could the consistently skeptical conclusions of Hume's philosophy leave us paralyzed? Hume himself reports, in an introspective moment, that after pursuing his research for a while, he finds himself

> ready to reject all belief and reasoning, and [to] look upon no opinion even as more probable or likely than another. Where am I, or what? From what causes do I derive my existence, and to what condition shall I return? Whose favor shall I court, and whose anger must I dread? What beings surround me? and on whom have I any influence, or who have any influence on me? I am confounded with all these questions, and begin to fancy myself in the most deplorable condition imaginable, inviron'd with the deepest darkness, and utterly depriv'd of the use of every member and faculty. (*T*, I, 4, 7, 175)

Reason has no answer to these questions. Depressing indeed!

What is the solution?

> Most fortunately it happens, that since reason is incapable of dispelling these clouds, nature herself suffices to that purpose, and cures me of this philosophical melancholy and delirium, either by relaxing this bent of mind, or by some avocation, and lively impression of my senses, which obliterate all these chimeras. I dine, I play a game of back-gammon, I converse, and am merry with my friends; and when after three or four hours' amusement, I wou'd return to these speculations, they appear so cold, and strain'd, and ridiculous, that I cannot find in my heart to enter into them any farther. (*T*, I, 4, 7, 175)

We need not worry, he assures us, that the results of philosophical study will paralyze us by taking away all our convictions. "Nature," he says, "is always too strong for principle" (*HU*, 207). Custom and habit, those nonrational instincts that are placed in our natures, will ensure that we don't sit shivering in terror at our lack of certainty.

But Hume does not mean that we should cease to pursue philosophy. Indeed, his conviction that nothing is more useful than the science of human nature remains untouched. Only such a science can free us from the natural tendency toward dogmatism and superstition that plagues human society. Recalling his classification of all knowledge into the relation of ideas and matters of experience, Hume ends his *Enquiry Concerning Human Understanding* with these words:

> When we run over libraries, persuaded of these principles, what havoc must we make? If we take in hand any volume of school metaphysics, for instance; let us ask, *Does it contain any abstract reasoning concerning quantity or number?* No. *Does it contain*

any experimental reasoning concerning matter of fact and existence? No. Commit it then to the flames: For it can contain nothing but sophistry and illusion. (*HU*, 211)

Hume represents a kind of crisis point in modern philosophy. Can anyone build anything on the rubble he leaves behind?

1. What sort of skepticism does Hume criticize? What sort does he advocate?
2. What does Hume hope his philosophizing will accomplish? Does it do that for you?

FOR FURTHER THOUGHT

1. Both Descartes and Hume can be compared to Robinson Crusoe. Each tries to construct "a world" out of the resources available only to an isolated individual. Sketch the similarities and differences in their projects, noting the materials they have available and the tools with which they work.
2. Does Hume's view of human liberty leave room for *responsibility*? Compare Descartes on free will.
3. How would du Châtelet explain Hume's skeptical-sounding conclusions? What mistake would she say he made? How do the differences in their views on the foundations of human knowledge account for their disagreement on this point?

KEY WORDS

enlightenment	complex ideas
Newton	simple ideas
analysis	association
synthesis	relations of ideas
framing hypotheses	matters of fact
Émilie du Châtelet	a priori
Republic of Letters	constant conjunction
perceptions	necessary connection
impressions	cause
ideas	subjective

self	fact/value gap
determinism	is/ought problem
necessity	projections
liberty	sentiment
compatibilism	agreeable
naturalism	useful
argument from design	sympathy
a posteriori	antecedent skepticism
reason	mitigated skepticism
passion	

NOTES

1. Immanuel Kant, "An Answer to the Question: What Is Enlightenment?," in *Perpetual Peace and Other Essays*, trans. Ted Humphrey (Indianapolis, IN: Hackett, 1983), 41.
2. Kant, "What Is Enlightenment?," 44.
3. From Newton's *Principia Mathematica*, General Scholium to Book III, reproduced in John Herman Randall, *The Career of Philosophy* (New York: Columbia University Press, 1962), 1:579.
4. Quotations and page numbers from du Châtelet's works are from Émilie du Châtelet, *Selected Philosophy and Scientific Writings*, ed. Judith P. Zinsser, trans. Isabelle Bour and Judith P. Zinsser (Chicago: University of Chicago Press, 2009). Quotations from the *Discourse on Happiness* are marked *DH*; those from *Foundations of Physics* are marked *FP*.
5. We have benefited from the excellent study of Hume by Barry Stroud: *Hume* (London: Routledge and Kegan Paul, 1977).
6. References to Hume's works are as follows: *HU*: *Enquiry Concerning Human Understanding*, ed. Tom L. Beauchamp (Oxford: Oxford University Press, 1999).
   D: *Dialogues Concerning Natural Religion*, in *Principal Writings on Religion*, ed. J. C. A. Gaskin (Oxford: Oxford University Press, 1993), cited by part and page number.
   T: *A Treatise of Human Nature*, ed. David Fate Norton and Mary J. Norton (Oxford: Oxford University Press, 2000). Citations are by book, part, section, and page number.
   PM: *An Enquiry Concerning the Principles of Morals*, ed. Tom L. Beauchamp (Oxford: Oxford University Press, 1998).
7. Bertrand Russell, *A History of Western Philosophy* (New York: Simon and Schuster, 1945), 567.

CHAPTER
20

IMMANUEL KANT
Rehabilitating Reason (Within Strict Limits)

David Hume had published *A Treatise of Human Nature* at the youthful age of twenty-three, whereas Immanuel Kant (1724–1804) published the first of his major works, *The Critique of Pure Reason*, in 1781, when he was fifty-seven. He enters the great conversation rather late in life because it has taken him some time to understand the devastating critique of Hume, "that acute man."

> Since the beginning of metaphysics, . . . no event has occurred which could have been more decisive in respect of the fate of this science than the attack which David Hume made on it. (*P*, 64)[1]

> I freely admit: it was David Hume's remark that first, many years ago, interrupted my dogmatic slumber and gave a completely different direction to my enquiries. (*P*, 67)

Kant sets himself to solve what he calls "Hume's problem": whether the concept of cause is indeed objectively vacuous, a fiction that can be traced to a merely subjective and instinctive habit of human nature. We have seen the skeptical consequences Hume draws

from his analysis; these, we can imagine, are what wake Kant from his "dogmatic slumber."

Human thought seems naturally to recognize no limits. It moves easily and without apparent strain from bodies to souls, from life in this world to life after death, from material things to God. One aspect of Enlightenment thought is the acute consciousness of how *varied* thoughts become when they move out beyond the ground of experience—and yet how *certain* most people feel about their own views. This is the dogmatism (or superstition) that Hume tries to debunk. Stimulated by Hume, Kant, too, feels this is a problem. It is true that in mathematics we have clear examples of knowledge independent of experience. But it does not follow (as thinkers such as Plato suppose) that we can extend this knowledge indefinitely in a realm beyond experience. Kant uses a lovely image to make this point.*

---

*Plato believes that the nonsensible, purely intelligible world of Forms is not only knowable but also more intelligible than the world of experience and more real, too. See pp. 152–155.

The light dove, cleaving the air in her free flight, and feeling its resistance, might imagine that its flight would be still easier in empty space. It was thus that Plato left the world of the senses, as setting too narrow limits to the understanding, and ventured out beyond it on the wings of the ideas, in the empty space of the pure understanding. He did not observe that with all his efforts he made no advance—meeting no resistance that might, as it were, serve as a support upon which he could take a stand, to which he could apply his powers, and so set his understanding in motion. (*CPR*, 47)

Could the dove fly even better in empty space? No, it could not fly there at all; it absolutely depends on some "resistance" to fly. In the same way, Kant suggests, human thought needs a medium that supplies "resistance" to work properly. In a resistance-free environment, everything is equally possible (as long as formal contradiction is avoided), and the conflicts of dogmatic believers (philosophical, religious, or political) are inevitable.

Kant is convinced that Hume is right to pinpoint *experience* as the only medium within which reason can legitimately do its work. But Kant doubts that Hume has correctly understood experience. Why? Because Hume's analysis has an unacceptable consequence. We did not explicitly draw this consequence when discussing Hume (because he does not draw it). But if Hume is right, Newtonian science itself is basically an irrational and unjustified fiction.* Recall that for Hume *all* our knowledge of matters of fact beyond present perception and memory is founded on the relation of cause and effect. And causes are nothing more than projections onto a supposed objective world from a feeling in the mind.

Kant is convinced that in Newtonian science we do have rationally justified knowledge. And if Hume's examination of reason forces us to deny that we have this knowledge, something must be

wrong with Hume's analysis. What we need, Kant says, is a better **critique of reason**—a critique that will lay out its *structure*, explain its *relationship to its objects*, and delineate the *limits* within which it can legitimately work. Hume thinks that we need a science of human nature. Kant agrees, but he sets out to do a better job of it than Hume did.

Awakened from his dogmatic slumber, recognizing that, like the dove, he can no longer try to fly in empty space, Kant makes an absolutely revolutionary suggestion:

> Hitherto it has been assumed that all our knowledge must conform to objects. But all attempts to extend our knowledge of objects by establishing something in regard to them *a priori*, by means of concepts, have, on this assumption, ended in failure. We must therefore make trial whether we may not have more success in the tasks of metaphysics, if we suppose that objects must conform to our knowledge. . . . We should then be proceeding precisely on the lines of Copernicus' primary hypothesis. Failing of satisfactory progress in explaining the movements of the heavenly bodies on the supposition that they all revolved round the spectator, he tried whether he might not have better success if he made the spectator to revolve and the stars to remain at rest. A similar experiment can be tried in metaphysics, as regards the *intuition* of objects. (*CPR*, 22)

This requires some explanation. Nearly all previous philosophy (and science and common sense, too) has made a very natural assumption—as natural as the assumption that the heavenly bodies revolve around us. But perhaps it is just as wrong.

What is that assumption? It is that we acquire knowledge and truth when our thoughts "conform to objects." According to this assumption, objects are *there*, quite determinately *being* whatever they are, completely independent of our apprehension of them. To know them our beliefs must be brought to *correspond* to these independently existing things. Aristotle's classical definition of truth expresses this assumption perfectly: to say of what *is* that it is, and of what *is not* that it is not, is true.* The assumption

---

*You can see that Hume ends up exactly where Descartes fears to be, with science indistinguishable from a dream. To escape this fate, Descartes thinks you need to prove the existence of a nondeceptive God. But by undermining such proofs, Hume finds himself unable to escape from solipsism—except by joining a game of backgammon and ignoring the problem.

---

*See Aristotle's discussion of this on p. 187.

is a basic part of the representational theory of knowledge and perception (p. 372).

But Hume has argued that you can't think about representation in this way. Ideas that have their origin in experience (e.g., green, warm, solid) can go no further than experience. And ideas that don't (e.g., cause) are mere illusions. By using such concepts, we can know nothing at all about objects. All this follows if (1) we are acquainted only with the ideas in our experience, (2) objects are thought to exist independent of our experience, and (3) knowledge requires that we ascertain a correspondence between ideas and objects.*

But what if this assumption has it exactly backward? What if, to be an object at all, a thing has to conform to certain concepts? What if objects couldn't exist unless they were related to a rational mind, set in a context of rational concepts and principles? Think about the motion of the planets in their zigzag course across the sky. On the assumption that this motion is *real*, accurate understanding remains elusive. Copernicus denies this assumption and suggests that the motion is only *apparent*. On this new assumption, we are able to understand and predict the behavior of these objects.

Perhaps, Kant is suggesting, the same is true in the world of the intellect. Perhaps the objects of experience are (at least in part) the result of a construction by the rational mind. If so, they have no reality independent of that construction. Like the apparent motions of the planets, the objects of our experience are merely apparent, not independently real. If this is so, it may well be that concepts such as causation, which cannot be *abstracted* from experience (the lesson of Hume), still *apply* to experience, simply because objects that are *not* structured by that concept are *inconceivable*. The suggestion is that the rational mind has a certain structure, and whatever is knowable by such a mind must necessarily be known in terms of that structure. This structure is not derived from the objects known; it is *imposed* on them—but not arbitrarily, because the very idea of an object not so structured makes no sense.

This is Kant's **Copernican revolution** in philosophy. To the details of this novel way of thinking we now turn.

Critique

If we are going to take seriously this possibility that objects are partially constituted by the rational mind, we must examine how that constitution takes place. We need to peer reflectively behind the scenes and catch a glimpse of the productive machinery at work—at the *processes* involved in knowing anything at all. A prior question, of course, is whether we *can* know anything at all, but Kant thinks that Newton's science has definitely settled that question. Assuming, then, that a rational mind can have some knowledge, we want to ask, How does it manage that? We need to engage in what Kant calls "critique." A "critical" philosophy is not one that criticizes, in the carping, censorious way where "nothing is ever right." *Critique* is the attempt to get behind knowledge claims and ask, What makes them possible?

The objects of human knowledge seem to fall into four main classes. We can see what Kant is up to if we frame a question with respect to each of these classes.

1. How is *mathematics* possible?
2. How is *natural science* possible?
3. How is *metaphysics* possible?
4. How is *morality* possible?

These are, in Kant's sense, "critical" questions. We are not going to develop mathematics, physics, metaphysics, or morality. But in each case we are going to look at the rational foundations on which these disciplines rest. What is it, for instance, about human reason that makes it possible to develop mathematics? What *structure*, *capacities*, and *concepts* must reason have for it to be *able* to do mathematics?

These are *reflective questions*, which together constitute a *critique of reason*, a critical examination of the way a rational mind works. Kant also

---

*Montaigne compares the problem to that of a man who does not know Socrates and is presented with a portrait of him. How can he tell whether it resembles Socrates?

calls this kind of investigation **transcendental.*** A *transcendental inquiry* reaches back into the activities of the mind and asks how it produces its results. If this kind of investigation succeeds, we'll know what the powers of reason are—and what they are not. We can, Kant thinks, determine the *limits* of rational knowledge. And if we can determine both the capacities and the limitations of human reason, we may be able to escape both of those evils between which philosophy has so often swung: *dogmatism* on the one hand and *skepticism* on the other. From Kant's point of view, these extremes are well illustrated by Descartes and Hume, respectively.

---

1. What is the problem with the *representational theory of knowledge and perception* that Kant thinks can be resolved by imitating Copernicus? How does a "Copernican turn" help?
2. What does a critique of reason try to uncover? In what sense will the answers be transcendental?

Judgments

Because all our claims to know are expressed in the form of judgments, the first task is to clarify the different kinds of judgments there are. Hume had divided our knowledge into relations of ideas and matters of fact.† Kant agrees that this is roughly right, but not precise enough. Hume's distinction runs together two quite different kinds of consideration. (1) There is an *epistemological* question involved: Does a bit of knowledge rest on experience or not? (2) There is also a *semantic* question: How do the meanings of the words we use to express that knowledge relate to each other? Kant sorts these matters out, and the result is a classification of judgments into *four* groups rather than into Hume's two.

1. Epistemological
   1a. A judgment is **a priori** when it can be known to be true without any reference to experience. "Seven plus five equals twelve" is an example.
   1b. A judgment is **a posteriori** when we must appeal to experience to determine its truth or falsity. For instance, "John F. Kennedy was assassinated" cannot be known independent of experience.

2. Semantic
   2a. A judgment is **analytic** when its denial yields a contradiction. Here is an example Kant gives: "All bodies are extended." This is analytic because the predicate "extended" is already included as part of the subject, "bodies." To say that there is some body that is *not* extended is, in effect, to claim there can be some extended thing that is not extended. And that is contradictory. If an analytic judgment is true, it is necessarily true. The opposite of an analytic judgment is not possible. Since it is analytic that every father has a child, it is not even logically possible that there should be a father without a child. Thus, every father necessarily has a child.
   2b. A judgment is **synthetic** when it does more than simply explicate or analyze a concept. Here are some examples: "Every event has a cause," "Air has weight," and "John F. Kennedy was assassinated." Consider the first example. The concept *having a cause* is not part of the concept *being an event*. This is something Hume teaches us.* So it is not contradictory, though it may be false, to say of some event that it has no cause. The opposite of every synthetic judgement is possibly true.

---

*The term "transcendental" must be carefully distinguished from the similar term "transcendent." See p. 480.
†Hume's discussion of these is found on pp. 445–446.

*Recall Hume's claim that "all events seem entirely loose and separate." Neither experience nor reason, he claims, ever discloses that necessary "connexion" that might link them inseparably together. See p. 450.

"Two things fill the mind with ever new and increasing admiration and awe . . . the starry heavens above me and the moral law within me."

—Immanuel Kant

These two pairs can be put together to give us four possibilities:

- *Analytic a priori*: "All bodies are extended." This is analytic, as we have seen, because "extended" is part of the definition of "body." It is a priori because we don't have to examine our experience of bodies to know it is true; all we need is to understand the meanings of the terms "body" and "extended."
- *Analytic a posteriori*: This class seems empty; if the test for analyticity is examining a judgment's denial for contradiction, it seems clear that we do not also have to examine experience. Every analytic judgment must be a priori.
- *Synthetic a posteriori*: Here belong most of our judgments about experience, from particular

judgments (e.g., "The water in the tea kettle is boiling") to general laws (e.g., "Water always boils at 100°C at sea level").

- *Synthetic a priori*: This is a puzzling and controversial class of judgments. If we were to know such a judgment as true, we would have to be able to know it quite independent of experience. This means that if such a judgment is true, it is true no matter what our experience shows us. Even if the events of experience were organized in a completely different way, a true judgment of this kind would remain true. And yet it is *not* true because it is analytic; its denial expresses a logical possibility.

We can represent these types in a matrix:

	A priori	*A posteriori*
Analytic	"Every mother has a child."	✕
Synthetic	"?"	"There is a Waterloo in both Iowa and Wisconsin."

There is something very odd about synthetic a priori judgments. Consider a judgment that is about experience. Suppose that it is synthetic, but that we can know it a priori. Because it is synthetic, its opposite is (from a logical point of view) a real possibility. And yet we can know—without appealing to experience—that this possibility is never realized! How can this be?

Kant believes that the solution to the dilemmas of past philosophy lies precisely in the recognition that we possess synthetic a priori judgments. It is his Copernican revolution in philosophy that makes this recognition possible. Think: On the assumption that objects are realities independent of our knowing them, it would be crazy to suppose that we could know them without experiencing them in some way; our thoughts about them would be one thing, the objects something quite different;

and they could vary independently.* What could possibly guarantee that things would match our thoughts a priori? On the traditional correspondence assumption, then, a priori knowledge that is synthetic would be impossible.

But suppose that objects *are* objects only because they are structured in certain ways by the mind in the very act of knowing them. Then it is plausible to think that there might be *principles* of that structuring and that some of these principles might be synthetic. And those principles could be known a priori—independent of the objects they are structuring. So if Kant's Copernican revolution makes sense, there will be a priori synthetic principles for every domain of objects.

Kant's examples of such principles may surprise you. He takes the following to be synthetic a priori:

- all the judgments of mathematics and geometry;
- in natural science, such judgments as "Every event has a cause";
- in metaphysics, "There is a God," and "The soul is a simple substance, distinct from the body";
- in morality, the rule that we should not treat others merely as means to our own ends.

This is not to say we *know* all these judgments or that they are all true. That remains to be seen. But if you examine them, you should be able to see that they are all examples of judgments that would have to be known a priori (i.e., not from experience), if at all. And examination should also confirm, Kant thinks, that they are all synthetic. None of them is true simply in virtue of how the terms are related to each other.

Kant wants to understand how mathematics, natural science, metaphysics, and morality are possible. In the light of his Copernican revolution, we can see that he is asking how the rational mind structures its objects into the objects of mathematics, natural science, metaphysics, and morality. Implicit in the foundations of all these disciplines, Kant thinks, are some judgments that do not arise out of experience but *prescribe* how the objects of experience *must be*. All four of these areas are

constituted by synthetic a priori judgments. The objects we encounter are—in part—*constructions*. And these judgments are *principles for the construction of objects*.

Kant sometimes calls a priori judgments "pure." By this, he means that they are not "contaminated" by experience. We can now restate his questions with a transcendental twist:

1. How is *pure* mathematics possible?
2. How is *pure* natural science possible?
3. How is *pure* metaphysics possible?
4. How is *pure* morality possible?

Let's examine his answers.

---

1. Can you give examples of your own for each of the four types of judgment?
2. Explain the idea of a synthetic a priori judgment, showing clearly both its semantic and its epistemological aspects.
3. What makes a priori synthetic judgments puzzling?

Geometry, Mathematics, Space, and Time

It would be useful to have a criterion by which we could distinguish a priori knowledge from a posteriori knowledge. Kant suggests that there are two tests we can use: **necessity** and **universality.**

> Experience teaches us that a thing is so and so, but not that it cannot be otherwise. First, then, if we have a proposition which in being thought is thought as *necessary*, it is an *a priori* judgment. . . . Secondly, experience never confers on its judgments true or strict, but only assumed and comparative *universality*, through induction. . . . Necessity and strict universality are thus sure criteria of *a priori* knowledge, and are inseparable from one another. (*CPR*, 43–44)

As Hume has taught us, necessity cannot be discovered by means of experience; as far as experience tells us, all events are "entirely loose and separate." Further, because experience is limited in extent, it cannot guarantee that a proposition is universally true (i.e., true everywhere and at all times). It follows that if we find a judgment that is either

---

*Compare Ockham's reflections on God's omnipotence, pp. 336–337.

necessarily true or universally true, we can be sure that it does not have its justification in experience. Such a judgment must be a priori.

Mathematical truths are both necessary and universal. They are, therefore, clear examples of a priori judgments. But are they analytic or synthetic?

> One might indeed think at first that the proposition 7 + 5 + 12 is a merely analytic proposition, which follows according to the principle of contradiction from the concept of a sum of seven and five. But if we look more closely, we find that the concept of the sum of 7 and 5 contains nothing further than the unification of the two numbers into a single number, and in this we do not in the least think what this single number may be which combines the two . . . and though I may analyze my concept of such a possible sum as long as I please, I shall never find the twelve in it. We have to go outside these concepts by resorting to the intuition which corresponds to one of them, our five fingers for instance . . . and thus add to the concept of seven, one by one, the units of five given in intuition. . . .
>
> Nor is any principle of pure geometry analytic. That the straight line between two points is the shortest is a synthetic proposition. My concept of the straight contains nothing of magnitude but only a quality. The concept of the shortest is therefore wholly an addition, and cannot be drawn by any analysis from the concept of the straight line. Intuition, by means of which alone the synthesis is possible, must therefore be called in here to help. (*P*, 74)

Hume suggests that the truths of mathematics are simply matters of how ideas are related to each other—that they are analytic and can be known by appeal to the principle of contradiction. Kant argues that this is not so. For "seven plus five equals twelve" to be analytic, the concept "twelve" would have to be included in the concept "seven plus five." But all that concept tells us, if Kant is right, is that two numbers are being added. It does not, of itself, tell us what the sum is.

What can tell us what the sum is? Only some **intuition,** Kant says.* An intuition is not anything mysterious or occult. By "intuition" Kant simply means the presentation of some sensible object to the mind, such as our five fingers. We must "add successively" the units presented in the intuition: We count, one finger at a time. Knowing that seven plus five equals twelve is a *process*. We *construct* mathematics by inscribing it on a background composed of objects or sets of objects.

But we need to understand these objects more clearly. If mathematics were only about the objects of experience, it could be neither necessary nor universal. We might know that these five oranges and those seven oranges happen to make twelve oranges. But we wouldn't know that *all* such groups of oranges (examined or not) make twelve and *must* make twelve. If we know this with necessity and universality (as we surely do), the objects that justify mathematical truths must themselves be known in a purely a priori manner. There must be *pure* intuitions, forms of *pure sensibility*. But what could they be?

> Now space and time are the two intuitions on which pure mathematics grounds all its cognitions and judgements. . . . Geometry is grounded on the pure intuition of space. Arithmetic forms its own concepts of numbers by successive addition of units in time. (*P*, 90)

Think about **space** a moment. According to our ordinary experience, space is filled with things. But suppose you "think away" all these things— all the household goods, the clothes, the houses, the earth itself, sun, moon, and stars. Have you thought away space? Kant thinks not. (Newton would have agreed.) But you have "subtracted" everything *empirical*—that is, everything that gives particular content to our experience. All that is left is a kind of container, a form or structure, in which empirical things can be put. But, since you have gotten rid of everything empirical, what is left is *pure*. And it can be known a priori. Geometry is the science of this pure intuition of space.*

---

*Kant is the ancestor of a school in the philosophy of mathematics that still has distinguished adherents. The viewpoint is called "intuitionism" but might more accurately be termed "constructivism."

---

*Kant is referring to Euclidean geometry, of course. Various non-Euclidean geometries were discovered—or constructed—in the nineteenth century.

But what is the status of the intuition itself? Could space simply be one more (rather abstract and esoteric) object independent of our perception of it? Kant doesn't think so. And the reason is this: The truths of geometry, like those of mathematics, are *necessary*. If you ask, "How *likely* is it that any given straight line is the shortest distance between its end points?" you demonstrate that you haven't understood geometry! Moreover, that a straight line in a plane is the shortest distance between two points is something we know to be universally true. If space were an object independent of our minds, knowing this would be impossible. We would have to say that this is true *for all the spaces we have examined*, but beyond that—who knows? Geometers do not proceed in this manner. They neither make experiments concerning space nor suppose that unexamined space could have a different structure. Yet geometry is the science of space. How can this be?

The explanation must be this: Space is not something "out there" to be discovered; space is a form of the mind itself. It is a pure intuition providing a "structure" into which all our more determinate perceptions *must fit*. When you handle an apple, your experience is constituted on the one hand by sensations (color, texture, weight, and so on) and on the other hand by a structure into which these sensations fit (the pure intuition of space). The apple is not an object entirely independent of our perception of it. Part of that perception is constituted by the intuition of space, which we do not *abstract from* the experience, but *bring to* the experience.

This has an important consequence. We cannot experience the apple as it is in itself, independent of our perception of it. Why not? Because part of what it is to *be* an apple is to be in space; and space is an aspect of our experience that comes from the side of the subject. So we know the apple as it *appears to us*, not the apple as it *is in itself*. What goes for the apple goes for the entire world. We can only know how things *appear*.

Things are given to us as objects of our senses situated outside us, but of what they may be in themselves we know nothing; we only know their appearances, i.e. the representations which they bring about in us when they affect our senses.

Consequently I do indeed admit that there are bodies outside us, i.e. things which, although wholly unknown to us, i.e. as to what they may be in themselves, we know through the representations which their influence on our sensibility provides for us, and to which we give the name of bodies. This word therefore merely means the appearance of that for us unknown but nonetheless actual object. (*P*, 95)*

Just as space is the pure intuition that makes geometry possible, **time** is the pure intuition that makes mathematics possible. Geometrical figures are constructed on the pure (spatial) intuition in which *external* objects are experienced. Numbers and their relations are constructed on the pure (temporal) intuition in which *any* objects (including mental events) are experienced. An elementary example of constructing in time is counting, where we construct one number *after* another.

Kant has now answered his first question. Pure geometry and mathematics are possible because their objects—space and time—are not independent of the mind that knows them; space and time are pure forms of sensible intuition. He has shown, moreover, that geometry and mathematics essentially involve judgments that are synthetic (because they are constructive) and a priori (because they are necessary and universal).

Because experience is always in time—and in space as well if it is of external objects—it is a *product* of contributions from two sides: the objective and the subjective. Nowhere can we know things as they are in themselves. It is not as Descartes thinks, that we know things-in-themselves in a confused and inadequate way that can be continually improved. We do not know them at all! Of the objects we do experience, we can know a priori just what we ourselves, as rational minds, necessarily supply in experiencing them.

---

*Note that this conclusion squares with Locke's belief about the unknowability of substance. Here, however, that conviction is set in a much more rigorous framework and is much more adequately argued for. See pp. 418–419 for Locke on substance.

1. Explain why Kant thinks that mathematical and geometrical propositions are both a priori and synthetic.
2. What is Kant's argument that space and time must be "pure" or a priori forms of intuition?
3. How do Kant's reflections on space and time lead to the conclusion that we can know things only as they appear to us, not as they are in themselves?

Common Sense, Science, and the A Priori Categories

Pure mathematics does not exhaust our knowledge. We know many things in the course of our ordinary life and through Newtonian science. What is the application of Kant's Copernican revolution in these spheres? One implication is that whatever common sense and science may reveal, they cannot penetrate the veil of our pure sensible intuitions, which structure all possible objects in space and time. Our knowledge will concern how these things *appear* to us, not how they are in themselves.

To deal with his second question, how pure natural science is possible, Kant needs to clarify a distinction between two powers of the mind. He calls them **sensibility** and **understanding.** The former is a passive power, the ability to receive impressions. The latter is an active power, the power to construct a representation of objects using concepts.

A **concept,** Kant tells us, is a kind of rule for operating on intuitions. In itself, it needn't have any sensuous content at all. To have a concept is to have an *ability*. And in the use of concepts the understanding is *active*, not passive. Think of the concept *viper*. To possess this concept is to be able to sort snakes into vipers and nonvipers. Having the concept is *not* having an image or a Lockean abstract idea in your mind, as the empiricists believed. To have the concept is to be able to use a rule for dividing the snakish parts of our experience into categories or classes of things. Kant says,

> Our knowledge springs from two fundamental sources of the mind; the first is the capacity of receiving representations (receptivity for impressions), the second is the power of knowing an

object through these representations. . . . Through the first an object is *given* to us, through the second the object is *thought*. . . . Intuition and concepts constitute, therefore, the elements of all our knowledge, so that neither concepts without an intuition in some way corresponding to them, nor intuition without concepts, can yield knowledge. Both may be either pure or empirical. When they contain sensation (which presupposes the actual presence of the object), they are empirical. When there is no mingling of sensation with the representation, they are pure. (*CPR*, 92)

Kant's general term for the contents of the mind is **representation.** He is here telling us that our representations can be of several different kinds: pure or empirical, intuitive or conceptual. In fact, this gives us a matrix of four possibilities; let us set them out with some examples:

Representations

	Pure	Empirical
Intuitions (from sensibility)	Space and time	Sensations of red, warm, hard, etc.
Concepts (from understanding)	Straight, cause, substance, God, the soul	Cherry pie, otter, water, the sun, unicorn, etc.

We have not determined whether all these representations actually *represent* something, but we know that any concept that does represent something will do so in tandem with some intuition. For "neither concepts without an intuition . . . nor intuition without concepts, can yield knowledge." The dove cannot fly in empty space.

Kant has contrasted sensibility with understanding, intuitions with concepts. But he is also convinced that they must work together.

> To neither of these powers may a preference be given over the other. Without sensibility no object would be given to us, without understanding no object would be thought. Thoughts without content

are empty, intuitions without concepts are blind. It is, therefore, just as necessary to make our concepts sensible, that is, to add the object to them in intuition, as to make our intuitions intelligible, that is, to bring them under concepts. . . . The understanding can intuit nothing, the senses can think nothing. Only through their union can knowledge arise. (*CPR*, 93)

In addition to the *pure* intuitions that can be known a priori (i.e., space and time), we have *empirical* intuitions—what Locke calls "sensations" and Hume calls "impressions." Kant thinks of sensations as the *matter* of sensible objects. We can illustrate by imagining a square cut out of wood. The spatial properties of a square (four equal straight lines, four right angles) can be known a priori, quite independent of its color or texture. But it can only be some *particular* square if it is either red or some other color, either smooth or less than smooth. Our sensations determine which it is. They provide the "filling" or content for the purely formal intuition of a square.*

Are concepts like this, too? Do we have pure concepts, as well as empirical concepts? Well, suppose there were concepts that we *necessarily* made use of whenever we thought of any object at all. Remembering that necessity is one of the marks of the a priori, we would have to conclude that we have pure or a priori concepts. This is, in fact, just what Kant thinks; he is convinced that we make use of pure concepts all the time. In fact, these concepts—these *a priori rules*—do for our understanding exactly what the pure intuitions of space and time do for sensibility: They give it structure and organization. They make it possible for us to experience *objects* and not just a chaos of impressions.

Just as there are empirical intuitions, there are empirical concepts. Just as there are pure intuitions, there are pure concepts.† Like sensibility,

the understanding brings something of its own to experience. In neither dimension is the mind just "white paper" on which experience writes, as Locke claimed. It is this rich source of structure in our experience, this transcendental organizing power, that Kant wants to uncover through his critique of reason.

The question then forces itself upon us: What concepts do we have that *apply* to objects but are not *derived* from them? We are searching for a set of concepts we use necessarily in thinking of an object. These will be a priori concepts. Kant calls them **categories** because they will supply the most general characteristics of things: the characteristics it takes to qualify as a thing or object at all.*

We discover these concepts through critical philosophy, which is reflective or transcendental in nature. So we need to reflect on our thinking, to see whether there are some features of our thinking about objects that must be present no matter what the object is.

Let's begin by asking, What is it to think of an *object*, anyway? Consider the contrast between these two judgments:

A: "It seems as if there is a heavy book before me."
B: "The book before me is heavy."

What is the difference? In a certain sense, they both have the same content: book, heavy, before me. Yet there is a crucial difference. *B* is a judgment about an *object*, whereas *A* pulls back from making a judgment about that object. *A* is a judgment, not about the book, but about *my perception*; it has only what Kant calls "subjective validity." *B*, however, is a judgment about *the book*. It is an "objective"

---

*The pattern of thought here should remind you of the distinction between matter and form in Aristotle and Aquinas; *sensation* plays the role of matter, and *concepts* play the role of form. Though there is a structural similarity, there is a fundamental difference: In Kant both members of the pair have their being only *relative to a mind*. In this Kant shows his debt to Locke and his successors. And in this Kant is characteristically "modern."

†Check the examples again in the preceding chart.

---

*You can see that Kant is embarked on a project similar to that of Aristotle: to discover the characteristics of being qua being. Aristotle also produces a set of categories, displaying the most general ways in which something (anything) can *be*. (See p. 185.) Kant goes about the project in a roughly similar way: He looks at the language in which we talk about objects. Between Kant and Aristotle, however, there stands the Kantian Copernican revolution—and that makes a tremendous difference. Kant's "categories," the universal and necessary features of objects, originate in the structure of *thinking* about those objects. They apply not to being *as such*, but to being *as it is knowable* by rational minds such as ours— that is, to appearance.

judgment; whether true or false, it makes a claim that an object has a certain characteristic.

What makes this difference? It can't be the empirical concepts involved, because "book" and "heavy" and "before me" are the same in *A* and *B*. Nor can the difference be anything derived from my experience in the two cases, since my experience may be exactly the same in each. So the difference must be an a priori one. It seems to be a difference in the *manner* in which the judgments are made, or in the *form* of the judgments. If we can isolate the feature that distinguishes *B* from *A*, we will have put our finger on the contribution the *understanding* makes to our experience of an objective world.

In this case, Kant tells us, the distinguishing feature is that in *B* we are thinking in terms of a **substance** together with its **properties.** These concepts are not derived from what is given in my sensations (since the sensations are exactly the same in *A*). These concepts are brought to the experience by the understanding in the very form of thinking of the book as an object. The book is a substance that has the property of being heavy. But this means that the concepts "substance" and "property" are a priori concepts—and that is just what we are looking for.

The point is this: In thinking of an objective world, thinking necessarily takes certain forms of organization. One of these forms consists of a kind of logical function or rule: *Structure experience in terms of substances having properties.** Unless thoughts take this logical form, Kant says, a world of objects simply cannot be conceived at all. Without the application of these a priori concepts, there can be no objective world for common sense or science to know. So a world of objects is, like the world of sensible intuitions, a composite. There is an empirical aspect to it (expressed in empirical concepts such as "book" and "heavy"). But there is also an a priori aspect to it (expressed in nonempirical concepts such as "substance" and "property"). Experience of an objective world requires both.

Kant works out an entire system of such a priori concepts or categories. He thinks he can do this by canvassing all the possible forms objective judgments can take. And he thinks he can do that because he assumes that logic (the science of the forms of judgment) is a closed and finished science; no essential changes, he observes, have occurred in it since Aristotle.* For each possible form of judgment, he finds an a priori concept that we bring to bear on sensations. In each case, the application of this concept produces an a priori characteristic of the objective world of our experience. Kant identifies twelve such categories—twelve general ways we know that any objective world *must* be. The fact that the world of our experience must be structured in terms of substances-having-properties is just one of these ways.

The a priori concept of substance gets an opportunity, so to speak, to apply to experience because sensations come grouped together in various ways in *space*. Considered just as sensations, my experience of what I call the book hangs together in a certain way; the color, texture, shape, and so on move together across my field of vision. If this were not so, I could scarcely unify these sensations under one concept and experience one object, the book. In a similar way, sensations also appear *successively in time*. This provides a foothold for another of the categories: **causation.**

We have examined Hume's powerful argument that our idea of cause is not an empirical idea—that it is not abstracted from our experience.† Because it contains the notion of a necessary connection between cause and effect, Hume concludes that the idea is a fiction, a kind of illusion produced in us by custom. So we cannot really know that objects are related to each other by cause and effect.

But what if there simply couldn't *be* objects at all unless they were set in causal relations with each other? What if the concept of causation (like the concept of substance) is a necessary aspect of any world of objects? This is the possibility that Kant's Copernican revolution explores. If nothing could *be* objective for us without *appearing* in a context of

---

*To see the importance of this rule, contrast it with the way that Buddhist philosophers understand the world around us. See p. 41.

*We now know that Kant's list of the possible forms of judgments is not, as he thinks, complete. Logic has gone through a revolution since Kant's time.

†Review this argument on pp. 447–451.

causal relations, we could know that every event has a cause—and avoid Hume's skeptical conclusions.

Can Kant convince us that this is so? Again Kant shows us that there is a difference between judgments that refer only to our perceptions and objective judgments. It may *seem* to us that one thing follows necessarily upon another, but once we affirm the idea of a world of objects, we are committed to there being a rule that it *must* be so. Suppose that something unusual happens. What will we do? We will search for its cause. Will we allow the possibility that this event had no cause? Certainly not. But what if we search and search and do not discover its cause? Will we finally conclude that it has no cause? Of course not. No degree of failure in finding its cause would ever convince us that it has no cause. *Every* event has a cause.

How do we know that? We have seen that it is not analytic. Nor can our confidence be based on an induction from past successes in finding causes, for as Hume argues, that would never justify our certainty that even unexamined events must have causes. If we know that every event has a cause, we know it because part of the very idea of an objective world is that events in it are structured by rules of succession we don't control. There *could not be* an objective world that was not organized by cause and effect.

The concept of causality *does* apply to the world we experience—not because we discover it there, but because we bring it with us to the experience.

> This complete solution to the Humean problem . . . thus rescues their a priori origin for the pure concepts of the understanding, and their validity for the universal laws of nature . . . but in such a way that it limits their use to experience only. (*P,* 117–118)

Let us sum up. The principle that every event has a cause is, as we have seen, synthetic (the concept of causation is not included in the concept of an event but is added to it). And Hume is right that the causal principle cannot be known a posteriori, from experience. But we know that the principle applies universally and necessarily to all experience. We know that because, as Kant says, experience is derived from it. The principle that every event has a cause is, then, one of the *synthetic a priori* judgments. Such purely rational, nonempirical

principles, Kant believes, lie at the root of both commonsense knowledge and Newtonian science.

This, Kant says, is how science of nature is possible. It is possible because nature itself (the objective world that is there to be known) is partially constituted by the concepts and principles that a rational mind must use in understanding it. We know a priori that nature is made up of substances-having-properties, though only through experience can we know which substances have what properties. We know a priori that the world is a causally ordered whole, though only through experience can we know which particular events cause what other events. Science, together with its pure or a priori part, is possible only because it is the knowledge of an objective world that is not independent of our minds. Natural science is possible only on the basis of Kant's Copernican revolution.

Let us just remind ourselves once more of the consequence: We have, and can have, no knowledge whatever about things as they are "in themselves." Do things-in-themselves—independent of how we know them—occupy space? *We have no idea.* Are they located in time, so that one event really does happen after another? *We have no idea.* Are there things (substances) at all? Does one event really cause another? *We have no idea.* Our knowledge is solely about the way things appear to us.

But, we must add, it does not follow that our knowledge is in any way illusory. It is not like a dream or a fancy of our imagination. The distinction, in fact, between illusion and reality is one drawn by us *within* this objective world of appearance—not *between* it and something else. We are not capable of knowing anything *more real* than the spatiotemporal world of our experience, structured as it is by the categories of the pure understanding. This world may be "transcendentally ideal" (that is, its basic features are not independent of the knowing mind), but it is *empirically real.*

This, perhaps, needs a bit more explanation.

Phenomena and Noumena

"Thoughts without content are empty," Kant says, and "intuitions without concepts are blind" (*CPR,* 93). Thoughts are made up of concepts united in

BARUCH SPINOZA

Expelled with curses from the Amsterdam synagogue in 1656, Baruch Spinoza (1632–1677) has been characterized both as a "God-intoxicated man" and as an atheistic naturalist. Fundamentally, he is one of the most rationalistic of philosophers. In his major work, *The Ethics*, Spinoza aims to attain a secure happiness by approaching as closely as possible an adequate understanding of absolutely everything.

He defines "substance" as what exists "in itself" and requires nothing beyond itself for its being. He argues that substance must be infinite and that there cannot be two such substances (otherwise each would limit the other and defeat the infinity). So there can be but one substance, which can equally well be called God or Nature. This means that the individuals of our experience—from stones to ourselves—are not substances, but modifications of the one infinite substance.

Mind and body are not substances, as Descartes thought, but attributes under which the one substance can be conceived. In fact, for every natural body, there is an idea; the idea corresponding to a human body is what we call the mind. It follows that every bodily change is a mental change and vice versa.

Because everything that happens is a necessary expression of the immutable divine nature, there is no free will in the ordinary sense. Freedom, Spinoza claims, is just the power to act from one's own nature, unconstrained by anything outside oneself. God (or Nature), then, is the only completely free being, since God is the only thing for which there is nothing outside itself.

We, for the most part, are in "bondage," since we are controlled by emotions (desire, love, hate) that we passively suffer; emotions are *caused* in us. But our freedom expands as we act from "adequate ideas" that are part of our own nature. Since the only truly adequate ideas are those in God's mind, we move toward freedom by the intellectual love of God, coming to see the necessities of the world as God sees them. Such knowledge is the source of power to act (rather than react), of virtue, and of joy. Thus we can approximate the blessed life of God.

---

various ways. But unless those concepts are given a content through some intuition, either pure (as in geometry) or empirical (as in physics), they are "empty"—sheer rules that for all we know may apply to nothing. They provide us with no knowledge. However, merely having an intuition of space, or of blue-and-solid, provides no knowledge either. Intuitions without concepts are "blind." To know, or to "see" the truth, we must have concepts that are applied to some matter.

Kant insists on this point again and again, for we are

> subject to an illusion from which it is difficult to escape. The categories are not, as regards their origin, grounded in sensibility, . . . and they seem, therefore, to allow of an application extending beyond all objects of the senses. (*CPR*, 266)

We have ideas of "substance," for example, and "cause." And it seems there is no barrier to applying them even beyond the boundaries of **possible experience.** In fact, nearly all previous philosophers think we can do that! Plato, for example, is convinced that reality is composed of *substances* (the Forms) that cannot be sensed but are purely intelligible. Descartes asks about the *cause* of his idea of God. One of the assumptions of traditional metaphysics is that these concepts *can* take us beyond the sphere of experience.* But, if Kant is right, these concepts

---

*Notice how Kant has turned completely upside down Plato's claim that knowledge is restricted to the purely intelligible world of Forms. For Kant, this realm beyond any possible sensory experience cannot be known at all; what we can know is the changing world of the senses, about which Plato thinks we can have only opinions. Here we have yet another example of the radical consequences of modern science for traditional epistemology and metaphysics; for Kant's confidence in knowledge of the sensory world rests ultimately on the achievement of Newton.

GOTTFRIED WILHELM VON LEIBNIZ

Mathematician, physicist, historian, theologian, and diplomat, Gottfried Wilhelm von Leibniz (1646–1714) wrote voluminously; among his most philosophically important works are *Discourse on Metaphysics* (1686) and *Monadology* (1714).

As an inventor of calculus, Leibniz was poised to make use of the principles of continuity and infinity in his philosophical work. He objected to the purely quantitative, geometrical account of matter (as extension) given by Descartes and Spinoza. Sheer extension does not account for resistance, solidity, and impenetrability, he argued, so there must be some real qualitative thing to be extended. A new concept of substance was needed, and Leibniz offered one: A substance is a being capable of action. This makes reality intrinsically dynamic; the ultimate substances are points of activity (force), each with an inherent tendency toward motion (in his view, rest is just infinitesimally small movement). He called these simple substances *monads*.

Though each monad is intrinsically simple, each has infinitely many properties—namely, the ways it is related to each of the infinitely many other monads. So each monad, in a way, mirrors or reflects the entire universe; in certain monads, this reflection is perception and the mind. If you knew any monad completely, you would know everything.

> "Flower in the crannied wall, . . .
>   if I could understand
> What you are, root and all, and all in all,
>   I should know what God and man is."
>   —*Alfred, Lord Tennyson (1809–1892)*

Because each monad mirrors all the others, a change in one would necessitate a change in all the others. The sum total of all the substances that are possible along with a given monad—mirrored in it—constitute a *possible world*. There are many possible worlds, many families of possible monads; this actual world is just one of the possibilities. Contrary to Spinoza, then, Leibniz held that the actual universe does not exist of necessity.

Why is *this* world, of all the many possible worlds, the actual one? We can figuratively imagine God—the one being that exists necessarily—contemplating all the possible worlds and choosing one to actualize. He would clearly choose the "best" one, the one most like God himself. This would be the universe that combines the most actuality (the richest variety of content) with the greatest simplicity of laws. In that sense, Leibniz believed, we live in the best of all possible worlds.

are nothing but *forms of thought*, which contain the merely logical faculty of uniting *a priori* in one consciousness the manifold given in intuition; and apart, therefore, from the only intuition that is possible for us, they have even less meaning than the pure sensible forms [space and time]. (*CPR*, 266)

The categories, Kant claims, cannot be used apart from sensible intuitions to give us knowledge of objects. Why not? Because they are merely "forms of thought." Compare them to mathematical functions, such as x^2. Until some number is given as x, we have no object. If a content for x is supplied, say two or three, then an object is specified—in these cases the numbers four or nine. The categories of substance, cause, and the rest are similar. They are merely operators, the function of which is to unite "in one consciousness the manifold given in intuition." If a certain manifold of sensations is given, our possession of the concept "substance" allows us to produce the thought of a book; a different manifold of sensations produces the thought of a printing press; and the category of "causation" allows us to think a causal relation between the two. Objects are the result of the application of the categories as operators to some sensible material.

As we have seen, a concept is just a formal rule for structuring some material. The material is supplied by our intuitions. Without the sensible intuitions, there are no *objects*. But it can *seem* as though there are. This is the illusion.

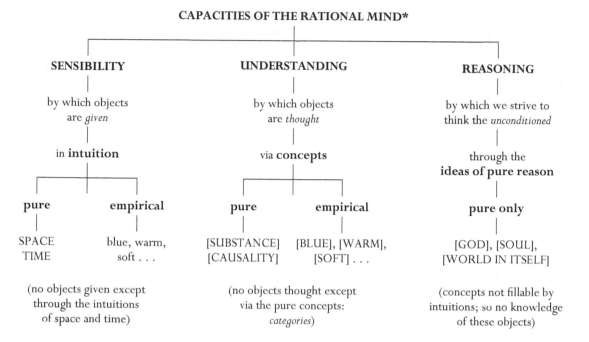

CAPACITIES OF THE RATIONAL MIND*

SENSIBILITY	UNDERSTANDING	REASONING
by which objects are *given*	by which objects are *thought*	by which we strive to think the *unconditioned*
in **intuition**	via **concepts**	through the **ideas of pure reason**
pure · empirical	pure · empirical	pure only
SPACE TIME · blue, warm, soft . . .	[SUBSTANCE] [CAUSALITY] · [BLUE], [WARM], [SOFT] . . .	[GOD], [SOUL], [WORLD IN ITSELF]
(no objects given except through the intuitions of space and time)	(no objects thought except via the pure concepts: *categories*)	(concepts not fillable by intuitions; so no knowledge of these objects)

The categories . . . extend further than sensible intuition, since they think objects in general, without regard to the special mode (the sensibility) in which they may be given. But they do not thereby determine a greater sphere of objects. (*CPR*, 271)

One common form of the illusion is the claim that we can know things as they are, apart from the way they appear to us. This is the illusion of speculative metaphysics. The illusion is reinforced because we do have the concept of **things-in-themselves.** Kant even gives it a name: Something as it is in itself, independent of the way it reveals itself to us, is called a **noumenon.** This contrasts with a **phenomenon,** its appearance to us.

But this concept of a noumenon is not a concept with any positive meaning. Its role in our intellectual life is purely negative; it reminds us that there are things we cannot know—namely what the things affecting our sensibility are like, independent of our intuitions of them. The phenomenal world of appearance is all we can ever know.

1. What does it mean that the dove cannot fly in empty space? Relate this aphorism to the notions of concept and intuition.

2. Explain the role Kant assigns to the categories, illustrating it with the examples of substance/properties and cause/effect. How are these a priori concepts related to the objects of our common experience?
3. Explain the famous Kantian dictum: "Thoughts without content are empty, intuitions without concepts are blind."
4. Explain the notion that our a priori concepts are the source of a powerful illusion—the illusion of speculative metaphysics.

Reasoning and the Ideas of Metaphysics: God, World, and Soul

Kant's third question concerns metaphysics. The term "metaphysics" has a precise meaning for Kant. Metaphysics contrasts sharply with both common sense and science. We have seen that the entire range of possible experience is governed by the pure *intuitions* of space and time, as well as by the *pure categories* of the understanding. These, together with *sensations*, constitute the way things appear to us, the realm of phenomena. Beyond this

*Concepts are indicated in square brackets.

realm, our understanding is without footing. We know there are things that appear to us, but we are completely at sea about what they may be in themselves. "Out there," the dove cannot fly.

Metaphysics looks in two directions. Understood in the traditional way, it tries to gain knowledge about things apart from their appearance to us. It is the attempt to go beyond experience in a *transcendent* direction, toward the *noumenal world*, which *transcends* all possible experience. But metaphysics can also look in the opposite direction: to the structures on the side of the subject that condition the being of objects. In this case, Kant calls it *transcendental*. It is just that critique of pure reason we have been examining; it tries only to discern the a priori conditions of experience.

Not surprisingly, Kant thinks the transcendent kind of metaphysics is impossible. But his discussion of the reasons for the impossibility are full of interesting insights. First, Kant claims to be able to explain why the quest for metaphysical knowledge recurs with such inevitability and why it is so difficult to give up. Second, he finds a positive use for the fundamental metaphysical ideas—God, the world, and the soul—even though he denies that these ideas can give us knowledge. Finally, Kant's examination of these ideas propels us into the fourth of his major concerns, the practical use of reason, or morality.

The notion we can get knowledge of things-in-themselves is, Kant says, "a *natural* and inevitable *illusion*" (*CPR*, 300). Something in the very structure of rationality gives us that notion; it has to do with *reasoning*. The aim of reasoning is to supply "the reason why" something is true. As we have seen numerous times already, the why question can always be repeated; we can ask for the reason for the reason. Kant talks of this process as one that seeks the *conditions* that account for a given truth. Grass is green. Why? In answering this question, we refer to some condition in the world that explains that fact. Why is that condition the way it is? Again, we can supply a condition that explains that condition. And we could go on.

As you can see, the quest for reasons will not be satisfied until it finds some condition that doesn't need to be explained by a further condition.

Reason is always searching for the *unconditioned*. We can think of this as Kant's version of the search for first principles. This has always been the task of first philosophy, or metaphysics. The search is for something intelligible in itself, which explains or makes intelligible all the rest.

> Reason can never be completely satisfied by any use of the rules of the understanding in experience, this use always remaining conditioned; and when reason demands completion of this chain of conditions, it drives the understanding out of its sphere, partly to represent objects of experience in a series so far extended that no experience whatever can comprehend it, partly even (in order to complete it), to seek *noumena* quite outside experience, to which the chain can be fastened; whereby reason, independent at long last of the conditions of experience, can nevertheless make its hold complete. (*P*, 137)

We can understand only what lies within the bounds of possible experience. But reason cannot be content with that. If those bounds are reached, reason still wants to ask why. Why is experience as a whole the way it is? Why is there experience at all? But this question can be answered only by transcending those boundaries. To ask for the condition that explains the absolute totality of all possible experience is no longer asking for the explanation of one phenomenon in terms of another. It is asking for something absolute, for the **unconditioned,** which will necessarily involve knowledge of things-in-themselves.

And so arise, naturally and inevitably, those concepts of God, the world in itself, and the knowing subject or soul. These concepts are different from all others. They are not empirical concepts abstracted from sensations. Nor are they a priori concepts structuring our experiences. Kant gives them a special name: **Ideas of Pure Reason.***

---

*Kant has Plato explicitly in mind here. In Plato the "Forms" or "Ideas" are purely intelligible entities that can be understood but not sensed. For Kant, of course, the Ideas are concepts, not realities; and they can give us no knowledge. But they are concepts that *aim* to present realities beyond sensory experience. For Plato on the Forms, see pp. 152–155.

Ideas lie in the nature of reason, as categories in the nature of the understanding, and if ideas carry with them an illusion which can easily mislead, this illusion is unavoidable, although "that it shall not seduce into error" can very well be achieved. (*P*, 133)

Reason can try to trace out the ultimate conditions in three different directions: back into the *subject* (trying to construct an absolute psychological Idea), out into the *world* (trying to discover the cosmological Ideas), and toward the *absolute condition of anything at all* (searching for the theological Idea). And so we find reason inevitably constructing the ideas of soul, world, and God.

THE SOUL

Descartes, we saw, finds he cannot doubt his own existence. And when he asks himself what he is, the answer seems obvious: a thing that thinks. He "knows" that he is a substance whose essential characteristic is to think. Descartes, as we have seen, further claims that this substance is simple (indivisible), distinct from the body, unchanging through time, and immortal.

It is clear that Descartes is not doing empirical psychology here; there are no experiments, and he gathers no data. Kant calls this kind of thing **rational psychology.** Rational psychology is an attempt to understand the fundamental nature of the self by rational reflection on what the self *must* be if experience is to be possible. It is a quest for the *unconditioned condition* on the side of the subject. Kant is convinced that rational psychology is illusory, that there can be no such knowledge. But he also thinks that the illusion is a powerful one and difficult to resist. It arises from what Kant calls "the sole text of rational psychology," the judgment "I think" (*CPR*, 330). Reflection on this judgment alone seems to be enough to yield all the conclusions desired by the rational psychologist.

Is the soul a substance? It seems as though you can conclude that you are a substance. Here is the argument. Every thought you have can be preceded (at least implicitly) by the phrase, "I think." When you say to yourself, "I think roses are lovely," this thought belongs to *you*; they are qualities or properties of your self. But what about the "I" in your thought? Could this "I" be simply a property or characteristic? Of what? The idea that *you* might be just a property of some other substance doesn't seem to make sense. *You* are the absolute subject of all these determinations. But this is just what we mean by substance; a substance is, by definition, that which cannot be predicated of anything else but is the subject of properties.* So you, as a thinking thing, must be a substance.

This seems a persuasive argument, but, if Kant is right, it is a mere sophism. Remember that "substance" is one of the a priori categories. This means that it is a concept that is purely formal in itself, without any content. Its whole function is to serve as a kind of rule for organizing sensible intuitions into experience. But where is the intuition that corresponds to the "I"? Kant agrees with Hume, who claims not to be able to find any perception of the self when he introspects.† When you say "I think," you are not peering at or describing your self. The whole content of what you think is expressed in what comes *after* that phrase.

> The "I" is indeed in all thoughts, but there is not in this representation the least trace of intuition, distinguishing the "I" from other objects of intuition.
>
> We do not have, and cannot have, any knowledge whatsoever of any such subject. (*CPR*, 334)

Reason is always searching for the conditions that make experience possible. In looking back and back into ourselves, we seem to come upon the idea that there is a substance to which all these mental activities belong. But this is a kind of grammatical or logical illusion. Just because you need to express your thinking by using subject/predicate forms in which the "I" occurs, you cannot infer that *noumenal reality* is structured that way. We cannot transform a *semantic* necessity in the way we represent

---

*This idea of substance can be traced back to Aristotle's discussion of the categories of being. Substance is basic in the sense that all other modes of being (qualities, relations, and so on) depend on substance. See pp. 186–187 for a brief discussion of this point.

†For Hume on the self, see "The Disappearing Self," in Chapter 19. See also the Buddhist doctrine of *anātman* (pp. 41–45).

ourselves into a *metaphysical* necessity concerning our natures.

Kant says that the "I" in "I think" is just a kind of formal marker. Concepts such as this (others are "now" and "here" and "this") are sometimes called "indexicals"; what is peculiar about them is that they have no determinate content but merely indicate something relative to the circumstances of utterance. About the term "I," Kant says, "we cannot even say that this is a concept, but only that it is a bare consciousness which accompanies all concepts" (*CPR*, 331). All knowledge, however, is through concepts. So the "I" is nothing more than an empty representation of an unknown *X*, "this I or he or it (the thing) which thinks" (*CPR*, 331). What we are in ourselves is completely unknown to us. For all that rational reflection can tell you, this *X* that you are may be anything at all. The self or soul, then, is merely that unknown *X* to whom the world appears and by which it is structured into objects.*

Similar reflections undermine the claims about the soul's simplicity, its unchanging nature, and its immortality. In each case a *merely subjective condition* of thinking is transformed into a concept of a *noumenal object*. The "I," however, the transcendental ego, is not an object and cannot be known as an object. The "I" is a *subject* and *resists objectification*. As far as rational knowledge goes, the subject of thinking remains merely an *X*, which must express itself *as if* it were a simple substance, continuously the same through time, and so on. But what it is in itself remains a complete mystery. The concept of "soul" is an empty idea.

The World and the Free Will

In seeking the conditions that explain what we experience, reason drives us back to more and more fundamental conditions and eventually to some condition that is supposed to explain the phenomenal world as a whole. This condition could only be something noumenal—the world in itself lying behind the world we experience.

As we have seen, we cannot know whether the categories by which we structure our experience also apply to the world in itself. In particular, we can have no idea whether that world is causally ordered. This opens an interesting possibility in the long debate about freedom of the will. Descartes argued that our wills are free because our souls lie outside the causal network of the physical world. This leaves our wills as absolutely free as God's. Hobbes and Hume locate our minds within the physical world, where they are as subject to the laws of nature as a stone is. They try to rescue freedom of the will by reanalyzing the idea of freedom. As long as you can do what you want to do, they say, then you are free, even if the causes of your action reach back and back and back in an unbroken chain to the time before you were born. In this way, they hope to reconcile freedom of action with the new physics.*

From Kant's point of view, Descartes, Hobbes, and Hume all share an important presupposition: they take themselves to be describing things (in this case the will, or human action) as they are, independent of our knowing them. What happens if we recognize that things-in-themselves are unknown to us and that all we can know is their appearance? Doing so, Kant thinks, will resolve this puzzle in the nicest possible way: We can agree with Descartes that freedom is exemption from causality, but we do not have to carve out a part of the world in which causal law does not apply.

This surely seems like the best of both views! We avoid Descartes' dubious exemption of the will from causal determination. But we also avoid Hobbes' and Hume's questionable definition of freedom. If Kant can preserve human freedom and still allow science unlimited scope, what more could we ask?

What makes this possible, of course, is the distinction between things as they appear to us and things-in-themselves.

---

*Remember that Locke says we do have the idea of ourselves as spiritual substances, but we don't know the real nature of those substances. (See p. 419.) Kant's analysis of a priori concepts forces him to go one step further: We don't know that the metaphysical concept of substance or soul applies to us at all!

---

*Review the discussion by Descartes in *Meditation IV*, p. 385. For Hume's view, see "Rescuing Human Freedom," in Chapter 19.

Is it a truly disjunctive proposition to say that every effect in the world must arise *either* from nature *or* from freedom; or must we not rather say that in one and the same event, in different relations, both can be found? (*CPR*, 466)

Every action, even every act of will, has two aspects: (1) It is something that appears in the world of our experience, and (2) it is something in itself. As an appearance, part of the world of nature, it is governed by all the principles that constitute that realm, including causality. In this aspect, every action is causally determined. But as a thing in itself, we cannot even say that it occurs in time! And the category of causality does not extend to what occurs beyond the bounds of experience. By considering actions under both of these aspects, we can say that an act can be both free and determined: free in itself (since the category of causality does not reach so far) and yet causal as it appears to us. The notion that an act couldn't possibly be both is simply due to considering the things we experience as things in themselves. And that is a mistake that critical philosophy can keep us from making.

> All actions of rational beings, insofar as they are appearances . . . stand under natural necessity; the same actions however, merely with respect to the rational subject and to its faculty of acting according to reason alone, are free. . . . Freedom thus hinders the law of nature . . . by as little as the law of nature takes away from the freedom of the practical use of reason. (*P*, 148)

The "practical use of reason" is freedom in action, freedom to decide what events should occur in the world. This freedom, Kant is convinced, is closely tied to reason and acting for reasons. We can act freely when we act *for a reason* and not just in response to nonrational causes. You can see that Kant is thinking of reason itself, in the form of a rational will, as a certain kind of (spontaneous) causality. When you act for good reasons, you bring into being events that *appear* in the causal order of the world, but *in themselves* may have a completely noncausal—but rational— origin. The *order of reasons* is not the same as the *order of causes*.

We need to be very careful, however. Kant does not claim he has proved that there are free actions or that he has evidence that such free actions exist. Remember, the will as free is the will considered noumenally, and about the noumenal world we can know nothing at all. Kant does not even claim to have proved that such freedom is possible; the most he will say is that "causality through freedom is at least *not incompatible with nature*" (*CPR*, 479). There is no contradiction in thinking of an act as free in itself, but determined as appearance.

This means that, from the viewpoint of critical theory, freedom remains merely an Idea of Reason. It is the Idea to which reason is driven when it asks about how it can itself make a difference in the world. Although no empirical filling of that concept is available to give us knowledge, we can say something more positive about freedom when we come to the topic of morality.

GOD

We have seen how reason, in asking the why question, runs through a series of conditions that aims at completeness. The endpoint of each such series must be the concept of some being that is, *in itself*, a foundation for phenomena and a natural stopping place. We have seen how this process generates the Ideas of the soul and of the world in itself. Kant's conclusion in both cases is, of course, that these Ideas are *merely ideas*. Because we have no intuitions providing content for these concepts, knowledge of them is impossible. Experience is the only soil our intellect can cultivate. And experience is essentially open ended; no closure, no completeness will be found there. So the Ideas are sources of illusion. We are drawn to think we can know something about them, but we are mistaken.

There is one more pattern of reasoning we simply cannot avoid. It leads to the concept of God. Kant agrees with Descartes and the tradition that the idea of God is the idea of an all-perfect being, but he has a very interesting analysis of the way reasoning leads us to that idea. Like the ideas of soul and world, the idea of God is not an arbitrary invention. Nor is it something we might or might not invent, as Hume claims. Nor is it, as some in the Enlightenment hold, a priestly or political trick foisted on people to keep them in subjection. For any being that reasons, it is an absolutely unavoidable concept.

Reason asks for the reason why and eventually asks, *Why is there anything at all?* It seems that there must be some being that is the foundation for *whatever* there is.

This is how reason inevitably comes upon the Idea of God. But the Idea is empty.* No experience, no intuition could ever fulfill the requirements of this Idea. Moreover, it is the Idea of something that cannot just be another phenomenal being; since it is the foundation for the determinate character of all phenomenal things, it must be noumenal—a thing-in-itself. But since things-in-themselves are unknowable, the concept of God is *just* an Idea of Reason.

Kant adds a critique of the major arguments that purport to prove the existence of God. He divides the arguments into three types: cosmological, design, and ontological. He argues that each of the first two types makes use of the principle of the ontological argument at a crucial stage. So let us focus on that.

The Ontological Argument

We met Descartes' version of this argument in the fifth meditation; the argument is originally presented by Anselm of Canterbury in the eleventh century.† You will remember that this argument presupposes nothing but our idea of God as a most perfect being. From that idea alone, a priori, as Kant would say, the existence of God is supposed to follow.

Kant's critique of this argument is famous and multifaceted, but we will examine only one part of it. That part of Kant's criticism rests on an analysis of what we are doing when we say that something exists.

> "Being" is obviously not a real predicate: that is, it is not a concept of something which could be added to the concept of a thing. It is merely the positing of a thing, or of certain determinations, as existing in themselves. (*CPR*, 504)

This is a difficult thought, but we can make it clear by reflecting on definitions. Suppose we have a certain concept x. If we want to know what that concept is, we are asking for a definition. And the definition will be given in terms of certain predicates, say *f*, *g*, *h*. So we will be told that an *x* is something that is *f*, *g*, and *h*. A triangle, for example, is a closed plane figure bounded by three straight lines. Could **"being"** or "existence" be on such a list of predicates? This is what Kant denies. To say that *a triangle is a figure* is one thing. To say that *a triangle exists* is to say something of an altogether different *kind*. If we say that a triangle exists, we are not expressing one of the properties of the triangle; existence is not the kind of thing that should be named in a list of those properties. To say that a triangle exists is to "posit" something that has *all* the properties of a triangle. It is to say that the concept (together with the properties that define it) *applies* to something.

If Kant is right, it follows that every judgment of existence is *synthetic*. None of them is simply analytic of the concept expressed by the subject of the judgment—because existence is not a normal predicate and cannot be part of the subject term's definition. And that means that *in no case* is the denial of a judgment asserting existence a contradiction. But this is exactly what the ontological argument claims.*

The fundamental mistake of the argument is the assumption that existence is a predicate like others and that the concept of a perfect being would have to include it. But if I say that God does not exist, I am not denying in the second part of the sentence

---

*Remember the slogan, "Thoughts without content are empty, intuitions without concepts are blind." The Ideas are thoughts without content.

†For a discussion of the original argument as given by Anselm, see pp. 412–415. Also see the argument as presented by Descartes in *Meditation V*.

---

*Modern logic agrees with Kant here. The two propositions "Dogs bark" and "Dogs exist" may look very much alike, but their logic is very different. In symbolic notation, the first is $(x)(Dx \supset Bx)$. The second is $(\exists x)(Dx)$.

what I have implicitly asserted in the first part. I am simply refusing to "posit" an object of the sort the sentence describes. Atheism may be wrong, but it is at least not a logically incoherent view. So the ontological argument fails.

> The attempt to establish the existence of a supreme being by means of the famous ontological argument of Descartes is therefore so much labour and effort lost; we can no more extend our stock of [theoretical] insight by mere ideas, than a merchant can better his position by adding a few noughts to his cash account. (*CPR*, 507)

Is it Kant's purpose to make atheism possible? Not at all. In another famous line, Kant says,

> I have therefore found it necessary to deny *knowledge*, in order to make room for *faith*. (*CPR*, 29)

What sort of faith he has in mind we will discover in examining his moral philosophy.

Let us sum up this section with some reflections on the positive function of these Ideas of Reason: soul, world, and God. We have seen that in no case can we have knowledge of the things-in-themselves these Ideas point to. Taken as sources of knowledge, the Ideas are illusory. But they do express an *ideal* that reason cannot disregard: the ideal of knowledge as a complete, unified, and systematic whole, with no loose ends and nothing left out. It is this that drives reason forward in asking its why-questions; and it is this goal that, in their various ways, the Ideas of soul, world, and God express. *If* reason could complete its search, it would have to end with such concepts. Because experience, the field in which reason can successfully labor, is essentially open ended, the search cannot be completed. But these ideals can serve a regulative purpose, representing the goal toward which rational creatures like ourselves are striving. We want to understand *completely*.

1. What is it about reasoning, in Kant's view, that drives us inevitably to the concepts of God, the soul, and the world in itself?
2. How does Kant attack the Cartesian claim that we are thinking things?

3. Explain how the distinction between noumena and phenomena allows Kant to claim that we can reconcile causality with freedom.
4. Why is it, according to Kant, that the idea of God is an unavoidable idea for any reasoning being?
5. Kant says, "'Being' is obviously not a real predicate." What does this mean? How does Kant use this principle to criticize the ontological argument for the existence of God?
6. If the Ideas of Pure Reason (God, the soul, the world in itself) are such powerful sources of illusion, what good are they?

Reason and Morality

So far, we have seen Kant examining in his critical way our capacities for knowing. The critical investigation into knowledge looks at reason in its *theoretical* aspect; it is concerned with the a priori foundations of mathematics and physics, together with the temptations of transcendent metaphysics. We are now turning to see what Kant has to say about our actions. The critical inquiry into action concerns reason in its *practical* aspect. It deals with the a priori foundations of morality.

Kant takes pains to distinguish his treatment from a common way to look at morality—as just one more empirical phenomenon to be understood. If we take this point of view, we examine what people *in fact* praise and blame and what motivations (e.g., sympathy) explain these facts. To look at morality this way, Kant says, is to do "*practical anthropology*" (*G*, 190). This is the way Hume looks at morality.*

There is nothing wrong with studying practical life this way, but Kant is convinced that a merely empirical study of morality will miss the contribution of *reason* to our practice; and it will be impossible to find the *moral law*. All you will get is a collection of different, probably overlapping, practices or customs. No *universality* can be

---

*To make sure you understand the contrast, look back at the way Hume does moral philosophy—as part of his science of human nature, pp. 460–462.

found this way; nor will the *necessity* that attaches to duty appear.*

Kant, of course, wants to apply his Copernican revolution to practice, as well as to theory. We need a transcendental inquiry into the foundations of our practical life to complement the critique of our theoretical life. Morality, he believes, is not just a set of practices in the phenomenal world. It has its foundation in *legislation by pure reason*. Morality, like mathematics and natural science, is constituted in part by a priori elements originating in the nature of reason itself. To work out a "pure moral philosophy" (*G*, 191), Kant aims

> to seek out and establish *the supreme principle of morality*. (*G*, 193)

This is an ambitious aim. You can see that if Kant succeeds, he will have undercut the moral relativism that seems to be the result of empirical anthropology. He will have found a *criterion* of moral value that is *nonrelative*.

THE GOOD WILL

One way into such a "pure moral philosophy" is to ask whether there is anything at all that could be called good not just in some respect, but *without qualification*.

> Intelligence, wit, judgement, and the other mental talents, whatever we may call them, or courage, decisiveness, and perseverance, are, as qualities of *temperament*, certainly good and desirable in many respects; but they can also be extremely bad and harmful when the will which makes use of these *gifts of nature . . .* is not good. It is exactly the same with *gifts of fortune*. Power, wealth, honour, even health and that total well-being and contentment with one's condition which we call "*happiness*," can make a person bold but consequently often reckless as well, unless a good will is present to correct their influence on the mind. (*G*, 195)

None of these things is good *without qualification*; they are good only if used well. Think of a healthy, wealthy, and smart terrorist!

It is impossible to imagine anything at all in the world, or even beyond it, that can be called good without qualification—except a *good will*. (*G*, 195)

Many earlier philosophers have suggested a connection between being a morally good person and being happy. Plato, for instance, argues that the just man *is* the happy man.* Kant, more realistic perhaps, disagrees. If happiness correlates (as Hobbes claims) with the satisfaction of desires, there is no guarantee that moral goodness will match perfectly with happiness. Think of the image in Plato's *Republic* of the perfectly just man languishing in prison; it is just too hard, Kant seems to suggest, to imagine that he is also perfectly happy! There is a relationship, however.

> It goes without saying that the sight of a creature enjoying uninterrupted prosperity, but never feeling the slightest pull of a pure and good will, cannot excite approval in a rational and impartial spectator. Consequently, a good will seems to constitute the indispensable condition even of our worthiness to be happy. (*G*, 195)

It may not be the case that happiness correlates perfectly with a good will in this world, but it *should* be so. Any "impartial spectator" will feel uneasy at the sight of some really rotten person who is really happy. Goodness may not guarantee happiness, but it seems to constitute the condition for deserving it. This opinion is reflected in common sayings, such as "She deserves better."†

We cannot, then, solve the problem about the nature of moral goodness by inquiring (as Aristotle, Epicurus, and Augustine do) into happiness. If the only thing good without qualification is a **good will,** we must examine that directly. So let us ask, What is a good will?

We need first to clarify the notion of will. We will not go far wrong if we think of an *act of will* as a kind of internal command with a content of

---

*For *universality* and *necessity* as marks of the a priori contributions of reason to experience, see p. 470. What goes for experience goes for action, too.

*See pp. 172–176. Plato is not the only one to pursue this tack. We find it in Aristotle (pp. 208–213), Epicurus (pp. 239–240), the Stoics (pp. 241–245), and Augustine (pp. 283–284).

†This connection between moral goodness and happiness is important for what Kant calls "rational religion." See pp. 493–494.

this kind: "Let me now do *A*!" But not every such imperative qualifies as an act of will. If I do *A* on a whim, just because I feel like it, this will be acting from *inclination*, not from will. Only internal commands that come at the end of a process of rational deliberation qualify as acts of will. In fact, it is not too much to say that *will is just reason in its practical employment*. In its theoretical employment, the outcome of a process of reasoning is a descriptive statement (e.g., "Bodies fall according to the formula $v = 1/2 \ gt^2$"). But when reason deliberates about practical matters, the outcome is an imperative (e.g., "Let me now help this suffering person").

As this example makes clear, every act of will has a certain content. If we spell out the "*A*" in one of the will's commands, we get what Kant calls a *maxim*. **Maxims** are rules that express the *subjective intention* of the agent in doing an action. For instance, we might get maxims of the following sort: "Let me now keep the promise I made yesterday" or "Let me now break the promise I made yesterday."

We can think of Kant's moral philosophy as the search for a criterion, a rule for sorting maxims into two classes: those that are morally okay and those that are not. If he can find such a rule, he will have found "the supreme principle of morality."

Now we return to the question, What makes an act of will *good*? Kant first makes a negative point. It is not the *consequences* of a good will that make it good. In determining what makes it good, we must altogether set aside what it actually accomplishes in the world.

> Even if it were to happen that, because of some particularly unfortunate fate or the miserly bequest of a step-motherly nature, this will were completely powerless to carry out its aims; if with even its utmost effort it still accomplished nothing, so that only good will itself remained, . . . even then it would still, like a jewel, glisten in its own right, as something that has its full worth in itself. (*G*, 196)

If Jane acts out of a truly good will, our estimation of her moral worth is unaffected even if an uncooperative nature frustrates the intended outcome.

Her will sparkles "like a jewel," even if the action it produces goes wrong.*

But this just raises the question with more urgency. What makes a will good? If a good will cannot be defined by anything external to it, something about the *willing itself* must make it good. We have seen that every act of will has an intelligible content, expressible as the maxim of that act. Only the maxim, in fact, differentiates one act of will from another. So a good will must be one with a certain kind of maxim. But what kind?

> "Always do right. This will gratify some people, and astonish the rest."
>
> *Mark Twain (1835–1910)*

Kant finds a clue in the concept of **duty.** We act out of a good will when we try to do the right thing. In trying to do what is morally right, we do not have our eyes on some advantage to ourselves, but only on the rightness of the action.† We want nothing else but to do our duty. What is duty?

> Duty is the necessity of an act done out of respect for the law. (*G*, 202)

Duty and law go together. The law tells us what our duties are. The law says, "You *must* do *A*"—the "must" expressing the "necessity" Kant refers to. If an action is done out of a good will, then, it is one that has a peculiar motivation: "respect for law." What law? The moral law, of course. But what does that law say? The answer to this question is the heart of Kant's moral philosophy, but we are not quite ready for it yet.

---

*Compare the Stoic story of the two slaves, p. 245.

†In T. S. Eliot's play *Murder in the Cathedral*, Thomas Becket, the archbishop of Canterbury, is meditating about his possible martyrdom. He says, "The last temptation is the greatest treason: / To do the right deed for the wrong reason." This is a very Kantian sentiment.

"Duty is the sublimest word in our language. Do your duty in all things. You cannot do more. You should never wish to do less."

Robert E. Lee (1807–1870)

Let us note that actions can be motivated in two quite distinct ways. We often act out of desires of various kinds. These are the kinds of motivations that Hobbes and Hume recognize.* Kant groups all these motivations under **inclinations.** But he recognizes one other motivator: **respect for law.** This is a purely rational motivation, quite different from and possibly opposed to even the strongest desire. For Kant, unlike Hume, reason is not just the slave of the passions. Like Plato, Kant thinks that reason can rule, can motivate us to override and control the desires.† And he believes his critical philosophy explains how this can be.

On the assumption that rational respect for law can motivate persons to do their duty, we can classify actions in four ways:

1. *As done from inclination, but contrary to duty*: I do not repay the ten dollars I borrowed because my friend has forgotten about it, and I would rather keep it.
2. *As done from calculated self-interest, but according to duty*: Common proverbs, such as "Honesty is the best policy," often express this (partial) overlap of prudence and morality.
3. *As done from a direct inclination, but according to duty*: If I act to preserve my life out of fear, or I am kind simply because I am overwhelmed with pity, I am doing the right thing, but not *because* it is right.
4. *As done from duty, even if it runs contrary to inclinations*: I keep my promise to take my children on a picnic, whether I want to or not.

Only the last is a case of acting from a good will.

We have an answer, then, to the question about what makes a will good. We act from a good will when we act out of a sense of duty, doing what is right solely because it is right, from respect for the moral law. Only such acts have true moral worth.

THE MORAL LAW

We now need to know what the moral law says. We already know that we cannot discover it by empirical investigation; the most we can get that way is anthropology—a description of the rules people *do* live by. We cannot get rules they *ought* to live by.* At best, one might be able to cite examples to imitate. But no one, Kant says, could

> give morality worse advice than by trying to derive it from examples. For every example of morality presented to me must itself first be assessed with moral principles to see whether it deserves to be used as an original example, i.e., as a model. By no means can it have the authority to give us the concept of morality. Even the Holy One of the Gospels must first be compared with our ideal of moral perfection before we can acknowledge Him to be such. (*G*, 210)

If there is going to be a moral law, its origin must be independent of experience. It must be a priori; it must be an aspect of practical reason itself.

To understand the content of the moral law, we need one more distinction, that between two kinds of *imperatives*:

1. A **hypothetical imperative** has this form: "If you want *x* in circumstance *C*, do *A*."
2. A **categorical imperative** has this form: "Do *A* (in circumstance *C*)."

Note that there is no reference to your wishes, wants, desires, ends, or goals in a categorical imperative. This is what it means to call it "categorical." Given that you are in *C*, it simply says, "Do *A*." It is not "iffy" or conditional.

---

*For Hobbes, you will recall, desire for pleasure and aversion to pain are the sole motivators. Hume adds a non-egoistic source of action in sympathy, but this, too, is simply a passion. See pp. 410–411 and 461–462.

†See pp. 458–460 for Hume's views of passion and reason. Plato's opposed views are discussed on pp. 170–171.

---

*Note that once more Kant is trying to solve a problem that Hume poses. He is trying to answer the question, Where does the "ought" come from? Review Hume's famous challenge on p. 461.

If the moral law expresses our duty and if there is something necessary about our duty, then it seems the moral law must be *categorical*. Hypothetical imperatives are neither necessary nor universal; they apply to you only if your wants are those specified in the if-clause. If you don't want to build a bridge, then the technical imperatives of engineering get no grip on you. But the moral law applies regardless of your wants.

We can sum up in this way. The moral law must

* abstract from everything empirical;
* make no reference to consequences of actions;
* be independent of inclinations;
* be capable of inspiring respect.

Now if we examine hypothetical imperatives, we find that they one and all

* make reference to empirical facts;
* concern consequences of actions;
* express our inclinations;
* inspire, at most, approval, not respect.

Therefore, the moral law must not be a hypothetical imperative; it must be a categorical imperative.

We are getting close. The moral law is a rule for choosing among maxims. It is supposed to be a sorting device, separating the morally acceptable maxims from those not acceptable. Kant's first approach is to look not to the *content* of maxims, but to their *form*. As an imperative, the morally acceptable maxim has the character of law, and the essential feature of a law is that it has a *universal* form.*

> There is therefore only one categorical imperative and it is this: "Act only on that maxim by which you can at the same time will that it should become a universal law." (*G*, 222)

Kant has reached his goal: "the supreme principle of morality." This is the first formulation of the famous categorical imperative. Note several features of this rule:

* It is clearly synthetic; no contradiction is produced by denying it.
* It is clearly a priori; it has no empirical content.
* It is therefore an example of pure reason at work—this time legislating for actions.

If pure reason in its theoretical employment provides principles according to which things *do in fact happen*, we can now see that in its practical employment pure reason provides a principle according to which things *ought to happen*.

Let us see how it works. There are two cases.* Here is the first. You are considering making a promise, but you have in mind not keeping it if it runs counter to your inclinations. The maxim of your action might be expressed this way: "Let me make this promise, intending not to keep it if I don't want to."

How does the categorical imperative get a grip on this? It tells you that this is a morally acceptable maxim only if you can *universalize* it. To universalize a maxim is to consider the case in which *everyone* acts according to it: "Let us all make promises, intending not to keep them if we don't want to."

Now the question to ask is, Could this be a universal law? It could not; for if everyone acted according to this rule, no one would trust others to keep their promises. And if no one ever trusted others to keep a promise, the very meaning of promising would vanish. Saying "I promise" would become indistinguishable from saying "Maybe." So your original maxim is not one that can be universalized; you cannot will that everyone should act on the principle you are considering for your own action. It could not be a *law*, and it must be rejected as an acceptable moral principle. Whenever you act according to this maxim, you are acting *immorally*.

Here is the second case. You are in the presence of someone who desperately needs your help, and you are considering the maxim: "Let me not help this person." Could you universalize this maxim? The first thing to note is that, unlike the promising case, universalizing this maxim will not produce incoherence; universal failure to provide help does not undermine the very maxim we are considering.

---

*Think of laws in science; if a proposition is claimed to be a law, but a counterinstance is found, we conclude that it is not a law after all—because it does not hold universally. Review what Kant says about universality and necessity being the criteria for the a priori. (See p. 470.)

---

*Kant considers four cases, but we will simplify.

JEAN-JACQUES ROUSSEAU

"Man is born free, and is everywhere in chains." Thus Rousseau (1712–1778) begins *The Social Contract*, one of his most famous works. He has in mind not just actual slavery, but also the constraints, expectations, oppressions, and inequalities generated in civilized societies. How did the transition from freedom to chains come about?

Rousseau paints a picture of "natural man" living a simple life, largely isolated from others, devoted to satisfying his few needs in an environment that makes that easy to do. His self-interest is moderated by compassion, he oppresses no one, and is exploited by none.* He feels no need to satisfy another's expectations. He is free.

But natural inequalities in strength, wit, or enterprise are amplified when men begin to live in society. Property ("mine," not "thine") comes into being. Inequalities in wealth and power are generated. Comparison raises its ugly head and everyone wants to appear esteemed by others. Hence arise vanity and contempt, shame and envy—and all the pretenses and hypocrisies of modern societies. Some become rulers, others slaves.

———

*Contrast this version of the state of nature with that of Hobbes, pp. 410–412.

It is not enough, however, to understand the degradation of man in society. Rousseau wants to find a remedy. In *Émile* he describes an education that will allow the preservation of a man's freedom and natural goodness. And in *The Social Contract* he searches for principles that will legitimate a government that will be neither oppressive nor corrupt.

Since might does not make right, actual control by force cannot justify a state. Only an agreement among free individuals could do that. This agreement would have to be one in which each individual surrenders his private right to do as he pleases to the whole community, which then expresses through law the "general will" of the community—that is, what is in the common interest.

No one individual will be privileged by laws that everyone must agree to, so the laws will tend toward equality. Such a contract each will enter into freely, and therefore in obeying the laws each will obey only himself, thus expressing in society the freedom of the natural man.*

———

*Kant admired Rousseau, and it is easy to see why. The idea of laws agreed to freely by all—obedience to which is freedom itself because they express the fundamental nature of human beings—is obviously a foreshadowing of the categorical imperative.

A world where no one offers another person help is a possible, if unattractive, world. There is no *logical* contradiction in considering it.

But if you universalize the maxim in question, you are in effect willing that *you* should not be helped, no matter how desperately you might need it. Since it is perfectly rational to will that another should help when you need it, your will is engaged in a kind of *practical* contradiction; you are saying, "Help me and don't help me." And that is not a rational thing to say. You *couldn't* universalize the promise-breaking maxim; you *wouldn't* universalize the no-aid maxim. And this is not simply an empirical fact about you. Rather, it would be unreasonable for you to will that nobody should

ever help you. Thus, neither maxim conforms to the moral law. Reason—in different ways—stands against both.

In either case it becomes clear that the essence of acting immorally is deciding to make an *exception for yourself* from rules that you (at the same time) will should be *obeyed by others*. You can see how close the categorical imperative comes to the traditional Golden Rule.

There is only one categorical imperative, but Kant thinks it can be expressed in a variety of ways. One of the most interesting makes use of the notion of an *end in itself*. All our actions have ends; we always act for the sake of some goal. If our end is prompted by desire, the end has only *conditional value.* That is, it is worth something *only* because someone desires it. Diamonds have that sort of worth. If no one wanted them, they would be worthless; and how much they are worth depends exactly on how much people want them (taking a certain supply of them for granted). All these ends are relative, not absolute.

> Suppose, however, there were something *whose existence in itself* had an absolute worth, something that, as an end *in itself*, could be a ground of definite laws. . . .
>
> Now, I say, a human being, and in general every rational being *does exist* as an end in himself, *not merely as a means* to be used by this or that will as it pleases. (G, 228–229)

Rational beings—including extraterrestrial rational beings, if there are any—are different from the ends that have worth only because somebody desires them. How could they fail to be different? They are the *source* of all the relative values there are. How could they just be another case of relative values? They are ends in themselves. In terms of value, then, there are two classes of entities:

1. **Things,** which have only a *conditional* value, which we can call *price*; their value is *relative* to the desires for them and correlates to their *use* as *means* to the satisfaction of those desires.
2. **Persons,** who have *absolute* worth, which we can call *dignity*; their value is *not relative* to what someone desires from them; they have value as *ends* and command *respect.*

In terms of this distinction, the categorical imperative can be stated this way:

> Act in such a way that you treat humanity, whether in your own person or in any other person, always at the same time as an end, never merely as a means. (G, 230)

Don't treat persons like things. Don't *use* people. Don't think of others simply as means to your own ends. These are all admonitions in the spirit of Kant's categorical imperative. You can see that this form of it is merely a variant of the first (universalizing) form: By restricting the maxims of your own actions to those to which *anyone* could subscribe (the first form), you are

extending to *everyone* the dignity of personhood (the second form) by respecting them as equal sources of the moral law.

AUTONOMY

The moral law as categorical imperative arises from pure reason. It imposes itself imperiously on me, saying, Do this—choose your maxims according to whether they can be universalized. But since it is a principle of reason and I am a rational being, I am not just subject to it. I am also the *author* of it. It expresses my nature as a rational being. And we are led naturally to

> the Idea of the *will of every rational being as a will that legislates universal law.* . . . The will is therefore not merely subject to the law, but subject in such a way that it must be considered as also *giving the law to itself.* (G, 232)

This leads Kant to the momentous conclusion that with regard to the moral law, each of us is **autonomous.** We each give the law to ourselves. A law to which I cannot give my rational consent according to the universalization principle cannot be a *moral* law.

There are nonmoral (and even immoral) laws; Kant calls them **heteronomous**—having their source outside ourselves. What is characteristic of such laws is that I have no intrinsic reason to obey them. If I find them binding on me, it is only because they appeal to some interest (perhaps by threatening punishment for violations). But with respect to the moral law, no such appeal to the inclinations can work. Not even promises of heaven or threats of hell are relevant. With respect to the moral law, I do not feel bound from without, for the moral law expresses my inmost nature as a rational creature.

As an autonomous legislator of the moral law, I find myself a member of a community of such legislators. Kant calls this community a **kingdom of ends.**

> For rational beings all stand under the *law* that each of them should treat himself and all others *never merely as a means* but always at *the same time as an end in himself.* But from this there arises a systematic union of rational beings through shared objective

laws—that is, a kingdom. Since these laws aim precisely at the relation of such beings to one another as ends and means, this kingdom may be called a kingdom of ends (admittedly only an ideal). (*G,* 234)

Note that Kant here calls certain laws "objective." These laws contrast with "subjective" rules. A *subjective rule* or *maxim* is relative to inclination, and inclinations differ from person to person. Consider the maxim "Let me run six miles per day." Is that a good maxim? We would all agree that this depends on what you *want*; it is a good maxim for someone who wants eventually to compete in a marathon, but it is a poor maxim for someone who wants only to maintain basic fitness. Such maxims are neither objective nor universal; they are implicitly hypothetical, relative, and personal. There are many such personal maxims, and Kant has no objection to them.

But, if Kant is right, not all rules are relative and subjective like this. A law legislated by the rational will, according to the categorical imperative, is "objective." He means it is a law that *any rational being* will agree to. The moral law for me is the moral law for you. Any maxim approved by the universalization test will be the same for all; it is simply not acceptable unless it is fit to be a *universal* law, one that each rational being can legislate for itself. Reason is not, despite Hume, just the "slave of the passions"; reason is the source of a criterion for judging the passions. The inclinations may propose actions, together with their maxims, but reason judges which are acceptable. Reason is legislative; it is autonomous; and its laws are *absolute.**

We can come back at last to the notion of a good will, the only thing good without qualification. We now see that a good will is governed by the categorical imperative; a good will is one that can be universalized. We can even imagine a will so much in harmony with reason that all its maxims are in natural conformity with the moral law. Such a will

Kant calls a "holy" will. A **holy will** would never feel that it *ought* to do something it didn't want to do because it would always *want* to do what was right. Though we can imagine such a will, we must confess that it is not the will we have. We experience a continual struggle between inclination and duty. So a good will is something we may aspire to, but we can never be completely confident that we have attained it.

> We like to flatter ourselves with the false claim to a nobler motive but in fact we can never, even with the most rigorous self-examination, completely uncover our hidden motivations. For when moral worth is the issue, what counts is not the actions which one sees, but their inner principles, which one does not see.
>
> I am willing to grant that most of our actions are in accord with duty; but if we look more closely at the devising and striving that lies behind them, then everywhere we run into the dear self which is always there; and it is this and not the strict command of duty . . . that underlies our intentions. (*G,* 209)

"In the moral life the enemy is the fat relentless ego."

Iris Murdoch (1919–1999)

As Aristotle said, "It is a hard job to be good."*

FREEDOM

Finally, we need to situate Kant's moral theory in the general critique of reason, to see how the moral law fits with his epistemology and metaphysics. The notion of *autonomy* is the key. An autonomous will must be one that is *free.*

> The will is a kind of causality that living beings have so far as they are rational. Freedom would then be that property whereby this causality can be active, independently of alien causes determining it. (*G,* 426)

---

*Note that in a certain way, Kant again agrees with Hume, this time about the fact/value distinction. There are no values just in facts per se. Value comes from the side of the subject. But it does not follow that it is always bestowed by desire or passion; reason has a crucial role that provides a kind of objectivity in morality parallel to the objectivity in science.

---

*See p. 215.

What else then can freedom of the will be but autonomy—that is, the property that a will has of being a law to itself? (*G*, 246)

You are not truly free when you are merely free to follow the whim of a moment, to indulge your desires, or to act capriciously. To act in these ways is to yield control to "alien causes," because in a *rational being* like yourself, *will* (reason in its practical employment) should be in control, not inclination. Freedom is "a kind of causality"—a power of producing actions according to a rule that you (rationally) legislate for yourself. To be free is to be true to your nature as a rational being by giving the law for your actions to yourself. This law is the moral law. So freedom is not lawlessness, nor is it freedom from duty. But then, duty is not something alien either, not something externally (heteronomously) imposed on you. So freedom is really autonomy, and "a free will and a will under moral laws are one and the same" (*G*, 246).

You should remember that from a theoretical point of view, freedom was declared to be one of the Ideas of Pure Reason, and Kant confessed that he couldn't prove we were free. Let us use the distinction between the phenomenal and noumenal worlds to remind ourselves of how the question of freedom might look from that point of view.

Phenomenally	Noumenally
I *appear* to myself as an *object* in the world.	I *am* the unknown *subject* to whom the world appears.
All objects are organized by the a priori category of causality.	The category of causality does not apply.
I appear to act under causal laws that I do not legislate for myself (*heteronomy*).	I may act under rational laws I legislate for myself (*autonomy*).
I do not appear to be free.	I am free, in that I can act on laws that I give to myself.

Given that the noumenal world is strictly unknowable, we do not know the propositions on the right to be true. We do know, however, that there is a world of things-in-themselves to which the category of causality does not apply. So those propositions are *possibly* true. From a theoretical point of view, then, Kant's Copernican revolution *creates room* for autonomy, freedom, and the moral law.

We are now in a position to go another step. As agents, Kant says, we

cannot act except under the Idea of freedom. . . . Reason must regard itself as the author of its own principles independently of alien influences. It follows that reason, as practical reason, or as the will of a rational being, must regard itself as free. (*G*, 247–248)

Whenever you face a decision, you cannot help but think that it is up to you to decide. You cannot help but regard yourself as free, able to choose for yourself despite whatever outside influences impinge on you. Now this still doesn't *prove* that you are free. Freedom of the will remains a mere Idea of Pure Reason. But it makes it not unreasonable to *believe* you are free. Recall Kant saying that he "found it necessary to deny *knowledge*, in order to make room for *faith*" (*CPR*, 29). Faith in freedom is one thing he has in mind—not an arbitrary faith, but one founded in that practical necessity to think of ourselves as agents "under the Idea of freedom." It is not knowledge, but it is a **rational faith.** And the distinction between things as they are in themselves and things as they appear to us is the metaphysical foundation that makes this faith possible. We *must assume* we are free; and we *may do so*. The assumption of freedom is a *practical necessity* and a *theoretical possibility*.

Morality is the foundation of other articles of a rational faith as well. We can think of morality as giving us the command, "*Do that through which thou becomest worthy to be happy*" (*CPR*, 638). As we have seen, being worthy of happiness does not guarantee that we will be happy, at least not in the world of our experience. Yet goodness and happiness *ought* to go together. It wouldn't make good sense if we were urged by reason to qualify for a condition that would ultimately be denied to us. It seems that reason is telling us that we have *a right to hope* for happiness. The fact that we belong to the noumenal, purely intelligible world opens up a possibility that it might be more than a mere hope.

For it to be more than a futile hope, however, it seems that a future life must be possible (since we see that goodness and happiness do not coincide in this life). It follows that we must believe in the immortality of the soul (which is, from the point of view of theoretical knowledge, a mere Idea of Reason). And we must also believe that a power exists sufficient to guarantee the eventual happiness of those who strive for moral goodness. This power, of course, is God (also, from the point of view of theory, merely an Idea).

> God and a future life are two postulates which, according to the principles of pure reason, are inseparable from the obligation which that same reason imposes upon us. (*CPR*, 639)

So Kant rounds off his critical philosophy. Wisdom, Kant tells us, requires indeed a certain modesty about our rational powers—as both Socrates and Hume, in their different ways, insist. But our powers are adequate to do mathematics and empirical science, and they provide a sure and certain guide for our practical life. For the rest, faith and hope are at least not irrational. But *knowledge* is limited to the realm of possible experience. After the incisive skeptical probes of Hume, "that acute man," Kant has grounds to claim that he has indeed rehabilitated reason—but only within strict limits.

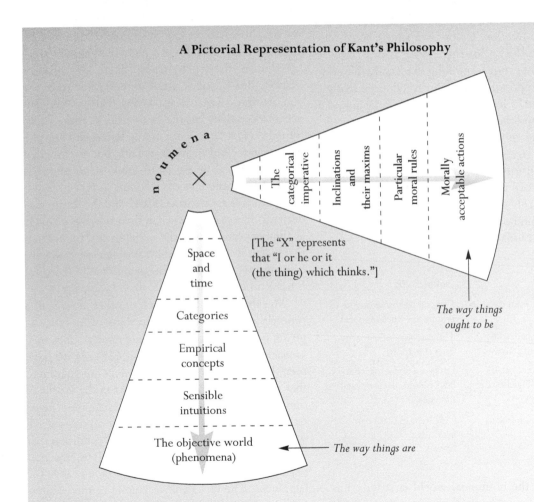

A Pictorial Representation of Kant's Philosophy

noumena

×

The categorical imperative

Inclinations and their maxims

Particular moral rules

Morally acceptable actions

[The "X" represents that "I or he or it (the thing) which thinks."]

The way things ought to be

Space and time

Categories

Empirical concepts

Sensible intuitions

The objective world (phenomena)

The way things are

Our task as knowers: To understand the phenomena of the objective world.

Our task as doers: To make the way things are coincide with the way they ought to be (to make the two cones overlap perfectly).

Kant's critical philosophy has a profound influence on the course of subsequent philosophy, and, as we will see, aspects of it are still alive today.

1. Why can't Kant be satisfied with the kind of view "practical anthropology" gives us of morality? What will be missing in such a view?
2. Kant says that the only thing good without qualification is a good will. What is the relation between will and rationality?
3. What is the connection between a good will and the concept of duty?
4. What is the supreme principle of morality? Why is it categorical (not hypothetical)? And why must it be a priori?
5. In what way does the distinction between conditional value and absolute value play a role in the moral law?
6. In what way are you autonomous (rather than heteronomous) in the realm of morality? Why doesn't individual autonomy precipitate social chaos?
7. Explain the connections among autonomy, rationality, and human freedom.
8. Kant says he has demonstrated the limits of knowledge, but that this makes room for faith. Faith in what? And on what grounds?

FOR FURTHER THOUGHT

1. Kant does seem to resolve certain puzzles concerning knowledge that are bequeathed to him by Descartes and Hume. But there is a high price to pay for these successes: We have to give up the hope of knowing reality as it really is. Can you think of a way to avoid paying this price?
2. Suppose you are talking things over with Kant and he says, "Lying is wrong, you know." And, in the way undergraduates are apt to these days, you reply, "Who's to say?" What would Kant have to say to you? And would you need to think again about that flippant, but very popular, question?

KEY WORDS

critique of reason	things-in-themselves
Copernican revolution	noumenon
transcendental	phenomenon
a priori	unconditioned
a posteriori	Ideas of Pure Reason
analytic	rational psychology
synthetic	being
necessity	good will
universality	maxims
intuition	duty
space	inclinations
time	respect for law
sensibility	hypothetical imperative
understanding	categorical imperative
concept	things
representation	persons
categories	autonomous
substance	heteronomous
properties	kingdom of ends
causation	holy will
possible experience	rational faith

NOTES

1. References to Kant's works are as follows:
   P: Prolegomena to Any Future Metaphysics, ed. Günter Zöller, trans. Peter G. Lucas and Günter Zöller (Oxford: Oxford University Press, 2004).
   G: Groundwork for the Metaphysics of Morals, trans. Arnulf Zweig, ed. Thomas E. Hill Jr. and Arnulf Zweig (Oxford: Oxford University Press, 2002).
   CPR: Immanuel Kant's Critique of Pure Reason, trans. Norman Kemp Smith (New York: St. Martin's Press, 1956).

CHAPTER

21

GEORG WILHELM FRIEDRICH HEGEL

Taking History Seriously

Since early Greek times, those seeking wisdom have aspired to give a general account of the universe and our place in it. One after another, philosophers announce to the world that they have succeeded in solving the riddle. But each attempt, though it builds on preceding efforts and tries to correct their shortcomings, seems to raise new occasions for doubt. The persistent jabs of Sophists and skeptics always find a target and keep generations of philosophers in business. Some assumptions, however, are taken for granted by most of these thinkers and by Western culture in general. We can set them out in the following way:

- There is a *truth* about the way things are.
- This truth is *eternal* and unchanging.
- This truth can, in principle, be *known* by us.
- It is the job of the *philosopher*, relying on reason and experience, to discover this truth.
- Knowing the truth about ourselves and the universe in which we live is *supremely important*, for only such truth can serve as a secure foundation on which culture can be built: science, religion, ethics, the state, and a good life for all.

As we have seen, both Hume and Kant argue for a severe limitation on these ambitions. Hume drives us toward a skeptical attitude regarding the powers of human reason, and Kant, though he rescues Newtonian science and offers us a rational morality, concedes that we can know things only as they appear to us, structured by our sensibility and rational faculties. What we really are, and what reality is in itself, is completely and forever hidden from us.

Still, in one important respect, Kant accepts the assumptions common to most of the Western philosophical tradition: that there is a truth about the way things are and that this truth is eternal. He thinks he has found it. Kant's central truths, of course, focus on what it is to be rational. The structures of a rational mind are the same for all rational creatures (and so, of course, for all humans). They are unchanging over time. The receptive structures of sensibility, the pattern-imposing categories of understanding, and the insatiable logical drive of reason are the given features of mind, identical in every age and every place.

496

Nineteenth-century thinkers transform this picture in surprisingly far-reaching ways. Chief among them is Georg Wilhelm Friedrich Hegel (1770–1831), a German philosopher of encyclopedic range who is sensitive to the exciting changes surrounding him in his world. It will be worth spending a little time setting the scene.

Historical and Intellectual Context

THE FRENCH REVOLUTION

July 14, 1789: A Paris mob storms the fortress-prison known as the Bastille, hated symbol of royal absolutism. Hegel is nineteen. Like youths all over Europe, he is enthralled. The revolution seems like a new start, an overthrow of the dead weight of centuries. Reason triumphs over tradition. The people are in control.*

This control turns into the Reign of Terror, spawns a series of wars, and leads ultimately to Napoleon's coup d'état and his assumption of the title of emperor. But something deep and remarkable has happened, and Europe will never be the same again. Hegel imbibes the sense of history being made, of real change, of the possibility of progress toward a more rational society. And he never loses it.

> It is not difficult to see that ours is a birth-time and a period of transition to a new era. Spirit has broken with the world it has hitherto inhabited and imagined, and is of a mind to submerge it in the past. Spirit is indeed never at rest but always engaged in moving forward. But just as the first breath drawn by a child after its long, quiet nourishment breaks the gradualness of merely quantitative growth—there is a qualitative leap, and the child is born—so likewise the Spirit in its formation matures slowly and quietly into its new shape, dissolving bit by bit the structure of its previous world, whose tottering state is only hinted at by isolated symptoms. The frivolity and boredom which unsettle the established order, the vague foreboding of something unknown, these are the heralds of approaching change. The gradual crumbling that left unaltered the face

*For the French Revolution, see https://en.wikipedia.org/wiki/French_Revolution.

"What is rational is actual and what is actual is rational."

—G. W. F. HEGEL

of the whole is cut short by a sunburst which, in one flash, illuminates the features of the new world. (*PS*, 6–7)[1]

Hegel's references to the revolution are obvious here, as is his sense of something new bursting into history. It is not, of course, absolutely new, any more than

> a new-born child; it is essential to keep this in mind. It comes on the scene for the first time in its immediacy or its Notion. Just as little as a building is finished when its foundation has been laid, so little is the achieved Notion of the whole the whole itself. When we wish to see an oak with its massive trunk and spreading branches and foliage, we are not content to be shown an acorn instead. (*PS*, 7)

Several crucial concepts are introduced in these two quotations, and it is important to get some preliminary understanding of them. The word translated as **"Spirit"** is the German *Geist*. Scholars disagree about whether the best English equivalent is "spirit," as this translator has it, or "mind."

Hegel's use of *Geist* surely includes everything we mean by mind, but it has implications that allow Hegel to see the revolution as spirit breaking with past traditions and maturing as it moves forward in history. The term **"Notion"** is a translation of *Begriff* and is often rendered "concept." It is the term Kant uses for concepts, including the a priori concepts he calls *categories*. Sometimes we use "concept" where it seems appropriate and sometimes "notion." In this second quotation we can understand Hegel to be saying that the *concept* of a people united in "Liberty, Equality, and Fraternity" has come on the scene. But that is not yet the *reality* of a society organized by those principles. That may take a long time, just as it takes a long time for the acorn to develop into the giant oak. Development, movement toward maturity, the sense of history going on—history with direction, purpose, aim—are central characteristics of Hegel's thought.

The Romantics

Hegel lives at a turning point in German culture. His generation rebels against what they see as the dry, cold rationality of the Enlightenment, championing feeling and imagination instead. The greatest writers, poets, and musicians of his day, such as Goethe, Schiller, and Beethoven, are known as **Romantics.** They agree with Kant that science and reason cannot reveal reality, but they look to other faculties to take us where reason falters: to intuition, to love, to passion.*

Like the Renaissance humanists, the Romantics look back to classical Greece. The *unity* and *harmony* of Greek life impresses them, especially the harmony they see there between rationality and feeling. They object to Kant's attempt to pit reason and morality against human passions. Many of them also oppose the Christianity they are familiar with, setting its pessimism about sin and evil in humanity against what they perceive as the sunny, optimistic outlook of the Greeks.† Some, including the young Hegel, explore the possibilities for a new folk religion that would express more adequately the ideals they hold dear.

Hegel himself is not a Romantic. As we'll see, he is himself a great champion of reason, and he criticizes Romanticism in some respects. But this ideal of harmony within and among human beings he makes thoroughly his own.

Hegel's thought is notoriously difficult, and what you will read here is a considerable simplification. But in an introduction to philosophy, that is quite in order. The main themes and something of Hegel's contribution to the great conversation should be intelligible. As you will surely see, the very idea of the history of philosophy *as* a great conversation owes much to Hegel. For him, this conversation *is* philosophy, and to study its history is to immerse oneself in the development of reason itself.

Epistemology Internalized

Hume calls for the construction of a science of human nature, and Kant attempts a critique of pure reason. In each case, the motivation is to examine the "instrument" by which we gain knowledge in order to understand the nature and limits of our cognitive capacities. This seems, on the face of it, a very reasonable thing. But Hegel has an objection.

> In the case of other instruments, we can try and criticize them in other ways than by setting about the special work for which they are destined. But the examination of knowledge can only be carried out by an act of knowledge. To examine this so-called instrument is the same thing as to know it. But to seek to know before we know is as absurd as the wise resolution of Scholasticus, not to venture into the water until he had learned to swim.[2]

If we want to know whether a chisel is an adequate instrument, we can use our sense of touch as a criterion, or we can observe with our eyes how easily it parts the wood. But if we want to know whether our knowledge is an adequate instrument—whether it gets us the truth—we have only our own knowledge to depend on. For coming to know how (and what) we know is an *instance* of knowing and cannot therefore *precede* it. How do we know that our "knowledge" about knowledge really is—*knowledge?*

---

*For more on the romantics, see https://en.wikipedia.org/wiki/Romanticism.

†But see Nietzsche, p. 570.

Hegel also thinks that Kant concedes too much to skepticism. Our aim at the outset is to know the way things *really are*, to discover the truth about reality as it exists *in itself*. Kant argues that all we can know is how things appear to us—that the truth about reality as it is in itself is forever hidden from our sight.

Some of Kant's successors find this unsatisfactory—indeed, self-contradictory. How can we know that there are things-in-themselves if we cannot know anything about them? Hegel agrees with this criticism and works out an alternative view in which the distinction between consciousness and its objects is seen to be a distinction *internal* to consciousness. This is a difficult notion, but a crucial one. Let us see if we can understand it.

Amazingly, Hegel thinks he can solve both problems at once: the problem of circularity and the problem of skepticism. As long as we think of a mind as *one* complete and finished entity and the object of knowledge as a *second* complete and finished entity, Hegel thinks there can be no solution to these problems. As long as subject and object are thought to be inherently unrelated, there can be no guarantee that they will correspond, and skepticism always looms large. Descartes and Locke do not defeat it, Hume resigns himself to it, and Kant cultivates the garden of phenomena in the midst of a vast sea of unknowables. For Hegel, the key to the solution is the idea of **development.** He proposes to show that consciousness moves through *stages* (he sometimes calls them "moments"), that it does this with a kind of *necessity*, driven by inadequacies at each stage, and that we can "watch" as it develops itself from the simplest and most inadequate consciousness to one that is completely adequate to its object. To "watch" in this way is to do what he calls **phenomenology**—to observe the *internal dialectic* through which consciousness moves toward ever more satisfactory relations with its objects. Phenomenology of mind (spirit) takes consciousness itself as a phenomenon; it tries to set out the *logos*—the logic or internal rationale—of its development.

Development, for Hegel, is not chaotic or random; though it zigzags toward its goal, it does have a direction. Consciousness, history, forms of life, and reality all develop

- from *implicit* forms to *explicit*;
- from the *potential* to the *actual*;
- from the *abstract* to the *concrete*;
- from *notion* to *reality*;
- from *partial truth* to *absolute knowledge*;
- from *less rational* to *more rational*.

Development, in short, is progress.

"The reasonable man adapts himself to the world; the unreasonable one persists in trying to adapt the world to himself. Therefore all progress depends on the unreasonable man."

George Bernard Shaw (1856–1950)

We have several times used the word "internal." This needs to be explained. You can see the significance of what Hegel is doing by comparing it to our "ordinary" way of thinking. Most of us think of knowledge as a certain state of mind that *represents* or *corresponds to* some object *external* to it. You have this idea that your bicycle is in the garage. That is one thing. You also have a bicycle. That is a second thing. These two things, idea and object, seem quite independent of one another and can vary independently.* That is why knowledge is a problem. You can believe your bicycle is in the garage when in fact it has been stolen. In the possibility of this discrepancy we have the origins of skepticism.†

Notice, though, that every time we are aware of an object, we take it *really to be* (in itself) what it *seems to be* (for us). As long as we are satisfied in our contemplation of this object, no dichotomy between what it really is and how it appears to us arises in our consciousness. But then how does the idea of *appearance* ever arise? How does the idea of the way something *is for us* ever get distinguished from the idea of what it *is in itself*? Hegel argues that this can happen because consciousness is conscious

---

*Again we note the key elements of the representational theory. See p. 372.

†If you review Descartes' first meditation, the classic modern source for skeptical problems, you will see that it depends on the absolute independence of idea and object.

not only of the object but also of itself (as related to the object); and it *does* happen whenever we become aware of some discrepancy between our "knowledge" of the object and our "experience" of the object.

> For consciousness is, on the one hand, consciousness of the object, and on the other, consciousness of itself; consciousness of what for it is the True, and consciousness of its knowledge of the truth. Since both are *for* the same consciousness, this consciousness is itself their comparison; it is for this same consciousness to know whether its knowledge of the object corresponds to the object or not. (*PS*, 54)

The crucial phrase here is this: "both are *for* the same consciousness." The object and our awareness of that object are given *together*—in the same consciousness! This is why Hegel thinks a critique of knowledge can be *internal* to consciousness and why it can proceed by means of phenomenology. The comparison between concept and object is made by the same consciousness that is aware of both. The object of consciousness is not, never has been, and *could not be* some completely independent thing-in-itself. Every object is an object *for a subject.* * The slogan "no object without a subject" expresses the key idea in what is called **idealism.**

What we discover if we just "watch" consciousness at work is that it reveals—by itself, and with a certain kind of inevitability—the discrepancies between its own awareness and its objects. It corrects itself to make its awareness more adequate to the object, but in changing itself, it finds that the object has not stayed put but has changed correspondingly. And what the object was previously taken to *be*, we now see it only *appears* to be. Its former status as thing-in-itself (a status it had only because the former consciousness *ascribed* that status to it) is now withdrawn, and it is now seen as having been only an object *for us.* Thus arises *within consciousness* the distinction between **appearance** and **reality,** that very distinction we naively thought existed between the realm of consciousness as a whole and something entirely independent of consciousness.

As an example, consider the 2014 film *Gone Girl.* When one of the main characters, Amy, disappears, police discover evidence that she has been murdered. As the plot develops, it comes to light that Amy is alive and well, having staged the whole thing. What you had taken to be reality is now seen to be merely appearance. But, of course, you are now taking something else to be real. And it is always possible that a larger picture may upset your convictions yet again.

Phenomenology is the discipline that traces the dialectical succession of these ever more adequate stages of consciousness.

> Consequently, we do not need to import criteria, or to make use of our own bright ideas and thoughts during the course of the inquiry; it is precisely when we leave these aside that we succeed in contemplating the matter in hand [knowledge] as it is *in and for itself.* (*PS*, 54)

There is no need for philosophers to come up with the criterion for knowledge, Hegel tells us, because the problem of the criterion is in the process of solving itself! Nor should we despair because it seems we cannot compare our thoughts with their objects and test them definitively for their correctness. In examining its own adequacy, consciousness is continually engaged in such comparison and testing; "all that is left for us to do is simply to look on" (*PS*, 54). Hegel claims that by pursuing philosophy this way, by simply "looking on," we will see the criterion for knowledge develop naturally and necessarily *from within consciousness itself.*

Hegel's *Phenomenology of Spirit* can be thought of as a kind of biography of consciousness, the story of its development toward maturity. As consciousness develops, it grows ever more adequate to its object (and its object to consciousness), until at the end we discover a stage that deserves to be called **absolute knowledge.** At this point there will be no more discrepancy between reality and the knower; what there is will *be* what it is *known to be*; and what we *know* will correspond perfectly to *what there is*—because there has been a long process of mutual adjustment of each to the other. At that point, reason will be satisfied because it will see

---

*Here Hegel agrees with Kant—indeed with Berkeley!

ARTHUR SCHOPENHAUER

Known for his pessimism, Arthur Schopenhauer (1788–1860) accepts the Kantian distinction between the phenomenal world presented to our understanding and the world as it is in itself. Schopenhauer holds that phenomena are organized by a *principle of sufficient reason*, which guarantees that everything we can experience has a cause or ground explaining why it must be as it is. This principle corresponds to the Kantian a priori machinery of the mind and entails that the experienced world, including even my body, is "my idea."

In *The World as Will and Idea* (1818), Schopenhauer claims to go beyond Kant; that is, he claims to be able to identify the character of the world as it is in itself. We ourselves, he argues, are part of the noumenal world, so we have the most direct and immediate knowledge of its nature. In us the world reveals itself to be "will," a blind, ceaseless striving, the desire for existence. The whole of the phenomenal world, with all its varied individuals, is but a manifestation in time and space of this will. Beneath the surface appearances of things, we see a never-ending struggle for existence, desire succeeding desire, until life finally ends in death.

Unsatisfied desire is painful, but when desire is satisfied, boredom sets in—until we want something else. So life continually swings between pain and ennui.

Is there any cure for the disease of life? Schopenhauer holds that art, and music in particular, can provide a temporary release from this cycle of frustration. In the peculiarly disinterested character of aesthetic experience, the clamor of the will is quieted. We are freed for a time from the wheel of suffering and lose ourselves in the contemplation of a beautiful object.

A more permanent salvation can be attained only by a denial of the will to live itself. Schopenhauer believes this is the goal of all religions and is found most explicitly in Buddhism. If we realize that individuality (including our own bodily life in the phenomenal world) is merely idea—a kind of illusion, and not reality—our striving for individual ends will cease, egoism will be defeated, and we can dwell in a kind of will-less, ascetic, compassionate harmony with all.

"Hope springs eternal in the human breast;
Man never is, but always to be blest."

Alexander Pope (1688–1744)

---

that *what is real is what is rational* and *what is rational is the real*.

> The series of configurations which consciousness goes through along this road is, in reality, the detailed *education* of consciousness itself to the standpoint of Science. (*PS*, 50)

There is an ambiguity in the way we have presented Hegel to this point, but it is an ambiguity present in Hegel's thought. Is this development to be thought of as a series of stages within the life of *each human consciousness*, as it matures toward adequacy, or is it to be regarded as a historical process, through which the *human race* travels from stages of primitive culture to the most advanced science, religion, and philosophy? The answer is that it is both. And in some sense it is a *logical* progression as

well. Individuals are manifestations of Spirit, but so are civilizations and cultures. And throughout all, Hegel holds, there is present the **World Spirit,** which develops in individuals and cultures toward self-knowledge, rationality, and freedom. But of this, more later.

So far, this is all rather abstract. We need to look at several examples. Let us begin where Hegel does in his book *Phenomenology of Spirit*, with the simplest sort of knowledge—what he calls **sense-certainty.***

---

*Philosophers have often looked to something like this to serve as the *foundation for knowledge*. It may be that you are deceived that there is a dagger before you. But, apparently, you cannot be mistaken that it is *as if* there were a dagger before you. How things *seem* to you, what you *sense* (as opposed to

Consider the simple presence of some object to your consciousness—for example, the paper on which this sentence is written. You may now be *thinking* of this experience. But in the *consciousness* of the piece of paper itself, there is no thinking going on. There is just the presence of the paper to your consciousness. You are just *sensing* the paper. The fact that there is no thinking involved—no use of concepts to characterize the paper—is crucial for the *certainty* of this kind of experience. It is a very basic kind of experience—an experience of the sheer presence of something to consciousness, without any input from consciousness itself. This sort of consciousness is wholly *receptive*. It is like one of Hume's impressions. There seem to be no Kantian "conceptual filters" at work organizing, relating, and structuring the material. That is why this kind of experience seems to exclude the possibility of mistake. Hegel calls this kind of experience **immediacy.**

We, of course, are using language and quite sophisticated concepts in doing this phenomenology of sense-certainty. But we want to characterize it "from the inside," so to speak, as it experiences itself. So we must be careful not to import our external descriptions into that consciousness. What, then, is it like? All we can say by way of description is that there is a "this" presented to an "I." And perhaps, to make the "this" more clear, we can add that it is presented *now* and *here*. Sense-certainty presents what philosophers have called a *particular* (the "this") in its sheer particularity, without attributing any *universal* characteristics to it.*

Sense-certainty does not know this page *as* white or *as* dotted with black marks—or, for that matter, *as* a page. Such characterizations import interpretive concepts into the experience, but it is wholly bare of such notions. There is just that sheer presence in your visual field. (Take a minute to see whether this description does capture an elementary aspect of your current experience.)

But now we notice that this "I" might direct its attention elsewhere, and a new "this" is presented—a can of Coke, perhaps. But the Coke can be characterized by "this" just as well as the paper. And there is a new "now" and "here," as well. The "this," "now," and "here" have not changed; they just apply to a different object. But what this shows us is that these are themselves *concepts*; they are, in fact, universals. And they are among the *most universal* of all universals because they can apply to *every* object.

Moreover, another consciousness might become aware of this piece of paper. In that case, there is another "I" involved. It is no less an "I" than the first. And this shows that the "I" is also a universal. Like the others, it is *universally* universal. And so it is essentially empty.* It reveals nothing at all about the nature of the "I" in question.

What does all this mean? We can observe, Hegel says, that this most fundamental kind of consciousness turns into its opposite. It seemed to be the most concrete, rich, dense, real kind of knowledge there is. It seemed to be "immediate," by which Hegel means uninterpreted, unconceptualized, and unmodified by any conscious activity. It seemed to be an apprehension of the pure particularity of things. But it turns out that this "knowledge" is the most bare, most abstract, most universal, and most empty of content imaginable.

> Because of its concrete content, sense-certainty immediately appears as the *richest* kind of knowledge. . . . Moreover, sense-certainty appears to be the *truest* knowledge; for it has not as yet omitted anything from the object, but has the object before it in its perfect entirety. But, in the event, this very *certainty* proves itself to be the most abstract and poorest *truth*. (*PS*, 58)

---

what objects you *perceive*), seems immune from doubt and so is fit to be a foundation. Recall what Descartes claims to be certain of even if his senses deceive him about external objects. Hume's impressions also play this role. There are later examples as well, right into the twenty-first century. But if Hegel is right in his critique of sense-certainty, a lot of modern epistemology is simply based on a mistake.

*The distinction between particulars and universals goes back at least to Plato, who notes that some things have properties in common—squareness, redness, humanity, and so on. These common features, Plato thinks, are (peculiar) things themselves; he calls them "Forms." (See p. 153.) Aristotle and the medieval philosophers call the common properties of things "universals." For Kant, it is *concepts* that supply this universal aspect. Hegel has this part of the great conversation clearly in mind here.

*There are echoes here of Kant's critique of rational psychology. Review pp. 481–482.

What does such a consciousness *know*? It *cannot say*. But is knowledge that cannot be expressed really knowledge at all? Imagine a world in which consciousnesses contains only such brute awareness; there would be no classification, no characterization, no comparison, no relating of one thing to another, no narratives, no laws, no explanations, no remembrance of things past or expectations of things to come—and virtually no language! Consciousness could not even be aware of a tree *as a tree*, for that involves the application of the concept "tree." Would such a world qualify as one in which *knowledge* exists? Hegel, for one, is sure that it would not.

So sense-certainty, which seemed to be the most secure form of knowledge, immune from the ravages of doubt, turns out not to be knowledge at all. And consciousness is impelled to go beyond it. Note well: It is consciousness itself that is forced beyond this minimal stage. Indeed, in necessarily using the universal concepts of "this" and "I," it is already beyond this stage. *We* are not imposing this from the outside. *We* are not supplying some criterion according to which this stage is unsatisfactory. There is an internal dialectic at work, forcing consciousness to recognize the inadequacy of sense-certainty and to move to a new level of sophistication. We are just "looking on."

Suppose that we "personalize" consciousness for a moment (as Hegel tends to do anyway) and think of it as having intentions and goals. We can then ask, What is it that "motivates" consciousness to develop beyond this primitive stage? Hegel answers that consciousness, in its "attempt to be" simply sense-certainty, *negates itself*. In the stage of sense-certainty, it "intends" to be nothing more than a knowledge of what is immediately present to it. But it fails. The insufficiency of this attempt is *displayed* to consciousness itself in its very attempt. It *cannot* be what it tries to be because it necessarily interprets even this minimal experience in terms of universal concepts ("this," "here," "now," and "I"), which, moreover, are completely inadequate to capture the experience.

But, Hegel points out, this negation of itself as certain knowledge is not a kind of blank rejection. It is not equivalent to skepticism (which

can be thought of as a *general* sort of negation of knowledge). It is a quite determinate and specific negation: the negation of the sufficiency of sense-certainty for knowledge. And this drives consciousness not into skepticism, but into a new form.

Consciousness has learned that it cannot find the certainty of true knowledge by retreating to elementary beginning points.* So it has no other alternative but to plunge ahead, making use of concepts to interpret its experience. If knowledge is to be possible, consciousness cannot be merely receptive, for what it has discovered is that any attempt to merely "register" what is present to it already makes use of universal concepts, but these are concepts so poor that *what* is being sensed cannot be expressed. Mind *must* play a more active role.

We can learn one more thing from this first bit of the dialectic of consciousness. Sense-certainty is negated. Its pretensions to knowledge are false. But when consciousness goes on to another stage, it will not leave the contents of sense behind, to start afresh. When consciousness begins to interpret in terms of richer concepts, it will *use* the very sense experience that it just recognized as inadequate for knowledge. So the earlier stage is not lost; what is *true* in it is preserved and incorporated in the next level.

Hegel finds this dialectical pattern repeated again and again, both in the progress of consciousness toward absolute knowledge and in the sequence of stages the human race goes through in history. A stage or "moment" of consciousness develops until it displays its own inadequacy. It is then negated and supplanted by a second (as the universally universal supplants the purely particular in sense-certainty). Then a third stage emerges that incorporates the valuable and true in each of these stages. That stage then begins to develop, and the process repeats itself.† It is this *internal* dialectic that Hegel thinks will supply at last the

---

*Contrast Descartes' project of discovering a foundation in simple certainties and Hume's recommendation to trace ideas back to impressions.

†Hegelians have often called these moments the *thesis*, the *antithesis*, and the *synthesis*. Hegel does not often use these terms, but this triadic structure is common in his analyses.

criterion for knowledge and close off the possibility of skepticism.

We cannot here follow the immensely elaborate and complex dialectic Hegel displays for us. Let us instead sketch briefly the progress of the next few stages, then discuss more fully several of the most famous and influential of them.

The inadequacy of sense-certainty leads consciousness on to the stage Hegel calls

- *perception*, in which objects (things) are characterized using concepts (universals) that describe their properties. But what is a thing? Is it a mere collection of the properties?* That hardly seems right since it misses the *unity* of a thing. Is it then something lying behind all the properties?† But then it becomes an unknowable *X*, since we perceive things only in terms of their properties. That can't be right either. This dilemma forces consciousness on to the next stage of
- *understanding*, in which things are understood in terms of laws, as in Newtonian science. These laws are thought to express the *truth of things*—their inner nature or essence. They explain the properties we ascribe to things in perception and give us an account of the unity of things—of why a given thing has just the properties it does have. But in producing such explanations, consciousness is *active*, not merely passive.‡ In recognizing this contribution by itself, consciousness reaches the stage of explicit
- *self-consciousness*.

What Hegel says here is justly famous; let's examine it more carefully.

---

1. How does the problem of the "instrument" called knowledge involve us again in circular reasoning?
2. In what sense does Hegel think Kant concedes too much to the skeptics?
3. How does the distinction between appearance and reality arise within consciousness, if Hegel is right?
4. What is phenomenology?
5. What would absolute knowledge be—if we could get it?

6. What is sense-certainty? What is it "certain" about? Can it say? Sketch Hegel's critique of sense-certainty.
7. Define the term "immediate," as Hegel uses it. Why is immediacy something that has to be surpassed?
8. Explain how perception and understanding are dialectical developments from sense-certainty.

Self and Others

There is, within the stage of self-consciousness, a dialectic that structurally resembles the one in sense-certainty. In a passage that is the despair of commentators, Hegel seems to suggest that the most basic form of self-consciousness is *desire*. Why should this be? Any answer, in view of the obscurity of Hegel's text here, is somewhat speculative, but perhaps this is what he has in mind.

Consciousness faces a world of objects that is *other* than itself. Yet, in the stage of understanding, it recognizes that the essence or truth of these objects (as revealed in scientific laws) is its own work. So the other isn't really other after all. And yet it obviously isn't just itself, either. It both *is* and *is not* other. What to do? Consciousness tries to resolve this unsatisfactory situation by making the other wholly its own. And isn't that exactly what desire is—a project to make mine what is not yet mine?

Such desire is not just conscious of the object, however. It is also, in a minimal way, *self*-conscious. Think about what it is like to want something. You say, "I want a fast car." The "I" (which doesn't have a fast car) is present explicitly in the expression of your desire for the car. In desiring something you experience a poignant contrast between yourself and what is not yourself.*

But there is something incomplete about this stage of self-consciousness because although I am present in it, I am not conscious of myself as a self that *is* self-conscious. All we have are these two poles—I and the other—together with a project to close the gap between them. But it remains unclear just what this I *is*.

---

*That is Berkeley's proposal. See pp. 432–433.
†That is Locke's idea. See pp. 418–419.
‡Here we have Kant's contribution. See pp. 474–475.

---

*Recall the Buddha's claim that there is no conception of the self that does not lead to attachment and craving (p. 41).

It might help to think of the way a child develops a consciousness of herself. At first no distinction is made between herself and the other. What breaks this seamless unity of the child's world is frustration (unsatisfied desire). She becomes aware of the difference between herself and Mama, herself and the bottle, herself and Teddy. But she is not yet conscious of herself *as a self-conscious being*. This comes much later and requires—as Hegel is among the first to recognize—another self-conscious being with which to contrast herself.

> Self-consciousness achieves its satisfaction only in another self-consciousness. (*PS*, 110)

Like everything in Hegel's world, **self-consciousness** doesn't appear complete at its first appearance; it *develops*. Its development requires recognition by another self-consciousness. This sort of recognition *creates* self-conscious beings. I become self-conscious when I am acknowledged as such by another self-conscious being and recognize this acknowledgment. Self-consciousness is a *social* fact.*

Again, like everything else, this development does not go smoothly; it is filled with conflict of the most desperate sort. It is a dialectical achievement that involves—no surprise—radical negation. How does it work? Let's consider two individuals, Jones and Smith.

Suppose that Jones, who has achieved self-consciousness, comes to recognize Smith as like himself—a self-consciousness constituted by desire. This is not a happy recognition. In a certain sense, it means that Jones has "lost himself," for he now recognizes himself as an "other"—for Smith. He is now an *object* for Smith. Moreover, remember that desire is an attempt to make one's own what is felt to be alien. The ominous aspect of this can be brought out in terms of *control*. Jones experiences Smith as someone who is trying to control him, define him, make him into what

Smith wants him to be. Naturally, Jones resists this objectification and control.

Meanwhile, from the other side, Smith is having analogous experiences. He feels himself to be the object of a hostile takeover attempt by Jones—to be nothing more than what Jones takes him to be and under the threat of control by Jones. He, too, struggles against this status.*

But even this does not bring out the full complexity of the situation. In recognizing each other as self-conscious beings, "They *recognize* themselves as *mutually recognizing* each other" (*PS*, 112). So their consciousness of each other is of a distinctive kind—different from their consciousness of things like stones or pencils.

Again there is development, and again it is tortuous because this mutual recognition is still inadequate. From each side, the situation is this: One is doing the *recognizing* and the other is *being recognized*. Look at it from the side of Jones, remembering that the same can be said for Smith's point of view. Jones recognizes Smith as both like himself and as other than himself, but he does not yet recognize Smith as a *pure* self-consciousness.† Smith appears as an embodied, living conscious individual—one who wants to control Jones. So Jones thinks,

---

*Contrast this with the views of Avicenna or Descartes, who think they can imagine being conscious of themselves in isolation (pp. 304 and 382, respectively). If Hegel is right, this individualism is simply impossible. Humans are made into self-conscious individuals, persons in the full sense, by their interactions with other human beings. No one is self-made.

---

*Kant's second formulation of the categorical imperative (p. 491) commands us to treat others as ends, not as means only. What Hegel is identifying here is an unavoidable tendency in self-conscious beings to treat each other precisely as means. Relations between the sexes often take this dialectical form, and complaints that someone is perceived only as a "sex object," or is being "used," get a natural interpretation in this Hegelian context. Hegel agrees, of course, with the rationality and rightness of Kant's imperative, but he is pointing out how difficult it is to achieve the state in which it is actualized.

†Hegel has a strong sense of "self-consciousness" in mind here. Think of it like this. You can become conscious of your height and weight, but that is a minimal self-consciousness indeed. You can go further and become aware of your inclinations, of your character, of your personality, of your thoughts. Indeed, for *any fact* about yourself, you could become conscious of it—make it into an *object* for yourself. By making every such fact into an object for yourself, you attain a kind of *pure* self-consciousness. To use the title of a book by Thomas Nagel, this is *The View from Nowhere* (New York: Oxford University Press, 1986).

- Smith is like me, an independent, self-conscious being.
- Smith is aware of me.
- Smith recognizes that I am aware of him.
- He realizes that *for me*, he is just another object in the world.
- Like me, Smith is constituted by desire.
- Hence, Smith will not be content to leave me in my independence because that will mean I may come to control him.
- So I had better not leave Smith in his independence, lest he control me.
- Therefore, if I cannot absolutely control him, I must kill Smith.

Smith, of course, has exactly parallel thoughts. Each consciousness is driven to negate the other, to control it, to turn it into a mere means for the satisfaction of its own desire.* And it is this negating that reveals to each consciousness its true nature as a *pure self-consciousness*.

Hegel's thought here is an extreme one. *Spirit* comes on the scene explicitly for the first time in pure self-consciousness; it cannot *realize itself* (become an actuality) except in mutual recognition by independent and free self-conscious individuals. But such mutual recognition is hazardous and tricky; on each side it involves tearing oneself away from everything immediate and merely natural. The only proof that I am not just an object for another, but a subject—a spirit, a being-for-myself, a person—is my willingness to risk *everything worldly* to gain such recognition. A struggle for domination ensues.

But what happens next is a surprise. Suppose Jones wins the struggle and kills Smith. Has he achieved what he wanted? Not at all. For in eliminating Smith, he deprives himself of precisely that source of recognition that he needs to realize himself as a self-conscious being! He has shattered the mirror in which he might have discovered who he is. In some fashion (either in the course of history

or in some dim way within each developing consciousness, or perhaps in both), self-conscious individuals become aware of this self-defeating character of the life-and-death struggle. And the result is a compromise.

What happens is this: The stronger makes the weaker into his slave.* Let us imagine that Jones makes himself the master. Then he has, in relation to Smith, a very real independence and freedom; and he experiences Smith as recognizing that independence. Jones, then, exists *for himself* and has apparently achieved what he needs: the recognition of himself as a free and independent self-consciousness. But has he really? Strangely enough, he has not. For consider the consciousness of the slave. It is a *dependent* consciousness—unfree and subject to the will of the master. But such a consciousness is not fit to provide the recognition that the master needs to confirm himself as free and independent. That can only be given by another free and independent individual. From Jones' own point of view, Smith (his slave) is almost indistinguishable from a mere brute. What could "recognition" by such a creature mean?

Consider now the consciousness of the slave, Smith. Suppose he is a cobbler; he takes leather and nails and transforms them into shoes. He does this to satisfy his master's desire, not his own desire. But in working on the things of the world, Smith expresses himself; he *puts himself into the products of his labor*.† These products exist independent of him; he recognizes himself in them and so achieves in his *work* a kind of self-realization that is denied the master. He *objectifies* himself and so can recognize himself in what he produces. "I," he can say, "am the one who made this; this object reveals what I can do and who I am; I have put *myself* into this object." Thus he achieves a definite kind of self-consciousness. In the independence of these

---

*There are echoes here of Hobbes' description of the state of nature. See again pp. 410–413. In Jean-Paul Sartre's play *No Exit*, we find three people engaged in just such control games. Eventually we discover they are in hell, from which there is "no exit," since they cannot die. One of the characters says, "Hell is other people."

---

*It is worth noting that many ancient societies, including Greek, Roman, and Hebrew, were slave societies. Muslim societies and many European colonies countenanced slavery, too, often up until relatively recently. Hegel's discussion here has a historical cast that the earlier, more purely epistemological studies lack.

†Compare Locke, on the origin of property, pp. 425–426.

objects, in the products of his labor, he recognizes his own independence.*

But that is not all. In addition to this "positive moment" in Smith's attainment of self-consciousness, there is a pervasive fear in the slave that constitutes a "negative moment."

This fear of the slave, a kind of universal dread, drives Smith back into himself, distances him from the master and even from the things on which he works. The entire material world is "negated"; the slave in his fear says "no" to it all—and discovers himself as a pure self-consciousness. He becomes aware of himself as something *other* than everything else that exists. So he becomes what the master can never become: a being who exists as an object *for himself*. He, rather than the master, is the bearer of spirit in its progress toward new heights of development!

---

1. Why does Hegel think desire is the first stage of self-consciousness?
2. Explain the role that recognition plays in the development of self-consciousness.
3. In the dialectic of master and slave, in what sense does the slave win?

Stoic and Skeptical Consciousness

Spirit progresses beyond this master–slave dialectic, according to Hegel, at a particular point in history. The world, Hegel thinks, entered a new era when Alexander's empire displaced the system of Greek city-states. Under the impersonal, bureaucratic weight of vast empires, including both Alexander's and Rome's, people felt helpless to shape their own destiny. And so spirit, now acutely conscious of itself, withdraws from everything that

it cannot control; in effect, it withdraws *into itself*, finding there an independence and freedom that is denied it in the hostile world.

Spirit's first move in this direction is toward Stoicism, which discounts everything outside of oneself as "what is not in one's power." And what is not in one's power, according to the Stoics, is not worth worrying about. This leaves only internal conscious states, such as "opinion, aim, desire, aversion," over which the Stoic claims we can exercise total control and so total freedom.*

As you might expect, though, Hegel aims to show that even though Stoicism is an advance in some respects, it is still one-sided and inadequate. The Stoic form of self-consciousness, he argues, is still too abstract.

> Freedom in thought has only *pure thought* as its truth, a truth lacking the fullness of life. Hence freedom in thought, too, is only the Notion of freedom, not the living reality of freedom itself. (*PS*, 122)

There is a lack of *reality* in the Stoic's freedom, according to Hegel. That is why he says the Stoic has only the notion (the concept) of freedom, not its "living reality." Stoicism captures a partial truth, but it cannot capture the whole truth because it does not lead to a unified life in which what thinking declares to be valuable is *actually realized in natural existence*.†

Again, the road toward such unity is tortuous and indirect. Things have to get worse before they can get better. The ancient skeptics pursue unity, on Hegel's view, by aspiring to live the negation that Stoics proclaim in thought.

> *Scepticism* is the realization of that of which Stoicism was only the Notion, and is the actual experience of what the freedom of thought is. This is *in itself* the negative and must exhibit itself as such. (*PS*, 123)

Skeptics suspend judgment about each and every claim concerning reality. Indeed, they actively use the resources of thought to make this possible by

---

*Some forty years later, Karl Marx would take up this dialectic of master and slave. For Marx, of course, it is not consciousness that is at stake, but real material life and well-being. He accepts Hegel's point that one objectifies oneself in one's labor and goes on to emphasize that if the product of one's labor is not one's own, if it belongs to another, then one becomes alienated *from oneself*. From this point arises his critique of capitalism. See "Marx: Beyond Alienation and Exploitation," in Chapter 22.

---

*See p. 242.

†It is worth comparing this critique of Stoicism with that of Saint Augustine. See p. 289. Note also that Hegel's internal critique of Stoicism (that it splits a person into two halves) is akin to the Romantics' critique of Kant (p. 498).

constructing equally plausible arguments on each side of every question.*

But once again, this stratagem on the part of Spirit proves unstable. Living a unified life requires *living*, which seems impossible without making judgments about what is real and what is good. The standard skeptical response is to "adhere to appearances," as Sextus Empiricus puts it, to "live in accordance with the normal rules of life, undogmatically, seeing that we cannot remain wholly inactive."† Hegel's analysis of this tactic exposes it as a sham. Skeptical self-consciousness at one time

> recognizes that its freedom lies in rising above all the confusion and contingency of existence, and at another time equally admits to a relapse into occupying itself with what is unessential. . . . It affirms the nullity of seeing, hearing, etc., yet it is itself seeing, hearing, etc. It affirms the nullity of ethical principles, and lets its conduct be governed by these very principles. Its deeds and its words always belie one another. (*PS*, 124–125)

In short, skeptical self-consciousness is mired deep in self-deception. Priding itself on its freedom, it becomes slave to the customs of the society in which it finds itself, whatever they happen to be.

Hegel's Analysis of Christianity

The next transition arises naturally out of this unsatisfactory state.‡ Spirit recognizes its split nature,

Hegel says, and it recognizes the split as a duality *within itself*. It no longer identifies itself only with the thinking, rational side but incorporates into itself both of the opposed aspects. This self-divided consciousness, aware nonetheless that it is *one*, Hegel calls the **Unhappy Consciousness.*** On the one side there is the experience of free and rational thinking, of pure universality, which nothing merely contingent or natural can touch. Hegel calls this the *Unchangeable*. On the other side, consciousness experiences itself as a changeable, unessential, particular individual, subject to the sheerest happenstance of accident. These two sides are "alien to one another" (*PS*, 127).

Under psychological pressure to resolve this dilemma, consciousness identifies itself with the changeable, experiencing the unchangeable as "an alien Being," as *not itself* (*PS*, 127). The Unhappy Consciousness is essentially a *religious* consciousness; as you can see, Hegel has in mind the two poles around which Augustine's thought revolves: God and the soul.† But there is an obviously radical twist in Hegel's story. The Unchangeable (experienced as God) is not *actually* a being independent of an individual's consciousness; it only seems so. Actually, it is one *pole* of Spirit's consciousness of itself in this unhappy stage of its dialectical development. And the desperately unhappy individual, cut off from the Unchangeable, does not *actually* exist independently; he only seems to.

Christianity appears to Hegel as a subtle and ingenious construction on the part of Spirit to reunite what has been split. Jesus, understood as truly man

---

*For an example of the techniques of the skeptics, see p. 250.

†See p. 249. For a modern version of the same principle, recall Montaigne's "defense" of Raymond Sebond and its outcome, pp. 351–353. A somewhat similar pattern is found in David Hume; see p. 463.

‡It is perhaps time to pause a moment and reflect. Recall that Hegel's strategy is to discover the criterion for knowledge *from within*. The dialectic we have been tracing can be thought of as a process of sloughing off one proposed but clearly unsatisfactory criterion after another. And by now the goal should be getting clearer, too, though the details still need to be filled in. Nothing will do but a state in which Spirit is not *alienated* from reality, but *identifies* with it and can see *itself* expressed in whatever it knows to be real. Moreover, you can see that we have moved from a purely theoretical sense of knowledge to one that incorporates the entire life of a knower. This correlates with the increasingly

---

historical cast to the story Hegel is telling. Hegel, for whom the truth is always the whole, will be satisfied with nothing less: *Reason governs all*.

*Compare Augustine's flirtation with Manicheanism (which located evil outside himself) and the essential move in its rejection—his recognition that the problem was his own divided will (pp. 263–264).

†Hegel's characterization of this stage as an *Unhappy Consciousness* brings to mind Saint Paul's despairing cry in Romans 7: "When I want to do the right, only the wrong is within my reach. In my inmost self I delight in the law of God, but I perceive that there is in my bodily members a different law, fighting against the law that my reason approves and making me a prisoner under the law . . . of sin." A quick review of Chapter 12 would be helpful at this point.

and truly God, manifests the unity of the Spirit. His existence demonstrates that *in principle* the two sides of spirit—eternal and temporal, infinite and finite, unchangeable and changeable—are one. The Christian believer participates in the Unchangeable through devotion, sacrifice, and thanksgiving and hopes for the completion of this process in the life to come.*

So Hegel regards Christianity as expressing truth, or at least partial truth, but it does so in mythological and imaginative forms. It takes philosophy—that is, reason—to understand its real significance.†

---

1. What is the "truth" in Stoicism? Why is Stoicism, in Hegel's view, nonetheless inadequate?
2. How does Stoicism lead to the pure negativity of skepticism? Why does Hegel think skepticism, too, is inadequate?
3. How does the inadequacy of skepticism lead to the unhappy consciousness? How does Hegel utilize this concept to try to understand Christianity?

Reason and Reality: The Theory of Idealism

Consciousness, by its own internal development, has now reached the stage of reincorporating its *other* into itself. It recognizes that what it took to be alien—the thing sensed and perceived, the world as understood by science, the object of desire and labor, the self-consciousness of the master and the dependence of the slave, the negatively valued world of Stoic and skeptic, and finally the projection of itself into the heavens as God—is all its own work. Wherever consciousness looks, it sees nothing but *itself*!*

> In grasping the thought that the *single* individual consciousness is *in itself* Absolute Essence, consciousness has returned into itself. (*PS*, 139)

Hegel calls this stage **reason.** It will help to understand why if we think back to Kant. For Kant, reason is the faculty that asks and tries to answer why-questions. The propensity to ask such questions sets us off in a search for the "condition" that explains the subject we are asking about. Because we can always ask again, we find ourselves driven toward the Idea (a technical term, for Kant, you recall) of a condition that is *unconditioned*, that neither has nor needs any further explanation. But in the realm of phenomena, nothing unconditioned can be found, and noumena are closed to our inspection. So reason is a drive that must remain forever unsatisfied. This is how Kant limits knowledge to make room for faith.

But for Hegel there is no need for faith. His elaborate dialectic *from within* has, he thinks, covered all the possibilities that any consciousness could ever be aware of. And everywhere, absolutely everywhere, consciousness discovers *itself*; in every explanation of an *other*, it finds meanings, laws, truths, and values it has itself supplied. It is

---

*Is Hegel a Christian theologian, explaining "the true meaning of the faith"? Or is he an atheist, proposing a secular interpretation of a religious tradition he does not accept? As is characteristic with Hegel, it is hard to answer this question unambiguously. He is convinced that every stage of consciousness has its truth (as well as its falsity) and that what is true in it will be preserved in successor stages. But there *are* successor stages, which will do more justice to the phenomena than the earlier ones do. Christianity, for Hegel, is one necessary, fruitful stage in the history of spirit. But it is no more than that. Marx and his followers will emphasize the aspect of surpassing religion and proclaim themselves atheists. Others—"liberal" theologians—will emphasize what is true and must be preserved. Kierkegaard takes offense at the whole notion that finite individuals could ever "surpass" the truth in Christianity. See Chapter 22.

†Compare al-Fārābī's and Averroës' views on the relation between revealed religion and truth. See pp. 297–298 and 317.

---

*Our natural resistance to this conclusion, our conviction that consciousness cannot be all there is, has its basis in "sense-certainty"—in the apparent brute-fact character of sensation. It seems absolutely *not up to us* to determine what we sense when we open our eyes. And the sense of something independent of our awareness—something *other*, something *alien*—is very powerful. Hegel does not deny this, but he asks you to consider that as soon as you try to say what it is that you sense, you are in the realm of concepts, interpretation, and reason. *What it is*—even this apparently independent fact—is relative to the consciousness that comprehends it.

true that there is process involved, but it is a process that consciousness now knows must have a close; for it knows that it—it, itself—is the Unconditioned. And that is why Hegel calls the stage in which this truth is recognized *reason*. It is Kantian reason with this difference: It can achieve its aim!

> Now that self-consciousness is Reason, its hitherto negative relation to otherness turns round into a positive relation. Up till now it has been concerned only with its independence and freedom, concerned to save and maintain itself for itself at the expense of the *world*, or of its own actuality, both of which appeared to it as the negative of its essence. But as Reason, assured of itself, it is at peace with them, and can endure them; for it is certain that it is itself reality, or that everything actual is none other than itself; its thinking is itself directly actuality, and thus its relationship to the latter is that of idealism. . . .
>   Reason is the certainty of consciousness that it is all reality; thus does idealism express its Notion. (*PS*, 139–140)

To put it in another typically Hegelian way, the *substance* of the world is a *subject* of consciousness!

This conclusion might seem to be outrageous. How could *you*, a "*single* individual consciousness," be *all reality*? Is this some sort of mysticism? Even if we grant Hegel's controversial claim that whatever you can be aware of is something you have constituted yourself, *you* are certainly not conscious of *all reality*!*

Two things can be said in Hegel's defense. First, his claim is to be understood only as the outcome of the entire dialectical story that has been told to this point. It is not something that you in your common sense should be expected to immediately assent to. Our feeling of outrageousness may be simply a manifestation of that stage of consciousness in which most of us mostly live; we may occupy a rather lowly rung on the dialectical ladder. Common sense may have its limits, and the question we need to address is this: How sound is the dialectical path that Hegel has sketched for us?

The second reply has to do with the *subject* of consciousness. Your outrage is predicated on the assumption that you are merely a single, finite, limited individual. If that were so, of course, the outrage would be justified. But is that so? One thing to consider is our earlier conclusion that mind and forms of consciousness are inherently social.* A completely isolated individual consciousness is not possible. So you, as a conscious subject, represent or manifest a more general consciousness: that of your community, those who share the same language and instruments of interpretation (concepts).

Moreover, Hegel agrees with Kant that reason is a principle of universality. What is rational cannot differ from mind to mind. If it is rational in *these* circumstances to do just exactly *that*, then it is rational for us, for you, and for anyone else. So when Hegel says that consciousness in its mode of reason is *all reality*, he does not mean the consciousness that you happen to display today. After all, the dialectic he has led us through has shown us one after another inadequate form of consciousness. And your form of consciousness today is no doubt inadequate in many ways. Hegel means that consciousness, reason *in itself* or *in its essence*, is identical with all reality. This consciousness is *implicit* in you, and each person is part of the historical process in which it is *becoming explicit*. In that (implicit) sense, even the single consciousness that *you* are is *all reality*.†

In this connection, Hegel often talks in terms of a *World Spirit*. The term has clear religious connotations, but it would be a mistake to identify it with the Christian concept of God. (Recall Hegel's critique of the "alienation" characteristic of traditional religious—unhappy—consciousness.) The World Spirit is consciousness and reason manifesting itself in the world. Indeed, Hegel thinks history is a process in which "God" is coming to comprehend itself through us. In a sense, then, you and I are God—but potentially, implicitly, and in essence, not yet in actuality.

---

*Compare Hegel's view to the Vedic claim that *ātman* is *Brahman* (p. 38).

*See p. 505.
†For an enlightening analogy, compare Aristotle's notion of potentiality. The tadpole is not yet actually a frog, but it already is a frog *potentially* (see pp. 196–197).

Consciousness will determine its relationship to otherness or its object in various ways, according to the precise stage it has reached in the development of the World Spirit into self-consciousness. How it *immediately* finds and determines itself and its object at any time, or the way in which it is *for itself*, depends on what it has already *become*, or what it already is *in itself*. (*PS*, 141–142)

The endpoint of this process, when subject and object correspond perfectly, is the stage Hegel calls *absolute knowledge*.

What is known in absolute knowledge? The Kantian *Idea*—the unconditioned explainer of all reality. But it is now known not just as an ever-receding goal serving to regulate our inquiries. It is known as it is *in itself*. For it is the World Spirit's rational consciousness of itself as constituting all reality. In absolute knowledge the problem of the criterion will be solved, because all possible grounds for skeptical doubt will have been analyzed and *surpassed* in the dialectical progression that gets us to that point. Spirit will not just know reality; it will know that it knows. It will *be* what it knows.

It is not for you or us, but for the World Spirit that objects are (or rather, will be) completely intelligible. For us there remains opacity and darkness and an alien character to the things of the world. They continue to be experienced as *other*. But if Hegel is right, this otherness is merely appearance; even now it is in the process of being surpassed. In themselves, things are illuminated by the light of reason and are comprehensible without remainder. There are no dark and unintelligible Kantian noumena hiding behind the face of appearance. Apart from being known, things do not even exist—*could not* exist; things have their reality only *for a subject*. That is what idealism means. Hegel's idealism is an **absolute idealism** because reality is thought to be constituted in the self-consciousness of the Absolute—in God, Reason, the World Spirit. For the World Spirit is all of reality.

1. Explain idealism as the theory of how reason and reality are related.
2. Relate, as Hegel might, the World Spirit, absolute knowledge, and yourself.

Spirit Made Objective: The Social Character of Ethics

The recognition on the part of reason that it encompasses all reality is not yet the end of the dialectic. For this is, as we might say, "mere" recognition and has a formal or abstract character to it. Hegel would say it merely expresses the *notion* of reason.* It remains for reason to *objectify* itself by expressing itself in its objects so that these objects are made to display explicitly the rationality that, so far, is theirs only implicitly. Reason must become practical reason and actually shape the life of the community of self-conscious beings. Reason must become ethics.

The realm of **objective spirit,** as Hegel calls it, is the realm of culture—of art, religion, custom, morality, the family, and law. Here Spirit externalizes itself into worldly objects and can comprehend itself in contemplating its products. But this, too, is a process involving complication, negativity, and inadequacy. Again we will simplify.

Hegel looks back to ancient Greece before the controversy between Socrates and the Sophists for an example of unity and harmony.† At this time, the judgments of individuals about what should and should not be done, what is valuable, and what the good life consists of reflect the "ethos" of the Greek city-state. Individuals simply absorb the standards of their city; these standards are theirs without question and without reflection. Citizens do not experience a conflict between their individual conscience and what is required of them by the state because they cannot be said to have an "individual" conscience at all.‡ Their desires are simply molded

---

*Compare the passage about the French Revolution, pp. 497–498.

†Hegel would not want to deny that there have been many such "traditional societies" (as they are often called); but the Greeks, whom Hegel here interprets in line with the Romantic view of them, are unique because he takes them to have been the first to move away from the "immediacy" of traditional modes of community to a more rational and reflective mode.

‡Hegel says, "An Athenian citizen did what was required of him, as it were from instinct" (*RH*, 53). Compare Heidegger on "the One" ("The 'Who' of Dasein," in Chapter 27).

by the customs of the community, which they take for granted. We must not think that there is anything sinister about this process. It is the most natural thing in the world since children grow up *necessarily* internalizing the standards of the society in which they live.

There are consequences: (1) Citizens naturally identify their own good with the good of the state to which they belong, so there is harmony between individual and community; and (2) they experience themselves as free in their actions—so free, indeed, that they need not even remark on it. We can call this the stage of **custom.**

But this stage, Hegel notes, is marked by an *immediate* identity between an individual and the community. And, as we should now know, immediacy is a state that needs to be overcome and will be overcome by producing some negative to itself. Immediacy is always simplistic, naive, and abstract for Hegel. In this case, it lacks the character of being *for itself*, which is essential to a developed consciousness; it is not a *self-conscious* harmony and freedom. It does not represent a rational decision, just an unexamined way of life that is taken for granted.

The negative "moment" in Greek history is represented by the Sophists and Socrates. Influenced by the wider knowledge of the non-Greek world brought about through trade and warfare, the Sophists express the view that Greek customs are not "natural," not matters of *physis*, but mere matters of "convention" or *nomos*.* This represents a giant step toward becoming self-conscious, for it suggests that customs and traditions have been invented and can be changed. Socrates, for his part, engages in his ceaseless questioning in order to discover the *reason why* something is considered just or pious or courageous.† It is self-consciousness as reason that comes on the scene with Socrates. The detachment of consciousness from its immersion in traditional customs is a fateful step; it undermines individuals' sense of natural solidarity with their

communities, and Western civilization is never the same again. Our history since has been an exploration of the consequences of this step.

This negative stage of increasing individual self-consciousness culminates, according to Hegel, in modern times, when the Reformation affirms the criterion of individual conscience, Enlightenment thinkers debunk everything based only on tradition and privilege, and the French Revolution tries overnight to reconstruct society according to the dictates of reason.* Philosophically speaking, Hegel sees this stage reaching a climax in the ethical thinking of Immanuel Kant. He calls this stage **morality.** We need to pay some attention to Hegel's discussion of Kant because he takes Kant to "typify" this second, self-conscious stage.

Hegel accepts much of Kant's analysis. Morality, he agrees, must be founded on reason, not desire. Reason, moreover, gives us universal laws telling us what our duties are. And to do one's duty is to act in a way that is both autonomous and free:†

> I should do my duty for duty's sake, and when I do my duty it is in a true sense my own objectivity which I am bringing to realization. In doing my duty, I am by myself and free. To have emphasized this meaning of duty has constituted the merit of Kant's moral philosophy and its loftiness of outlook. (*PR*, 253)

In all these respects, Kant's thought is the culmination of that tradition of self-reflective rationality begun by Socrates. In fact, Hegel gives the Kantian emphasis on the role of reason additional support.

Think about the claim that you are free when you can do—without hindrance or constraint—what you want to do.‡ It is a view of freedom that

---

*See the debate about *nomos* and *physis* (Chapter 4).

†Any of the earlier dialogues of Plato will give you the flavor of his questions, *Euthyphro* being a particularly good example.

---

*Take a quick look back at the discussions of conscience in the Reformation (p. 347), Kant on enlightenment (p. 438), and Hume on superstition (p. 441). The French revolutionaries consciously aimed at a rational society; to this end, they introduced a new religion of reason, rationalized the calendar, adopted the metric system, and cut off the king's head.

†For Kant's theory of morality, see "Reason and Morality," in Chapter 20.

‡See Hume's endorsement of this view, pp. 453–455. It is the natural companion of the view that reason is and must be the slave of the passions.

has been espoused by many "liberal" thinkers, from Hume and John Stuart Mill to present-day "liberal" economists. What is characteristic of the view is that desires are simply accepted as a given; according to this view, the question a person faces in seeking happiness is just this: What shall I do to satisfy maximally the desires I in fact have? A person is free to the degree that no one interferes with his or her pursuit of that satisfaction.

It is Hegel's view that this is a very shallow kind of freedom, no more satisfactory than the abstract view of Stoic and skeptic. Indeed, it is equally abstract, but in a precisely opposite direction. Just as the Stoic and skeptic abstract themselves from "living reality" and identify themselves with pure thought, so the "liberal" theorists about freedom identify themselves solely with their nonreflective, given desires. The former experience themselves as possessing an "infinite will," since their decisions range freely over any alternatives presented to them.* The will of the latter is wholly finite, being simply a set of naturally given (or culturally instilled) inclinations, hankerings, wants, and so on. Hegel calls this an "arbitrary will."

> Arbitrariness implies that the content is made mine not by the nature of my will but by chance. Thus I am dependent on this content, and this is the contradiction lying in arbitrariness. The man in the street thinks he is free if it is open to him to act as he pleases but his very arbitrariness implies that he is not free. When I will what is rational, then I am acting not as a particular individual but in accordance with the concepts of ethics in general. (*PR*, 230)

To be truly free, Hegel claims, we must not be at the mercy of whatever happens to influence and form us, lest we be simply the pawns of irrational interests and forces. To be free we must be *rational*. And, since rationality is intrinsically *universal*, to be rational is to be *ethical*. This is already argued by Kant, and Hegel emphatically agrees. Reason is not, and cannot be, simply the slave of the passions; reason must be a determining factor in action.

Hegel thinks that the Stoic/skeptic view on the one hand and the "liberal" Humean view on the other constitute *two abstract moments* that need to interact and interpenetrate each other. Abstract reason must become concrete in action, and the arbitrary will needs to be disciplined by reason. In this way, Hegel buttresses the Kantian view of reason, freedom, morality, and action.

But, in Hegel's view, Kant does not show us how to make reason actual in the world. Recall that Kant's criterion for the moral acceptability of a principle of action is the categorical imperative.* Suppose we are thinking of acting on a certain maxim; the categorical imperative bids us examine it by asking, Can it be universalized? The maxim will be morally acceptable as a basis for acting only if it passes this universalization test. Otherwise, it would be morally wrong to act on that principle. It is important to note that the categorical imperative is a purely formal rule; by itself, it does not bid us do anything in particular. What it does is test proposed maxims (and hence actions) for moral acceptability.

One of Kant's clearest examples is the proposal to make a promise, intending all the while to break it if it proves inconvenient to keep. Kant argues that this cannot be a moral maxim because if universalized, promising would simply disappear.

This seems a strong argument. What is Hegel's objection? In effect, Hegel asks, And then what? Suppose we grant the entire argument; what are we to do now? We see that the practice of false promising cannot be institutionalized in a society, but that still leaves us with two options:

1. We can make promises, intending sincerely to keep them.
2. We can dispense with the institution of promising altogether.

There seems to be no way the categorical imperative, as a purely formal rule, can decide between these two possibilities, for there seems nothing impossible or contradictory about a society that

---

*Compare Descartes' claim in *Meditation IV* that even God's will is not more free than our own.

*The content of the categorical imperative, together with an examination of two examples, is set out on pp. 489–491.

simply does not have the institution of promising. Kant's formal principle is *too abstract* because it cannot choose between these two alternatives.*

The criticism can be put in a more politically sensitive way if we consider another example: stealing. Can a maxim that I may steal my neighbor's property be universalized? It again seems clear that it cannot, for were it universalized, the institution of private property would disappear. Hegel grants that there is a contradiction between the institution of private property and the maxim "Thou mayest steal." You cannot consistently have both. But again, we seem to be left with two consistent possibilities:

3. A society with private property and rules against stealing
4. A society without private property

Kant's purely formal imperative, Hegel argues, is helpless to choose between them.† And the reason is that in itself it has no *content*.

> The absence of property contains in itself just as little contradiction as the non-existence of this or that nation, family, etc., or the death of the whole human race. But if it is already established on other grounds and presupposed that property and human life are to exist and be respected, then indeed it is a contradiction to commit theft or murder; a contradiction must be a contradiction of something, i.e., of some content presupposed from the start as a fixed principle. (*PR*, 90)

The inadequacy of this stage of morality was made dramatically clear, Hegel believes, in the French Revolution. This was an attempt to impose on society abstract principles of a universal sort, to *force* recalcitrant reality to be rational and free. But this freedom was a purely *negative* freedom; and the result was the Reign of Terror. When negative freedom

> turns to actual practice, it takes shape in religion and politics alike as the fanaticism of destruction—the destruction of the whole subsisting social order—as the elimination of individuals who are objects of suspicion to any social order, and the annihilation of any organization which tries to rise anew from the ruins. Only in destroying something does this negative will possess the feeling of itself as existent. Of course it imagines that it is willing some positive state of affairs, such as universal equality or universal religious life, but . . . what negative freedom intends to will can never be anything in itself but an abstract idea, and giving effect to this idea can only be the fury of destruction. (*PR*, 22)

The stage of morality is supplanted by what Hegel calls **ethics,** just as morality had previously supplanted custom in ancient Greece. (The terms *ethics* and *morality* are often used synonymously, but they are quite distinct for Hegel.)

What is required for Spirit to become fully rational, self-conscious, and free is for it to be able to recognize itself in its cultural expressions. So ethics is the recognition of rationality in institutions—in property, contracts, the family, and the state. Spirit, alienated from its products by setting itself apart from them, must reappropriate them, see itself in them, express itself in the social dimension—but now critically, rationally, freely. The abstraction of Kantian morality is to be overcome by the objectification of reason in society.

---

*Would a Kantian be able to reply to this argument? Might one say that if faced with the prospect of legislating for society a set of practices that either includes or excludes the practice of promising, the rational choice would be in favor of promising? If so, the same move might be possible for stealing and private property (see the following). In either case, however, rationality would probably have to mean more than just absence of contradiction.

†This is obviously another one of the points Karl Marx picks up from Hegel. If a purely formal and individualistic morality like Kant's cannot be a guide in selecting institutions, then a guide for life must be given by society, and doing that is politics.

CUSTOM →	MORALITY →	ETHICS
Pre-rationality	Abstract rationality	Concrete rationality
Nonreflective	Reflective	Reflection satisfied
Individual identifies with community	Individual alienated from community	Individual identifies with rational community
Individual feels free	Individual is free (in abstract sense)	Individual is free (in actuality)

For Hegel, ethics is virtually indistinguishable from social and political philosophy. Or rather, it is not philosophy at all, but the *realization* of philosophy in an actual community. As he says, "the system of right is the realm of freedom made actual, the world of mind brought forth out of itself like a second nature" (PR, 20). What kind of social system will this incarnation of Spirit be? How will right, duty, rationality, and freedom all manage to coalesce in the society of Spirit objectified?

We won't go into the details of Hegel's social thought; he tends too much to see his own society as approaching or having reached the ideal, and much of his discussion is thus of interest only to historians. But we need to indicate his general idea and to point out one of its consequences.

As we have already noted, an individual must be thought of as socially shaped and constructed; no one is an island. Hobbes' view that the state originates in a contract made by isolated individuals is, for Hegel, simply another instance of undue abstraction.* The relation between an individual and the community is more like that between a leg and the body it belongs to. If the leg were to say, "I am an independent entity, and I will go my own way," this would be manifestly absurd. It is no less absurd for individuals to consider themselves distinct from the community that nourishes, educates, shapes, and forms them. Indeed, an individual per se is an *abstraction* (there's that word again) from the whole. As separate from the community, a person lacks reality. It is the community, which Hegel calls the **State,** that is the bearer of the objective reality of spirit and as such is "higher" than the individual. The state is like an organism, and individuals are like its organs. Hegel goes as far as to say,

> A single person . . . is something subordinate, and as such he must dedicate himself to the ethical whole. Hence if the state claims life, the individual must surrender it. . . .
>
> It is false to maintain that the foundation of the state is something at the option of all its members. It is nearer the truth to say that it is absolutely

necessary for every individual to be a citizen. (PR, 241–242)

But what kind of state is it that can rightly subordinate persons like this? It must be, Hegel says, a rational state. And that means that it must be one in which laws are universal and impartial, one to which free and rational individuals can give their free and rational consent.* Citizens will be able to live freely and rationally in such a state because the state is the objective correlate of that reason which is the essence of their very being. Here we see how Hegel thinks to surpass, and yet incorporate, the "moments" of unthinking harmony (custom) and rational abstraction from that harmony by individuals (morality). There is to be a new harmony, founded self-consciously on rational principles. After being merely implicit in traditional societies, and after long estrangement from a reality that was less than fully rational, Spirit is now to find itself mirrored in the institutions and laws of the organic community.

> If men are to act, they must not only intend the good but must know whether this or that particular course is good. What special course of action is good or not, right or wrong, is determined, for the ordinary circumstances of private life, by the laws and customs of a state. It is not too difficult to know them. . . . Each individual has his position; he knows, on the whole, what a lawful and honorable course of conduct is. To assert in ordinary private relations that it is difficult to choose the right and good, and to regard it as a mark of an exalted morality to find difficulties and raise scruples on that score indicates an evil and perverse will. It indicates a will that seeks to evade obvious duties or, at least, a petty will that gives its mind too little to do. (RH, 37)

The empty form of Kantian morality is thus to be given content by the laws and customs of the state one grows up in. It is true that "each individual is also the child of a people at a definite stage of its development" (RH, 37) and that none of us lives

---

*For Hobbes' view of the social contract, see pp. 414–415. See also Locke, pp. 424–426.

*It does not necessarily mean one in which each citizen has a vote; Hegel's picture of a rational state is a constitutional monarchy where decisions are made by discussion among large-scale interests, such as the landed class and corporations.

in a perfectly rational society. But Hegel seems to say that this is no excuse for trying to go off on our own individualistic tangents. Our ethical life is only realized by actualizing the norms of our society. An individual "*must bring the will demanded by his people to his own consciousness, to articulation*" (*RH*, 38). Nor can societies as a whole attempt to sweep the board clean and start again, as the French attempted to do in the revolution. That way lies only destruction. Instead, societies must build on whatever rationality is already embodied in their stage of development, however inadequate and one-sided it may be.

When Spirit completes this task, when its objective expression in culture matches perfectly its rational essence, then individuals—the subjective bearers of self-consciousness—will recognize themselves in the laws and institutions of their society without hesitation. At that point they will be fully free. All will be, as in the stage of custom, a harmony. But now it will be a rationally founded harmony, approved by the self-conscious, rational citizens of that state.

There is an uneasy ambiguity in Hegel's treatment of the ideal community. On the one hand, there is some basis for a radical critique of nearly any given society; insofar as its institutions lack rationality—and when will they not?—they are subject to criticism and potential change. On the other hand, Hegel can seem terribly conservative, for whatever there is in the way of social arrangements has *some* rationality to it, is in some way a stage on the way to the absolute. The state at that stage, moreover, is the shaper of all the individuals who make it up; apart from it, they are mere abstractions, unrealities. Moreover, that stage is in some sense, he tells us, necessary. If it is necessary and is simply working its own way out toward a more adequate embodiment of reason and freedom, what sense does it make to interfere? His emphasis that the philosopher must not prescribe, but must simply "look on," seems to indicate that in the social setting, as in epistemology, Spirit takes care of itself.

This ambiguity runs throughout Hegel's thought and explains how after his death there could form two groups of Hegelians, radical and conservative,

each claiming to represent the master.* It permeates, moreover, his thought about history, with which we will end our much simplified consideration of this complex system of ideas.

---

1. What does Hegel mean by *objective spirit*?
2. What transition in our history does Hegel believe Socrates represents?
3. What does Hegel praise in Kant's account of morality? What, nonetheless, is his critique of the categorical imperative?
4. What is Hegel's critique of an arbitrary will?
5. How does Hegel understand ethics?
6. How does Hegel think that individuals are related to the state?
7. What is there in Hegel's thought that explains why both conservatives and radicals could claim him as their ancestor?

History and Freedom

The concept of development plays a central role in Hegel's thought. The development of spirit is complex and dialectical because spirit, unlike nature, is intrinsically in relation to itself; that is why there is always negativity involved: always (1) an object standing in opposition to the subject, (2) typically experienced as *other* (alien), and (3) needing to be recovered so that the subject can recognize itself in its object. As an observer of the development of spirit, Hegel sees this dialectical process at work everywhere: in the consciousness of the individual, in society, even in concepts themselves. Unlike nearly all previous philosophers, Hegel sees *reason itself* developing its own tools, its concepts and notions, in this dialectical and historical process. That is why it has not been possible previously to solve the problem of the criterion: Each philosopher has necessarily been working in a certain stage of the development of reason and necessarily expresses the way things look at that stage. But each of these stages has been inadequate. The criterion for knowledge and action, Hegel believes, is in the

---

*The most famous of the "left-wing," or radical, Hegelians is Karl Marx.

process of *working itself out in history*. And we "phe-nomenological" observers need only "look on" to see it happening.

History has a direction and a purpose; it is going somewhere. And Hegel claims to know where it is going. Its goal is **freedom.** In a schematic way, Hegel claims we can actually see this process going on. In ancient Asian societies (for example, the Persian), he says, only *one* was free (the ruler); in Greek and Roman societies, *some* were free (the citizens, but not the slaves); and in his own time, it has been realized that *all* are free (though the work-ing out of this realization may take a long time yet). But to understand this fully, we need to say a bit more about freedom and its relation to reason.

> The sole thought which philosophy brings to the treatment of history is the simple concept of *Reason*: that Reason is the law of the world and that, there-fore, in world history, things have come about ra-tionally. (*RH*, 11)

Reason, here, seems to be simply another term for the Absolute, for the World Spirit. History un-folds as reason works out the dialectical stages from implicit to explicit self-consciousness and from a naively traditional to a self-consciously rational and organic society.

How is reason related to freedom? Well, what is freedom? Freedom, Hegel tells us, is

> self-contained existence. . . . For when I am dependent, I refer myself to something else which I am not; I cannot exist independently of something external. I am free when I am within myself. This self-contained existence of Spirit is self-consciousness, consciousness of self. (*RH*, 23)

You can see that if there isn't anything in reality *but* Spirit (or reason)—its objects having exis-tence only relative to it,* so that when Spirit be-comes conscious of them, it is becoming conscious of itself in them—and if to be free is to be "self-contained," then Spirit is essentially free. But being *essentially* free and being *actually* free are two dif-ferent things. The former is merely the abstract es-sence; the latter is the concrete reality. History is

the dialectical tale by which the former becomes the latter.

> World history is the exhibition of spirit striving to attain knowledge of its own nature.
>
> World history is the progress of the conscious-ness of freedom. . . .
>
> We have established Spirit's consciousness of its freedom, and thereby the actualization of this Free-dom as the final purpose of the world. (*RH*, 23–24)

This sounds glorious, but how does it fit the facts of history, where there is so much that seems irrational and evil? Is Hegel just a "cockeyed op-timist" about history? On the contrary, Hegel is acutely conscious of the negative side of the story, only, as always, he sees this negativity as an es-sential aspect of the dialectic leading to freedom. Reason triumphs eventually, but only with agoniz-ing slowness and indirection. He is under no illu-sions about the motivations behind the acts that make history.

> Passions, private aims, and the satisfaction of selfish desires are . . . tremendous springs of action. Their power lies in the fact that they respect none of the limitations which law and morality would impose on them; and that these natural impulses are closer to the core of human nature than the artificial and troublesome discipline that tends toward order, self-restraint, law, and morality.
>
> When we contemplate this display of passions and the consequences of their violence, the unrea-son which is associated not only with them, but even—rather we might say *especially*—with *good* de-signs and righteous aims; when we see arising there-from the evil, the vice, the ruin that has befallen the most flourishing kingdoms which the mind of man ever created, we can hardly avoid being filled with sorrow at this universal taint of corruption. And since this decay is not the work of mere nature, but of human will, our reflections may well lead us to a moral sadness, a revolt of the good will (spirit)—if indeed it has a place within us. Without rhetori-cal exaggeration, a simple, truthful account of the miseries that have overwhelmed the noblest of na-tions and polities and the finest exemplars of private virtue forms a most fearful picture and excites emo-tions of the profoundest and most hopeless sadness, counterbalanced by no consoling result. We can endure it and strengthen ourselves against it only by

---

*This is the key element in Hegel's absolute idealism.

thinking that this is the way it had to be—it is fate; nothing can be done. (*RH*, 26–27)

Hegel compares history to a "slaughter bench," on which the happiness, wisdom, and virtue of countless individuals and peoples have been sacrificed. When this image takes hold, the question forces itself on us:

> To what principle, to what final purpose, have these monstrous sacrifices been offered? (*RH*, 27)

Hegel's answer, of course, is freedom. But we need to say a bit more about how he thinks freedom will come out of this protracted and bloody process.

He is under no illusions, as we have noted, about individuals acting from reason. In fact, he goes as far as to say,

> we assert then that nothing has been accomplished without an interest on the part of those who brought it about. And if "interest" be called "passion" . . . we may then affirm without qualification that *nothing great in the world* has been accomplished without passion. (*RH*, 29)

But that is only half the story. The other half is equally important: reason, or what Hegel calls the *Idea*.

> Two elements therefore enter into our investigations: first the Idea, secondly, the complex of human passions; the one the warp, the other the woof of the vast tapestry of world history. (*RH*, 29)

Individuals, then, act out of their passions and desires. Like the threads in a tapestry that run in one direction only, they are unaware that they are held in place by a rationality that, fixing their actions into a pattern they can scarcely discern, works out a purposeful progress toward absolute knowledge and freedom.

The burden of historical development is carried particularly, Hegel thinks, by certain persons, whom he calls **"world-historical individuals."** Alexander, Caesar, and Napoleon are examples he cites. What is true of them is that

> their own particular purposes contain the substantial will of the World Spirit.
>
> Such individuals have no consciousness of the Idea as such. They are practical and political men.

But at the same time they are thinkers with insight into what is needed and timely. They see the very truth of their age and their world, the next genus, so to speak, which is already formed in the womb of time. It is theirs to know this new universal, the necessary next stage of their world, to make it their own aim and put all their energy into it. (*RH*, 40)

They do not pursue this "new universal" consciously, of course. They are simply pursuing their private aims, often ruthlessly; "so mighty a figure must trample down many an innocent flower, crush to pieces many things in its path" (*RH*, 43). But in doing so, they unknowingly serve a larger purpose. There are unintended effects to their actions, and whether they will it or not, they serve the purposes of reason. This Hegel calls the

> *cunning of Reason*—that it sets the passions to work for itself, while that through which it develops itself pays the penalty and suffers the loss. . . . The particular in most cases is too trifling as compared with the universal; the individuals are sacrificed and abandoned. The Idea pays the tribute of existence and transience, not out of its own funds but with the passions of the individuals. (*RH*, 44)

Individuals, then, are the *means* by which the World Spirit actualizes its reason in the world. And if we see this, we can be reconciled to the agony and the tragedy of world history. It is all worthwhile because it is necessary to realize the goal.

> The insight then to which . . . philosophy should lead us is that the actual world is as it ought to be, that the truly good, the universal divine Reason is the power capable of actualizing itself. This good, this Reason, in its most concrete representation, is God. God governs the world. (*RH*, 47)

What Hegel gives us in his reflections on history is a **theodicy,** a justification of the ways of God to human beings; it is one solution to the old problem of evil. Hegel's is perhaps the most elaborate theodicy since Augustine wrote *The City of God* in the early fifth century.* But notice the

---

*See the discussion of Augustine's view of history, pp. 285–287. One crucial difference is that for Augustine the justification of history lies *beyond* it in the life to come, whereas for Hegel it lies *within* history itself in an attainable

price that is paid: The actual world *is as it ought to be*. Remembering Hegel's own lament over the "slaughter bench" of history, this is a remarkable conclusion. All this is worthwhile because it leads to a supremely valuable end.

> *"World history is the world's court."*
> *Friedrich von Schiller (1759–1805)*

And what, in particular, is that end to be? It is "the union of the subjective with the rational will; it is the moral whole, the *State*" (*RH*, 49). Once again, note that the state does not exist for the sake of satisfying the desires of its citizens.

> Rather, law, morality, the State, and they alone, are the positive reality and satisfaction of freedom. The caprice of the individual is not freedom. . . . The Idea is the interior; the State is the externally existing, genuinely moral life. It is the union of the universal and essential with the subjective will, and as such it is *Morality*. (*RH*, 50)*
>
> It is the realization of Freedom, of the absolute, final purpose, and exists for its own sake. All the value man has, all spiritual reality, he has only through the state. . . . For the True is the unity of universal and particular will. And the universal in the state is in its laws, its universal and rational provisions. The state is the divine Idea as it exists on earth. (*RH*, 52–53)

Here again we find that ambivalence between conservative and radical points of view. When Hegel says the state is the "divine Idea as it exists on earth," does he mean *any* state or does he mean only the ideal, perfectly rational state?

---

historical condition. A second difference is that Augustine looks for the *peace* of the blessed, whereas Hegel justifies everything in terms of the rational *freedom* to be enjoyed by citizens of a rational state. A third difference is in the conception of God. For Augustine, God is a being quite independent of the world he created, having his being even outside of time; for Hegel, the world *is* God coming to self-actualization in time through self-conscious knowers such as ourselves.

*Hegel here uses the term "morality" to designate what he elsewhere has called "ethics," perhaps to indicate that only in the actuality of the state does Kantian morality realize its inner nature.

But perhaps this ambivalence can be reduced if we note that Hegel is quite self-consciously *not* a "world-historical individual." He is a philosopher. And it is not the job of philosophy, he holds, to change the world; it is the philosopher's job simply to understand it. Remember that we began our consideration of Hegel's philosophy with the problem of the criterion. Hegel suggests that this problem does not need to be solved by the philosopher because it is in process of solving itself; all the philosopher needs to do is "look on" and describe. Near the end of his life, Hegel comes back to that same point in a memorable image.

> One more word about giving instruction as to what the world ought to be. Philosophy in any case always comes on the scene too late to give it. As the thought of the world, it appears only when actuality is already there cut and dried after its process of formation has been completed. . . . When philosophy paints its grey in grey, then has a shape of life grown old. By philosophy's grey in grey it cannot be rejuvenated but only understood. The owl of Minerva spreads its wings only with the falling of the dusk. (*PR*, 12–13)

---

1. What is the goal of history, according to Hegel? What all does it justify?
2. Explain the notion of the *cunning of reason*. What are world-historical individuals?
3. How does Hegel think of God? How is God related to the world? To us?
4. Explain the image of the owl of Minerva. What does it say about the task of the philosopher?

FOR FURTHER THOUGHT

If you were to understand yourself in terms of Hegel's philosophy, how would you characterize (a) your real nature, (b) your relation to society, and (c) your place in history? Would you find this satisfactory?

KEY WORDS

Spirit	development
Notion	phenomenology
Romantics	idealism

appearance
reality
absolute knowledge
World Spirit
sense-certainty
immediacy
self-consciousness
Unhappy Consciousness
reason
absolute idealism

objective spirit
custom
morality
ethics
State
freedom
world-historical
   individuals
cunning of Reason
theodicy

NOTES

1. References to Hegel's works are as follows:
   PS: Phenomenology of Spirit, trans. A. V. Miller
   (Oxford: Clarendon Press, 1977).

   PR: Hegel's Philosophy of Right, trans. T. M. Knox
   (Oxford: Oxford University Press, 1952).
   RH: Reason in History, trans. Robert S. Hartman
   (New York: Liberal Arts Press, 1953).

2. Quoted from *The Logic of Hegel*, trans. William
   Wallace (Oxford: Clarendon Press, 1892),
   in Richard Norman, *Hegel's Phenomenology: A
   Philosophical Introduction* (Published for Sussex
   University Press by Chatto and Windus, London,
   1976), 11.

KIERKEGAARD AND MARX

Two Ways to "Correct" Hegel

Hegel's influence was enormous. Everywhere, he was read and discussed, dissected and analyzed, damned and admired. The synthesis of so much learning and the forging of so many insights could hardly help but shape the next generation of philosophers.

Despite the range and depth of Hegel's thought, some readers had the sense (which perhaps you share) that this magnificent system was extravagant, that it promised more than it could deliver. In a certain way, moreover, and contrary to Hegel's explicit intentions, it seemed too *abstract*; it did not seem to deal concretely enough with the actuality of people's lives as they led them, making specific choices in specific circumstances. This was an ironic complaint indeed because abstraction is Hegel's great enemy.

In this chapter, we glance at two thinkers who are deeply in Hegel's debt. They can both be considered Hegelians, but they are renegade Hegelians, each in his own way. Both have contributed in lasting ways to our thinking in many spheres of human life, from religion to politics,

from art to economics, from the anxieties of individual psychology to the sociology of class struggle. Their intellectual progeny in our time go by the names of **existentialist** and **Marxist.** Thus, we examine some of the central contributions of Søren Kierkegaard and Karl Marx to the great conversation.

Kierkegaard: On Individual Existence

The authorship of Søren Kierkegaard (1813–1855) is exceedingly varied and diverse. For one thing, about half of it is pseudonymous (written under other names—and quite a number of them, too). Why? Not for the usual reason, to hide the identity of the author; nearly everyone in little Copenhagen knew Kierkegaard, and they knew he had written these books. There is a deeper reason: the various "authors"—a romantic young man known simply as A, Judge William (a local magistrate), Johannes *de silentio* (John the silent), the Seducer (who writes a famous diary), Victor Eremita (the Hermit), Johannes Climacus (the Climber), to name only a few—represent different views. Through their voices, Kierkegaard expresses certain possibilities for managing the problem of having to exist as a human being. This problem, he believes, cannot be solved in the abstract, by thinking about it—though it cannot be solved without thinking about it either! One works out a solution to the problem in one's own life through the choices one makes, which define and create the self one becomes. Kierkegaard's pseudonymous authors "present themselves" to the reader as selves in the process of such self-creation. They thereby function as models for possibilities that you or I might also actualize in our own lives; they awaken us to alternatives and stimulate us to self-examination.

Kierkegaard adopts this technique, which he calls **"indirect communication,"** because of his conviction that most of us live in varying forms and degrees of self-deception. We are not honest with ourselves about the categories that actually structure our lives. He attempts to provoke the shock of self-recognition by offering characters with which the reader may identify and then revealing slowly, but inexorably, what living in that way really means. He is particularly concerned with an "illusion" he discerns in many of his contemporaries in nineteenth-century Denmark: the impression that they are *Christians*. He wants to clarify what it means actually to live as a Christian and, in particular, to distinguish such a life from two things: (1) from the average bourgeois life of a citizen in this state-church country, where everyone is baptized as a matter of course, and (2) from the illusion that intellectual speculation of the Hegelian type is a modern successor to faith.

In the course of this elaborate literary production, Kierkegaard offers us insights that many recent philosophers, psychologists, and theologians have recovered and used in their own work. For our present purposes, we sketch three of these life possibilities and then draw some conclusions about how Hegel needs to be modified if Kierkegaard is right. Following Kierkegaard, we call these possibilities the aesthetic, the ethical, and the religious.

THE AESTHETIC

In the first part of a two-part work called *Either/Or*,* we find the somewhat chaotic papers of an unknown young man whom the editor of the volume (himself a pseudonymous character) elects simply to call "A." The fond desire of A's life is simply to *be* something. His ideal is expressed in a line by the twentieth-century poet T. S. Eliot: "You are the music while the music lasts."[1] This kind of complete absorption, which we experience occasionally in pleasurable moments, seems wonderful to him. If only the whole of life could be like that! If only he could evade reflection, self-consciousness, thought, the agony of choice, and this business of always having to *become* something! If he could just enjoy life in its **immediacy.**† A's dream is to live unreflectively a life of pleasure.

But A is a clever and sophisticated young man. He realizes that this is not possible. For one thing, immediacy never exists where it is sought; to take it as one's aim or ideal entails directly that one has missed the goal. As soon as you think, "What I really want is a life of pleasure," you prove that you are already beyond simply *having* such a life. You are reflecting on how nice that would be. No human, in fact, can attain the placid, self-contained immediacy of the brutes. And it is clear to A that pleasure is not his life, but the chief preoccupation of his life.

This becomes clear to A through his reflections on the figure of Don Juan. As A imagines him, he is pure, undifferentiated, unreflective desire—nothing more than embodied sensuality. Don Juan wants women wholesale, and he gets what

---

*Already in the title of this early work, we see an attack on central themes in Hegel, for whom "both/and" might be an appropriate motto. As we have seen, the progress of Hegelian dialectic is a successively reiterated synthesis, gathering in the truth contained in earlier stages until we reach in the end a stage of absolute knowledge. Kierkegaard is convinced that such a stage is impossible for existing human beings. We'll see why.

†"Immediacy," of course, is a Hegelian category. Look back to pp. 501–504 for Hegel's phenomenological critique of immediacy as a foundation for knowledge.

he wants. In Mozart's opera *Don Giovanni*,* the Don's servant keeps a list of his "conquests," which he displays in a comic aria, informing us that they number 1,003 in Spain alone. Don Juan represents something analogous to a force of nature—an avalanche or hurricane—but for this very reason there is something subhuman about him.† A thereby concludes that this "pure type" can exist only in art and that music is the appropriate vehicle for its expression. Sensuality (together with its associated pleasure) is not human reality, but an aspect of human reality. Considered in itself, it is an abstraction.‡

What, then, to do? To A, there seems to be one obvious solution: to make one's life itself into a work of art. Then one could enjoy it as one enjoys any fine aesthetic object. The pleasures of immediacy may be vanishing, but the pleasures of aesthetic appreciation are all the more available. The most damning comment on a movie or novel is—boring! So one wants above all to keep life interesting.

◆

"The only obligation to which in advance we may hold a novel, without incurring the accusation of being arbitrary, is that it be interesting."

Henry James (1843–1916)

Toward this end, A writes a little "how-to" manual called *Rotation of Crops*.

> People with experience maintain that proceeding from a basic principle is supposed to be very reasonable; I yield to them and proceed from the basic principle that all people are boring. Or is there anyone

who would be boring enough to contradict me in this regard? . . . Boredom is the root of all evil.

> This can be traced back to the very beginning of the world. The gods were bored; therefore they created human beings. Adam was bored because he was alone; therefore Eve was created. Since that moment, boredom entered the world and grew in quantity in exact proportion to the growth of population. Adam was bored alone; then Adam and Eve were bored together; then Adam and Eve and Cain and Abel were bored *en famille*. After that, the population of the world increased and the nations were bored *en masse*. To amuse themselves, they hit upon the notion of building a tower so high that it would reach the sky. This notion is just as boring as the tower was high and is a terrible demonstration of how boredom had gained the upper hand. (*EO* 1, 285–286)[2]

"*The biggest danger, that of losing oneself, can pass off in the world as quietly as if it were nothing; every other loss, an arm, a leg, five dollars, a wife, etc. is bound to be noticed.*"

—Søren Kierkegaard

---

*Kierkegaard admired this opera extravagantly, attending many performances of it.

†The figure of Don Juan can be understood as a representation of the aspect of reality Nietzsche calls "Dionysian" in his *Birth of Tragedy*. See pp. 564–566, but also compare Nietzsche's later (and different) concept of the Dionysian on p. 590.

‡Here A is echoing, of course, Hegel's own critique of immediacy. These considerations also constitute a criticism of the hedonistic ideal of Epicurus and Hobbes. See pp. 236–237, 410.

Here we have an expression of the categories under which A organizes his life. Everything is evaluated in terms of the pair of concepts,

interesting/boring.

The rotation method is a set of techniques for keeping things interesting. Let us just note a few of the recommendations.

Variety, of course, is essential. But it is no use trying to achieve variety by varying one's surroundings or circumstances, though this is the "vulgar and inartistic method."

> One is weary of living in the country and moves to the city; one is weary of one's native land and goes abroad; one is europamüde [weary of Europe] and goes to America, etc; one indulges in the fanatical hope of an endless journey from star to star. (*EO* 1, 291)

What one must learn to do is vary *oneself*, a task that A compares to the rotation of crops by a farmer. The key idea is a developed facility for remembering and forgetting. To avoid boredom, we need to remember and forget artistically, not randomly as most of us do. Whoever develops this art will have a never-ending source of interesting experiences at hand.

> No part of life ought to have so much meaning for a person that he cannot forget it any moment he wants to; on the other hand, every single part of life ought to have so much meaning for a person that he can remember it at any moment. (*EO* 1, 293)

In addition, one requires absolute freedom to break away at any time from anything, lest one be at the mercy of something or someone boring. Thus, one must beware of entanglements and avoid commitments. The rule is no friendships (but acquaintances aplenty), no marriage (though an occasional affair adds to the interest), and no business (for what is so boring as the demands of business?).

The key notion is to stay in control. As A writes in one of a series of aphoristic paragraphs,

> Real enjoyment consists not in what one enjoys but in the idea. If I had in my service a submissive jinni who, when I asked for a glass of water, would bring me the world's most expensive wines, deliciously blended, in a goblet, I would dismiss him until he learned that the enjoyment consists not in what I enjoy but in getting my own way. (*EO* 1, 31)

This project of living for the interesting is explored in a variety of ways in A's papers, but its apex is surely the fictional diary within *Either/Or* known as *The Seducer's Diary*. The essentials of the diary's plot are simple. Johannes, the diarist, manipulates a young woman, Cordelia, into an engagement to marry. He then manipulates her into breaking off the engagement, after which they spend a passionate night together before he leaves her.

Johannes arranges the whole affair to intensify the interesting. As a result, the focus is on the psychological rather than the physical. And it must be so, for the seducer is the polar opposite of Don Juan (within the sphere of the aesthetic).* Whereas the latter is supposed to be wholly nonreflective, an embodiment of pure immediacy, the seducer lives so completely in reflection that he seems to touch down in reality only occasionally. All is planning, arranging, scheming, plotting, and enjoying the results, as one would enjoy a play at the theater. Johannes is at once the playwright, the actor, and the audience in the drama of his life. It is not the actual seduction that matters to him, but the drama leading up to that moment. That is what is really interesting. And to preserve the aesthetic character of his experience, he must keep the necessary aesthetic distance, even from himself.

Other aspects of this project to treat one's life like an aesthetic object reveal themselves subtly in the diary. The project must be carried out in secret. To reveal his intentions to Cordelia would ruin the whole enterprise, so he must, necessarily, deceive Cordelia. He is, in terms Kant and Hegel would find appropriate, *using* her for ends she not only does not consent to, but also of which she has not the slightest hint.

Johannes reflects on his feelings for Cordelia.

> Do I love Cordelia? Yes! Sincerely? Yes! Faithfully? Yes—in the esthetic sense. (*EO* 1, 385)

He flatters himself that he is benefiting her. In what sense? Why, in the only sense he recognizes: He is making her life more interesting! He found her a naive young girl; he will leave her a sophisticated

---

*Remember that the aesthetic is defined as that style of life in which everything is judged in terms of the pair of categories, interesting/boring.

woman. She was innocent, uninitiated into *possibility*; he has taught her the delights and the terrors of the possible. He found her nature; he will leave her spirit. So, at least, he tells himself.

Whether Cordelia agrees is another matter. *Either/Or* contains a letter she sent to Johannes after the break, which Johannes had returned unopened:

> Johannes,
>
> Never will I call you "my Johannes," for I certainly realize you have never been that, and I am punished harshly enough for having once been gladdened in my soul by this thought, and yet I do call you "mine": my seducer, my deceiver, my enemy, my murderer, the source of my unhappiness, the tomb of my joy, the abyss of my unhappiness. I call you "mine" and call myself "yours," and as it once flattered your ear, proudly inclined to my adoration, so shall it now sound as a curse upon you, a curse for all eternity. . . . Yours I am, yours, yours, your curse.
>
> Your Cordelia (*EO* 1, 312)

It appears that even within the sphere of the aesthetic there might be no clear answer to whether Johannes has benefited Cordelia. But, as we'll see, that is not the only kind of question that can be asked.

---

1. What is "indirect communication"? Why did Kierkegaard write so much under pseudonyms?
2. Under what categories does an aesthete organize his or her life? Describe two ways this might work out, using the examples of Don Juan and the seducer.

THE ETHICAL

The bulk of the second part of *Either/Or* consists of long letters from a magistrate in one of the lower courts, a certain Judge William. They are addressed to A. The main topic is love, but the judge has his eye on a larger issue: what it means for an existing human being to be a *self*.

To see the relevance of this issue, let us look back to another of A's aphorisms. He says,

> My life is utterly meaningless. When I consider its various epochs, my life is like the word *Schnur* in the dictionary, which first of all means a string, and second a daughter-in-law. All that is lacking is that

in the third place the word *Schnur* means a camel, in the fourth a whisk broom. (*EO* 1, 36)

A recognizes that his life lacks continuity. It is as if he were a succession of different people, one interested in this, another in that. The different periods of his life have no more relation to each other than do the meanings of the word *Schnur*. In a sense, A has no self—or rather, he is splintered into a multiplicity of semiselves, which comes to much the same thing. The judge has a remedy.

Taking his cue from A's own preoccupations, the judge gives us an analysis of **romantic love.** Its "mark" is that it is *immediate*. Its watchword is "To see her was to love her." And indeed, that is how we think about love, too; we talk about "falling in love"—something that can *happen* to one, a condition in which one may, suddenly, just find oneself. Falling in love is not something one *does* deliberately after reflection.

> Romantic love manifests itself as immediate by exclusively resting in natural necessity. It is based on beauty, partly on sensuous beauty. . . . Although this love is based essentially on the sensuous, it nevertheless is noble by virtue of the consciousness of the eternal which it assimilates, for it is this that distinguishes all love from lust: that it bears a stamp of eternity. The lovers are deeply convinced that in itself their relationship is a complete whole that will never be changed. (*EO* 2, 21)

This conviction, however, because it is based on something that *happens* to one, is an illusion. If you can fall into love, you can fall out of it again. For this reason, it is easy to make romantic love look ridiculous; it promises what it cannot deliver: faithfulness, persistence, *eternity*.* The judge notes that a lot of modern literature expresses cynicism about love. The culmination of this cynicism is either (1) giving in to the transience of nature, resigning the promise of lasting love, and making do

---

*Popular love songs testify to this "stamp of eternity" that distinguishes romantic love from sheer lust. Think, for example, of Irving Berlin's 1925 classic, "Always," or Elvis Presley's "Love Me Tender," in which we hear, "I love you / And I *always* will," "*Never* let me go," and "Till the *end of time*" (italics added), or Adele's "Daydreamer," in which she sings that "he'll be there *for life*" (italics added). Of course, many pop and rock songs do celebrate lust.

with a series of affairs; or (2) the marriage of convenience, which gives up on love altogether.

The judge deplores both alternatives. He believes A is right in valuing romantic love. But, he says to A, what you want, you can't have on your terms. The promise of eternity in romantic love can be realized, but not if you simply "go with the flow" (as we say). What is required is choice, a determination of the will that is precisely what one finds in conjugal love—that is, in **marriage.** The bride and groom *make promises* to each other, including the promise to *love.* The judge argues that what one hears from the Romantic poets, that marriage is the enemy of romantic love, is simply false. For what romantic love seems to offer, but cannot deliver, is exactly what the engagement of the will can provide: the continuity and permanence of love. Marriage, as an expression of the will, is not the death of romantic love; it comes to its aid and provides what it needs to endure. Without the will, love is simply inconstant and arbitrary nature.*

It is true, the judge admits, that conjugal love is not a fit subject for art. Love stories usually go like this: The handsome prince falls in love with the beautiful maiden, and after much opposition and struggle (ogres and dragons, wicked uncles and unwilling fathers), they are married; the last line of the story is "And they lived happily ever after." But, says the judge, these stories end just where the really interesting part begins. Nevertheless, the marriage cannot be represented in art, "for the very point is time in its extension." The married person "has not fought with lions and ogres, but with the most dangerous enemy—with time."

> The faithful romantic lover waits, let us say for fifteen years; then comes the moment that rewards him. Here poetry very properly perceives that the fifteen years can easily be concentrated; now it hastens to the moment. A married man is faithful for fifteen years, and yet during these fifteen years he has had possession; therefore in this long succession he has continually acquired the faithfulness he possessed, since marital love has in itself the first love and thereby the faithfulness of the first love. But an

ideal married man of this sort cannot be portrayed, for the point is time in extension. . . .

> And although this cannot be portrayed artistically, then let your consolation be, as it is mine, that we are not to read about or listen to or look at what is the highest and the most beautiful in life, but are, if you please, to live it.

> Therefore, when I readily admit that romantic love lends itself much better to artistic portrayal than marital love, this does not at all mean that it is less esthetic than the other—on the contrary, it is more esthetic. (*EO 2,* 138–139)

❧

"Popular literature and film argue the dullness of the good, the charm of the bad."

Iris Murdoch (1919–1999)

Note that the judge is defending the *aesthetic* validity of marriage. You want something really *interesting*? Commit yourself to making romantic love last a lifetime. Moreover, the judge sees marriage as an example of a style of life quite other than that which A has been leading. The ethical life requires the development of the **self.**

The crucial difference between the aesthetic and the ethical is **choice.** In a certain sense, of course, the aesthetic life is full of choices. But, with that clear-sighted irony that an intelligent aesthete brings to his experience, A sees that none of them is a significant choice. Any choice might as well have been the opposite—and can be tomorrow. After all, if your aim is "the interesting," you must not get stuck in commitments. None of these aesthetic choices really means anything for the self doing the choosing. Among A's papers, this is expressed in "An ecstatic lecture."

> Marry, and you will regret it. Do not marry, and you will also regret it. . . . Whether you marry or do not marry, you will regret it either way. . . . Trust a girl, and you will regret it. Do not trust her, and you will also regret it. . . . Whether you trust a girl or do not trust her, you will regret it either way. Hang yourself, and you will regret it. Do not hang yourself, and you will also regret it. . . . Whether you hang yourself or do not hang yourself, you will regret it either way. This, gentlemen, is the quintessence of all the wisdom of life. (*EO 1,* 38–39)

---

*Compare what Hegel has to say about the "arbitrariness" of a will (by which he means merely natural or conditioned desires) that has not been subjected to reason. See p. 513.

Why will you regret it either way? Because you will see that your choice has closed off other interesting possibilities. You marry, but within a week you think of the fun you could be having as a bachelor. A's life is full of choices, but none of them is decisive. And often enough he stands like Buridan's ass, unable to choose at all.

> Imagine a captain of a ship the moment a shift of direction must be made; then he may be able to say: I can do either this or that. But if he is not a mediocre captain he will also be aware that during all this the ship is ploughing ahead with its ordinary velocity, and thus there is but a single moment when it is inconsequential whether he does this or does that. So also with a person . . . there eventually comes a moment where it is no longer a matter of Either/Or, not because he has chosen, but because he has refrained from it, which also can be expressed by saying: Because others have chosen for him—or because he has lost himself. (*EO* 2, 164)

And so it is with us; if we drift, if we fail to decisively take hold of our lives, if we treat every either/or as indifferent, we will lose our selves; there will be nobody who we are.*

So the judge pleads with A to adopt a different either/or, the mark of which is *seriousness of choice*. When one chooses seriously, when one *engages oneself*, one chooses *ethically*.†

> Your choice is an esthetic choice, but an esthetic choice is no choice. On the whole, to choose is an intrinsic and stringent term for the ethical. Wherever in the stricter sense there is a question of an Either/Or, one can always be sure that the ethical has something to do with it. The only absolute Either/Or is the choice between good and evil, but this is also absolutely ethical. (*EO* 2, 166–167)

And yet the judge is not—at least not directly—urging A to choose the good. He just wants him to *choose*.

> What, then, is it that I separate in my Either/Or? Is it good and evil? No, I only want to bring you to the point where this choice truly has meaning for you. . . .
> Rather than designating the choice between good and evil, my Either/Or designates the choice by which one chooses good and evil or rules them out. Here the question is under what qualifications one will view all existence and personally live. That the person who chooses good and evil chooses the good is indeed true, but only later does this become manifest, for the esthetic is not evil but the indifferent. And that is why I said that the ethical constitutes the choice. Therefore, it is not so much a matter of choosing between willing good or willing evil as of choosing to will, but that in turn posits good and evil. (*EO* 2, 168–169)

The judge's either/or, then, has to do with the categories under which things are evaluated. One will lead a radically different life if everything is decided according to

good/evil (ethical choice)

rather than

interesting/boring (aesthetic choice).

And the basic either/or, the really significant or deep one, is not either one of these alternatives, but that which poses this question:

aesthetic *or* ethical?

> "Nothing is so beautiful and wonderful, nothing so continually fresh and surprising, so full of sweet and perpetual ecstasy, as the good. No desert is so dreary, monotonous, and boring as evil. This is the truth about authentic good and evil."
>
> *Simone Weil (1909–1943)*

If the judge is right, the mark of making that choice is the *way* one chooses: with seriousness and passion of the will (in which case the categories of good and evil *automatically* arise), or in that ironic, detached,

---

*This thought is developed by Martin Heidegger, who holds that without a resolute seizing of oneself, one's life is dominated by what "they" say, or what "One" does or doesn't do. See "The 'Who' of Dasein," in Chapter 27.

†This does not mean that one necessarily chooses the right, but that one's choice, whether right or wrong, lies within the domain of the ethical; it is a choice subject to ethical evaluation. From the aesthetic point of view, such evaluation is simply not meaningful (since the categories of evaluation are restricted to "interesting/boring").

amoral way in which one can say, "Choose either, you will regret both."

We can now see why marriage is, for the judge, an example and symbol of the ethical. What one says at the altar is a decisive expression of the will, a choice that one makes for the future, a choice of *oneself*. One chooses to be the sort of self who will continue to nurture and come to the aid of romantic love. It is no longer a matter of what happens to you; it is a matter of what you *do* with what happens to you. The ethical person gives up the futile project of simply trying to *be* something and takes up the project of *becoming* something—of becoming a *self*.

It will be helpful before moving on to summarize some of the chief differences between these two ways of life.

- *Immediacy*, which in the aesthetic stage has the status of a condition to be aspired to, looks from the ethical point of view like *nature*—that is, material for the will to act on, to shape and form.
- The possibility of *reflection* in the aesthetic (the spectator's view of one's own life) takes on in the ethical the aspect of *practical freedom* (the ability to take the givens of one's life and make something of them).
- The necessity for *secrecy* in the aesthetic life (remember the seducer) is supplanted by a requirement of *openness* in the ethical.
- The prominence of the *accidental* in the aesthetic (what happens to one) finds its ethical contrast in the notion of the *universal* (what duty requires of every human being).
- The *abstraction* of the aesthetic, hung as it is between the impossible immediacy of Don Juan and the incredible reflectiveness of the seducer, is contrasted with the *concreteness* of an individual's self-construction, where the accidental givens are taken over and shaped by the universal demands of duty.
- The attempt to *be* is given up in favor of the striving to *become*.
- The emphasis on the *moment* is superseded by the value of the *historical* (as in an affair versus a marriage).
- The *fragmentariness* of an aesthetic life stands in contrast to the *continuity* of the ethical.

These contrasts pave two distinct avenues for human life. The question arises, Are there any other possibilities?

1. Explain Judge William's fundamental Either/Or. How does it relate to choice? And how is this choice different from the many choices made by an aesthete?
2. What is the judge's view of the relation between romantic love and marriage?

THE RELIGIOUS

If the key characteristic of the aesthetic style of life is enjoying (and perhaps arranging) what happens to one and that of the ethical stage is taking oneself in hand and creating oneself, it seems apparent that human existence involves a tension between two poles. Kierkegaard characterizes them differently in various works: immediacy and reflection; nature and freedom; necessity and possibility; the temporal and the eternal; the finite and the infinite. On the one hand, we simply *are* something: a collection of accidental facts. On the other hand, we are an awareness of this, together with some attitude toward these facts and the need to do something about them. This aspect of ourselves seems to elude all limitation, since it is not definitely this or that. It seems to be a capacity for distancing ourselves from anything finite, temporal, and given.*

From the ethical point of view, this duality defines the task facing an individual: to *become oneself*. The task is to bring these two poles together so that they inform each other: The immediate and finite takes a definite shape, and the reflective and infinite loses its abstract indefiniteness. One becomes a definite and unique thing: oneself.†

---

*See the note on p. 505, where we discuss Hegel's notion of pure self-consciousness. See also Pico della Mirandola on the dignity of human beings, pp. 349–350.

†We need to be careful here. Kierkegaard does not present the ethical self as unique in the sense that it defines itself as *different from other selves*, for that would be to define it in terms external to itself. Becoming oneself involves the embodiment of those rational and universally human aspects that Kant and Hegel focus on in their treatment of morality and ethics. These are shared by all. But the *way* in which these are embodied will depend on the particular given facts about oneself, and in that respect, no one individual will be exactly like any other.

If you listened only to the judge, you might think that this is an achievable, if difficult, task. Further reflection, however, casts doubt on that optimistic assumption. These two sides of a person, the raw material from which a self is to be constructed, have a disconcerting tendency to drift apart. We slide into identifying ourselves now with one aspect, now with another. We often end up acquiescing in this tendency, even cooperating with it. We refuse the anxiety-filled role of having to hold the two poles together. Our problem is that we are *not willing to be ourselves* and always want to be something more or something less: *either* something approaching God *or* something analogous to an unthinking brute.

As soon as we discover this tendency, we are beyond the ethical. What use is more determination to succeed in the task of being yourself if you continually undermine this determination by your unwillingness to be yourself?* All this huffing and puffing and moral seriousness begin to look like impossible attempts to lift yourself by your own bootstraps.

Even the judge seems to have an inkling of this; the last thing we hear from him concerns a "sermon" that he sends along to A. The judge tells A that the sermon has caused him to think about himself and also about A. The sermon was composed by an "older friend" of the judge's, a pastor out on the heaths of Denmark; it is a meditation on the thought that "as against God, we are always in the wrong." The pastor says that this is an edifying thought, a helpful thought, a thought in which we can find rest. Struggling with the ethical task, we inevitably discover ourselves failing. What then should we do? Perhaps, the pastor says, we try to console ourselves by saying, "I do what I can." But, he asks, doesn't that provoke a new anxiety?

> If a person is sometimes in the right, sometimes in the wrong, to some degree in the right, to some degree in the wrong, who, then, is the one who makes that decision except the person himself, but

in the decision may he not again be to some degree in the right and to some degree in the wrong?
>
> Doubt is again set in motion, care again aroused; let us try to calm it by deliberating on:

THE *UPBUILDING* THAT LIES IN THE THOUGHT THAT IN RELATION TO GOD WE ARE ALWAYS IN THE WRONG. (*EO* 2, 345–346)

These thoughts take us into the domain of religion; it is no coincidence that they are presented in a sermon. Kierkegaard's views on religion are complex and extensive; he expresses some of them under still other pseudonyms and some under his own name. He distinguishes two levels of religion: a basic level of religious consciousness (shared by pagan figures such as Socrates and Old Testament patriarchs like Abraham) and a more intense level distinctive, he thinks, of Christianity. One of his "authors" calls the first **"religiousness A"** and the second **"religiousness B."** Let us look at each in turn.

In a haunting little book by Johannes *de silentio* (John the silent) called *Fear and Trembling*, he asks, Is there anything beyond the ethical? If so, what would it be like? Johannes meditates on a story in Genesis 22, where God asks Abraham to take his only son, Isaac, to Mount Moriah and offer him up as a sacrifice. Abraham does what God asks, and only at the last moment, as Abraham raises the knife, is Isaac spared. If there is a stage of life beyond the ethical, this seems an appropriate story to contemplate. As Johannes makes clear, from a strictly ethical point of view,* Abraham is the moral equivalent of a murderer; he was willing to do the deed. Yet he is remembered as the *father of faith*. What can this mean?

Johannes says that he cannot understand Abraham. Before Abraham he is "silent." The reason is that Abraham seems to do two contradictory things at once. On the one hand, he apparently gives up Isaac, resigns any claim to him, emotionally lets him

---

*Compare what Augustine has to say about the bondage of the will. See pp. 265 and 280. The "Unhappy Consciousness" of Hegel, at once self-liberating and self-perverting, is another expression of this stage. See pp. 508–509.

*The ethical is here understood as the highest that human thought can reach with respect to our duties to one another. Johannes, like Kant, takes ethics to be composed of rules that we rationally understand to be binding on us all. From the ethical standpoint, then, taking one's son out to slaughter him is clearly forbidden. No one could rationally universalize this rule.

go; how else could he travel those three long days to Moriah? On the other hand, he clearly continues to love Isaac as dearly as ever and even to believe that the sacrifice of Isaac will not be required of him! The proof, Johannes says, is that Abraham was not embarrassed before Isaac after having raised the knife—that he received him back with joy. How could anyone do both things? It seems impossible, paradoxical, absurd.

But, Johannes suggests, this absurdity is precisely the secret life of faith. If there is anything beyond the ethically human, it must be something like this. It must be a state in which one lives in an absolute relationship to God, where even the universally human requirements of the ethical drop away into relative insignificance.* Yet it is not an escape from this world, but a life wholly engaged in the concrete finitude of one's earthly being.

Johannes illustrates these two internal movements by describing two "knights." The **Knight of Infinite Resignation** withdraws into the interior chambers of the spirit, makes no claims on anyone, asks for nothing worldly. Like the Stoic philosopher or the monk, this knight identifies not with his body but with the infinite, reflective side of himself, with his "eternal consciousness":

> In infinite resignation there is peace and rest; every person who wills it . . . can discipline himself to make this movement, which in its pain reconciles one to existence. Infinite resignation is that shirt mentioned in an old legend. The thread is spun with tears, bleached with tears; the shirt is sewn in tears—but then it also gives protection better than iron or steel. The defect in the legend is that a third person can work up this linen. The secret in life is that each person must sew it himself, and the remarkable thing is that a man can sew it fully as well as a woman. (*FT*, 45)

Johannes stresses how difficult it must be to make this movement. It would seem to require all one's energy, all one's strength, all one's passion. What could be left over to make still another movement? Yet that is just what the **Knight of Faith** does. He also resigns everything, sets himself adrift from the world, takes refuge in the eternal side of himself. But as he is making the movements of infinite resignation, the Knight of Faith comes back again into the world. How does he do that? Where does he find the strength? Johannes doesn't know. He can't understand it.

He admires the Knight of Resignation; he can understand, he says, how someone could resign everything, thinks he might even be capable of it himself, difficult though it is. But faith he can't understand. It seems absurd to him that this should be possible. And yet, if there is to be anything beyond the ethical, it would have to be something like this paradoxical life, simultaneously beyond and totally within this world. Johannes imagines that he meets a Knight of Faith.

> The instant I first lay eyes on him, I set him apart at once; I jump back, clap my hands, and say half aloud, "Good Lord, is this the man, is this really the one—he looks just like a tax collector!" But this is indeed the one. I move a little closer to him, watch his slightest movement to see if it reveals a bit of heterogeneous optical telegraphy from the infinite, a glance, a facial expression, a gesture, a sadness, a smile that would betray the infinite in its heterogeneity with the finite. No! I examine his figure from top to toe to see if there may not be a crack through which the infinite would peek. No! He is solid all the way through. . . . He belongs entirely to the world; no bourgeois philistine could belong to it more. . . . He finds pleasure in everything, takes part in everything. . . . He attends to his job. . . . He goes to church. . . . In the afternoon, he takes a walk to the woods. He enjoys everything he sees, the swarms of people, the new omnibuses. . . . Toward evening, he goes home, and his gait is as steady as a postman's. On the way, he thinks that his wife surely will have a special hot meal for him when he comes home—for example, roast lamb's head with vegetables. If he meets a kindred soul, he would go on talking all the way to Østerport about this delicacy with a passion befitting a restaurant operator. It so happens that he does not have four shillings to his name, and yet he firmly believes that his wife has this delectable meal waiting for him. If she

---

*It is not, of course, that a religious life of faith is an *unethical* life. Just as the judge argues that an ethical life is *more* aesthetic than a life lived specifically for aesthetic enjoyments, so does a relation to God preserve and enhance whatever is of value in the ethical life. As Johannes points out, Abraham did not become the father of faith by *hating* his son.

has, to see him eat would be the envy of the elite and an inspiration to the common man, for his appetite is keener than Esau's. His wife does not have it—curiously enough, he is just the same. . . . And yet, yet—yes, I could be infuriated over it if for no other reason than envy—and yet this man has made and at every moment is making the movement of infinity. He drains the deep sadness of life in infinite resignation, he knows the blessedness of infinity, he has felt the pain of renouncing everything, the most precious thing in the world, and yet the finite tastes just as good to him as one who never knew anything higher. (*FT*, 38–40)

Several points stand out in this portrait. The first is that faith is not something to be understood, not a doctrine to be memorized and accepted. Faith is something to be lived. Second, the life of faith is not a particularly ascetic sort of life. There are, of course, many sorts of lives that someone who is every moment making the movement of infinite resignation would simply not be interested in, but it is definitely a life *in* the world. Third, it is not easy to recognize a knight of faith. What distinguishes such knights from other people is not external but a matter of their "inwardness"; it concerns not so much what they do but how and why they do what they do. Fourth, because of its interiority, it may seem easy to "have faith"; it may seem to be something everybody and her brother has already got. But that is an illusion. In fact, no other sort of life is as difficult, as demanding, as strenuous as the life of faith. For, Johannes tells us, faith is a **passion,** the highest passion of all.

Johannes is full of scorn for Hegelian philosophers who think they have "understood" faith and now want to "go further." Here, he says, there is nothing to understand, nothing that can be learned in a formula from someone else. Here we have a way of life. To aspire to get beyond it is to show that you haven't the slightest idea what sort of life is lived by knights of faith. In an entire lifetime, he says, Abraham did not get further than faith. If it is possible at all, it is apparent that the life of faith is the greatest and most arduous life one could live.

In a large and difficult book, *Concluding Unscientific Postscript*, the philosopher among the pseudonyms, Johannes Climacus, says that an individual cannot be in two places at the same time, but "when he is nearest to being in two places at the same time he is in passion" (*CUP*, 178). What does he mean?

Suppose you are facing an important chemistry exam tomorrow. Here are two possibilities: (1) You have been keeping up with the course but want to study a little more; (2) you have been neglecting the course but are hoping an all-nighter will pull you through. It is as if you were in two places at once, the place you actually are and the place you want to be. And it is clear that the "distance" between these two points is greater in situation (2) than in (1). Correspondingly, passion is heightened in situation (2): fear, anxiety, and panic set in. The greater the distance between where you are and where you want to be, the greater the passion.

We can apply this principle to the sorts of lives that Kierkegaard's pseudonymous authors are presenting for our consideration. There is certainly passion in the aesthete's life, but there is no *great* passion because the aesthete is wholeheartedly committed to nothing. If we live this way, we fritter life away pursuing momentary passions; there is nothing for which we are willing to live or die.

There is much greater passion, much greater intensity in the life the judge recommends. Why? Because the distance between where the judge is and where he genuinely wants to be is much greater: His aim is to construct himself as a concrete ethical individual over a lifetime, making his moment-to-moment particularity an exemplary instance of what is universally required of all. That's quite a task! And that's why the judge insists that the way to reach it is committed, passionate, whole-hearted choice.

Johannes *de silentio* tells us that faith is the highest of the passions. Can we understand what he means by this? Let us take Socrates as an example, remembering that the first religious stage is exemplified in paganism as well as in Old Testament patriarchs such as Abraham. Socrates dedicates his life to seeking the truth. He knows that he does not yet have what he wants, but he perseveres right up until the end, never flagging in his quest for the right answers to questions about virtue and the right way to live.*

---

*For a discussion of Socrates' character and philosophical convictions, see Chapters 6 and 7.

Johannes Climacus understands Socratic passion in this way: Existing individuals like ourselves cannot grasp the eternal truths that Socrates sought. So if we want what Socrates wanted, we are in two places that are very far from each other—much farther from each other than you are from an A in chemistry, even if you haven't been studying. So the passion is intensified. Like Abraham's faith in God (maintained though he can't understand God's asking for the sacrifice of his son), Socrates' life exemplifies a passionate faith in the existence of a truth about human existence. This faith manifests itself in a lifelong search.

Is it possible that the passion guiding a life should be still more intense than that? The sermon that caused the judge to rethink his own life has already given us a hint. Suppose, Climacus says, that the situation is worse than it seems to Socrates. Suppose that we are not just lacking the truth but also that we are continually obscuring it—hiding it from ourselves, deceiving ourselves, pretending that we are other than in fact we are. If that were our situation, we would be even further from the eternal truth than Socrates thinks. Once again, passion would be intensified.

❖

> "The easiest person to deceive is one's own self."
> *Edward Bulwer-Lytton (1803–1873)*

Now this is precisely, he says, the possibility Christianity puts before us; this is what distinguishes Christianity from all sorts of paganism, from mysticism, and from Socratic and Abrahamic religion. Christianity (religiousness B) tells us that we are sinners. But what is sin? It is a very shallow view of sin to think of it as rule-breaking, as occasional lapses from the straight and narrow. No, sin is a condition of the self. **Sin is despair.** And what is despair? We already know; despair is *not being willing to be oneself.*

The varieties of despair are examined in a book by Anti-Climacus, *The Sickness unto Death.** Being

---

*Johannes Climacus tells us that he is not a Christian, but he claims to know what it is to be or become a Christian. Anti-Climacus writes from the perspective of a sort of super-Christian. Together they give us a view from beneath and a view from above of what a Christian life would be like.

---

able to be in despair is our advantage over other animals, but actually *to be* in despair is "the greatest misfortune and misery" (*SUD*, 45). Despair is a sickness in the self; unless cured, it leads to the worst sort of death—not the death of the body, but the death of the self.

We usually think of despair as something produced in us by unfavorable events.

> Someone in despair despairs over *something*. So, for a moment, it seems, but only for a moment. That same instant the true despair shows itself, or despair in its true guise. In despairing over *something* he was really despairing over *himself*, and he now wants to be rid of himself. (*SUD*, 49)

A man' wife leaves him or the stock market crashes, and he is in despair. Is he in despair over his wife leaving or over the market crash? No, Anti-Climacus says; he is in despair over himself. His despairing is his not being willing to be this self that he now is—this self whose wife has left him, whose stock portfolio is worthless. He would rather be someone else. That is his sickness. That is the essence of despair.

But what is a self? In an obscure passage, Anti-Climacus says,

> The self is a relation which relates to itself, or that in the relation which is its relating to itself. The self is not the relation but the relation's relating to itself. A human being is a synthesis of the infinite and the finite, of the temporal and the eternal, of freedom and necessity. In short a synthesis. (*SUD*, 43)

Here we have our old friends, the duality of (1) what we immediately, factually, are and (2) the possibility of reflecting on that and (freely) doing something about it. But this duality does not yet makes us selves, Anti-Climacus says. No, being a self is having to relate these factors to each other and create a harmony between them. Being a self, as the judge says, is a task—one we can fail at. And there is more than one way to fail at this, leading to different kinds of despair.

In one kind of despair, which Anti-Climacus calls the **Despair of Infinitude,** I drift away from the concrete, finite facts about myself and my situation in the world and become "fantastic." I lack finitude. My *emotions* slide in a kind of abstract sentimentality; I melt with sympathy for suffering mankind, but I cannot stand my next-door neighbor. My *understanding* squanders itself in the pursuit of useless knowledge; I know all about the lives of the movie stars, but don't care to know about the troubles of my roommate. My *will* fantasizes by building castles in the air; I aspire to many wonderful deeds, but do not focus on the nearest act at hand that would move me one step along the way. All this is despair. All this is not being willing to be myself. All this is sin.

"Those who have given themselves the most concern about the happiness of peoples have made their neighbors very miserable."

Anatole France (1844–1924)

In another kind of despair, the **Despair of Finitude,** I lack possibility. I go along with the crowd, doing what is expected, assuming that my path is already set by "the others."*

> By seeing the multitude of people around it, by being busied with all sorts of worldly affairs, by being wise to the ways of the world, such a person forgets himself . . . finds being himself too risky, finds it much easier and safer to be like the others, to become a copy, a number, along with the crowd.
> Now this form of despair goes practically unnoticed in the world. Precisely by losing oneself in this way, such a person gains all that is required for . . . making a great success out of life. Here there is no dragging of the feet, no difficulty with his self and its infinitizing, he is ground smooth as a pebble, as exchangeable as a coin of the realm. Far from anyone thinking him to be in despair, he is just what a human being ought to be. . . .
> Yes, what we call worldliness simply consists of such people who, if one may so express it, pawn themselves to the world. They use their abilities, amass wealth, carry out worldly enterprises, make prudent calculations, etc., and perhaps are mentioned in history, but they are not themselves. (*SUD*, 63–65)

---

*Martin Heidegger's more recent discussion of human existence as "falling-in-with-the-One" is obviously indebted to Kierkegaard's discussion of despair. See Chapter 27.

All this is despair. All this is not being willing to be myself. All this is sin.

There is yet another form that despair can take—a rather surprising one given the general definition of despair. In the **Despair of Defiance,** I defiantly will to be myself. We can perhaps light up this form of despair by contrasting *being willing* to be oneself with *willing* to be oneself. In the latter there is something proud, arrogant, Promethean. Here

> the self wants in despair to rule over himself, or create himself, make this self the self he wants to be, determine what he will have and what he will not have in his concrete self. . . . He does not want to don his own self, does not want to see his task in his given self, he wants . . . to construct it himself. (*SUD*, 99)

This self wants to be its own god, to create itself completely. That is why Anti-Climacus says such a person "does not want to don his own self" but to construct it—out of nothing, as it were.

Defiance can take several forms.

1. *Active defiance.* I will make myself whatever I want to be. I am self-made, and if I don't like what I turn out to be, I'll become something else. In this mode, the self

> can, at any moment, start quite arbitrarily all over again. . . . So, far from the self succeeding increasingly in being itself, it becomes increasingly obvious that it is a hypothetical self. The self is its own master, absolutely (as one says) its own master; and exactly this is the despair, but also what it regards as its pleasure and joy. But it is easy on closer examination to see that this absolute ruler is a king without a country, that really he rules over nothing; his position, his kingdom, his sovereignty, are subject to the dialectic that rebellion is legitimate at any moment. . . . Consequently, the despairing self is forever building only castles in the air. (*SUD*, 100)

If we refuse to start with what we immediately are, we have no real foundation on which to build our selves, and so we can build nothing more than "castles in the air."

2. *Passive defiance.* Perhaps I find something objectionable about myself. I notice a flaw, and because of it I am filled with resentment. But I don't want to be changed or healed—oh no! In passive defiance the self uses the flaw

as an excuse to take offense at all existence; he wants to be himself in spite of it. (*SUD*, 102)

The demonic despair . . . wants to be itself in hatred toward existence. . . . Rebelling against all existence, it thinks it has acquired evidence against existence, against its goodness. The despairer thinks that he himself is this evidence. . . . It is, to describe it figuratively, as if a writer were to make a slip of the pen, and the error became conscious of itself as such—perhaps it wasn't a mistake but from a much higher point of view an essential ingredient in the whole presentation—and as if this error wanted now to rebel against the author, out of hatred for him forbid him to correct it, and in manic defiance say to him: "No, I will not be erased, I will stand as a witness against you, a witness to the fact that you are a second-rate author." (*SUD*, 104–105)

In wanting to be its own creator, to begin "a little earlier than other people," the defiant self imagines that it can establish itself from the ground up. But no one can do that. There is much about each of us that we simply have to accept. So even defiance is despair. Even this is not being willing to be myself—the self that I actually am. Even this is sin.

❧

"Miserable, wicked me. How interesting I am."
W. H. Auden (1907–1973)

But all this analysis raises an urgent question: What would a self be like that did not despair?

This then is the formula which describes the state of the self when despair is completely eradicated: in relating to itself and in wanting to be itself, the self is grounded transparently in the power that established it. (*SUD*, 43)

What does Anti-Climacus mean by saying that such a self is "grounded transparently in the power that established it"? We can call this power *God*. But what does *transparent grounding* come to? We think he means to say that there are not *two* things to do: (1) be willing to be oneself and (2) establish a relationship with God. No, doing the first *is* doing the second and vice versa. You cannot do one without doing the other. Being willing to be the self that God created *is* being grounded in God.

What should we call this state of a self without despair? Virtue? No, says Anti-Climacus, not virtue. The proper name for the state of the self opposite to despair is **faith.** So we come back again to that passion of inward intensity we met earlier in the Knight of Faith. Only now the passion is ever so much more intense because now we can see how much we are actually despairing—how far from a true way of life we really are.

But how could we come to accept ourselves as we are, knowing what we now know about despair, about sin? What we require is forgiveness. And this, too, Christianity has a word about. But it is a word that once more intensifies the passion, for it is the word about Christ, the God-Man who makes our forgiveness possible. Kierkegaard and his pseudonyms all agree that this pushes the truth out beyond all understanding. If, with Socrates, the relation between an existing individual and the eternal truth had an element of paradox about it, Christianity makes it far worse. If there is any truth in Christianity, it is absolutely paradoxical, paradoxical in itself. If we know anything about God, we know God is not human. Yet Christianity proclaims our healing through the life and death of the God-Man.

What does this mean? It means, Kierkegaard is certain, that faith should never be confused with knowledge. (Philosophy is just confused, a subject for ridicule, if it thinks that by human reason it can "go further" than faith; faith is not a matter of understanding anything, for the absolute paradox rebuffs our understanding.) It means that proofs for the existence of God and evidence for the divinity of Jesus are beside the point; faith is not a matter of accepting certain propositions as true or understanding them, but of *existing* in a certain manner, of living a certain form of life. It means that a life trusting in the forgiveness of sins, a life in imitation of Christ, is inherently risky—that there are no guarantees that it will "pay off." Such a life is the ultimate risk, stretched as it is between recognition of one's sinfulness and the paradox of possible forgiveness. But such is the life of faith; for faith is the highest passion.

But does Christianity present us with the truth about ourselves, about our sickness and its healing—or not? That is not a question Kierkegaard thinks he can answer for us. That is something we all have to answer for ourselves. And answer it we will—one way or another—in our lives.

---

1. What two "movements" does the Knight of Faith make? Why does Johannes *de silentio* think this is "absurd," or beyond human understanding?
2. Characterize in several ways the two aspects of human life that fascinate Kierkegaard and his "authors."
3. How do these two aspects look to the aesthete, to the ethical person, and to someone who lives in religious categories?
4. What is despair? What is the condition of a self when despair is completely eradicated? How can this be attained?
5. What, according to Kierkegaard and Johannes Climacus, is distinctive about Christianity? Why is it characterized as "the highest passion"?

THE INDIVIDUAL

You might think that the pattern we have seen in the relations between aesthetic, ethical, and religious forms of life is just the Hegelian pattern all over again. Inadequacies in earlier stages are exposed and remedied by later stages, toward which consciousness moves with inexorable logic. But this would be a serious mistake. To see why, we must examine the way Kierkegaard understands the position of the individual human being.

One reason he resorts to indirect communication is to combat the Hegelian view of the natural and necessary evolution of consciousness to ever higher levels. Each pseudonymous "author" presents to the reader a "possibility" for life; in that respect, they are all on the same level. Each invites the reader to identify with him.

- *The aesthete*: You only have one life to live, so you might as well make it interesting. It is true that the kind of ironic detachment this requires means that life is ultimately meaningless and that there are no serious choices, but that's just how life is.
- *The ethicist*: You *are* what you *make* of yourself. And that is a matter of choice, the sort of serious choice that constitutes a continuing self. Making those choices is what gives life meaning.
- *The Christian*: We all inevitably fail at creating ourselves. We must acknowledge this fact and have faith in God's forgiveness through Christ. In this way we can come to accept ourselves despite our unacceptability; only thus can we be free simply to *be* ourselves.*

Kierkegaard claims that human beings must *choose* among possibilities like these. And they must choose without being able know for certain which choice was the right or best one. For humans, the key concepts are choice, decision, and *risk*. A move from one kind of life to another is less like the result of rational persuasion and more like conversion.

It is true that *within* each of these frameworks each occupant thinks he can characterize and explain the others. To the judge, A looks like a man who has lost himself; to A, the judge's marriage looks overwhelmingly boring. The Christian sees them both as examples of despair—of not willing to be oneself; and no doubt the Christian could be accused, from some other framework, of irrationality and of going beyond the evidence. Where does the truth lie? To determine this, it seems one would have to take up a point of view outside them all. But it is Kierkegaard's conviction that no such point of view is available to an existing human being. There is no such vantage point for us as Hegel imagines absolute knowledge to be—no coincidence of subjectivity and objectivity, no identification of ourselves with Absolute Spirit, no *good reason* to choose one life rather than another, and no *knowledge* here at all. You and I, he thinks, are free to choose among the possibilities, but we are not free to choose for objective reasons. Neither are we free *not* to choose. Simply by living, we are making our choices; we cannot help it.

---

*It is worth noting that Kierkegaard's stage of *faith* is worlds away from the sort of "self-esteem" urged on us by so much contemporary psychology (and advertising!). The "I'm OK, you're OK" syndrome is basically aesthetic, in Kierkegaard's terms. It lacks both the seriousness of the ethical and the consciousness of sin.

"What a chimera then is man! What a novelty! What a monster, what a chaos, what a contradiction, what a prodigy! Judge of all things, feeble earthworm, depository of truth, a sink of uncertainty and error, the glory and shame of the universe."

Blaise Pascal (1632–1662)

Hegel and the Hegelians whom Kierkegaard knew suppose that the process of living well can be organized in an objective and rational way. In particular, they think that philosophy can construct a *system* that gives every aspect of life and reality its proper place. But Johannes Climacus distinguishes between a *logical system* and what he calls an *existential system*. He claims that a logical system is possible, but an existential system is not. Geometry is a good example of a **logical system;** it is founded on axioms, postulates, and definitions, from which we can prove theorems using the rules of logic. Because the theorems of a logical system are already implicit in the premises, the system has a kind of "finality" to it: given a certain set of axioms, the set of derivable theorems is also given; no new truths can be added later, and none of the theorems can be altered. But this finality is bought with a price; a logical system tells us nothing about existence. With respect to what actually exists, it presents only a *possibility*.

An **existential system,** in contrast, is not possible (at least for us) because "existence is precisely the opposite of finality" (*CUP*, 107). The problem is that in constructing a system that supposedly captures existence, the speculative philosopher supposes that he can be finished with existence before existence is finished with him! As long as he lives, he must choose; his own existence is precisely not something finished. To suppose that at some point in his life, he (or we, or the human race in its history) could attain the finality that comes with a system is simply comic.

We have seen that the problem of the criterion has plagued philosophers since at least Sextus Empiricus. By what mark can we tell when we have latched onto truth and goodness? Hegel answers that we will know *in the end*—that is, when we see how everything hangs together in a systematic way. Kierkegaard denies that this kind of sight is possible for existing human beings. Perhaps that *would* do as a criterion, but we can't get there from here. So we have to live without a criterion, without certainty, without good reason. We live by a *leap*.

The essential task for an existing human being, then, is not to speculate philosophically about absolute knowledge, but to become himself. As we have seen, this is a task involving risky choices, choices that must be made without the comfort of objective certainty. Speculative philosophers who try to present a *system* explaining existence imagine they can reach such a degree of objectivity that they revoke the risk in living; but this is sheer illusion. As Climacus plaintively asks, "Why can we not remember to be human beings?" (*CUP*, 104).

Kierkegaard endorses a saying by G. E. Lessing (a noted eighteenth-century German dramatist) to this effect: If God held in his right hand the truth and in his left hand the striving for the truth and asked the existing individual to choose one, the appropriate choice would be the left hand.

With respect to the individual's relation to the truth, there are two questions: (1) whether it is indeed the truth to which one is related; and (2) whether the mode of the relationship is a true one. Call the former an *objective question* and the latter a *subjective question*. The former concerns *what* is said or believed and the latter *how* it is said or believed.

For an existing individual, there is no way to settle that first question definitively. As a result, the *how* is accentuated.* For an individual, the quality of life depends on the intensity, the passion, the decisiveness with which this relation is maintained. Climacus offers a formula that expresses the appropriate relation of the individual to the **truth.**

---

*Here Climacus is thinking of truth about the best life choices. But an analogy from general epistemology might be helpful. Knowledge is commonly defined as *justified true belief*. Unless our belief is true—that is, objectively correct—it cannot constitute knowledge. But the best we can do is believe for good reasons. Nothing we can do will guarantee truth.

An objective uncertainty held fast in an appropriation-process of the most passionate inwardness is the truth, the highest truth available for an existing individual. (*CUP*, 182)

Objectively speaking, the individual never has more than "uncertainty"; this uncertainty correlates subjectively with the riskiness of the choice made, and the riskier the choice, the more intense the "passionate inwardness" with which it is made. For the individual, living in this subjectivity *is* living in the truth.

Kierkegaard is interested in two questions: (1) What is it to be an existing human being? and (2) What is it to be a Christian? He is convinced that unless we get an adequate answer to the first question, we will get the second answer wrong. He believes most people do get it wrong. In an age in which everyone considers himself a Christian as a matter of course, Kierkegaard means to unsettle this complacency by drawing our attention back to the first question.

If the problem that faces each individual is this problem of how to manage the duality implicit in being a self, then it becomes evident that being a Christian must be a certain way of solving the problem. It cannot be just a matter of church membership, or of being baptized, or of having the right (i.e., orthodox) beliefs, or of "understanding" oneself and one's place in the "system" (in the manner of Hegelian philosophy). It is a problem that cannot be solved in any other way than by the construction of the self through the choices, momentous and trivial, that one makes when faced with life's multifarious possibilities.

In a whimsical passage, Johannes Climacus tells us how he became an author. He was smoking his cigar on a Sunday afternoon in a public garden and ruminating on how he might best spend his life to be of benefit to mankind. He was thinking about all those

"celebrated names and figures, the precious and much heralded men who are coming into prominence and are much talked about, the many benefactors of the age who know how to benefit mankind by making life easier and easier, some by railways, others by omnibuses and steamboats, others by the telegraph, others by easily apprehended compendiums and short recitals of everything worth knowing, and finally the true benefactors of the age who make

spiritual existence in virtue of thought easier and easier, yet more and more significant. And what [he asks himself] are you doing?" Here my soliloquy was interrupted, for my cigar was smoked out and a new one had to be lit. So I smoked again, and then suddenly this thought flashed through my mind: "You must do something, but inasmuch as with your limited capacities it will be impossible to make anything easier than it has become, you must, with the same humanitarian enthusiasm as the others, undertake to make something harder." This notion pleased me immensely, and at the same time it flattered me to think that I, like the rest of them, would be loved and esteemed by the whole community. For when all combine in every way to make everything easier, there remains only one possible danger, namely, that the ease becomes so great that it becomes altogether too great; then there is only one want left, though it is not yet a felt want, when people will want difficulty. Out of love for mankind, and out of despair at my embarrassing situation, seeing that I had accomplished nothing and was unable to make anything easier than it had already been made, . . . I conceived it as my task to create difficulties everywhere. (*CUP*, 165–166)

What sort of difficulties? Those that remind us of what a hazardous and risky business it is, this business of having to be an existing human individual.

---

1. What is characteristic of a system? What would an existential system be? How does Kierkegaard attack this notion?
2. What, according to Johannes Climacus, is the proper relation of an existing human individual to the truth?

Marx: Beyond Alienation and Exploitation

Several themes become prominent at the close of the Enlightenment and the beginning of the nineteenth century. They are most systematically developed in Hegel. We can summarize these themes as follows:

- *The significance of history.* The classical quest for eternal truths, knowable at any time and in any circumstances, is replaced by the notion of the development of culture and of reason itself, which is thought of as *progress* toward a more encompassing truth, rationality, and freedom.

- *The role of opposition and antagonism in this progress.* Hegel emphasizes the role of the *negative* in development: struggle and loss are an essential part of any move forward.* William Blake, the English Romantic poet, puts it this way: "Without contraries is no progression."³
- *The attainment of the goal by the race, not the individual.* Because the progress is a historical one, the goal (self-consciousness, rationality, freedom) must be one toward which the race is moving, rather than one that an individual could completely attain.
- *The justification of the evil that accompanies this progression.* Hegel acknowledges the suffering that individuals endure on the "slaughter bench" of history but argues that all is worthwhile because of the incomparable value of the realization of Absolute Spirit in the wholly rational state.

Karl Marx (1818–1883) accepts these Hegelian views. As a young man, Marx was self-consciously one of the left-wing Hegelians. Like Kierkegaard, he complains that Hegelian philosophy is speculative and abstract. But unlike Kierkegaard, his remedy for this abstraction is not to focus on the plight of the anxious individual; such a focus on "subjectivity" would seem to him an abstraction of a different, but still deplorable, kind. Marx develops his critique along other lines.

Hegel believes (1) that reality is Spirit, (2) that the human being is Spirit unknown to itself, alienated from its objects (and so from itself), and (3) that the cure for this **alienation** is the knowledge that there is nothing in the object that is not put there by the subject—by Spirit itself. The human being is God coming to consciousness of himself through history. Marx comes to believe that this is exactly right, but only in a funny kind of way. For what Hegel has done, Marx thinks, is to take reality and "etherealize" it. It is as though the real world has been transposed into another key and played back to us—all there,

but with everything looking weirdly distorted. Marx thinks that Hegel has turned philosophy on its head, and he is determined to put philosophy back on its feet again. In an early work written with Friedrich Engels, Marx expresses this determination:

> In direct contrast to German philosophy which descends from heaven to earth, here we ascend from earth to heaven. That is to say, we do not set out from what men say, imagine, conceive, nor from men as narrated, thought of, imagined, conceived, in order to arrive at men in the flesh. We set out from real, active men, and on the basis of their real life-process we demonstrate the development of the ideological reflexes and echoes of this life-process. The phantoms formed in the human brain are also, necessarily, sublimates of their material life-process, which is empirically verifiable and bound to material premises. Morality, religion, metaphysics, all the rest of ideology and their corresponding forms of consciousness, thus no longer retain the semblance of independence. They have no history, no development; but men, developing their material production and their material intercourse, alter, along with this their real existence, their thinking and the products of their thinking. Life is not determined by consciousness, but consciousness by life. (*GI*, 118–119)⁴

Consider the last sentence. Hegel writes as if the forms of consciousness are independent of the material world. Forms of life, Hegel holds, depend on forms of consciousness, the level to which knowledge has evolved: sense-certainty, perception, understanding, desire, the unhappy consciousness, morality, and so on. But to Marx and Engels, this puts the cart before the horse. Those forms of consciousness do not have the kind of independence Hegel ascribes to them, so they do not, in themselves, have a history. There is, however, an underlying reality that does have a history. This *material reality* has to do first and foremost with *economic* matters—with putting bread on the table. It is the reality of "real, active men" and their "life processes." Hegel's forms of consciousness are simply "sublimates" or ideological reflections of this more basic reality.

The most essential need of real people is the sustenance of their material life. Marx calls this the

---

*In a way, this is a very old thought. See Heraclitus on the necessity for opposition and strife, pp. 18–19.

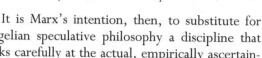

"From each according to his ability, to each according to his needs!"

—KARL MARX

first premise of all human existence, and therefore of all history, the premise, namely, that men must be in a position to live in order to be able to "make history." But life involves before everything else eating and drinking, a habitation, clothing and many other things. The first historical act is thus the production of the means to satisfy these needs, the production of material life itself. (*GI*, 119–120)

This premise is followed by other no less basic points: that producing the means of subsistence requires instruments of production; that this multiplies needs; that people propagate their own kind and so create families; and, most important, that these activities involve people from the start in social relationships.

> It follows from this that a certain mode of production or industrial stage is always combined with a certain mode of co-operation, or social stage, and this mode of co-operation is itself a "productive force." (*GI*, 121)

It is Marx's intention, then, to substitute for Hegelian speculative philosophy a discipline that looks carefully at the actual, empirically ascertainable facts about human beings. Marx is an influential figure in the history of both sociology and economics. He holds that if you want to understand a certain form of consciousness—of religion, perhaps, or of literature—you need to understand the material (economic and social) conditions in which it is produced. He also believes that certain forms of intellectual and spiritual life are merely compensations for an unsatisfactory life here on earth; religion, for instance, an opiate of the people, will simply vanish if we can get society straightened out.

Understanding is not enough, however. What Marx calls for is action. Perhaps no one has put the philosopher in such a central role since Plato had proposed that philosophers should become kings and kings philosophers.* In a famous line, Marx writes,†

> The philosophers have only *interpreted* the world,
> in various ways; the point, however, is to *change* it.
> (*TF*, 109)

To understand what changes Marx wants philosophy to produce, we must consider what Marx sees when he undertakes to describe "real" people in their actual existence.

ALIENATION, EXPLOITATION, AND PRIVATE PROPERTY

In an early work (1844), Marx analyzes the condition these "real" people had reached in the middle of the nineteenth century. This is the heyday of the **Industrial Revolution**—of the steam engine, the coal mine, and the knitting mill, of the twelve- or fourteen-hour workday, of child labor, and of a widening gap between those who own the means of production and the masses who give their labor in

---

*For the rationale behind this proposal of Plato's, see "The State," in Chapter 8. In a way, Marx proposes a similar role for the intellectual in the struggles of his time.

†Look once more at the "Owl of Minerva" passage in Hegel (p. 519). This is what Marx is attacking.

factories they have no stake in.* Here is how Marx sees things.

> *Wages* are determined through the antagonistic struggle between capitalist and worker. Victory goes necessarily to the capitalist. The capitalist can live longer without the worker than can the worker without the capitalist. (*EPM*, 65)

The **capitalist,** of course, owns the means of production—the factories and tools. A separation of ownership from labor is characteristic of the industrial age. In the days when cobblers made shoes, virtually all cobblers had their own shops and tools; perhaps they had an apprentice or two and maybe even a servant, but ownership and labor were typically combined in the same person. In the industrial age, however, there is a split between the class of people who own the very large and expensive means of industrial production and the class that provides the labor, a split that takes on the characteristics of a "struggle."

To increase their profits and compete with other industrial entrepreneurs, the capitalists pay the workers no more than is necessary to keep the workers alive, working, and reproducing. This is possible in part because there are typically more workers than jobs. So the worker takes on the characteristic of a **commodity** in the system; as with other commodities, like coal or cotton, the capitalist tries to buy it as cheaply as possible. As a commodity, of course, the worker is not thought of as a human being, but "only as a working animal—as a beast reduced to the strictest bodily needs" (*EPM*, 73). The worker could be (and often is) replaced by a machine.

The worker must face not only the capitalist but also the landlord. Formerly, the landed gentry could live solely by the productivity of the land. But the activity of the capitalist has forced competition here, too; and landowners are either driven out of this class altogether or become capitalists in their own right, seeking a profit from the land. They, therefore, seek to make rents as high as possible, and tenant farmers join the industrial workers as commodities on the market.

Political economists like Adam Smith and David Ricardo take **private property** for granted, but Marx sets out to *explain* it, leaning heavily on his Hegelian background. For example, suppose you take a piece of wood from the floor of the forest, sit down, and painstakingly carve into it the face of Lincoln. We can say that you have "put something of yourself into it." No longer raw nature, it now is an expression of yourself. It is, in fact, your labor *objectified*. In confronting it, you are confronting yourself: You are the person who *did that*. In contemplating this object, you become aware at one and the same time of it and of yourself, for part of what you are stands there in objectified form before you. Before you put your labor into it, you would not have been harmed had someone taken it, but now, if it is stolen, the thief steals part of *you*.*

We humans are active, productive, creative beings. The products of our labor show us to ourselves as in a mirror. Do you want to know what humans are? Look not just at their bodies or minds, but also at their art, their laws, their religion, their societies, their technologies, their industrial products; these things will tell you because they are humanity itself in objectified form. It is in such *externalization* that we make ourselves fully, self-consciously human.

The industrial age has perverted this process, for the worker labors and produces a *commodity*. What does that mean?

1. It means that workers do not experience their work as an affirmation of themselves. On the contrary, they feel *alienated* from their work. Their labor is not an expression of their lives but external to their lives. As Marx puts it, the worker

> does not affirm himself but denies himself, does not feel content but unhappy, does not develop freely his physical and mental energy but mortifies his body and ruins his mind. . . . His labor is therefore not voluntary, but coerced; it is *forced labor*. It is therefore not the satisfaction of a need; it is merely a *means* to satisfy needs external to it. Its alien

---

*For the Industrial Revolution, see https://en.wikipedia.org/wiki/Industrial_Revolution.

---

*This is, of course, a development of Locke's views on property. See pp. 425–426. Compare also Hegel on master and slave, pp. 506–507.

character emerges clearly in the fact that as soon as no physical or other compulsion exists, labor is shunned like the plague. (*EPM*, 110–111)

Rather than being fulfilled in their work, workers experience a loss of themselves. They are *dehumanized*; they feel active and productive only in their animal functions. In what should be their highest human functions (productive, creative labor), they become no more than animals, or worse, machines.*

2. Workers are also alienated from the *products* of their labor, which belong not to them but to the capitalist. The workers have just their wages, which are necessarily only enough for bare subsistence. Although they have put themselves into the products they make, they have no control over them.

3. In the early days of the Industrial Revolution, there was no solidarity among workers, no labor union, no force to rival the superior power of the employer. Without enough jobs to go around, workers competed against each other for employment. As a result, workers were also alienated from each other and, of course, from the capitalist, who was making money from exploiting them.

This is all more intelligible if we note that according to the economists of the day, *value* is defined in terms of labor. The value of something (including money) represents a certain amount of labor. The worker produces value, but for another: the one with the means to purchase the labor of the worker—that is, the capitalist.

Workers, then, are alienated from their labor and from the products of their labor; in neither can they find themselves. If we return now to the question about the origin of private property, we can see, Marx says, that it has its foundation in *alienated labor*. Because the classical political economists formulate their laws in terms of private property, we can see that they are formulating the laws of estranged labor—the laws of a condition of society in which workers are exploited, dehumanized.†

All these consequences result from the fact that the worker is related to the *product of his labor* as to an *alien* object. For on this premise it is clear that the more the worker spends himself, the more powerful becomes the alien world of objects which he creates over and against himself, the poorer he himself—his inner world—becomes, the less it belongs to him as his own. . . . The *alienation* of the worker in his product means not only that his labor becomes an object, an *external* existence, but that it exists *outside him*, independently, as something alien to him. . . .

It is true that labor produces for the rich wonderful things—but for the worker it produces privation. It produces palaces—but for the worker, hovels. It produces beauty—but for the worker, deformity. It replaces labor by machines, but it throws a section of the workers back to a barbarous type of labor, and it turns the other workers into machines. It produces intelligence—but for the worker stupidity, cretinism. (*EPM*, 108–110).

"Property is theft."

Pierre Joseph Proudhon (1809–1865)

In the condition of alienated labor—of private property—people's natural human needs become perverted. "Man becomes ever poorer as man, his need for *money* becomes ever greater if he wants to overpower hostile being" (*EPM*, 147). The need for money, of course, is insatiable. The process is fueled by *greed*. Greed and the money system, Marx says, are corollaries; devotion to money becomes a kind of secular religion.

---

1. What does Marx mean when he says that "life is not determined by consciousness, but consciousness by life"?
2. Characterize the struggle between capitalist and worker.
3. What is the origin of private property, according to Marx?
4. Describe some forms of worker alienation.

---

*Those of you who have worked on an assembly line or in a fast-food restaurant can perhaps verify from your own experience Marx's description of such work.

†Notice how Marx differs here from Locke, who believes there would be property even in a state of nature where no exploitation existed.

COMMUNISM

Private property, then, is not a natural, given fact; it is the result of alienated labor. This alienation of labor has a history. Marx sketches his view of this history in the *Manifesto of the Communist Party*, which he wrote with Engels in 1848.

> The history of all hitherto existing society is the history of class struggles.
>
> Freeman and slave, patrician and plebeian, lord and serf, guild-master and journeyman, in a word, oppressor and oppressed, stood in constant opposition to one another, carried on an uninterrupted, now hidden, now open fight, a fight that each time ended, either in a revolutionary reconstitution of society at large, or in the common ruin of the contending classes. . . .
>
> Our epoch, the epoch of the bourgeoisie, possesses, however, this distinctive feature: it has simplified the class antagonisms. Society as a whole is more and more splitting up into two great hostile camps, into two great classes directly facing each other: Bourgeoisie and Proletariat. (*CM*, 3)

The **bourgeoisie** is the class of owners, including both capitalists (in the narrower sense) and landlords. Marx characterizes it in the following way:

> The bourgeoisie, wherever it has got the upper hand, has put an end to all feudal, patriarchal, idyllic relations. It has pitilessly torn asunder the motley feudal ties that bound man to his "natural superiors," and left remaining no other nexus between man and man than naked self-interest, than callous "cash payment." It has drowned the most heavenly ecstasies of religious fervor, of chivalrous enthusiasm, of philistine sentimentalism, in the icy water of egotistical calculation. It has resolved personal worth into exchange value, and in place of the numberless indefeasible chartered freedoms, has set up that single, unconscionable freedom—Free Trade. In one word, for exploitation, veiled by religious and political illusions, it has substituted naked, shameless, direct, brutal exploitation. (*CM*, 5)

In pursuit of wealth, the bourgeoisie constantly revolutionizes the instruments of production and thus transforms relations among people in society into competitive relations. It produces a world market and interdependence among nations. It converts all other nations, on pain of extinction, into bourgeoisie as well. It concentrates property in a few hands, and it produces its own opposition: the proletariat.

> In proportion as the bourgeoisie, *i.e.*, capital, is developed, in the same proportion is the proletariat, the modern working class, developed—a class of labourers, who live only so long as they find work, and who find work only so long as their labour increases capital. (*CM*, 9)

The **proletariat** is the class of nonowners, of workers who have nothing but their labor to call their own. We have already characterized the life of the worker, as Marx sees it. We can now add that the lower strata of the middle classes—small tradespeople, shopkeepers, craftsmen, peasants—tend to sink gradually into the proletariat. As the proletariat grows in size, it begins to feel its strength and becomes the only really revolutionary class. As Marx sees it,

> The development of Modern Industry . . . cuts from under its feet the very foundation on which the bourgeoisie produces and appropriates products. What the bourgeoisie, therefore, produces, above all, is its own grave diggers. Its fall and the victory of the proletariat are equally inevitable. (*CM*, 15–16)

Historical development, as Marx sees it, has led us to the point where society is divided into two great classes whose interests are diametrically opposed. The interests of the proletariat, Marx believes, are best represented by the communists, "the most advanced and resolute section of the working class parties of every country," who have "the advantage of clearly understanding the line of march, the conditions, and the ultimate general results of the proletarian movement" (*CM*, 17). (This insight is the result of taking Hegelian dialectical philosophy off its head and setting it back on its feet.)

"Every man has by nature the right to possess property as his own."

Pope Leo XIII (1810–1903)

What **communism** stands for, then, is the abolition of private property. About this claim, Marx and Engels make the following remarks:

> The distinguishing feature of Communism is not the abolition of property generally, but the abolition of bourgeois property. But modern bourgeois private property is the final and most complete expression of the system of producing and appropriating products, that is based on class antagonisms, on the exploitation of the many by the few. . . .
>
> Hard-won, self-acquired, self-earned property! Do you mean the property of the petty artisan and of the small peasant, a form of property that preceded the bourgeois form? There is no need to abolish that; the development of industry has to a great extent already destroyed it, and is still destroying it daily. . . .
>
> You are horrified at our intending to do away with private property. But in your existing society, private property is already done away with for nine-tenths of the population; its existence for the few is solely due to its non-existence in the hands of those nine-tenths. You reproach us, therefore, with intending to do away with a form of property, the necessary condition for whose existence is, the non-existence of any property for the immense majority of society.
>
> In one word, you reproach us with intending to do away with your property. Precisely so; that is just what we intend. . . .
>
> Communism deprives no man of the power to appropriate the products of society; all that it does is to deprive him of the power to subjugate the labour of others by means of such appropriation. (*CM*, 18–20)

If the history of the world has, as Marx says, been the history of class struggles, then there seems to be something final and apocalyptic about this division of society into bourgeoisie and proletariat, into the few who have all and the many who have nothing. If this picture is taken seriously, it seems as though a final revolution, in which the workers take control of the means of production, might be the goal toward which history is moving. This is, in fact, the "theoretical advantage" that the communists claim—that they can see this line of development.

Marx agrees with Hegel about the character of the end: All this suffering is worthwhile only

for **freedom.*** But it is not the freedom of pure self-consciousness—knowing itself to be all there is, both subject and object—that Marx praises. Rather, it is the freedom of real, active, working men and women, who no longer find themselves alienated from their work, the products of their work, and their fellow workers.

> When, in the course of development, class distinctions have disappeared, and all production has been concentrated in the hands of a vast association of the whole nation, the public power will lose its political character. Political power, properly so called, is merely the organized power of one class for oppressing another. If the proletariat during its contest with the bourgeoisie is compelled, by the force of circumstances, to organize itself as a class, if, by means of a revolution, it makes itself the ruling class, and, as such, sweeps away by force the old conditions of production, then it will, along with these conditions, have swept away the conditions for the existence of class antagonisms and of classes generally, and will thereby have abolished its own supremacy as a class.
>
> In place of the old bourgeois society, with its classes and class antagonisms, we shall have an association, in which the free development of each is the condition for the free development of all. (*CM*, 26)

It is indeed not enough to understand the world; what is required is to change it. The *Manifesto* ends with a ringing call to action:

> The Communists disdain to conceal their views and aims. They openly declare that their ends can be attained only by the forcible overthrow of all existing social conditions. Let the ruling classes tremble at a Communistic revolution. The proletarians have nothing to lose but their chains. They have a world to win.
>
> WORKING MEN OF ALL COUNTRIES, UNITE! (*CM*, 39)

If things have not worked out as Marx and Engels expected, it must nonetheless be allowed that their vision of a world without exploitation and without class antagonisms has done as much actually to change the world (for better or worse) as any system of thought has ever done.

---

*See Hegel's discussion of freedom as the goal of history, pp. 516–519.

1. Characterize the bourgeoisie and the proletariat as Marx saw them in the mid-nineteenth century. How did he think they were related?
2. What does communism intend? Why?

FOR FURTHER THOUGHT

1. Does the pattern of your life seem to match (more or less) that of any of Kierkegaard's pseudonymous writers? Write a brief story to illustrate.
2. Argue for one or another of the following theses:
   a. If we could satisfactorily meet people's material needs (whether through communism or in some other way), the sorts of concerns expressed by Kierkegaard would seem merely neurotic symptoms to us and would probably vanish.
   b. Even if we completely satisfied everyone's material and bodily needs, the spiritual and existential questions that concerned Kierkegaard would be as lively as ever.
3. Argue for one of the following propositions:
   a. In a state of nature without exploitation, rights of private property would naturally develop (Locke).
   b. Private property essentially depends on the exploitation of some by others (Marx).

KEY WORDS

Kierkegaard

existentialist	religiousness B
Marxist	Knight of Infinite
indirect	Resignation
communication	Knight of Faith
immediacy	passion
interesting/boring	sin
romantic love	Despair of Infinitude
marriage	Despair of Finitude
self	Despair of Defiance
choice	faith
good/evil	logical system
aesthetic *or* ethical	existential system
religiousness A	truth

Marx

alienation	bourgeoisie
Industrial Revolution	proletariat
capitalist	communism
commodity	freedom
private property	

NOTES

1. T. S. Eliot, *Four Quartets: The Dry Salvages*, V, in *The Complete Poems and Plays 1909–1950* (New York: Harcourt, Brace, 1958), 136.
2. References to the works of Søren Kierkegaard are as follows:
   EO: *Either/Or*, vols. 1 and 2, trans. Howard V. Hong and Edna H. Hong (Princeton, NJ: Princeton University Press, 1987). References are to volume numbers and page numbers.
   FT: *Fear and Trembling*, trans. Howard V. Hong and Edna H. Hong (Princeton, NJ: Princeton University Press, 1983).
   SUD: *The Sickness unto Death*, trans. Alistair Hannay (London: Penguin Books, 1989).
   PF: *Philosophical Fragments*, trans. Howard V. Hong and Edna H. Hong (Princeton, NJ: Princeton University Press, 1985).
   CUP: *Concluding Unscientific Postscript*, trans. David F. Swenson and Walter Lowrie (Princeton, NJ: Princeton University Press, 1944).
3. William Blake, "The Marriage of Heaven and Hell," in *William Blake*, ed. J. Bronowski (New York: Penguin Books, 1958), 94.
4. References to the works of Karl Marx are as follows:
   GI: *The German Ideology*, in *The Marx–Engels Reader*, ed. Robert C. Tucker (New York: W. W. Norton, 1972).
   TF: *Theses on Feuerbach*, in Tucker (ed.), *The Marx–Engels Reader*.
   EPM: *The Economic and Philosophic Manuscripts of 1844*, ed. Dirk J. Struik (New York: International Publishers, 1964).
   CM: *The Communist Manifesto* (with Friedrich Engels), trans. Samuel Moore, ed. David McLellan (Oxford: Oxford University Press, 1992).

CHAPTER

23

MORAL AND POLITICAL REFORMERS

The Happiness of All, Including Women

At about the time Marx is arguing for radical social and economic changes, a group of British philosophers advocate for different kinds of reforms in their own country. The utilitarians, as they come to call themselves, are much more empirical than Kant or Hegel and, in their own way, nearly as radical in their critique of society as Marx. We will begin by examining the utilitarians' overall approach to ethics and political philosophy. Afterward, we will turn to the question of women's rights, as addressed by both the utilitarians and a somewhat earlier British philosopher, Mary Wollstonecraft.

The Classic Utilitarians

Two thinkers stand out in connection with **utilitarianism:** Jeremy Bentham (1748–1832) and John Stuart Mill (1806–1873) set out its principal tenets. We begin our investigation of this still-influential view of morality with a pair of quotations, one from Bentham's *Introduction to the Principles of Morals and Legislation* (1789) and the second from Mill's booklet *Utilitarianism* (1861).

The principle of utility is the foundation of the present work. . . . By the principle of utility is meant that principle which approves or disapproves of every action whatsoever according to the tendency it appears to have to augment or diminish the happiness of the party whose interest is in question: or, what is the same thing in other words to promote or to oppose that happiness. (*PML*, 1)[1]

The creed which accepts as the foundation of morals, Utility, or the Greatest Happiness Principle, holds that actions are right in proportion as they tend to promote happiness, wrong as they tend to produce the reverse of happiness. (*U*, 137)[2]

Note the *teleological* or **consequentialist** orientation in both definitions.* The **principle of utility,** which Mill calls the "Greatest Happiness Principle," characterizes the rightness or

---

*You may recall that this word comes from the Greek *telos*, meaning "end" or "goal." Something is *teleological* if it points to an outcome. See the earlier discussion on p. 196. See also pp. 210–211.

wrongness of an action in terms of the outcome or consequences of that action.*

Notice also that both definitions direct our attention to a specific *kind* of consequence. Every act always has many, many consequences. Which of them are morally relevant? Bentham and Mill answer this question by claiming that in everything we do, no matter what the particular end, we are aiming at a single thing: happiness. But does this help? Aristotle has already noted that people disagree widely over what happiness is. What do the utilitarians think it is?

> By happiness is intended pleasure, and the absence of pain; by unhappiness, pain, and the privation of pleasure. To give a clear view of the moral standard set up by the theory, much more requires to be said. . . . But these supplementary explanations do not affect the theory of life on which this theory of morality is grounded—namely, that pleasure, and freedom from pain, are the only things desirable as ends; and that all desirable things . . . are desirable either for the pleasure inherent in themselves, or as means to the promotion of pleasure and the prevention of pain. (*U*, 137)

Its exclusive focus on pleasure and pain makes utilitarianism a type of hedonism.† But unlike some other hedonistic ethical systems, utilitarianism does not tell each of us to concern ourselves with our *own* happiness. The utilitarians insist that what is ethically relevant is not my happiness or yours, but happiness itself. So the utilitarian standard, as Mill tells us,

> is not the agent's own greatest happiness, but the greatest amount of happiness altogether. (*U*, 142)

Suppose you are facing a choice between actions and wondering which, morally speaking, you ought to do. What determines which choice is the right one? It is the sum total of pleasure and pain that each alternative action will produce for you

"The happiness which forms the utilitarian standard of what is right in conduct is not the agent's own happiness, but that of all concerned."

—JOHN STUART MILL

and everyone concerned. The action that produces the best pleasure/pain ratio overall is the one you ought to perform. You may not have the time or ability to calculate this pleasure/pain ratio at the moment of choice, of course. The utilitarians allow that you may fall back on other methods of choosing, such as relying on established rules of conduct. But what *makes* one choice the right choice is the fact that it would produce the most happiness.

What makes this a recipe for ethical and political reform? Notice first that the principle of utility is an *impartial* principle. Your own happiness is neither more nor less important in this determination than anyone else's. The happiness of each is to be weighed equally. Mill quotes Bentham as saying,

> Everybody to count for one, nobody for more than one. (*U*, 199)

---

*Contrast this with Kant's ethics, in which the morally relevant facts concern our intentions and motives. *Why* do I choose to act in some way—to promote someone's happiness, for instance? Is it because I respect the moral law—or for some other reason? See p. 488.

†The term "hedonism" is discussed on p. 236.

Even established rules of conduct, then, are to be rejected if, on consideration, we conclude that they do more harm than good, counting everyone's happiness equally.

Even more important, the utilitarians were not thinking just of private actions by individual citizens. They were one and all active in politics, in the reform of law, and in trying to produce better legislation. The principle of utility was to function not just as a moral guide, but also as a tool of social criticism and reform. In the early nineteenth century, many felt that the law in England was a mess—a tangled skein of contradictory precedents originating in forms of society very different from the one in which these thinkers were living. The law seemed designed chiefly to secure a livelihood for the lawyers.* The utilitarians used the principle of utility to criticize this maze by asking, Does this law, this institution, this way of doing things contribute to happiness or misery? This tool was sufficiently sharp to earn them the appellation "philosophical radicals." In the name of general happiness, they demanded parliamentary reform, prison reform, the extension of the right to vote, full legal rights for women, greater democracy, ways of making government officials accountable, changes in punishments, and so on.

Bentham believes that one of the great advantages of the principle of utility is the detail and precision of thought it makes possible in these moral and political issues. In fact, he tries to work out something like a calculus of pleasures and pains, so that one can simply *calculate* the right thing to do by taking into account the various amounts of happiness each alternative course of action or law would produce. Though Mill and other utilitarians have doubts about how strictly this method can work, a brief glance will help us get an understanding of the movement.

Bentham lists the various kinds of pleasures and pains that need to be taken into account. There are a great many; among the pleasures are those of sense, wealth, skill, a good name, piety, power,

happy memories, and so on. Among the pains are those of privation, the senses, awkwardness, a bad name, unhappy memories, expectation, and so on.

In considering any given pleasure, however, we see that it differs in several ways from another pleasure of the same kind; the same is true of pains. Pleasures and pains differ in

- *intensity* (some toothaches hurt worse than others);
- *duration* (some last longer);
- *certainty* or *uncertainty* (some are avoidable or indefinite, others not);
- *propinquity* or *remoteness* (some are expected tomorrow, others not for several years);
- *fecundity* (some pleasures or pains bring further pleasures or pains in their wake; others do not);
- *purity* (the degree to which a pleasure [or pain] is *not* tainted by accompanying pain [or pleasure]);
- *extent* (how many people are affected by it).

You can see how these considerations might be brought to bear on a practical problem. A more intense pleasure is preferable to one less intense. The longer pains last and the more people they affect, the worse they are judged to be. So if a law will produce quite intense pleasure for a few people but condemn a great many to pains of long duration, it is sure to be a very bad law. Actual cases are usually more complicated, but this gives the basic idea.

Bentham believes that legislation and moral judgment alike can approximate a science. Given the principle of utility and these rules, one can *discover* which law or action is best. He assumes that pleasure can be quantified; if this assumption is correct, the legislator or moral agent could, at least in principle, simply add up the sums to arrive at the right answer.

But can pleasures and pains be quantified in this exact way? Here is a point on which Mill differs from Bentham.* Though full of admiration

---

*Charles Dickens, Mill's contemporary, details the terrible effects of interminable suits dragging through the courts in his novel *Bleak House*.

*To understand why, it helps to know something of Mill's life. You may enjoy Mill's very readable *Autobiography*, in which he recounts his childhood and remarkable education at the hands of his father, his nervous breakdown and the cure of it, and his twenty-year platonic love of Harriet Taylor, who became his wife only after the death of her husband. Mill's active involvement with the intellectual and political movements of the day are also detailed.

for the older man, Mill says that Bentham is like a "one-eyed man," who sees clearly and far, but very narrowly.[3] To Bentham, pleasure is pleasure, and that's the end of it. In a famous line, Bentham declares that "quantity of pleasure being equal, push-pin [a children's game] is as good as poetry."[4] But Mill thinks this is obviously not true. Some pleasures are better than others, even if the *amount* of pleasure in each is the same. Pleasures, he wants to say, differ not only in quantity, but also in quality.

> It is quite compatible with the principle of utility to recognize the fact that some kinds of pleasure are more desirable and more valuable than others. It would be quite absurd that, while in estimating all other things quality is considered as well as quantity, the estimation of pleasure should be supposed to depend on quantity alone. (*U*, 138–139)

This may well be right, but it raises two problems. First, it seems to undermine Bentham's claim that legislation and morality might be made scientific, for even if you agree that one could compare *amounts* of pleasure and pain, *qualities* are not quantifiable. If they were, they would just be quantities again, and we would be back with Bentham. The second problem is whether there is any way to *tell* which pleasures are more desirable. To this question, Mill has an answer:

> Of two pleasures, if there be one to which all or almost all who have experience of both give a decided preference, irrespective of any feeling of moral obligation to prefer it, that is the more desirable pleasure. (*U*, 139)

Consult the person of experience, Mill tells us, someone who has tried both. Setting aside moral considerations, that person's preference is a sign that one exceeds the other in quality and is more desirable.*

But, you might object, is there any reason to think that people will agree about which pleasure is better? Suppose we take a survey of those who have experienced each of two kinds of pleasure—a day

in an amusement park, let us say, and a day spent reading poetry. Do you think we will find anything approaching unanimity? If we don't, how are we going to take the principle of utility as a practical rule to make decisions? We are supposed to maximize pleasure, but if different things please different people, how are we going to decide whether to build more amusement parks or more libraries?

> From this verdict of the only competent judges, I apprehend there can be no appeal. On a question which is the best worth having of two pleasures, or which of two modes of existence is the most grateful to the feelings, . . . the judgement of those who are qualified by knowledge of both, or if they differ, that of the majority among them, must be admitted as final. (*U*, 141)

So, Mill tells us, democratic politics is the way to decide about quality in pleasures. In fact, he thinks there will be a large measure of agreement because of the similarities among people. But where there are differences, the majority must rule.

A key concept of utilitarian moral philosophy is its **consequentialism:** Actions are sorted into the morally acceptable and the morally unacceptable by virtue of their consequences. The early utilitarians identify as relevant the consequences bearing on happiness, understanding happiness to be pleasure and the absence of pain. More recent utilitarians, while preserving the consequentialism, have sometimes looked to other features than pleasure to justify moral judgments.*

We have seen how Bentham and Mill understand the principle of utility. But is that principle the right one to use in making a choice? Is it, as the utilitarians hold, the criterion for the morally right? It is not the only option available, as we already know. Aristotle would ask whether the action contributes to our excellence (virtue). Jesus, Saint Paul, and Augustine would have us ask whether what we propose to do is in accord with the will

---

*We have to set moral consideration aside in making this judgment, lest we beg the question. After all, we are trying to discover where the greatest happiness lies precisely in order to determine what our moral obligations are!

*G. E. Moore, for instance, holds that a certain quality of *goodness* is what the moralist is to look to; while pleasure is one good thing, he says, there are numerous other goods, such as knowledge, not reducible to pleasure. R. M. Hare takes as fundamental what people *prefer*; whether that is always a matter of pleasure is an open question.

of God. Kant would urge us to submit the maxim of our action to the test of universalization. And Hegel would presumably have us look to the standards present in our current cultural situation.* What could the utilitarians say to convince us that the principle of utility is what Kant said he was searching for: the "supreme principle of morality"?

Both Bentham and Mill address this question. Both insist that because the principle of utility is held to be the first principle of morality, it is not subject to ordinary kinds of proof. Nonetheless, each thinks he can provide arguments to convince us.

Bentham thinks the alternatives are either impossible to apply consistently or amount simply to what some individual "feels" is right. He asks you to consider an individual (call him Jones) who says, "Action A is right; I *know* it is right even though I don't know whether it will bring happiness or misery." Suppose, Bentham says, that the consequences of A amount in fact to unmitigated misery. Could you agree that A is the right thing to do? Would you say this is something Jones "knows"?

Mill adds arguments of his own. Though he agrees that questions of ultimate ends do not admit of proof, he thinks convincing considerations can be brought forward. Among these considerations, unfortunately, are two arguments that seem so obviously flawed that it is hard to believe he expects anyone to take them seriously. They are famous (perhaps even infamous) for that reason alone. We examine them briefly.

> The only proof capable of being given that an object is visible is that people actually see it. The only proof that a sound is audible is that people hear it; and so of the other sources of our experience. In like manner, I apprehend, the sole evidence it is possible to produce that anything is desirable is that people do actually desire it. (*U*, 168)

What Mill needs to show is that the general happiness is desirable, that it is what we ought to strive for. But his analogies do not work. "Visible" means "can be seen," and "audible" means "can be heard."

But "desirable" means not "can be desired," but "should be desired." So the fact that something *is* desired doesn't mean it *ought* to be desired. Mill's defenders suggest that the analogies are inapt, but the real point is that the fact that people desire happiness is *evidence*, though not conclusive evidence, that happiness is desirable.

Mill's second argument is even harder to defend. The conclusion he needs to support is that each of us should (morally speaking) take the general happiness as our end; when we act, that is what we ought to be trying to bring about. He argues that

> happiness is a good, that each person's happiness is a good to that person, and the general happiness, therefore, a good to the aggregate of all persons. (*U*, 169)

We can, perhaps, grant the premises of this argument: Happiness is a good, and for each person, that person's own happiness is a good to that person. But all that follows from this premise is that each person's happiness is a good to *someone*. It does not follow that *your* happiness is a good to *someone else*, just because their own happiness is a good to them. Each and every bit of the general happiness is a good to *some* person, but it may not be, for all the premises tell us, that the general happiness is a good to *each and every* person. Yet that is what the principle of utility claims.*

How important are these errors? Both Bentham and Mill, after all, admit that their first principle cannot be proved. Perhaps, then, it is a mistake to try to prove it. We may feel that their consequentialist morality is pointing to something important even if it cannot be proved correct. The lack of proof does leave open the possibility that there is more to morality than utility, but it may be hard to deny that utility plays an important role.

Let us set aside this attempt at a positive proof and look at another kind of defense of the utilitarian creed. Mill considers various sorts of objections to it and tries to show that they all rest on misunderstandings. Let us review some of those objections.

---

*See pp. 212–213 (Aristotle); p. 256 (Jesus); pp. 282–283 (Augustine); p. 489 (Kant); and p. 515 (Hegel).

*Logicians have a name for this kind of mistake. They call it a *fallacy of composition* because what applies to every part is erroneously applied to the whole.

1. Some accuse utilitarians, especially utilitarians who set pleasure as the good, of aiming too low. It is the old objection aimed already at the Epicureans. Since pleasure and pain are something we share with the animals, to make these the standard of right and wrong is to espouse a philosophy for pigs.* To this, Mill replies that human beings, having higher faculties than pigs, require more to make them happy; but their happiness is still just pleasure and their unhappiness pain. In this connection, Mill pens a famous line:

> It is better to be a human being dissatisfied than a pig satisfied; better to be a Socrates dissatisfied than a fool satisfied. And if the fool, or the pig, are of a different opinion, it is because they only know their own side of the question. (*U*, 140)

2. Some hold that the utilitarian standard is unrealizable. Is it possible that everyone should be happy? First, Mill replies, even if that were impossible, the principle of utility would still be valid. We can do much to minimize unhappiness, even if we cannot attain its opposite. Second, it is an exaggeration to say that happiness—even the general happiness—is impossible. The happiness that utilitarians favor is not, after all, a life of constant rapture, but

> moments of such, in an existence made up of few and transitory pains, many and various pleasures, with a decided predominance of the active over the passive, and having as the foundation of the whole not to expect more from life than it is capable of bestowing. (*U*, 144)

He believes that even now a great many people live this way. If it were not for the "wretched education and wretched social arrangements" prevailing in his society, he thinks, such a life would be attainable by almost all. And he adds,

> When people who are tolerably fortunate in their outward lot do not find in life sufficient enjoyment to make it valuable to them, the cause generally is caring for nobody but themselves. (*U*, 144)

This point is so important to Mill that it is a little surprising he doesn't make more of it in *Utilitarianism*. In his *Autobiography*, Mill tells us about a period of severe depression that he suffered in his early twenties. He came out of it, he says, with a new certainty.

> I never, indeed, wavered in the conviction that happiness is the test of all rules of conduct, and the end of life. But I now thought that this end was only to be attained by not making it the direct end. Those only are happy (I thought) who have their minds fixed on some object other than their own happiness; on the happiness of others, on the improvement of mankind, even on some pursuit, followed not as a means, but as itself an ideal end. Aiming thus at something else, they find happiness by the way. The enjoyments of life (such was now my theory) are sufficient to make it a pleasant thing, when they are taken *en passant*, without being made a principal object. Once make them so, and they are immediately felt to be insufficient. . . . Ask yourself whether you are happy, and you cease to be so. The only chance is to treat, not happiness, but some end external to it, as the purpose of life. . . . This theory now became the basis of my philosophy of life.[5]

❦

> "Many persons have a wrong idea of what constitutes true happiness. It is not attained through self-gratification but through fidelity to a worthy purpose."
>
> *Helen Keller (1880–1968)*

A later utilitarian, Henry Sidgwick (1838–1900), calls this the **paradox of hedonism:** we cannot ensure our own happiness by aiming directly at it. Instead, we can find happiness only by devoting ourselves to projects aimed at something else.*

3. Some critics object that in making happiness the end, utilitarians undercut the most noble motives and the most admirable character. Do we

---

*See the discussion of Epicurus on pp. 236–240. You might also look at Aristotle's remark about pleasure on p. 209.

*If we take seriously this idea that happiness is a byproduct of other, nonhedonistic aims, strivings, and successes, this would to some extent reconcile the differences between utilitarians and those who (like Kant, Aristotle, and the Stoics) stress virtue as the key to ethics.

not, they ask, admire the individual who is willing to sacrifice personal happiness? Wouldn't this human virtue be destroyed if we all became happiness seekers?

Mill admits that we admire those who give up their personal happiness for the sake of something they prize even more. But what do they renounce their happiness *for*?

> After all, this self-sacrifice must be for some end; it is not its own end; and if we are told that its end is not happiness but virtue, which is better than happiness, I ask, would the sacrifice be made if the hero or martyr did not believe that it would earn for others immunity from similar sacrifices? . . . All honor to those who can abnegate for themselves the personal enjoyment of life when by such renunciation they contribute worthily to increase the amount of happiness in the world; but he who does it or professes to do it for any other purpose is no more deserving of admiration than the ascetic mounted on his pillar. (*U*, 147)

Utilitarians, Mill says, can admire self-sacrifice as much as any. They only refuse to recognize that it is good in itself. It is admirable only if it tends to increase the total amount of happiness in the world. And that is exactly what the principle of utility urges.

4. Other critics object that it is asking too much of people to aim at general happiness in all their actions. You can think of this as the opposite of the first objection; instead of holding that the standard is too low, some claim it is impossibly high.

To this Mill replies that it is the business of ethics to tell us what our duties are, what is right and what is wrong. But ethics does not go as far as to require that everything we do should be done from a certain *motive*.* From a utilitarian point of view, the rightness of an action is judged by what it brings about; why the agent acted in that way is irrelevant. Mill gives an example:

> He who saves a fellow creature from drowning does what is morally right, whether his motive be duty or the hope of being paid for his trouble. (*U*, 149)

Does this make ethics seem altogether *too external*? Are people's motives really that irrelevant to what is right and wrong? In a footnote added in response to criticism of that sort, Mill allows that the agent's *intention* (his aim to bring about the consequence of a person saved from drowning) is morally relevant. And our estimate of the *worth of the agent* may vary, depending on whether he was motivated by duty or greed. In the latter case we will think less of the man and be less likely to trust him in similar circumstances. But, Mill insists, the right thing was done, whatever the motive.

5. To the objection that utilitarianism, which counts only worldly happiness as the mark of moral rightness, is a "godless" doctrine, Mill replies that it all depends on how you think of God.

> If it be a true belief that God desires, above all things, the happiness of his creatures, and that this was his purpose in their creation, utility is not only not a godless doctrine, but more profoundly religious than any other. (*U*, 153)

6. It seems as if the principle of utility is impractical. It requires something there is usually no time to do. Very often we are called on to act quickly in making a choice; there is no time to do the exhaustive calculations required to determine the consequences of all the alternatives available. To this, Mill has a very interesting reply:

> This is exactly as if anyone were to say that it is impossible to guide our conduct by Christianity because there is not time, on every occasion on which anything has to be done, to read through the Old and New Testaments. The answer to the objection is that there has been ample time, namely the whole past duration of the human species. During all that time mankind have been learning by experience the tendencies of actions. (*U*, 155)

The fact that utility functions as a first principle does not in any way rule out secondary principles. These intermediate generalizations, Mill holds, are readily available to us in the common wisdom of our culture and in the law. We do not need to calculate each time whether *this* murder would be

---

*This is exactly what Kant thinks morality does require; that every morally right action be one that is done out of duty, from respect for the moral law. Actions done out of mere inclination are not worth anything, morally speaking. See p. 488.

all right, or whether *that* lie would be justified, or whether making *this* contribution to the relief of the homeless fits with the first principle. We learn the basic moral rules as children. Such secondary rules may be subject to gradual improvement. They may be more and more perfectly adapted to produce happiness. There may be occasional exceptions to them, too, but a *moral* justification for an exception must be decided by appeal to utility.

> Nobody argues that the art of navigation is not founded on astronomy because sailors cannot wait to calculate the Nautical Almanac. Being rational creatures, they go to sea with it ready calculated; and all rational creatures go out upon the sea of life with their minds made up on the common questions of right and wrong. (*U*, 157)

It is indeed not possible to calculate the utility of each of our actions on the occasion of their performance. But we don't need to. We cannot do without secondary rules in society, which can be learned and relied on. But these can be improved by bringing them more closely in line with the first principle: utility. For Mill, Bentham's great value lies in his attempt to improve these subordinate principles, particularly in social institutions and the law.

7. A seventh objection begins from the observation that we can imagine actions that promote the general happiness but are nonetheless wrong. Mill's example is a white lie told to avoid some minor embarrassment or gain something useful. It is wrong to lie, but the principle of utility seems to imply that *this* lie is not only permissible, but also required. Mill responds that there is so much utility in being able to trust one another that anything that undermines that mutual trust—either by weakening our own aversion to lying or by weakening others' trust in us—is contrary to the principle of utility. Whatever minor benefit one hopes to gain by telling a white lie is outweighed by the harm done by undermining social trust. In short, following the *rule* against lying has a utility of its own, which is outweighed only in the most unusual circumstances.*

---

*Making the utility of specific rules the criterion of right and wrong, rather than the utility of individual acts, is called

8. This leads to a final objection, perhaps the most important of all, to which Mill devotes an entire chapter. The objection concerns **justice.** Can the demands of justice be incorporated into the utilitarian framework, or is justice something different, something that resists the calculation of consequences?

It is easy to dream up cases where there is at least the appearance of conflict between justice and utility. Executing an innocent person may, in certain circumstances, quell a riot and prevent many deaths. It is clear that to execute the innocent is *unjust.* Yet a utility calculation seems to tell us that in this circumstance, executing the person is the morally right thing to do because it would produce more pleasure and less pain overall.† So it seems there is a clash between the claims of justice and the claims of utility. In circumstances like this, justice tells us one thing, utility another. Mill tries to argue that this clash is merely apparent and that justice rightly understood can be seen to be just a special case of utility. If his argument is successful, justice and utility are reconciled.

Mill allows that the subjective feeling attached to judgments about justice is different from, and stronger than, feelings about utility. We think it more serious to violate justice than to fail to bring about as much happiness as we can. Why? Because, Mill believes, justice concerns the protection of someone's rights; injustice involves the violation of those rights. These might be legal rights, but they could also be moral rights—rights that the law should protect, but may not. When one person violates another's rights, we feel indignant and often want the perpetrator to be punished.

---

rule utilitarianism—provided the rules themselves are justified in terms of their utility in producing the desired consequences. Mill generally seems to regard the utility of acts as the criterion of right and wrong, but some scholars interpret him as an early rule utilitarian.

†Discussion of such cases has made it clear that from a utilitarian standpoint, it is not so easy to be sure that the circumstances justifying an innocent person's execution ever exist. For instance, we would have to be certain that the fact of the person's innocence would never be known, lest even worse events ensue. And could we ever be certain of that?

PETER SINGER

Peter Singer (b. 1946) is an Australian philosopher, lately teaching at Princeton. He is famous (or infamous) because of several conclusions to which his ethical reasoning leads him. We are interested not only in his conclusions, of course, but also in the arguments he puts forward for them.

Singer is a utilitarian, but like many twentieth-century and contemporary utilitarians, he gives up the classical utilitarians' understanding of happiness strictly in terms of pleasure and pain. Like his mentor at Oxford, R. M. Hare, Singer calls himself a "preference utilitarian," meaning by this that ethical reasoning should focus on the preferences or interests of the individuals involved. Of course, we all try to satisfy our own interests, but when we think ethically, we must consider all interests alike. Pain and suffering are bad, and that's true no matter who experiences it—even if the individual who suffers is of another species, such as a chimpanzee or a chicken.

Singer is perhaps most famous for his 1975 book, *Animal Liberation*. Here he argues that "there can be no reason—except the selfish desire to preserve the privileges of the exploiting group—for refusing to extend the basic principle of equal consideration to members of other species. I ask you to recognize that your attitudes to members of other species are a form of prejudice no less objectionable than prejudice about a person's race or sex" (*AL*, v). Failure to consider the interests of nonhuman animals he calls "speciesism," in analogy with racism or sexism.

It does not follow that all lives are of equal worth, since the interests of a being that is self-aware and has a sense of its past and future are more extensive than those of a being that lacks these features. But pain is pain and, ethically speaking, we must "bring nonhuman animals within our sphere of moral concern and cease to treat their lives as expendable for whatever trivial purposes we may have" (*AL*, 20).

This universal perspective leads him to a number of significant conclusions. For example, Singer condemns many factory-farming practices as cruel and insensitive to the interests of the animals involved. Animals live in cramped quarters where they cannot engage in their ordinary behaviors. They get sick. They harm each other. They suffer brutal mutilations and gruesome deaths. And what is all this suffering for? To give people something they enjoy eating at the lowest possible price. Could this be ethically right? Surely not, says Singer. Furthermore, Singer says, similar arguments apply not just to factory farms, but also to virtually all consumption of animals. He concludes that we should all be vegetarians.

Singer draws an even more striking conclusion about the global distribution of wealth. He begins from the premises that "suffering and death from lack of food, shelter, and medical care are bad" (*FAM, WEL,* 106) and that "if it is in our power to prevent something bad from happening, without thereby sacrificing anything of comparable moral importance, we ought, morally, to do it" (*FAM, WEL,* 107). It follows that spending money trivially is wrong whenever it could instead relieve the suffering and death that results from the extreme poverty in which hundreds of millions of people around the world still live. Buying luxuries—a bracelet, a new coat, or a BMW, for example—is morally wrong when so many are suffering. We usually think of donating money to fight poverty as charity, which means that we are praised if we do it but not condemned if we don't. Singer, however, thinks that such donations are simply our duty. If we took this seriously, Singer admits, "our lives, our society, and our world would be fundamentally changed" (*FAM, WEL,* 107).

Perhaps Singer's most controversial conclusions concern abortion and infanticide. Recall that he places the satisfaction of preferences at the foundation of his utilitarianism. A fetus, unlike a person, is not self-conscious, nor does it have well-developed preferences for its future life. He therefore suggests "that we accord the life of a fetus no greater value than the life of a nonhuman animal at a similar level of rationality, self-consciousness, awareness, capacity to feel, etc." (*PE*, 136). This means, he believes,

(continued)

PETER SINGER   *(continued)*

that a fetus does not have the same right to life as an adult and that abortion is sometimes justified.

He applies the same reasoning to newborns. "A week-old baby is not a rational and self-conscious being, and there are many nonhuman animals whose rationality, self-consciousness, awareness, capacity to feel, and so on, exceed that of a human baby a week or a month old. If the fetus does not have the same claim to life as a person, it appears that the newborn baby does not either" (*PE,* 151). If it is not wrong to abort a defective fetus, he concludes, it cannot be wrong to kill a defective newborn.

NOTE:
Abbreviations: *AL*—*Animal Liberation*, 2nd ed. (New York: Random House, 1990); *VP*—"A Vegetarian Philosophy" in *Consuming Passions*, Sian Griffiths and Jennifer Wallace, eds. (New York: Manchester University Press, 1998); *FAM*—"Famine, Affluence, and Morality," reprinted from *Philosophy and Public Affairs*, 1972, in Singer, (*WEL*) *Writings on an Ethical Life* (New York: Ecco Press, 2000); *PE*—*Practical Ethics*, 3rd ed. (New York: Cambridge University Press, 2011).

But, Mill asks, what is it to have a **right** in the first place?

> When we call anything a person's right, we mean that he has a valid claim on society to protect him in the possession of it. (*U,* 189)

I have a right to walk peaceably down a city street without being molested. To have such a right, Mill tells us, is to have a "valid claim" to protection in the exercise of this right. Society *owes* it to me to see that this right is not violated, has a **duty** to guarantee my safety in such circumstances.

But where do rights like this come from? On what grounds can I claim that society owes me such protection? Mill's argument is that such claims come from something that is so basic, so fundamental, that in its absence everything else making for happiness is in jeopardy: **security.**

> All other earthly benefits are needed by one person, not needed by another; and many of them can, if necessary, be cheerfully foregone or replaced by something else; but security no human being can possibly do without; on it we depend for all our immunity from evil and for the whole value of all and every good, beyond the passing moment, since nothing but the gratification of the instant could be of any worth to us if we could be deprived of everything the next instant by whoever was momentarily stronger than ourselves. (*U,* 190)

Security, being safe in our persons and possessions, is the "most indispensable of all necessaries," Mill says (*U,* 190).* Because it is so basic to our happiness, the feelings that attach to its protection are particularly strong. That is why justice *feels* different from utility. But in fact, utility lies at the very foundation of justice.

> I account the justice which is grounded on utility to be the chief part, and incomparably the most sacred and binding part, of all morality. Justice is a name for certain classes of moral rules which concern the essentials of human well-being more nearly, and are therefore of more absolute obligation, than any other rules for the guidance of life; and the notion which we have found to be of the essence of the idea of justice—that of a right residing in an individual—implies and testifies to this more binding obligation. . . . a person may possibly not need the benefits of others, but he always needs that they should not do him hurt. (*U,* 195–196)

In this way, Mill argues there is no conflict between justice and utility. If we return to our example of executing an innocent man for the sake of avoiding a riot, we can see what Mill would say. It is unjust to take his life, so it ought not to be done. To

—————
*You would be right to hear echoes of Hobbes here. See Hobbes on the deplorable "state of nature" in which no one can feel safe (pp. 410–413).

acquiesce in the violation of that man's security imperils the security of us all. And that none of us will tolerate.* The appearance of conflict can be overcome if we reflect that justice is the name we give to the deepest condition for securing our happiness.

1. What makes utilitarianism a teleological or consequentialist theory?
2. Explain the principle of utility.
3. What makes classic utilitarianism a form of hedonism?
4. What is happiness, according to the utilitarians, and what does it have to do with morality? (Pieces of their view of happiness are scattered through the chapter; gather them together to form your answer.)
5. How does a person apply the principle of utility to determine whether a particular action is morally right or wrong?
6. How do Bentham and Mill differ in their methods of calculating happiness? How does Mill propose to determine the quality of pleasures?
7. Mill presents two arguments in favor of utilitarianism. Explain each argument. Identify the fallacy in each.
8. How does Mill defend utilitarianism against the charges that (a) pleasure is too low a standard to be appealed to in morality and (b) the general happiness is too high a standard?
9. Contrast Mill and Kant on the question of whether an agent's motivation is relevant to an appraisal of the morality of an action.
10. What problem is justice thought to raise for the utilitarians? How does Mill argue that, at bottom, there is no conflict between justice and utility?

*Critics of utilitarianism will push the point, however, that it is *possible*—however unlikely—that such an execution will actually increase the general happiness. And if one could be sure that the circumstances were right, then utility would prescribe the execution. Since this could in no case be a just act, there is in principle an unresolved conflict between justice and utility, and Mill's attempt at reconciliation fails. A contemporary utilitarian, Brad Hooker, suggests that one advantage of rule utilitarianism is that it allows us to set aside such extreme cases to focus on the *general* benefit of rules against injustice. Otherwise, we will have to look elsewhere for the grounds of justice—perhaps in something like the Kantian imperative that one is never to use a person as a means to an end. See again Kant's discussion of this on p. 491.

The Rights of Women

Mill and his fellow utilitarians advocated for many different political reforms in the nineteenth century. Let us look at one particularly important example: women's rights. By the time Mill wrote *The Subjection of Women*[6] in 1869, slavery had been abolished in the United States and, indeed, in most of the world. But one form of bondage, Mill said, remained: that in which half the world's population, the female half, was still held. Our situation today is so much changed from the circumstances in which Mill wrote (though it is still far from ideal) that we need to exert our imaginations to grasp the **"woman question,"** as the controversy over women's rights was then known.

Mill, of course, was not the first or only one to write on these issues. Nearly two hundred years earlier, the English philosopher Mary Astell (1666–1731) had argued that women were intellectually

"Let there be then no coercion established in society, and the common law of gravity prevailing, the sexes will fall into their proper places."

—MARY WOLLSTONECRAFT

equal to men and deserved a real education. She had also criticized the way English society handled marriage, arguing that it worked to the detriment of women. And just a few years after Bentham published his *Principles of Morals and Legislation*, another English philosopher, Mary Wollstonecraft (1759–1797), published *A Vindication of the Rights of Woman* (1792). Wollstonecraft is not clearly a utilitarian, though much of what she writes is in the same spirit. Because Mill and Wollstonecraft take a similar view of the "woman question" and recommend similar remedies, we will consider them together.[7]

Writing in 1869, Mill reminds us of the state of English law concerning women. (It was scarcely better anywhere else.) Society assumed that women generally would marry, and most did. For this reason, the laws concerning marriage were the crucial ones. Here is what those laws held (*SW*, 502–506):

- A married woman can have no property except in her husband. Whatever is hers is his, but not vice versa.
- There is a way for a woman to secure "her" property from her husband, but even so, if he by violence takes it from her, he cannot be punished or compelled to return it to her.
- Her children are by law *his* children. She can do nothing with them except by his delegation. On his death, she does not become their legal guardian, unless he by will makes her so.
- If she leaves her husband, she can take nothing with her, not even her children. He can—by force, if it comes to that—compel her to return.

And, of course, women were excluded from voting, from running for Parliament, and (at least by custom) from nearly all nondomestic professions. Mill considers the question of why this should be so. Is it, he asks, because society has experimented with alternative social arrangements and discovered that, all in all, this is best? Of course not. The adoption of this system

> never was the result of deliberation, or forethought, or any social ideal, or any notion whatever of what conduced to the benefit of humanity or the good order of society. It arose simply from the fact that

from the very earliest twilight of human society, every woman (owing to the value attached to her by men, combined with her inferiority in muscular strength) was found in a state of bondage to some man. (*SW*, 475)

Mill stresses that the situation now sanctioned by law was simply the situation that was in place when laws were first written. This amounts to an adoption of the **law of the strongest,** a law that led to kingship and slavery, as well as to the subjection of women. So the fact that the subjection of women has been a custom nearly everywhere for ages is no more an argument in its favor than is a similar argument in support of absolute monarchy or slavery—both of which have been done away with in the modern world.

Moreover, it is not hard to explain why this custom has outlasted monarchy and slavery. Each of these had the attractions of power; the same is true of the relation between women and men. But there is an important difference:

> Whatever gratification of pride there is in the possession of this power, and whatever personal interest in its exercise, is in this case not confined to a limited class, but common to the whole male sex. . . . It comes home to the person and hearth of every male head of a family, and of everyone who looks forward to being so. The clodhopper exercises, or is to exercise, his share of the power equally with the highest nobleman. . . . We must consider, too, that the possessors of the power have facilities in this case, greater than in any other, to prevent any uprising against it. Every one of the subjects lives under the very eye, and almost, it may be said, in the hands, of one of the masters— in closer intimacy with him than with any of her fellow-subjects; with no means of combining against him, and, on the other hand, with the strongest motives for seeking his favour and avoiding to give him offence. (*SW*, 481, 482)

The fact that women don't complain about this inequality might constitute an argument in its favor; women consent to it, it is said, and even contribute to its continuance. But Mill notes several things: (1) Some women do complain. (2) The common pattern is that those subjected to power of an ancient origin begin by complaining not about the power itself, but only about its abuse; and there is plenty of complaint by women about their husbands' ill use of them. But most important, (3)

> men do not want solely the obedience of women, they want their sentiments. All men, except the most brutish, desire to have, in the woman most nearly connected with them, not a forced slave but a willing one, not a slave merely, but a favourite. They have therefore put everything in practice to enslave their minds. The masters of all other slaves rely, for maintaining obedience, on fear, either fear of themselves, or religious fears. The masters of women wanted more than simple obedience, and they turned the whole force of education to effect their purpose. (*SW*, 486)

To us, this may sound exaggerated. But Wollstonecraft cites passages from popular books about how to bring up young women that suggest this is no exaggeration. Let's look at some of her evidence.

The theme running through the popular literature of her time is that a woman exists for the sake of a man. Because of that, a **woman's virtues** are different from a man's and a woman's daily life is oriented toward **pleasing.** One of Wollstonecraft's sources is *Émile*, an influential book on education by Jean-Jacques Rousseau.* Here is Rousseau on the education of women. (We cite Wollstonecraft's quotations from Rousseau at some length to stimulate the imagination we need to re-create the situation of the time.)

> It being once demonstrated that man and woman are not, nor ought to be, constituted alike in temperament and character, it follows, of course, that they should not be educated in the same manner. . . .
>
> Woman and man were made for each other, but their mutual dependence is not the same. The men depend on the women only on account of their desires; the women on the men both on account of their desires and their necessities. We [men] could subsist better without them than they without us. . . .
>
> For this reason the education of women should be always relative to the men. To please, to be

useful to us, to make us love and esteem them, to educate us when young, and take care of us when grown up, to advise, to console us, to render our lives easy and agreeable—these are the duties of women at all times, and what they should be taught in their infancy. . . .

> Boys love sports of noise and activity; to beat the drum, to whip the top, and to drag about their little carts; girls, on the other hand, are fonder of things of show and ornament; such as mirrors, trinkets, and dolls: the doll is the peculiar amusement of the females; from whence we see their taste plainly adapted to their destination. . . . And, in fact, almost all of them learn with reluctance to read and write; but very readily apply themselves to the use of their needles. They imagine themselves already grown up, and think with pleasure that such qualifications will enable them to decorate themselves. . . .

> Girls . . . should also be early subjected to restraint. This misfortune, if it really be one, is inseparable from their sex; nor do they ever throw it off but to suffer more cruel evils. They must be subject, all their lives, to the most constant and severe restraint, which is that of decorum; it is, therefore, necessary to accustom them early to such confinement, that it may not afterwards cost them too dear; and to the suppression of their caprices, that they may the more readily submit to the will of others. . . .

> There results from this habitual restraint a tractableness which women have occasion for during their whole lives, as they constantly remain either under subjection to the men, or to the opinions of mankind; and are never permitted to set themselves above those opinions. The first and most important qualification in a woman is good nature or sweetness of temper: formed to obey a being so imperfect as man, often full of vices, and always full of faults, she ought to learn betimes even to suffer injustice, and to bear the insults of a husband without complaint; it is not for his sake, but her own, that she should be of a mild disposition. . . .

> Woman has everything against her, as well our faults as her own timidity and weakness; she has nothing in her favour, but her subtility and her beauty. Is it not very reasonable, therefore, she should cultivate both? . . . In infancy, while they are as yet incapable to discern good from evil, they ought to observe . . . as a law never to say anything disagreeable to those whom they are speaking to. (Quoted in *VRW*, 88–95)

---

* See the Sketch of Rousseau on p. 490.

There is more to the same effect in Wollstonecraft, quoted from other popular authors of the time. Mill and Wollstonecraft not only agree that this subjection of women to men is unjust, but also argue that it has many bad consequences. In particular, Wollstonecraft argues that many of the faults attributed to women by the writers of her time are not innate to women, but the result of their upbringing and social conditions. Let us examine what she and Mill have to say.

The idea that there are special virtues for a woman and that these are all oriented around pleasing men, results in morality being

> very insidiously undermined, in the female world, by the attention being turned to the show instead of the substance. A simple thing is thus made strangely complicated; nay, sometimes virtue and its shadow are set at variance. (*VRW*, 148)

A woman is persuaded to value trivial things: attractiveness, dress, decorum, the short-term pleasures of sex. Thus are women turned toward sensuality and away from understanding.

> They who live to please—must find their enjoyments, their happiness, in pleasure! (*VRW*, 129–130)

It is this emphasis on pleasing—and pleasing men particularly—that accounts for the fact that the term "a virtuous woman" has such a narrow connotation. Why should that term direct the mind immediately to sexual behavior, when the term "a virtuous man" does not? Because a woman is regarded as first and foremost a pleaser!

"Women have been trained to speak softly and carry a lipstick. Those days are over."

Bella Abzug (1920–1998)

Furthermore, everything is focused on the opinions of others, on how a woman is *regarded*. This constant attention to maintain an appearance of respectability often supersedes actual moral obligations. With respect to reputation, Wollstonecraft says,

The attention is confined to a single virtue—chastity. If the honour of a woman, as it is absurdly called, be safe, she may neglect every social duty; nay, ruin her family by gaming and extravagance; yet still present a shameless front—for truly she is an honourable woman! (*VRW*, 150)

Thus the social order makes women worse than they ought to be; this narrow view of their nature gives them the status of secondary beings whose very existence is justifiable only in terms of a relation to another.

> Pleasure is the business of woman's life, according to the present modification of society; and while it continues to be so, little can be expected from such weak beings. Inheriting in a lineal descent from the first fair defect in nature—the sovereignty of beauty—they have, to maintain their power, resigned the natural rights which the exercise of reason might have procured them, and chosen rather to be short-lived queens than labour to obtain the sober pleasures that arise from equality. (*VRW*, 61)

Not much can be expected from such weak beings, Wollstonecraft says. But, of course, they have been deliberately created weak. Mill puts the argument this way:

> All women are brought up from the very earliest years in the belief that their ideal of character is the very opposite to that of men; not self-will, and government by self-control, but submission, and yielding to the control of others. All the moralities tell them that it is the duty of women, and all the current sentimentalities that it is their nature, to live for others; to make complete abnegation of themselves, and to have no life but in their affections. And by their affections are meant the only ones they are allowed to have—those to the men with whom they are connected, or to the children who constitute an additional and indefeasible tie between them and a man. When we put together three things—first, the natural attraction between the sexes; secondly, the wife's entire dependence on the husband, every privilege or pleasure she has being either his gift, or depending entirely on his will; and lastly, that the principal object of human pursuit, consideration, and all objects of social ambition, can in general be sought or obtained by her only through him, it would be a miracle if the object of being attractive to men had not become

the polar star of feminine education and formation of character. And, this great means of influence over the minds of women having been acquired, an instinct of selfishness made men avail themselves of it to the utmost as a means of holding women in subjection, by representing to them meekness, submissiveness, and resignation of all individual will into the hands of a man, as an essential part of sexual attractiveness. (*SW*, 486–487)

Wollstonecraft speaks of women having to resign reason and their natural rights "to maintain their power" (*VRW*, 61). And this leads to further bad consequences. Women become, of necessity, *cunning.*

Only employed about the little incidents of the day, they necessarily grow up cunning. My very soul has often sickened at observing the sly tricks practised by women to gain some foolish thing on which their silly hearts were set. Not allowed to dispose of money, or call anything their own, they learn to turn the market penny; or, should a husband offend, by staying from home, or give rise to some emotions of jealousy—a new gown, or any pretty bauble, smooths Juno's angry brow.

But these *littlenesses* would not degrade their character, if women were led to respect themselves, if political and moral subjects were opened to them; and, I will venture to affirm that this is the only way to make them properly attentive to their domestic duties. An active mind embraces the whole circle of its duties, and finds time enough for all. (*VRW*, 187)

On narrowness of education another female fault is built: meddlesomeness. Wollstonecraft argues that

women cannot by force be confined to domestic concerns: for they will, however ignorant, intermeddle with more weighty affairs, neglecting private duties only to disturb, by cunning tricks, the orderly plans of reason which rise above their comprehension. (*VRW*, 12)

Mill adds that men who are considerate of their wives' opinions are often made worse, not better, by the wife's influence.

She is taught that she has no business with things out of that [domestic] sphere; and accordingly she seldom has any honest and conscientious opinion on them; and therefore hardly ever meddles with them for any legitimate purpose, but generally for an

interested one. She neither knows nor cares which is the right side in politics, but she knows what will bring in money or invitations, give her husband a title, her son a place, or her daughter a good marriage. (*SW*, 512)

Many women do manage to "govern" their husbands, of course. Their weakness and lack of straightforward rationality, however, cause them to do this indirectly, sneakily, with what Rousseau calls "subtility." In fact, Wollstonecraft argues, it is this very weakness that entices women to become tyrants in their families.

Women are, in fact, so much degraded by mistaken notions of female excellence, that I do not mean to add a paradox when I assert that this artificial weakness produces a propensity to tyrannize, and gives birth to cunning, the natural opponent of strength, which leads them to play off those contemptible infantine airs that undermine esteem even whilst they excite desire. (*VRW*, 7)

Either women use their beauty, their desirability, to tyrannize men or they become shrewish. But what is the alternative?

"Educate women like men," says Rousseau, "and the more they resemble our sex the less power will they have over us." This is the very point I aim at. I do not wish them to have power over men; but over themselves. (*VRW*, 69)

In this last remark we come near to the heart of the matter. Such, then, are the consequences of restricting the education and dulling the reason of women, of teaching them that their only concern must be to please a man.

What do Wollstonecraft and Mill want for women? **Equality** with men before the law, independence, **freedom** to make their own decisions, strength of body, a real **education** that broadens understanding and doesn't just heighten sensitivity, and the capacity for friendship with men rather than submissive fawning. Wollstonecraft sums it up by declaring that there should be no sexually based virtues. Virtue—moral goodness—is a *human* matter; only evil comes from assuming that there is one virtue for a man and another for a woman, with its corollary that the woman's virtue exists only relative to the man's. True, men and women may to some extent have different duties, but they are one and all, she says, human duties.

> I here throw down my gauntlet, and deny the existence of sexual virtues, not excepting modesty. For man and woman, truth, if I understand the meaning of the word, must be the same. (*VRW*, 57)

As things are, a woman is denied the independent use of reason and must see everything through her husband's eyes. But the question is, does she have as much capacity for reason and understanding as a man?

> If she have, which, for a moment, I will take for granted, she was not created merely to be the solace of man, and the sexual should not destroy the human character. (*VRW*, 59)

Very well. But should we take that for granted? How could we tell whether her reason would be as strong as a man's if it were given a chance? Both Mill and Wollstonecraft argue that you can't tell by looking at contemporary society or history because both are tainted by the corrupting influence of the education and upbringing women have received. The only way to tell is to make the experiment. Wollstonecraft says,

> I have not attempted to extenuate their faults; but to prove them to be the natural consequence of their education and station in society. If so, it is reasonable to suppose that they will change their character, and correct their vices and follies, when they are allowed to be free in a physical, moral, and civil sense.
>
> Let woman share the rights, and she will emulate the virtues of man; for she must grow more perfect when emancipated, or justify the authority that chains such a weak being to her duty. (*VRW*, 214–215)

Mill adds,

> I consider it presumption in anyone to pretend to decide what women are or are not, can or cannot be, by natural constitution. They have always hitherto been kept, as far as regards spontaneous development, in so unnatural a state, that their nature cannot but have been greatly distorted and disguised; and no one can safely pronounce that if women's nature were left to choose its direction

as freely as men's, and if no artificial bent were attempted to be given to it except that required by the conditions of human society, and given to both sexes alike, there would be any material difference, or perhaps any difference at all, in the character and capacities which would unfold themselves. (*SW*, 532)

> There are no means of finding what either one person or many can do, but by trying. (*SW*, 499)

Suppose the trial is made and we find that women are not by nature the inferior beings they have been made to be. Suppose that the reforms in law and custom Mill and Wollstonecraft urge come to pass. What good can we expect to come of them? First, Mill says, we will have justice rather than injustice, and that is no insignificant gain (*SW*, 558). Second, we would virtually double "the mass of mental faculties available for the higher service of humanity" (*SW*, 561). Third, women would have a more beneficial influence, though not necessarily a greater influence, on general belief and sentiment (*SW*, 563). Fourth, there will surely be a great gain in happiness for women (*SW*, 576).

We can close this brief consideration of the "woman question" in the nineteenth century with an appeal by Wollstonecraft:

> I then would fain convince reasonable men of the importance of some of my remarks; and prevail on them to weigh dispassionately the whole tenor of my observations. I appeal to their understandings; and as a fellow-creature, claim, in the name of my sex, some interest in their hearts. I entreat them to assist to emancipate their companion, to make her a *helpmeet* for them.
>
> Would men but generously snap our chains, and be content with rational fellowship instead of slavish obedience, they would find us more observant daughters, more affectionate sisters, more faithful wives, more reasonable mothers—in a word, better citizens. We should then love them with true affection, because we should learn to respect ourselves. (*VRW*, 164)

If our situation is very different from the situation in which these two philosophers wrote, one reason is the impact their thoughts have had on successive generations down to the present day.

1. What principles for the education of women does Rousseau advocate?
2. What bad consequences do Wollstonecraft and Mill see flowing from the differential treatment of women?
3. What ideals do they recommend in place of the current beliefs about the position of women in society?
4. What benefits will result from such a change, according to Wollstonecraft and Mill?

FOR FURTHER THOUGHT

1. What implications would Kant's categorical imperative have for the "woman question"? Would they differ from those of the utility principle?
2. To a considerable degree, we have made the experiment that Wollstonecraft and Mill recommend. Look at what they anticipate the outcome to be and estimate to what degree we have achieved their ends.

KEY WORDS

utilitarianism
principle of utility
consequentialism
paradox of hedonism
justice

right
duty
security
woman question
law of the strongest

woman's virtues
pleasing
equality

freedom
education

NOTES

1. References to Jeremy Bentham, *An Introduction to the Principles of Morals and Legislation* (Oxford: Clarendon Press, 1907), are cited in the text by the abbreviation *PML*. References are to page numbers.
2. References to John Stuart Mill's *Utilitarianism,* in *On Liberty and Other Essays*, ed. John Gray (Oxford: Oxford University Press, 1991), are cited in the text by the abbreviation *U*. References are to page numbers.
3. John Stuart Mill, "Bentham," in *Utilitarianism and Other Essays*, ed. Alan Ryan (New York: Penguin Books, 1987), 151.
4. Quoted in *The Encyclopedia of Philosophy*, ed. Paul Edwards (New York: Macmillan, Free Press, 1967), 1:283.
5. John Stuart Mill, *Autobiography,* in *Essential Works of John Stuart Mill*, ed. Max Lerner (New York: Bantam Books, 1961), 88.
6. References to John Stuart Mill's *The Subjection of Women*, ed. John Gray (Oxford: Oxford University Press, 1991), are cited by the abbreviation *SW*. References are to page numbers.
7. References to Mary Wollstonecraft, *A Vindication of the Rights of Woman*, ed. Mary Warnock (London: J. M. Dent, Everyman's Library, 1986), are cited by the abbreviation *VRW*. References are to page numbers.

CHAPTER

24

FRIEDRICH NIETZSCHE

The Value of Existence

Born to a German Lutheran minister's family, Friedrich Nietzsche (1844–1900) lost his father when he was five years old. He was strictly brought up in a household of five women where religion, according to reports, was less practiced than preached. He went to excellent schools and studied classical philology at the universities of Bonn and Leipzig. At the unheard-of age of twenty-four, Nietzsche became a full professor in philology at the University of Basel, Switzerland.

He served as a medical orderly in the Franco-Prussian War and returned in poor health, but he continued working and published his first book in 1872. In 1879, he resigned his professorship on grounds of ill health and spent the next nine years in lonely apartments in Switzerland and Italy. He was severely ill for a long time, racked with pain and weakness that would have put most men in the hospital. But throughout his illness he kept working, producing book after book. He was deeply disappointed in the reception of his work; very few copies of his books were purchased, the few reviews were based on misunderstandings, and he was generally ignored. In the late winter of 1888,

he broke down and spent the next eleven years insane, cared for by his sister.*

Nietzsche is famous, or infamous, as an influence on the Nazi movement. There is no doubt that he wrote things that easily lent themselves to the distortions of Nazi propagandists, and he is certainly no friend of Christianity, democracy, or equal rights for all. But there is also no doubt that he would have been sickened by the whole Nazi business. He was no friend of nationalism either, thinking of himself always as a "good European." Scarcely any other writings contain such malicious attacks on "the Germans." And anti-Semitism was

---

*Walter Kaufmann, famous as a Nietzsche translator, writes, "His madness was in all probability an atypical general paresis. If so, he must have had syphilis; and since he is known to have lived a highly ascetic life, it is supposed that, as a student, he had visited a brothel once or twice. This has never been substantiated, and any detailed accounts of such experiences are either poetry or pornography—not biography. Nor has the suggestion ever been disproved that he may have been infected while nursing wounded soldiers in 1870" (*The Portable Nietzsche* [New York: Viking Press, 1954], 13–14).

diagnosed by Nietzsche as a particularly reprehensible form of resentment (about as bad a thing as he could say about anything). But the Nazis made him over in their own image and used perverted versions of his concepts of the *overman* and *will to power* to their advantage.

Like Kierkegaard (whom he did not know), Nietzsche is concerned primarily with the individual, not with politics. His basic question is this: In a fundamentally meaningless world, what sort of life could justify itself, could show itself to be worth living? Around that issue all his work circles.*

Pessimism and Tragedy

Appropriately enough for a classically trained philologist, Nietzsche's first book, *The Birth of Tragedy*,† is about the Greeks. Both its style and its content were shocking to his scholarly colleagues. It is not a dry historical treatise filled with footnotes and Greek quotations; it is a passionately argued account of how tragedy allowed an ancient people to solve the problem of "the value of existence" (*BT*, 17), together with a plea for the relevance of that solution today.[1] Nietzsche challenges the received view of the Greeks, that everything they did expressed a noble simplicity and grandeur, a calm and measured naivete, a spirit in which everything was harmonious and beautiful. Though this spirit fits Greek statues and temples, Nietzsche argues

"We want to be the poets of our life."
—Friedrich Wilhelm Nietzsche

that it doesn't fit tragedy—in particular, it doesn't fit what we know of the origins of tragedy.*

What is the problem that tragedy is supposed to solve? Nietzsche finds it expressed by Sophocles in the play *Oedipus at Colonus*.

According to an ancient legend, King Midas had long hunted the forest for the wise *Silenus,* the companion of Dionysus, without catching him. When Silenus finally fell into his hands, the king asked him what is the very best and most preferable of all things for man. The stiff and motionless daemon refused to speak; until, forced by the king, he finally

---

*Interest in Nietzsche is intense these days, and controversy rages over the proper interpretation of his thought. One source of dispute concerns what weight to give to the mass of notes that were published posthumously under the title *Will to Power*; to put our cards on the table, we believe it best to stick to what Nietzsche himself approved for publication, using the rest only to illuminate that.

†Published in 1872, its title was originally *The Birth of Tragedy from the Spirit of Music*. In the second half of the book, Nietzsche praises Richard Wagner's music dramas as an indication that the spirit of tragedy might be reborn. But by 1886, when a later edition came out, Nietzsche had despaired of Wagner as a "romantic" and a "decadent." This later edition contains Nietzsche's severe appraisal of the book in a preface called "Attempt at a Self-criticism."

---

*By tragedy Nietzsche means above all the dramas of Aeschylus and Sophocles. Representative examples are the *Oresteia* trilogy by Aeschylus and the well-known plays of Sophocles, *Oedipus Rex* and *Antigone*. The third great Athenian tragedian, Euripides, is thought by Nietzsche to preside over the death of tragedy.

burst into shrill laughter and uttered the following words: "Miserable ephemeral race, children of chance and toil, why do you force me to tell you what is best for you not to hear? The very best of all things is completely beyond your reach: not to have been born, not to *be*, to be *nothing*. But the second best thing for you is—to meet an early death." (*BT*, 3, 27)

The problem is **pessimism.** Contrary to the accepted view of Greek cheerfulness, Nietzsche believes that the Greeks looked into the abyss of human suffering without blinking, that they experienced the terrors and misery of life—and they *did not look away*. All things considered, said Greek folk wisdom, Silenus is right; the best of all is not to be. And yet the Greeks found a way to live, to affirm life, even to rejoice in life. How did they do that? Nietzsche finds the key to this puzzle in their art, especially in their tragedies.

The first thing to note is that the tragedies were performed at religious festivals. Attending these performances was serious business, more like going to a papal mass than taking in the latest hit movie. The second thing to note is that prizes were given for the best plays at each festival, so playwrights were continually challenged to excel.* But most important, the tragedies unite two opposing powers in human life. Nietzsche designates these powers with the names of two Greek gods, Apollo and Dionysus; each is the patron of a certain kind of art.

Apollo is the god of order and measure, the god of reason and restraint and calm composure. He is the god who says, "Nothing too much" and "Know thyself." It is the spirit of Apollo that reigns supreme in the harmonious sculptures on the Parthenon, where each individual being reaches a divine perfection without denying the perfection of any other. This spirit also pervades Homer's portrayal of Olympus and its radiant gods. Zeus, Hera,

Athena, Poseidon, and the rest are a magnificent dream of the human spirit.* In the Homeric epic, then, the wisdom of Silenus was

> continually overcome anew, in any case veiled and removed from view by the Greeks through that artistic *middle world* of the Olympians. In order to be able to live, the Greeks were obliged to create these gods, out of the deepest necessity. . . . So the gods justify the life of men by living it themselves—the only adequate theodicy! (*BT*, 3, 28)†

In this way, Nietzsche accounts for the epic, for the glories of Homer's *Iliad* and *Odyssey*. But tragedy is something else. In **tragedy,** the suffering in human life is not "veiled and removed from view"; it is presented, explored, and given weight. Tragedy *shows* us the terror.

To account for tragedy, Nietzsche believes we need to bring in another kind of god. **Dionysus** (Bacchus) is the god of wine, of intoxication, of excess and loss of control. Where Dionysus lives, order, form, and measure break down. Women are caught up in long lines, dancing beyond the civilized towns to orgies in the countryside.‡ Individual consciousness is drowned in a sea of feelings; primal nature overcomes conventions. This god, too, has his art. Lyric poetry and folk song express passions without reserve—desire, anguish, hate, contempt, frenzy, joy. But lyric and folk song are, by themselves, no more tragedy than is the epic. For the birth of tragedy, Dionysus must meet Apollo.

To understand how Nietzsche thinks tragedy solves the problem of the value of existence, we need to grasp one more thing: the metaphysics of **Schopenhauer.**§ In *The Birth of Tragedy* Nietzsche

---

*Nietzsche says that for the Greeks, everything was a contest. Characteristically, he sees envy, ambition, and the struggle to prevail flaring out in every sphere of Greek life, from athletics to poetry. What distinguishes the Greek ethos from our own, he thinks, is that this competitive spirit is *affirmed* and not condemned; "Every talent must unfold itself in fighting" ("Homer's Contest" in *PN*, 37).

*See Chapter 1 on the Homeric gods as portrayed in *The Iliad*.

†In his later thought, after all gods have disappeared, Nietzsche reaffirms this principle. The only satisfactory justification for human life lies in *living* it. The question then becomes, What sort of life could constitute such a justification? The answer turns out to be a life rather like the one the Greek gods themselves lived.

‡Such festivals are chronicled in Euripides' late play, *The Bacchae*.

§See the Sketch of Schopenhauer on p. 501.

accepts Schopenhauer's view of reality, though not Schopenhauer's evaluation of it. For Schopenhauer, as for Kant, the world of our experience is merely appearance, not reality. But unlike Kant, Schopenhauer thinks he knows what it is that appears. *In itself*, this world we are so familiar with is nothing but **will**—endless striving, desiring, wanting. The principles that *individuate* things—that make you different from me, one stone different from another—are space, time, and causality (as Kant taught). But these principles apply only in the realm of phenomena. Reality in itself is not cut up into individual things by our intuitions and concepts.*

As you should be able to see, Schopenhauer's realm of individuated, orderly phenomena fits neatly with Apollo, the god of order, measure, and knowledge. And his image of the raging depths of urgent reality accords with Dionysus, whose intoxications break down all distinctions and overwhelm all rules. Apollo governs the world of *appearance.* Dionysus represents the *in itself.*

We are now ready to understand how Nietzsche thinks tragedy can, at one stroke, solve the problem of existence and overcome pessimism. The key, he believes, is the role of the chorus in Greek tragedy. If you are familiar with these plays, you know that in them a chorus often speaks (or chants) in unison. Nietzsche notes three facts here. (1) In early Greek drama there were no actors; there was only the chorus. (2) The chorus was composed of **satyrs,** those half-human, half-goat companions to Dionysus. (3) Tragedy has a religious dimension. In some way that we need to understand, tragedy *redeems.* Through tragedy we can be *saved.*

What does it mean that the chorus was originally made up of satyrs?

Nature before knowledge has set to work on it . . . that is what the Greek saw in his satyr. . . . What he saw was the archetype of man,

the expression of his highest and strongest impulses. . . . The satyr was something sublime and divine. (*BT,* 8, 47)

In the songs, the chants, the dances of the satyrs, Greek spectators recognized something deep and natural in themselves. Their spirits sang, too, in the Dionysian rhythms of the chorus, which seemed to well up directly from primordial reality—from the *will.**

But tragedy as we have it is not just music and dance. There is drama, a story, individual characters who act and suffer. So far we have not accounted for that. But the explanation is not far away: The drama, Nietzsche tells us, is the *dream of the chorus.* The Dionysian chorus dreams an Apollonian dream, and the spectators, identifying with the chorus, dream it too.

A play, after all, is rather like a dream, isn't it? It's all imagination, appearance, phenomenon. The tragedies present (apparent) individuals whose (apparent) actions have (apparent) effects. Oedipus searches out the riddle of the Sphinx, Jocasta hangs herself, Clytemnestra murders Agamemnon in the bath. Yet no one rushes on stage to prevent Agamemnon's death or to save Antigone from being buried alive. Experiencing a tragic drama, Nietzsche says, is like having a dream in which you say to yourself, "This is a dream! I want to dream on!" (*BT,* 1, 21).

And now we are ready to understand how Nietzsche thinks tragedy overcomes the pessimistic wisdom of Silenus to solve the problem of existence. Tragedy does not deny the pessimism. It revels in the *destruction of individuals.* Oedipus blinds himself with his wife's brooches. Clytemnestra dies at the hand of her son. Prometheus is chained to a mountain peak where every day, an eagle eats at his liver.

But now we can see that tragedy acts as a window into reality. Just as the drama is the Apollonian dream of the Dionysian chorus, so—given

*Note the similarities between Schopenhauer's metaphysics and Buddhist metaphysics (pp. 41–45). Knowledge of Buddhist thought was just seeping into Germany when Schopenhauer was writing.

*For a modern counterpart, you might think of the audience at a rock concert. In Oliver Stone's movie *The Doors,* one of the musicians says to Jim Morrison, "I played with Dionysus, man."

Schopenhauer's metaphysics—*our individual lives are merely appearance* and not reality. We ourselves are a dream—a dream of the will. Reality is found in the Dionysian depths, where no individuation by space, time, or causality is possible. And just as the chorus affirms the dream, *including* the suffering and destruction, so the spectators affirm life. They affirm it passionately and joyously, including the suffering and destruction, for they know themselves to be other than, more than—infinitely more than—the petty individualities of the apparent world. They experience themselves in fusion with primal being as the eternal, nonindividualized, primordial root of the world. They experience themselves as willing the creation of the drama—and the creation of their lives.

Tragedy is terror and ecstasy in one. Everything that pessimism can say is true—and yet those truths concern only the dream world of appearance. There is also another truth,

> and this is the most immediate effect of Dionysian tragedy, that state and society, indeed the whole chasm separating man from man, gives way to an overpowering feeling of unity which leads back to the heart of nature. The **metaphysical consolation**—with which . . . all true tragedy leaves us—that life at the bottom of things, in spite of the passing of phenomena, remains indestructibly powerful and pleasurable, this consolation appears in embodied clarity in the chorus of satyrs, of creatures of nature who live on as it were ineradicably behind all civilization and remain eternally the same in spite of the passing of generations and of the history of peoples. (*BT*, 7, 45)

The metaphysical joy in the tragic is a translation of the instinctively unconscious Dionysian wisdom into the language of images: the hero, the greatest phenomenon of the will, is negated for our pleasure, because he remains only phenomenon and the eternal life of the will remains untouched by his annihilation. "We believe in eternal life," such is the cry of tragedy. . . . In Dionysian art and in its tragic symbolism, this same nature speaks to us in its true undistorted voice: "Be as I am! Beneath the incessantly changing phenomena, I am the eternally creative original mother, eternally

compelling people to exist, eternally finding satisfaction in this changing world of phenomena!" (*BT*, 16, 90)

Nietzsche distinguishes two kinds of pessimism: one of weakness and one of strength. The former he finds in Schopenhauer, who wants nothing more than Buddhist relief from willing—rest, escape from life. But in their tragedies the Greeks show us another way: *joyous affirmation in the face of the terror*. Like a primordial artist, the will ceaselessly creates the dreamscape of the phenomenal world. And we, identifying with this Dionysian power, can experience our lives, too, as art. Our lives may turn out as tragic as the lives of Oedipus and Agamemnon. This art work, in which we individuals are like actors on a stage, is not created for our happiness or our improvement. And yet we

> have our greatest dignity in our meaning as works of art—for only as an *aesthetic phenomenon* are existence and the world *justified* to eternity. (*BT*, 5, 38)

In what do we find our dignity and value? What is it that makes life worth living? Not anything moral, Nietzsche says, not *another* life (the "life of the world to come"), or our relation to God. Only its **aesthetic value** justifies our life and makes it worth living. There is something intrinsic to *Oedipus Rex* that leads us to value it, to continue to perform and experience it even after 2,500 years. If *our lives* had that same sort of aesthetic value, that would be enough to justify the living of them. If we come to experience ourselves as images and artistic projections for the true author of our lives—for the primordial unity, the will, that Dionysian power projecting the dream of the world drama—pessimism can be overcome. We can accept our lives even if our eyes are wide open to the wisdom of Silenus. We must think of ourselves as works of art! That is the way to solve the problem of "the value of existence." That is the only way it *could* be solved.* And that is what tragedy shows us.

---

*Compare Kierkegaard's aesthetic mode of life, pp. 522–525.

1. What is the "wisdom" of Silenus?
2. Distinguish the human powers symbolized by the gods Apollo and Dionysus.
3. How does Nietzsche use the metaphysics of Schopenhauer in his analysis of tragedy?
4. What is the role of the chorus in a Greek tragedy, according to Nietzsche?
5. What "metaphysical consolation" does tragedy provide?

Goodbye Real World

In *The Birth of Tragedy,* Nietzsche uses metaphysics to solve the problem of existence. Spectators at a tragedy, he thinks, experience the "metaphysical consolation" of realizing that they are infinitely more than the limited and suffering individuals they normally appear to be. Behind the appearance they discover *reality* in the Dionysian exuberance of the one true will's self-affirmation. They identify with their "true" self and rejoice. This solution is *metaphysical* in its appeal to "another world," a **real world** beneath the familiar world of everyday experience. Philosophers have long assured us that things are not really as they seem; from the ancient Greeks and Indians to Descartes, Kant, and Hegel, we hear that reality is not what we think—that *we* are not what we think! Nietzsche's reliance on Schopenhauer's metaphysics of the will is just another example of the same pattern.

But in the period after writing *The Birth of Tragedy,* Nietzsche comes to believe that no such metaphysics is possible for us. So another solution has to be found for the problem of the value of existence. All of Nietzsche's later work is oriented around this problem. Before we can grasp that solution, however, we need to understand why he thinks we must abandon the traditional philosophers' dream: to tell us what there really is.

> Little by little I came to understand what every great philosophy to date has been: the personal confession of its author, a kind of unintended and unwitting memoir; and similarly, that the moral (or immoral) aims in every philosophy constituted the actual seed from which the whole plant invariably grew. Whenever explaining how a philosopher's most far-fetched metaphysical propositions have come about, in fact, one always does well

(and wisely) to ask first: "What morality is it (is *he*) aiming at?" (*BGE,* 6, 8–9)

What we need is a psychology of the great philosophers that uncovers what really motivates their work. Nietzsche prides himself on his psychological acuity and thinks he has discovered that it is not *reality* that philosophical theories display, but the *philosophers themselves:* what sorts of people they are, how weak or strong they are, how sick or how healthy. Philosophy is "confession." Philosophers, Nietzsche says, want us to believe that they want truth, that their sole interest is knowledge. But

> they are not honest enough, however loud and virtuous a racket they all make as soon as the problem of truthfulness is touched upon, even from afar. For they act as if they had discovered and acquired what are actually their opinions through the independent unraveling of a cold, pure, divinely unhampered dialectic. . . . They are using reasons sought after the fact to defend a pre-existing tenet, a sudden idea, a "brainstorm," or in most cases a rarefied and abstract version of their heart's desire. They are all of them advocates who refuse the name, . . . in most cases wily spokesmen for their prejudices, which they dub "truths"; and they are *very* far from having a conscience brave enough to own up to it. (*BGE,* 5, 8)

> "To do philosophy is to explore one's own temperament, and yet at the same time to attempt to discover the truth."
>
> *Iris Murdoch (1919–1999)*

Nietzsche means to apply this critique to all the central conceptions of Western philosophy: to "soul," "free will," "the 'real' world," "God," "immortality," and "morality"—to say nothing of "cause," "substance," "unity," and "sameness of things." Nietzsche senses dishonesty in such notions.* What philosophers create is a world

---

*This suspicion toward traditional philosophizing, which Nietzsche in the nineteenth century shares with Kierkegaard, finds numerous echoes in the twentieth century. Compare the variously motivated rejections by Peirce (p. 604), Dewey (pp. 606–607), and Wittgenstein (pp. 633, 638, 648–649).

that satisfies "their heart's desire"; their "reasons" come later.

> But this is an old, eternal story . . . [Philosophy] always creates the world according to its own image, it cannot do otherwise; philosophy is this tyrannical drive itself, the most spiritual form of the will to power, to "creation of the world" to the *causa prima* [first cause]. (*BGE*, 9, 11)

Nietzsche's notion of "will to power," that "tyrannical drive" displayed in philosophizing, is a central idea for him; we explore it more fully later. Here we only note that this will to power expresses itself in philosophers through their attempts to create the world in their own image— and that means according to what they value, what they *need*. The Stoics, for example, needed order, law, control; they needed to be safe from disorder, chaos, and helplessness. So they created a world of providential orderliness, organized by the *logos,* the divine reason present in it. To cohere with such a world was virtue, happiness, and perfect freedom. But is nature really like that? Nietzsche doesn't think so. So the Stoics read into nature what they *need* it to be. And *all* the philosophers have done the same.

In addition to such personal needs, Nietzsche thinks there are *common* factors that influence metaphysical views. These factors may be grounded in the language we speak or simply in our human nature.

> Over immense periods of time the intellect produced nothing but errors. A few of these proved to be useful and helped to preserve the species. . . . Such erroneous articles of faith . . . include the following: that there are enduring things; that there are equal things; that there are things, substances, bodies; that a thing is what it appears to be; that our will is free; that what is good for me is good in itself. It was only very late that truth emerged— as the weakest form of knowledge. (*GS*, 110)

Even today, these "articles of faith" seem to be just common sense. But Nietzsche tells us they are *errors*. Kant's famous *categories,* Nietzsche holds, are also errors.* The concept of substance, for instance,

---
*See pp. 473–474.

"is indispensable for logic, although in the strictest sense nothing real corresponds to it" (*GS*, 111). The same is true of the a priori concept of causality.

> Cause and effect: such a duality probably never exists; in truth we are confronted by a continuum out of which we isolate a couple of pieces, . . . An intellect that could see cause and effect as a continuum and a flux and not, as we do, in terms of an arbitrary division and dismemberment, would repudiate the concept of cause and effect and deny all conditionality. (*GS*, 112)

You can see that Nietzsche accepts the Kantian point that we must judge the world in terms of such very general concepts. But Nietzsche's view differs radically from Kant's on two scores: (1) These concepts do *not* apply correctly to the phenomenal world, and (2) there is no noumenal world of things-in-themselves that these concepts fall short of. Their necessity for us is a purely practical necessity; without such "errors" we couldn't survive in the world as it is. So these errors are not arbitrary or capricious inventions; they serve *life*. But the fact that they are useful doesn't mean that they are true. "The conditions of life might include error" (*GS*, 121).

Human beings as they now are have been formed by their errors; we depend on them. Expanding on the general character of these errors, Nietzsche writes,

> The four errors.——Man has been educated by his errors. First, he always saw himself only incompletely; second, he endowed himself with fictitious attributes; third, he placed himself in a false order of rank in relation to animals and nature; fourth, he invented ever new tables of goods and always accepted them for a time as eternal and unconditional. (*GS*, 115)

Note that all four errors concern our knowledge of ourselves. Though they have taken "Know thyself" as their motto, philosophers go wrong most often just here. They see themselves "incompletely," they endow themselves with "fictitious attributes," they conclude that they are higher in "rank" than the other animals. They endow themselves with immortal souls. And they call this wisdom. But we, Nietzsche says, have learned differently. We have become more modest in every way. We no longer derive man from "the spirit" or "the deity"; we have placed him back among the animals. We consider him the strongest animal because he is the most cunning: his spirituality is a consequence of this. On the other hand, we oppose the vanity that would raise its head again here too—as if man had been the great hidden purpose of the evolution of the animals. Man is by no means the crown of creation: every living being stands beside him on the same level of perfection. And even this is saying too much: relatively speaking, man is the most bungled of all the animals, the sickliest, and not one has strayed more dangerously from its instincts. But for all that, of course, he is the most *interesting*. (*A*, 14)

It is clear that Nietzsche accepts a naturalistic, scientific picture of the world and of our place in it—with the qualification that science, too, must use those same falsifying concepts. Science cannot avoid this degree of error because it must be expressed in language, and language necessarily simplifies and falsifies. The universe of which we are a part is indifferent to good and evil, wasteful beyond measure, without mercy and justice, fertile and desolate, without purpose or reason, composed of mere processes in continuous flux. And we are just animals of a sickly sort, mechanisms governed by instincts that we are scarcely conscious of. Consciousness itself is scarcely our "essence"; it is "the last and latest development of the organic and hence also what is most unfinished and unstrong" (*GS*, 11). To focus on consciousness is bound to mislead.

◆

"A man said to the universe:
  'Sir, I exist!'
'However,' replied the universe,
  'The fact has not created in me
A sense of obligation."

Stephen Crane (1871–1900)

This view of things, Nietzsche thinks, results from centuries of training in truthfulness; *honesty* has brought us to this point. Philosophers have thought otherwise, but

how could we reproach or praise the universe? . . . None of our aesthetic and moral judgments apply to it. . . . When will all these shadows of God cease to darken our minds? When will we complete our de-deification of nature? When may we begin to "*naturalize*" humanity in terms of a pure, newly discovered, newly redeemed nature? (*GS*, 109)

The last words in this quotation are extremely important to Nietzsche, but we are not yet ready to understand them. For the moment, let us focus on the situation Nietzsche thinks we have come to: the view of the universe that—unless we continue to deceive ourselves—we *must* come to. Nature is "de-deified," vacant of all purposiveness and value; "nature is always value-less, but has been *given* value at some time as a present—and it was *we* who gave and bestowed it" (*GS*, 301).* In such a world we live; of such a world are we a part.

In *Twilight of the Idols*, Nietzsche offers a capsule history of philosophical conceptions of reality. He calls it "HOW THE 'REAL WORLD' FINALLY BECAME A FABLE: *History of an Error*":

1. The real world attainable for the wise man, the pious man, the virtuous man—he lives in it, he is it.

    (Most ancient form of the idea, relatively clever, simple, convincing. Paraphrase of the proposition: "I, Plato, am the truth.")†

2. The real world unattainable for now, but promised to the wise man, the pious man, the virtuous man ("to the sinner who repents").

    (Progress of the idea: it becomes more cunning, more insidious, more incomprehensible—it becomes a woman, it becomes Christian . . .)‡

3. The real world unattainable, unprovable, unpromisable, but the mere thought of it a consolation, an obligation, an imperative.

---

*Compare the early Wittgenstein, pp. 629–630. The difference is that for Wittgenstein we are *not* a part of the world.

†In *The Antichrist*, Nietzsche interprets Jesus according to the same formula. The kingdom of God, Jesus says, is "within you." And it is, of course, Jesus who says, "I am the way, the truth, and the life" (John 14:6). Compare the Indian notion that *ātman* is Brahman (p. 38).

‡Christianity, Nietzsche thinks, has *betrayed* the spirit of Jesus.

(The old sun in the background, but seen through mist and skepticism; the idea become sublime, pale, Nordic, Königsbergian.)*

4. The real world—unattainable? At any rate unattained. And since unattained also unknown. Hence no consolation, redemption, obligation either: what could something unknown oblige us to do? . . .

   (Break of day. First yawn of reason. Cockcrow of positivism.)

5. The "real world"—an idea with no further use, no longer even an obligation—an idea become useless, superfluous, therefore a refuted idea: let us do away with it!

   (Broad daylight; breakfast; return of *bon sens* and cheerfulness; Plato's shameful blush; din from all free spirits.)

6. The real world—we have done away with it: what world was left? the apparent one, perhaps? . . . But no! with the real world we have also done away with the apparent one!

   (Noon; moment of the shortest shadow; end of the longest error; pinnacle of humanity; IN-CIPIT ZARATHUSTRA.) (*TI*, 20)

Little by little, the real world vanishes: Parmenides' One, Plato's Forms, Aristotle's God, Augustine's soul, the Christian heaven, Descartes' free and immortal mind, Kant's world of things-in-themselves, Hegel's Absolute Spirit, Schopenhauer's will. All gone. Evaporated by a heightened honesty about ourselves and our place in the scheme of things. But what is left? Only the **apparent world?** Proposition 6 tells us that when the contrast between real and apparent vanishes, so does all reason to disparage this world—the one and only world—by calling it "apparent" (or, as many philosophers have said, "*merely* apparent"). There is just the world, and we a part of it.

> The "true world" and the "apparent world"—that means: the mendaciously invented world and reality. (*EH*, 218)

Nietzsche's estimate of his own importance can be gathered from the phrase that characterizes

stage 6, the stage of his own philosophy; he calls it the "pinnacle of humanity." He truly believes that he has seen through the shams and pretenses of all our previous philosophical history. Zarathustra, as we shall see soon, is the fictional "prophet" in whose mouth Nietzsche puts his own deepest philosophical thoughts. "INCIPIT ZARATHUSTRA" means "Zarathustra begins." And the time of Zarathustra is noon—when the shadows are shortest, when everything is in light and can be seen for what it is.

Now we see why Nietzsche has to rethink the problem of the meaning of life. In *The Birth of Tragedy*, he had relied on one version of the "real world" to solve the problem of pessimism. But now the real world has disappeared. And the question about the value of existence is posed anew, in an even more stark and dramatic way. How *can* life have any meaning in a world such as we now believe in? But before we can get ourselves out of this hole, we have to dig it still deeper. We must *look into the chasm* if we are to be saved.

The Death of God

The disappearance of the "real world" is not an obscure and remote event of interest only to a few philosophers. We all need a sense for the meaning of life, and for centuries most people have found it in religion*—in the West, primarily through Christianity. We have solved the problem of meaninglessness by setting our lives in the larger context of creation and salvation, God's plan, immortality, heaven and hell. So the whole culture—and certainly every Christian, Jew, and Muslim—has been committed to a metaphysics involving a "real world." If "real worlds" vanish like smoke in a clear sky, what will happen?

---

*Kant lived in Königsberg. Nietzsche obviously is thinking of the unknowable noumenal world and the categorical imperative.

---

*Remember that the Greek tragedies had precisely this function—to answer the question (in the face of pessimism) about the value of existence. Remember, too, that they were performed at *religious* festivals. Note also the religious language Nietzsche uses when he talks about this problem. Art "saves" us, he says; our lives are "redeemed" when we see them in an aesthetic perspective.

In one of his best known parables, Nietzsche gives us his answer:

The madman. —Have you not heard of that madman who lit a lantern in the bright morning hours, ran to the market place, and cried incessantly: "I seek God! I seek God!" —As many of those who did not believe in God were standing around just then, he provoked much laughter. Has he got lost? asked one. Did he lose his way like a child? asked another. Or is he hiding? Is he afraid of us? Has he gone on a voyage? emigrated? —Thus they yelled and laughed.

The madman jumped into their midst and pierced them with his eyes. "Whither is God?" he cried; "I will tell you. *We have killed him*—you and I. All of us are his murderers. But how did we do this? How could we drink up the sea? Who gave us the sponge to wipe away the entire horizon? What were we doing when we unchained this earth from its sun? Whither is it moving now? Whither are we moving? Away from all suns? Are we not plunging continually? Backward, sideward, forward, in all directions? Is there still any up or down? Are we not straying as through an infinite nothing? Do we not feel the breath of empty space? Has it not become colder? Is not night continually closing in on us? Do we not need to light lanterns in the morning? Do we hear nothing as yet of the noise of the gravediggers who are burying God? Do we smell nothing as yet of the divine decomposition? Gods, too, decompose. God is dead. God remains dead. And we have killed him.

"How shall we comfort ourselves, the murderers of all murderers? What was holiest and mightiest of all that the world has yet owned has bled to death under our knives: who will wipe this blood off us? What water is there for us to clean ourselves? What festivals of atonement, what sacred games shall we have to invent? Is not the greatness of this deed too great for us? Must we ourselves not become gods simply to appear worthy of it? There has never been a greater deed; and whoever is born after us—for the sake of this deed he will belong to a higher history than all history hitherto."

Here the madman fell silent and looked again at his listeners; and they, too, were silent and stared at him in astonishment. At last he threw his lantern on the ground, and it broke into pieces and went out. "I have come too early," he said then; "my time is not yet. This tremendous event is still on its way, still wandering; it has not yet reached the ears of men. Lightning and thunder require time; the light of the stars requires time; deeds, though done, still require time to be seen and heard. This deed is still more distant from them than the most distant stars—*and yet they have done it themselves.*"

It has been related further that on the same day the madman forced his way into several churches and there struck up his *requiem aeternam deo.* Led out and called to account, he is said always to have replied nothing but: "What after all are these churches now if they are not the tombs and sepulchers of God?" (*GS*, 125)

Perhaps what Nietzsche means to say in these dramatic paragraphs is clear enough, but some questions and answers might be in order.

- Why is the message concerning the **death of God** put into the mouth of a madman? Because anyone who brings this message to a culture dominated by Christianity is bound to seem mad.
- Why does the madman announce the "death" of God rather than merely his nonexistence? Because a death is something that *happens* at a particular time. Nonexistence is just not ever having been. God's death, Nietzsche thinks, is something that happened recently.
- What does it mean that God died? It means that people no longer believe—though they may not have noticed this fact. "The greatest recent event—that 'God is dead,' that the belief in the Christian god has become unbelievable—is already beginning to cast its first shadows over Europe" (*GS*, 343).
- Who are the clowns standing around that make fun of the madman? Those who don't take these things seriously; they think God can disappear and everything can go along as it always has.
- Who are the murderers of God? We all are.
- What are the consequences of God's death? We have lost our moorings. We don't know anymore where we are, where we are going—or where we should be going. We are without a goal. The one who for centuries supplied the rules for living, the goal to strive for, has died.
- Why does the madman say, "I have come too early"? Because though the deed is done, people are not ready to recognize what they have done. And they certainly are not aware of the

consequences. "God is dead; but given the way of men, there may still be caves for thousands of years in which his shadow will be shown" (*GS*, 108).

Can we say anything more precise about how God died? Zarathustra says, "When gods die, they always die several kinds of death" (*Z* 4, 373). Nietzsche offers several explanations. For example, in the account we canvassed in the last section, Nietzsche claims that the whole idea of a metaphysical "real world" simply became incredible to us. Christianity, which Nietzsche calls "Platonism for the 'common people'" (*BGE*, preface, 4), disappears with the rest of the "real worlds" killed by "the decline of the faith in the Christian god, the triumph of scientific atheism" (*GS*, 357).

But there are other explanations. In the fourth book of *Thus Spoke Zarathustra,* the prophet meets "the last pope," who says that though he is now "retired," he served the old god "until his last hour." Zarathustra asks him how God died. The old pope replies,

> When he was young, this god out of the Orient, he was harsh and vengeful and he built himself a hell to amuse his favorites. Eventually, however, he became old and soft and mellow and pitying, more like a grandfather than a father, but most like a shaky old grandmother. Then he sat in his nook by the hearth, wilted, grieving over his weak legs, weary of the world, weary of willing, and one day he choked on his all-too-great pity. (*Z* 4, 373)

Zarathustra understands pity as the opposite of a life-affirming emotion. In **pity,** one *deplores* the condition of someone's existence.* Because the Christian God pities mankind, it is possible that his "all-too-great" pity might in the end undermine even his own will to live, and he might simply wither away. Pity, Zarathustra thinks, is a very bad thing.

------

*The thing Nietzsche holds most adamantly against Christianity is that it is (as he sees it) a religion of pity. If pity is the appropriate reaction to human life as a whole—is even the reaction of *God!*—then one is virtually saying it would be better if life did not exist at all. And then one is back with Silenus. Nietzsche is of the opinion that Christianity gives in to pessimism instead of overcoming it.

> "Religion is an illusion and it derives its strength from the fact that it falls in with our instinctual desires."
>
> *Sigmund Freud (1856–1939)*

Zarathustra tells the old pope that it might have happened that way, but perhaps also in another way. Perhaps it was just intellectual honesty that finally did away with God; integrity, intellectual conscience, cleanliness of spirit, honesty—and finally just good taste—eventually reject the comforts of such a god. And where did we learn such honesty? From Christianity itself. Nietzsche calls this atheism

> a triumph achieved finally and with great difficulty by the European conscience, being the most fateful act of two thousand years of discipline for truth that in the end forbids itself the *lie* in faith in God.
>
> You see what it was that really triumphed over the Christian god: Christian morality itself, the concept of truthfulness that was understood ever more rigorously, the father confessor's refinement of the Christian conscience, translated and sublimated into a scientific conscience, into intellectual cleanliness at any price. (*GS*, 357)

Paradoxically, God, the source of Christian morality, is finally done in by that morality itself!

There are also less praiseworthy explanations for the death of God. Nietzsche puts one of them into the mouth of "the ugliest man," whom Zarathustra meets and recognizes as *"the murderer of God"* who "took revenge on this witness" (*Z* 4, 376). The ugliest man confesses,

> But he *had* to die: he saw with eyes that saw everything; he saw man's depths and ultimate grounds, all his concealed disgrace and ugliness. His pity knew no shame: he crawled into my dirtiest nooks. This most curious, overobtrusive, overpitying one had to die. He always saw me: on such a witness I wanted to have revenge or not live myself. The god who saw everything, *even man*—this god had to die! Man cannot bear it that such a witness should live. (*Z* 4, 378–379)

Nietzsche does not admire such motives for killing off the Christian god. Nietzsche wants a life that, unlike the ugliest man's life, can bear examination—especially one's own examination. Moreover, he considers revenge a particularly bad motive (although one that is hard to get beyond). Motives such as these, Nietzsche tells us, have also played a role in the death of God.

"A little philosophy inclineth man's mind to atheism, but depth in philosophy bringeth man's minds about to religion."

Francis Bacon (1561–1626)

Reactions to this great event will differ. Some people will deny that it has happened; others will despair. But, Nietzsche says, the consequences for himself and others like him

> are quite the opposite of what one might perhaps expect: They are not at all sad and gloomy but rather like a new and scarcely describable kind of light, happiness, relief, exhilaration, encouragement, dawn.
>
> Indeed, we philosophers and "free spirits" feel, when we hear the news that "the old god is dead," as if a new dawn shone on us; our heart overflows with gratitude, amazement, premonitions, expectation. At long last the horizon appears free to us again, even if it should not be bright; at long last our ships may venture out again, venture out to face any danger; all the daring of the lover of knowledge is permitted again; the sea, *our* sea, lies open again; perhaps there has never yet been such an "open sea." (*GS*, 343)

Despite such cheerful thoughts, Nietzsche sees that the death of God poses a serious problem. If religious roots have nourished our culture has for two thousand years, what happens when those roots no longer sustain its life? When the source of our values dries up, what happens to them? When the lawgiver disappears, what happens to our law? As the madman says, "Is there still any up or down?" The threat is **nihilism.** Zarathustra meets a soothsayer who expresses the danger of nihilism this way:

> —And I saw a great sadness descend upon mankind. The best grew weary of their works. A

doctrine appeared, accompanied by a faith: "All is empty, all is the same, all has been!" And from all the hills it echoed: "All is empty, all is the same, all has been!" Indeed we have harvested: but why did all our fruit turn rotten and brown? What fell down from the evil moon last night? In vain was all our work; our wine has turned to poison; an evil eye has seared our fields and hearts. . . . Verily, we have become too weary even to die. We are still waking and living on—in tombs. (*Z* 2, 245)

When Zarathustra hears the soothsayer, he himself becomes "sad and weary"; he becomes "like those of whom the soothsayer had spoken" (*Z* 2, 246). Weariness of life—finding everything empty, shallow, meaningless, the same—that is the mood of nihilism.* Into such a state we might be cast by the death of God. It is against nihilism that Zarathustra and Nietzsche must now struggle. A new meaning must be forged for life. But the fight for meaning, as we shall see, will take a surprising turn: Christianity itself—the factor that until now had saved us from nihilism—is accused of the greatest nihilism of all.

---

1. Philosophers claim to tell us about reality, but what do they really reveal, if Nietzsche is right?
2. In what ways can errors be useful? What are some of the errors Nietzsche identifies?
3. What is Nietzsche's "nonmetaphysical" view of the world and human nature?
4. Sketch the stages by which Nietzsche thinks the "real world" became a fable.
5. What does Nietzsche mean when he says, "God is dead"?
6. In what ways might God have died?

Revaluation of Values

As we have seen, Nietzsche believes that nature is "value-less." Whatever values we might think are

---

*Theodore Dalrymple refers to a "bitter Argentinian tango" that includes the words "everything is the same, nothing is better"—a doctrine, he says, "as barbaric and untruthful . . . as has yet emerged from the fertile mind of man" (*Life at the Bottom* [Chicago: Ivan R. Dee, 2001], 194).

present have been "bestowed" on nature by us.* He claims that

> *there are no moral facts at all.* Moral judgement has this in common with religious judgement, that it believes in realities which do not exist. Morality is merely an interpretation of certain phenomena, more precisely a *mis*interpretation. . . . In this respect moral judgement should never be taken literally. (*TI,* 33)

Our current values, then, are *interpretations* that were formed in a context that takes God and a "real world" for granted. But if God is dead for us and we no longer believe in any world but the one revealed by our senses and interpreted by the sciences, we surely need to look again at the received values. Nietzsche asks himself, "*In what do you believe?*" and answers, "In this, that the weights of all things must be determined anew" (*GS,* 269).

But how do we do this? Nietzsche thinks that philosophers have not been much help; they have typically busied themselves with the task of providing rational foundations for morality.† But in doing so they have simply taken a certain morality for granted. This prevented them from even laying eyes on

> the real problems of morality—all of which come to light only by comparing *many* moralities. As strange as it may sound, in every previous "science of morality" the problem of morality itself was *missing;* there was no suspicion that it might be something problematic. (*BGE,* 186, 74–75)

If we are going to determine the "weights" of things anew, we obviously cannot just take the present "weights" for granted. So Nietzsche calls

---

*Contrast this view with that of Plato, Aristotle, and (especially) Augustine. Compare the diagram on p. 272.

†Think of Plato (pp. 172–177) and Aristotle (pp. 208–213), who try to show that living virtuously is the way to live happily; of the Stoics (pp. 243–245), who try to demonstrate that the good life is integration into the order of the universe; of Aquinas (pp. 332–335), who argues for a natural moral law; of Kant (pp. 488–491), who claims that morality is a requirement of pure reason alone; of Hegel (pp. 514–515), for whom morality is realized in a perfectly rational state; and of the arguments for utilitarianism (pp. 548–549).

for "a *taxonomy* of morals" (*BGE,* 186, 74) and makes a contribution to this project in his book *On the Genealogy of Morals.* Just as genealogy traces the ancestry of a person, a genealogy for a certain morality will trace its ancestry by revealing the historical and psychological conditions out of which it grew. Nietzsche thinks that our present morality is the result of a "revaluation of values" that took place a long time ago. And he believes he can tell us the story of how that happened.

MASTER MORALITY/ SLAVE MORALITY

It is a mistake, Nietzsche says, to identify the good with the useful or beneficial, as the utilitarians do. It is equally a mistake to identify it with good will or right intention, as Kantians do. Besides, neither utilitarians nor Kantians ask the radical questions about morality that Nietzsche wants to press: Why have morality at all? What good is it? Would we be better off without it?

Pursuing his genealogical project, Nietzsche asks, What did the word "good" originally mean?

> The judgement "good" does *not* derive from those to whom "goodness" is shown! Rather, the "good" themselves—that is, the noble, the powerful, the superior, and the high-minded—were the ones who felt themselves and their actions to be good—that is, as of the first rank—and posited them as such, in contrast to everything low, low-minded, common, and plebeian. (*GM,* 1, 2, 12)

Here is a morality—the morality of the aristocrats, the well-born, the powerful, the masters. These people of the "first rank" call themselves "noble," "commanders," "the rich," the "happy," the "truthful"—what *need* do they have to lie? They affirm their lives; they say yes to their being. They *feel* themselves to be good. To them, "good" means "what *we* are."

> The knightly-aristocratic value-judgements presuppose a powerful physicality, a rich, burgeoning, even overflowing health, as well as all those things which help to preserve it—war, adventure, hunting, dancing, competitive games, and everything which involves strong, free, high-spirited activity. (*GM,* 1, 7, 19)

IRIS MURDOCH

Iris Murdoch (1919–1999), one of the few philosophers about whom a commercially successful movie has been made,* wrote twenty-six novels in addition to significant philosophy. Her small book, *The Sovereignty of Good* (1970), sketches a philosophy at odds with prevailing views of mind and morality.

How should we decide what to do? Here is a common picture. We must be as rational as we can be in discovering the facts. And then, in the light of the facts, we decide. There is no value in the facts to sway our wills one way or another, so nothing in the facts can ever show that we have chosen wrongly. Since beliefs about reality are separate from will and action, we are free to decide whatever we wish. Because there is no objectivity to value, there is no valid way to critique choices. The only virtues left are sincerity and authenticity.† The worst vice is hypocrisy.

It is not only in philosophy that this image is common. Murdoch says the "man" pictured here is the hero of almost every recent novel. And it doesn't take much imagination to see here the root of frequently heard remarks such as these: We must not judge, Everyone has their own values, and Who's to say what's good anyway? Just get in touch with your inner self, identify with your feelings, and be yourself. The inevitable consequence is a shallow moral relativism.

Now Murdoch thinks this is all wrong—wrong as a picture of the mind, wrong as metaphysics, and wrong as a theory of morals. The right picture of the mind is not one of our will plunking for one or another set of neutrally described facts, but of our *seeing* things in one way or another. Consider, Murdoch suggests, a woman, M, who believes

---

Iris (2001), starring Judi Dench, portrays the philosopher and novelist in her later days, as she struggles with Alzheimer's disease.

†The essentials of this view can be found in such disparate thinkers as Hume (p. 461), Kant—with qualifications (p. 486), Kierkegaard (p. 535), Nietzsche (p. 574), Wittgenstein (p. 629), the positivists (p. 635), Heidegger (p. 676), Sartre (p. 684), and de Beauvoir (p. 687). It might almost define the modern world.

her son has married beneath him. She finds her daughter-in-law, D, common, unpolished, lacking in dignity and refinement. She seems pert and familiar, sometimes rude, and always tiresomely juvenile. But M is intelligent, well-intentioned, and capable of self-criticism; she begins to wonder whether she herself might not be a bit snobbish, perhaps old-fashioned, and—very likely—jealous. She begins to suspect that her own biases are distorting the way she sees D and engages in the effort to see her more justly. She *pays attention* to D; she tries to see her with a loving eye, rather with a resentful eye. And as she engages in this mental struggle to see D fairly, she begins to see that D is not common but refreshingly simple, not undignified but spontaneous, not juvenile but delightfully youthful. She replaces fantasy with reality.

Existentialism pictures "the fearful solitude of the individual marooned upon a tiny island in the middle of a sea of scientific facts, and morality escaping from science only by a wild leap of the will. But our situation is not like this" (27).* Our *freedom* is not like this. Utilitarianism aims to maximize the satisfaction of desires overall. But because every desire embodies a certain way of seeing things— with a greedy eye, an envious eye, a hateful eye, a lustful eye—the moral task is to purify desire. Our freedom is exercised in small, piecemeal ways when we attempt to *see things more lovingly*—or not. When we then choose, we find that most of the business of choosing is already over—determined by the nature of our attention. In fact, if we attend properly, we will have no choices—and that is the ultimate condition to be aimed at. It is the moral quality of our vision, not an arbitrary act of will, which determines how we act. "Freedom, we find out, is not an inconsequential chucking of one's

---

*Quotations are from *The Sovereignty of Good* (London: Routledge and Kegan Paul, 1970).

(continued)

IRIS MURDOCH   *(continued)*

weight about, it is the disciplined overcoming of self" (95).

Reality is what is revealed to the patient eye of *love*. Discerning things as they are is a slow business, perhaps never-ending, and so moral change and moral achievement are difficult and slow. "Man is not a combination of an impersonal rational thinker and a personal will. He is a unified being who sees, and who desires in accordance with what he sees, and who has some continual slight control over the direction and focus of his vision" (40).

We can be helped along the moral way by the appreciation of beauty—"a completely adequate entry into . . . the good life, since it *is* the checking of selfishness in the interest of seeing the real"—and by great art, which "teaches us how real things can be looked at and loved without being seized and used, without being appropriated into the greedy organism of the self. . . . Selfish concerns vanish; nothing exists except the things that are seen. Beauty is that which attracts this particular sort of unselfish attention" (65). The experience of beauty in nature and art shows that will is not the creator of value, as so much of modern philosophy insists. The world is *flooded* with value.

As Plato saw, beauty and goodness are closely allied; indeed, beauty is the visible image of a goodness that draws us toward itself but cannot itself be represented. Loving beauty, as we naturally do, we come to love reality unselfishly. We "discover value in our ability to forget self, to be realistic, to perceive justly" (90). And so we are on the road to virtue. "Ignorance, muddle, fear, wishful thinking, lack of tests often make us feel that moral choice is something arbitrary, a matter for personal will rather than for attentive study. The difficulty is to keep the attention fixed upon the real situation and to prevent it from returning surreptitiously to the self with consolations of self-pity, resentment, fantasy and despair" (91).

The general name for our attachments is love. Love is "capable of infinite degradation and is the source of our greatest errors; but when it is even partially refined it is the energy and passion of the soul in its search for Good, the force that joins us to Good and joins us to the world through Good" (103). Our attachments "tend to be selfish and strong, and the transformation of our loves from selfishness to unselfishness is sometimes hard even to conceive of. . . . The love which brings the right answer is an exercise of justice and realism and really *looking*" (91). Its correlate is humility, which "is not a peculiar habit of self-effacement, rather like having an inaudible voice, it is selfless respect for reality and one of the most difficult and central of all virtues" (95).

Some of us are conventionally religious, some of us are not. But "there is a place both inside and outside religion for a sort of contemplation of the Good, . . . an attempt to look right away from self towards a distant transcendent perfection, a source of uncontaminated energy, a source of *new* and quite undreamt-of virtue. . . . This is the true mysticism which is morality, a kind of undogmatic prayer which is real and important, though perhaps also difficult and easily corrupted" (101–102). True morality has its source in selfless love of the Good.

The noble type of person feels *himself* as determining value—he does not need approval, he judges that "what is harmful to me is harmful per se," he knows that he is the one who causes things to be revered in the first place, he *creates values.* (*BGE,* 260, 154)

This is the morality of conquerors. They may "help the unfortunate, but not, or not entirely, out of pity" (*BGE,* 260, 154). Among themselves, they are held in check "by custom, respect, usage, gratitude, even more by circumspection and jealousy," and in their relations with one another they express "consideration, self-control, tenderness, fidelity, pride, and friendship" (*GM,* 1, 11, 25). But once they go beyond their community where foreigners are found, they behave in a manner not much better than predators on the rampage. There they enjoy freedom from all social constraint, in the wilderness they make up for the tension built up over a long period of confinement and enclosure within a peaceful community, they *regress* to the innocence of the predator's conscience, as rejoicing monsters, capable of high spirits as they walk away without qualms from a horrific succession of murder, arson, violence, and torture, as if it were nothing more than a student prank, something new for the poets to sing and celebrate for some time to come. (*GM*, 1, 11, 25–26)

Nietzsche obviously has the heroes of Homer's great poems in mind.* These magnificent and terrible human beings claim the right to define goodness—and its opposite. Those who are not good are *below* them—the common, plebeian, pitiable, unhappy, lying ones. The nobles call these weak, shifty, untrustworthy people "bad." They are despicable, contemptible, almost beneath notice. They are slaves or fit to be slaves. Toward them the nobles have no duties. The "bad" have no dignity, no worth—no *goodness.*

So we have a first type of morality, **master morality.** It is characterized by a certain sort of value discrimination. Its categories are

good / bad,

and moral judgments are made in those terms. Notice that all the weight lies in the first term. "Bad" is just a contrast term; it designates only a shadow of the good. The masters affirm themselves and find themselves good; others hardly matter. It is clear that this sort of moral evaluation is made *from the point of view* of the masters: "we the noble, we the good, we the beautiful, we the happy ones!" (*GM*, 1, 10, 22).

Nietzsche also identifies a second type of morality: **slave morality.** Here there is a value contrast, too—not "good/bad," but

good / evil,

and its psychological dynamics are very different. Here "evil" is the primary concept and is driven not by affirmation, but by negation—not by a yes to life, but by a no. So "evil" and "bad" are very

different from each other. Correspondingly, the "goods" in the two moralities are also different. But this requires explanation.

Slaves are by definition the powerless. They find themselves at the mercy of those noble "predators on the rampage" who call themselves "the good." They suffer from them—and they *resent* it.

> —The slave revolt in morals begins when **ressentiment*** itself becomes creative and ordains values: the *ressentiment* of creatures to whom the real reaction, that of the deed, is denied and who find compensation in an imaginary revenge. While all noble morality grows from a triumphant affirmation of itself, slave morality from the outset says no to an "outside," to an "other," to a "non-self": and *this* no is its creative act. The reversal of the evaluating gaze—this *necessary* orientation outwards rather than inwards to the self—belongs characteristically to *ressentiment.* In order to exist at all, slave morality from the outset always needs an opposing, outer world;—its action is fundamentally reaction. (*GM*, 1, 10, 22)

So the slave basically says, "No!" And to whom does the slave say no? Why, to the masters, of course—to those who say of themselves that they are the *good.* There is no way a slave will agree with the master's self-evaluation; such rapacious monsters are experienced as *evil.*

This negation of what is other than themselves, Nietzsche says, is the "creative deed" in slave morality. The fundamental concept is that of the enemy, the *evil* man. As a kind of afterthought, the slave derives its opposite—the *good* one, himself. Just as "bad" is the shadow of "good" for the masters, so is "good" a shadow of the primary word "evil" for the slaves.

Let us ask: What is such a good person like? Can there be any doubt? The good would have to be such as they themselves are: poor, weak, humble, serving. Being powerless, slaves cannot overtly express their outrage over the actions of the strong. So their resentment simmers in them. It becomes a longing for revenge and colors their lives with

---

*See Chapter 1.

---

*Nietzsche consistently uses the French term because there is no German word with just that nuance. We will use the corresponding English term, "resentment."

rancor. What sort of revenge, Nietzsche asks, would be most appropriate for those who cannot simply overpower their enemies? What sort would be *possible?* The most subtle, shrewd, and insidious **revenge** of all would be this: to persuade the strong they should adopt the values of the weak, to give them a bad conscience about their "goodness," to get *them* to say of their natural impulses, "These are evil; they must be suppressed. We are sinful. We must become 'good' (as the slaves define good)." What a triumph that would be! How delicious the revenge! How satisfying! And, Nietzsche tells us, *that is just what happened.*

Nietzsche identifies the Jews as the source of this slave revaluation of values. Having actually been slaves in Egypt and thereafter continually dominated by the powerful nations around them (Egypt, Assyria, Babylon, Greece, Rome), the Jews are the world-historical origin of the most powerful revision in moral values the Western world has seen.

> It has been the Jews who have, with terrifying consistency, dared to undertake the reversal of the aristocratic value equation (good = noble = powerful = beautiful = happy = blessed) and have held on to it tenaciously by the teeth of the most unfathomable hatred (the hatred of the powerless). It is they who have declared: "The miserable alone are the good; the poor, the powerless, the low alone are the good. The suffering, the deprived, the sick, the ugly are the only pious ones, the only blessed, for them alone is there salvation. You, on the other hand, the noble and the powerful, you are for all eternity the evil, the cruel, the lascivious, the insatiable, the godless ones. You will be without salvation, accursed and damned to all eternity!" (*GM,* 1, 7, 19–20)

This act of "*most intelligent revenge*" originated a tremendous revaluation of values, a "revolt which has a two-thousand-year history behind it and which has today dropped out of sight only because it— has succeeded" (*GM,* 1, 7, 19). And Nietzsche adds: "There is no doubt as to *who* inherited this Jewish transvaluation" (*GM,* 1, 7, 20). He means, of course, the Christians.

> This Jesus of Nazareth, as the gospel of love incarnate, this "redeemer" bringing victory and salvation to the poor, the sick, the sinners—did he not

represent the most sinister and irresistible form of the very same temptation, the indirect temptation to accept those self-same *Jewish* values and new versions of the ideal?* (*GM,* 1, 8, 20)

Jesus' love, of course, takes him to the cross— for the salvation of mankind. But, Nietzsche asks, in the service of what values? Certainly not on behalf of master morality! In this way, through the influence of Christianity, "Israel's revenge and transvaluation of all values has so far continued to triumph over all other ideals, over all *nobler* ideals" (*GM,* 1, 8, 21). Our values, Nietzsche believes, are Judeo–Christian values.

And now we are ready for the big question, the question Nietzsche thinks he is the first to ask: *What value do these values have?*

OUR MORALITY

Think again about Kant and the utilitarians, the sponsors of the two most powerful moral theories of modern times. Although they have many differences, they have something in common: Both assert the equal dignity and value of each individual human being. For Kant, this equality is grounded in the fact that every one of us is equally rational and that *the same moral law* is legislated categorically for each of us. Utilitarianism specifies that when we calculate the greatest happiness, *each one is to count for one.* In either case, no basic inequality of value is allowed to exist between humans; there is no "order of rank" that would allow moral privileges to certain persons and not others. This emphasis on basic **equality** in our values, Nietzsche believes, can be traced back to the slave revolt in morality; after all, it is the slaves, not the masters, who have an interest in leveling things out. This insistence on equality is a (more or less secular) consequence of the Christian theme that we are all children of God, equally precious in his sight.

But is this egalitarianism something we should prize, or is it a symptom of decadence, weakness,

---

*For Nietzsche's interpretation of Jesus as someone *incapable* of resisting evil, see The Antichrist, sections 27–35. The sections following 35 give Nietzsche's view of how Christianity betrayed the spirit of Jesus.

illness, resentment—of a basic dissatisfaction with life? Our morality, Nietzsche thinks, is the morality of the *herd*.

> *Morality in Europe today is herd animal morality*—and thus, as we understand things, it is only one kind of human morality next to which, before which, after which many others, and especially *higher* moralities, are or should be possible. But this morality defends itself with all its strength against such "possibilities," against such "should be's." Stubbornly and relentlessly it says, "I am Morality itself, and nothing else is!" (*BGE,* 202, 89)

In this context, Nietzsche calls himself an "immoralist" and a **"free spirit."** Nietzsche assails "modern ideas" and "modern men," with their claims to equality and equal rights and their advocacy of democracy and socialism. Zarathustra says,

> I do not wish to be mixed up and confused with these preachers of equality. For, to *me* justice speaks thus: "Men are not equal." Nor shall they become equal! (*Z* 2, 213)

Why should men not *become* equal? Because the only way that could happen is by leveling down to the average or below the average: to the level of the herd. And to do that is to give in to the morality of resentment, of revenge—the morality of slaves.

Zarathustra's story begins with the prophet high on a mountain, outside his cave, where he has lived alone for ten years. He believes he has some wisdom to share and descends from the heights to impart it to men. He speaks to a crowd in a village marketplace about a superior kind of human being he calls "the **overman**" (see the next section), but they don't want to hear it. Then he tries to motivate their interest with a description of "what is most contemptible." Zarathustra calls this "the *last man*":

> Alas, the time is coming when man will no longer give birth to a star. Alas, the time of the most despicable man is coming, he that is no longer able to despise himself. Behold, I show you the *last man*.
>
> "What is love? What is creation? What is longing? What is a star?" thus asks the last man, and he blinks.
>
> The earth has become small, and on it hops the last man, who makes everything small. His race is

as ineradicable as the flea-beetle; the last man lives longest. . . .

> No shepherd and one herd! Everybody wants the same, everybody is the same: whoever feels differently goes voluntarily into a madhouse.
>
> "Formerly, all the world was mad," say the most refined, and they blink.
>
> One is clever and knows everything that has ever happened: so there is no end of derision. One still quarrels, but one is soon reconciled—else it might spoil the digestion.
>
> One has one's little pleasure for the day and one's little pleasure for the night: but one has a regard for health.
>
> "We have invented happiness," say the last men, and they blink. (*Z* 1, 129–130)

Zarathustra is obviously full of contempt for such a safe, cautious, careful, timid, excessively prudent form of life. He sneers at the idea that *here* one finds happiness. But what happens? The crowd interrupts him with "clamor and delight":

> "Give us this last man, O Zarathustra," they shouted. "Turn us into these last men! Then we shall make you a gift of the overman!" (*Z* 1, 130)

Our morality, Nietzsche believes, has turned us into such "last men." Or, if we are not yet quite "last men," that is what we long to be: comfortable, easily satisfied, without pain and suffering—"happy." Everyone has an equal right to this, we think. Nietzsche's Zarathustra means to teach us (or those of us with ears to hear) to *despise* such a life.

"The mass of men lead lives of quiet desperation."

Henry David Thoreau (1817–1862)

Zarathustra compares the preachers of equality to tarantulas. He says of them,

> Thus I speak to you in a parable—you who make souls whirl, you preachers of *equality*. To me you are tarantulas, and secretly vengeful. But I shall bring your secrets to light; therefore I laugh in your faces with my laughter of the heights. Therefore I tear at your webs, that your rage may lure you

out of your lie-holes and your revenge may leap out from behind your word justice. For *that man be delivered from revenge*, that is for me the bridge to the highest hope, and a rainbow after long storms. (*Z* 2, 211)

Nietzsche hopes to bring to light the dark and dirty secrets hidden in our highest values—to show us that behind such words as "equality" and "social justice" stand hatred, revenge, resentment, weakness, and spite. And why does he want to expose those secrets? So that we might at last "be delivered from revenge," from negation and saying, "No!" Our "highest values" have been inherited from that first revaluation of values, but now we can see that they are based on lies.

> If, out of the vindictive cunning of impotence, the oppressed, downtrodden, and violated tell themselves: "Let us be different from the evil, that is, good! And the good man is the one who refrains from violation, who harms no one, who attacks no one, who fails to retaliate, who leaves revenge to God, who lives as we do in seclusion, who avoids all evil and above all asks little of life, as we do, the patient, the humble, the just." When listened to coldly and without prejudice, this actually means nothing more than: "We weak men are, after all, weak; it would be good if we refrained from doing anything *for which we lack sufficient strength*" . . . as if the weakness of the weak man itself . . . were a free achievement, something willed, chosen, a *deed*, a *merit*. (*GM*, 1, 13, 30)

> "Our virtues are most frequently but vices in disguise."
>
> *Francois de La Rochefoucauld (1613–1680)*

The "virtues" of slave morality are really just what the weak *cannot help* but do. The weak, however, interpret these virtues as something they *choose*—something for which they deserve praise. But, Nietzsche says, this is self-deception. And, Nietzsche claims, it is this morality based on revenge and lies that is *our* morality. Jerusalem has overcome Rome; "consider before whom one bows down today in Rome itself" (*GM*, 1:16).

◆

> "He who says there is no such thing as an honest man, you may be sure is himself a knave."
>
> *George Berkeley (1685–1753)*

There is one additional, absolutely crucial, lie that Nietzsche believes the weak and impotent tell. They tell it to themselves—and to their enemies. It is the lie about **free will.** In truth, Nietzsche holds, there is no such thing as a free will. Human beings are body entirely; they are animals. As we have seen, he even calls us mechanisms. But unless there were a free will, how could the weak take credit for their "virtues"? And, even more important, how could they blame the strong for their "crimes"? Nietzsche holds that the concept of "free will" is

> the most disreputable piece of trickery the theologians have produced, aimed at making humanity "responsible" in their sense, i.e. at *making it dependent on them.* . . . Wherever responsibilities are sought it is usually the instinct for *wanting to punish and judge* that is doing the searching. Becoming is stripped of its innocence once any state of affairs is traced back to a will, to intentions, to responsible acts: the doctrine of the will was fabricated essentially for the purpose of punishment, i.e. of *wanting to find guilty.* . . . People were thought of as "free" so that they could be judged and punished—so that they could become *guilty:* consequently every action *had* to be thought of as willed, the origin of every action as located in consciousness. (*TI*, 31)

The idea of "free will" is an invention, an interpretation of the facts by those who wanted very much to be able to hold people accountable, to persuade people they were guilty, sinful, and evil in the sight of God—because *they could have done otherwise!*

The truth is quite to the contrary, Nietzsche believes:

> *No one* is responsible for simply being there, for being made in such and such a way, for existing under such conditions, in such surroundings. . . . *No one* is the result of his own intention, his own will,

his own purpose. . . . One is necessary, one is a piece of fate, one belongs to the whole, one *is* in the whole—there is nothing which could judge, measure, compare, condemn our Being. . . . We deny God, we deny responsibility in God: *this* alone is how we redeem the world. (*TI,* 32)

One of Nietzsche's aims is to restore a sense of the "innocence" of life, freed from the slanders of sin and guilt. "Atheism and a kind of **second innocence** belong together" (*GM,* 2:20, 71). Christians believe the world is redeemed by the sacrifice of Christ on the cross for human sin. Nietzsche thinks to redeem the world by denying sin, Christ, and God altogether. As he sees it, the concepts of free will, sin, guilt, and responsibility are part and parcel of the revolution in values he calls "slave morality." And Nietzsche calls for a new "revaluation of values" in which none of these concepts that taint existence has a place.

We would get Nietzsche wrong, however, if we thought that he simply wants to get back again to the master morality of Homer's epic heroes. Despite their love of life, their self-affirmation and yes-saying, there is something simple-minded, naive, and slightly stupid about these "nobles." The long history of resentment and self-deception has also been a history of self-examination, self-discipline, training, obedience, and hardness toward oneself and others. Through it we have become subtler, deeper, more—human. Through this long process, Nietzsche says, everything became more dangerous,

> not only cures and therapies, but also arrogance, revenge, perspicacity, extravagance, love, the desire to dominate, virtue, illness. With some fairness, admittedly, it might also be added that it is only on the basis of this *essentially dangerous* form of human existence, the priestly form, that man has at all developed into an *interesting animal,* that it is only here that the human soul has in a higher sense taken on *depth* and become *evil*—and these have certainly been the two fundamental forms of man's superiority over other animals up to now! (*GM,* 1, 6, 18)

There is no going back. We need to go forward— "beyond good and evil." And with that thought we are ready to consider Nietzsche's concept of the overman.

1. In what ways might God have died?
2. What does Nietzsche understand by a "genealogy" of morals?
3. What is master morality like? Who devised it? What do the central terms "good" and "bad" mean?
4. What is slave morality like? Who devised it? What do the central terms "good" and "evil" mean?
5. What is *our* morality like?
6. In what ways does Nietzsche criticize our morality?
7. Who is the "last man"?
8. How did the idea of free will arise?

The Overman

"*Dead are all gods,*" Zarathustra says; "*now we want the overman to live*" (*Z* 1, 191). When Zarathustra arrives at the village, fresh from his ten-year retreat on the mountain, his first words to the crowd in the marketplace concern the overman.*

> *I teach you the overman.* Man is something that shall be overcome. What have you done to overcome him?
>
> All beings so far have created something beyond themselves; and do you want to be the ebb of this great flood and even go back to the beasts rather than overcome man? What is the ape to man? A laughing-stock or a painful embarrassment. And man shall be just that for the overman: a laughing-stock or a painful embarrassment. You have made your way from worm to man, and much in you is still worm. Once you were apes, and even now, too, man is more ape than any ape. . . .
>
> Behold, I teach you the overman. The overman is the meaning of the earth. Let your will say: the overman *shall be* the meaning of the earth! I beseech you, my brothers, *remain faithful to the earth,* and do not believe those who speak to you of otherworldly hopes! (*Z* 1, 124–125)

---

*This is the point at which it must be acknowledged that "overmen" do not seem to include women. Only males, for instance, are among the "higher men" in Zarathustra's cave at the end of his quest for wisdom. Nietzsche writes quite a lot about women, of which this is a representative sample: "Women want to be autonomous: and to that end they have begun to enlighten men about 'women per se'—*that* is one of the worst signs of progress in Europe's overall *uglification*" (*BGE,* 232, 124).

Let us remind ourselves of the drama so far. In his early book, *The Birth of Tragedy*, Nietzsche tries to solve the problem of the meaning of life (the value of existence) by using Schopenhauer's metaphysical theory—that reality in itself is *will*. The idea is that through tragedy, we identify ourselves with the surging, nonindividualized, eternal reality of the will and are saved from pessimism about life. Later Nietzsche comes to believe that philosophy cannot guarantee any metaphysical theory and Schopenhauer's real world disappears. But though God is dead, otherworldly values continue to hold sway; the morality of "good and evil" is still our morality. By saying no to life as it expresses itself in the strong, this morality levels down to the mediocre herd and so sets itself *against life itself*. The result: pessimism and nihilism remain undefeated, and the problem of the meaning of life is still unsolved.

Zarathustra proposes to solve it, and the overman is the key. The overman, he says, "is the meaning of the earth." Human beings as they now are cannot be what all these eons of evolution have been for. That would be too petty, too small, too absurd. It could not be that all the while *life* has been driving at *us!* No, "man is something that shall be overcome."

> Man is a rope, tied between beast and overman—a rope over an abyss. A dangerous across, a dangerous on-the-way, a dangerous looking-back, a dangerous shuddering and stopping.
>
> What is great in man is that he is a bridge and not an end: what can be loved in man is that he is an *overture* and a *going under*. (*Z* 1, 126–127)

Nietzsche clearly has in mind some mode of life that is not "human, all-too-human" (as our lives typically are) but human, *more than human*. Zarathustra is the prophet of the overman. In the life of the overman, the earth itself will find its meaning, and the problem of "the value of existence" will find its solution.

We need to try to understand what sort of life Nietzsche imagines this to be. What is an overman like? Nietzsche returns to this question again and again, though not always under the rubric of "overman"; for instance, the last section in *Beyond*

Good and Evil, "What Is Noble," addresses this same issue. What he says is exceptionally rich and complex, often expressed in poetic form that a brief treatment can hardly do justice to. But here we set out a number of the principal themes:

1. An overman will "remain faithful to the earth." There will be no hankerings for a "real world"—for the soul, God, immortality, heaven. None of these fictions can solve the problem of the value of existence.

> It was suffering and incapacity that created all afterworlds—this and that brief madness of bliss which is experienced only by those who suffer most deeply.
>
> Weariness that wants to reach the ultimate with one leap, with one fatal leap, a poor ignorant weariness that does not want to want any more: this created all gods and afterworlds. . . .
>
> Listen rather, my brothers, to the voice of the healthy body: that is a more honest and purer voice. More honestly and purely speaks the healthy body that is perfect and perpendicular:* and it speaks of the meaning of the earth. (*Z* 1, 143–145)

Belief in "afterworlds" is a symptom of suffering and sickness and weariness with life. The overman will have none of it.

2. There is a "physiological presupposition" for the overman (*EH,* 298). The overman will be possessed of "*the great health,* . . . a new health, stronger, more seasoned, tougher, more audacious, and gayer than any previous health" (*GS,* 382). The healthy body, Zarathustra says, speaks true, and what it says reveals the meaning of the earth. But how can that be? How can a *body* say anything at all?

> "Body am I, and soul"—thus speaks the child. And why should one not speak like children?
>
> But the awakened and knowing say: body am I entirely, and nothing else; and soul is only a word for something about the body. . . .
>
> Behind your thoughts and feelings, my brother, there stands a mighty ruler, an unknown

---

*"Perpendicular," no doubt, because it is not on its knees praying.

sage—whose name is self. In your body he dwells; he is your body.

There is more reason in your body than in your best wisdom. (*Z* 1, 146–147)

If we are "body entirely," then in all our thinking and reasoning, the *body* thinks and reasons. But why would a *body* invent stories about a soul and an afterlife? Because it is at war with itself; it is ill, "angry with life and the earth" (*Z* 1, 147). Sick bodies create "real worlds" as compensation. A body possessing "the **great health**," by contrast, would need no compensation. An overman would trust the body, and in so doing would trust himself—but then the body of someone who could be called an overman would be a body that *could* be trusted.

❧

"I have said that the soul is not more than the body. And I have said that the body is not more than the soul. And nothing, not God, is greater than oneself is."

Walt Whitman (1819–1892)

Someone possessed of this "great health" would be able to experience in his own body all the drives to wisdom that *any* body could experience—the tendencies to lie and deceive oneself, as well as the exuberance of great health and strength. Such a person could diagnose illness, expose pretense, distinguish the true from the false. Nietzsche says such a person will confront

> an as yet undiscovered country whose boundaries nobody has surveyed yet, something beyond all the lands and nooks of the ideal so far, a world so overrich in what is beautiful, strange, questionable, terrible, and divine that our curiosity as well as our craving to possess it has got beside itself—alas, now nothing will sate us any more.
>
> After such vistas and with such a burning hunger in our conscience and science, how could we still be satisfied with *present-day man*? (*GS,* 382)

This "undiscovered country" is where the overman lives. A prerequisite for living there—indeed, even for discovering its existence—is the great

health. Nietzsche clearly thinks of himself as one of those "argonauts of the ideal" who has sailed many a sea to find this place.* He describes it this way:

> Another ideal runs ahead of us, a strange, tempting, dangerous ideal to which we should not wish to persuade anybody because we do not readily concede *the right to it* to anyone: the ideal of a spirit who plays naively—that is, not deliberately but from overflowing power and abundance—with all that was hitherto called holy, good, untouchable, divine . . . ; the ideal of a human, superhuman well-being and benevolence that will often appear *inhuman*—for example, when it confronts all earthly seriousness so far. (*GS,* 382)

Note that Nietzsche is not eager to persuade us to adopt this ideal. We probably do not have the right to it. The chances are overwhelming that we are not overmen, and if we tried to put on this ideal, if *we* thought we could easily go "beyond good and evil," we would almost certainly become mere "actors" of that ideal. And for such "actors" Nietzsche has the greatest contempt.†

3. The notion that the overman "plays naively" with what has hitherto been called good and divine parallels what Zarathustra says about the necessary

---

*The first section of Nietzsche's quasi-autobiographical book *Ecce Homo* (which means "Behold, the man"—the phrase taken from Pilate's words as he presents the scourged Jesus to the crowd) is titled, "Why I Am So Wise." Here Nietzsche tells us of his long illness, of his weakness, of the incredible pains he suffered. But never to complain. No, he is *grateful* for it. "I took myself in hand, I made myself healthy again: the condition for this—every physiologist would admit that—is *that one be healthy at bottom*. A typically morbid being cannot become healthy, much less make itself healthy. For a typically healthy person, conversely, being sick can even become an energetic *stimulus* for life, for living *more*. This, in fact, is how that long period of sickness appears to me *now*: as it were, I discovered life anew, including myself; I tasted all good and even little things, as others cannot easily taste them—I turned my will to health, to *life*, into a philosophy. For it should be noted: it was during the years of my lowest vitality that I ceased to be a pessimist; the instinct of self-restoration *forbade* me a philosophy of poverty and discouragement" (*EH*, 224).

†It has happened that people read Nietzsche, decide to go "beyond good and evil," to become overmen, and end up merely absurd—and sometimes as murderers (not exactly what Nietzsche has in mind).

"metamorphoses of the spirit." He tells us "how the spirit becomes a **camel;** and the camel, a **lion;** and the lion, finally, a **child**" (*Z* 1, 137).

> What is difficult? asks the spirit that would bear much, and kneels down like a camel wanting to be well loaded. What is most difficult, O heroes, asks the spirit that would bear much, that I may take it upon myself and exult in my strength? (*Z* 1, 138)

The easy path, the soft life of pleasure and indulgence, is not for an overman. An overman seeks out what is "most difficult" and loads it on his back. Discipline, obedience, and bearing heavy burdens is part of an overman's training. An overman is someone who is hard on himself and others. A spirit that would attain great heights cannot *begin* on the heights, any more than an apprentice cabinetmaker can begin as a master craftsman.*

> In the loneliest desert, however, the second metamorphosis occurs: here the spirit becomes a lion who would conquer his freedom and be master in his own desert. Here he seeks out his last master: he wants to fight him and his last god; for ultimate victory he wants to fight with the great dragon.
>
> Who is the great dragon whom the spirit will no longer call lord and god? "Thou shalt" is the name of the great dragon. But the spirit of the lion says, "I will." "Thou shalt" lies in his way, sparkling like gold, an animal covered with scales; and on every scale shines a golden "thou shalt."
>
> Values, thousands of years old, shine on these scales; and thus speaks the mightiest of all dragons: "All value of all things shines on me. All value has long been created, and I am all created value. Verily, there shall be no more 'I will.'" (*Z* 1, 138–139)

The spirit that would attain to overman status cannot be content with bearing the burdens of the camel. In the guise of a lion, the spirit says "No!" to all "Thou shalts" and thus opens up a space for freedom—a space in which new values can be created.

> But say, my brothers, what can the child do that even the lion could not do? Why must the preying lion still become a child? The child is innocence and forgetting, a new beginning, a game, a self-propelled wheel, a first movement, a sacred "Yes." For the game of creation, my brothers, a sacred "Yes" is needed: the spirit now wills his own will, and he who had been lost to the world now conquers his own world. (*Z* 1, 139)

The "naive play" of the overman is the play of a child—a yes to his own life that grows out of great health. It is the "innocence" of the child "willing his own will."* The child plays "the game of creation." And what does the child create? Values.

4. So the overman is a creator of values. And creation cannot take place without a corresponding destruction—the "No!" of the lion. "Whoever must be a creator always annihilates" (*Z* 1, 171). But the overman does not create heedlessly or arbitrarily. The child does not play dice with values. The principal thing the overman creates is *himself*. And his values are simply expressions of who he is.†

> We, however, *want to become those we are*—human beings who are new, unique, incomparable, who give themselves laws, who create themselves. (*GS*, 335)

In *Ecce Homo,* Nietzsche says a surprising thing.

> To become what one is, one must not have the faintest notion *what* one is. (*EH*, 254)

The danger is that one gets an idea of *what one is* and then tries to conform to that idea. But in that case one has almost certainly got it *wrong,* and one will become merely the ape of an ideal that is not one's own. One must not decide too soon what one is or take the idea of what one is from others; this is good advice for everyone, Nietzsche thinks. And it

---

*Nietzsche began his career by learning the demanding craft of philology. Students sometimes think they should be able to skip the camel phase—not have to bear the burden of tracing out the arguments of Plato, Aristotle, and Kant—and become philosophers immediately, without effort. But one way or another, in everything worthwhile, one must first be a camel. Great pianists have practiced many scales.

---

*But see Augustine on the "innocence" of children, p. 278.

†Compare Kierkegaard on being willing to be oneself, pp. 532–534.

is essential advice for those few who are possessed of the great health and are capable of becoming overmen. For it is *themselves* they want to create, not some cracked and misshapen image of themselves.

It is not the case, however, that an overman can just lie back and wait for what he is to unfold itself. That way one will get nothing worthwhile. All creators, Nietzsche tells us, are *hard*—most of all, hard on themselves.

> Among the conditions for a *Dionysian* task are, in a decisive way, the hardness of the hammer, *the joy even in destroying.* The imperative, "become hard!" the most fundamental certainty *that all creators are hard,* is the distinctive mark of a Dionysian nature.*
> (*EH,* 309)

An overman demands much, has a right to demand much. He demands most of all *from himself.* Zarathustra warns,

> But the worst enemy you can encounter will always be you, yourself; you lie in wait for yourself in caves and woods.
> Lonely one, you are going the way to yourself. . . . You must wish to consume yourself in your own flame: how could you wish to become new unless you had first become ashes! . . .
> Lonely one, you are going the way of the lover: yourself you love, and therefore you despise yourself, as only lovers despise. The lover would create because he despises. What does he know of love who did not have to despise precisely what he loved? (*Z* 1, 176–177)

Not for the overman a sweet contentment with his present state—no feeling good about himself or easy self-esteem. He climbs over himself on his way to himself. Love of himself is inseparable from contempt—contempt of whatever in himself has not yet become perfect. The overman overcomes himself, "giving style" to his character:

> A great and rare art! It is practiced by those who survey all the strengths and weaknesses of their

nature and then fit them into an artistic plan until every one of them appears as art and reason and even weaknesses delight the eye. Here a large mass of second nature has been added; there a piece of original nature has been removed—both times through long practice and daily work at it. Here the ugly that could not be removed is concealed; there it has been reinterpreted and made sublime. . . . In the end, when the work is finished, it becomes evident how the constraint of a single taste governed and formed everything large and small. (*GS,* 290)

So the overman is the **poet** of his life, the artist who both creates the work and lives it. In *The Birth of Tragedy,* Nietzsche says that existence and the world can be justified only as an aesthetic phenomenon. On this point Nietzsche has not changed his mind. If the overman is going to become the meaning of the earth, he will do it by creating himself as a work of art. Zarathustra considers those who are "sublime." By the "sublime," he means those who have struggled hard for the heights and have attained them, but who still have "tense souls" filled with the exertion of control. He admires them but considers that they have not yet reached the pinnacle.

> To stand with relaxed muscles and unharnessed will: that is most difficult for all of you who are sublime.
> When power becomes gracious and descends into the visible—such descent I call beauty.
> And there is nobody from whom I want beauty as much as from you who are powerful: let your kindness be your final self-conquest.
> Of all evil I deem you capable: therefore I want the good from you.
> Verily, I have often laughed at the weaklings who thought themselves good because they had no claws. (*Z* 2, 230)

It is the *beauty* of the overman that makes life worthwhile.

5. The overman loves himself. In deliberate opposition to the morality of "good and evil," Nietzsche praises **selfishness.** Zarathustra, for the first time,

> pronounced *selfishness* blessed, the wholesome, healthy selfishness that wells from a powerful

---

* Here we see that Dionysus does not disappear when the "real worlds" of *The Birth of Tragedy* are left behind. But the conception of the god deepens and changes substantially, as we shall see. An overman is clearly a "Dionysian nature." In his last book, *Ecce Homo,* Nietzsche identifies *himself* with Dionysus.

soul—from a powerful soul to which belongs the high body, beautiful, triumphant, refreshing, around which everything becomes a mirror—the supple, persuasive body, the dancer whose parable and epitome is the self-enjoying soul. The self enjoyment of such bodies and souls calls itself "virtue." (*Z* 3, 302)

It is important to note that it is the selfishness of "a powerful soul" in a "high body" that is praised—not every kind of selfishness. Only an overman has a *right* to such selfishness.

There is also another selfishness, an all-too-poor and hungry one that always wants to steal—the selfishness of the sick: sick selfishness. With the eyes of a thief it looks at everything splendid; with the greed of hunger it sizes up those who have much to eat; and always it sneaks around the table of those who give. Sickness speaks out of such craving and invisible degeneration; the thievish greed of this selfishness speaks of a diseased body. (*Z* 1, 187)

Because we know what Nietzsche thinks of sickness and diseased bodies, there is no question about his attitude toward this kind of selfishness. But what can we say of the higher selfishness, the kind appropriate to the higher man?

Perhaps above all, the higher selfishness is the overman's determination not to be drawn *away from himself.* If the *task* is to become who we are, then all sorts of enticements to betray that task must be resisted—for the sake of the self! There is one mode of being drawn away from oneself that Zarathustra particularly pillories: what Christians call love of the **neighbor.***

You crowd around your neighbor and have fine words for it. But I say unto you: your love of the neighbor is your bad love of yourselves. You flee to your neighbor from yourselves and would like to make a virtue out of that: but I see through your "selflessness." . . .

Do I recommend love of the neighbor to you? Sooner I should even recommend flight from the neighbor and love of the farthest. . . . But you are afraid and run to your neighbor. (*Z* 1, 172–173)

_____
* Compare Jesus' parable of the good Samaritan, p. 257.

As Zarathustra interprets it, neighbor love is another one of those virtues "lied" into existence by the weak; they are dissatisfied with themselves, and they "flee" to the neighbor. Being occupied with the sufferings of others, Zarathustra thinks, is a way of avoiding the hard task of creating oneself. Selflessness is praised by those who have no self worth prizing. Neighbor love is part of the "morality of timidity" that the herd praises to thwart "everything that raises an individual above the herd and causes his neighbor to fear him" (*BGE*, 201, 88).

"Selfishness is the greatest curse of the human race."

William E. Gladstone (1809–1898)

But once again, as with selfishness generally, there can be a bad and a good form of loving one's neighbor.

"Do love your neighbor as yourself, but first be such as *love themselves*—loving with a great love, loving with a great contempt." Thus speaks Zarathustra the godless. (*Z* 3, 284)

As we have seen, loving yourself is being *hard* on yourself, loving yourself "with a great contempt" for all in your life that has not yet been "given style." Loving your neighbor "as yourself" would involve the same hardness and contempt.

6. Zarathustra praises not the accidental and anonymous "neighbor," but the **friend.**

I teach you not the neighbor, but the friend. The friend should be the festival of the earth to you and an anticipation of the overman. I teach you the friend and his overflowing heart. . . .

Let the future and the farthest be for you the cause of your today: in your friend you shall love the overman as your cause. (*Z* 1, 173–174)

A friend is not *someone who needs you,* and you should not "flee" to your friend out of some need of your own. A true friend is one with an "overflowing heart," which, of course, requires the "great health." A friend shares what is highest—the passion for self-overcoming. Friends are not just good-time buddies, occasions for enjoyment. Friends stimulate each other to excel; each demands more and ever more from the other—more, that is, of the other's nobility and self-mastery.

> In a friend one should have one's best enemy. You should be closest to him with your heart when you resist him. (*Z* 1, 168)
>
> Let us be enemies too, my friends! Let us strive against one another like gods. (*Z* 2, 214)

7. As the prophet of the overman, Zarathustra is also the prophet of the **will to power.**

> Where I found the living, there I found will to power; and even in the will of those who serve I found the will to be master. . . .
>
> And life itself confided this secret to me: "Behold," it said, "I am *that which must always over-come itself.* Indeed, you call it a will to procreate or a drive to an end, to something higher, farther, more manifold: but all this is one, and one secret. . . .
>
> "Whatever I create and however much I love it—soon I must oppose it and my love; thus my will wills it. And you too, lover of knowledge, are only a path and footprint of my will; verily, my will to power walks also on the heels of your will to truth." (*Z* 2, 226–227)

In every kind of overcoming, every will to a higher state, in every valuation and esteeming, Zarathustra detects the will to power.* It is will to power that seeks truth.† It is will to power that creates tablets of values—as a means to self-control and mastery, to more power!

> A tablet of the good hangs over every people. Behold, it is the tablet of their overcomings; behold, it is the voice of their will to power. (*Z* 1, 170)

Will to power drives the revenge of the weak and motivates the slave rebellion in morality. And will to power points us toward the overman as the one in whom power is at its peak. That is why the overman can be the meaning of the earth. Overman is what life—all life—is driving toward.

> "Where love rules, there is no will to power; and where power predominates, there love is lacking."
>
> *Carl Gustav Jung (1877–1962)*

The power of the overman is primarily *self*-mastery, *self*-overcoming; it is the enjoyment of an overfull, overflowing, abundant life in which one is no longer dominated by need, aching, longing, or wishing that things might be otherwise. The life of an overman is a life *beyond revenge* and *without resentment.*

> One needs only to do me some wrong, I "repay" it—you may be sure of that: soon I find an opportunity for expressing my gratitude to the "evil-doer" (at times even for his evil deed). (*EH*, 229)

No blaming, no accusations, no complaining. No victim-think. No self-pity. *No pity at all.* The life of an overman will not be without suffering, pain, and struggle, but an overman is strong enough for that, too. More to the point, an overman is *grateful* for it. That, too, can be overcome.

All this may sound attractive; we might like to be overmen, too. But we should not be naive about the power of an overman. It is a life, after all, *beyond good and evil.* And Nietzsche on numerous occasions takes pains to tell us how dangerous overmen can be. In the chapter on "What Is Noble," Nietzsche says,

> To refrain from injuring, abusing, or exploiting one another; to equate another person's will with our

---

*You may be wondering how Nietzsche can identify will to power as the key drive in all existence, when he has attacked the will as superficial and hardly the sort of thing that can serve as a cause. The answer is that will to power is not the *conscious* will; it is not the intention to which we normally ascribe action. Will to power is simply *life itself* climbing over itself, overcoming every plateau, always seeking mastery and control—whether consciously or not. Needless to say, this is not Schopenhauer's *metaphysical will* either; will to power is meant to be a characterization of life in *this* world.

† In an important speech called "On Immaculate Perception," Zarathustra attacks the idea that there can be any disinterested, purely contemplative, spectatorlike knowledge. *All* our knowing and pursuit of truth is driven by desire, interest, will. The trick is not to pare these passions away, but to multiply them (as "great health" makes possible), to add perspectives so as to gain the *height* from which an overman can survey the truth. "How much truth does a spirit *endure,* how much truth does it *dare*? More and more that became for me the real measure of value. Error (faith in the ideal) is not blindness, error is *cowardice*" (*EH*, 218).

own: in a certain crude sense this can develop into good manners between individuals, if the preconditions are in place (that is, if the individuals have truly similar strength and standards and if they are united within one single social body). But if we were to try to take this principle further and possibly even make it the *basic principle of society,* it would immediately be revealed for what it is: a will to *deny* life, a principle for dissolution and decline. We must think through the reasons for this and resist all sentimental frailty: life itself *in its essence* means appropriating, injuring, overpowering those who are foreign and weaker. . . . "Exploitation" is not part of a decadent or imperfect, primitive society: it is part of the *fundamental nature* of living things, . . . a consequence of the true will to power, which is simply the will to life.* (*BGE,* 259, 153)

An aristocracy of overmen will *of course* exploit those beneath them. Again Nietzsche displays his hostility to "modern ideas" of equality and equal rights for all. All this is superficiality and sentimental weakness. Worse, it is "a will to *deny* life, a principle for dissolution and decline." Men are *not* equal. And a clear view of the very "*essence*" of life should convince us of that.

8. An overman will know what he is worth. Under no illusions about equality, the noble soul of an overman will sense the immense distance between himself and others. He will be conscious of the "*order of rank,* and of how power and right and spaciousness of perspective grow into the heights together" (*HA,* preface, 9). Very much like Plato,† Nietzsche thinks there are roughly three classes of human beings.

> The highest caste—I call them *the fewest*—being perfect, also has the privileges of the fewest: among them, to represent happiness, beauty, and graciousness on earth. Only to the most spiritual human beings is beauty permitted: among them alone is graciousness not weakness. . . .
> The *second:* they are the guardians of the law, those who see to order and security, the noble

warriors, and above all the king as the highest formula of warrior, judge, and upholder of the law. . . .

> A high culture is a pyramid: it can stand only on a broad base; its first presupposition is a strong and soundly consolidated mediocrity. Handicraft, trade, agriculture, *science,* the greatest part of art, the whole quintessence of *professional* activity, to sum it up, is compatible only with a mediocre amount of ability and ambition. (*A,* 57)

"Choose equality."

Matthew Arnold (1822–1888)

Nietzsche emphasizes that in this pyramid, with the few at the top, there is nothing unnatural.

> In all this, to repeat, there is nothing arbitrary, nothing contrived; whatever is *different* is contrived—contrived for the ruin of nature. The order of castes, the *order of rank,* merely formulates the highest law of life; the separation of the three types is necessary for the preservation of society, to make possible the higher and the highest types. The *inequality* of rights is the first condition for the existence of any rights at all. (*A,* 57)

The overman, then, will look *down.* The *many* will be below him—perhaps far below. But what attitude will these highest few have toward those who are lower in the order of rank? The overman will be filled with contempt, loathing, and nausea wherever he sees resentment and revenge in those lower ranks, deception and self-deception, the rancor of the ill-constituted, the demand for equality (where there *is* none)—in short, the morality of good and evil. But for those mediocre ones who are content, who find their happiness in mediocrity, the situation is different:

> It would be completely unworthy of a more profound spirit to consider mediocrity as such an objection. In fact, it is the very *first* necessity if there are to be exceptions: a high culture depends on it. When the exceptional human being treats the mediocre more tenderly than himself and his peers, this is not mere politeness of the heart—it is simply his *duty.* (*A,* 57)

---

*Remember Nietzsche's description of the "uncaged beasts of prey" who created master morality (pp. 574–577). Is Nietzsche here celebrating what Marx deplores?

†For Plato's ideal ordering of a state, see pp. 177–179.

There is certainly more to be said about the life of an overman, but in a word, the overman is one who says "Yes!" to his life, to life itself—who is strong enough for such a yes, healthy enough for such a yes. In such self-affirmation and in continual self-overcoming, the overman finds his joy. And in individuals like that the earth finds its meaning.

There is one problem still facing the overman, a problem Zarathustra faces, too. Can one who has reached these heights really say "Yes!" to *everything*? With that question we come to the crucial test for those who aspire to greatness.

---

1. What does it mean that man is "a bridge and not an end"?
2. What does it mean to "remain faithful to the earth"?
3. Explain the parable of the camel, the lion, and the child.
4. How does one "become what one is"?
5. In what sense is selfishness a virtue? In what sense not?
6. What is the contrast Nietzsche draws between the neighbor and the friend?
7. Explain the notion of an "order of rank."

Affirming Eternal Recurrence

Thus Spoke Zarathustra tells us not only of Zarathustra's speeches but also of his visions, dreams, and adventures. Most important, it chronicles Zarathustra's own growth toward overman status. By the end of the book, if Zarathustra is not yet an overman, he is close. As we have seen, an overman says "Yes!" to his life; an overman turns his back on spite and revenge and all no-saying; an overman remains faithful to the earth. But how could one tell whether one has done that? Self-deception is such a common human characteristic; perhaps one is kidding oneself.

In *The Gay Science,* Nietzsche devises a test.

The greatest weight.—What, if some day or night a demon were to steal after you into your loneliest loneliness and say to you: "This life as you now live it and have lived it, you will have to live once more and innumerable times more; and there will be nothing new in it, but every pain and every joy

and every thought and sigh and everything unutterably small or great in your life will have to return to you, all in the same moonlight between the trees, and even this moment and I myself. The eternal hourglass of existence is turned upside down again and again, and you with it, speck of dust!"

Would you not throw yourself down and gnash your teeth and curse the demon who spoke thus? Or, have you once experienced a tremendous moment when you would have answered him: "You are a god and never have I heard anything more divine." If this thought gained possession of you, it would change you as you are or perhaps crush you. The question in each and every thing, "Do you desire this once more and innumerable times more?" would lie upon your actions as the greatest weight. Or how well disposed would you have to become to yourself and to life *to crave nothing more fervently* than this ultimate eternal confirmation and seal? (*GS,* 341)

The **eternal recurrence** of all things:* At one point, Zarathustra faces that prospect (*Z* 3, 269–272), but he sets it aside. He speaks of an "abysmal thought," which, apparently, he cannot bear to face. Some time later he calls it forth.

Up, abysmal thought, out of my depth! I am your cock and dawn, sleepy worm. Up! Up! My voice shall crow you awake! . . .

I, Zarathustra, the advocate of life, the advocate of suffering, the advocate of the circle; I summon you, my most abysmal thought!

Hail to me! You are coming, I hear you. My abyss speaks. I have turned my ultimate depth inside out into the light. Hail to me! Come here! Give me your hand! Huh! Let go! Huhhuh! Nausea, nausea, nausea—woe unto me! (*Z* 3, 327–328)

What could this thought be that so terrifies Zarathustra, that fills him with such nausea? Remember the prospect that the demon puts before us: that *all* things should recur—eternally—exactly

---

*Scholars are divided about whether Nietzsche believed in recurrence as a fact. There is some evidence that he did, but many think it inconclusive. Whether he did or did not, however, it is clear that its principal importance for him is not as a truth, but as a thought experiment to test the level of yes-saying in a person's life.

as they are. Zarathustra's abysmal thought is that this means the small man, the herd man, the "last" man, the man of resentment and revenge, the weak, the priest, the slaves with their nihilistic morality, Christianity—all this would recur again and again and again. . . .

> The great disgust with man—*this* choked me and had crawled into my throat; and what the soothsayer said: "All is the same, nothing is worth while, knowledge chokes." A long twilight limped before me, a sadness, weary to death, drunken with death, speaking with a yawning mouth. "Eternally recurs the man of whom you are weary, the small man"— thus yawned my sadness and dragged its feet and could not go to sleep. . . . "Alas, man recurs eternally! The small man recurs eternally!" (*Z* 3, 331)

The prospect of eternal recurrence brings the soothsayer's nihilism back with a vengeance. What is life for, if it isn't going anywhere? If there is no hope for ultimate improvement, for progress, for getting beyond the small and the great—for overcoming man once and for all—what would be the point? Man would be a bridge leading nowhere! If it all repeats itself, how could one bear it? But that is just the question the demon asks, isn't it? Suppose this prospect of the eternal recurrence of everything were offered to you. Would you "throw yourself down and gnash your teeth," or would you say, "Never have I heard anything more divine"? The way you answer this question shows "how well disposed" you are "to yourself and to life." It is a test of your yes-saying. Would you say "Yes!" even to this? Would you affirm the eternal recurrence of all things?*

❧

"'Tis all a checkerboard of Nights and Days
Where Destiny with Men for Pieces
     plays;
Hither and thither moves, and mates, and
     slays,
And one by one back in the closet lays."
The Rubaiyat of Omar Khayyam, 49

---

* Of the Holocaust, too, you ask? Of the events on 9/11? Yes, even of those.

What the thought of eternal recurrence teaches Zarathustra is that the meaning of life cannot be sought in anything beyond it. Eternal recurrence is the ultimate denial of all "real worlds"; there is just *this world*—over and over and over again. With "real worlds" gone, life must justify itself as it is, or it cannot be justified at all. Not every life, Nietzsche thinks, can stand this thought. Only the strongest can bear this "greatest weight"—only an overman who says "Yes!" to everything, who affirms life and remains faithful to the earth, who overcomes himself, who gives style to his life, who creates his own values in the very living of his life. The overman says "Yes!" to eternal recurrence. And it is in the life of the overman that the problem of the meaning of life is solved. In *that* life, it doesn't seem a problem!

In *Ecce Homo,* a late work, Nietzsche says, "I am a disciple of the philosopher Dionysus" (*EH,* 217). The *philosopher* Dionysus? When we meet Dionysus in *The Birth of Tragedy,* he is a god; in fact, he is just *one* of the gods, symbolizing a certain feature of human life, of passion unconstrained by reason, measure, and order (these being Apollo's domain). But something interesting has happened in the course of Nietzsche's development. With the disappearance of "real worlds," any contrast between distinct ultimate realities also vanishes. Every aspect of human life, therefore—virtues, vices, values, science—has to be accounted for in terms of the same fundamental reality. And what is that? Will to power.

We have seen that Nietzsche interprets intelligence and "spirit" as no more than an aspect of body. And each body (slave and master alike) expresses the will to power, the will to overcome. So what Nietzsche thinks of as Apollo in *The Birth of Tragedy*—the powers of reason, order, measure (and philosophy, too)—is now seen to be just a manifestation of a body's will to power. So all these Apollonian powers are not *opposed* to Dionysus; they are an *aspect* of Dionysus, a manifestation of the Dionysian will to power. Will to power *sublimated into reason*—that is how Dionysus can be a philosopher and not just the god of irrational intoxication. And that is why at the end only Dionysus remains. A philosophy that remains *faithful to the earth* must be a philosophy of the will to power that says yes to everything earthly—and so is willing to affirm the eternal recurrence of everything. But to affirm life, to rejoice in life, *is* Dionysian.

The affirmation of eternal recurrence is identical with a formula that Nietzsche calls "my formula for greatness in a human being: *amor fati*" (*EH*, 258), that is, love of fate. He explains it in this way:

> that one wants nothing to be different, not forward, not backward, not in all eternity. Not merely bear what is necessary, still less conceal it . . . but *love* it. (*EH*, 258)

Because everything that happens in this world is, Nietzsche believes, necessary and a manifestation of the will to power, to love it is to affirm it. And to affirm it is to say yes even to its eternal recurrence. Whoever can truly do that is an overman—and a disciple of the god and philosopher Dionysus.

What is the "best sign" of a "redeemed" life? Gratitude. Gratitude for *everything*—just as Nietzsche himself was grateful for his illness and pain and for those who did him wrong. That gratitude covers everything is a sign of affirming life— even to the point of willing it all again.*

What is the temptation most to be avoided? Pity. To pity is to say, *would it were not so.* "Pity is the *practice* of nihilism" (*A,* 7). To pity is to give in to suffering, to hallow suffering, to suffer oneself. But Zarathustra believes that suffering and pain are no objection to life! They are, rather, stimulants to self-overcoming, and for them, too, one must be grateful. In the end, Zarathustra is like a convalescent recovering from a long illness—from his wandering in search of wisdom, from his nausea, his pity, his lack of ability to affirm life. Zarathustra is approaching the life of an overman.

Nietzsche tells us, out of his own experience, what such a convalescence is like.

> The free spirit again draws near to life—slowly, to be sure, almost reluctantly, almost mistrustfully.

It again grows warmer about him, yellower, as it were; feeling and feeling for others acquire depth, warm breezes of all kind blow across him. It seems to him as if his eyes are only now open to what is *close at hand.* He is astonished and sits silent: where *had* he been? These close and closest things: how changed they seem! what bloom and magic they have acquired! He looks back gratefully—grateful to his wandering, to his hardness and self-alienation, to his viewing of far distances and bird-like flights in cold heights. What a good thing he had not always stayed "at home," stayed "under his own roof" like a delicate apathetic loafer! He had been *beside himself:* no doubt of that. Only now does he see himself—and what surprises he experiences as he does so! What unprecedented shudders! What happiness even in the weariness, the old sickness, the relapses of the convalescent! How he loves to sit sadly still, to spin out patience, to lie in the sun! Who understands as he does the happiness that comes in winter, the spots of sunlight on the wall! They are the most grateful animals in the world, also the most modest, these convalescents and lizards again half turned towards life:—there are some among them who allow no day to pass without hanging a little song of praise on the hem of its departing robe. And to speak seriously: to become sick in the manner of these free spirits, to remain sick for a long time and then, slowly, slowly, to become healthy, by which I mean "healthier," is a fundamental *cure* for all pessimism. (*HA,* 8–9)

Such a convalescent could wish for it all again.

---

1. What does it mean to affirm eternal recurrence? What does one's reaction to the prospect of eternal recurrence reveal about oneself?
2. How has the conception of Dionysus changed from Nietzsche's early work to his late work?
3. Explain *amor fati* and indicate how this could be Nietzsche's "formula for greatness in a human being."

---

*Here Nietzsche, the great opponent of Christianity, strangely ends on a note that echoes Paul, the greatest of Christian missionaries, who says, "Give thanks in all circumstances" (1 Thess. 5:18), and "Always and for everything [give] thanks" (Eph. 5:20).

FOR FURTHER THOUGHT

1. Suppose that you want to resist Nietzsche's attacks on equality and equal rights. How much else in Nietzsche would you have to reject?
2. Nietzsche believes the interpretation of human beings as sinful is based on a lie, whereas

Kierkegaard takes it to be the very truth. Nietzsche pins his hopes for "redemption" on *amor fati* and affirming eternal recurrence; Kierkegaard pins his on faith. Compare these analyses of the problem of human life and its solution.

3. Gladys asks Gordon, "If you had it to do all over again, would you still marry me?" Is that a good question? Relate it to Nietzsche's claim about eternal recurrence.

KEY WORDS

pessimism	ressentiment
Apollo	revenge
tragedy	equality
Dionysus	free spirit
Schopenhauer	overman
will	last man
satyrs	free will
metaphysical	second innocence
consolation	great health
aesthetic value	camel
real world	lion
apparent world	child
death of God	poet
pity	selfishness
nihilism	neighbor
master morality	friend
good/bad	will to power
slave morality	eternal recurrence
good/evil	

NOTES

1. References to Nietzsche's works are as follows:

PN: The Portable Nietzsche, trans. Walter Kaufmann (New York: Viking Press, 1954). References are to page numbers.

BT: The Birth of Tragedy, trans. Douglas Smith (Oxford: Oxford University Press, 2000). References are to sections and page numbers.

HA: Human, All Too Human, trans. R. J. Hollingdale (Cambridge: Cambridge University Press, 1986). References are to page numbers.

GS: The Gay Science, trans. Walter Kaufmann (New York: Vintage Books, 1974). References are to sections.

Z: Thus Spoke Zarathustra, in *The Portable Nietzsche.* References are to part and page number.

BGE: Beyond Good and Evil, trans. Marian Faber (Oxford: Oxford University Press, 1998). References are to section and page numbers.

GM: On the Genealogy of Morals, trans. Douglas Smith (Oxford: Oxford University Press, 1996). References are to essay, section, and page numbers.

A: The Antichrist, in *The Portable Nietzsche.* References are to sections.

TI: Twilight of the Idols, trans. Duncan Large (Oxford: Oxford University Press, 1998). References are to page numbers.

EH: Ecce Homo, in *On the Genealogy of Morals and Ecce Homo,* trans. Walter Kaufmann (New York: Vintage Books, 1967). References are to page numbers.

25

THE PRAGMATISTS
Thought and Action

The nineteenth century is a tumultuous century, socially, politically, and intellectually. It is the century of the railroad, the newspaper, and the factory. It is the century of the British Empire, colonialism, and the conquest of the American continent. And it is the century of the principle of the conservation of energy, of non-Euclidean geometries, of non-Aristotelian logic, and of evolution. It is a topsy-turvy century, indeed, but one convinced on the whole that progress is being made every day.

Nothing bolsters this conviction more substantially than the progress of science, and among the accomplishments of nineteenth-century science, none stands out more prominently than that of **Darwin.** A cause for controversy to the present day, Darwin's theory of evolution offers a basically mechanistic explanation for the forms of living things, for their variety, and for their tendency to alter over long spans of time. The basic outlines of Darwin's theory of evolution are well known: Sexual selection and the mechanisms of inheritance produce small variations in offspring; some of these changes are beneficial to individuals who possess

them; under the pressures of population and scarce resources, these individuals are more likely to reproduce, passing their advantage to their offspring, thus leading eventually to differentiation of species in different ecological niches. The core ideas are those of *random variation* and *natural selection*. Like the revolutions of Copernicus and Newton, Darwin's revolution in biology is a momentous and influential shift, affecting intellectuals of all kinds—not least those philosophers who come to call themselves pragmatists.

Charles Sanders Peirce

Charles Sanders Peirce (1839–1914), the son of a Harvard mathematician, was trained in the techniques of science from an early age. For a good part of his adult life, he worked as a scientist for the US Coast and Geodetic Survey. He made some contributions to the theory of the pendulum and was concerned with problems of accurate measurement. But he was early attracted to problems in logic and probability theory and studied the philosophies of Kant and Hegel. He helps extend logic beyond the Aristotelian syllogism. Besides contributions to the theory of deductive and inductive inference, he explores the sort of inference that starts from certain facts and leaps to a hypothesis that explains them. He calls this last sort *abductive inference*, though it is nowadays usually called *inference to the best explanation*.

Peirce is also a metaphysician of some power, combining in his later thought a version of evolutionary theory with absolute idealism.* But it is not his metaphysics that has been influential, so we concentrate on what he calls his **pragmatism.** The word comes from a Greek root meaning "deed" or "act" and is chosen to accentuate the close ties that Peirce sees between our intellectual life (concepts, beliefs, theories) on the one hand and our practical life of actions and enjoyments on the other. Peirce also occasionally calls it *practicalism* and sometimes *critical commonsensism*. We'll see that John Dewey thinks of "instrumentalism" as a term nearly equivalent in force, this term bringing out the tool-like character of the intellectual conceptions we use.

FIXING BELIEF

In the late 1870s, Peirce published a series of articles in *Popular Science Monthly*, in which the influence of scientific practice on this lifelong researcher is evident. He distinguishes four ways of coming to a fixed belief about some subject matter, four methods of settling opinion. These are techniques that can be used (indeed, are used) to arrive at what we *think* is true. They are ways of resolving doubt.

First there is the *method of* **tenacity.** If the aim is settlement of opinion, one might ask oneself,

> Why should we not attain the desired end, by taking as answer to a question any we may fancy, and constantly reiterating it to ourselves, dwelling on all which may conduce to that belief, and learning to turn with contempt and hatred from anything that might disturb it? (*FB*, 233–234)[1]

Those who adopt this technique enjoy certain benefits. It cannot be denied, Peirce says, "that a steady and immovable faith yields great peace of mind" (*FB*, 249).

Nonetheless, Peirce believes that this is not a satisfactory method of settling opinion. His reason is an interesting one and sheds light on his pragmatism. One might think that the proper objection to the method of tenacity is that it is bound to leave one with too many false beliefs. But that is not Peirce's objection. The trouble with this method is that it

> will be unable to hold its ground in practice. The social impulse is against it. The man who adopts it will find that other men think differently from him, and it will be apt to occur to him, in some saner moment, that their opinions are quite as good as his own, and this will shake his confidence in his belief. (*FB*, 235)

The right objection is that tenacity *doesn't work!** This thought, that others may well be as right as oneself, arises from the "social impulse," Peirce says, "an impulse too strong in man to be suppressed" (*FB*, 235). We are in fact influenced by the opinions of others. So some method must be found that will fix belief not only in the individual, but also in the community.

This thought leads us to the second method: **authority.**

> Let an institution be created which shall have for its object to keep correct doctrines before the attention of the people, to reiterate them perpetually, and to teach them to the young; having at the same time power to prevent contrary doctrines from being taught, advocated, or expressed. Let all possible causes of a change of mind be removed from men's apprehensions. Let them be kept ignorant, lest they should learn of some reason to think otherwise than they do. Let their passions be enlisted, so that they may regard private and unusual opinions with hatred and horror. Then, let all men who reject the established belief be terrified into silence. Let the people turn out and tar-and-feather such

---

*For an account of absolute idealism in its Hegelian guise, see pp. 509–511. The key feature in Peirce's version is that the entire universe has the distinguishing features of mind and that it is moving toward a rational end out of love. But such a brief account hardly does it justice.

---

*Experience with certain sorts of "fanatics" may make one doubt whether Peirce is altogether correct here.

men, or let inquisitions be made into the manner of thinking of suspected persons, and, when they are found guilty of forbidden beliefs, let them be subjected to some signal punishment. When complete agreement could not otherwise be reached, a general massacre of all who have not thought in a certain way has proved to be a very effective means of settling opinion in a country. (*FB*, 235–236)

This method, Peirce judges, is much superior to the first; it can produce majestic results in terms of culture and art. He even allows that for the mass of humankind, there may be no better method than that of authority. But this method is also unstable: There will always be some people who see that in other ages or countries, different doctrines have been held on the basis of different authorities. And they will ask themselves whether there is any reason to rate their beliefs higher than the beliefs of those who have been brought up differently.* These reflections "give rise to doubts in their minds" (*FB*, 238). In the long run, authority does not work any better than tenacity in settling opinion.

The unsatisfactory character of the first two methods gives rise to the third, which Peirce calls both *the method of* **natural preferences** and the *a priori method*. Here we accept what seems "obvious," or "agreeable to reason," or "self-evident," or "clear and distinct." Our opinions are neither those we just happen to have nor those imposed by an authority; they are those we arrive at after reflection and conversation with others.

The best examples of such a method, Peirce thinks, are the great metaphysical systems from Plato through Hegel. But history seems to show that one person's self-evidence is another's absurdity, and the method

makes of inquiry something similar to the development of taste; but taste, unfortunately, is always more or less a matter of fashion, and accordingly metaphysicians have never come to any fixed agreement, but the pendulum has swung backward and forward between a more material and a more spiritual philosophy, from the earliest times to the latest. (*FB*, 241)

"The whole function of thought is to produce habits of action."

—Charles Sanders Peirce

Again we have an unstable and hence unsatisfactory method for settling our opinions.*

What we need is some method

by which our beliefs may be determined by nothing human, but by some external permanency—by something upon which our thinking has no effect. . . . It must be something which affects, or might affect, every man. And, though these affections are necessarily as various as are individual conditions, yet the method must be such that the ultimate conclusion of every man shall be the same. Such is the method of science. Its fundamental hypothesis, restated in more familiar language, is this: There are Real things, whose characters are entirely independent of our opinions about them; those Reals affect our senses according to regular laws, and, though our sensations are as different as our relations to the objects, yet, by taking advantage of the laws of perception, we can ascertain by reasoning how things really and truly are, and any man, if he have sufficient experience and he reason enough about it, will be led to the one true conclusion. (*FB*, 242–243)

---

*Compare once again the example cited by Herodotus so long ago, p. 63. Peirce, however, does *not* draw the conclusion of Herodotus, that "custom is king over all."

---

*Compare Hume's impatience with intuition as a foundation for knowledge, pp. 441–443.

Several features of the fourth method, the *method of science,* are distinctive. First, there is the attempt to make our beliefs responsive to something *independent* of what any of us thinks— or would like to think; in various ways, the first three methods lack precisely this feature. Second, we see that the method of science is decidedly a *public* method: There is to be no reliance on what is peculiar to you or to me; our beliefs are to be determined by what can affect you *and* me *and* anyone else who inquires. Again, this public character is lacking in the first three methods. Third, because of this essentially public character, the *social impulse* (which wrecks the first three methods) will not undermine opinion that is settled in this scientific way.

Peirce's conception of science, however, rests on the assumption that there actually is some reality independent of our thinking about it. Suppose we ask, Why should we grant this assumption?* For one thing, the practice of science does not lead us to doubt the assumption; indeed, Peirce holds, the method "has had the most wonderful triumphs in the way of settling opinion" (*FB*, 249). In this regard, too, it is strikingly different from the other methods: It works! But the fundamental reason to grant this assumption has to do with the very nature of belief and doubt. Peirce's thoughts on this score are original and deep. We need to look at them.

BELIEF AND DOUBT

We have been examining methods of "fixing" belief or settling our opinions. But what is it to have a **belief?** And what is it like to **doubt?** Doubting and believing are clearly different, but how? Peirce finds three differences: (1) The sensation of believing is different from that of doubting; they just feel different. (2) We are strongly disposed to escape doubt but are content when we have a belief—at least until something provokes doubt about that belief. (3) The most profound difference, however, gets us to the very nature of belief and doubt,

for a belief is a **habit,** and doubt is the lack of such a habit. This needs explaining.

Let's assume you believe the world is (roughly) round. What is it to have this belief? It is not a matter of having a thought in your mind; presumably, you have believed this for a long time, although you have not been constantly thinking that thought. And it would be wrong to say that you believe it only when you have this thought actively in mind. Rather, belief "puts us into such a condition that we shall behave in a certain way, when the occasion arises" (*FB*, 231). So if you believe the world is round, you are in a "condition" that leads you to behave in the following ways: If someone asks you whether the world is flat, you say, "No, it is round"; if you win a trip "around the world," you accept it gladly; if you see a picture of the world taken from a satellite, you say, "Yes, that is what I expected it would look like." If you are on the highway in Kansas, you drive confidently and do not worry about running your car off the edge. Being *disposed to behave* in these various ways— and more—is what it is to have the belief that the world is round. To have a belief is to have a habit that guides your actions in the world.

Doubt, in contrast, is an uncertain state; doubting is the lack of a settled habit and so involves not knowing what to do in a given situation. The resulting anxiety is why we struggle to escape doubt. Peirce calls the struggle to escape doubt and attain belief **inquiry,** though he admits that sometimes it is not a very apt term. Inquiry, then, is an attempt to recover the calm satisfactoriness of *knowing what to do when,* which is characteristic of belief. Peirce is convinced that only the public, intersubjective methods of scientific inquiry will work in the long run to carry us from doubt to fixed belief.

Three things are essential to inquiry: a stimulus, an end or goal, and a method. Here is how Peirce thinks about these things:

- stimulus: doubt
- end: settlement of opinion
- method: science

We need to explore further each of the first two factors. Let us begin with some reflections on doubt.

*After all, this seems to be the central issue in modern epistemology; it is what Descartes' methodical doubt undermines and what Hegel's idealism denies. How can Peirce be so naive?

According to all the pragmatists, inquiry (indeed, thinking in general) always begins with a felt problem. But, they say, not everything that has been thought by philosophers to be problematic really is so.

> Some philosophers have imagined that to start an inquiry it was only necessary to utter a question whether orally or by setting it down upon paper, and have even recommended us to begin our studies with questioning everything! But the mere putting of a proposition into the interrogative form does not stimulate the mind to any struggle after belief. There must be a real and living doubt, and without this all discussion is idle. (*FB*, 232)

Peirce obviously has Descartes in mind.* Perplexed by the contradictory things he had been taught, Descartes decides to "doubt everything" until he should come upon something "so clear and distinct" that he could not possibly doubt it. Descartes is embarked on what Dewey is to call "the quest for certainty."

But Peirce simply cannot take this methodical doubt seriously. This is not, he thinks "a real and living doubt"; it is only a "make-believe" (*WPI*, 278). To propose that one begin by doubting everything, Peirce remarks, is to suppose that doubting is "as easy as lying."

> We cannot begin with complete doubt. We must begin with all the prejudices which we actually have when we enter upon the study of philosophy. These prejudices are not to be dispelled by a maxim, for they are things which it does not occur to us *can* be questioned. Hence this initial skepticism will be a mere self-deception, and not real doubt; and no one who follows the Cartesian method will ever be satisfied until he has formally recovered all those beliefs which in form he has given up. . . . A person may, it is true, in the course of his studies, find reason to doubt what he began by believing; but in that case he doubts because he has a positive reason for it, and not on account of the Cartesian maxim. Let us not pretend to doubt in philosophy what we do not doubt in our hearts. (*SCFI*, 156–157)

Do you call it *doubting* to write down on a piece of paper that you doubt? If so, doubt has nothing to do with any serious business. But do not make believe;

if pedantry has not eaten all the reality out of you, recognize, as you must, that there is much that you do not doubt, in the least. (*WPI*, 278)

Peirce condemns "make-believe" doubt because of his analysis of belief. To believe, as we have seen, is to have a habit, a disposition to behave in certain ways in certain situations; to doubt is to be without such a habit—not to know what to do when. But if that is so, to say "I doubt everything" while going about eating bread rather than stones, opening doors rather than walking into them, and carrying on all the normal business of living is "a mere self-deception." There is much we do not doubt at all, and we should not "pretend to doubt in philosophy what we do not doubt in our hearts."

It is quite possible, of course, that our experiences will lead us to doubt things that we had not doubted before; the world often surprises us. But then these are *real doubts*, posing real problems and urging us on to inquiry because we no longer know how to act. This is very different from a philosopher who sits in his dressing gown before the fire and says, "I doubt everything."

Peirce's critique of Descartes' starting point, then, comes to this: (1) It is impossible, since we cannot suspend judgment about everything while continuing to live; and (2) it is futile.* What we need is not an absolutely certain starting point, but a method of improving the beliefs we actually have; only *real* doubts are to count in nudging us away from them. As long as our beliefs work for us, we will have no motivation to question them.

We might also wonder whether Peirce has correctly identified the end of inquiry. Should we really settle for the mere fixation of belief as the end or goal of our inquiries? Surely, we are inclined to think, what we are after in science and philosophy is the *truth*. Couldn't we settle our opinions and still be *wrong*?

TRUTH AND REALITY

Peirce points out first that we invariably think each of our beliefs to be true as long as we have

---

*Review Descartes' first meditation.

*Compare Hume's critique of "antecedent skepticism," p. 462. The similarities are striking, but Peirce's criticism is based on a deeper conception of belief.

no cause to doubt it.* It is only in that uneasy state of doubt that we wonder about the truth of our beliefs. Second, when doubt ceases, so does inquiry. If we are satisfied with the belief we come to, what sense does it make to wonder, abstractly, whether it might still be false? If our belief is fixed, we wouldn't know what else to do to determine whether it is true or false.

Finally, Peirce asks us to consider what we mean by "true":

> If your terms "truth" and "falsity" are taken in such senses as to be definable in terms of doubt and belief and the course of experience (as for example they would be if you were to define the "truth" as that to a belief in which belief would tend if it were to tend indefinitely toward absolute fixity), well and good: in that case, you are only talking about doubt and belief. But if by truth and falsity you mean something not definable in terms of doubt and belief in any way, then you are talking of entities of whose existence you can know nothing, and which Ockham's razor would clean shave off. (*WPI*, 279)

What motivates those "doubts" that we raise occasionally even when we are, for all practical purposes, satisfied with our beliefs? It is the suspicion that our beliefs may not, for all their practical usefulness, *correspond* with reality—that reality may, for all our care and investigation, still be quite different. And this might be the case, we suspect, even if we could in no way discover the discrepancy. But if that is what we mean, Peirce says, then we "are talking of entities of whose existence [we] can know nothing." **Ockham's razor,** that principle of parsimony in theorizing, would shave them clean off.†

We do not and cannot stabilize our beliefs, Peirce argues, by noticing they are true—by seeing that they correspond with a fact. His argument for this is complicated, but we can appreciate the gist by considering what it would take to compare

a belief directly with reality. Consider again your belief that the world is round. You could only compare that belief to reality itself if your belief were independent of any other beliefs or cognitions. But that is never the case. For example, to point to a photograph taken by a satellite involves beliefs about satellites and photographs. More generally, all our cognitions, beliefs, hypotheses, theories, and understandings are dependent on other items of that same kind; none of them provides a *test* of correspondence with a fact independent of the beliefs we already have when we experience that fact.*

It would be easy to draw the wrong conclusion from this claim, however.† We should not suppose that those "external permanencies"—those things "upon which our thinking has no effect" (*FB*, 242)—are therefore beyond our understanding. Peirce remarks that although

> everything which is present to us is a phenomenal manifestation of ourselves, this does not prevent its being a phenomenon of something without us, just as a rainbow is at once a manifestation both of the sun and the rain. (*SCFI*, 169)

What Peirce's argument does do, however, is to undercut any claim to be *certain* about a belief on the grounds that it represents a "pure intuition," uncontaminated by prior beliefs. This is an implication Peirce is happy to welcome since, as we have seen, he has given up the project of basing our knowledge on a foundation of certain truths. What counts, again, is whether we have a method to *improve* our beliefs, not whether we can be *certain* of them.

But now we must ask, How does Peirce think of **truth?** If we cannot understand fixation of belief in terms of attaining truth, he suggests we define

---

*Compare Hegel for a similar point, pp. 499–500.

†William of Ockham, the fourteenth-century theologian and philosopher, formulates this principle: Do not multiply entities beyond necessity. It is a rule that bids us to make do with the simplest hypothesis in explaining the facts.

---

*Here Peirce agrees with Hegel's attack on immediacy. To try to say what an experience is *of* without relying on the concepts and theories we bring to that experience is impossible. There is no unmediated knowledge, no "theory-free" apprehension of "the facts." Wilfrid Sellars has called the opinion to the contrary a myth, "the myth of the given." For the Hegelian view, see pp. 499–504. For Sellars', see pp. 730–731.

†So easy that it is regularly done these days.

truth in terms of belief and doubt. He offers several attempts at such a definition:

> The opinion which is fated to be ultimately agreed to by all who investigate, is what we mean by the truth. (*HMIC*, 268)

> that to a belief in which belief would tend if it were to tend indefinitely toward absolute fixity. (*WPI*, 279)

> a state of belief unassailable by doubt. (*WPI*, 279)

Note that each of these definitions makes truth dependent on the states of belief and doubt, not the other way around. A true belief, according to them, is a fixed belief—not fixed just for the moment, but *absolutely* fixed, not just undoubted, but *unassailable* by doubt. The truth about some subject matter is what investigators using scientific methods, if they were persistent, would eventually come to agree upon. That is what truth *means*.

Let's draw out some consequences. The truth is a kind of *ideal*, one for which we strive in our inquiries. Because it is what investigators *will* agree upon, no present agreements (no matter how broad and deep) can suffice to give us absolute confidence that what we *now* believe is true. It is always possible that further investigation will upset present beliefs. Nonetheless, it is quite possible that many of our present beliefs are true. What does this mean? It means that many of our beliefs are ones that future investigators will continue to reaffirm in the light of their inquiries; these beliefs are in fact "unassailable by doubt" because the world holds no surprises that will upset them, though again we can never be certain that this is so for any given belief.

Note, moreover, the truth is something *public*. It is not the case that truth is relative to individuals or cultures. The **community of inquirers** defines what is true—though it is not any particular community here and now, but rather the whole community of inquirers over time.

We can see how this understanding of truth fits in with Peirce's pragmatism by noting a further implication:

> For truth is neither more nor less than that character of a proposition which consists in this, that belief in the proposition would, with sufficient experience and reflection, lead us to such conduct as would tend to satisfy the desires we should then have. To say that truth means more than this is to say that it has no meaning at all.[2]

Beliefs, being habits, invariably lead to conduct when combined with desires that move us to act. For example, you believe there is a hamburger before you and, being hungry, pick it up and take a bite. The belief is a true one if, when you act on it, your desire can be satisfied and not frustrated. If you bite into a Big Mac, then the belief that it was a hamburger is a true one. If your teeth meet a rubber imitation, your belief is a false one; the falsity is testified to by the fact that your action does not satisfy your desire to eat.* True beliefs, then, are those that can be relied on in our practical activity in the world (including the world of the scientific laboratory). William James puts it this way: They are the beliefs that *pay*. But Peirce would be quick to add that they must pay *for the community of inquirers* and in the *long run*.

It is in terms of truth, so understood, that Peirce thinks we must also understand the concept of **reality.** What do we mean by "the real"? Peirce says that we may define it as

> that whose characters are independent of what anybody may think them to be. (*HMIC*, 266)

But though that is a perfectly correct definition, it is not, he thinks, a very helpful one. It does not tell us how to recognize reality or give us any instructions about how to find it.

A more satisfactory explanation can be given in terms of truth (which, remember, is itself defined in terms of belief fixed by the methods of scientific investigation). Peirce remarks that scientists are convinced that different lines of inquiry into the same subject matter will come eventually to the same result:

---

*This notion of satisfaction is an important one for the pragmatists. In the thought of William James, it is subject to certain ambiguities and provoked the outcry of critics: "What? Do you mean to say that any belief that *satisfies you* is to be counted a true one?" But you can see that in Peirce's hands the public nature of truth, together with the requirement of agreement by a community of scientific inquirers, makes this rebuke inapplicable to him.

Different minds may set out with the most antagonistic views, but the progress of investigation carries them by a force outside of themselves to one and the same conclusion. This activity of thought by which we are carried, not where we wish, but to a foreordained goal, is like the operation of destiny. No modification of the point of view taken, no selection of other facts for study, no natural bend of mind even, can enable a man to escape the predestinate opinion. This great hope is embodied in the conception of truth and reality. The opinion which is fated to be ultimately agreed to by all who investigate, is what we mean by the truth, and the object represented in this opinion is the real. That is the way I would explain reality. (*HMIC*, 268)

According to this view, reality is *what true opinion says it is*. And true opinion is an opinion that further scientific inquiry will never upset. But here is a problem. Doesn't this understanding of reality make it dependent on us in a way that the former definition (in terms of what is independent of what anyone may think) does not? Hasn't Peirce contradicted himself here? He considers this objection and says that

reality is independent, not necessarily of thought in general, but only of what you or I or any finite number of men may think about it,* . . . though the object of the final opinion depends on what that opinion is, yet what that opinion is does not depend on what you or I or any man thinks. Our perversity and that of others may indefinitely postpone the settlement of opinion; it might even conceivably cause an arbitrary proposition to be universally accepted as long as the human race should last. Yet even that would not change the nature of the belief, which alone could be the result of investigation carried sufficiently far; and if, after the extinction of our race, another should arise with faculties and disposition for investigation, that true opinion must be the one which they would ultimately come to. "Truth crushed to earth shall rise again," and the opinion which would finally result from investigation does not depend on how anybody may actually think. But the reality of that which is real does depend on the real fact that investigation is destined to lead, at last, if continued long enough, to a belief in it. (*HMIC*, 269)

Reality, then, can be independent of the inquiries of any finite number of individuals and yet be what would be revealed in inquiry, provided inquiry is scientific and carried "sufficiently far." For Peirce, then, *science* is the *criterion of the real*; not science as it exists at any given stage, of course, but that ideal science toward which scientific activity is even now moving.*

The real, then, is that which, sooner or later, information and reasoning would finally result in, and which is therefore independent of the vagaries of me and you. Thus the very origin of the conception of reality shows that this conception essentially involves the notion of a COMMUNITY, without definite limits, and capable of a definite increase of knowledge. . . . Now, a proposition whose falsity can never be discovered, and the error of which therefore is absolutely incognizable, contains, upon our principle, absolutely no error. Consequently, that which is thought in these cognitions is the real, as it really is. There is nothing, then, to prevent our knowing outward things as they really are, and it is most likely that we do thus know them in numberless cases, although we can never be absolutely certain of doing so in any special case. (*SCFI*, 186–187)

Two comments: (1) Peirce is here denying the Kantian doctrine that we cannot know things as they really are, but only as they appear to us.† There is no essentially hidden thing-in-itself; things are as they reveal themselves to inquiry. (2) His ground

---

*Compare Parmenides saying that "thought and being are the same," p. 24.

*Here we have a decisively different conception of the *problem of the criterion*; it is not a criterion from which to start—as though we had to solve that problem first, before we could do any intellectual work. Peirce would agree that if we think of the problem of the criterion in that way, it is unsolvable; it requires that we know something before we can know something, and skepticism will be the result. According to Peirce's view, however, we know enough about the nature of the criterion to know that we do not now have it in hand; yet we also know how to make definite and regular progress toward it. Peirce's view has certain similarities to Hegel's idea that "absolute knowledge" lies at the end of a process of historical development and that nothing prior to that point can be certain; it differs in recommending empirical science as the method by which to arrive at "fixed beliefs." (See the discussion of Hegel, pp. 500–504).

†Review Kant's distinction between noumena and phenomena, pp. 476–479.

for affirming that we can know things "as they really are" is the "principle" that there is no error possible where it is impossible to discover it. Why does he believe this? To understand his reasoning here, we must turn to what Peirce has to say about *meaning*.

First let us summarize a main theme in all we have examined so far. It goes by the name of **fallibilism:** a readiness to acknowledge that one's knowledge is not yet completely satisfactory, together with an intense desire to find things out.* Peirce would wholeheartedly agree with an aphorism formulated in the early twentieth century by Otto Neurath, one of a group of thinkers known as logical positivists.

> We are like sailors who must rebuild their ship on the open sea, never able to dismantle it in dry-dock and to reconstruct it there out of the best materials.³

There is, perhaps, no belief of ours immune from possible revision. But, like the sailors on the open sea, we cannot replace all our beliefs at once. If we revise certain convictions, we do it only by standing on some others, which, for the time being, we must regard as stable.

---

1. Why, according to Peirce, is the method of science superior to the methods of tenacity, authority, and natural preferences for arriving at fixed beliefs?
2. What is it, actually, to believe something? To doubt something? And what is the function of intellectual inquiry?
3. What is Peirce's critique of Descartes' project of arriving at certainty through doubting?
4. How does Peirce understand truth? How is this different from the way, say, Aristotle (and most of the tradition) understands it? (See p. 187.)
5. How does Peirce understand reality? If you asked him, "Do we now know reality?" what would he say?
6. What is fallibilism? How is it related to the quest for certainty?

---

*Compare Socrates' confession of ignorance, together with his passionate search for the truth, pp. 97–98. And note the similarity to Kierkegaard's view of our relation to the truth, pp. 536–537

MEANING

Peirce says that

> pragmatism is, in itself, no doctrine of metaphysics, no attempt to determine any truth of things. It is merely a method of ascertaining the meanings of hard words and of abstract concepts. (*SP*, 317)

We have already, as a matter of fact, seen this method at work on the concepts of belief and doubt, truth and reality. But now we must examine it directly.

Peirce restricts his doctrine of **meaning** to what he calls *intellectual concepts*, which he contrasts with *mere subjective feelings*. An **intellectual concept** is any concept "upon the structure of which, arguments concerning objective fact may hinge" (*SP*, 318). Examples are concepts such as "hard," "ten centimeters," "lithium," and "believes." By contrast, consider what Peirce has to say about **subjective feelings.**

> Had the light which, as things are, excites in us the sensation of blue, always excited the sensation of red, and *vice versa*, however great a difference that might have made in our feelings, it could have made none in the force of any argument. In this respect, the qualities of hard and soft strikingly contrast with those of red and blue; because while red and blue name mere subjective feelings only, hard and soft express the factual behaviour of the thing under the pressure of a knife-edge. . . . My pragmatism, having nothing to do with qualities of feeling, permits me to hold that the predication of such a quality is just what it seems, and has nothing to do with anything else. Hence, could two qualities of feeling everywhere be interchanged, nothing but feelings could be affected. Those qualities have no intrinsic significations beyond themselves. (*SP*, 318)

Peirce here presents a version of a thought experiment called the **inverted spectrum.** It is often given in a two-person setting. Suppose the sensation you have when you see a ripe tomato is qualitatively identical to the sensation your friends have when they look at the sky on a clear day and vice versa. Could you discover this? Apparently you could not, since you cannot directly access your friends' sensations, nor they yours—and everything else would be the same. You would have learned to call ripe tomatoes "red" (doesn't everybody?) despite the fact that the sensation they produce in you is the sensation your friends call blue. If someone asked you to bring them something red, you might bring a tomato. And you would call the sky "blue," even though the sensation you have when you look at it is the same as the sensation your friends have when looking at a ripe tomato. Such an inversion of qualities would make absolutely no difference to our behavior, our language, our reasoning, or our science. They are "mere subjective feelings only." Such sensations have no *meaning*. Nothing else depends on them.

Contrast such a sensation with the quality of hardness. Whether something is hard makes a difference to all those things sensations do not affect: our behavior (we cannot crush it in our hand like a sponge), our language (if we call something hard, we communicate something definite to our hearers), our reasoning (from the premise that an item is hard, we can conclude that a knife edge will not easily divide it), and our science. "Hard" is an intellectual concept. It has *implications* that must be understood if we are to understand the concept. If you do not understand that a knife edge will not easily divide a hard object, you do not understand what "hard" means.

These implications have to do with the *behavior* of the objects that are correctly called "hard" under different circumstances. Even if a knife edge is never actually drawn across an object, to call it "hard" is to imply that *if* a knife edge *were* put to it, it *would not* divide easily. So the implications of an intellectual concept include what Peirce calls the "would-be's" and the "would-do's" of objects. These would-be's and would-do's are, of course, simply habits or dispositions. The rock has a disposition to resist a knife edge; and by virtue of this disposition it is rightly called "hard."

We have looked at one example of an intellectual concept and have noted the ways in which it contrasts with pure subjective sensations. But now we should ask, How can we decide what an intellectual concept means? That is, how can we make our ideas clear?

The very first lesson that we have a right to demand that logic shall teach us is, how to make our ideas

clear; and a most important one it is, depreciated only by minds who stand in need of it. To know what we think, to be masters of our own meaning, will make a solid foundation for great and weighty thought. . . . It is terrible to see how a single unclear idea, a single formula without meaning, lurking in a young man's head, will sometimes act like an obstruction of inert matter in an artery, hindering the nutrition of the brain, and condemning its victim to pine away in the fullness of his intellectual vigor and in the midst of intellectual plenty. (*HMIC*, 251–252)

Peirce distinguishes three grades of clearness in ideas. We may first "have such an acquaintance with the idea as to have become familiar with it, and to have lost all hesitancy in recognizing it in ordinary cases" (*HMIC*, 252). If we can identify samples of quartz, for example, from among a variety of stones presented to us, then "quartz" is clear to us to this first degree. A second grade of clearness is provided by a verbal definition, such as one finds in a dictionary and could memorize (or write down in an exam, perhaps). But to attain the third grade of clearness we must follow this rule:

Consider what effects that might conceivably have practical bearings, we conceive the object of our conception to have. Then, our conception of these effects is the whole of our conception of the object. (*HMIC*, 258)

Let us examine this rule carefully. The first thing to note is that the meaning of an intellectual concept is always something that itself has meaning. Meanings are not things; they are not brute facts; they are not sensations or actions. You do not learn what "hard" means by knocking yourself on the head with a rock. Or, if you do, then the meaning of "hard" is still not the rock; nor is it the sensation you felt when you were struck. The word "hard" is a *sign*, and its meaning must be another sign. (We will examine the nature of signs in a moment.)

Next, consider the idea of "effects, which might conceivably have practical bearings." If we ask what "hard" means, we are asking for a conception that can apply to objects that are hard; we are asking what effects these objects have that we can notice, that is, have some impact on us—for instance, that they will not be scratched by many other substances.

Finally, note that Peirce holds that the whole of our conception of these effects is the whole of the conception we are trying to clarify. There is nothing in our conception of "hard" beyond our conception of these effects. Peirce offers a procedure for identifying these effects:

> Proceed according to such and such a general rule. Then, if such and such a concept is applicable to such and such an object, the operation will have such and such a general result; and conversely. (*SP*, 331)

This is a formula for what is sometimes called **operational definition.** Note that applications of this procedure will always have two parts: There will be an operation performed and a result observed. Let us see how it might work in the case of "hard." We can define "*x* is hard" in this way:

- If you apply a knife edge to *x*, you will not cut it.
- If you throw *x* forcefully at a window, the window will (probably) break.
- If you press your hand on *x*, *x* will resist the pressure of your hand.

Note that in each case the structure is the same; an operation is specified, and a result is observed. Some action is performed and in consequence we have an experience of some kind. Note also that an indefinite number of such tests can be made, and all of them together make up the meaning of the concept "hard."

By employing such operational definitions, we can attain the third grade of clearness in ideas. With such clarity we can not only apply the concept to familiar examples or give a verbal definition, but also clear away the fogginess that so often seems to surround our ideas. We sometimes hear that we know how gravity *works*—that is, we know its laws—but we don't know what it *is*. The same is sometimes said of force—that we understand its effects, but not what it *is*. But if Peirce is right about the structure of clear ideas, this is just confusion. Once you know the laws of gravity and the equations of force, once you can predict the results of certain operations correctly so that

your experience confirms your predictions, you *do know* what gravity and force are; for there is nothing more in your ideas of them than these effects, which you admit you are clear about. What else could you possibly mean?

> The idea which the word force excites in our minds has no other function than to affect our actions, and these actions can have no reference to force otherwise than through its effects. Consequently, if we know what the effects of force are, we are acquainted with every fact which is implied in saying that a force exists, and there is nothing more to know. (*HMIC*, 265)

We have already seen operational definitions at work, clarifying our ideas of belief and doubt, truth and reality. Let's review. In what does your *belief* that the earth is round consist? The answer is given in terms of operation and result: If you are offered a trip around the world, you will not say, "What? Are you crazy?" What does it mean to *doubt* whether a certain food is spoiled? If it is offered to you, you will be uncertain whether to eat it. What is it for a belief to be *true*? If the community were to inquire sufficiently long about it, there would come a point where the belief would stabilize. What do we mean when we claim that something is *real*? That inquiry concerning it would survive all possible tests. In each case, Peirce has been striving all along for that third grade of clearness, and in each case he applies that hypothetical structure of operation and result. In each case, the operations are such as any member of the community might (in principle) perform, and the results are public in the sense that anyone might observe them. There might, of course, be private associations or feelings associated with these terms—especially with "truth" and "reality"—but these are not part of the meaning of the terms. Language, after all, is a social convention we learn as children and teach others. Were its meanings not founded in something public and common, neither the learning nor the teaching of language would be explicable.

We should note one other consequence of Peirce's discussion of meaning. Consider two beliefs that seem to be different; perhaps they just have a different feel to them or are expressed in different words. Are they really different? If the practical consequences of the two are not different, "then no mere differences in the manner of consciousness of them can make them different beliefs, any more than playing a tune in different keys is playing different tunes" (*HMIC*, 255). William James was later to put this point in terms of a slogan:

Every difference must make a difference.

If there is no difference in practical effects, then there is no difference in meaning. Peirce draws out the radical consequence of this principle:

It will serve to show that almost every proposition of ontological metaphysics is either meaningless gibberish—one word being defined by other words, and they by still others, without any real conception ever being reached—or else is downright absurd; so that all such rubbish being swept away, what will remain of philosophy will be a series of problems capable of investigation by the observational methods of the true sciences. (*WPI*, 282)

This seems to be an announcement of the end of philosophy, its true work being taken over by the empirical sciences. Indeed, some twentieth-century thinkers draw just that conclusion from similar premises about meaning.* Peirce himself, however, goes on to argue for a metaphysics of absolute idealism in which mind is the fundamental fact in reality. Because he thinks this conclusion can be warranted on the basis of methods continuous with those of the sciences, he believes that his metaphysics conforms to this radical principle.

Signs

A consideration of some elements of Peirce's doctrine of signs will bring us full circle. The entities that have meaning Peirce calls **"signs."** Here again Peirce is extremely original. His discussion is very complex and never systematically worked out. We concentrate on several central features.

Peirce gives the term "sign" (as he does "habit") a very wide sense. He means to include the simplest cases of communication in the animal world as well as the most sophisticated language of science. He

believes there is one property that is common to all signs and that differentiates them from anything not a sign. All signs have a certain *triadic structure*: A *sign* stands for an *object* to an *interpretant*.* Being a sign, then, requires all three of these elements. We do, of course, sometimes just say that "*a* means *b*," but Peirce holds this is an incomplete formulation; if it is spelled out in full, we must say that "*a* means *b* to *c*."

It is from this triadic structure that modern linguistics and philosophy of language has grown. We may consider language simply as a set of markers or tokens and investigate the permissible relations among them; such an investigation of rules relating signs to each other is called **syntax.** Second, we may pay attention to the relation between words and what they are about—that is, what they stand for: the "word–world" relation. When we do this, we are considering the **semantics** of language. Finally, we may think about the way signs affect their users and hearers, and this is known as **pragmatics.**

Let us think for a moment of the semantic aspect of signs. Peirce notes three different ways that a sign can be related to its object. (1) The significance of the sign may depend on an actually existing *causal relation* between it and what it signifies. Thus does Robinson Crusoe infer that he is not alone on his island, for footprints in the sand *mean* another person. Signs that work in this way Peirce calls **indexes.** A weather vane, for example, is an index of the direction of the wind. (2) Some signs work because they *resemble* their object. Peirce calls these **icons.** The face in the rock at the Delaware Water Gap is an icon of an Indian. Photographs, as you should be able to see, are both indexes and icons. (3) Some signs are related to their objects in purely *conventional* or *arbitrary* ways. Peirce calls such signs **symbols.** Most words in human languages are like

---

*We would normally speak here of an "interpreter," thinking primarily, no doubt, of a human who understands the sign. Peirce uses this odd term "interpretant" because he wants to be able to say that there are a variety of ways in which the meaning of a sign can be apprehended, interpretation by a human mind being only one. The behavior of bees in response to a bee dance indicating the direction of nectar (they fly in a certain direction) is, in his terms, an interpretant of the dance. But it would be strange to think of the flight of bees as an "interpreter" of the dance.

---

*Compare the logical positivists, pp. 634–635.

this. There is no natural relation between the color red and the word "red"—or, for that matter, "rojo" or "rouge." These words stand for red things, rather than for square or heavy things, because a custom or convention of using them in that way has grown up.*

But they stand for red things only *to* some interpretant. Without an interpretant, a sign is just a brute fact; nothing, in short, is a sign unless it is used as a sign. What kinds of interpretants can there be? Peirce distinguishes three important kinds. (1) There are *emotional interpretants* for signs. Some words, for instance, produce a lot of feeling when heard or uttered ("freedom," for example), others very little. But the feeling itself is not just a brute fact; it has itself the nature of a sign; it is itself significant. A feeling of pride on observing the flag refers to one's nation just as surely as does the flag itself. (2) There are also *energetic interpretants*. Peirce gives the example of a drill sergeant's order, "Ground arms!" One interpretant of this command is the actual movement by the troops as they lower their muskets to the ground. But by far the most important kind of interpretant is (3) the *logical*. And we need to examine this in more detail.

The first thing to be noted about a logical interpretant is that it is itself a sign. In fact, it is a sign that has the same meaning as the sign it interprets. A dictionary definition might be a good example: "vixen" is defined as "female fox." The latter is the interpretant, and you can see it is about the same class of objects as the former. But, Peirce says, such an interpretant cannot be the final or *ultimate* interpretant; because it is itself a sign, it calls for further interpretants of the same kind. And those interpretants require still others, and so on. Can this potential regress be brought to a halt?†

There is an ultimate interpretant, Peirce says. It is a *habit*. Though Peirce's discussion of these matters is somewhat obscure, we can understand his point in this way. One understands a word best when one goes beyond the first and second grades of clearness to the third.*That third grade of clearness, you recall, is given by a set of "if–then" sentences that specify a series of operations together with the results experienced in consequence of performing them. For example, "*x* is hard" means "if you try to cut *x* with a knife, you will fail," and so on. A habit or disposition is itself precisely such a set of "if–thens." So having the *third grade of clearness* with respect to a concept is having a *habit with respect to the word* that expresses the concept. For example, if you understand "hard," then your behavior is such that *if* you want something you can cut with a knife, *then* you will select a stick rather than a stone to practice whittling.

> Consequently, the most perfect account of a concept that words can convey will consist in a description of the habit which that concept is calculated to produce. But how otherwise can a habit be described than by a description of the kind of action to which it gives rise, with the specification of the conditions and of the motive? (*SP*, 342)

We saw earlier that belief has the nature of a habit; we now see that coming to master the meaning of a word is itself a matter of attaining a habit. So the meaning of an intellectual concept is given by a logical interpretant, and each logical interpretant is subject to further interpretations until anchored finally in a habit of behavior. Two things follow: (1) A linguistic or conceptual sign can function *as a sign* only in the context of an entire working system of signs; nothing can be a sign in isolation; all by itself, a word has *no meaning*. This view is often called **"holism."** (2) Our entire intellectual life is tied to matters of behavior and experience, to action, and to the quest to establish habits (concepts and beliefs) that will serve us well. To this end, we modify the concepts and beliefs we begin with (and cannot help having), hoping to attain intellectual concepts that will prove ever more adequate to living in our community and in

---

*This is a point Zhuangzi made long before Peirce. (See p. 86.) So did Locke (p. 420), though unlike Locke, Peirce denies that such general terms stand for *ideas* in the mind— unless, of course, they are terms *for* such ideas.

†You should be reminded here of Descartes' second rule, which prescribes analysis into simples that are clear and distinct ideas requiring no further analysis (p. 362). And Hume, worried about the same problem, traces ideas back to their origin in sensations. Both are ways to halt the regress of meaning-giving. Peirce's way to halt this regress is distinctively different.

---

*See p. 602.

the world. As we have seen, Peirce recommends the methods of science as the way to attain more adequate habits—to "fix" our beliefs. And with this thought we have come full circle.

---

1. Contrast intellectual concepts with what Peirce calls mere subjective feelings. Could you be experiencing something different from what I am experiencing when we both look at lush grass? Would that matter? Could we find out?
2. What is Peirce's rule for attaining the "third grade of clearness" about our ideas?
3. What does James' slogan "Every difference must make a difference" mean?
4. Contrast Peirce's theory of meaning with that of Hume.
5. Distinguish syntax, semantics, and pragmatics.
6. Distinguish various kinds of signs. Of what sort is most of language composed?

John Dewey

John Dewey was born in the year that Darwin published *On the Origin of Species by Means of Natural Selection*. He took seriously Darwin's incorporation of human life into nature and tried to work out its consequences for epistemology, metaphysics, and ethics. He lived a long life, from 1859 to 1952, and wrote voluminously on social, educational, and political matters, as well as on these more traditional philosophical topics. He was born in Vermont on the eve of the Civil War and lived through the time of tremendous industrial growth in America, the expansion westward, and both world wars. He lived through the revolution in physics that we associate with Einstein and contributed to theories that made scientific methods applicable also in sociology and psychology. He said of himself that the forces that influenced him and stimulated him to think came not from books, but "from persons and from situations" (*FAE*, 13).[4] He is one of the classic sources of pragmatic ideas in philosophy.

THE IMPACT OF DARWIN

We are scarcely able to canvas everything Dewey contributed, even to pragmatic philosophy. But an examination of his *naturalism* in epistemology and metaphysics, together with his *theory of value*, will supplement our discussion of Peirce and give a good overview of the leading pragmatic themes. A 1909 lecture, "The Influence of Darwinism on Philosophy," sets the stage:

> That the publication of the "Origin of Species" marked an epoch in the development of the natural sciences is well known to the layman. That the combination of the very words origin and species embodied an intellectual revolt and introduced a new intellectual temper is easily overlooked by the expert. The conceptions that had reigned in the philosophy of nature and knowledge for two thousand years, the conceptions that had become the familiar furniture of the mind, rested on the assumption of the superiority of the fixed and final; they rested upon treating change and origin as signs of defect and unreality. In laying hands upon the sacred ark of absolute permanency, in treating the forms that had been regarded as types of fixity and perfection as originating and passing away, the "Origin of Species" introduced a mode of thinking that in the end was bound to transform the logic of knowledge, and hence the treatment of morals, politics, and religion. (*IDP*, 3)

The ancient Greeks assume that to really know something, one has to grasp its essence, its form (*eidos*).* Scholastic philosophy in the Middle Ages, sharing this assumption, translates *eidos* as "species." The cardinal principle is that species (forms) are fixed, an assumption that would shape philosophy, science, ethics, and theology for two thousand years.

> The influence of Darwin upon philosophy resides in his having conquered the phenomena of life for the principle of transition, and thereby freed the new

---

*This is clearest in the work of Plato (see "Knowledge and Opinion," in Chapter 8); for him, knowledge has to be certain and its objects eternal and unchanging: the Forms. For Aristotle, form is always embedded in concrete substances, but he is no less insistent than his teacher Plato that the object of knowledge is always the form of a thing, and, as we have noted before, the dominant form is the one toward which a substance develops: its final cause. The final cause of all things, for Aristotle, is that pure actuality he calls the *unmoved mover*, or God.

logic for application to mind and morals and life. When he said of species what Galileo had said of the earth, *e pur se muove* [and yet it moves], he emancipated, once for all, genetic and experimental ideas as an organon of asking questions and looking for explanations. (*IDP*, 8)

The new philosophy inspired by Darwin's work

forswears inquiry after absolute origins and absolute finalities in order to explore specific values and the specific conditions that generate them. . . . Interest shifts from the wholesale essence back of special changes to the question of how special changes serve and defeat concrete purposes. . . . To idealize and rationalize the universe at large is after all a confession of inability to master the courses of things that specifically concern us. As long as mankind suffered from this impotency, it naturally shifted a burden of responsibility that it could not carry over to the more competent shoulders of the transcendent cause. But if insight into specific conditions of value and into specific consequences of ideas is possible, philosophy must in time become a method of locating and interpreting the more serious of the conflicts that occur in life, and a method of projecting ways for dealing with them: a method of moral and political diagnosis and prognosis. (*IDP*, 10–13)

Dewey sees the result of Darwin's evolutionary theory as the prospect of applying scientific, experimental methods to all the pressing, practical human problems. This can't happen overnight, he acknowledges; but he does see it happening and devotes himself to helping the process along.

Old ideas give way slowly; for they are more than abstract logical forms and categories. They are habits, predispositions, deeply engrained attitudes of aversion and preference. Moreover, the conviction persists—though history shows it to be a hallucination—that all the questions that the human mind has asked are questions that can be answered in terms of the alternatives that the questions themselves present. But in fact intellectual progress usually occurs through sheer abandonment of questions together with both of the alternatives they assume—an abandonment that results from their decreasing vitality and a change of urgent interest. We do not solve them: we get over them. Old questions are solved by disappearing, evaporating, while new questions corresponding to the changed

"At the best, all our endeavors look to the future and never attain certainty."

—JOHN DEWEY

attitude of endeavor and preference take their place. (*IDP*, 14)

We have not solved all the old problems of philosophy, but that's all right. Those are problems, Dewey says, that we should just "get over." When we see how the "new methods" of the latest scientific revolution can be applied to the practical problems we already face, the old problems will simply "evaporate."

Dewey thus sets himself against any philosophy that would pose an impassable gulf between knowers and what is known, between subject and object, self and nonself, experience and nature, action and the good.* Human beings are to be understood as embedded without residue in the flux of natural processes—indeed, as a product of such

---

*This theme Dewey adapts from Hegel; see p. 498.

processes. The vaunted cognitive abilities of the human species, including its capacity for sophisticated science, are to be understood as abilities developed through the evolutionary process. This view is often called **naturalism,** and John Dewey is one of its most vigorous exponents.

An epistemological corollary of this naturalistic vision in metaphysics is *giving up the quest for certainty.* All our knowledge is understood to be revisable in the light of future experience. What we know depends as much on our interests and capacities as it does on the objects of knowledge; if our interests shift, so will our concepts, and with them the "world" of our experience.

The same is true of our *values,* Dewey believes. Here, too, no certainty is possible, but it does not follow that all values are on a par or that whatever an individual happens to like is valuable. Dewey believes that some views about value are superior to others and that we can improve our opinions about morals and values. The situation here is parallel to that in the sciences. Let us explore these matters in more detail.

Naturalized Epistemology

Like Peirce, Dewey thinks of intelligence or inquiry as a matter of problem solving.

> The function of reflective thought is to transform a situation in which there is experienced obscurity, doubt, conflict, disturbance of some sort, into a situation that is clear, coherent, settled, harmonious. (*HWT,* 100–101)

This is the process: We face a difficulty or perplexity; we take stock of the situation (the facts of the case); we imagine possible courses of action. This leads us to reflect on the facts; we may then consider other possibilities for action and then investigate the situation further. This interaction between the discovered facts and suggested solutions goes on until we find what moves us toward a more satisfactory state.

> Suppose you are walking where there is no regular path. As long as everything goes smoothly, you do not have to think about your walking; your already formed habit takes care of it. Suddenly you find a ditch in your way. You think you will jump it

(supposition, plan); but to make sure, you survey it with your eyes (observation), and you find that it is pretty wide and that the bank on the other side is slippery (facts, data). You then wonder if the ditch may not be narrower somewhere else (idea), and you look up and down the stream (observation) to see how matters stand (test of idea by observation). You do not find any good place and so are thrown back upon forming a new plan. As you are casting about, you discover a log (fact again). You ask yourself whether you could not haul that to the ditch and get it across the ditch to use as a bridge (idea again). You judge that idea is worth trying, and so you get the log and manage to put it in place and walk across (test and confirmation by overt action). . . .

> The two limits of every unit of thinking are a perplexed, troubled, or confused situation at the beginning and a cleared up, unified, resolved situation at the close. (*HWT,* 105–107)

Dewey means this example to represent the pattern of *all* our intellectual endeavors. Three points are particularly important. First, human knowers are not passive spectators of the world they come to know, as traditional theories of knowledge maintain. Knowers are involved participants in the world. Dewey rejects the key idea in the representational theory of knowledge (p. 372): that we have direct access only to the world of our own mental states. His own theory, by setting human beings firmly within the natural world, claims to avoid many of the traditional problems of epistemology.* Second, he also rejects the rule that we should "not frame hypotheses."† The mind "leaps forward" to possible solutions. Such leaps should be encouraged, not condemned. Third, what is crucial is not whether a proposition represents a leap beyond present evidence, but whether it stands up

---

*The solipsism and skepticism that haunt Descartes and Hume, for instance, simply cannot arise in this view; they *begin* with the possibility that *my* experience might be all there is and face the problem of justifying belief in anything else. For Dewey, this is not a real possibility because we are in *constant interaction* with the world around us from the very start. Compare this to the Vaiśeṣika idea that our multiple interactions with the world imply the reality of external objects (p. 47).

†For the role of this thought in the views of Newton and David Hume, see pp. 439–443.

WILLIAM JAMES

Often called America's greatest psychologist, William James (1842–1910) was also a distinguished contributor to pragmatist philosophy. In addition to the classic *Principles of Psychology* (1890), James is noted for *The Will to Believe* (1896), *The Varieties of Religious Experience* (1902), *Pragmatism* (1907), and *The Meaning of Truth* (1909).

Like the other pragmatists, James stressed the connection between our beliefs and our practical life. But more than the others, he emphasized the practical consequences of actually believing one thing or another. Because our beliefs are shaped as much by our needs and interests as by the world, we are justified in taking those needs and interests into account when deciding what to believe. With respect to our conception of reality as a whole, James held that the crucial question is this: Does our conception give us cause to hope or cause to despair?

The great philosophical systems, James believed, are in part a reflection of the temperaments of those who devised them, and in this light he sorted philosophies into the *tender-minded* (rationalistic, idealistic, optimistic, religious, and free-willist) and the *tough-minded* (empiricist, materialist, pessimistic, irreligious, and fatalistic). James viewed pragmatism as a middle way between these extremes.

The key to pragmatism, James said, is a revised notion of truth as a human thing; to an unascertainable degree, our truths are a product of our interests. A belief is true when it works for us—not just here and now, but overall and in the long run. The true is just the useful in the way of ideas. In cases where the evidence does not clearly decide the issue (and he thought nearly all the large questions of philosophy are like that), we are within our rights to believe what will make for a more satisfying life. The question of fatalism is such a case. We are justified in believing that the universe is open to new possibilities of improvement, not a closed system where each future event is already determined by the ancient past, because this belief will have better consequences in our lives than the other.

Nor is there any reason, according to James, why religious faith should be rationally forbidden. If belief in God works to make life more satisfying—offering hope rather than despair—then it is true. And James thought it does work that way.

---

to future tests by experience and action. A good hypothesis is one that *works*.*

There is an intimate connection between this way of conceiving human knowledge and the futility of a **quest for certainty.** If the correctness of our beliefs lies open to future tests, to possible correction by future experience (mediated by actions we have not yet taken), then any claim to certainty *now* must be unjustified. Even the most firmly grounded beliefs of science and common sense may need to be modified as human experience grows more extensive and complex.†

---

*Compare this to Émilie du Châtelet's endorsement of framing hypotheses (pp. 440–441).

†You can see that Dewey, like Hegel, takes time seriously. Not only our beliefs but also our methods, concepts, and logical tools are part of history. But unlike Hegel, he does not envision a stage in which the progression comes to completion; there is no such thing as *absolute knowledge*

"Certitude is not the test of certainty."
Oliver Wendell Holmes Jr. (1841–1935)

Dewey carries on a constant dialectical debate with traditional philosophy and especially with empiricism. Like William James, he believes that pragmatism is a middle way between the extremes of empiricism and rationalism, incorporating what is best in both. The main problem with these traditional rivals, he believes, is that each operates with an impoverished notion of experience.

(i) In the orthodox view, experience is regarded primarily as a knowledge-affair. But to eyes not looking

---

for Dewey. In this regard, he resembles Kierkegaard more than Hegel (though he would not have liked Kierkegaard's supernatural religion or the emphasis on nonrational choice). Compare pp. 534–536.

through ancient spectacles, it assuredly appears as an affair of the intercourse of a living being with its physical and social environment. (ii) According to tradition experience is (at least primarily) a psychical thing, infected throughout by "subjectivity." What experience suggests about itself is a genuinely objective world which enters into the actions and sufferings of men and undergoes modifications through their responses. (iii) So far as anything beyond a bare present is recognized by the established doctrine, the past exclusively counts. Registration of what has taken place, reference to precedent, is believed to be the essence of experience. Empiricism is conceived of as tied up to what has been, or is, "given." But experience in its vital form is experimental, an effort to change the given; it is characterized by projection, by reaching forward into the unknown; connection with a future as its salient trait. (iv) The empirical tradition is committed to particularism. Connections and continuities are supposed to be foreign to experience, to be by-products of dubious validity. An experience that is an undergoing of an environment and a striving for its control in new directions is pregnant with connections. (v) In the traditional notion experience and thought are antithetical terms. Inference, so far as it is other than a revival of what has been given in the past, goes beyond experience; hence it is either invalid, or else a measure of desperation by which, using experience as a springboard, we jump out to a world of stable things and other selves. But experience, taken free of the restrictions imposed by the older concept, is full of inference. There is, apparently, no conscious experience without inference; reflection is native and constant. (*NRP*, 23)

Important points are made here. Let us review them in order.

- Point (i) denies that the knower is a disinterested spectator.
- Point (ii) rejects any notion of experience that would locate it exclusively in a subject.
- Point (iii) captures the inherent purposiveness of experience, the fact that it is always oriented toward the future.*

- Point (iv) attacks the Humean notion that experience presents all events as "loose and separate."*
- Point (v) notes that conceiving of reason as a faculty for making inferences distinct from experience restricts experience to a purely subjective realm. This leaves us unable to escape skepticism if we base our knowledge on experience. But if we characterize experience adequately, we recognize it as a matter of interactions between an organism and its environment; it is "full of inference" and presents itself in intimate contact with the objective world. All experience is already involved in the world.

Once we grasp these points, many of the traditional problems of philosophy (such as the problem of the "reality" of the "external" world) simply "evaporate"; we "get over" them.

NATURE AND NATURAL SCIENCE

Experience, then, is an affair of nature because human beings are wholly natural creatures. But what is nature? Dewey resists the imperialism, so to speak, of sciences that claim a unique title to reveal the essence of nature. Galileo and Descartes agree that (material) reality is what mathematical physics can tell us about, and Hobbes tries to extend that claim to human nature. The result seems to Dewey an unpalatable dichotomy: Either human experience is not a part of the world of nature at all (as in Descartes' dualism) or Hobbesian materialism reigns. But neither seems able to do justice to all we value and hold dear. If we identify science with the *physical* sciences (as traditionally understood), we cut ourselves off from the uses of intelligence in the more human spheres.

But what counts as intelligent intervention, Dewey holds, is a matter of *method*. And a method is legitimate if it succeeds in transforming confused situations into clear ones in *any* sphere.

> The result of one operation will be as good and true an object of knowledge as any other, provided it is good at all: provided, that is, it satisfies the conditions which induced the inquiry. . . . One might even go as far as to say that there are as many kinds

---

*Contrast Hume's rule about ideas: To discover whether a purported idea is a genuine one, trace it *back* to an impression. Here experience is assumed to be *given* whole and complete at any moment, and "the past exclusively counts." Compare Peirce, pp. 601–604.

*See p. 450.

of valid knowledge as there are conclusions wherein distinctive operations have been employed to solve the problems set by antecedently experienced situations. . . .

There is no kind of inquiry which has a monopoly of the honorable title of knowledge. (*QC*, 197, 220)

Intelligence can be applied in any field that is a matter of human concern.

In fact the painter may know colors as well as the meteorologist; the statesman, educator and dramatist may know human nature as truly as the professional psychologist; the farmer may know soils and plants as truly as the botanist and mineralogist. For the criterion of knowledge lies in the method used to secure consequences and not in metaphysical conceptions of the nature of the real. . . .

That "knowledge" has many meanings follows from the operational definition of conceptions. There are as many conceptions of knowledge as there are distinctive operations by which problematic situations are resolved. (*QC*, 221)

If we add one more ingredient, we will be ready to see why Dewey thinks that intelligence can be as effective in the realms of value and morality as it is in science. That ingredient is his **instrumentalism.** Because the basic cognitive situation is the problem situation, and because hypotheses are created to resolve such situations satisfactorily, the concepts involved in hypotheses are necessarily relative to our concerns and interests. Without interests and concerns there would be no problems! Ideas, concepts, and terms, then, are intellectual *tools* we use as long as they serve our purposes and discard when they no longer do. They are *instruments* for solving problems.

Physicists and chemists create concepts that serve the purposes of these sciences: explanation, prediction, and control. But these concepts, too, are merely instruments serving certain purposes; there is nothing prior or more basic about them that should cast a disparaging shadow on concepts serving other purposes. Dewey believes that many philosophers have been misled in thinking that modern physics alone reveals the true nature of reality. Making that assumption seems to shunt the qualities manifest in experience (all those

"secondary qualities," whose loss was mourned by John Donne) off the main line onto a siding. But, Dewey says, that is to mistake the purport of scientific knowledge.

True, physical science treats the world as just a sequence of *events* in certain relations to each other. But we needn't conclude that the world *really* is just such a sequence of events, bare of every quality we prize and delight in. Scientific concepts, like all concepts, are merely tools we use to satisfy certain interests. But the interests served by physical science are not all the interests we have; they are not even our primary interests. In fact, treating nature as physics does (in terms of events and relations between events) serves larger purposes: our interest in controlling change, "so that it may terminate in the occurrence of an object having desired qualities" (*QC*, 105). The concepts of science owe their very being to *values* we have.

"Event" is a concept about as bare and stripped of all that is precious to us as we can find. Yet it applies to everything that happens. Even tables and chairs can be considered extended, slowly unfolding events. But as we experience them, they are not "bare" events, but *events with meanings*. Consider, Dewey suggests, a piece of paper. We call it "a piece of paper," when we are interested in it in a certain way—as something to write on, perhaps, or something to wrap the fish in. But if we consider it in terms of an event (a kind of extended happening), it is clear that it

has as many other explicit meanings as it has important consequences recognized in the various connective interactions into which it enters. Since the possibilities of conjunction are endless, and since the consequences of any of them may at some time be significant, its potential meanings are endless. It signifies something to start a fire with; something like snow; made of wood-pulp; manufactured for profit; property in the legal sense; a definite combination illustrative of certain principles of chemical science; an article the invention of which has made a tremendous difference in human history, and so on indefinitely. There is no conceivable universe of disclosure in which the thing may not figure, having in each its own characteristic meaning. And if we say that after all it is "paper" which has all these different meanings, we are at bottom but asserting that . . . paper is its ordinary meaning for human intercourse. (*EN*, 7)

Suppose we insist on asking, But what is it *really*? Is it really wood pulp? Or a white surface for writing on? Or atoms and the void? What would Dewey say? He would tell us that we were asking a question to which there is no answer. It is all of these things—and more—because the applicability of any of these concepts merely reflects certain purposes and interests. No one of them can be singled out as the *essence* of the event.

We can see that for Dewey there is no sharp line demarcating science from common sense. Both are ways of dealing with recalcitrant situations; science and common sense are different because they serve different purposes, but they are alike in using concepts as *tools* for the realization of those purposes. The same is true of philosophy. Dewey proposes

> a first-rate test of the value of any philosophy which is offered us: Does it end in conclusions which, when they are referred back to ordinary life-experiences and their predicaments, render them more significant, more luminous to us, and make our dealings with them more fruitful? Or does it terminate in rendering the things of ordinary experience more opaque than they were before, and in depriving them of having in "reality" even the significance they had previously seemed to have? (*EN*, 319–320)

---

1. What, according to Dewey, is the significance of Darwin for philosophy?
2. What is naturalism? Should we be naturalists? Are you one?
3. What are the stages in problem solving?
4. Why must we give up the quest for certainty?
5. What are Dewey's criticisms of empiricism? Of spectator theories of knowledge?
6. What is instrumentalism?
7. In what way are tables and chairs events with meanings? Is there one meaning, or are there more?

VALUE NATURALIZED

Let us apply this criterion to Dewey's own philosophy by looking at what he has to say about values.

He notes that the modern problem about values arises with the expulsion of ends and final causes from nature, which takes place with the rise of modern science.

> For centuries, until, say, the sixteenth and seventeenth centuries, nature was supposed to be what it was because of the presence within it of *ends*. . . . All natural changes were believed to be striving to actualize these ends as the goals toward which they moved by their own nature. Classical philosophy identified *ens* [being], *verum* [truth], and *bonum* [goodness], and the identification was taken to be an expression of the constitution of nature as the object of natural science. In such a context there was no call and no place for any *separate* problem of valuation and values, since what are now termed values were taken to be integrally incorporated in the very structure of the world. But when teleological considerations were eliminated from one natural science after another, and finally from the sciences of physiology and biology, the problem of value arose as a separate problem. (*TV*, 2–3)

Our earlier discussions of Hildegard, Dante, and the consequences of Galilean science fit this analysis.* The problem of how to understand values in a world of sheer fact is acute. As Dewey sees it, there are two tendencies in modern thought that accept the value-neutral character of nature. On the one hand, value is thought to originate in something above or beyond nature: in God, perhaps, or in pure reason, as Kant claims. On the other hand, value is identified with purely subjective satisfactions, such as pleasure.

Neither of these alternatives is attractive to Dewey, who wants to account for values in a wholly *naturalistic* way, but without identifying goodness with the arbitrary preference of an individual. What he wants is a way of treating values parallel to the way a scientist treats hypotheses—a way that will make *progress* in valuations possible but without claiming *certainty* at any point.

> The problem of restoring integration and cooperation between man's beliefs about the world in which he lives and his beliefs about the values and purposes that should direct his conduct is the deepest problem of modern life. (*QC*, 255)

---

*See Chapter 16.

It is this "integration and cooperation" between facts and values that is disturbed by the rise of modern science in the sixteenth and seventeenth centuries.* Dewey thinks a pragmatic approach can best restore such integration and solve this "deepest problem." The key idea is this:

> Escape from the defects of transcendental absolutism is not to be had by setting up as values enjoyments that happen anyhow, but in defining value by enjoyments which are the consequences of intelligent action. Without the intervention of thought, enjoyments are not values but problematic goods, becoming values when they re-issue in a changed form from intelligent behavior. (*QC*, 259)

Let us explore this idea. Like Peirce, who holds that we must begin reflection with the beliefs we already have, Dewey thinks we all cannot help but begin with certain values. We do so simply by virtue of the fact that there are things we *like* or *prize*. Some of these likings may be biologically determined, some culturally produced. But wherever they come from, we always have such likings, desirings, and prizings. In accord with his general theory of experience, Dewey denies that these are purely subjective states. To *like* something is to have a certain disposition to behavior; if you like chocolate ice cream, you have tendencies to choose it when buying ice cream, to eat it when it is served to you, and so on. Liking is a matter of interactions between an organism and its environment; it is a transactional matter. To like *X* is to be disposed to try to get it; or, if we already have *X*, liking it is a matter of attempts to preserve, keep, or protect it.

Now, given that we all have such likings, do they constitute values? In one sense they do, Dewey says, but in another sense not. They do represent what we antecedently or *immediately* value (to use a word of Hegel's); but it would be a big mistake to identify these values with values per se. And the reason is that there is a big difference between what we find **satisfying** and that which is **satisfactory,** between what we *desire* and what is *desirable,* between those things we *think good* and the things that *are good.* Dewey is here trying to do justice to

the fairly common experience of wanting a certain thing, getting it, and discovering (once we have it) that it does not live up to expectations.

What makes the difference between the satisfying and the satisfactory is the intervention of intelligence.

> The fact that something is desired only raises the *question* of its desirability; it does not settle it. . . . To say that something satisfies is to report something as an isolated finality. To assert that it is *satisfactory* is to define it in its connections and interactions. The fact that it pleases or is immediately congenial poses a problem to judgment. How shall the satisfaction be rated? Is it a value or is it not? Is it something to be prized and cherished, *to be* enjoyed? Not stern moralists alone but everyday experience informs us that finding satisfaction in a thing may be a warning, a summons to be on the lookout for consequences. To declare something *satisfactory* is to assert that it meets specifiable conditions. It is, in effect, a judgment that the thing "will do." (*QC*, 260–261)

The ultimate sources of value, then, are our likings, prizings, esteemings, desirings. If we never liked anything, value would not even be on our horizon. But the things we like are always involved in a network of relations to other things. It might be that if we could just have *Y*, we would be satisfied. But *Y* never comes isolated and alone. It requires *X* as a precondition and brings along *Z* as a consequence. And *X* might require such effort and sacrifice that the luster of *Y* is considerably diminished. And *Z* might be so awful that it disqualifies *Y* as a value altogether. (The use of methamphetamines or opioids might be a good example.) Discovering these relations is the work of inquiry, intelligence, and scientific methods, for causal conditions and consequences are matters of fact. So science and values are not two realms forever separated from each other. Finding what is valuable involves the use of methods similar to those used in the sciences.*

---

*See, for instance, Hume on the gap between fact and value, p. 461.

*Note that in a way, Dewey agrees here with the classical tradition from Socrates through Aquinas that it is *reason* that judges what is good. There are two differences: (1) He understands reason in terms of scientific inquiry; (2) The ultimate "measure" of the good is what we like (after suitable investigation), not a value inherent in things.

It follows, then, that value judgments can be true and false, for they involve a prediction. To say that something is *good* or to urge that an action *ought* to be done is to say that it *will do*—that we will continue to like it in the light of the entire context in which it is embedded. To call something satisfactory is to say not only that it *does*, but that it *will* satisfy, given its causal conditions and consequences. And whether that is so is a matter of fact. What is desirable, then, is what is desired after intelligent inquiry and experience have had their say. So not only can value judgments be true and false, they can also be supported by methods of intelligent inquiry analogous to scientific methods.

Let us consider a typical objection to this way of looking at things. Suppose we allow that intelligence and the methods of science might have bearing on *means* and on *consequences*; we might nonetheless hold that this does not show how these methods can get any grip at all on what is *good in itself*, what is *intrinsically valuable*.* Or we might say that science (sociology or anthropology) can indeed tell us what people do in fact value, but it cannot tell us what is valuable.

What is Dewey's reply? To suppose that there are such things as **ends in themselves** or things that are good no matter what is to make an illegitimate abstraction from the real context in which things are liked and enjoyed. Every end is itself a means to some further end, simply because it is located in time and has consequences. Ends, then, are never absolute; they are what Dewey calls

ends-in-view. We may take a certain state of affairs to be an end, but that is always provisional and subject to revision in the light of further experience. In fact, there is a *continuum* of ends and means, each means being a means in the light of some end and each end a means to some further end. Furthermore, there is a *reciprocity* between ends and means; any actual end is what it is only as the culmination of those specific means that lead to it, and the means are means only as they lead to that particular end.

You simply cannot have ends apart from means, and every means qualifies the end you actually get.* This fact has implications, Dewey believes, for the maxim "the end justifies the means" and also for the popular objection to it. The maxim clearly involves the notion of something which is an end-in-itself, apart from the conditions and consequences of its actual existence. That end is supposed to justify the use of whatever means are necessary to its attainment—no matter how awful they may be. The maxim is plausible, however, only because we wrongly assume that only *that* end will be brought into existence. You always get more than you intend—for better or worse. Thus, the maxim is true in one sense (nothing *could* justify a means except a certain end) but false in another sense (no end in isolation from its context could ever justify terrible means to it, simply because there are no such ends). Dewey says that

> nothing happens which is final in the sense that it is not part of an ongoing stream of events. . . . Every condition that has to be brought into existence in order to serve as means is, *in that connection*, an object of desire and an end-in-view, while the end actually reached is a means to future ends as well as a test of valuations previously made. Since the end attained is a condition of further existential occurrences, it must be appraised as a potential obstacle and potential resource. If the notion of some objects as ends-in-themselves were abandoned, human

---

*This objection is a version of Hume's principle that reason is and can only be the slave of the passions. (See p. 459.) According to this principle, reason can tell you how to get what you want (means), but it cannot tell you what to want (ends). We have already seen, however, that Dewey challenges just this exclusivity of reason and experience; if he is right, there is no experience that is not already interpreted in terms of certain concepts and no reason apart from experience. In a way, this echoes Kant's famous motto about concepts and intuitions (see p. 473), but with this difference: that there are no absolutely a priori concepts; all concepts are instruments invented to serve certain purposes—which themselves are not absolute but develop reciprocally as a result of the application of the methods of intelligence. Again, the closest historical parallel is Hegel (see "Epistemology Internalized," in Chapter 21).

---

*This is a fact that nations are apt to forget in wartime, to their own detriment. And individuals who take it as their end to be, let us say, rich, sometimes discover that in the process they have created themselves as persons they are not happy to be. Means enter into, that is, help determine, the character of the ends you actually get.

beings would for the first time in history be in a position to frame ends-in-view and form desires on the basis of empirically grounded propositions of the temporal relations of events to one another. (*TV*, 43)

It is clear that Dewey has no use for the idea of something good in itself—at least not prior to intelligent reflection. If any pragmatic sense can be made of that notion at all, it will have to be along Peircean lines: that which the intelligent community ultimately comes to agree on as desirable or good.* We have no hotline to either truth or goodness, and certainty has to be given up with respect to values, as well as knowledge. But by inquiring into the conditions and consequences of ends-in-view, we bring our values more and more in line with what we ultimately *would* be satisfied with, if we knew everything there is to know about the facts. If we were to treat our values the same way we treat our scientific beliefs, then

> standards, principles, rules . . . and all tenets and creeds about good and goods, would be recognized to be hypotheses. Instead of being rigidly fixed, they would be treated as intellectual instruments to be tested and confirmed—and altered—through consequences affected by acting upon them. They would lose all pretense of finality—the ulterior source of dogmatism. . . . Any belief as such is tentative, hypothetical; it is not just to be acted upon, but is to be *framed* with reference to its office as a guide to action. Consequently, it should be the last thing in the world to be picked up casually and then clung to rigidly. When it is apprehended as a tool and only a tool, an instrument of direction, the same scrupulous attention will go to its formation as now goes into the making of instruments of precision in technical fields. Men, instead of being proud of accepting and asserting beliefs and "principles" on the ground of loyalty, will be as ashamed of that procedure as they would now be to confess their assent to a scientific theory out of reverence for Newton. (*QC*, 277–278)

This theme, that thought and action are reciprocally dependent on each other, that no knowledge worth the name is without implications for practice, and that no action is irrelevant to the utility of our intellectual tools, may be considered the distinctive and essential theme of pragmatism.

---

1. What is the origin of value? How does Dewey argue that despite this origin, the valuable is not identical to what I happen to like?
2. What is the difference between ends-in-view and absolute ends? How does Dewey think that means and ends should be related?
3. If modern science gives rise to the peculiarly modern problem about values, how does pragmatism claim to resolve that problem? And what role does science itself have in the resolution?

FOR FURTHER THOUGHT

1. Peirce and Dewey both urge fallibilism, giving up the quest for certainty. Imagine that our culture took that advice. What would be the result? Do you think that would be mostly good or mostly bad?
2. Naturalism holds that we human beings are, without remainder, parts of the natural world explored by the sciences—not thinking souls (Plato, Descartes), bundles of perceptions (Hume), noumenal selves (Kant), or the World Spirit on its way to self-realization (Hegel). Why should we think so, in the light of all this philosophical history?

KEY WORDS

Peirce

Darwin	truth
pragmatism	community of inquirers
tenacity	reality
authority	fallibilism
natural preferences	meaning
science	intellectual concept
belief	subjective feelings
doubt	inverted spectrum
habit	operational definition
inquiry	signs
Ockham's razor	syntax

---

*Review what Peirce says about truth, pp. 598–599.

semantics

pragmatics

indexes

icons

symbols

holism

Dewey

naturalism

quest for certainty

instrumentalism

satisfying

satisfactory

ends in themselves

ends-in-view

NOTES

1. References to the works of Charles Sanders Peirce are as follows:

    FB: "The Fixation of Belief"; *HMIC*: "How to Make Our Ideas Clear"; *WPI*: "What Pragmatism Is"; *SCFI*: "Some Consequences of Four Incapacities"; and *SP*: "Survey of Pragmatism," in *Collected Papers of Charles Sanders Peirce*, vol. 5, ed. Charles Hartshorne and Paul Weiss (Cambridge, MA: Harvard College, 1934).

2. Note added by Peirce in 1903 to "The Fixation of Belief," in Hartshorne and Weiss, *Collected Papers*, 232.

3. Epigraph (translated from the German) to W. V. O. Quine's *Word and Object* (New York: John Wiley and Sons, 1960).

4. References to the works of John Dewey are as follows:

    FAE: "From Absolutism to Experimentalism," and *NRP*, "The Need for a Recovery of Philosophy," in *Dewey: On Experience, Nature, and Freedom*, ed. Richard Bernstein (Indianapolis, IN: Bobbs–Merrill, 1960).

    IDP: "The Influence of Darwinism on Philosophy," in *John Dewey: The Middle Works (1899–1924)*, vol. 4, ed. Jo Ann Boydston (Carbondale: Southern Illinois University Press, 1977).

    QC: *The Quest for Certainty: A Study of the Relation of Knowledge and Action* (1929; New York: G. P. Putnam's Sons, Capricorn Books, 1960).

    HWT: *How We Think* (Boston: D. C. Heath, 1933).

    EN: *Experience and Nature* (New York: W. W. Norton, 1929).

    TV: *Theory of Valuation* (Chicago: University of Chicago Press, 1939).

CHAPTER

26

LUDWIG WITTGENSTEIN

Linguistic Analysis and Ordinary Language

One of the major interests in twentieth-century Western philosophy is language. At first glance, this may seem puzzling, but a second look suggests that it is not so surprising. Our scientific theories, our religious and philosophical views, and our commonsense understandings are all expressed in language. Whenever we try to communicate with someone about a matter of any importance, it is language that carries the freight. What if there were something *misleading* about the language in which we think? What if it sets traps for us, catapults us into errors without our even realizing it? Perhaps we ought not to trust it at all.

Actually, this suspicion is a sort of subtext running through modern philosophy, but in the twentieth century this attention to language becomes a major preoccupation of philosophers. The interest in language has been so dominant that some speak of "the linguistic turn" in philosophy.

In this chapter we examine two phases of this interest in language. These two phases are often called *analytic philosophy* and *ordinary language philosophy*. Both are complex movements involving many thinkers, and one could get a taste of these

styles of doing philosophy in a number of ways. We have chosen to focus on one remarkable thinker, Ludwig Wittgenstein (1889–1951), whom many would cite as one of the greatest philosophers of the twentieth century. Surprisingly, he can stand as an emblem for *both* phases because Wittgenstein changes his mind. As we follow his severe critique of his own earlier analytic thought, we can see how attention to language in its *ordinary* employment tends to supplant the earlier attraction of an *ideal* language. Wittgenstein is also interesting because he is not just interested in language; his passionate concern from first to last is, *How shall we live?* But first we need a little background.

Language and Its Logic

To understand analytic philosophy, we need to know at least a bit about modern **logic.** It is a tool of very great power, incredibly magnified in our day by the speed and storage capacities of the digital computer. Every college and university now teaches this "formal," or "symbolic," logic, which was developed in the period near the beginning of the twentieth century by Gottlob Frege, Bertrand Russell, Alfred North Whitehead, and others.

The power of the new logic derives from abstracting completely from the meaning or semantic content of assertions. It is a *formal* logic in just this sense: The rules governing transformations from one symbolic formula to another make reference only to the syntactical structures of the formulas in question and not at all to their meaning. Aristotle's logic of the syllogism, of course, is formal in this same sense.* But the new logic provides a symbolism for the internal structure of sentences that is enormously more powerful than Aristotle's. It can also deal with a more complex set of relations among sentences. For the first time, it really seems plausible that whatever you might want to say can be represented in this formalism. Because this logic abstracts entirely from content, it can be used with equal profit in any field, from operations research to theology. It can show us what follows from certain premises, explain why assertions are inconsistent with each other, and diagnose errors in reasoning. Being formal in this sense, it sets out a kind of logical skeleton that can be fleshed out in any number of ways, while preserving the logical relations precisely.

The prospect opened up by the new logic is that of a language more precise and clear than the language we normally speak—a purified, *ideal language,* in which there is no ambiguity, no vagueness, no dependence on emphasis, intonation, or the many other features of our language that may mislead us. Bertrand Russell expresses the appeal of such a language in this way:

> In a logically perfect language the words in a proposition would correspond one by one with the components of the corresponding fact, with the exception of such words as "or," "not," "if," "then," which have a different function. In a logically perfect language, there will be one word and no more for every simple object, and everything that is not simple will be expressed by a combination of words, by a combination derived, of course, from the words for the simple things that enter in,

one word for each simple component. . . . It is a language which has only syntax and no vocabulary whatever. Barring the omission of a vocabulary, I maintain that it is quite a nice language. It aims at being that sort of a language that, if you add a vocabulary, would be a logically perfect language. Actual languages are not logically perfect in this sense, and they cannot possibly be, if they are to serve the purposes of daily life.[1]

Two complementary ideas make the new logic of particular interest to philosophers. The first is the conviction that natural language, such as ordinary English, does not in fact possess this sort of perfection. The second is that our natural languages tend to lead us astray, especially when we think about philosophical matters.

So the dazzling idea of applying the new logic to traditional philosophical problems takes root in the imagination of many philosophers. Perhaps, if we could formulate these problems using the crystalline purity of these formal logical structures, they could finally—after all these centuries—be definitively solved. The excitement is great. And indeed some very impressive analyses of puzzling uses of language are produced.

As an example, let us consider Russell's "theory of definite descriptions." A *definite description* is a phrase of the form, "the so-and-so." Some sentences containing phrases of this form have a paradoxical character. Consider this sentence: "The golden mountain (that is, a mountain wholly made of pure gold) does not exist." We think this is a true sentence, don't we? You couldn't find a mountain made of gold anywhere. But now ask yourself: How can it be *true* that the golden mountain doesn't exist unless this definite description, "the golden mountain," is *meaningful*? (Meaning is a prerequisite for truth; if a term lacks meaning you don't even know *what it is* that might be true!) And how can that phrase be meaningful unless there is something that it means? And if there *is* something that it means—why, then, there must be a golden mountain after all. So the original sentence seems to be *false,* not true. So it looks as if the sentence, if true, is false. And that's a paradox.

Russell applies the new logic to this puzzle and shows how it can be made to disappear. The

---

*See pp. 188–189. For the distinction between syntax and semantics, see p. 604.

solution goes like this. We go wrong in thinking of the phrase "the golden mountain" as a *name*. It is true that for a name such as "Socrates" to be meaningful, there must be something that it names.* Although definite descriptions *look* like names, they actually have the *logic* of predications. If we can get clear about the logic of such phrases, we will clear up our confusion.

According to Russell, to say "The golden mountain does not exist" is equivalent to saying, "There exists no thing that has both of these properties: being golden and being a mountain." In the language of formal logic, this is expressed as follows: $\sim(\exists x)(Gx \ \& \ Mx)$. In this formula, it is clear that the *G* (for golden) and the *M* (for mountain) are in the predicate position. There are, in fact, no names in it at all—not even the occurrences of the letter *x*, which function as variables ranging over everything. In effect, the formula invites you to consider each and every thing and assures you with respect to it: This is not both golden and a mountain. And that statement is both true and unparadoxical.

So by getting clear about the *logic* of the language in which the puzzle is stated, we get ourselves into a position to understand the sentence in a clear and unpuzzling way. We see that it is just a confusion to think that this language commits us to the existence of a golden mountain. Of great importance, however, is that we also identify the *source* of the confusion—which lies very naturally in the language itself. Phrases such as "the golden mountain" *do* look like names.

---

*You might think at this point, "Whoa—I know that's not true; 'Santa Claus' is a name, but there isn't anything that it names!" But Russell holds that "Santa Claus" is not a true name; it is shorthand for "the fat, jolly, bearded man who flies through the air on a sleigh and brings presents to children at Christmas time." And that is a definite description, subject to the same analysis as "the golden mountain." True names *do* name something. (In some moods, Russell thinks that even "Socrates" is not a true name, but a disguised description; when he is thinking along these lines, he is inclined to say that the only true names are terms such as "this" and "that.")

> "Beware of language, for it is often a great cheat."
> —*Peter Mere Latham (1789–1875)*

This analysis has a great impact on many philosophers, and a sort of cottage industry develops in which bits of language are analyzed in similar fashion, trying to show how we are misled by misreading the logic of our language. The suspicion grows that many of the traditional problems of philosophy have their origin in such misreadings. The prospect opens up that some, at least, of these problems in epistemology, metaphysics, and ethics can be cleared up and perhaps even be made to completely disappear.*

Tractatus Logico-Philosophicus

In 1889 a son was born into the wealthy and talented Wittgenstein family of Vienna. He grew up in an atmosphere of high culture; the most prominent composers, writers, architects, and artists of that great city were regular visitors to his home. His father was an engineer and industrialist, his mother very musical, and Ludwig was talented both mechanically and musically. But it was a troubled family; there were several suicides among his siblings, and he himself seems to have struggled against mental illness most of his life.

Having decided to study engineering, he went first to Berlin and then to Manchester, England, where he did some experiments with kites and worked on the design of an airplane propeller. This work drew his interests toward pure mathematics and eventually to the foundations of mathematics and logic.

---

*Think, for example, of what might happen to Plato's semantic argument for the reality of the Forms (p. 154), if understood in this light. His argument is that terms such as "square" and "equal" do not name anything in the visible world, yet they are meaningful. So they must name something in the intelligible world. But if what Plato takes to be a *name* has the logic of a *predicate*, the whole argument for the Forms on this basis falls to the ground.

BERTRAND RUSSELL

Over a long lifetime (1872–1970), Bertrand Russell wrote on nearly every conceivable topic. His books range from *The Principles of Mathematics* (1903) and *Human Knowledge, Its Scope and Limits* (1948) to *The Conquest of Happiness* (1930) and *Common Sense and Nuclear Warfare* (1959). In 1950 he was awarded a Nobel Prize for literature. A pacifist during World War I, Russell was active in social causes all his life. Three passions, he said, governed his life: a longing for love, the search for knowledge, and unbearable pity for the suffering of mankind.

Though his views changed and developed on some topics, he was consistent in wishing philosophy to become more scientific. As one of the major contributors to the new logic, he held that traditional philosophical problems either are not properly the business of philosophy at all (and should be farmed out to the sciences) or are problems of logic. As a maxim for scientific philosophizing, Russell recommended that logical constructions replace inferences whenever possible.

Consider, for example, our knowledge of the external world; suppose you think you are now seeing a table. What you have directly in your acquaintance is a "sense datum"—some brownish, trapezoidal, visual figure or a tactual feeling of resistance. Common sense (and philosophy, too) characteristically *infers* from such data the existence of a table quite independent of my evidence for it. But such inferences are notoriously unreliable and lead easily to skeptical conclusions.

Russell suggested that your knowledge of the table should rather be *constructed* in terms of logical relations among all the sense data (actual and possible) that, in ordinary speech, we would say are "of" the table. Thus the inference to the table external to your evidence is replaced by a set of relations among the data constituting that evidence—a view known as *phenomenalism*. About those items, skeptical problems do not arise.

In matters of ethics, Russell took a utilitarian line, holding that right actions are those that produce the greatest overall satisfaction. With respect to religion, he was an agnostic. He was once asked what he would say if after his death he found himself confronted with his Maker. He replied that he would say, "God, why did you make the evidence for your existence so insufficient?"

In the fall of 1911 he went to Cambridge to study with Russell, who tells a story about Wittgenstein's first year there.

> At the end of his first term at Cambridge he came to me and said: "Will you please tell me whether I am a complete idiot or not?" I replied, "My dear fellow, I don't know. Why are you asking me?" He said, "Because, if I am a complete idiot, I shall become an aeronaut; but if not, I shall become a philosopher." I told him to write me something during the vacation on some philosophical subject and I would then tell him whether he was a complete idiot or not. At the beginning of the following term he brought me the fulfillment of this suggestion. After reading only one sentence, I said to him: "No, you must not become an aeronaut."[2]

When the war broke out in 1914, Wittgenstein was working on a manuscript that was to become the *Tractatus Logico-Philosophicus*. He served in the Austrian army and spent the better part of a year in an Italian prisoner-of-war camp, where he finished writing this dense, aphoristic little work that deals with everything from logic to happiness. After the war, he gave away the fortune he had inherited from his father, designating part of it for the support of artists and poets. He considered that he had set out in the *Tractatus* the final solution of the problems addressed there and abandoned philosophy to teach school in remote Austrian villages. He lived, at that time and afterward, in severe simplicity and austerity.

His days as a schoolmaster did not last long, however, and for a time he worked as a gardener in a monastery. Then he took the lead in designing and building a mansion in Vienna for one of his sisters. Eventually, through conversations with friends, he came to recognize what he thought

"At some point one has to pass from explanation to mere description."

—Ludwig Wittgenstein

were grave mistakes in the *Tractatus* and to think he might be able to do good work in philosophy again. He was invited back to Cambridge in 1929, where he submitted the *Tractatus*—by then published and widely read—as his dissertation.

He lectured there (except for a time during the Second World War) until shortly before his death in 1951. He published nothing else in his lifetime, though several manuscripts circulated informally. A second major book, *Philosophical Investigations,* was published posthumously in 1953. Since then, many other works have been published from notes and writings he left.

Subsequent developments leave no doubt that Wittgenstein is one of the century's deepest thinkers. He is also one of the most complex and fascinating human beings to have contributed to philosophy since Socrates.[3] Wittgenstein's concerns early in life are fundamentally moral and spiritual; the most important question of all, he believes, is *how to live.* As we'll see, however, he also thinks there is very little one can *say* about that problem. In fact, he thinks getting clear about what one *cannot* say is just

about the most important thing we can do. In the preface to the *Tractatus,* he writes,

> The book deals with the problems of philosophy, and shows, I believe, that the reason why these problems are posed is that the logic of our language is misunderstood. The whole sense of the book might be summed up in the following words: what can be said at all can be said clearly, and what we cannot talk about we must pass over in silence. (*Tractatus,* preface, 3)[4]

Wittgenstein's thought here is a radical one indeed: The *posing* of the problems of philosophy is itself the problem! If we can just get clear about "the logic of our language," these problems will *disappear.* They will be part of "what we cannot talk about." About them we must be silent.*

How will getting clear about the logic of our language produce such a startling result? If we get clear about the logic of our language, Wittgenstein thinks, we will see what the *limits* of language are. We will also see that thinkers violate those limits whenever they pose and try to answer the sorts of problems we call philosophical.

> Thus the aim of the book is to set a limit to thought, or rather—not to thought, but to the expression of thoughts: for in order to be able to set a limit to thought, we should have to find both sides of the limit thinkable (i.e., we should have to be able to think what cannot be thought).
>
> It will therefore only be in language that the limit can be set, and what lies on the other side of the limit will simply be nonsense. (*Tractatus,* preface, 3)

You will recall that Kant sets himself to uncover the limits of rational knowledge and thinks to accomplish that by a critique of reason. The domain of knowledge is *phenomena,* the realm of possible experience. Beyond this are things-in-themselves (*noumena*), thinkable, perhaps, but unknowable by

---

*Those of you who know something of Zen may detect a familiar note here. Wittgenstein never discusses Zen—his concern is for problems, not schools of thought. But you would not go far wrong to think of him as a kind of Zen master for the West—especially in his later thought.

us. Knowledge, Kant believes, has definite limits; and we can know what these are.*

Wittgenstein's strategy in the *Tractatus* bears a family resemblance to this Kantian project, but it is more radical on two counts: (1) It aims to set a limit not just to *knowledge*, but also to *thought itself*; and (2) what lies on the other side of that limit is *not even thinkable*. Wittgenstein calls it "nonsense."

Wittgenstein's ingenious notion is that this limit setting must be done in language—and *from inside* language. He thinks he has found a way to draw the line between meaning and nonsense that doesn't require having to *say* what is outside the limit. One can set this limit, he thinks, from the inside, by working outward from the central *essence of language* through everything that can be said in language. What lies out beyond the boundary simply *shows itself* to be linguistic nonsense.

Here are the first two sentences in Wittgenstein's youthful work, the *Tractatus Logico-Philosophicus*:

1.   The world is all that is the case.
1.1   The world is the totality of facts, not of things.†

These sayings, announced so bluntly, may seem dark, but the key to unlock these mysteries is at hand: the new logic. Wittgenstein believes that he can use this logic to reveal the *essence of language,* and language *shows* us what the *world* must be. But this needs explanation.

PICTURING

What is language? We are told that Wittgenstein's thinking about this question takes a decisive turn when he sees a diagram in a magazine story about an auto accident. Let us suppose it looked like this:

---

*A quick review of Kant's Copernican revolution and the idea of critique will bring this back to mind. See pp. 466–468.

†The *Tractatus* is arranged in short, aphoristic sentences, or small groups of sentences that express a complete thought. These sentences are numbered according to the following scheme. There are seven main aphorisms, 1, 2, 3, and so on; 1.1 is supposed to be a comment on or an explanation of 1; 1.11 is to play the same role with respect to 1.1. It must be admitted that this elegant scheme is sometimes difficult to interpret.

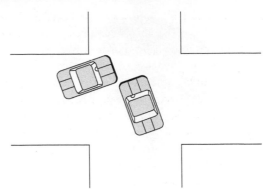

This diagram, we can say, pictures a **state of affairs.** It may not, of course, accurately represent what really happened. Let us call the actual state of affairs the **facts.** We can then say that this is a picture of a **possible state of affairs**—a picture of what might have been the facts. (We can imagine the lawyers on each side presenting contrasting pictures of the accident.)

2.1   We picture facts to ourselves.
2.12   A picture is a model of reality.
2.131   In a picture the elements of the picture are the representatives of objects.
2.14   What constitutes a picture is that its elements are related to one another in a determinate way.
2.141   A picture is a fact.

The preceding diagram is itself a fact: It is made up of actual elements (lines on the page) that are related to each other in certain ways. Moreover, each element in the diagram *represents* some object in the world (the edges of the streets, cars). So this fact pictures another (possible) fact: the way the objects here represented were actually (or possibly) related to each other at a certain time and place.

Every picture has a certain *structure*. By "structure," Wittgenstein means the way its elements are related to each other. Two pictures that are different in many ways might still have a similar structure. Imagine, for instance, a color photograph taken from a helicopter hovering over the corner just after the accident. The elements of this picture (blobs of color) are quite different from the elements of our drawing (black lines on a white background). But if our drawing is accurate, the two pictures have similar structures: Their elements are related to each other in similar ways.

Furthermore, the two pictures not only have similar structures but also have something in common: what Wittgenstein calls **pictorial form.** Pictorial form is the *possibility* that a picture might actually have just this structure, that elements of some sort might actually be arranged in just this way. There needn't ever have been a picture, or a fact, with elements related to each other like this. But even if there never had been, there *could* have been. This possibility, actualized in our diagram, might also be actualized in many more pictures of the same state of affairs. All these pictures would have the *same* pictorial form.

But it is not just similar pictures that share the same form.

2.16   If a fact is to be a picture, it must have something in common with what it depicts. . . .

2.17   What a picture must have in common with reality, in order to be able to depict it—correctly or incorrectly—in the way it does, is its pictorial form.

Pictures and *what is pictured* by them must also share the same form.

So far we have been thinking of spatial pictures of spatial objects. But there are other kinds of pictures, too. We can, for instance, think of an orchestra score as a picture; this is a spatial picture (the notes are laid out next to each other on a page), but what it primarily pictures is not spatial, but temporal: the succession of sounds the orchestra plays in a performance. So while we tend to use the word "picture" rather narrowly, the concept applies very widely. Wherever there are objects in relation representing other objects, there is a Wittgensteinian picture. Every picture, Wittgenstein claims, is a *logical* picture. And logical pictures can depict the world (*Tractatus,* 2.19).

If we think of a certain two-dimensional *physical* space, such as a desktop, we can see that there are a variety of possible ways the books on it can be arranged. Analogously, we can think of **logical space.** Logical space consists of all the *possibilities*

there are for all the *objects* there are to be related to each other in all the *possibly different ways* there are. Logical space, then, comprises the form not only of all the actual states of affairs but also of all possible states of affairs. Given this notion of logical space, we can say,

2.202   A picture represents a possible situation in logical space.

Some pictures represent reality correctly and others don't. How can we tell whether what a picture tells us is true?

2.022   What a picture represents it represents independently of its truth or falsity, by means of its pictorial form.

2.223   In order to tell whether a picture is true or false we must compare it with reality.

2.224   It is impossible to tell from the picture alone whether it is true or false.

2.225   There are no pictures that are true a priori.

You can't tell just by looking at our accident diagram whether it represents the accident correctly. And this is the case with *all* pictures, Wittgenstein says. A *true* picture is one that represents a possible state of affairs that is also actual. And actual states of affairs are *facts*. So a true picture depicts the facts. If there were a picture that was true a priori (independent of experience), you wouldn't have to "compare it with reality" to tell whether it was true; you could discover the facts just by examining the picture. But that, Wittgenstein says, is precisely what is not possible. To tell whether a picture is true (represents the facts correctly), you have to check its fit with the facts. In no case can we tell a priori whether a picture is true. This is an extremely important feature of pictures.*

―――――――――
*If Wittgenstein is right, rationalist attempts to say what the world must be like based on reason alone must be mistaken. No matter how "clear and distinct" one of Descartes' ideas is, for instance, one can't deduce from this that it is true. By stressing that there are no pictures that are true a priori, Wittgenstein expresses one version of empiricism. Compare Hume, pp. 443–444.

THOUGHT AND LANGUAGE

Among the logical pictures, there is one sort that is of particular significance:

3.   A logical picture of facts is a thought.

3.001 "A state of affairs is thinkable": what this means is that we can picture it to ourselves.

3.01   The totality of true thoughts is a picture of the world.

Our thoughts, then, are pictures, too. And, being pictures, they have all the characteristics of pictures we noted earlier: They are composed of elements in a certain arrangement, so they are facts with a certain structure; in virtue of that, they possess pictorial form; they represent possible states of affairs; and they share their pictorial and logical form with what they represent.

And now comes a crucial point:

3.1   In a proposition a thought finds an expression that can be perceived by the senses.

This is why Wittgenstein thinks he can set a limit to thought by finding the limits of language. It is in language that thought is expressed. If there are limits to what language can express, these will be the limits of thought as well.

A perceptible expression of a thought is a **proposition**—in fact, a sentence. But what is a sentence? Like all pictures, it is a fact, an arrangement of objects.

3.1431 The essence of a propositional sign is very clearly seen if we imagine one composed of spatial objects (such as tables, chairs, and books) instead of written signs. Then the spatial arrangement of these things will express the sense of the proposition.

For instance, suppose you want to picture the fact that Sarah is standing to the east of Ralph. You might use a table to represent Sarah and a chair to represent Ralph. By putting the table to the east of the chair, you can picture the fact in question. This shows us, Wittgenstein says, "the essence of a propositional sign." What he means is that written or spoken sentences are like this, too; they are made up of elements standing in certain relations.

But it is not obvious that they are like this.

4.002 Everyday language is a part of the human organism and is no less complicated than it. It is not humanly possible to gather immediately from it what the logic of language is. Language disguises thought.

The *essence* of language is hidden, "disguised." Yet it is something that can be disclosed, or shown. What reveals the hidden essence of language? *Logic.* Wittgenstein agrees with Russell that the superficial grammar of what we say may not be a good indication of the logic of what we say. And he holds that the new logic displays for us the internal structure, the essence of language. Still, he is not tempted to discard our natural languages (German or English, for example) in favor of some artificially created "ideal" language. Because the languages we speak are *languages,* they too must exemplify the essence of language. What we need is not to junk them in favor of some ideal, but to understand them.

5.5563 In fact, all the propositions of our everyday language, just as they stand, are in perfect logical order.

If they weren't, they wouldn't constitute a language!

But because "language disguises thought," the logical structure of our language is not apparent. To bring it to light we need *analysis.* What sort of analysis, then, can we give of a sentence? We already have the elements of an answer in hand. A sentence is a picture, and we know that a picture, like all facts, is composed of elements set in a certain structure. So there must be elements and a structure in every sentence. It only remains to determine what they are.

Let's consider again the sentence "Sarah is to the east of Ralph." We saw that this could be represented by one object in relation to another, a table and a chair, for instance. The table would in effect be a kind of name for Sarah and the chair a name for Ralph. Wittgenstein concludes that the *only* elements needed in a language are names. Everything else—all the adjectives and prepositions, for instance—are inessential. If sentences were completely analyzed into their basic elements, all this would disappear. We would be left with **names** in a structure.*

> 3.202 The simple signs employed in propositions are called names.
>
> 3.203 A name means an object. The object is its meaning. . . .
>
> 3.26 A name cannot be dissected any further by means of a definition: it is a primitive sign.

As you can see, there would be a very great difference between the "look" of a completely analyzed propositional sign and our ordinary sentences. One might have a hard time even recognizing the complete analysis of a familiar sentence, particularly because the names in question have to be *simple* signs. What we take to be names in ordinary language are invariably complex; "George Washington," for instance, is a shorthand expression for "the first president of the United States" (and many other descriptions). These descriptions themselves need to be analyzed if we are to understand how language pictures the world.

Sentences are essentially composed of names in a logical structure. And names are *simple.* They cannot be further analyzed or "dissected." The meaning of a name cannot be given in a definition using other linguistic elements; the meaning of a name is the object it stands for.†

Now we are ready to go back to the beginning and understand those first mysterious propositions of the *Tractatus.* Just as sentences represent possible states of affairs, true sentences represent facts. True sentences, moreover, are made up of names, and names stand for objects. But a sentence isn't just a list of names; it has an internal structure. So a fact isn't just a jumble of things; it has the same structure

as the true sentence that pictures it. The **world,** then, is what is pictured in the totality of *true sentences.* The world is not a random collection of objects, but "the totality of facts, not of things" because it shares the same logical form as the true sentences.

> 1.13 The facts in logical space are the world.

So the world is "all that is the case."

But we do not yet see how to solve the main problem Wittgenstein poses: to set a limit to thought. To do this, we have to look more closely at the logic of propositions.* Ordinary language often disguises the logical form of our sentences, but analysis can reveal it. A complete analysis would leave us with sentences that could not be further analyzed—simple sentences sometimes called **atomic propositions.** They would have constituents (names in a structure of possibility), but they could not be further broken down into other sentences.

> 4.221 It is obvious that the analysis of propositions must bring us to elementary propositions which consist of names in immediate combination.

But how are these simple sentences related to each other? Wittgenstein holds that

> 5.134 One elementary proposition cannot be deduced from another.

What this means is that the truth-value of each is independent of the truth-value of any other. An elementary proposition can remain true while the truth-values of any others (or even all the others) change. This has consequences for our view of the world as well.

> 2.061 States of affairs are independent of one another.
>
> 2.062 From the existence or non-existence of one state of affairs, it is impossible to infer the existence or non-existence of another.

---

*Here is a rough analogy. Certain notations in mathematics are merely a convenience and could be eliminated without diminishing the science. For instance, x^3 is just $x \cdot x \cdot x$, and $4y$ can be defined as $y + y + y + y$. So Wittgenstein thinks names standing in certain relations will express whatever we want to express, though we usually use more economical means.

†It is worth noting that Wittgenstein does not offer any examples of these simple names in the *Tractatus.* He argues that such names must be implicit in our language and ultimately reachable by analysis; but just what they are—and what they name—is something of a mystery.

---

*We do not here distinguish sentences from propositions, though some philosophers do; a *proposition* is often thought of as an abstract feature several sentences can share when they mean the same thing. For example, "Mary hit Sally" and "Sally was hit by Mary" are different sentences but can be said to express the same proposition. Another example is "Snow is white" and "Schnee ist weiss."

Recall once more the beginning of the *Tractatus:*

| 1.2 | The world divides into facts. |
| 1.21 | Each item can be the case or not the case while everything else remains the same. |

This view, called **logical atomism,** is reminiscent of Hume's remark that "all events seem entirely loose and separate."* It means that relations existing between atomic facts cannot be *logical* relations. Given one true elementary proposition, it is never *necessary* that another one be true—or false.

There are, of course, logical relations between complex propositions. If we are given the truth-value of *p* and of *q*, we can infer something about the truth of the conjunction, *p and q*. To display these logical relations, Wittgenstein devises *truth tables.* A truth table for a complex proposition sets forth all the logically possible combinations of truth-values for its components and then displays the corresponding truth-values for the whole. Here, for example, are truth tables for conjunctive, disjunctive, and negative propositions.

p	q		p and q	p or q	not p
T	T		T	T	F
T	F		F	T	F
F	T		F	T	T
F	F		F	F	T

The two columns on the left set out the possibilities: They show us that two propositions may both be true, one or the other may be true, or neither one may be true. The truth table for the *conjunction* shows us that the conjunction is true only when both components are true and false otherwise. The truth table for the *disjunction* (an "or" statement) shows us that the disjunction is true unless both components are false. And the truth table for *negation* shows that negating a proposition changes its truth-value.

Propositions may be of any degree of complexity. There may be a very large number of elementary propositions in its makeup, and the logic of their relations may be extremely complicated. The truth table for a proposition such as

if [if (p and q) then not (r or s)]
then (t if and only if not u)

is very large, but it is calculable. A computer could calculate it in a fraction of a second. The truth-value of a complex proposition is a function of the truth-values of the component parts; this feature is called *truth functionality.* The logic of the *Tractatus* is a truth-functional logic.

LOGICAL TRUTH

We noted that no pictures are true a priori. To determine whether a proposition is true or false, then, we must compare it to the world. From the point of view of logic, any elementary proposition might be true or it might be false. Such propositions are called *contingent:* Their truth depends on the facts, and there is never any necessity in the facts. The negation of any true elementary proposition always pictures a possibility. Suppose it is true that it is now raining where you are; then it is false that it is not raining there (see the preceding truth table), but it is not necessarily false. Given the configuration of the objects in the world, it is raining. But the objects of the world *could have been* otherwise configured.

We might like to ask, Just how far do these unrealized possibilities extend? How many possibilities are there? The answer is that this is what logic shows us. Our experience of the world can tell us what the actual facts are. Logic shows us what they *might be.* Logic is the science of the possible. And everything that it shows us is *necessary.*

Consider, for example, the truth table for a proposition like this:

Either it is raining or it is not raining.

p	not p	p or not p
T	F	T
F	T	T

The first column gives us the possibilities for the truth of *p*. The next column shows us what is the case when *p* is negated. And the third displays the results of disjoining the first two. The crucial thing to notice is that whatever the truth of *p* (and there are just these two possibilities), *p or not p* is true.

---

*See p. 450.

In other words, there is no possibility that this proposition could be false. It is *necessarily* true; it is a **logical truth.** Such a proposition Wittgenstein calls a **tautology.***

There are three important points to notice here.

1. The sentence represented by *p or not p* is a complex, not an elementary, proposition; *p* may or may not be elementary, but in this complex proposition, it is set in a structure defined by the logical operators, "not" and "or."† Only propositions that are logically complex in this way can be necessarily true or false.

2 .Logical words such as "not," "and," "or," and "if–then" are not *names*. These terms do not stand for objects; they have an entirely different function. They are part of the *structure* of sentences, not part of the content. Their function is to produce propositions from other propositions.

> 4.0312 My fundamental idea is that the "logical constants" are not representatives; that there can be no representatives of the *logic* of facts.

Wittgenstein illustrates this "fundamental idea" by considering double negation. There is a law of logic stating that negating the negation of a proposition is equivalent to asserting the proposition.

To say that *it is not the case that it is not raining* is equivalent to saying *that it is raining*. If the logical operator "not" were a name of something, the left side of this equivalence would picture something quite different from what the right side pictures (because it contains two "nots"), and the law would

be false. But it doesn't. And the proof of this is that a truth table for this principle is a tautology. So the logical operators are not names.

3. Why is it that the proposition *p* can tell us something? It can be informative because it picks out one of several possibilities and says, That is how things are. In picking out that possibility, it excludes another. It tells us something about the world by shutting out one possibility and allowing another; *p or not p,* by contrast, excludes nothing. It does not rule out any possibilities, so it does not *say* anything.

> 4.462 Tautologies and contradictions are not pictures of reality. They do not represent any possible situations. For the former admit *all* possible situations, and the latter *none.*

SAYING AND SHOWING

Wittgenstein draws a distinction that is very important to him: the distinction between **saying** and **showing.** Propositions do two things; they show something and they say something.

> 4.022 A proposition *shows* its sense. A proposition *shows* how things stand *if* it is true, and it *says that* they do so stand.

The proposition "All crows are black" shows or presents its sense. To grasp its sense is to understand what *would be* the case if it *were true*. So understanding the sentence is knowing *what would make it either true or false*. And that—its sense—is what a proposition *shows*.

But a proposition such as this not only shows its sense. It also *says* that things are this way, that crows actually are black. It makes an assertion and so is true or false, depending on the facts of the world. According to Wittgenstein, this is the most general propositional form, what all propositions have in common:

> 4.5 This is how things stand.

Propositions *show* (display) their sense; they *say* how things are.

But tautologies and contradictions *show* that they *say nothing*. If these limiting cases of propositions say

---

*There are two limiting cases of propositions: *tautologies* and *contradictions*. While tautologies are necessarily true, contradictions are necessarily false. Tautologies do not rule out any possibilities, whereas contradictions rule them all out. In a sense, it is not strictly correct to call tautologies and contradictions "propositions" because propositions are pictures of reality; tautologies and contradictions do not picture states of affairs. They have a different role to play.

†A *logical operator* is a term that has the function of producing propositions from other propositions. Additional examples are "and" and "if–then."

nothing, however, we might wonder whether they have any importance. Couldn't we just ignore them? No. They are of the very greatest importance because they show us what is possible and what is impossible. They display for us the structure of logical space.

But they have another importance as well.

6.1   The propositions of logic are tautologies.

What Wittgenstein here calls the "propositions" of logic are sometimes called the laws of logic. Consider as an example the very basic law called the *principle of noncontradiction:* No proposition can be both true and false. We can represent this as

not both p and not p.

If we write a truth table for this formula, we can see that it is a tautology—that is, necessarily true no matter what the truth-values of *p* are.

p	not p	p and not p	not (p and not p)
T	F	F	T
F	T	F	T

So the device of truth tables provides a justification for the laws of logic. Showing they are tautologies is equivalent to demonstrating their necessary truth. The truth table shows that there is no alternative to the laws of logic—no possibility that they might be false.* The *Tractatus* doctrine is that every principle of logical inference can be reduced to a tautology.†

Moreover,

6.113   It is the peculiar mark of logical propositions that one can recognize that they are true from the symbol alone, and this fact contains in itself the whole philosophy of logic.

---

*Of course this also shows that the laws of logic *say* nothing—that is, are *about* nothing. The laws of logic are purely formal and empty of content. And that is exactly why they can be noncontingently true.

†In fact this claim is not correct. Truth tables constitute a decision procedure for validity only in propositional logic, where the analysis of structure does not go deeper than whole propositions. Alonzo Church later proves that in quantificational (or predicate) logic, where the analysis reveals the internal structure of propositions, there is no such decision procedure.

What this means is that the propositions of logic can be known a priori. As we saw previously, we can know about the actual world only by comparing a proposition with reality. It is the mark of logical propositions that this is not only unnecessary, but also impossible; because they say nothing, they cannot say anything we could check out by examining the facts.

So the propositions of logic are one and all tautologies. And every valid form of inference can be expressed in a proposition of logic. This means that all possible logical relations between propositions can be known a priori. And in knowing them, we know the logical structure of the world—logical space, what Wittgenstein calls "the scaffolding of the world" (6.124).

SETTING THE LIMIT TO THOUGHT

Finally, we are ready to understand how Wittgenstein thinks he can show us the limits of language. An operation discovered by Wittgenstein can be performed on a set of elementary propositions to produce all the possible complex propositions (truth functions) that can be expressed by that set. Suppose we have just two elementary propositions, *p* and *q*. Using this operator, we can calculate that there are just sixteen possible truth functions combining them: *not p, not q, p or q, p and q, if p then q,* and so on. Now imagine that we were in possession of *all* the elementary propositions there are; using this operation on that enormous set, one could simply calculate all the possible truth functions there are and so *generate each and every possible proposition.*

Remembering the picture theory of meaning, we can see that this set of propositions pictures all the possible states of affairs there are and in all their possible combinations. So, it represents the entirety of logical space; it pictures everything that there could possibly be in reality—every "possible world." Notice that there would be no proposition saying that these are all the possible facts. That these are all the facts there are *shows itself* in these propositions being all there are.

This very large set of propositions contains *everything it is possible to say,* plus the tautologies and contradictions (which say nothing). Beyond this set of possible propositions lies only *nonsense*. So the limit of thought is indeed set from inside. Thought is expressed in language. The essence of language is picturing. And, given this, we can work out from the center to the periphery of language by means of logic. We do not need to take up a position outside the thinkable to draw a line circumscribing it. The limit *shows itself* by the lack of sense that pseudopropositions display when we try to say something unsayable. It is indeed, then, only "in language that the limit can be set, and what lies on the other side of the limit will simply be nonsense" (*Tractatus,* preface, 3).

---

1. What is Wittgenstein's aim in his *Tractatus*? And what motivates that aim—that is, why does he want to do that? If he had succeeded, would that have been significant?
2. Explain how a picture is a "model of reality." In what sense is a picture itself a fact?
3. Explain the concepts of pictorial form, possible state of affairs, and logical space.
4. Why are there no pictures that are true a priori?
5. In what way does language "disguise" thought? What is the essential nature of a proposition?
6. What is the meaning of a simple name? What are atomic propositions composed of? And why is this view correctly called "logical atomism"?
7. What, then, is the world? And how is it related to logic? To language? To the truth?
8. How do truth tables work? What is truth functionality?
9. What domain does logic reveal to us? In what way does logic "show itself"?
10. Contrast contingent truth with necessary truth. How do necessary truths reveal themselves in a truth table?
11. Why do tautologies and contradictions "say nothing"? What do they "show"?
12. Explain: "A proposition *shows* its sense" and it *says* "This is how things stand." Give an example.
13. How is the limit to thought set?

VALUE AND THE SELF

We noted earlier that the young Wittgenstein's concerns were mainly spiritual and moral, but we have just seen that the bulk of the *Tractatus* deals with quite technical issues in logic and the philosophy of language. How are we to understand this apparent discrepancy? In a letter to a potential publisher for the *Tractatus*, Wittgenstein writes,

> The book's point is an ethical one . . . : My work consists of two parts: the one presented here plus all that I have *not* written, and it is precisely this second part that is the important one. My book draws limits to the sphere of the ethical from the inside as it were, and I am convinced that this is the ONLY *rigorous* way of drawing those limits. In short, I believe that where many others today are just *gassing*, I have managed in my book to put everything firmly in place by being silent about it.[5]

What could this mean—that the really important part of the book is the part he did not write? Why didn't he write it? Was he too lazy? Did he run out of time? Of course not. He didn't write the important part because he was convinced it *couldn't be written*. What is most important—the ethical point of the book—is something that *cannot be said*.

Nonetheless, and again paradoxically, he does have some things to "say" about this sphere, which he also calls "the mystical."* Before we examine his remarks—brief and dark sayings, as many have noted—it will be helpful to set out a consequence of what we have already learned.

4.11   The totality of true propositions is the whole of natural science.

The essence of language is **picturing;** and to picture is to say, "This is how things are." The job of natural science is to tell us how things are. And if natural science could finish its job, we would then have a *complete* picture of reality.† Nothing—no object, no fact—would be left out. Science would include all the true propositions there are.

But natural science does not contain any propositions like these: one ought to do *X*; it is wrong to *Y*; the meaning of life is *Z*. It follows that these are

---

*It is obviously a problem how we are to understand what he "says" about the unsayable. He makes a suggestion we consider later.

†Compare Peirce's similar conviction, pp. 599–600.

not really propositions at all; they look a lot like propositions, but, if Wittgenstein is right, they lie *beyond the limits of language*. Strictly speaking, they are unsayable. Those who utter them may be "just *gassing*." Or they may be trying to say the most important things of all but failing because they "run against the boundaries of language." In a "Lecture on Ethics" Wittgenstein gave in 1929 or 1930 he says,

> This running against the walls of our cage is perfectly, absolutely hopeless. Ethics so far as it springs from the desire to say something about the ultimate meaning of life, the absolute good, the absolute valuable, can be no science. What it says does not add to our knowledge in any sense. But it is a document of a tendency in the human mind which I personally cannot help respecting deeply and I would not for my life ridicule it.[6]

Ethics "can be no science" because science consists of propositions, and

> 6.4   All propositions are of equal value.
> 6.41   The sense of the world must lie outside the world. In the world everything is as it is, and everything happens as it does happen: *in* it no value exists—and if it did exist, it would have no value. If there is any value that does have value, it must lie outside the whole sphere of what happens and is the case.
> 6.421   It is clear that ethics cannot be put into words.

The vision of the *Tractatus* is one where everything in the world is flattened out, where nothing is of more significance than anything else because nothing is of any significance at all. In the world is no **value** at all, nothing of importance. There are just the facts.

So ethics "cannot be put into words," and yet it is the most important thing of all. To understand this, we need to consider Wittgenstein's views of the subject, the self, the "I." He suggests that if you wrote a book called *The World as I Found It*, there is one thing that would not be mentioned in it: *you*. It would include all the facts you found, including all the facts about your body, your character, personality, dispositions, and so on. But you—the

subject, the one to whom all this appears, the one who *finds* all these facts—would not be found.*

> 5.632   The subject does not belong to the world; rather, it is a limit of the world.
> 5.641   The philosophical self is not the human being, not the human body, or the human soul, with which psychology deals, but rather the metaphysical subject, the limit of the world—not a part of it.

The self is not a *fact*. Wittgenstein calls it the **"limit of the world."** Think about the relation between an eye and its visual field. The eye is not itself part of the visual field; it is not seen. In the same way, all content, all the facts, are "out there" in the world, which is the "totality of facts" (1.1).

> 5.64   Here it can be seen that solipsism, when its implications are followed out strictly, coincides with pure realism. The self of solipsism shrinks to a point without extension, and there remains the reality co-ordinated with it.

---

*Among thinkers we have studied, this should remind you most of Kant. It is not identical with Kant's view, however. Kant believes that, though we can't come to know the nature of "this I or he or it (the thing) which thinks," we can know a lot about it—that it is the source of the pure intuitions, the categories, and the a priori synthetic propositions, all of which explain the structure of the empirical world. For Wittgenstein, none of this is possible. The structure of the world is not dictated by the structure of rational minds because the structure of reality is just logic; and logic, consisting as it does of empty tautologies, neither has nor needs a source. Kant's world needs a structure-giver because its fundamental principles are thought to be synthetic. But logic is analytic. It requires no source beyond itself because it has no content requiring explanation. This "scaffolding of the world" is neither a fact in the world, nor a fact about the world, nor a fact about rational minds. It is not a fact at all! It *shows itself*. Look again at the relevant discussions of Kant on pp. 481–482, including the diagram on p. 494.

†Compare Descartes' struggles to overcome solipsism by proving the existence of God in *Meditation III*; see also pp. 382 and 402. Wittgenstein acknowledges there is a truth in solipsism, but such truth as there is already involves the reality of the world—of which the self is aware. So there is no need to *prove* the world's existence—or that of God, about whom in any case nothing can be said.

5.62 For what the solipsist *means* is quite correct; only it cannot be *said*, but makes itself manifest.*

What the solipsist wants to say is that only he exists and the world only in relation to himself. But this cannot be *said*. Why not? Because to say it would be to use language—propositions—to picture facts. And in picturing facts we are picturing the world, *not* the transcendental self to whom the world appears. So this self "shrinks to a point without extension." And if we ask *what there is*, the answer is the world—"all that is the case" (*Tractatus*, proposition 1). And this is just the thesis of radical **realism,** the antithesis of solipsism.

The concern of ethics is good and evil. But, as we have seen, there is no room for good and evil in the world, where everything just is whatever it is. What application, then, do these concepts have? Ethics must concern itself with the self, the subject. But how? Here is a clue.

6.373 The world is independent of my will.

6.374 Even if all that we wish for were to happen, still this would only be a favour granted by fate, so to speak.

You may will to do something, such as write a check to pay a telephone bill. And usually you can do it. But it is clear that paying a bill by check depends on the cooperation of the world: The neurons have to fire just right, the nerves must transmit the neural signals reliably, the muscles must contract in just the right way, the bank must not suddenly crash, and so forth. And none of that is entirely in your control. That is what Wittgenstein means when he says the world is independent of my will. If you intend to pay your telephone bill, getting it done is, in a way, a "favour granted by fate." In a strict sense, your willing *is* your action; what follows is just the result of your action.

"For us there is only the trying. The rest is not our business."

—*T. S. Eliot* (1888–1965)

Good and Evil, Happiness and Unhappiness

Good and evil, then, cannot attach to any facts; they must pertain to the will. But what sort of willing would be good? Wittgenstein suggests an analogy with our attitude toward works of art:

> The work of art is the object seen *sub specie aeternitatis*; and the good life is the world seen *sub specie aeternitatis*.† This is the connection between art and ethics.
>
> The usual way of looking at things sees objects as if it were from the midst of them, the view *sub specie aeternitatis* from outside. (*N*, 84c)[7]

Most of us, most of the time, do not occupy the position of the transcendental subject, even though that is what we essentially are—the limit of the world, not some entity within the world. We identify ourselves with a body, with certain desires, hopes, and fears—and our focus narrows. We suffer from tunnel vision and our world is no longer *the* world; it is merely the world of our concerns. But when we are lost in a great work of art—a Mozart symphony, a Shakespeare play, *The Lord of the Rings*—our world and the world of the artwork coincide. For a time we forget our selfish worries. The world of the story is all there is, and we are just a vanishing point to which it appears. Now Wittgenstein asks,

> Is it the essence of the artistic way of looking at things, that it looks at the world with a happy eye? (*N*, 86e)

He doesn't answer the question, but obviously means us to answer yes. And it's true, isn't it, that we are happy when we are caught up in aesthetic experience? What's true in aesthetics is true in life.

6.421 (Ethics and aesthetics are one and the same.)

6.43 If the good or bad exercise of the will does alter the world, it can alter only the limits of the world, not the facts—not what can be expressed by means of language.

†From the viewpoint of eternity.

In short the effect must be that it becomes an altogether different world. It must, so to speak, wax and wane as a whole.

The world of the happy man is a different one from that of the unhappy man.

Bad willing is dominated by selfish fears and hopes—worrying about our past and our future, living in the constricted world of our private concerns. So the bad person's world narrows, wanes. But to live life from the viewpoint of eternity is to live in the present, and "whoever lives in the present lives without fear and hope" (*N*, 76e). A life lived *sub specie aeternitatis*, then, is the good life, and—in parallel with aesthetic experience—the ethical person is also the happy person. To live ethically is to be opened up to the world. When we identify with the transcendental self, our world waxes larger. We see it just as it is—a limited whole and the totality of facts, none of which is of such importance to us that it crowds out any other. *Our* world becomes *the* world. Although the *facts* of the world don't change, it is really true that the world of the happy person is a different world from that of the unhappy. The happy experience the world *as it is*.*

❖

"Every man takes the limits of his own field of vision for the limits of the world."

—*Arthur Schopenhauer (1788–1860)*

In a "Lecture on Ethics," Wittgenstein describes an experience that he has had, which, he says, is an experience of "absolute value."

I believe the best way of describing it is to say that when I have it *I wonder at the existence of the world.* And I am then inclined to use such phrases as "how extraordinary that anything should exist" or "how extraordinary that the world should exist."[8]

---

*Compare Heraclitus, who says, "To those who are awake the world order is one, common to all; but the sleeping turn aside each into a world of his own." The *Tractatus* might almost be read as an extended commentary on this and related sayings by Heraclitus, with logic—the "scaffolding" of the world—playing the role of the *logos*. See the discussion of these matters on pp. 17–20.

Now, according to the doctrine of the *Tractatus*, this can only be nonsense. One can wonder that the world contains kangaroos, perhaps; but there is no meaningful proposition that can express the "fact" that the world exists. Why not? Because this is no fact. Beyond the totality of true propositions—and these, remember, describe the totality of the facts, all that is the case—there is no further proposition that says, "Oh yes, and don't forget, the world exists." And yet that is what Wittgenstein very much wants to say. It points to the important part of the book—the part he couldn't write. To "wonder at the existence of the world" is to experience it as a limited whole. And that is what Wittgenstein calls "the **mystical.**"

6.44 It is not *how* things are in the world that is mystical, but *that* it exists.

6.45 To view the world *sub specie aeterni* is to view it as a whole—a limited whole. Feeling the world as a limited whole—it is this that is mystical.

It is tempting to think that we can ask, Why does the world exist? or Why is there anything at all rather than nothing? But

6.5 When the answer cannot be put into words, neither can the question be put into words.

The riddle does not exist.

If a question can be framed at all, it is also *possible* to answer it.

The *answer* cannot be put into words because to say why the world exists would be to state a fact—and the world itself is already the totality of facts. So the *question*, "Why does the world exist?" which has exercised so many philosophical minds and has produced so many arguments for God's existence, is *no question at all*. It seems like a question—but that is an *illusion* generated by language.

What we can say is *how* the world is. And that is the job of natural science. But

6.52 We feel that even when *all possible* scientific questions have been answered, the problems of life remain completely untouched. Of course there are then no questions left, and this itself is the answer.

6.521   The solution of the problem of life is seen in the vanishing of the problem. . . .

6.522   There are, indeed, things that cannot be put into words. They *make themselves manifest*. They are what is mystical.

🔸

"The most beautiful thing we can experience is the mysterious. It is the source of all true art and science."

—Albert Einstein (1879–1955)

THE UNSAYABLE

If you have been following carefully, you have no doubt been wondering how Wittgenstein can manage to say all this that he so explicitly "says" cannot be said. This is indeed a puzzle we must address. What he has been writing is clearly philosophy. But if, as he (philosophically) says, the totality of true propositions is science, what room is there for philosophy?

4.111   Philosophy is not one of the natural sciences. . . . Philosophy aims at the logical clarification of thoughts. Philosophy is not a body of doctrine but an activity. A philosophical work consists essentially of elucidations. Philosophy does not result in "philosophical propositions," but rather in the clarification of propositions. Without philosophy thoughts are, as it were, cloudy and indistinct: its task is to make them clear and to give them sharp boundaries.

The key thought here is that philosophy is an activity; its business is clarification. It follows that we should not look to philosophy for *results*, for truths, or for "a body of doctrine." To do so is to mistake the nature of philosophizing altogether. It has been one of the major failings of the philosophical tradition, Wittgenstein believes, that it has tried to produce "philosophical propositions"— that it has thought of itself as in the same line of work as science. But it is *altogether different* from science. It lies, one might say, at right angles to science. Wittgenstein's view of his predecessors is severe:

4.003   Most of the propositions and questions to be found in philosophical works are not false but nonsensical. Consequently we cannot give any answer to questions of this kind, but can only establish that they are nonsensical. Most of the propositions and questions of philosophers arise from our failure to understand the logic of our language. . . . And it is not surprising that the deepest problems are in fact *not* problems at all.

6.53   The correct method in philosophy would really be the following: to say nothing except what can be said, i.e., propositions of natural science—i.e., something that has nothing to do with philosophy—and then, whenever someone else wanted to say something metaphysical, to demonstrate to him that he had failed to give a meaning to certain signs in his propositions.

Plato and Aristotle, Hume and Kant all think they are revealing or discovering truth. But, if Wittgenstein is right, all of their most important claims are nonsensical. They aren't even *candidates* for being true! Their theories are pseudoanswers to pseudoquestions. Just *gassing*. Such theories arise because these philosophers don't understand the logic of our language; Wittgenstein thinks he has, for the first time, clearly set this forth.

But there is still a worry. Wittgenstein is himself not utilizing "the correct method" in writing the *Tractatus*. How, then, are we to take his own "propositions" here?

6.54   My propositions serve as elucidations in the following way: anyone who understands me eventually recognizes them as nonsensical, when he has used them—as steps—to climb up beyond them. (He must, so to speak, throw away the ladder after he has climbed up it.) He must transcend these propositions, and then he will see the world aright.

To "see the world aright" is to see it from the viewpoint of eternity, from the point of view of the **philosophical self.** It is not too far-fetched to be reminded of that ladder the mystics talk about as leading to oneness with God. Having climbed Wittgenstein's ladder, we too can wonder at the

THE LOGICAL POSITIVISTS

The *Tractatus* was painstakingly studied by a group of scientifically oriented philosophers in Vienna (a group that came to be known as the Vienna Circle). They admired its logic and philosophy of language, but had no sympathy for what Wittgenstein himself thought most important. These *logical positivists*, as they were called, began a movement that had a significant impact on scientists, on philosophy of science, and on the general public. **Logical positivism** is identified with three claims:

1. Logic and mathematics are *analytic*. The positivists accept Wittgenstein's analysis of the basic truths of logic: They are all tautologies and so are factually empty, providing no knowledge of nature. They are, however, very important because they provide a framework for moving from one true factual statement to another. That is, they license inferences, just as Wittgenstein says they do.

2. Meaningful propositions can be distinguished from meaningless ones by the **verifiability principle.** Here is Moritz Schlick's explanation of verifiability:

> The meaning of a proposition consists, obviously, in this alone, that it expresses a definite state of affairs. One can of course, say that the proposition itself already gives this state of affairs.* This is true, but the proposition indicates the state of affairs only to the person who understands it. But when do I understand the meanings of the words which occur in it? These can be explained by definition. But in the definitions new words appear whose meanings . . . must be indicated directly: the meaning of a word must in the end be *shown*, it must be *given*.[9]

Wittgenstein never specifies what the elementary names stand for, but for the positivists these basic terms indicate items in perceptual experience—green, hot, hard, etc. This is what is "given." The bite of the verifiability principle is this: Unless you can point to a perceptual difference that a proposition's being true or false makes, it is *meaningless*. Clearly, positivism is a kind of empiricism.*

The positivists have no tolerance for a "good" kind of nonsense that might point to something important, but is "unsayable." They talk about the *elimination* of metaphysics. What is to be left as meaningful is science alone. Out with Plato's Forms, Aristotle's entelechy, Augustine's God, Descartes' mind, Kant's noumena, Hegel's Absolute Spirit—and Wittgenstein's mystical! Whatever cannot be verified by the senses is to be purged from human memory.†

3. Like Wittgenstein, they hold that the business of philosophy is the clarification of statements, but they are convinced that philosophy itself doesn't have to be classified as nonsense. Clarification has certain definite results: It issues in definitions. Much of what the positivists write concerns what they call "the logic of science," so they are interested in the concepts of *law* and *theory*, of *hypothesis* and *evidence*, of *confirmation* and *probability*. Under their influence, the *philosophy of science* becomes a recognized part of philosophy, and most university philosophy departments now teach courses in that area.

The fate of ethical statements on positivist principles is particularly interesting. What kind of statement is a judgment that stealing is wrong? In an explosive book titled *Language, Truth, and Logic*, the English philosopher A. J. Ayer sets out the positivist view of ethics. Ethical concepts, he says, are "mere pseudoconcepts."

> Thus if I say to someone, "You acted wrongly in stealing that money," I am not stating anything more than if I had simply said, "You

_____

*Wittgenstein says, "A proposition *shows* its sense" (4.022).

_____

*Like David Hume, the positivists want to base all nonanalytic knowledge on the data our senses provide. See again Hume's rule, "No impression, no idea" (p. 444). It has been said, with some justice, that logical positivism is just Hume plus modern logic.

†Compare Hume's trenchant remarks at the end of his *Enquiry* (pp. 463–464).

THE LOGICAL POSITIVISTS

stole that money." In adding that this action is wrong I am not making any further statement about it. I am simply evincing my moral disapproval of it. It is as if I had said, "You stole that money," in a peculiar tone of horror, or written it with the addition of some special exclamation marks. The tone, or the exclamation marks, adds nothing to the literal meaning of the sentence. It merely serves to show that the expression of it is attended by certain feelings in the speaker.

If I now generalize my previous statement and say, "Stealing is wrong," I produce a sentence which has no factual meaning—that is, expresses no proposition which can be either true or false. It is as if I had written "Stealing money!!"—where the shape and thickness of the exclamation marks show, by a suitable convention, that a special sort of moral disapproval is the feeling which is being expressed.[10]

This is pretty radical stuff, at least as judged by the philosophical tradition.* Socrates' search for the nature of piety, courage, and justice must be misguided. Plato's Form of the Good, Aristotle's virtues as human excellences, Epicurus' pleasure, the Stoics' will in harmony with nature, Augustine's ordered loves, Hobbes' social contract, Kant's categorical imperative, Mill's greatest happiness principle—all these, if Ayer is right, are just expressions of personal preferences, no more than how these individuals *feel* about things.†

---

*But see the motto of Protagoras on p. 62 and the relevance of rhetoric to justice as developed by Gorgias, Antiphon, and Callicles, discussed on pp. 64–67. A major portion of rhetoric might be thought of as techniques for "expressing moral sentiments" in persuasive ways.

†Note that the Wittgenstein of the *Tractatus* would think this turn of events about as awful as could be imagined. While he would agree that value is not a matter of fact, he locates ethics—what really matters—in the life of the *transcendental self*. Positivist ethics construes

> "The idea that 'good' is a function of the will stunned philosophy with its attractiveness, since it solved so many problems at one blow: metaphysical entities were removed, and moral judgments were seen to be, not weird statements, but something much more comprehensible, such as persuasions or commands or rules."
> —*Iris Murdoch (1919–1999)*

It is important to note that this **emotivist theory of ethics,** with its dramatic contrast between the factually meaningful and the meaningless, depends on the adequacy of the verifiability principle. But there are problems with that principle. Suppose we ask, What sort of statement is the principle itself? There seem to be three possibilities, none of them satisfactory. (1) It doesn't itself seem to be verifiable by sense experience, so it cannot be a *factual* statement. (2) It doesn't seem to capture the ordinary sense of meaningfulness, since there are lots of unverifiable statements we think we understand perfectly well: For example, "The last word in Caesar's mind, unuttered, before he died, was 'tu.'" So it doesn't seem to be a *definition*. (3) If it is taken as a *recommendation*, it is open to the objector to simply say (on positivist grounds), "Well, I feel different about it."

We need a better theory of meaning.

---

value as no more than the way some *empirical self* happens to feel. What greater difference could there be? From Wittgenstein's point of view, if Ayer is right, all we ever get in morality is "just *gassing*." See p. 629.

existence of the world, experience happiness and beauty—and do our science. But we would always have to keep in mind the last "proposition" of the *Tractatus*:

> 7.   What we cannot speak about we must pass over in silence.

Yet, the things we must "pass over in silence" are the most important of all.

1. Why couldn't the "important" part of the *Tractatus* be written?
2. Why must the sense of the world lie outside the world? Why cannot there be "propositions of ethics"?
3. Suppose you wrote a book entitled *The World as I Found It*. Would you appear in the book?
4. How does solipsism coincide with pure realism?
5. In what way is the world of the happy person different from the world of the unhappy person? What does it mean to see the world *sub specie aeternitatis*?
6. Could a person be absolutely safe? (Compare Socrates in his defense to the jury in *Apology* 41c–d, p. 129.)
7. What is the "mystical"? Why does it have absolutely nothing to do with the "occult"?
8. Why won't science solve the problems of life? Why does "the riddle" not exist?
9. What is philosophy? What is its "correct method"? What is the ladder analogy?

Philosophical Investigations

The analysis of language in terms of the new logic yields some impressive results, but not everyone is convinced that this is the way to go. Logical atomism has some problems (see the following section). And the ambitious program of the logical positivists doesn't seem to be working out even for their favorite case of meaningful discourse: science.

These problems suggest that instead of looking to some "ideal" language inspired by logic, we might be better advised to pay closer attention to how our own language actually functions. Maybe it's not that language itself is to blame so much as that we—philosophers particularly—misuse it or misdescribe its use. Perhaps all goes smoothly

when we talk about minds or truth in everyday life, but when the philosopher reflectively asks himself, "Just what is a mind?" or "What is truth?" things start to go all wobbly.

This suspicion is deepened by the later Wittgenstein. In the preface to his youthful work, *Tractatus Logico-Philosophicus,* Wittgenstein had written,

> The *truth* of the thoughts that are here set forth seems to me unassailable and definitive. I therefore believe myself to have found, on all essential points, the final solution of the problems. (*I*, Preface, 5)

With great consistency and in perfect conformity with his inexpressible ethics, he then leaves philosophy. As the years pass, though, he engages in conversations with other philosophers and scientists, including members of the Vienna Circle. Eventually he comes to believe that he has not, after all, found "the final solution" of all the problems he had addressed. The vision expressed in his *Tractatus* is powerful and elegant, but Wittgenstein gradually becomes convinced that it is not *true*. In the first fifty pages of *Philosophical Investigations* he subjects his earlier views to devastating criticism.*

There are certainly difficulties in the *Tractatus*. For one thing, his view that logic consists solely of tautologies is proved by Alonzo Church to be too simple. Furthermore, there is that strange consequence of the picture theory—that all his own philosophical propositions are nonsensical, despite the fact that many of us seem to understand at least some of them rather well. But it is neither of these things that moves Wittgenstein to criticize the doctrines of the *Tractatus*. He begins to feel difficulties in connection with its central thesis—that the essence of language is picturing, together with the correlated doctrine of names and simple objects. Think of requests like "Shut the door," or

---

*Published posthumously in 1953, two years after his death, *Philosophical Investigations* is written in two parts, the first of which is organized in numbered sections, most of which are a paragraph or two long. Like the *Tractatus*, it is a difficult book, but in quite a different way. Whereas you can read a sentence in the *Tractatus* half a dozen times and still be puzzled about what it means, the *Investigations*, for the most part, reads with some ease. But then you find yourself asking, What does this all amount to?

exclamations like "Phooey!" Bits of language? Of course. But what is their logical form? And of what simple names are they composed? And what possible states of affairs do they picture? Just to ask such questions shows up a deficiency in the *Tractatus* doctrine. Even if you were to grant that the picture theory correctly analyzes an important part of language (e.g., the propositions of natural science), it would be at best only partial; it would not reach the essence of language.

PHILOSOPHICAL ILLUSION

Wittgenstein allows that his *Tractatus* does express a possible way of seeing things. We can climb the ladder of his "nonsensical" propositions and get a certain vision of things. He had said in the *Tractatus* that we would then "see the world aright" (*Tractatus* 6.54). But he now thinks this way of seeing things is a mistake. Yet, "mistake" is not quite the right word; it is more like an illusion, he suggests, or even a superstition that held him in thrall (*PI*, 97, 110).[11] But how could he have been so deceived? What is the source of this illusion that the *Tractatus* presents with such clarity and power?

We sometimes find that others misunderstand what we mean when we talk to them. These misunderstandings can often be removed by paraphrasing, by substituting one form of expression for another. It is often helpful to use simpler terms to explain what we mean:

> This may be called an "analysis" of our forms of expression, for the process is sometimes like one of taking a thing apart. (*PI*, 90)
>
> But now it may come to look as if there were something like a final analysis of our forms of language, and so a *single* completely resolved form of every expression. That is, as if our usual forms of expression were, essentially, unanalyzed; as if there were something hidden in them that had to be brought to light. When this is done the expression is completely clarified and our problem is solved.

The Wittgenstein of the *Tractatus* was committed to all these notions: to the idea that there is "something hidden" in our ordinary language that can be "completely clarified" by a "final analysis" into "a *single* completely resolved form of every

expression." The slide to these conclusions is so subtle we scarcely notice it, but it is a slide into illusion.

Language, propositions—these seem mysterious, strange. We are encouraged to suppose that there *must* be an essence of language—*one* essence—because it is all called by one name, "language." Further, we assume that every instance of it must have something in common with all the rest. This is a supposition that goes way back; Socrates, in asking about piety, is not content with answers that give him examples of pious behavior. What he wants is the essence of piety—that is, something common to all examples that *makes* them instances of piety.*

About this seductive idea, Wittgenstein now says,

> A *picture* held us captive. And we could not get outside it, for it lay in our language and language seemed to repeat it to us inexorably. (*PI*, 115)

This picture is not a *Tractatus* picture. It is a picture in an ordinary, though metaphorical, sense, as when we say, "I can't help but picture her as happy." It is a picture of language as a *calculus*, as something possessing "the crystalline purity of logic" (*PI*, 107). Captive to a picture, we cannot shake off the conviction that language *must* have an essence, that hidden in the depths of our ordinary sentences must be an exact logical structure in which simple names stand for simple objects. Logic, which is the "scaffolding of the world" (*Tractatus* 6.124), *requires* it. Propositions *must* have pictorial form and an isomorphism with what they picture. Never mind that they don't actually look like that! That is the way it *must* be—we think.

But that is just what is wrong with the *Tractatus* vision. It doesn't *describe* the way language works; it *prescribes*. Once we become aware of that, we can also see our way out of the illusion. We can get out of the grip of this superstition by confining ourselves solely to *description*.

> We must do away with all *explanation*, and description alone must take its place. And this description

---

* See p. 112.

gets its light, that is to say its purpose, from the philosophical problems. These are, of course, not empirical problems; they are solved, rather, by looking into the workings of our language, and that in such a way as to make us recognize those workings. . . . The problems are solved, not by giving new information, but by arranging what we have always known. Philosophy is a battle against the bewitchment of our intelligence by means of language. (*PI,* 109)

Note that philosophy is still something quite different from the sciences: Its problems are "not empirical." And philosophy's job is not to produce theories or explanations. Philosophy is still an activity of clarification rather than a set of results. But Wittgenstein no longer thinks that all philosophical problems can be solved at once, by analyzing "the essence of language." We must proceed in a piecemeal fashion, working patiently at one problem after another by "looking into the workings of our language," by "arranging what we have always known." It is not "new information" that we need to resolve philosophical problems. We need the ability to find our way through the many temptations to misunderstand.

When philosophers use a word—"knowledge," "being," "object," "I," "proposition," "name"—and try to grasp the *essence* of the thing, one must always ask oneself: is the word ever actually used in this way in the language-game which is its original home?—
　　What we do is to bring words back from their metaphysical to their everyday use. (*PI,* 116)

The notion of a *language-game* is one we will have to examine closely. It is clear that philosophical theories of knowledge, reality, the self, and the external world are regarded with great suspicion by Wittgenstein, just as they were in the *Tractatus.* Such theories, we may imagine, he still regards as "just *gassing.*" But the reason for suspicion is now different. The words that are being used in these theories—"know," "object," "I," "name"—all are words with common uses. Wittgenstein now suspects that as they are used in these philosophical theories, the words lose their anchors in the activities that make them meaningful. They float free, without discipline, and lose their meaning; yet, it is just *because* they have no anchors in concrete life

that they seem to indicate deep problems. This appearance of depth, however, is just part of the illusion. What is needed is to "bring words back from their metaphysical to their everyday use."
　　Philosophical problems are baffling:

A philosophical problem has the form: "I don't know my way about." (*PI,* 123)

But the solution is not to construct a philosophical theory about the baffling topic. What we need is to clarify the language in which the problem is posed.

Philosophy may in no way interfere with the actual use of language; it can in the end only describe it.
　　For it cannot give it any foundation either.
　　It leaves everything as it is. (*PI,* 124)

The work of the philosopher consists in assembling reminders for a particular purpose. (*PI,* 126–128)

This is surely a radical view of philosophy, as radical in its way as that of the *Tractatus.* According to this view, the aim of the philosopher is not to solve the big problems about knowledge, reality, God, the soul, and the good. These are not real problems at all; they arise only out of misunderstanding our language. The task of the philosopher is to unmask the ways in which these problems are generated and, by putting "everything before us" and "assembling reminders," bring us back to home ground. What is the purpose of the reminders? To show us how the language in which these "deep" questions are framed is actually used in those human activities in which they get their meaning. If we understand that, we will be freed from the temptation to suppose these are real questions. Wittgenstein offers the following rule:

Don't think, but look! (*PI,* 66)

Here are two more striking remarks on this theme.

The philosopher's treatment of a question is like the treatment of an illness. (*PI,* 255)

What is your aim in philosophy? To shew the fly the way out of the fly-bottle. (*PI,* 309)

The first remark suggests that philosophy is itself the illness for which it must be the cure. There is that old saying by Bishop Berkeley about raising a dust and then complaining that we cannot see. The posing of philosophical problems, Wittgenstein is saying, is like that. Being possessed by a philosophical problem is like being sick; only it is we who make ourselves sick—confused, trapped, perplexed by paradoxes. We foist these illusions on ourselves by misunderstanding our own language. It *easy* to do that because language itself suggests these illusions to us. Philosophy, then, is a kind of therapy for relieving mental cramps.

With the second remark we get the unforgettable image of a fly having gotten itself trapped in a narrow-necked bottle, buzzing wildly about and slamming itself against the sides of the bottle, unable to find the way out that lies there open and clear if only the fly could recognize it. We get into philosophical problems so easily but then can't find our way out again.

> "But *this* isn't how it is!"—we say, "Yet *this* is how it has to *be!*" (*PI*, 112)

Just like the fly in the bottle! It is Wittgenstein's aim to show the fly the way out of the bottle—to help us put philosophical problems behind us, not to devise theories to solve them.

LANGUAGE-GAMES

Let us look in more detail at the way Wittgenstein uses the prescription "Don't think, but look!" in criticizing the characteristic theses of the *Tractatus*. We begin with one of the most basic notions in that work, the notion of a *name*.

Wittgenstein makes use of a device he calls "language-games." A **language-game** is an activity that involves spoken (or written) words. These words have a natural place in the activity; it is this place, the role they play in the activity, that makes them mean what they do mean. It is sometimes helpful, Wittgenstein suggests, to imagine a language-game more primitive than the ones we engage in. Here is such a primitive language-game.

> The language is meant to serve for communication between a builder A and an assistant B. A is building with building-stones: there are blocks, pillars, slabs and beams. B has to pass the stones, and that in the order in which A needs them. For this purpose they use a language consisting of the words "block,"
> "pillar," "slab," "beam." A calls them out;—B brings the stone which he has learnt to bring at such-and-such a call.—Conceive this as a complete primitive language. (*PI*, 2)

The words in this language-game can very naturally be thought of as names. To each word there corresponds an object. Here we have an example of a language that the theory of the *Tractatus* fits. This theory

> does describe a system of communication; only not everything that we call language is this system. And one has to say this in many cases where the question arises "Is this an appropriate description or not?" The answer is: "Yes, it is appropriate, but only for this narrowly circumscribed region, not for the whole of what you were claiming to describe." (*IPI*, 3)

In the following language-game, the *Tractatus* view that names exhaust the meaningful symbols shows itself to be inadequate—if we only *look*.

> I send someone shopping. I give him a slip marked "five red apples." He takes the slip to the shopkeeper, who opens the drawer marked "apples"; then he looks up the word "red" in a table and finds a colour sample opposite it; then he says the series of cardinal numbers . . . up to the word "five" and for each number he takes an apple of the same colour as the sample out of the drawer.—It is in this and similar ways that one operates with words. (*PI*, 1)

What is interesting in this little example is the very different way in which the shopkeeper operates with each of the three words. "Apple" seems to be a name, like "slab." But what of "red"? And, even more significantly, what of "five"? Both words are used in ways completely different from "apple" and completely different from each other. Can they all be *names?** Suppose we ask,

> But what is the meaning of the word "five"?
> —No such thing was in question here, only how the word "five" is used. (*PI*, 1)

---

*Consider again Plato's theory of Forms (pp. 152–155). Is Plato someone who falls into the trap of thinking that meaningful words are all names and that there must be something each one names? Or think of Locke on general terms, pp. 428–430.

The point of this language-game, this little "reminder," is to cure us of the hankering to ask about the meaning of this word, especially since we are inclined to think its *meaning* must be an *object* analogous to apples—only a very mysterious object. We are brought back to the way in which we actually *use* the word. We say the numbers and take an apple for each number. And there is nothing deep or mysterious here to puzzle us. Note that this example shows us Wittgenstein doing just what he says the job of the philosopher is: dispelling puzzlement by bringing words "back from their metaphysical to their everyday use" (*PI*, 116). There is no explanation given, just description. Wittgenstein is merely "arranging what we have always known" (*PI*, 109). The quest for general explanations is likely to lead us into illusions about meaning and language—illusions into which the author of the *Tractatus* was led.

In the *Tractatus*, Wittgenstein had held that the proposition was the basic unit and that each proposition pictured a possible state of affairs. Now he asks,

> But how many kinds of sentence are there? Say assertion, question, and command?—There are *countless* kinds: countless different kinds of use of what we call "symbols," "words," "sentences." And this multiplicity is not something fixed, given once for all: but new types of language, new language-games, as we may say, come into existence, and others become obsolete and get forgotten. . . .
>
> Here the term "language-*game*" is meant to bring into prominence the fact that the speaking of language is part of an activity, or of a form of life. (*PI*, 23)

Think how different from each other these language games are: giving orders, describing an object, testing a hypothesis, playacting, making a joke, translating, asking, cursing, greeting, praying. In all these ways—and more—we use language. It *is* absolutely unhelpful—and worse, dangerous!—to suppose that language is everywhere all alike. It leads into pseudoproblems and illusions, the sorts of dead ends where we are likely to say, This isn't how it *is*, but this is how it *must* be.

1. How is philosophy now conceived? What are "philosophical problems" like? What is to happen to them?
2. What is a language-game? What does Wittgenstein think the notion can do for us, and why does he think this is important?
3. How does the example of shopping for five red apples undermine some basic theses of the *Tractatus*?
4. What now happens to the notion of an essence of language? How many kinds of sentences are there, anyway?

NAMING AND MEANING

We are tempted to think, as the *Tractatus* suggests, that "a name means an object. The object is its meaning." We are tempted to think that naming is fundamental and that the rest of language can be built on that foundation. We teach the child "ball," "blue," "water." But how do we do this? We present a ball to a child and repeat "ball," "ball." This might lead us to form a general theory that says names are learned via such **ostensive definitions**—basically by pointing to objects.

But if we *look* at what is going on, we see that this cannot be right. If someone tries to teach you what a watch is (supposing you don't know) by pointing to the device on his or her wrist, you may take it that "watch" means a color, a material, a device for keeping time, or an indicated direction. An ostensive definition, Wittgenstein says, "can be variously interpreted in *every* case" (*PI*, 28). He does not deny that such ostensive definitions can sometimes be useful. But because such definitions can always be understood in a variety of ways, they cannot be the key to the essence of language. They cannot give us a *foundation* on which language can be built.

This person could help you out by saying, "This device on my wrist is a watch." But that presumes, as you can clearly see, that you are already in possession of large portions of the language. You must already understand "device" and "on" and "wrist" if what the person says is going to be helpful. Language, then, cannot *begin* with names ostensively defined, and a name cannot have its meaning provided independent of other bits of language. And that means an ostensive definition is no help in getting into the game in the first place.

But that leaves us with a problem. How do we ever get started with language, if acquiring the use of even such a basic name as "ball" presupposes an understanding of language in general? It seems impossible. Again Wittgenstein advises us to *look*. And if we look, what we see is that teaching a child the basic words is simply *training*. We set up "an association between the word and the thing" (*PI*, 6). It's like teaching your dog to come when you say "Come!"

Suppose that such an "association" is established between "apple" and apples by "training" little Jill in that way. Does she now *understand* the word "apple"? Well, does your dog understand "Come!" when it comes at that command? The process is similar, Wittgenstein suggests, and so are the results. Jill, of course, has only the most rudimentary understanding at that stage. The difference between Jill and Rover is that Jill can eventually go on to learn a lot more about apples by internalizing an ever more complex language in which to talk about them. Understanding comes in degrees. Jill is capable of understanding more than Rover, but they start in the same way. It is not by definitions (ostensive or not) that we enter the gate of language, but by *training*.

These simple associations that training sets up are not, however, themselves the meanings of words. But if neither the object named nor an association between a word and the object is the meaning of a name, what can meaning be?

> For a *large* class of cases—though not for all—in which we employ the word "meaning" it can be defined thus: the meaning of a word is its use in the language. (*PI*, 43)

The meaning of a word (by and large) is its having a specific place in a particular language-game, a certain form of life. This "place" is defined by how the word is related to other words, to activities and objects—and the positions it can occupy in sentences. To understand a word, you have to understand what *role* it plays in the language-games where it has its home—what jobs it does. The **meaning** is the **use.** And that is why it is important not to think, but to *look*—look and see how a word is actually being used.

FAMILY RESEMBLANCES

These are strong criticisms of the *Tractatus*. But we need to ask again: Is it really true that there is no essence of language? Wittgenstein asks us to consider an example: *games*.

> I mean board-games, card-games, ball-games, Olympic games, and so on. What is common to them all?—Don't say: "There *must* be something common, or they would not be called 'games'"—but *look and see* whether there is any-thing common to all.—For if you look at them you will not see something that is common to *all*, but similarities, relationships, and a whole series of them at that. To repeat: don't think, but look!—Look for example at board-games. . . . When we pass next to ball-games, much that is common is retained, but much is lost.—Are they all "amusing"? . . . Or is there always winning and losing, or competition between players? Think of patience [solitaire]. In ball-games there is winning and losing; but when a child throws his ball at the wall and catches it again, this feature has disappeared. Look at the parts played by skill and luck; and at the difference between skill in chess and skill in tennis. Think now of ring-a-ring-a-roses; here is the element of amusement, but how many other characteristic features have disappeared! . . .
>
> And the result of this examination is: we see a complicated network of similarities overlapping and criss-crossing: sometimes overall similarities, sometimes similarities of detail.
>
> I can think of no better expression to characterize these similarities than "family resemblances"; for the various resemblances between members of a family: build, features, colour of eyes, gait, temperament, etc. etc. overlap and criss-cross in the same way.—And I shall say: "games" form a family. (*PI*, 65–67)

Recall that at the beginning of the Western philosophical tradition, dominating it with the kind of power that only unexamined assumptions can have, stands Socrates with his questions: What is piety? Courage? Justice? And what Socrates wants is a definition, the essence of the thing. What he wants to discover are those features that (1) any act of justice has, (2) any nonjust act lacks, and (3) *make* the just act just. Are acts A and B both just? Then it seems natural to suppose that there must be something they have in *common*, some *essential* *characteristic* they share, some feature by virtue of which they are just. Unless we understand what that is, we will not understand justice.*

It is difficult to exaggerate the impact this assumption has had. It certainly lies beneath the *Tractatus* quest for the essence of language; it accounts for the author's certainty that there must be such a thing. But now that we are looking rather than thinking, we discover that, in very many cases, there is no such thing. There is no essence of games or of language. And almost surely there is no essence of justice or piety. All are matters of instances, examples, and cases loosely related to each other by crisscrossing and overlapping similarities. What we find when we look are **family resemblances.** What we find is exactly the kind of thing that Socrates so curtly dismisses when it is offered by Euthyphro!

It follows from this new picture that there may be no sharp boundaries for many of our concepts.

> How should we explain to someone what a game is? I imagine that we should describe *games* to him, and we might add: "This and *similar things* are called 'games.'" And do we know any more about it ourselves? Is it only other people whom we cannot tell exactly what a game is? But this is not ignorance. We do not know the boundaries because none have been drawn. To repeat, we can draw a boundary— for a special purpose. Does it take that to make the concept usable? Not at all! (Except for that special purpose.) (*PI,* 69)

> Frege compares a concept to an area and says that an area with vague boundaries cannot be called an area at all. This presumably means that we cannot do anything with it.—But is it senseless to say: "Stand roughly there"? (*PI,* 71)

We may understand Wittgenstein's point more clearly by examining another example. What, people sometimes ask, is a religion? Is belief in a supreme being essential to religion? Then early Buddhism is not a religion. How about belief in life after death? But early Judaism seems to lack that feature. Some people suggest that communism is

essentially religious in character. But how can that be, if it lacks so many of the features of Presbyterianism? If we search for the conditions that are both necessary and sufficient to define "religion," we will probably search in vain. But suppose we proceed this way: Do you want to know what a religion is? Consider Roman Catholicism; this and similar things are called "religions." To treat the question this way is to think of "religion" as a family resemblance concept.

Someone might ask, "How similar to Roman Catholicism does something have to be if it is to qualify as a religion?" We would be right to reply that there is no exact answer to that question. And the absence of a clear boundary does not mean that the concept is unusable, any more than "Stand roughly there" is a useless instruction just because it isn't perfectly precise.*

When he was writing the *Tractatus,* Wittgenstein thought that every proposition had to have a determinate sense and that therefore a completely analyzed proposition would be free of all vagueness and ambiguity. How could it be otherwise, when it was composed of simple names, each standing for a simple object? But if we look, without seeking to prescribe how it *must* be, we see that language is not everywhere exact, like a logical calculus. Like "game," many of our concepts are governed by relationships of family resemblance rather than essences.† And they are none the worse for that. So Wittgenstein assembles his reminders of how our language actually functions, bringing us back to the activities (forms of life) in which it does its varied jobs. And in so doing, he shows us the way out of various fly bottles we get ourselves into by misunderstanding the logic of our language.

---

*Notice how this sort of thing undercuts Descartes' requirement (*Meditation IV*) that we should assent only to ideas that are clear and distinct. Most of our ideas, Wittgenstein holds, are not clear and distinct. And that is not something we should try to fix. On the contrary, our concepts are "in order" as they are.

†But not all. We do have concepts that are governed by strict rules. Many scientific concepts—"triangle," for example, or "force"—are like that. We should not think of the family resemblance claim as a *theory* about the essence of meaning!

---

*Euthyphro on piety is a good example. For other examples, see Plato on knowledge (pp. 149–152) and Descartes on clear and distinct ideas (p. 362).

1. Why cannot ostensive definitions be basic in language use? And if they are not, how do language-games get started? (How do children learn a language?)
2. Explain the motto "The meaning of a word is its use in the language."
3. Must usable concepts have sharp boundaries? What are family resemblances? What are we supposed to learn from the example of games?

The Continuity of Wittgenstein's Thought

As you can see, virtually every one of the principal theses of the *Tractatus* is undermined and rejected by the later Wittgenstein.

- There is an essence of language.
- The essence of language is picturing facts.
- There is a complete and exact analysis of every sentence.
- The basic elements of language are names.
- The meaning of a name is its bearer.
- Names are simple.
- Names name simple objects.
- The world is pictured as the totality of facts in logical space.

Other thinkers have changed their ways of thinking—Augustine after his conversion to Christianity, Kant after reading Hume—but Wittgenstein's turnabout is as deep and dramatic as any. Is there any line of continuity that one can trace through this shift? Let us suggest that three interrelated themes and a motivation persist.

The first theme is an opposition, amounting almost to a personal revulsion, to what Wittgenstein calls "just *gassing*." A more contemporary term for this phenomenon might be "bullshitting."[12] The second is the idea that one might "set a limit to thought" (*Tractatus*, preface, 3). The third is the notion that some things cannot be said, but only shown. The motivation that persists is a quest for a life that is worth living.

1. The whole point of the *Tractatus*, you will recall, was to "set a limit to thought" by delineating what can and cannot be said. Whatever can be said can be said clearly. The rest is "nonsense," which we must "pass over in silence" (*Tractatus*, preface, 3). Wittgenstein felt that most talk about the meaning of life, about value and God and the soul, was "just *gassing*"—an attempt to put into words questions and answers that cannot be put into words. But it is crucial to remember that he also thought that these matters were *far and away the most important*. The revulsion he felt was grounded in his conviction that prattle about them demeans them, takes them out of the realm in which they properly exist. A good man, for instance, is not someone who *talks* about goodness, but someone who "shows" it, displays it in his life. "It is clear that ethics cannot be put into words" (*Tractatus* 6.421). But it can be put into a life!

2. His project—to set a limit to thought by identifying nonsense, gassing, and bullshit—is still a driving force in Wittgenstein's later thought. The aim has not changed, but the method by which he thinks it can be done has changed. In the *Tractatus*, he tried to do it all at once—with one stroke, as it were—by constructing a *theory* of language and meaning that would expose nonsense for what it is. But now having come to see that he had been prescribing to language, that he had been held captive by the picture of language as a logical calculus, he gives up the attempt to create a theory. Instead, he "assembles reminders" (*PI*, 127) that bring us back from nonsense to the actual uses of language in those varied activities (forms of life) in which words get their meaning. This is something that cannot be done all at once; it requires the careful examination of case after case where language "goes on holiday" (*PI*, 38) and misleads us. And so we get the little stories, the language-games, the questions and answers, and the multitudinous examples of the *Philosophical Investigations*.

3. The *Tractatus* tells us there are some things that cannot be said. These things *show* themselves. Among them are these:

- the logical structure of language (which displays itself in every proposition);
- the nature of logical truth (manifest in tautologies);
- the relation of the philosophical subject to the world (the coincidence of solipsism and realism);

- the happiness of the good person (who has a different world from that of the unhappy person);
- "the mystical" (that the world is).

Are there still, in *Philosophical Investigations,* things that can only be shown, not said? There are, and one suspects they are still the most important things. But it is no longer so easy to list them. Rather, the *showing* has become identical with the style of the book. Even the samples we have examined display a most unusual style.* The book is full of questions (often unanswered), conversations between the author and an interlocutor, instructions ("Compare . . . ," "Imagine . . ."), little stories, suggestions, reminders, and so on. Surely no other book in the history of philosophy contains so many questions! Wittgenstein is reported to have said that he thought an entire book of philosophy could be written containing nothing but *jokes.*

The aim of all this is still, as in the *Tractatus,* to get us to "see the world aright" (*Tractatus,* 6.54). But that no longer means a flight of the metaphysical self to that point without extension from which the entire world looks like a limited whole of valueless facts. Seeing the world aright now means to see it, and language especially, in all its lush richness. And we are invited to see it that way—or, better, to let it *show itself* to us—through the very structure of the book. It is no accident that in the preface Wittgenstein compares his book to an album of sketches:

> The philosophical remarks in this book are, as it were, a number of sketches of landscapes which were made in the course of . . . long and involved journeyings.
> . . . Thus this book is really only an album. (*PI,* ix)

We could compare what Wittgenstein is doing here to the work of an artist. He is trying in as many ways as he can to help us appreciate the "landscapes" of our language so that we no longer get lost in them, confused by them. The book *shows* us a way of investigating puzzles and problems.

> It is not our aim to refine or complete the system of rules for the use of our words in unheard-of ways.
>
> For the clarity that we are aiming at is indeed *complete* clarity. But this simply means that the philosophical problems should *completely* disappear. . . .
>
> The real discovery is the one that makes me capable of stopping doing philosophy when I want to.—The one that gives philosophy peace, so that it is no longer tormented by questions which bring *itself* in question. . . . Problems are solved (difficulties eliminated), not a *single* problem.
>
> There is not a philosophical method, though there are indeed methods, like different therapies. (*PI,* 133)

Here we come to the motivation that persists from the early work through the last. By bringing our words back from their metaphysical to their everyday use, he wants to show us how to be *content* here—in the everyday. It's not just that we misunderstand our language; because language structures a form of life, we also fail to understand our *lives.* We are *driven* to these illusions because we are not satisfied with our lives. Metaphysical theories are a kind of compensation, an attempt to find peace *beyond the world* because we have not been able to find it here. (The *Tractatus,* too, was an attempt to find peace that way.)*

Wittgenstein wants to show us a form of life that is so worthwhile we can simply stop doing philosophy when we want to. As in the *Tractatus,* "philosophical" problems should simply *disappear.* But the form of life shown us in the *Investigations* is not something "unheard-of." It is our own life! A student asks a Zen master, "What must I do to gain enlightenment?" The master asks, "Have you eaten?" "Yes," says the student. "Then wash your bowl."

---

*One is reminded of Kierkegaard's indirect communication, or of Nietzsche's aphorisms, or maybe of Heraclitus or Zhuangzi, or perhaps of the stories about how Zen masters proceed. It is not accidental that the earlier book is called a *treatise* and the later book *investigations.* The former suggests completeness and a theoretical character that is altogether lacking in the latter.

*Compare Nietzsche on "real worlds," pp. 570–571. See also Kierkegaard's characterization of the "Knight of Faith," pp. 530–531. Wittgenstein once said that Kierkegaard was the greatest philosopher of the nineteenth century. The relation between the Knight of Infinite Resignation and the Knight of Faith in Kierkegaard is remarkably like the relation between the *Tractatus* and the *Investigations.* It is significant, I think, that Wittgenstein wanted them printed together, though this has not happened.

These investigations are profoundly subversive of the traditional ways of doing philosophy. Doctrines found in Plato, Descartes, Locke, Hume, Kant, Hegel, and so on are undercut, not by *argument* but by the examples, stories, questions, and language-games—all designed to get us to see things in a different (though familiar) light. Wittgenstein aims to show us how to give up the temptation to formulate philosophical *theories* about reality, mind, perception, or understanding. He aims to show the fly the way out of the bottle.

There is a theme in Wittgenstein's later work, closely connected to the idea of a language-game, that we can perhaps pull out. It is a theme directly relevant to a matter that has come up repeatedly in our account of the great conversation: the question about relativism. Recall that this issue originates in the dispute between Socrates and the Sophists (see those earlier chapters) and is expanded on by most of our philosophers. Can Wittgenstein throw any new light on that old perplexity?

1. What continuities exist between the thoughts of the early and the late Wittgenstein?
2. How has the project of setting a limit to thought changed in Wittgenstein's later philosophy?

Our Groundless Certainty

Think about the ubiquitous arrow, indicating to us which way to go—to the exit, on the one-way street, to Philadelphia. How do you know which way you are being directed to go? Why, for instance, don't you go toward the tail of the arrow? Or why don't you go in different directions on different days of the week?

> What has the expression of a rule—say a signpost—got to do with my actions? What sort of connexion is there here?—Well, perhaps this one: I have been trained to react to this sign in a particular way, and now I do so react to it. (*PI*, 198)

Training again. Rather like we train a dog to heel, perhaps. And because we *all* go the way the arrow points, we can see that the training initiates us into a common way of doing things—a *practice*. In fact

a person goes by a sign-post only in so far as there exists a regular use of sign-posts, a custom. (*PI*, 198)

Without such a custom, such a "regular use," there would be no such thing as obeying the sign. If that is right, some interesting consequences follow.

> It is not possible that there should have been only one occasion on which someone obeyed a rule. It is not possible that there should have been only one occasion on which a report was made, an order given or understood; and so on.—To obey a rule, to make a report, to give an order, to play a game of chess, are *customs* (uses, institutions). (*PI*, 199)

We are not to understand this as an empirical remark, as something that we conclude on the basis of *observing* cases of rule following. Rather, Wittgenstein means to say that it is *not possible* that there should be a purely private rule. Because obeying a rule is part of a custom, it presupposes a community in which such practices exist.

But suppose you were asked, "How *do* you *know* that is the way to go?"

> Well, how do I know?—If that means "Have I reasons?" the answer is: my reasons will soon give out. And then I shall act, without reasons. (*PI*, 211)
>
> "How am I able to obey a rule?"—If this is not a question about causes, then it is about the justification for my following the rule in the way I do.
>
> If I have exhausted the justifications I have reached bedrock, and my spade is turned. Then I am inclined to say: "This is simply what I do." (*PI*, 217)

In this striking metaphor, Wittgenstein brings us back to the communal practices in which our language-games have their home. It is as if the philosophical why-questions have made us dig deeper and deeper. But there comes a point when we can dig no more, find no more justifications for our beliefs, our knowledge claims, or our scientific methods. At that point we reach bedrock, and our "spade is turned." What is **bedrock?** Is it some Cartesian clear and distinct idea? Is it some Humean private impression? Is it a Kantian synthetic a priori truth? No. None of these things. Bedrock is "simply what I do." And what I do is part of what we do, we who live this form of life, engage in these activities, play these language-games, grow up in these customs. There comes a point where explanations and justifications

ZEN

"Usually thinking is rather self-centered. In our everyday life, our thinking is ninety-nine percent self-centered: 'Why do I have suffering? Why do I have trouble?'" (*SS*, 118). Zen, a form of Buddhism brought from India to China and developed in Japan, presents a radical cure for this self-centeredness and promises, in consequence, release from suffering.

The key is to see into our own nature. But the aim is not to develop a theory of the mind or gain an intellectual understanding. Paradoxically, the goal is to have no goal, to be free of "attachments," as the Zen masters put it. That is not easy, however, cluttered as our minds are with desires, concerns, and anxieties. Something dramatic has to happen, a kind of explosion that blows our usual ways of thinking into smithereens. The result of that explosion is enlightenment, or **satori.**

To stimulate that explosion, Zen masters often assign students a **koan** to meditate on—a puzzling statement that seems at first to make no sense. Here are several famous *koans*:

- All things return to the One, but where does this One return?
- Who is it that carries for you this lifeless corpse of yours?
- Who is the Buddha? Three pounds of flax.
- What are your original features, which you have even prior to your birth?

Kao-feng (1238–1285) has left us an account of his wrestling with the *koan* about the One. While deep in sleep one night, he found himself fixing his attention on it. For the next six days and nights,

> while spreading the napkin, producing the bowls, or attending to my natural wants, whether I moved or rested, whether I talked or kept silent, my whole existence was wrapped up with the question "Where does this one return?" No other thoughts ever disturbed my consciousness; no, even if I wanted to stir up the least bit of thought

irrelevant to the central one, I could not do so. . . . From morning till evening, from evening to morning, so transparent, so tranquil, so majestically above all things were my feelings! Absolutely pure and not a particle of dust! My one thought covered eternity.

But this was not yet satori. After the sixth day, he happened to glance at a poem written on a wall and *suddenly* he awoke from the spell, and

> the meaning of "Who carries this lifeless corpse of yours?" burst upon me. (*DTS*, 101)

But, significantly, he doesn't tell us what the meaning is. He doesn't tell us because he can't. What he experienced then, what he *knew*, is the kind of thing that words cannot capture. He has seen into his own nature, and the result is a transformed life.

Words can, however, *indirectly* indicate the reality experienced there, and Zen masters are not at a loss for words to point us in the right direction. One clue is that there are two stages in Kao-feng's enlightenment. In the first stage of intense concentration, the mind is polished, like a mirror freed from dust, and he feels himself eternal. What happens in the second stage? Something exotic, marvelous, intensely dramatic? No.

> Zen is not some kind of excitement, but concentration on our usual everyday routine. (*SS*, 57)
> It is a kind of mystery that for people who have no experience of enlightenment, enlightenment is something wonderful. But if they attain it, it is nothing. But yet it is not nothing. (*SS*, 47)

Zen gives a radical interpretation to what the Buddha found when he gained enlightenment. The Buddha nature, which all existing things share and express, is actually *emptiness*. Our mind is no-mind, our self is no-self. And the intense realization of this frees us from the imperious demands of the ego. The result, surprisingly, is nothing extraordinary.

ZEN

It is just our everyday life, but played now in a new, selfless key.*

> When we are hungry we eat; when we are sleepy we lay ourselves down; and where does the infinite or the finite come in here? . . . Life as it is lived suffices. (*DTS*, 9)
>
> . . . when your practice is calm and ordinary, everyday life itself is enlightenment. (*SS*, 59)

If a student displays his lack of enlightenment, a Zen master will sometimes strike him with a staff. This illustrates that the transition from self-centered everydayness to true everyday life is a violent matter. The two lives may look very similar from the outside, but inwardly no difference could be greater. Moreover, this change never just happens; it requires intense effort and activity.

The truth is that our nature has been the Buddha nature all along. (Everything arises from the same emptiness.) All along, everything needed for enlightenment has been ours; we have just been too dim-witted to see it. After satori is ours, we are amazed to discover that

_____

*Compare Kierkegaard's Knight of Infinite Resignation with his Knight of Faith (pp. 530–531). Compare also Wittgenstein's *Tractatus* with his *Philosophical Investigations* (pp. 643–645). Philosophy, the later Wittgenstein says, "leaves everything as it is."

we have been led astray through ignorance to find a split in our own being, that there was from the very beginning no need for a struggle between the finite and the infinite, that the peace we are seeking so eagerly after has been there all the time. (*DTS*, 13)

The path to enlightenment is not easy. It is leaving home on a dangerous journey and coming back again. But the home to which you return is very different— and yet exactly the same—as the home you left.

> Before a man studies Zen, to him mountains are mountains and waters are waters; after he gets an insight into the truth of Zen through the instruction of a good master, mountains to him are not mountains and waters are not waters; but after this when he really attains to the abode of rest, mountains are once more mountains and waters are waters. (*DTS*, 14)

It is as though upon attaining enlightenment, you suddenly "see the world aright" (*Tractatus* 6.54).

NOTE:
References are as follows:
   DTS: D. T. Suzuki, *Zen Buddhism*, ed. William Barrett (New York: Doubleday, 1956).
   SS: Shunryu Suzuki, *Zen Mind, Beginner's Mind*, ed. Trudy Dixon (New York: Weatherhill, 1970).

---

for behaving in a certain way come to an end. Then one just acts. We do as our linguistic community has trained us to do. In the end, it comes down to this:

> When I obey a rule, I do not choose.
>   I obey the rule *blindly*. (*PI*, 219)

In the *Tractatus*, we found the distinction between what can be said and what can only be shown. In the *Investigations*, we find that when we get to bedrock, there is no more to say. At that point you can only *display* my form of life, the language-game you play. Here, where the spade is turned, you just *show* you what you do: This is what you do—how you live, the way you understand, mean things, and follow

rules; this is your (our) form of life. In the *Tractatus*, it was the logical hardness of tautologies that turned the spade, that could only be shown. Here it is the practice of a certain set of language-games.

But this bedrock cannot, as we have seen, be a purely private form of life, governed by private rules. And Wittgenstein now pushes this point by asking, "What does it mean to 'agree in language'?"

> If language is to be a means of communication there must be agreement not only in definitions but also (queer as this may sound) in judgments. (*PI*, 242)

Are there some particular judgments that we need to agree about to communicate with one another in a language? In an essay titled "A Defense of Common Sense," English philosopher G. E. Moore claims to "know with certainty" a large number of propositions.[13] And he thinks we all know them, too. For instance, he claims each of us knows that

- there exists a living human body that is my body.
- my body was born at a certain time in the past.
- my body has been at various distances from other things, which also exist.
- there have been many other human bodies like my own.
- I have had many different experiences.
- so have other human beings.

This is not Moore's complete list, but you get the idea. It is a list of what seem to be *truisms*.

Wittgenstein tends to think the word "know" is inappropriately used here. But our interest is directed to his idea that these "judgments" might form the basis for an agreement defining a language or a form of life.

How is it that we are so *certain* of these "facts"? Have we carefully investigated each of them and found that the evidence is in their favor? No. They do not have that kind of status. Taken together they are more like a picture we accept.

> But I did not get my picture of the world by satisfying myself of its correctness; nor do I have it because I am satisfied of its correctness. No: it is the inherited background against which I distinguish between true and false. (*OC,* 94)[14]

Wittgenstein compares this "inherited background" to a kind of mythology, by which he means that though the truisms of the picture are empirical, they are not acquired by empirical investigation.* He also compares our world picture to the banks of a river within which the water of true and false propositions can flow. The mythology can change; the banks of the river are not unalterable. And in some ways, at least, different pictures are possible for us even at a given time.

---

*Here you should keep in mind the Kantian a priori synthetic principles. Wittgensteinian "world pictures" play a similar role. They define a world for us. They are as anchored for us as the categories. But they are neither universal nor necessary— nor are they unchangeable. They function like the *paradigms* in Thomas Kuhn's influential book, *The Structure of Scientific Revolutions* (Chicago: University of Chicago Press, 1962).

Very intelligent and well-educated people believe in the story of creation in the Bible, while others hold it as proven false, and the grounds of the latter are well known to the former. (*OC,* 336)

How are we to account for this? Suppose the doubter talks to the believer. If the reasons for doubt are already well known to someone who believes the biblical story, what could the doubter say to convince the believer? All the doubter's reasons are already on the table—and they don't convince!

Different language-games (different forms of life) are possible. And arguments in favor of one of them *presuppose* the standards of argument and evidence characteristic of that very form of life. So reasons do not get a grip on a different form of life with different standards and rules of reasoning. Reasons, Wittgenstein reminds us, come to an end.

World pictures, then, may differ; but there is *always some* framework within which we come to believe and think certain things.

> If you tried to doubt everything you would not get as far as doubting anything. The game of doubting itself presupposes certainty. (*OC,* 115)

> Why do I not satisfy myself that I have two feet when I want to get up from a chair? There is no why. I simply don't. That is how I act. (*OC,* 148)

> How does someone judge which is his right and which his left hand? How do I know that my judgment will agree with someone else's? How do I know that this colour is blue? If I don't trust *myself* here, why should I trust anyone else's judgment? That is to say: somewhere I must begin with notdoubting; and that is not, so to speak, hasty but excusable; it is part of judging. (*OC,* 150)

Can you doubt—Descartes notwithstanding— that you have a body? That you have parents? That you have never been to the moon? These things "stand fast" for us. It is hard to imagine anything *more certain* than these judgments that could cast doubt on them. Is it, for example, *more certain* that my senses have sometimes deceived me than that the sky I'm looking at is blue?*

---

*Wittgenstein's critique here should remind you of Peirce on doubt and belief. (See again pp. 596–597.)

Much seems to be fixed, and it is removed from the traffic. It is so to speak shunted onto an unused siding. (*OC*, 210)

Now it gives our way of looking at things, and our researches, their form. Perhaps it was once disputed. But perhaps, for unthinkable ages, it has belonged to the *scaffolding* of our thoughts. (Every human being has parents.) (*OC*, 211)

The use of the *Tractatus* word "scaffolding" in this connection cannot be an accident. In his earlier view, logic (that transparent and absolutely rigid medium) was the *scaffolding* of the world. Now, in dramatic contrast, what grounds our system of beliefs are such apparently empirical and logically accidental facts as that I have parents or even that motor cars don't grow out of the earth (*OC*, 279).

But the complex system of certainties that make up a world picture does not function like an ordinary foundation. The foundation of a house is that on which everything else rests, yet the foundation could stand alone. Our certainties, however, form a *system* of interrelated judgments.

> When we first begin to *believe* anything, what we believe is not a single proposition, it is a whole system of propositions. (Light dawns gradually over the whole.) (*OC*, 141)

> I have arrived at the rock bottom of my convictions. And one might almost say that these foundation-walls are carried by the whole house. (*OC*, 248)

Here the atomism of the *Tractatus* is most thoroughly repudiated. We do not first believe a single isolated proposition, then a second, a third, and so on. "Light dawns gradually over the whole." In a striking metaphor, Wittgenstein suggests that the foundation walls are themselves borne up by their connection with the rest of the house.

We may still want to ask, What makes us so certain of this picture? What guarantees for us that these judgments are fixed, that they do stand fast? Wittgenstein's answer is that *nothing* guarantees this. There is no guarantee. We are, indeed, certain of these things; but our certainty cannot be anchored in anything objective, in anything more certain than they.

> To be sure there is justification; but justification comes to an end. (*OC*, 192)

And in what does it come to an end?

> At the foundation of well-founded beliefs lies belief that is not well-founded. (*OC*, 253)

> The difficulty is to realize the groundlessness of our believing. (*OC*, 166)

> Giving grounds . . . , justifying the evidence, comes to an end;—but the end is not certain propositions' striking us immediately as true, i.e., it is not a kind of *seeing* on our part; it is our *acting*, which lies at the bottom of the language-game. (*OC*, 204)*

> My *life* consists in my being content to accept many things. (*OC*, 344)

If the Western philosophical tradition has been a quest for certainty, we can say that Wittgenstein satisfies that quest, for he acknowledges that there are many, many things of which we are certain (many more things than most philosophers ever imagined!). But if philosophy is a quest for objective certainty, for a foundation that *guarantees the truth* of the edifice of knowledge, then, in a certain sense, if Wittgenstein is right, philosophy is over. Epistemology is *over*. For there comes a point where the spade is turned, where one cannot dig any deeper. And bedrock comes sooner than most philosophers have wanted it to come. We find it in our form of life. Our life *consists* in "being content to accept many things." This is, Wittgenstein holds, a difficult realization; we keep wanting to ask that good old why-question. Can't we, we yearn to ask, *somehow justify our form of life?* No, says Wittgenstein. It is *groundless*. It is "simply what we do." And what we do may not be what *they* do. Philosophy cannot dig deeper than the practices and customs that define our form of life. We do have our certainties, but they are groundless.[15]

> Philosophy may in no way interfere with the actual use of language; it can in the end only describe it.
> For it cannot give it any foundation either.
> It leaves everything as it is. (*PI*, 124)

---

1. When we see the sign EXIT, how do we know which way to go to find the exit?
2. Could there be just one occasion on which someone obeyed a certain rule? Explain.
3. When reasons give out, what do we do then? In what sense do we obey rules blindly?

---

*See Kierkegaard on the unavoidability of a leap (p. 536).

4. What is bedrock? And what does Wittgenstein mean by "agreement in language"? Why is that important?

5. What kind of status does your "world picture" have? Are you certain about it? What guarantees its correctness?

6. What does it mean to say that our believing is groundless?

FOR FURTHER THOUGHT

1. The young Wittgenstein thought he had found a unique solution to the problem of the meaning of life—the problem disappears! Try to explain this "solution" in terms that could be meaningful to your own life and then decide whether you accept it.

2. If Wittgenstein is right, philosophy as a quest for foundations, for the absolute truth of things, has suffered shipwreck. Do you think he is right? If so, what should we do now?

3. Several times, a similarity to Zen themes has been suggested. See whether you can work out this parallel more fully. Are there differences, too?

KEY WORDS

logic	limit of the world
states of affairs	realism
facts	mystical
possible state of affairs	philosophical self
pictorial form	logical positivism
logical space	verifiability principle
proposition	emotivist theory of
names	ethics
world	language-game
atomic propositions	ostensive definitions
logical atomism	meaning as use
logical truth	family resemblances
tautology	satori
saying/showing	koan
picturing	bedrock
value	

NOTES

1. Bertrand Russell, "Logical Atomism," in *Logic and Knowledge* (London: Allen and Unwin, 1956), 197–198.

2. Bertrand Russell, "Philosophers and Idiots," *Listener* 52, no. 1354 (February 10, 1955): 247. Reprinted in Russell's *Portraits from Memory* (London: Allen and Unwin, 1956), 26–27.

3. A brief and very readable account of Wittgenstein's life can be found in Norman Malcolm's *Ludwig Wittgenstein: A Memoir* (Oxford: Oxford University Press, 1958).

4. Ludwig Wittgenstein, *Tractatus Logico-Philosophicus*, trans. D. F. Pears and B. F. McGuiness (London: Routledge and Kegan Paul, 1961). Quotations from the main text of the *Tractatus* are identified by the paragraph numbers found in that work.

5. Paul Englemann, *Letters from Ludwig Wittgenstein, with a Memoir* (Oxford: Basil Blackwell, 1967), 143–144.

6. Ludwig Wittgenstein, "Lecture on Ethics," *Philosophical Review* 74 (1965): 12.

7. Quotations from Ludwig Wittgenstein's *Notebooks, 1914–1916* (Oxford: Basil Blackwell, 1961), are cited in the text using the abbreviation N. References are to page numbers.

8. Wittgenstein, "Lecture on Ethics," 8.

9. Moritz Schlick, "Positivism and Realism," in *Logical Positivism*, ed. A. J. Ayer (New York: Macmillan, 1959), 86–87.

10. A. J. Ayer, *Language, Truth, and Logic* (New York: Dover, n.d.), 107–108.

11. Quotations from Ludwig Wittgenstein's *Philosophical Investigations* (New York: Macmillan, 1953) are cited in the text using the abbreviation *PI*. References are to section numbers.

12. Wittgenstein is mentioned in Harry D. Frankfurt's interesting piece, "On Bullshit," in his *The Importance of What We Care About* (Cambridge: Cambridge University Press, 1988). Frankfurt identifies the essence of *bullshit* as the lack of any concern for the truth.

13. G. E. Moore, "A Defense of Common Sense," in *Contemporary British Philosophy*, 2nd ser., ed. G. Muirhead (London: Allen and Unwin, 1925).

14. Quotations from Ludwig Wittgenstein's *On Certainty* (Oxford: Basil Blackwell, 1969) are cited in the text using the abbreviation *OC*. References are to paragraph numbers.

15. We have learned much about reading Wittgenstein from Gordon Bearn's *Waking to Wonder: Wittgenstein's Existential Investigations* (New York: State University of New York Press, 1996).

CHAPTER

27

MARTIN HEIDEGGER
The Meaning of Being

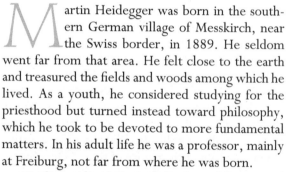

Martin Heidegger was born in the southern German village of Messkirch, near the Swiss border, in 1889. He seldom went far from that area. He felt close to the earth and treasured the fields and woods among which he lived. As a youth, he considered studying for the priesthood but turned instead toward philosophy, which he took to be devoted to more fundamental matters. In his adult life he was a professor, mainly at Freiburg, not far from where he was born.

Heidegger lived through both world wars and for a time in the 1930s supported the Nazi Party. This disreputable episode has been the occasion for much debate: Was it, or was it not, essentially connected to his philosophy? Opinion is divided. Although Heidegger was not in all respects an admirable person, he is nevertheless a philosopher of great power. He died in 1976.*

The difficulty of his writing is legendary. Heidegger's aim is to try to say things that our

tradition—the great conversation since Plato—has made it hard to say. Heidegger thinks the tradition has "hidden" precisely what he is most interested in, so he devises new terms to express what he wants to say.* Often these inventions have Greek etymological roots. Sometimes they are ordinary words put together in extraordinary ways or given extraordinary meanings. The difficulty is compounded because translators do not always agree on the best English rendering of a German term, so the same term may be translated several ways.†

In 1927, Heidegger published a book called *Being and Time*. The work Heidegger projected was in two parts, and *Being and Time* constituted just two-thirds of the first part. The rest was never published. Why? Apparently he came to believe that

---

*For a brief discussion of the Heidegger/Nazi case, see http://www.sophia-project.org/uploads/1/3/9/5/13955288/quirk_heidegger1.pdf.

*Early in our story we see thinkers struggling to find (or invent) language adequate to what they want to say. Compare Anaximander (p. 12), Heraclitus (p. 18), and Democritus (p. 30).

†We have had to make some terminological decisions; where a translation is at variance with our decision, we have put the translation we are using in brackets.

the edifice for which *Being and Time* was to provide a foundation could not be built on that foundation. Consequently, there was a "turn" in his thinking, so that (as with Wittgenstein) we can speak of the early and the late philosophy. Heidegger's thought after this "turn" is important, but notoriously difficult. Here we will restrict ourselves to his early thought, examining the influential themes in *Being and Time*.

What Is the Question?

Heidegger's thought has from the beginning a remarkable single-mindedness. There is one question, and only one, to which all his intellectual effort is directed. Heidegger calls it the question of the meaning of **Being**.* How to understand this question is itself a question. The concern it expresses will become richer and clearer as we explore his philosophy, but we should now address it in a preliminary way.

You have before you a piece of paper on which some words are written. The paper can be described in a variety of ways. When we describe it, we are saying *what* it is—what kind of thing it is, what its characteristics and functions and uses are. But there is also this curious fact: *that it is*. I call it a curious fact because it tends to remain in the background, taken for granted—even, perhaps, hidden. But it is just this fact Heidegger wishes to ask about. What does it mean for the piece of paper to *be*? Kant, you will recall, urges that "being" is no ordinary predicate, and we have noted that this insight is incorporated into the quantifier of modern logic.† To say that the piece of paper *exists*, Kant claims, is not further to describe it or to elaborate its concept, but to assert that something *corresponds* to the description we have given.

So far, so good. But what does this "corresponding" come to? What is it for the piece of paper to *be*? It is hard, perhaps, to get that question clearly in mind. Heidegger is convinced that Kant doesn't satisfactorily answer this question, nor has anyone else in Western philosophy answered it. But that is precisely the question Heidegger is addressing. What does that *mean*—that the paper *is*?

Heidegger begins *Being and Time* with a quotation from Plato's dialogue *The Sophist*, in which a stranger remarks,

> For manifestly you have long been aware of what you mean when you use the expression "being." We, however, who used to think we understood it, have now become perplexed. (*BT*, 1)[1]

That, Heidegger thinks, precisely describes *our* situation. You might think that this is odd. Even if Plato is perplexed, how can it be that all the intervening centuries of thought haven't cleared the matter up? Heidegger's answer is that philosophical reflection about Being has *hidden* as much as revealed the phenomenon—and for deep and interesting reasons, as we will see.

We tend to have conflicting intuitions about the nature of Being. On the one hand, it seems the most obvious thing in the world: It applies to everything! We ourselves and every entity we meet *are*. How could we not know what Being is? On the other hand, if you are asked to define it, your response will probably be like that of Augustine when asked about the nature of time.* One thing is clear, Heidegger says: Being is not itself an entity; it is not one more thing along with all the other things in the world. Imagine that you write down on a long, long list all the things that there are. Would you write down "apples, planets, babies, dirt, . . . , and Being"? No, you would not. Each of the entities on that list, in a strange way, has carried its Being along with it.† But what is this Being

---

*We follow the usual convention and capitalize the word when it is *Being* that is in question. The word "being" of course has other uses in English. Occasionally we may speak of *a being* or of *beings;* when uncapitalized, the term is the equivalent of "entity" or "item" or "thing" in a very broad sense (not just a physical thing)—that is, whatever can *be,* or have *Being*.

†See again Kant's discussion of the ontological argument (pp. 484–485).

---

*See p. 275.

†The early Wittgenstein's contrast between (a) the totality of facts that make up the world and (b) *that* the world exists is essentially the same as Heidegger's contrast between entities (beings) and Being. (See p. 632.) Wittgenstein, of course, believes nothing can be said about this "*that* it is"; this is the "unsayable" about which we must be silent—the

that puts humans and hammers and rocks and stars on the list but unicorns and square circles off? That is the question.

In saying that Being—the object of his inquiry—is not itself *a* being (not a thing, an entity, one of the items that exist), Heidegger means to make clear that he is not engaging in that traditional quest for *the* being who is responsible for all the rest. Heidegger is not searching for or trying to prove the existence of God—at least as God has traditionally been conceived. Heidegger is not asking about the *highest being*, but about what it is that accounts for the fact that there is *anything at all* (rather than nothing). This question seems on the one hand to be so abstract and distant from us as to be of purely academic interest. Yet on the other hand, because we ourselves exist, it seems so intimate and near to us as to be almost too close to examine.* How could we make any progress in answering this question about the meaning of Being?

The Clue

> Any inquiry, as an inquiry about something, has *that which is asked about*. But all inquiry about something is somehow a questioning of something. So in addition to what is asked about, an inquiry has *that which is interrogated*. . . . Furthermore, in what is asked about there lies also *that which is to be found out by the asking*. (*BT*, 24)

The inquiry about the meaning of Being is *asking about* Being; that is the focus of our question. And what we want to find out by our asking is the meaning of Being. But what will we examine? If our investigation is to be a real, concrete one, it can't just hang in the air; it must tie down to something. There must be something that we *interrogate*.

> Being is always the Being of an entity. (*BT*, 29)

Being, in other words, is not like the smile of the Cheshire cat, which can remain mysteriously after the cat has vanished. As we have seen, Being comes along with the entities that *are*. What Heidegger is now saying is that apart from entities, there "is" no Being.* So we can't investigate Being directly; we must do it in connection with some entity. But which entity shall we choose? In principle, any might do, from quarks to gophers to black holes. But is there some entity that would be *best* to interrogate with respect to its Being?

At this point, Heidegger notes that an inquiry like this is itself something that has Being. (Asking questions is not just *nothing*, after all.) And we would not have answered our question about the meaning of Being unless we also got clear about the Being of items such as inquiries—and of the entities that inquire! This suggests that *we ourselves* might be the entity to interrogate in our inquiry, the focus of our investigation.

Heidegger recognizes, of course, that many sorts of investigation concern themselves with human beings: physics, chemistry, biology, history, psychology, anthropology. But none of these sciences takes the perspective on humans that is relevant to our question. To focus attention on the relevant aspect, he refers to the entity we will interrogate by a term that is usually left untranslated: **Dasein.** This German term can be used to refer to almost any kind of entity, though it is usually used for human beings. Literally the term means "being there." ("Da" means "there" or sometimes "here"; "sein" is "being.") And Heidegger chooses this term to highlight the aspect of humans he is interested in: not the chemistry of the body or the history of human society, but their Being.†

The suggestion that Dasein should be the focus of our investigation—the entity to be

---

mystical. But it is just this that Heidegger commits all his intellectual energy to trying to say. A caution: What Heidegger means by "world" is very different from what the *Tractatus* means by it, and our relationship to it is correspondingly different.

*Again Wittgenstein comes to mind: Recall the analogy of the visual field that does not include the eye that sees it (see p. 630).

---

*Heidegger's notion of *Being*—something distinct from *beings*—is obviously indebted to the claim by Aquinas that existence (*esse*) is "something added." (See p. 302.) But Aquinas would not agree that there can be no Being without *a* being, because that's precisely what *God* is!

†Like the term "person" in Kant, this term doesn't specify whether human beings are the only beings with the particular *way of Being* we have. Perhaps in other galaxies. . .

"What is strange in the thinking of Being is its simplicity. Precisely this keeps us from it."

—MARTIN HEIDEGGER

interrogated—is further supported by noting that we are distinctive among entities in an interesting way.

> Dasein is an entity which does not just occur among other entities. Rather it is ontically distinguished by the fact that, in its very Being, that Being is an *issue* for it. But in that case, this is a constitutive state of Dasein's Being, and this implies that Dasein, in its Being, has a relationship towards that Being—a relationship which itself is one of Being. And this means further that there is some way in which Dasein understands itself in its Being, and that to some degree it does so explicitly. It is peculiar to this entity that with and through its Being, this Being is disclosed to it. *Understanding of Being is itself a definite characteristic of Dasein's Being.* Dasein is ontically distinctive in that it *is* ontological. (*BT*, 32)

This important paragraph no doubt needs some explanation. Heidegger employs a distinction between two levels at which an entity can be described; he calls them **ontic** and **ontological**. We can think of the *ontic level* as that of ordinary facts. Each Dasein has a certain physical size, grows up in a certain culture, experiences moods, uses language and tools, remembers and intends, often fears death, and usually thinks its way of life is the right way: These are all ontic facts.

But there is also a deeper level at which Dasein can be described: in its *way of Being*—in the way it is "there," present to things, in the world, together with others. We can think of this level as a matter of structural features of Dasein that make possible all the ontic facts we are ordinarily aware of.* This is the *ontological level*.

Heidegger holds that, ontically considered, Dasein is unique among entities. And what makes it distinctive is that its own Being "is an *issue* for it." What he means is that Dasein is the being that is concerned about its own Being; it *matters* to Dasein how things are going with it, how it is doing, what the state of its Being is and will become. So Dasein already has a certain understanding of Being. Its own Being is always, at any given point, "disclosed to it." Because this feature of Dasein is so fundamental, Heidegger asserts that Dasein "*is* ontological." What does this mean? Ontology is the discipline concerned with Being. So to say that Dasein *is* ontological is to say that Dasein's way of Being involves having an *understanding* of its own Being.

This feature of Dasein is so central that Heidegger points to it as the *essence* of Dasein. In each case—yours, ours—Dasein "has its Being to be" (*BT*, 33). It is as though Dasein can't just *be* (the way spiders are, for example); Dasein has to *decide* about its Being. How it will *be* is an *issue*; its Being this way or that is not just a given fact. Being, for Dasein, is a *problem* to be solved; but it cannot be

---

*It might be helpful to recall that Kant is asking about the "transcendental" conditions on the side of the subject that must be assumed, so that science, or mathematics, or morality, or metaphysics is possible. In a similar way, Heidegger is asking, What must Dasein be for the ontic facts to be what they are?

solved in a disinterested and theoretical way; it is solved only by living—by existing.*

Heidegger searches for a term to designate the way of Being that is characteristic of Dasein. He settles on "existence." Dasein *exists*. As he uses this term, dogs and cats *are*, but they do not *exist*. Stones and stars are, but they do not exist. They have a different *kind* of Being. "Existence," then, is a technical term for Dasein's way of being. The term "exist" has etymological roots that suggest a kind of projection out from or away from the given situation. Heidegger sometimes writes it as "ek-sist" to emphasize this transcending of the given.† As we will see, Dasein ek-sists: It is always projecting itself beyond the present circumstance to future possibilities. We are aware of the *present* in the light of what we have been (the past) and could become (the future); we are not simply confined in it. It is this feature that makes it possible for Dasein to be concerned about its own Being. (Already we hear intimations of the importance of *time* to the question about the meaning of Being.)

Heidegger can say, then, that the essence of Dasein—what Dasein most essentially is—is its existence. And his first task is an "analytic" of Dasein. If we can get clear about Dasein's way of Being, this should be a step toward the larger question of the meaning of Being in general. Dasein is the best entity to interrogate because Dasein, in existing, already has an understanding of Being. To some degree, Being is "in the open" in Dasein, available in a way it would not be in a chemical compound. Dasein's self-understanding does not yet amount to the clear and comprehensive ontological understanding Heidegger is seeking; it is only an average, everyday kind of understanding, which (as we will see) may hide as much as it discloses. But Heidegger has found the clue as to where to begin.

Heidegger calls an analysis of Dasein's existence a *fundamental* ontology. It should provide a basis for the ontology of anything else. Since the essence of Dasein is its existence, this will be an *existential*

analysis. And what Heidegger will be looking for is something analogous to the traditional *categories*, that is, concepts setting out the most basic sorts of ways that things can be.* Heidegger uses the term **existentials** for the existential concepts that correspond to the traditional categories.

Let us summarize:

- What we are after is the meaning of Being. The name for such an inquiry is "ontology."
- The place to begin is where Being is "in the open."
- Dasein, because it is constituted by an understanding of its own Being, is such a "place."
- So, Dasein is the entity to be interrogated.
- Dasein's way of Being is existence.
- So we want an existential analysis of Dasein.
- This analysis will be formulated in terms of concepts called "existentials," which play the role for Dasein that the traditional categories play for other entities—that is, they give the most general characterizations of its way of Being.
- And this analysis will provide a fundamental ontology, from which the meaning of Being in general can be approached.

This focus on Dasein and its existence has led many to classify Heidegger as an **existentialist,** and perhaps there is no harm in that. But it must be clearly kept in mind that the analysis of existence is not what he is mainly interested in. Heidegger is, from first to last, intent on deciphering the meaning of Being.

Phenomenology

We now know what the aim is. But we do not yet have a very clear idea of how to pursue that goal. Even though Dasein is the kind of being that has an understanding of its own Being, we must not think that philosophy can just take over that understanding—far from it. For one thing, there are many ways in which Dasein has been interpreted in the great conversation, and any of these

---

*Compare Kierkegaard, p. 522.
†"Ek" is a Greek particle that suggests a standing out away from some origin, as in "ecstasy"—standing outside one's normal self.

*Compare Aristotle on the categories, p. 185, and Kant, p. 474. Heidegger agrees that "Being can be said in many ways." But he thinks neither of them has discovered the appropriate "categories" for Dasein, the language adequate to our existence.

are available for Dasein to use: as a soul temporarily imprisoned in a body (Plato), as a rational animal (Aristotle), as a creature of God (Augustine), as the *ego cogito* (Descartes), as a material mechanism (Hobbes), as a transcendental ego (Kant), or as the absolute subject (Hegel). *None* of these interpretations, Heidegger thinks, is adequate. In one way or another, they all miss the *existence* of Dasein. And even the everyday, unsophisticated way in which Dasein understands itself may hide as much as it reveals about Dasein's true existential nature.

You can see, however, that we have a serious problem. How are we going to approach Dasein? With what method? Heidegger suggests that the analysis should proceed in two stages. In the first stage, we should set aside all the sophisticated theories of the tradition and try just to look at Dasein's "average everydayness."* We want to grasp Dasein as it exists most obviously and naturally. Still, the results of this analysis of everyday Dasein will be merely provisional, because we suspect that Dasein understands itself to some degree *inauthentically*, self-deceptively, hiding its way of Being from itself.

For this reason, the second stage is necessary; we must ask what it would be for Dasein to own up to what it really is, to exist and understand itself *authentically*. In such an adequate self-understanding of its Being, Dasein will reveal the existentials that define it, and we will have an authentic **fundamental ontology.**

But we are still faced with the problem of how to go about investigating everyday existence. This must be done, Heidegger tells us, *phenomenologically*. Hegel's use of the term **phenomenology** can serve as a clue to its meaning here.† There, the key idea is that we can "watch" consciousness as it develops through its stages toward more adequate forms. This idea of observing is central for Heidegger, too.‡ It has nothing to do with bodily eyes,

of course; this "watching" is more a matter of attitude, of not imposing preconceived notions on the subject in question. Phenomenology is the disclosing, or uncovering, of a phenomenon by means of discourse about it. We can think of it as the attempt to *let* entities manifest themselves as they truly are.

"I am a camera with its shutter open, quite passive, recording, not thinking."

Christopher Isherwood (1904–1986)

Phenomena are understood to be "the totality of what lies in the light of day or can be brought to light" (*BT*, 51). A phenomenon, Heidegger says, is "*that which shows itself in itself*, the manifest" (*BT*, 51). Phenomena are not "mere appearances," then. Nor are they illusions or signs for something else. They are "the things themselves" as they show themselves "in themselves." And that is why phenomenology can be ontology—because it lets Being *itself* appear, as it is.

Notice that Heidegger makes a subtle distinction: Some matters, he says, "lie in the light of day," and others "can be brought to light." Roughly speaking, entities are what lie in the light of day—the tableware we use at lunch, the daily newspaper, the family dog. But (and this should be no surprise by now) their Being is not so clearly apparent to us. Their Being must be *brought* to light, uncovered, disclosed. And this is just what phenomenology is designed to do.

Heidegger suggests three ways in which the phenomenon of Being might be hard to discern: (1) Being might be "hidden," in the sense that it is just too close to us for us to focus on it easily; (2) it might be "covered up," an idea that suggests Being was once known but has been made inaccessible by the tradition; and (3) Being might be "disguised,"

---

*Compare the later Wittgenstein's motto "Don't think, but look!" (p. 638).

†See p. 499.

‡Heidegger's phenomenological method actually owes most to his teacher, Edmund Husserl, who develops phenomenological methods of inquiry. For Husserl, phenomenology is (1) a *science* that is (2) purely *descriptive*, rather than deductive or explanatory, (3) that *sets aside* all prior

assumptions and *presuppositions*, (4) the subject matter of which is *consciousness*—its structure, its contents, and its "intended" objects—and (5) the outcome of which is *a description of essences*—for example, an account of *what it is to be* an act of perception or the object of a remembering. Husserl's motto is "to the things themselves!"

in the sense that Dasein, unable to face the awful truth about its existence, might draw a veil of camouflage over it (*BT*, 59–60). So the data we are after might not simply be there "in the light of day," manifesting themselves for us to see. We will have to engage in some *interpretation* to bring the phenomena to light. This interpretation Heidegger calls **"hermeneutics,"** drawing this term from the tradition of interpreting texts, particularly Scripture. The meaning of a text is often obscure; to understand it requires an interpretation. Similarly, the meaning of Being is obscure. To get to the meaning of Dasein, then, will require a method that is phenomenological and hermeneutical at the same time. Our aim is to let the phenomenon of Being shine forth, as it is in itself.

---

1. Indicate the difference between Being and beings. Why does Heidegger say that Being is not *a* being?
2. Why does Heidegger choose *us* as the beings to "interrogate" in his quest for the meaning of Being? And why does he designate us with the term "Dasein"?
3. What does it mean to say that Dasein exists? And what will an existential analysis provide for us?
4. Why does Heidegger recommend we begin our search by examining Dasein's average everydayness? And why is phenomenology the appropriate method?
5. What is hermeneutics? And why must our phenomenology of existence be hermeneutical?

Being-in-the-World

We are now ready to begin the analysis of Dasein's existential structure. Remember, what we are aiming at is an explicit understanding of Dasein's way of Being, the way that Heidegger calls "existence." The *basic state* of Dasein, he tells us, is this: Dasein essentially, necessarily, *is-in-the-world*. The hyphens in this odd phrase are not accidental; they tell us that we are dealing here with a *unitary* phenomenon. It is not possible to understand Dasein apart from its world; indeed, Dasein without the world would not be "da"—that is, *there*. To be in a world—to "have" a world—is constitutive for Dasein.

We can already see that Heidegger's phenomenological analysis of Dasein's Being is completely at variance with the view expressed most clearly by Descartes, that it is a real possibility that I might be the only thing that exists.* As we have seen, this ego (or mind) gets trapped inside itself and has a hard time finding the world again. In supposing that such an independent existence is possible for the soul, Heidegger claims, Descartes misses precisely the *Being* of Dasein—namely, its **Being-in-the-world.** Heidegger thinks that Descartes' notion of the *ego*, of "the *thing* which thinks," in fact attributes to Dasein a kind of Being that belongs rather to a different sort of entity, which he calls the present-at-hand (which we will discuss subsequently). This is just one dramatic example of how the Western philosophical tradition has gone wrong—one example, Heidegger thinks, of how our forgetfulness of Being has warped our perception of things. One finds this pattern, he believes, in the whole history of the conversation since Descartes. Locke's spiritual substance, Berkeley's spirit, Hume's bundle theory, Kant's transcendental ego, and Hegel's infinite subject—all understand the subject as a peculiar kind of *thing*.

Our tradition, Heidegger holds, has succumbed to a tendency toward *objectification*. As a result, we have taken the world to be made up of substances, things, objects; and the self or soul or mind has been understood as just another substance or thing. No wonder the crucial question seemed to be the epistemological one: whether the subject (a thinking thing) can *know* the object (a different kind of thing). Can a subject *transcend* its subjectivity and know the truth about objects existing independent of it? All this, Heidegger believes, is a result of our having "covered over" the phenomenon of Being. And, most crucially, it has distorted our understanding of *our own* Being. This covering over is what Heidegger means to combat. And the first shot in this battle is the notion that the basic state of Dasein (which, you will recall, is in each case *mine*) is Being-in-the-world.

---

*Review *Meditation I* with its skeptical arguments from sense deceptions, dreams, and the evil demon.

What does this mean? For one thing, it means that the fundamental relation between Dasein and the world is not epistemological, but ontological. Knowing is not basic; Being is. We *are* in-the-world, and we are so in a way that is deeper and richer than any propositional knowledge could completely express. What is it to be *in* the world? We can't fully answer this question until we understand more clearly what a "world" is. But in a preliminary way, we can say this: It is not the same as the coffee being *in* the cup or the pencil being *in* the box. In these cases, we have one thing spatially contained in another. Heidegger does not want to deny that Dasein can be regarded like this: When you go through the front door, you are *in* your house in exactly this sense.

But this is not the basic fact about the way you are in the world. (It is not the basic fact, for that matter, about the way you are in your house.) Dasein is *in-the-world* more in the sense in which your sister is *in* the navy or your brother is *in* love. Dasein's way of Being-in-the-world is a matter of being engaged in projects, using tools, being involved with others. Dasein *dwells* in the world; it is not just *located* there. Dasein's

> Being-in-the-world has always dispersed itself or even split itself up into definite ways of Being-in. The multiplicity of these is indicated by the following examples: having to do with something, producing something, attending to something and looking after it . . . accomplishing, evincing, interrogating, considering, discussing, determining. . . . All these ways of Being-in have *concern* as their kind of Being—a kind of Being we have yet to characterize in detail. (*BT*, 83)

Concernfully—that is the way Dasein is *in*-the-world. What this means is that there is a more basic mode of relating to the things in the world than knowing them. Knowledge we might have or lack. But Being-in is something we cannot *be* without.

> From what we have been saying, it follows that Being-in is not a "property" which Dasein sometimes has and sometimes does not have, and *without* which it could be just as well as it could with it. It is not the case that man "is" and then has, by way of an extra, a relationship-of-Being towards the

"world"—a world with which he provides himself occasionally. (*BT*, 84)

Being-in-the-world, in other words, is one of the *existentials* that characterizes the fundamental ontology of Dasein. It is one aspect of the essence of Dasein. The world is *given with* Dasein. But what a *world* is we are not yet clear about.

Remember that we are trying to disclose the Being of Dasein by an investigation of "average everydayness." So we now have to ask, How does this phenomenon of Being-in-the-world show itself in Dasein's average everydayness? What form does our Being-in normally take? We can get an answer, Heidegger suggests, via an interpretation of the *entities in the world* "closest" to us.

> We shall call those entities which we encounter in concern "*equipment*." In our dealings we come across equipment for writing, sewing, working, transportation, measurement. The kind of Being which equipment possesses must be exhibited. (*BT*, 97)

If we try to give a phenomenological description of our everyday mode of Being, what we find is that we dwell in a world of gear, of equipment for use. We do not first understand a pen as a "mere thing" and thereafter apprehend its use as a writing instrument. We grasp it *to write with*, usually without a thought. It is "on hand," or, as Heidegger puts it, **ready-to-hand.**

We simply turn the knob to open the door, often with our mind entirely on other matters—don't we? We deal with the things around us in an engaged, not a detached, manner. We cope with them in a variety of ways. They are elements in our ongoing projects. The things that are phenomenologically "closest" to us are not, then, neutral "objects" that we first stare at in a disinterested way and to which we must subsequently assign some "value."

It is in this engaged manner that we are most primordially in-the-world. Descartes worries about the problem of a transcendent reality: Is there anything "out there" beyond my mind's ideas? But if Heidegger is right, that is not a problem at all. Dasein *is* a kind of transcendence—in its very Being! Dasein is essentially *in-the-world*, engaged with the entities of the world in a concernful fashion. Kant says that the scandal of philosophy is that philosophers have not solved this problem of transcendence. Heidegger thinks the scandal is that philosophy has thought there is a problem here! That there seems to be a problem about "the reality of the external world" is just a sign of how distant we are from an understanding of our own mode of Being.*

But we still need to clarify the mode of Being of these entities "closest" to us in-the-world. Let us ask, What is it to *be* a hammer? In what does its *being-a-hammer* consist? There is a certain characteristic shape for a hammer, and a hammer is usually made out of certain definite materials, though both shape and materials can vary. But it is neither shape nor composition that *makes* a hammer a hammer. What it is for something to be a hammer is for it to have a certain definite use—a function, a purpose. A hammer is (to oversimplify slightly) *to-drive-nails-with*. That is what a hammer *is*. A hammer *hammers*.

It is important to note that the Being of the hammer involves a reference to something else—to nails. What is it to be a nail? To be a nail is to be something that can be driven into boards to fasten them together. Another reference!

> Taken strictly, there "is" no such thing as *an* equipment. To the Being of any equipment there always belongs a totality of equipment, in which it can be this equipment that it is. Equipment is essentially "something in-order-to . . . ."
>
> In the "in-order-to" as a structure there lies an *assignment* or *reference* of something to something. (*BT*, 97)

It is not possible, in other words, that there should exist just one item of equipment. Being a hammer involves a context of other equipment and, ultimately, the world.†

_____

*Heidegger's analysis of Being-in-the-world is a radical rejection of what we have called the *representational theory* (p. 372), the central claim of which is that we are directly or immediately acquainted only with ideas in the mind. If Heidegger is right, what we are directly and immediately acquainted with are functionally understood items in the world around us.

†Compare the antiatomistic remarks of the later Wittgenstein, pp. 648–649.

Let us ask a related question. When do we *understand* something to be a hammer? In what does this understanding consist? Most basically, I understand a hammer when I know how to hammer with it—when I can use it to drive the nails into the boards. The Being of the hammer does not reveal itself to a disinterested observation of its appearance or to a scientific investigation of its weight and material properties. Its Being is manifest primarily and fundamentally in a skill I have, particularly when I actualize this skill in actually hammering. That is how the hammer *shows itself* to be what it is. Hammers are understood in virtue of a kind of "know-how," not (primarily) by way of a "theory of hammers." Its being a hammer reveals itself to my *circumspective concern*—to my care-full involvements with it in the projects I am engaged in. Heidegger calls this kind of Being "readiness-to-hand."

Tools, gear, and equipment in general have this kind of Being. And dealing with the ready-to-hand is the most fundamental mode of our Being-in-the-world. We find it on all sides if we only have eyes to look. Our fundamental mode of understanding is not theoretical or scientific, but practical. We *understand how* to drive a car, use a fork, put on a pair of pants, open a can. And we manifest that understanding in actually driving, hammering, using the computer, combing our hair, and so on.

It cannot be emphasized too much that this concernful dealing with the ready-to-hand is *basic*. If Heidegger is right about this, the question of whether there "really" are hammers and cars and cans simply cannot arise. Philosophers have thought this is a real problem only because they have missed the Being of Dasein as Being-in-the-world and Dasein's relation to the ready-to-hand.

We are making some progress, but we do not yet know what it is to be a *world*. A clue can be derived from the fact that the ready-to-hand never comes alone, but always in a context of references and assignments to other entities. The hammer is to pound the nails; there would be no nails if there were no boards to join; the boards are shaped the way they are to build a house; houses are for sheltering and for dwelling in. All these things are meaningful together—or not at all. Each has the structure of an in-order-to. But if we pay close attention to this phenomenon of interlocking in-order-tos, we can see that three other things are also manifest.

1. Though we do not usually pay attention to the hammer directly—what we are involved in is the *work*, and the hammer is used "transparently"—the work involves *making use of something* for a purpose. Consider a cobbler making shoes.

> In the work there is also a reference or assignment to "materials": the work is dependent on leather, thread, needles, and the like. Leather, moreover, is produced from hides. These are taken from animals, which someone else has raised. . . . Hammer, tongs, and needle, refer in themselves to steel, iron, metal, mineral, wood, in that they consist of these. In equipment that is used, "Nature" is discovered along with it by that use—the "Nature" we find in natural products. (*BT*, 100)

As Heidegger is careful to point out, the "Nature" that presents itself in this way is nature as a resource: "the wood is a forest of timber, the mountain a quarry of rock; the river is water-power, the wind is wind 'in the sails'" (*BT*, 100). This nature is part of the world of equipment "in" which Dasein essentially is. So it is not quite the "Nature" of the scientist (to which we will come shortly). Along with the ready-to-hand Being of equipment, then, there is revealed the world of nature.

2. Other entities having the same kind of being as Dasein are also manifest. I, after all, did not make the hammer I pound with, nor did I manufacture the nails, nor did I shape the boards I join with them. These entities reveal that I am not alone in the world but live in the world with others who are like me.* This world, moreover, shows itself to be a *public* world. Hammers are mass produced; they are designed specifically so that *anyone* can hammer with them. The instruments in a car are intentionally designed so that the *average person* can easily read them.

3. There is a third phenomenon that is evident together with the ready-to-hand: Heidegger calls

it a "for-the-sake-of-which." Let's go back to the hammer. The hammer has its Being as equipment; it is ready-to-hand for hammering. As we have seen, there is a whole series of references or assignments in which the hammer is involved: It is essentially related to nails, which "refer" to boards, which "point" toward building houses. Does this set of functional relations have a terminus? Does it come to an end somewhere? Is there anything *for the sake of which* this whole set of relations exists? Yes. The totality of these involvements

> goes back ultimately to a "towards-which" in which there is *no* further involvement: this "towards-which" is not an entity with the kind of Being that belongs to what is ready-to-hand within a world; . . . The primary "towards-which" is a "for-the-sake-of-which." But the "for-the-sake-of-which" always pertains to the Being of *Dasein*, for which in its Being, that very Being is essentially an issue. (*BT*, 116–117)

Dasein, concerned for its own Being, understands the possibility that it might freeze in the winter and provides for itself a house. It is in terms of the possibilities of Dasein's Being that the entire set of functional relations attains its structure and Being. We get the image of an immensely complicated, crisscrossing network of functional assignments in which all the entities in the world are caught up and have their Being. This network is anchored in the Being of Dasein, that Being for whom its own Being is a matter of concern and whose Being has the structure of Being-in-the-world.

It is important to note that the **world** is not an entity; nor is it a collection of entities; nor is it a totality of facts, as the early Wittgenstein thinks.* Heidegger's thought is as far removed from the atomism of the *Tractatus* as you can imagine. It is only within the context of the world that something can *be* a hammer. The world is a prior whole, presupposed by the Being of the ready-to-hand; it is not the *sum* of lots and lots of things, each of which might equally well exist alone. There would be no hammers in a world without

---

*Just as the "external world" problem seems like a pseudoproblem from Heidegger's point of view, the same is true of the problem of "other minds." It just doesn't arise!

*See the discussion of the first sentences of the *Tractatus*, pp. 622 and 625–626.

nails to drive; there would be no nails without boards to join; there would be no boards without houses to build; and there would be none of these entities without Dasein—that for-the-sake-of-which they all exist and whose mode of Being is Being-in-the-world.

But if we are clear about what the world is *not*, we are still not clear about what it *is*. The world in which Dasein has its Being is one of those all-too-familiar, too-close-to-be-observed phenomena. The world is not, for instance, the earth. It would sound very odd indeed to talk about Being-in-the-earth (as though one lived underground). Nor is the world the same as the universe. (Christians talk of the "sins of the world," but "sins of the universe" makes no sense at all.) What, then, is this familiar, but strange, phenomenon of the world?

Though our immediate focus is usually on the things *in* the world, Heidegger suggests that there are certain experiences in which the phenomenon of the world itself—the *worldhood* of the world—comes to the fore. Consider working with a lever, trying to move a large and heavy box. What is manifest is the work, the project—to get *this* over *there*—and in a subsidiary (but not explicitly focused) way, the lever. Suddenly the lever breaks. It is no longer ready-to-hand. It takes on the character of *conspicuousness*. Whereas we had hardly noticed the lever before, just using it in that familiar transparent way, suddenly it announces itself, forces itself into awareness.

Two things happen. For one thing, "pure presence-at-hand announces itself in such [damaged] equipment" (*BT*, 103). There occurs a transition to another mode of Being. The functionality that defined the lever *as* a lever vanishes; the item is disconnected from that series of references and involvements that made it be—as a lever. It no longer *is* a lever. It just *lies there*. We no longer seize hold of it in that familiar way to use in our project. Rather, it stands over against us. We observe it, stare at it. It has become an *object*. It now *is* merely **present-at-hand**.

This glimpse into the present-at-hand is a revelation of another whole *mode of Being*: a realm of pure objects, suitable for contemplation and scientific investigation. It is important to note that in some sense, it is the same entity as before: but revealed in this way, it can be a theme for investigation by the natural sciences. In fact, nature—in the sense dealt with by modern physics—now first makes its appearance. This is not nature as a resource, part of the equipment of the world; it is nature disconnected from Dasein's concern—a sheer presence.

Here we have the *origin* of that objectifying way of understanding the world, which has so dominated our tradition. The important thing to note is that the present-at-hand is not primordial, or basic. The objects of natural science have their Being in a *modification* of the more fundamental entities that are ready-to-hand.

This claim has its bite in the notion that no matter how much of the world we "objectify," we always, necessarily, do so on a background of circumspective concern, of practices that involve the ready-to-hand. Dasein cannot, if Heidegger is right, totally objectify itself. Yet, that is just the way our tradition has treated Dasein—as an *object* with *properties* of a certain sort (distinctive properties, perhaps, but an object nonetheless). That is why we tend to think that explanations of a *scientific* sort can be given for human behavior: explanations in terms of conditioning, or complexes, or drives, or peer "pressure," or any number of other analogues to explanation in physical science. And that is why the question of the meaning of Being is so obscure to us; in assimilating our own Being to that of the present-at-hand, we have lost the sense of what it is to *exist*. Because existence is our own mode of Being, a misunderstanding here turns everything topsy-turvy. It is no wonder that clarifying the meaning of Being is so difficult a task.

But what is it to be a world? That is the second thing that shows up in those experiences where tools go wrong in some way. When the lever breaks, not only does the present-at-hand light up, but also the whole network of relations in which it was transparently embedded now comes into view. The *worldhood of the world* is constituted by this system of references, within which Dasein and the ready-to-hand have their Being. To be a world, in other words, is to be a structure within which entities *are* and have their meaning.* This entire *network of in-order-tos and toward-whichs and for-the-sake-ofs*—that is the phenomenon of the world. So the world is neither a thing nor a collection of things. It is that wherein entities have their Being, whether that Being is existence, readiness-to-hand, or presence-at-hand.

You should now have a fairly clear understanding of that basic *existential*, that most fundamental characteristic of Dasein: Dasein's Being-in-the-world.

The "Who" of Dasein

Who is Dasein?

That may sound like a strange question, and in fact it is. Not because the term "Dasein" is a strange one, but because the answer seems so straightforward. If Dasein is in each case "mine," then it would seem that, in your case anyway, the answer would be *you yourself*, this *person* named John or Mary, this *individual,* this *self* or *subject*; *you* are who Dasein is in this case. What could be more obvious?

But Heidegger thinks this easy and familiar answer covers up or disguises the ontological reality. To talk of self or subject is to fall prey to the temptation to suppose that you are a *thing*—either a kind of soul substance (perhaps in the way Descartes thinks) or a body (as Hobbes thinks). But the *Being* of Dasein in its everydayness is not illuminated by this kind of answer; rather, it is hidden. So let us ask: Who is Dasein as it exists in its averageness? The answer Heidegger gives to this question is extraordinary.

> It could be that the "who" of everyday Dasein just is *not* the "I myself." (*BT*, 150)

Heidegger's phenomenological answer to the question about the "who" of Dasein in everydayness is *das Man*. This phrase is based on an ordinary German term that occurs in contexts such as "*Man*

sagt," which can be rendered as "One says," or "It is said that," or perhaps as "They say." A woman in the supermarket says to another, "I think I'll try this; they say that's good." You might ask, Who is this "they"? If you had put this question to her, she probably wouldn't have been able to tell you.*

So Heidegger finds that Dasein in its average everydayness is this "They" or "the One."† But what does that mean? We have already seen that *Others* are "given" along with the ready-to-hand (e.g., with this shirt, which was cut and sewn in a factory somewhere). And if our account is to be phenomenologically adequate, it must record the fact that Others are encountered as themselves Being-in-the-world. The Others, too, *exist* with that same concernful Being-in-the-world as you do.

Moreover, the existence of Others like you is not something that has to come as the conclusion of an argument, as the old problem of "other minds" suggests. You do not first start with *yourself* and then conclude on the basis of similarity between observable aspects of yourself and Others that they must be persons, too.‡ That would not be an accurate description of your experience of Others.

> By "Others" we do not mean everyone else but me—those over against whom the "I" stands out. They are rather those from whom, for the most part, one does *not* distinguish oneself—those among whom one is too. . . . The world of Dasein is a *with-world*. Being-in is *Being-with* Others. (*BT*, 154–155)

---

*Heidegger's conception of "the world" is something like that "scaffolding of the world" that the early Wittgenstein thinks logic provides. (See p. 629.) The enormous difference, of course, is that Wittgenstein's scaffolding supports only sheer meaningless facts—what Heidegger would call the present-at-hand—whereas the worldhood of the world is rich in functionality, usefulness, meaning.

---

*The translators of *Being and Time* render "*das Man*" as "the They." Hubert Dreyfus argues in an unpublished commentary that it is much better to bring it into English as "the One" (*Being-in-the-World: A Commentary on Heidegger's Being and Time, Division I*, June 1988). We will sometimes use one locution and sometimes the other.

†Dreyfus argues convincingly that Heidegger does not always distinguish clearly two facets of his own account of "the One": a positive function Dreyfus calls "conformity" or "Falling-in-with" and a negative function he calls "conformism" or "Falling-away-from." The latter, but not the former, correlates with Dasein in the mode of *inauthentic existence*. We try to keep these aspects distinct.

‡To proceed in this way would be to assume that I *first* have an ontologically adequate grasp of myself and *thereafter* extend this understanding to others. But that is just the (very Cartesian) assumption that Heidegger says we cannot make.

Being-with, like Being-in-the-world, is an *existential*—one of the characteristics that defines Dasein's Being. This means that Dasein could not exist without Others, any more than it could exist without the world. It is part of Dasein's very *Being* to be with-Others-in-the-world. This is true even when Dasein is alone or neglects the Others or is indifferent to them. The anchorite in the cave is *with* Others, if only in the mode of seeking to avoid them. The anchorite carries the Others with her into the cave in her ability to speak a language, to think, to meditate in the way she does; this "carrying with" is what it means to say that Being-with is an *existential*.

The discovery of Being-with is an important step. But it does not yet get us clearly to the "who" of Dasein. There is a clue, however, in the phrase, "those from whom . . . one does *not* distinguish oneself." We could paradoxically put it this way: One is, oneself, one of the Others. In fact, Heidegger tells us, we are so much one of the "they" that we are constantly concerned lest we differ too much from them.

> In one's concern with what one has taken hold of, whether with, for, or against, the Others, there is constant care as to the way one differs from them, whether that difference is merely one that is to be evened out, whether one's own Dasein has lagged behind the Others and wants to catch up in relation to them, or whether one's Dasein already has some priority over them and sets out to keep them suppressed. (*BT*, 163–164)

We can think of this as the existential foundation for the familiar (ontic) phenomenon of "keeping up with the Joneses." Heidegger calls it **distantiality** (still another of those invented words!); he uses this term to signify the constant concern of Dasein that it might get too far away from the norm—from what "they say" or what "one does." (Compare: "One just doesn't *do* that!") Either one doesn't want too large a "distance" to open between oneself and the Others or one takes care to preserve a certain "appropriate distance."

Heidegger suggests that this phenomenon is "hidden" from Dasein. And, indeed, we think that is so. If we suggest to young people that an enormous part of their lives is governed by norms they participate in but are hardly aware of, we usually get a lot of resistance. They all want to think of themselves as unique, self-made individuals! But we all hold our forks the same way, a way different from that of the English; and we North Americans all stand roughly the same distance from others when we converse with them, a distance farther away than Latin Americans stand. If you spell "existence" as "existance," you will be corrected. And if you want to "be your own person" by dyeing your hair green or wearing a ring in your nose, you are merely rejecting one They for another, falling in with Others who say, "That's cool."

> One belongs to the Others oneself and enhances their power. . . . The "who" is not this one, not that one, not oneself, not some people, and not the sum of them all. The "who" is the neuter, the "they" [the One]. . . .
>
> We take pleasure and enjoy ourselves as *they* take pleasure; we read, see, and judge about literature and art as *they* see and judge; likewise we shrink back from the "great mass" as *they* shrink back; we find "shocking" what *they* find shocking. The "they" [the One], which is nothing definite, and which all are, though not as the sum, prescribes the kind of Being of everydayness. (*BT*, 164)

Consider the "proper" distance to stand from someone you are talking with. Social scientists will tell you that there is a "norm" here based on your cultural background. You almost certainly behave according to your cultural norm, and you are uncomfortable if it is violated. Is this something you *decided*? Certainly not. What is its ground, its reason, its justification—its *logos*? There really doesn't seem to be any. Is it "natural"? No, though it feels natural to us, just as other distances feel natural to people of other cultures. Where does it come from, this "naturalness"—this "rightness," even—that we are uncomfortable violating? Can there be any other answer than "that is what we do?"* This is how *One* does it. That is all the foundation it has!

Along with distantiality, the phenomenon of **averageness** is an existential characteristic of the One. And this involves a kind of *leveling down*, in

---

*Compare the later Wittgenstein, pp. 645–646 and 649.

which every kind of uniqueness, oddness, or priority is smoothed out as much as possible. We noted the *public* character of the world as manifest in ready-to-hand items. Now we see that the world is a common, public world in another sense, too. The "way things are done" is set by the One, not by each Dasein privately for itself. The world of the One is a *public* world from the start. It is into that world, moreover, that Dasein comes from the very beginning; the One shapes and makes Dasein's "who" what it is. We are all *das Man*. In a striking phrase, Heidegger puts it this way:

> Everyone is the other, and no one is himself.
> (*BT*, 165)

The public character of the world of the One—the world of everyday Dasein (our world)—has an interesting consequence:

> It deprives the particular Dasein of its answerability. The "they" . . . can be answerable for everything most easily, because it is not someone who needs to vouch for anything. It "was" always the "they" who did it, and yet it can be said that it has been "no one." . . .
>
> Thus the particular Dasein in its everydayness is *disburdened* by the "they." (*BT*, 165)

Who is responsible for the way everyday life goes? No one. It is just the way One does it. Dasein conforms to this *way of Being*; Dasein *Falls-in-with-it*. Notice that this is not—so far—something for which Dasein is to *blame*; distantiality and averageness are *existentials*; that is, they are aspects of the very *essence* of Dasein's existence. It couldn't be otherwise for Dasein. And isn't this fortunate? To have to bear the burden of responsibility for the whole of the way one lives would be too much; the "they" is there to help out.

Heidegger distinguishes three modes in which Dasein can relate itself to itself: **inauthenticity, authenticity,** and an undifferentiated mode, which is neither. We have so far been trying to describe the undifferentiated mode of Dasein's existence—though the eagerness with which Dasein accepts the "disburdening" is a hint of what inauthenticity amounts to. As a being for whom its own Being is always at issue, Dasein is always

facing the *decision* between existing inauthentically and existing authentically; it always exists predominantly in one mode or the other. We will explore these modes more fully later, but we can now say that authentic existence is not a grasping of some nature or essence of oneself quite different from the "they-self"; it is, rather, a matter of coming to terms with the fact that this is what one is and that one is *no more than this*. And inauthentic existence is a way of hiding this truth from oneself. Existing as "the One" is not yet inauthentic. But "the One" constantly presents to Dasein the possibility of evading the disquieting aspects of *having to Be the being that it is* by fleeing into the security of what "they say." Thus the One is both a constitutive factor in Dasein and a temptation to inauthenticity.

For now, though, we can see that the answer to the question about the "who" of Dasein is this: In its average everydayness, Dasein exists in the mode of "the One." Dasein (each of us in our way of existing) belongs to "the They."

---

1. How does the notion of Dasein's Being-in-the-world undercut the philosophical tradition about the nature of the self or subject? What does it mean to be in-the-world? And why is epistemology not fundamental?
2. Contrast, using an example, the ready-to-hand with the present-at-hand. Which is basic?
3. What is the world? Contrast Heidegger's answer with that of Wittgenstein's *Tractatus*.
4. What does it mean to say that Dasein is (in its average everydayness) the One? Explain in terms of distantiality and averageness.
5. Explain how the One is both an existential (i.e., is essential to or constitutive of Dasein) and a temptation to inauthenticity.

Modes of Disclosure

Dasein has an understanding of its own Being, though it is not explicitly worked out. But what sort of understanding is this? In what ways is Dasein *always* already disclosed to itself? Think of a dense and dark forest, and in the midst of it imagine a clearing. The clearing opens a space within which flowers and trees can appear; in fact, it is the clearing that is the condition for anything at all being visible. And now, with this analogy in mind, let us ask, Is there such a clearing in the *world*? Does Dasein exist in such a clearing? Not exactly, Heidegger answers. Rather, he wants to say, Dasein *is* such a clearing.*

> Dasein brings its "there" along with it. If it lacks its "there," it is not factically† the entity which is essentially Dasein; indeed, it is not this entity at all. *Dasein is its disclosedness.* (*BT*, 171)

A human that was not this kind of openness to beings and to Being would, perhaps, be a corpse. In any case, it would not be "there." Disclosedness is part of the existential constitution of Dasein. And that is what we now have to bring more clearly to light.

Heidegger discusses this "thereness" of Dasein under three headings: **attunement,** understanding, and discourse. These are very rich pages in *Being and Time*, and we must be content with omitting much. But it is essential to grasp something of these modes of disclosure.

ATTUNEMENT

We are sometimes asked, "How are you doing?" The surprising thing is that we can always answer. And in answering, we report our *mood*. We say, "Fine," or "Awful—I think I failed the calculus exam." Heidegger holds that moods don't *just happen*; they are not just meaningless present-at-hand items we undergo, the way our heart sometimes beats faster and sometimes slower. Moods are *cognitive*. They are disclosive. But what do they disclose? They reveal how we are coping with this business of having to exist—that is, how we are bearing the burden of having to be here. Dasein is "attuned" to its own Being.

Moreover, moods are not experienced as private states or feelings, independent of the world

out there. Suppose you are in a bad mood, that (as we say) you got out of bed on the wrong side this morning. Where, phenomenologically speaking, does this mood reveal itself? In your head, while the world goes on its sunny way? Not at all. *Nothing*, you are likely to say, is going right. *Everything* seems to be against you. Your *world* is dark. And why should it not be so, if your Being is indeed Being-in-the-world? Moods are pervasive, coloring everything. Suppose you have been watching a horror movie on a DVD all alone, late at night. Thereafter, every creak in the house, every hoot of an owl, and every gust of wind in the trees takes on an ominous quality. You anxiously check the locks and make sure the windows are closed. The *world* is now a scary place! How are you now bearing the burden of having to be there? Not very well.

Dasein never exists without a mood. Even the flat, calm, easygoing character of an average day is a mood. Dasein *is*, remember, its disclosedness. In revealing its "thereness," Dasein's mood discloses how Dasein is attuned to its world. In this disclosure is revealed a further aspect of Dasein's Being: **thrownness.** We find ourselves "thrown" into our Being-in-the-world in the following sense. None of us chose to be born. Nor did we decide to be born recently, rather than in the thirteenth century. Nor were we consulted about whether we would be American or Chinese or Mexican. Nor if we preferred being male or female. Nor black nor white nor any other color. Nor to be born to just *these* parents in just *that* town with just *those* relatives and neighbors, with a certain very specific kind of housing, transportation, and tools at hand. (Lucy says to Snoopy: "You've been a dog all your life, haven't you? I've often wondered what made you decide to become a dog." Snoopy, lying on his doghouse roof, replies, "I was fooled by the job description." But that is a joke, isn't it? It *belongs* in the comics!) We just *find ourselves* in existence—in a world of a particular sort, having one language rather than another and one characteristic way of looking at things, rather than another. We are, as Heidegger says, "delivered over" to our "there," to our world (*BT*, 174).

We could put this idea in another way: *Who* we are is a very particular sort of *One*; there is no help

---

*The German word here translated as "clearing" is "Lichtung." It is important that the word comes from the word for *light*—"Licht." Dasein is in itself the "light of nature" (Descartes, *Meditation III*), the condition for uncovering the truth.

†See p. 666 and the Glossary for a discussion of facticity.

for it, for we are "thrown" into one "they" rather than another. Even if we eventually reject certain features of this One, as characteristically happens when human beings mature, we do so drawing on the resources available in *this* world; we cannot make use, for instance, of the psychological and technological discoveries of the twenty-third century. We are *thrown* into the world.

This throwness is a fact. It is a fact about our Being. So it is an *ontological* fact. Heidegger uses two words for facts. Ordinary facts (that the kiwi is a bird native to New Zealand, for instance, or that this book is written in English) he calls *factual*. Facts about things present-at-hand, for instance, are factual. Ontological facts about Dasein, facts about us not as beings, but about our Being (or *way* of Being), he calls *factical*. Our being a "clearing," for instance, is factical; our Being-in-the-world is factical; our throwness is part of our **facticity.** In attempting a "fundamental ontology" of Dasein, then, Heidegger is investigating its facticity: the facts about its Being. The facticity of our being thrown is one of the things that moods reveal.

A phenomenologist could go through mood after mood and display the character of each as revealing an aspect of Dasein's Being. But Heidegger focuses on one mood in particular, which he thinks has far-reaching implications. Let us sketch his analysis of **anxiety.**

Like all moods, anxiety is cognitively significant; that is, it discloses something. Anxiety is rather like fear, but it would be a big mistake to confuse them. Fear discloses the fearful: some particular threat to a future possibility of Dasein (the charging bull, the assassin relentlessly hunting one down). Anxiety, by contrast, reveals a very general feature of Dasein's Being. Anxiety is directed, not to a particular threatening entity, but to something more fundamental and far-reaching.

> That in the face of which one has anxiety is Being-in-the-world as such. (*BT*, 230)

What is Being-in-the-world? We already know; it is the most basic existential characteristic of Dasein. So what Dasein is anxious-in-the-face-of is *itself!* Heidegger is suggesting that anxiety reveals in a peculiarly conspicuous way Dasein's

having-to-Be. Ordinarily, average Dasein goes along "absorbed" in the world of its concern, engaged in projects that seem unquestionably to have a point and meaning. But if we remember that the self of everyday Dasein is the *One*, we can see that these projects are those set down by the public world; they have their meaning dictated by the "they." And normally Dasein does not notice this. In its average everydayness, Dasein is delivered over to Being-in-the-public-world-of-already-assigned-significances. Dasein has "fallen-in" with the world of what "One says," what "One does and doesn't do."*

If a person suffering from anxiety is asked what she is afraid of, she replies, "Nothing." And that, Heidegger says, is exactly right; nothing *in the world* is the object of this mood. Rather, anxiety

> takes away from Dasein the possibility of understanding itself, as it falls, in terms of the "world" and the way things have been publicly interpreted. Anxiety throws Dasein back upon that which it is anxious about—its authentic potentiality-for-Being-in-the-world. Anxiety individualizes Dasein. . . .
>
> Anxiety makes manifest in Dasein its *Being towards* its ownmost potentiality-for-Being—that is, its *Being-free* for the freedom of choosing itself and taking hold of itself. (*BT*, 232)

The world doesn't exactly become meaningless; it is still the *world* (i.e., a set of in-order-tos). But in anxiety, one is detached from it; it means nothing to the particular Dasein gripped by anxiety. One can still see others going through the motions, but it seems absurd.† Anxiety distances us from our ordinary everyday *Being-in*. It makes clear that how you are to be is a matter of *choice*—that you are *responsible* for your Being. As Heidegger

---

*It is important to remember that this feature is an *existential*; it is not something Dasein could be without, so it is not something to *blame* Dasein for or to *regret*.

†"Absurd" is a word that we don't believe Heidegger uses in this context, but it plays a large role in the thought of French existentialist thinkers, such as Sartre and Camus. See, for instance, Sartre's novel *Nausea* and Camus' *The Myth of Sisyphus* and *The Stranger*. Heidegger does not like Sartre's version of existentialism; it essentially preserves rather than overcomes Cartesian dualism, he maintains. But the Heideggerian influence in these thinkers is strong.

says, anxiety "individualizes." It separates us out from the One.

Wrenched out of the familiar "falling-in" with the way of the world, Dasein experiences itself as *not-at-home-in-the-world*. Yet, it is essentially nothing but Being-in-the-world! Dasein has no other reality; it cannot repair to its own "substance" or enjoy its own "essence" apart from the world. "Just be *yourself*," we are often advised. But, if Heidegger is right, there is no one for us to be apart from our falling in with the world of the One! In anxiety, then, Dasein is made aware of that fact, but in the mode of not being absorbed in that world. There is no home but that home, yet, anxiously, we are homeless.*

On the one hand, anxiety reveals with penetrating clarity the nature of Dasein's Being. But on the other hand, it provides a powerful motivation for Dasein to hide itself from itself—to flee back into the comfortable, familiar, well-ordered, meaningful world of the One, to avoid the risky business of taking up responsibility for one's own Being. That is why Heidegger says that Dasein is anxious about its "authentic potentiality-for-Being-in-the-world." Anxiety presents Dasein with the clear choice between existing authentically or inauthentically. The temptation is to flee back into the world, to be reabsorbed in it, to shut one's eyes to the fact that a *decision* about one's way of life is called for. The temptation is to think that our lives are as antecedently well ordered as the career of a hammer—that the meaning of life is *given* and doesn't have to be *forged*. To flee back into the predecided life of the One would "disburden" Dasein and quiet anxiety. But such fleeing on the part of Dasein would be "falling-away-from" itself, the *inauthentic* kind of **falling.**† Falling-away-from oneself is the same as

falling-prey-to the One. So Dasein "tranquilizes" itself in the familiar world of significance, fleeing *away from* its freedom and its not-at-homeness *into* the world of the One; thus it disguises from itself its true Being (that its Being is an *issue*). We crave a world in which we can say, "I had no choice." And behold, in the world of the One, all crucial decisions are already made, dictated by the norms of what One does and doesn't do. The possibilities open to Dasein are "disposed of" beforehand. One's life is *settled*. And anxiety is covered up.

Moods, then, are cognitively significant; they always tell us something about ourselves and, in particular, about our Being. Among the moods, anxiety most clearly reveals the Being of Dasein—that it is thrown-Being-in-the-world-of-the-One. And in doing so, it both distances Dasein from that Being and provides a motivation for falling back into that world in an inauthentic way.

UNDERSTANDING

In one way or another, Dasein is always "attuned" to its world. But every attunement carries with it an **understanding** of that world (and every understanding has its mood). We have already met "understanding," of course. Dasein from the beginning has been held to be that being who—simply by virtue of Being—has an understanding of its Being. To be "there," in fact, *is* to understand. But this is hard to—understand. Let us see if we can do so.

We can begin in a familiar way by examining what we mean when we say that Jane understands carburetors. We mean that she is competent with respect to carburetors, that she can adjust, tune, and repair them. It need not be that Jane could write a book about carburetors. But if you are having carburetor troubles, Jane is the one for you. She really *understands* carburetors! Now it is crucial to note that *possibility* or *potentiality* is involved in

---

*The German word here is "Unheimlichkeit," literally "not-at-homeness." The translators of *Being and Time* bring it into English as "uncanniness." It is perhaps this same sense of homelessness that Augustine has in mind when he prays, "Our hearts find no peace until they rest in you" (p. 283). Unlike Augustine, Heidegger cannot believe that there is a home for us *beyond* the world.

†Remember that there are two kinds of "falling": *falling-in-with* is one of the essential characteristics of Dasein, an *existential*. Dasein's "who" is invariably and inevitably the

One. The second kind of falling, *falling-away-from*, is Dasein's fleeing from the anxious realization of its own essential homelessness into the illusory security that the life of the One seems to offer. Such fleeing is the mark of *inauthentic* existence, of not appropriating the Being that is *one's own*. Simone de Beauvoir calls this flight from authenticity "seriousness." (See pp. 681–683.)

this kind of understanding. Jane can do more than just describe the current present-at-hand state of your carburetor; she can see *what's wrong* with it. And this means that she has in view a potential state of the device that is different from its current state; a possibility that it might function properly. And she has the *know-how* to produce that state. Jane's understanding is a matter of being able to bring it from a condition of not working well to one of satisfactory performance, a possibility not now realized.

This notion of possibility is also involved in the existential understanding that belongs to Dasein. For what does Dasein essentially understand? Itself, in its own Being. Suppose someone (God, maybe) had a list of everything factually true of you at this moment: every hair on your head, the state of every neuron in your brain, and every thought and feeling. Would this list tell us who you are? It would not. It wouldn't, even if it listed every fact about you since you were born. Why not? Because you, as a case of Dasein, are not something present-at-hand, a mere collection of facts; you are essentially *what you can be.* You are a certain "potentiality-for-Being," to use Heidegger's language. Unless someone understands your *possibilities*, he or she will not understand you.

> Dasein is constantly "more" than it factually is, supposing that one might want to make an inventory of it as something-at-hand and list the contents of its Being. . . . But Dasein is never more than it factically is, for to its facticity its potentiality-for-Being belongs essentially. (*BT*, 185)

But now let's think about what is needed for you to understand yourself. Here is the somewhat startling answer: nothing—beyond your Being-there. To exist *is* to understand.* Understanding (as an *existential*) is having competence over one's Being; that is not something added on "by way of an extra" (*BT*, 183). That is what it is to exist. And this understanding is an understanding of possibility.

Right now, at this very moment, you *are* a certain understanding of your possibilities (e.g., the possibility of continuing to read this chapter, of going to the refrigerator for a cold drink, of calling a friend, of becoming an engineer or accountant, perhaps of dropping out of school and bumming around the world). You exist these potentialities in your every thought and movement. And this understanding, which you *are*, is not something that you need to conceptualize or explicitly think about. It just is a certain *competence* with respect to your Being that you cannot help manifesting.

Understanding has the structure of *projection.* We are always projecting ourselves into possibilities. Again, we must be careful not to think of this as a matter of reflecting on possibilities, of reviewing or deliberating, or of having them "in mind." It is more primordial than that. To understand a chair, for instance, is to be prepared to sit in it rather than wear it. To understand oneself as a student is to *project* oneself into potentially mastering Chinese or statistics or into the possibility of becoming a college graduate. Understanding oneself as a student *permeates* one's Being. To exist in a specific situation *is* to have an understanding (or a misunderstanding) of the promise or menace of what is impending. Understanding in this fundamental sense is a matter of our *Being.* It is an aspect of what it means to *exist.* Since we are what we *can be*, possibility is even more fundamental to our Being than the actuality of the facts about us. And these possibilities are not something external to our Being. They are possibilities that we *are.*

❦

> "Man is the entity that makes itself."
>
>   *José Ortega y Gasset (1883–1955)*

This understanding, as a kind of preparedness to act, tends to be tacit. But it can be developed more explicitly; it then takes the form of **interpretation.** Interpretation is not something different from understanding; it is understanding itself come to fruition. Consider the light switch in your room, something you understand very well in one sense; you operate with it in such a familiar way

---

*This is quite compatible, of course, with your *misunderstanding* yourself; a misunderstanding is a kind of understanding. That is why inauthentic existence is one of your possibilities.

that you scarcely notice it; you probably couldn't say what its color is. But suppose one day it fails to function. Now its "place" in the functional ordering of the world is disturbed; you had all along been taking its role as equipment for granted—that is, understanding it implicitly. But now it comes to the fore, and you understand it explicitly—*as* a device to transmit electricity. This "as" structure is already implicit in your everyday and familiar understanding, but now it is expressed; it becomes explicit in an *interpretation*. Interpretation always lays bare "the structure of *something as something*" (*BT*, 189).

The fact that interpretation (whether of a device, a text, the meaning of someone's action, and so on) is always founded on a prior understanding has an important implication for Heidegger. There is no way we can disengage ourselves from our Being-in-the-world sufficiently to guarantee a completely "objective" view of anything. Every interpretation *always* takes something for granted; it is worked out on some background that is not itself available for inspection and decision. That does not mean that truth is unavailable to Dasein, but it does mean that Dasein is involved in a kind of circle it cannot get out of.* Interpreting is understanding *x as y*—for example, the switch *as* a device for controlling the flow of electricity. But interpretation just makes explicit that prior understanding of it *as* a switch in the first place. That understanding is a matter of having a certain competence with respect to it. Such competent understanding is a matter of (largely unreflective) projection, of ways of behaving toward what *could be*. And all this exists only on the background of our Being-in-the-world in general, which involves understanding the potentialities of such equipment as light switches.

This circle is usually called the **hermeneutic circle;** all interpretation is caught up in what is understood beforehand. It is not a vicious circle,

Heidegger maintains, but it is one that should be recognized.

> If the basic conditions which make interpretation possible are to be fulfilled, this must . . . be done by not failing to recognize beforehand the essential conditions under which it can be performed. What is decisive is not to get out of the circle, but to come into it in the right way. (*BT*, 194–195)

"The right way" is to come without illusions (that is, without imagining that one can get a kind of "bare" look at the object of interpretation) and to be as clear and explicit as possible about what one is bringing to the interpretive task. Part of Heidegger's conviction is that this background can never be made *completely* explicit, for it is this background that Dasein *is*. To get a completely explicit interpretation of ourselves, we would have to stand completely outside ourselves, and it is obvious that we cannot do that.

Let us summarize. Understanding, like attunement, is an *existential*. There is no Being-there that does not involve understanding. The primordial mode of understanding is a kind of know-how or competence with respect to things, particularly with respect to Dasein's own Being. This is largely implicit, but it can be spelled out in an interpretation. It is just such an interpretation that Heidegger is striving to construct with respect to the meaning of Dasein's Being and ultimately for the meaning of Being in general.

DISCOURSE

Because the world of Dasein is a world of significations (in-order-tos, toward-whichs, and for-the-sake-ofs, to put it in Heideggerese), Dasein exists in an *articulated* world; like a turkey, it has "joints" at which it may be readily carved. The hammer is distinct from the nails but is *for* pounding them into the boards, which are a third articulated item. In understanding how to use a hammer, Dasein displays a primordial understanding of this articulation. As we have seen, this primitive kind of understanding can be made explicit in interpretation. And now we must add that interpretation itself is a phenomenon *in-the-world* only in terms of *discourse*.

Discourse, Heidegger says, is *equiprimordial* with attunement and understanding. (This means

---

*It is interesting to compare this point with the pragmatist claim that we must give up the quest for certainty. See the image of sailors on a ship, p. 601; and the summary of Dewey's view of experience, pp. 609–610. There is some justice in viewing the history of modern philosophy as a conversation between the rationalists, the empiricists, and the pragmatists. In this (oversimplified) schema, Heidegger would line up with the pragmatists.

that while it cannot be reduced to either of them, it is equally basic.) Discourse, too, is an *existential*. There is no Dasein that doesn't *talk*.* In talk, or **discourse,** the articulations of the world of Dasein are expressed in *language*. Moreover, we talk *with one another*, so discourse essentially involves Being-with. Discourse involves communication.

Again, Heidegger warns against a misunderstanding.

> Communication is never anything like a convey-ing of experiences, such as opinions or wishes, from the interior of one subject into the interior of another. Dasein-with is already essentially mani-fest in a co-state-of-mind [co-attunement] and a co-understanding. In discourse Being-with becomes "explicitly" *shared*; that is to say, it *is* already, but it is unshared as something that has not been taken hold of and appropriated. (*BT*, 205)

This remark should be understood as part of Heidegger's continuing polemic against the Carte-sian picture of the isolated subject shut up within the walls of the mind and forced to find some way to "convey" a message across an empty space to an-other such subject. As Being-with, we already live in a common world with others—the public world of equipment and its structural articulation. In dis-course we "take hold" of this common legacy and express it in language.

---

1. What do moods reveal? How are they related to what Heidegger calls *thrownness*?
2. What does anxiety reveal? How is it related to responsibility? To inauthenticity?
3. In what way is possibility or potentiality involved in Dasein's understanding of itself?
4. Explain why understanding is necessarily involved in the hermeneutic circle. Does this have any implications for how certain you should feel about your opinions?

Falling-Away

With the analysis of the modes of disclosure, the general shape of Heidegger's fundamental ontol-ogy is coming into view. Dasein is

- Being-in-the-world;
- Being-with-others;
- Falling-in-with-the-One;
- Thrown;
- A clearing, manifesting itself in attunement, understanding, and discourse.

We also know that Dasein has the potentiality for existing in either an authentic or an inauthen-tic fashion. We need to understand these alter-natives more clearly. Let us begin by discussing inauthenticity.

Dasein *is* Being-in-the-world and as such "falls-in-with" the "Others" who constitute "the One." Dasein has no secret, private essence *out of which* it could fall; nor is Dasein initially "innocent," later falling into sin. As long as we are talking about the first kind of falling—falling-in-with—questions of innocence or guilt are not yet in order. This kind of falling is a constitutive, ontological characteristic of what it is to be Dasein.*

In discussing anxiety, we noted that Dasein is tempted to flee its anxious homelessness and *lose itself* in the tranquilizing security of the public world. But Heidegger now wants to go a step fur-ther and claim that simply Being-in-the-world is itself *tempting*. For the world is, after all, the world of the One. And to understand why this might by its very nature tempt Dasein toward inauthentic-ity, we need to understand the modes of disclosure characteristic of *the One*. How does One under-stand? How are "they" attuned to their Being? What sort of discourse is Dasein thrown into as it takes up its Being-in-the-world?

---

*What about newborn babies, you ask? The answer seems to be that while they are clearly human, they are not a case of Dasein. They are not (yet) *there* in that way character-istic of Dasein. As they are socialized, Dasein slowly dawns in them.

*Despite Heidegger's protestations, some theologians suggest that we might have here the basis for an interpreta-tion of what the Christian tradition has called "original sin." If there is no "pure" essence of Dasein to be corrupted in the first place, and if—as we will shortly see—the One that becomes the "who" of Dasein is itself inauthentic, how could Dasein *not* be "conceived and born in sin"? For Augustine on original sin, see pp. 277–278.

IDLE TALK

As we have seen, discourse has its Being in language, which expresses the articulations making up the world. Discourse is essentially revealing, disclosing. It opens up the world. But in average everydayness, discourse tends toward being just **idle talk.**

> We do not so much understand the entities which are talked about; we already are listening only to what is said-in-the-talk as such. What is said-in-the-talk gets understood; but what the talk is about is understood only approximately and superficially. (*BT*, 212)

This is something you can test for yourself. Listen carefully to the conversations that go on among your acquaintances; see how much of their "everyday" talk is just a matter of latching on to "what-is-said" as such, without any deep commitment to the subject matter being discussed or to the truth about it. How much of it is just chatter, or an attempt to impose opinions on others? How much is what Wittgenstein calls "just *gassing*"?*

> And because this discoursing has lost its primary relationship-of-Being towards the entity talked about, or else has never achieved such a relationship, it does not communicate in such a way as to let this entity be appropriated in a primordial manner, but communicates rather by following the route of *gossiping* and *passing the word along*. What is said-in-the-talk as such, spreads in wider circles and takes on an authoritative character. Things are so because one says so. . . .
>
> Idle talk is the possibility of understanding everything without previously making the thing one's own. (*BT*, 212–213)

When Dasein is thrown into the world, it is into idle talk that Dasein is thrown.

> There are many things with which we first become acquainted in this way, and there is not a little which never gets beyond such an average understanding. (*BT*, 213)

Dasein is a talking entity. But when Dasein falls-in-with the others in its world, as it must, it

also falls-in-with this degenerate form of discourse. Note that there is no possibility of extricating ourselves from idle talk. It is the milieu in which we exist. The best we can do is to struggle against it—from within it—toward "genuine understanding."* But as long as we remain inauthentically content with what-is-said, idle talk will cover over the meaning of Being, including the meaning of our own Being. That is why Heidegger can say, "Being-in-the-world is in itself tempting" (*BT*, 221).

CURIOSITY

Dasein, we have said, is a "clearing" in the midst of the world because *understanding* is an aspect of its essence. But in its average everydayness, understanding, too, tends to become shallow and disconnected from Being. As long as we are absorbed in our work, hammering away on the roof, our understanding is engaged in the project. But when we take a rest, understanding idles. And then it becomes **curiosity.** Curiosity is a concern just to see—but not to understand what one sees.

> Consequently it does not seek the leisure of tarrying observantly, but rather seeks restlessness and the excitement of continual novelty and changing encounters. In not tarrying, curiosity is concerned with the constant possibility of *distraction*. Curiosity has nothing to do with observing entities and marvelling at them. . . .† To be amazed to the point of not understanding is something in which it has no interest. Rather it concerns itself with a kind of knowing, but just in order to have known. (*BT*, 216–217)

One is reminded of those folks who visit the Grand Canyon primarily to bring back slides to show their friends. Curiosity and idle talk, Heidegger says, reinforce each other; "*either* of these ways-to-be drags the other one with it" (*BT*, 217). You can see why this is so. If one never tarries anywhere, one's understanding is bound to be expressed in idle talk about what one has "seen."

---

*See pp. 629, 635, and 643.

*Idle talk seems to correspond pretty nearly with the way Plato describes life in the cave. See his myth on pp. 162–165.

†Look again at the "rotation method" from the first part of Kierkegaard's *Either/Or* (pp. 523–524).

Together, Heidegger wryly remarks, they are supposed to guarantee a "life" that is genuinely "lively."

"The public have an insatiable curiosity to know everything. Except what is worth knowing. Journalism . . . supplies their demands."

Oscar Wilde (1854–1900)

AMBIGUITY

Because of the predominance of idle talk and curiosity, ambiguity pervades Dasein's Being-in-the-world. It

> soon becomes impossible to decide what is disclosed in a genuine understanding, and what is not. . . .
> Everything looks as if it were genuinely understood, genuinely taken hold of, genuinely spoken, though at bottom it is not; or else it does not look so, and yet at bottom it is. (*BT*, 217)

Genuine understanding of something is, of course, difficult. It takes time, patience, and careful attention. But in a day when the results of the most mathematically sophisticated physics are reported in the daily paper in a way that is supposed to inform the average person, who can tell what is truly understood and what is not? Since understanding is the "light of nature" in which beings and Being are "cleared," and since understanding is essential to the very Being of Dasein, a deadly **ambiguity** seeps into Dasein's existence.

◆

"A true account of the actual is the rarest poetry, for common sense always takes a hasty and superficial view."

Henry David Thoreau (1817–1862)

In its average everydayness, Dasein is the *One*. But the average everydayness of the One is characterized by idle talk, curiosity, and ambiguity. It follows that Dasein

> has, in the first instance, fallen away from itself as an authentic potentiality for Being its Self, and has

fallen into the "world." "Fallenness" into the "world" means an absorption in Being-with-one-another, in so far as the latter is guided by idle talk, curiosity, and ambiguity. (*BT*, 220)

In falling-in-with the way of the world, Dasein tends to fall-away-from itself. While it is important to keep these two notions distinct, one gets the definite impression that Heidegger believes the first invariably brings the second with it. Dasein falls away from itself by failing to grasp its own Being clearly. It understands itself the way "they" understand. It even takes its moods, its way of being attuned, from the One—what matters to Dasein is what "they say" matters. Dasein does not decisively seize itself for itself; it lets itself float, lost in the interpretations of the public "they." It is this *not being one's own*, belonging only to the One, that is the heart of inauthenticity. And we all *are* inauthentic in this way.

This idea is driven home by a further reflection about *thrownness*. To this point, we have talked about being "thrown" into the world as if it were an event that happened to us once, at birth. But Heidegger maintains that we are constantly being thrown into the world.

> Thrownness is neither a "fact that is finished" nor a Fact that is settled. Dasein's facticity is such that *as long as* it is what it is, Dasein remains in the throw, and is sucked into the turbulence of the "they's" inauthenticity. (*BT*, 223)

Dasein remains "in the throw" as long as it is. We are constantly being thrown into the world, and the world is always the world of the One. This has important implications for what **authentic existence** might be.

> *Authentic* existence is not something which floats above falling everydayness; existentially, it is only a modified way in which such everydayness is seized upon. (*BT*, 224)

We will return to that shortly.

Care

Heidegger's interpretation of the ontology of Dasein is rich and complex. We have explored quite a number of the *existentials*, or "categories" that define its way of Being. At this point, Heidegger asks whether this multiplicity of concepts is founded in a deeper unity. He thinks he can point to a unifying ontological concept, in the light of which all the rest makes sense.

The single phenomenon that lies at the root of Dasein's Being, Heidegger tells us, is **Care.** Care is understood as the ontological structure that makes possible Dasein's everyday *concerns* for its projects, its *solicitude* for Others, even its *willing* and *wishing.* In typical Heideggerian fashion, Care is spelled out as

- Being-ahead-of-itself by projecting toward its possibilities, while
- Being-in-the-world, and
- Being engaged with entities encountered within-the-world.

(This kind of talk should now be making some sense to you; go over these phrases carefully, making sure that it is not simply "idle talk" to you.)

It is important to note that Care is not some special "ontic" attitude that Dasein might occasionally display. Care is the *Being* of Dasein: without Care, no Being-there. Care is manifest in all understanding, from the intensely practical to the most purely theoretical. It is present in attunement and in all discourse. Dasein is not fundamentally the rational animal, not basically the *ego cogito*, not primarily a *knower.* What is most fundamental to Dasein's Being is caring: Dasein is the being for whom things *matter.** And that brings us right back to the very beginning, where we noted that Dasein is that being for whom its own Being is an *issue.*

We know a woman who was sitting on the living room sofa as she was recovering from a severe case of flu. She looked about and said, "I must be alive; I'm beginning to care that the house is a mess." Heidegger would have liked that.

---

*Some years ago, the rock group Queen recorded a song in which this phrase was repeated: "Nothing really matters." Is this an argument against Heidegger's claim that Care is the essence of Dasein? Not at all. If it were *true* that nothing really mattered, Queen would not bother to sing it in that poignant and nostalgic way they do. They *care* that "nothing matters," thereby proving that something *does* matter.

We have in Care, then, a single, unitary, simple foundation for all the complexities we have so far discovered in the Being of Dasein—and for those still to come. But we now need to consider Dasein *as a whole.* Because Dasein is always projecting itself into a future, we must think about *death.*

---

1. Explain idle talk, curiosity, and ambiguity as inauthentic modes of Dasein's Being.
2. What does it mean to say that Care is the Being of Dasein?

Death

Despite the extensive analysis we have been following, Heidegger is not satisfied that he has explored all the dimensions of Dasein's Being. In particular, it is not clear that we have an understanding of the *totality* of Dasein. Nor has much been said about the character of *authenticity.* So these topics remain. We first explore the idea of totality.

We have seen that Dasein's existence is characterized by projection toward possibilities: at every stage, Dasein is what it is *not yet*; there are always potentialities-for-Being that are yet unrealized. As Heidegger now puts it, this means that there is always "something *still outstanding*," something "*still to be settled*" with respect to Dasein's Being (*BT,* 279). Can that be brought into our understanding in a way that will give us an interpretation of Dasein as a *whole*? This obviously brings us to the topic of the *end* of Dasein: to death. It is death that makes Dasein a whole.

In one sense, of course, death is just the end of Dasein's life. But if we are to understand it, we must also see it in light of that basic existential, Care. As a *possibility* for Dasein, death is something that, in a strange sense, Dasein *lives,* because Dasein *is* its possibilities. This is an unusual possibility because it is one that Dasein is *bound* to realize. Unlike other possibilities, this is one about which Dasein has no choice. As Heidegger puts it, death is "not to be outstripped" (*BT,* 294). As soon as a man is born, he is old enough to die. We are *thrown* into this possibility, with never a chance of extrication.

"Xerxes did die,
    And so must I."

                    The New England Primer

One of the aspects of Dasein, however, is *falling*. And in falling-away-from itself into the world of the "they," Dasein evades coming to grips with this possibility, turns away, flees-in-the-face of it. In its "everyday" mode, Dasein covers over this possibility, hides from itself the fact that it is destined for death. And so Dasein becomes inauthentic, no longer truly itself. How does Dasein do this? By interpreting death as a mishap, an event, as something present-at-hand—but not yet!

> This evasive concealment in the face of death dominates everydayness so stubbornly that, in Being with one another, the "neighbors" often still keep talking the "dying person" into the belief that he will escape death and soon return to the tranquillized everydayness of the world of his concern. Such "solicitude" is meant to "console" him. . . . In this manner the "they" provides a *constant tranquillization about death*. (*BT*, 297–298)

Everydayness transforms **death** from one's ownmost possibility into an event that is distant and then says it is nothing to be *afraid* of. But in so tranquilizing Dasein, it closes off the *anxiety* a genuine appropriation of this possibility generates.* Dasein's fleeing in the face of death takes the form of evasion. Our Being is a **Being-toward-death,** but everydayness *alienates Dasein from this Being*.

🜚

"Do not fear death so much, but rather the inadequate life."

                    Bertolt Brecht (1898–1956)

So, our ontological interpretation of Dasein *can* get hold of Dasein as-a-whole; Dasein's Being is a Being-toward-death, in which Dasein's death is understood as a possibility that in each moment is a defining characteristic of Dasein. Any adequate interpretation of Dasein will necessarily have grasped Dasein's death. Being-toward-death, too, is an *existential*.

The evasion and alienation from oneself typical of absorption in the "they" is a form of inauthentic existence. Is, then, an authentic appropriation of death possible? We know what it would be like. There would be no evasion, no explaining away, no misinterpreting of the mode of Being of death. Death would be steadily apprehended as a possibility of Dasein's Being—not in brooding over it or thinking about it, but existing in every moment in the *anticipation* of death.

This authentic anticipation of death wrenches Dasein away from the One. It *individualizes* Dasein, brings each Dasein before a possibility that belongs to it alone: It says, "I must die." Anticipation forces the realization that one is finite and so lights up all the possibilities that lie between the present and death. Anticipation grasps both the certainty of death and the uncertainty about when it will come. This understanding of itself on the part of Dasein is accompanied by an attunement. (Remember that every understanding has its mood, every mood an understanding.) The mood that accompanies anticipation is *anxiety*. Again, anxiety is displayed as the mood in which Dasein comes face to face with itself—and *doesn't* flee. Anticipation

> reveals to Dasein its lostness in the they-self, and brings it face to face with the possibility of being itself, primarily unsupported by concernful solicitude, but of being itself, rather in an impassioned freedom towards death—a freedom which has been released from the illusions of the "they" and which is factical, certain of itself, and anxious. (*BT*, 311)

Because anticipation releases us from bondage to the interpretations of the One, we are "freed" to *be ourselves* as a whole—but only as Being-toward-death. Any evasion casts us back into the "they" and inauthenticity.

Conscience, Guilt, and Resoluteness

Authentic existence is now our theme. But there is a problem. Dasein is caught up in the life of the

---

*See again the contrast between fear and anxiety, pp. 666–667.

One, living wholly by what "they say." Remember that there is no private essence to Dasein, no "interior" self with contents of its own. In everydayness, Dasein acquiesces in the way "they" understand its possibilities; it goes along with the mood and understanding and discourse of the One; it has not "taken hold" of itself. How then does Dasein know there is anything *but* the life of the "they-self"? How does it become *aware* that it is not being *itself* but is fleeing itself by falling-into-the-world inauthentically? What resources does Dasein have to enable it to come to itself in authentic existence?

> Because Dasein is *lost* in the "they," it must first find itself. In order to find *itself* at all, it must be "shown" to itself in its possible authenticity. In terms of its possibility, Dasein is already a potentiality-for-Being-its-Self, but it needs to have this potentiality attested. (*BT*, 313)

What is it that can "show" Dasein to *itself* as a possibly authentic Self? What "attests" to this possibility? The voice of **conscience,** Heidegger says (*BT*, 313). But we have to be careful here, as elsewhere, not to interpret this "voice" in the way it is ordinarily understood. By now we should be sufficiently on guard: conscience, like understanding, attunement, and discourse, has an everyday form that hides as much as it discloses. What we are looking for is the *existential ground* on the basis of which ordinary experiences of conscience are *possible.*

So conscience in this existential or ontological sense is not to be identified with that nagging little voice that occasionally tells us we have done something wrong. The deep sense of conscience must have the same sort of Being as Dasein; it is not occasional, but constant. It is, moreover, a mode of disclosure, in which something is presented to be understood. So we need an interpretation of this phenomenon that makes clear where this "voiceless voice" comes from, to whom it is addressed, and what it "says."

In the mode of average everydayness, Heidegger says, Dasein is constantly listening. But it "listens away" from itself and hears only the voice of the "they." As a result, it "fails to hear" itself. As we have seen, Dasein *is* the One; each of us is

one of "the others" (from whom, for the most part, we do not distinguish ourselves); and this indefinite One is what generally determines how life goes in the world.

Conscience is a "call" to this One (who we are).

> *What* does the conscience call to him to whom it appeals? Taken strictly, nothing. The call asserts nothing, gives no information about world-events, has nothing to tell. Least of all does it try to set going a "soliloquy" in the Self to which it has appealed. "Nothing" gets called to this Self, but it has been *summoned* to itself—that is, to its ownmost potentiality-for-Being. (*BT*, 318)

As we have seen, Dasein *is* just such a potentiality-for-Being. But this Being of Dasein is hidden to itself as long as it is governed by the "they." What conscience does is to disclose Dasein to itself as such a potentiality-for-being. So conscience "calls Dasein forth to its possibilities" (*BT*, 319). In effect, it says, "You cannot hide behind the 'they' any longer; *you* are responsible for your existence!" (In putting words in the mouth of conscience, we are of course falsifying somewhat Heidegger's insistence that the call is "wordless," but not in a damaging way, we hope.)

We now know to whom the call of conscience is addressed: to Dasein in its everydayness. And we know what the call "says": *You must become yourself*!* The call, then, summons inauthentic Dasein to take hold of itself, to take itself over, and in so doing to be itself authentically. But who is doing the calling?

> In conscience Dasein calls itself. (*BT*, 320)

Well, we might have known! Still, that is not exactly clear. How can Dasein call itself in this way? If it is Dasein to whom the call comes, how can it be Dasein who is doing the calling? Indeed, as Heidegger acknowledges, the call typically seems to come from *beyond* oneself. It seems to be

> something which *we ourselves* have neither planned for nor prepared for nor voluntarily performed, nor have we ever done so. "It" calls, against our

---

*Compare Nietzsche, pp. 584–585, and Kierkegaard, pp. 530–532.

expectations and even against our will. On the other hand, the call undoubtedly does not come from someone else who is with me in the world. The call comes *from* me and yet *from beyond me.* (*BT*, 320)

This seems phenomenologically accurate; it is the basis, Heidegger suggests, for interpretations of the call as the voice of God or for attempts to give a sociological or biological interpretation of conscience. None of these will do, however, since these causal accounts all try to locate conscience in *something*—that is, in something present-at-hand. And the call has to have the kind of Being of Dasein.

The puzzle can be solved if we recall the not-at-homeness that is revealed in the mood of anxiety. Anxiety, you will remember, individualizes Dasein, pulls it out of the "they," and makes clear that it is its own *having to be.* In anxiety, Dasein feels alienated from the world of the One, yet recognizes that it has no other home. It comes to understand itself as *thrown into existence.* With this contrast between Dasein as *at home in the world on terms set out by the "they"* and *Dasein as cast out of that familiar home* we can solve the problem. The "it" that calls is "uncanny" Dasein in its mode of not-being-at-home-in-the-world; and "it" calls to Dasein in the mode of the "they," summoning it *to itself.*

And now we can also see why authentic existence is not a wholly different kind of existence from inauthentic but just a modified way in which such everydayness is seized on. To exist authentically is to take responsibility for the self that one is. And that is—inevitably, inextricably, and for as long as one lives—the self that has been (and is being) shaped by the particular "they" into which one has been "thrown." There is no "true self" other than this.

Conscience, then, summons Dasein, lost in the "they," to take up responsibility for itself. It is true that you are not responsible for yourself "from the bottom up," so to speak; you are not responsible for how and where you were "thrown" into existence. But in authentic existence you shoulder the burden. The authentic self does not excuse itself, blaming parents, society, or circumstance for its shortcomings. Authentic Dasein *makes itself*

responsible; it says, "Yes, this is who I am, who I have been; and this is who I will become."[*]

Conscience summons Dasein to be itself, to turn away from the rationalizations and self-deceptions of the "they." It summons lost Dasein back to its thrownness and forth into existence—into an understanding that projects itself into the peculiar possibilities of its own future. The summons issues from Dasein itself, and Dasein hears the verdict: **guilty.** Why "guilty"? Because Dasein, in fleeing itself into the world of the "they," has not been what it is called to; Dasein has not been *itself.* Yet we are not summoned to a kind of wallowing around in self-recrimination; we are to realize our essence—that is, for the first time truly to *exist.*

Conscience, then, "attests" to inauthentic Dasein that there is another possibility and calls it to exist authentically by taking over this having-to-be-itself into which it has been thrown. Dasein takes it over in a certain *understanding* of its own authentic possibilities, in the *mood* of anxiety (since the tranquilizing "they" is set aside), and with a reticence that answers to the wordless *discourse* of conscience. There is nothing to be said; there is everything to be done.

> This distinctive and authentic disclosedness, which is attested in Dasein itself by its conscience—*this reticent self-projection upon one's ownmost Being-guilty, in which one is ready for anxiety*—we call "resoluteness." . . .
>
> In resoluteness we have now arrived at that truth of Dasein which is most primordial because it is *authentic.* (*BT*, 343)

"Resoluteness" is the term for authentic Being-in-the-world. To be resolute is to *be oneself.* In resoluteness, Dasein exists in that disclosedness that puts it "in the truth." But since what Dasein grasps in the understanding of resoluteness is its own Being-guilty, it understands that in truth it has been, and perhaps will soon again be, "in untruth."

We can put the results of this section and the preceding one together in the following

---

[*]Contrast Kierkegaard's despair of defiance, pp. 533–534. Heidegger's *authentic existence* seems a secular interpretation of what Kierkegaard understands by *faith* (pp. 534–535).

way: In *anticipation*, authentic Dasein grasps its Being-toward-death. In answering the call of conscience, Dasein sets aside the temptations of the One and *resolutely* takes up the burden of Being-itself as thrown, existing, falling, guilty Being-in-the-world. But in resolutely Being-itself, a finite whole, Dasein must anticipate its death. And anticipation, for its part, is not a kind of free-floating imagination, but a way of Being that has come to itself and has become transparent to itself. So anticipation and resoluteness, if understood deeply enough, imply each other.

In **anticipatory resoluteness,** Dasein comes at last authentically to itself. We don't often hear Heidegger speak of "joy," but in the section where he discusses anticipatory resoluteness, he writes,

> Along with the sober anxiety which brings us face to face with our individualized potentiality-for-Being, there goes an unshakable joy in this possibility. (*BT*, 358)

◆

"That it will never come again
Is what makes life so sweet."

Emily Dickinson (1830–1886)

Temporality as the Meaning of Care

Imagine that you know a secret and are very sure that Peter doesn't know it. But on Thursday afternoon he makes an extremely puzzling remark. At first you can't figure out what his remark *means* nor (which is not the same) what it *means* that Peter made the remark. But as you think about it, you realize that he must know the secret, too. Only on that background does his remark make any sense. What Peter said is *intelligible* only on that assumption. It is that background—Peter knowing the secret—that made it *possible* for him to say what he did.

This everyday example brings us to Heidegger's sense of **meaning.** Heidegger's interest, of course, is directed to the meaning of Being. That is the fox we have been hunting through all these

hills and dales and twisty paths. It is for the sake of uncovering the meaning of Being that Heidegger engages in the analysis of Dasein. But so far we have merely been asking, What is the meaning of *Dasein's* Being? In asking this, we have been constructing an *ontology*. This ontology (the *existentials*) serves as a *background* against which the phenomena of average everydayness become *intelligible*. We can now say that it is the articulated structure of Care that makes everyday Dasein *possible*. And we can summarize this structure:

- existence (Being-ahead-of-itself-in projecting possibilities);
- facticity (thrownness into-the-world and toward-death);
- falling (in-with-the-Others and away-from-itself).

Taken together as a totality, these features define Care as the essence of Dasein's Being. But have we reached rock bottom with the concept of Care? Or can we ask once again, What is the *meaning of Care*? At this point, we need to pay explicit attention to meaning.

> What does "*meaning*" signify? . . . meaning is that wherein the understandability of something maintains itself. . . . "Meaning" signifies the "upon-which" of a primary projection in terms of which something can be conceived in its possibility as that which it is. (*BT*, 370–371)

That is hard to understand. But if you think back to our example, you should be able to grasp it. What did Peter mean by making this remark? To uncover the meaning, we "project" his remark onto a background (or larger context) that makes it understandable—namely, that Peter knows the secret. This background is that "upon which" we project Peter's remark. In this larger context, Peter's remark makes perfect sense; it is meaningful. So meaning is "that wherein the understandability" of the remark "maintains itself." Moreover, it seems that *only* if Peter knows the secret is it possible for him to say what he does.

Here is another analogy. Some people think that human life is meaningful only if it is projected onto a larger background, perhaps of immortality or divine purposes. In that context, life has, perhaps, the meaning of a *test*. Without such a background, they say, life is meaningless—pointless. The meaningfulness of life is possible only if it is embedded in a larger context. Whether this is so is an interesting question we do not directly address. But the sense of meaning is the same as the one in Heidegger's question about the meaning of Care—and, ultimately, of the meaning of Being.

So if we are now asking about the meaning of Care, we are asking about a deeper background, or larger context, in the light of which the phenomenon of Care becomes intelligible. We are asking about that on which Care can be projected to make it understandable and to show it as possible. Is there a still more fundamental (more primordial) structure to Dasein's Being that makes it possible? That is the question.

Heidegger takes as his clue the Being of Dasein when it is most "true," or most itself: authentic existence. We have seen authentic existence spelled out in terms of anticipatory resoluteness. Anticipatory resoluteness, for its part, is

> Being towards one's ownmost, distinctive, potentiality-for-Being. (*BT*, 372)

What makes this "Being towards" possible? **Time**—and in particular, the future.

For anticipatory resoluteness to be *possible*, it must be that Dasein is, in its very Being, *futural*—temporal. This doesn't mean that Dasein is "located" in time, any more than Dasein's Being-in-the-world means that Dasein is "located" in an objective space.* Dasein is "futural" in that it *comes toward itself* in that projecting of possibilities that defines existence. Dasein is always ahead-of-itself-in-time.

We have seen that anticipatory resoluteness also fastens onto itself as Being-guilty. Dasein takes over its facticity—makes its thrownness its own—by taking responsibility for itself. You "are" your possibilities. But what these possibilities are depends on what you have been. You can only project yourself authentically into the future by "coming back" to yourself as having been something. What you have been (and now are, as a result) is not just a set of dead facts. These facts take life and

meaning from your projects. You are now, let us say, a college student; as each moment slips away, this is something you have been. But *have you been* preparing for a job? Or *have you been* learning to understand yourself? Or laying a foundation for a scholarly life? Or inching up the ladder of monetary reward? Four people who answer these questions differently might have taken exactly the same courses and read exactly the same books to this point. But the *meaning* of what they have done is radically different; it is projected against a different background (and notice that each background essentially makes reference to the future!). Because the meaning of what they have done is different, what they "have been" is also different. The difference is defined by the different futures they project. We can now see that because it is futural, Dasein also essentially has a past. But once again we must be careful. This is an *existential* past, not one that is composed of moments that have added up and then dropped away into nothingness. It is a past that one constantly *is*.

Finally, anticipatory resoluteness plants one firmly in the current situation. It does not live in daydreams or fantasy; it is not lost in nostalgia. Authentic Dasein resolutely takes *present* action in the light of an attuned understanding of its *future* potentialities and its *past* having been. An unblinkered, clear, disclosive *sight* of what is present is essential to Dasein's authentic appropriation of itself.

And now we can say that

> Temporality reveals itself as the meaning of authentic care. (*BT*, 374)

So that "on which" Care becomes intelligible is the structure of temporality. Temporality involves projecting into the future, coming back to one's past, and making present. It is important to note that this structure is not itself an entity; it is not a thing or a being. Most important, it is not like an empty container into which temporal items can be placed. Temporality is the most fundamental structure of Dasein's Being-there. Dasein is essentially temporal and essentially *finite*, since authentic Dasein anticipates its end in death. Time, in the sense of existential temporality, is the framework within which Care is possible. Time is, to put it in

---

*Review the discussion of Being-in on p. 657.

Heidegger's terms, the *horizon* of Dasein's Being. Just as whatever is visible to you now is within the horizon, the framework of temporality defines the horizon for Dasein. All the features of Dasein's Being we have examined are possible only against this background.

Heidegger's analysis of Dasein is now virtually complete. Dasein is at any moment not just what it is *then*, but also what it has been and will be. This "connectedness" of Dasein in its stretching along Heidegger calls **historicality.** And he thinks the proper understanding of that phenomenon—enlightened by the entire analysis of the Being of Dasein—is essential to the proper writing of "history."

After the "turn" in his thinking, Heidegger leaves the analysis of Dasein and tries to focus directly on Being itself. He has interesting things to say about art (as a way in which Being manifests itself) and about technology (into which we are "thrown," as Dasein was thrown into what "they say" in *Being and Time*). Technology is a mode of revealing Being. Heidegger looks forward, in almost mystical fashion, to a time when people will no longer experience Being as something to be technologically exploited and used, but can just let Being *be*. But these are themes that we will not explore here.

---

1. Why is a consideration of death necessary if we are to understand Dasein as a totality? Why is Being-toward-death one of the existentials?
2. How does average everydayness manage to "tranquilize" itself about death? Contrast with an authentic appropriation of death.
3. In what way does the call of conscience call Dasein to itself? Relate this to authenticity, responsibility, and guilt.
4. "Temporality reveals itself as the meaning of authentic care." Explain.

FOR FURTHER THOUGHT

1. Contrast the notion of "world" in the early Wittgenstein and Heidegger. Which do you think is the more basic notion? Why?
2. Write a short story in which the main character exemplifies some aspects of inauthenticity as Heidegger understands that notion.

KEY WORDS

Being	facticity
Dasein	anxiety
ontic	falling
ontological	understanding
existentials	interpretation
existentialist	hermeneutic circle
fundamental ontology	discourse
phenomenology	idle talk
hermeneutics	curiosity
Being-in-the-world	ambiguity
ready-to-hand	authentic existence
world	Care
present-at-hand	death
das Man	Being-toward-death
Being-with	conscience
distantiality	guilty
averageness	resoluteness
inauthenticity	anticipatory resoluteness
authenticity	meaning
attunement	time
thrownness	historicality

NOTE

1. Quotations from Martin Heidegger's *Being and Time*, trans. John Macquarrie and Edward Robinson (Oxford: Basil Blackwell, 1967), are cited in the text using the abbreviation *BT*.

CHAPTER

28

SIMONE DE BEAUVOIR

Existentialist, Feminist

I "am an existentialist" (*ELA*, 307), proclaims Simone de Beauvoir (1908–1986).[1] Deeply influenced by her longtime companion, Jean-Paul Sartre, she wrote novels, essays, a play, and philosophical works, along with many occasional articles and, later in life, an autobiography. Her big 1949 book, *The Second Sex*, is generally acknowledged to be one of the classics of feminism. A newspaper headline on the day after her death proclaimed, "Women, you owe her everything."[2] Before we consider her discussion of the status of women, we first need to understand her view of the *human* condition.

Ambiguity

De Beauvoir's term for the human condition is **ambiguity**.* By this she means that we are all

- bodies, objects entrenched in the world of objects, yet transcending our objectness toward an open future,

- destined for death, yet aware of that fact,
- embedded in time, yet conscious of that embedding,
- a unique subjectivity, seemingly the center of the world, yet among others who experience themselves the same way,
- an agent who acts in the world, yet faced with our objectified acts which others interpret as it suits them,
- an object for others, as they are for us.

On every side we find ourselves to be this, yet not this, unstable, drawn between two poles. What are you? A consciousness? Yes. A body? Yes. Free? Yes. Conditioned? Yes. Solitary? Yes. Among others? Yes—all those things, so different from each other, so opposed. Your very existence is ambiguous.

Like Kierkegaard, Heidegger, and Sartre, de Beauvoir realizes that this status poses problems to the human being, and she agrees that these problems cannot be solved just by constructing a theory. They have to be solved by living. "In truth," she says, "there is no divorce between philosophy and life" (*EPW*, 217). Like them, she is aware, too,

---

*Note that this is not the Heideggerian ambiguity, one of the modes of inauthenticity. Here ambiguity is a structural feature of human existence.

that there are wrong turns that can be taken.* Let's begin by looking at several.

One is taken by the "hero" of Albert Camus' novel, *The Stranger*. After killing an Arab on an Algerian beach—almost as though he himself were not involved ("The trigger gave, and the smooth underbelly of the butt jogged my palm.")—Meursault is convicted and sentenced to death. A chaplain visits him; Meursault rejects the comfort he is offered and says,

> Nothing, nothing had the least importance, and I knew quite well why. . . . From the dark horizon of my future a sort of slow, persistent breeze had been blowing toward me, all my life long, from the years that were to come. And on its way that breeze had leveled out all the ideas that people tried to foist on me in the equally unreal years I then was living through. What difference could they make to me, the deaths of others, or a mother's love, or his God; or the way a man decides to live, the fate he thinks he chooses?[3]

We hear in these words the unmistakable voice of **nihilism,** and this is one way to resolve the ambiguity: withdraw into your consciousness, observe passively, make everything into an object, and all importance, all significance, all value flattens out. De Beauvoir comments,

> Mr. Camus's Stranger is right to reject all those ties that others want to impose upon him from the outside. . . . No possession is given, but the foreign indifference of the world is not given either. (*PC*, 92–93)

She is saying that this "view from nowhere" is not a privileged point from which to see *the truth* about existence. Rather, it is a vain attempt to evade the ambiguity that we *are* so as not to have to *live* it. It is escape; it is inauthentic.

> The nihilist is right in thinking that the world *possesses* no justification and that he himself *is* nothing [i.e., does not have the solid reality of a rock]. But he forgets that it is up to him to justify the world and to make himself exist validly. (*EA*, 57)

Analogous to the nihilist is the **cynic** who disparages everything equally and the **humorist** who makes everything look comical. De Beauvoir begins one of her philosophical essays with a story about an ancient king of Epirus (in northwest Greece).

> Plutarch tells us that one day Pyrrhus was devising projects of conquest. "We are going to subjugate Greece first," he was saying. "And after that?" said Cineas. "We will vanquish Africa." —"After Africa?" —"We will go on to Asia, we will conquer Asia Minor, Arabia." —"And after that?" —"We will go on as far as India." —"After India?" —"Ah!" said Pyrrhus, "I will rest." — "Why not rest right away?" said Cineas. (*PC*, 90)

It is so easy to make things look absurd! What is the trick here? Cineas takes a series of goals, which Pyrrhus lists one after the other, and interprets them as if he intended to do each of them *in order to* eventually accomplish the last. Since it is so easy to do the last, why go through the trouble of all the rest? Two more examples: "Isn't the tennis player absurd to hit a ball in order for someone to send it back to him and the skier absurd to climb a slope in order to immediately come back down?" (*PC*, 99).*

A more common way of denying the ambiguity of human life is by what de Beauvoir calls **seriousness.** It is more common because we all begin life as children.

> The child's situation is characterized by his finding himself cast into a universe which he has not helped to establish, which has been fashioned without him, and which appears to him as an absolute to which he can only submit. In his eyes, human inventions, words, customs, and values are given facts, as inevitable as the sky and the trees. This means that the world in which he lives is a serious world, since the characteristic of the spirit of seriousness is to consider values as ready-made things. (*EA*, 35)[4]†

The child takes his parents to be "the divinities which they vainly try to be," and he thinks that he, too, "has

---

*Compare Kierkegaard on the varieties of despair (pp. 532–535) and Heidegger on inauthentic existence (p. 672).

*Can you find the trick in these examples?
†Here we see echoes of Heidegger on "the One." See pp. 662–664.

being in a definite and substantial way. He is a good little boy or a scamp; he enjoys being it" (*EA*, 35, 36).

Ordinarily, this solid, comfortable world develops cracks during adolescence. The teenager

> discovers his subjectivity; he discovers that of others . . . he notices the contradictions among adults as well as their hesitations and weakness. Men stop appearing as if they were gods, and at the same time the adolescent discovers the human character of the reality about him. Language, customs, ethics, and values have their source in those uncertain creatures. The moment has come when he too is going to be called upon to participate in their operation; his acts weigh upon the earth as much as those of other men. He will have to choose and decide. (*EA*, 39)

He discovers his freedom but finds that this is a mixed blessing. While there is joy in his liberation, there is much confusion, too. The adolescent

> finds himself cast into a world which is no longer ready-made, which has to be made; he is abandoned, unjustified, the prey of a freedom that is no longer chained up by anything. . . . Freedom is then revealed, and he must decide upon his attitude in the face of it. (*EA*, 39–40)

Because childhood conceals freedom, a man will all his life be nostalgic for the time when he did not know its demands and anxieties. What happens often enough is that—afraid of his freedom, afraid of having to choose, afraid of *himself*—a man takes refuge again in the serious world.

> The serious man gets rid of his freedom by claiming to subordinate it to values which would be unconditioned. He imagines that the accession to these values likewise permanently confers value upon himself. Shielded with "rights," he fulfills himself as a *being* who is escaping from the stress of existence. . . .
>
> He chooses to live in an infantile world, but to the child the values are really given. The serious man must mask the movement by which he gives them to himself, like the mythomaniac who while reading a love-letter pretends to forget that she has sent it to herself. (*EA*, 46–47)*

---

*De Beauvoir uses the term "man" in both the generic and the sexed sense. It is generally easy to tell from the context which is meant. In this chapter we will sometimes, though not always, follow suit.

But this is dishonest. The serious person may think that values are given—authorized perhaps by God, perhaps by the laws of history, perhaps by the Communist Party. But wherever she claims to find them, the truth is that she chooses them.

De Beauvoir accepts Sartre's argument that there is no God, that the very concept of God is incoherent. (See the Sartre profile, pp. 684–685.) But she has arguments of her own.

> "Let us listen to the voice of God," says the believer. "He will tell us himself what he expects of us." But such a hope is naive. God could manifest himself only through an earthly voice because our ears can hear no other. But how, then, does one recognize its divine nature? Upon asking a hallucinating woman who that interlocutor was who spoke to her by mysterious waves, she responded cautiously, "He says that he is God, but *I* don't know him." . . . Kafka describes the same uncertainty in *The Castle* [1926]. Man can receive messages and even see the messenger. But isn't this one an impostor? And does *he* know who sends him? Hasn't he forgotten half the message along the way? Is this letter that he hands over to me authentic, and what is its meaning? The Messiah says that he is the Messiah; the false Messiah also says it. Who will distinguish one from the other?
>
> One will be able to recognize them only by their works. But how will we decide whether these works are good or bad? We will decide in the name of a human good. . . . Man cannot enlighten himself through God. . . . Man is never in situation except before men, and this presence or this absence way up in heaven does not concern him. (*PC*, 104–106)

🔹

"Can one be a saint if God does not exist? That is the only concrete problem I know of today."

Albert Camus (1913–1960)

The serious person claims to subordinate his freedom to values that are of nonhuman origin. He says, "This is serious business" and judges by values he thinks are unconditioned. But he *makes himself* serious; "he is no longer a man, but a father, a boss, a member of the Christian Church or the Communist Party" (*EA*, 48). These identifications supply him with *rights*, and paradoxically he becomes the *slave* of ends that he himself has set up. He serves these values unquestioningly. They become

> inhuman idols to which one will not hesitate to sacrifice man himself. Therefore, the serious man is dangerous. It is natural that he makes himself a tyrant. (*EA*, 49)

Ignoring the subjectivity of his own choice, it comes naturally to him to ignore the subjectivity and freedom of others. Seriousness easily leads to fanaticism. It produces the Inquisition, the lynchings of blacks in the Old South, the cruelties of colonialism, the Holocaust, and the gulag. (Today de Beauvoir would certainly add that it produces jihad.)

More or less midway between the nihilist and the serious man is a character de Beauvoir calls *the* **adventurer.**

> He throws himself into his undertakings with Zest, into exploration, conquest, war, speculation, love, politics, but he does not attach himself to the end at which he aims; only to his conquest. He likes action for its own sake. He finds joy in spreading through the world a freedom which remains indifferent to its content. (*EA*, 58)

Unlike the serious man and the nihilist, the adventurer accepts, affirms his existence in all its inherent ambiguity. He rejoices in its exercise. He does not expect justification of his life from values already given, but he remains "indifferent" to the content of his adventures. How they affect others is no concern of his.

> The massacres of the Indians meant nothing to Pizarro; Don Juan was unaffected by Elvira's tears. Indifferent to the ends they set up for themselves, they were still more indifferent to the means of attaining them; they cared only for their pleasure or their glory. . . . Thus, nothing prevents [the adventurer] from sacrificing these insignificant beings to his own will for power. He will treat them like instruments; he will destroy them if they get in his way. (*EA*, 61)

Adventurism seldom appears in its purity, however, for two reasons: First, because the adventurer needs others—for money, allies, or enjoyment—he usually must submit to established power to get what he wants, sacrificing some of his own freedom. (When he can get what he wants without submission, he becomes a dictator, a tyrant.) Second, he usually pursues certain goals—fame, fortune, or glory—*in all seriousness*. He does not regard *those* ends as a game; he takes them very seriously.

De Beauvoir describes still more varieties of inauthenticity, but it is time to see what an authentic life would be like. To begin, recall that for de Beauvoir, a human being is not just a *thing* with a given *nature*. De Beauvoir often puts it this way: In comparison with a full and completed thing, like a rock—which just is whatever it is—a person is always incomplete. There is always something left to be filled in. She is not just *being*, but *disclosure* of being, consciousness of being.

But—and this is very important for de Beauvoir—this disclosure is not something passive; it is not mere registration of an object, not just a reflection of the world. "I am not first a thing but a spontaneity that desires, that loves, that wants, that acts" (*PC*, 93). Existence is dynamic, active, always engaged in projects. And what is the aim of these projects? To create being, to fill in the lack, to justify my existence by making myself a being of undoubted value, something absolute.* This, of course, I cannot do in its entirety, but de Beauvoir insists that this is no cause for despair; nor is it a reason to retreat into apathy. While "I must resign myself to never being entirely saved" (*PC*, 130), I can "take delight in this very effort toward impossible possession" (*EA*, 12).

> This means that man, in his vain attempt to *be* God, makes himself exist *as* man, and if he is satisfied with this existence, he coincides exactly with himself. It is not granted him to exist without tending toward this being which he will never be. But it is possible for him to want this tension even with the failure which it involves. His being is lack of being, but this lack has a way of being which is precisely

_____

*Augustine and Luther would consider this the apex of "works righteousness." Justified as they believe we are—against all expectation—by the grace of God, proper motivation is not supplied by this futile effort to justify *ourselves*, but by *gratitude* for all we have been given. (See pp. 282–284.)

JEAN-PAUL SARTRE

Perhaps the best known of the existentialist philosophers, Jean-Paul Sartre (1905–1980) was a novelist, playwright, biographer, and short-story writer, as well as a philosopher. His most influential philosophical work is *Being and Nothingness* (1943), which was followed in 1960 by another large book, *Critique of Dialectical Reason*. Influenced by the phenomenology of Husserl and Heidegger, the early Sartre investigated the structures of consciousness. He notes that in ordinary unreflective awareness, the ego or self does not appear; what is present is just an object—this tree, that melody. The ego appears when I reflect on my thoughts— *I am seeing the tree*—but then the *I* is an object, too! Consciousness itself escapes objectification. It is, Sartre says, a pure function, an emptiness: **nothingness.** All **being** is located in the object of consciousness, which is full, opaque, dense: the **in-itself.**

Yet even unreflective consciousness has a kind of diaphanous self-awareness. It is always **for-itself.** As such, no consciousness is ever completely coincident with itself; there is nothing that it definitively *is*. Human reality (Sartre's term for Heidegger's *Dasein*) is the place where in-itself and for-itself meet. We humans are undeniably objects; we have being. But we are also awareness of ourselves and not just a collection of facts. So we *are not* what we are (because we are conscious of what we are and separated from it by a film of nothingness), and we *are* what we are not (because what we are conscious *of* is indeed our being).

Consider, he says, the waiter in the café:

> His movement is quick and studied, a little too precise, a little too rapid. He comes toward the patrons with a step a little too quick. He bends forward a little too eagerly; his voice, his eyes express an interest a little too solicitous for the order of the customer. Finally there he returns, trying to imitate in his walk the inflexible stiffness of some kind of automaton while carrying his tray with the recklessness of a tightrope walker. . . . All his behavior seems to us a game. . . . He is playing with himself. But what is he playing? We need not watch long before we can explain it: he is playing *at being* a waiter in a café. (*B&N,* 151–152)

And so it is, inevitably, with all of us. None of us can be just *what we are*. We are always **playing a role.** We are always free, however, to decide to change that role or abandon it for another one. One of Sartre's most famous claims is that **"existence precedes essence,"** by which he means that there is no given essential nature to a human being; we first exist, and then by our free choices and actions make ourselves into something. This is, moreover, something that we are doing at every moment. Condemned to be free, we experience anguish, and to avoid it we slide into various forms of self-deception or **bad faith.**

JEAN-PAUL SARTRE

Here is a famous example. Think of a woman, Sartre says, who goes out with a man for the first time. The situation is rich with future possibilities, but when he says, "I find you so attractive," she chooses to strip the words of their suggestiveness and consider them only in their most literal meaning. She "disarms this phrase of its sexual implications; she attaches to the conversation and to the behavior of the speaker, the immediate meanings which she imagines as objective qualities. The man who is speaking to her appears to her sincere and respectful as the table is round or square." Yet all the while it is the sense of future risk that makes the moment magical, and in denying that she is in bad faith.

But then he takes her hand. Now what will she do? "To leave the hand there is to consent in herself to flirt, to involve herself. To withdraw it is to break the troubled and unstable harmony which gives the hour its charm. . . . We know what happens next; the young woman leaves her hand there, but she does not notice that she is leaving it." By chance, she is at this moment wholly spiritual, drawing her companion "up to the most lofty regions of sentimental speculation," speaking of life, of her life. She is wholly a personality, a consciousness. She is *fleeing herself* by regarding the elements of the situation now as sheer in-itself facts, now as absolute transcendence, quite independent of the facts. She trades on the duality in human life to avoid the necessity of making a choice—which necessity, however, she cannot ultimately escape. "We shall say," says Sartre, "that this woman is in bad faith" (*B&N*, 146–148).

Underlying all the various projects in human life is a fundamental project, Sartre says: to fill the emptiness, the lack, the not-yet-being-anything. Human reality aims at *being*. Yet we would not be satisfied to have the solid, unconscious being of a stone or a corpse. What we want is simultaneously to *be* something and to *enjoy* being it. We want our being to be the result of our conscious choice; we want to be an in-itself/for-itself. But this concept of a self-caused, completely full, yet conscious being is just the traditional notion of God. The ultimate project of human beings, then, is to be God. Unfortunately, Sartre believes, the concept of God is self-contradictory. So man, he concludes, is a futile passion.

NOTE:

The quotation in this section is from *Being and Nothingness* (*B&N*), as presented in *The Philosophy of Jean-Paul Sartre*, ed. Robert Denoon Cumming (New York: Modern Library, 1965).

---

existence. . . . The failure is not surpassed, but assumed. . . . To attain his truth, man must not attempt to dispel the ambiguity of his being but, on the contrary, accept the task of realizing it. (*EA*, 12–13)*

Human life is not inherently absurd. Ambiguity is not absurdity. Nor does death make life absurd. It is not death that makes us finite, either—the existence of others suffices for that. Even our **projects** are inherently finite.

Man has to be his being. Every moment he is seeking to make himself be, and that is the project. The human being exists in the form of projects that are not projects toward death but projects toward singular ends. He hunts, he fishes, he fashions instruments, he writes books: these are not diversions or flights but a movement toward being. . . .

Pyrrhus would be absurd if he left in order to return home, but it is the humorist who introduces this finality here. . . . Pyrrhus is not leaving in order to return; he is leaving in order to conquer. That undertaking is not contradictory. A project is exactly what it decides to be. It has the meaning that it gives itself. (*PC*, 115, 100)

It is by way of these projects that value appears in the world. Renouncing the "given" values of the serious man, the existentialist realizes that

it is desire which creates the desirable, and the project which sets up the end. It is human existence

---

*Here we have de Beauvoir's version of Heidegger's "authenticity."

"The fact that we are human beings is infinitely more important than all the peculiarities that distinguish human beings from one another."

—Simone de Beauvoir

which makes values spring up in the world on the basis of which it will be able to judge the enterprise in which it will be engaged. (*EA*, 15)*

It is a fact that any project of mine can be, and almost certainly will be, surpassed. I invent a new form of internal combustion engine even while I know that eventually it will be improved upon. I devise a scientific theory, sure all the while that it will not be the last word. But this doesn't make invention or theorizing absurd. Here is no good reason for pessimism. Human existence just *is* this process of setting goals and striving to achieve them. To want it to be something else, something final and complete, is to wish for the moon.

The key notion in an existentialist understanding of the human being is **freedom.** Man *is* free, but he must

---

*One might expect that on this basis de Beauvoir would endorse a rather extreme relativism in ethics. As we shall see, that is far from the case.

also continually be *making* himself free. Although it is not possible to *will ourselves not free*, it is possible to *fail to will ourselves free*. The temptations of nihilism and seriousness exercise a constant pull, and it is so easy to deny our freedom. "In laziness, heedlessness, capriciousness, cowardice, impatience, one contests the meaning of the project at the very moment that one defines it" (*EA*, 25). But in contesting it one undermines himself. Freedom—this active projecting ourselves into the world, seeking this end or another, trying in one way or another to justify our existence—that is *what we are.*

The adventurer knows this. That is his superiority over the serious person and the nihilist. "If existentialism were solipsistic, as is generally claimed, it would have to regard the adventurer as its perfect hero" (*EA*, 59). But de Beauvoir's existentialism is not solipsistic, and we now have to think about ethics.

---

1. List some aspects of our ambiguous nature.
2. How do the nihilist, the cynic, and the humorist deny the ambiguity?
3. How does seriousness evade the ambiguity of human life?
4. In what way is the adventurer closer to authenticity than either the nihilist or the serious person?
5. What flaws does de Beauvoir reveal in the adventurer's character?
6. Why can we not rely on God to set our values?
7. How can one justify one's life? And why cannot we be entirely saved?
8. Why must humans be continually making themselves free?

Ethics

As soon as a child has finished a drawing or a page of writing, he runs to show them to his parents. He needs their approval as much as candy or toys; the drawing requires an eye that looks at it. These disorganized lines must become a boat or a horse for someone. . . .

I walk in the country, I break off a stem, I kick a pebble, I climb a hill; all that without witnesses. But no one is satisfied with such solitude for his entire life. As soon as my walk is completed, I feel the need to tell a friend about it. (*PC*, 116)

Our life is always a life with others. Even the adventurer, the hero of his own story, needs others to pursue his goals, to remember his deeds. Most of us need others, of course, because we do not grow our own food or build the homes we live in. We do not sew our own clothes or assemble the cars that we drive. All this is important, but de Beauvoir has more than this in mind. You act in the world and your action makes something *be*. Suppose you decide to write a book. You work over it for six years and finally it *is*. But there was no void in the world shaped exactly like it, crying out in advance for just this production. The book is there, and then we see what *others* will make of it. A person's life has no antecedent justification; there is no guarantee that it will be worthwhile; but if others take up your book and use it, your life is (to that extent) vindicated.*

> In order for the object that I founded to appear as a good, the other must make it into his own good, and then I would be justified for having created it. The other's freedom alone is capable of necessitating my being. My essential need is therefore to be faced with free men. (*PC*, 129)

Feeling gratuitous, unnecessary, superfluous, faced with the necessity of creating ourselves by creating objects, we wish to escape the pure contingency of our existence and "need others in order for our existence to become founded and necessary" (*PC*, 129).

"Nothing worth doing is completed in our lifetime; therefore, we must be saved by hope. Nothing true or beautiful or good makes complete sense in any immediate context of history; therefore, we must be saved by faith. Nothing we do, however virtuous, can be accomplished alone; therefore we are saved by love. No virtuous act is quite as virtuous from the standpoint of our friend or foe as from our standpoint. Therefore, we must be saved by the final form of love which is forgiveness."

Reinhold Niebuhr (1892–1971)

Notice that it is *free* human beings that I need.† Coerced acceptance, drugged approval, or slavish applause mean nothing. Only the tyrant already mired in self-deception will enjoy the crowds who are forced to shout their praises. Moreover, if the other appears only as a limited and unfree object, the place he creates for me is as contingent and useless as himself.

> I don't wish to be recognized by just anyone, because in communication with others, we look for the completion of the project in which our freedom is engaged, and therefore others must project me toward a future that I recognize as mine. For me it would be a bitter failure if my action were perpetuated by becoming useful to my adversaries. The project by which others confer necessity upon me must also be my project. (*PC*, 133)

What I need is that my projects do not die a quick death by being universally ignored, opposed, or used for purposes I do not share. The ideal would be for all of humanity to extend my project into the indefinite future toward ends that I approve of; that would be the ultimate justification. But there is no hope for that; men are separate, opposed, and the goal of making my project last thus takes on the aspect of a struggle.

But how can I struggle here? I can't obtain admiration or love by violence; that would be absurd.

> I can only appeal to the other's freedom, not constrain it. I can invent the most urgent appeals, try my best to charm it, but it will remain free to respond to those appeals or not, no matter what I do. . . . Respect for the other's freedom is not an abstract rule. It is the first condition of my successful effort. (*PC*, 136)

In fact, two conditions must be met: (1) I must be free to appeal to the future for my vindication; and (2) I must have people who are free to respond to my appeals.

> I must therefore strive to create for men situations such that they can accompany and surpass my transcendence. I need their freedom to be

---

*While working on this chapter I was listening to music. Samuel Barber's Adagio for Strings was playing. I paused, paying close attention, and this thought came to me: To have written that—that alone would justify a life.

†Compare Hegel on the necessity for self-consciousness that it be confronted by other self-conscious individuals.

available to use and conserve me in surpassing me. I ask for health, knowledge, well-being, and leisure for men so that their freedom is not consumed in fighting sickness, ignorance, and misery. (*PC*, 137)

So here we have the foundation of an ethics. **Ethics** is grounded in the freedom of human existence. Others need you to be free to affirm their projects as you need them and their freedom.

> Freedom is the source from which all significations and all values spring. It is the original condition of all justifications of existence. The man who seeks to justify his life must want freedom itself absolutely and above everything else. . . . To will oneself moral and to will oneself free are one and the same decision. (*EA*, 24)

Morality cannot be obedience to God; there is no God. Nor can it be conformity to an abstract rule like Kant's categorical imperative; abstract rules do not help in particular situations because the *meaning* of the situation is determined by us. Nor can one be moral by seeking another's happiness, as the utilitarian claims, or by seeking only one's own happiness, as the egoist claims; no one can make another person happy and no one can be happy if others are too miserable to be free. The goal of ethical action is freedom—one's own and the other's.

> Freedom can not will itself without aiming at an open future, . . . but only the freedom of other men can extend [our ends] beyond our life.
>
> Man can find a justification of his own existence only in the existence of other men. Now, he needs such a justification; there is no escaping it. (*EA*, 71–72)

To will myself free is to take up the burden of justifying my life. Since I cannot do that without others who are free to continue to affirm my projects,

> to will oneself free is also to will others free. This will is not an abstract formula. It points out to each person concrete action to be achieved. (*EA*, 73)

This sounds noble and ideal, but de Beauvoir is under no illusions about how difficult this is to realize. Trying to make it work immediately encounters "concrete and difficult problems" (*EA*, 73). Her awareness of these problems was intensified by the situation of France during the Second World War. In May 1940, the German army invaded France, whose forces were quickly overwhelmed. There was much confusion and debate about what to do, but the outcome was German occupation of the northern two-thirds of France with a collaborationist French government, headquartered in Vichy, nominally controlling the south. While a "Free French" government-in-exile was proclaimed by Charles de Gaulle in London, the Vichy government, under the leadership of Marshal Petain, cooperated with German policies, including the arrest and deportation of Jews to Nazi concentration camps. Many Frenchmen considered these collaborators traitors, and an active Resistance movement played a significant role in sabotage and harassment of the occupiers throughout the rest of the war. Resistance fighters rescued many Allied airmen who were shot down over France and diverted German forces so as to aid the invasion at the beaches of Normandy on June 6, 1944. After the war some of the collaborationist leaders were put on trial and executed for treason and war crimes.*

De Beauvoir was sympathetic to the Resistance and had close contacts with many in that movement. Because the conflict pitted not just the French against the Germans, but also the French against each other, it was a wrenching time for all. An ethics that made freedom its centerpiece clearly had something to say in these circumstances, but it couldn't be simple. The goal is freedom for all; but what is one to do when some use their freedom to deny the freedom of others? You can't have both the freedom of the Jew to live her life as she thinks best and the freedom of the Nazi to deport her to Buchenwald. You have to choose. "A freedom which is interested only in denying freedom must be denied" (*EA*, 91).

As we have seen, freedom for de Beauvoir is nothing abstract; nor is it merely the Stoic freedom

---

*A discussion of occupied France during World War II, with many links to other sites, can be found at http://en.wikipedia.org/wiki/Vichy_France.

to withdraw into one's consciousness and say, "This means nothing to me." Freedom "realizes itself only by engaging itself in the world: to such an extent that man's project toward freedom is embodied for him in definite acts of behavior" (*EA*, 78). Often enough in this world, the free acts of a person meet obstacles and her ends cannot be attained. But there are two different ways this happens. It can happen, first, because of the natural resistance of things: "Floods, earthquakes, grasshoppers, epidemics and plague" can frustrate our desires and turn our projects back on themselves, but these material obstacles do not *oppress* us; "man is never oppressed by things" (*EA*, 81). Even death does not oppress us; it is the natural limit of life—the price we pay for the privilege of being alive.

❧

"The love of liberty is the love of others; the love of power is the love of ourselves."

William Hazlitt (1778–1830)

Oppression occurs when some people use their freedom to take away others' freedom.

> Only man can be an enemy for man; only he can rob him of the meaning of his acts and his life because it also belongs only to him alone to confirm it in its existence, to recognize it in actual fact as a freedom. . . . One does not submit to a war or an occupation as he does to an earthquake: he must take sides for or against, and the foreign wills thereby become allied or hostile. (*EA*, 82)

Oppression denies to a person what is most central to human existence; it denies a chance to justify one's life through acts that create oneself by transcending one's current being through projects that others can take up and extend into the indefinite future. Oppression comes in many forms, occupation by a foreign power being only one. Slavery may be the most extreme. Women, too, have been oppressed, de Beauvoir holds (as we shall see in the next section). And workers are oppressed by employers when

> they are condemned to mark time hopelessly in order merely to support the collectivity; their life

is a pure repetition of mechanical gestures; their leisure is just about sufficient for them to regain their strength; the oppressor feeds himself on their transcendence and refuses to extend it by a free recognition. (*EA*, 83)

There are echoes of Marx here; de Beauvoir finds congenial the Socialist ideal that Communists supposedly serve, but she is severely critical of the Communist Party, whether in France or the Soviet Union.* It is truly hateful, she says, when life is forced to occupy itself solely with maintaining itself, when there is no chance to reach out toward new vistas, to project oneself toward ends of one's own choosing. Such circumstances call for rebellion, not resignation.

Again, rebellion cannot be just *saying*, "I don't accept this." Like every free act, it must be realized in behavior. And this means **violence.** It would be nice if the oppressor, realizing his own need for the freedom of others, would simply give up oppressing. A purely moral transition away from oppression would have to come by way of a conversion of the oppressors, but de Beauvoir, schooled in the brutality of the Nazi occupation, dismisses this notion as a mere "utopian reverie" (*EA*, 97). To use the title of a play by Sartre, if you want to fight oppression, you have to reconcile yourself to "dirty hands." You cannot "enter into solidarity with all the others, because they do not all choose the same goals. . . . One will always work for certain men against others" (*PC*, 108).

But what can justify violence? Here de Beauvoir uses a word that does not come easily to her; she says there is something that is an "absolute" **evil.**

> We think that such an evil exists. One can excuse all the offenses, even the crimes by which individuals assert themselves against society. But when a man deliberately tries to degrade man by reducing him to a thing, nothing can compensate for the

---

*She objects to the groupthink demanded of party members, the historical determinism in Communist doctrine that denies individual freedom, and the hypocrisy that doctrine produces when Communists excoriate their enemies in moral language that makes sense only on the assumption that their opponents' acts are freely chosen.

abomination he causes to erupt on earth. There resides the sole sin against man. When it is accomplished no indulgences are permitted and it belongs to man to punish it. (*EE*, 257)

These words appear in an essay she wrote following the trial of Robert Brasillach, the French editor of a fascist newspaper who contributed to the arrest and deportation of Jewish citizens during the war. During the trial a petition was circulated among intellectuals pleading for his pardon. De Beauvoir refused to sign it. Brasillach was convicted of treason and executed. The essay "An Eye for an Eye" is a justification of her refusal and of the moral right to punish such evils.

> For to punish is to recognize man as free in evil as well as in good. It is to distinguish evil from good in the use that man makes of his freedom. It is to will the good. (*EE*, 259)

She supported the use of violence by Resistance fighters trying to undermine the German occupation, but she does not glorify it and demands in every case that it justify itself. It is true that violence involves a kind of paradox. To oppose those who would treat human beings as mere things, they themselves will "have to be treated like things" (*EA*, 97).* It is

> necessary to choose to sacrifice the one who is an enemy of man; but the fact is that one finds himself forced to treat certain men as things in order to win the freedom of all.
>
> A freedom which is occupied in denying freedom is itself so outrageous that the outrageousness of the violence which one practises against it is almost cancelled out. . . . (*EA*, 97)
>
> In any event, it is evident that we are not going to decide to fulfill the will of every man. There are cases where a man positively wants evil, that is, the enslavement of other men, and he must then be fought. (*EA*, 136)

Every struggle, moreover, "obliges us to sacrifice people whom our victory does not concern, people who, in all honesty, reject it as a cataclysm: these people will die in astonishment, anger or despair" (*EA*, 108). To put it in contemporary terms, in every struggle there will be "collateral damage." And that is still not the worst, because we will need to sacrifice not only those who oppose us,

> but also those who are fighting on our side, and even ourselves. Since we can conquer our enemies only by acting upon their facticity, by reducing them to things, we have to make ourselves things; in this struggle in which wills are forced to confront each other through their bodies, the bodies of our allies, like those of our opponents are exposed to the same brutal hazard: they will be wounded, killed, or starved. (*EA*, 99)

Here we are faced with the difficult problem of **means and ends** in action. We know that "the supreme end at which man must aim is his freedom" (*EA*, 113), but there is there a limit to the means that can be chosen to achieve it, even though we cannot devise a formula to decide the matter for every case.

> The means can be understood only in the light of the desired end, but inversely, the end is inseparable from the means by which it is carried out, and it is a fallacy to believe that the end can be achieved by just any means.*
>
> It is not possible to act for man without treating certain men, at certain times, as means.
>
> However, treating man as a means is committing violence against him; it means contradicting the idea of his absolute value that alone allows the action to be fully founded. . . . The moralist who wants both to act and to approve of himself would want to use only means that are in themselves ethical, that is to say, only those whose meaning is in keeping with the end he is aiming for. However, this dream is impossible, and if he insists, he will only vacillate between heaven and earth without being able to engage himself in this world. To come down to earth means accepting defilement, failure, horror; it means admitting that it is impossible to save everything; and what is lost is lost forever. . . .
>
> Whatever I may choose to do, I will be unfaithful to my profound desire to respect human life; and yet, I am forced to choose. (*MIPR*, 184, 189–190)

---

*Compare Kant on treating people as things, p. 491.

*This is similar to John Dewey's view of ends and means. See pp. 614–615. De Beauvoir, however, is less optimistic than Dewey about the possibilities for reconciling means and ends into a morally approvable synthesis.

Ethics can show us the end that deserves our unconditional respect: the transcendence and freedom of each individual. But it provides no neat recipes for accomplishing that end. We must face each situation with an unblinking eye for the facts and an understanding of their meaning in the light of the ultimate end. And then we must choose, keeping in mind that "an action which wants to serve man ought to be careful not to forget him on the way" (*EA*, 153).

Existentialist ethics recommends a "lucid generosity" (*PC*, 124): generous in framing our projects so that they maximize freedom for all, but lucid in understanding that others may oppose these projects and in any case—in their own freedom—will make of them what they will. The justification of our lives is ultimately not in our control.

But despite life's risk and incompleteness, there is joy in existence. Liberation has a concrete meaning only in "individual and living joy." If "the satisfaction of an old man drinking a glass of wine" or "the laugh of a child at play" counts for nothing, then all the rest is worthless. "If we do not love life on our own account and through others, it is futile to seek to justify it in any way" (*EA*, 135–136).

---

1. Why do we need others?
2. Why do we need others who are free?
3. In what way is ethics grounded in the nature of human existence?
4. Why is freedom the supreme value?
5. Define oppression.
6. In what circumstances is violence justified?
7. When is punishment justified?
8. How are means and ends properly related?

Woman

"What is a woman?" de Beauvoir asks. "Everyone agrees there are females in the human species; today, as in the past, they make up about half of humanity. And yet we are told that 'femininity is in jeopardy.' . . . So not every female human being is necessarily a woman" (*SS*, 3).

The question suggests that there is an *ideal* of woman that existing women are failing to live up to. But what is that ideal? Where does it originate? Where does it get its power? And is it something that we should cherish or repudiate? De Beauvoir addresses these questions in a passionately written, wide-ranging book titled *The Second Sex*, published in 1949.[5] The key to de Beauvoir's answer is summed up in one very influential sentence: "One is not born, but rather becomes, a woman" (*SS*, 283).

The first chapter is a survey of the data of biology with respect to male and female. "These biological data are of extreme importance; they play an all-important role and are an essential element of woman's situation" (*SS*, 44). Like all humans, a woman *is* her body; all people experience the world, express themselves, and act through the body. But there are differences; to a much greater degree than a man, a woman feels alienated from her body; ". . . a hostile element is locked inside, . . . the species is eating away at [her]" (*SS*, 42).

> From puberty to menopause she is the principal site of a story that takes place in her and does not concern her personally. . . . She feels most acutely that her body is an alienated opaque thing; it is the prey of a stubborn and foreign life that makes and unmakes a crib in her every month; every month a child is prepared to be born and is aborted in the flow of the crimson tide. (*SS*, 40, 41)

Pregnancy and gestation are female processes that demand heavy sacrifices.

> Childbirth itself is painful; it is dangerous. This crisis shows clearly that the body does not always meet the needs of both the species and the individual; the child sometimes dies, or while coming into life, it kills the mother; or its birth can cause her a chronic illness. (*SS*, 42)

A man, of course, is also a bearer of the species; but his species burden is much lighter, and "by comparison, is infinitely more privileged: his genital life does not thwart his personal existence; it unfolds seamlessly without crises and generally without accident" (*SS*, 44). The female, in addition to having to bear these extra sexual burdens, is typically shorter than the male and lighter, with less muscular strength and with a smaller respiratory capacity. On average, women are less robust and more delicate than men.

> These biological data are of extreme importance: they play an all-important role and are an essential element of woman's situation. . . . Because the body is the instrument of our hold on the world, the world appears different to us depending on how it is grasped. . . . But we refuse the idea that they form a fixed destiny for her. They do not suffice to constitute the basis for a sexual hierarchy . . . they do not condemn her forever to this subjugated role. (*SS*, 44)

Mere facts have, in themselves, little significance. What matters is what human beings do with the facts. For example, although a woman is in greater bondage to the species than a man, how much that matters depends a great deal on (1) how many children society demands and (2) the quality of care given in pregnancy and childbirth.

"The definition of man," de Beauvoir says, "is that he is a being who is not given, who makes himself what he is. . . . Woman is not a fixed reality but a becoming; she has to be compared with man in her becoming; that is, her *possibilities* have to be defined" (*SS*, 45).*

We can see here that existentialist themes are going to play a large role in de Beauvoir's feminism. Individuals are not abandoned to the dictates of their biological nature. Values cannot be based on physiology. Past choices have created the situation women find themselves in today; "biology alone cannot provide an answer to this question that concerns us: why is woman the *Other*? The question is . . . what humanity has made of the human female" (*SS*, 48).

Woman has been defined, de Beauvoir says, as **the Other.** What does this mean? Otherness, she says, is a fundamental category of human thought. No group ever sets itself up as a distinctive group, a One, without setting up an Other by contrast. What has happened in our history, and almost universally, is that male human beings have been understood as human beings par excellence, as the

One, while females have been understood only relative to them, as the Other. This One/Other pattern is symbolized in Genesis, where Adam is created whole and entire, but Eve is made from Adam's flesh as "a helper" for him. Man is taken as representative of humanity, the absolute, while woman has only a relative existence. Philosophers, for their part, have usually reflected this view rather than criticizing it, though there have been a few exceptions; de Beauvoir mentions John Stuart Mill (see pp. 555–561).

In the standard case, this One/Other relationship is reciprocal. Jones, as subject, takes Smith as object, and Smith does the same to Jones. Each tends to consider himself as the essential while thinking of the other as inessential. As Hegel and Sartre both argue, this is a formula for conflict, each trying to dominate the other. (One of the characters in Sartre's play *No Exit* says, "Hell is other people.") But, says de Beauvoir, the male/female case is different; although there is conflict, there is little reciprocity. Woman has always been dependent; "the two sexes have never divided the world up equally" (*SS*, 9). This raises an obvious question.

> Why do women not contest male sovereignty? No subject posits itself spontaneously and at once as the inessential from the outset; it is not the Other who, defining itself as Other, defines the One; the Other is posited as Other by the One positing itself as One. But in order for the Other not to turn into the One, the Other has to submit to this foreign point of view. Where does this submission in woman come from? (*SS*, 7)

Why has male dominance been so widespread and persistent? "If woman discovers herself as the inessential and never turns into the essential, it is because she does not bring about this transformation herself. . . . Women . . . do not posit themselves authentically as Subjects." (*SS*, 8); they do not assert themselves as a One against the male Other. But why is *that*?

De Beauvoir discusses several reasons. For one thing, women have lacked the economic and educational resources allotted to men. For another, they feel the species tie to men. And there are the biological differences in strength and robustness

---

*Here is a good example of de Beauvoir using the term "man" in both the generic and the sexed senses. Within three sentences she uses the term both ways.

(though these had more importance ages ago than they do today). But two factors are crucial, she says, one on each side of the divide. As we saw in the discussion of *ambiguity*, human beings face constant temptations to evade the anxiety of existing, together with its freedom and its demands for choice and responsibility. From the woman's side it looks like this:

> Refusing to be the Other, refusing complicity with man, would mean renouncing all the advantages an alliance with the superior cast confers on them. Lord-man will materially protect liege-woman and will be in charge of justifying her existence: along with the economic risk, she eludes the metaphysical risk of a freedom that must invent its goals without help. Indeed, beside every individual's claim to assert himself as subject—an ethical claim—lies the temptation to flee freedom and to make himself into a thing: it is a pernicious path because the individual, passive, alienated, and lost, is prey to a foreign will, cut off from his transcendence, robbed of all worth. But it is an easy path: the anguish and stress of authentically assumed existence are thus avoided. (*SS*, 10)

Woman has been content to be the "second sex," then, because "she often derives satisfaction from her role as *Other*" (*SS*, 10).

From the man's side it can be seen that this arrangement has suited him very well. Not only do men get a "helper" in their projects and a subservient sexual partner, but even "the most mediocre of males believes himself a demigod next to women" (*SS*, 13).

This pattern of regarding woman as the Other, then, has lasted so long because each party to it has seen advantages in it for itself. Both parties are guilty of "bad faith" (to use Sartre's term), of evading the true nature of their existence by "falling away" (to use Heidegger's term) from their freedom into given roles that allow an escape into "the serious" (to use de Beauvoir's term). However,

> the perspective we have adopted is one of existentialist morality. Every subject posits itself as a transcendence concretely, through projects; it accomplishes its freedom only by perpetual surpassing toward other freedoms; there is no other justification for present existence than its expansion toward

an indefinitely open future. Every time transcendence lapses into immanence, there is degradation of existence into "in-itself," of freedom into facticity; this fall is a moral fault if the subject consents to it; if this fall is inflicted on the subject, it takes the form of frustration and oppression; in both cases it is an absolute evil. (*SS*, 16)*

Woman is a free and autonomous being like all humans, but she has been—partly through compulsion, partly through her own acquiescence—degraded to the status of an object and doomed to immanence. "Woman's drama lies in this conflict between the fundamental claim of every subject, which always posits itself as essential, and the demands of a situation that constitutes her as inessential. How, in the feminine condition, can a human being accomplish herself?" (*SS*, 17). Consistent with her existentialist ethics, de Beauvoir says that the criterion for fulfillment is not happiness, but liberty. So the question is, how can women become *free*?

By far the larger part of this big book, however, is not devoted to that question (we shall return to it), but to an analysis of the current situation of women (as of 1949) and an account of how things came to be that way. She discusses not only biology, but also **psychoanalysis** and historical materialism. She looks back in history to nomadic peoples, early tillers of the soil, and the situation of women from classical times through the Middle Ages to the French Revolution and beyond, dissecting myths and analyzing the portrayal of women in literature. She sketches "woman's life today," from childhood to old age, in great detail. Because it is impossible to do justice to these riches in this short chapter, we shall just present a sample of her thoughts on a number of topics.

On Early History The early days of the species were hard, and a man's superior strength must have been of tremendous importance in guaranteeing

---

*"In itself" (*en-soi*) is Sartre's term for the being that just is what it is, with no opening to possibilities, no freedom to choose among them, and no future but the past. He contrasts it with the *pour-soi*, the for-itself that is conscious of itself and its openness to multiple futures.

mere survival. Men, moreover, were oriented beyond themselves in the world, transforming it by means of tools, while women submitted to their biological fate and bore children. Man "tests his own power; he posits ends and projects paths to them: he realizes himself as existent. . . . This is the reason fishing and hunting expeditions have a sacred quality" (*SS*, 73).

But there was something even more important. Man's activity had a dimension that gave it "supreme dignity: it is often dangerous" (*SS*, 73).

> The warrior risks his own life to raise the prestige of the horde—his clan. This is how he brilliantly proves that life is not the supreme value for man but that it must serve ends far greater than itself. . . . It is not in giving life but in risking his life that man raises himself above the animal; this is why throughout humanity, superiority has been granted not to the sex that gives birth but to the one that kills. (*SS*, 73, 74)

This is, she says, "the key to the whole mystery" (*SS*, 74). A species is continued by creating itself anew, but this is only repeating the same again. In transcending mere animal life through existence, a species creates *values*; by contrast with these values mere repetition is diminished to nothing more than a *means*. Thus did men attain a superior status even in the eyes of women, who are biologically destined for the repetition of life.

Yet women, too, feel the urge to surpass and create a new future. "It is above and beyond all sexual specification that the existent seeks self-justification in the movement of his transcendence. . . . Today what women claim is to be recognized as existents, just like men, and not to subordinate existence to life" (*SS*, 74, 75).

On Patriarchy Many of the most ancient gods are female. This has led some to suppose that there was a time when women ruled, but de Beauvoir says that "this golden age of Woman is only a myth. . . . Society has always been male; political power has always been in men's hands" (*SS*, 80). The time of female gods was a time when men had not yet become masters of technique, tool users, conquerors of the earth. But even then, men understood their equals to be other men; woman

has always been the Other. A sure sign of her inferiority is that almost always she goes to live under her husband's roof and often takes his name. In primitive times "marriage is sometimes founded on abduction, real or symbolic: because violence done to another is the clearest affirmation of another's alterity. Taking his wife by force, the warrior proves he is able to annex the riches of others and burst through the bounds of the destiny assigned to him at birth" (*SS*, 83). Woman, for her part, "maintains the life of the tribe by providing children and bread, nothing more" (*SS*, 82).

When men began to work with tools, to *make* tools with which to work, they claimed responsibility for what they made.

> The worker fashions a tool according to his own design he imposes on it the form that fits his project; facing an inert nature that defies him but that he overcomes, he asserts himself as sovereign will. . . . His movement, adroit or maladroit, makes it or breaks it; careful, skillful, he brings it to a point of perfection he can be proud of: his success depends not on the favor of the gods but on himself. . . . He finds cause and effect in the relationship between his creating arm and the object of his creation. . . . This world of tools can be framed in clear concepts: rational thinking, logic, and mathematics are thus able to emerge. (*SS*, 84)

Woman, by contrast, "could not obtain the benefits of tools for herself." Thus she "remained enslaved to the mysteries of life" (*SS*, 86). So she "did not participate in his way of working and thinking" (*SS*, 86). She did not think logically.* In consequence, man did not recognize in her an equal. Given her incapacity, he *had* to recognize her as Other; and given his will to power, he could not be anything but her oppressor.

When men began to own land, they also claimed ownership of women. At the time of patriarchal power, man wrested from woman all her rights to possess and bequeath property. Because she does not own anything, "woman is not raised to

---

*Here are found the origins of what Derrida and other deconstructionists call "logocentrism," which "privileges" logic, rationality, and objectivity—all traditionally male ways of engaging the world. See pp. 700–701.

the dignity of a person; she herself is part of man's patrimony, first her father's and then her husband's. . . . Under the **patriarchal** regime, she was the property of a father who married her off as he saw fit" (*SS*, 90, 91). Inheritance passed through the male line and it was important to ensure that sons were legitimate heirs. Thus were women hedged about with restrictions on their movements and behaviors, and the virgin and the faithful wife were honored in both law and religion.

> Thus the triumph of patriarchy was neither an accident nor the result of a violent revolution. From the origins of humanity, their biological privilege enabled men to affirm themselves alone as sovereign subjects; they never abdicated this privilege; . . . the place of woman in society is always the one they assign to her; at no time has she imposed her own laws. (*SS*, 86)

On the Myth of the Feminine One reason woman is a puzzle is that her image is constantly confused with myth; "to the dispersed, contingent, and multiple existence of *women*, mythic thinking opposes the **Eternal Feminine, unique and fixed**" (*SS*, 266). Even worse, this myth is itself ambivalent and many-sided. There is woman as "the Praying Mantis, the Mandrake, or the Demon, . . . the Muse, the Goddess Mother, and Beatrice as well. . . . The saintly mother has its correlation in the cruel stepmother, the angelic young girl has the perverse virgin" (*SS*, 267). She is Eve and Pandora, benefactor and disperser of troubles, life and death, priestess and sorcerer, temptation and release from temptation—each aspect chosen by the fears and desires of the moment.

But what is she *really*? Men say they can't understand women, but even women do not know. No aspect of the myth is more firmly anchored than the notion of woman as *mystery*. In truth, says de Beauvoir, there is mystery on both sides, male and female. Each subjectivity is impenetrable to the other; no existent can *be* another, experience the world as he or she does. But in another sense, deciding what one *is* is difficult because "in this area there is no truth. An existent *is* nothing other than what he does; the possible does not exceed the real, essence does not precede existence; in his pure subjectivity the human being *is nothing*. He is measured

by his acts" (*SS*, 270).* This holds for men and women alike. But for women, oppressed through most of history, the mystery is magnified because

> they *do* nothing, they do not make themselves *be* anything; they wonder indefinitely what they *could have* become, which leads them to wonder what they *are*: it is a useless questioning; if man fails to find that secret essence, it is simply because it does not exist. (*SS*, 271)

Perhaps the myth of woman will someday be extinguished; the more women assert themselves as human beings, the more the quality of the Other will die out in them.

Character and Situation De Beauvoir is severe in her judgment on woman's character, calling woman

- contrary, prudent, and petty,
- lacking in a sense of fact and accuracy,
- false, theatrical, self-seeking,
- passive,
- without a grasp on reality,
- a believer in magic—in telepathy, astrology, clairvoyants, faith healers, answered prayers,
- unfamiliar with the use of logic,
- a believer in intuitions,
- servile, lacking in real pride,
- resigned, but also resentful.

But why is that? It is not because of her hormones or womanly body. It is not because these characteristics manifest the *essence* of woman. It is because of her situation,

> because she has no choice but to devote her existence to preparing food and cleaning diapers: she cannot draw the meaning of grandeur from this. She must ensure the monotonous repetition of life in its contingence and facticity. . . . Her life is not directed toward goals: she is absorbed in producing or maintaining things that are never more than means—food, clothes, lodging. . . . A woman is shut up in a kitchen or a boudoir, and one is surprised her horizon is limited; her wings are cut, and then she is blamed for not knowing how to fly. (*SS*, 644–645)

---

*The "existence precedes essence" slogan was made famous by Sartre in his 1945 lecture, "Existentialism Is a Humanism," published as *Existentialism*, trans. Bernard Frechtman (New York: Philosophical Library, 1947).

But "let a future be open to her and she will no longer be obliged to settle in the present" (*SS*, 645). Women must "refuse the limits of their situation and seek to open paths to the future; resignation is only a surrender and an evasion; for woman there is no other way out than to work for her liberation" (*SS*, 664).*

Labor and Independence   De Beauvoir's claim that throughout history women have not *done* anything, and so have not *become* anything, itself contains the clue to their emancipation.†

> It is through work that woman has been able, to a large extent, to close the gap separating her from the male; work alone can guarantee her concrete freedom. The system based on her dependence collapses as soon as she ceases to be a parasite. (*SS*, 721)

What needs to be changed is women's situation, and nothing more urgently than her **economic dependence** on men. Let women *do* something and they will transcend their captivity in the immanence of nature, exercise their freedom, and join men in equality as existing human beings—no longer just the Other, no more merely the "second sex." In fact, this has been happening, but it has been a slow process. The Industrial Revolution did more to change women's situation than anything else. With the invention of machine tools, sheer strength was less important, and manufacturers eagerly sought female labor. True, women workers were shamefully exploited—even more than male workers; they would do more work for less pay and were more docile than male workers. "In 1831, silk workers work in the summer from as early as three o'clock in the morning to eleven at night" (*SS*, 133). It was not until 1900 that "the workday is limited to ten hours; in 1907 the woman worker is granted free disposal of her income; in 1909 maternity leave is granted" (*SS*, 134). Woman's status as worker slowly improved, though it was a long and tortuous process. Nonetheless, it is evident

that "it is through labor that woman won her dignity as a human being" (*SS*, 133). Only through labor has she become a person in her own right.

Two other developments helped this along. Varieties of birth control allowed woman to "reduce the number of pregnancies and rationally integrate them into her life, instead of being their slave. . . . Relieved of a great number of reproductive servitudes, she can take on the economic roles open to her, roles that would ensure her control over her own person" (*SS*, 139). And little by little, woman has gained political equality. Women got the vote in New Zealand in 1893 and in Australia in 1908. It was not until 1920 that woman suffrage became the law of the land in the United States and not in France until 1945. But it is economic independence that is the key.

Liberty, Equality, Friendship   With economic independence, at least for many, women are in a position to do more than simply maintain life. They can devise projects, act on the world, and envision a future that is different from the past. And they can begin, for the first time, to meet men as equals. De Beauvoir is under no illusions that this will be easy and conflict-free, however. Women will now have to struggle with the fate of all human existents—"the tragedy of the unhappy consciousness; each consciousness seeks to posit itself alone as sovereign subject. Each one tries to accomplish itself by reducing the other to slavery" (*SS*, 159). With these echoes of Hegel, de Beauvoir reminds us that women liberated now face the hard work of having to be good human beings.

It is possible to rise above conflict, though never to eliminate it altogether, and some men and women have managed true friendship, whether within marriage or out of it.

> The conflict can be overcome by the free recognition of each individual in the other, each one positing both himself and the other as object and as subject in a reciprocal movement. But friendship and generosity, which accomplish this recognition of freedoms concretely, are not easy virtues; they are undoubtedly man's highest accomplishment; this is where he is in his truth: but this truth is a struggle endlessly begun, endlessly abolished; it

---

*Compare this to Wollstonecraft's explanation of the faults attributed to women (pp. 558–559).

†Some feminists hold that de Beauvoir underestimates what women *do* in rearing children and maintaining a home and so neglects the choice, responsibility, and self-definition that come with those traditional roles.

demands that man surpass himself at each instant. Put into other words, man attains an authentically moral attitude when he renounces *being* in order to assume his existence; through this conversion he also renounces all possession, because possession is a way of searching for being; but the conversion by which he attains true wisdom is never finished, it has to be made ceaselessly, it demands constant effort; . . . life is a difficult enterprise whose success is never assured. (*SS*, 159–160)

Although economic independence is a crucial step in securing for women the dignity of human beings, it is not enough. Only when men and women both assume the ambiguity of the human condition will they be able to live together in amity.

> The fact of being a human being is infinitely more important than all the singularities that distinguish human beings; it is never the given that confers superiority: "virtue," as the ancients called it, is defined at the level of "what happens depends on us." The same drama of flesh and spirit, and of finitude and transcendence, plays itself out in both sexes; both are eaten away by time, stalked by death, they have the same essential need of the other; and they can take the same glory from their freedom; if they knew how to savor it, they would no longer be tempted to contend for false privileges; and fraternity could then be born between them. (*SS*, 763)

1. In what sense is woman more burdened by the demands of the species than man?
2. What does it mean that woman has been defined as "the Other"?
3. How have women and men both fallen into inauthenticity in their relationships with each other?
4. What are some of the features of patriarchy?
5. What is the key to understanding woman as mystery?
6. What aspect of woman's situation must be changed if she is to be liberated from oppression?
7. What challenges will a liberated woman still face?

FOR FURTHER THOUGHT

1. Write a short story that illustrates the ambiguity of human existence and its temptations.

2. How much of what de Beauvoir hoped for for women has been accomplished, in your view? What remains to be done?
3. Write an essay on some aspect of more recent feminist thought, comparing it to de Beauvoir. A good starting place is the survey by Robin May Schott, *Discovering Feminist Philosophy* (New York: Rowman and Littlefield, 2003).

KEY WORDS

ambiguity	bad faith
nihilism	projects
cynic	freedom
humorist	ethics
seriousness	oppression
adventurer	violence
nothingness	evil
being	means and ends
in-itself	the Other
for-itself	psychoanalysis
playing a role	patriarchal
existence precedes	Eternal Feminine
essence	economic dependence

NOTES

1. Individual writings collected in *Simone de Beauvoir: Philosophical Writings*, ed. Margaret A. Simons (Urbana: University of Illinois Press, 2004), are referenced by page numbers as follows:
   PC: *Pyrrhus and Cineas*
   MIPR: *Moral Idealism and Political Realism*
   EPW: *Existentialism and Popular Wisdom*
   EE: *An Eye for an Eye*
   ELA: *An Existentialist Looks at Americans*
2. Quoted in Elizabeth Fallaise, ed., *Simone de Beauvoir: A Critical Reader* (London: Routledge, 1998), 7.
3. Quoted in Conor Cruise O'Brien, *Albert Camus of Europe and Africa* (New York: Viking Press, 1970), 17–18.
4. Simone de Beauvoir, *The Ethics of Ambiguity* (New York: Citadel Press, 1948, 1976). References are given as *EA* by page numbers.
5. Simone de Beauvoir, *The Second Sex*, trans. Constance Borde and Sheila Malovany-Chevallier (New York: Vintage Books, 2011). References are given as *SS* by page numbers.

POSTMODERNISM

Derrida, Foucault, and Rorty

Some say that the postmodern era began in architecture. The modernist sensibility in architecture dominated most of the twentieth century. Its patron saint was Le Corbusier, and its prime symbol was the steel and glass skyscraper—austere, mathematical, rational. Postmodernist architecture, by contrast, emphasized human interactions and playful imagination, using pastiche (borrowing elements from other times, traditions, and cultures) to enhance engineering requirements.*

Modernist architecture stands as a visible symbol of enlightenment promise, where science and rationality would rule and happiness would prevail. As disillusionment with that ideal set in, migrations of people across the globe and the rise of the Internet made awareness of other cultures inescapable. Just as in ancient Greece, where increasing familiarity with other cultures brought the sophists to prominence, multiculturalism and moral relativism seem an inescapable consequence.* Postmodernists in philosophy are suspicious of claims to truth, objectivity, rationality, and universality. They are dubious about the idea that natural science is an apt model for knowledge in general. They doubt that philosophy as it has been practiced in the Descartes, Hume, Kant tradition can serve as a judge of the true and the good. And they want to leave behind (or destroy) all metaphysical pretensions to grasp some absolute reality beyond appearance.

Just as the sophists came up against Socrates, so **postmodernism** has spawned its critics. Philosophically speaking, we are recapitulating that old quarrel. In a recent book, Thomas Nagel (b. 1937) deplores the postmodern influence:

> The worst of it is that subjectivism is not just an inconsequential intellectual flourish or badge of

---

*Compare the Seagram building, lacking all extraneous decoration (http://www.archdaily.com/59412/seagram-building-mies-van-der-rohe/), to Philip Johnson's AT&T building, with its grandfather clock top (https://en.wikipedia.org/wiki/550_Madison_Avenue).

---

*Look again at Herodotus on how the Greeks and the Persians care for their dead (p. 63) and review the arguments between the sophists and Socrates (pp. 95–97).

theoretical chic. It is used to deflect argument, or to belittle the pretensions of the arguments of others. Claims that something is without relativistic qualification true or false, right or wrong, good or bad, risk being derided as expressions of a parochial perspective or form of life—not as a preliminary to showing that they are mistaken whereas something else is right, but as a way of showing that nothing is right and that instead we are all expressing our personal or cultural points of view. The actual result has been a growth in the already extreme intellectual laziness of contemporary culture and the collapse of serious argument throughout the lower reaches of the humanities and social sciences, together with a refusal to take seriously, as anything other than first-person avowals, the objective arguments of others.[1]

Is that a just critique? To wrestle with that question, we will look at three postmodernist ideas: deconstruction as formulated by Jacques Derrida, Michel Foucault's historical studies of knowledge and power, and the liberal ironism of Richard Rorty.[2]

Deconstruction: Jacques Derrida

The idea of "deconstructing texts" has had a very wide influence. On the assumption that language structures all our thought and action—not just speech and literature, but also social institutions and political structures—the notion of a **"text"** seems applicable everywhere. If all our understandings are structured by the specific language we speak, and without that structuring would be impossible, then all of culture is a kind of *text* to be read, interpreted, understood (or misunderstood)—and deconstructed. No one has been more influential in working out the idea of deconstruction than the French philosopher, Jacques Derrida (1930–2004).

To understand **deconstruction,** it will help to get as clear as we can about what it aims to deconstruct. And to do that let us remind ourselves of certain themes in Heidegger. In *Being and Time* Heidegger adopts (or adapts) Husserl's method of phenomenology to lay bare the essence of human existing—what he calls *Dasein*. To proceed phenomenologically is to try to set aside the assumptions, presuppositions, and interpretations that are

normally brought to experience; the aim is to let what is experienced—the phenomenon—simply *show itself as it is* and then describe it with care by identifying its essential features. Notice that he takes for granted that there *is* something—something prior to all description—in which Dasein's Being consists. There is a *truth* about our being here, and that truth is revealed phenomenologically via these existential concepts. Human existence as a phenomenon is laid bare—self-evident, undeniable—a *presence* to be recognized and described.

In his later work Heidegger turns away from the claim that discovering the essence of human existence will lead us directly to the meaning of Being itself. But he does not turn away from the idea that the goal is still *presence*. If we could allow the *presencing of beings* itself to be present, that might change us, save us, rescue us from this long era of blindness to Being and deliver us into the "truth of Being."

It is precisely this notion of **presence** that Derrida has in his sights. To make it more clear, let us cite some other examples.

- In Plato's allegory of the cave, the prisoner turns away from mere shadows of reality and clambers into the sunlight outside the cave, where she will eventually *see* the truth of things. This "seeing," toward which Plato's epistemology drives, is a case of the Forms being *present* to the knower. (See pp. 159–160.)
- Aristotle argues that not everything can be demonstrated—on pain of an infinite regress—so the first principles just have to be *seen* to be true, seen as they *present* themselves to the mind. (See pp. 190–192.)
- Descartes, seeking something he cannot doubt, finds it in the *cogito*, the "I think, therefore I am" principle. This is so clearly and distinctly *present* to his mind that it can play the role of a first certainty; on this he can build. (See pp. 362–364.)
- Hume may be skeptical about external things, causality, the self, and God; but impressions are just *there*!—present in experience. You can't doubt the blue triangle when it *presents* itself in your visual field. (See pp. 443–444.)
- Kant's transcendental critique of reason *presents* us with the constitutive principles of any rational mind, both theoretical (causality, for

example) and practical (the categorical imperative). We simply have to *recognize* that the buck stops there. (See pp. 468–470.)

- For Hegel such presence is not available to us here and now, but it is what the dialectic of history is driving toward: absolute knowledge, where the gap between the knower and the known is overcome—pure *presence*. (See pp. 498–500, 509–511.)

These examples give you the sense that Derrida is concerned with something central in the Western philosophical tradition. The assumption at work is that at some point we come face to face with undeniable, clear, self-evident truth because the object of that truth is immediately present to our consciousness. At that point we can think the truth, express the truth, speak the truth. The object reveals itself as it is and all we have to do is *signify* its nature in language. Derrida calls this assumption **logocentrism.*** This logocentric presumption, Derrida thinks, pervades our tradition. We could put it this way: *Presence* can guarantee the truth of basic propositions, thus providing *foundations* to build on, and *argument* can guarantee the solidity of the building built on those foundations. As deconstructionists sometimes put it, logocentrism "privileges" reason as an avenue to truth and goodness.

But of course these truths must be expressed in language, and there's the rub. Derrida notes that language takes two forms, spoken and written. For the most part we think that **speaking** has a kind of priority over **writing,** and many philosophers have thought so, too. Plato, for instance, sees writing as a secondary and inherently dangerous form of language. After all (so the thought goes), when I speak I am simply expressing my thought, and what I think is immediately present to my consciousness. There is no *gap*, as it were, between the *presence* of a yellow patch in my visual field and the thought, "Yellow here now." And if I *say* what I think, this speaking is a direct expression of the thought. My language is transparent to my meaning; it doesn't need interpretation. What I mean is obvious on the

"There is nothing outside the text."

—JACQUES DERRIDA

face of it.* In speech, then, my language is directly "in touch" with my meaning, which is just what it is, unquestionable and present in all its fullness. What I say has an authentic *origin* in what is present to me; with respect to what I *mean*, I have a **privileged access.**

Writing, however, is different. The link to presence is broken. Writing escapes my control. It is a set of mere marks—arbitrary, lifeless signs—sent out there in the world; who knows what someone will make of them? The reader is not present to what I intend to communicate, but *absent*. This absence is accentuated by the reproducibility of writing. What Plato wrote has been cited, quoted, copied over and over, and is now read by endless

---

*The Greek term *logos* is rich with connotations, all of which Derrida means to draw on. It can mean "word" or "speech" or "discourse" or "argument" or "rational account."

---

*Hegel, of course, long ago expressed doubts about this "immediacy." See pp. 501–504 for his critique of "sense-certainty."

numbers of readers unknown to him in contexts unimagined by him. This absence of readers to what Plato intended to say is an essential feature of writing.

> In order for my "written communication" to retain its function as writing, i.e., its readability, it must remain readable despite the absolute disappearance of any receiver, determined in general. My communication must be repeatable—iterable—in the absolute absence of the receiver or of any empirically determinable collectivity of receivers. Such iterability . . . structures the mark of writing itself, no matter what particular type of writing is involved. . . . A writing that is not structurally readable—iterable—beyond the death of the addressee would not be writing. (*SEC*, 7)

In this contrast between speech and writing we have one of a number of **binary oppositions** that Derrida thinks have dominated the Western philosophical tradition.* One side of each opposition is given primacy; the other is its shadow, derivative from the first and dependent on it. Logocentrism gives priority to speaking (*logos*), while regarding writing as a derived, secondary, insecure, "bad" form of language. Speaking is associated with certainty, with finality, with the truth; when we speak we merely bring forth in an external way what we *know* internally; we *represent* the truth in language. Writing lacks this immediate certification in consciousness. All of the philosophers cited in the above list, Derrida thinks, are logocentric in this sense.

To those brought up in the Western philosophical tradition, this may seem just common sense. But Derrida now pushes this thought in a radical direction.

> I would like to demonstrate that the traits that can be recognized in the classical, narrowly defined concept of writing are generalizable. They are valid not only for all orders of "signs" and for all languages in general but . . . for the entire field

of what philosophy would call experience, even the experience of being: the above-mentioned "presence." (*SEC*, 9)

To demonstrate this, Derrida does two things. He brings to bear certain aspects of the linguistic theory developed by a Swiss linguist, Ferdinand de Saussure, and he tries to show that this opposition undermines itself even in the texts of the most logocentric philosophers—that is, he *deconstructs* their texts. Let us look at each of these in turn.

Writing, Iterability, *Différance*

Saussure notes that the signs of which language is composed, whether spoken or written, are arbitrary. There is no natural connection between the word "goat" and goats.* The existence of (what we call) a goat does not necessitate that we have just this word expressing just this concept, for there is no necessity that we parcel up the world in precisely this way: into goats and all the rest. In fact, some languages, such as Mandarin, use a single word to refer to goats and sheep. Because language is arbitrary, either way of classifying is also arbitrary. So the English word "goat" doesn't mean what it does because of goats. But what, then, makes a word the word that it is, meaning what it does, expressing the concept that it expresses? Saussure's answer is its differences from all other words.

Language forms a system of differences. Its signs are not linked directly to immediately present objects—or even to meanings—but mean what they do because of the way they are related to and differ from other signs. Let us speak of a term like "goat" as a **signifier.** Then we can call both the meaning of that term (the concept) and an actual goat (the referent) the **signified.** Because language is constituted by a system of differences rather than by direct signification of meanings or objects,

> the signified concept is never present in and of itself, in a sufficient presence that would refer only to itself. Essentially and lawfully, every concept is inscribed in a chain or in a system within which it

---

*Others are presence/absence, soul/body, form/matter, one/many, reality/appearance, literal/metaphorical, nature/culture, male/female, light/darkness, good/evil. Such binary oppositions are among the main things that deconstruction aims to deconstruct.

---

*Compare the views of Peirce (pp. 604–606) and Zhuangzi (p. 86).

refers to the other, to concepts, by means of the systematic play of **differences.** (*D*, 11)

Think of it this way. What makes the word "goat" refer to goats is not a simple arrowlike relation between the word and the reality, but a many-faceted, many-layered system of relationships that the word has to other things: to other words like "sheep" and "animal" and "livestock," to actual critters, to human intentions and behavior, and to the contexts in which the word is uttered or written, heard or read. It is the ways it is *different* from all these related factors that makes it mean what it does. This principle of difference, Derrida says, "affects the *totality* of the sign, that is the sign as both signified and signifier" (*D*, 10). To an unspecifiable degree, both words and their meanings float free of the world we normally think they are anchored to.

If Derrida is right, then the situation is *not* like this: I first have a meaning in mind; then I search for language to express it. On the contrary, meanings are not entities with natures of their own; they do not exist independent of language in some Platonic realm of essences. The *meaning* of the word "goat" (the signified) is completely dependent on the signifier—this conventional sign, "goat," that is part of the language. And this signifier is what it is because of the role it plays in a larger economy of language uses.*

Derrida calls the words you use, even those you use in speaking the "present" contents of your mind, **traces.** A word is not an atomic unity isolated from everything else. Rather, a word is simply a trace of all those relationships in all those networks that make it signify what it does. A word is like a footprint or a mark showing that something else responsible for it is in the neighborhood. So what determines the identity of a word is largely *absent* from the occasion of utterance. And the same is true, for the above reasons, for the meaning it expresses.

Moreover, one's language (English in our case) is not something one controls; it is a system of signifiers that has a reality independent of any single user. Since the words of one's language are not constituted by anything one does, but rather by these differential relationships to other things, there can never be what the logocentric tradition assumes: language that expresses directly, in its plenitude or fullness, solely what is *present* to an individual's consciousness. One's language is always already caught up in a network of associations that go far beyond the present moment. What determines what a person means is not wholly in that person's power.

The consequence is that speaking is no better off than writing. In fact, Derrida holds that what has been held to be characteristic of writing is true also of speech: It is unstable, separated by an unbridgeable gap from what it is about, and subject to various possible interpretations. It is no longer possible to claim that what someone says has its origin solely in what is present to the speaker, since what one says depends as well on what the speaker does not say but is in the background of what is said—all of which helps to constitute the meaning of what the speaker says.

Speaking, just like writing, is iterable, repeatable, quotable, capable of being "grafted" into other contexts, its meaning subject to "drift" (*SEC*, 9). Like writing, a spoken utterance can be "repeated in the absence not only of its 'referent,' which is self-evident, but in the absence of a determinate signified or of the intention of actual signification" (*SEC*, 10). It is obvious, Derrida says, that we can use a term in the absence of what it refers to: we can talk about a goat when no goat is present and we can talk about the absent past and the absent future. But Derrida adds that a term can be used even in the absence of intention. What does that mean?

We usually think that the meaning of what someone says (given a language) is determined by two factors: the speaker's intention and the context. But Derrida argues that neither one can make what someone says completely determinate. Meaning something is itself language-permeated. You can no more intend to say that you'll return your neighbor's lawn mower without making use of your linguistic skills than you can manage the actual return without physical skills. Being linguistic in character, however, even intentions are

---

*There are similarities here to Wittgenstein's slogan, "The meaning is the use." See p. 641.

not *wholly present* to the meanings they purport to convey; they, too, are made up of traces of what is absent; so even intentions cannot *anchor* a speaker's meaning securely; they cannot eliminate the inevitable drift because they, too, are textlike, requiring interpretation—more like writing than we ordinarily think. Intentions, too, can be grafted into alternative contexts and get different readings. There is a certain **absence,** then, that permeates even the simplest intending-to-say, a fissure that opens between one's intention and one's meaning.* This does not mean that one's intentions are irrelevant to what one says. The category of intention, Derrida says, "will not disappear; it will have its place, but from that place it will no longer be able to govern the entire scene and system of utterance" (*SEC*, 18).

The same is true of contexts. The contexts that are relevant, of course, are contexts *as they are understood* (by speaker, hearer, quoter, and so on). And so long as understanding comes into it, language comes into it. The same iterability, then, will potentially destabilize any characterization of the context. So neither intention nor context can freeze the flow of meaning into something absolutely, perfectly, completely definite. It's a matter of interpretation all the way down.

This means that the traditional privileging of speech over writing is undone, that in fact writing—or the features ascribed to writing—is more fundamental, more "original" than speech. Derrida does not mean, of course, to make a historical claim here—to say that writing chronologically predated speech. The claim is rather that the characteristics of what was held to be secondary and derivative are already, and necessarily, found in what was thought to be basic and primary. It is not, then, that the speech/writing

dichotomy is simply overturned, so that it becomes writing/speech, with writing now in the primary spot, but that a deeper sense of "writing" is discovered that underwrites both terms.* Derrida sometimes calls this deeper sense *archewriting* to signify that the system of differences Saussure found in language infects all of thought and speech—and always has. Thus does Derrida deconstruct the traditional binary opposition between speech and writing.

Derrida's most characteristic term for this nonpresence of what is meant by a bit of language is *différance.* The French term for the English "difference" is "*différence*"—spelled the same but pronounced "dee-fer-ahnz." In a Heidegger-like move, Derrida changes the second "e" to an "a," thus creating a technical term that borrows from the ordinary but—well, differs from it. Derrida delights in the fact that this change of a letter shows up in writing but doesn't change the pronunciation. As Derrida uses the term, "*différance*" expresses a double meaning. It signifies (1) *to differ* (to be other than) and (2) *to defer* (to postpone, to put off). *Différance* accounts for the fact that a word means what it does in virtue of differing from other words; *différance* also separates a word from its meaning, assures its difference from that very meaning. Moreover, what a word means is never absolutely present at the time of its use, so its meaning is deferred, delayed, put off to an interpretation—to a different set of words that, of course, don't *present* its meaning either. If you long to find what Plato calls "traveller's rest" and "journey's end" (see p. 159), you are bound to be disappointed. There is no point at which "the eye of the soul" can stop and behold truth, or beauty, or Being. Every sign is merely the sign of another sign; every sign is a detour on the way to presence.

---

*This is why deconstructionists say an author may not always be the best interpreter of his own works. In a sense, the author occupies exactly the same position with respect to what he has written as the reader; both offer interpretations of a text that escapes their control. Some deconstructionists have gone so far as to speak of "the death of the author," as though what the author intends by what she writes is completely irrelevant and the reader rules. As we see, however, Derrida does not go so far.

---

*This structure is common to deconstructionist treatments of all those binary oppositions mentioned earlier. It is similar to the surpassing of opposites in Hegel (see pp. 498–501 for examples), except that there is not even the temporary illusion of completion in the third term or any hope of eventually attaining *presence* via a unity of subject and object. This kind of metaphysical hope Derrida means to put beyond us forever.

For the "unveiling of truth," *différance* substitutes "incessant deciphering" (*D*, 18).

🔶

"If a poet interprets a poem of his own he limits its suggestibility."

William Butler Yeats (1865–1939)

Différance applies to itself, too—a point that Derrida emphasizes. He says, paradoxically, that *différance* is "neither a word nor a concept" (*D*, 3, 5), meaning that we should not suppose that here, at last, we have the *truth* about meaning, reference, truth, and Being. *Différance*, he goes on to say, "is never presented as such" and "has neither existence nor essence" (*D*, 6). He goes so far as to say that *différance* "is not" (*D*, 6, 21).

> What is written as *différance*, then, will be the playing movement that "produces"—by means of something that is not simply an activity—these differences, these effects of difference. This does not mean that the *différance* that produces differences is somehow before them, in a simple and unmodified—in-different—present. *Différance* is the non-full, non-simple, structured and differentiating origin of differences. Thus, the name "origin" no longer suits it (*D*, 11).

> It governs nothing, reigns over nothing, and nowhere exercises any authority. It is not announced by any capital letter. Not only is there no kingdom of *différance*, but *différance* instigates the subversion of every kingdom. Which makes it obviously threatening and infallibly dreaded by everything within us that desires a kingdom, the past or future presence of a kingdom. (*D*, 22)

Note that Derrida isn't claiming that all words are ambiguous or polysemic (having more than one meaning). Even if you straighten out an ambiguity by saying, "No, I mean the sort of bank you put your money in, not the sort that you fish from," *différance* does its work on that clarification. There is nothing in this clarifying sentence that a hearer may not inscribe in other contexts, no words that aren't mere traces of other words, no meaning that isn't deferred. Derrida's term for this phenomenon is **dissemination.** Meaning is spread, scattered, distributed widely, disseminated rather than gathered all in one spot to be grasped in a simple act of understanding a word.

> What we know, or what we would know if it were simply a question here of something to know, is that there has never been, never will be, a unique word, a master-name. (*D*, 27)

Derrida notoriously declares that "there is nothing outside the text." Some have thought that Derrida means that in offering an interpretation of some text (written or spoken) one should restrict oneself to that text—that in understanding Shakespeare, for instance, one needn't take into account the conditions of life in Elizabethan England. But the dissemination of meaning indicates that there are in principle no limits to what may be relevant in understanding a text. Derrida says that

> the concept of text I propose is limited neither to the graphic, nor to the book, nor even to discourse, and even less to the semantic, representational, symbolic, ideal, or ideological sphere. What I call "text" implies all the structures called "real," "economic," "historical," socio-institutional, in short: all possible referents. [To say that there is nothing outside the text] does not mean that all referents are suspended, denied, or enclosed in a book . . . , but it does mean that every referent, all reality has the structure of a differential trace, and that one cannot refer to this "real" except in an interpretive experience. The latter neither yields meaning nor assumes it except in a movement of differential referring. That's all. (*LI*, 148)

Does "nothing outside the text" amount to a kind of linguistic idealism, then, a theory that there is nothing more to the world than our language says there is?* Derrida wants to deny that, but the claim that "every referent, all reality has the structure of a differential trace" strongly suggests it. Why, we might ask, should "all reality" have just the structure that Derrida finds in the *language* we use to describe it? He clearly means to say that everything we could possibly understand is infected by undecidability because understanding is necessarily

---

*Compare Hegel's idealism, where being is always *for* a conscious subject (pp. 509–511). If we substitute "language" for "conscious subject" do we get Derrida's idea?

expressed in language. But so understood, the claim comes to this: that language about reality is linguistic in character. And that is a tautology that is neither very interesting nor very exciting. Most commentators remain puzzled by this provocative remark.

Note that Derrida denies claiming that there is nothing to a text but what a reader finds there. For one thing, the idea of "complete" freedom goes against the grain of his insistence that there can be no completeness anywhere. But more important, he emphasizes that not all readings are equally good. To read Rousseau well, for instance (Derrida has a book on Rousseau),

> one must understand and write, even translate French as well as possible, know the corpus of Rousseau as well as possible, including all the contexts that determine it (the literary, philosophical, rhetorical traditions, the history of the French language, society, history, which is to say, so many other things as well). Otherwise, one could indeed say just anything at all, and I have never accepted saying, or encouraging others to say, just anything at all, nor have I argued for indeterminacy as such. (*LI*, 144, 145)

Derrida believes his reflections on language will make possible *better* ways to read texts, *better* ways of discovering both the relative stabilities that exist there and the internal inconsistencies, the gaps, the slips and slides that *différance* makes possible.

> Let it be said in passing how surprised I have often been, how amused or discouraged, depending on my humor, by the use or abuse of the following argument: Since the deconstructionist (which is to say, isn't it, the skeptic-relativist-nihilist!) is supposed not to believe in truth, stability, or the unity of meaning, in intention or "meaning to say," how can he demand of us that we read *him* with pertinence, precision, rigor? How can he demand that his own text be interpreted correctly? How can he accuse anyone else of having misunderstood, simplified, deformed it, etc.? In other words, how can he discuss, and discuss the reading of what he writes? The answer is simple enough: this definition of the deconstructionist is *false* (that's right: false, not true) and feeble; it supposes a bad (that's right: bad, not good) and feeble reading of numerous texts, first of all mine, which therefore must finally be read or reread. (*LI*, 146)

So it is not the case that anything goes. The recognition of *différance* and all its multifarious effects does not do away with rigor, Derrida urges, but enables a new and enlarged kind of rigor. He does believe, however, that his analysis of language means the end of the logocentric era. This long history of searching for sure and certain foundations, of trying to base a theory of reality and moral goodness on the very presence of Being itself, this reliance on rationality to deliver the *truth*, is over. Metaphysics is over, finished, done for. There is no firm ground to stand on to distinguish appearance from reality, rhetoric from argument, or metaphor from a literal use of language. If "modernism" is a continuation of that logocentric quest in those who share Enlightenment hopes, then Derrida is definitely a "postmodernist."

DECONSTRUCTING A TEXT

We now have the main themes of deconstruction in hand. Let us briefly turn to an example of what deconstruction looks like when applied to a text. We can think of a text, whether spoken or written or embedded in some institutional context (a constitution, a legal system, a religion), as an attempt to construct an edifice that will withstand the winds of criticism and the earthquakes that might shake its foundations. Reading a text is like observing the building under construction. You read Plato or Aristotle or Nietzsche, or you study the US Constitution or the mores of family life in Fiji, and as you go along it looks good. It looks solid, well-grounded, consistent, and persuasive. It has obviously been well thought out, carefully planned, assembled with attention to detail.

But if you look more closely you begin to see cracks in the walls, parts that do not fit well with other parts, some aspects that tend to undermine others, and you can begin to see that the building trembles. It is not as secure as it first looked. This instability is inevitable, given the structures of *différance*, since nowhere is it possible to find absolutely firm ground to build on. The lack of stability tends to show up in what Derrida calls the **"margins,"** in things that don't seem central to the argument or thesis—in footnotes, prefaces, rhetorical devices, parentheses, metaphors. Just where everything looks firm and solid, things begin to slip and slide.

Let us take as an example Derrida's analysis of Plato's dialogue, *Phaedrus*, in which Socrates recounts an ancient Egyptian myth. In this myth, an Egyptian god, Thoth, offers writing to King Thamus as a gift that will benefit his people. Thoth says that writing will make them wiser and improve their memory. But the king refuses the gift. He says that it will, on the contrary, increase forgetfulness, since people won't have to exercise their memories. Writing will substitute *reminding* for *remembering*, and people will have only a semblance of wisdom rather than the real thing.* They will think they know what they do not really know,† and this will make them arrogant and difficult to get along with. Writing, the king says, is composed of marks external to the soul and is a poor substitute for the direct apprehension of the truth. Writing is just a ghost of true knowledge.

All these themes we have already explored, and here we find them right at the beginnings of the Western philosophical tradition. What can a deconstructive reading of this text reveal? One is struck by the fact that it is *in writing* that Plato warns of the dangers of writing! Plato writes a myth that tells us that writing (in contrast with speaking) is simply repeating without knowing. So it is the written myth that repeats without knowing the definition of writing—which is to repeat without knowing (*PP*, 75). Here we see a rhetorical device, the writing of a myth, cutting away at the very substance of the argument that the myth is devised to express. Suddenly the argument wobbles.

Derrida sometimes says that deconstruction is not a method and not a technique, by which he seems to mean that there is nothing mechanical or rule-governed about it. Yet it is a certain way of reading a text or of understanding institutions and customs. Deconstruction is above all

suspicious—suspecting that all is not as cheery and solid as it is made out to be and looking for signs of instability and slip. Often enough, though perhaps not as often as some deconstructionists think, it is right.

---

1. In what sense can everything we experience be thought of as a "text"?
2. Explain the way in which *presence* appears in three or four different philosophies.
3. What are the central features of *logocentrism*?
4. Explain the traditional way of understanding the difference between speaking and writing.
5. Saussure says that language is "a system of differences." Explain.
6. Explain the terms "signified" and "signifier." In what ways, if Derrida is right, does the former depend on the latter?
7. How does *iterability* insert drift and play into language and undercut its ability to represent in full the *presence* of the signified?
8. Why can neither intention nor context completely determine the meaning of a linguistic item?
9. How is the speech/writing binary opposition deconstructed by Derrida?
10. Explain *différance*.
11. What is *dissemination*? Why does he call a word a *trace*?
12. Why do deconstructionists think it is especially profitable to pay attention to the *margins* of a text?
13. What does Derrida find in the margins of Plato's *Phaedrus* that offers a foothold to deconstruction?

Knowledge and Power: Michel Foucault

One of the central themes of postmodernism was formulated by Jean-François Lyotard (1924–1988) in *The Postmodern Condition* (1979). "Simplifying to the extreme," he wrote, "I define postmodern as incredulity towards metanarratives." By **metanarratives,** he understands grand overarching theories of history or the world. Here are some examples of what he has in mind: Enlightenment views of inevitable progress based on reason and the sciences; Marxist views of history as determined by economic forces driving toward a pregiven goal; the Christian story

---

*Compare Heidegger on "idle talk," "curiosity," and "ambiguity" as modes of inauthentic existence (pp. 671–672). Also see Wittgenstein on "just *gassing*" (pp. 629, 643).

†Recall how Socrates at his trial characterizes his own wisdom: He does not claim to know what he in fact does not know. Socrates calls this "human" wisdom. (See p. 130.)

"The soul is the prison of the body."

—MICHEL FOUCAULT

looking especially for what is shared, taken for granted, and perhaps even unconscious. He calls such a form of life an *"episteme,"* putting the emphasis on what is known—or thought to be known—at a certain time, since these underpinnings of "knowledge" define what is possible in the way of thinking and acting.

A comparison with Kant may be instructive. Kant's critique seeks a priori structures that make mathematics or science or morality possible; he finds them in universal and necessary features of every rational mind—space and time, the categories, and the categorical imperative.* Foucault seeks something similar, except that what he finds is not universal, not present in each rational mind, and never necessary. An episteme is a kind of **historical a priori,** something that conditions and limits what it is possible for a people to think in a given historical era. It functions in the background, not explicitly formulated, and scarcely conscious.

> What I am attempting to bring to light is the epistemological field, the *episteme* in which knowledge, envisaged apart from all criteria having reference to its rational value or to its objective forms, grounds its positivity and thereby manifests a history which is not that of its growing perfection, but rather that of its conditions of possibility. (*OT*, xxii)

of creation, the fall, and salvation through Christ; Muslim beliefs in a final revelation to Mohammed, leading to the dominance of Islam over the entire world; the Hegelian dialectic necessarily working its way toward absolute knowledge. He thinks of these metanarratives as fundamentally authoritarian in nature. In place of them, Lyotard favors "little narratives"—stories, interpretations, and ways of understanding situations that are focused on particular problems and have specific achievable goals in mind.

This suspicion of grand narratives is exemplified perfectly in the work of Michel Foucault (1926–1984). Foucault says that he wants to write the history of the present, that is, to understand our present situation in light of its historical antecedents. In his early works, he characterizes his method as "archeological." He means that he is looking for the underpinnings of our current cultural practices in past forms of thought and life,

Rather than seeing our history as progress toward increasing truth, he wishes to discern the fundamental "truths," the "knowledge" accepted by the ages preceding ours. "Each society has its régime of truth, its 'general politics' of truth: that is, the types of discourse which it accepts and makes function as true" (*P/K*, 131). He is skeptical about current claims to truth, especially in the human sciences of psychology, psychiatry, medicine, and economics.† What interests him is not their truth, but what effect the *assumption* of their truth has on our lives. He examines certain deep and fundamental, and

---

*Kant's program for philosophical critique can be reviewed at pp. 467–468.

†Critics sometimes complain that Foucault does not acknowledge the progress and relative objectivity achieved in the "hard" sciences—physics and chemistry, for example. This is largely true, although he gives them an occasional nod.

often sudden, shifts in accepted *epistemes* in an effort to show how our current one came about.

---

1. What are "metanarratives," and what is the postmodern objection to them?
2. Describe the aim of "archaeology" as practiced by Foucault.
3. What is an *episteme*?

Archaeology of Knowledge

His *Madness and Civilization* (1965) offers an example of this **archaeological method.** Up to the end of the Middle Ages, the mad were generally believed to be possessed by gods or demons. Madmen were accorded different senses (they could hear voices unheard by others) and a different rationality, and they were objects of both fear and awe. In the Renaissance, these religious interpretations were supplanted by the concept of folly; the mad were possessed not by gods, but by a crazy foolishness. Erasmus wrote *In Praise of Folly*. Don Quixote's tilting at windmills was paradigmatic.

But then, Foucault says, a curious thing happened. Leprosy, a scourge of humanity for centuries, virtually disappeared from the Western world. As a result, a large number of institutions for the care of lepers suddenly became vacant. It was not long until a new use was found for them. Beginning in 1656, orders were given by the king to round up all the idle, the unemployed, the vagabonds, and the beggars and place them in these now empty buildings. Foucault calls this "the great confinement," and indeed it included a surprisingly large portion of the population. Among those confined in the "poor houses," of course, were the mad.

Society shut these idlers away and required them to work, both for the benefit of the community and for their own moral improvement. Foucault emphasizes that this requirement was not merely an economic measure. It had a moral meaning—that work was an intrinsic part of virtue. Confinement, thus, "will have not only the aspect of a forced labor camp, but also that of a moral institution responsible for punishing, for correcting a certain moral 'abeyance'" (*M&C*, 59). The essential thing is that "men

were confined in cities of pure morality, where the law that should reign in all hearts was to be applied without compromise, without concession, in the rigorous forms of physical constraint. Morality permitted itself to be administered like trade or economy" (*M&C*, 60, 61). Thus was inscribed in law the "great bourgeois . . . idea that virtue, too is an affair of state, that decrees can be published to make it flourish, that an authority can be established to make sure it is respected" (*M&C*, 61). Here we have "the civil equivalent of religion for the edification of a perfect city" (*M&C*, 63).

The next crucial step came after the French Revolution, when these "prisons" were emptied of all but criminals and the mad. This left great confusion. Edicts ordered the insane to be separated from the convicts, but what was to be done with them? No hospitals existed for their care, and families were often unable to cope with them. They constituted chaos in the prisons and a danger outside them. This conundrum led to the birth of the asylum.

Foucault discusses two early experiments in isolating the insane from normal society, one in England by the Quakers and one in France by the rationalists. Differences exist, certainly, but in both cases the structure of care is the same: close observation, clear rules, promises of liberty upon observance of the rules but punishments for their violation. The aim was to get the patients to internalize the rules to the point where they would be their own guardians.

> Madness escaped from the arbitrary only in order to enter a kind of endless trial for which the asylum furnished simultaneously police, magistrates, and torturers; a trial whereby any transgression in life, by a virtue proper to life in the asylum, becomes a social crime, observed, condemned, and punished. . . . The asylum . . . is not a free realm of observation, diagnosis, and therapeutics; it is a juridical space where one is accused, judged, and condemned, and from which one is never released except by the version of this trial in psychological depth—that is, by remorse. . . . For a long time to come, and until our own day at least, [madness] is imprisoned in a moral world. (*M&C*, 269)

These reforms, lauded as humane, enlightened, and liberating, have quite a different meaning for

Foucault. They set up authoritarian, totalizing environments that control in a subtler, more effective fashion than the scaffold or the lash because they are designed to internalize control in the madmen themselves. The image of being "imprisoned in a moral world" is striking. For Kant, morality was freedom, the freedom of autonomy and self-legislation. For Foucault, morality is a prison. The insane will be made their own jailers.

Are these changes progress? Does this parade of interpretations—from contact with the supernatural, to the unreason of folly, to moral disorder, and then, finally, in the nineteenth century, to mental illness—constitute a move toward the truth? Foucault will not say. When psychiatry finally announces that the mad are just ill, mentally ill, this (like the rest) may be no more than a product of ethical and social commitments that are far from obvious. Each stage manifests a certain *episteme* at work, and an archaeological understanding of them makes no judgments. There is discontinuity in their succession, but no explanation is offered, and no evaluation is given.

---

1. Sketch the stages of understanding madness.
2. Why does Foucault say that the mad were "imprisoned in a moral world"?

GENEALOGY

In 1971 Foucault published an essay on Nietzsche that signaled a shift in emphasis. Without leaving the archaeological method behind, he turned to **genealogy.** Nietzsche famously wrote a genealogy of morality, finding the historical and psychological roots of our morality in the life of slaves, in weakness, hatred, lies, and resentment.* Foucault now aims to give an analogous account of the way *epistemes* are constituted and succeed one another. Genealogy looks neither back to a golden age nor forward to some meaningful culmination. Its task, rather, is to "maintain passing events in their proper dispersion; . . . to discover that truth or being does

---

*For Nietzsche's critique of modern morality, see pp. 578–581.

not lie at the root of what we know and what we are, but the exteriority of accidents" (*NGH*, 81). The successive stages in human history are but a series of interpretations, ultimately ungrounded in anything other than further interpretations.

Moreover, **interpretation** doesn't just float free in the speculations of the intellectuals. It structures life. The task of genealogy "is to expose a body totally imprinted by history" (*NGH*, 83). An *episteme* is now understood to be embodied in social relationships and institutions, in dominations and subjections—in short, in power relationships. Like Foucault's archeology, genealogy traces historical shifts, but with special attention to the mechanisms by which such shifts are accomplished. It looks for "the entry of forces, . . . their eruption, the leap from the wings to center stage, each in its youthful strength" (*NGH*, 84).

The shift to genealogy marks *Discipline and Punish* (1975). Here Foucault traces the history of the prison and tries to show how the principles of its establishment are at work throughout modern society—in the military, factories, hospitals, and schools. We haven't always had prisons. In earlier days there was just the law, expressive of the sovereign's will, and punishments for its violation. These punishments were often public, violent, and accompanied by tortures of the most extreme kind.

Punishment in those days was occasioned by acts that were understood as attacks on the king and his law and was intended both to take vengeance on the criminal and to impress the spectators. Thus, punishment was savage and spectacular, but intermittent. It was an occasional display of power that reached down from above and wreaked havoc on the body of the miscreant.

Reformers in both England and France aimed to make punishments more humane, and so was born the prison as we know it. The aim was not necessarily to punish less, but to punish better. Social contract theories of the state led to thinking of crime not as an assault on the monarch, but as breaking the implicit promise that binds society together. Punishments were to "fit the crime," and a kind of "micro-physics" of power developed. It is always, Foucault says, "the body that is at issue—the body and its forces, their utility and their docility, their distribution and their submission" (*DP*, 25). Power over the body of the condemned can only be effective, of course, if it is combined with knowledge—knowledge of the body. But we must not think of this knowledge as something distinct from the power to use it. Rather,

> there is no power relation without the correlative constitution of a field of knowledge, nor any knowledge that does not presuppose and constitute at the same time power relations. . . . In short, it is not the activity of the subject of knowledge that produces a corpus of knowledge, useful or resistant to power, but **power-knowledge,** the processes and struggles that traverse it and of which it is made up, that determines the forms and possible domains of knowledge. (*DP*, 27, 28)

What develops is a kind of "political **technology of the body**" (*DP*, 26), the aim of which is a body that is both docile and productive (i.e., useful). Foucault stresses the fact that disciplinary mechanisms operate on the body; but we should not be misled by this emphasis on the body.

> It would be wrong to say that the soul is an illusion, or an ideological effect. On the contrary, it exists; it has a reality; it is produced permanently around, on, within the body by the functioning of a power that is exercised on those punished—and in a more general way, on those one supervises, trains, and corrects; over madmen, children at home and at school, the colonized, over those who are stuck at a machine and supervised for the rest of their lives. This is the historical reality of this soul, which, unlike the soul represented by Christian theology, is not born in sin and subject to punishment, but is born rather out of methods of punishment, supervision, and constraint. . . . The soul is the effect and instrument of a political anatomy; the soul is the prison of the body. (*DP*, 29, 30).*

A striking idea, that the body is imprisoned in the soul. The technology of power-knowledge obviously works on a body. But its aim is to instill certain attitudes, preferences, goals, beliefs, values, and constraints—just the mental characteristics traditionally ascribed to the soul. Insofar as this

technology is successful, it produces a "soul" that governs the behavior of a body and is, in a sense, its jailer. The aim is the moral transformation of the criminal, straightening out a crooked soul.

Genealogy illuminates how this power-knowledge technology works, and Foucault looks back to a proposal for an ideal prison by Jeremy Bentham.* Bentham called it the **Panopticon.** The plan was to have cells arranged in a circle around a central tower. A guard in the tower could see into each cell, but the inhabitants of the cells could not see each other, nor could they see into the tower. Because they could never be sure whether they were being observed, the effect was equivalent to always being watched. Knowing that you are observed is itself a powerful means of control.

Observation has other effects as well. It enables the construction of a "dossier," a file documenting the details of a life. The one observed becomes "a case," an object to be understood, controlled, improved, reformed—known. The focus of attention shifted from occasional acts that violated the law to the person of the criminal. He was to be "understood" in all his various details. And so was born the concept of the **delinquent**—the repeat offender, the recidivist, the individual for whom the door of the prison is a revolving door. The ideology of the prison held that they were places of reform, where improved souls could be returned to normal society. In fact, Foucault holds, the prison is a system for manufacturing delinquents.

These technologies of control, institutionalized in the prison, infiltrated other sectors of society. Power no longer descended from the king like a thunderbolt; it was diffused, horizontal, everywhere. The microphysics of power generated techniques of **discipline** aimed at a body "that may be subjected, used, transformed, and improved" (*DP*, 136). The growth of what we call "the disciplines" of psychiatry and criminology played an important role in this new power-knowledge complex.

> What was then being formed was a policy of coercions that act upon the body, a calculated

---

*Compare Aristotle on the soul as the form of the body, pp. 205–206.

*A discussion of Bentham's utilitarianism can be found on pp. 545–548.

manipulation of its elements, its gestures, its behavior. The human body was entering a machinery of power that explores it, breaks it down and rearranges it. A "political anatomy," which was also a "mechanics of power," was being born; it defined how one may have a hold over others' bodies, not only so that they may do what one wishes, but so that they may operate as one wishes, with the techniques, the speed and efficiency that one determines. Thus discipline produces subjected and practiced bodies, "docile" bodies. (*DP*, 138)

Gradually there came into being a "blueprint of a general method" that spread throughout society. The aim of all these control technologies was **normalization.**

The workshop, the school, the army were subject to a whole micropenality of time (latenesses, absences, interruptions of tasks), of activity (inattention, negligence, lack of zeal), of behavior (impoliteness, disobedience), of speech (idle chatter, insolence), of the body ("incorrect" attitudes, irregular gestures, lack of cleanliness), of sexuality (impurity, indecency). At the same time, by way of punishment, a whole series of subtle procedures was used, from light physical punishment to minor deprivations and petty humiliations. It was a question both of making the slightest departure from correct behavior subject to punishment, and of giving a punitive function to the apparently indifferent elements of the disciplinary apparatus: so that, if necessary, everything might serve to punish the slightest thing; each subject find himself caught in a punishable, punishing universality. (*DP*, 178)

As Foucault sees it, the prison reforms of the eighteenth and nineteenth centuries were generalized, and their techniques were widely adopted in other spheres of society. Panopticism, the gaze that sees and knows all, subtle and minute punishments aimed at deviations from societal norms, micropower widely distributed—all this has produced a **carceral society.** It is not only criminals who are incarcerated; we all live in a prison.

The judges of normality are present everywhere. We are in the society of the teacher-judge, the doctor-judge, the "social worker"-judge; it is on them that the universal reign of the normative is based; and each individual, wherever he may find himself, subjects to it his body, his gestures, his behavior, his aptitudes, his achievements. The carceral network, in

its compact or disseminated forms, with its systems of insertion, distribution, surveillance, observation, has been the greatest support, in modern society, of the normalizing power. (*DP*, 304)*

"Is it surprising," Foucault asks, "that prisons resemble factories, schools, barracks, hospitals, which all resemble prisons?" (*DP*, 228)

Following in the footsteps of that "master of suspicion," Nietzsche, Foucault suspects that the high ideals of the prison reformers, their humanitarian proposals, were mostly a mask for a far more disreputable project.

Historically, the process by which the bourgeoisie became in the course of the eighteenth century the politically dominant class was masked by the establishment of an explicit, coded and formally egalitarian juridical framework, made possible by the organization of a parliamentary, representative regime. But the development and generalization of disciplinary mechanisms constituted the other, dark side of these processes. The general juridical form that guaranteed a system of rights that were egalitarian in principle was supported by these tiny, everyday, physical mechanisms, by all those systems of micro-power that are essentially non-egalitarian and asymmetrical that we call the disciplines. (*DP*, 97)

Again, as in Nietzsche, what drives historical change is power. But in modern societies it is not the individual's will to power. It is all those microtechniques of control, largely anonymous, widely distributed, and ruled by no one that constitute the power-knowledge—our *episteme*—that coerces the soul by a kind of invisible hand. Genealogy is a history of power relations.

One may think that the situation is hopeless for the individual, entangled as he is by coercive forces on all sides. But in fact it is not so. Power is never, in Foucault's view, unidirectional. While he rejects any attempt to forge a general theory of resistance, power can be resisted by power, and we

---

*It is instructive to compare Foucault's notion of normalization with Nietzsche's description of "the last man" (p. 579) and with Heidegger's concept of "the One" (pp. 662–664). Nietzsche proposes to surpass normalized individuals with the overman and Heidegger with authentic existence. Foucault does not seem to propose a way out.

all, individuals and groups alike, have some power. Power is never a matter of one-way repressions, but of struggle, conflict, and war. Distrustful of large-scale revolutions (which typically end up as bad or worse than what they replace), he endorses local struggles to change some of the most oppressive practices of the carceral society.

In the later volumes of his *History of Sexuality*, Foucault looks to practices of self-formation by the Greeks and Romans. We are not just objects, molded into docile bodies by the disciplinary society. We are also, or at least we can become, subjects in control of our lives. He would deplore current tendencies to "discover who we are" by looking inside; who we are at present is simply a result of the operations of power not in our control. To be satisfied with that would be to acquiesce in what the disciplines have made us. But technologies of self-formation are possible, many of them already explored by the ancient Epicureans and Stoics. Again like Nietzsche, he believes we can create a kind of relation to ourselves and forge for ourselves an aesthetically pleasing life.* And in doing that we can achieve a kind of personal freedom.

---

1. How does genealogy differ from archaeology?
2. Why does Foucault see an intimate connection between knowledge and power?
3. How can operations on the body create a soul that takes the body prisoner?
4. In what way is Bentham's Panopticon a symbol of the disciplinary society?
5. How do prisons create delinquents?
6. What is the carceral society?
7. Can one escape from the carceral society?

Liberal Irony: Richard Rorty

Richard Rorty (1931–2007) considers Wittgenstein, Heidegger, and Dewey the greatest philosophers of the twentieth century; of these three, he ranks John Dewey first.* Like Dewey, he considers that he is working out the consequences of taking Darwin seriously. We are "exceptionally clever animals," nothing more (*PSH*, 72). As Rorty sees it, Darwin's evolutionary theory is one more step in the long process of **"de-divinizing"** the world. Rorty aims to complete that process. We consider him under the rubric of postmodernism because he exemplifies most of the major themes of that diffuse movement.

Here is how the story goes, according to Rorty. People—even intellectuals—used to believe in God. The pragmatic "cash-value" of such belief was that we felt ourselves responsible to something beyond ourselves, to a being greater than we. When the sciences began to give us more control over the world and our lives, belief in God began to wane.† But there still seemed to be something beyond ourselves to which we had to adjust our beliefs, something with an "essential nature" that our theories had to "correspond" to. We owed it to reality—to the world and to the self—to make our theories *true* of it. And so was born modern philosophy with its focus on epistemology.

Philosophy was now supposed to take over that "priestly" function mediating between us and reality. Philosophers became authorities, supplying criteria for "truth" and "knowledge" and "objectivity," getting us in touch with the metaphysical depths and revealing who we really are, what the world is, and how we ought to live. But philosophy based on these "metaphysical" assumptions, Rorty thinks, has played itself out; the lesson we should draw from Wittgenstein, Heidegger, and Dewey is that this tradition is over. And in any case, we can now see that this history has been a history of immaturity, of infantilism—based on the thought that we humans cannot take responsibility for ourselves but must bow to some power, some reality beyond us. Rorty aspires to a culture in which no trace of divinity remains,

---

*For Epicurean techniques, see pp. 239–240; for the Stoics, see pp. 241–243. Nietzsche on "giving style" to one's life is worth a look; see p. 585.

*He also expresses (qualified) admiration for Derrida and Foucault.

†Compare Nietzsche's tale of "How the Real World Finally Became a Fable," pp. 569–570.

either in the form of a divinized world or a divinized self. Such a culture would have no room for the notion that there are nonhuman forces to which human beings should be responsible. It would drop, or drastically reinterpret, not only the idea of holiness but those of "devotion to truth" and of "fulfillment of the deepest needs of the spirit." The process of de-divinization . . . would, ideally, culminate in our no longer being able to see any use for the notion that finite, mortal, contingently existing human beings might derive the meanings of their lives from anything except other finite, mortal, contingently existing human beings. (*CIS*, 45)

Rorty wants us to grow up, and in his view that means getting to the point where "we no longer worship *anything*, where we treat *nothing* as a quasi divinity, where we treat *everything*—our language, our conscience, our community—as a product of time and chance" (*CIS*, 22). It is this determination to see everything about us as subject to this **contingency** that is Rorty's leading theme.

---

1. What does Rorty mean by "de-divinizing" the world?
2. What does it mean to think of ourselves, our beliefs, and our language as completely contingent?

CONTINGENCY, TRUTH, AND ANTIESSENTIALISM

Rorty offers arguments along with this story of a certain kind of historical "progress." To aspire to the *truth* about things is to assume that we can take truth as a goal. But Rorty argues that this makes no sense. There is no way we could ever determine the difference between a belief that is *true*—in the sense that it corresponds to reality—and a belief we think is *justified by the evidence*. After providing all the justification we can, taking into account what everyone has to say about the matter, what more could we do to discover whether it is true? Citing William James' pragmatic adage that every difference must make a difference, Rorty concludes that

> we cannot regard truth as a goal of inquiry. The purpose of inquiry is to achieve agreement among human beings about what to do, to bring about

consensus on the ends to be achieved and the means to be used to achieve those ends. Inquiry that does not achieve coordination of behavior is not inquiry but simply wordplay. (*PSH*, xxv)

Rorty's denial that truth is correspondence to some independent reality is part of a general attack on the notion of representation. We have noted the rise of a *representational theory of knowledge and perception* in the views of Descartes, Locke, and their followers.* According to this theory, ideas in the mind can represent items external to the mind but can also misrepresent them. Modern epistemology sought a *criterion* for distinguishing correct from incorrect ideas. Philosophers worked to assure us that by using suitable methods and taking suitable care, we can be confident that our ideas do not misrepresent reality. This image of the **mind as a mirror** of the world beyond it has dominated philosophical imagination from Descartes down to recent times—and Rorty thinks that for the most part it still does.†

> The picture which holds traditional philosophy captive is that of the mind as a great mirror, containing various representations—some accurate, some not—and capable of being studied by pure, nonempirical methods. Without the notion of the mind as a mirror, the notion of knowledge as accuracy of representation would not have suggested itself. Without this latter notion, the strategy common to Descartes and Kant—getting more accurate representations by inspecting, repairing, and polishing the mirror, so to speak—would not have made sense. Without this strategy in mind, recent claims that philosophy could consist of "conceptual analysis" or "phenomenological analysis" or "explication of meanings" or examination of "the logic of our language" . . . would not have made sense. (*PMN*, 12)

A whole nest of terms cluster around this mirror image, this "glassy essence" of the mind: representation, truth, knowledge, objectivity, universal validity, essential nature, appearance versus

---

*The central theses of this theory can be found on p. 372.

†Using Derrida's terminology, we could say that Rorty aims to *deconstruct* this image.

reality, and rationality. Rorty wants to leave them all behind or at least to redescribe them in ways consistent with his Darwinian pragmatism. Following Peirce and Dewey, Rorty says that words are tools and beliefs are habits of action. Tools and habits are not the sorts of things that represent; they are not appraised as true or false, but as useful or not useful.

Words and beliefs, Rorty says, do not have a representational relationship to the world at all, but merely a causal one. Language is a set of tools for coping with the environment, tools that other animals do not have (or have only minimally). These tools are shaped in part by human purposes and in part by causal interactions with the world. We cannot disentangle, as Kant wanted to do, what we bring to our experience from what the world supplies. Nor do we need to.

> No matter whether the tool is a hammer or a gun or a belief or a statement, tool-using is part of the interaction of the organism with its environment. To see the employment of words as the use of tools to deal with the environment, rather than as an attempt to represent the intrinsic nature of that environment, is to repudiate the question of whether human minds are in touch with reality—the question asked by the epistemological sceptic. No organism, human or non-human, is ever more or less in touch with reality than any other organism. The very idea of "being out of touch with reality" presupposes the un-Darwinian, Cartesian picture of a mind which somehow swings free of the causal forces exerted on the body. The Cartesian mind is an entity whose relations with the rest of the universe are representational rather than causal. So to rid our thinking of the vestiges of Cartesianism, to become fully Darwinian in our thinking, we need to stop thinking of words as representations and to start thinking of them as nodes in the causal network which binds the organism together with its environment. (*PSH*, xxiii)

The world, then, in conjunction with our language-using community, causes us to hold certain beliefs; and we continue to hold those beliefs that prove to be reliable guides to getting what we want. That's all there is to it. The very idea of representation is pointless.

Language is not a medium of representation. Rather, it is an exchange of marks and noises, carried out in order to achieve specific purposes. It cannot fail to represent accurately, for it never represents at all. (*PSH*, 50)*

Basic to any language is a vocabulary, in terms of which we identify things and distinguish one kind of thing from another. Each of us speaks with what Rorty calls a **"final vocabulary,"** meaning those terms that are basic for us, foundational for the way we look at the world. But if we now understand the language we speak in terms of "time and chance," it seems radically *contingent* that we should have just the final vocabulary that we have. We speak as we do because of the causal history of the language and not because of the nature of the objects we deal with.† We could be expressing our science and common sense, our law and morality, our literature and religion, in ways quite different from the way we do. Our vocabulary is not *dictated* by the realities we mean to talk about.

Given that our vocabulary is a contingent set of tools for coping, rather than written on the mind by the very nature of things, a variety of such tools may be possible. Rorty takes this to be one of the lessons of history. No vocabulary has any metaphysical backing; there is nothing outside a language by which to judge it. Like any tool, language can be changed and perhaps improved. If we find that some part of our vocabulary has lost its usefulness, if it is getting in the way of attaining our purposes, we can invent new ways of speaking.‡

Suppose we were convinced of the complete contingency of our final vocabulary. We would then be the sort of person Rorty calls an **ironist.** An ironist, he says, fulfills three conditions.

---

*This is Rorty's way of dealing with what Derrida calls "logocentrism."

† Other philosophers ask why it should be a matter of "either/or" at this point. Why cannot we speak as we do *both* because of the history of the language *and* because of the objects we deal with? Why cannot a belief be at once a node in a causal network *and* a representation? See Peirce's analogy of the rainbow (p. 598) and Quine on pp. 725–728.

‡ Compare this to Zhuangzi's warning against being misled by words (p. 86).

(1) She has radical and continuing doubts about the final vocabulary she currently uses, because she has been impressed by other vocabularies, vocabularies taken as final by people or books she has encountered; (2) she realizes that argument phrased in her present vocabulary can neither underwrite nor dissolve these doubts; (3) insofar as she philosophizes about her situation, she does not think that her vocabulary is closer to reality than others, that it is in touch with a power not herself. . . . I call people of this sort "ironists" because their realization that anything can be made to look good or bad by being redescribed, and their renunciation of the attempt to formulate criteria of choice between final vocabularies, puts them in the position which Sartre called "meta-stable": never quite able to take themselves seriously because always aware that the terms in which they describe themselves are subject to change, always aware of the contingency and fragility of their final vocabularies and thus of their selves. (*CIS*, 73, 74)

An ironist believes that nothing has an essence that demands a certain vocabulary. No description is a matter of getting the object's *intrinsic* characteristics correctly registered, since there is no reason to believe in such characteristics. Descriptions always (explicitly or implicitly) relate an object to something else.* In particular, every description is formulated in a vocabulary that is relative to human purposes and interests. For an ironist, not even science should be understood as disclosing the "true nature" of things. The replacement of Aristotelian final causes by mechanistic explanations, for instance, was not a move to a finally true picture of the world; it simply replaced a less useful vocabulary by one more useful—for certain purposes, of course, such as prediction and control.

In short, languages are made rather than found (*CIS*, 7, 77). Given a certain vocabulary, speakers will find some sentences expressible in it to be "true" and others not; but there is no neutral criterion for choosing a language as a whole. Which language we prefer depends on what our purposes are. Furthermore, a person may have

various purposes, and these may not always fit neatly together. One may speak the language of evolutionary biology during a week's work in the laboratory and the language of the Catholic Mass on Sundays. These languages may even be incommensurable—impossible to make a coherent whole of. But there is no requirement in the nature of things that says a final vocabulary has to be coherent.

For an antiessentialist like Rorty,

> there can be no such thing as a description which matches the way X really is, apart from its relation to human needs or consciousness or language. The term "objective" is defined by antiessentialists not in terms of a relation to intrinsic features of objects but rather by reference to relative ease of attaining consensus among inquirers. Just as the appearance–reality distinction is replaced by distinctions between relative utility of descriptions, so the objective–subjective distinction is replaced by distinctions between relative ease in getting agreement. To say that values are more subjective than facts is just to say that it is harder to get agreement about which things are ugly or which actions evil than about which things are rectangular. (*PSH*, 50, 51)

Here we have several examples of Rorty's attempt at redescription. The objective notion of *getting it right*, for instance, is to be "redescribed" as *getting agreement* among inquirers. We have, Rorty says, no distinctive use for the former notion.

Note that Rorty resists giving an *explanation* for why it is harder to get agreement about values than facts. Philosophers are regularly tempted to explain this difference by saying that facts are objective while values are not. But from Rorty's point of view, this move is perfectly useless. The only difference that makes a difference is the surface difference. The rest is just unverifiable metaphysics that is better discarded.

Even humans lack an essential nature, according to Rorty. There are no metaphysical depths to the self, any more than there are metaphysical depths to the world. "On our view," Rorty says, "human beings are what they make themselves" (*PSH*, 61). We cannot, of course, create ourselves *de novo*. We are as contingent, as much the result of blind causes, as the world around us. And yet,

---

*Compare Dewey's example of the piece of paper (p. 611). Derrida, too, using the notion of *différance*, attacks the notion of knowing the intrinsic natures of things.

as language users, we can re-create ourselves by choosing or inventing a new vocabulary.

What if we were to ask, "But is it *true* that human beings are what they make themselves?" Rorty amiably replies that to think of ourselves this way is useful for certain purposes—in particular for the purposes of realizing a certain kind of person or society—but if you don't share those purposes, you won't find it useful. Putting this description of human beings to someone whose interests are religious or metaphysical is like "putting a bicycle pump in the hands of a ditch digger, or a yardstick in the hands of a brain surgeon" (*PSH*, 62).

Thus, Rorty must not intend even his basic claims about the contingency of our vocabulary to be mirroring the facts. It is not recognition of some objective fact that catapults us into agreeing with Darwin or into an ironic stance with respect to our final vocabulary. To put it that way would be to fall back into thinking that there were facts independent of the way they are described—to relapse into the representational, metaphysical kind of thinking from which Rorty is trying to free us. When he recommends irony to us, he is in effect saying that it is more fruitful, more useful, and altogether better to think of ourselves and our final vocabularies in this ironic way than in any other. Try it on, we can hear him saying, and see whether it doesn't suit.

> Interesting philosophy is rarely an examination of the pros and cons of a thesis. Usually it is, implicitly or explicitly, a contest between an entrenched vocabulary which has become a nuisance and a half formed new vocabulary which vaguely promises great things. . . .
>
> The method is to redescribe lots and lots of things in new ways, until you have created a pattern of linguistic behavior which will tempt the rising generation to adopt it, thereby causing them to look for appropriate new forms of nonlinguistic behavior, for example, the adoption of new scientific equipment or new social institutions. This sort of philosophy does not work piece by piece, analyzing concept after concept, or testing thesis after thesis. Rather, it works holistically and pragmatically. It says things like "try thinking of it this way." . . . It does not pretend to have a better candidate for doing the same old things which we did when we spoke in the old way. Rather, it suggests that we

might want to stop doing those things and do something else. But it does not argue for this suggestion on the basis of antecedent criteria common to the old and the new language games. For just insofar as the new language really is new, there will be no such criteria.

> Conforming to my own precepts, I am not going to offer arguments against the vocabulary I want to replace. Instead, I am going to try to make the vocabulary I favor look attractive by showing how it may be used to describe a variety of topics. (*CIS*, 9)

By taking this rhetorical task on himself, Rorty signals that the old quarrel between philosophy and rhetoric, between Socrates and the Sophists, is one of those binary oppositions he wants to overcome. And after all, if words are tools for coping rather than representations of reality, whatever techniques that work will do. What we want is a vocabulary that we will find satisfying; whether we arrive at it by rational argument or rhetorical persuasion is of little importance.

---

1. Why does Rorty believe we cannot take truth as a goal? What is the appropriate goal, in his view?
2. What is a vocabulary? What is an ironist's relationship to the vocabulary she uses?
3. What does Rorty want to substitute for the notion of "representation"?
4. Why are there no *essential natures* to be known?

LIBERALISM AND THE HOPE OF SOLIDARITY

Rorty calls himself not merely an ironist but a *liberal* ironist. This signals the *kind* of utility by which he chooses to assess his new vocabulary. For what ends is it useful?

As Rorty understands the term, a **liberal** is someone for whom "cruelty is the worst thing we do" (*CIS*, xv). By "cruelty" Rorty does not mean just deliberate infliction of physical pain by one person on another, but also humiliation, neglect, and the sorts of institutional and political arrangements that disadvantage certain groups. A liberal ironist, then, is someone whose final vocabulary is oriented around minimizing the amount of cruelty in the world, realizing all the while that this very conviction of hers is entirely contingent. An ironist does not fight cruelty because it violates the dignity of human nature (she believes there is no human nature) or because cruelty is something bad in itself (she can make no sense of that). There are no deep facts about humans or their suffering, no absolute good or bad to appeal to, no criteria that don't beg the question. A liberal ironist admits that

> a circular justification of our practices, a justification which makes one feature of our culture look good by citing still another, or comparing our culture invidiously with others by reference to our own standards, is the only sort of justification we are going to get. (*CIS*, 57)

Neither common sense nor metaphysics can supply justifications for the ironist's values because she realizes that "anything can be made to look good or bad by being redescribed" (*CIS*, 73). She understands that she just happens, for historical reasons, to have been produced as the sort of person who believes that being cruel is the worst thing. But for all that, her firm commitments remain firm; she sticks to her final vocabulary. She is an ironist *and* a liberal. She could say, with Rorty,

> *Our* moral view is, I firmly believe, much better than any competing view, even though there are a lot of people whom you will never be able to convert to it. It is one thing to say, falsely, that there is nothing to choose between us and the Nazis. It is another thing to say, correctly, that there is no neutral, common ground to which an experienced Nazi philosopher and I can repair in order to argue out our differences. That Nazi and I will always strike one another as begging all the crucial questions, arguing in circles. (*PSH*, 15)

In rejecting the possibility of some neutral basis on which to argue the superiority of democratic liberalism, Rorty is trying to shift the ground on which a good society is justified. We should not try to base our argument on a foundation of antecedently existing facts recognizable by all parties; as we have seen, Rorty thinks there is no such common ground.

Philosophers should get to work, Rorty says, substituting **hope** for *knowledge*—hope in the future realization of a utopian ideal. They should busy themselves "redescribing humanity and history in terms which make democracy seem desirable," making it seem that "the ability to be a citizen of the full-fledged democracy which is yet to come . . . is what is important about being human" (*RC*, 3).

> To say that one should replace knowledge by hope is to say . . . that one should stop worrying about whether what one believes is well grounded and start worrying about whether one has been imaginative enough to think up interesting alternatives to one's present beliefs. (*PSH*, 34)
>
> I do not much care whether democratic politics are an expression of something deep, or whether they express nothing better than some hopes which popped from nowhere into the brains of a few remarkable people (Socrates, Christ, Jefferson, etc.) and which, for unknown reasons, became popular. (*RC*, 14)

If we ask about the content of this democratic liberalism that Rorty hopes for, he refers us to J. S. Mill's little book, *On Liberty*. Here we find "a world in which nothing remains sacred save the freedom to lead your life by your own lights, and nothing is forbidden which does not interfere with the freedom of others" (*PSH*, 271). Freedom, rather than truth, should be our principal goal.

If the only limitation on freedom is the requirement that we not "interfere with the freedom of others," this, Rorty says, demands that we make a sharp distinction between the **private** and the **public.***

> The ironist's final vocabulary can and should be split into a large private and a small public sector, sectors which have no particular relation to one another. (*CIS*, 100)
>
> In our public role as citizens, we should be guided by the maxim to reduce the amount of cruelty in the world—cruelty being understood as interference with another person's pursuit of happiness. But we ought to refrain from imposing our version of happiness on anyone else.

---

*Although Rorty combats traditional "binary oppositions" (appearance/reality, knowledge/opinion, morality/prudence, absolute/relative), this is one distinction he thinks it important to insist on.

. . . there is a potential infinity of equally valuable ways to lead a human life, and . . . these ways cannot be ranked in terms of degrees of excellence, but only in terms of their contribution to the happiness of the persons who lead them and of the communities to which these persons belong. (*PSH*, 268)

In our private lives we should be free to pursue the creation of ourselves and our idiosyncratic loves in any way we find satisfactory. Since there is no such thing as a given human nature, variety and individuality should be cherished. Rorty wishes to encourage "an ever-expanding profusion of new sorts of human lives, new kinds of human beings" (*PSH*, 269). The watchword here should be *pluralism*, refusing to set any limits to the sorts of selves and communities that individuals might wish to create, save those that prevent cruelty. Those who are able to pursue Nietzschean self-overcoming should be allowed to do so; only let them not try to turn their private projects into a politics that elevates an elite few—the noble, the overmen—to a privileged place in society. "We should stop trying to combine self-creation and politics, especially if we are liberals" (*CIS*, 14). Our responsibilities to others

constitute *only* the public side of our lives, a side which competes with our private affections and our private attempts at self-creation, and which has no *automatic* priority over such private motives. Whether it has priority in any given case is a matter for deliberation, a process which will usually not be aided by appeal to "classical first principles." Moral obligation is, in this view, to be thrown in with a lot of other considerations, rather than automatically trump them. (*CIS*, 194)*

And how is "moral obligation" understood on Rorty's view? It is obvious by now that Rorty cannot hope to ground morality in human nature (as Aristotle did), or in the degrees of goodness inherent in things (as Augustine did), or in the unconditional demands of reason (as Kant did). **Morality,** rather, is simply a term for what the members of a certain community understand is "not done"—not among *them*, that is. Morality is a matter of

"the sort of thing *we* don't do." An immoral action is, on this account, the sort of thing which, if done at all, is done only by animals, or by people of other families, tribes, cultures, or historical epochs. If done by one of us, or if done repeatedly by one of us, that person ceases to be one of us. She becomes an outcast, someone who doesn't speak our language, though she may once have appeared to do so. (*CIS*, 59, 60)

This parochialism about morality, Rorty thinks, is just part of the general contingency of human life. This is ironism applied to morality. But that isn't his last word on the subject, since he is, after all, a *liberal* ironist. Speaking for himself, he believes in moral progress—both that it is possible and that we have made substantial moral progress over the centuries.† Progress means enlarging the "we," the people whose pain we feel as we feel our own or that of those we dearly love. Rorty's term for this enlarged sense of our community is **solidarity.**

The right way to take the slogan, "We have obligations to human beings simply as such," is as a means of reminding ourselves to keep trying to expand our sense of "us" as far as we can. . . . We should stay on the lookout for marginalized people—people whom we still instinctively think of as "they" rather than "us." We should try to notice our similarities with them. The right way to construe the slogan is as urging us to *create* a more expansive sense of solidarity than we presently have. The wrong way is to think of it as urging us to *recognize* such a solidarity, as something that exists antecedently to our recognition of it. (*CIS*, 196)

In my utopia, human solidarity would be seen not as a fact to be recognized by clearing away "prejudice" or burrowing down to previously hidden depths but, rather, as a goal to be achieved. It is to be achieved not by inquiry but by imagination, the imaginative ability to see strange people as fellow sufferers. . . .

This process of coming to see other human beings as "one of us" rather than as "them" is a matter of detailed description of what unfamiliar

---

*It is not entirely clear how this view of moral obligation as just one of a number of factors to consider fits with Rorty's view that cruelty is the "worst" thing we do.

†Contrast this rather cheerful appraisal with the dark view of Foucault, for whom modern society resembles nothing so much as a prison. See p. 711.

people are like and of redescription of what we ourselves are like. This is a task not for theory but for genres such as ethnography, the journalist's report, the comic book, the docudrama, and, especially, the novel. (*CIS*, xvi)

The value of increasing our sensitivity to cruelty, of enlarging the boundaries of those we count as "one of us," is not something that can be demonstrated. We cannot prove, for instance, that there is something *inhuman* in "the audiences in the Coliseum, . . . the guards at Auschwitz, and the Belgians who watched the Gestapo drag their Jewish neighbors away" (*CIS*, 189).

> We decent, liberal humanitarian types . . . are just luckier, not more insightful, than the bullies with whom we struggle. (*PSH*, 15)
>
> It is neither irrational nor unintelligent to draw the limits of one's moral community at a national, or racial, or gender border. But it is undesirable—morally undesirable. So it is best to think of moral progress as a matter of increasing *sensitivity*, increasing responsiveness to the needs of a larger and larger variety of people and things. (*PSH*, 81)

Why is that best? Because, Rorty believes, thinking that way is our best hope for increasing human happiness in the future.

RELATIVISM

It should be no surprise by now to hear that Rorty is often called a *relativist*. In response, he admits that "if **'relativism'** just means failure to find a use for the notion of 'context-independent validity,' then this charge [is] entirely justified" (*RC*, 24). The total contingency of our vocabulary, its dependence on the history of the language and on the innovations of previous "redescribers" of things, means that everything we say is dependent on other things we say. We cannot get free of our "thrownness" (Heidegger) or our "form of life" (Wittgenstein) to see things as they are independent of that context. Whatever we say is relative to our linguistic and cultural milieu. But that said, Rorty goes on the attack.*

---

*A perusal of *Rorty and His Critics* shows that many philosophers are unconvinced by his rebuttal of the charge.

We so-called "relativists" refuse, predictably, to admit that we are enemies of reason and common sense. We say that we are only criticizing some antiquated, specifically philosophical dogmas. But, of course, what we call dogmas are exactly what our opponents call common sense. Adherence to these dogmas is what they call being rational. (*PSH*, xvii)

We have seen that Rorty recommends trashing much of our traditional vocabulary—not only the appearance/reality distinction, but also the distinctions between finding and making, discovery and invention, argument and rhetoric, objective and subjective, morality and expediency, philosophy and literature, and indeed that between absolutism and relativism itself. All these, Rorty claims, depend on assumptions that we would be better off without. The charge of relativism, then,

> should not be answered, but rather evaded. We should learn to brush aside questions like "How do you *know* that freedom is the chief goal of social organization?" in the same way as we brush aside questions like "How do you *know* that Jones is worthy of your friendship?" . . . Such choices are not made by reference to criteria. (*CIS*, 54)

Rorty believes that the liberal democracies of the West, despite their faults, are the best societies humanity has devised to date. Coming from a member of such a society, of course, this can sound awfully ethnocentric. But Rorty cheerfully admits the **ethnocentrism.** His defense is that *every* view is ethnocentric, since no one can escape from the social and cultural forces that formed her.

> There is no *neutral,* non-circular way to defend the liberal's claim that cruelty is the worst thing we do, any more than there is a neutral way to back up Nietzsche's assertion that this claim expresses a resentful, slavish attitude. . . . We cannot look back behind the processes of socialization which convinced us twentieth-century liberals of the validity of this claim and appeal to something which is more "real" or less ephemeral than the historical contingencies which brought those processes into existence. *We* have to start from where *we* are. . . . What takes the curse off this ethnocentrism is . . . that it is the ethnocentrism of a "we" ("we

liberals") which is dedicated to enlarging itself, to creating an ever larger and more varied *ethnos*. (*CIS*, 198)

Many who identify themselves as "postmoderns" share major themes with Rorty: the emphasis on contingency; doubts about truth, objectivity, and knowledge; blurring the line between rhetoric and argument. But like Nagel and Derrida, Rorty is disturbed by some of the more extreme versions of postmodernist thinking.

> Insofar as "postmodern" philosophical thinking is identified with a mindless and stupid cultural relativism—with the idea that any fool thing that calls itself culture is worthy of respect—then I have no use for such thinking. But I do not see that what I have called "philosophical pluralism" entails any such stupidity. The reason to try persuasion rather than force, to do our best to come to terms with people whose convictions are archaic and ingenerate, is simply that using force, or mockery, or insult, is likely to decrease human happiness.
>
> We do not need to supplement this wise utilitarian counsel with the idea that every culture has some sort of intrinsic worth. We have learned the futility of trying to assign all cultures and persons places on a hierarchical scale, but this realization does not impugn the obvious fact that there are lots of cultures we would be better off without, just as there are lots of people we would be better off without. To say that there is no such scale, and that we are simply clever animals trying to increase our happiness by continually reinventing ourselves, has no relativistic consequences. The difference between pragmatism and cultural relativism is the difference between pragmatically justified tolerance and mindless irresponsibility. (*PSH*, 276)

Whether this distinction will hold up in the continuing human conversation is something that Rorty himself would be content to leave to the future.

---

1. How does Rorty understand liberalism?
2. What sort of justification of her position can a liberal ironist give? What kind of justification is ruled out for her?
3. What does it mean that Rorty wants to substitute hope for knowledge?
4. Why does Rorty say that if we take care of freedom, truth will take care of itself?
5. Explain Rorty's sharp distinction between the public and the private. Why is it important to him?
6. How does Rorty understand morality? What is the goal of liberal morality?
7. How does Rorty respond to the charge of relativism?

FOR FURTHER THOUGHT

1. Find examples of postmodernism in recent culture: movies, music, literature, politics, or university classes.
2. Do we live in a carceral society? Compare Foucault and Rorty on this question. What do you say?
3. Is morality just a power play (Foucault) or only a matter of what "we" do or don't do (Rorty)? Is there a viable alternative?
4. Is there a way to escape the relativism of "true-for-me" and "true-for-you"?

KEY WORDS

postmodernism	genealogy
text	interpretation
deconstruction	power-knowledge
presence	technology of the body
logocentrism	Panopticon
speaking	delinquent
writing	discipline
privileged access	normalization
binary oppositions	carceral society
signifier	de-divinizing
signified	contingency
differences	mind as mirror
traces	final vocabulary
absence	ironist
différance	liberal
dissemination	hope
margins	public/private
metanarratives	morality (for Rorty)
episteme	solidarity
historical a priori	relativism
archaeological method	ethnocentrism

NOTES

1. Thomas Nagel, *The Last Word* (Oxford: Oxford University Press, 1997), 5, 6.

2. References to the following works are all to page numbers.

   References to the works of Jacques Derrida are as follows:

   D: "Différance" in *Margins of Philosophy* (1972), trans. Alan Bass (Chicago: University of Chicago Press, 1982).

   LI: "Limited Inc a, b, c . . ." (1977), trans. Samuel Weber, in *Limited Inc* (Evanston, IL: Northwestern University Press, 1988).

   PP: "Plato's Pharmacy" in *Dissemination* (1972), trans. Barbara Johnson (Chicago: University of Chicago Press, 1981).

   SEC: "Signature, Event Context" (1972), trans. Samuel Weber and Jeffrey Mehlman, in *Limited Inc* (Evanston, IL: Northwestern University Press, 1988).

   References to the works of Michel Foucault are as follows:

   OT: *The Order of Things* (London: Tavistock, 1970).

   M&C: *Madness and Civilization*, trans. Richard Howard (New York: Vintage Books, 1988).

   NGH: *Nietzsche, Genealogy, History*, trans. Donald F. Bouchard and Sherry Simon, reprinted in *The Foucault Reader*, ed. Paul Rabinow (New York: Pantheon Books, 1984).

   DP: *Discipline and Punish*, trans. Alan Sheridan (New York: Vintage Books, 1997).

   References to the works of Richard Rorty are as follows:

   CIS: *Contingency, Irony, and Solidarity* (Cambridge: Cambridge University Press, 1989).

   PSH: *Philosophy and Social Hope* (London: Penguin Books, 1999).

   PMN: *Philosophy and the Mirror of Nature* (Princeton, NJ: Princeton University Press, 1979).

   RC: *Rorty and His Critics*, ed. Robert B. Brandom (Oxford: Blackwell, 2000).

PHYSICAL REALISM AND THE MIND

Quine, Dennett, Searle, Nagel, Jackson, and Chalmers

N**ot** every philosopher is caught up in the postmodern fervor. There are those who think that what is truly ironic is giving up on the search for truth and objective knowledge just when we are actually beginning to understand the world around us and the mind within. There are, moreover, those old objections to relativism that perhaps cannot just be shrugged off the way Rorty does. If we turn each of our convictions into merely one more contingent product of history, we need to ask, "From what point of view can we be making such a judgment about our point of view?" As Thomas Nagel puts it, "the claim 'Everything is subjective' must be nonsense, for it would itself have to be either subjective or objective. But it can't be objective, since in that case it would be false if true. And it can't be subjective, because then it would not rule out any objective claim, including the claim that it is objectively false."[1]

Even apart from postmodernist skepticism, we have seen philosophy in a kind of retreat from its traditional objectives. Especially since Kant,

philosophers have tended to think of their discipline as distinctively different from science. As the sciences continued to triumph in one field after another, some began to wonder whether there was anything left for philosophers to do. By the middle of the twentieth century, many concluded that philosophy had to give up its grand aims and pretensions to knowledge. The watchword was "analysis," the aim was clarity of language, and the mode of procedure was piecemeal analysis of well-defined, small problems.

But as the century wore on, some philosophers began once again to turn to the traditional problems centered on the nature of human beings and their place in the larger scheme of things. In the words of Karl Popper (1902–1994),[2]

Language analysts believe that there are no genuine philosophical problems, or that the problems of philosophy, if any, are problems of linguistic usage, or of the meaning of words. I, however, believe that there is at least one philosophical problem in which all thinking men are interested. It is the problem of cosmology: *the problem of understanding the world—including ourselves, and our knowledge, as part of the world.**

Wilfrid Sellars (1912–1989) puts it this way:

> The aim of philosophy, abstractly formulated, is to understand how things in the broadest possible sense of the term hang together in the broadest possible sense of the term. Under "things in the broadest possible sense" I include such radically different items as not only "cabbages and kings," but numbers and duties, possibilities and finger snaps, aesthetic experience and death. To achieve success in philosophy would be, to use a contemporary turn of phrase, to "know one's way around" with respect to all these things, not in that unreflective way in which the centipede of the story knew its way around before it faced the question, "how do I walk?" but in that reflective way which means that no intellectual holds are barred.[3]

I will call the viewpoint to be discussed here **"physical realism,"** a term used earlier by Sellars' father, Roy Wood Sellars;[4] it is also called "naturalism," or sometimes "scientific realism" or simply "realism."† The central ideas of physical realism are that human beings are wholly a part of nature and that our best account of nature is presented in the sciences. A philosopher working in this way will try to understand "how things hang together" by making use of everything we believe that we know from whatever source—and especially from the sciences. This construction of a synoptic (seeing together) view is a job that no special

science claims—not physics or psychology or any science in between. Philosophy, understood in this way, is integrative and holistic and in certain areas becomes part of a multifaceted interdisciplinary approach to problems.

Science, Common Sense, and Metaphysics: Willard van Orman Quine

Interestingly, this turn to a broader scope for philosophy was signaled by an attack on traditional empiricism. It may seem strange that a viewpoint taking science seriously should begin with a critique of the empiricists. Surely the methods of the sciences are decidedly empirical—tied at crucial points to observation and experiment—so how can this be?

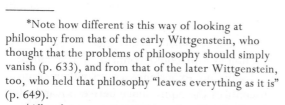

"I see the question of truth as one to be settled within science, there being no higher tribunal."

—WILLARD VAN ORMAN QUINE

---

*Note how different is this way of looking at philosophy from that of the early Wittgenstein, who thought that the problems of philosophy should simply vanish (p. 633), and from that of the later Wittgenstein, too, who held that philosophy "leaves everything as it is" (p. 649).

†All such terms are imprecise, rather like signposts pointing in a certain direction. Serious thought, rigorous argument, can scarcely be carried on in terms of such "isms," which is why they occur seldom in the writings of good philosophers and have not featured prominently in this book. But they do have a use, and in this chapter we take them to point to themes found in thinkers who can reasonably be grouped together but who are by no means always in agreement about everything.

According to Willard van Orman Quine (1908–2000), a logician of distinction and for many years a professor of philosophy at Harvard, traditional empiricists—David Hume and the logical positivists, for example—have been *dogmatic*, just the opposite of what they advertise themselves to be. Quine has a double critique of such philosophy, two objections that he says ultimately come to the same thing. Empiricists have been dogmatic (1) in believing that there is a sharp distinction between analytic and synthetic truths and (2) in thinking that each meaningful statement is equivalent to some (perhaps very complicated) statement that refers only to immediate experience.

The first dogma allowed a neat division of labor that gave philosophers something to do. Scientists were to do the empirical work of formulating synthetic truths about the world, while philosophers could clarify notions used in science and common sense by way of definitions that were analytically true. The second dogma is expressed in Hume's advice to trace every idea back to an impression, as well as in the positivists' verifiability criterion of factual meaningfulness.* Quine characterizes this second dogma as **"reductionism"** (*TDE*, 20),[5] since its goal is to "reduce" talk of objects in the world to talk that mentions only the data of sensation.

These may seem arcane and merely technical issues, but abandoning these dogmas has far-reaching consequences. For one thing, Quine says, we will no longer have any reason to draw a sharp line distinguishing philosophy from science, or, for that matter, speculative metaphysics from natural science. These boundaries get blurred. Since eliminating metaphysical speculation had been one of the main goals of the empiricist movement from Hume to the logical positivists, this effect is quite dramatic. Second, common sense and science will be seen as alike in their basic structure. And third, this critique will mark a move toward pragmatism. Let us examine these consequences.

HOLISM

Ever since Hume had distinguished "relations of ideas" from "matters of fact," empiricists had insisted on a sharp difference between them. Analytic truths were supposed to be true just in virtue of the meanings of their terms, telling us nothing about the world. You don't have to consult experience to know that two plus two is four or that no bachelor can be married; these are analytically true—so the story goes—and all that is required is that you understand the language. But if you want to know whether it is raining in Brooklyn now, or how fast objects fall near the surface of the earth, just understanding the sentences won't tell you. For that sort of truth you need confirmation by sensory experience. This divide was supposed to be both exclusive (no statement could be both analytic and synthetic) and exhaustive (if a statement was neither analytically true nor confirmable by sense experience, it was declared to be meaningless). That was how you got rid of metaphysics.*

The two dogmas are related in the following way. Suppose you have an ordinary factual statement about the world: "Water boils at 100°C at sea level." Call this *p* (for physical world statement). According to the early positivists, *p* was meaningful because it could be "reduced to" (or defined in terms of) a set of statements that did not talk about water or the sea at all, but only about our experiences—experiences, as we say, "of" water, thermometers, altimeters, and so on. Call this latter set of statements *e* (for statements about our experience). This reduction would yield a statement of the form "*p* if and only if *e*" that would be analytically true—true in virtue of the meanings of *p* and *e*. What *p* really means, supposedly, is *e*. Though you could confirm or disconfirm *p* empirically, no experience could either confirm or disconfirm the equivalence between *p* and *e* because that was true by definition.

But consider the correlation between the physical fact of water boiling and the relevant experiences. Given an observer in normal circumstances,

---

*See pp. 634–635.

*See p. 634 for the way positivists use this distinction for precisely this purpose.

when you have the one you have the other. But is that correlation a matter of *meaning*? Or is it a *fact* we discover by empirical methods? Quine argues that there is no nonarbitrary, noncircular way of determining the answer to these questions. No appeal to sameness of meaning, or to synonymy, or to definition, or to more sophisticated semantic rules will distinguish analytic from synthetic statements.* He concludes that the idea that *individual* statements of fact (*p* statements) are made meaningful by definitions reducing them to statements mentioning only immediate experience (*e* statements) cannot be sustained. To continue to think so is to accept a dogma. Our knowledge does depend on experience, but not in that atomistic sort of way.

Quine suggests, to the contrary, that

> our statements about the external world face the tribunal of sense experience not individually but only as a corporate body. . . . In taking the statement as unit we have drawn our grid too finely. The unit of empirical significance is the whole of science. (*TDE*, 41, 42)

We can see the sense in this claim if we reflect a moment on the way hypotheses are tested in science. Suppose some scientists come across an unfamiliar material. They hypothesize that its chemical composition is XYZ. How can that hypothesis be tested? Relying on theory they already are confident of, they deduce that if it is XYZ, then it will turn green when heated to 200°C. So they heat it and observe what happens.

What can they learn from this experiment? There are two cases. Suppose first that they observe it turning green. Do they now know that the substance is XYZ? No, not for certain, for there may be other reasons why this substance will turn green in the experimental circumstances. At best they have been given some reason to believe it is XYZ and other tests might confirm it further.

Now suppose that they make the experiment and it doesn't turn green. Do they know that the substance *isn't* XYZ? The perhaps surprising answer

is no—though in this case they have discovered a reason for believing that it is not XYZ, and in most cases that is what they will conclude. But why can't they conclude that their hypothesis is false, period?

Here is the logical situation. The observation sentence, "This substance turns green at 200°C," does not follow from the hypothesis that this substance is XYZ alone, but only in conjunction with certain other propositions. The scientists are also relying on a law correlating XYZ with turning green and a set of sentences describing the experimental situation—for example, that the temperature has in fact reached that level. We can represent this schematically in the following argument:

L: When XYZ is heated to 200°C, it turns green.
S: This substance is heated to 200°C.
H: This substance is XYZ.
Therefore *O*: This substance turns green.

A little reflection will convince you that the observation sentence *O* follows deductively from the *conjunction* of *L* (the law), *S* (the situation description), and *H* (the hypothesis). Suppose now that *O* is not observed. Then we know that the conjunction of the premises (*L and S and H*) is false. Because a conjunction as a whole is true only if each of its constituent propositions is true, it must be that at least one of the conjuncts is false, but the experiment does not tell us which one it is! In light of the failure to observe *O*, we have to retract *some* premise of the argument, but it is logically open which one it would be best to take back.

We can now see why Quine says that our statements about the world "face the tribunal of sense experience . . . only as a corporate body" and not individually. Evidence that any one of them is false will necessarily have implications for others, but it won't be determinate which others are at fault. Quine, then, endorses a version of **holism** in epistemology parallel to that favored by Peirce with respect to meaning.†

---

*It is also a fact that no one ever produced an actual example of successful reduction of physical language to purely experiential language.

†See Peirce's claim that a sign has meaning only in the context of a system of signs, p. 605. Quine's insight is also shared by the later Wittgenstein, p. 649. There is also a resemblance to Derrida's idea of traces, though Quine does not accept that the undecidability *goes all the way down*.

The totality of our so-called knowledge or beliefs, from the most casual matters of geography and history to the profoundest laws of atomic physics or even of pure mathematics and logic, is a man-made fabric which impinges on experience only along the edges. Or, to change the figure, total science is like a field of force whose boundary conditions are experience. A conflict with experience at the periphery occasions readjustments in the interior of the field. Truth values have to be redistributed over some of our statements. Reevaluation of some statements entails reevaluation of others, because of their logical interconnections—the logical laws being in turn simply certain further statements of the system, certain further elements of the field. Having reevaluated one statement we must reevaluate some others, which may be statements logically connected with the first or may be the statements of logical connections themselves. But the total field is so underdetermined by its boundary conditions, experience, that there is much latitude of choice as to what statements to reevaluate in the light of any single experience. No particular experiences are linked with any particular statements in the interior of the field, except indirectly through considerations of equilibrium affecting the field as a whole.

If this view is right, it is misleading to speak of the empirical content of an individual statement—specially if it is a statement at all remote from the experiential periphery of the field. Furthermore it becomes folly to seek a boundary between synthetic statements, which hold contingently on experience, and analytic statements, which hold come what may. Any statement can be held true come what may, if we make drastic enough adjustments elsewhere in the system. Even a statement very close to the periphery can be held true in the face of recalcitrant experience by pleading hallucination or by amending certain statements of the kind called logical laws. Conversely, by the same token, no statement is immune to revision. (*TDE*, 42, 43)*

To the metaphors of the "man-made fabric" and the "field of force," Quine adds yet another. Human

cognition yields a **web of belief.**[5] Our beliefs, he suggests, are like the strands of a spider's web, each related to the others, none able to stand alone, and most of them anchored to the world beyond the web only indirectly. Yet there are (quite) firm attachments, as we shall see, in what he calls "observation sentences."

This picture of our intellectual life poses a problem. Consider the example again and suppose that green is not observed. How shall we decide whether to (a) reject the hypothesis, (b) revise the law, or (c) reconsider our description of the experimental situation? As Quine notes, there is even a fourth option: we could reestablish logical equilibrium by dismissing the observation report as illusory.

This is a puzzle that goes to the heart of scientific practice and it hardly seems credible that we should make such a choice randomly. Quine's solution is that we should follow "our natural tendency to disturb the total system as little as possible" (*TDE*, 44), a rule he also calls "the **maxim of minimum mutilation**" (*PT*, 14). Applied to our example, this conservative principle would probably mean that the hypothesis (that the substance is XYZ) would be the thing to go, though that would depend on the particular case and could not be predicted in advance. We should also scrutinize the experimental situation to determine whether we have described it correctly. But to revise the law in question would mutilate the system to a much greater degree. Because a law is located nearer the center of the web of theory, changing it would force a great many other changes as well.

Yet "no statement is immune from revision," and even a law or a theory with a long history of success can be upset. That is what happens in scientific revolutions. Whatever choice is made at this point, Quine says, it should be such as to "maximize future success in prediction," as that is the test by which success in science is judged (*PT*, 2, 15). Prediction may not be our main *goal* in pursuing the game of science—we aim at understanding, he says, and control of the environment—but predictive success is "what decides the game, like runs and outs in baseball" (*PT*, 20).

---

* Here Quine expresses agreement with Peircean fallibilism (p. 601) and joins the pragmatists in rejecting Descartes' quest for certainty based on an unquestionable foundation.

⬧

"The whole of science is nothing more than a refinement of everyday thinking."

Albert Einstein (1879–1955)

We have been talking about science, but in fact Quine believes that no sharp line divides science from common sense. The same considerations that motivate the postulation of electrons are at work in positing tables and chairs as objects independent of our experience of them.

> Our acceptance of an ontology is, I think, similar in principle to our acceptance of a scientific theory, say a system of physics: we adopt, at least insofar as we are reasonable, the simplest conceptual scheme into which the disordered fragments of raw experience can be fitted and arranged.
>
> By bringing together scattered sense events and treating them as perceptions of one object, we reduce the complexity of our stream of experience to a manageable conceptual simplicity. The rule of simplicity is indeed our guiding maxim in assigning sense data to objects: we associate an earlier and a later round sensum with the same so-called penny, or with two different so-called pennies, in obedience to the demands of maximum simplicity in our total world picture. (*OWTI*, 16, 17)*

Quine talks here of "the disordered fragments of raw experience" and of **"sense data."** You may be reminded of Hume's characterization of experience as "a bundle or collection of different perceptions, which succeed each other with an inconceivable rapidity, and are in a perpetual flux and movement."† Quine's idea is that common sense postulates the reality of physical objects for the same reasons that science posits atoms: to explain the course of our experience and to simplify our

account of the world. Tables and chairs, then, can be thought of as "theoretical entities" posited to make sense of experience.

This notion presupposes, of course, that we can isolate and identify the elements of experience. And that in turn seems to require a language in which the course of experience can be reported and described—"play-by-play," as it were. Other philosophers have doubted that such a "private" language is really conceivable,* and in later works we find Quine characterizing the "data" that we have to work with in a much less subjective way. In *The Pursuit of Truth* (1990), for instance, he talks instead of the stimulation of our sense organs, a matter that can be characterized in as objective and public a manner as you like. He characterizes **observation sentences** as

> sentences that are directly and firmly associated with our stimulations. Each should be associated affirmatively with some range of one's stimulations and negatively with some range. The sentence should command the subject's assent or dissent outright, on the occasion of a stimulation in the appropriate range, without further investigation and independently of what he may have been engaged in at the time. A further requirement is intersubjectivity: unlike a report of a feeling, the sentence must command the same verdict from all linguistically competent witnesses of the occasion.
>
> Examples are "It's raining," "It's getting cold," "That's a rabbit." (*PT*, 3)

Although Quine admits that "observationality is vague at the edges," it is observation sentences that provide "a final checkpoint" for theory and make science objective. It is worth noting that although they are occasioned by stimulation of the sense organs, observation sentences are not *about* that stimulation; they speak of objective facts like rain, temperature, and rabbits. Observation sentences constitute "the link between language, scientific or

---

*Quine here stresses simplicity as the rule, but elsewhere he offers additional criteria for judging whether a theory does a good job: Does it conserve as much as possible of previous theories? Does it generalize? Is it refutable? Does it go too far?

†For Hume's description, and the consequences he derives from it, see p. 453.

---

*Wittgenstein is a case in point. In *Philosophical Investigations*, pp. 258ff, he presents a critique of the very idea of such a "private language." Derrida's critique of *presence* in terms of language as a system of differences has the same effect; see pp. 701–704.

not, and the real world that language is all about" (*PT*, 4, 5).*

Though no statement is in principle unrevisable, some statements are *very resistant* to revision; observation statements do anchor the web of belief quite securely. Although holistic matters of overall coherence govern the formulation of our theories, they must be balanced by the tenacious hold that observation sentences have. Quine says of himself that he "does indeed combine foundationalism with coherentism, as I think it is evident that one must."[6]

It is this foundationalist aspect that both distinguishes Quine's view from that of Rorty, for whom coherence is everything, and allows him to resist the claim that science is just another ideology. Though all our theories are "underdetermined" by the evidence the world supplies, it is because experimental science is tied tightly to observation sentences that it has a superior degree of objectivity; it lets the world have a decisive say in the theories we accept.† Common sense shares this feature, though to a lesser extent.

ONTOLOGICAL COMMITMENT

In response to what is imprinted on our senses, then, we "project" or "posit" a more or less stable world of objects. These posits constitute our **ontology**—our view of *what there is*.‡ Every theory or systematic set of beliefs has its ontology, expresses some commitment as to what there is. The tie between these posits and experience is not to be found by defining one in terms of the other, but in the way the posits organize, simplify, and predict our experiences. There is always surplus meaning in our conception of these posits—meaning that they cannot be reduced to subjective experience or sense organ stimulation—and that is true whether we posit divine beings or physical objects. That is why Quine believes that there is no deep gulf between science and common sense or between science and metaphysics.

> Physical objects are conceptually imported into the situation as convenient intermediaries—not by definition in terms of experience, but simply as irreducible posits comparable, epistemologically, to the gods of Homer. For my part I do, qua lay physicist, believe in physical objects and not in Homer's gods; and I consider it a scientific error to believe otherwise. But in point of epistemological footing the physical objects and the gods differ only in degree and not in kind. Both sorts of entities enter our conception only as cultural posits. The myth of physical objects is epistemologically superior to most in that it has proved more efficacious than other myths as a device for working a manageable structure into the flux of experience.
>
> Science is a continuation of common sense, and it continues the common-sense expedient of swelling ontology to simplify theory. (*TDE*, 44, 45)

❧

> "Physical concepts are free creations of the human mind, and are not, however it may seem, uniquely determined by the external world."
>
> *Albert Einstein (1879–1955)*

Most physical realists resist talking of physical objects as a "myth," and that way of referring to them disappears in Quine's later work as well. But the idea remains that entities such as Zeus and Athena cannot be ruled out on principle as meaningless. If you think these gods are real, Quine might say, here is a challenge: Formulate a theory about them, deduce some observation sentences, and see whether this theory passes the prediction test better than its rivals. Quine bets that it won't.

---

*It is the character of observation sentences that allows Quine to reject the Derridean claim that no sentence has a completely firm meaning. Note the structural similarity of this "realist" view with that of St. Thomas Aquinas, p. 330.

†In postmodernist terminology, Quine "privileges" science as a source of truth about the world. What might Quine say about logocentrism? Insofar as logocentrism is identified with a commitment to *presence* and immediate certainty about the truth, he would distance himself from it. No statement is immune from revision. But insofar as logocentrism means commitment to reason, logic, argument, and observation, Quine would hold that logocentrism is a *good* thing.

‡Quine prefers the term "ontology" to the similar but more historically freighted term "metaphysics," though he uses both terms.

Every theory, then, commits us to an ontology, to some view about what exists. How are we to know what the sentences of a theory commit us to? Consider a sentence like "Some dogs are white." It seems clear enough that in uttering this sentence we express commitment to the existence of dogs. But how about "white"? Are we signaling that we also believe in an additional something named *whiteness*? And for that matter, how about *doghood*? As we know, Plato thinks that in addition to the particular sensible things we are familiar with, there is an intelligible world of Forms—eternal and unchangeable realities that sensible entities "participate" in. Only by positing the Forms, he thinks, can we explain the fact that this dog and that dog are both white: Both partake of whiteness. Medieval philosophers called these items *universals*.

Quine proposes that we make use of the techniques of modern logic to clarify these matters. When we say that some dogs are white, we are actually saying that there is at least one thing that is both a dog and white: $(\exists x)$ (Dog x & White x). This sentence commits us to the existence of some x that is a dog, but it doesn't assert that there is yet another thing that exists, doghood, and still a third thing, whiteness. So we have a clear way of determining what ontology a certain sentence or theory assumes. "To be assumed as an entity is, purely and simply, to be reckoned as the value of a variable" (*OWTI*, 13). Note that the criterion Quine proposes does not tell us what there *is*, but only what a certain theory or point of view or sentence says that there is.

> We look to bound variables* in connection with ontology not in order to know what there is, but in order to know what a given remark or doctrine, ours or someone else's, *says* there is; and this much

is quite properly a problem involving language. But what there is is another question. (*OWTI*, 15, 16)

Our language does not determine what there is, but it does signal what we commit ourselves to in the way of entities. The question of whether to believe in the existence of these entities comes down to the question, Will postulating those entities make sense of our experience, simplify our story of the world, and increase predictive power? Judged that way, Quine thinks, it is right to be committed to the existence of dogs, but not to doghood—or to most other Platonic Forms or to the Homeric gods. But even so, in questions of ontology Quine counsels "tolerance and an experimental spirit" (*OWTI*, 19).

Note that the question about what there is and the question about what theory of the world we should adopt become one question on this view. What is there? Our best theory will tell us (fallibly and subject to correction, of course). And how do we find the best theory? By adopting roughly scientific methods—by testing refutable theories to see which ones survive. What this means is that science becomes the criterion of what there is, the arbiter of ontology.

NATURAL KNOWING

Suddenly that sounds revolutionary. Think back to the problem Descartes posed for himself and tried to solve in his *Meditations*. Descartes was a scientist of some distinction, but the question that worried him was this: Could all of my science be but a dream? Could it be an illusion foisted on me by a demon deceiver? How do I know that science portrays the world as it really is? In short, he felt himself faced with the formidable problem of the "external" world.

As we have seen, this problem is intimately tied to the *representational theory* of knowledge. According to this theory, we are directly acquainted only with the contents of our own minds—with patches of color in a visual field, noises in an auditory field, and so on. Do these correspond to anything external to the mind? That seems to be something that requires proof. You will recall that Descartes himself thought that our belief in an external world

---

*A bound variable is contrasted with a free variable. The formula "x is green" contains the free variable x. Such formulae have no truth value until we either specify a particular value for x (for instance, x = grass) or make it a general sentence about some or all things by attaching a "quantifier." In $(\exists x)$ (Green x) the variable x is said to be "bound" by the existential quantifier that means "There exists at least one x such that. . . ." This sentence says that some things are green; it does have a truth value and is, in fact, true.

could be justified only by proving the existence of an infinitely good God who would never deceive us about it.

For several hundred years this problem took center stage in epistemology. Berkeley thought it could be solved by denying the independent existence of a material world—turning ideas into things. Hume despaired of solving the problem and ended in skepticism. Kant divided the question, proposing that the objective world of our experience (the world of science) was a merely phenomenal world—a world relative to us—and that reality in itself was unknowable. Hegel thought the world was truly knowable only by the World Spirit, for whom the distinction between "external" and "internal" will disappear at the end of history, though humans were in the process of developing more and more of that comprehensive view of things.

The problem survives in the twentieth century in Bertrand Russell's attempt to define physical object concepts in terms of sense data (his logical atomism) and in **phenomenalism,** the "reductive" view that we earlier saw Quine criticizing. Even the early Quine is not entirely free of entanglement with the representational theory; his talk of physical objects as a *myth*, the aim of which is to simplify and orchestrate "the disordered fragments of raw experience," fits the pattern perfectly.

In a complete reversal, Wilfrid Sellars argues that it is the representational theory that depends on a myth: the **Myth of the Given.**[7] According to this myth, the quest to justify our knowledge comes to rest on data that are simply *given* to us, *presented* to us.* The classical empiricists believed that what is given are sensory states—impressions of blue, warm, hard, sweet, loud, and so on. These states were thought to be basic and unanalyzable, like Hume's simple impressions or the early Wittgenstein's simple objects. They were supposedly theory-neutral and could serve as a sure and certain **foundation** for knowledge.

Sellars argues to the contrary that what is and must be basic in our conceptual scheme are

objective claims like "This apple is red." It is in such terms that we learn the language. Children learn "This is a ball," "That is yellow," "Get the yellow ball"; they don't learn a private sense-datum language and then infer from that foundation to something about the external world. It is a myth, Sellars says, that we are first and foremost directly acquainted with our own subjective states. Beliefs and desires are focused from the start on the so-called external world. If anything is "posited," it is raw experiential feelings, not tables and chairs.

In fact, Sellars says, belief that there are such states can best be understood in analogy with the postulation of theoretical entities (such as atoms) in science. Jones sometimes says, for instance, "This thing looks red," when we can clearly see that it is not. We *explain* this utterance by positing a subjective state in Jones analogous to the state he is in when he is actually observing something red. When sense-datum theorists, phenomenalists, and empiricists assume that knowledge must begin with those private sensory states, they have it precisely backward.*

This strongly suggests that epistemology, as it has been pursued throughout most of the modern period, needs a drastic overhaul. The central problem since Descartes has been how to avoid skepticism about the "external" world. But now that problem looks artificial—one of those problems created by the way it is stated. If we begin with *human beings* (entities in thoroughgoing interaction with the world around them) rather than with *minds*, epistemology will look very different. And, indeed, that is what both Sellars and Quine claim. As Quine understands the epistemological problem, it concerns "the relation between the meager

---

*Compare Derrida's critique of the notion of presence, pp. 699–701, and Heidegger on Being-in-the-world, pp. 657–662.

---

*It may seem that Sellars' talk of positing sensory states on the basis of Jones' behavior is in direct conflict with Quine's claim that what we posit are objective entities. But not so, for two reasons: (1) to talk as Quine does of stimulation of the sense organs is already to be talking objectively of the world, and (2) although sensory states may be *causally* prior to our knowledge of the world, they are not *epistemologically* prior; that is, we do not build up our knowledge of the world on the basis of subjective foundations. Remember that the content of an observation sentence is not about subjective experience.

input and the torrential output" (*EN*, 24). That is, how does it happen that we humans produce utterances that are about the world, not about "fragments of raw experience" or surface stimulations of sense organs? What accounts for the fact that we construct both common sense and incredibly complex scientific theories, given the paucity of our evidence?

> The old epistemology aspired to contain, in a sense, natural science; it would construct it somehow from sense data. Epistemology in its new setting, conversely, is contained in natural science, as a chapter of psychology. We are studying how the human subject of our study posits bodies and projects his physics from his data, and we appreciate that our position in the world is just like his.
>
> Epistemology, or something like it, simply falls into place as a chapter of psychology and hence of natural science. It studies a natural phenomenon, viz., a physical human subject. (*EN*, 24)

Here is the situation as Quine sees it in this newly **naturalized epistemology.*** We observe Sally looking at a tree. We are cognizant (let us suppose) of the ways in which the rods and cones in her eyes are stimulated by the light reflected from the tree. We hear Sally say, "There's a tree." In normal circumstances we would say that Sally knows there is a tree before her. What we want to understand is how the stimulation of her eyes produces the knowledge expressed in Sally's utterance. Let's further suppose that psychology (perhaps combined with physiology and linguistics) can trace the processes in Sally that yield the utterance. This would give us the understanding we are seeking.

We then apply the same understanding to ourselves. If that's how Sally attains knowledge of the world around her, then that's how we do it, too. In fact, we can now say that our own perception of Sally, of the tree, and of the way Sally comes to know of the tree is *itself* a product of the very same

kind of process we detected in Sally. And the epistemological question turns out to be scientifically solvable.

Note that this way of thinking about epistemology begins with observation of the world—of Sally and the tree. We could call it **"third-person epistemology,"** or an "epistemology of the other." Only when the problem is (scientifically) solved with respect to humans or other animals generally is the solution deemed to apply also to me. We, too, after all, are human animals. Here we have a dramatic contrast with the way traditional epistemology—with its problem of the "external" world—has been conceived. Traditionally, epistemology has been thought to be a "first-person" problem.* How do I know that there is a tree before me, that I'm not deceived or dreaming? How do I know I can *trust* the processes (whatever they are) that lead me to say, "There's a tree" or "There's Sally"? How do I know that even the best psychology isn't simply an illusion? The basic problem, from this point of view, is not a factual question at all, but a normative one: Am I *justified* in believing there are things independent of my experience? Do I have a *right* to believe that?

From this point of view, there is an obvious objection to Quine's program.† Quine is simply begging the question, *assuming* we know that Sally sees the tree, when what is at issue is whether any one of us knows anything at all. The third-person and the first-person cases are not parallel. In the Sally case we can see both Sally and the tree—or at least we think we can. But in your own case what you have are simply your experiences (or stimulations), and you can't *compare* these items with an actually existing tree.‡ That your situation is just like

---

*We already used the phrase "naturalized epistemology" to describe John Dewey's theory of knowledge. A look back to this section (pp. 608–610) would provide a richer understanding of the viewpoint and indicate the ways in which Quine adapts pragmatic themes.

---

*Remember Descartes sitting before the fire, wondering whether it is *true* that he holds a piece of paper in his hand, as he surely seems to.

†By Barry Stroud, for instance. See "The Significance of Naturalized Epistemology," in Kornblith, *Naturalizing Epistemology*.

‡Here the pattern of the representational theory repeats itself. Notice that Quine does not want to get rid of representations altogether, but to naturalize them. The aim is to account for representations in terms that do not put them outside the natural world.

Sally's is not something to be taken for granted; whether that is so or not is precisely the problem. The problem is not the scientific one of discovering the causal processes that lead me to my belief, but the problem of whether you are justified in trusting either your perceptions or your science—just as Descartes says.

What can a naturalized epistemologist say to this? One thing that Quine says is that this epistemological anxiety is merely a symptom of the quest for certainty, and like Peirce and Dewey, he thinks we have to give that up.* This old problem of the "external" world, trying to guarantee that our knowledge isn't deceptive, should simply be dismissed. Perhaps it will always be possible to pull back from our natural commitments and raise the skeptical worry, but we ought to go with the best knowledge we have, fallible though it may be; and our best knowledge is found in the sciences. Philosophy has no privileged place from which to judge the whole of that.

There is a second reply that can be made. The story that science tells of our history is an evolutionary one—a story of the environment selecting organisms (and hence species) that survive long enough to reproduce. Consider a deer calmly drinking from a water hole. A mountain lion approaches. Suddenly the deer tenses, raises its head, and in full alertness mode looks to the left. There must be something right about this reaction. It is not much of a stretch to say that there is something *true* in it. The deer's reaction *means* "Danger near—get ready to flee!" And what it means is correct.

No doubt this sort of reaction is built into a deer's central nervous system. But suppose it weren't. Suppose a deer's input–output circuits were insensitive to the scent of a mountain lion. Deer reactions in the presence of a lion would then signify "All is well, continue feeding," deer would be easy prey, few would survive to reproduce their kind, and deer as a species would soon disappear. It is not much of a stretch to say that such a reaction would be in error; given a deer's innate goal of preserving its life, there would be something *false*

about it. As John Dewey might say, such a reaction "will *not do*."

This suggests that a member of a species that has survived the winnowing process of evolutionary selection is *guaranteed* a certain fit with its environment. Its reactions to items that are crucial for its continued existence must be at least roughly right. Since we ourselves are such creatures, we can have some confidence that in basic matters that concern survival our expectations, our anticipations, and indeed our beliefs track the truth. Were such a capacity for truth not built into us by our genes, our ancestors would have perished long ago. As Daniel Dennett says, "Evolution has designed human beings to be rational, to believe what they ought to believe and want what they ought to want. . . . The capacity to believe would have no survival value unless it were a capacity to believe truths" (*TB*, 33; *IS*, 17).[8] On basic matters, then, such as whether another person is nearby, we have a *right* to trust our senses. Evolutionary considerations provide a *justification* of such beliefs.

It is true that there is something circular about this justification. We begin by assuming we can know the relation between the deer and the mountain lion; we construct a theory explaining how the deer comes to know about the lion; and we then apply this theory to ourselves and think we are justified in claiming to know about the deer and the mountain lion—just what we were assuming at the start. But once we give up thinking that philosophy has some special insight, some argument that is in principle beyond the sciences, once we give up the quest for certainty and resolve to make do with what looks like our best knowledge, this circle may not seem so forbidding. Perhaps it is only a matter of making the circle as comprehensive as possible—and resigning ourselves to fallibility as the human predicament.*

In helping itself to great gobs of the so-called external world in framing its explanations, **evolutionary epistemology** does not, and probably cannot, defeat traditional skepticism. Depending on your point of view, that may or may

---

*For Peirce, see p. 601; for Dewey, see p. 609.

*There is a similarity at this point between naturalized epistemology and the *hermeneutic circle*. Compare Heidegger on understanding, pp. 668–669.

not be a problem for it. There are, however, several more specific problems that such an evolutionary epistemology faces. Let us briefly state three objections and see what might be said in reply.

First objection: It is unclear how far beyond basic needs relating directly to survival such truth-tracking extends; perhaps not very far. Some evolutionary epistemologists, however, suggest that there is an analogy between (a) an organism displaying a novel behavior in an unfamiliar situation and (b) a scientist hypothesizing a cause for a puzzling occurrence. Both involve "guesses." Both are cases of trial and error. In the first case nature decides whether the organism's guess ("I can jump that chasm") is correct; if incorrect, it may be the end of the organism. In the second case, the scientist puts nature to the test to see, via observations of experimental results, whether her hypothesis ("Introducing gene X into corn DNA will make it resistant to rot") deserves to survive. Popper cleverly says that we humans have an advantage over simpler organisms because we can "make our theories, our conjectures, suffer in our stead in the struggle for the survival of the fittest."[9] Surviving species and unfalsified theories have something in common: Both have passed stringent tests of adequacy.

Second objection: False beliefs can also have survival value—as when you avoid contact with plague victims because you think they are possessed by demons. The evolutionary epistemologist must admit this. But the cure for such false beliefs is more and better science, more ingenious experimentation to cull out the falsehoods. There will never be a guarantee that the hypotheses that survive are the true ones, but in eliminating one possible account after another, we can have some confidence that we are circling around and in toward the truth of the matter.

Third objection: There is evidence that we humans naturally make use of "inference rules" or heuristics that lead us astray.* Assuming that these

tendencies to make mistakes have also been developed by evolutionary pressures, how can evolution be used to argue that as a rule we believe truly? In reply it must be admitted that humans are prone to make certain kinds of errors based on data available to them. But this admission shows that we have also developed to the point where we can identify these misleading shortcuts and temptations to find the nonobvious obvious. Knowing this, we can take precautions against being led down the garden path. Although there can be no certainty that we have identified all the possible slips and slides away from rationality, it is hard to see this as an objection to a naturalized, evolutionary theory of knowledge.

Physical realism, as we are understanding that term, does not necessitate naturalized epistemology, but they are harmonious, and each reinforces the other.

---

1. In what two ways does Quine believe that traditional empiricism has been dogmatic?
2. Explain why Quine thinks that our statements face the tribunal of experience "only as a corporate body."
3. What can we learn from an experiment that fails to produce a predicted observation?
4. How does Quine think of the distinction between science and metaphysics? Between science and common sense?
5. Explain "the maxim of minimum mutilation."
6. What is an *observation sentence*, and what role does such a sentence play for Quine?
7. What is an *ontology*? How do we determine what ontology we are committed to in accepting a certain belief or theory?
8. Contrast first-person epistemology with third-person epistemology.
9. How might evolutionary considerations provide a (partial) justification for our claims to know the world?
10. List three objections to the use of evolutionary considerations to justify our knowledge. List three replies.

---

*For a fascinating catalogue of such misleading procedures, see Richard Nisbett and Lee Ross, "Judgmental Heuristics and Knowledge Structures," in Nisbett and Ross, *Human Inference: Strategies and Shortcomings of Social Judgment* (Englewood Cliffs, NJ: Prentice Hall, 1983), reprinted in Kornblith, *Naturalizing Epistemology*.

The Matter of Minds

It is obvious that a physical realist will need a theory of the mind. It is no less obvious that constructing such a theory will pose problems for the physical realist. He will have to give an account of mind that is consistent with science; and science seems to tell us that our minds are the wholly natural, evolutionary products of a world that is fundamentally material in character. There have been materialists in our tradition—Democritus, Epicurus, Hobbes, and Marx come to mind—but they have been a minority and their theories of the mind have not been very persuasive. The majority view, expressing what is sometimes called the "perennial philosophy," has been that mind cannot be reduced to matter but has some sort of independent status, perhaps in an immaterial soul (as in Plato, Aquinas, and Descartes), as a transcendental ego surpassing the categories of soul and body altogether (as in Kant), or as spirit (Hegel).

INTENTIONALITY

This problem for physical realists acquired a particularly sharp set of teeth in the late nineteenth century with the work of Franz Brentano (1838–1917), a German psychologist and philosopher. Brentano identifies the essential feature of mental phenomena as their **Intentionality.*** Each mental act, he says, is Intentional, by which he means that it is *about* something, directed on some object. You can't think without thinking *of* something, you can't hope without hoping *for* something, you can't fear without being afraid *of* something, you can't dream without dreaming *about* something, you can't remember without remembering something, and so on. There is always this "intended object" that is the focus of your mental acts. Mental acts are relational—as though there is something independent of themselves that they are aiming at.

The relation is a peculiar one, however, quite different from the relations that hold between physical objects and events. Consider the following

facts. If *a* is next to *b*, it must be the case that both *a* and *b* exist. Nor could event e_1 occur before event e_2, unless both events existed. Moreover, if e_1 causes e_2, then again both must be real events. Here we have examples of relations that are spatial, temporal, and causal—arguably the fundamental characteristics of the physical world—and in each case the relation cannot hold unless both terms of the relation are existent.

But you can think about Santa Claus, dream of flying, and want a time travel machine. In each of these cases the relation holds, although one of the terms doesn't exist. There is no Santa Claus, you can't fly, and time travel machines are mere fictions. Mental acts may be directed on existing things; but they don't cease to be the acts they are, directed to the objects they are directed on, just because those "objects" aren't there. This is very strange. It is so strange that it led Brentano to believe that mental phenomena were totally different in kind from physical phenomena. It looks like mental phenomena, having the property of Intentionality, are not identical to physical phenomena that lack that property. Apparently, the mental cannot be reduced to the physical. And if that is so, then—apparently—physical realism is false. That's the problem.

Philosophers of mind in the second half of the twentieth century wrestle with this problem, many of them trying to reconcile the Brentano thesis with physicalism. Thinking about the problem has been given a boost by the advent of the computer, as well as by advances in neuroscience. These developments pose anew the old question: Can a machine think? How could a physical thing exhibit that sort of property? How could it be *about* something?

The many dimensions of this problem have led to the creation of an interdisciplinary research program known as **cognitive science.** Philosophers, linguists, psychologists, computer scientists (especially those in artificial intelligence research), and neuroscientists meet together regularly, read each other's papers, and work cooperatively, sharing results and criticisms in an attempt to solve the mysteries of the mind. This is an extremely vigorous and ongoing conversation and no brief treatment can pretend to do it justice. What we shall do here

---

*Note that this is a technical term (deriving from medieval philosophy) and is to be distinguished from "intention" in the normal sense of the word. The latter refers to an antecedent of actions that are done for a purpose, actions that are (for that reason) intentional. Intentionality, in Brentano's sense, applies to every mental act, not only to intentional actions in the usual sense of the word. When the technical term is at stake, we will capitalize the word.

is just dip a toe into the waters at the philosophical end of this large pond, looking at two problems that some philosophers—but not others—believe are quite distinct: Intentionality and consciousness.

Intentional Systems: Daniel Dennett

Daniel Dennett's most famous concept is that of an Intentional System (*IS*, 3–22). Dennett (b. 1962) suggests that we think about a chess-playing computer. We can understand such a machine, he says, in three fundamentally different ways. Suppose we are observing it in the middle of a game and we want to predict its next move. We can take up a *design stance* and make the prediction on the basis of its program, relying on how it is designed to operate. If we know how it is programmed, we can predict the next move on the basis of that program and the current state of play. This sort of prediction will work as long as the machine does not malfunction, in which case all bets from the design stance are off.

But even a malfunctioning computer's next move can be predicted if we adopt the *physical stance*. From this point of view we look at the actual physical constitution of the computer, the physical states the computer is in, and the causal transitions from state to state. On this basis, prediction of one state from another is possible in principle, but given the complexity of computers these days no one can make such predictions in an ongoing game.

Suppose, now, that our chess-playing computer has a program that modifies itself in the light of its wins and losses—that is, it improves with "experience"—and that we have sent it abroad for a series of games with Russian chess masters. When it comes back, no one—not even its original designers—will know its program, so prediction from the design stance will be impossible. Prediction from the physical stance remains impracticable. Is there any way, then, that we can predict its behavior? Yes. We can adopt the **Intentional Stance** with respect to it.

We do this when we look at the computer as a *rational* system designed to realize certain *goals*. We are then apt to say things like this: "It wants to

protect its king," and "It believes that attacking with the knight is the best way to do that." Now "wants" and "believes" are Intentional notions, of course, so in effect we are ascribing mental states to the machine. Predictions from this stance are somewhat chancy, but there isn't any better strategy available for playing such a machine. We play the computer as we would play another human being, expecting it to rationally choose the most effective move from those available in the current situation. Doing this is treating it as an **Intentional System.**

So does a computer have a mind? It is very natural at this point to resist, to say that these mental ascriptions are only a manner of speaking, that the computer doesn't *really* want things and believe things—not the way *we* do. It's only *useful* to speak *as if* it did. We can't take that *literally*. Surely there is nothing *in* the computer that would count as an actual desire or belief. But that reaction, of course, puts us face to face with the question: What is there in *us* that counts as one of these mental states? Supposing that we are physical systems "designed" by the evolutionary process—that our brain and central nervous system work on purely natural principles—how do we differ in this respect from the programmed chess-player? How can *we* be Intentional Systems? Yet we do have minds, don't we?*

Wilfrid Sellars calls this a clash between the "scientific" image of ourselves and the "manifest" image of ourselves. Can this conflict be resolved? A physical realist is likely to think that the key to reconciliation is the notion of **function.** The function of a thing is what it is for; the function of the heart, for instance, is to pump blood through the body. But notice that "function" is a *formal* notion, one that does not specify in detail what sort of item is suited to perform that function. Consider the idea of a fuel-delivery system for an internal combustion engine. These days most car engines are equipped with fuel injection, yet not so long ago carburetors were the norm. Carburetors and

---

*This seems a perfect example of what Wittgenstein calls the "form" of a philosophical problem: "I don't know my way about." "*This* isn't how it is!"—we say, "Yet *this* is how it has to *be*!" (See p. 639.)

fuel-injection systems are constructed along very different lines, but they perform the same function of delivering a mix of air and fuel to the engine.

Could *belief* be a functional concept like this? That is what the physical realist claims. Ascribing a belief to a system—whether machine or human—is not attributing to the system something that is intrinsically mental, as opposed to physical; it is claiming that something in the system plays a certain *role*, performs a certain function. Exactly what that is remains unspecified from the Intentional point of view, just as one doesn't specify carburetors or fuel injection when talking about a fuel-delivery system. It could be, then, that believing, desiring, hoping, fearing, and even thinking itself—for all these concepts tell us—are just processes going on in the brain, processes that are wholly physical in nature.

Understood in this way, the lesson we should draw from Brentano's Intentionality thesis is that the mental cannot be *reduced* to the physical—just as Quine argued that talk of physical objects cannot be *defined* in terms of sense data—but that does not mean that mental talk brings with it an ontology of its own incompatible with the ontology of the physical sciences. Adopting the Intentional Stance is a matter of understanding and explaining the behavior of a system by attributing to it internal states that are functional in nature.

On this view, for a system to believe that it is raining is for it to be in a state that is connected in various functional ways to its input and output, as well as to other functionally defined internal states. For instance, when Jones *believes* it is raining, Jones *expects to see* the streets wet, she is *inclined to reach* for the umbrella before going out, and she may *think* that she doesn't have to water the grass tonight.* Such an internal state, having multiple connections to other states— perceptual, behavioral, and mental—may well be a state of the central nervous system in a highly developed organism such as we are. Having such a state resident in one's brain just *is* to believe that it is raining.

Intentional ascriptions, then, constitute an overlay, an interpretation in mentalistic terms of a system that may well be physical in nature. Many questions arise at this point and debate has been vigorous about how they should be answered. For example, how far down the evolutionary scale does it make sense to ascribe Intentionality? Do ants have beliefs? Do clams? Or how about a simple mechanism like a thermostat? Does the thermostat *want* to keep the temperature at a certain level? Does it now *believe* that the room is too cool and in light of that *choose* to turn on the furnace? It certainly seems like we could adopt the Intentional Stance with regard to it, ascribe these properties to it, and explain its behavior in these terms. But, we are inclined to say, it doesn't *really* have beliefs and desires—not like we do.

If we do say that, however, it seems we should specify just what is so different about us and where the line should be drawn between those systems

"I propose to see . . . what the mind looks like from the third-person, materialistic perspective of contemporary science."

—DANIEL DENNETT

---

*This view of belief has obvious affinities with that of Peirce. See pp. 596–597.

that are truly Intentional and those that are not. For his part, Dennett refuses to draw such a line.

> There is no magic moment in the transition from a simple thermostat to a system that *really* has an internal representation of the world about it. The thermostat has a minimally demanding representation of the world, fancier thermostats have more demanding representations of the world, fancier robots for helping around the house would have still more demanding representations of the world. Finally you reach us. . . .
>
> The differences are of degree, but nevertheless of such great degree that understanding the internal organization of a simple intentional system gives one very little basis for understanding the internal organization of a complex intentional system, such as a human being. (*TB*, 32, 33)

Dennett is content to let Intentional interpretation range far and wide and simply says that it is less *useful* to apply it to clams and thermostats than to humans and chess-playing computers. The former can be understood from the design and physical standpoints well enough. It is the complexity of the latter that makes it virtually impossible to understand, explain, and predict their behavior *except* from the Intentional point of view.

But this appeal to usefulness raises another question: Is Intentional ascription *merely* a pragmatic device having no more than an instrumental use? Does it have no ontological implications whatsoever?* Although he confesses that he has written some things that suggest this, Dennett claims to be a kind of realist about belief and the other Intentional attitudes. Belief ascriptions, he says, trace out *real patterns* in the world—even though those patterns won't be visible unless we use Intentional interpretation.† Dennett imagines

some Martians who are superphysicists, so super that it is no trick for them to predict human behavior from the physical stance. But suppose

> that one of the Martians were to engage in a predicting contest with an Earthling. The Earthling and the Martian observe (and observe each other observing) a particular bit of local physical transaction. From the Earthling's point of view, this is what is observed. The telephone rings in Mrs. Gardner's kitchen. She answers, and this is what she says: "Oh, hello dear. You're coming home early? Within the hour? And bringing the boss to dinner? Pick up a bottle of wine on the way home, then, and drive carefully." On the basis of this observation, our Earthling predicts that a large metallic vehicle with rubber tires will come to a stop in the drive within the hour, disgorging two human beings, one of whom will be holding a paper bag containing a bottle containing an alcoholic fluid. The prediction is a bit risky, perhaps, but a good bet on all counts. The Martian makes the same prediction, but has to avail himself of much more information about an extraordinary number of interactions of which, so far as he can tell, the Earthling is entirely ignorant. For instance, the deceleration of the vehicle at intersection A, five miles from the house, without which there would have been a collision with another vehicle—whose collision course had been laboriously calculated over some hundreds of meters by the Martian. The Earthling's performance would look like magic! How did the Earthling know that the human being who got out of the car and got the bottle in the shop would get back in? (*TB*, 26, 27)

The Earthling's knowledge is not magic, of course. But it depends absolutely on his making use of Intentional Stance concepts to interpret what is going on. Our lives are bound up in these Intentional patterns; we not only rely on them in anticipating the actions of others, but also find them indispensable in understanding ourselves as both knowers and doers. "Knowing" is an Intentional notion, of course (as is "understanding"), and if we regard ourselves as knowing anything we are viewing ourselves from the Intentional Stance. "Choosing to do *A*" is likewise Intentional; it involves knowing what you are aiming at, believing that doing *A* will achieve that aim, and (in the appropriate circumstances) trying to do *A*. Although for limited purposes (medical

---

*Paul Churchland argues that so-called "folk psychology"—the way we naturally understand ourselves and others in Intentional terms—could be eliminated altogether in favor of neuroscience. Strictly speaking, he thinks, there are no such things as beliefs. See "Eliminative Materialism and the Propositional Attitudes," *Journal of Philosophy* 78, no. 2 (February 1981).

†Dennett compares the concept of belief to that of a center of gravity. Although it isn't an item installed at the factory or requiring periodic service, a car's center of gravity is real enough, as is proved when it rolls over in a sharp curve.

purposes, perhaps) you can regard yourself purely as a physical mechanism, you cannot restrict yourself to the physical stance when you act.* It is Intentionality that makes our lives *human*.

Granting that Intentionality is a level of interpretation beyond that of the design and physical stances, granting that it is useful—even indispensable for our form of life—and granting that it cannot be reduced to the physical, the question remains: Why does Intentional ascription work? That is, what is actually going on in complex Intentional Systems such as ourselves that allows such interpretation to succeed in providing explanations and predictions?

Here a number of options are being actively pursued. Taking a cue from logic, linguistics, and computer science, some think that there must be analogues in the brain to the parts of a sentence—a kind of **language of thought**.† One of the striking characteristics of thought and belief, after all, is that they can be expressed in language, and language has a grammatical and logical structure. So one can argue that distinctions between verbs and noun phrases, logical connectives, quantifiers, and grammatical transition rules must all be represented in the functioning brain if mental states are to be physically real and effective in controlling behavior. On this model, the brain is thought of as a kind of syntactic engine, a computational device operating on language-like items that in themselves are purely physical but that play functional roles that guarantee their meaningfulness.

Other philosophers find more promise in a different form of computation called *parallel distributed processing* or **connectionism**.‡ So-called

neural nets do not operate in a linear fashion on well-defined atomistic units according to explicit rules, but can accept large amounts of data simultaneously and process it holistically. Models of the mind based on these principles are efficient in doing things that brains are very good at, such as recognizing patterns—faces, for instance. Moreover, they have other nice features: They tolerate ambiguity well, they pick up on analogies, they can complete incomplete data sets, and they degrade slowly rather than crash all at once when some component fails. Connectionism shows much promise, but whether it will be superseded by yet another model remains to be seen.

---

1. What property of mental acts does the term "Intentionality" refer to?
2. Why is Intentionality a problem for a physicalist account of mind?
3. Explain the notion of an Intentional System by contrasting Dennett's three stances: design, physical, and Intentional.
4. How does the notion of *function* help to reconcile Intentionality with the physical basis of mind?
5. If Intentionality cannot be "reduced" to the physical, does it follow that minds are something other than matter? Why or why not?
6. What does Dennett say about the question, Does a thermostat have a mind?
7. Is ascribing Intentional properties to things merely a matter of a useful strategy? Or do mental concepts like *belief* pick out something real?
8. Contrast the "language of thought" hypothesis with the "connectionist" hypothesis.

THE CHINESE ROOM: JOHN SEARLE

You may be acquainted with Siri, the Apple program that answers questions and obeys your commands. On the Apple website, we read, "It understands what you say. And knows what you mean." Is this true? Understanding and knowing are, of course, Intentional notions, and we have seen that Intentionality is one of the marks of the mental. Does Siri have a mind?

Apple's claim is an expression of what is called "strong AI." This strong version of artificial intelligence holds that the brain is just a flesh-and-blood

---

*Questions about the freedom of the will are relevant here. In *Elbow Room: The Varieties of Free Will Worth Wanting* (Oxford: Oxford University Press, 1984), Dennett makes use of the Intentional Stance to develop a quasi-Kantian, compatibilist view of human freedom, identifying increasing freedom with increasing rationality.

†Jerry Fodor has defended this option vigorously. See, for instance, *The Language of Thought* (New York: Thomas Y. Crowell, 1975) and "Propositional Attitudes," *Monist* 61, no. 4 (October 1978): 501–523.

‡One of the most engaging treatments of the mind using these principles is Paul Churchland's book, *The Engine of Reason, the Seat of the Soul* (Cambridge, MA: MIT Press, 1995).

computer, and a mind is no more than its program. There is nothing special about a brain; it's just a programmed meat machine. Given the right program, any physical device could be given a mind, complete with beliefs, wants, understanding, and perhaps even consciousness.

The most famous objection to strong AI was formulated by John Searle (b. 1932) in a thought experiment known as the **Chinese room.**[10] Suppose that we have a kind of super-Siri, a few generations on from the present-day Siri, but designed in Chinese. If you ask it a question in Chinese, it will search its database and produce an answer in Chinese. Imagine, furthermore, that its answers are indistinguishable from the answers that a native Chinese speaker would give. Question: Does it understand Chinese?*

Well, suppose that you, understanding no Chinese at all, were locked in a room containing baskets of Chinese symbols and a rulebook in English for manipulating these symbols.

> So the rule might say: "Take a squiggle-squiggle sign out of basket number one and put it next to a squoggle-squoggle sign from basket number two." Now suppose that some other Chinese symbols are passed into the room, and that you are given further rules for passing back Chinese symbols out of the room. Suppose that unknown to you the symbols passed into the room are called "questions" by the people outside the room, and the symbols you pass back out of the room are called "answers to the questions." Suppose, furthermore, that the programmers are so good at designing the programs and that you are so good at manipulating the symbols, that very soon your answers are indistinguishable from those of a native Chinese speaker. (*MBS*, 32)

The question now is: Do you understand Chinese? Of course not. "But if going through the appropriate computer program for understanding Chinese is not enough to give *you* an understanding of Chinese, then it is not enough to give *any other digital*

computer an understanding of Chinese" (*MBS*, 33). And it seems to follow that Siri does *not* understand what you say and does *not* know what you mean. Siri is as empty of real understanding as you are in the Chinese room. Siri does not have a mind.

The literature discussing the Chinese room is extensive, and not everyone is convinced. Searle's own view is that while minds can be simulated on a computer, a computer program cannot *be* a mind any more than a computer simulation of a hurricane can *be* a hurricane. Minds, with their Intentionality and consciousness, are biological phenomena and are caused by brains. Could a machine think? Well, replies Searle, in one sense of "machine," obviously yes. If a machine is simply a physical system capable of performing certain operations, then the brain is a machine; we have brains; we can think; so a machine can think. But strong AI claims that merely having a computer program of the right sort is sufficient to have a mind. And that's wrong. If Searle is right about this (and this is contentious), then only a machine with the causal properties of a living brain, whatever those are, could produce a mind.

1. Describe the Chinese room.
2. What does Searle think that his thought experiment proves?
3. Does Siri have a mind?

CONSCIOUSNESS: NAGEL, JACKSON, CHALMERS

When you are awake, you are conscious, and so are other people. And so, we usually assume, is your dog. Descartes thought that nonhuman animals, having no soul, were mere automatons, but that is hard to believe. Consciousness certainly seems to be widespread in the animal world, but what, exactly, is it? In a now-classic article, **"What is it like to be a bat?"** Thomas Nagel says, "the fact that an organism has conscious experience *at all* means, basically, that there is something it is like to *be* that organism . . . something it is like *for* the organism" (*WLB*, 166).[11]

This subjective, first-person character of experience seems to escape the grasp of a third-person

*This is a version of the famous Turing Test. In 1950, Alan Turing addressed the question, "Can Machines Think?" by devising a test involving a machine answering questions put to it. If the answers couldn't be distinguished from those given by a human being, he suggested that we would have to say yes.

point of view. The functional analysis of mental concepts we have just been examining, of course, is just such a third-person view. Understood in this functionalist way, thought and belief, desire and hope, could be completely empty of experience, go on in the dark, as it were, quite unconscious. Or so it seems. And yet there is something that it *feels like* to be thirsty, to love someone, to be jealous, or to remember last summer at the beach. This is a fact, but it seems to be a most peculiar fact. To bring out its strange character, Nagel suggests we think about bats. Bats are mammals, and there is no more reason to doubt that they have experience than to doubt that your dog does. But their experience must be very different from our own.

> Now we know that most bats . . . perceive the external world primarily by sonar, or echoloca-tion, detecting the reflections, from objects within range, of their own rapid, subtly modulated, high-frequency shrieks. Their brains are designed to cor-relate the outgoing impulses with the subsequent echoes, and the information thus acquired enables bats to make precise discriminations of distance, size, shape, motion, and texture comparable to those we make by vision. But bat sonar, though clearly a form of perception, is not similar in its op-eration to any sense that we possess, and there is no reason to suppose that it is subjectively like anything we can experience or imagine. (*WLB*, 168)

When we imagine something we have not our-selves experienced, we rely on experiences we have actually had. We often say, "I know how you feel." But we can do so only if we have experienced something similar. But here is something so radi-cally different that it seems impossible to imagine or conceive what it must be like to *be* a bat. What is the bat's world like—*for the bat*? There must be facts about the inner life of bats, facts about what it is like, subjectively, to experience the world that way. But Nagel suggests that these facts may be "beyond our ability to conceive." There may be facts "beyond the reach of human concepts, . . . facts which *could* not ever be represented or compre-hended by human beings, . . . facts that do not consist in the truth of propositions expressible in a human language" (*WLB*, 170, 171). We seem to be in the strange position of knowing *that* there are

certain facts about reality, but we can't know *what* those facts are.

Reflecting on the experience of bats dramatizes the contrast between objective and subjective. We know a lot about bat behavior, bat brains, and how echolocation works. But all this scientific, third-person knowledge seems to leave something out— *what it is like for the bat*. And there does not seem to be any way, by pursuing more science, to fill it in. But now we can see that the situation is exactly the same with me. There is something it is like to be *me*, something subjectively experienced, felt, known "from the inside," so to speak. And third-person objective science can't get a hold on that either. Consciousness seems to be not a puzzle, but a mystery.

There are other ways to illustrate the subjective character of experience and its opaqueness from the objective point of view. Frank Jackson asks us to consider the (imaginary) case of Mary.

> Mary is a brilliant scientist who is, for whatever reason, forced to investigate the world from a black and white room *via* a black and white television monitor. She specialises in the neurophysiology of vision and acquires, let us suppose, all the physi-cal information there is to obtain about what goes on when we see ripe tomatoes, or the sky, and use terms like "red," "blue," and so on. She discovers, for example, just which wave-length combinations from the sky stimulate the retina, and exactly how this produces *via* the central nervous system the contraction of the vocal chords and expulsion of air from the lungs that results in the uttering of the sentence "The sky is blue."
>
> What will happen when Mary is released from her black and white room or is given a colour tele-vision monitor? Will she *learn* anything or not? It seems just obvious that she will learn something about the world and our visual experience of it. But then it is inescapable that her previous knowledge was incomplete. But she had *all* the physical infor-mation. Ergo there is more to have than that, and Physicalism is false. (*EQ*, 275)[12]

Suppose that on leaving her black-and-white room, Mary sees a ripe tomato. For the first time its redness will be apparent to her. She knew all about seeing red from a third-person point of view, but now she sees it from her own point of view. What, then, will Mary learn? She will learn *what it is like* to see red—something that all her science couldn't tell her. She won't just *know about* seeing red, she will *experience* seeing red. And that's different.

This is known as the **knowledge argument,** and it is an argument for **qualia** and against physicalism. A quale is an immediately experienced quality—the blue that is present to you when you look up at a clear sky, for instance, or the unmistakable smell of bacon frying. We have met qualia before in the impressions of Hume, in Hegel's immediacy, and in the "mere subjective feelings" of Peirce. They are sometimes called "raw feels," meaning that qualia aren't contaminated by any concepts or interpretations.

Physicalism can be understood as the claim that whatever exists is physical in nature and could be understood in a completed physical science. It is roughly equivalent to what has traditionally been known as materialism. Functionalism in the philosophy of mind is usually taken to be a case of physicalism. What Jackson's argument seems to yield is the conclusion that there is more to reality than either physical science or a functional analysis of mental states can tell us. If Mary, who knows all the physical facts about vision, says, "Wow! I had no idea red looked like *that*," there must be facts about reality that are not physical facts, and, as he says, physicalism must be false.

"It seems to me that we are surer of the existence of conscious experience than we are of anything else in the world."

—David Chalmers

Before we turn to what a physicalist might say, let's look at one more challenge from "the friends of qualia." The Australian philosopher David Chalmers (b. 1966) is known for distinguishing the "hard problem" in philosophy of mind from the "easy problems." By easy problems he means those that can be analyzed in roughly functionalist terms. These problems may be hard enough, in a way, but we know roughly how to solve them and have made substantial progress in their solution. How does the brain process information? How does what the eye sees get registered in the visual centers of the brain? Why does a pinprick on the arm produce the "ouch" response? We know a lot about all this and can learn more. We have seen how Dennett's Intentional Stance accounts for understanding intelligent behavior and have suggested that connectionist programs might give us a handle on how the internal processing might go. But what about consciousness itself? Why does the physical brain give rise to those subjectively experienced smells, colors, and pains? There is clearly an intimate relation between experience and the brain, but there seems to be an *explanatory gap*. Nothing in neuroscience seems to give the slightest clue as to why a brain state should give rise to qualia, to what it is like to be me. That's **the hard problem:** consciousness. Chalmers wants to take consciousness seriously.

> I have assumed that consciousness exists, and that to redefine the problem as that of explaining how certain cognitive or behavioral functions are performed is unacceptable. . . . Some say that consciousness is an "illusion," but I have little idea what this could even mean. It seems to me that we are surer of the existence of conscious experience than we are of anything else in the world. . . . This might be seen as a Great Divide in the study of consciousness. If you hold that an answer to the "easy" problems explains everything that needs to be explained, then you get one sort of theory; if you hold that there is a further "hard" problem, then you get another. (*CM*, xii, xiii)[13]

Chalmers wants a theory of consciousness, and he emphasizes that such a theory would not overturn our scientific picture of the world, but broaden it. He adds that he has no "strong spiritual or religious inclinations." "Materialism," he says, "is a beautiful and compelling view of the world, but to account for consciousness, we have to go beyond the resources it provides" (*CM*, xiv).

> Physical explanation is well suited to the explanation of *structure* and *function*. . . . But the explanation of consciousness is not just a matter of explaining structure and function. Once we have explained all the physical structure in the vicinity of the brain, and we have explained how all the various brain functions are performed, there is a further sort of explanandum: consciousness itself. Why should all this structure and function give rise to experience? The story about the physical process does not say. (*CM*, 107)

Chalmers has a number of arguments and thought experiments to support this conclusion. We'll look at just one: the case of the **zombies.** Chalmers isn't thinking about Hollywood zombies, the "undead." These are usually deformed human beings with significant impairments. Quite to the contrary, Chalmers is imagining an exact physical duplicate of, say, himself.

> So let us consider my zombie twin. This creature is molecule for molecule identical to me, and identical in all the low-level properties postulated by a completed physics, but he lacks conscious experience entirely. . . . He will certainly be identical to me *functionally*; he will be processing the same sort of information, reacting in a similar way to inputs, with his internal configurations being modified appropriately and with indistinguishable behavior resulting. . . . It is just that none of this functioning will be accompanied by any real conscious experience. There will be no phenomenal feel. There is nothing it is like to be a zombie. (*CM*, 94, 95)

There is no reason to believe that zombies actually exist in our world. But the question is whether zombies in this sense are conceivable, possible. Is there any contradiction in imagining them? Is the notion of a zombie conceptually coherent? If so, then consciousness is something extra, something not entailed by the physical constitution of a human being. The question of their conceivability is not a simple question, and Chalmers has a lot to say about it. But he also says that "the logical possibility of zombies seems . . . obvious to me.

A zombie is just something physically identical to me, but which has no conscious experience—all is dark inside. While this is probably empirically impossible, it certainly seems that a coherent situation is being described; I can discern no contradiction in the description" (*CM*, 96).

If Chalmers is right, you are unlike you zombie twin in one crucial respect: There is something it is like to be you. You have first-person, subjective experiences; you really smell the roses, feel the grittiness of sand on the beach, and am afraid in the dark. All these qualia are immediately present to you in yur consciousness. And despite the structural and functional similarities, all are absent in your zombie twin. There is nothing it is like to be a zombie. A complete physical description could be given of your zombie twin, and it would leave nothing out, whereas a complete physical description of you will not really be complete. It will leave out *what it is like to be* you.

Dennett notes an odd consequence, however. Chalmers' zombie twin, being physically, functionally, and behaviorally similar to him, will also claim to have first-person experiences. (If not, he wouldn't be his exact twin.) If Chalmers says, "Ah, smell that fragrance; isn't that delightful?" his zombie twin, in the same circumstance, will say, "Ah, smell that fragrance; isn't that delightful?" Since, from a third-person point of view, Chalmers' zombie twin will be indistinguishable from Chalmers, none of us could tell the difference. But here comes the zinger: How could Chalmers tell the difference? Perhaps Chalmers himself is a zombie! He certainly believes he experiences raw feels that are not accessible from a third-person point of view. But then, so does his twin. He believes it is just *obvious* that he has subjective experiences. But so does his zombie twin. Perhaps Chalmers is right and his zombie twin is mistaken. Or maybe it's the other way around. But how could either of them know which is the case?

This is certainly a relevant question. As you might guess, the debate about functionalism and qualia is vigorous and ongoing—one more episode in the great conversation. Where do you think the truth lies?

1. Why does Nagel take bats as his prime example?
2. What does reflection on the inner life of bats mean for philosophy of mind?
3. Describe the thought experiment concerning Mary.
4. Why is the Mary story known as the "knowledge argument"?
5. What are qualia?
6. What is physicalism? How does the Mary story pose a problem for the physicalist?
7. What is the "hard problem," according to David Chalmers?
8. What is a zombie?
9. What moral does Chalmers draw from the case of his zombie twin?
10. Why would Chalmers' zombie twin believe he has subjective experiences?

FOR FURTHER THOUGHT

1. Is science our best avenue to truth about the world, as Quine and the physical realists believe? Or is it just one more narrative in a multicultural world, with no more claim to truth than any other?
2. Could a machine think? In light of the Intentional Stance on the one hand and the Chinese room on the other, justify your answer.
3. Can heterophenomenology yield all the truths there are about minds? Or does it leave something out? Explain.

KEY WORDS

physical realism
reductionism
holism
web of belief
maxim of minimum mutilation
sense data
observation sentences
ontology
phenomenalism
Myth of the Given
foundationalism
naturalized epistemology
third-person epistemology
evolutionary epistemology
Intentionality
cognitive science
Intentional Stance
Intentional System
function
language of thought
connectionism
Chinese room
"What is it like to be a bat?"
knowledge argument
qualia
physicalism
the hard problem
zombies

NOTES

1. Thomas Nagel, *The Last Word* (Oxford: Oxford University Press, 1997), 15.
2. Karl Popper, *The Logic of Scientific Discovery* (London: Hutchinson, 1959), 15.
3. Wilfrid Sellars, "Philosophy and the Scientific Image of Man," in *Science, Perception, and Reality* (London: Routledge and Kegan Paul, 1963), 1.
4. Roy Wood Sellars, *The Philosophy of Physical Realism* (New York: Macmillan, 1932).
5. References to the works of W. V. Quine are as follows:
   TDE: "Two Dogmas of Empiricism," *Philosophical Review* 60 (1951): 20–43. Reprinted in W. V. Quine, *From a Logical Point of View* (Cambridge, MA: Harvard University Press, 1953). Page references are to *From a Logical Point of View*.
   WB: W. V. Quine and J. S. Ullian, *The Web of Belief* (New York: Random House, 1970).
   PT: *Pursuit of Truth* (Cambridge, MA: Harvard University Press, 1990).
   OWTI: "On What There Is," *Review of Metaphysics* 2 (1948): 21–38. Reprinted in W. V. Quine *From a Logical Point of View* (Cambridge, MA: Harvard University Press, 1953). Page references are to *From a Logical Point of View*.
   EN: "Epistemology Naturalized," in *Ontological Relativity and Other Essays* (New York: Columbia University Press, 1969).
6. W. V. Quine, "Comment on Haack," in *Perspectives on Quine*, ed. R. B. Barrett and R. F. Gibson (Oxford: Blackwell, 1990), 128.
7. Wilfrid Sellars, "Empiricism and the Philosophy of Mind," in *Science, Perception and Reality* (London: Routledge and Kegan Paul, 1963), 127–196.
8. References to works by Daniel Dennett are as follows:
   TB: "True Believers: The Intentional Stance and Why It Works," in *Scientific Explanation*, ed. A. F. Heath (Oxford: Oxford University Press, 1991).

IS: The Intentional Stance (Cambridge, MA: MIT Press, 1987).

9. Karl Popper, *Conjectures and Refutations: The Growth of Scientific Knowledge* (London: Routledge and Kegan Paul, 1963), 52.

10. (*MBS*) John Searle, *Minds, Brains, and Science* (Cambridge, MA: Harvard University Press, 1984), 28–41.

11. (*WLB*) Thomas Nagel, "What Is It Like to Be a Bat?" in Nagel, *Mortal Questions* (Cambridge: Cambridge University Press, 1979).

12. (*EQ*) Frank Jackson, "Epiphenomenal Qualia," in David Chalmers, ed., *Philosophy of Mind* (Oxford: Oxford University Press, 2002).

13. (*CM*) David Chalmers, *The Conscious Mind* (Oxford: Oxford University Press, 1996).

AFTERWORD

This book is mainly a history of the Western philosophical tradition that begins in Greece. It is also an introductory book, touching only on highlights of this Western tradition. There are other vigorous traditions, too, as shown by the discussions of Indian, Chinese, and Islamic philosophy, though these are mere hints of riches that lie beyond the scope of the book. There is no doubt that the participants in these different conversations have much to learn from one another. But we inheritors of the Western tradition will only be shallow partners in cross-cultural conversations if we do not understand *ourselves*; and the way to understand ourselves is to understand our history.

The book also gives a very inadequate hint of the lively and interesting philosophical work being done today. New problems provoke novel thinking. New technologies bring new possibilities, and these may promise good or threaten evil. Ethical problems are posed by genetic manipulation, cloning, and computing. Problems of global warming, terrorism, genocide, poverty, the environment, abortion, and euthanasia call for philosophical reflection about ends and means and about human nature. The resurgence of religion keeps the tension with reason and science alive. Reflection continues on the challenges of skepticism and the extent and character of human knowledge. We can hardly say that Kant's four questions (What can we know? What ought we to do? For what can we hope? And what is man?) have been definitively answered.

Nor has the question about relativism been settled to the satisfaction of everyone. The rise of multiculturalism raises questions about the extent to which every culture deserves equal respect; are there some cultures that are better than others? If so, how would one tell? Is it all just a matter of opinion, as the ancient Sophists thought? Must might make right? Though the problem sometimes seems intractable, it is impossible to avoid taking up a point of view on the question. Some are struggling to see whether there is a way to acknowledge a truth in relativism without giving up the Socratic quest altogether.[1]

---

[1] For a look at recent arguments about relativism, see Norman Melchert, *Who's to Say? A Dialogue on Relativism* (Indianapolis: Hackett, 1994).

Philosophy isn't everything. Daniel Dennett has said that if the unexamined life is not worth living (Socrates), the overexamined life is nothing to write home about either. But philosophy has the peculiar characteristic of being inescapable for us all. So we should try to think about these matters with something approaching Aristotelian "excellence," remembering what one of our professors once said: "Whether you will philosophize or won't philosophize, you *must* philosophize."

APPENDIX
Writing a Philosophy Paper

It is not enough, when studying philosophy, to master the arguments of the philosophers. You must try your own hand at "doing philosophy," as the phrase goes, and the very best way to do that is to write a philosophical essay of your own. Here we give you some suggestions, and a few rules, for writing a good paper.

A philosophy essay is not a research paper, needing time spent in the library or on the Internet. Your aim should not be to gain still more information, but to formulate and defend (at least provisionally, for now) an answer to some philosophical problem that you think important. What this requires is not research, but thinking—trying to figure out what can be said for and against a certain position. Is pleasure the good for humans, as Epicurus and Bentham think, or are the criticisms of Aristotle, Augustine, and Kant conclusive? Are our wills free? (Think of Democritus, Aquinas, Descartes, Hume, and de Beauvoir.) Is one or another argument for the existence of God cogent? Your aim should be to write a paper giving good reasons—*your reasons*—supporting your conclusion on some such problem.

In writing this paper, you need to have an audience in mind. Don't write it for your instructor. In particular, don't write it to please him or her; that will surely skew your results in a way that will be less than authentically you. We suggest that you keep in mind an intelligent person about your own age, someone not a philosophy major, but with an interest in the problem you are addressing—perhaps a sibling at another university. You want to convince this person that your conclusion on the matter in question is the most reasonable one.

You should begin with a statement of the problem you mean to address. Since you will not be writing a book, you need to narrow the problem down to something you can handle in five or ten pages. Don't try to answer the question "Does God exist?" but you might intend to show that Hume's critique of the design argument is fatally flawed. Don't address the question "Is human knowledge possible?" but you could try "Can I know that this apple exists independent of my perception of it?" Whatever your problem, it may require some clarification, perhaps including a summary of several ways other philosophers have answered it. Within the first few paragraphs, you should state clearly the view that you intend to support. Let us call this the *thesis* of the paper. You should give your audience an indication of this thesis early on so they can appreciate the relevance of the arguments you put forward in the body of the paper.

These arguments will present the premises that you think make it reasonable to believe your conclusion. You should strive to set forth premises that are true, if possible, or at least plausible, keeping your target audience in mind. It may well be that some of your premises are not themselves obvious, and you may need to offer support for them. Thus you may need to develop subarguments for these premises, trying again to find reasons that are acceptable.

One persuasive tactic in argument is to consider objections to your thesis and show why they are not well founded. Here you should seek out the strongest objections; to consider only weak objections leaves your support for the thesis itself weak, since an opponent could easily cite the stronger objections. The way Plato deals with the Sophists is a good model; Thrasymachus and Callicles are not "straw men" that are easy to blow down, but worthy opponents whose defeat would indeed be a victory.

You may certainly get help from the philosophers you have studied if you agree with some of their arguments. Here you need to be careful, though. You can't just borrow a philosopher's words without indicating that you are doing so. The way to do that is to use quote marks around the sentences you are borrowing and indicate in a footnote the source from which they come. Even close paraphrases should be acknowledged this way. If you use sources other than this text (and your instructor will tell you whether that is desired or required), you should indicate that in a bibliography at the end.

You will find an outline a great help in writing a philosophy paper. Some experts recommend a full outline in complete sentences; they say that if you do this, the paper pretty much writes itself. Others find a less full outline more helpful—a list of topics that need to be covered in more or less the desired order. In either case, you will find that continual revision will be necessary as you write. Perhaps Mozart could have a sonata completely in mind before he wrote down the first notes, but there are few Mozarts among us. Computers and word processors make moving text around, adding, and deleting deliciously easy, so make use of the technology. After you get a draft that you are fairly satisfied with, set it aside for a day or two. When you come back to it, you will certainly find things that can be improved. (This, of course, means that you shouldn't try to write the paper the night before it is due!)

The paper should close with a summary of the argument, recalling the problem to be solved, the solution proposed, and the main premises used to establish the conclusion.

Here are a few basic rules to observe:

1. Write clearly. Keep your sentences short and don't use fancy words. Write as simply as the subject allows. You are not out to impress anyone, but to convince your readers of your conclusion.

2. Don't use up space with obvious trivialities or broad generalizations. Don't begin by writing, "Since the dawn of time human beings have puzzled over the meaning of life."

3. Don't appeal to authority. If you are trying to prove that mind and body are distinct entities, it will not help to note that Descartes thought so. Descartes might be mistaken.

4. Don't fall back on "I believe" or "I feel." Your reader is interested not in your autobiography, but in the argument for your conclusion.

5. Avoid padding and repetitiveness. Saying the same thing six different ways will not strengthen your case.

6. Never make excuses. Don't say, "Of course, I'm only a college freshman. . . ." Just do your best.

7. Don't depend only on spellcheck; if you type "buy" instead of "but," no spell checker will find the error. Proofread your paper carefully before turning it in. Sloppiness in spelling and grammar gives a bad impression of carelessness.

Your instructor will try not to evaluate your argument according to whether he or she agrees with your conclusion. You should pay no attention to the instructor's views on the topic in question. The important thing is the relevance, clarity, and strength of your premises relative to the conclusion you are supporting. The quality of the argument is what counts.

It should be unnecessary to stress that your paper should be your own work and represent the thinking that you have put into it. Plagiarism—passing off someone else's work as your own—is wrong. It involves lying, fraud, and cheating, and it undermines the trust that is the foundation on which a community of scholars can function.

If these moral reasons do not convince you, you may want to remember that plagiarism is harshly punished in the academy. If you were discovered to have cheated in this way—a very real possibility—you would certainly be failed for this assignment, perhaps be failed for the course, and possibly even be expelled from the school.

Writing a philosophy paper can be challenging, especially the first time you try it. But it is an excellent exercise for developing clarity of thought, self-criticism, and a sense for what rationality is really like.

GLOSSARY

Here you will find brief explanations of difficult or unfamiliar terms, sometimes followed in parentheses by the names of philosophers with whom the term is especially—though not solely—associated.

absolute knowledge A term in HEGEL's philosophy, designating the state of consciousness when everything "other" has been brought into itself and Spirit knows itself to be all of reality.

Active Intellect An independent, immaterial intellect that plays an important role in human cognition in Islamic philosophy. (AL-KINDĪ, AL-FĀRĀBI, AVICENNA, AVERROËS)

aesthetic KIERKEGAARD's term for the style of life that aims at keeping things interesting; the pursuit of pleasurable experiences. **Aesthetics** (also spelled "esthetics") is the theory of art and of the experience of the beautiful or sublime.

alienation HEGELian term appropriated by MARX to describe the loss of oneself and control over what properly belongs to oneself in capitalist social structures, such as one's labor. Existentialism stresses the feeling of alienation among modern human beings.

ambiguity A term applied to human reality, indicating its immanence and transcendence. (SIMONE DE BEAUVOIR)

analytic A term applied to statements the denial of which is a contradiction (for example, "All bachelors are unmarried"). (KANT, **logical positivists**)

anātman The doctrine that there is no permanent, unchanging self (BUDDHA, NĀGASENA). See also *ātman*.

anticipatory resoluteness HEIDEGGER's term for authentically facing the fact that one is destined for death.

a posteriori A term applied primarily to statements, but also to ideas or concepts; knowledge of the a posteriori is derived from (comes *after*) experience (for example, "Trees have leaves"). (KANT)

appearance The way things present themselves to us, often contrasted with the way they really are. KANT holds that all we can ever come to know is how **things-in-themselves** *appear* to our senses and understanding; appearance is the realm of **phenomena** versus **noumena.**

a priori A term applied primarily to statements, but also to ideas or concepts, that can be known *prior to* and independent of appeal to experience (for example, "Two and three are five," or "All bodies are extended"). (KANT)

argument A set of statements, some of which (the premises) function as reasons to accept another (the conclusion).

ātman The permanent, unchanging self posited in the Upaniṣads and endorsed by the Brahmanical schools of Indian philosophy. (Vaiśeṣika, Nyāya)

atomism From a Greek word meaning "uncuttable"; the view that reality is composed of tiny indivisible bits and empty space. (DEMOCRITUS, Vaiśeṣika, HOBBES, CAVENDISH) See also **logical atomism**.

attachment A term for inappropriately strong desires and aversions (BUDDHA).

attunement In HEIDEGGER's thinking, the term for a mode of disclosure that manifests itself in a mood; for example, the mood of anxiety discloses **Dasein**'s not-being-at-home in the world of its ordinary concern.

authenticity Being oneself, taking responsibility for oneself in accepting the burden of having to "be here"—that is, thrown into this particular existence with just these possibilities. (HEIDEGGER)

autonomy Self-rule or giving the law to oneself, as opposed to *heteronomy*, being under the control of another. A key principle in KANT's **ethics**.

Being The fundamental concept of **metaphysics**. Doctrines of **categories** such as those of ARISTOTLE and KANT attempt to set forth the most general ways that things can *be*. The meaning of Being is the object of HEIDEGGER's quest.

Being-in-the world The most general characteristic of **Dasein**, according to HEIDEGGER; more fundamental than knowing, it is being engaged in the use of gear or equipment in a world functionally organized.

binary opposition A pair of terms, each of which lives on its opposition to the other. Examples are appearance/reality, knowledge/opinion, one/many, speaking/writing, and good/evil. Often a target for deconstruction by postmodernists. Also prominent in LAOZI's thought.

carceral society The character of current society, according to FOUCAULT, where everything is formed by technologies analogous to those used in a prison.

categorical imperative The key principle in KANT's moral theory, bidding us always to act in such a way that the maxim (principle) of our action could be universally applied.

categories Very general concepts describing the basic modes of being. ARISTOTLE distinguishes ten, including "**substance**," "quantity," and "quality." KANT lists twelve, the most important of which are "substance" and "causality." The Vaiśeṣikas recognizes six, including "substance," "attributes," "**particularity**," and "universals."

causation What accounts for the occurrence or character of something. ARISTOTLE distinguishes four kinds of cause: material, formal, efficient, and final. Recent theories, influenced by HUME, see causation as a relationship between events, where the first is regularly or lawfully related to the second. (AL-GHAZĀLĪ)

Chinese room A thought experiment by John Searle constituting an argument that a computer program alone cannot produce understanding or a mind.

compatibilism The view that human liberty (or freedom of the will) can coexist with determinism—the universal **causation** of all events. Classic sources are HOBBES and HUME.

conclusion That part of an argument for which evidence (in the form of the premises) is presented.

contingency What might be or might not be, depending; the opposite of necessity. RORTY emphasizes the historical contingency of our language and point of view.

convention The Sophists contrast what is true by nature (*physis*) with what is true by convention or agreement (*nomos*) among humans.

correspondence A view of truth; a statement is said to be true, provided that it "corresponds" with what it is about—that is, it *says* that reality is such and such, and reality *is in fact* such and such. (ARISTOTLE, AQUINAS, LOCKE)

criterion A mark or standard by which something is known. The "problem of the criterion" is posed by skeptics, who ask by what criterion we can tell that we know something and, if an answer is given, by what criterion we know that this is the correct criterion. (MOZI, ZHUANGZI, SEXTUS EMPIRICUS, MONTAIGNE, DESCARTES, HEGEL)

Dào Literally, "way" or path. In Chinese thought, the proper way of living. LAOZI also uses the term to describe the ineffable source of all things. (ZHUANGZI)

Dasein Literally, "being there." HEIDEGGER's term for the way of being that is characteristic of humans. It designates that way to be in which one's own **Being** is a matter of concern.

dé Literally, "potency" or "power." For CONFUCIUS, MENCIUS, and XUNZI, a kind of moral charisma needed for good leadership.

deduction A kind of argument, aiming at validity, in which the premises purport to prove the conclusion; a successful or valid deductive argument.

dependent origination The view that all things and events are fully caused by the conditions that preceded them. (BUDDHA)

determinism The view that there is a causal condition for every event, without exception, sufficient to produce that event just as it is. (DEMOCRITUS, EPICURUS, HUME, KANT) See also **compatibilism**.

dialectic A term of many meanings. For SOCRATES, it is a progression of questions and answers, driving toward less inadequate opinions. For PLATO, it is the sort of reasoning that moves from **Forms** to more basic Forms and at last to the Form of the Good. For HEGEL, it is the progress of thought and reality by the reconciliation of opposites and the generation of new opposites. MARXists apply the Hegelian doctrine to the world of material production.

différance DERRIDA's term for the destabilizing of meaning and reference by language as a system of differences; a word is what it is because it *differs* from other words, and it fails to *present* its signified meaning because it *defers* it to other interpretations.

dogmatism A term applied by philosophers to the holding of views for no adequate reason.

dualism The metaphysical view that there are two basically different kinds of things in reality; the most common dualism is that of mind and body, as in DESCARTES, for instance. (Compare **monism**.)

empiricism The view that all knowledge of facts must be derived from sense experience; a rejection of **rationalism**, the view that any knowledge of nature is innate or constructable by reasoning alone. Exemplified by HUME, LOCKE, BERKELEY, and the **logical positivists**.

entelechy A goal or end residing within a thing, guiding its development from potentiality to the actuality of its **essence**. (ARISTOTLE)

epiphenomenalism The view that consciousness is an effect of physical happenings in the body but has no causal powers itself. It is just "along for the ride."

episteme FOUCAULT's terms for the background assumptions of a given historical era.

epistemology Theory of knowledge, addressing the questions of what knowledge is, whether we have any, what its objects may be, and how we can reliably get more.

essence The set of properties that makes each thing uniquely the kind of thing that it is. (ARISTOTLE, AQUINAS, DESCARTES)

ethics The study of good and evil, right and wrong, moral rules, virtues, and the good life; their status, meaning, and justification.

ethnocentrism Judging everything by the standards current in one's own society.

eudaemonia Greek term for happiness or well-being. (PLATO, ARISTOTLE, EPICURUS, the Stoics, the skeptics)

existentialism The philosophy that focuses on what it means to exist in the way human beings do—usually stressing choice, risk, and freedom. (KIERKEGAARD, HEIDEGGER, DE BEAUVOIR)

facticity The way of **Being** of **Dasein**. One aspect of our facticity, for instance, is our **Being-in-the-world**; another is our **thrownness**—simply finding ourselves in existence in some particular way. (HEIDEGGER)

fallibilism The view that though we may know the truth in certain cases, we can never be certain that we do. (PEIRCE, XENOPHANES)

falling HEIDEGGER's term for the phenomenon of being defined by others.

family resemblance WITTGENSTEIN's term for the way many of our concepts get their meaning, via overlapping resemblances rather than a set of necessary and sufficient conditions.

filial piety Respect and obedience to one's parents. (CONFUCIUS, MENCIUS, XUNZI)

Forms Those ideal realities PLATO takes to be both the objects of knowledge and the source of the derived reality of the sensible world: the Square Itself, for instance, and the Forms of Justice and the Good. Used uncapitalized for the forms of ARISTOTLE and AQUINAS, which have no being apart from the particular things that exemplify them.

four sprouts The four emotional dispositions from which virtues grow. (MENCIUS)

free spirit A term used by certain late nineteenth-century thinkers, such as NIETZSCHE, to symbolize their freedom from the inherited tradition—particularly the religious tradition.

genealogy A search for the historical antecedents of current cultural assumptions. (NIETZSCHE, FOUCAULT)

Great Chain of Being The view that reality is stretched between God (or **the One**) and nothingness, with each kind of thing possessing its own degree of being and goodness. Found in PLOTINUS and AUGUSTINE; widespread for many centuries.

hedonism The view that pleasure is the sole objective of motivation (psychological hedonism) or that it is the only thing good in itself (ethical hedonism). (EPICURUS, BENTHAM, MILL)

hermeneutic circle The idea that any interpretation takes something for granted; for example, understanding part of a text presupposes an understanding of the whole and vice versa. Every understanding lights up its objects only against a background that cannot at the same time be brought into the light. It follows that complete objectivity is impossible. (HEIDEGGER)

historical a priori What is so taken for granted at a time that it could hardly be imagined that one could question it. May change over time. (FOUCAULT)

hubris A Greek word meaning arrogance or excessive self-confidence, particularly of mortals in relation to the gods.

hylomorphism The theory that every material object is a composite of matter (*hyle*) and form (*morphe*); matter is the potentiality of a thing, form its actuality. (ARISTOTLE, AVICENNA, AQUINAS—with qualifications)

idealism The view that objects exist only relative to a subject that perceives or knows them. There are many forms; in HEGEL's *absolute idealism*, for instance, mind or Spirit (the Absolute) is the only ultimate reality, everything else having only a relative reality. (also BERKELEY)

inauthenticity HEIDEGGER's word for **Dasein**'s fleeing from itself into the average everyday world of what "they" say and do; not being oneself.

induction A method of reasoning that infers from a series of single cases to a new case or to a law or general principle concerning all such cases.

inherence A relationship that obtains between a whole and its parts, an attribute and a substance, a universal and a particular, etc., in Vaiśeṣika thought.

innate ideas Ideas that any mature individual can acquire independent of experience. Defended in different ways by PLATO and by DESCARTES; attacked by LOCKE and the empiricists.

instrumentalism DEWEY's term for his own philosophy, according to which all our intellectual constructions (concepts, laws, theories) have the status of tools for solving problems.

karma In Indian thought, a lawlike connection between the performance of good (or bad) actions and good (or bad) consequences for the person who performs the actions. (BUDDHA)

language-games Comparing words to pieces in a game such as chess. What defines a rook are the rules according to which it moves; what characterizes a word are the jobs it does in those activities and forms of life in which it has its "home." (the later WITTGENSTEIN)

light of nature DESCARTES' term for reason, in the light of which things can appear so clear and distinct that they cannot possibly be doubted.

logical atomism A view expressed by the early WITTGENSTEIN, in which language is thought of as a logical calculus built up from simple unanalyzable elements called *names*. Names stand for simple objects, which are the substance of the world.

logical positivism A twentieth-century version of **empiricism**, which stresses the **tautological** nature of logic and mathematics, together with the criterion of **verifiability** for factual statements.

logical truth Truths that are true by virtue of logic alone. WITTGENSTEIN explains logical truths as **tautologies**.

logocentrism The view DERRIDA finds dominant in our tradition, where knowledge finds a foundation in its objects being present to consciousness and reason and logic are thought to be reliable avenues to the extension of truth.

logos Greek term meaning word, utterance, rationale, argument, structure. In HERACLITUS, the ordering principle of the world; in the Gospel of John, that according to which all things were made and that became incarnate in Jesus.

materialism The view that the fundamental reality is matter, as understood by the sciences—primarily physics; mind or spirit has no independent reality. (HOBBES)

metaphysics The discipline that studies being as such, its kinds and character, often set out in a doctrine of **categories**.

monism The metaphysical view that there is only one basic kind of reality; materialism is one kind of monism, HEGELian idealism another. (Compare **dualism**.)

mutual care The doctrine that we should be equally concerned with each person's well-being. (MOZI)

naturalism A view that locates human beings wholly within nature and takes the results of the natural and human sciences to be our best idea of what there is; since DARWIN, naturalists in philosophy insist that the human world is a product of the nonpurposive process of evolution.

natural law Law specifying right and wrong, which is embedded in the very nature of things, independent of custom and convention. (Stoics, AQUINAS, LOCKE)

nihilism The view that nothing really matters, that distinctions of value have no grounding in the nature of things; what threatens, according to NIETZSCHE, when God dies.

nirvāṇa Escape from **attachment** and the cycle of rebirth (*saṃsāra*). (BUDDHA)

nominal essence An essence that is determined not by the true nature of things, but by the words we have for them. (LOCKE)

nomos The way things are insofar as they depend on human decision, custom, or convention. (Compare *physis*.) (Sophists)

normalization In FOUCAULT, the goal and effect of disciplinary technologies; making all alike.

noumena KANT's term for things as they are in themselves, independent of how they may appear to us; he believes they are unknowable. (Contrasted with **phenomena** or **appearance**.)

nous Greek term usually translated as "mind." In ARISTOTLE, *nous* is the active and purely formal principle that engages in thinking and contemplation; he argues that *nous* is more than just the form of a living body; it is a reality in its own right and is eternal.

objective spirit That realm in which Spirit expresses itself externally, giving rationality to institutions, law, and culture. (HEGEL)

Ockham's razor A principle stated by WILLIAM OF OCKHAM, demanding parsimony in positing entities for the purpose of explanation; often formulated as "Do not multiply entities beyond necessity."

One, the 1. In PLOTINUS and Neoplatonic thought, the source from which the rest of reality emanates. 2. A translation of HEIDEGGER's term "das Man," designating **Dasein** as not differentiated from the "Others," the crowd, the anonymous many who dictate how life goes and what it means.

ontic HEIDEGGER's term for the realm of ordinary and scientific facts. (Compare **ontological**.)

ontological 1. Having to do with **Being**, with what there is in the most general sense. 2. In HEIDEGGER, having to do with the deep structure of **Dasein's Being** that makes possible the **ontic** facts about average everydayness; disclosed in *fundamental ontology*.

ontological argument An argument for God's existence that proceeds solely from an idea of what God is, from his **essence**. Different versions found in ANSELM, AVICENNA, and DESCARTES; criticized by AQUINAS, HUME, and KANT.

particularity (*viśeṣa*) In Vaiśeṣika thought, the thing that makes each individual substance distinct from all other things.

phenomena What appears, just as it appears. In KANT, contrasted with *noumena*. The object of study by **phenomenology**.

phenomenology The attempt to describe what appears to consciousness; a science of consciousness, its structures, contents, and objects. (HEGEL, HUSSERL, HEIDEGGER)

physicalism The view that reality is through and through material in nature. (DEMOCRITUS, DENNETT)

physis The way things are, independent of any human decision. (Compare *nomos*.) (Sophists)

pictorial form What a picture and the pictured have in common, which allows the first to picture the second. (early WITTGENSTEIN)

possible state of affairs In early WITTGENSTEIN, the way in which objects could relate to each other to constitute a fact.

power-knowledge FOUCAULT's idea that knowledge and power are inextricably linked.

pragmatism A view developed by PEIRCE, JAMES, and DEWEY in which all of our intellectual life is understood in relation to our practical interests. What a concept means, for instance, depends wholly on the practical effects of the object of our concept.

pramāṇa A knowledge source, such as perception or inference. (Nyāya)

premise Statement offered in support of a conclusion; the evidentiary part of an argument.

present-at-hand A HEIDEGGERian term for things understood as bereft of their usual functional relation to our interests and concerns; what "objective" science takes as its object. A modification of our usual relation to things as **ready-to-hand**.

primary qualities In GALILEO and other early moderns, qualities that a thing actually has—for example, size, shape, location—and that account for or explain certain effects in us (**secondary qualities**), such as sweetness, redness, warmth. (DESCARTES, LOCKE, BERKELEY)

qualia The immediate qualities of experience, private and subjective. Sense data. Green, warm, loud, sweet.

quiddity Latin-origin term for *what* a thing is; its essence, in contrast to its actual existence. (AQUINAS)

rationalism The philosophical stance that is distrustful of the senses, relying only on reason and rational argument to deliver the truth. (PARMENIDES, DESCARTES)

rational psychology KANT's term for the discipline that attempts to gain knowledge of the self or soul in nonempirical ways, relying on rational argument alone.

ready-to-hand HEIDEGGER's term for the mode of **Being** of the things that are most familiar to **Dasein**; gear or equipment in its functional relation to **Dasein**'s concerns.

realism A term of many meanings; central is the contention that reality is both logically and causally independent of even the best human beliefs and theories.

rectification of names The process of ensuring that names (i.e., words) match reality (CONFUCIUS).

relativism A term of many meanings; central is the view that there are no objective standards of good or bad to be discovered and that no objective knowledge of reality is possible; all standards and knowledge claims are valid only relative to times, individuals, or cultures. (Sophists)

rén The central virtue in Confucian ethics. Sometimes translated as "humanheartedness" or "Goodness" (CONFUCIUS) or "benevolence" (MENCIUS, XUNZI).

representational theory The view that our access to reality is limited to our perceptions and ideas, which function as representations of things beyond themselves. (DESCARTES, LOCKE, BERKELEY)

rhetoric The art of persuasive speaking developed and taught by the **Sophists** in ancient Greece, whose aim was to show how a persuasive *logos* could be constructed on each side of a controversial issue.

rites Rituals and rules of etiquette in ancient Chinese society (CONFUCIUS, MENCIUS, XUNZI, MOZI).

saṃsāra The cycle of birth, death, and rebirth in Indian thought.

secondary qualities Those qualities, such as taste and color, produced in us by the **primary qualities** of objects—size, shape, and so on. (GALILEO, DESCARTES, LOCKE, BERKELEY)

semantics Study of word–world relationships; how words relate to what they are about. (PEIRCE)

sense-certainty What is left if we subtract from sensory experience all interpretation in terms of concepts, for example, the blueness we experience when we look at a clear sky; the immediate; where HEGEL thinks philosophy must start.

showing Contrasted in WITTGENSTEIN's early philosophy with *saying*; logic, for instance, shows itself in every bit of language; a proposition *shows* (displays) its sense, and it *says* that this is how things stand.

skandhas The momentary physical and mental phenomena that make up all things. Often translated as "aggregates." (BUDDHA)

skepticism The view that for every claim to know, reason can be given to doubt it; the skeptic suspends judgment about reality (ZHUANGZI, SEXTUS EMPIRICUS, MONTAIGNE). DESCARTES uses skeptical arguments to try to find something that cannot be doubted.

social contract The theory that government finds its justification in an agreement or contract among individuals. (HOBBES, LOCKE)

solipsism The view, which must be stated in the first person, that only I exist; the worry about falling into solipsism motivates DESCARTES to try to prove the existence of God.

Sophist From a Greek word meaning "wise one"; in ancient Greece, teachers who taught many things to ambitious young men, especially **rhetoric**.

sound In logic a sound **argument** is one that is **valid** and has true **premises**.

Stoicism The view that happiness and freedom are possible if we simply distinguish clearly what properly belongs to ourselves and what is beyond our power, limiting our desires to the former and thus keeping our wills in harmony with nature.

substance What is fundamental and can exist independently; that which has or underlies its qualities. There is disagreement about what is substantial: PLATO takes it to be the **Forms**, ARISTOTLE the individual things of our experience. Some philosophers (for example, SPINOZA) argue that there is but *one* substance: God. (also Vaiśeṣika, LOCKE, BERKELEY, KANT, HEGEL)

sūtra In Indian thought, an aphorism or a set of aphorisms setting out the doctrines of a school of thought. (BUDDHA, Vaiśeṣika, Nyāya)

syllogism An **argument** comprising two **premises** and a **conclusion**, composed of categorical subject–predicate statements; the argument contains just three terms, each of which appears in just two of the statements. (ARISTOTLE)

synthetic A term applied to statements the denial of which is not contradictory; according to KANT, in a synthetic statement the predicate is not "contained" in the subject but adds something to it (for example, "Mount Cook is the highest mountain in New Zealand").

tautology A statement for which the truth table contains only T's. WITTGENSTEIN uses the concept to explain the nature of logical truth and the laws of logic.

tawḥīd In Islam, the absolute unity or oneness of God. (AL-KINDĪ)

teleology Purposiveness or goal-directedness; a teleological explanation for some fact is an explanation in terms of what end it serves. (ARISTOTLE, HEIDEGGER)

theodicy The justification of the ways of God to man, especially in relation to the problem of evil: What would justify an all-powerful, wise, and good God in creating a world containing so many evils? (AUGUSTINE, LEIBNIZ, HEGEL)

things-in-themselves In KANT's philosophy, things as they are, independent of our apprehension of them, of the way they appear to us; *noumena*.

Third Man Term for a problem with PLATO's **Forms**: We seem to be forced into an infinite regress of Forms to account for the similarity of two men.

thrownness HEIDEGGER's term for **Dasein**'s simply finding itself in existence under certain conditions, without ever having a choice about that.

transcendental Term for the conditions on the side of the subject that make knowing or doing possible. KANT's critical philosophy is a transcendental investigation; it asks about the **a priori** conditions for experience and action in general.

utilitarianism Moral philosophy that takes consequences as the criteria for the moral evaluation of action; of two choices open to one, it is right to choose the one that will produce the most happiness for all concerned.

validity A term for logical goodness in deductive arguments; an **argument** is valid whenever, if the **premises** are true, it is not possible for the conclusion to be false. An argument can be valid even if the premises are false.

verifiability principle The rule adopted by the **logical positivists** to determine meaningfulness in factual statements; if no sense experience can count in favor of the truth of a statement—can verify it at least to some degree—it is declared meaningless.

wúwéi Often translated as "nonaction." A way of accomplishing something effortlessly or by following nature. (LAOZI, ZHUANGZI)

zombie An exact physical duplicate of a human being, but without conscious experience. (CHALMERS)

CREDITS

Text Credits

From Hesiod, "Theogony," in *Hesiod and Theognis*, translated by Dorothea Wender (Penguin Classics, 1973), copyright © 1973 by Dorothea Wender.

Excerpts from *The Iliad* by Homer, translated by Robert Fagles, translation copyright © 1990 by Robert Fagles. Used by permission of Viking Books, an imprint of Penguin Publishing Group, a division of Penguin Random House LLC. All rights reserved.

From *The Odyssey* by Homer, translated by Robert Fagles, copyright © 1996 by Robert Fagles.

From John Mansley Robinson, *An Introduction to Early Greek Philosophy*, copyright © 1968 by Houghton Mifflin Company.

From Franklin Edgerton, *The Beginnings of Indian Philosophy*, copyright © 1965 by George Allen and Unwin.

From Patrick Olivelle, translator, *Upaniṣads*, copyright © 1996 by Patrick Olivelle, Oxford University Press.

From W. J. Johnson, translator, *The Bhagavad Gita*, copyright © 1994 by W. J. Johnson, Oxford University Press.

From Bhikkhu Ñanamoli and Bhikkhu Bodhi, translators, *The Middle-Length Discourses of the Buddha*, Fourth Edition. Copyright © 2015 by Bikkhu Bodhi, Wisdom Publications in Sommerville, MA.

From I. B. Horner, translator, *Milinda's Questions*, copyright © 1964 by I. B. Horner.

From Matthew Dasti and Stephen Phillips, translators, *The Nyāya-sūtra: Selections with Early Commentaries*. Copyright © 2017 by Hackett Publishing. Reprinted with the permission of Hackett Publishing Company, Inc. All rights reserved.

Excerpts from *The Clouds* by Aristophanes, translated by William Arrowsmith, translation copyright © 1962 by William Arrowsmith. Used by permission of New American Library, an imprint of Penguin Publishing Group, a division of Penguin Random House LLC. All rights reserved.

From Herodotus, *The Histories* (New York: Penguin Books, 1972).

Excerpts from *Thucydides: The Reinvention of History* by Donald Kagan, copyright © 2009 by Donald Kagan. Used by permission of Viking Books, an imprint of Penguin Publishing Group, a division of Penguin Random House LLC. All rights reserved.

From Euripides, *Hippolytus*, in *Euripides I*, copyright © 1955 by University of Chicago Press.

From Plato, *Gorgias*, translated by Robin Waterfield. Copyright © 1994 by Oxford University Press.

From *Mozi*, by Ian Johnston, translator. Copyright © 2010 Columbia University Press. Reprinted with the permission of the publisher.

From *The Complete Works of Zhuangzi*, by Burton Watson, translator. Copyright © 2013 by Columbia University Press. Reprinted with the permission of the publisher.

From René Descartes, *Meditations on First Philosophy*, translated by Ronald Rubin, copyright © 1986 by Areté Press.

From Edwin A. Burtt (Ed.), *The English Philosophers from Bacon to Mill* (New York: Modern Library, 1939).

From John Locke, *An Essay Concerning Human Understanding*, ed. Alexander Campbell Fraser (New York: Dover Publications, 1959).

From John Locke, *Of Civil Government, Two Treatises* (London: J. M. Dent and Sons, 1924).

From John Locke, *A Letter Concerning Toleration* (Indianaplos: Hackett, 1983).

From George Berkeley, *Principles of Human Knowledge and Three Dialogues*, edited by Howard Robinson. Copyright © 1996 by Oxford University Press.

From Emilie Du Châtelet, *Selected Philosophy and Scientific Writings*, edited by Judith P. Zinsser, translated by Isabelle Bour and Judith P. Zinsser. Copyright © 2009 Judith P. Zinsser and Isabelle Bour.

From David Hume, *A Treatise of Human Nature*, edited by David Fate Norton and Mary J. Norton. Copyright © 2000 by Oxford University Press.

From David Hume, *Enquiry Concerning Human Understanding*, edited by Tom L. Beauchamp. Copyright © 1999 by Oxford University Press.

From Immanuel Kant, *Groundwork for the Metaphysics of Morals*, translated by Arnulf Zweig, edited by Thomas E. Hill Jr. and Arnulf Zweig. Copyright © 2002 by Oxford University Press.

From Immanuel Kant, *Prolegomena to Any Future Metaphysics*, edited by Günter Zøller, translated by Peter G. Lucas and Günter Zøller. Copyright © 2004 by Oxford University Press.

From Immanuel Kant, *Critique of Pure Reason*, translated by Norman Kemp Smith (New York: St. Martin's Press, 1956).

From Hegel, *Reason in History*, translated by Robert S. Hartman, copyright © 1953 by Prentice-Hall, Inc.

From Hegel, *Phenomenology of Spirit*, translated by A. V. Miller, copyright © 1977 by Oxford University Press. Reprinted with permission from the publisher.

From Hegel, *Philosophy of Right*, translated by T. M. Knox, copyright © 1952 by Oxford University Press.

From Søren Kierkegaard, *The Sickness unto Death,* translated by Alastair Hannay (Penguin Classics, 1989), translation copyright © 1989 by Alastair Hannay.

From Søren Kierkegaard, *Concluding Unscientific Postscript*, translated by David F. Swenson and Walter Lowrie, copyright © 1941 by Princeton University Press.

From Søren Kierkegaard, *Fear and Trembling*, translated by Howard V. Hong and Edna H. Hong (Princeton: Princeton University Press, 1983).

From Søren Kierkegaard, *Either/Or, Parts I & II*, translated by Howard V. Hong and Edna H. Hong (Princeton University Press,

1987), copyright © 1987 by Howard V. Hong. Reprinted with permission.

From *The Marx–Engels Reader*, ed. Robert C. Tucker (New York: W. W. Norton , 1972).

From Karl Marx, *The Economic and Philosophic Manuscripts of 1844*, ed. Dirk J. Struik (New York: International Publishers, 1964).

From Karl Marx (with Friedrich Engels), *The Communist Manifesto*, translated by Samuel Moore. Copyright © 1992 by Oxford University Press.

From John Stuart Mill, *On Liberty and Other Essays*, edited by John Gray. Copyright © 1991 by Oxford University Press.

From Mary Wollstonecraft, *A Vindication of the Rights of Woman*, edited by Mary Warnock, J. M. Dent Ltd., and Charles E. Tuttle Co. Inc., Everyman's Library, 1986.

Excerpts from *The Portable Nietzsche* by Friedrich Nietzsche, edited by Walter Kaufmann, translated by Walter Kaufmann, translation copyright 1954, © 1968, renewed © 1982 by Penguin Random House LLC. Used by permission of Viking Books, an imprint of Penguin Publishing Group, a division of Penguin Random House LLC. All rights reserved.

From Friedrich Nietzsche, *On The Genealogy of Morals*, translated by Douglas Smith. Copyright © 1996 by Oxford University Press.

From Friedrich Nietzsche, *Beyond Good and Evil*, translated by Marion Faber. Copyright © 1998 by Oxford University Press.

Excerpts from *The Gay Science* by Friedrich Nietzsche, translated by Walter Kaufmann, copyright ©1974 by Penguin Random House LLC. Used by permission of Random House, an imprint of Penguin Publishing Group, a division of Penguin Random House LLC. All rights reserved.

From Friedrich Nietzsche, *The Birth of Tragedy*, translated by Douglas Smith. Copyright © 2000 by Oxford University Press.

From Friedrich Nietzsche, *Twilight of the Idols*, translated by Duncan Large. Copyright © 1998 by Oxford University Press.

From Friedrich Nietzsche, *Human, All Too Human*, translated by R. J. Hollingdale (Cambridge: Cambridge University Press, 1986).

From *The Collected Papers of Charles Sanders Peirce, Volume V: Pragmatism and Pragmaticism*, edited by Charles Hartshorne and Paul Weiss, pp. 169, 186–187, 231–236, 238, 241–243, 249, 251–252, 255, 258, 265–266, 268–269, 278–279, 282, 317–318, 342, Cambridge, MA: The Belknap Press of Harvard University Press, Copyright © 1934 by the President and Fellows of Harvard College.

From *The Collected Works of John Dewey: The Middle Works, 1899–1924*, Volume 4: 1907–1909 © 2008 by the Board of Trustees, Southern Illinois University, reproduced by permission of the publisher.

From John Dewey, *How We Think* (Boston: D. C. Heath, 1933).

From John Dewey, *Experience and Nature* (New York: W. W. Norton, 1929).

Photography Credits

INDEX